LANGUAGE FILES

TWELFTH EDITION

Editors of Previous Editions

11th edition, 2011
Vedrana Mihalicek
Christin Wilson

10th edition, 2007
Anouschka Bergmann
Kathleen Currie Hall
Sharon Miriam Ross

9th edition, 2004
Georgios Tserdanelis
Wai Yi Peggy Wong

8th edition, 2001
Thomas W. Stewart, Jr.
Nathan Vaillette

7th edition, 1998
Nick Cipollone
Steven Hartman Keiser
Shravan Vasishth

6th edition, 1994
Stefanie Jannedy
Robert Poletto
Tracey L. Weldon

5th edition, 1991
Monica Crabtree
Joyce Powers

4th edition, 1987
Carolyn McManis
Deborah Stollenwerk
Zhang Zheng-Sheng

3rd edition, 1985
Anette S. Bissantz
Keith A. Johnson

2nd edition, 1982
Carol Jean Godby
Rex Wallace
Catherine Jolley

1st compilations, 1977–79
Deborah B. Schaffer
John W. Perkins
F. Christian Latta
Sheila Graves Geoghegan

Language Files

Materials for an Introduction to Language and Linguistics

Twelfth Edition

Editors

Hope C. Dawson
Michael Phelan

**Department of Linguistics
The Ohio State University**

The Ohio State University Press
Columbus

Library of Congress Cataloging-in-Publication Data
Names: Dawson, Hope, editor. | Phelan, Michael, 1980– editor.
Title: Language files : materials for an introduction to language and linguistics / editors, Hope C. Dawson,
    Michael Phelan (Department of Linguistics, The Ohio State University).
Description: Twelfth edition. | Columbus : The Ohio State University Press, [2016] | Includes bibliograph-
    ical references and index.
Identifiers: LCCN 2016015920 | ISBN 9780814252703 (pbk. ; alk. paper) | ISBN 0814252702 (pbk. ; alk.
    paper)
Subjects: LCSH: Linguistics.
Classification: LCC P121 .L3855 2016 | DDC 410—dc23
LC record available at https://lccn.loc.gov/2016015920

Cover design by Laurence J. Nozik
Text design by Juliet Williams
Type set in ITC Stone Serif

9 8 7 6 5 4 3 2 1

CONTENTS

....

Chapter 16: Language and Computers   623

Chapter 17: Practical Applications   651

Symbols Used Throughout the Book

The following symbols are used throughout this book; many are also conventionally used in the field of linguistics. For a comprehensive guide to the phonetic symbols used in the book, please refer to the last page.

italics	Indicates that the relevant text is a particular linguistic item being referred to (e.g., The word *platypus* is a noun).
bold sans serif	Indicates that the relevant text is an item in the glossary.
ALL CAPS	With regard to signed languages, indicates that the capitalized text is a sign. In phonetics, indicates that a word in an utterance receives a pitch accent.
'x'	Signifies that x is a meaning.
"x"	Signifies that x is an utterance.
<x>	Signifies that x is an orthographic representation.
/x/	Signifies that x is a phoneme or a phonological form.
[x]	In phonetics, signifies that x is a phone or allophone or a phonetic form. In syntax, indicates that x is a constituent.
XP	Denotes a phrase of type X.
*	In synchronic linguistics, designates an ungrammatical form. In historical linguistics, marks a reconstructed form.
#	In pragmatics, designates an infelicitous utterance. In phonology, marks a word boundary.
·	Marks a syllable boundary.
+	Marks a morpheme boundary.
Ø	In phonology, indicates an allophone or a phoneme that has been deleted. In semantics, indicates a set with no members.
→	In phonology, denotes 'becomes.' In syntax, denotes 'may consist of' (or, in more formal theories, 'dominates' or 'is the mother of').
>	In historical linguistics, denotes 'changes into.'
<	In historical linguistics, denotes 'derives from.'
C	Represents any consonant.
V	Represents any vowel.
N	Represents any nasal.
👍	Indicates that an answer to a particular question in a Practice file can be found in the appendix.
🔗	Indicates that a relevant URL can be found at http://linguistics.osu.edu/ research/pubs/lang-files/links.
🔊	Indicates that a relevant sound file can be found at http://linguistics.osu.edu/ research/pubs/lang-files/sounds.
🎥	Indicates that a relevant video file can be found at http://linguistics.osu.edu/ research/pubs/lang-files/videos.

PREFACE TO THE TWELFTH EDITION

An Introduction to *Language Files*

Since its inception almost forty years ago, *Language Files* has grown from a collection of materials designed simply as a supplement for undergraduate courses into a full-fledged introductory textbook. The scope of the text makes it suitable for use in a wide range of courses, while its unique organization into instructor-friendly files allows for tremendous flexibility in course design.

Language Files was originally the idea of Arnold Zwicky, who was among its first authors. Since the first edition, many editors have contributed to the development of *Language Files*; the current edition is the result of this cumulative effort.

Changes in the Current Edition

In this edition, we have revised, clarified, and updated many of the existing files and the accompanying exercises. We have also substantially updated the accompanying online resources, and we have added icons next to the text to inform the reader of particular places where additional resources are available on our website. The speaker icon 🔊, video icon 🎥, and link icon 🔗 indicate that sound files, video files, and relevant URLs can be found at

> http://linguistics.osu.edu/research/pubs/lang-files/sounds,
> http://linguistics.osu.edu/research/pubs/lang-files/videos, and
> http://linguistics.osu.edu/research/pubs/lang-files/links, respectively.

The cartoons accompanying each file have also been replaced with original artwork by Julia Porter Papke.

In addition to these global changes, the following chapters have undergone significant revision or changes.

Chapter 1: Introduction

- **File 1.1 Introducing the Study of Language** now includes a section providing helpful hints on how to use this book.
- **File 1.3 Other (Non-Essential) Aspects of Knowing a Language** has been renamed and revised to clarify the relationship of writing and prescriptive grammar to the study of language. The discussion of writing has also been updated to reflect the prevalence of electronic communication, and the discussion of prescriptive grammar has been revised to clarify the distinction between prescriptive and descriptive grammars, among other things.

Chapter 2: Phonetics

- **File 2.2 Articulation: English Consonants** has been revised in places to clarify the descriptions of consonant articulations and to better align some of the terminology with that of the IPA.
- **File 2.3 Articulation: English Vowels** has been revised in places to more explicitly discuss variation among speakers.
- **File 2.5 Suprasegmental Features** has an updated discussion of intonation.

Chapter 3: Phonology

- **File 3.1 Phonotactic Constraints and Foreign Accents** has been revised in places to clarify the roles of phonetic inventory and phonotactic constraints in foreign accents and the connection to phonology as a whole.
- **File 3.2 Phonemes and Allophones** has been substantially rewritten to clarify, among other things, the notions of predictability, distributions of sounds, and the distinction between allophones and phonemes.
- **File 3.3 Phonological Rules** has replaced the example of multiple rule application with one that does not involve an allomorphic distribution.

Chapter 4: Morphology

- Various minor updates have been made to clarify differences between inflection and derivation; to remove possessive -'s from the list of English inflectional suffixes; to better explain bound roots; and to acknowledge the lack of clear boundaries in morphological typology.

Chapter 5: Syntax

- **File 5.3 Syntactic Constituency** has replaced the coordination test with the pro-form substitution test.
- **File 5.4 Syntactic Categories** and **File 5.5 Constructing a Grammar** now include more overt discussion of the simplified nature of the system presented here and further issues for readers to consider.

Chapter 6: Semantics

- **File 6.2 Lexical Semantics: The Meanings of Words** clarifies types of antonyms.

Chapter 7: Pragmatics

- **File 7.2 Rules of Conversation** has been revised to clarify the role of Grice's maxims in conversation and particularly their relevance for the listener; the discussion of flouting and violating maxims has also been revised to show the important difference between the two.
- **File 7.4 Speech Acts** has been revised to clarify the nature of speech acts, performative speech acts, and the distinction between sentence types and speech acts.

Chapter 8: Language Acquisition

- **Files 8.2 and 8.3 First-Language Acquisition: The Acquisition of Speech Sounds and Phonology** and **The Acquisition of Morphology, Syntax, and Word Meaning** have updated tables providing an overview of the development of child language abilities from birth to four years old.

Chapter 9: Psycholinguistics

- This chapter has been substantially updated, expanded, and revised to reflect recent research and updated theories of language processing.
- **File 9.1 Language and the Brain** has been updated to give a more detailed view of the brain regions involved in language processing and the flow of information between these regions.
- **File 9.2 Language Disorders** has been expanded to include information on specific language impairment, Williams syndrome, and their relevance to theories of language acquisition.
- **File 9.3 Speech Production** now includes discussion of factors affecting speech production and the use of speech errors in psycholinguistics.
- **File 9.4 Speech Perception** has been revised and expanded to include discussion of factors affecting speech perception.
- **File 9.5 Lexical Access** is a new file replacing the previous 9.5. This file is reorganized around the idea of lexical access and includes discussion of neural network models.
- **File 9.6 Sentence Processing** has been revised to include constraint-based models of sentence processing.
- **File 9.7 Experimental Methods in Psycholinguistics** has been updated and expanded with several more methodologies and includes new images of these methods and the data obtained from them.

Chapter 10: Language Variation

- **File 10.3 Factors Influencing Variation: Regional and Geographic Factors** now clarifies characteristics of the Mid-Atlantic dialect that are different from the rest of the Midland dialect.

Chapter 11: Language and Culture

- **File 11.4 Politeness** now clarifies the relationship between different politeness strategies and face-threatening acts.

Chapter 16: Language and Computers

- This chapter has had minor updates to reflect more recent technological developments.

Further Resources for Using *Language Files*

The *Language Files* home page can be found at

http://linguistics.osu.edu/research/publications/languagefiles/

This home page includes links to the pages hosting sound files, video files, and relevant URLs, which can be found at

http://linguistics.osu.edu/research/pubs/lang-files/sounds,
http://linguistics.osu.edu/research/pubs/lang-files/videos, and
http://linguistics.osu.edu/research/pubs/lang-files/links, respectively.

All of these pages are organized by chapter and topic.

A password for instructors to access the instructor's guide and answer key can be obtained at

https://ohiostatepress.org/

by locating the web page for the 12th edition of *Language Files* and filling out the online form provided there.

In order to facilitate the receipt of feedback from users of *Language Files,* we also provide an email address,

files@ling.ohio-state.edu

to which any suggestions, questions, or requests for clarification concerning this edition may be directed.

The home page for the Department of Linguistics at The Ohio State University can be found at

http://linguistics.osu.edu/.

Contributors to the 12th Edition

Many people have contributed to this edition, including students and faculty of the Department of Linguistics at The Ohio State University and colleagues at other institutions.

We are particularly appreciative of Kiwako Ito and Shari Speer (Department of Linguistics, The Ohio State University) for their contributions to the revised Psycholinguistics chapter.

We would additionally like to thank the following individuals for their contributions of data and examples and for their advice regarding various aspects of the book: Lifeng Jin, Brian Joseph, Yusuke Kubota, Julia McGory, Vedrana Mihalicek, Julia Porter Papke, Judith Tonhauser, Kodi Weatherholtz, Chris Worth, and Murat Yasavul (Department of Linguistics, The Ohio State University), Bill Vicars (Department of ASL and ASL University, Sacramento State College: www.Lifeprint.com), and various people who have emailed us with errata and suggestions over the years.

We are also grateful to our department chair and the supervisor for this edition, Shari Speer, who has provided insight and support throughout the entire process of preparing the book.

Finally, we would like to thank the people at The Ohio State University Press, especially Tara Cyphers, Tony Sanfilippo, and Juliet Williams, for their care and attention in this project. We appreciate their advice, patience, flexibility, and cooperation throughout the production of this edition.

Hope C. Dawson
Michael Phelan

Department of Linguistics
The Ohio State University

ACKNOWLEDGMENTS

The editors and publisher are grateful to the following sources.

We are grateful to Julia Porter Papke for providing cartoons for the first page of each chapter, along with figure (1) in File 1.2 and figure (3) in File 6.2. All © 2015 by Julia Porter Papke.

File 1.5
Figure (3) © 2006, William Vicars, www.Lifeprint.com. Used with permission.

File 2.2
Figure (1) from *Speech physiology, speech perception, and acoustic phonetics,* by Philip Lieberman and Sheila E. Blumstein. © 1988, Cambridge University Press. Used with permission.

File 2.7
Figures (2), (3), (4), (6), (7), and (9) © 2006, William Vicars, www.Lifeprint.com. Used with or adapted by permission.

File 2.8
Images of ASL in Exercises 36 and 37 © 2006, William Vicars, www.Lifeprint.com. Used with permission.

File 3.1
Figures (4)–(6) © 2006, William Vicars, www.Lifeprint.com. Used with permission.

File 3.3
Figure (12) © 2006, William Vicars, www.Lifeprint.com. Used with or adapted by permission.

File 3.6
Images of ASL in Exercise 20 © 2006, William Vicars, www.Lifeprint.com. Used with permission.
Exercises 30 (Totonac), 31 (Tojolabal), and 35 (Farsi) republished with permission of Cengage Learning SO, from *Workbook in descriptive linguistics,* by Henry A. Gleason, Jr., © 1955; permission conveyed through Copyright Clearance Center, Inc.
Exercise 37 (Greek) adapted from *Workbook in linguistic concepts,* by Bruce L. Pearson. © 1977, McGraw-Hill Education Material. Reproduced with permission.

File 4.2
Figures (2), (3), and (4) © 2006, William Vicars, www.Lifeprint.com. Adapted by permission.

File 4.6

Exercises 8 (Bontoc), 38 (Swahili), and 42 (Hanunoo) republished with permission of Cengage Learning SO, from *Workbook in descriptive linguistics,* by Henry A. Gleason, Jr., © 1955; permission conveyed through Copyright Clearance Center, Inc.

Images of ASL in Exercises 13 and 33 © 2006, William Vicars, www.Lifeprint.com. Used with or adapted by permission.

Exercises 29 (Isthmus Zapotec), 40 (Zoque), and 44 (Popoluca) from *Morphology: The descriptive analysis of words,* 2nd edn., by Eugene A. Nida. © 1949, University of Michigan Press.

Exercise 35 (Cebuano) adapted from *Workbook in linguistic concepts,* by Bruce L. Pearson. © 1977, McGraw-Hill Education Material. Reproduced with permission.

File 8.1

List in (1) adapted from Lenneberg's characteristics in *The articulate mammal: An introduction to psycholinguistics,* by Jean Aitchison, p. 60. Routledge Classics Edition, 2011. © 1976, Jean Aitchison. Reproduced with permission of Taylor & Francis Group.

Examples (5) and (6) reproduced with permission of Thomas Wadsworth, from *Psycholinguistics,* by Jean Berko Gleason and Nan Bernstein Ratner, 2nd edn., © 1998; permission conveyed through Copyright Clearance Center, Inc.

File 8.4

Example (2) from "The development of conversation between mothers and babies," by Catherine E. Snow. *Journal of Child Language* 4.1–22. © 1977, Cambridge University Press. Used with permission.

File 8.5

Example (1) from *Language acquisition of a bilingual child: A sociolinguistic perspective (to age 10),* by Alvino E. Fantini. © 1985, Channel View Publications Ltd./Multilingual Matters. Used with permission.

File 8.6

Data in Exercise 3 republished with permission of Blackwell Publishing, Incorporated, from "Later lexical development and word formation," by Eve V. Clark. *The handbook of child language,* ed. by Paul Fletcher and Brian MacWhinney, © 1995; permission conveyed through Copyright Clearance Center, Inc.

Data in Exercise 4 from "The acquisition of language in infant and child," by Martin D. S. Braine. *The learning of language,* ed. by Carroll E. Reed. © 1971, National Council of Teachers of English. Used with permission.

Data in Exercises 9 and 12d from *An introduction to language and linguistics,* by Ralph Fasold and Jeffrey Connor-Linton. © 2006, Cambridge University Press. Used with permission.

Data in Exercises 12e, f and 16a from *The study of language,* by George Yule, 2nd edn. © 1996, Cambridge University Press. Used with permission.

Data in Exercise 16b from *The lexicon in acquisition,* by Eve V. Clark. © 1993, Cambridge University Press. Used with permission.

Data in Exercise 17 from "The development of conversation between mothers and babies," by Catherine E. Snow. *Journal of Child Language* 4.1–22. © 1977, Cambridge University Press. Used with permission.

File 9.1

Figure (1) reprinted from *Cognition,* Vol. 92, Gregory Hickok and David Poeppel, "Dorsal and ventral streams: A framework for understanding aspects of the functional anatomy of language," pp. 67–99, © 2004, with permission from Elsevier.

Figure (2) from "Dynamic processing in the human language system: Synergy between the arcuate fascicle and extreme capsule," by Tyler Rolheiser, Emmanuel A. Stamatakis, and Lorraine K. Tyler. *The Journal of Neuroscience* 31(47).16949–57. © 2011, republished with permission of the Society for Neuroscience.

File 9.2

Example (2) republished from Howard Poizner, Edward Klima, and Ursula Bellugi, *What the hands reveal about the brain,* p. 120, © 1987 Massachusetts Institute of Technology, by permission of the MIT Press.

Examples (4), (5), and (6) from "Neuropsychological studies of linguistic and affective facial expressions in deaf signers," by David P. Corina, Ursula Bellugi, and Judy Reilly. *Language and Speech* 42(2–3).307–31, © 1999 by SAGE Publications. Reprinted by permission of SAGE Publications, Ltd.; permission conveyed through Copyright Clearance Center, Inc.

File 9.7

Figure (1) adapted from "Functional MRI in the investigation of blast-related traumatic brain injury," by John Graner, Terrence R. Oakes, Louis M. French, and Gerard Riedy. *Frontiers in Neurology* 4:16. © 2013 by the authors. Creative Commons Attribution 3.0 Unported License.

Figure (2) adapted from image provided by Aaron G. Filler, MD, PhD, via Wikicommons (https://commons.wikimedia.org/wiki/File:DTI_Brain_Tractographic_Image_Set.jpg). Creative Commons Attribution—Share Alike 3.0 Unported License.

File 9.8

Data in Exercise 8b from "Linguistics and agrammatism," by Sergey Avrutin. *GLOT International* 5.87–97. © 2001, Blackwell Publishers Ltd. Reprinted with permission of John Wiley & Sons, Inc.

Data in Exercises 8c and 8d are excerpts from *The shattered mind,* by Howard Gardner, © 1974 by Howard Gardner. Used by permission of Alfred A. Knopf, an imprint of the Knopf Doubleday Publishing Group, a division of Penguin Random House LLC. All rights reserved.

File 10.1

Sections adapted from "Styles," by Ann D. Zwicky. *Styles and variables in English,* ed. by Timothy Shopen and Joseph M. Williams. © 1981, Winthrop Publishers (Prentice-Hall).

File 10.2

Figure (1) © 2006, William Vicars, www.Lifeprint.com. Used with permission.

File 10.3

Figure (1) from *Signs across America,* by Edgar H. Shroyer and Susan P. Shroyer, pp. 96, 97. © 1984, Gallaudet University Press. Reproduced with permission.

Figure (2) adapted from *American regional dialects,* by Craig M. Carver. © 1987, University of Michigan Press. Figure originally from *A word geography of the eastern United States,* by Hans Kurath, Fig. 5a. © 1949, University of Michigan Press.

File 10.6

Images of ASL in Exercise 13 from *Signs across America,* by Edgar H. Shroyer and Susan P. Shroyer, p. 3. © 1984, Gallaudet University Press. Reproduced with permission.

File 11.1

Example (7) adapted from "Strategies of status manipulation in the Wolof greeting," by Judith Irvine. *Explorations in the ethnography of speaking,* ed. by Richard Bauman and Joel Sherzer, p. 171. © 1974, Cambridge University Press. Used with permission.
Figure (8) by Jake Berman, via Wikicommons (https://en.wikipedia.org/wiki/File:NYC_subway-4D.svg). Creative Commons Attribution—Share Alike 3.0 Unported License.

File 12.3

Example (1) adapted from *Some day been dey: West African Pidgin folktales,* by Loreto Todd. © 1979, Routledge and Kegan Paul.

File 12.4

Table (1) from "Creole languages," by Derek Bickerton, pp. 120–21. *Scientific American* 249(1).116–22. Reproduced with permission. © 1983, Scientific American, a division of Nature America, Inc. All rights reserved.

File 12.5

Examples (1) and (2) from "Intersections between social motivations and structural processing in code-switching," by Carol Myers-Scotton. *Papers for the Workshop on Constraints, Conditions, and Models: London, 27–29 September 1990.* © 1991, European Science Foundation. Reproduced with permission.

File 12.7

Example (3) from"The role of English in Pennsylvania German development: Best supporting actress?," by Janet M. Fuller. *American Speech* 74(1).38–55. © 1999, the American Dialect Society. Republished by permission of the copyrightholder, and the present publisher, Duke University Press. www.dukeupress.edu.
Examples (4) and (6) from "Language contact phenomena in Pennsylvania German: A literature review," by Steven Hartman Keiser. © 1999, unpublished manuscript, Columbus, OH.
Example (5) from "Linguistic structure and sociolinguistic identity in Pennsylvania German society," by Mark Louden. *Language and lives: Essays in honor of Werner Enninger,* ed. by James R. Dow and Michèle Wolff, 79–91. © 1997, Peter Lang. Reproduced with permission.

File 12.8

Data in Exercise 18 adapted from "On the pidgin status of Russenorsk," by Ernst Håkon Jahr. *Language contact in the Arctic: Northern pidgins and contact languages,* ed. by Ernst Håkon Jahr and Ingvild Broch, 107–22. © 1996, Mouton de Gruyter. And from "Russenorsk: A new look at the Russo-Norwegian pidgin in northern Norway", by Ingvild Broch and Ernst Håkon Jahr. *Scandinavian language contacts,* ed. by P. Sture Ureland and Iain Clarkson, 21–65. © 1984, Cambridge University Press.
Data in Exercise 19 from *The present state of Australia,* 2nd edn., by Robert Dawson. 1831, Smith, Elder and Co.
Data in Exercise 24 from "Negotiations of language choice in Montreal," by Monica S. Heller. *Language and social identity,* ed. by John J. Gumperz, 108–18. © 1982, Cambridge University Press. Used with permission.

Data in Exercise 25 adapted from "The pragmatics of code-switching: A sequential approach," by Peter Auer. *One speaker, two languages: Cross-disciplinary perspectives on code-switching,* ed. by Lesley Milroy and Pieter Muysken, 115–35. © 1995, Cambridge University Press. Used with permission.

File 13.8

Data in Exercise 30 republished with permission of Cengage Learning SO from *Problems in the origins and development of the English language,* by John Algeo, 3rd edn. New York: Harcourt, Brace, and World, © 1982, pp. 245–46. Permission conveyed through Copyright Clearance Center, Inc.

Data in Exercise 38 (Proto-Western Turkic) adapted from *Introductory workbook in historical phonology,* 5th edn., by Frederick Columbus. © 1974, Slavica Publishers. Used with permission.

File 14.2

Figure (4) reprinted by permission from Macmillan Publishers Ltd.: *Nature,* "Neuroperception: Facial expressions linked to monkey calls," by Asif A. Ghazanfar and Nikos K. Logothetis, Vol. 423, pp. 937–38. © 2003, Nature Publishing Group.

Parts of Sections 14.2.2 adapted from "The birds and the bees," *An introduction to language,* 2nd edn., by Victoria Fromkin and Robert Rodman, 41–45. © 1978, Holt, Rinehart and Winston.

File 14.3

Example (1) reproduced with kind permission from Springer Science+Business Media: *Animal Learning & Behavior,* "Cognition in the African Grey parrot: Preliminary evidence for auditory/vocal comprehension of the class concept," Vol. 11, 1983, page 181, by Irene M. Pepperberg, Table 1.

Last Page

IPA Chart from http://www.internationalphoneticassociation.org/content/ipa-chart. Creative Commons Attribution—Share Alike 3.0 Unported License. © 2015, International Phonetic Association.

CHAPTER

1

....

Introduction

FILE 1.0

....

What Is Language?

Language touches every part of our lives: it gives words to our thoughts, voice to our ideas, and expression to our feelings. It is a rich and varied human ability—one that we can use effortlessly, that children seem to acquire automatically, and that linguists have found to be complex yet systematic and describable. In this book, language will be the object of our study.

Contents

....

Introducing the Study of Language

1.1.1 Why Study Language?

Language makes us uniquely human. While many species have the capacity to communicate using sounds and gestures, and a few can even acquire certain aspects of human language, no other species is comparable to humans with respect to the creativity and complexity of the systems that humans use to express thoughts and to communicate. We can manipulate elements in our language to express complex thoughts and ideas, and we can understand words and sentences that we have never spoken or heard. This capacity is shared by hearing people and deaf people, and it emerges very early in the development of children, who acquire adult linguistic competence in an astonishingly short period of time. It is the human language faculty that makes this possible. Used as a probe into the human mind, language provides us with a unique window through which we can investigate a fundamental aspect of what it is to be human.

Language also reflects one's self-identity and is indispensable for social interactions. We perform different roles at different times in different situations in society. Consciously or subconsciously, we speak differently depending on where we come from, whom we talk to, where the conversation is carried out, what purposes we have, etc. For example, southerners in America tend to speak with an accent different from, say, that of native New Yorkers; a conversation between two buddies likely would not be the same as a conversation between business associates; two lawyers would speak differently in a café than they would in a courtroom; and a middle-aged person might imitate younger speakers in order to sound younger. All languages vary, and they reflect a speaker's individual identity as well as social and cultural aspects of a society.

Not only does studying language reveal something interesting about human society, but there are also many practical applications of the study of language that can have a significant effect on people's everyday lives. For example, studying languages allows us to develop better teaching tools for language instruction, design computers that can interact with humans using language, and more effectively treat people with speech and language disorders.

1.1.2 Some Surprising but True Things about Language

You have been speaking one or more languages for most of your life, and therefore you may think that you know most of what there is to know about language. However, you will likely find some of the following facts about language surprising.

(1) Grammar is actually a much more complex phenomenon than anything that could ever be taught in school, but nevertheless every human being masters the grammar of some language.

(2) There are languages that don't have words for *right* and *left* but use words for cardinal directions (like *north* and *west*) instead (see Chapter 11).

(3) Some aspects of language appear to be innate (see Chapter 8).

(4) There are more than 7,000 languages spoken in the world, but 90% of the population speaks only 10% of them.

(5) Some languages, such as Turkish, have special verb forms used for gossip and hearsay.

(6) Many of the sentences that you hear and utter are novel; they have never been uttered before.

(7) Some languages structure sentences by putting the object first and the subject last (see Chapter 5).

(8) In some communities, such as the Al-Sayyid Bedouin tribe, all or most members of the community can use a signed language (see File 1.5).

(9) There is nothing inherent about most words that gives them their meaning; any group of speech sounds could have any meaning.

(10) There are specific structures in your brain that process language (see Chapter 9).

(11) The language you speak affects whether or not you distinguish between certain sounds.

(12) Rules like "don't split infinitives" were propagated by people in the eighteenth century who believed that English should be more like Latin.

(13) The same words in the same order don't always mean the same thing.

(14) No language is more or less logical than any other.

1.1.3   Some Common Misconceptions about Language

In addition to not knowing some of the facts in the list above, you may also have ideas about language that are not true. The following is a list of common misconceptions. It's understandable that people might have come to hold some of these beliefs, because they are often propagated throughout societies (and a few of them even have an element of truth to them); however, the scientific investigation of language has revealed them to be false.

(1) People who say *Nobody ain't done nothin'* aren't thinking logically.

(2) Swearing degrades a language.

(3) Many animals have languages that are much like human languages (see Chapter 14).

(4) Writing is more perfect than speech.

(5) The more time parents spend teaching their children a language, the better their children will speak (see Chapter 8).

(6) You can almost always recognize someone's background by the way he talks (see Chapter 10).

(7) The rules in grammar textbooks are guidelines for correct language use and should be followed whenever possible.

(8) Women tend to talk more than men (see Chapter 10).

(9) There are "primitive" languages that cannot express complex ideas effectively.

(10) People from the East Coast talk nasally (see Chapter 10).

(11) Some people can pick up a language in a couple of weeks (see Chapter 8).

(12) It's easier to learn Chinese if your ancestry is Chinese.

(13) Native Americans all speak dialects of the same language.

(14) Every language has a way to mark verbs for the past tense (see Chapter 4).

(15) Correct spelling preserves a language.

1.1.4   Underlying Themes of Linguistic Study

These two lists illustrate that there is much more to know about language than is obvious to those who use it. Human language is an enormously complex phenomenon. The task of a **linguist** is to tease apart the patterns of various aspects of human language in order to discover how language works.

Below is a list of some very general principles of human language that will be explained and illustrated throughout this book. We present them here not because we expect you to see the full significance of each of these ideas all at once, but rather because they are underlying themes in the study of linguistics and will come up repeatedly throughout the book. During your studies, you may find it useful to refer to this list to see how these ideas interact with the topic that you are currently studying.

(1) Language is systematic in spite of its enormous complexity, and it can therefore be studied scientifically.
(2) Not only is language systematic, but it is systematic on many levels, from the system of individual sounds to the organization of entire discourses.
(3) These systematic rules allow us to express an infinite number of ideas in an infinite number of ways.
(4) Language varies systematically from person to person, region to region, and situation to situation. There is variation at every level of structure.
(5) Languages are diverse, often astonishingly so.
(6) Despite this diversity, there are a great many universal properties of languages. That is, there are characteristics shared by all languages as well as characteristics that no language has.
(7) Many properties of language are arbitrary, in the sense that they cannot be predicted from other properties or from general principles.
(8) Although a great many complex rules govern our speech, we are no more aware of them than we are of the principles that govern walking or picking up an object.
(9) Children acquire language without being taught; language acquisition is (at least partly) innate.
(10) All languages change over time, whether speakers desire change or not.

This book will introduce you to some of the properties of language and basic principles of the study of linguistics. We hope to lead you to examine your own beliefs and attitudes about language, to make you more aware of the diversity of language systems as well as their fundamental similarities, and to introduce you to some of the applications of linguistic investigation. The study of language and linguistics will not disappoint the challenge seekers, the scientific investigators, or those who are simply inquisitive.

1.1.5   How to Use This Book

Here are some helpful hints on how to use this book. Note that a guide to the general symbols used throughout the book is provided immediately after the table of contents on p. ix, and the full chart of the International Phonetic Alphabet (IPA) is given at the end of the book on p. 743, with the two preceding pages giving the IPA for Standard American English along with example words for each sound.

This book is structured as modularly as possible so that the various chapters and files can be used in different orders to best fit the needs of any individual class. Note the following about each chapter's structure: the first file is a very basic introduction to the topic of the chapter and includes an expanded table of contents. The last file in each chapter contains various practice materials for use by students and instructors: exercises, discussion questions, activities, and further readings are given, with a section of such practice materials devoted to each individual file within the chapter. A few example exercises, marked with a thumbs-up icon ⊙, have answers provided in the Appendix found at the back of the book.

Three other icons are used in the book. The speaker icon 🔊, video icon ▣, and link icon 🔗 indicate that sound files, video files, and relevant URLs can be found at http://linguistics.osu.edu/research/pubs/lang-files/sounds, http://linguistics.osu.edu/research/pubs/lang-files/videos, and http://linguistics.osu.edu/research/pubs/lang-files/links, respectively. All icons are direct links in the electronic versions of this book. Definitions for all terms given in boldface throughout the book are given in the Glossary and also are directly linked in the electronic versions. A Selected Bibliography, Language Index, and Subject Index are also found at the back of the book.

FILE **1.2**

What You Know When You Know a Language

1.2.1 Linguistic Competence and Linguistic Performance

As a speaker of English (or any other language that you may be a speaker of), you know a great deal about your language. Suppose, however, that someone were to ask you to put all of that knowledge into a textbook that would be used to teach English to others. You would soon find that although you know perfectly well how to speak English, you are not consciously aware of most of that knowledge.

If you think about it, we are really unaware of many of the things we do every day. For example, most people know how to walk and do so without thinking about it. Most of us can describe walking as well: we pick up one foot and put it in front of the other. However, there are many nuances and individual motor tasks involved in walking that we don't ever think about and that only a very small set of people (kinesiologists, for example) understand: exactly how you shift your balance between steps, how speed affects your stride, and so on. You modulate these things all the time when you walk without thinking about them, and very few people know exactly how they do so. The same holds true for our knowledge of language: for the most part, it is hidden. Linguists are interested in this "hidden" knowledge, which they refer to as **linguistic competence.**

Not all of your knowledge about **language** is hidden, however. People reveal some of their knowledge through their linguistic **performance**—the way that they produce and comprehend language. You can think of linguistic competence as a person's unseen potential to speak a language, while linguistic performance is the observable realization of that potential: our performance is what we do with our linguistic competence. Put another way, your linguistic competence is stored in your mind, and your linguistic performance is revealed in your speech (though keep in mind that revealing it does not mean that we are conscious of how it works).

Consider again the case of walking. If you are able to walk, you have the ability to do so even when you are sitting down (and not actively using it). That ability is your walking competence. When you stand up and walk across the room, that's walking performance. Now, suppose that you stumble or trip on occasion. That doesn't mean that you aren't a competent walker: you still have your walking competence, but your performance was impaired. Maybe you just weren't paying attention to where you were going, or the ground was uneven, or it was dark and you couldn't see clearly, or perhaps there was nothing unusual at all but for some reason you simply lost your balance. In the same way, you may make **performance errors** when you use language, such as being unable to remember a word, mispronouncing something, or jumbling the words in a sentence. Sometimes there is an apparent reason: you may be tired or distracted, or you may be trying to produce a particularly difficult utterance. Other times, however, there is no apparent reason at all: you simply make a mistake. Nonetheless, you still have your linguistic competence.

Since competence can't be observed directly, linguists must use linguistic performance as a basis for making hypotheses and drawing conclusions about what linguistic competence must be like. However, in most cases they try to disregard imperfections in performance (the inevitable speech errors, incomplete utterances, and so on) and focus on consistent patterns in their study of linguistic competence.

1.2.2 The Speech Communication Chain

When you use language, you use it to communicate an idea from your mind to the mind of someone else. Of course, language is not the only way to do this; there are many types of communication systems, such as honking a horn on a car, drawing a picture, screaming wordlessly at the top of your lungs, or using semaphore flags. The key elements in any communication system (as outlined by Claude Shannon and Warren Weaver in 1949) are an information source, a transmitter, a signal, a receiver, and a destination. When we use language as our communication system, one person acts as the information source and the transmitter, sending a signal to another person, who acts as a receiver and the destination. In order to act either as the source and transmitter or as a receiver and destination, you must know a lot about your language. The diagram in (1) outlines the **communication chain** as it relates to language.

(1) The speech communication chain

This illustration shows the numerous steps that must be carried out in order for an idea to be communicated from one person to another. First, an idea of something to be communicated must be thought of; this is not necessarily a function of language per se, but it is certainly the first step in communicating any idea. Once the idea is there, you have to put the idea into words that have the meaning you want to communicate and that are expressed in a particular way. These steps form the backbone of much of traditional linguistic research. Note that these first four steps represent the "information source" in the communication system. Step 5 is the transmitter; in this step, the speaker actually gives physical expression to the idea of the message to be conveyed. Step 6 is the signal itself. Here, the sounds generated by the speaker travel through the air to the listener. The listener acts as the receiver in step 7, sensing the sound signal and sending it to her own brain. Step 8 in the diagram is particularly simplified, in that it really encompasses steps 2–4 in reverse. That is, to "decode" the signal that has been perceived and to interpret the signal as language, the listener must understand and break down the order of words (and parts of words) and what the words mean. Finally, step 9 represents the destination: the listener has received the communicated idea.

Note that in the diagram, the listener in fact receives exactly the same idea that the speaker tried to convey. This, as you have probably experienced, is an idealization: in real life, the listener doesn't always get the right message. All of these steps take place in a particular context that can either add to the ability of all participants to understand the communication or interfere with the success of the communication (interference in the chain is known as **noise**).

The diagram in (1) is rather simplified in terms of how it summarizes each step; the rest of this book will go into far more detail about how each part of this communication chain works with respect to language. However, the next section briefly explains each part, showing you what it is that you know when you know a language. As you read about each component, try to think about where it fits into the diagram of the speech communication chain.

1.2.3 What You Know When You Know a Language

One of the most basic things that you know when you know a language, assuming that you use spoken language, is speech sounds. (If you use a signed language, you know a great deal about speech gestures in an analogous way. For information about the difference between spoken and signed languages, refer to File 1.5.) First, you know which sounds are speech sounds and which sounds are not; if you hear a dog bark or a door slam, you will not confuse it with the sounds of language. You also know which speech sounds are sounds of your language as opposed to some other language. Not only do you hear and recognize these sounds, but you also know how to produce them, even though you may have never had to think about the mechanics of doing so. Suppose you had to explain the differences between the vowels in the words *bat, beat,* and *boot.* You have probably been producing these sounds for years without thinking twice about them, but clearly you do have competent knowledge of how to do so. All of this knowledge has to do with the area of language known as **phonetics** (discussed in Chapter 2).

You have more knowledge than this about the sounds of your language, though: you also know how these sounds work together as a system. For instance, you know which sequences of sounds are possible in different positions. In words like *pterodactyl* or *Ptolemy,* English speakers normally do not pronounce the /p/ because /pt/ is not a sound combination that can occur at the beginning of English words. There is nothing inherently difficult about the sequence; it occurs in the middle of many English words such as *captive.* And in other languages, such as Greek, /pt/ appears at the beginning of words. This language-specific knowledge about the distribution of speech sounds is part of your **phonology** (discussed in Chapter 3). Your knowledge of phonology allows you to identify that *spaff* and *blig* could be possible words of English but that *fsap* and *libg* could not. Additionally, phonology allows you to recognize sounds and words spoken by different speakers, even though most people do not pronounce them in exactly the same way.

For the most part, speech consists of a continuous stream of sound; there are few if any pauses between words. Speakers of a language, however, have little trouble breaking this stream of sound down into words. For example, an English speaker can easily analyze the sequence in (2a) as containing the individual words in (2b); this is what we must do all the time when we hear speech.

(2) a. thedogisplayinginthebackyard
    b. the dog is playing in the back yard

You also know how to break individual words down into smaller parts that have a particular meaning or function (how many parts are there in the word *unbelievability*?), and how to create words by combining these smaller parts. That is, you can both produce and comprehend newly composed words that you haven't heard before, for example, *ungiraffelike*. You also know which combinations are words and which ones aren't: *baker* is a word, but **erbake* is not. *Nicely* is a word, but **bookly* is not. (The * is used to mark that something is ungrammatical—in this case, it indicates that these are not possible words of English.) Your knowledge of these and other facts about word formation comprises your knowledge of **morphology** (discussed in Chapter 4).

You also know a great deal about your language's **syntax** (discussed in Chapter 5): how words combine to form phrases and sentences. This fact is evidenced by your ability to construct and use sentences that you have never heard before, and to recognize when a sentence is well-formed.

(3) a. I will pick the package up at eight o'clock.
    b. At eight o'clock, I will pick up the package.
    c. *Package up pick at o'clock will the eight I.
    d. *I will picks the package up at eight o'clock.

In (3) above, sentences (a) and (b) are both **grammatical**, even though they have different word orders. On the other hand, (c) and (d) are **ungrammatical**: (c) is nonsense, and (d) violates a rule of verb agreement. It's possible that you have thought at some point about the fact that verbs must agree with their subjects and that random orderings of words don't make sentences. But what about the sentences in (4)?

(4) a. I have a cup of pebbles.
    b. *I have a cup of pebble.
    c. *I have a cup of gravels.
    d. I have a cup of gravel.

Your internal knowledge of English syntax gives you the information necessary to know that (4a) and (4d) are grammatical while (4b) and (4c) are not, although it is likely (especially if you are a native speaker of English) that you have never thought explicitly about this fact.

Another part of your linguistic competence has to do with your ability to determine the meaning of sentences. When you interpret meanings, you are appealing to your knowledge of **semantics** (discussed in Chapter 6). When you hear a word, such as *platypus* or *green* or *dawdle,* you have some idea of a meaning that goes with that word. You know when two words mean the same thing—e.g., *sofa* and *couch*—and when one word has two (or more) meanings—e.g., *duck.* You also know how words combine together to form larger meanings.

(5) a. The green duck dawdled around the cactus.
 b. The duck dawdled around the green cactus.

(6) a. The platypus ducked under the sofa.
 b. The sofa ducked under the platypus.

Each of the two sentences in (5) contains the same words, yet they have different meanings. The same is true of the pair of sentences in (6), but here the second seems semantically anomalous, because part of your knowledge of English semantics includes the fact that a sofa is not the sort of thing that is able to duck.

Your understanding of the meaning of sentences also involves an understanding of how the context of those utterances influences their meaning. Suppose that, while you are sitting in class, your instructor says to you, "Can you close the door?" Taken quite literally, you have been asked a yes-no question about your door-closing abilities, but you would probably not even think of interpreting the question in that way; instead, you would understand it as a request to close the door. Your ability to use context in order to interpret an utterance's meaning is part of your knowledge of **pragmatics** (discussed in Chapter 7). Your knowledge of pragmatics also helps you figure out which utterances are appropriate or inappropriate in any given situation.

Each of these elements of language—phonetics, phonology, morphology, syntax, semantics, and pragmatics—is part of your linguistic competence and is therefore an integral part of the way that you communicate linguistically. These are the things that you know when you say that you know a language.

1.2.4 How Your Linguistic Competence Is Stored

Now that we have considered some of the kinds of knowledge involved in knowing a language, it is appropriate to give some thought to the question of **where** this knowledge is. This is a difficult question to answer, because although people produce language all the time, it isn't tangible. If I make a hammer, then afterwards I can pick it up and show it to you. I cannot, on the other hand, show you a sentence that I have created. That sentence exists only in my mind (and, after I have uttered it, it exists in your mind as well). Although I may write it down, the string of letters that appears on the page is only a visual representation of the sentence: it isn't the sentence itself (a concept that will be further elaborated on in File 1.3). So where does language exist? It exists only in the minds of its speakers. In some ways, you can think of your linguistic competence not only as your ability to use language but also as being language itself!

There are two parts of this knowledge. The first part is called the **lexicon**, which consists of the collection of all the words that you know: what functions they serve, what they refer to, how they are pronounced, and how they are related to other words.

The second part of your knowledge is made up of all the **rules** you know about your language, which are stored in the form of a **mental grammar**. A word of caution may be in order here: The words *grammar* and *rule* mean something rather different to a linguist than they do to most people in casual conversation (for more on the common understanding of the term *grammar,* see File 1.3). For a linguist, a **grammar** is a language system. It is the set of all the elements and rules (about phonetics, phonology, morphology, syntax, and semantics) that make up a language. A rule, then, is just a statement of some pattern that occurs in language. The rules in your mental grammar help you to produce well-formed utterances and to interpret the utterances of others.

The rules in your mental grammar are not necessarily the sorts of rules that are written down or taught anywhere; rather, they are the rules in your head that tell you how to combine sounds and words to create well-formed utterances. In the first years of their lives, children work very hard to acquire these rules by paying attention to the language being used around them. All humans (excepting those with the most severe cases of mental retardation or significant brain damage) are capable of acquiring the language that they are exposed to as children, and they will do so naturally, without being taught. In Chapter 8, we will discuss **language acquisition** and how children go about constructing mental grammars of their native languages.

Although everyone becomes a fully competent speaker of their native language, with a complete mental grammar that allows them to communicate effectively with other people in their speech community, the details of mental grammars do vary among speakers. Variation occurs among speakers from different language and dialect groups and even among speakers of the same dialect. No two speakers have exactly the same mental grammar, and therefore no two speakers will find exactly the same set of sentences well-formed. However, our mental grammars are similar enough that we disagree very seldom and are able to understand one another most of the time. More information about **language variation** can be found in Chapter 10.

In sum, your linguistic competence is stored in a lexicon and a mental grammar, which you access in order to both produce and comprehend utterances. Though you may not be actively aware of all of the linguistic knowledge that you have stored away, you nonetheless use it all the time; it forms the backbone of the communication chain.

1.2.5   Uncovering and Describing What You Know

One of the jobs of linguists is to figure out all of the hidden knowledge that speakers have stored in their mental grammars: to objectively describe speakers' performance of language and, from their performance, to deduce the rules that form the speakers' competence. This process is analogous to a situation in which you see nurses, doctors, ambulances, and people in wheelchairs coming from a building you are unfamiliar with, and you hypothesize that the building is a hospital. You use the evidence you can see in order to draw conclusions about the internal structure of what you cannot see.

In order to discover the internal structure of language—that is, the lexicon and the mental rules—linguists must first describe language as it is used. This involves listening to spoken language, finding generalizations, and then making descriptive statements about what has been observed. For example, a linguist describing English might make the observations in (7).

(7) Examples of descriptive observations about English
    a. The vowel sound in the word *suit* is produced with rounded lips.
    b. The sequence of sounds [bɪt] is a possible word in English.
    c. The plural of many nouns is the same as the singular but with an -*s* at the end.
    d. Adjectives come before the nouns they describe: *green shirt*, not *shirt green*.
    e. The words *sofa* and *couch* mean roughly the same thing.

These generalizations and others like them describe what English speakers do. By analyzing such collections of generalizations, known as **descriptive grammars**, linguists can begin to determine what the mental grammar must consist of. That is, a mental grammar contains all of the rules that an individual speaker uses to produce and comprehend utterances, while a descriptive grammar contains the rules that someone has deduced based on observing speakers' linguistic performance.

FILE 1.3

....

Other (Non-Essential) Aspects of Knowing a Language

1.3.1 What Language Inherently Is and Is Not

In File 1.2, we talked about what it means to know a language: anyone who knows a language has a vast amount of mental knowledge, or competence, about how to use this language to communicate ideas. But there are a number of non-essential aspects of language common in societies that are often so closely linked with language use that they sometimes cloud the issue of what it means to say that someone knows a language.

Two of those aspects—writing and prescriptive grammar—are discussed in this file. Our goal is to help you see that, while these topics are both interesting and related to knowledge of language, they are not a fundamental or necessary part of "what you know" when you know a language, and thus are not central to the study of linguistics. For this reason they are not a primary focus of this book (though see Chapter 15 for a discussion of writing systems), and it will be useful for you as readers and students to regularly remind yourself of this, since writing and prescriptive rules often have a prominent role in other classes about language(s).

1.3.2 Writing Is Secondary to Speech (And Not Necessary for Knowledge of a Language)

Speaking and signing, on the one hand, and writing, on the other, are two different forms of communication that serve different functions, though both are related to language. Neither is superior or inferior to the other—writing is not a more perfect way of communicating through language. Language, as we saw in File 1.2, consists of the knowledge in speakers' minds; this knowledge is made up of a lexicon and a mental grammar. In order to reveal their knowledge of language, speakers must perform it in some way. While speech and writing are both expressions of linguistic competence, speech is a more immediate (and typically the primary) manifestation of language. One of the basic assumptions of modern linguistics (as opposed to linguistics before the beginning of the twentieth century), therefore, is that speech—whether spoken orally or signed manually (see File 1.5)—is the primary object of linguistic study.

Writing is the representation of language in a physical medium different from sound. Both spoken language and writing encode thought into forms that allow those thoughts to be communicated to others. At some level, one could think of speech as an immediately physically transmittable form, while writing is a physically preservable form. Modern technology has blurred this distinction, however, since one can (almost) immediately transmit writing (e.g., text messaging, email, Internet chat), and speech can easily be physically preserved through audio- and video-recording. But writing adds another step to the process of communication: a person thinks of an idea, expresses it using mental grammar, and then has to transfer it to written form. All units of writing, whether letters or characters, are based on units of speech, e.g., words, morphemes, syllables, or sounds (more on writing systems will be discussed in Chapter 15): so, for a thought to be written, it must first be processed by the speech system and then put into writing. This last step no longer necessarily requires a person (the speaker or the transcriber) to put the ideas into writing—many people have phones and computers that can automatically transcribe speech (see Chapter 16)—but the extra step is still there, and it is usually necessary to check the results of such programs for errors and to make corrections, as we all know.

Because linguists' goal is to understand mental language competence using performed language, it makes sense to get as close to the original as possible. So when linguists study language, they typically take the spoken language as their best source of data and their object of description (except in instances of languages like Latin, for which there are no longer any native speakers and the written form **is** thus the closest they can come; see also File 16.5 on corpus linguistics). Our primary concern throughout this book is therefore with spoken language. While ideally we would prefer to give all of our examples in audio form to make this point clearer, for practical reasons we instead use conventional written transcriptions of the audio form, with the understanding that it is always the spoken form that is intended (the conventions used for specifically phonetic transcription are given in Chapter 2; other transcriptions where the phonetic details are not at issue follow standard writing or transliteration conventions for the languages involved). But do pay special attention to the icons that appear throughout the text, which often indicate that recordings of these examples are available (see File 1.1.5).

There are several additional reasons why speech is considered a more basic form of language than writing. The most important ones are the following:

a. Writing must be taught, whereas spoken language is acquired naturally. All children (except children with serious learning disabilities) naturally learn to speak the language of the community in which they are brought up. They acquire the basics of their native language before they enter school, and even if they never attend school, they become fully competent speakers. Spoken languages can even develop spontaneously in societies where a full language does not exist (see File 8.1). All writing systems must be taught explicitly.

b. Writing does not exist everywhere that spoken language does. This may seem hard to imagine in our highly literate society. But the fact is that there are still many communities in the world where a written form of language is not used. According to SIL International, among the approximately 7,100 languages in the world today, an estimated 3,535 languages (or 50%) are unwritten (*Ethnologue*, Lewis et al. 2015). Note that this estimate says nothing about literacy percentages or fluency, but only whether a writing system exists. Even in cultures that use a writing system, there are individuals who do not learn the written form of their language. In fact, the majority of human beings are illiterate, though quite capable of spoken communication. However, no naturally occurring society uses only a written language with no spoken form.

c. Neurolinguistic evidence (studies of the brain "in action" during language use) demonstrates that the processing and production of written language is overlaid on the spoken language centers in the brain. Spoken language involves several distinct areas of the brain; writing uses these areas and others as well.

d. Writing can be edited before it is shared with others in most cases, while speech is usually much more spontaneous. This is further evidence of the immediacy of speech as a communication signal, compared to the delayed nature of writing.

e. Archeological evidence indicates that writing is a later historical development than spoken language. Writing was first used in Sumer (modern-day Iraq) about 6,000 years ago. The Sumerians probably devised written characters for the purpose of maintaining inventories of livestock and merchandise. As far as physical and cultural anthropologists can tell, spoken language, by contrast, has probably been used by humans for hundreds of thousands of years.

The reason why we want to be clear on this point is that there is often a misconception that writing is more perfect than speech, or that it is more appropriate to study written language than spoken. Part of this is simply due to the fact that written language is the focus of many language classes throughout elementary, primary, and secondary education, whether language arts, grammar, composition, literature, or even foreign languages. Note, however, that the goals of these classes are quite different from those of linguistic study. In addition, writing can seem more correct and more stable, in contrast to speech, which can be careless, corrupted, and susceptible to change. Some people even go so far as to identify "language" with writing and to regard speech as a secondary form of language used imperfectly to approximate the ideals of the written language. What gives rise to the misconception that writing is more perfect than speech? There are several reasons for this misconception, some of which ironically are the same as the ones listed above:

a. Writing can be edited, and so the product of writing is usually more aptly worded and better organized, containing fewer errors, hesitations, pauses, filler words, false starts, and incomplete sentences than are found in speech. This "perfection of writing" can be explained by the fact that writing is often the result of deliberation, correction, and revision, while speech is the spontaneous and simultaneous formulation of ideas; writing is therefore less subject to the constraint of time than speech is. (Think back also to the distinction between linguistic competence and linguistic performance discussed in File 1.2.1.)

b. Writing must be taught and is therefore intimately associated with education and educated speech. Since the speech of the educated is more often than not perceived as the "standard language," writing is associated indirectly with the varieties of language that people tend to view as "correct." However, the association of writing with the standard variety is not a necessary one. Some writers attempt to transcribe faithfully the speech of their characters, as in Zora Neale Hurston's *Their Eyes Were Watching God* or Harper Lee's *To Kill a Mockingbird,* among many others. In addition, "nonstandard" language is very common in texting, Internet memes, tweeting, blog and discussion board posting and commenting, emailing, etc., which for many people make up a large proportion of the written language to which they are exposed daily.

c. Writing is more physically stable than spoken language, which consists of nothing more than sound waves traveling through the air and is therefore ephemeral and transient, if it is not captured by audio- or video-recording. Writing tends to last, because of its physical medium (characters on some surface, in its basic form) and can be preserved for a very long time. Spelling, especially in the modern era, does not seem to vary from individual to individual or from place to place as easily as pronunciation does. Thus writing has the appearance of being more stable. (Of course, spelling does vary, as exemplified by the official differences between the American ways of spelling, for example, *gray, color,* and words with the suffix *-ize,* and the British spellings *grey, colour,* and *-ise;* spelling variation is again also seen frequently in Internet-based written language.) Writing could also change if it were made to follow changes in speech. The fact that people at various times try to carry out spelling reforms amply illustrates this possibility. (For instance, *through* is sometimes spelled as *thru,* or *night* as *nite,* to reflect their modern pronunciations more closely.)

While these characteristics of writing may make it seem more polished and permanent at times, they clearly do not make it a more primary indication of a speaker's linguistic competence. It is for these reasons that linguists focus on spoken language as the object of their study and why we say that writing is a non-essential aspect of knowing a language. Even so, writing relates to language in fascinating ways, which will be discussed in Chapter 15.

1.3.3   Language Is Not Prescriptive Grammar

We said in File 1.2 that part of knowing a language is having a system of rules about phonetics, phonology, morphology, syntax, semantics, and pragmatics that tell you how to combine sounds and words into well-formed, meaningful utterances that someone else can understand. Linguists try to discover these mental rules by observing, describing, and analyzing speech as it is performed.

There are, therefore, several uses of the term *grammar* that need to be clarified. Linguists recognize at least three distinct things called "grammar": (a) what the linguist is actually trying to understand—the mental grammar, whether of an individual speaker or of a group of speakers of that language variety, (b) the linguist's description of the rules of a language as it is spoken—the descriptive grammar, and (c) the socially embedded notion of the "correct" or "proper" ways to use a language—the **prescriptive grammar.**

The first two have been described in detail in the previous file and will be explored throughout the rest of this book. But the third meaning of grammar is unfortunately the most common in everyday speech, so it is worth taking the time to explain what prescriptive grammar is, and why it is not an inherent part of language and therefore not the object of our study here.

To most people, the word *grammar* means the sort of thing they learned in English class or in other language classes, when they were taught about subjects and predicates and parts of speech and were told not to dangle participles or strand prepositions. (1) shows some examples of this sort of grammar for English.

(1)   Examples of prescriptive rules
   a. Do not end a sentence with a preposition.
      NO: Where do you come <u>from</u>?
      YES: <u>From</u> where do you come?

   b. Do not split infinitives.
      NO: . . . <u>to</u> boldly <u>go</u> where no one has gone before
      YES: . . . <u>to go</u> boldly where no one has gone before

   c. Do not use double negatives.
      NO: I <u>don't</u> have <u>nothing.</u>
      YES: I <u>don't</u> have <u>anything.</u> I have <u>nothing.</u>

As you can see from these examples, prescriptive rules tell you how you "should" speak or write, according to someone's idea of what is "good" or "bad." This is why it is called "prescriptive": it is being **prescribed** like a doctor's prescription of a medicine. Of course, there is nothing inherently good or bad about any use of language; prescriptive rules serve only to mold your spoken and written English to some norm.

Notice that prescriptive rules make value judgments about the correctness of an utterance. But the rules in any individual's mental grammar are what actually exist as the foundation of language and **cannot**—by definition—be incorrect, even if they differ in some respect from the rules of the mental grammar of some other speakers of that language variety, or from general descriptive grammatical statements about the language variety as a unified entity. Descriptive grammatical statements, in contrast to prescriptive rules, simply describe what happens in spoken language and therefore accept the patterns different speakers use, without judgment. Descriptive grammars allow for different varieties of a language; they don't ignore a construction simply because some prescriptive grammarian doesn't like it, and they don't describe what speakers "should" or "shouldn't" do—just what they actually do. For example, some descriptive statements of English grammar would include those in (2).

(2) Examples of descriptive grammar statements
     a. Some English speakers may end sentences with prepositions.
     b. Some English speakers may split infinitives.
     c. Some English speakers use double negatives for negation.

These descriptive statements are simply descriptions of what happens, not guidelines for what ought to happen. They provide a much closer picture of the competence of a language's speakers than prescriptive rules. After all, just like writing, prescriptive rules must be taught, and they often conflict with what native speakers of a language (who are clearly competent language users) really do. Note, however, that descriptive grammars of individual speakers or groups of speakers can differ from those of other speakers. For example, a descriptive grammar of typical Ohio State University undergraduate students would note that constructions like *The room needs painted* are perfectly grammatical for some speakers (i.e., are produced by their mental grammars), while they are not grammatical for other speakers (i.e., their mental grammars would only produce constructions like *The room needs to be painted* or *The room needs painting*). In situations like this, people in the second group may not be sure of exactly what is meant upon first hearing something like *needs painted* or may think that it results from a performance error on the part of the speaker, but if those people continue to hear such constructions on a regular basis, their mental grammars will adapt to processing and understanding this construction, and may eventually add a rule to allow them to produce the construction (and vice versa, for speakers in the first group). So a descriptive statement like "Constructions like *needs painted* are grammatical for some speakers, even though they are ungrammatical for me" is merely describing a situation of differences between mental grammars, with no judgment of intrinsic correctness, and is fundamentally different from a prescriptive rule that says "Constructions like *needs painted* are never correct in English; one should say *needs to be painted* or *needs painting* instead."

If prescriptive rules such as those in (1) are not based on actual use, how did they arise and become so familiar to many speakers of English? In many cases, these rules were formulated by people on the basis of something other than the actual language being spoken around them. During the seventeenth and eighteenth centuries, scholars became preoccupied with the art, ideas, and language of ancient Greece and Rome. The classical period was regarded as a golden age and Latin as the perfect language. The notion that Latin was somehow better or purer than contemporary languages was strengthened by the fact that Latin was by then strictly a written language and had long ceased to undergo the changes natural to spoken language. For many writers of the seventeenth and eighteenth centuries, the rules of Latin became, whenever remotely feasible, the rules of English. The rules in (1a) and (1b) above result from this phenomenon.

With regard to (1a), speakers of English have been freely ending sentences with prepositions since the beginning of the Middle English period (about 1100 C.E.). There are even some instances of this construction in Old English. In modern English, speakers who attempt to avoid it often sound stilted and stuffy (e.g., see the quote, some variation of which is often attributed to Winston Churchill, rejecting this rule: *This is the sort of English up with which I will not put*). The fact that ending sentences with prepositions is perfectly natural in English did not stop seventeenth-century poet, playwright, and literary critic John Dryden from forbidding it, because he found it to be non-Latin. His rule has been with us ever since.

Concerning the rule in (1b), English has had a two-word infinitive composed of *to* plus an uninflected verb (e.g., *to write*) since the early Middle English period as well. English speakers have always been able to split this two-word infinitive by inserting words (usually adverbs) between *to* and the verb (e.g., *to quickly write*). There have been periods in English literary history when splitting infinitives was very fashionable. However, eighteenth-century grammarians noticed that Latin infinitives were never split. Of course, it was impossible to split a Latin infinitive because it was a single word (e.g., *describere* 'to write down'). But that fact did not prevent the early grammarians from formulating this as another prescriptive rule of English grammar.

The double negative rule (see (1c)) has a different source. In Old and Middle English, double and triple negatives were common, and even quadruple negatives were used, usually for the purposes of emphasis. The sentence in (3) from Old English illustrates this. It contains two negative words and was entirely grammatical.

(3)   The use of the double negative in Old English

ne	bið	ðær	**nænig**	ealo	gebrowen	mid	Estum
not	*is*	*there*	*not-any*	*ale*	*brewed*	*among*	*Estonians*

'No ale is brewed among the Estonians.'

By Shakespeare's time, however, the double negative was rarely used by educated speakers, although it was still common in many dialects. In 1762, Bishop Robert Lowth attempted to argue against the double negative by invoking rules of logic: "Two negatives in English destroy one another or are equivalent to an affirmative" (204). Of course, language and formal logic are different systems, and there are many languages, such as Russian and Spanish, in which multiple negation is **required** in some cases for grammaticality. Certainly no one misunderstands the English-speaking child or adult who says, "I don't want none." Lowth ignored the fact that it is **usage,** not logic, that must determine the descriptive rules of a grammar—but his prescriptive rule has persisted in classrooms and "grammar" books to this day.

Again, it may well be true for many speakers that their mental grammars do not have rules that produce double negatives (particularly in formal speech or writing), but for many other individual speakers and speakers of certain dialects of English, such constructions are perfectly regular, and there is certainly nothing inherent to English or any other language that would rule out constructions like this as being necessarily ungrammatical, which is how prescriptive rules often present the situation.

You may think it somewhat surprising that rules that do not reflect actual language use should survive. One of the most important reasons that they do survive is that such rules are associated with a particular social status. Nonstandard dialects are still frowned upon by many groups and can inhibit one's progress in society: for example, trying to get a job while speaking with a nonstandard, stigmatized dialect may be difficult. The existence of prescriptive rules allows a speaker of a nonstandard dialect to explicitly learn the rules of the standard dialect and employ them in appropriate social circumstances (for more discussion of language varieties, see Chapter 10). Therefore, prescriptive rules are used as an aid in social identity marking and mobility. This does not mean, however, that these judgments about dialects are linguistically valid. The idea that one dialect of a language is intrinsically better than another is simply false; from a strictly linguistic point of view all dialects are equally good and equally valid. To look down on nonstandard dialects is to exercise a form of social and linguistic prejudice. It is for these reasons that linguists do not make use of prescriptive grammars, but rather only descriptive grammars, which are used as a tool for discovering mental grammars.

In other cases, prescriptive rules arise as a reaction against, and an attempt to stop, the natural course of language change. A fact about language is that **all** living languages (i.e., those spoken natively) change (see Chapter 15), but such changes in progress are often not well received by current speakers of a language. An illustration of such a change and the reactions against it can be found in "progressive passive" constructions like modern-day English *The house is being painted today.* No grammar teacher or prescriptivist in the twenty-first century would have a problem with this sentence, but they would almost certainly frown upon a sentence like *The clock struck ten while the trunks were carrying down* (i.e., *were being carried down,* in modern English). Such a sentence would no doubt cause confusion among most English speakers and easily be judged as ungrammatical. But this sentence, which appears in Jane Austen's 1818 novel *Northanger Abbey,* was perfectly grammatical at that time, though the current way of saying such things had begun to appear a few decades earlier in English. Richard Grant Wright, in his 1882 fifth edition of *Words and Their Uses,* devotes an entire chapter to this construction, which, he says, "about seventy or eighty years ago, began to affront the eye, torment the ear, and assault the common sense of the speaker of plain and idiomatic English." He does note that "to check its diffusion would be a hopeless undertaking," but spends thirty pages discussing the history and grammatical background of this "monstrosity, [of] illogical, confusing, inaccurate, unidiomatic character," which today we consider to be completely grammatically correct. This provides a good example of how ideas about grammaticality can undergo drastic changes over time since they are not inherent to a language.

FILE 1.4

....

Design Features of Language

1.4.1   How to Identify Language When We Come across It

Before we discuss language in any more depth, it will be useful if we first have some idea of what people mean when they say "language." So far, we have discussed what you know when you know a language, and we have explored various commonly held ideas about language that are both true and untrue. We haven't yet defined language, though.

Defining language turns out to be a remarkably difficult task: nobody seems to be able to find a definition of *language* that captures its fundamental nature. But if we cannot define *language,* then we must come up with some other solution because we still must have some way to identify language when we come across it. One possibility is to identify the features that something must have in order to be a language. Linguist Charles Hockett designed one such list that identifies descriptive characteristics of language. While his list does not tell us the fundamental nature of language, it does tell us a great deal about what language is like and what we can do with it.

Hockett's descriptive characteristics of language are known as the **design features** of language. The list has been modified over the years, but a standard version is provided below. While there are many kinds of communication systems in the world, all of which follow some form of the communication chain outlined in File 1.2, only communication systems that display all nine of these design features can be called a "language." The order in which the design features are presented is also significant: the features proceed from most universal to most particular. All communication systems have the first three design features, while human language alone has the final two.

1.4.2   Mode of Communication

The very nature of a system of communication is that messages must be sent and received. The term **mode of communication** refers to the means by which these messages are transmitted and received. For most human languages, speakers transmit messages using their voices; however, a significant number of human languages are also transmitted gesturally—via hand, arm, head, and face movement. Both are viable systems for transmitting the complex sorts of messages required of language. Language **modality** will be discussed in considerably more depth in File 1.5.

1.4.3   Semanticity

Another aspect of language that is universal across all communication systems is **semanticity.** Semanticity is the property requiring that all signals in a communication system have a meaning or a function. It is critically important to successful linguistic communication that, for example, if your friend says to you "pizza," you both have a similar idea of what he is talking about. It would not be good for communication if your friend said "pizza" and you

20

thought, "There's that word with the /p/ sound again. Wonder why he keeps saying it all the time."

Even if you hear a word you don't know, you nevertheless assume that it must have some meaning. For example, if you heard the sentence *There was a large amount of frass in the tubes with the fruit flies,* you might not recognize the word *frass,*[1] but you would not assume that it was meaningless. If words or sentences didn't have meaning, then we would be unable to use them to communicate!

1.4.4 Pragmatic Function

Communication systems must also have a **pragmatic function:** that is, they must serve some useful purpose. Some functions of human language include helping individuals to stay alive, influencing others' behavior, and finding out more about the world. For example, a person who needs food might use language to ask for more mashed potatoes; more dramatically, a person trapped in a burning house might stay alive by calling for help. A politician communicates certain messages to try to influence people's voting behavior. People ask questions in order to learn the information they need to get through their days.

Sometimes people may question the usefulness of a certain communicative act, for example, in the case of gossip. However, even gossip fulfills a useful purpose in societies. It helps us to understand our social environment and plays an important role in social bonding and establishing social relationships. The same is true of set phrases such as "nice weather today" or the question, "Hey, what's up?" and its typical response, "Not much. How about you?" These set phrases serve to acknowledge the other person or initiate a conversation, which are both necessary tasks for the maintenance of our social structure.

1.4.5 Interchangeability

Interchangeability refers to the ability of individuals to both transmit and receive messages. Each individual human can both produce messages (by speaking or signing) and comprehend the messages of others (by listening or watching).

1.4.6 Cultural Transmission

Another important feature of human language is that there are aspects of language that we can acquire only through communicative interaction with other users of the system. This aspect of language is referred to as **cultural transmission.** Even though children's ability to learn language seems to be innate, they must still learn all of the specific signals of their language through interaction with other speakers. In fact, a child who is never spoken to will not learn language (see File 8.1). Furthermore, children will learn the language(s) or dialect(s) that other people use to interact with them. Thus, children of Russian parents will learn Russian if their parents interact with them in Russian, but they will learn English if their parents interact with them in English. Our genetic or hereditary background in and of itself has no influence whatsoever on the language that we acquire as children.

1.4.7 Arbitrariness

a. Arbitrariness in Language. It is generally recognized that the words of a language represent a connection between a group of sounds or signs, which give the word its **form,** and a **meaning,** which the form can be said to represent. The combination of a form and

---

[1]The word *frass* means 'the debris or excrement of insects.'

a meaning is called a **linguistic sign**: Form + Meaning = Linguistic Sign. For example, one word for 'the inner core of a peach' is represented in English by the sounds [pɪt][2] (which we spell as <pit>), occurring in that order to give the sound (i.e., the form) that we make when we say the word *pit*.

(1) [pɪt] +   = the word *pit*

An important fact about linguistic signs is that the connection between form and meaning is typically **arbitrary.** The term *arbitrary* here refers to the fact that the meaning is not in any way predictable from the form, nor is the form dictated by the meaning. Note that there **is** a relationship between form and meaning: you don't have a different meaning in mind every time that you say [pɪt]. If there were no relationship at all, then you could say [pɪt] one time and mean 'licorice' and say it again and mean 'courageous' and say it another time and mean 'mandolin.' Clearly language doesn't work this way. This relationship is an arbitrary **convention** of English, which tells you that a certain group of sounds goes with a particular meaning.

The opposite of arbitrariness in this sense is **nonarbitrariness,** and there are some nonarbitrary aspects of language, which will be discussed below. The most extreme examples of nonarbitrary form-meaning connections, where the form represents the meaning directly, are said to be **iconic** (or "picture-like"). For linguistic signs in general, however, the connection between form and meaning is not direct, nor is it derivable from laws of nature.

b. Evidence for Arbitrariness. The fact that the inner core of a peach may be called a *stone* or even a *seed* as well as a *pit* points to arbitrariness. If the connection between the form and the meaning were nonarbitrary (because the form determined the meaning, or vice versa), there would not be many possible forms to express a single meaning. Likewise, there is nothing intrinsic in the combination of the sounds represented by [pɪt] that suggests the meaning 'inner core of a peach'; the same sequence of sounds can represent 'a large, deep hole in the ground.'

Evidence of arbitrariness in language can also be seen in cross-linguistic comparisons. Words with the same meaning usually have different forms in different languages, and similar forms usually express different meanings, as the examples in (2) illustrate. If there were an inherent, nonarbitrary connection between forms and meanings, with the meaning being determined by the form or vice versa, then such cross-linguistic differences should not occur. There would be universally recognized forms for each meaning.

---

[2]Symbols in square brackets "[ ]" are transcriptions in the International Phonetic Alphabet (or IPA), which is a standardized set of symbols devised to indicate pronunciations for all languages. For more details, see Chapter 2 ("Phonetics") and the guides to the sounds of English and the IPA Chart on pp. 741–43.

(2)   Arbitrary form-meaning connections of linguistic signs as seen cross-linguistically

Form	Meaning	Language
[wɑtɹ] [o] [vasɐ] [søy]	'water'	English French German Cantonese
[li]	proper name, 'Lee' 'bed' 'borrowed/lent' 'this'	English French German Cantonese

Finally, arbitrariness in language is shown in names for inventions and new products. For example, new cars come on the market every year. Many of them are very similar to each other: they all have four tires, a cabin that can seat some number of people, an engine, and so on. Yet despite their similarities, makes of cars have startlingly different names. Some of them are very long words while others are quite short, and they begin with all kinds of different sounds. A person naming a new car will certainly think of a sequence of sounds that she likes, but she will not be constrained in any way by the nature of the car or the nature of the sounds themselves—only by her own arbitrary preferences.

c. Onomatopoeia. It is clear that arbitrariness is the norm in language, at least as far as the basic relationship between the form of a word and its meaning is concerned. At the same time, though, it turns out that there are some nonarbitrary aspects to language. In the vocabulary of all languages, there is a small degree of nonarbitrariness involving items whose forms are largely determined by their meanings. Most notable and obvious are the so-called **onomatopoetic** (or onomatopoeic) words, i.e., words that are imitative of natural sounds or have meanings that are associated with such sounds of nature.

Examples of onomatopoetic words in English include noise-words such as *bow-wow* [baʊwaʊ] for the noise a dog makes, *splat* [splæt] for the sound of a rotten tomato hitting a wall, and *burble* [bṛbl̩] for expressing the rushing noise of running water. In all of these words, the matchup between the form of the word and the meaning of the word is very close: the meaning is very strongly suggested by the sound of the word itself.

Even in such onomatopoetic words, however, an argument for arbitrariness can be found. While the form is **largely** determined by the meaning, the form is not an exact copy of the natural noise; roosters, for instance, do not actually "say" [kɑkədudl̩du]—English speakers have just arbitrarily **conventionalized** this noise in that form. Different languages can have different onomatopoetic words for the same sounds. For example, a rooster "says" [kɑkədudl̩du] in English but [kukuku] in Mandarin Chinese, even though (presumably) roosters sound the same in China and the United States. If there were an inherent and determined connection between the meaning and the form of onomatopoetic words, we would expect the same meaning to be represented by the same sounds in different languages. The table in (3), which lists eleven natural sounds represented by onomatopoetic words in nine languages, shows that this is not the case.

(3)   Cross-linguistic examples of onomatopoeia (see Chapter 2 and the IPA chart in the back of the book for aid on IPA symbols)

Sound	English	German	French	Spanish	Hebrew	Hindi	Mandarin	Japanese	Greek
Dog barking	[baʊwaʊ]	[vaʊvaʊ]	[wafwaf]	[waʊwaʊ]	[haʊhaʊ]	[bʰɔbʰɔ]	[waŋwaŋ]	[waɴwaɴ]	[ɣavɣav]
Rooster crowing	[kakə-dudl̩du]	[kikəʁiki]	[kokoʁiko]	[kikiɾiki] or [kokoɾiko]	[kukuɣikuku]	[kukukuku]	[kukuku]	[kokekokkoː]	[kikiriku]
Cat meowing	[miaʊ]	[miaʊ]	[miaʊ]	[miaʊ]	[miaʊ]	[miaʊ]	[miaʊ]	[niaɯ]	[ɲaʊ]
Cow lowing	[muː]	[mu]	[məː]	[mu]	[mu]	[mũː]	[məɹ]	[moːmoː]	[muː]
Sheep bleating	[bɑː]	[mɛː]	[bɛː]	[beː]	[mɛ̃ː]	[mɛ̃ːmɛ̃ː]	[miɛ]	[meːmeː]	[beː]
Bird chirping	[twittwit]	[pippip]	[kɥikɥi]	[piopio] or [pippip]	[tsuitstsuits]	[tʃiːtʃiː]	[tɕitɕi]	[tʃitʃi]	[tsiutsiu]
Bomb exploding	[bum]	[bum] or [vʁum]	[bum]	[bum]	[bum]	[bʰɔɖaːm]	[bɔŋ]	[baɴ]	[bum]
Laughing	[hɑhɑ]	[haha]	[haha]	[xaxa]	[haha]	[haha]	[xaxa]	[haha]	[xaxa]
Sneezing	[atʃu]	[hatʃi]	[atʃum]	[atʃu]	[aptʃi]	[atʃũː]	[aʔtʰi]	[hakɯʃoɴ]	[apsu]
Something juicy hitting a hard surface	[splæt]	[platʃ]	[flɔk]	—	—	—	[pyaʔ]	[guʃaʔ]	[plats]
Clock	[tɪktɑk]	[tɪktak]	[tiktak]	[tiktak]	[tɪktak]	[tiktik]	[ti?taʔ]	[tʃiktakɯ]	[tiktak]

d. Sound Symbolism. A second apparent counterexample to arbitrariness is **sound symbolism**: certain sounds occur in words not by virtue of being directly imitative of some sound but rather simply by being evocative of a particular meaning. That is, these words, or parts of these words, more abstractly suggest some physical characteristics by the way they sound. For instance, in many languages, words for 'small' and words that have smallness as part of their meaning often contain the vowel [i]. We observe this in English words such as *teeny* 'extra small,' *petite* and *wee* 'small,' and dialectal *leetle* for 'little,' in Greek *mikros* 'small,' and in Spanish diminutive nouns (i.e., those with the meaning 'little X') such as *perrito* 'little dog,' where *-ito* is a suffix indicating 'little.' Such widespread sound symbolism—with the sound [i] suggesting 'smallness'—seems to be motivated because [i] is a high-pitched vowel and so more like the high-pitched sounds given off by small objects. Thus the use of [i] in 'small' words creates a situation in which an aspect of the form, i.e., the occurrence of [i], is influenced by an aspect of the meaning, i.e., 'smallness.' We may thus characterize the appearance of [i] in such words as somewhat nonarbitrary—the "small" vowel [i] has a connection to the meaning 'small(ness).'

e. Nonarbitrary Aspects of Language. The above examples show that nonarbitrariness and iconicity have at best a somewhat marginal place in language. At the same time, though, it cannot be denied that they do play a role in language and moreover that speakers are aware of their potential effects. Poets often manipulate onomatopoeia and sound symbolism in order to achieve a specific phonic impression in their poetry. For example, Alfred Tennyson in his poem *The Princess* utilized nasal consonants to mimic the noise made by the bees he refers to:

(4)   The **m**oa**n** of doves i**n** i**mm**e**m**orial el**m**s
       And **m**ur**m**uring of i**nn**u**m**erable bees   (v. 11.206–7)

1.4.8 Discreteness

Consider the English sentence *He is fast.* It is not one unified sign that always appears exactly as it is. Rather, it is composed of many discrete units. First, there are the independent words *he, is,* and *fast.* These words, in turn, are composed of even smaller discrete units: the individual sounds [h], [i], [ɪ], [z], [f], [æ], [s], and [t]. The property of language (among other communication systems) that allows us to combine together discrete units in order to create larger communicative units is called **discreteness.**

Every language has a limited number of sounds, between roughly 10 and 100. English, for example, has about 50 sounds. The sounds themselves are for the most part meaningless—the sound [f] in *fish* or *foot* does not have any meaning by itself—but we can combine a very small number of sounds to create a very large number of meaningful words. For example, we can combine the sounds [f], [u], and [l] to create the word *fool*; [t], [u], and [l] to create the word *tool*; [p], [u], and [l] to create the word *pool*; [k], [u], and [l] to create the word *cool,* etc. We can then reorder the sounds in [kul] *cool* to get [klu] *clue* or [luk] *Luke.* We can thus generate a large number of meaningful elements (words) from a few meaningless units (sounds). We can further combine words into phrases and sentences. Thus, from a selection of only 100 or fewer units, we can create a very large number of meanings (an infinite number, actually). A communication system that can put pieces together in different ways has much more expressive capability than one that does not. If we were limited to only 100 or so meanings, then language would not be nearly so useful as it turns out to be!

1.4.9 Displacement

Displacement is the ability of a language to communicate about things, actions, and ideas that are not present in space or time while speakers are communicating. We can, for example, talk about the color red when we are not actually seeing it, or we can talk about a friend who lives in another state when he is not with us. We can talk about a class we had last year or the class we will take next year. We can also talk about things that do not exist, such as unicorns and fictional characters.

1.4.10 Productivity

The last of Hockett's design features is productivity, which is closely related to discreteness. **Productivity** refers to a language's capacity for novel messages to be built up out of discrete units. Note how productivity differs from discreteness. For a communication system to have discreteness, the only requirement is that there be recombinable units; however, it would be possible for there to be a fixed set of ways in which these units could combine. Indeed, some communication systems do work that way. Because language is productive, though, there is no fixed set of ways in which units can combine.

The productivity of human language grants people the ability to produce and understand any number of novel sentences that they have never heard before, thereby expressing propositions that may never have been expressed before. In fact, in any language it is possible to produce an infinite number of sentences, so many of the sentences that you hear are ones you have never heard before. For example, you probably have never read the following sentence before, but you can still understand what it means: *Funky potato farmers dissolve glass.* You understand what it means even though you may not know why the potato farmers are funky or how glass can be dissolved, and you know this even though you have never seen or heard the sentence before.

We are able to construct and understand novel forms such as this one based on the fact that the discrete units of language (sounds, morphemes, and words) can be put together in regular, systematic, and rule-governed ways. The way that you come to understand the meaning of a new sentence is by applying what you know about the rules for how words combine in your language to the new string of words, together with the meanings of the words themselves (see Chapter 5 and File 6.4).

Rules at all levels of linguistic structure are **productive**. That is, they allow creation of new forms, tell which new forms are allowed, and tell how they can be used. The rules of language, rather than limiting us, are in fact what grant us the ability to communicate about such a broad range of ideas.

1.4.11   What the Design Features Tell Us, and What They Don't Tell Us

All languages exhibit all nine design features: any communication system that does not is therefore not a language. Furthermore, as far as we know, only human communication systems display all nine design features. (File 14.1 discusses Hockett's design features with respect to animal communication systems.)

Because all languages exhibit the nine design features, does this mean that any communication system that exhibits all nine features should be considered a language? For example, there are **formal languages,** such as the formal logic used to write mathematical proofs and various computer languages. While these formal languages display all of the design features, they nevertheless differ in critical ways from languages such as English, Spanish, Mandarin, and Apache. For example, no child could ever acquire a computer language like C++ as his native language! Furthermore, a number of people engage in constructing languages that imitate human language as a hobby. There are many reasons that people might choose to do this. For example, the created language could be used in some sort of fictional universe, such as Klingon in the television series *Star Trek* or Dothraki and Valyrian in the series *Game of Thrones*. Or it might be designed to facilitate international communication, which was the goal of the designers of the language Esperanto. Other people, such as J.R.R. Tolkien, have constructed artificial languages just for fun.

Do we want to make a distinction between languages such as English, Spanish, Mandarin, and Apache, on the one hand, and Esperanto, Elvish, Dothraki, Valyrian, and Klingon, on the other? And how should we classify "formal" languages? Although many of these questions are still open to debate and research, we will make the following distinctions for the purposes of this book. The object of our linguistic study here will be confined to what we call **natural languages,** those languages that have evolved naturally in a speech community. The lexicon and grammar of a natural language have developed through generations of native speakers of that language. A **constructed language,** on the other hand, is one that has been specifically invented by a human and that may or may not imitate all the properties of a natural language.

Some constructed languages have the potential to become natural languages, if they are learned by native speakers and adopted by a speech community. This is the case with Modern Hebrew, which was reconstructed from Ancient Hebrew and then adopted by a particular community. The distinction between constructed languages and formal languages is that formal languages are not the sort of system that a child can acquire naturally.

Because we want to confine most of our discussion to natural languages, we will often shorten the term to "language" in the rest of the book. You should keep in mind, however, that other types of language do, in fact, exist. Thus the design features help us distinguish language from other nonlinguistic communication systems, but we need more criteria to ensure that a system is a natural language and not an artificial language.

FILE 1.5

....

Language Modality

1.5.1 Auditory-Vocal and Visual-Gestural Languages

In File 1.2, we saw that language is a cognitive system. That is, language exists only insofar as people who use a particular language have a set of grammatical rules for it in their heads. However, it isn't enough to say merely that we have grammatical rules in our heads. In order for language to be a system of communication—a system that allows us to share our thoughts with others—we have to be able to use it to transmit messages. We must be able to use those grammatical rules to produce something in the world: something that others are able to perceive and interpret. Therefore, every language must have a **modality** or a mode of communication. A language's modality tells us two things: how it is produced, and how it is perceived.

It is likely that most of the languages with which you are familiar are **auditory-vocal** (sometimes also called **aural-oral**), which means that they are perceived via hearing and produced via speech. Auditory-vocal languages include English, Russian, Portuguese, Navajo, Korean, and Swahili, among many others. Auditory-vocal languages may also be referred to as **spoken languages.** Throughout history there has been a commonly held—though entirely incorrect—view that language is inseparable from speech. This misconception is often spread when the terms *speech* and *language* are used interchangeably. From this confusion, people may conclude that only spoken languages may properly be described as being languages.

There are also human languages that are **visual-gestural.** In fact, there are hundreds of visual-gestural languages in use all over the world. Visual-gestural languages, which may also be referred to as **signed languages**, are those that are perceived visually and produced via hand and arm movements, facial expressions, and head movements.[1] Although visual-gestural languages are often used by individuals who are deaf or hard of hearing, many hearing people also communicate via one of the world's many signed languages. And, as with spoken languages, signed languages may be acquired in childhood as a person's first language or much later, through either instruction in school or immersion in a culture that uses a particular signed language.

------

[1]Auditory-vocal and visual-gestural languages represent the two most predominant modes of communication for human language. There are, however, some less commonly used language modalities. For example, individuals who are deaf-blind may use a tactile-gestural modality. That is, they use their hands to feel another person's signing. Within a particular signed language, there may be certain conventions or modifications to signs when they are being interpreted by touch, creating a different dialect of the signed language for use among the visually impaired. When two individuals, each of whom is both deaf and blind and communicates in this way, have a conversation, the entire conversation will take place using the tactile-gestural modality. But this alteration in modality does not represent a new type of language. Thus we may say that signed languages have a primary modality that is visual-gestural and a secondary modality that is tactile-gestural.

With the exception of their modality, signed languages are similar to spoken languages in every way. (See File 1.2.) Signed languages are made up of words that can be put together in sentences according to particular grammatical rules. In fact, every kind of linguistic analysis that may be performed on spoken languages may also be performed on signed languages. Examples of linguistic phenomena from various signed languages will be presented throughout the rest of *Language Files*.

1.5.2   Some Common Misconceptions about Visual-Gestural Languages

Unfortunately, there is a great deal of misinformation that has been spread about the nature of visual-gestural languages. Few, if any, people believe all of these misconceptions—indeed, some of the misconceptions contradict one another—but each is repeated often enough to bear discussing here.

a. Signed Language vs. Manual Codes. There is a myth that signed languages derive from spoken languages, rather than being languages in their own right. According to this myth, one would expect that deaf signers in America would have a signed language that was structurally identical to English, while signers in Japan would have a signed language that was structurally similar to Japanese, and so on. In other words, this myth suggests that signed languages are merely codes for the languages spoken in the surrounding area.

Codes and languages are radically different kinds of systems in several ways. A **code** is an artificially constructed system for representing a natural language; it has no structure of its own but instead borrows its structure from the natural language that it represents. Morse code is a well-known example of a code. Signed languages, on the other hand, evolve naturally and independently of spoken languages. They are structurally distinct from each other and from spoken languages. Note, in addition, that codes never have native speakers (i.e., people who learn them as children as their primary form of communication) because they are artificial systems. Languages, of course, do have native speakers. Signed languages are learned natively by both hearing and deaf people all over the world.

A strong piece of evidence that sign languages do not derive from the surrounding spoken language is that British Sign Language and American Sign Language are unrelated; someone who is fluent in only one of these languages cannot understand a person using the other. This is true despite the fact that speakers of American English and British English can generally understand each other quite well.

It is worth noting that manual codes for spoken languages do exist. These codes use certain gestures to represent letters, morphemes (parts of words), and words of a spoken language and follow the grammar of that spoken language. For example, to communicate the concept 'indivisible' in American Sign Language (ASL) requires only one gesture, as seen in (1b), whereas a manual code for English, Signed Exact English II (SEE II) requires three separate gestures, as seen in (1a), because of the way that it mirrors English morphology.

(1)   The meaning 'indivisible' represented in two manual systems
     a. SEE II: 'indivisible'   b. ASL: INDIVISIBLE

    in-   divide   -ible

The differences between the two systems shown in example (1) relate to how morphemes are represented, but there are also differences in word order, because the word order for versions of signed English mirror those of English, while ASL has its own rules for word order.

An indication that manual codes are not natural languages is the striking difference between manually coded English and natural languages such as English and ASL in the rate of transmission of information. These rates can be measured by rendering the same proposition into different languages or codes and measuring the time it takes for someone to produce the proposition in each language or code. A comparison of these rates showed an average seconds-per-proposition rate of 1.5 for both English and ASL, whereas SEE II scored at a distant 2.8. This suggests that true language, whether it is spoken or signed, is a much more efficient means of communicating than signed codes.

Both manual codes and signed languages have been used for communication with and among deaf individuals. However, because the manual codes are based on natural languages rather than being languages themselves, they do not share many of the properties of language that linguists study, so they will generally be ignored in this book.

b. Signed Language vs. Pantomime. There is a second belief that is entirely counter to the view that signed languages are manual codes, but that is equally incorrect. This second myth states that signed languages don't consist of words at all but rather involve signers using their hands to draw pictures in the air or to act out what they are talking about. There are two misconceptions here masquerading as one.

The first misconception is that signed languages do not have any internal structure. In fact, signed languages are governed by the same sorts of phonological, morphological, and syntactic rules that govern spoken languages.

The second misconception is that the words in a signed language are completely iconic. Were this the case, one would expect that it would not be necessary to learn signed languages at all; we would be innately able to understand them because every word would clearly show its meaning. Like spoken languages, however, the forms of words in signed languages are predominantly arbitrary in their relationship to meaning (see File 1.4). The sound sequence /hugar/ means 'to play' in Spanish and 'he lives' in Hebrew and has no meaning at all in English. Similarly, the gestures shown in (2) mean 'possible' in ASL and 'weigh' in Finnish Sign Language. There is no obvious reason why the ideas of 'possible' and 'weigh' should be represented in the same way. Furthermore, if you look at the form of this sign, there is no particular reason that this gesture should or shouldn't be associated with either of these meanings. They are merely arbitrary conventions of the language users: one convention for one linguistic community, and a different convention for the other.

 (2)   POSSIBLE (ASL) and WEIGH (Finnish SL)

This point is even clearer when we consider the signs for 'possible' in a different language. In Taiwan Sign Language, the sign for 'possible' is made entirely with one hand: first the pinky touches the chin, and then a bent hand touches one side of the chest and then the other. As you can see in (2), this is nothing like the sign for 'possible' in ASL!

There are signs in any given signed language that appear to have a certain degree of iconicity. For example, (3) shows the ASL sign for KNOW. The form in (3a) is the version generally shown in dictionaries and taught in classrooms. Notice how the speaker's hand touches his forehead, where one may think of thought occurring. However, this iconicity does not extend to the regular use of the sign by the signing community; the form in (3b) is a common pronunciation of KNOW in which the hand instead touches the cheek. (Just as with spoken languages, signed languages are often pronounced slightly differently in casual conversation.)

(3) a. KNOW (indexical form)   b. KNOW (casual pronunciation)

© 2006, William Vicars, www.Lifeprint.com. Used with permission.

The key point here is that the way that the sign is modified makes the sign less iconic and more arbitrary. In fact, there is a general trend across signs in signed languages that, while they may be somewhat iconic when introduced into the language, over time they change and become more arbitrary.

In any event, if signed language were about drawing pictures or pantomime, then signers would have their communication restricted to concrete objects and events. In reality, signed languages can convey abstract concepts as well. Displacement is every bit as available to signers as to those who use a spoken language.

c. Universality of Signed Languages. A third myth, which is related to the myth that signed languages are pantomime, is that there is only one signed language that is used by deaf speakers all over the world. One might expect a certain degree of universality in pantomime; after all, pantomime must be iconic. Signed languages, however, are arbitrary. There are many distinct signed languages, and they are not mutually intelligible.

In fact, there are more than 150 documented signed languages, each of which is as distinct from every other as are the various spoken languages that you may have heard of. Two individuals who knew two different signed languages would have as much trouble communicating with one another as you would have while communicating with someone who spoke a language that you did not speak.

1.5.3   Who Uses Signed Languages?

Signed languages are used all over the world. Wherever there is a sizable community of deaf individuals, there is a signed language in use. In some cases, when deaf children are born to deaf parents, the children learn a signed language from their parents. More often, when a deaf child is born to hearing parents who do not sign, the child may learn a signed language at an institution such as a school for the deaf.

Interestingly, there have been multiple times throughout history when the deaf population has composed such a large percentage of some community's overall population that the entire community—both hearing and deaf individuals—have used a signed language to communicate. One such case was the northern part of Martha's Vineyard Island during the eighteenth and early nineteenth centuries. Although English was used as well, everyone in the community signed, regardless of whether they were deaf or had deaf family members. Hearing individuals would at times have conversations with one another in Martha's Vineyard Sign Language even if there were no deaf individuals present—the signed language was that pervasive in the community. (The sign language that they used was one that was spoken only on Martha's Vineyard Island. Since that time, the language has been completely lost; see File 12.6 for more information about language death.) Something similar is going on today in the Al-Sayyid Bedouin tribe in Israel; again, such a large portion of the community is deaf that many hearing individuals sign fluently, even if they do not have deaf family members. In fact, the ability to sign fluently is considered a kind of status symbol among the hearing individuals. Thus, a person need not be deaf in order to be a signer.

Furthermore, just because a person has a hearing loss does not mean that that person will necessarily choose to communicate using a signed language. In the United States, the Deaf community (notice the capital <D>) comprises individuals who are deaf or hard of hearing and who further identify themselves as Deaf, subscribe to a particular Deaf culture with its own values and customs, and use ASL to communicate. These individuals take pride in their language and in being Deaf, just as people from many other cultural backgrounds feel pride for their own languages and cultures. However, there are numerous other deaf individuals who do not associate themselves with Deaf culture, who communicate in some other way, for example, by reading lips. There is no outside compulsion for deaf individuals to become signers or members of the Deaf community, and whether they do or don't is determined by diverse and complicated social and practical factors.

Thus, while signed languages are by and large associated with deaf people, it is neither the case that only deaf individuals sign nor the case that deaf individuals must sign. Rather, both auditory-vocal and visual-gestural modalities are viable options for human language, and the choice between them will depend in any given circumstance on both physical and social parameters.

1.5.4 Representing Signs in a Two-Dimensional Format

There is a point worth making here that is not about signed languages themselves but rather about the way that we present the signs in this book. Of course, a sign cannot be written straightforwardly using the Roman alphabet (the characters that English is written in and that you are reading right now) because these characters represent sounds, which are an irrelevant property for signed languages. We therefore adopt the convention that you have already seen above of using capitalized letters spelling out an English word to represent the sign for that word. For example, we might say that the sign for 'dog' is DOG.

Sometimes, however, it is not sufficient merely to give the meaning of a sign. Often it will also be necessary to specify the form of a sign: the way that it is produced. There are three kinds of images used throughout this book to accomplish that task: photographs of signers, drawings of people producing signs, and drawings that show only the hands (but not the signer). Each of these types of illustration is useful in a different way and highlights a different aspect of the sign being illustrated. However, none of them completely captures the way that a sign is produced in three-dimensional space and in real time. Thus, while the images are a useful guide to various linguistic properties of the signs being discussed, they cannot be taken to be a completely reliable guide for how to produce the signs.

For this reason, we have included icons indicating that there are relevant URLs available on our webpage (http://linguistics.osu.edu/research/pubs/lang-files/links) with all such images. Several online ASL dictionaries, with pictures and videos, are freely available and provide the public with wonderful resources on this language, and we encourage you to make use of these sites. Some of these websites can be found at the following links: http://www.lifeprint.com/, http://www.handspeak.com/, http://www.aslpro.com/, and http://www.signingsavvy.com/.

1.5.5   The Importance of Studying Different Modalities

While certain linguistic principles may be expressed differently in signed languages than they are in spoken languages, they are there! With the exception of the physical principles of how the languages are articulated and perceived, both visual-gestural and auditory-vocal languages have the same characteristics. This similarity says something remarkable about the nature of human language and its universality. On the other hand, the fact that the physical principles of how spoken and signed languages are articulated and perceived differ allows us to investigate which aspects of language are universal and which are modality specific.

For example, studies of spoken language have found that pauses in continuous spontaneous speech have a certain minimum length, even when people are told to speak rapidly. To find out whether this is because of the need to breathe (and the minimum amount of time required to take a breath) or whether this is related to cognitive processes (maybe we pause because we haven't yet planned the next part of our utterance), we can study pause length in the production of signed languages compared with pause length in spoken languages (since breathing doesn't interfere with signing as it does with speech). Studies on pause duration in signed languages (e.g., Grosjean 1979) showed that pauses do exist in signed languages but that they do not have a certain minimum length. So we can conclude that the minimum pause length in spoken languages is not a fact about linguistic processing ability, but rather a fact about auditory-vocal languages.

The majority of examples in this book will come from spoken languages (most often English) only because we are assured that our readers are familiar with English. However, in terms of linguistic research more generally, considering languages with different modalities is of the utmost importance. By observing the sorts of effects that different modalities do and do not have on languages, we can come to learn profound truths about language itself.

....

Practice

File 1.1—Introducing the Study of Language

Discussion Questions

    1. Look at the list of "surprising but true" facts about language given in Section 1.1.2. Which items on the list were things you had heard before, and which were new to you? Which really were surprising? What about those items surprised you?

    2. Look at the list of "common misconceptions" about language given in Section 1.1.3. How many of these beliefs are ones you have held at some point or have heard other people express? For each, how do you think that it came to be widely believed? What sort of evidence do you think linguists might have that causes them to say that each is false?

File 1.2—What You Know When You Know a Language

Exercises

    3. Why do linguists tend to ignore speech performance errors in their study of linguistic competence?

    4. Look back at the illustration at the beginning of this chapter. What is missing from this picture from a communication standpoint? What has to happen in order for the person on the right to receive the message "There is a platypus in the bathtub"?

    5. Look back at the illustration at the beginning of this chapter. List at least three messages other than "There is a platypus in the bathtub" that the person on the left might be trying to convey, based on the illustration of the concept he has in his mind.

    6. What are five descriptive statements about your native language?

Discussion Questions

    7. Look back at the illustration at the beginning of this chapter. We have already talked about how language can be used to convey the message "There is a platypus in the bathtub." What other sorts of ways could this message be communicated? Do you think they would be less effective or more effective than using language? Explain.

    8. We said in File 1.2 that it's more likely that you have thought explicitly about examples such as the data given in (4) if you are a non-native speaker of English than if you are a native speaker. Why would a non-native speaker be more likely to have thought about a particular grammatical rule of English than a native speaker? What does this tell you about the relationship between mental grammar and the sorts of grammars that we learn in school (either for a first language or for a second language)?

9. Suppose that you are chaperoning a group of kindergarten students on a trip to the zoo. One of these children walks up to you, pulls on your sleeve, and exclaims, "Look at all the **aminals**!" (Please note: the spelling of "aminals" is intended to indicate the child's pronunciation.) Has this child necessarily made a speech performance error? How do you know? If you do not know, how might you find out? What sort of additional evidence might you need? What would you do to test your hypothesis?

10. What might be some of the difficulties linguists encounter because they use speech as the primary data for finding out the grammatical rules of a language?

File 1.3—Other (Non-Essential) Aspects of Knowing a Language

Exercise

11. For each of the following statements:
    i. Identify which ones are prescriptive and which are descriptive.
    ii. Give an example of how each statement could be written the other way (that is, write the prescriptive ones as descriptive and the descriptive ones as prescriptive).

    a. *It's me* is ungrammatical; *it's I* is the only correct way to express this idea.
    b. Though *ain't* is regularly used in many dialects and informal styles of English, and English speakers generally understand its meaning, people who use this form may suffer some negative social consequences since *ain't* is often associated with lack of education and deemed to be ungrammatical by many speakers.
    c. In casual styles of speaking, English speakers frequently end sentences with prepositions; ending sentences with prepositions is often avoided in formal styles, however.
    d. For any sentence beginning with *There is/There's* or *There are,* the verb must agree in number with what comes after it, the "logical subject." For example, *There's something I want to say* and *There are a few things I want to say* are both correct, but *There's a few things I want to say* is always ungrammatical.
    e. Some speakers of English accept *My mother loved* as a grammatical sentence.

Discussion Questions

12. Some of the reasons that linguists believe speech is more basic than writing overlap with the reasons that some people think writing is more basic. Explain how this could be, keeping in mind that linguists might have goals different from those of other members of society.

13. Why do you think linguists are more concerned with descriptive grammars than with prescriptive grammars?

14. "Since speech is more basic than writing, it is not worthwhile to study writing in any way." Do you agree with this statement? Why or why not?

15. Give a prescriptive rule and a descriptive statement regarding the placement of adjectives with respect to the nouns they modify in English. Explain how each type of statement

might change if, at some point in the future, younger speakers of English began saying things like *shirt green* or *idea brilliant*.

16. Would language change if we put effort into advocating prescriptive rules? Give evidence from what you have learned in this file, and/or from your personal experience, to support your view.

17. Explain briefly in your own words the difference between a prescriptive grammar and a descriptive grammar. Use one or two grammar books of any language that are accessible to you as examples, saying whether they are descriptive or prescriptive and why.

 18. Go to the Links page for Chapter 1 and listen to "Grammar Girl" (free podcasts). Decide whether she's talking about prescriptive or descriptive grammar. How do you know?

File 1.4—Design Features of Language

Exercises

19. Consider this sign ⊗ meaning 'no-smoking.' The sign has two components: ⊘ meaning 'no,' and a picture of a cigarette meaning 'cigarette/smoking.' Does each of the components have an arbitrary or an iconic relation with its meaning? Please briefly explain your answer. Be sure to discuss each of the two elements separately.

20. Traffic signals and signs are an example of a communication system that combines both arbitrary and nonarbitrary elements. Give two examples of traffic signs that are arbitrary and two that are iconic. Explain why you think each of your examples is arbitrary or iconic.

21. In Chinese, expressions for moving from one city to another by way of yet another city must take the form 'from X pass-through Y to Z' and cannot be expressed as 'from X to Z pass-through Y'; this is illustrated in the examples below (remember that the * indicates that a sentence is unacceptable in a language).

  a. ta   cong   Sanfanshi   jingguo   Zhijiage   dao   Niuyue
     he   from   San Francisco pass-through Chicago   to   New York
     'He went from San Francisco through Chicago to New York'

  b. *ta cong   Sanfanshi   dao   Niuyue   jingguo   Zhijiage
     he   from   San Francisco to   New York pass-through Chicago
     'He went from San Francisco to New York through Chicago'

How would you characterize the form-meaning relationship exhibited by these Chinese expressions? (*Hint:* Look at the ordering of places in the sentences, and compare that to the journey being described.)

Discussion Questions

22. Consider the compound words *blackboard* and *outfox* and the relationship of their meanings to the meanings of the words that make them up. In what ways do these compound words show a degree of nonarbitrariness in their form-meaning connection? Will this be true for all compound words? (*Hint:* Think about the color of objects we call *blackboards*.)

23. Onomatopoetic words often show a resistance to change in their pronunciation over time; for example, in earlier stages of English the word *cuckoo* had roughly the same pronunciation as it has now [kuku], and it failed to undergo a regular change in the pronunciation of vowels that would have made it sound roughly like *cowcow* [kɑʊkɑʊ] (compare the word *house* [hɑʊs], which used to be pronounced as [huːs] before this change). Similarly, the word *babble* has had *b* sounds in it for over 2,000 years and did not undergo the sound shift characteristic of all the Germanic languages by which original *b* came to be pronounced as *p*. Can you suggest a reason for this resistance to change with respect to these (and similar) words?

24. Try to imagine what would happen if we suddenly lost one of the design features of language. How would our communication change? What abilities would we lose? Discuss each of the following design features with respect to these questions.

   a. Displacement   **d.** Pragmatic Function
   b. Interchangeability   **e.** Discreteness
   c. Productivity

Activities

25. Productivity refers to our ability to produce and understand messages that have never been expressed before. To understand how frequently we deal with messages that have never been expressed before or that we have never heard or uttered before, go to an Internet search engine and type in a number of sentences, using quotation marks around the sentence. For example, you could type in <"People can produce and understand messages that have never been expressed before."> Type in at least 10 sentences. For each sentence, write down the number of documents that the search engine found containing your sentence. How many of your sentences have not been expressed at least once on the World Wide Web? Try to use sentences of different lengths and compare the results. With short sentences, you may get more hits—but be sure to see whether you have in fact found the same sentence in each case, rather than just part of a sentence. Longer sentences, like the sentence you're reading right now, are less likely to result in as many hits.

26. One piece of evidence for sound symbolism is the often quite consistent responses that speakers of a language give when asked the relative meanings of pairs of nonsense words, where the only clue to work from is the sound (i.e., the form) of the words. For example, speakers of English typically judge the nonsense word *feeg* to refer to something smaller than the nonsense word *foag*.

   Pronounce the words below according to regular English spelling, and for each pair of words decide which member of the pair could refer to something heavy and which to something light. Compare your answers with those of others in your class. Are they consistent?

   a. lat—loat   **d.** toos—tace   **g.** poas—poat
   b. foon—feen   **e.** fleen—feen   **h.** toos—tood
   c. mobe—meeb   **f.** seeg—sleeg

File 1.5—Language Modality

Exercises

27. Over the years, many people have (mistakenly) associated signed languages with pantomime. Give three arguments that this association is unwarranted.

28. The following are illustrations of the signs for 'me' in both American Sign Language and Taiwan Sign Language. What about these signs is similar, and what is different? To what extent is each sign iconic, and to what extent is it arbitrary?

a. ME in ASL
(The signer is touching his chest.)

b. ME in Taiwan Sign Language
(The signer is touching his nose.)

Discussion Question

29. Consider again the list from File 1.2 of what you know when you know a language. Speculate about how each of the items in this list might be manifested in the same way for spoken and signed languages and how each of the items might be manifested differently.

Activities

 30. Go to the Links page for Chapter 1 and click on the link for The British Museum's British Sign Language (BSL) object descriptions. On this page you can view BSL descriptions of over 200 items from the museum's collection. Select two or three items from the galleries on the page and watch their descriptions. You can also watch children describing several items.

i. Describe your impressions of watching these signers. In general terms, describe how they use their hands, their bodies, and their faces.

ii. Based on what you have observed in the videos, discuss why static images (such as those we use in this book) are inadequate for describing the way that a signed language is produced.

iii. Do you understand any of what the signers are saying? If so, how do you know (what cues are you using)? If not, why do you not know?

Further Readings

Crystal, David. 2010. *The Cambridge encyclopedia of language.* 3rd edn. Cambridge: Cambridge University Press.

Groce, Nora Ellen. 1985. *Everyone here spoke sign language: Hereditary deafness on Martha's Vineyard.* Cambridge, MA: Harvard University Press.

Hall, Christopher J. 2006. *An introduction to language and linguistics: Breaking the language spell.* New York: Continuum.

Lewis, M. Paul; Gary F. Simons; and Charles D. Fennig (eds.). 2015. *Ethnologue: Languages of the world.* 18th edn. Dallas, TX: SIL International. Online version: http://www.ethnologue.com/.

Valli, Clayton; Ceil Lucas; Kristin J. Mulrooney; and Miako Villanueva. 2011. *Linguistics of American Sign Language: An introduction.* 5th edn. Washington, DC: Gallaudet University Press.

CHAPTER
2
Phonetics

FILE **2.0**

What Is Phonetics?

Phonetics is the study of the minimal units that make up language.[1] For spoken language, these are the sounds of speech—the consonants, vowels, melodies, and rhythms. As described in File 1.2, the process of communicating has several steps. Within this chain, there are three aspects to the study of speech sounds: **articulatory phonetics,** the study of the production of speech sounds; **acoustic phonetics,** the study of the transmission and the physical properties of speech sounds; and **auditory phonetics,** the study of the perception of speech sounds. In this chapter, we will discuss the articulation and acoustics of speech sounds, as these branches are better understood than auditory phonetics at this point.

One of the most basic aspects of phonetics is figuring out which sounds are possible in speech. You can make a plethora of different noises with your mouth, but only a subset of these noises are used in human language. In this chapter, we will describe some of the features that characterize the speech sounds of the world's languages. We'll see that breaking speech sounds into their component parts reveals similarities among even the most exotic-seeming sounds.

Contents

------

[1]While phonetics is traditionally the study of the **sounds** of speech, the study of phonetics is not actually limited to spoken modalities (see File 1.5). Because *phonetics* has come to refer to the study of the minimal units that make up language in general, phoneticians may also study the minimal units (the phonetics) of signed languages (see File 2.7).

FILE **2.1**

Representing Speech Sounds

2.1.1 Studying Pronunciation

"You're not from around here, are you?" Sometimes you can tell by the way a person pronounces words that he or she speaks a dialect that is different from yours. For example, some people do not pronounce *pin* differently from *pen*. In some parts of Ohio the word *push* is pronounced with a vowel sound like the one in *who*. If you hear someone say *poosh*, you can guess where they are from. Such pronunciation differences have been noted for many thousands of years. For example, there is a story in the Bible (Judges 12:4–6) about a group who, after winning a battle, used a password to identify their fleeing attackers. The password they used was *shibboleth,* since their enemies couldn't pronounce the <sh> sound. This group then killed anyone with the telltale pronunciation *sibboleth.* These illustrations show that pronunciation is a part of what we know when we know a language.

There are numerous ways of studying pronunciation in spoken language. In recent years, phoneticians have begun to employ some very sophisticated instrumental techniques to study spoken language.

In articulatory phonetics, we want to know the way in which speech sounds are produced—what parts of the mouth are used and in what sorts of configurations. To investigate these aspects of sound production, phoneticians have used **X-ray photography** and cinematography, among other techniques. More recently, to avoid methods that expose talkers to dangerous amounts of radiation, phoneticians have used point-tracking devices such as the X-ray microbeam or the electromagnetic articulograph to track the locations of small receptors glued onto the lips, tongue, and jaw. Articulatory phonetics is also done with **palatography** (see Section 2.2.6) to observe contact between the tongue and the roof of the mouth, and instruments to measure airflow and air pressure during speech. Ultrasound is also used and is particularly useful for imaging the full tongue during articulation.

In acoustic phonetics, we are more interested in the characteristics of the sounds produced by these articulations. To study acoustic phonetics, phoneticians use pictures of the sounds, using tools such as the **sound spectrograph.** These pictures help acoustic phoneticians explore the physical properties of sounds. These days, you can download sound editing and analysis software from the web. Try searching for a "waveform editor" or an "audio spectrograph," or simply for "phonetics analysis software," and see what free software is available that will to enable you to look at and edit speech sounds on your computer.

The third branch of phonetics, auditory phonetics, focuses on how humans process speech sounds: how we perceive pronunciation. While the fundamentals of perception can be explored by using fairly simple experimental methods that look at human responses to particular stimuli, advanced study of this field depends on more modern equipment such as magnetic resonance imaging (MRI) and computerized tomography (CT).

All of these techniques give us great insight into the details of phonetics. But the simplest and most basic method of phonetic analysis—**impressionistic phonetic transcription**—is still a vital tool for phoneticians. Phonetic transcription is a method of writing down speech sounds in order to capture what is said and how it is pronounced. An example of phonetic transcription is the line "you say tomato, I say tomahto" from Ira Gershwin's lyrics to the song "Let's Call the Whole Thing Off." The word *tomato* is pronounced differently by different people, and we can symbolize two of the pronunciations as "tomato" and "tomahto" as Gershwin did. Or we could follow the pronunciation guide in *Webster's Third New International Dictionary* and write the two pronuncations as təˈmātō and təˈmåto. Or we could refer to the *American Heritage Dictionary,* where the two pronunciations are written təmāʹtō and təmäʹtō. Confusing, isn't it? Yet we need to use phonetic transcription because the normal spelling of the word doesn't tell us enough about how it is pronounced by different people. Spelling is conventionalized, and it symbolizes the word that is meant, rather than how it is pronounced.

Spelling	Gershwin	*Webster's*	*Amer. Heritage*
tomato	tomato	təˈmātō	təmāʹtō
tomato	tomahto	təˈmåtō	təmäʹtō

2.1.2 The "Right" Phonetic Alphabet

Did Gershwin write the two pronunciations of *tomato* correctly? Or does one of the dictionaries have the right way to symbolize the difference? It should be clear that there is no one "right" answer about how to write pronunciation in a phonetic transcription. The choices we make are largely arbitrary or influenced by typographical or historical considerations. However, it is absolutely crucial that both the reader and the author agree on the sound qualities that are assigned to the symbols in a phonetic alphabet. This is why almost all dictionaries give some guide to the pronunciation symbols where they list familiar words as examples of the sounds. For example, *father* is used to illustrate the sound intended by <å> in *Webster's* and by <ä> in the *American Heritage*. Whether the <a> has one mark or two is an arbitrary decision. This is fine, so long as we have a pronunciation guide.

If the goal of having a phonetic transcription system is to be able to unambiguously convey the important aspects of the pronunciation of a given set of sounds, using a written system of symbols, then such a system must have certain characteristics.

First, each symbol should represent one sound (or **phone**) only, and there should be only one symbol for each sound. The letter <c> violates this principle in English spelling because it represents two sounds (the [k] sound in *cat*, and the [s] sound in *cymbal*, and both the [k] and [s] in *cynic*, for example). Hence, using a <c> does not unambiguously tell the reader which sound is intended.

Second, if two sounds can distinguish one word from another, they should be represented by different symbols. The letters <th> in English violate this principle because the difference between the <th> sounds in *thy* and *thigh* is not captured by using <th> for both words. That is, there is an important difference in pronunciation that is not captured with these letters.

Third, if two sounds are very similar and their difference arises only from the context they are in, we should be able to represent that similarity (see Chapter 3 for how sounds influence surrounding sounds). For example, the [k] sounds in *keep* and *cool* are different from each other in that the exact places they are articulated are dependent on the following vowel. The [k] in *keep* is produced farther forward in the mouth than the [k] in *cool* because the sounds of the words are made using a single flowing action. The influence of one sound on a neighboring sound is known as **co-articulation.** If we are not interested in representing this variation, because it is reasonably predictable in English, we want to make sure that these [k] sounds are not written with different symbols in our transcription system.

Based on the criteria above, the English spelling system is not a good phonetic alphabet because:

- sometimes the same sound is spelled using different letters, such as the [i] sound in *sea, see, scene, receive, thief, amoeba,* and *machine;*
- sometimes the same letters can stand for different sounds, as in *sign, pleasure,* and *resign,* or *charter* and *character,* or *father, all, about, apple, any,* and *age;*
- sometimes a single sound is spelled by a combination of letters, as in *lock, that, book, boast, mountain, shop, apple,* or *special;*
- sometimes a single letter represents a combination of sounds, as in *exit* or *use;*
- sometimes letters stand for no sound at all, as in *know, doubt, though, island, rhubarb,* or *moose.*

A good phonetic transcription system is consistent and unambiguous because there is always a one-to-one correspondence between sounds and symbols. This is even true across languages, so that the symbols you will be learning can be used to transcribe the sounds of any language.

In this book we use the International Phonetic Alphabet (IPA for short). This phonetic alphabet is the right one to use because it is applicable to all spoken human languages, rather than just English, and it has all of the properties of a "useful phonetic alphabet" discussed above. That is, there is a one-to-one correspondence between sounds and symbols, so that each symbol represents only one sound and each sound is represented by only one symbol. In addition, the IPA can be used to transcribe different levels of detail, from broad transcriptions to a very fine level of phonetic detail.

2.1.3   Types of Speech Sounds

In order to create a good phonetic transcription system, we need to know what types of sounds we are trying to transcribe. Phoneticians divide the speech stream into two main categories: **segments** and **suprasegmentals**. Segments are the discrete units of the speech stream and can be further subdivided into the categories consonants (File 2.2) and vowels (File 2.3). These sounds are transcribed easily using discrete symbols like [p] and [i]. Suprasegmentals, on the other hand, can be said to "ride on top of" segments in that they often apply to entire strings of consonants and vowels—these are properties such as stress, tone, and intonation (File 2.5). These properties are somewhat more difficult to represent using an alphabetic-like transcription system, and there are many different ways they can be transcribed.

From an articulatory point of view, consonants and vowels are both made by positioning the vocal tract in a particular configuration. However, **consonants** are distinguished from vowels in that consonants are produced with a constriction somewhere in the vocal tract that impedes airflow, while **vowels** have at most only a slight narrowing and allow air to flow freely through the oral cavity. We can also distinguish consonants and vowels acoustically.

Yet another way we can distinguish vowels and consonants is the role each one plays in a **syllable.** A syllable is a unit of speech—every utterance contains at least one syllable. A syllable may contain only a single sound, as in the **monosyllabic** word *uh* [ʌ], or several sounds, as in *sprints* [spɹɪnts]. A syllable can be broken down into an **onset** and a **rhyme.** The rhyme consists of the vowel and any consonants that come after it—the segments that match in words that we think of as rhyming (such as *man, can,* and *plan*)—while any consonants that occur before the rhyme within the syllable form the onset (such as *man, can,* and *plan*). All syllables have a rhyme, but onsets are optional in some languages. The rhyme

(1) Syllable structure

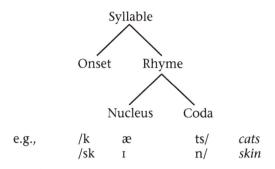

e.g.,	/k	æ	ts/	*cats*
	/sk	ɪ	n/	*skin*

can be further broken down into the **nucleus,** the vocalic part of rhyme, and the **coda,** which consists of any final consonants. The structure of a syllable is shown in (1).

The syllable nucleus is the "heart" of the syllable, carrying suprasegmental information such as stress, volume, and pitch, which vowels are much better suited to do than consonants. Consonants usually do not function as the nucleus of the syllable (but see Section 2.2.5 for syllabic consonants), while vowels do not function as onsets of syllables.

Vowels in turn are often divided into two categories: **monophthongs** ([mɑnəpθɑŋz]) and **diphthongs** ([dɪfθɑŋz] or [dɪpθɑŋz]). You can think of monophthongs as simple vowels, composed of a single configuration of the vocal tract, while diphthongs are complex vowels, composed of a sequence of two different configurations. We consider diphthongs to be "single" vowels, however, because the sequence of two configurations acts as the nucleus to a single syllable. To conceptualize this better, think of the two words *knives* and *naive.* The actual vowel sounds in these two words are essentially the same, but in *knives,* there is just one syllable nucleus (the diphthong [ɑɪ]), while in *naive,* there are two separate syllables with two separate nuclei (the monophthong [ɑ] in the first syllable, followed by the monophthong [i] in the second syllable). The differences between monophthongs and diphthongs will be discussed in more detail in File 2.3.

2.1.4 Phonetic Symbols for English

This section lists the IPA symbols for English segments that we will be using in this book. Phonetic symbols are written in square brackets, [ ], to distinguish them from letters or words written in ordinary spelling. It is important to remember that these symbols are not the same as letters of English. Rather, they represent the sounds of language. The following table gives the phonetic symbols for the sound inventory of Standard American English, and the example words make use of Standard American English pronunciations. (Other sounds and symbols will be introduced in File 2.4.) There are recordings of these words available on the Sounds page for Chapter 2.

Symbol	Sample Words	Name of Symbol
Consonants:		
[p]	pit, tip, spit, hiccough, appear	
[b]	ball, globe, amble, brick, bubble	
[t]	tag, pat, stick, pterodactyl, stuffed	
[d]	dip, card, drop, loved, batted	

(cont.)

Symbol	Sample Words	Name of Symbol
[k]	kit, scoot, character, critique, exceed[1]	
[g]	guard, bag, finger, designate, Pittsburgh	
[ʔ]	uh-oh, hatrack, Batman, button, curtain	glottal stop
[f]	foot, laugh, philosophy, coffee, carafe	
[v]	vest, dove, gravel, anvil, average	
[θ]	through, wrath, thistle, ether, teeth	theta
[ð]	the, their, mother, either, teethe	eth, [εð]
[s]	soap, psychology, packs, descent, peace, excruciating[1]	
[z]	zip, roads, kisses, Xerox, design	
[ʃ]	shy, mission, nation, glacial, sure	esh, [εʃ]
[ʒ]	measure, vision, azure, casualty, decision	yogh, [joʊg] or ezh, [εʒ]
[h]	who, hat, rehash, hole, whole	
[ʧ]	choke, match, feature, constituent	
[ʤ]	judge, George, Jell-O, region, residual	
[m]	moose, lamb, smack, amnesty, ample	
[n]	nap, design, snow, know, mnemonic	
[ŋ]	lung, think, finger, singer, ankle	engma or eng
[l]	leaf, feel, Lloyd, mild, applaud	
[ɹ]	reef, fear, Harris, prune, carp	
[ɾ]	butter, udder, cuter, Adam, bottle, ready	flap
[w]	with, swim, mowing, queen, twilight	
[w̥][2]	which, where, what, whale, why (for those dialects in which *witch* and *which* do not sound the same)	voiceless 'w'
[j]	you, beautiful, feud, use, yell	lower-case 'j'

Syllabic Consonants:

Symbol	Sample Words	Name of Symbol
[m̩]	possum, chasm, Adam, bottomless	syllabic 'm'
[n̩]	button, chicken, lesson, kittenish	syllabic 'n'
[l̩]	little, single, simple, stabilize	syllabic 'l'
[ɹ̩][3]	ladder, singer, burp, percent, bird	syllabic 'r'

---

[1]The letter <x> in *exceed* and *excruciating* represents a series of two sounds: [ks].
[2]An alternative symbol for this sound is [ʍ], the upside-down 'w.'
[3]Another symbol that is sometimes used for this sound when unstressed (as in *ladder,* but not *burp*) is [ɚ], schwar.

Symbol	Sample Words	Name of Symbol

Vowels:
i. Monophthongs (Simple Vowels)

Symbol	Sample Words	Name of Symbol
[i]	beat, we, believe, people, money, dean	
[ɪ]	bit, consist, injury, malignant, business, gym	small capital 'i'
[ɛ]	bet, reception, says, guest, bend	epsilon
[æ]	bat, laugh, anger, comrade, rally, hand	ash
[u]	boot, who, brewer, duty, through, dune	
[ʊ]	put, foot, butcher, could, boogie-woogie	upsilon
[ɔ]	bought, caught, wrong, stalk, core, law	open 'o'
[ɑ]	pot, father, sergeant, honor, hospital, bomb	script 'a'
[ʌ]	but, tough, another, oven, fungus	wedge or turned 'v'
[ə]	among, Asia, eloquent, famous, harmony	schwa

ii. Diphthongs (Complex Vowels)

Symbol	Sample Words	Name of Symbol
[ɑɪ]	I, abide, Stein, aisle, choir, island, fine	
[ɑʊ]	bout, brown, doubt, flower, loud	
[ɔɪ]	boy, doily, rejoice, perestroika, annoy	
[oʊ]	oh, boat, beau, grow, though, over	
[eɪ]	bait, reign, great, they, gauge, age	

In the list in the table above, we have given you examples of individual sounds in individual words. When we actually use language on a day-to-day basis, however, we speak in phrases and sentences, with all the words run together. This type of speech is known as **running speech** or **continuous speech**, and, although as linguists we sometimes need to break speech into its component parts of words and sounds, you should bear in mind that most everyday speech is not separated out into these pieces. In running speech, the pronunciations of words may be affected by the surrounding words (see Section 2.1.2 on phonetic co-articulation or File 3.3 on phonological assimilation), and one of the open research questions in the study of language processing is how the human mind processes running speech into its meaningful component parts (see Chapter 9).

FILE **2.2**

Articulation: English Consonants

2.2.1 Introducing Articulatory Phonetics

Say the word *hiss* and hold the [s]. Now inhale while holding the tongue position of [s]. What part of your tongue is cooled by the incoming airstream? What part of the roof of your mouth is cooled? Simple, intuitive observations such as these (bolstered by careful X-ray and palatography studies) lead to an **articulatory description** of speech sounds like the consonants of English. **Articulation**, also called an **articulatory gesture**, is the motion or positioning of some part of the vocal tract (often, but not always, a muscular part like the tongue and/or lips) with respect to some other part of the vocal tract in the production of a speech sound (more on this below).

The focus of this file is the articulation of English consonants. Recall from Section 2.1.3 that consonants are speech sounds that are produced with a constriction somewhere in the vocal tract that impedes the airflow. When describing a consonant, it is therefore necessary to provide information about three different aspects of its articulation:

- Is the sound voiced or voiceless?
- Where is the airstream constricted (i.e., what is the place of articulation)?
- How is the airstream constricted (i.e., what is the manner of articulation)?

The voicing, place, and manner of articulation are known as **segmental features.** Please remember that in this file and elsewhere, whenever we say things like "[p] is voiceless" or "the [p] in *pan*," what we really mean is "the sound represented by the symbol [p]." Remember that we are talking about **speech sounds,** symbolized by phonetic transcription, not letters like <p>, <j>, etc.

2.2.2 Anatomy of Human Speech Production

In order to answer the three questions listed above, we first need to know more about the anatomy of speech production. There are three basic components of the human anatomy that are involved in the production of speech (see (1)). The first is the **larynx** (sometimes called the voice box), which contains the vocal folds and the glottis and is located in the throat, at the Adam's apple.[1] The second is the **vocal tract** above the larynx, which is composed of the oral and nasal cavities. The third is the **subglottal system,** which is the part of the respiratory system located below the larynx. When air is inhaled, it is channeled through the nasal or oral cavity, or both, through the larynx, and into the lungs. When air is exhaled, it is forced out of the lungs and through the larynx and the vocal tract.

English speech sounds are formed when exhaling, forcing a stream of air out of the lungs through the oral or nasal cavity, or both. This airstream provides the energy for sound

---

[1]Yes, everyone has an Adam's apple! It is a protrusion of the cartilage protecting the vocal folds and is usually larger and more prominent in men than in women.

(1) The speech production mechanism.

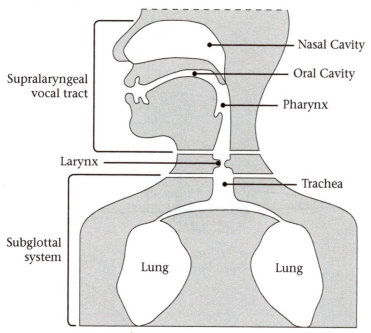

From Lieberman and Blumstein, *Speech physiology, speech perception, and acoustic phonetics* (1988), p. 4. Copyright 1988 Cambridge University Press. All rights reserved. Reprinted with permission.

production—either by making the vocal folds vibrate or by making hissing or popping noises as air escapes through narrow openings in the mouth. Sounds created by exhaling are said to be made by using a **pulmonic** (= lung) **egressive** (= blowing out) **airstream mechanism**. All English speech sounds are made using this mechanism, although it is not the only way to produce speech. Other **airstream mechanisms** used in other languages are discussed briefly in Section 2.4.6.

2.2.3 States of the Glottis: Voicing

Humans have a larynx at the top of the **trachea** (or windpipe). Within the larynx are folds of muscle called **vocal folds** (these are popularly known as vocal cords, but they are not really cords). In the diagram in (2) we are viewing the larynx as if looking down a person's throat. A flap of tissue called the epiglottis is attached at the front of the larynx and can fold down and back to cover and protect the vocal folds, which are stretched horizontally along the open center of the larynx. The opening between these folds is called the **glottis.** At the front of the larynx, the vocal folds are attached to cartilage and can't be moved, but at the back of the larynx, the vocal folds are attached to two small movable cartilages that can close or open the glottis. When the two free ends are brought together ("approximated"), the vocal folds can be nearly or completely closed, impeding airflow through the glottis (2b). When the folds are wide open, the glottis has roughly the shape of a triangle, as can be seen in (2a). There is also an intermediate position, in which the vocal folds are partially open, as shown in (2c). This is the position of the vocal folds when you whisper.

When the vocal folds are open, the flow of air coming up from the lungs passes through freely, and when the folds are held close together, they vibrate as air from the lungs forces its way through them. Try putting your hand lightly on your throat, or putting your

(2) Three states of the glottis. The view is of the larynx (from above), looking down the throat.

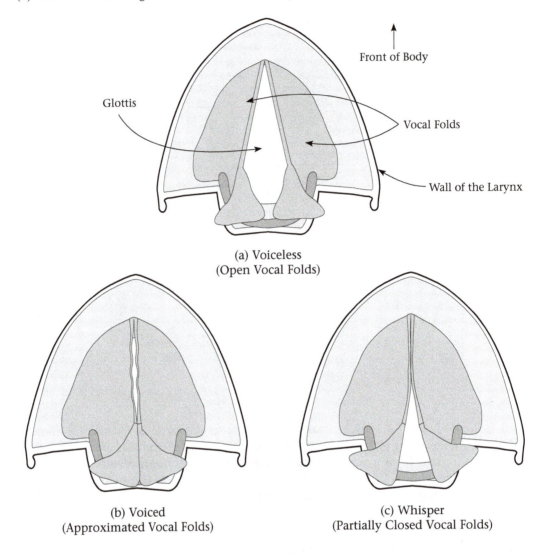

Front of Body

Glottis

Vocal Folds

Wall of the Larynx

(a) Voiceless
(Open Vocal Folds)

(b) Voiced
(Approximated Vocal Folds)

(c) Whisper
(Partially Closed Vocal Folds)

fingers in your ears, and then making a drawn-out [s]. Your vocal folds are separated to open the glottis, as in (2a), so you should feel no vibration. But now make a [z] (again, draw it out), and you will feel a vibration or buzzing feeling. This is due to the vibration of the vocal folds—your glottis is now as in the shape of (2b). This vibration is called **voicing**.

Sounds made with the vocal folds vibrating are called **voiced** sounds, and sounds made without such vibration are called **voiceless** sounds. The underlined sounds in the following pairs of words (see (3)) differ only in that the sound is voiceless in the first word of each pair and voiced in the second. Try saying these words, but don't whisper when you do, because the vocal folds don't vibrate when you whisper.

 (3) Voiceless versus voiced sounds

a. [f] <u>f</u>at	c. [θ] <u>th</u>igh	e. [s] <u>s</u>ip	g. [ʃ] dilu<u>ti</u>on
[v] <u>v</u>at	[ð] <u>th</u>y	[z] <u>z</u>ip	[ʒ] delu<u>si</u>on
b. [tʃ] ri<u>ch</u>	d. [p] <u>p</u>at	f. [t] <u>t</u>ab	h. [k] <u>k</u>ill
[dʒ] ri<u>dge</u>	[b] <u>b</u>at	[d] <u>d</u>ab	[g] <u>g</u>ill

In making an articulatory description of a consonant, it is therefore first necessary to state whether a sound is voiced (there is vocal fold vibration; see (2b)) or voiceless (there is no vocal fold vibration; see (2a)). A chart of the voiced and voiceless consonants of English is provided in Section 2.2.7.

Phoneticians can determine if a given segment is voiced or voiceless using a number of different techniques. The simplest is one we described earlier: feeling for vibration of the vocal folds while you produce a sound. This technique, however, is very limited in its ability to determine voicing in running speech (try saying *ice cream* while placing your fingers lightly on your throat—is it obvious that the [s] and [k] in the middle are both voiceless?). One alternative is to examine a picture of the acoustic signal called a **spectrogram,** which will be discussed in more detail in File 2.6. The **voicing bar** on a spectrogram can indicate whether vocal fold vibrations are present in a sound. Another method of studying voicing is to look at the vocal folds directly, using high-speed video. A very thin fiberoptic line is inserted through the speaker's nostril and nasal cavity, down into the upper part of the pharynx. This line conveys a strong white light through the vocal tract to illuminate the vocal folds. A tiny camera, attached to the line and connected to a computer, records movements of the vocal folds. As the subject speaks, the extremely fast vibrations of the vocal folds are filmed so that one can later look at and analyze the recordings frame by frame. While this method allows the speaker to talk freely, with no obstacles in the mouth, and gives a very clear picture of the adjustments and movements of the vocal folds, it is invasive and requires the presence of well-trained medical personnel.

2.2.4 Place of Articulation

The second aspect of describing consonants is stating where in the vocal tract the constriction is made—that is, where the vocal tract is made narrower. This is referred to as the **place of articulation** of a sound. When reading about each of the following points of articulation, refer to (4), which shows a schematic view of the vocal tract as seen from the side (called a **sagittal section**). To see how this diagram matches up with an actual human head, you may find it helpful to refer to the picture to the lower left, which shows this same diagram superimposed on a photograph. We begin our descriptions with the front of the mouth—the left side of the diagram—and work our way back toward the throat.

Bilabial consonants are made by bringing both lips close together. There are five such sounds in English: [p] *p̲at*, [b] *b̲at*, [m] *m̲at*, [w] *w̲ith*, and [ʍ] *w̲here* (for some speakers).

Labiodental consonants are made with the lower lip against the upper front teeth. English has two labiodentals: [f] *f̲at* and [v] *v̲at*.

Interdentals are made with the tip of the tongue protruding between the front teeth. There are two interdental sounds in most varieties of American English: [θ] *thigh* and [ð] *thy*.

Alveolar sounds are made with the tongue tip at or near the front of the upper **alveolar** [ælvilɹ] **ridge.** The alveolar ridges are the bony ridges of the upper and lower jaws that contain the sockets for the teeth. (Think of the inside of a baby's mouth before teeth grow in.) The front of the upper alveolar ridge, which is the most important area in terms of describing alveolar consonants, is the part you can feel protruding just behind your upper front teeth. From now on, any reference to the alveolar ridge means specifically the upper alveolar ridge. English has eight alveolar consonants: [t] *t̲ab*, [d] *d̲ab*, [s] *s̲ip*, [z] *z̲ip*, [n] *n̲oose*, [ɾ] *a̲tom*, [l] *l̲oose*, and [ɹ] *r̲ed*.

Post-alveolar sounds are made a bit farther back. If you let your tongue or finger slide back along the roof of your mouth, you will find that the front portion is hard and the back portion is soft. Post-alveolar sounds are made with the front of the tongue just behind the alveolar ridge, right at the front of the hard palate. English has four post-alveolar sounds: [ʃ] *lea̲sh*, [ʒ] *mea̲sure*, [tʃ] *chur̲ch*, and [dʒ] *ju̲dge*.

Palatal sounds are made with the body of the tongue near the center of the hard portion of the roof of the mouth (the '**hard palate**'). English has only one palatal sound: [j] _yes_.

Velar consonants are produced at the **velum,** also known as the soft palate, which is the soft part of the roof of the mouth behind the hard palate. Sounds made with the back part of the tongue body raised near the velum are said to be velar. There are three velar sounds in English: [k] _kill_, [g] _gill_, and [ŋ] _sing_.

Glottal sounds are produced when air is constricted at the larynx. The space between the vocal folds is the glottis. English has two sounds made at the glottis. One is easy to hear: [h], as in _high_ and _history_. The other is called a glottal stop and is transcribed phonetically as [ʔ]. This sound occurs before each of the vowel sounds in _uh-oh_ and in the middle of a word like _cotton_.

(4) Sagittal section of the vocal tract

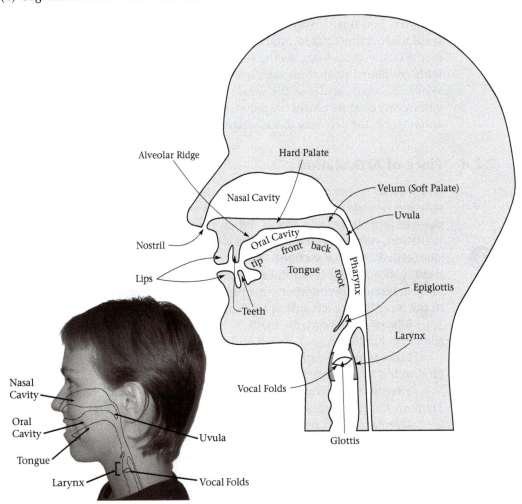

2.2.5   Manner of Articulation

The third aspect of consonant description, in addition to stating whether a consonant is voiced or voiceless and giving the consonant's place of articulation, is its **manner of articulation**; that is, it is necessary to describe how the airstream is constricted or modified in the vocal tract to produce the sound. The manner of articulation of a consonant depends largely on the degree of closure of the articulators (how close together or far apart they are).

Stops are made by obstructing the airstream completely in the oral cavity. (Stops can also be referred to as plosives, a term that references the release of built-up air pressure when the constriction is opened.) Notice that when you say [p] and [b], your lips are pressed together for a moment, stopping the airflow. [p] and [b] are bilabial stops. [b] is a voiced bilabial stop, while [p] is a voiceless bilabial stop. [t], [d], [k], and [g] are also stops. What is the three-part description (voicing, place, and manner) of each? The glottal stop, [ʔ], is a little different because the closure is not in the oral cavity but in the larynx: the vocal folds momentarily close tight, stopping the airflow. If you press your fingertips lightly on your Adam's apple while saying *uh-oh*, you can feel movement with the closure and then the release in the glottis. And if you stop halfway through *uh-oh*, holding all of your articulators in place, then you should be able to feel a catch in your throat, which is the glottal stop (note that if you keep holding it, you will run out of air, as with all stops!).

Fricatives are made by forming a nearly complete obstruction of the vocal tract. The opening through which the air escapes is very small, and as a result a turbulent noise is produced (much as air escaping from a punctured tire makes a hissing noise). Such a turbulent, hissing mouth noise is called **frication**, hence the name of this class of speech sounds. [ʃ], as in *ship*, is made by almost stopping the air with the tongue just behind the alveolar ridge. It is a voiceless post-alveolar fricative. How would you describe each of the following fricatives: [f], [v], [θ], [ð], [s], [z], [ʒ], and [h]?

Affricates are complex sounds, made by briefly stopping the airstream completely and then releasing the articulators slightly so that frication noise is produced. They can thus be described as beginning with a stop and ending with a fricative, as reflected in the phonetic symbols used to represent them. English has only two affricates, [t͡ʃ], as in *church*, and [d͡ʒ], as in *judge*.[2] [t͡ʃ] is pronounced like a very quick combination of a [t], pronounced somewhat farther back in the mouth, followed by [ʃ]. It is a voiceless post-alveolar affricate. [d͡ʒ] is a combination of [d] and [ʒ]. What is its three-part description (voicing, place, and manner)?

Nasals are produced by relaxing the velum and lowering it, thus opening the nasal passage to the vocal tract. In most speech sounds, the velum is raised against the back of the throat, blocking off the nasal cavity so that no air can escape through the nose. These sounds are called oral, because the air flows through the oral cavity instead. So when the velum is lowered and air escapes through the nasal cavity, like it is with [m], as in *Kim*, [n], as in *kin*, and [ŋ], as in *king*, the sounds are referred to as nasals. These are sometimes called nasal stops, because there is a complete obstruction of the airflow in the oral cavity, but unlike oral stops, the air continues to flow freely through the nose. For [m], the obstruction is at the lips; for [n], the obstruction is formed by the tongue tip and sides pressing all around the alveolar ridge; and for [ŋ], the obstruction is caused by the back of the tongue body pressing up against the velum. In English, all nasals are voiced. Thus [m] is a voiced bilabial nasal (stop); the only difference between [m] and [b] is that the velum is lowered for the articulation of [m], but raised for the articulation of [b]. How would you describe [n] and [ŋ]?

Approximants, like all consonants, involve constriction of the vocal tract, but the constrictions are not narrow enough to block the vocal tract or cause turbulence. Approximants can be further divided into liquids and glides. We separate these categories mostly because they pattern differently in English, but we will also point out some minor articulatory differences.

Liquids are formed with slightly more constriction than glides, and their quality changes (is "liquid") depending on where they occur in a word, e.g., the beginning or end

---

[2]Affricates can also be represented with the two individual symbols that make up the sound, either just next to each other ([tʃ], [dʒ]) or with a tie bar connecting them ([t͡ʃ], [d͡ʒ]). We use the connected versions of the symbols ([t͡ʃ], [d͡ʒ]) in this book to make it clear that affricates function as a single sound.

of a syllable (see the discussion of clear versus dark [l] in Section 2.4.6). The first liquid we have in English is the alveolar lateral liquid [l]. In this sound, the front of the tongue is pressed against the alveolar ridge, as in [d], but unlike in a stop, where the tongue is sealed all the way around the ridge, the sides of the tongue are relaxed (lateral = side), letting the air flow freely over them. You can feel this by starting to say *leaf* and pausing your tongue at the [l], and then inhaling sharply. The air will cool the side(s) of your tongue, showing you the airflow pattern. (Not everyone has the same pattern: do you feel air on the left or right side of your tongue? or both?) Liquids are usually voiced in English, so [l] is a voiced alveolar lateral liquid.

The other liquid in English is [ɹ]. There is a great deal of variation in the ways speakers of English make r-sounds; most are voiced and articulated in the general alveolar region, and a common type also involves curling the tip of the tongue back behind the alveolar ridge to make a **retroflex** sound. Another common type involves "bunching" the tongue up near the roof of the mouth, but for our purposes [ɹ] as in *red* may be considered a voiced alveolar retroflex liquid.

Nasals and liquids are classified as consonants, so we would not normally expect them to be syllabic. (See Section 2.1.3.) However, they sometimes act like vowels in that they can function as syllable nuclei. Pronounce the following words out loud, and listen to the liquids and nasals in them: *prism, prison, table,* and *hiker.* In these words the nucleus of the second syllable consists only of a syllabic nasal or liquid; there is no vowel in these second syllables. In order to indicate that these are **syllabic consonants**, a short vertical line is placed below the phonetic symbol. The final *(o)n* of *prison* would be transcribed [n̩]; likewise [m̩], [l̩], and [ɹ̩] in *prism, table,* and *hiker.*

Glides are made with only a slight closure of the articulators (so they are fairly close to vowel sounds), and they require some movement (or "gliding") of the articulators during production. [w] is made by raising the back of the tongue toward the velum while rounding the lips at the same time, so it is officially classified as a voiced **labial-velar** glide, though we will usually categorize it as bilabial for the sake of simplicity. (Notice the similarity in the way you articulate the [w] and the vowel [u] in the word *woo*: the only change is that you open your lips a little more for [u].) [ʍ] is produced just like [w], except that it is voiceless; not all speakers of English use this sound. Speakers who use it say it in, for example, the word *which* [ʍɪtʃ], making it distinct from *witch* [wɪtʃ]. [j] is made with a slight constriction in the palatal region. It is a voiced palatal glide. Compare the pronunciation of *yawn* [jɔn] and *eon* [iɑn], and notice the similarity between [j] and the vowel [i].

The last manner of articulation that we will discuss here is the **flap**. A flap (sometimes called a tap) is similar to a stop in that it involves the complete obstruction of the oral cavity. The closure, however, is much faster than that of a stop: the articulators strike each other very quickly. In American English, we have an alveolar flap, in which the tip of the tongue is brought up and simply allowed to quickly strike the alveolar ridge before it moves into position for the next sound. This voiced sound is symbolized by the IPA character [ɾ] and occurs as the middle sound in the words *writer* and *ladder.*

2.2.6 Investigating Place and Manner of Articulation: Palatography

The average speaker is able to feel at least approximately where and how particular consonant sounds are made; however, phoneticians have developed a number of methods for looking more precisely at the place and manner of articulation. One of the most common methods is **palatography.** In palatography, a picture is made that shows where the tongue touches the roof of the mouth during a particular articulation.

One way to do this, **static palatography,** involves painting the tongue black with a (tasteless) mixture of olive oil and charcoal powder. When the speaker produces the sound [s] as in *see,* the tongue leaves a black trace wherever it touched to make the constriction.

The speaker can then produce the sound [ʃ] as in *she* (after rinsing off and repainting the tongue), so that the place of articulation (e.g., on the alveolar ridge or the hard palate) for [s] versus [ʃ] can be studied. This method, in addition to being rather messy, works only if the speaker produces a single isolated sound and the contact pattern is photographed or examined immediately.

In order to observe the interplay between articulations, that is, how one consonant's place of articulation affects another consonant's place of articulation, you can use **dynamic palatography**. This method is similar to static palatography but more sophisticated because it allows the experimenter to record sequences of contacts that the tongue makes with the hard palate in the course of the production of an utterance. The places where contact is made are directly recorded into a computer. Once the recordings are made, you can align a specific point in time of the acoustic display of the utterance with a specific dynamic palatography display. This way you can measure exactly where, how much, and how long contact between the tongue and the roof of the mouth is produced at any given time in the utterance.

The speaker in such a study is required to use an artificial hard palate (similar to a retainer) that is custom made to fit his or her hard palate exactly. This artificial palate has many small embedded electrodes that record contact as soon as the tongue moves against them. Thus, for any given moment in time during the recording, the researcher knows exactly where the tongue contacts the roof of the mouth. Since the retainer covers only the hard palate, the exact amount of contact made in the soft palate region for velar consonants, such as [g] or [k], is sometimes hard to see. Nevertheless, this method provides fairly exact data about where and at what point in time within an utterance the tongue touches the hard palate.

You can compare the two types of images made using static versus dynamic palatography in (5). Both of these images show the contact pattern for a [d], spoken by different speakers. The one on the left is the result of static palatography; the one on the right is from dynamic palatography. In both cases, the speaker's teeth are toward the top of the page, and we are looking at the roof of the mouth. In the static palatography picture, the black marks indicate where the tongue touched the roof of the mouth during the production of the nonsense word *ahdah* [ɑdɑ]. In the dynamic palatography picture, the cross-marks indicate the locations of all the sensors on the artificial hard palate; the black boxes indicate sensors that were contacted by the tongue during the [d] of the phrase *bad guy* [bædgɑɪ].

In both cases, it is clear that the tongue made full contact with the alveolar ridge and part of the hard palate, completely closing off the airflow. This is consistent with how we have described the manner of articulation of [d], as a stop.

(5) Comparing images from static and dynamic palatography for the production of [d]

The contact was made at the front of the mouth in both cases—right along the alveolar ridge, as expected from our description of the place of articulation for [d]. There are differences in the two pictures, however: the one on the left also clearly shows that this speaker produced the word with the tongue far enough forward that it also partly touched the teeth—hence this particular production could be characterized as also **dental**, not purely alveolar. Meanwhile, the image on the right shows that the speaker's tongue was slightly farther back, on the alveolar ridge but not up against the front teeth. These kinds of minor pronunciation variations are not something that we can capture using our standard transcriptions.

Notice that palatography tells you only about the position of the tongue within the mouth: the pictures in (5) say nothing about the voicing or nasality of the sounds produced. These pictures are thus completely consistent with the articulations we expect for not only [d] but also [t] and [n].

2.2.7 The Consonant Chart

The chart of the consonants of English in (6) can be used for easy reference. As seen in our descriptions throughout, the three-part articulatory description of consonants is conventionally given in this order: Voicing-Place-Manner, e.g., voiced palatal glide or voiceless bilabial stop. To find the description of a sound, first locate the phonetic symbol on the chart. You can find out the state of the glottis by checking whether the sound is in the shaded part of the box or not—the shaded boxes show voiced consonants, while the non-shaded ones show voiceless consonants. Then check the label at the top of the vertical column that contains the sound to see what its place of articulation is. Finally, check the manner of articulation label at the far left of the sound's horizontal row. Locate [ð], for example. It lies in a shaded region, indicating that this sound is voiced. Now look above [ð]. It is in the vertical column marked "interdental." Looking to the far left you see it is a fricative. [ð], then, is the voiced interdental fricative.

You can also use the chart to find a symbol that corresponds to a particular phonetic description by essentially reversing the above procedure. If you want to find the voiced post-alveolar fricative, first look in the fricative row, and then under the post-alveolar column, and locate the symbol in the shaded part of the box: this is [ʒ].

The chart can also be used to find classes of sounds—that is, groups of sounds that share one or more characteristics. For instance, to find all the alveolars, just read off all the sounds under the "alveolar" column. Or, to find all the stops, read off all the sounds in the "stop" row. (See Section 3.3.2 on natural classes.)

You should familiarize yourself with the chart so that you can easily recognize the phonetic symbols. The list of phonetic symbols for consonants, which was presented in File 2.1.4, should also help you remember which symbol represents which consonant. This chart and the list are also printed on the last two pages of this book, for easy reference. Remember that we are talking about **speech sounds** and not letters in the English spelling system.

(6) English consonant chart

	Place of Articulation													
	Bilabial		Labio-dental		Inter-dental		Alveolar		Post-Alveolar		Palatal		Velar		Glottal	
Stop	p	b					t	d					k	g	ʔ	
Fricative			f	v	θ	ð	s	z	ʃ	ʒ					h	
Affricate									ʧ	ʤ						
Flap							ɾ									
Nasal		m					n							ŋ		
Lateral Liquid							l									
Retroflex Liquid							ɹ									
Glide	w̥	w³										j				

State of the Glottis │ Voiceless │ Voiced

---

³As noted above, [w] (along with its voiceless counterpart) is specifically a labial-velar rather than a purely bilabial sound, but we include it in this column for simplicity of representation.

··

Articulation: English Vowels

2.3.1 Articulatory Properties of Vowels

In Section 2.1.3, we explained the difference between consonants and vowels, and in File 2.2, we discussed the articulation of consonants. Here we discuss the articulation of vowels. Vowels are the most sonorant, or intense, and the most audible of sounds in speech. Unlike consonants, they usually function as syllable nuclei, and the consonants that surround them often depend on the vowel for their audibility. For example, in the word *pop* [pɑp], neither [p] has much sound of its own; the [p]s are heard mainly because of the way they affect the beginning and end of the vowel sound. (See Section 2.6.5 for more information about this.)

Because vowels are produced with a relatively open vocal tract, they do not have a consonant-like place or manner of articulation (constriction). They are also almost always voiced. This means that the three standard descriptors for consonants (place, manner, and voicing) are not helpful when we want to describe vowels. What should we use instead?

Hold your jaw lightly in your hand. Now say *he* [hi], *who* [hu], and *ha* [hɑ]. Did your jaw move for *ha*? The tendency for the jaw to open and the tongue to lie low in the mouth for [ɑ] is why we will call [ɑ] a **low** vowel. It is usually pronounced with the jaw quite open—lowering the tongue body away from the roof of the mouth. The contrast in jaw position between [i] and [u] as opposed to [ɑ] is large because both [i] and [u] are pronounced with the tongue body close to the roof of the mouth—hence they are called **high** vowels.

Vocal fold vibration is the sound source for vowels. The vocal tract above the glottis acts as an acoustic resonator affecting the sound made by the vocal folds. The shape of this resonator determines the quality of the vowel: [i] versus [u] versus [ɑ], for example.

There are four main ways in which speakers can change the shape of the vocal tract and thus change vowel quality:

- raising or lowering the body of the tongue
- advancing or retracting the body of the tongue
- **rounding** or not rounding the lips
- making these movements with tense or lax gestures

Therefore, when describing a vowel, it is necessary to provide information about these four aspects of the articulation of the vowel. Refer to the chart in (1) as each aspect is discussed in the following section.[1]

Broadly speaking, there are two types of vowels in English, namely, monophthongs and diphthongs. Diphthongs are two-part vowels, whereas monophthongs have only one part (see Section 2.1.3). We will discuss the four aspects of the articulation of the vowels

---

[1]Although this textbook uses IPA symbols for transcription, the classification of English vowels is presented in a more traditional style, with only three levels of height and a tense-lax distinction. The standard IPA vowel chart is printed on the last page of the book for comparison purposes.

(1) The vowels (monophthongs) of English

(2) The vowel chart in a sagittal section of the vocal tract, for the articulation of [i], [u], and [ɑ].

using monophthongs; articulation of diphthongs will be discussed in the next section. Note that recordings of many of the following contrasts are available on the Sounds page for Chapter 2, as indicated by the speaker icon.

2.3.2 Tongue Height

The first two of these aspects have to do with the position of the tongue in the mouth. Figure (2) shows the position of the tongue for the three vowels discussed above. The highest point of the tongue body is considered to be the place of the vowel, as you can see by comparing the tongue position in (2) with the placement of the symbols in (1).

If you repeat to yourself the vowel sounds of *seat, set, sat*—transcribed [i], [ɛ], [æ]—you will find that you open your mouth a little wider as you change from [i] to [ɛ], and then a little wider still as you change from [ɛ] to [æ]. These varying degrees of openness correspond to different degrees of tongue height: high for [i], mid for [ɛ], and low for [æ].

High vowels like [i] are made with the front of the mouth less open because the tongue body is raised, or high. The **high** vowels of English are [i], [ɪ], [u], and [ʊ], as in _leak, lick, Luke, look_, respectively. Conversely, **low** vowels like the [æ] in _sat_ are pronounced with the front of the mouth open and the tongue lowered. The low vowels of English are [æ] as in _cat_ and [ɑ] as in _cot_. **Mid** vowels like the [ɛ] of _set_ are produced with an intermediate tongue height.[2] In the inventory of English monophthongs, these mid vowels are [ɛ, ʌ, ɔ], as in _bet, but, bought_, respectively. Note that an unstressed vowel in English is often pronounced as the mid vowel [ə], as in _above_ and _atomic_.[3]

In many American dialects, words like _caught_ and _cot_, or _dawn_ and _Don_, are pronounced differently, with an [ɔ] and [ɑ], respectively. In other American dialects, these words are pronounced the same. If you pronounce these pairs the same, you probably use the unrounded vowel [ɑ] in all of these words. For most speakers of English, however, even those who pronounce _caught_ and _cot_ the same, the vowel [ɔ] appears in words such as _law_ and _saw_, as well as in words like _core_ and _more_.[4]

2.3.3 Tongue Advancement

Besides being held high or mid or low, the tongue can also be moved forward or pulled back within the oral cavity. For example, as you can see in (2), in the high **front** vowel [i] as in _beat_, the body of the tongue is raised and pushed forward so it is just under the hard palate. The high **back** vowel [u] of _boot_, on the other hand, is made by raising the body of the tongue in the back of the mouth, toward the velum. The tongue is advanced or moved

forward for all the front monophthongs, [i], [ɪ], [ɛ], [æ], as in _seek, sick, sec, sack_, and retracted or pulled back for the back monophthongs, [u], [ʊ], [ɔ], [ɑ], as in _ooze, look, draw, dot_. The central vowels, [ʌ] as in _luck_ or [ə] as the first vowel in the word _another_, require neither advancement nor retraction of the tongue.[5]

---

[2]Some of you may be wondering about the vowel sounds in words like _ate_ and _oat_. These sounds begin as the mid front and back tense vowels [e] and [o], respectively. But in most dialects of American English, these vowels are almost always pronounced as the diphthongs [eɪ] and [oʊ], respectively, so they have not been included in the chart of monophthongs. They will be discussed along with the other diphthongs in Section 2.3.6.

[3]We should point out that there is, of course, variation in the pronunciation of all speech, even if we are talking about "Standard American English" (see Chapter 10 on language variation; vowels in particular vary a lot in English). If at any point your pronunciations don't exactly match those presented here, you're certainly not wrong! For consistency we will be using particular transcriptions to represent sounds throughout the book, but we will make note of specific variations where appropriate. For example, some speakers of American English make further distinctions among unstressed vowels. If you pronounce _roses_ differently from _Rosa's_, or the first vowel of _enough_ differently from that of _another_, then the underlined vowel in the first word of each pair is likely a high lax vowel, either the front [ɪ] or the central "barred 'i'" [ɨ], while that in the second is the mid [ə] (e.g., [ɪnʌf] vs. [ənʌðɹ̩]). To keep things simple, we just use [ə] for these unstressed vowels.

[4]Note that vowel characteristics like tense versus lax can be difficult to tell apart before certain consonants in syllable coda position, particularly [ɹ] and [l]. For some speakers, especially those who have a strong contrast between [ɔ] and [ɑ], the vowel in words like _core_ and _cold_ is closer to a monophthongal [o] than [ɔ], and the vowel in words like _there_ is closer to [e] than [ɛ]. We have chosen to use [ɔ] and [ɛ] throughout in these contexts, but the other symbols may well be more appropriate for certain speakers' pronunciations.

[5]You may notice that the vowel symbol [ʌ] is given as back rather than central on the standard IPA chart on the last page of the book. We categorize it as central here based on its pronunciation in most varieties of American English, but it is pronounced as a back vowel in some other varieties, such as New Zealand English.

2.3.4 Lip Rounding

Vowel quality also depends on lip position. When you say the [u] in *two,* your lips are **rounded.** For the [i] in *tea,* they are **unrounded,** or spread. English has three rounded monophthongs: [u], [ʊ], [ɔ], as in *loop, foot, paw;* all other monophthongs in English are unrounded. In the vowel chart in (1), the rounded vowels are enclosed by the dashed line.

2.3.5 Tenseness

Vowels that are called **tense** are said to have more extreme positions of the tongue and/ or the lips than vowels that are **lax.** The production of tense vowels involves bigger changes from a mid-central position in the mouth. That is, they require a more extreme tongue gesture of raising, lowering, advancing, or retracting in order to reach the periphery (outer edges) of the possible **vowel space.** This means that the tongue position for the tense high front vowel [i] is higher and fronter than for the lax high front vowel [ɪ]. Lax vowels, then, are not peripheral to the degree that tense vowels are. Compare tense [i] in *meet* with lax [ɪ] in *mitt,* or tense [u] in *boot* with lax [ʊ] in *put.* In the latter case you will find that the tense rounded vowel [u] is also produced with more and tighter lip rounding than the lax counterpart [ʊ]. In the vowel chart in (1), you can clearly see that the distance between the tense vowels [i] and [u] is bigger than the distance between the lax vowels [ɪ] and [ʊ]. Additionally, tense vowels in English usually have a longer duration (in milliseconds) than lax vowels.

We can use these four characteristics to create the descriptions of English vowels.

(3) Sample descriptions of English vowels
    a. [i], as in *beat,* is high, front, unrounded, and tense.
    b. [ɔ], as in *caught* or *thaw,* is mid, back, rounded, and lax.
    c. [ɑ], as in *cot,* is low, back, unrounded, and lax.
    d. [ʌ], as in *cut,* is mid, central, unrounded, and lax. (Note that "central" and "mid" refer to the same general area in the vocal tract but along different dimensions.)

2.3.6 Describing Vowels: Diphthongs

As mentioned in Section 2.1.3, diphthongs are complex vowel sounds, as opposed to monophthongs, which are simple vowel sounds. They are "complex" because they are two-part sounds, consisting of a transition from one vowel to the other in the same syllable. The diphthong in *buy,* which consists of two articulations and two corresponding vowel sounds, is thus written as a two-part symbol: [ɑɪ] as in *buy* [bɑɪ].[6] Although a diphthong consists of a sequence of sounds, it is considered one sound, similar to an affricate (discussed in Section 2.2.5).

If you try saying the word *eye* slowly, concentrating on how you make this vowel sound, you should find that your tongue starts out in the low back position for [ɑ][7] and then moves toward the high front position for [ɪ] (see (4)). If you have a hard time perceiving this

[6]There are other analyses of the structure of diphthongs. The most common alternative to the one presented here views diphthongs as two-part vowel sounds consisting of a vowel and a glide (see Section 2.2.5) within the same syllable. The correspondence for [ɪ], as in [ɑɪ], is then the palatal glide [j], hence, [ɑj]. The diphthongs we present as [ɑɪ], [ɑʊ], [ɔɪ], [oʊ], and [eɪ] would be written as [ɑj], [ɑw], [ɔj], [ow], and [ej], respectively, in this system.

(4) Two-part articulations of the diphthongs of English (the arrows indicate the transitions)

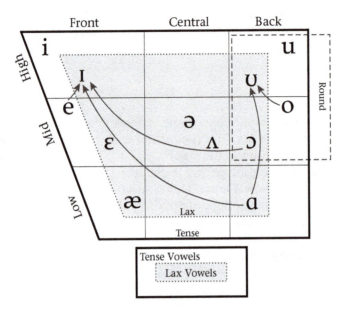

as two sounds, try laying a finger on your tongue and saying *eye*. This should help you feel the upward tongue movement.

To produce the vowel in the word *bow (down)*, the tongue starts in the low back position for [ɑ] and moves toward the high back position for [ʊ] while the lips round, so this diphthong is written [ɑʊ], as in [bɑʊ]. In the vowel of the word *boy*, the tongue moves from the mid back position for the rounded vowel [ɔ] toward the high front position for [ɪ]; so the diphthong of *boy* is written [ɔɪ], as in [bɔɪ]. To say the vowel in the word *bow (and arrow)*, the tongue starts in the mid back position for the rounded vowel [o] and moves toward the high back position for the rounded vowel [ʊ]; so the diphthong is written [oʊ], as in [boʊ]. For the production of the vowel of the word *bay*, the tongue starts in the mid front position for [e] and moves toward the position for [ɪ]; so this diphthong is written [eɪ], as in [beɪ] *bay*. The chart in (4) illustrates the tongue movements involved in the production of these diphthongs.

2.3.7   Investigating Vowel Articulations

In Section 2.2.6, we described several ways to determine the place and manner of articulation of consonants, using different types of palatography. These methods won't tell us much about vowel articulations, however, because, of course, vowels are produced with a relatively open vocal tract, and the tongue doesn't touch the roof of the mouth. Instead, studying vowels usually involves imaging techniques that allow investigators to look at the whole mouth and the tongue's position in it.

---

[7]There is a great deal of variation in the production of both the low back vowel [ɑ] as in *cot* and the beginning of the diphthongs. While we use the symbol [ɑ] here for both, for many speakers the vowel in *cot* and the first part of the diphthong in *eye* are pronounced differently, and the diphthongs would be more accurately transcribed [aɪ] and [aʊ], representing a more fronted pronunciation of the low vowel. Other variations in diphthong pronunciation include, for example, the production of the vowel in *eye* as more like [ɑi], of the vowel in the word *toy* as more like [oi], and of the vowels in *about* and *write* as more like [əʊ] and [əɪ], respectively.

One technique is to use X-ray movies of people talking. These X-ray films can be played over and over again to see tongue, lip, and jaw movements as they occur over time. Although you can find some old example films of X-ray speech online, this methodology is not used anymore because it turned out to be harmful for the speakers.

Instead, researchers now use safer methods such as ultrasound, Magnetic Resonance Imaging (MRI), or Electromagnetic Articulography (EMA). Ultrasound and MRI (like X-rays) both make use of invisible rays that "bounce off" hard structures in their path to create visual images of those structures (in the case of ultrasound, these are sound waves; in the case of MRI, these are radio waves). EMA, on the other hand, involves placing small sensors on a subject's tongue, teeth, and other articulators; these sensors then transmit information back to a computer about their relative locations, allowing researchers to collect precise information about how the articulators move and interact in speech.

Of course, all of the techniques mentioned here can be also used to study consonant articulations, and all are especially useful for consonants that are produced without contact on the hard palate (e.g., [b] or [g]). This makes these techniques particularly well-suited for studying the interaction of consonants and vowels in running speech.

FILE 2.4

Beyond English: Speech Sounds of the World's Languages

2.4.1 Beyond English?

In File 2.1, we said that the phonetic alphabet used in this book can be used for any language. The parts of the phonetic alphabet that we have employed up to this point may seem Anglocentric—no different really from *Webster's* pronunciation symbols for English, or any other reasonably consistent method of writing English sounds. To "de-anglicize" our phonetic alphabet so that it is truly useful for describing the pronunciation of other languages, we must add more symbols to it.

It is not the goal of this file, however, to discuss all of the speech sounds that can be used in human language. Rather, we restrict ourselves to some of the common phonetic symbols that you may encounter. Yet even this partial look at phonetic diversity highlights the fact that English uses only a small subset of the possible sounds found in human language. We should note that if you run across a symbol you are not familiar with, you are now in a position to interpret it using the IPA chart on the last page of this book.

2.4.2 Vowels

The most straightforward additions to our phonetic alphabet can be made by filling in some holes. There are certainly other sounds that are possible given the features we've identified for English sounds, but these correspond to combinations of the features that happen not to occur in English. Consider, for example, the vowel chart in File 2.3. In connection with that chart we noted that the only rounded vowels in English are the back vowels [u], [ʊ], and [ɔ] and the diphthong [oʊ] (as in *who'd*, *hood*, *awed*, and *owed*, respectively). You might have thought that these are the only rounded vowels in other languages as well. But if you have studied German or French, you know that this is not true. In addition to the back rounded vowels [u] and [o], German and French both have front rounded vowels, such as [y] and [ø]. The high front rounded vowel [y] is pronounced with a tongue position very similar to that for [i], but instead of spread lips, the vowel is pronounced with rounded lips. Similarly, the mid front rounded vowel [ø] is produced with a tongue position as in [e], but with rounded lips. (1) gives some examples of the contrast between front and back rounded vowels in French and in German.

Another vowel distinction that does not come up in English is the distinction between [ɑ] and [a]. [ɑ] is used for low back unrounded vowels, which may contrast with [a], a more central or front low unrounded vowel. Links to additional examples that you can listen to can be found on our website.

All of the vowels we have discussed so far have been oral vowels—that is, they are produced with the velum raised and hence the nasal passage closed. All languages have oral vowels, and many have only oral vowels. Some languages, however, also have **nasalized vowels.**

A nasalized vowel is in nearly every respect identical to its oral vowel counterpart—the only exception is that the velum is lowered and the nasal passage is open, letting air escape through the nose as well as the mouth (cf. Section 2.2.5). This is very much like the

(1) Examples of the contrast between front and back rounded vowels

	Front			**Back**	
		French			
[ty]	'you (familiar)'		[tu]	'all'	
[vy]	'seen'		[vu]	'you (formal)'	
[nø]	'knot'		[no]	'our (plural)'	
[fø]	'fire'		[fo]	'false'	
		German			
[gytə]	'benevolence'		[gutə]	'good (masc. sg.)'	
[grys]	'greet'		[grus]	'greeting'	
[ʃøn]	'beautiful'		[ʃon]	'already'	
[bøgen]	'arches'		[bogen]	'arch'	

distinction between an oral stop [b] and a nasal stop [m]. Nasalized vowels are written with a tilde [~] over the corresponding oral vowel symbol. So, a nasalized mid front vowel is written [ẽ], and a nasalized mid back rounded vowel is written [õ].

While vowels can be nasalized in English, we do not use the nasality to distinguish words. We don't have to look very far, however, to find vowel nasalization used as the only feature to distinguish words in language, as the following examples from French illustrate:

(2) Examples of the contrast between oral and nasal vowels in French

	Oral			**Nasalized**	
[mɛ]	'but'		[mɛ̃]	'hand'	
[ʃas]	'hunt'		[ʃãs]	'luck'	
[bo]	'beautiful' (masc.)		[bõ]	'good' (masc.)	

2.4.3 Fricatives

Take a look at the fricative row of the English consonant chart (6) in File 2.2. In this row there are seven empty cells—bilabial voiceless and voiced, palatal voiceless and voiced, velar voiceless and voiced, and glottal voiced. It turns out that all seven of these possible sounds occur in other languages. The symbols that belong in those cells are shown below in (3).

(3) Examples of fricatives

Description	**Symbol**	**Example**	**Gloss**	**Language**
voiceless bilabial fricative	[ɸ]	[éɸá]	'he polished'	Ewe
voiced bilabial fricative	[β]	[èβè]	'Ewe'	Ewe
voiceless palatal fricative	[ç]	[çeri]	'hand'	Modern Greek
voiced palatal fricative	[ʝ]	[ʝut]	'good'	Dutch
voiceless velar fricative	[x]	[xɔma]	'soil'	Modern Greek
voiced velar fricative	[ɣ]	[ɣɔma]	'eraser'	Modern Greek
voiced glottal fricative	[ɦ]	[pluɦ]	'plough'	Ukrainian

Though English does not contrast voiced and voiceless glottal fricatives, we do have the voiced glottal fricative [ɦ] when the *h* sound comes between vowels, as it does in the word *ahead*. We also often pronounce the voiceless fricative at the beginning of words like *huge* as the palatal [ç] rather than the glottal [h]. Both of these pronunciations are due to co-articulation (see Section 2.1.2 and File 3.3).

In theory it should be easy to say the other fricatives in this list because they simply combine features that already exist in English. [ɸ] is a bilabial sound like [p], and a fricative with a noise sounding much like [f]. Voilà, now you can say [ɸ], right? Well, not if you are like most people. It takes practice to master these new, non-English sounds. However, you may have some experience with some of them if you've studied other languages. The voiceless velar fricative [x] is found in German, Yiddish, and Mandarin Chinese. It is the last sound in the German pronunciation of *Bach* [bɑx], the first sound in the Yiddish word *chutzpah* [xʊtspə] 'brazenness, utter nerve,' and the first sound in the Mandarin Chinese word [xɑu²¹⁴] 'good.' The voiced bilabial fricative [β] is found in Spanish (*Cuba* [kuβa]), as is the voiced velar fricative [ɣ] (*amigo* [amiɣo] 'friend').

2.4.4 Filling in Other Blanks in the Consonant Chart

We can continue to fill in other empty cells in the English consonant chart. For example, looking at the affricate row, you will notice that English has only post-alveolar affricates. As you might guess, others are possible. For example, the voiceless alveolar affricate [t͡s] occurs in a variety of languages including Canadian French ([abut͡si] 'ended'). Similarly, a voiceless labial affricate [pf] is a familar sound from German ([pfɛnɪk] 'penny'). The phonetic symbols for these sounds give a good indication of how to say them because we already know how to say [t], [s], [p], and [f].

In addition to the palatal glide [j], it should come as no surprise that some languages make use of palatal stops and nasals. For example, the voiceless palatal stop [c] is used in Greek ([ceri] 'candle'), and the voiced palatal nasal [ɲ] is a familiar consonant in Spanish ([kaɲa] 'pipe') and Italian ([ɲoki] *gnocchi*). These palatal sounds are made with the body of the tongue, like a [k] or [ŋ], but with the middle of the tongue pressing into the roof of the mouth. You can get the feel of palatal sounds by contrasting your pronunciation of *key*, in which the tongue is fronted, versus *coo*, in which the tongue contact is farther back. It would be reasonable to transcribe English *key* as [ci] and *coo* as [ku]. The four new sounds that we discussed in this section are listed in (4).

(4) Examples of affricates and palatals

Description	Symbol	Example	Gloss	Language
voiceless alveolar affricate	[t͡s]	[abut͡si]	'ended'	Canadian French
voiceless labial affricate	[pf]	[pfɛnɪk]	'penny'	German
voiceless palatal stop	[c]	[ceri]	'candle'	Modern Greek
voiceless palatal nasal stop	[ɲ]	[kaɲa]	'pipe'	Spanish

2.4.5 Places of Articulation Not Used in English

So far we have seen that the phonetic alphabet contains symbols for non-English sounds that are composed of the same basic phonetic features that are found in English. We now turn to some consonants that are made at places of articulation that we don't find in English.

The voiceless uvular stop [q] is used in Farsi, for example, in the word [qædri] 'a little bit.' The **uvula** is at the very back of the roof of the mouth—that thing that hangs down in your throat. Uvular stops are produced by making a stop closure between the back of the tongue and the uvula. This is like a [k] but with the tongue pulled farther back than normal. The voiced counterpart of [q] is [ɢ].

The voiceless pharyngeal fricative [ħ] is used in Maltese, for example, in the word meaning [sħab] 'clouds.' The voiced pharyngeal fricative [ʕ] is used in some dialects of Hebrew, as in the word [ʕor] 'skin.' The pharyngeal place of articulation seems exotic indeed if you thought that the uvular stop was pronounced far back in the mouth, because the **pharynx** is even further back and lower in the vocal tract. However, it is fairly easy to say a pharyngeal fricative if you start with the vowel [ɑ] of *father* and just open your jaw wider to pull the tongue back in the mouth. For many people this maneuver causes a frication noise—a voiced pharyngeal fricative. The new sounds that we discussed in this section are listed in (5).

(5) Examples of places of articulation not used in English

Description	Symbol	Example	Gloss	Language
voiceless uvular stop	[q]	[qædri]	'little bit'	Farsi
voiceless pharyngeal fricative	[ħ]	[sħab]	'clouds'	Maltese
voiced uvular stop	[ɢ]	[ihipɢeoqteq]	'explore'	Inuktitut
voiced pharyngeal fricative	[ʕ]	[ʕor]	'skin'	Yemenite Hebrew

2.4.6 Manners of Articulation Not Used in English

Just as some languages use places of articulation that are not used in English, some languages use manners of articulation not found in English. In this section we will describe four non-English manners of articulation.

The American English [ɹ] sound is an exotic speech sound. This sound is very unusual in the languages of the world. It is also very difficult for children to master (e.g., many children pronounce the word *train* as [twein] instead of [tɹein]), and it is also a cause of difficulty for adult learners of English. Many languages that have an /r/ sound have a tongue-tip trilled [r]. If you have studied a language other than English, you may have run into the voiced alveolar **trill** [r]. For example, the sound that corresponds to the Spanish spelling <rr> is trilled ('dog' [pero]).

Another manner of articulation not used in English may be familiar from the Russian word for 'no' [nʲɛt]. The **palatalized** nasal in this word is indicated by the superscript small [ʲ]. To American ears [nʲ] sounds like the sequence [nj], but in X-ray movies of Russian we see that the tongue body position for the glide [j] is simultaneous with the tongue tip position for [n]. So instead of a sequence [nj], the Russian palatalized [nʲ] involves a secondary articulation [ʲ] that is simultaneous with the primary constriction [n]. Many consonants can be palatalized. In the exercises later in this book you will find the palatalized voiceless bilabial stop [pʲ], the palatalized voiceless alveolar stop [tʲ], the palatalized voiceless velar stop [kʲ], the palatalized voiceless alveolar fricative [sʲ], and the palatalized voiceless post-alveolar fricative [ʃʲ].

The phenomenon of secondary articulation helps explain a difference in how [l] is pronounced in English. At the beginnings of words (and as the first sound in stressed syllables within words) [l] is pronounced with the tongue-tip touching the alveolar ridge and the tongue body held rather low in the mouth. But at the ends of words (or as the last sound in a syllable) [l] is pronounced with the tongue body higher in the mouth, and sometimes the tongue-tip does not touch the roof of the mouth at all. Compare the way you say [l] in *laugh* and *Al* (where the [l] is before and after the vowel [æ]). Traditionally these two pronunciations of English [l] are called **clear** (tongue body down, tongue-tip up) and **dark** (tongue body up and tongue-tip down), respectively. We can add to this rough description by noting that in dark [l] (as in *Al*) there is a secondary articulation in which the tongue body moves toward the velum. The dark [l] is therefore more accurately described as **velarized,** and we write this velarized alveolar lateral liquid as [ɫ]. In Macedonian the contrast between velarized [ɫ] and plain [l] distinguishes words: for example, [bela] means 'trouble' while [beɫa] means 'white (fem. nom. sg.).'

The final non-English manner of articulation we want to discuss here is **glottalization,** which produces **ejective** sounds. In ejectives, a glottal stop [ʔ] is produced simultaneously with the primary oral closure in the vocal tract. This simultaneous glottal gesture is symbolized by an apostrophe after the symbol for whatever consonant is glottalized (e.g., [p'] for a glottalized voiceless bilabial stop).

At first, glottalization may seem quite comparable to a secondary articulation. The name for the phenomenon, "glottalization," parallels the names of the secondary articulations "palatalization" and "velarization." Unlike palatalization and other secondary articulations, however, glottalization affects the **airstream mechanism** of speech. That is, unlike all of the other sounds we have discussed, the main airstream for glottalized sounds is not the exhaled air from the lungs. Instead, the air pressure that makes the stop release noise (the pop when you release a stop closure) is made by compressing the air in the mouth cavity with the larynx. This is done by closing the glottis (and forming an oral closure like [k]) and then raising the larynx in the throat. This compresses the air in the mouth—you can think of the rising larynx as a piston in a car engine. Then the stop release noise is made by this compressed air when the [k] closure is released. And then the glottal stop is released. This high-pressure release may make quite a "pop," giving these consonants the name ejectives. These consonants may seem very exotic, but they can be fun and easy once you learn them. They occur in 15%–20% of all languages. The sounds that we have discussed in this section are listed in (6).

(6) Examples of manners of articulation not used in English

Description	Symbol	Example	Gloss	Language
voiced alveolar trill	[r]	[pero]	'dog'	Spanish
palatalized consonants	[pʲ] etc.	[pʲatʲ]	'five'	Russian
velarized alveolar lateral liquid	[ɫ]	[beɫa]	'white'	Macedonian
ejective consonants	[p'] etc.	[p'o]	'foggy'	Lakhota

FILE 2.5

Suprasegmental Features

2.5.1 Segmental vs. Suprasegmental Features

So far we have studied the characteristics of the **segments** (i.e., individual sounds) of speech: place and manner of articulation and voicing for consonants; tongue height and advancement, lip rounding, and tenseness for vowels. In this file we will consider other features that speech sounds may also have: length, intonation, tone, and stress. These features are called **suprasegmental** features because they are thought of as "riding on top of" other segmental features (*supra-* means 'over, above'). Suprasegmental features are different from the segmental features we've studied so far in that it is often difficult or even impossible to identify the quality of a suprasegmental feature if you hear just a single segment. Instead, for suprasegmentals, you have to compare different segments and different utterances to see what the features are. In addition, some suprasegmental features can extend across numerous segments in an utterance, rather than belonging to a single phonetic segment.

2.5.2 Length

The first suprasegmental feature we will talk about is **length**: some speech sounds are longer than others. However, the actual duration of a segment may vary for a number of different reasons (e.g., speaking quickly to a friend as you run out the door versus speaking slowly as you read a story to a young child). Because of this variation, we can't just look at a particular segment and say "that was a long [i]" or "that was a short [i]." Instead, we have to compare the durations of segments within a given utterance (e.g., "this is a long [i] compared to that one").

In some languages, differences in the durations of segments can be as meaningful as the difference between having your tongue body in a high versus a mid front position ([i] versus [e]). Substituting a long segment for an otherwise identical short segment (or vice versa) can result in a different word. For example, consider the data from Finnish shown in (1). In Finnish, both vowels and consonants may be either long or short, and the contrast can make a difference in the meaning of a word. Long vowels and consonants are marked with a following [ː]; segments without this symbol are assumed to be short.

(1) Examples of using length to contrast word meaning in Finnish

    a. i.   [muta] 'mud'
        ii. [muːta] 'some other'
       iii. [mutːa] 'but'

    b. i.   [tapan] 'I kill'
        ii. [tapaːn] 'I meet'

    c. i.   [tule] 'come!'
        ii. [tuleː] 'comes'
       iii. [tuːleː] 'is windy'

The difference between a long [uː] and a short [u] in Finnish is dependent on the overall speech rate; you have to compare the duration of any given segment with the durations of the other segments to figure out if it was long or short. This is what makes length a suprasegmental feature.

In addition to this type of length contrast that can make the difference between two words, speech sounds also vary in duration inherently. For example, all else being equal, high vowels are shorter than low vowels, and voiceless consonants are longer than voiced consonants. Voiceless fricatives are the longest consonants of all.

The duration of a speech sound may also be influenced by the sounds around it. For example, say the words *beat* and *bead* aloud. In which word is the [i] longer? In English, a vowel preceding a voiced consonant is about 1.5 times longer than the same vowel before a voiceless consonant. The place and manner of articulation of a following consonant can also affect vowel length. Try saying the word *bees*. How does the length of the [i] in *bees* compare to that in *bead*?

2.5.3   Intonation

Voiced speech sounds, particularly vowels, may be produced with different pitches. Pitch is the psychological correlate of fundamental frequency, which depends on the rate of vibration of the vocal folds (see File 2.6). The pattern of pitch movements across a stretch of speech such as a sentence is commonly known as **intonation.** The intonation contour of an utterance plays a role in determining its meaning. For example, you can read the same words with different intonations and mean different things. Try reading the words in (2) out loud with different pitch patterns, and see if you can get this effect. You might try reading them with either a rising or a falling pitch at the end, or with any other intonation patterns you can think of.

(2)   a. You got an A on the test
      b. Yes

Using a rising intonation at the end of the utterance tends to make it sound more like a question, while using a falling intonation makes it sound like a statement.

Although there are multiple systems available for analyzing the intonation of an utterance, one of the most common systems assumes that there are two different intonational phenomena involved in marking the intonation contours of sentences: **pitch accents** and **phrase tones.**

Pitch accents usually involve a change in fundamental frequency in the middle of an utterance: a word may be produced with a pitch that is particularly higher or lower than the surrounding words. Words that receive a pitch accent are perceived as very prominent in an utterance—not all words in an utterance get a pitch accent. Pitch accents are therefore used to highlight important information in an utterance, for example.

Read the examples in (3) aloud. The word that receives a pitch accent, that is, the word that is especially prominent, is written in capital letters. You can see that by putting the prominence on different words, you can use the same string of words to answer different questions.

(3) a. Speaker 1: Who kissed Peter?
     b. Speaker 2: MARY kissed Peter.

     a. Speaker 1: Who did Mary kiss?
     b. Speaker 2: Mary kissed PETER.

     a. Speaker 1: What did Mary do to Peter?
     b. Speaker 2: Mary KISSED Peter.

Like pitch accents, phrase tones usually involve changes in fundamental frequency, but unlike pitch accents, they occur at the end of a phrase instead of in the middle of an utterance. Phrase tones have two major functions. First, they affect the overall meaning of an utterance, distinguishing, for example, between a statement, where the speaker provides information, and a question, where the speaker is requesting information. Read the examples in (4a) and (4b) aloud.

(4) a. You got an A on the test.
     b. You got an A on the test?
     c. You got an A on the test, a C on the homework, and a B on the quiz.

How did you read the last word of each sentence? Did you read it with a falling pitch or a rising pitch? The first sentence is a statement and is thus usually produced with falling pitch at the end. This is called sentence-final intonation. The second sentence is a yes/no question, which is usually said with rising pitch, so-called question intonation, at the end.

Second, phrase tones group words into linguistic units called phrases.[1] A short utterance will usually have just one phrase tone at the end, as in (4a) and (4b), but a longer utterance will usually be broken up into smaller phrases. Read (4c) aloud. Did you notice the perceptual breaks at the commas? (While punctuation coincides with the breaks in these examples, this is not always the case—however, phrase tones can be thought of as the "punctuation" of spoken language.) The pitch before these breaks first falls and then rises again slightly. This is called a continuation rise; it indicates that the speaker is not done speaking. Thus, the intonation on the word *test* does two things: it marks both the end of a phrase and the speaker's intention to continue talking. An example can show how differently a string of syllables will be interpreted depending on the use of phrase tones: say *What's that in the road ahead?* out loud, and then *What's that in the road? A head?* All of the phonetic segments should be exactly the same both times, but a listener will understand the two utterances to have very different meanings!

2.5.4 Tone

In many languages, the pitch at which the syllables in a word are pronounced, called the **tone,** can make a difference in the word's meaning. Such languages are called **tone languages** and include Thai; Mandarin and other "dialects" of Chinese (cf. File 10.1 for an explanation of the notion "dialect"); Vietnamese; languages in New Guinea such as Skou; many of the Bantu languages of Africa such as Zulu; other African languages such as Yoruba and Igbo; and many North and South American Indian languages such as Apache, Navajo, Kiowa, Mazotec, and Bora. To see how the tone of a word can make a difference in meaning, consider the Mandarin Chinese words in (5).

---

[1]Phrases will also be discussed in Chapter 5 on syntax. While the general meaning of the word is the same in both cases—i.e., linguistically relevant groups of words—note that there is not a one-to-one correspondence between the phrases that are marked by phrase tones and syntactic phrases.

(5)   Examples from Mandarin Chinese: different tones, different meanings

Segments	Tone Numbers[2]	Tone Pattern	Gloss
[ma]	55	high level	'mother'
[ma]	35	high rising	'hemp'
[ma]	214	low falling rising	'horse'
[ma]	51	high falling	'scold'

As you can see, the same segments in a word (in this case, the syllable [ma]) can be pronounced with different tones and as a result correspond to different meanings.

In tone languages, tones can be of two types: either level or contour. All tone languages have level tones; in these tones a syllable is produced with a relatively steady tone such as a high tone, a mid tone, or a low tone. Some tone languages also have contour tones, where a single syllable is produced with tones that glide from one level to another. These are analogous to diphthongs in that they have two parts. For example, a rising tone might glide from a low tone to a high tone, while a falling tone might glide from a high tone to a low tone.

There are multiple systems for transcribing tones; the choice of system often has to do with the number and type of tonal contrasts the transcriber needs to make, as well as the history of the systems traditionally used to transcribe tones in a particular set of languages. As seen in (5) above, for example, tone numbers are often used to indicate the different levels of tone in Mandarin. In Kikerewe (a Bantu language spoken in Tanzania), on the other hand, tones are often transcribed using accent marks over the vowel in a syllable, where [´] indicates a high tone, [¯] indicates a mid tone, [`] indicates a low tone, [ˇ] indicates a rising tone, and [ˆ] indicates a falling tone (see (6)). See the IPA chart on the last page of the book for the standard IPA symbols used to mark tone.

(6)   Examples of level and contour tones in Kikerewe.

Word	Tone Pattern	Gloss
[kùsàlà]	low-low-low	'to be insane'
[kùsálà]	low-high-low	'to cut off meat'
[kùʃǐːngà]	low-rise-low	'to defeat, win'
[kùsìːngà]	low-low-low	'to rub, apply ointment'
[kùzúmà]	low-high-low	'to insult, scold'
[kùzùmà]	low-low-low	'to rumble, be startled'
[kùkālâːŋgà]	low-mid-fall-low	'to fry'

It is important to note that the tones in a tone language are at least partially relative, rather than absolute. This is part of what makes them suprasegmental features. For example, the pitch of a high-level tone spoken by a Mandarin speaker with a deep or low-pitched voice will be considerably lower than the pitch of the same tone spoken by a female speaker with a higher-pitched voice. To determine whether a given syllable has a high or a low tone, you must compare it to other syllables spoken by the same speaker—and even then, different utterances may be produced with different tonal ranges! Further, tone and intonation are not mutually exclusive; tone languages also use intonation.

---

[2]The tone numbers used in this table were devised by a Chinese linguist named Y. R. Chao to describe the tones of all dialects of Chinese. In this commonly used system for Chinese, '5' indicates the highest pitch and '1' indicates the lowest pitch in the pitch range.

At the same time, however, there are certain constants in tone production that can help listeners process tones. Some languages tend to be "higher pitched" overall than others: for example, Cantonese tends to be spoken on a higher pitch than Taita (a Bantu language spoken in Kenya), which gives listeners at least some sort of baseline to expect for the tonal range. And, of course, a listener's knowledge about the speaker's physical characteristics (male versus female, tall versus short, etc.) will help him correctly identify the tones he hears.

2.5.5 Stress

The last suprasegmental feature we will examine is **stress**. Stress, like tone, is a property of entire syllables, not segments, though the syllable nucleus, which is usually a vowel, carries most of the information about stress (see File 2.1.3). A stressed syllable is more prominent than an unstressed one. This prominence is due to a number of factors, including the fact that stressed syllables are longer and louder than unstressed syllables and usually contain full vowels. Full vowels are produced with more extreme positions of the tongue than reduced vowels, which are produced closer to the mid central position in the mouth and often occur in unstressed syllables.

For example, compare the first vowels in the words *photograph* and *photography*; how are they different? In *photograph*, the first syllable is the most stressed and would be transcribed with the full vowel [oʊ]. But in *photography*, the second syllable is the most stressed, and the vowel in the first syllable has been "reduced" to [ə].

English uses several stress levels, as illustrated by a word like *photography*: in this word, the second syllable is most prominent (has primary stress), the final syllable is next most prominent (has secondary stress), and the other syllables are unstressed (have tertiary stress). In IPA, we transcribe stress using a mark before the beginning of a syllable: primary stress is marked with [ˈ], and secondary stress is marked with [ˌ]. Tertiary stress is not marked. So, for example, the word *photography* would be transcribed as [fəˈtɑɡɹəˌfi].

In some languages the placement of stress on a word is predictable; for example, stress almost always falls on the first syllable of a word in Czech, on the next to last syllable of a word in Welsh, and on the last syllable of a phrase in French. In other languages such as Russian and English, stress placement is not predictable and must be learned for each word. In such languages the placement of stress can cause a difference in meaning. For example, what is the difference between a *bláckboard* and a *black bóard*? a *white hóuse* and the *White House*? (Note that in these phrases, an acute accent is placed over the word or syllable that receives primary stress.) Consider also the words *record, perfect,* and *subject.* How are their meanings different when stress falls on the first syllable as opposed to the second? Compare also the words *incite* and *insight,* which differ phonetically only in stress placement but which mean different things.

Much of our emphasis in the previous files has been on the transcription of speech sounds with a series of symbols. Suprasegmental features, however, prove to be difficult to transcribe this way because they are "superimposed" on the other features. For example, while the symbol [ɑ] always represents the same speech sound whenever we write it, the symbol [ː] has no meaning in isolation. Its meaning is a function of the meaning of the symbol (such as [ɑ]) with which it is used, and even then it indicates only that a segment is long relative to the length of a similar sound transcribed without the [ː]. Similarly, marking stress indicates only that the segments of the stressed syllables are louder and longer than their neighboring sounds. And you can change the intonational pattern of an English utterance radically without changing the segments on which the intonation rides. As you can see, our transcription system doesn't express these facts very well. Perhaps because of this, suprasegmental features remain an important topic in contemporary phonetic research.

FILE 2.6

....

Acoustic Phonetics

2.6.1 Articulatory vs. Acoustic Phonetics

So far we have been concerned with articulatory phonetics, the study of how speech sounds are produced. In this file, we will examine many of the exact same speech sounds. This time, however, we will focus on the physical aspects of the sound wave, i.e., the acoustic characteristics of the sounds.

One of the main difficulties in studying speech is that speech is fleeting; as soon as a sound is uttered, it's gone. One of the ways to capture it is to transcribe it using phonetic symbols, as we've seen in previous files. But transcription runs the risk of involving endless debate about what a speaker actually said (e.g., did she say short [ɑ] or long [ɑː]?). However, modern technology has made it possible to conquer the fleeting nature of speech, at least to some degree, by making records of the acoustic properties of sounds.

2.6.2 Simple Sound Waves

Before we look at speech sounds, it is important to understand something of the nature of sound waves. Sound waves, unlike letters on a page, are not permanent things. They are disturbances in the air set off by a movement of some sort. One kind of movement that can set off a sound wave is vibration, such as that produced by violin strings, rubber bands, and tuning forks—or vocal folds. In this kind of sound wave, a vibrating body sets the molecules of air surrounding it into vibration.

In order to understand how this works, imagine that air molecules are like people in a crowded room trying to keep a comfortable distance from one another: if one person moves toward another person, that second person may step back away from the first person. By stepping back, this new person may move closer to yet another person, and so the reaction continues throughout the room. Similarly, if one person suddenly moves away from another person, that second person may realize she could have more space on either side by moving back toward the first person. Again, the result may be a chain of movements throughout the crowd while everyone tries to stay equally far apart from everyone else.

There are two physical phenomena resulting from this tendency toward equidistance that make it possible for sound waves to move through the atmosphere. These are **compression,** in which air molecules are more crowded together than usual, and **rarefaction,** in which air molecules are spread farther apart than usual. Because of a tendency for air molecules to remain equidistant from one another, whenever they are placed in compression or rarefaction, a certain instability is set up. Compressed molecules tend to move away from one another so that they are no longer compressed. Likewise, when air is rarefied, there is a tendency for the molecules to move nearer together, as they were before rarefaction occurred. This continues until a stable distance is reached.

When the string of a guitar is vibrating, it causes a sound wave in the following way: as the string moves away from its rest position, it pushes the adjacent air molecules closer to neighboring molecules, causing compression. The neighboring, compressed molecules

74

(1) 440 Hertz sine wave, the tone A

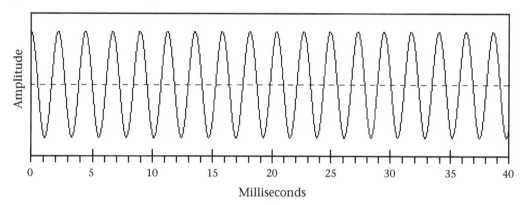

move away from the first "uncomfortably close" molecules, toward others. Those other molecules in turn do the same, and the chain reaction continues.

As the vibrating guitar string moves in the other direction, back to its rest position and beyond, a rarefaction is created. This pulls the air molecules that had been pushed away back toward the string, which creates a rarefaction between them and the molecules on their other side, which pulls those molecules back, and so on. Note that the consequences of the movement (the crowding of the molecules) may be transmitted over a large distance while each individual molecule simply vibrates in place. This chain reaction, which is the consequence of the movement of the string, is the sound wave. When the string moves back and forth at a certain frequency (that is, a certain number of times per second), a group of air molecules that are at some distance from the string will alternately be compressed and rarefied at that frequency. If this chain reaction involving compression and rarefaction is repeated at a rate of 440 times a second, we will hear a musical tone known as "A above middle C." A sound wave such as this, which repeats at regular intervals, is called a **periodic wave.**

If we plot the energy with which the air molecules press against or pull away from one another in such a sound, the resulting plot looks like the one shown in (1). You can think of the figure in (1) as a plot of the movement (vertical axis) of some air molecules across time (horizontal axis), or, more accurately, you can think of it as being the amount of pressure exerted by the air molecules across time. That is, if the dashed line in the figure represents the resting location of a molecule, you can think of the wavy line (the sine wave) as representing the molecule being pushed away from the resting position, then back toward it, and then away from it in the other direction. The plot in (1) has a frequency of 440 Hz ("Hertz," abbreviated Hz, is a unit of measurement meaning 'cycles/second'), meaning that the molecule moves away from, back toward, away from in the opposite direction, and back toward its original resting position 440 times in a single second.

Air molecules can vibrate at many different frequencies. When they vibrate at rates from 20 to 20,000 times a second, we perceive the vibration as sound. It is interesting to note, however, that we don't really use this whole range for speech. In fact, the highest frequency that can be transmitted by a telephone is 3500 Hz, and yet little essential information about the speech signal is lost by cutting off frequencies above this. And, of course, air molecules vibrate at higher or lower frequencies that we do not hear as sound at all. (But some animals do hear them as sound!)

2.6.3 Complex Sound Waves

Our discussion of sound waves up to this point has been very basic and somewhat simplified. In fact, simple sound waves such as those discussed in the previous section are not

(2)   A point on a guitar A string

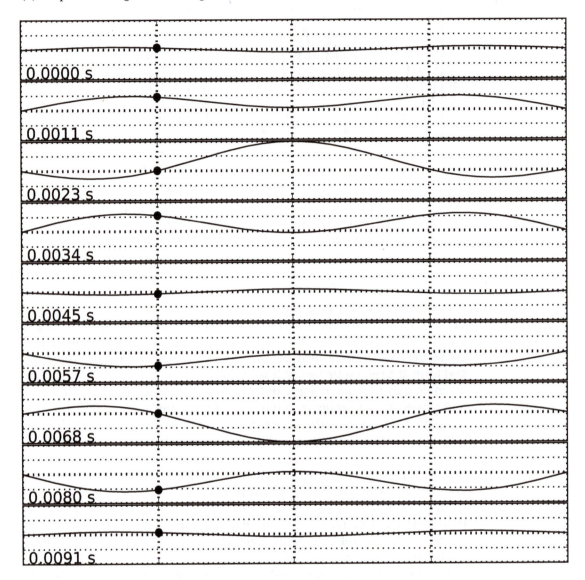

necessarily produced by guitar strings or human vocal folds. Most things can vibrate at many frequencies at the same time. Figure (2) shows a particular point of a guitar A string: moving up, then part of the way back down, then back up again, then all the way down, then part of the way back up, then back down again, and finally all the way up again to start over. This pattern is repeated 110 times per second. But, since the motion of the string is more complex than just going all the way up and all the way back down, you can describe the string as vibrating both at 110 Hz (the number of times per second the entire pattern repeats) and at 330 Hz (the number of times per second a partial pattern is repeated).

Very complex waves can result from this sort of combination of movements, but the complex movements can always be broken down into simple movements at simple frequencies. These simple movements at single frequencies in turn generate simple sound

(3)   Two simple waves combining to form a complex wave

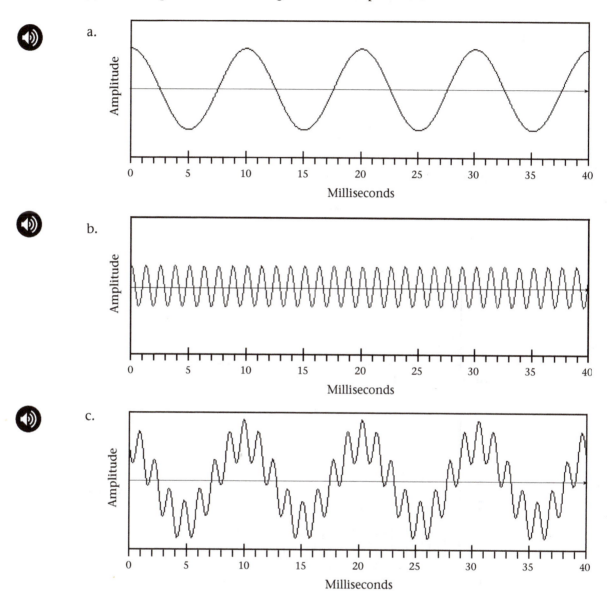

waves at single frequencies that combine to make complex sound waves. For example, in Figure (3), you can see a plot of two simple sound waves, (a) and (b), and the complex sound wave (c) resulting from their combination. Thus (3a) and (3b) illustrate the simple wave components of the complex wave in (3c).

The sound wave that is produced by the vocal folds is a complex wave. This complex wave is composed of a fundamental wave, which repeats itself at the frequency of the opening and closing of the vocal folds, and a set of **harmonics,** which repeat at frequencies that are multiples of the fundamental. Thus, if the vocal folds open and close at a rate of 100 cycles per second, the fundamental frequency of the resulting sound wave is 100 Hertz (cycles/second), the second harmonic is 200 Hz, the third harmonic is 300 Hz, and so on. Note that the first harmonic is the **fundamental frequency** (pitch).

(4)   Source plus filter equals speech sound

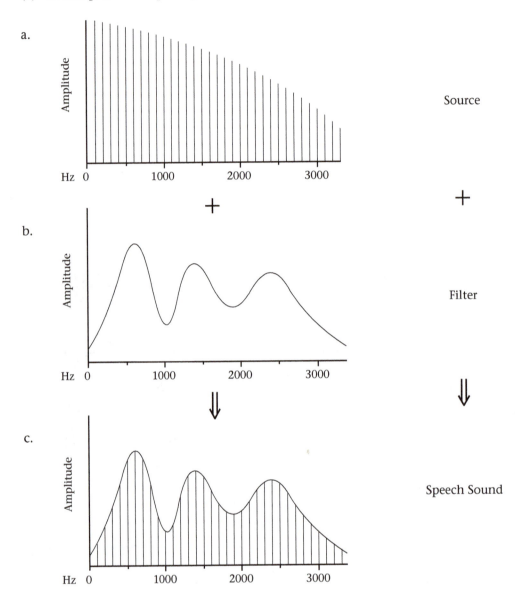

The complex wave produced by the vocal folds is known as the source wave, because the vocal folds are the source of the sound wave: it is their movement that creates the wave. It can be represented in a histogram as in (4a), where the horizontal axis represents frequency, and the vertical axis represents the amplitude of the wave. Each line represents one component wave (or harmonic) in the complex vocal wave. Note that the relative amplitude of each wave gets progressively smaller at higher frequencies.

As this sound wave passes through the vocal tract, the articulators shape it, or filter it, boosting the energy at some harmonic frequencies and damping the energy at others. This filter action is similar to the effect of room acoustics on a speaker's voice. Some rooms enhance the voice so that no amplification is needed, while others seem to absorb the voice, muffling the sound. In a similar way, the vocal tract acts as a filter on the source wave. In (4), the vocal tract positioned for the vowel [ɑ] has a filtering effect as in (4b), and harmonics at about 600 Hz, 1380 Hz, and 2500 Hz are enhanced, while harmonics at other positions are damped, yielding the output wave in (4c).

Thus a speech sound (wave) is the result of two independent things: the source wave (the contribution of the vocal folds) and the filter (the contribution of the articulators and the vocal tract).

2.6.4 Vowels

In the production of vowels, the filtering effect of the vocal tract produces amplitude peaks at certain frequencies by enhancing the harmonics (the component waves of a complex waveform, produced by the vocal folds) at those frequencies while damping harmonics at other frequencies, as discussed above. These peaks in the filter function are called **formants** (resonant frequencies of the vocal tract). For example, just as a trombone has particular resonant frequencies (determined by the length of the tube) that shape the sound produced by the vibration of the lips, in vowel sounds the vocal tract has resonant frequencies (determined by the length and configuration of the vocal tract) that shape the sound produced by vocal fold vibration. Vowels have several formants, the first three of which are the most important for speech perception (see File 9.4 for a discussion of speech perception). The values of these formants differ from vowel to vowel, which allows us to distinguish between vowels we hear. The table in (5) lists typical formant frequencies for eight American English vowels.

(5) Typical frequencies in Hz of the first, second, and third formants for American English vowels

Vowel	F1	F2	F3
[i]	280	2250	2890
[ɪ]	400	1920	2560
[ɛ]	550	1770	2490
[æ]	690	1660	2490
[u]	310	870	2250
[ʊ]	450	1030	2380
[ɔ]	590	880	2540
[ɑ]	710	1100	2540

We can plot these vowels by the frequencies of their first two formants, as shown in (6). Note that if we put the origin (0,0) in the upper right-hand corner, the resulting diagram looks strikingly similar to the vowel chart in (1) in File 2.3. Thus we can see that the first formant corresponds inversely to the height dimension (high vowels have a low F1, and low vowels have a high F1), and the second formant corresponds to the advancement (front/back) dimension (front vowels have a high F2, and back vowels have a low F2).

A common method of visually representing acoustic properties of speech sounds is to use a **spectrogram.** Spectrograms are graphs that encode three acoustic dimensions: the vertical axis represents frequency, and the horizontal axis represents time. A third dimension is represented by degree of darkness, which indicates the amount of acoustic energy present at a certain time and at a certain frequency. Dark horizontal bands usually represent formants because formants are enhanced bands of energy at particular frequencies. In (7) we see spectrograms for the three vowels [i], [u], and [ɑ]. The arrows point out only the first three vowel formants, although there are more formants visible in these spectrograms. The horizontal lines in each of these displays mark off frequency in Hz by the 1000s. These spectrograms show visually the differences that we hear when we listen to these three vowels.

(6)   Plot of the first formant (F1) against the second formant (F2) of some English vowels

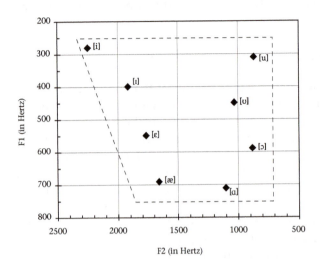

(7)   Spectrograms of the vowels [i], [u], [ɑ]

Frequency (Hz)

[i]   [u]

[ɑ]

If you compare the spectrograms of [i] and [u] in (7), you will notice that while the first formant is very similar, the second formant is much higher for [i] than for [u]. This is because the second formant corresponds to tongue advancement; your tongue is much farther forward when pronouncing [i], so the corresponding formant is much higher. You can also see that the first formant of [i] and [u] is much lower than the first formant of [ɑ] because the former are high vowels while the latter is a low vowel (the first formant corresponds inversely to vowel height).

2.6.5 Stops

Spectrograms can clearly show other types of segments as well. In File 2.2, we described the articulatory properties of consonants in terms of their voicing and their manner and place of articulation. Stop consonants are produced by completely closing off the oral cavity with the lips or tongue, blocking the flow of air. This lack of airflow makes stops easy to detect on spectrograms because they are characterized by a lack of energy—hence a gap—in the display, as illustrated in (8). So, the acoustic characteristic of a stop (the silence we hear, or the blank space on the spectrogram) reflects its manner of articulation.

If a stop is voiced, the vocal folds will actually be vibrating during the closure, and some low-frequency noise is produced. This noise can be seen in (8) as the dark band at the very bottom of the spectrogram during the "silence" of the stop. This band is called the **voice bar.**

Voiceless stops never have this voice bar. In English, voiceless stops are also often further characterized by a period of **aspiration,** during which air rushes out of the mouth after the release of the stop closure and before the onset of the vowel. This aspiration, transcribed with a superscript [ʰ], as in [pʰ], can be clearly seen as the messy shading without clear formants that occurs between the gap of the consonant and where the formants of the vowel begin in the spectrogram of the word *pat* in (9).

The acoustic information corresponding to place of articulation for a stop is found mostly in the vowels around it since, after all, the stop itself is essentially silence. When we pronounce a sequence like [ɑdɑ], the tongue can't move instantaneously from a low back tongue position to the alveolar ridge for the voiced alveolar stop and back to the vowel position. Rather, the tongue glides from one position to the next. Therefore, there are points in time when the tongue is in transition from the vowel to the consonant or the consonant to the vowel. Of course, this changing vocal tract shape affects the formants; as a result, during the early part of the second vowel the formants are also in transition toward their usual values. The spectrograms in (8) show vowel-stop-vowel sequences in which we can see moving formants reflecting the moving articulator. (The horizontal lines in each of these displays mark off frequency in Hz by the 1000s.)

We can determine the place of articulation of a stop by examining the frequency of the second formant at the juncture of the vowel and the consonant. For alveolar stops, the second formant of the vowel will be around 1700–1800 Hz going into or coming out of the consonant. Thus, in the spectrogram of [ɑdɑ] in (8), the second formant rises from the formant value of the vowel (the F2 of [ɑ] is about 1100 Hz) to about 1800 Hz just before the consonant [d] and falls back down afterward. For velar stops, the pattern will depend on what kind of vowel precedes or follows the consonant. For example, if the consonant is followed by a front vowel, the F2 will start high and then fall, but if the consonant is followed by a back vowel, the F2 will start fairly low, around 900 Hz or lower. In addition, just before the consonant, the second formant will rise and the third formant will lower, as if they would meet in the consonant. You can see this in the spectrogram of [ɑgɑ] in (8). This is sometimes called a "velar pinch." For bilabial stops, F2 will be lower at the juncture between the consonant and the vowel than it is in the vowel itself. As the spectrogram of [ɑbɑ]

(8)   Spectrograms of [adɑ], [agɑ], [abɑ]

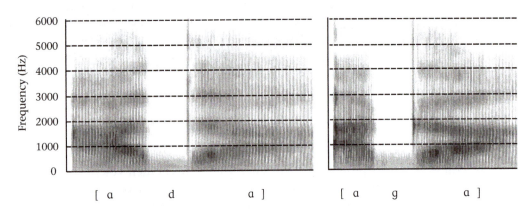

[ɑ   d   ɑ]   [ɑ   g   ɑ]

[ɑ   b   ɑ]

(9)   Spectrogram of [pʰæt]

[p   ʰ   æ   t   ]

shows, the second formant lowers slightly just before the [b] and rises just afterward. These patterns allow us to distinguish the place of articulation of stops visually. The placement of the burst of air that follows the stop when the stop is released also gives information about the place of articulation of the stop.

2.6.6 Fricatives

Fricatives involve a new kind of sound that we have not dealt with up to this point. The difference between the noise found in vowels and in fricatives is that the sound in vowels has its source in the periodic vibration of the vocal folds (as discussed in Sections 2.6.2 and 2.6.3), while the sound in fricatives comes from the aperiodic, or random, turbulence of the air rushing through a small opening. Note in (10) that during the vowels there is a regular repetition (seen in the vertical stripes), while in the fricative portions there is no apparent pattern; it looks like static on a TV screen. In addition, note that this is the same kind of noise as that of the aspiration discussed in the previous section.

We find differences among English fricatives in the relative frequency of the noise (e.g., [s] has a higher frequency energy concentration in the frication noise than [ʃ]), in the amplitude (e.g., [s] is louder than [f]), which appears as darker shading on a spectrogram, and in the duration (e.g., [s] is longer than [z]). In Figure (10), you can see that the static-like coloring denoting the aperiodic energy of the fricative is centered between 6000 and 9000 Hz for [s], but is much lower, centered between 2000 and 4000 Hz, for [ʃ]. As with stops, the formant transitions from the consonant into the vowel are also used by listeners to determine the place of articulation.

Voiced fricatives are interesting in that they combine periodic noise (the vocal folds are vibrating in a regular cycle) and aperiodic noise (there is turbulence from the air being forced through a small opening). Affricates are sequences of stop plus fricative both in their articulation and in their acoustic characteristics. A spectrogram of an affricate begins with a gap in the waveform, which is immediately followed by the aperiodicity of a fricative.

2.6.7 Nasals, Liquids, and Glides

In the production of nasal consonants, the oral cavity is closed as if for a stop, but air escapes past the lowered velum through the nasal cavity. In acoustic terms, the nasal passage serves as the filter for the vocal source, just as the oral cavity acts as a filter in vowels. All nasal consonants have quite similar formants (see (11)), reflecting the shape of the nasal passage, which enhances some harmonics and damps others. Nasal formants are usually somewhere around 250, 2500, and 3250 Hz. The place of articulation of nasal consonants, however, is still cued by the transitions from the nasal into the vowel. Note that in (11), there is a lighter area (a lack of energy, caused by the damping of the nasal cavity) at around 1250 Hz for [mi] and around 1750 Hz for [ni].

Like nasals, liquids and glides have formants. Both nasals and liquids are characterized by an abrupt change in the spectrogram just before the consonant, which is very different from the gradual changes that mark the transition into stops and glides. The glide [w] has formants very similar to those of [u] (and [j] to [i]), but because consonants are shorter than vowels, the formants do not have time to reach those positions and stay there. Glides are sometimes appropriately called **semivowels**.

(10) Spectrograms of [lis] and [liʃ]

(11) Spectrograms of [mi] and [ni]

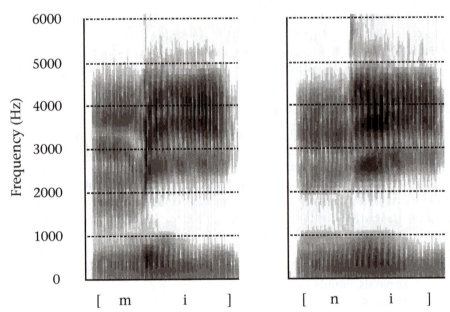

2.6.8 Interpreting Spectrograms

All of the sounds shown thus far in this chapter were recorded in a sound booth, spoken quite distinctly and almost in isolation, with few other sounds. But we do not usually speak this way and hardly ever listen to such speech. Most of the time, our speech is connected, and neighboring sounds can impact the cues of a sound a great deal (see Chapter 3). Sometimes our speech is rushed or mumbled, and conversations often take place with a great deal of background noise, making the sounds even harder to distinguish from one another. Therefore, while extremely useful for preserving, analyzing, and comparing speech, sound spectrograms of naturally occurring speech can be very difficult to interpret. For example, (12) shows the spectrogram of a recording made in the audience at a rock concert. Instead of the careful speech of one person, the 2.5-second spectrogram represents sounds produced by four singers, two guitars, a piano, drums, and thousands of screaming fans. It would be next to impossible to use this spectrogram for analysis of the singers' consonants and vowels, but fans in the audience would have little trouble understanding the lyrics and following along with the complex musical patterns made by the instruments while subconsciously filtering out the background noise of their cheering neighbors. This should highlight once again how incredibly talented our ears are at picking out speech sounds!

 (12) Spectrogram from rock concert

FILE **2.7**

....

The Phonetics of Signed Languages

2.7.1 Extending *Phonetics* to Signed Languages

Phonetics was originally coined as a term used specifically to talk about the study of the sounds of language. However, phonetics has come to be the name of the subfield that deals with how language is produced, regardless of the modality of that production. Signs, which serve the same function as words in spoken languages, likewise have internal structure. Therefore, signs in any signed language are composed of discrete components, just like words in spoken language, and these components can be studied in the same way that vowels and consonants can be.

As has been the case for most of the preceding files of this chapter, the focus of this file will be on articulatory phonetics: how signs are produced. However, in the same way that phoneticians also study acoustic phonetics—the sounds themselves—and auditory phonetics—how sounds are perceived—linguists who are working on signed language phonetics may also take an interest in how signs are perceived or in the structure of the signs themselves, independent of how they are articulated.

2.7.2 The Parameters of Articulation in Signed Languages

The study of the phonetics of signed languages is relatively new. Thus, whereas linguists speak fairly confidently when they say, for example, that a significant feature in describing a consonant is place or manner of articulation, there is still some discussion about which attributes of a sign are significant. Nonetheless, there is a canonical set of parameters that are generally recognized in one way or another as being linguistically significant.

How do you know that a parameter is significant? Well, in evaluating spoken languages (if you speak one), the task is relatively easy. You know, for example, that *mitt* and *bit* are different words, and therefore the feature nasal must be important (because you are able to distinguish between [m] and [b], and they differ only in nasality). When we want to know whether some particular parameter is significant in a signed language, we can do much the same thing: we look to see whether a change to the articulation of that parameter can influence the identity of a sign. (This notion of how discrete yet meaningless units of language can come to affect meaning will be readdressed in Section 3.2.3.)

By performing this set of observations, we can conclude that there are five key **parameters** of articulation in signed languages: place of articulation, movement, handshape, hand orientation, and non-manual markers, each of which will be discussed in more detail below. The way that these features are organized, though, does not correspond directly to the way that features like nasal or rounded are organized. Rather, they themselves are segments. In the same way that a word will have some number of vowels and some number of consonants, a sign will have some number of movements and some number of places of articulation.

One fascinating difference between signed and spoken language is the manner in which their fundamental elements, called phones or **primes,** are combined into utterances.

In spoken languages, owing both to the nature of the speech mechanism and to the way that our brains process auditory input, phones are organized in linear temporal order; several phones cannot be produced at the same time. (Imagine trying to produce all the phones of a word at the same time! Furthermore, think about how difficult it is to understand three different people talking to you at the same time.) In contrast, a prime in ASL always occurs simultaneously with other primes. Primes cannot stand alone but must co-occur with primes from the other parameters. For example, one could not simply have a hand movement without also having the hand in a particular handshape or location. (It is possible not only to produce multiple primes at the same time, but also to interpret them. Imagine that you are shown a photograph, but that it flashes in front of you and then disappears immediately. You will be able to tell many things about the photograph, because our visual processing, unlike auditory processing, does allow us to clearly perceive multiple different things going on at the same time.) Because all five of the parameters of signing articulation discussed below are superimposed, they interact with one another in complex ways. One parameter may change while another stays the same, or two may change at the same time.

In the following sections we will describe each of the five parameters in more detail and provide several examples of each. Although the examples given in this file come from only one language, the same parameters are relevant for all signed languages.

2.7.3   Location

The first parameter of sign articulation that we will consider is **location.** Clearly it is impossible to articulate a sign if the hands aren't somewhere! And we could imagine a system in which all gestures could be made anywhere at all and still have the same meaning (just as you can say a word at any volume at all and it still has the same meaning). How, then, do we know that location is important? We find pairs of words like the following. In the ASL signs for 'apple' (1a) and 'lucky' (2a), the location where the sign is made is at the chin. The sign for 'onion' in (1b) is the same in every way as the sign for 'apple' except that it is made near the eye. Similarly, the sign for 'clever' in (2b) is the same in every way as the sign for 'lucky' except that it is made starting at the forehead. Evidence like this tells us that location is significant.

(1)   a. ASL: APPLE

b. ASL: ONION

(2) a. ASL: LUCKY

© 2006, William Vicars, www.Lifeprint.com. Adapted by permission.

b. ASL: CLEVER

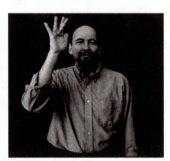

© 2006, William Vicars, www.Lifeprint.com. Adapted by permission.

The examples in (1) and (2) have places of articulation that differ between the upper and lower halves of the face. Examples such as these are particularly clear in pictorial two-dimensional form; however, there are certainly other locations that contrast.

Every signed language has a particular "signing space": a general area in which signs may be produced. Obviously the outside range might be determined by how far away from your body you can stretch your arms, but most languages have a smaller space than this. For example, ASL has very few signs that are articulated below the waist. But place of articulation is a much more specific feature than just identifying a general area. A sign's place of articulation tells exactly where, relative to the signer's body, that sign must be articulated. Examples include [the front of the shoulder of the arm opposite from the hand making the sign], [the top of the bridge of the nose], [above the shoulder of the hand articulating the sign, but touching neither the shoulder nor the ear], and so on.

Interestingly, signing space can be expanded or reduced. If a signer is "whispering," he will reduce the signing space, bringing all places of articulation in closer to his center. This may also involve altering the location of some signs, articulating them in places closer in front of the torso than they normally would be. However, the places of articulation will still have the same sort of positions relative to each other. That is, in whispering, signs normally produced on the forehead will be lowered, while signs normally produced on the chin will also be lowered; every sign will come in toward the signer's center an equivalent amount. Similarly, if a signer is "yelling," he will increase his signing space and the amount of movement in his signs.

2.7.4 Movement

The second parameter is **movement**. The examples in (3) and (4) show two pairs of signs that are distinguished by the kind of movement they involve. In TOUGH, one hand begins higher than the other and moves rapidly downward until it is lower; PHYSICS is similar in many ways but involves the two hands moving toward each other.

(3) a. ASL: TOUGH (difficult)

© 2006, William Vicars, www.Lifeprint.com. Adapted by permission.

b. ASL: PHYSICS

© 2006, William Vicars, www.Lifeprint.com. Adapted by permission.

The signs CAN and SHOES likewise distinguish between vertical and horizontal movement (see (4)), though the vertical motion in CAN is different from the vertical motion in TOUGH. (Try to describe the difference in movement between these two signs.)

(4) a. ASL: CAN   b. ASL: SHOES

© 2006, William Vicars, www.Lifeprint.com. Used with permission.

Some signs have movements that are designed to take a hand from one place of articulation to another. For example, the ASL sign for KING moves from the shoulder opposite the signing hand to the top of the hip on the same side as the signing hand. This is different from, for example, the sign for TOUGH above, because in TOUGH what matters is the type of movement itself, more than the precise starting and stopping location.

A third type of movement has to do with ways that the wrist or fingers move and does not actually require any change in place at all. For example, in the ASL sign for YES, the wrist moves up and down (as though it were a head nodding), and in the ASL sign for WAIT, the fingers waggle back and forth, but the hands do not move. Other such movements may include finger circling or one hand tapping another body part.

One interesting thing about movement is that it functions a little bit like vowels in spoken language. You can often understand a word or sentence (in its written form) without vowels; similarly, a signer can often understand a sign or sentence without movement. Nonetheless, just like vowels in spoken languages, movement is a critical part of articulation in signed languages.

2.7.5   Handshape

Third, we will look at **handshape.** In (5) you see four signs of American Sign Language, each with no movement and with the same place of articulation (touching the chin). What differs is the shape of the hand: which fingers are extended, whether the fingers are bent or straight, the position of the thumb, whether fingers are touching, and so on. In (5), the four different handshapes give four different meanings to the four signs that they are a part of.

(5)   Examples of signs in ASL differing only in handshape

a. COLOR

b. ORANGE

c. MISS

d. WRONG

In order to see one way that handshape can interact with movement, consider the two ASL signs in (6). Here, although both LIKE and WHITE begin with the same handshape, they end with different handshapes, because the handshape changes during the movement.

(6)   a. ASL: LIKE

© 2006, William Vicars, www.Lifeprint.com. Adapted by permission.

b. ASL: WHITE

© 2006, William Vicars, www.Lifeprint.com. Adapted by permission.

The two signs in (6) also serve to make the point that one sign can contain more than one handshape.

2.7.6 Orientation

The fourth parameter that has to do with the way that the hands are used is **orientation**: the direction that the palm of the hand is facing. In both (7a) and (7b), the hands are facing toward each other; however, in (7a) the two hands are pointing left and right, whereas in (7b) they are facing toward the speaker and away from the speaker.

(7) a. ASL: MEET (the uninflected verb)

© 2006, William Vicars, www.Lifeprint.com. Adapted by permission.

b. ASL: I MEET YOU

© 2006, William Vicars, www.Lifeprint.com. Adapted by permission.

Of course, even in two-handed signs, the hands need not face each other; in the signs for CAN and SHOES in (4), the palm orientation is [facing down]. In the signs for LUCKY and CLEVER in (2), there is a change of orientation during the sign: these two signs begin with the palm facing the speaker and end with the palm facing away from the speaker.

2.7.7 Non-Manual Markers

The fifth and final parameter of signed language is the use of non-manual markers. Non-manual markers include any gestures, such as facial expressions or head movements, that are not made with the hands. The examples in (8) show the ASL signs for LATE and NOT YET. While the location, movements, shape, and orientation of the hands are the same in the two signs, NOT YET also includes non-manual markers: a slight negative shake of the head and the tongue sticking out slightly.

(8) a. ASL: LATE

b. ASL: NOT YET

Another example of this parameter is the use of pursed lips in the ASL sign REALLY-SKINNY. The sign in question also has a manual component: two hands, each with the pinkies extended, begin with the pinkies touching and then move away from each other. However, if just this manual part is performed, without the lips being pursed, then the entire word hasn't been articulated. It would be like leaving a segment out of some spoken word: saying [fut] instead of [flut] for *flute,* for example. If somebody were to say, "I play the [fut] in the school orchestra," you would know what they meant, but you would also know that they hadn't articulated the word properly. A second example would be not producing a tone change in a word that required one in a language like Mandarin Chinese, in which tones are components of word production.

In other cases, non-manual markers act as more of a suprasegmental feature like intonation. For example, there is a particular intonation that we associate with questions like *Where do you live?* In ASL there is also a suprasegmental feature that indicates such a question: it includes inclining the head forward and lowering the eyebrows.

Non-manual markers can be used to modify signs in other ways as well; for example, compare the signs for HOT in (9a) and VERY HOT in (9b). Notice how the signer's face is different when he articulates VERY HOT from when he articulates HOT. (There are other differences in the production of these two signs as well, but for now just pay attention to the signer's facial features.)

(9) a. HOT

© 2006, William Vicars, www.Lifeprint.com. Adapted by permission.

b. VERY HOT

© 2006, William Vicars, www.Lifeprint.com. Adapted by permission.

Sometimes, the non-manual marker/facial expression is the only way a sign is indicated. For instance, just the non-manual marker of NOT YET (the tongue sticking out a bit and a slight shake of the head) can carry the full meaning of NOT YET.

2.7.8 Phonetic Inventories in Signed Languages

In File 2.4, it became clear that different languages make use of different inventories of sounds. Some languages have front rounded vowels or consonants with a uvular place of articulation, but English has neither; English is rather unusual in having a retroflex liquid; and so on. All spoken languages have some kinds of consonants and vowels, but the sets of consonants and vowels differ from language to language. The same is true of signed languages. Every language has handshapes, kinds of movements, places of articulation, orientations, and non-manual markers, but not every one is available in every sign language.

For example, in Taiwan Sign Language (TSL), there is a handshape that is called the "dragon" handshape, formed by sticking the pinky and index finger up while bending the middle finger and ring finger in to meet the thumb. If you try to make this handshape, you will find that it is not terribly difficult to produce. Nonetheless, this handshape is not available in the inventory of handshapes that are used in ASL. A second example is the handshape formed by making a fist and extending your ring finger: TSL makes use of it, but ASL does not. Conversely, the ASL "T" handshape, which is formed by making a fist and sticking the thumb between the index finger and middle finger (as though you were playing "I got your nose" with a young child), is a handshape that is not available in TSL. There are other handshapes that appear in neither ASL nor TSL but that do occur in other sign languages. A more profound difference is that in TSL, the elbow can be an active articulator, whereas in ASL the forearm and elbow can only be used as passive articulators. (To conceptualize what this means, think about your mouth: your tongue is an active articulator because it moves, but your alveolar ridge is a passive articulator because it is involved in articulation only when your tongue touches it.)

The same sort of thing (primes that are available in one signed language but not another) occurs for kinds of movement and places of articulation. Some languages have a movement that is a side-to-side twisting of the wrist; others do not. Some sign languages have [crown of the head] as a place of articulation; others do not.

There are many things, of course, that you can do with your hands and arms—just as there are many things you can do with your mouth. Some of these, such as swallowing, whistling, throwing a ball, or brushing at a mosquitos, are nonlinguistic, while others may be linguistic. It is important to remember, though, that just because a certain kind of articulatory gesture may have linguistic applications does not mean that any given language necessarily uses it.

2.7.9   Studying and Analyzing the Phonetics of Signed Languages

In the previous files, a number of innovations have been described that help researchers to discuss, describe, and research the articulation of spoken languages. There have been fewer technological innovations for the study of phonetics in signed languages, in part because the sign language articulators are large, slow, and not covered by your cheeks. In other words, they are a lot easier to study in a straightforward way than are the articulators of spoken languages!

Another reason, though, is that, as we mentioned above, the study of the phonetics of signed languages is simply newer than the study of spoken language phonetics. Of course, one tool that has been very helpful is simple video recording, which allows researchers to look at the same segments over and over again. More sophisticated technology involves attaching sensors to various parts of signers' hands, arms, face, and so on. The sensors' positions and movements can then be recorded and sent to a computer to allow precise measuring of, for example, amount of movement, precise tilt and orientation, exact distance between hands and between hands and the body, and so on. Of course, as this field of study continues to grow, more instruments and tools are certain to follow.

FILE **2.8**

Practice

Note: Several of the activities in this chapter (e.g., 28 and 29 below) and later chapters call for the use of phonetics analysis software. These days, it is possible to find free software to download onto your computer that allows you to fairly easily record and look at speech sounds. To find some, try searching for "phonetics analysis software" or "waveform editor." Some that are available include Praat, WaveSurfer, Speech Analyzer, and Waveforms Annotations Spectrograms and Pitch (WASP), among others. We have included links to some of these on our website. None of the activities in this book crucially depend on using one or the other—all of these packages are excellent for our purposes. Occasionally, however, we think that it is helpful to beginning students to give specific instructions on how to complete an activity; when we do so, the instructions will be for Praat. You should, however, be able to complete any activity using whatever package you choose; ask your instructor for more resources if you need help.

File 2.1—Representing Speech Sounds

Exercises

    1. What are the three different areas of phonetics, and how do they fit into the communication chain?

    2. Why is it useful to have a phonetic transcription system?

    3. What is meant by having a "one-to-one correspondence between sounds and symbols"? Why would this property be desirable?

File 2.2—Articulation: English Consonants

Exercises

    4. Looking back at Figure (2) of File 2.2, explain why your vocal folds don't vibrate when you whisper.

    5. Write the phonetic symbol representing each of the following sounds (don't forget to use square brackets). The first one is given as an example.

    Example: voiced palatal glide: [j]

    a. voiceless post-alveolar affricate   **e.** voiced interdental fricative
    b. voiced velar nasal   **f.** voiced post-alveolar fricative
    c. voiced glottal fricative   **g.** voiced alveolar lateral liquid
    d. voiced labiodental fricative

6. Write the three-part articulatory descriptions for the consonant sounds represented by the following symbols. The first one is given as an example.

   Example: [j]: voiced palatal glide

   a. [f]   **f.** [ɹ]
   b. [z]   **g.** [ʒ]
   c. [n]   **h.** [ʧ]
   d. [ŋ]   **i.** [g]
   e. [ʃ]   **j.** [ʔ]

7. For each group of sounds, identify the segment that differs in place of articulation from the other three.

   a. [s], [n], [ɹ], [v]
   b. [k], [n], [ŋ], [g]
   c. [m], [p], [l], [w]
   d. [ʃ], [ʤ], [d], [ʧ]
   e. [t], [n], [d], [k]

 8. This exercise is designed to help you become more familiar with the shapes of the vocal tract connected with the production of different consonant sounds. For each drawing presented on page 97, there is only one consonant sound of English that could be produced by a vocal tract positioned as shown; you are to figure out which stop, nasal, or fricative sound is represented (either by referring to the descriptions of different sounds or by experimenting with your own vocal tract—some of each is recommended). Be sure that you take into account the voicing, manner, and place of articulation of each sound. Write the phonetic symbol for that sound between the brackets below the appropriate drawing. Note that voicing is shown by two wavy or bumpy lines (representing vocal fold vibration) where the larynx would be, whereas voiceless sounds are represented by two lines shaped like an ellipse at the larynx level, indicating an open glottis. Take care also to note whether the air passage to the nasal cavity is open or closed (i.e., if the velum is lowered or raised). The first drawing is labeled to start you off.

9. Given the articulatory descriptions of consonants in this file, what would you expect the difference between a [t] and an [s] to look like in static palatography pictures? Of the two pictures below, which do you think could be an instance of [t] and which an instance of [s]? How do you know? What other sounds would make the pattern seen in (a) and (b)?

   a.   **b.**

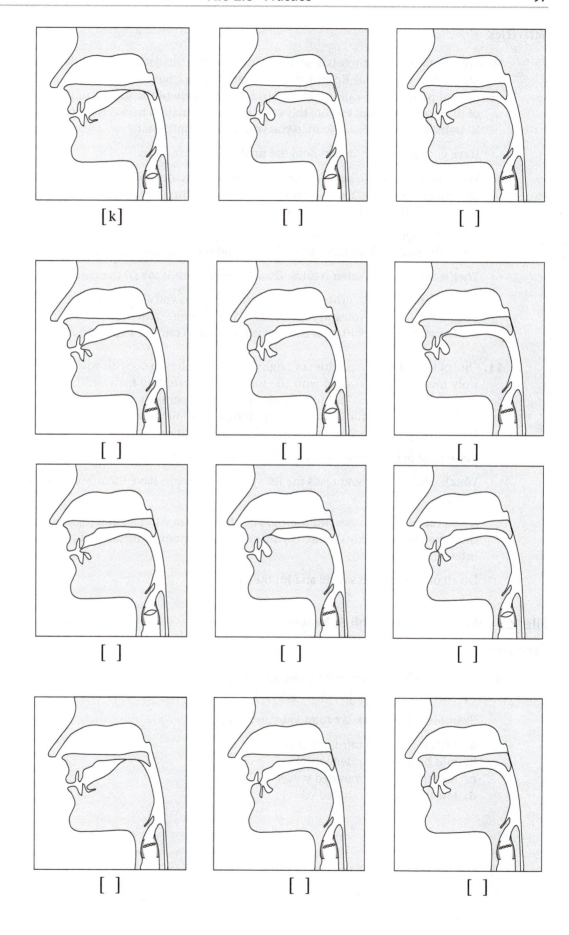

[k]   [ ]   [ ]

[ ]   [ ]   [ ]

[ ]   [ ]   [ ]

[ ]   [ ]   [ ]

Activities

10. We mentioned that there is a lot of variation in the articulation of English [ɹ]. Many people say [ɹ] with the tongue tip curled up (the retroflex [ɹ]). But there are also many people who instead produce a so-called bunched [ɹ] with the body of the tongue pulled up to the roof of the mouth. You can explore this variation in articulation between retroflex and bunched [ɹ] by asking some friends to help you with the toothpick test.

Have your friend say *far* and hold the final [ɹ], as in [faɹɹɹɹɹ].

While holding the [ɹ], have him/her carefully insert a toothpick into the space between the upper and lower front teeth (try not to point the toothpick at an angle up or down, but keep it level with the space between the teeth).

If the toothpick pokes the top of the tongue, your friend is producing a bunched [ɹ]; if it pokes the underside of the tongue, your friend is producing a retroflex [ɹ].

Try the same test on other friends. Do all of your friends say [ɹ] the same way?

Try the same test with other words containing [ɹ]. Do you always produce [ɹ] the same way in all the words? Do you and your friends have the same patterns of variation across words? (Note that language variation is discussed in more detail in Chapter 10.)

11. One of the other complexities of English phonetics has to do with whether [θ] and [ð] are truly interdental (produced with the tongue tip protruding between the front teeth). For many people they are, but for a sizable number of perfectly good speakers of English, [θ] and [ð] are dental (produced with the tongue tip touching the back of the upper front teeth). Ask your friends to help you look at this variation.

Make a list of words that contain [θ] and a list of words that contain [ð].

Watch while your friend reads the list (you may have to have them hold the list up at eye level).

If you can see the tongue protruding, your friend is making [θ] and [ð] interdental. If not, then they are probably dental. Is your friend consistent in making all [θ]s and [ð]s either interdental or dental?

Do all of your friends say [θ] and [ð] the same way?

File 2.3—Articulation: English Vowels

Exercises

12. Write the phonetic symbol representing each of the following sounds (don't forget to use square brackets). The first one is given as an example:

Example: high back lax rounded vowel: [ʊ]

  a. high front tense unrounded vowel
  b. mid back lax rounded vowel
  c. mid front lax unrounded vowel
  d. low back lax unrounded vowel

13. Write the four-part articulatory descriptions for the vowel sounds represented by the following symbols. The first one is given as an example.

Example: [ə]: mid, central, unrounded, and lax

a. [ɪ]   **d.** [u]
b. [ʌ]   **e.** [æ]
c. [ɛ]   **f.** [ʊ]

14. Give the IPA symbol for the vowel that occurs in each word.

a. sues   **f.** sows
b. sis   **g.** says
c. sees   **h.** sighs
d. suss   **i.** sauce
e. sews   **j.** sass

Supplemental Exercises: Consonants and Vowels Combined

15. Circle all the symbols below that represent voiced sounds:

[s]   [d]   [g]   [ð]   [tʃ]   [b]   [t]   [ʔ]   [ɹ]   [θ]   [p]

[oʊ]   [f]   [ʃ]   [z]   [k]   [i]   [m]   [v]   [h]   [w]   [ɪ]

16. Give the conventional spelling for the following phonetically transcribed words. (Note that some may have more than one possible spelling.) The first one (a) is given as an example.

a. [sloʊp] *slope*   **k.** [peɪn]   **u.** [pitsə]   **ee.** [fɹ̩m]
b. [sʌni]   **l.** [wɛnzdeɪ]   **v.** [ækʃn̩]   **ff.** [pɹaɪd]
c. [seɪl]   **m.** [kanʃəs]   **w.** [bjuɾi]   **gg.** [ðoʊ]
d. [wɔɹm]   **n.** [θaʊznd̩]   **x.** [ʃuleɪs]   **hh.** [gɹeɪs]
e. [ɹut]   **o.** [fʌdʒ]   **y.** [kɹɔld]   **ii.** [sɹ̩veɪ]
f. [liʒɹ̩]   **p.** [kaɪt]   **z.** [pɔɪnt]   **jj.** [lʊk]
g. [sɹ̩tʃt]   **q.** [kɹaʊd]   **aa.** [kloʊð]   **kk.** [neɪʃn̩]
h. [kɹud]   **r.** [ɹat]   **bb.** [ɹoʊt]   **ll.** [bæŋ]
i. [ɹɪdʒ]   **s.** [dʒɔ]   **cc.** [θæŋk]   **mm.** [eɪɹə]
j. [ɹitʃ]   **t.** [ɹɪtʃ]   **dd.** [ʃak]   **nn.** [baks]

17. Transcribe the following words. The first one (a) is given as an example.

a. touch [tʌtʃ]   **p.** punched   **ee.** leather   **tt.** cringe
b. woman   **q.** lather   **ff.** Godzilla   **uu.** pushed
c. women   **r.** Cairo   **gg.** raspberry **vv.** isn't
d. flood   **s.** vision   **hh.** slyly   **ww.** rhythm
e. wrapped   **t.** price   **ii.** calves   **xx.** January
f. prays   **u.** monkey   **jj.** wove   **yy.** mother
g. brood   **v.** huge   **kk.** mustache   **zz.** pure
h. ghoul   **w.** cough   **ll.** carrot   **aaa.** February
i. torch   **x.** batch   **mm.** child   **bbb.** bathtub
j. stood   **y.** whale   **nn.** sugar   **ccc.** union
k. move   **z.** easy   **oo.** cane   **ddd.** hoodlum
l. breathe   **aa.** hour   **pp.** said   **eee.** icy
m. breath   **bb.** carton   **qq.** larynx   **fff.** July
n. lose   **cc.** though   **rr.** love   **ggg.** cookies
o. loose   **dd.** circus   **ss.** sewn   **hhh.** August

18. Correct the mistakes in the following phonetic transcriptions of English words, if there is a mistake.

a. [ʃut] shut   **c.** [falʊ] follow   **e.** [lɛft] left   **g.** [ðim] theme   **i.** [ɹæn] rang
b. [swit] swift   **d.** [tɹɑd] trod   **f.** [ʧild] child   **h.** [voıs] voice   **j.** [hɛlθ] health

19. Read the phonetically transcribed sentences below and write them out in ordinary spelling. These transcriptions represent the pronunciation of a particular speaker on a particular occasion and thus may differ from your own pronunciation of the same passages in certain minor details, but this should not cause you any difficulty. These passages are from Woody Allen's book *Without Feathers*.

a. [dʌbz æskt hɪz bɹʌðɹ̩ wʌt ɪt wʌz laɪk ɪn ði ʌðɹ̩ wɹ̩ld n̩d hɪz bɹʌðɹ̩ sɛd ɪt wʌz nɑt ənlaɪk klivln̩d] ([dʌbz] "Dubbs" is a proper name.)

b. [ɪtɹ̩n̩l̩ nʌθɪŋnɛs ɪz oʊkeı æz lɔŋ æz jɹ̩ dɹɛst fɔɹ ɪt]

c. [ɪf ju ɑɹ sɪkstin ɔɹ ʌndɹ̩ tɹaı nɑt tə goʊ bald]

d. [mʌni ɪz nɑt ɛvɹiθɪŋ bʌt ɪt ɪz bɛɹɹ̩ ðæn hævɪŋ wʌnz hɛlθ]

e. [ðə ɡɹæshɑpɹ̩ pleıd al sʌmɹ̩ waıl ði ænt wɹ̩kt n̩ seɪvd wɛn wɪntɹ̩ keım ðə ɡɹæshɑpɹ̩ hæd nʌθɪŋ bʌt ði ænt kəmpleınd əv ʧɛst peınz]

f. [ðə sæfaɹɹ̩ wʌz ɹɹɪʤənəli oʊnd baı ə sʌltn̩ hu daɪd ʌndɹ̩ mɪstɹɹiəs sɹ̩kəmstænsəz wɛn ə hænd ɹiʧt aʊt əv ə boʊl əv sup hi wʌz itɪŋ n̩ stɹæŋɡl̩d hɪm]

g. [ðə ɡɹeıt ɹoʊ ɪz ə mɪθəkl̩ bist wɪθ ðə hɛd əv ə laıɹ̃ ænd ðə badi əv ə laıɹ̃ bʌt nɑt ðə seım laıɹ̃] ([ɹoʊ] "Roe" is a nonsense name.)

Discussion Question

20. **i.** What is the difference between a consonant and a vowel?
 ii. Why can't we use palatography to study vowel height?

Activities

21. How loud are vowels and consonants? For this activity, you'll need two people and a large open space with either little background noise (like a quiet woods) or steady background noise (like a beach). Stand back to back, as for a duel. One person is the speaker. His/her job is to say a speech sound at normal volume repeatedly, with minimal volume change over repetitions. The other person is the listener. His/her job is to slowly walk away from the speaker, counting the number of steps it takes until the speech sound can no longer be heard.

Write down the number of steps it takes for different speech sounds to become inaudible. Is the number of steps the same for consonants and vowels? Is it the same for all consonants?

Here are some good sounds to try (be sure that you don't say a vowel with the consonants (e.g., don't say [ɛf] when you mean [f]): [f], [θ], [s], [n], [i], [ɪ], [u], [ɑ], [æ].

File 2.4—Beyond English: Speech Sounds of the World's Languages

Exercises

22. Write the IPA symbol for each of the following sounds (don't forget to use square brackets). The first one is given as an example.

Example: voiced alveolar trill   [r]

a. voiced bilabial fricative
b. mid front rounded vowel
c. voiceless palatal stop

d. voiceless uvular stop
e. velarized alveolar lateral liquid
f. voiceless ejective alveolar stop

23. Write out the description of each of the following IPA symbols or combinations of symbols. The first one is given as an example.

Example: [x]   voiceless velar fricative

a. [y]   **d.** [ɲ]
b. [ɦ]   **e.** [t͡s]
c. [sʲ]   **f.** [ħ]

Discussion Question

24. Refer to the IPA consonant chart on the last page of the book. Note that there are two types of empty boxes in this chart: some are gray and some are white. What is the difference between the two types of empty boxes?

File 2.5—Suprasegmental Features

Exercises

25. Read the following pairs of sentences aloud. Words in capital letters indicate the presence of a pitch accent and should be said with special prominence. Both sentences in each pair contain exactly the same words, but they differ in intonation and have different meanings. Paraphrase what the two sentences in each pair mean. How are the meanings different?

a. John called Paul a Republican and then he INSULTED him.
John called Paul a Republican and then HE insulted HIM.

b. John even gave his daughter a new BICYCLE.
John even gave his DAUGHTER a new bicycle.

c. Maxwell didn't kill the JUDGE with a silver hammer.
Maxwell didn't kill the judge with a silver HAMMER.

d. Of the three men, John hates BILL the most.
Of the three men, JOHN hates Bill the most.

26. In File 2.5, you learned that where a break occurs in a sentence can change its meaning. Turn each of the strings of words below into two sentences with different meanings by adding punctuation or other visual markers of phrase tones that can serve to differentiate the two meanings. Then paraphrase the different meanings.

a. when danger threatens your children call the police
b. I met Mary and Elena's mother at the mall yesterday
c. turn right here

27. Using your knowledge of English, indicate which syllable of each of the following words receives primary stress. Is the placement of English stress predictable for these words? Why or why not?

a. cat   f. category

b. catsup   g. caterpillar

c. cattle   h. catastrophe

d. catalogue   i. catastrophic

e. cathedral   j. categorical

Activities

28. In the text, we said that the duration of a speech sound may be influenced by the sounds around it. To test this for yourself, first record the following words using a microphone and some sort of phonetics software (see the note at the beginning of File 2.8).

heat / heed / he's
hit / hid / his
hate / hayed / haze
hat / had / has
height / hide / hies
hoot / who'd / whose

Notice that in each set of three words, only the final consonant changes: it is a voiceless alveolar stop, a voiced alveolar stop, or a voiced alveolar fricative.

Measure the duration of the vowel in each word. (You can use Praat to record by clicking on *New* and *Record mono Sound . . .* or *Record stereo Sound. . . .* After you have recorded and saved your sentences, you can look at the spectrograms by opening the recording [*Read* and *Read from file*] and clicking on *Edit.* A window will open with the spectrogram of your sound in the lower section. You can highlight the vowels using the cursor and get their duration by clicking on *Query* and then *Get selection length.*)

   i. For which context is each vowel the shortest? The longest? (That is, are vowels longer before voiceless or voiced alveolar stops? voiced alveolar stops or fricatives?) Is the answer the same for every vowel?

  ii. Within a context, which vowel is the shortest? The longest? (That is, is the vowel in *heed* shorter or longer than the vowel in *hid*, etc.?)

 iii. Based on your observations, which of the following words do you think would have longer vowel: *boat* or *bode*?

29. Record yourself saying the sentence *Mary had a little lamb* (using a microphone and some sort of phonetics software (see the note at the beginning of File 2.8). Say the sentence with as many different intonational patterns as you can think of. You should record at least five sentences. After you have recorded and saved your sentences, you should be able to look at the pitch movements of your voice graphically in the speech editor. (You can use Praat to record by clicking on *New* and *Record mono Sound . . .* or *Record stereo Sound. . . .* After you have recorded and saved your sentences, you can look at the pitch movements by opening the file (click on *Read* and *Read from file*) and clicking on *Edit.* A window will open with the pitch movements of your utterance in the lower part of the picture represented by a blue line on top of the spectrogram. You can adjust the pitch range that is shown in the picture by clicking on *Pitch* and *Pitch settings. . . .*) Now answer the following questions.

(cont.)

    i. What meaning did you intend for each of the sentences you recorded? For example, the sentence could have been a question or a correction that Mary (and not someone else) had a little lamb; or it could have been sarcastic; etc.

    ii. How are the pitch movements for each of the sentences different? To answer this, just describe what you see and hear. You could, for example, write that the pitch peaks on a certain word or goes down at the end.

    iii. Can you draw any conclusions as to which pitch movement you used to convey which meaning? For example, if you say the sentence in order to correct a certain word, what is your pitch movement for the correction?

File 2.6—Acoustic Phonetics

Exercises

30. Describe in your own words how vowels are "shaped" by the vocal tract.

31. What information does a spectrogram give you?

32. Match each of the following words to the appropriate spectrogram.

    a. shoe
    b. hippo
    c. ow!

33. Following is a spectrogram showing the formants of five vowels from a language of Mexico called Mazotec. (Each vowel in the spectrogram is preceded by a fricative.) Mazotec has five vowels: [i], [e], [a], [o], and [u]. Your task is to measure the vowel space.

    i. Find the center value for the first and the second formants (in Hertz). Be sure to take the value from the middle of the formant (on both the time axis and the frequency axis).

    ii. Then plot the first formant values against the second formant values in the graph provided below. In other words, for each vowel, its first formant frequency will be the vertical (the *y*) value, and its second formant frequency will be the horizontal (the *x*) value of a point.

    iii. How does the Mazotec vowel space compare with the vowel space of English (cf. (6), File 2.6)? Are the vowels in the same place relative to each other, or are there differences in the way that English distributes its vowels compared to how Mazotec distributes its vowels?

(cont.)

Activity

34. You may be able to learn something interesting about vowels by whistling. Whistling high-lights the second vowel formant, which is highest when the tongue is in the high front position and lowest when the tongue is in the high back position. Whistle down a scale until you get to the lowest note you can whistle. Now let your vocal folds vibrate (as if you were humming while whistling). What vowel sound are you making? Try it again, but this time whistle up a scale until you get to the highest note you can make. Try unrounding your lips (smile!) and see if it sounds like a vowel of English when you hum. You may have found that your highest note has a tongue position like [i] and your lowest note has a tongue position like [u].

File 2.7—The Phonetics of Signed Languages

Exercises

35. The following two ASL signs differ in one parameter. Which parameter distinguishes them?

THINK   WONDER

36. The following two signs, both of which are articulated in front of the torso, differ in two parameters and are the same in two parameters. Which two are the same? Which two differ? How do they differ? (Try to describe the differences as specifically as possible.)

CHOCOLATE   CHURCH

© 2006, William Vicars, www.Lifeprint.com. Used with permission.

37. Describe the five parameters of articulation for each of the following signs of ASL.

a. DEAF   b. GRANDMA   c. BAD

© 2006, William Vicars, www.Lifeprint.com. Used with permission.

Discussion Questions

38. Suppose that you were assigned to a team that was responsible for creating a sort of IPA to represent signed languages using written characters. What sorts of characters might this alphabet need to have? How might you want to organize such an alphabet? What would be some of the challenges that you would run into with this project?

39. What does signed "yelling" have in common with yelling in spoken languages; what does signed "whispering" have in common with whispering in spoken languages? Are there any differences (aside, obviously, from the modality itself)?

Further Readings

Johnson, Keith. 2012. *Acoustic and auditory phonetics.* 3rd edn. Malden, MA: Wiley-Blackwell.

Ladefoged, Peter, and Keith Johnson. 2015. *A course in phonetics.* 7th edn. Stamford, CT: Cengage Learning.

Ladefoged, Peter, and Sandra Ferrari Disner. 2012. *Vowels and consonants: An introduction to the sounds of languages.* 3rd edn. Malden, MA: Wiley-Blackwell.

Ladefoged, Peter, and Ian Maddieson. 1996. *The sounds of the world's languages.* Oxford: Blackwell.

CHAPTER

3

Phonology

FILE 3.0

What Is Phonology?

Like phonetics, phonology has to do with the study of speech sounds ("phones"), but important differences exist between these related fields. As we saw in Chapter 2, phonetics is the study of speech sounds as physical entities: how they are produced in the vocal tract, what their articulatory and acoustic properties are, and how they are interpreted. **Phonology**, on the other hand, is the study of how sounds are organized within a language and how they interact with each other. Phonologists ask the following kinds of questions: What is the organization of sounds in a given language? Within a language, are there particular sounds whose distribution with regard to other sounds is predictable in some way? Which sounds are used in a language to distinguish between words?

Contents

FILE 3.1

Phonotactic Constraints and Foreign Accents

3.1.1 Phonotactic Constraints

In Chapter 2, we focused on the sounds of language as entities in the physical world: the particular combinations of movements involved, the articulatory and acoustic properties that distinguish sounds, etc. But language is not just individual sounds. When we know a language, we also need to know how its sounds work together as a system. Can any sounds appear in any order in a word? Are sounds always produced exactly the same way? What are our mental perception and categorization of the sounds? Do sounds influence each other when they occur together? These are the sorts of questions we will be dealing with in this chapter.

To introduce the idea of how languages organize sounds, we begin here by looking at the restrictions languages have on the kinds of sounds and sound sequences possible in different positions in a word (particularly at the beginning and end). We know that languages "sound different" from each other. Some of this is due to differences in their **phonetic inventories** (i.e., the sounds that are produced as part of the language) and suprasegmental features. When we described the consonants and vowels of Standard American English in Chapter 2, we were describing its phonetic inventory, and we also looked at some sounds found in other language inventories. But languages can sound quite different from each other even when their phonetic inventories are very similar. This is often due to differences in the rules governing which sound sequences are possible in a language and which are not. These restrictions on possible combinations of sounds are known as **phonotactic constraints.**

We can investigate these restrictions in more detail by considering some in a language we know very well—English. We start with the question of which consonants are permitted at the beginning of a word, noting that any consonant of English may occur word-initially except for two: [ʒ] and [ŋ]. While some speakers do pronounce these sounds in borrowed words such as *Jacques* and *Nguyen,* no native English word begins with them. A large number of two-consonant combinations also occur word-initially, with a stop or fricative being followed by a liquid or glide:

(1) [bɹ] bring   [gl] glean   [mj] music   [kw] quick
     [θɹ] three   [fl] fly   [hj] humor   [sw] sweet

In addition, [s] can also be followed by voiceless and nasal stops (as in *stay, small*) and by [f] and [v] in a small number of borrowed words (*sphere, svelte,* etc.). [ʃ] can be followed by a nasal stop or a liquid, but only [ʃɹ] is a cluster native to English (e.g., *shrink*). The others are present only in borrowings from Yiddish and German (e.g., *Schlemiel* 'clumsy person,' *Schnook,* 'fool,' *Schwinn*). (See activity (6) in File 3.6 to explore these patterns more thoroughly.)

In addition to having constraints concerning which particular sounds are permitted to occur together or in certain positions, languages have phonotactic constraints regarding syllable types (see File 2.1 for syllable structure). Languages generally prefer syllables made up of a consonant (C) first and a vowel (V) second, but some languages allow a syllable to begin with more than one consonant. For instance, English allows up to three consonants to start a word, provided the first is [s], the second [p], [t], or [k], and the third [l], [ɹ], [j], or [w] (see below). There is a wide variety of syllable types in English, as illustrated in (2).

(2)
V	*a*	CV	*no*	CCV	*flew*	CCCV	*spree*
VC	*at*	CVC	*not*	CCVC	*flute*	CCCVC	*spleen*
VCC	*ask*	CVCC	*ramp*	CCVCC	*flutes*	CCCVCC	*strength*
VCCC	*asked*	CVCCC	*ramps*	CCVCCC	*crafts*	CCCVCCC	*strengths*

Other languages, however, do not have such a large number of permitted syllable structures, as the lists in (3) illustrate. (Hebrew CVCC syllables are allowed only at the end of a word, and only if the final consonant is [t].)

(3)

Hawaiian	Indonesian	Hebrew
CV	CV	CV
V	V	CCV
	VC	CCVC
	CVC	CVC
		CVCC

Notice that this means that Indonesian has clusters only in the middle of words; that is, there are no clusters initially or finally. Hawaiian does not permit clusters in any position. Meanwhile, even though Hebrew permits both initial and final clusters, it does not allow a single vowel to be a syllable by itself. Every language has its own set of permitted segmental sequences.

The phonotactic constraints of a language will generally apply to every word in the language, native or not. Therefore, languages seek to overcome problems of borrowing a foreign word that violates their phonotactics. For instance, in English, two stops cannot come at the beginning of words, nor can stop plus nasal combinations. So, in order to pronounce the borrowed words *Ptolemy* and *gnostic* more easily, English speakers simply drop the first consonant and pronounce the words as [tɑləmi] and [nɑstɪk], respectively. Alternatively, speakers may insert a vowel between the two consonants, as in the pronunciation of the words *Gdansk* and *knish* as [gədænsk] and [kənɪʃ]. Both of these alterations eliminate violations of the phonotactic constraints of English.

As these examples from English illustrate, there are different ways of handling phonotactic problems. Japanese and Finnish, which generally avoid syllables containing sequences of consonants, provide us with additional examples. When a foreign word with a consonant cluster is borrowed, it must be changed somehow to fit the language's syllable structure. As seen in English above, the first "repair" option is to drop or delete one of the consonants, and the other is to insert a vowel to separate the consonants. Finnish opts for deletion, dropping the first of a series of consonants in loanwords that do not conform to its phonotactics. Thus, Germanic *Strand* (CCCVNC; N = nasal) ends up as *ranta* 'beach' (CVNCV) in Finnish, and *glass* becomes *lasi*. Note also the addition of a final vowel to avoid a consonant in syllable-final position.

Japanese uses the other option, inserting vowels into the cluster, so that, for example, a CCC sequence will end up as CVCVCV. The vowel insertion is predictable and rule-governed: the vowel [o] is inserted after [t] and [d], while the high back unrounded vowel [ɯ] is inserted after all other consonants. Thus, we can predict the form of new words in Japanese that have been borrowed from English. For example, when the English word *birth control* was borrowed into Japanese, it became [baːsɯ kontoɾoːɾɯ]. Note that the nasals [n] and [m] are allowed to occur syllable-finally in Japanese, although no other consonants are.

/bəɹθ/	→	[baːsɯ]
/kəntɹol/	→	[kontoɾoːɾɯ]

[ɯ] is inserted at the end of [baːsɯ] and [kontoɾoːɾɯ] to keep the word-final syllables from ending in a consonant. The second [o] in [kontoɾoːɾɯ] is inserted to prevent [t] and [ɾ] from forming a consonant cluster. Notice also that Japanese substitutes other sounds for some of the English sounds, such as [s] for [θ]. This will be discussed in Section 3.1.3.

3.1.2 Phonotactic Constraints in Signed Languages

There are similar kinds of constraints on what sorts of segment combinations are and are not allowed in various signed languages. As with the phonotactic constraints for syllable structures and for consonants and vowels in spoken languages described above, constraints on syllable structure and on what sorts of handshapes and movements can appear adjacent to one another in signed languages differ from language to language. The phonotactic constraints discussed in this section are specific to ASL.

First we will consider restrictions on syllable structure; there will be two examples.[1] It was mentioned above that in Hebrew, a vowel alone cannot serve as a syllable: there is a minimum requirement that a syllable in Hebrew contain at least two segments. There is a similar minimum requirement for ASL syllables: a monosyllabic sign cannot consist of just one handshape, one location, and one orientation; at least one of these elements is required to change during the sign in order to form a grammatical syllable.

The second example we will consider is when changes of handshape are allowed. Many signs include a change of handshape during movement of the hands from one location to another; other signs involve handshape changes that occur while the hands are held stationary at some particular place. In ASL, handshape changes may always occur during movement. The sign WHITE, shown in (4), provides a good example of this.

(4) ASL: WHITE

© 2006, William Vicars, www.Lifeprint.com. Adapted by permission.

Likewise, if a sign comprises only one place of articulation without movement to another place of articulation, handshape change can occur while the hand is kept at that

---

[1]It probably seems very peculiar to think about signs as having syllables! Nonetheless, signs can be broken down into prosodic units just like spoken words. If you are not a signer, though, it is very difficult to figure out what might comprise a signed syllable. (We also lack intuitions about syllable structure of spoken languages that we do not know.) Therefore, we will simply take it as an underlying assumption that signed languages have syllables, and go from there.

location. However, if a sign involves the hands being at some place and then moving, or moving and then winding up at some place, then the change of handshape must take place during the movement. It is not permitted in ASL for handshape to change while the hands are held at some particular location if there is a movement component of that sign.

Not only do signed languages have syllable structure constraints, but there are also constraints on which segments can be adjacent to one another in the same way that certain sound combinations are not allowed in some languages (like word-initial [fk] in English). For example, in any given signed language, there may be certain handshapes that—though parts of the system of handshapes in that language—are not allowed by the grammar to appear adjacent to one another within a word.

An interesting phonotactic constraint that does not have any obvious direct parallel in spoken languages but that seems fairly uniform among signed languages pertains to the fact that in signed languages there are two possible primary articulators, namely, the right hand and the left hand. In all signed languages studied to date, a signer may be right-hand dominant or left-hand dominant (which roughly corresponds to whether the signer is right- or left-handed). The dominant hand is the one that the signer will use to perform all one-handed signs. (If a right-handed signer were to injure her right arm or happened to be carrying a large box under her right arm, she might temporarily switch and use her left hand to sign with, but no signer switches back and forth between hands as a matter of course: this would be considered extremely aberrant to any native speaker of a signed language.) Interestingly, there are very specific restrictions on what the non-dominant hand may do in any given two-handed sign. If both hands are moving, then the non-dominant hand must have the same handshape, orientation, and motion as the dominant hand; that is, in signs where both hands are moving, there is a symmetry constraint. It is important to note that although the motion must be the same, the direction of the motion may be parallel or anti-parallel. An example of an ASL sign that follows the symmetry constraint is CAN 'be able to,' illustrated in (5). Although the non-dominant hand does move in this sign, it mirrors exactly the shape, orientation, and movement of the dominant hand.

 (5) ASL: CAN

© 2006, William Vicars, www.Lifeprint.com. Used with permission.

The non-dominant hand may also participate in a sign by remaining stationary while the dominant hand moves. This is exemplified in the ASL sign CHOCOLATE in (6): the two hands have different handshapes, but the non-dominant hand (the lower hand, which is held flat) is not moving.

 (6) ASL: CHOCOLATE

© 2006, William Vicars, www.Lifeprint.com. Used with permission.

A grammatical sign in any signed language cannot have both hands moving unless they both have the same handshape and orientation and are performing the same kind of movement. Interestingly, in Signed Mandarin (which is not a signed language, but rather a signed code for Mandarin Chinese; see File 1.5) there are certain signs that have been introduced by hearing (non-native signer) instructors at schools for the deaf that do not follow this rule. The fact that the Signed Mandarin words do not follow the universal rule for signed languages is yet more evidence that signed codes and signed languages differ! For example, in the Signed Mandarin sign for 'ink,' both hands are moving, so the sign should follow the symmetry constraint. However, in this sign the dominant hand is facing toward the signer, and the non-dominant hand away from the signer, so they have different orientations. The dominant hand moves in a path away from the body while the non-dominant hand moves from side to side, so they have different movement; and the dominant hand has one finger extended while the non-dominant hand has three fingers extended, so they have different handshapes. Thus this sign is ungrammatical for three reasons.

There has been an attempt (again by non-native signers) to introduce such signs from Signed Mandarin into Taiwan Sign Language, but the reaction among the native signers is that these signs are not possible in their language. It is exactly as though somebody told you that [kpflus] was a new word of English; you wouldn't accept it!

3.1.3 Foreign Accents

Applying the phonotactic constraints of one language while speaking another is an important source of foreign accents. A Spanish speaker, for example, may pronounce *student* as [ɛstudɛnt], because in Spanish, the consonant clusters [st], [sk], and [sp] are not permitted to occur at the beginning of a word without being preceded by a vowel—as in the words *estudiante* 'student,' *escuela* 'school,' and *espalda* 'shoulder.' The speaker who says [ɛstudɛnt] is simply applying the phonotactic constraints of Spanish when speaking English words.

As noted above, another source of foreign accents is differences in phonetic inventories. Just as there are many speech sounds in other languages that English does not use, so also there are sounds in English's inventory that are not used by other languages. We can detect this when we hear non-native speakers of English pronounce English words. For example, since the phonetic inventory of French does not contain [ð] or [θ], French speakers often pronounce *this* [ðɪs] as [zɪs] and *thin* [θɪn] as [sɪn]. This process is called **sound substitution**: speakers use sounds of their native language to replace non-native sounds when pronouncing the words of a foreign language.

Notice that the sounds that French speakers use to replace [ð] and [θ] are very similar to the sounds replaced. [ð] is replaced by [z], another voiced fricative that is pronounced at a similar place of articulation, and /θ/ is replaced by the corresponding voiceless fricative [s]. In most cases, speakers will substitute the most similar sound available in their inventory. Similarly, speakers of signed languages have accents when signing in a second signed language, sometimes carrying over primes like handshape and movement from their first language.

Another familiar example involves the pronunciation of German by some speakers of English. German has a voiceless velar fricative [x]. The phonemic inventory of English, of course, lacks this sound, though we do have a voiceless velar stop [k]. Most speakers of English substitute [k] for [x] in a German word like *Bach* [bɑx], producing [bɑk] instead. Another example of the same substitution is the way most American English speakers pronounce *Lebkuchen* [lebkuxən] 'Christmas cookie' as [leɪbkukən]. Some English speakers, striving for a more "German-like" pronunciation, will pronounce it instead as [leɪbkuhən]. Why do you suppose an English speaker might substitute [h] for [x]?

Phonotactic constraints are thus one important way that languages organize their phonetic inventories into phonological systems. In the next file, we look at other ways that the sounds of languages are organized with respect to one another and the rules that govern where they appear.

....

Phonemes and Allophones

3.2.1 Different Sounds Have Different Distributions

As discussed in File 3.1, languages have restrictions on which sounds can occur in certain environments. To illustrate this, say *tan* [tæn] and *gnat* [næt] out loud several times quickly. Did you have any difficulty with this task? Probably not. Now try the same thing with *gang* [gæŋ] and an imaginary new word *ngag* [ŋæg]. Was this any harder? Most likely [ŋæg] was quite difficult! But these tasks were very similar: the first involved producing sequences of an alveolar nasal and stop with a low vowel, and the second involved sequences of a velar nasal and stop with a low vowel. The problem, then, does not lie with these sequences in general. The problem is also not with a sequence of a nasal followed by a velar stop, since *nag* [næg] should cause no problems for you. So what is it about [ŋæg] that makes it so hard to pronounce? The problem here is specifically with where [ŋ] occurs: as noted in the previous file, one of the phonotactic restrictions of English is that [ŋ] cannot occur at the beginning of a word. When we say "cannot," again, we are not talking about some rule that the "grammar police" enforce—your mental grammar is where this rule resides, and you can feel its strong effects when you try to pronounce [ŋæg]. This, then, is a very basic way that sounds have different distributions in languages.

On the basis of this distributional pattern, we could make some predictions: first, we can predict that an English speaker would have a difficult time with a word beginning with [ŋ] in a foreign language and would likely replace the [ŋ] with [n]. We could also predict that no unfamiliar or new words in English will begin with [ŋ].

We see a different situation in comparing the distributions of the oral velar stops [k] and [g] in English. Are there any restrictions on where they can occur? Can we predict which of the two sounds might occur in any given new word? We can easily think of word pairs like *cot–got*, *crab–grab*, *tack–tag*, *wick–wig*, *backer–bagger*, and *hunker–hunger*, in which the only sound that differs between the two words is [k] and [g]. (Remember: we are talking about sounds, not spelling! It may help you to phonetically transcribe these words if you have doubts.) And since both sounds occur at the beginning, middle, and ends of words, between vowels and after [ŋ], there do not appear to be any particular restrictions on where they may appear. What this tells us is that the voicing difference between these two sounds is **meaningful** in English. Changing the sound from voiced to voiceless (or vice versa) changes the word produced. Because of this, we cannot predict where either of these sounds will occur in a word.

Does the fact that [k] and [g] are meaningfully different sounds in English tell us anything about their distribution in another language? No. Just as the constraint against word-initial [ŋ] in English tells us nothing about whether other languages allow it word-initially (many do), so also English's contrast between [k] and [g] tells us nothing about their relationship in other languages. Each language must be investigated independently.

Kikamba is a Bantu language spoken in Kenya, and, like English, it has [k] and [g] as part of its phonetic inventory, as seen in its word for 'to guard' [kosuuŋga]. But if we look more closely at where these sounds can appear in Kikamba words, we would notice patterns that are different from those in English. The voiced velar stop [g] is quite restricted: it only occurs immediately after the velar nasal [ŋ]. The voiceless stop [k] is not restricted in the same way—it can occur at the beginning of a word, as seen above, as well as in the middle of a word between vowels, as in [kwaaka] 'to build.' The one place it does not occur, however, is after the velar nasal [ŋ] (see Roberts-Kohno 2000): no [ŋk] sequences are permitted. To illustrate how strong this distributional pattern is in Kikamba, consider the word *katala* 'to count.' To say 'if you count,' you add an [o] to the beginning of the word: [okatala]. But to say 'if I count,' you must add an [ŋ], and the word is then pronounced as [ŋgatala].

What this tells us is that the difference between these two sounds is **not** meaningful in Kikamba, in contrast to English. Changing which sound is produced will not change the meaning of the word. If someone learning Kikamba were to use [k] after [ŋ] (e.g., [ŋkatala] for 'if I count'), a native speaker of Kikamba might think that the speaker sounded funny, had an accent, or had mispronounced the word, but the meaning would not change.

3.2.2 Allophones and Phonemes

In every language, certain sounds pattern together as if they were simply variants of the "same" sound, instead of different sounds that can be used to distinguish words. This was the case for [k] and [g] in Kikamba in Section 3.2.1: the voicing difference between these two sounds is not meaningful in that language. It can't be used to distinguish words, and there is a clear pattern of where one versus the other appears, which makes these two sounds completely predictable. Therefore, these sounds can be thought of as variants of the "same" sound in Kikamba: the 'k' sound is pronounced with voicing when it appears after [ŋ], and without voicing everywhere else.

We have similar relationships between "same" and "different" sounds in English. One of the major goals of this file is to help you understand this distinction more clearly, and we can begin by building on some of what we learned about English sounds in Chapter 2. First, look at the list of words in (1): if you asked someone who had not studied phonetics if the underlined sound was the same in each word, what do you think their answer would be?

(1) <u>t</u>op s<u>t</u>op li<u>tt</u>le ki<u>tt</u>en

Most people would say "yes," identifying all of the words as containing the sound 't.' But now that you have learned about the phonetics of English, would you answer the same way? If you transcribe the words on a separate piece of paper according to what you learned in the previous chapter, you will probably wrote them as follows:

(2) [tɑp] [stɑp] [lɪɾl̩] [kɪʔn̩]

So here we have three sounds: the voiceless alveolar stop [t], the voiced alveolar flap [ɾ], and the voiceless glottal stop [ʔ]. We did not talk much about how these sounds were related to each other in the previous chapter, but most English speakers, with a little practice, are able to hear the difference between very carefully enunciated pronunciations like [lɪtl̩] and [kɪtn̩] (such as some people produce when doing formal speaking or singing) and the everyday pronunciations [lɪɾl̩] and [kɪʔn̩], with the flap and glottal stop. So what is the relationship among these sounds? If someone says [lɪtl̩], does that mean something different from [lɪɾl̩], or is a [kɪtn̩] a different kind of animal from a [kɪʔn̩]? For native English speakers, the answer is "no": both are the same word, and if we notice the difference in pronunciation at all, we may think someone saying [kɪtn̩] is not from the United States or is perhaps being a bit pretentious in exaggerating the pronunciation. This tells us that the three sounds [t], [ɾ], and [ʔ] are not meaningfully different in English: they are different pronunciations of the "same" sound.

What about the 't' sounds in *top* and *stop*? Many of you likely transcribed them the same, as the difference between these sounds was not focused on in Chapter 2. Say these words out loud, carefully, focusing on the 't' sound while holding your palm in front of your mouth. You should be able to detect a short burst or puff of air after the 't' in *top* that is absent in *stop*. That puff of air is what we call **aspiration** (see Section 2.6.5), and it is transcribed with a superscripted [ʰ]. These words can thus more accurately be transcribed as [tʰɑp] and [stɑp], respectively (and *kitten* as [kʰɪʔn̩]). Is this a meaningful difference? Our first indication that it is not is that native English speakers have a very difficult time hearing these as different sounds (more so than is usually the case with the [ɾ] and [ʔ] pronunciations of 't'). More importantly, however, switching the sounds does not change the meaning of the word: [stʰɑp] sounds odd, but it does not sound like any word other than *stop*.

So here we have four different sounds in the American English inventory ([t, tʰ, ɾ, ʔ]) that are somehow the "same" sound 't.' This is the essence of the difference between phonetics and phonology: physically (articulatorily and acoustically), there are four different sounds, but at some psychological level[1] these are all the same sound to a native speaker. A similar pattern of aspirated versus non-aspirated stops is seen with 'k' (*kit* [kʰɪt] versus *skit* [skɪt]) and 'p' (*pit* [pʰɪt] versus *spit* [spɪt]).

As we saw with [k] and [g] above, the patterning of aspirated versus unaspirated voiceless stops in English doesn't tell us how they are categorized in other languages, however, and we see a different pattern in Hindi, for example. A native speaker of Hindi does not (and cannot) ignore the difference between aspirated and unaspirated sounds. Hindi contains many words that are pronounced almost exactly the same way, except that one word will have an aspirated stop where the other has an unaspirated stop. The data in (3) illustrate this.

 (3)

Hindi	Gloss
[pʰəl]	'fruit'
[pəl]	'moment'
[bəl]	'strength'

So for a Hindi speaker, pronouncing the voiceless stop in the word for 'moment' with aspiration would change the word being said, just as in English changing the voiceless stop in *pit* to voiced would give *bit,* a different word and meaning. For the native Hindi speaker, then, aspirated [pʰ] is as different from unaspirated [p] as [pʰ] is from [b] to our ears. But since, unlike voicing, aspiration never makes a difference in the meanings of English words (e.g., [mæp] and [mæpʰ] would simply be recognized as different pronunciations of the word *map*), native speakers of English are usually not consciously aware of the difference between aspirated and unaspirated stops.

The different ways that [p] and [pʰ] affect meaning distinctions in English and Hindi tells us that these sounds are categorized differently in the phonological systems of the two languages. We say that these two sounds are **noncontrastive** in English, because interchanging the two does not result in a change of meaning, while in Hindi [p] and [pʰ] are **contrastive,** because replacing one sound with the other in a word can change the word's meaning.

---

[1]The reasons for this may be manifold, including phonetic similarities, phonological patterning, different pronunciations across language varieties, or spelling.

The meaning of a word with [p] (e.g., [pəl] 'moment') contrasts with the meaning of a similar word with [pʰ] (e.g., [pʰəl] 'fruit'). We will have more to say about this terminological distinction below.

Linguists attempt to characterize these different relations between sounds in language by grouping the sounds in a language's phonetic inventory into sets. Each set contains all of the sounds that a native speaker considers to be the "same" sound. For example, [t] and [tʰ] in English would be members of the same set. By contrast, speakers of Hindi would not classify [t] and [tʰ] as members of the same set, because they perceive them as different. That is, they are contrastive in Hindi, as seen in the words [tal] 'beat' and [tʰal] 'plate.'

A set of speech sounds that are perceived to be variants of the same sound is called a **phoneme.** Each member of a particular phoneme set is called an **allophone,** which corresponds to an actual phonetic segment produced by a speaker. That is, the various ways that a phoneme is pronounced are called allophones. For example, then, the 't' sounds in words like *stop, top, little,* and *kitten* ([t, tʰ, ɾ, ʔ]) all belong to a single set, a phoneme that we will label with the symbol /t/. From now on, pay special attention to the difference between square brackets and slashes: a sound given in square brackets ([tʰ]) is an allophone (a phonetic segment), while a sound given in slashes (/t/) is a phoneme (a psychological category). So by saying that *stop* and *top* each have the phoneme /t/, we are saying that the sounds [t] and [tʰ] are related—that they are the "same" sound.

In (4) we see how the phoneme /t/ is related to its allophones [t], [tʰ], [ɾ], and [ʔ] in English, and how the Hindi phonemes /t/ and /tʰ/ are related to their allophones [t] and [tʰ]. Since [t] and [tʰ] contrast in Hindi, they are therefore allophones of different phonemes, unlike in English.

(4)

	English				Hindi	
Phonemes:	/t/				/t/	/tʰ/
Allophones:	[t]	[tʰ]	[ʔ]	[ɾ]	[t]	[tʰ]

By providing a description like this, linguists attempt to show that the phonological system of a language has two levels. The more concrete level involves the physical reality of phonetic segments pronounced in everyday speech, the allophones, whereas phonemes are something more abstract, which can be described as the form in which we store sounds in our minds. So phonemes are abstract psychological concepts, and they are not directly observable in a stream of speech; only the allophones of a phoneme are. It is important to note that any sound that is pronounced, then, is an allophone of some phoneme; the phoneme itself is never pronounced.

The phoneme is a unit of linguistic structure that is just as significant to the native speaker as the word or the sentence. Native speakers reveal their knowledge of phonemes in a number of ways. When an English speaker makes a slip of the tongue and says [ʧeɪn ɹek] for *rain check,* reversing [ʧ] and [ɹ], he or she has demonstrated that [ʧ] functions mentally as a single unit of sound, just as [ɹ] does. Recall from File 2.2 that [ʧ] is phonetically complex, consisting of [t] followed immediately by [ʃ]. Yet, since [ʧ] represents the pronunciation of a single phoneme /ʧ/ in English, no native speaker would make an error that would involve splitting up its phonetic components; you will never hear [tɹeɪn ʃɛk] as a slip of the tongue (see File 9.3).

Knowledge of phonemes is also revealed in alphabetic spelling systems (see File 15.2). For example, English does not have separate letters for [pʰ] and [p]; they are both spelled with the letter *p*. Examples like this show that the English spelling system ignores differences in pronunciation that don't result in meaning distinctions. For the most part, the English spelling system attempts to provide symbols for phonemes, not phonetic segments. In general, alphabetic writing systems tend to be phonemic rather than phonetic, though they achieve this goal with varying degrees of success. As noted in File 2.1, of course, there are multiple ways to represent the same sound (e.g., the [k] sound is written with a <k> in the word *kitten* but with a <c> in the word *cool*). What's crucial here, though, is that both of these spellings represent /k/, and not, for example, the difference between [k] and [kʰ].

3.2.3   Identifying Phonemes and Allophones: The Distribution of Speech Sounds

In order to determine whether particular sounds in a given language are allophones of a single phoneme or whether they contrast and are allophones of separate phonemes, we need to consider the distribution of the sounds involved, as we saw above. The **distribution** of a phone is the set of **phonetic environments** in which it occurs, that is, the sounds that come before and after it in a word. For example, nasalized vowels in English occur only in the environment of a nasal consonant. More precisely, a linguist would describe the distribution of English [ĩ], [æ̃], etc., by stating that the nasalized vowels always and only occur immediately preceding a nasal consonant, as in *bean* and *brand*.

Once we have examined the phonetic environments of any two or more given sounds, we can determine a type of distribution by comparing the sets of phonetic environments. In this book we will mainly be concerned with two types of distribution—contrastive distribution and complementary distribution—though a third distribution, free variation, will also be introduced in the following section.

Let us consider **contrastive distribution** first. Contrastive distribution is simply a case in which the two sounds occur in the same phonetic environment, and using one rather than the other changes the meaning of the word (thus the sounds can also be referred to as contrastive, as above). [p] and [pʰ] in Hindi have a contrastive distribution because when they occur in exactly the same phonetic environment, they give two different words: [pʰəl] 'fruit' and [pəl] 'moment.'

Thus when we look at the distribution of particular sounds in a language, we can determine that two sounds contrast or are in contrastive distribution by identifying a **minimal pair.** A minimal pair is defined as two words (with different meanings) whose pronunciations differ by exactly one sound. If you find a minimal pair, you know that the two sounds that differ are contrastive in that language. So, [pʰəl] 'fruit' and [pəl] 'moment' are a minimal pair, showing that [p] and [pʰ] are contrastive in Hindi, as are [pʰəl] 'fruit' and [bəl] 'strength,' showing that [pʰ] and [b] are also contrastive.

If you try, you can easily think of many minimal pairs in English, or any other language you know well. For example, the minimal pair [tʰiːm] *team* and [tʰiːn] *teen* shows that [n] and [m] are contrastive in English, and we have mentioned various others above.

The second type of distribution we need to consider is **complementary distribution.** To understand better what we mean by complementary distribution, think about what the term complementary means: two complementary parts of something make up a whole. For example, the set of people in your class at any given moment can be divided into the set of people who are under 5'5" tall and the set of people who are 5'5" tall or taller. These two sets of people complement each other. They are mutually exclusive (one person can't simultaneously be both shorter and taller than 5'5"), but together they make up the whole class. So also with sounds: sounds that are in complementary distribution do not occur in the same phonetic environments—their distributions complement each other. So, if you look at the set of environments in which sound A occurs and compare it with the set of environments in which sound B occurs, you see that sound A never occurs in one of B's environments, and

B never occurs in one of A's environments (just like a person can't be in both the group of people taller than 5'5" and the group of people shorter than 5'5").

So when sounds are in complementary distribution, you will not find a minimal pair. Such sounds are never contrastive with respect to each other; they will not be used in the same phonetic environment to produce words with different meanings. If sounds are in complementary distribution, they are therefore considered to be allophones of the same phoneme.

Let us look back at some examples we have seen in English. We mentioned above that nasalized vowels in English always and only occur immediately preceding a nasal consonant. We can see an example of this by looking at the distribution of the sounds [i] and [ĩ] in English.

(5) dean [dĩn]   lean [lĩn]   mean [mĩn]   team [tĩm]   scream [skɹĩm]
    deed [did]   leap [lip]   mere [miɹ]   seat [sit]   see   [si]

If we analyze the sets of phonetic environments where [i] and [ĩ] occur here (more detail on how to do this will be presented File 3.5.2), we can summarize their distributions as follows: [i] appears before the sounds [d, p, ɹ, t] and at the end of a word; [ĩ] appears before [n, m]. Furthermore, [i] never appears before [m, n], and [ĩ] never appears before [d, p, ɹ, t] or at the end of the word. Their distributions are therefore complementary, which means that they do not contrast in English. We thus can say that the sounds [i] and [ĩ] are allophones of the same phoneme /i/.

Consider another linguistic example mentioned above: the distribution of the English sounds [p] and [pʰ], as seen in (6).

(6) spat   [spæt]   pat   [pʰæt]
    spool   [spul]   pool   [pʰul]
    speak   [spik]   peek   [pʰik]

As you can see, there are no minimal pairs involving a [p]–[pʰ] contrast, and [p] and [pʰ] do not occur in the same phonetic environments. We can summarize their distributions as: [p] occurs after [s] but never word-initially, and [pʰ] occurs word-initially but never after [s]. Since these sounds appear in different phonetic environments, there can be no pair of words composed of identical strings of sounds except that one has [p] and the other has [pʰ] (e.g., saying [spʰat] does not give a different word; it's just an odd pronunciation of *spot*). The sounds [p] and [pʰ] are in complementary distribution in English and are therefore allophones of a single phoneme /p/.

For both of these phonemes, we can also see that the appearance of their allophones in any specific context is predictable. For example, for any of the many other words with /i/ in English not listed in (5), we can predict that the allophone [ĩ] (and never [i]) will appear before [m] or [n] (e.g., *gleam, seen*), and that [i] (and never [ĩ]) will occur before other sounds (e.g., *tree, reek*). Similarly, we can predict that the allophone [pʰ] (but never [p]) will occur at the beginning of any word not listed in (6), such as *pot* or *pin*.[2] Similarly, we can predict that [p] (but never [pʰ]) will follow [s] in other words, such as *spot* and *spin*.

We find complementary distribution of sounds in other languages too, of course. For example, in File 3.1, we saw that the sounds [k] and [g] in Kikamba have a different distribution from what is found in English. They are in contrastive distribution in English (as evidenced by the minimal pair *back–bag*), which means that they are allophones of separate phonemes /k/ and /g/. But in Kikamba, we described the distribution as follows: [g] only

---

[2]In point of fact, this is true not just at the beginning of a word but at the beginning of any stressed syllable. That is, in English, [pʰ] but not [p] can appear as the first consonant of a stressed syllable.

occurs immediately after the velar nasal [ŋ], while [k] can occur at the beginning of a word or in the middle of a word between vowels, but never after [ŋ]. The two sounds are therefore in complementary distribution in Kikamba, indicating that they are allophones of the same phoneme /k/, or are both the same sound to speakers of Kikamba. We will see many more examples of sounds in contrastive and complementary distribution throughout the rest of this chapter, and in File 3.5, we will discuss how to analyze data sets in other languages in order to determine the relationships of particular sounds.

We can summarize the difference between sounds that are contrastive (e.g., [p] and [pʰ] in Hindi, or [k] and [g] in English) and sounds that are allophones of the same phoneme (e.g., [p] and [pʰ] in English, or [k] and [g] in Kikamba) as shown in (7).

(7)

	Contrastive	**Allophonic**
Relation to phonemes	Allophones of separate phonemes	Allophones of the same phoneme
Predictability of distribution	Unpredictably distributed	Predictably distributed
How you can tell	Contrastive distribution; minimal pairs	Complementary distribution

3.2.4   Free Variation

Most phonological distributions can be described as either contrastive or complementary. Remember that the hallmark of a contrastive distribution is that the two sounds can occur in the same phonetic environments but will produce different words. The hallmark of a complementary distribution is that the two sounds will not occur in the same environments but can be predicted to occur in specific phonetic contexts.

In some contexts, however, more than one pronunciation of a given sound may be possible without changing the meaning of the word. In these cases, you may not be able to predict exactly which sound will occur, but the choice does **not** affect the meaning of the word. Consider, for example, the pronunciations of some English words in (8) (note that [p˺] represents an unreleased voiceless bilabial stop).

(8) leap   [lip]   leap   [lip˺]
    soap   [soʊp]   soap   [soʊp˺]
    troop   [tɹup]   troop   [tɹup˺]
    happy   [hæpi]   —   *[hæp˺i]

These words show that [p] and [p˺] both share some of the same phonetic environments; specifically, they can both appear at the ends of words. Unlike the case of English [b] versus [pʰ], or [m] versus [n], however, there are no minimal pairs involving these sounds in the language. Why not? Although there are pairs of words in (9) that differ in only one sound, none of these words contrast in meaning. Thus, the choice between [p] and [p˺] in *leap*, *soap*, and *troop* does not make a difference in meaning; that is, the sounds are noncontrastive. Rather, they are interchangeable in word-final position. Sounds with this type of patterning are considered to be in **free variation**. To a native speaker, sounds like [p] and [p˺] that are in free variation are perceived as being the "same" sound. We can conclude that they are allophones of the same phoneme, because they are perceived as the same and do not serve to distinguish the meanings of words.

Because [p] and [pˀ] can occur in the same environment, they are in what is called **overlapping distribution;** they can occur in the same environment. Sounds that are in contrastive distribution and sounds that are in free variation are therefore both considered to have an overlapping distribution; only sounds that are in complementary distribution do not overlap. For example, in English, the sounds [d] and [t] are in overlapping distribution because they can occur in the same phonetic environment. The words *lid* and *lit* form a minimal pair, and both [d] and [t] can occur after [lɪ]; that is, the environment [lɪ_] is one where [d] and [t] overlap. Similarly, [t] and [tˀ] have an overlapping distribution because they can also both occur after [lɪ_], as two different pronunciations of the word *lit*. The difference between [d] and [t] on the one hand, and [t] and [tˀ] on the other, is that interchanging [d] and [t] changes the meaning of the words, while interchanging [t] and [tˀ] does not.

We can thus extend our table in (8) to include the characteristics of free variation, as shown in (9).

(9)

	Contrastive	**Allophonic**	**Free Variation**
Relation to phonemes	Allophones of separate phonemes	Allophones of the same phoneme	Allophones of the same phoneme
Predictability of distribution	Unpredictable	Predictable	Unpredictable
How you can tell	Contrastive distribution; minimal pairs	Complementary distribution	Overlapping distribution with no difference in meaning

FILE **3.3**

....

Phonological Rules

3.3.1 Phonological Rules

In File 3.2, we discussed the fact that phonemes and (allo)phones belong to different levels of structure in language—that is, phonemes are abstract mental entities, and phones are physical events. In this file we consider the connection between these two levels.

The mapping between phonemic and phonetic elements can be described using **phonological rules** (recall from Section 1.2.3 that a rule of grammar expresses a pattern in a language). A speaker's knowledge of phonological rules allows him or her to "translate" phonemes into actual speech sounds; knowledge of these rules forms part of the speaker's linguistic competence. The mapping between the phonemic form, also called the **underlying form,** and the actual phonetic form of a word by means of phonological rules can be represented with the diagram in (1).

(1) phonemic form
         ⇓
       rules
         ⇓
    phonetic form

As an example, consider the English words *seat* /sit/ and *loot* /lut/. These words have a final /t/ sound in their phonemic form that is often pronounced as [t], at least in careful speech.[1] Now compare the pronunciation of /t/ in the forms of these words when the suffix *-ed* is added, as shown in (2).[2]

(2) seat   [sit]   seated   [siɾəd]
     loot   [lut]   looted   [luɾəd]

As discussed in File 3.2, the phoneme /t/ is pronounced as the flap [ɾ] when it occurs between two vowels, specifically when the preceding vowel is in a stressed syllable and the following vowel is in an unstressed syllable. This observation about English can be stated as the descriptive rule in (3). (Note that this rule is simplified; as we know from File 3.2, there are more allophones of /t/ than just [t] and [ɾ].)

---

[1]In linguistic analysis, we often have to distinguish between "careful" and "casual" speech. Careful speech is when a speaker speaks more slowly and clearly than usual, while casual speech is when a speaker speaks more quickly and with more co-articulation (see Section 2.1.2) than usual. Of course, these are really endpoints on a scale of speech styles (see File 10.1), and people actually talk at many different styles in between. The pronunciations listed in (2) are used in all but the most careful styles of speech.

[2]Here and throughout this file, we use a fairly broad transcription system, recording phonetic detail only if relevant for the segments under discussion.

122

(3) /t/ is pronounced as   [ɾ] after a stressed vowel and before an unstressed vowel
                            [t] everywhere else

Notice that a phonological rule has three parts: the sound(s) affected by the rule, the environment where the rule applies, and the result of the rule. In the rule in (3), /t/ is affected by the rule. The rule applies when /t/ occurs after a stressed vowel and before an unstressed vowel. The result of the rule is that /t/ is "flapped"; that is, it is pronounced as [ɾ].

We can write this rule using shorthand of the form X→Y / C _ D. Here, 'X' is the sound that is affected by the rule, 'Y' is the result of the application of the rule, and 'C _ D' is the environment in which the rule applies. 'C _ D' is also called the **conditioning environment**. By "C _ D," we mean that C comes before the sound affected by the rule and D comes after it; the blank represents where the sound that is affected by the rule appears. You can read these rules in the following way: "X becomes Y when it comes after C and before D." Thus, if you see CXD, you know that it will become CYD when the rule applies. So, for the rule in (3), we would write:

(4)

X	→	Y	/	C	_	D
/t/	→	[ɾ]	/	stressed vowel	_	unstressed vowel
/t/	→	[t]	/	everywhere else		

In (5), we illustrate how the phonetic forms of the examples in (2) are derived from the phonemic forms. You can see that the rule applies to the phonemic forms of *seated* and *looted* because /t/ occurs in the correct context for the rule, as defined in (4). However, in *seat* and *loot* the rule does not apply since /t/ does not occur in the context for flapping.

(5)

phonemic form:	/sit/	/sit + əd/	/lut/	/lut + əd/
apply rule	—	siɾəd	—	luɾəd
phonetic form	[sit]	[siɾəd]	[lut]	[luɾəd]

The derivation in (5) illustrates what happens in speaking. In listening, a hearer reverses this process: he or she perceives the phonetic form of an utterance, then sends it "backwards" through the phonological rules, and finally obtains a phonemic form that matches a form stored in memory.

3.3.2 Natural Classes

We have observed that the phoneme /t/ can be pronounced as a flap. In fact, it is not only /t/ that can be flapped, but /d/ as well, as shown in (6). For speakers of American English, the middle /d/ in *seeded* and *seated* are both pronounced as a flap, making these words sound very similar, if not identical.

(6) seed [sid]   seeded [siɾəd]

Since /d/ also undergoes flapping, we can modify our rule in (4) as follows:

(7) /t, d/   →   [ɾ] / stressed vowel __ unstressed vowel

Given the observation that both /t/ and /d/ are subject to the same phonological rule, we can now ask whether it is random chance that these two sounds are both subject to the flapping rule or if there is a more principled reason for their similar patterning.

To answer this question, let's consider the articulatory descriptions of the two sounds:

(8) /t/   voiceless alveolar (oral) stop
     /d/   voiced alveolar (oral) stop

Not only are both sounds alveolar stops; they are the **only** oral alveolar stops in English.[3] Therefore, we can make the description more general by removing some of the properties:

(9) /t, d/   alveolar (oral) stop

With respect to English, saying "alveolar (oral) stop" is the same as saying /t/ and /d/. These two sounds are the only oral phonemes in English that are produced by stopping the flow of air at the alveolar ridge. Thus, they are the **natural class** of alveolar (oral) stops. A natural class is a group of sounds in a language that share one or more articulatory or auditory property, **to the exclusion of all other sounds in that language.** That is, in order for a group of sounds to be a natural class, it must include all of the sounds that share a particular property or set of properties, and not include any sounds that don't.

All of the properties used in Files 2.2, 2.3, and 2.4 to describe individual sounds can also be used to describe natural classes. For example, in the English vowels the monophthongs [i, u] and the first part of the diphthongs [eɪ] and [oʊ] are tense vowels, and there are no other tense vowels in English. Thus, these four vowels are members of the natural class of tense vowels in English. Likewise, the consonants [k, g, ŋ] are all described as velar consonants, and they are the only velar consonants used in English; thus they constitute the natural class of velar consonants in English. Natural classes can be used to describe both the sounds affected by a rule **and** the environments where a rule applies.

In talking about groups of sounds, we must use a few properties in addition to those needed to describe individual sounds. One new property that we will need is **sibilant.** Sibilants are segments that have a high-pitched, hissing sound quality. The natural class of sibilants in English is [s, ʃ, ʧ, z, ʒ, ʤ].

In addition, if you look at the consonant chart at the end of this book, you will notice that the only labiodental consonants in English are the fricatives [f] and [v], while the bilabial fricative slots are left empty. In many situations it is advantageous to refer to [f] and [v] together with [p, b, m, w] and [w̥] as belonging to the same natural class. For this purpose we use the property **labial.**

Another property used to describe natural classes divides the segments into two groups, **obstruents** and **sonorants.** Obstruents are produced with an obstruction of the airflow. The sounds in this category are stops, fricatives, and affricates. Sonorants, on the other hand, are segments produced with a relatively open passage for the airflow. Sonorant segments include nasals, liquids, glides, and vowels. Thus, the class of labial obstruents in English is [p, f, b, v], while the class of labial sonorant consonants is [m, w, w̥].[4] The class of labial consonants is the union of both sets: [p, f, b, v, m, w, w̥]. As we will see, being able to divide consonants into obstruents and sonorants is quite useful in stating phonological rules.

---

[3]We say that /t/ and /d/ are the only **oral** alveolar stops because nasal /n/ can also be classified as an alveolar nasal stop (see Section 2.2.5).

[4]As already mentioned, the class of sonorants also includes vowels, because they do not have an obstruction of airflow. Some linguists treat rounded vowels as "labial," in which case the entire class of English labial sonorants would be [m, w, w̥, u, ʊ, o, ɔ], and the entire class of English labials would be [p, f, b, v, m, w, w̥, u, ʊ, o, ɔ].

3.3.3 Types of Phonological Rules

Every language has many phonological rules. In addition to seeing that they apply to natural classes of segments, we can classify phonological rules according to the kind of process that they involve. Seven major types of processes are discussed here, along with examples from the phonology of English and other languages.

a. Assimilation. Rules of **assimilation** cause a sound (or gesture) to become more like a neighboring sound (or gesture) with respect to some phonetic property. In other words, the segment affected by the rule assimilates or takes on a property from a nearby (often adjacent) segment. Rules of assimilation are very common in languages. An example of assimilation is the pronunciation of the prefix *un-* in English. Words like *unbelievable, unstable,* and *unclear* are often pronounced [ʌmbəlivəbl̩], [ʌnsteɪbl̩], and [ʌŋkliɹ]. That is, the nasal /n/ is often pronounced as a bilabial nasal when it occurs before a bilabial sound, as in *unbelievable,* and as a velar nasal when it occurs before a velar sound, as in *unclear.* This is called Nasal Place Assimilation because the nasal /n/ changes its place of articulation:

(10) **Nasal Place Assimilation** (English): An alveolar nasal assimilates to the place of articulation of a following consonant.

Thus, when a sound having the properties alveolar and nasal immediately precedes a labial consonant, this rule causes the alveolar nasal to take on the property labial (thereby replacing its specification for alveolar).

We can see a similar sort of phenomenon taking place across word boundaries in certain ASL handshapes. We will consider the handshape that is used in the sign ME, which is a pointing index finger, as shown in (11).

(11) The unassimilated sign for ME in ASL

The sign ME may take on features of other handshapes, however, depending on the sign that follows it. For example, in order to say "I am named . . . ," a speaker of ASL would sign "ME NAME . . . ." In order to say "I know," a speaker of ASL would sign "ME KNOW." The signs NAME and KNOW have different handshapes: NAME is articulated with two fingers (index finger and middle finger) extended; KNOW is articulated with a bent hand and all four fingers extended.

When the sign ME is produced before one of these other words, it can take on the handshape of the word that follows it, as shown in (12).

(12) a. The phrase 'I am named . . .' in ASL, formed from the lexical items ME NAME

b. The sentence 'I know' in ASL, formed from the lexical items ME KNOW

© 2006, William Vicars, www.Lifeprint.com. Adapted by permission.

Notice that in both (12a) and (12b), the signer touches his chest with his hand facing the same way as he would in the unassimilated form. That is, the place of articulation, the orientation, the movement, and the non-manual marker for ME do not change. But the handshape used for ME in (12a) is the handshape of NAME, and the handshape used in (12b) is the handshape of KNOW.

Another assimilation process is **palatalization.** Palatalization refers to a special type of assimilation in which a consonant becomes like a neighboring palatal. For example, when American English speakers say *Did you?* rapidly, they very often pronounce it as [dɪdʒu]. The sounds [d] (the alveolar stop from the end of *did*) and [j] (the palatal glide from the beginning of *you*) combine to form the post-alveolar affricate [dʒ]. In this case, the palatal nature of the glide has been assimilated by the stop, making it a post-alveolar affricate. High and mid front vowels such as [i] and [e] also cause this change. The most common types of palatalization occur when alveolar, dental, and velar stops or fricatives appear before a front vowel. So the following are all common types of palatalization: [t] → [tʃ]; [d] → [dʒ]; [s] → [ʃ]; [k] → [tʃ]; [g] → [dʒ]. While there are variants on palatalization, and other sounds can be palatalized, the main things to look for are a sound becoming a palatal or post-alveolar and/or a phonological rule conditioned by a high or mid front vowel.

The rules of assimilation that we've discussed so far cause sounds to assimilate to **adjacent** sounds. This is a common way that assimilation occurs. However, long-distance assimilation also exists, and a relatively common type of long-distance assimilation is called **vowel harmony.** This typically causes all the vowels in a word to "harmonize" or agree in some property such as rounding or backness.

Finnish has a common type of vowel harmony rule, which can be stated as follows:

(13) **Vowel harmony** (Finnish): A back vowel becomes front when preceded by a front vowel in the same word.

By this rule, Finnish words have, with few exceptions, either all front vowels or all back vowels, but not both in the same word. We can see the vowel harmony rule in action when a suffix is added to the end of a word. In this case, the suffix vowel changes to match the quality of vowels in the word. For example, the suffix meaning 'in' has the form [-ssɑ] when added to a word where the last vowel is back, as in [tɑlo] 'house,' [tɑlossɑ] 'in the house.' However, the suffix takes the form [-ssæ] when it attaches to a word with a final front vowel, as in [metsæ] 'forest,' [metsæssæ] 'in the forest.' In cases like this, we can say that the vowel of the suffix harmonizes with, or assimilates to, the preceding vowel.

b. Dissimilation. Unlike assimilation, which makes sounds more similar, rules of **dissimilation** cause two close or adjacent sounds to become less similar with respect to some property, by means of a change in one or both sounds. An example of dissimilation in Greek is the following:

(14) **Manner dissimilation** (Greek): A stop becomes a fricative when followed by another stop.

For example, in fast speech especially, the form /epta/ 'seven' can be pronounced as [efta], and /ktizma/ 'building' can be pronounced as [xtizma] ([x] is a voiceless velar fricative).

c. Insertion. Phonological rules of **insertion** cause a segment not present at the phonemic level to be added to the phonetic form of a word. An example of this kind of rule from English is voiceless stop insertion.

(15) **Voiceless stop insertion** (English): Between a nasal consonant and a voiceless fricative, a voiceless stop with the same place of articulation as the nasal is inserted.

Thus, for instance, the voiceless stop insertion rule may apply to the words *dance* /dæns/ → [dænts], *strength* /stɹɛŋθ/ → [stɹɛŋkθ], and *hamster* /hæmstɹ/ → [hæmpstɹ].

d. Deletion. **Deletion** rules eliminate a sound that was present at the phonemic level. Such rules apply more frequently to unstressed syllables and in casual speech. English examples include:

(16) **/h/-Deletion** (English): /h/ may be deleted in unstressed syllables.

The /h/-deletion rule would apply to a sentence such as *He handed her his hat* /hi hændəd hɹ hɪz hæt/ to yield [hi hændəd ɹ ɪz hæt]. Deletion is common in fast speech because it saves time and articulatory effort. Sounds like [h] that are not very perceptible are often the "victims" of deletion because speakers can save time and effort by deleting them without sacrificing much information. That is, the listener may not be relying on these sounds in order to understand what the speaker is saying.

Another common type of deletion is dissimilatory deletion. Like dissimilation, this process involves two close or adjacent sounds, but rather than one sound becoming less similar, as in dissimilation, one of the sounds is simply deleted. This often affects [ɹ] in English, as in the pronunciations of *prerogative* /pɹɪɹɑgətɪv/ as [pəɹɑgəɹv], *governor* /gʌvəɹnəɹ/ as [gʌvənɹ], or *library* /laɪbɹɛɹi/ as [laɪbɛɹi].

e. Metathesis. Rules of **metathesis** change the order of sounds. In many instances, sounds metathesize in order to make words easier to pronounce or easier to understand. In Leti, an Austronesian language, consonants and vowels switch places when a word that ends in a consonant is combined with a word that starts with two consonants. The last two sounds in the first word trade places to avoid having three consonants in a row.

(17) **CV metathesis** (Leti): When three consecutive consonants occur, the first consonant trades places with the preceding vowel.

By this rule, /danat + kviali/ 'millipede' undergoes metathesis to become [dantakviali], and /ukar + ppalu/ 'index finger' becomes [ukrappalu]. On the other hand, /ukar + lavan/ 'thumb' does not undergo metathesis and so is pronounced as [ukarlavan] because there are not three consecutive consonants.

f. Strengthening. Rules of **strengthening** (also called fortition) make sounds stronger. The rule of English aspiration, as stated below, provides an example:

(18) **Aspiration** (English): Voiceless stops become aspirated when they occur at the beginning of a stressed syllable.

The pronunciations of *pat* [pʰæt] and *top* [tʰɑp], as discussed in File 3.2, illustrate the application of the English aspiration rule. Aspirated stops are considered to be stronger sounds than unaspirated stops because the duration of voicelessness is much longer in aspirated stops (since it extends through the period of aspiration).

g. Weakening. Rules of **weakening** (also called lenition) cause sounds to become weaker. The "flapping" rule of English, discussed in 3.3.1, is an example of weakening. [ɾ] is considered to be a weaker sound than [t] or [d] because it is shorter and it obstructs air less.

(19) **Flapping** (English): An alveolar (oral) stop is realized as [ɾ] when it occurs after a stressed vowel and before an unstressed vowel.

Note that voicing assimilation is also involved in the change of /t/ to [ɾ]: the /t/ takes on the "voicedness" of the vowels surrounding it.

Another common weakening process in English is the reduction of unstressed vowels. As we saw in Chapter 2, in unstressed syllables vowels are often pronounced as the mid central [ə], or the syllable's nucleus becomes a syllabic consonant. We have seen many examples of this already, but note in particular the pronunciation of, for example, the words *atom* /ætəm/ → [ˈæɾm̩] and *atomic* /ætɑmɪk/ → [əˈtʰɑmɪk], in which vowel reduction can be seen, along with flapping or aspiration of /t/, depending on which syllable is stressed.

3.3.4   Multiple Rule Application

To this point we have mostly talked about examples where only one phonological rule applies. In reality, there is often more than one process that occurs between a given phonemic form and the phonetic output. This can be seen particularly easily with regard to the English rules that involve stress, such as flapping, aspiration, /h/-deletion, and vowel reduction. In most of these cases, since the processes are independent of each other, we can conceive of multiple rules applying at the same time without a problem. For example, in (20) we can see that there is no need to order flapping and vowel reduction with respect to each other in the pronunciation of *photograph*. Since flapping does not affect the environment in which vowel reduction takes place, nor vowel reduction the environment in which flapping takes place, applying one rule before the other does not change the outcome.

(20) a. **phonemic form:** /ˈfoʊtoʊgɹæf/   b. **phonemic form:** /ˈfoʊtoʊgɹæf/
    flapping: ˈfoʊɾoʊˌgɹæf   **vowel reduction:** ˈfoʊtəˌgɹæf
    vowel reduction: ˈfoʊɾəˌgɹæf   **flapping:** ˈfoʊɾəˌgɹæf
    phonetic form: [ˈfoʊɾəˌgɹæf]   **phonetic form:** [ˈfoʊɾəˌgɹæf]

But there are other cases in which the interaction among phonological rules is more complex. We can illustrate this by looking at the interaction of flapping in English with the following rule that affects the pronunciation of the diphthong /aɪ/ in some dialects.

(21) **Diphthong-raising** (some English dialects): The diphthong /aɪ/ is pronounced as [əɪ] when it occurs before a voiceless sound (i.e., the initial low vowel /a/ of the diphthong /aɪ/ is "raised" to the mid vowel [ə] before a voiceless consonant).

For speakers with this rule, the vowels in the words *write* [ɹəɪt] and *ride* [ɹaɪd] differ because of the voicing contrast between [t] and [d]. But in the related words *writer* and *rider*, the /t/ and /d/ appear between a stressed vowel and an unstressed vowel, which is the environment in which the flapping rule applies. Since flapping changes /t/ from a voiceless sound to a voiced one, if flapping were to apply first, then /aɪ/ would no longer be before a voiceless sound, and diphthong-raising should not apply. If diphthong-raising were to apply first, however, flapping would not be affected. In this case, applying the rules in different orders would result in two different pronunciations, as seen in (22) for the word *writer.*

(22) a. **phonemic form:** /ˈɹaɪtəɹ/   b. **phonemic form:** /ˈɹaɪtəɹ/
    flapping: ˈɹaɪɾəɹ   **raising:** ˈɹəɪtəɹ
    raising: —   **flapping:** ˈɹəɪɾəɹ
    phonetic form: *[ˈɹaɪɾəɹ]   **phonetic form:** [ˈɹəɪɾəɹ]

As the asterisk before the phonetic form in (22a) indicates, for speakers who have this diphthong-raising rule, the order in (22b) gives the correct phonetic form; the phonetic form in (22a) is the pronunciation of *rider* [ˈɹaɪɾəɹ] in these dialects, but not *writer* [ˈɹəɪɾəɹ]. This indicates that diphthong-raising must apply before flapping in these situations (or the phonological system must somehow be organized so that both rules apply).

3.3.5 Obligatory and Optional Rules

Notice that phonological rules may be **obligatory** or **optional**. Obligatory English rules include aspiration, vowel nasalization, vowel lengthening (see Section 2.5.2), and liquid and glide devoicing. Such a rule always applies in the speech of all speakers of a language or dialect having the rule, regardless of style or rate of speaking. The effects of obligatory rules are often very subtle and difficult to notice, but they are an important part of a native accent. For instance, it may be difficult for native speakers to tell that a vowel is nasalized in English, but not applying the rule of vowel nasalization would make someone sound like a non-native speaker of English.

The existence of obligatory rules is part of what causes people to have foreign accents. It is easier to learn the rules of a new language than to "turn off" the obligatory rules of your native language. The very fact that we are often unaware of these rules causes us to apply them when they are not appropriate. When speakers of American English learn other languages, they often apply rules such as flapping and vowel reduction, in addition to the phonotactic constraints discussed in File 3.1, even though the other language may not have these rules.

Optional phonological rules, on the other hand, may or may not apply in any given utterance. Optional rules are responsible for variation in speech; for example, we can pronounce *He handed her his hat* as [hi hændəd h̥ɹ hɪz hæt] or [hi hændəd ɹɪz hæt], depending on whether the /h/-deletion rule is applied or not. The use of optional rules depends in part on rate and style of speech.

Implicational Laws

3.4.1 Recurring Phonological Patterns

In studying phonetics, you saw that human languages use a wide variety of sounds. In spite of this variety, some sounds are more common than others. Thus, while it is true that almost all human languages use the stop consonants [p] and [t] and the vowel [a], relatively few languages use pharyngeal fricatives ([ħ] and [ʕ], the "throaty" sounds used in Arabic), voiceless vowels (like in whispered speech), and clicks (*tsk, tsk!* and horse-calling sounds are American examples). So [p], [t], and [a] are **more common** in languages, while pharyngeal fricatives, voiceless vowels, and clicks are **less common** speech sounds. The purpose of this file is to explain why some sounds are more common than others. Before attempting an explanation, however, we will consider four aspects of more common and less common speech sounds.

3.4.2 Sound Inventories

The first observation has to do with the inventories of sounds in languages. The observation is basically this: if a language uses a less common sound, it is generally the case that one of its more common counterparts will also be used. Two parts of this statement need clarification. First, when we say that a language uses a particular sound, we mean that the sound is in the inventory of **phonemes** in the language. In other words, that sound is contrastive relative to other sounds in the language.

The second part of the statement that needs clarification is the phrase "one of its more common counterparts." This phrase refers to the fact that for each less common sound in the inventory there tends to be a more common sound in the inventory that is very similar to the less common sound, differing in only one or two phonetic features. For instance, the more common counterpart of a voiceless vowel is a voiced vowel of the same tongue height, tongue advancement, and lip rounding. Likewise, the more common counterpart of a voiceless pharyngeal fricative is a voiceless velar fricative.

The table in (1) presents some (relatively) less common sounds and their (relatively) more common counterparts.

One thing to notice about this chart is that [s] appears both as a more common sound (as opposed to [x]) and as a less common sound (as opposed to [t]). This illustrates the fact that in using the terms "more common" and "less common" to designate the sounds in an implicational relationship, we are not referring to an absolute standard. Rather, "more common" and "less common" are used in a **relative** way. In other words, [s] is less common than [t], but more common than [x].

If a language uses a less common sound, one of its more common counterparts will usually also be included in that language's inventory of contrastive sounds. In terms of the chart presented in (1), this means that any language that uses [ã] will also use [a], any language that uses [a̱] will also use [a], any language that uses [d] will also use [t], and so on. This type of observation is called an **implicational law** because the presence of the less common sound

(1)

Less common	More common
[ã]	[a]
[a̧]	[a]
[x]	[k] or [s]
[s]	[t]
[d]	[t]
[ð]	[d] or [z]
voiced stops	voiceless stops
fricatives in place X	stops in place X

implies that the more common sound will also be used in the language. Of course, the implication cannot be reversed. In other words, the fact that English uses the sound [k] does not imply that we also use [x].

Implicational laws can be stated for natural classes of sounds in addition to individual pairs of sounds. For instance, the class of voiceless consonants is relatively more common than the class of voiced consonants. In other words, if a language makes use of voiced stops, it will also make use of voiceless ones. The reverse is not true; there are some languages that have only voiceless stops. Thus, the presence of voiced stops implies the presence of their voiceless counterparts, while the presence of voiceless stops does not imply the presence of voiced ones.

In the same way, the presence of fricatives in a language implies the presence of stops with the same place of articulation as the fricatives in that language. Thus, if a language uses an [s], then it also uses a [t].

3.4.3 Frequency and Distribution

The second observation concerning more common and less common sounds is related to the **degree** to which sounds will be used in a particular language and to the **range of distribution** of the sounds in the words of the language. Thus, even if a language makes use of a pharyngeal fricative, this less common sound will be used in fewer words than will the more common velar fricative. In other words, the pharyngeal fricative will have limited usage compared with the velar fricative.

More common sounds also have a wider distribution within a language—i.e., they are used in more phonetic environments than less common sounds. So, for instance, Cantonese Chinese has both stops and fricatives in its inventory of sounds, but fricatives may occur in only one position in the syllable: as the first sound. Stops have wider distribution: they occur both syllable-initially and syllable-finally in Cantonese.

An English example of the limited usage and limited distribution of less common sounds is the phoneme [ð]. The sound [ð] can be classified as less common because it is relatively rare in the languages of the world, and anywhere [ð] occurs in English, [z] can also occur. If you try to think of words that contain [ð], you will probably find that your list is limited to "grammatical" words like *this, that, those, them,* and *they,* and a few other words like *mother* and *lathe.* Furthermore, [ð] occurs as the last sound in English words less often than [z] does. Compared with the number of words that contain [z], it is obvious that [ð] has limited use in English.

3.4.4 Acquisition of Sounds

A third type of observation related to more common and less common sounds has to do with the order of their acquisition: children learning a language acquire the use of more common sounds before they acquire the use of less common ones. As a result, children who have not yet mastered the complete sound inventory of their native language will substitute more common sounds when trying to say less common sounds. When a little girl says [dɪs wʌn] for *this one,* she is replacing the relatively less common [ð] with [d], a much more common sound. This is an indication that the child has not yet fully acquired the use of [ð], although [d] is readily available for use. When the language development of a child is followed from babbling through maturity, a characteristic order of acquisition appears. This order in the acquisition of sounds is relatively constant for children around the world, no matter what language they are learning. Once again, the implicational laws capture a generalization about language: namely, that the acquisition of a relatively less common sound implies that its more common counterpart has already been acquired.

3.4.5 Sound Change

The fourth and last type of observation related to more common and less common sounds involves language change: less common sounds tend to be less stable than more common ones. Thus, in the course of language change, if any sound is going to be lost, it is more likely to be a less common one rather than its more common counterpart.

An illustration of this can be drawn from the history of English. In the Old English pronunciation of the word *knight* there was a voiceless velar fricative [x] between the vowel and the [t]. As you can see, the letters <gh> indicate where this consonant used to be. During the development of English, this velar fricative was lost (so *knight* now rhymes with *quite*). In fact, all instances of the velar fricative sound (as in *height, sight, fight, might,* and so on) were lost. English speakers just stopped using velar fricatives altogether, so now we find it hard to learn how to say them when we are trying to learn a language like German that uses them. This observation fits in with the implicational law that says that fricatives are less common than stops. Therefore, the fricative [x] is less stable and more likely to be lost or changed to a more common sound than the corresponding stop consonant [k]. For more on sound change, see File 13.3.

3.4.6 Explaining Implicational Laws

We might be tempted to say that the implicational laws discussed in 3.4.2 are themselves the explanations of these observations. Thus, we might say that [x] is more likely to be lost in language change than [k] is because [k] is more common than [x]. Or we might want to say that [k] is acquired by children before [x] because [k] is more common than [x]. This type of explanation is circular, however. The circularity stems from the fact that we distinguished between common and less common sounds by making the observations.

The alternative to this circular form of explanation is to explain the above observations (and thus the implicational laws) in terms of the communicative nature of language. It is important to realize that when people use language, their goal (generally speaking) is to communicate—that is, to successfully transmit a message from a speaker to a hearer (refer to diagram (1) in File 1.2). Focusing on the function of language leads us to ask what sounds are most useful for transmitting a message from speaker to hearer.

First of all, if a sound is difficult to produce, speakers will be somewhat inconsistent in pronouncing it, and this inconsistency may result in confusion on the part of the hearer.

To avoid being misunderstood, speakers may avoid words with difficult sounds (resulting in limited usage), and if enough speakers avoid a difficult sound, it may disappear from the language entirely (language change). In addition, sounds that are difficult to produce (such as fricatives, whose production involves delicate control of muscles) are not likely to be mastered by children before easier sounds are. As you can see, there are at least some instances where the observation that sound X is more common than sound Y is directly tied to the fact that sound X is easier to produce than sound Y. Thus, [k] is more common than [x] because stops are easier to produce than fricatives. Alveolar fricatives are more common than pharyngeal fricatives because the tip of the tongue is more agile than the back of the tongue; hence alveolar consonants are easier to produce than pharyngeal ones. Thus, ease of production is an explanation for at least some of the implicational laws.

Another way to answer the question of what sounds are most useful for transmitting a message from speaker to hearer focuses on the hearer's point of view. It is reasonable to suppose that if a sound blends into the surrounding sounds too much, its distinctive qualities may become difficult to hear. So, for example, if Morse code were made up of long dashes and not-so-long dashes, or dots and somewhat shorter dots, rather than dots and dashes, it would be difficult to use. In the same way, the consonants and vowels that make up syllables are most usable when they are quite different from each other. So, the kind of syllable that is most useful in transmitting messages in language is composed of **maximally distinct** consonants and vowels. By this we mean that the consonants have very few qualities in common with the vowels, and the vowels are likewise very different from the consonants. The value of maximally distinct carriers of information is obvious when we think about Morse code. If you can't tell the difference between dots and dashes, then little communication can take place. In the same way, if you can't tell the difference between consonants and vowels, then communication using language is likely to be very inefficient.

Perhaps a couple of examples of the ways that consonants can be more vowel-like, or vowels can be more consonant-like, are in order. One implicational law that we noticed is that the use of voiced consonants in a language implies the use of voiceless ones (thus voiceless consonants are more common than voiced ones). One explanation for this implicational law is that voiceless consonants have fewer qualities in common with vowels than do voiced consonants; thus, in syllables containing consonants and vowels, voiceless consonants are perceptually more salient (or noticeable) than voiced ones.

One way that vowels can be less consonant-like is to be pronounced with the mouth wide open, as in the vowel [ɑ]. Because consonants are made by obstructing the vocal tract in some way, a vowel that is pronounced with the mouth wide open will be more distinct from surrounding consonants than will be a vowel like [i] or [u] that is pronounced with the mouth somewhat closed. It just so happens that there is an implicational law corresponding to this distinction between [i], [u], and [ɑ]. The presence of a closed vowel ([i], [u]) implies the presence of an open vowel ([ɑ]). Thus, syllables with maximally distinct consonants and vowels are easier to perceive than syllables with consonants and vowels that resemble each other, and therefore some implicational laws exist for the sake of the listener, to make language easier to perceive.

In this file we have seen that although there is great variety in the sounds that can be employed in language, there are universal tendencies: to restrict the inventory of sounds to certain more common sounds, to restrict the degree of utilization and distribution of less common sounds in languages that do use them, to acquire more common sounds earlier than less common ones, and for less common sounds to be unstable in the face of language change. These implicational laws can at least sometimes be explained by assuming that people are using language in order to communicate and that this produces a need for efficiency that leads to the use of easily produced and perceived sounds.

··

How to Solve Phonology Problems

3.5.1 Goals of Phonemic Analysis

Because phonemes are important units of linguistic structure, linguists must have a general method for identifying them in all languages. But the task of determining what the phonemes of a language are and what allophones are assigned to them is not always straightforward. For one thing, the set of phonemes differs from language to language, and so a separate analysis is required for each language. Moreover, phonemes are psychological units of linguistic structure and are not physically present in a stream of speech. As a result, it is not possible to identify the phonemes of a language simply by taking physical measurements on a sample of language. Nor is it always easy to identify phonemes by investigating a native speaker's intuitions, because the minute phonetic details on which decisions about phonemes are made are often precisely those that speakers are not accustomed to noticing.

To get around these problems, linguists have developed an objective procedure by which the phonemes of a language can be discovered through examination of a set of words written in phonetic transcription. This procedure is based on two main observations about patterns of sounds.

First, as discussed in File 3.2, phonemes make distinctions in meaning. If two sounds are members of separate phonemes, minimal pairs can almost always be found. For example, the minimal pair *led* and *red* is evidence that [l] and [ɹ] contrast and are allophones of separate phonemes in English. But if two sounds are allophones of the same phoneme, minimal pairs differing only in those sounds will not exist. For example, [bʌʔn̩] and [bʌtʰn̩] are both possible pronunciations of the English word *button* (though [bʌtʰn̩] may sound a little stilted). This is because the sounds [ʔ] and [tʰ] are both allophones of the phoneme /t/. Thus, the meaning doesn't change.

Second, the allophones of a phoneme are not a random collection of sounds but are a set of sounds that have the same psychological function—they are the "same" sound. Accordingly, allophones of the same phoneme are systematically related to one another: they often share many phonetic properties, and it is possible to predict which allophone will appear in a word on the basis of phonological rules.

By analyzing the patterns of sounds that are physically present, it is possible to draw conclusions about the psychological organization of a language, which is not directly observable.

3.5.2 How to Do a Phonemic Analysis

Although a phonemic analysis can be performed successfully on any language, we will begin with a problem based on English. Look over the data in (1), which are given in a fairly detailed phonetic transcription. Recall that an open circle under a segment indicates that it is voiceless.

(1) 'pray'   [pʰɹ̥eɪ]   'fresh'   [fɹ̥ɛʃ]
     'gray'   [gɹeɪ]   'regain'   [ɹigeɪn]
     'crab'   [kʰɹ̥æb]   'shriek'   [ʃɹ̥ik]
     'par'   [pʰɑɹ]   'tar'   [tʰɑɹ]
     'broker' [bɹoʊkɹ̩]

Consider the sounds [ɹ] and [ɹ̥]: are these sounds constrastive or allophones of the same phoneme? (Of course, native speakers of English may intuitively know that they are allophones of the same phoneme. However, the procedure for doing a phonemic analysis should produce the same answer without appealing to the intuitions of speakers.)

In order to answer this question, it is necessary to examine scientifically the **distribution** of sounds within these data. That is, for each sound in question we need to determine the set of phonetic environments in which it can occur. But just what do we mean by *environment*? For the time being, we can define the **environment** of a sound as the sounds that immediately precede and follow it within a word. For example, in the word [gɹeɪ], [ɹ] is in the environment [g __ eɪ]; that is, [ɹ] is preceded by [g] and followed by [eɪ].

The best way to begin a phonemic analysis is to look first for minimal pairs. Suppose for a moment we were interested in the sounds [pʰ] and [tʰ] in the data in (1). These sounds do appear in a minimal pair: [pʰɑɹ] and [tʰɑɹ] have different meanings and differ phonetically by only a single sound in the same position. This tells us that [pʰ] and [tʰ] are in overlapping distribution and, more specifically, that they are in contrastive distribution, because the difference between them causes a difference in meaning. Therefore, they are allophones of different phonemes. We can also look for pairs of words that differ phonetically by only a single sound in the same position but that have exactly the same meaning. If we find any, we know that the sounds are in free variation and are allophones of the same phoneme.

Returning to the status of [ɹ] versus [ɹ̥], we see that there are no minimal pairs in the data that differ only by these two sounds. Since [ɹ] and [ɹ̥] are not in overlapping distribution in our data,[1] we can assume that they are in complementary distribution. However, we must prove that this is so by making a generalization about where [ɹ] (but not [ɹ̥]) may appear, and vice versa. In order to do so, we need to compare the phonetic environments of each of these sounds. The easiest way to do this is to make a list for each sound, as follows. (Note that "#" indicates a word boundary.)

(2)   [ɹ]   [ɹ̥]

       [g __ eɪ]   [pʰ __ eɪ]
       [ɑ __ #]   [kʰ __ æ]
       [b __ oʊ]   [f __ ɛ]
       [# __ i]   [ʃ __ i]

Once you have collected the list of phonetic environments for each sound from all of the data, you can proceed as follows:

1. *Look at the environments to find natural classes.* As a beginner, you may find it helpful to begin by giving the phonetic description for each of the sounds in the environments listed. This will help you to see any generalizations. (As you become more familiar with the IPA and the features it represents, it will become easier to see generalizations just

---

[1]You can always assume that the data you are given are representative of the language pattern you are asked to analyze for the purposes of solving phonology problems in this book. Sometimes we have selected a particular subset of the data from a language to illustrate a particular analytical point; this should not be taken as a sign that every word in the language will follow exactly the same pattern. However, the patterns we present are representative of basic phonological distributions.

from looking at the list of sounds.) So, for example, we could look at the sounds that appear before [ɹ̥] in (2), which are [pʰ], [kʰ], [f], and [ʃ], and describe them as follows: aspirated **voiceless** bilabial stop; aspirated **voiceless** velar stop; **voiceless** labiodental fricative; **voiceless** post-alveolar fricative. This lets you see that all of these sounds share the feature of being voiceless consonants. This generalization permits us to simplify the description of the environment for [ɹ̥]; instead of listing each sound separately, it is now possible to say:

(3)   [ɹ̥] appears after voiceless consonants.

Now look at the environments in which [ɹ] appears. Are there any natural classes? Yes and no. Certainly [b] and [g] are voiced consonants, and [ɑ] is also voiced, but the set that includes [b], [g], [ɑ], the beginnings of words, and the ends of words does not form a natural class. Thus, the critical observation to make here is that there is no single natural class of environments in which [ɹ] can be found.

We have looked at the sounds preceding [ɹ] and [ɹ̥], but what about the sounds that follow them? As you can see, only [ɹ] may occur word-finally, but either [ɹ] or [ɹ̥] can occur before a vowel. Because the environment that follows either [ɹ] or [ɹ̥] can be the same (for example, [eɪ]), this alone can't tell us about when you get [ɹ] versus [ɹ̥]. Thus, the environments that condition the appearance of [ɹ] or [ɹ̥], i.e., the conditioning environments of these particular allophones, are their immediately preceding sounds.

It is important to keep in mind that the relevant part of the environment will differ based on the particular phonological rule involved. Sometimes the conditioning environment is the preceding environment, sometimes it is the following environment, and sometimes it is a combination of the two (think back to the environment for the flapping rule in English). It is also the case that some of the natural classes involved will be quite broad (e.g., "voiceless consonants," "vowels") and some will be more narrow (e.g., "alveolar stops," "front high and mid vowels").

2. *Look for complementary gaps in the environments.* So far, we have shown that [ɹ̥] appears after voiceless consonants, while [ɹ] appears in an apparently random set of environments. Yet, it is possible to make one more critical observation by comparing the two sets of environments. [ɹ] does not appear in the environments in which [ɹ̥] appears, namely, after voiceless consonants. Moreover, [ɹ̥] does not appear where [ɹ] does; there is no [ɹ̥] after voiced consonants or at the beginnings or ends of words. Since the environments of [ɹ] and [ɹ̥] have systematic and complementary gaps, we say that [ɹ] and [ɹ̥] are in complementary distribution. We can predict, based on the preceding sound, which one will occur. Therefore, they are allophones of the same phoneme. Note that any kind of complementary gap—any environment where one sound can occur but not the other—results in predictability.

3. *State a generalization about the distribution of each of these sounds.* In other words, write a rule that will make predictions about where each of the sounds can occur. Actually, we've done the hard part of this already by observing that [ɹ̥] occurs following voiceless consonants. How should we state the distribution of [ɹ]? We could try formulating our rule as follows:

(4)   [ɹ̥] appears following voiceless consonants;
      [ɹ] appears following voiced consonants or vowels, or at the beginning or end of a word.

However, that's not a very succinct formulation of the rule. To simplify it, recall that wherever [ɹ̥] occurs, [ɹ] can't, because their possible environments form complementary sets. Therefore, we can revise our rule this way:

(5) [ɪ̥] appears following voiceless consonants;
    [ɪ] appears elsewhere.

4. *Determine the identity of the phoneme and its allophones.* This next step in writing the rule involves deciding what the phoneme to which these sounds belong should be. In order to do so, we need to decide which of the allophones is the **basic allophone** and which is the **restricted allophone.** We have determined that the conditioning environment for [ɪ̥] consists of a single natural class of sounds. [ɪ̥] is restricted to occurring only there, whereas [ɪ] may appear anywhere else. Therefore, we can identify [ɪ̥] as the restricted allophone and [ɪ] as the basic one.

It makes sense to name the phoneme after the basic allophone, since it is the one that can show up in a wider variety of contexts. Furthermore, the basic allophone is assumed to be the closest approximation of the mental "sound" that speakers store in memory. In choosing a name for the phoneme, we have made the leap from observable phonetic reality to unobservable psychological reality. (It is not always possible to choose one allophone as basic, however. In that case the phonology exercise's instructions will not tell you to do so, and any of the allophones would serve equally well as the name of the phoneme.)

We can improve on our rule once more by writing it to show the process of going from the phoneme to each of the allophones, as in (6). This notation was introduced in Section 3.3.1. The arrows in the rule in (6) mean 'is pronounced as.' We use slashes around symbols that represent phonemes, and a single slash indicates the beginning of the environment specification.

(6) /ɪ/ → [ɪ̥] / after voiceless consonants;
    /ɪ/ → [ɪ] / elsewhere.

Now that we have formulated the necessary phonological rule, we can see which phonological process it involves (see File 3.3). In this rule a voiced phoneme changes into a voiceless sound when it follows another voiceless sound. In other words, /ɪ/ becomes more like a preceding sound with respect to the feature of voicelessness. Therefore, we can conclude that the process of assimilation is involved in this phonological rule.

3.5.3 Some Potential Trouble Spots

The procedure outlined in the previous section will work for any language for which reliable phonetic transcriptions exist. However, beginners are often confused by certain questions.

For instance, if you discover that no minimal pairs exist for two sounds, is it possible to automatically conclude that they are allophones of the same phoneme? No. It is still necessary to show that the sounds are in complementary distribution, since allophones are predictable variant pronunciations of the same phoneme.

Consider what happens if you make a decision too soon. Using the data presented in (1) at the beginning of the previous section, suppose you wanted to know whether [g] and [ʃ] are allophones of the same phoneme. Since there are no minimal pairs differentiated by these sounds in the data set, it might seem reasonable to conclude that they are. (Of course, a speaker of English should have no trouble thinking of a minimal pair involving these two sounds, for example, *gag* and *gash.* The exercises, however, are designed to be self-contained; that is, in all of the problems in the book, you will be given enough data **within** the problem set to solve the problem. This means that you should not rely on outside knowledge you may have of the language you are analyzing to answer the question.) But a careful examination of the data reveals that this is the wrong conclusion. Listing the data and the relevant environments, you find what is shown in (7).

(7) [g] appears in *gray* [gɹeɪ], *regain* [ɹɪgeɪn]
       generalization: [g] appears between vowels or at the beginning of a word;
   [ʃ] appears in *fresh* [fɹɛʃ], *shriek* [ʃɹ̥ik]
       generalization: [ʃ] appears at the beginning or end of a word.

As these data illustrate, [g] and [ʃ] are not in complementary distribution because their distributions overlap: either may occur at the beginning of a word. Furthermore, either may be followed by the phoneme /ɹ/. As a result, no phonological rule can be responsible for their distribution. In general, when no generalization can be made about where a group of sounds can occur, it is possible to conclude that they are contrastive and are allophones of separate phonemes. A conclusion based on such a demonstration is just as valid as showing that minimal pairs exist. This alternative way of showing that sounds are members of separate phonemes is useful because it's not always possible to find minimal pairs for all distinctive sounds. For example, there are no minimal pairs involving [ŋ] and [h] in English. But it is reasonable to assume that they belong to separate phonemes because they share few phonetic properties, and no phonological rule determines where they can occur.

The range of tests for identifying phonemes can be broadened somewhat by the use of **near-minimal pairs.** Recall that a minimal pair is a pair of words differing in meaning but phonetically identical except for one sound in the same position in each word. The definition of near-minimal pairs is the same, except that the words are **almost** identical except for the one sound. For example, *heard* [hɹ̩d] and *Bert* [bɹ̩t] form a near-minimal pair involving [h] and [b]. We are justified in saying that [h] and [b] are allophones of separate phonemes because no conceivable phonological rule would permit only [h] at the beginnings of words ending in [d], and only [b] at the beginnings of words ending in [t]. (This conclusion is partly based on extensive study of how phonological rules work: experience does play a role in being able to do phonological analysis.)

One final point about minimal pairs: notice that we have not defined them as pairs of words that rhyme. It is not necessary for two words to rhyme in order to form a minimal pair. Consider the English minimal pairs *state* [steɪt] and *steak* [steɪk], for example, or *boat* [boʊt] and *beat* [bit]. Nor is rhyming sufficient to qualify a pair of words as a minimal pair: *gray* [gɹeɪ] and pray [pʰɹ̥eɪ] from the list of data above rhyme, but differ in two sounds. And to take another example, *glitter* and *litter* rhyme but do not form a minimal pair because they do not contain the same number of sounds.

Another question that often troubles beginners is this: when describing the environment in which a sound appears, how do you know where to look? In the problem we solved in the previous section, we focused on the sounds that preceded [ɹ] and [ɹ̥]. But as we noted above, this is certainly not the only possibility. In fact, identifying conditioning environments is the most challenging part of doing a phonemic analysis.

Recall that in many cases, the relevant conditioning environment consists of the sounds immediately surrounding the sound in question. However, it is sometimes necessary to look beyond the sound's immediate environment. As we saw for Finnish vowels in Section 3.3.3, if you are examining the distribution of a vowel allophone, it is quite common that the conditioning environment involves a vowel in an adjacent syllable, even though consonants may intervene. It may also be necessary to consider preceding or following sounds even when they belong to another word that is adjacent in the stream of speech. However, it is best to start by examining the immediate environment of an allophone when you are trying to determine what its conditioning environment is.

Since there are many logically possible environments to consider, the task is made easier by eliminating all of those except the most plausible. This can be accomplished by using strategies like the following:

a. *Formulate hypotheses about the allophones.* Investigation of the world's languages has revealed that some sounds are more common than others (see File 3.4 for a relevant discussion). For example:

- Voiced nasals and liquids are more common than voiceless ones.
- Oral vowels are more common than nasal vowels.
- Short consonants are more common than long consonants.
- "Plain" consonants are more common than those with secondary articulations like velarization, palatalization, and labialization.

On the basis of these generalizations, it is possible to speculate that if a less common sound appears in a language, it is likely to be a restricted allophone. But these tendencies should be used only as a guide for forming hypotheses, not as a basis for jumping to conclusions, since some languages exhibit exceptions. For example, French has both nasal and oral vowel phonemes.

b. *Keep in mind that allophonic variation results from the application of phonological rules.* Also remember that rules usually involve some phonological process, such as assimilation or deletion. It is thus often helpful to compare the allophones themselves to get an idea of what kind of phonological process may be involved and then check the environments in which they appear for evidence. For example, if the sounds differ only in voicing, as with [ɪ] and [ɪ̥] above, a reasonable guess would be that voicing assimilation is involved, so you will want to look for voiced and voiceless sounds in the relevant environments, as we did. Similarly, if one of the allophones is a palatal or post-alveolar consonant, and the other is alveolar or velar, a palatalization process may be involved, so you would look for front high and mid vowels and/or the palatal glide in the environments following the palatal allophone. The more familiar you are with the phonological processes in Section 3.3.3, the easier this task will be. Even if it is not obvious that a phonological process has been at work, you should be able to write a phonological rule and, thus, state a generalization about where the allophones of the phoneme occur.

3.5.4   Flowchart for Discovering the Distribution of Sounds

The flowchart in (8) should help you to identify the type of distribution two (or more) sounds in a language have. The rectangular boxes ask you to do something or give you some information that your working through the flowchart has revealed. The diamond-shaped boxes pose a question. Try reading through the flowchart before you attempt to analyze the languages in the next file (File 3.6, "Practice"); it may help you to understand the relationship between the different types of distributions of sounds in a language.

(8)   A flowchart for identifying the distribution of sounds

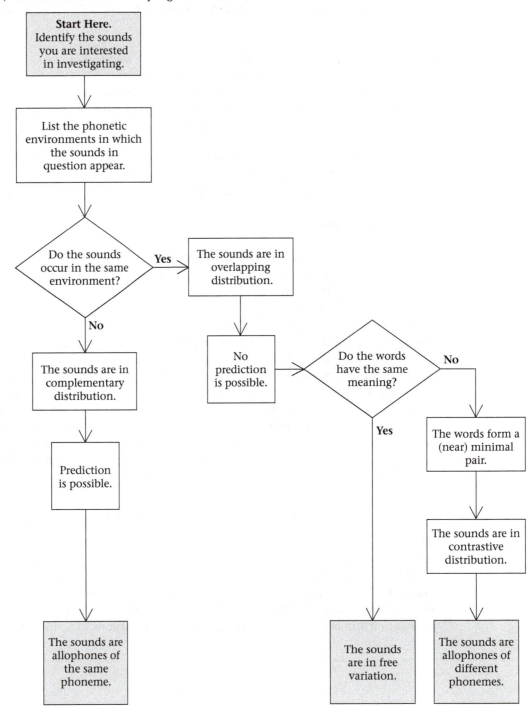

FILE 3.6

....

Practice

File 3.1—Phonotactic Constraints and Foreign Accents

Exercises

1. According to the phonotactic constraints on English syllable structure given in Section 3.1.1, is [bljust] a possible word in English? Why or why not? Does this match your own intuition?

2. List three different ways an English speaker might make the borrowed Polish place name Szczebrzeszynie [ʃʧɛbʒɛʃɲɛ] fit within English phonotactics.

Discussion Questions

3. If a consonant cluster occurs in a language, do you think that it should automatically be considered a legal phonotactic sequence in the language? For example, do you think that [ʃl] should be considered phonotactically legal in English because it occurs in the words *schlep* and *schlocky*? Why or why not?

4. Why do you think it is difficult for people to learn the phonotactics of another language? That is, why do people use "repair" strategies or substitutions rather than just pronouncing the foreign word the way it is pronounced by native speakers of the foreign language?

5. In File 3.1, we discussed the process by which some individuals are trying to introduce new signs into Taiwan Sign Language.

   i. Why do you think the hearing instructors came up with signs that violate a universal principle of signed languages? If it is a universal principle, then why didn't the instructors create signs that followed it?

   ii. Now that these signs have been created, do you think they will catch on in TSL? Why or why not?

   iii. Do you think that if they do catch on, they will be modified in any particular way, or do you think that they will keep the same form that they had in Signed Mandarin? (Be sure to refer to the information about foreign accents also discussed in File 3.1.) If you think they will change, what are some possible sorts of changes that could take place?

   iv. What do you think about the Mandarin-speaking instructors creating new signs? In general, should people who are not speakers of a particular language be allowed to introduce new words into that language? Is this case different, since the creators of the new signs have a native language with a different modality?

Activities

6. In the following chart, which of the combinations occur at the beginning of an English word? For these combinations think of (or find) words that begin with the consonant cluster and write them in the box. If the consonant combination violates the phonotactic constraints of English, leave it blank.

	[w]	[l]	[n]	[ɹ]	[t]	[s]
[t]	twenty					
[m]						
[p]						
[ʃ]						
[s]						
[k]						

7. Using the chart in Activity 6, list which consonant combinations can occur at the ends of English words (e.g., *apt*).

8. Find a few words that have been borrowed into English (there are lists in File 12.2), and identify the original form of each word before it was borrowed into English. What changes did English speakers make to the foreign words when they were borrowed?

File 3.2—Phonemes and Allophones

Exercises

9. **Ukrainian**
   Look at the following Ukrainian words containing the sounds [s], [sʲ], [ʃ], and [ʃʲ]. The sounds [sʲ] and [ʃʲ] are palatalized variants of [s] and [ʃ]; see the discussion in Section 2.4.6. The words have been arranged to help you identify minimal pairs.

	[s]		[sʲ]		[ʃ]		[ʃʲ]	
a.	[lɪs]	'fox'	[lɪsʲ]	'sheen'	[lɪʃ]	'lest'		
b.	[mɪska]	'bowl'			[mɪʃka]	'little mouse'	[mɪʃʲi]	'mice'
c.	[sapka]	'little hoe'			[ʃapka]	'hat'		
d.	[sɪla]	'strength'			[ʃɪla]	'she sewed'	[ʃʲistʲ]	'six'
e.	[sum]	'sadness'			[ʃum]	'rustling'		
f.	[sudɪ]	'trials'	[sʲudɪ]	'hither'			[koʃʲi]	'baskets'
g.	[sosna]	'pine'	[sʲomɪj]	'seventh'	[ʃostɪj]	'sixth'		
h.	[posadu]	'job' (acc.)	[posʲadu]	'I will occupy'				

   i. What minimal pairs can you identify in these words?

   ii. Is there a minimal triplet (like a minimal pair, but involving three sounds and three words)? What is it?

   iii. Which three of these four sounds are in contrastive distribution?

   iv. One of these sounds occurs only before a particular vowel. What is this sound, and what is the vowel? Which words indicate this?

Discussion Questions

10. We have said that both contrastive distribution and free variation involve a context where it is impossible to predict which of two or more sounds belongs. However, these two are not the same thing. Consider the context [pʰlɑ__]. Of the sounds [p, pʼ, b, t, tʼ, d], only one doesn't form a real word of English when inserted in this context—which one? Of the rest of these sounds, which ones are in contrastive distribution? Which ones are in free variation? How do you know?

11. Fill in the following table using the three terms "contrastive distribution," "complementary distribution," and "free variation" as defined in this chapter, with respect to two sounds in a given context. (For example, the upper left-hand cell of the table should contain the name of the type of distribution that occurs when two sounds are contrastive and predictable in a certain context.) Which cell in the table is blank? Why is it blank?

	Predictable	Unpredictable
Contrastive		
Non-Contrastive		

Activity

12. Obtain a dictionary or textbook for some signed language from your library, or go to an online sign language dictionary. (Some are included on the Links page for Chapter 3, although there are many others.) Look through the lists of words and try to find a minimal pair. The two words that you select should be the same in four of the following parameters and different in one: place of articulation, movement, handshape, orientation, and non-manual marker. For your minimal pair, specify which parameter the two signs differ in, and describe the difference.

File 3.3—Phonological Rules

Exercises

13. List the members of the following natural classes of English sounds.

    a. alveolar obstruents
    b. voiced labial consonants
    c. velar oral stops
    d. interdental fricatives
    e. high tense vowels
    f. low vowels
    g. palatal sonorants
    h. voiced sibilants

14. Describe the following natural classes of English sounds.

    a. [ɪ, l]   **d.** [i, u]
    b. [f, θ, s, ʃ, h]   **e.** [p, b]
    c. [w, j, w̥]   **f.** [n, ɹ, l]

15. Identify what type(s) of phonological rule(s) applies in each of the following derivations.

a. little	/lɪtl̩/	→	[lɪɾl̩]
b. late bell	/leɪt bɛl/	→	[leɪp bɛl]
c. park	/pɑɹk/	→	[pʰɑɹk]
d. lance	/læns/	→	[lænts]
e. it's her car	/ɪts hɹ̩ kɑɹ/	→	[ɪts ɹ̩ kʰɑɹ]
f. prescription	/pɹiskɹɪpʃən/	→	[pʰəɹskɹɪpʃn̩]
g. February	/fɛbɹuɛɹi/	→	[fɛbjuɛɹi]

Discussion Questions

16. Consider the following paragraphs and answer the questions about natural classes.

i. The English indefinite article is *a* [ə] before most words: *a lion, a peanut, a map,* a *unicorn,* etc., but it is *an* [æn] before words like *apple, onion, icicle, evening, eagle,* and *honor.* To what natural classes do the sounds at the beginning of each set of words belong? (That is, before what class of sounds do you use [ə]? [æn]?)

ii. Some American English speakers (largely in the Midwest and the South) pronounce [ɪ] in words like *then, Kenny, pen, Bengals, gem, lengthen, Remington,* and *temperature* (where other speakers have [ɛ]). But, like others, they have [ɛ] in words like *pet, bell, peg,* and *tech.* What natural class of sounds follows the vowel in words in which these speakers have [ɪ]?

iii. Some midwestern American speakers in casual speech drop the unstressed vowel in the first syllable of words like *police, believe, parade, Columbus, pollution, terrific,* and *collision,* but do not drop it in words like *detective, dependent, majestic,* or *pedantic.* What natural class of sounds follows the unstressed vowel in the first syllable in the first group of words?

iv. At some time during a child's language development, he or she might pronounce certain words as follows: *that* [dæt], *these* [diz], *this* [dɪs], and *three* [fɹi], *think* [fɪŋk], *bath* [bæf]. What natural class of sounds is being affected? Do the sounds used as replacements form a natural class?

17. The traditional sign for TOMATO in ASL involves one hand with the index finger extended, moving from the lips down in front of the body, while the other hand is in a flat O handshape and remains still in front of the body. Some signers now produce it without the O handshape, instead extending the index finger on the hand that stays still. What type of phonological process is this? Why do you think such a change might have happened?

File 3.4—Implicational Laws

Exercises

18. Explain why it doesn't make sense to ask the question, "Is [s] a common sound in the world's languages?"

19. Given the explanations for implicational laws given in Section 3.4.6, why do you think that clicks are relatively rare in the world's languages? Do you think it is related more to production or to perception? Why?

20. The explanations for implicational laws given in Section 3.4.6 have also been used to explain other phenomena, especially in the domains of language variation and change. Look at the following pictures of the ASL word LEARN. One set shows the formal version of the sign; the other shows a more casual version. Speculate as to why the sign might have changed from the formal version to the informal version, given considerations of perception and production.

a. ASL LEARN (more formal register)

© 2006, William Vicars, www.Lifeprint.com. Adapted by permission.

b. ASL LEARN (more casual register)

© 2006, William Vicars, www.Lifeprint.com. Adapted by permission.

Discussion Question

21. Referring to the phonotactic constraints on syllable structure in File 3.1, do you think that there is an implicational hierarchy of syllable types? If so, what do you think it might look like? If not, why not?

File 3.5—How to Solve Phonology Problems

The exercises for this file are designed to give you practice in doing phonemic analysis at the beginning, intermediate, and more advanced levels. The instructions to each exercise are somewhat different in each case, so read them carefully before proceeding. However, each exercise requires that you follow the step-by-step procedure for doing a phonemic analysis outlined in the text of File 3.5. The exercises are designed to introduce you to problems involving minimal pairs, complementary distribution, and free variation. A linguist doing a phonemic analysis of an unknown language would, of course, examine hundreds of words in order to be sure to have enough data to find the relevant minimal pairs, complementary distributions, etc. But to save you time, the data in the exercises below have been carefully selected to give you all the relevant information you will need in a very small set of words. As you approach each problem, consider all of the data before you answer the questions, rather than considering only (a), then only (b), and so on.

Exercises

22. Mokilese

Mokilese is an Austronesian language of the Malayo-Polynesian family, spoken in Micronesia. Examine the distribution of the voiced and voiceless vowel pairs: [i, i̥] and [u, u̥] (voiceless vowels have a circle under the phonetic vowel symbol). For each pair, determine whether they are allophones of different phonemes or allophones of the same phoneme. Provide evidence for your answer. If they are allophones of one phoneme, state the contexts in which each sound occurs and decide which sound is the basic sound. Can any generalizations be made? (*Hint:* Refer to natural classes.)

a.	[pi̥senmoŋ]	'hair'	**h.**	[masak]	'hard'
b.	[tu̥pu̥kda]	'bought'	**i.**	[liŋ]	'beautiful'
c.	[pu̥ko]	'basket'	**j.**	[pilda]	'to choose'
d.	[pi̥tʃumene]	'this pig'	**k.**	[poki]	'to strike something'
e.	[su̥pwo]	'firewood'	**l.**	[ludʒ]	'to jump'
f.	[si̥ko]	'to talk about'	**m.**	[kurdʒ]	'to grind'
g.	[uduk]	'flesh'	**n.**	[rik]	'to gather'

Beginning Exercises

23. Sindhi

The following data are from Sindhi, an Indo-European language of the Indo-Aryan family, spoken in Pakistan and India. Examine the distribution of the phones [p], [pʰ], and [b]. Determine if the three are allophones of separate phonemes or allophones of the same phoneme. What is your evidence? Is the relationship among the sounds the same as in English? Why or why not? [ɳ] and [ɖ] are the voiced retroflex nasal and oral stop.

a.	[pənʊ]	'leaf'	**g.**	[barʊ]	'weight'
b.	[ɖakʰə]	'grape'	**h.**	[kʰirʊ]	'milk'
c.	[ɖəpʊ]	'fear'	**i.**	[putʰi]	'back'
d.	[pʰəɳu]	'hood of snake'	**j.**	[bənʊ]	'forest'
e.	[kənʊ]	'ear'	**k.**	[pʰərʊ]	'arrow head'
f.	[perʊ]	'foot'	**l.**	[abʊ]	'water'

24. Standard Italian

Consider the following data from Standard Italian, an Indo-European language of the Romance family, spoken in Italy. Answer the questions that follow.

a.	[tinta]	'dye'	**g.**	[tiŋgo]	'I dye'
b.	[tɛnda]	'tent'	**h.**	[tɛŋgo]	'I keep'
c.	[dantsa]	'dance'	**i.**	[fuŋgo]	'mushroom'
d.	[neɾo]	'black'	**j.**	[bjaŋka]	'white'
e.	[dʒɛnte]	'people'	**k.**	[aŋke]	'also'
f.	[sapone]	'soap'	**l.**	[faŋgo]	'mud'

  i. Are there any minimal pairs? If so, what are they, and what can you conclude to be true of Italian from those minimal pairs?

  ii. State the phonetic environments in which the sounds [n] and [ŋ] appear. Identify any natural classes of sounds that appear in the environments you've provided.

  iii. Given what you know about the distribution of sounds and the environments you listed in (ii), are [n] and [ŋ] in complementary or contrastive distribution? Please explain your answer.

25. Standard Spanish

Standard Spanish is an Indo-European language of the Romance family. Examine the phones [d] and [ð]. Determine whether they are allophones of one phoneme or of separate phonemes. If they are allophones of one phoneme, identify the type of distribution. If they are in complementary distribution, state a rule that describes the distribution. If [d] and [ð] are allophones of separate phonemes, give minimal pairs that prove this.

a.	[dɾenar]	'to drain'		**g.**	[duða]	'doubt'
b.	[dentɾo]	'within'		**h.**	[bendito]	'blessed'
c.	[dia]	'day'		**i.**	[laðear]	'to tilt'
d.	[aðonde]	'where'		**j.**	[aldea]	'village'
e.	[ajuða]	'help'		**k.**	[deðo]	'finger'
f.	[iðioma]	'language'		**l.**	[toldo]	'canopy'

26. Russian

Russian is an Indo-European language of the Slavic family, spoken in Russia. Determine from the following Russian data whether the low front [a] and the low back [ɑ] complement each other as allophones of the same phoneme or whether they are in contrast as allophones of separate phonemes. If they are allophones of separate phonemes, provide evidence for your claim. If they are in complementary distribution, pick one allophone as the basic sound, and give the conditioning phonetic contexts for its allophones. [pʲ], [tʲ], [dʲ], [zʲ], and [lʲ] are palatalized consonants.

a.	[alʲt]	'viola'		**f.**	[trʌvɑ]	'grass'
b.	[tɑk]	'so'		**g.**	[dʲadʲə]	'uncle'
c.	[pʲatkə]	'heel'		**h.**	[mʲatʲ]	'to crumple'
d.	[mɑtʲ]	'mother'		**i.**	[vaʃ]	'your (plural)'
e.	[pʲatʲ]	'five'		**j.**	[zʲatʲ]	'son-in-law'

27. Burmese

Burmese is a Sino-Tibetan language of the Tibeto-Burman family, spoken in Myanmar. The following Burmese data contain both voiced and voiceless nasals. The latter are indicated by a small circle placed under the phonetic symbol. Are [m] and [m̥] allophones of the same phoneme, or are they different phonemes? What about [n] and [n̥]? Is the same also true for [ŋ] and [ŋ̊]? Give evidence for your answer. If there is a phonological process involved, state what it is and give the conditioning environment. What is it about this environment that triggers this rule? *Note:* Burmese is a tone language, where [ˊ] indicates a high-toned vowel, [ˋ] a low-toned vowel, [ˆ] a falling-toned vowel. No tone marking indicates that the vowel is mid-toned. The sequence of sounds [eɪ] is a diphthong.

a.	[mî]	'fire'		**n.**	[niè]	'fine, small'
b.	[mwêɪ]	'to give birth'		**o.**	[nwâ]	'cow'
c.	[mjiʔ]	'river'		**p.**	[ŋâ]	'five'
d.	[mjâwn]	'ditch'		**q.**	[ŋouʔ]	'stump (of tree)'
e.	[mjín]	'to see'		**r.**	[mîn]	'old (people)'
f.	[nê]	'small'		**s.**	[m̥í]	'to lean against'
g.	[njiʔ]	'dirty'		**t.**	[m̥wêɪ]	'fragrant'
h.	[nwè]	'to bend flexibly'		**u.**	[m̥jaʔ]	'to cure (meat)'
i.	[m̥jawʔ]	'to multiply'		**v.**	[m̥òwn]	'flour, powder'
j.	[n̥êɪ]	'slow'		**w.**	[n̥jiʔ]	'to wring, squeeze'
k.	[n̥wêɪ]	'to heat'		**x.**	[n̥jeɪʔ]	'to nod the head'
l.	[n̥jaʔ]	'to cut off (hair)'		**y.**	[ŋ̊â]	'to borrow'
m.	[ŋ̊eʔ]	'bird'		**z.**	[hîn]	'curry'

28. Korean

Korean is a "language isolate," meaning that it is not linguistically related to other languages. It is spoken in Korea. In the following Korean words, you will find the sounds [s] and [ʃ]. Determine whether the sounds [s] and [ʃ] are allophones of the same phoneme or separate phonemes. If the sounds are allophones of the same phoneme, give the basic and derived allophones and the environment in which the derived allophone occurs.

a.	[ʃi]	'poem'	**j.**	[sal]	'flesh'
b.	[miʃin]	'superstition'	**k.**	[kasu]	'singer'
c.	[ʃinmun]	'newspaper'	**l.**	[sanmun]	'prose'
d.	[tʰaksaŋʃige]	'table clock'	**m.**	[kasəl]	'hypothesis'
e.	[ʃilsu]	'mistake'	**n.**	[miso]	'smile'
f.	[oʃip]	'fifty'	**o.**	[susek]	'search'
g.	[panʃik]	'method'	**p.**	[tapsa]	'exploration'
h.	[kanʃik]	'snack'	**q.**	[so]	'cow'
i.	[kaʃi]	'thorn'			

29. English

English is an Indo-European language of the Germanic family. In the following dialect of English, common in Canada and parts of the United States, there is a predictable variant [əʊ] of the diphthong [aʊ]. What phonetic segments condition this change? What feature(s) characterize the class of conditioning segments?

a.	[əbəʊt]	about	**f.**	[dəʊt]	doubt	**k.**	[naʊn]	noun
b.	[kaʊ]	cow	**g.**	[baʊ]	bough	**l.**	[məʊθ]	mouth
c.	[laʊd]	loud	**h.**	[əʊst]	oust	**m.**	[aʊns]	ounce
d.	[ɹaʊz]	rouse	**i.**	[vaʊl]	vowel	**n.**	[bɹaʊz]	browse
e.	[əʊt]	out	**j.**	[həʊs]	house	**o.**	[kəʊtʃ]	couch

30. Totonac

Examine the classes of voiced versus voiceless vowels in Totonac, a Totonacan language spoken in Mexico. Are voiced and voiceless vowels in Totonac in contrast, in free variation, or in complementary distribution? If the sounds are in complementary distribution, pick one sound as the basic sound and give the phonetic contexts for its allophones. (Note that [ts] represents a voiceless alveolar affricate, and [ɫ] a velarized [l].)

a.	[tsapsḁ]	'he stacks'	**g.**	[snapapḁ]	'white'
b.	[tsilinksḁ]	'it resounded'	**h.**	[stapu̥]	'beans'
c.	[kasitti̥]	'cut it'	**i.**	[ʃumpi̥]	'porcupine'
d.	[kuku̥]	'uncle'	**j.**	[taːqhu̥]	'you plunged'
e.	[ɫkakḁ]	'peppery'	**k.**	[tihaʃɫi̥]	'he rested'
f.	[miki̥]	'snow'	**l.**	[tukʃɫi̥]	'it broke'

Intermediate Exercises

31. Tojolabal

Tojolabal is a Mayan language of the Kanjobalan-Chujean family, spoken in Mexico. Determine whether plain [k] and ejective [k'] are allophones of a single phoneme, in free variation, or in contrast. Support your answer with specific examples. (*Hint:* Don't forget that near-minimal pairs can be as convincing as minimal pairs.)

a.	[kisim]	'my beard'	**g.**	[sak]	'white'
b.	[ʦak'a]	'chop it down'	**h.**	[k'iʃin]	'warm'
c.	[koktit]	'our feet'	**i.**	[skutʃu]	'he is carrying it'
d.	[k'ak]	'flea'	**j.**	[k'uːtes]	'to dress'
e.	[p'akan]	'hanging'	**k.**	[snika]	'he stirred it'
f.	[k'aʔem]	'sugar cane'	**l.**	[ʔak']	'read'

32. **Spanish**

   Examine the following data from Spanish and answer the questions that follow. Note that [β] represents a voiced bilabial fricative, and [ɣ] a voiced velar fricative.

a.	[beβer]	'to drink'	**h.**	[blusa]	'blouse'	**o.**	[teŋgo]	'I have'
b.	[laβar]	'to wash'	**i.**	[oβliɣaðo]	'obligated'	**p.**	[iɣlesia]	'church'
c.	[buskar]	'to seek'	**j.**	[ambos]	'both'	**q.**	[aɣrio]	'sour'
d.	[suβtitulo]	'subtitle'	**k.**	[gloria]	'glory'	**r.**	[tiɣɾe]	'tiger'
e.	[ambɾe]	'hunger'	**l.**	[reɣalar]	'to present'	**s.**	[saŋgɾe]	'blood'
f.	[aβɾasar]	'to hug'	**m.**	[graβar]	'to engrave'	**t.**	[gama]	'range'
g.	[aβlar]	'to talk'	**n.**	[reɣla]	'rule'	**u.**	[goβernar]	'to govern'

   i. The allophones [b] and [β] are in complementary distribution, as are [g] and [ɣ]. Determine the conditioning environments for each pair, and state a rule that describes the distribution of the allophones.

   ii. Refer to Exercise 25 (Standard Spanish) and the rule for the distribution of the allophones [d] and [ð]. Describe the distribution of [b], [d], [g] and [β], [ð], [ɣ] in the most general terms possible, assuming each pair of allophones follows the same pattern.

33. **Canadian French**

   In the dialect of French (an Indo-European language of the Romance family) spoken in Canada, consider the distribution of [d] and [ʣ] (a voiced alveolar affricate) in the data below. State their distribution and determine if they are allophones of one phoneme or of separate phonemes. [y] is a high, front, tense, rounded vowel, and [ø] and [œ] are the mid, front, tense and lax rounded vowels, respectively.

a.	[akademɪk]	'academic'	**g.**	[gidɔ̃]	'handlebars'
b.	[ʣifisɪl]	'difficult'	**h.**	[miʣi]	'noon'
c.	[ʣɪsʊt]	'dissolved (f)'	**i.**	[dø]	'two'
d.	[ineʣɪt]	'unpublished (f)'	**j.**	[ʣy]	'some'
e.	[duʃ]	'shower'	**k.**	[dœ]	'of'
f.	[vãʣy]	'sold'	**l.**	[vɪd]	'empty'

34. **German**

   German is an Indo-European language of the Germanic family, spoken in Germany. Examine the voiceless velar fricative represented by [x] and the voiceless palatal fricative represented by [ç] in the German data below. Are the two sounds in complementary distribution or are they contrastive? If the sounds are allophones in complementary distribution, state the phonetic contexts for each allophone. (Remember that <ː> marks vowel length, so [uː] is a long vowel, not a sequence of two segments.)

a.	[buːx]	'book'	**f.**	[ɛçt]	'real"
b.	[lɔx]	'hole'	**g.**	[ʃpreːçə]	'(he/she/it) would speak'
c.	[hoːx]	'high'	**h.**	[lɛçəln]	'to smile'
d.	[flʊxt]	'escape'	**i.**	[riːçən]	'to smell'
e.	[ɪç]	'I'	**j.**	[fɛçtən]	'to fence'

35. Farsi

Farsi is an Indo-European language of the Indo-Iranian family, which is the most widely spoken language in Iran. In the following data, do [r], [r̥], and [ɾ] belong to one, two, or three different phonemes? If they belong to different phonemes, give the pairs of forms that show this. If they are allophones of one (or two) phonemes, state the rule for their distribution. Which one would you choose to represent the phonemic form, and why?

[r] voiced trill		[r̥] voiceless trill		[ɾ] voiced flap	
a. [ærteʃ]	'army'	**g.** [ahar̥]	'starch'	**m.** [ahaɾi]	'starched'
b. [farsi]	'Persian'	**h.** [behtær̥]	'better'	**n.** [bæɾadær]	'brother'
c. [qædri]	'a little bit'	**i.** [hærntowr̥]	'however'	**o.** [beɾid]	'go'
d. [rah]	'road'	**j.** [tʃar̥]	'four'	**p.** [biɾæŋg]	'pale'
e. [ris]	'beard'	**k.** [tʃedʒur̥]	'what kind'	**q.** [tʃeɾa]	'why'
f. [ruz]	'day'	**l.** [ʃir̥]	'lion'	**r.** [daɾid]	'you have'

36. Bukusu

Bukusu is a Niger-Congo language of the Bantu family, spoken in Kenya. The nasal prefix [n-] indicates that the verb is in the first person ('I eat, go, sing,' etc.). Two different processes occur when [n] stands before another consonant. Look at these words and think about what is happening. The symbols [β], [ɲ], and [x] represent, respectively, a voiced bilabial fricative, a palatal nasal, and a voiceless velar fricative. (Remember that <ː> marks vowel length, so [iː] is a long vowel, not a sequence of two segments.)

a. [ndiːla]	'I hold'		**j.** [ɲdʒina]	'I scream'
b. [seːnda]	'I move'		**k.** [suna]	'I jump'
c. [ɲdʒuːŋga]	'I watch'		**l.** [xala]	'I cut'
d. [ŋgaβa]	'I divide'		**m.** [ŋgeta]	'I pour'
e. [mbiːma]	'I weigh'		**n.** [ndasa]	'I add'
f. [xola]	'I do'		**o.** [mbula]	'I roam'
g. [mbuka]	'I perish'		**p.** [ndula]	'I trample'
h. [fuka]	'I cook'		**q.** [fwaːra]	'I dress'
i. [funa]	'I break'		**r.** [mbala]	'I count'

    i. How does the behavior of a nasal differ when it stands before the different types of obstruents (stops, fricatives, and affricates)?

    ii. There are two phonological processes at work here. What are they?

    iii. Write phonological rules to capture the facts about the nasal prefix /n-/ in Bukusu.

Advanced Exercises

37. Greek

Modern Greek is an Indo-European language spoken in Greece. Examine the sounds [x], [k], [ç], and [c] in the following data. [k] represents a voiceless velar stop, [x] a voiceless velar fricative, [ç] a voiceless palatal fricative, and [c] a voiceless palatal stop. Which of these sounds are in contrastive distribution, and which are in complementary distribution? State the distribution of the allophones.

a. [kano]	'do'	**g.** [çeli]	'eel'	**m.** [krima]	'shame'
b. [xano]	'lose'	**h.** [ceri]	'candle'	**n.** [xufta]	'handful'
c. [çino]	'pour'	**i.** [çeri]	'hand'	**o.** [kufeta]	'bonbons'
d. [cino]	'move'	**j.** [kori]	'daughter'	**p.** [çina]	'goose'
e. [kali]	'charms'	**k.** [xori]	'dances'	**q.** [cina]	'china'
f. [xali]	'plight'	**l.** [xrima]	'money'		

38. Ebira

Examine the sounds [e] and [a] in the following data from Ebira, a Niger-Congo language of the Nupoid family, spoken in Nigeria. Do they appear to be allophones of separate phonemes or allophones of the same phoneme? If the two sounds are in complementary distribution, state the conditioning environments for the allophones.

a.	[mezi]	'I expect'		**e.**	[mazɪ]	'I am in pain'
b.	[meze]	'I am well'		**f.**	[mazɛ]	'I agree'
c.	[meto]	'I arrange'		**g.**	[matɔ]	'I pick'
d.	[metu]	'I beat'		**h.**	[matʊ]	'I send'

39. Ukrainian

Ukrainian is an Indo-European language of the Slavic family, spoken in Ukraine. Compare the masculine nominative singular forms of nouns with the vocative forms (nominative is used for the subject of a sentence, and vocative is used when calling to or addressing someone, as in "Hey, Robin."). There is a phonological change between the nominative and the vocative, which adds the ending [-e] to the nominative form. Three pairs of sounds are in allophonic variation. What are these pairs of sounds? What sort of phonological process is at work here? (There is a special name for it; see File 3.3.) What do you think is conditioning this alternation? (The symbols [ɦ] and [x] stand for a voiced glottal fricative and a voiceless velar fricative, respectively.)

	Nominative	*Vocative*	*Gloss*
a.	[rak]	[ratʃe]	'lobster'
b.	[junak]	[junatʃe]	'young man'
c.	[ʒuk]	[ʒutʃe]	'beetle'
d.	[pastux]	[pastuʃe]	'shepherd'
e.	[ptax]	[ptaʃe]	'bird'
f.	[boɦ]	[boʒe]	'God'
g.	[pluɦ]	[pluʒe]	'plough'

40. Maltese

Maltese is an Afro-Asiatic language of the Semitic family, spoken on the island of Malta in the Mediterranean. Consider how the indefinite (*a, some*) and the definite (*the*) are formed in the following words. Maltese forms the definite of a noun by attaching either /il-/ or /l-/ to it. Examine the data below and answer the questions that follow. (The symbol [ħ] represents a voiceless pharyngeal fricative.)

a.

Indefinite		*Definite*	
[fellus]	'chicken'	[ilfellus]	'the chicken'
[aria]	'air'	[laria]	'the air'
[mara]	'woman'	[ilmara]	'the woman'
[omm]	'mother'	[lomm]	'the mother'
[kelb]	'dog'	[ilkelb]	'the dog'
[ʔattus]	'cat'	[ilʔattus]	'the cat'
[ħitan]	'walls'	[ilħitan]	'the walls'
[abt]	'armpit'	[labt]	'the armpit'
[ispaniol]	'Spanish (language)'	[lispaniol]	'the Spanish (language)'

i. How can you predict the form of the definite marker?

ii. What natural classes of sounds are involved?

(cont.)

Now look at these nouns in the indefinite and the definite:

b.   *Indefinite*   *Definite*

[tiːn]	'a fig'	[ittiːn]	'the fig'
[dawl]	'a light'	[iddawl]	'the light'
[sħab]	'some clouds'	[issħab]	'the clouds'
[natura]	'nature'	[innatura]	'the nature'

The definite marker has the same phonemic form in these words as it had in part (a), but a phonological process has changed its phonetic form.

iii. What type of process is responsible for the change? How did it affect the definite marker?

iv. What natural class of sounds causes the change from the phonemic form to the various phonetic forms in part (b)?

v. Give the definite form of the following nouns:

        Indefinite   *Definite*

[daːr]	'a house'	_____	'the house'
[zift]	'a pitch'	_____	'the pitch'
[azzar]	'a piece of steel'	_____	'the steel'
[iŋgliz]	'English'	_____	'the English (lang.)'
[belt]	'a city'	_____	'the city'

Further Readings

Hayes, Bruce. 2009. *Introductory phonology.* Oxford: Wiley-Blackwell.

Odden, David. 2013. *Introducing phonology.* 2nd edn. Cambridge: Cambridge University Press.

Spencer, Andrew. 1996. *Phonology.* Oxford: Blackwell.

CHAPTER
4

....

Morphology

FILE 4.0

....

What Is Morphology?

Morphology is the component of mental grammar that deals with types of words and how words are formed out of smaller meaningful pieces and other words. Every speaker of English knows that *wind* is an English word, as are *unwind, re-wind, winding, windable, windy*, etc. However, even though *woman* is also an English word, none of the following are possible: *unwoman, rewoman, womaning, womanable, womany*, etc. Why is it that you can add *re-* to *wind* and get another word, but adding *re-* to *woman* does not result in a word?

Morphology as a subfield of linguistics studies the internal structure of words. It tries to describe which meaningful pieces of language can be combined to form words and what the consequences of such combinations are on the meaning or the grammatical function of the resulting word. For example, the addition of *re-* to *wind* modifies the meaning of *wind* in a certain way, and in fact, it does so in the same way when added to *unite* (*reunite*), or *play* (*replay*).

Contents

154

··

Words and Word Formation: The Nature of the Lexicon

4.1.1 What Are Words Like?

Every language has some (large) number of words available for its users to choose from as they need. This stock of words can be thought of as a sort of mental dictionary that language users—both speakers and hearers—have internalized as part and parcel of acquiring their particular language. We call this mental dictionary the **lexicon.** But what exactly are the sorts of things we might have in our lexicon?

In the study of morphology, one topic we will consider is how words are made, but first we must answer the question of what words are. Most everyone has an idea of what a word is. However, not all words are equally distinct from all other words. To begin, consider the following question:

• Are *cat* and *dog* the same word or different words?

Your answer, like that of almost anyone familiar with English, is very probably "Of course they are different words! Isn't it obvious?" The reasons that this is obvious include both differences in **form,** that is, what a word sounds like when spoken (/kæt/ is quite distinct from /dɑg/; refer to the chart at the end of the book for help with any unfamiliar symbols) and differences in **meaning,** such as the fact that you cannot simply use *cat* and *dog* interchangeably to mean the same thing. On the other hand, you might say *cat* and *dog* are both kinds of pets, so the words aren't 100% different; they do have something to do with each other. These sorts of similarities, however, are not enough to lead us to claim that *cat* and *dog* are the same word.

Now consider this question:

• Are *cat* and *catalog* the same word or different words?

Based on the discussion above, some readers might hesitate before answering this question. These two words share some elements of form, the /kæt/ part, but *catalog* doesn't seem to have the meaning of *cat* anywhere in it. Similarly, the words *kid* and *kidney* may sound partly the same, but it seems that they are not actually related in their meaning. Even though it sounds like there **could** be a *cat* and a *log* in *catalog,* or a *kid* in *kidney,* and such a connection might even be used as a source of humor in a joke or cartoon, English speakers consistently distinguish these pairs as each containing two unrelated words. Thus, when looking to see whether two items are the same word, we must consider both their phonological form and their meaning. Nevertheless, the thought that one word could be found "inside" another word is an important one.

4.1.2 Derivation

In order to get at the idea of words being inside one another, consider this third question.

- Are *cat* and *catty* ('spiteful') the same word or different words?

Here, the connection is a good bit closer than in the preceding word comparisons. Cats have gained a reputation for sometimes being vicious fighters, and it is most probably in this context that the word *catty* came into existence as part of the English language, meaning something like 'behaving like a cat in a certain respect.' So the words *cat* and *catty* are similar not only in terms of their form (the /kæt/ part) but also in terms of their meaning, since both (at least potentially) engender the image of nasty fighting. Is this enough to say that *cat* and *catty* are instances of the same word?

Apart from having a certain phonological form and a meaning, words also belong to **lexical categories,** which are also sometimes called parts of speech. Lexical categories are classes of words that differ in how other words can be constructed out of them. For example, if a word belongs to the lexical category **verb,** it is possible to add *-ing* or *-able* to it to get another word (e.g., *wind* and *drink* are verbs). If a word belongs to the lexical category **adjective,** you can add *-ness* or *-est* to it to get another word (e.g., *quick* and *happy* are adjectives). If a word belongs to the category **noun,** you can usually add *-s* to it to make it plural (e.g., *desk* and *dog* are nouns). You can add *-like* to nouns to form an adjective (e.g., *woman-like, city-like,* etc.). You can also add *-ly* to many adjectives and form an **adverb** (e.g., *quickly, happily,* and *readily*).

Nouns, verbs, adjectives, and adverbs are also called **open lexical categories** because new words added to the language usually belong to these categories. In contrast, **closed lexical categories** rarely acquire new members. Closed lexical categories include **pronouns** (e.g., *we, she, they*), **determiners** (e.g., *a, the, this, your*), **prepositions** (e.g., *on, of, under, for*), and **conjunctions** (e.g., *and, or, but*).[1]

Now we can consider whether *cat* and *catty* belong to the same lexical category. The answer is no—*cat* is a noun, while *catty* is an adjective. Even though *cat* and *catty* share elements of form and elements of meaning, the fact that the words belong to different parts of speech classes is a pretty clear sign that we are in fact dealing with two different words, rather than two "versions" of one word. There remains the feeling, however, that *cat* and *catty* are related in a way that *cat* and *dog,* on the one hand, and *cat* and *catalog,* on the other, are not. What is the nature of this relation? Let's compare some of the attributes of the two words.

(1) | | *CAT* | *CATTY* |
|---|---|---|
| Form: | /kæt/ | /kæti/ |
| Meaning: | 'domesticated feline' | 'spiteful, (fighting) like a domesticated feline' |
| Lexical Category: | noun | adjective |

With respect to form, *cat* is obviously a shorter word (i.e., contains fewer sounds) than *catty.* The meaning of *catty* also seems to be based on the meaning of *cat,* rather than the

---

[1]See File 5.4 for a discussion of syntactic categories. Lexical and syntactic categories may, but do not necessarily, coincide—for example, verb is a lexical but not a syntactic category. Lexical categories are distinguished based on how you can construct other words out of the words that belong to that category—their morphological properties. Syntactic categories are distinguished by how you can construct sentences and other phrases out of expressions that belong to that category—their syntactic properties. This is why they are not necessarily the same thing. Also note that words and larger multi-word expressions belong to a syntactic category, but only words belong to lexical categories. For example, *likes* belongs to a lexical and a syntactic category, but *likes Bob a lot* has only a syntactic category associated with it.

other way around. This suggests that *catty* is based on *cat* or, in other words, that *cat* is the **root** on which *catty* is built. This process of creating words out of other words is called **derivation.** Derivation takes one word and performs one or more "operations" on it, the result being some other word, often of a different lexical category. When the resulting new word is not of a different lexical category, the meaning of the root word is usually changed. For example, while *playable* is an adjective derived from the verb *play*, *replay* is a verb derived from a verb, and *unkind* is an adjective derived from an adjective, but with altered meanings: *re-* derives verbs meaning 'Verb again' (where "Verb" stands for the meaning of the root verb, e.g., *replay* 'play again'), and *un-* derives adjectives meaning 'not Adjective' (e.g., *unkind* 'not kind'). In the simplest case, the root is used "as-is," and one or more additional pieces are tacked onto it (but see the discussion of allomorphy in Section 4.5.1). The added pieces are called **affixes.** The thing to which the affixes attach is called the **stem.** In the case of *catty*, *cat* /kæt/ is both the root and the stem, and the affix is /i/, spelled <y>, which is attached to the end of the stem.[2] Affixes such as /i/ are called derivational affixes since they participate in derivational processes.

4.1.3 Inflection

At this point, there is one more question for you to consider:

• Are *cat* and *cats* the same word or different words?

In terms of phonological form, the difference between /kæt/ and /kæts/ is exactly the same in degree (that is, one additional sound) as the difference we saw between /kæt/ and /kæti/. With respect to meaning, however, *cat* and *cats* seem to refer to the same kind of thing, the difference being whether we want to talk about one (singular) or more than one (plural) of that thing. Moreover, these are both of the same lexical category, noun:

(2)	*CAT*	*CATS*
Form:	/kæt/	/kæts/
Meaning:	'domesticated feline'	'domesticated feline' (plural)
Lexical Category:	noun	noun

This time the answer to the "same or different" question is not as obvious as it was in the earlier cases. *Cats* represents a different grammatical form of the word *cat,* used just in case we need to talk about more than one member of the class of *cat.* The creation of different grammatical forms of words is called **inflection.** Inflection uses the same sorts of pieces, such as stems and affixes, or processes (see File 4.2) that derivation does, but the important difference is the linguistic entity that inflection creates—forms of words, rather than entirely new words. For example, in contrast to derivational affixes, inflectional affixes such as *-s* typically do not change the lexical category of the word—both *cat* and *cats* are nouns. Similarly, both *wind* and *winding* are considered verbs. The forms that result from inflection are often required by the grammar, regardless of any meaning difference. For example, while *cats* means 'more than one cat,' the plural ending is always required in English, even if the plural meaning is conveyed elsewhere: **I have four cat* is ungram-

---

[2]If you are wondering about the second "t" in *catty,* something not present in *cat,* it is important to notice that the 't' is purely a spelling convention and is not reflected directly in the pronunciation, that is, the /t/ in *catty* is not "twice as long" as the /t/ in *cat.* Although in many cases it does not cause any problems to refer to the spelling when talking about the structure of words, there are cases where the spelling can be misleading about what is actually going on with morphological processes. By and large we will disregard spelling; see File 1.3.

matical, even though the meaning is clear (see Files 5.1 and 5.2 for more on this topic), in contrast to the meaning differences of derived forms, e.g., *She is kind/She is unkind/She is not kind.* In sum, we find that the idea of "same" or "different" with respect to words can be unexpectedly complicated since words have a number of different properties that need to be considered; at the very least, these include phonological form, meaning, and lexical category.

There are actually very few inflectional affixes in English, so it may help to collect them in one table for easy reference (see (3)). (Table (3) shows all of the functions of inflectional affixes of English and most of the common forms that those affixes take. However, there are some less common affixes that do not appear in the table. For example, the plural of *ox* is formed with the suffix *-en,* but because the plural marker *-en* appears on very few words, it is not listed below.) Notice that all of the inflectional affixes in the table—and all of the inflectional affixes of English—are attached after the stem. (Derivational affixes in English may attach either before or after the stem.) This generalization does not hold for all languages, however.

(3) Inflectional affixes of English[3]

Function	Affix(es)	Attaches to	Example
3rd per. sing. present	*-s*	verbs	She wait**s** there at noon.
past tense	*-ed*	verbs	She wait**ed** there yesterday.
progressive aspect	*-ing*	verbs	She is wait**ing** there now.
past participle	*-en, -ed*	verbs	Jack has eat**en** the cookies.
			Jack has tast**ed** the cookies.
plural	*-s*	nouns	The chair**s** are in the room.
comparative	*-er*	adjectives,	Jill is tall**er** than Joe.
		adverbs	Joe runs fast**er** than Jill.
superlative	*-est*	adjectives,	Ted is the tall**est** in his class.
		adverbs	Michael runs fast**est** of all.

4.1.4   Some Notes about Morphemes

So far we have seen words that cannot be broken down into smaller parts, like *cat* and *catalog,* and words that contain two parts—a root and an affix—like *catty* and *cats.* Roots and affixes are called **morphemes**. A morpheme is typically defined as the smallest linguistic unit with a meaning (e.g., the morpheme *cat*) or a grammatical function (e.g., the morpheme *-ed* that indicates past tense). Of course, a morpheme also has a certain phonological form. Thus, there are no smaller forms that carry their own meaning or grammatical function than morphemes.

A few notes are in order about the terminology that we use to discuss morphemes. First, while a root by definition contains only one morpheme, a stem may contain more than one morpheme. For example, in *cattiness,* the root is *cat,* but the stem to which the derivational affix *-ness* is added is *catty,* which itself contains two morphemes, as we have

---

[3]The possessive suffix *-'s,* as in *My friend's house is gorgeous,* is sometimes given as an inflectional affix in English. However, this suffix attaches to noun phrases, not nouns (e.g., in [*My friend from China*]*'s house is gorgeous,* though *-'s* may look like it is suffixed to *China, China* is not what possesses the house, but rather *my friend from China*), and the result is a different syntactic category, so we do not include it here.

already observed. Each affix is also a single morpheme. Affixes that follow a stem are called **suffixes,** whereas affixes that precede a stem are called **prefixes.**

Another thing to notice about affixes is that sometimes different meanings or functions can be marked by the same phonetic shape (note the two -*s* affixes in table (3)). Affixes that sound alike but have different meanings or functions are **homophonous** (see Section 5.5.3). (Different words that sound the same are likewise said to be homophonous.) Another example is the case of -*er,* which can be either inflectional or derivational. As an inflectional suffix, it marks comparative degree on adjectives and adverbs (like in *taller, faster* in the table), but the same phonetic shape can be used to derive an agent noun from a verb, as in *speak, speak**er**.* These two -*er* affixes are homophonous with each other, and it is therefore important to consider not only form but also meaning when you are analyzing morphological structures.

Further evidence that both form and meaning are necessary when identifying morphemes comes from cases of words that merely appear to contain multiple morphemes, but in fact do not. Look again at the word *catalog.* In terms of both its orthography and its pronunciation, it appears to contain the words *cat, a,* and *log.* Neither felines nor sections of tree limbs have anything to do with 'inventories,' though. Thus, we conclude that *catalog* is monomorphemic: it is made of only one part.

As a final caution, do not confuse word length with number of morphemes. Some words, such as *Madagascar, lugubrious,* or *pumpernickel,* are quite long but contain only one morpheme; other words, such as *ads,* are very short but contain two morphemes.

4.1.5 Classifying Elements in Morphology

In morphology, the most basic act of analysis is a comparison of words based on form, meaning, and lexical category. Such comparisons allow for the segmentation of words into the smaller parts that they contain, i.e., morphemes. From such an analysis, it becomes apparent that words and affixes do not share the same status in the language overall. Simple words like *cat, dog, book,* and *walk* cannot be broken down into smaller meaningful pieces—they consist of exactly one morpheme. Affixes like -*ing* or -*y* also consist of only one morpheme but cannot stand alone like single-morpheme words.

Morphemes such as the simple words above are called **free morphemes** because they can be used as words all by themselves. Affixes, on the other hand, always have to be attached to the stem of some word in order to be used. Because they cannot stand alone, affixes are called **bound morphemes.** Affixes are not the only things that can be bound. There are some roots that do not have stand-alone forms; that is, they only appear with one or more affixes attached. For example, the words *infer, confer, refer, defer, prefer,* and *transfer* all seem to have a root -*fer* (stem /fɹ/) with a prefix attached to its left. This root, however, does not correspond to any free morpheme in English. The same is true of *boysen-* and *rasp-* in *boysenberry* and *raspberry.* While *berry* is a free morpheme, neither *boysen-* nor *rasp-* can stand alone. Morphemes of this sort are called **bound roots** because although they do seem to have some associated basic meaning (in the case of -*fer,* the meaning is something like 'carry, bring'), they are unable to stand alone as words in their own right. Other examples are -*ceive* (*conceive, receive, deceive*) and -*sist* (*resist, desist, consist, subsist*). Can you think of a single basic meaning for each of these bound roots?

Note that bound roots, while fairly common in English, are not necessarily morphological analyses that all English speakers will agree on. Many of the bound roots, including -*fer,* -*sist,* and -*ceive,* are the result of English borrowings from Latin (often via Old French; see also File 12.2), and are not **productive** (i.e., currently used to make new words; this is also true of some affixes in English). For many speakers of English, words such as *transfer* and *transport* or *boysenberry* cannot usually be broken down any further into morphemes, but speakers are able to make the generalization that words beginning with *trans-* must consist of a prefix plus a root of some sort, since *trans-* is productive; and since *boysenberry* is obviously a *berry* of some sort, it is likely to be a compound like *blueberry* or *blackberry,* even if we're not sure what *boysen* means.

Traditionally, a distinction is also made between **content** and **function morphemes.** Content morphemes are said to have more concrete meaning than function morphemes. Function morphemes, on the other hand, contain primarily grammatically relevant information. Sometimes, it is said that content morphemes carry semantic content (roughly, they refer to something out in the world), while function morphemes do not. A free root like *cat* is a prototypical content morpheme with a fairly concrete meaning. It carries semantic content in the sense that it refers to certain feline individuals out in the world. The affix *-ing*, on the other hand, is a prototypical function morpheme; it marks aspect[4] on a verb but doesn't have semantic content in the way that *cat* does.

Content morphemes include all derivational affixes, bound roots, and free roots that belong to the lexical categories of noun, verb, adjective, and adverb. Free content morphemes, that is, nouns, verbs, adjectives, and adverbs, are also called **content words.**

Function morphemes include all inflectional affixes and free roots that belong to lexical categories preposition, determiner, pronoun, or conjunction. Free function morphemes, that is, prepositions, determiners, pronouns, and conjunctions, are also called **function words.**

(4) Possible kinds of morphemes

	Content Morphemes	**Function Morphemes**
Free Morphemes	• Content words:	• Function words:
	• Nouns	• Determiners
	• Verbs	• Prepositions
	• Adjectives	• Pronouns
	• Adverbs	• Conjunctions
Bound Morphemes	• Bound roots	• Inflectional affixes
	• Derivational affixes	

While it may be useful to maintain the distinction between content and function morphemes, we must warn you that the distinction is not always clear-cut, and the classification of morphemes into these two classes may seem counterintuitive at times. For example, the preposition *under* is classified as a function morpheme, yet it seems to have a pretty concrete meaning—so concrete, in fact, that it would be easy to draw a picture to represent its meaning. On the other hand, the derivational affix *-ness* is classified as a content morpheme, but it is difficult to spell out what its meaning is. Its function seems to be to turn adjectives into nouns. While this is grammatically relevant, it would be difficult to draw a picture to capture the meaning of *-ness*. It can also be difficult to appreciate the meaning contribution of bound roots, which are classified as content morphemes. If anything, *under* may seem to be more meaningful than *-ness*, but their classification does not

---

[4]Aspect refers to how some event unfolds in time, for example, whether it is completed, ongoing, frequently occurring, etc., but it does not specify the actual time at which this event unfolds. For example, *was eating* and *will be eating* have different tense marking (past vs. future), but the same aspect (progressive, meaning that the eating event is depicted as ongoing or in progress); *was eating* and *has eaten* have different aspect, the former indicating that the action was in progress, the other that the action was completed.

necessarily support that intuition. If you are having trouble determining whether a morpheme is classified as a content or a function morpheme, refer to the table in (4) for help.

Given any particular morpheme, the diagram in (5) may help you decide what sort of morpheme it is.

(5) A flowchart for identifying the status of morphemes

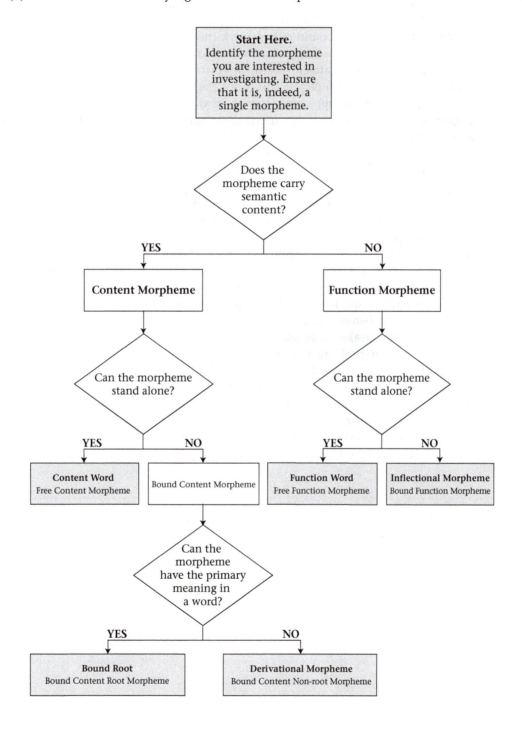

4.1.6   Derived and Inflected Words in the Lexicon

We have said that both derivation and inflection are ways of forming words, but in what sense is it meant that new words are being "formed"? Do we mean that every time a speaker uses a morphologically complex word, the brain reconstructs it? Some linguists maintain that this is the case. They claim that in a speaker's mental dictionary, the lexicon, each morpheme is listed individually along with other information such as its meaning, its lexical category (if it is a free morpheme), and rules for how and when it is allowed to attach to stems (if it is a bound morpheme). Indeed, that does seem to be what happens for some morphological processes in some languages. Thus, each time a word is used, it is re-formed from the separate entries in the lexicon of the parts that make it up. There is evidence, however, that indicates this is not the case for all languages; even morphologically complex words can apparently have a separate entry in the adult lexicon. That is, as English speakers, when we hear a morphologically complex word, such as *nonrecyclable,* we do not have to pull together the meanings of *non-, re-, cycle,* and *-able.* Rather, we by and large access the whole word together. (Refer to File 9.5 for more information about how words are stored in the lexicon.)

Even if not all language users do "build" morphologically complex words and word-forms every time they use them, there are still other reasons to consider derivation a process of word formation. In describing a language, the term *formation* refers to the **systematic relationships** between roots and the words derived from them on the one hand, and, on the other hand, between a word and its various inflected (i.e., grammatical) forms.

Furthermore, speakers of a given language also are often aware of these relationships. We see evidence of this when new words are formed based on patterns that exist in the lexicon. For example, a speaker of English may never have heard words such as *unsmelly, smell-ability,* or *smellful* before, but he or she would certainly understand what they mean. The fact that English speakers may use a word like *stick-to-it-ive-ness* illustrates that speakers of a language have no problem accessing the patterns in their lexicons and applying them for interpreting unfamiliar words . . . and even for creating them!

Rules that speakers are able to apply to form novel words are termed productive rules. (Refer to File 1.4.) English has examples of both nonproductive morphemes and productive ones; for example, the suffix *-tion* is generally not used by speakers to form new nouns, whereas the suffix *-ness* is. Over long periods of time, different affixes or other morphological processes may become more or less productive (see File 13.4).

FILE 4.2

....

Morphological Processes

4.2.1 The Processes of Forming Words

In the previous file, we looked at how words are put together and marked for grammatical features such as number and tense. We have seen that English makes use of derivational affixes to create more words than would exist with free morphemes alone. Of course, English is not the only language that enlarges its vocabulary in this way. When linguists observe a language that uses affixation to form additional words, they note that the occurring combinations are systematic, i.e., rule-governed. Because these combinations are rule-governed, we can say that a process is at work—namely, a **word formation process**—since new words or forms of words are being formed. What we will consider in this file are the ways in which languages create new words from existing words, and the grammatical forms of words. We shall see that many languages employ affixation but that many other languages employ other processes. (See Files 12.1 and 13.4 for still more ways in which new words come into use in a language, and note that some of the processes discussed here for English are not currently productive.)

4.2.2 Affixation

To this point, our morphological discussion has been limited to the process of **affixation.** Although English uses only **prefixes** (affixes that precede the stem they attach to) and **suffixes** (affixes that follow the stem they attach to), many other languages use **infixes** as well. Infixes are inserted within the root morpheme. Note that English has no regular infixes. At first glance, some students think that *-ful* in a word like *doubtfully* is an infix because it occurs in the middle of a word; File 4.4 will provide a more thorough account of how affixation works and show why this must be an incorrect analysis. In some colloquial speech or slang, there is some evidence of English infixes, but although some of these forms may be moderately productive, they are far from routinized. Tagalog, on the other hand, one of the major languages of the Philippines, uses infixes quite extensively. For example, the infix *-um-* is used to form the infinitive form of verbs:

(1) | *Verb Stem* | | *Infinitive* | |
|---|---|---|---|
| lakad | 'walk' | lumakad | 'to walk' |
| bili | 'buy' | bumili | 'to buy' |
| kuha | 'take, get' | kumuha | 'to take, to get' |

4.2.3 Affixation in Signed Languages

Signed languages make use of affixation as well: in the same way that a certain phonological form may either precede or follow a stem in spoken languages, so may a particular gesture precede or follow another gesture in a signed language. As an example, consider a suffix used in American Sign Language used to indicate negation. Recall from Section 2.7.1 that

163

phonetic parameters of sign language gestures include place of articulation, handshape, movement, hand orientation, and non-manual markers. This particular suffix is a movement: a rapid turning over of the hand, affixed to the end of the root sign that it is negating. The result of turning the hand is that the hand orientation in the suffix is reversed from the hand orientation in the root word. Therefore, the suffix is called the REVERSAL-OF-ORIENTATION suffix. Examples follow. Notice that in each case the two signs begin in the same way, but in the negated form there is an additional step of turning the hand away from its original orientation.

 Examples of the REVERSAL-OF-ORIENTATION suffix in ASL

(2) a. LIKE

© 2006, William Vicars, www.Lifeprint.com. Adapted by permission.

b. DON'T-LIKE

© 2006, William Vicars, www.Lifeprint.com. Adapted by permission.

(3) a. WANT

© 2006, William Vicars, www.Lifeprint.com. Adapted by permission.

b. DON'T-WANT

© 2006, William Vicars, www.Lifeprint.com. Adapted by permission.

(4) a. KNOW

b. DON'T-KNOW

By looking at (2)–(4), you will see that the exact form of the negation suffix differs in different environments. That is, although the movement is the same in each case (a turning of the hand(s) away from where it was originally facing), the location and orientation of the suffix are borrowed from the stem. Therefore, DON'T-LIKE and DON'T-WANT are articulated in front of the torso where LIKE and WANT are articulated, but DON'T-KNOW is articulated on the side of the head, where KNOW is articulated. This is no different from spoken languages, in which the form of an affix may assimilate to some aspect of the form of the stem. For example, in English we find the *in-* prefix which changes its form in such words as *irresponsible, impossible,* and *illogical.* Although the REVERSAL-OF-ORIENTATION suffix assimilates to a root word, the affix is clearly a second gesture that follows the root sign. Thus, so far, we have seen only cases where affixation in signed languages works very similarly to the way that it does in spoken languages.

Additionally, signed languages allow a kind of affixation that is not possible in spoken languages. For spoken languages, we considered affixes that can appear at the beginning, in the middle, and at the end of a stem. What we have not considered are affixes that are articulated at the same time as the stem. The reason is that in spoken language it is not possible to articulate two morphemes at the same time! In many cases, however, it is possible to articulate two morphemes in a visual-gestural language at the same time. (Recall from File 2.7 that phonemes in signs also routinely co-occur.) When affixes appear at the same time as each other, we say that they are **simultaneous**. Examples of simultaneous morphology have been found in every signed language that has been studied. This concept seems rather foreign to individuals who have studied only spoken languages, but it is not terribly complicated. Although signed languages allow affixation to be manifested in a way that spoken languages do not, by and large the rules for affixation are exactly the same for simultaneous morphology as for the linear morphology we have considered so far.

Most simultaneous morphology—from every signed language that has been studied—is inflectional rather than derivational. A form of simultaneous affixation that is very common across signed languages is verb inflection: morphological marking of subject and object on the verb. The general idea is that the sign for the verb originates in one location in order to mark the identity of the individual performing the action (the subject) and terminates in another location to indicate the object, while other aspects of the sign remain the same. This type of verbal inflection is used extensively in some signed languages (e.g., Idioma de Signos Nicaragense, a signed language of Nicaragua) and hardly at all in others (e.g., Kata Kolok, a signed language of Bali). In (5) is an example from American Sign Language. Although direction of movement differs depending on subject and object, handshape and the general type of movement (an arching path from one location to another) are consistent regardless of particular inflection.

(5) GIVE (inflected for various subjects and objects)

'I give to you'   'I give to him/her/it.'   'You give to him/her/it.'

'You give to me.'   'She/he/it gives to me.'   'She/he/it gives to you.'

A number of other verbs in ASL show similar patterns, including MEET, which can be found in (7) in File 2.7. Others include SHOW, ASK, and SEE. Note that while many signed languages have very similar verbal inflection systems, they are not entirely the same. Furthermore, different languages have different sets of verbs that inflect in this way: the Taiwan SL sign for 'teach' does inflect in this way, while the ASL sign for 'teach' does not.

A second example of simultaneous inflectional morphology in ASL is adverbial inflection of adjectives. For example, the sign HOT can be modified to mean VERY HOT by holding the first location of the sign for a small amount longer and then releasing it very quickly, as shown in (9) of Section 2.7.7. (Notice that the signer is moving his hand so quickly in the third cell of VERY HOT that the image of his hand is completely blurred!)

To articulate the VERY morpheme, handshape, orientation, location, and path of movement remain the same, but the way that the movement is performed is different.[1] This "rapid release" morpheme can apply to many ASL adjectives.

4.2.4 Compounding

Compounding is a process that forms new words not by means of affixes but from two or more independent words. The words that are the parts of the compound can be free morphemes, words derived by affixation, or even words formed by compounding themselves. Examples in English of these three types are shown in (6).

---

[1]The signer also can use non-manual markers for emphasis; this is equivalent to a speaker using features of his voice such as pitch or volume to alter the interpretation of a word. Imagine an English speaker saying, "I accidentally touched the pot right after it came from the oven, and it was HOT!"

(6) Examples of English compounds

Compounding of Free Morphemes	Compounding of Affixed Words	Compounding of Compounded Words
girlfriend	air-conditioner	lifeguard chair
blackbird	ironing board	aircraft carrier
textbook	watch-maker	life-insurance salesman

Notice that in English, compound words are not represented consistently in writing. Sometimes they are written together, sometimes they are written with a hyphen, and sometimes they are written separately. We know, however, that compounding forms words and not syntactic phrases, regardless of how the compound is written, because the stress patterns are different for compounds. Think about how you would say the words *red neck* in each of the two following sentences:

(7) a. The wool sweater gave the man a red neck.
 b. If you want to make Tim really angry, call him a redneck.

Compounds that have words in the same order as phrases have primary stress on the first word only, while individual words in phrases have independent primary stress. Some other examples are listed in (8). (Primary stress is indicated by ´ on the vowel.)

(8) *Compounds*   *Phrases*
 bláckbird   bláck bírd
 mákeup   máke úp

Because English does not consistently write compounds as one word or joined with hyphens, speakers are sometimes unaware of how productive compounding is and how complex the structures can be (even if linguists may not always agree on the analysis of longer compounds as resulting from morphological processes versus syntactic processes). Some examples of longer compounds in English are given in (9). Can you think of others?

(9) a. income tax preparation fees
 b. mint chocolate chip ice cream waffle cone

German is one of the many other languages that use compounding to form new words. Some examples of the numerous compounds in German are listed in (10).

(10)

Compound	*Meaning*	*Meanings of Individual Morphemes*
Muttersprache	'native language'	< mother language
Schreibtisch	'desk'	< write table
stehenbleiben	'stand (still)'	< stand remain
Wunderkind	'child prodigy'	< miracle child
Parkzeitüberschreitung	'exceeding of the amount of time one is allowed to park'	< park time exceedance

4.2.5 Reduplication

Reduplication is a process of forming new words by doubling either an entire free morpheme (**total reduplication**) or part of it (**partial reduplication**). English makes no systematic use of reduplication as a part of the language's grammar. There are a very few nonsystematic cases of lexical reduplication, however, such as "bye bye." Furthermore, in colloquial speech, we may often see reduplication used to indicate intensity; this can happen with verbs, adjectives, and nouns. Consider examples (11)–(13): what does the reduplicated word mean in each case?

(11) Do you just like him as a friend, or do you like-like him?

(12) That shirt isn't what I had in mind; it's much too pale of a green. I want a shirt that is green-green.

(13) Yesterday we just went out for coffee, but this weekend we're going on a date-date.

As you can see, though, each of these uses is very restricted to the context in which it appears. We wouldn't want to say that *green-green* is a word of English. On the other hand, there are some languages that make extensive use of reduplication. In these languages, reduplication can serve some of the same functions that affixation serves in English.

Indonesian uses total reduplication as an inflectional process to form the plurals of nouns:

(14) | *Singular* | | *Plural* | |
|---|---|---|---|
| rumah | 'house' | rumahrumah | 'houses' |
| ibu | 'mother' | ibuibu | 'mothers' |
| lalat | 'fly' | lalatlalat | 'flies' |

ASL also uses reduplication for some (though not all) of its plural formation and for other derivational and inflectional purposes.

Tagalog uses partial reduplication for both inflection and derivation. For example, partial reduplication is used inflectionally to indicate the future tense of verbs:

(15) | *Verb Stem* | | *Future Tense* | |
|---|---|---|---|
| bili | 'buy' | bibili | 'will buy' |
| kain | 'eat' | kakain | 'will eat' |
| pasok | 'enter' | papasok | 'will enter' |

Notice that the reduplicated piece, the **reduplicant,** can be described phonologically as the first syllable of the stem.

In conjunction with the prefix *maŋ-* (which often changes the initial consonant of a following morpheme to a nasal with the same place of articulation as the original initial consonant), Tagalog also uses reduplication to derive words for occupations:[2]

(16) | *Occupation* | *Morphemes* | *Verb* | | |
|---|---|---|---|---|
| [mamimili] | 'buyer' | < /maŋ+bi+bili/ | [bili] | 'buy' |
| [manunulat] | 'writer' | < /maŋ+su+sulat/ | [sulat] | 'write' |
| [maŋʔiʔisda] | 'fisherman' | < /maŋ+ʔi+ʔisda/ | [ʔisda] | 'fish' |

---

[2]Since the phonological content of the reduplicated piece (the reduplicant) depends on the phonological shape of the stem it attaches to, the "morpheme" in reduplication is the presence of the reduplicant, rather than the phonological shape of the reduplicant.

4.2.6 Alternations

Besides adding an affix to a morpheme or copying all or part of the morpheme to make new words or make morphological distinctions, it is also possible to make morpheme-internal modifications, called **alternations.** While alternations have to do with the sounds in a particular word pair or larger word set, these alternations mark morphological distinctions, whereas the rules in the phonology files (see File 3.3) dealt with pronunciation independent of meaning. The following are examples of morphological alternations in English:

(17) Although the usual pattern of plural formation is to add a suffix, some English plurals make an internal modification for this inflected form:

man	men	[æ]	~ [ɛ] ([æ] alternates with [ɛ] in these forms)
woman	women	[ʊ]	~ [ɪ]
goose	geese	[u]	~ [i]
foot	feet	[ʊ]	~ [i]

(18) The usual pattern of past and past participle formation is to add an affix, but some verbs show an internal alternation:

ring	rang	rung	[ɪ]~[æ]~[ʌ]
drink	drank	drunk	
swim	swam	swum	
feed	fed	fed	[i]~[ɛ]~[ɛ]
hold	held	held	[oʊ]~[ɛ]~[ɛ]

Some verbs show both an alternation and the addition of an affix to one form:

(19)
Root	*Alternation*	*Alternation and Affixation*
break	broke	broken
speak	spoke	spoken
bite	bit	bitten
fall	fell	fallen
give	gave	given

Although the above examples are all inflectional, sometimes a derivational relation such as a change in part of speech class can be indicated by means of alternations. In the case of (20), the final consonant of a noun voices in order to become a verb.

(20)
Nouns		*Verbs*	
strife (n)	[stɹaɪf]	strive (v)	[stɹaɪv]
teeth (n)	[tiθ]	teethe (v)	[tið]
breath (n)	[bɹɛθ]	breathe (v)	[bɹið]
use (n)	[jus]	use (v)	[juz]

Alternation is also a fairly common phenomenon in languages of the world. The following data come from Hebrew and show derivational alternation between nouns and verbs:

(21) **Verbs**   **Nouns**
       [limed]   'he taught'   [limud]   'lesson'
       [sijem]   'he finished'   [sijum]   'end'
       [tijel]   'he traveled'   [tijul]   'trip'
       [bikeɣ]   'he visited'   [bikuɣ]   'visit (noun)'
       [dibeɣ]   'he spoke'   [dibuɣ]   'speech'

4.2.7 Suppletion

Languages that employ morphological processes to form words will usually have a regular, productive way of doing so according to one or more of the processes discussed above. They might also have some smaller classes of words that are irregular because they mark the same morphological distinction by another of these processes. Sometimes, however, a root will have one or more inflected forms phonetically unrelated to the shape of the root. This completely irregular situation is called **suppletion.**

A small number of English verbs have suppletive past tenses:

(22) **Present**   **Past**
       [ɪz]   is   [wʌz]   was
       [goʊ]   go   [wɛnt]   went

Interestingly, verbs derived from the irregular *go* also show similar suppletion in their past stems: *undergo*, [past] *underwent.* Two common English adjectives—*good* and *bad*—have suppletive comparative and superlative forms.

(23) **Adj**   **Comparative**   **Superlative**
       [gʊd]   good   [bɛɹ̩]   better   [bɛst]   best
       [bæd]   bad   [wɹ̩s]   worse   [wɹ̩st]   worst

Note that there is simply no systematic similarity between the stems of these various inflected forms. That is, we could not write a productive or general rule that would account for the forms we find.

Noun inflection in Classical Arabic provides another example of suppletion:

(24) **Singular**   **Plural**
       [marʔat]   'woman'   [nisaːʔ]   'women'

The usual plural form for Classical Arabic nouns ending in [at], however, involves the lengthening of the vowel of this ending (a morphological alternation):

(25) **Singular**   **Plural**
       [diraːsat]   '(a) study'   [diraːsaːt]   'studies'
       [harakat]   'movement'   [harakaːt]   'movements'

Any given language will likely have some example(s) of suppletion, but these typically constitute a minority class within the lexicon.

FILE 4.3

Morphological Types of Languages

4.3.1 Classifying Languages by Morphological Type

So far, we have considered a number of processes that a language might utilize in order to form words: affixation, compounding, reduplication, alternation, and suppletion. Some languages make use of a number of these processes; others make use of very few; still others make use of none at all. Languages can be classified according to the way in which they use or don't use morphological processes. There are two basic morphological types, **analytic** and **synthetic,** the latter having several subtypes.

4.3.2 Analytic Languages

Analytic languages are so called because they are made up of sequences of free morphemes—each word consists of a single morpheme, used by itself with meaning and function intact. Purely analytic languages, also called **isolating** languages, do not use affixes to compose words. Semantic and grammatical concepts that are often expressed in other languages through the use of affixes are expressed by the use of separate words in analytic languages.

    Mandarin Chinese is an example of a language that has a highly analytic structure. In the example sentences below, for instance, the concept of plurality and the concept of the past tense are communicated in Mandarin through the use of invariant function words rather than the use of a change of form (cf. English, *I* to *we* to indicate plurality) or the use of an affix (cf. English *-ed* for past tense).

  (1) [wɔ   mən   tan   tɕin]   (tones omitted)
      I   *plural play   piano*
     'We are playing the piano'

  (2) [wɔ   mən   tan   tɕin   lə]   (tones omitted)
      I   *plural play   piano past*
     'We played the piano'

    Note that the form of 'we' (I-plural) that is used in the subject position is [wɔ mən] and that the pronoun has the same form when it is used as the object, placed after the verb:

  (3) [ta   da   wɔ   mən]   (tones omitted)
      s/he hit(s) I   plural
     'S/he hits us'

Only the position of a word in a sentence shows its function. English is unlike Mandarin in this respect, at least for some words, since the personal pronoun *we* is changed in form to *us* when it is used as the object of a verb. But English is like Mandarin in that word order is used to show the functions of nouns in a sentence, and in that nouns (unlike pronouns) are not marked by affixes to show their functions. For example, in the sentence *Girls like cats* the noun *girls* functions as the subject, and the noun *cats* as the direct object, but just the opposite is true of *Cats like girls*; these differences in function are signaled only by the order of words in the sentence in both English and Mandarin. Nonanalytic languages may use morphology to mark these differences.

Although only affixation has been explicitly mentioned in this section, recognize that prototypical analytic languages make use of no morphological processes at all.

4.3.3 Synthetic Languages

In **synthetic languages,** bound morphemes are attached to other morphemes, so a word may be made up of several meaningful elements. The bound morphemes may add another element of meaning to the stem (derivation) or indicate the grammatical function of the stem in a sentence (inflection). Recall that the term *stem* refers to that part of the word to which affixes are added. It may consist of one or more morphemes: for instance, in *reruns, -s* is added to the stem *rerun,* which is itself made up of two morphemes: *re-* and the root *run.*

Hungarian is a synthetic language. In the examples below, bound morphemes show the grammatical functions of nouns in their sentences:

(4) [ɔz   ɛmber   laːtjɔ   ɔ   kucaːt]
     the   man-(subject)   sees   the   dog-(object)
     'The man sees the dog'

(5) [ɔ   kucɔ   laːtjɔ   ɔz   ɛmbɛrt]
     the   dog   sees   the   man-(object)
     'The dog sees the man'

As mentioned above, in English it is the position in the sentence of the noun phrase *the man* or *the dog* that tells one whether the phrase is the subject or object of the verb, but in Hungarian, a noun phrase may appear either before or after the verb in a sentence and be recognized as the subject or object in either position because it is marked with a bound morpheme (the suffix [t]) if it is the direct object. (Many synthetic languages behave similarly.) Therefore, both examples below mean the same thing, even though the position of the noun phrase meaning 'the man' is different with respect to the verb meaning 'sees.'

(6) [ɔ   kucɔ   laːtjɔ   ɔz   ɛmbɛrt]
     the   dog   sees   the   man-(object)
     'The dog sees the man'

(7) [ɔz   ɛmbɛrt   laːtjɔ   ɔ   kucɔ]
     the   man-(object)   sees   the   dog
     'The dog sees the man'

Synthetic languages like Hungarian may also use bound morphemes to indicate some concepts that English signals by means of free morphemes. For example, Hungarian indicates personal possession and location by the use of suffixes attached to the stem ([haːz], 'house'), whereas in English these concepts are expressed by the use of free morphemes. Examples are given in (8) and (9).

(8) [ɔ   haːzunk   zøld]
the   house-our   green
'Our house is green'

(9) [ɔ   seːkɛd   ɔ   haːzunkbɔn   vɔn]
the   chair-your   the   house-our-in   is
'Your chair is in our house'

4.3.4 The First Type of Synthetic Language: Agglutinating Languages

To be more specific, the kind of synthesis (putting together) of morphemes we find in Hungarian is known as **agglutination**. In agglutinating languages, like Hungarian, the morphemes are joined together relatively "loosely." That is, it is usually easy to determine where the boundaries between morphemes are, as shown in (10) and (11).

(10) [haːz↓unk↓bɔn] [haːz-od-bɔn]
house-our-in   house-your-in
'in our house'   'in your house'

(11) [haːz-unk]   [haːz-ɔd]
house-our   house-your
'our house'   'your house'

Swahili is another example of an agglutinating language. Swahili verb stems take prefixes to indicate the person of the subject of the verb (first, second, or third) and also to indicate the tense of the verb, as in the following list of forms for the verb 'read':

(12) [ni-na-soma]   *I-present-read*   'I am reading'
[u-na-soma]   *you-present-read*   'You are reading'
[a-na-soma]   *s/he-present-read*   'S/he is reading'
[ni-li-soma]   *I-past-read*   'I was reading'
[u-li-soma]   *you-past-read*   'You were reading'
[a-li-soma]   *s/he-past-read*   'S/he was reading'
[ni-ta-soma]   *I-future-read*   'I will read'
[u-ta-soma]   *you-future-read*   'You will read'
[a-ta-soma]   *s/he-future-read*   'S/he will read'

A second characteristic feature of agglutinating languages is that each bound morpheme (ordinarily) carries only one meaning: *ni* = 'I,' *u* = 'you,' *a* = 's/he,' *na* = 'present,' etc.

4.3.5 The Second Type of Synthetic Language: Fusional Languages

In **fusional languages,** another subtype of synthetic language, words are formed by adding bound morphemes to stems, just as in agglutinating languages, but in fusional languages the affixes may not be easy to separate from the stem. It is often rather hard to tell where one morpheme ends and the next begins; the affixes are characteristically fused with the stem, and there are often alternations to the forms of both the stems and affixes (see the discussion of allomorphs in Section 4.5.1).

Spanish is a fusional language that has suffixes attached to the verb stem to indicate the person (I/you/he/she/it) and number (singular/plural) of the subject of the verb. It is often difficult to analyze a verb form into its stem and suffix, however, because there is often a fusion of the two morphemes. For example, in the following forms:

(13) [ablo] 'I am speaking'
     [abla] 'S/he is speaking'
     [able] 'I spoke'

the morphemes in (14) can be isolated:

(14) [-o]   first-person singular present tense
     [-a]   third-person singular present tense
     [-e]   first-person singular past tense

However, although these forms would suggest a stem *abl-* that means 'speak,' such a form never appears in isolation in Spanish. There is no Spanish free morpheme *abl*.

Fusional languages often differ from agglutinating languages in another way as well: agglutinating languages usually have only one meaning indicated by each affix, as noted above, but in fusional languages a single affix more frequently conveys several meanings simultaneously. Russian is a fusional language in which bound morphemes attached to verb stems indicate both the person and the number of the subject of the verb and the tense of the verb at the same time. For example, in (15) the bound form [-jɛt] signifies third person as well as singular and present tense:

(15) [ʧitajɛt]   's/he is reading'

In (16) the suffix [-l] means singular, masculine, and past tense, simultaneously. (Compare the Swahili examples in (12), in which person and tense are signaled by separate affixes.)

(16) [ʧital] 'he was reading'

4.3.6 The Third Type of Synthetic Language: Polysynthetic Languages

In some synthetic languages, highly complex words may be formed by combining several stems and affixes; this is usually a matter of making nouns (subjects, objects, etc.) into parts of the verb forms. Such languages are called **polysynthetic.** Sora, a language spoken in India, allows such **incorporation** of objects (subjects, instruments, etc.) into verbs:

(17) [aninɲamjɔten]   —word of Sora
     [anin - ɲam - jɔ   - te   - n]   —the same word divided into morphemes
     he   catch   fish   non-past   do
     'He is fish-catching'
     i.e., 'He is catching fish'

(18) [ɲamkɪdtenai]   —word of Sora
     [ɲam - kɪd - te   - n   - ai]   —the same word divided into morphemes
     catch   tiger   non-past   do   first person agent
     'I will tiger-catch'
     i.e., 'I will catch a tiger'

Such verbs are roughly comparable to an English construction like *baby-sit* or *trout-fish*, but the polysynthetic constructions may be more complex, including several nouns as well as a variety of other affixes:

(19) [pɔpoʊŋkoʊntam]   —word of Sora
     [pɔ   - poʊŋ - koʊn - t   - am]   —the same word divided into morphemes
     stab   belly   knife   non-past   you (sg.)
     '(Someone) will stab you with a knife in (your) belly'

(20) [ɲɛnədʒdʒadarsiəm]   —word of Sora
     [ɲɛn - ədʒ - dʒa   - dar   - si   - əm] —the same word divided into morphemes
     I   not   receive   cooked rice   hand   you (sg.)
     'I will not receive cooked rice from your hands'

The incorporated or "built-in" form of the noun is not necessarily identical to its free form. For example, in Sora, the free form of 'tiger' is [kɨna], that of 'hand' is [siʔi], and that of 'knife' is [kondi].

While these are the basic ways languages can be classified typologically, keep in mind that the boundaries are often not clear-cut, and languages can be more accurately described as residing somewhere along a continuum between analytic and synthetic, or between agglutinating, fusional, and polysynthetic, rather than fitting neatly into one specific category. Languages often show a mixture of features and can also change over time. English, for example, used to be much more synthetic than it currently is (like many Indo-European languages, it was fusional). Old English made use of much more inflectional morphology than Modern English—for example, marking nouns for case, number, and gender. Present-day English is much more analytic than older stages of the language were, but it still can be considered to be fusional, since it makes use of many highly productive inflectional and derivational affixes, and a single affix is able to represent more than one meaning (e.g., in *it runs*, the *-s* indicates third person, singular, and present tense).

The Hierarchical Structure of Derived Words

4.4.1 How Words Are Put Together

When we examine words composed of only two morphemes, a stem and an affix, we implicitly know something about the way in which the affix combined with its stem. That is, the word was formed via the addition of the affix to the stem. By itself, this fact seems neither particularly significant nor particularly interesting. After all, there are no other options. However, when a word comprises more than two morphemes, the order in which the morphemes are put together becomes a more significant question. In order to consider such questions, we first will note two facts about morphemes and lexical categories.

First, the stems with which a given affix may combine (its **input**) normally belong to the same lexical category. For example, the suffix *-able* attaches freely to verbs, but not to adjectives or nouns. Thus, we can add this suffix to the verbs *adjust, break, compare,* and *debate,* but not to the adjectives *asleep, lovely, happy,* and *strong,* nor to the nouns *anger, morning, student,* and *success.* Second, all of the words that are formed when an affix attaches to a stem (its **output**) also normally belong to the same lexical category. For example, the words resulting from the addition of *-able* to a verb are always adjectives. Thus, *adjustable, breakable, comparable,* and *debatable* are all adjectives.

It turns out that these two facts have an important consequence for determining the way in which words with more than one derivational affix must be formed. What it means is that you can trace the derivational history of words as though they were formed in steps, with one affix attaching to a stem at a time. Words with more than one affix can be represented as forming by means of several steps. For example, consider the word *reusable,* which is composed of a prefix *re-,* a stem *use,* and a suffix *-able.* One possible way this morphologically complex word might be formed is all at once: *re + use + able,* where the prefix and the suffix attach at the same time to the stem *use.* This cannot be the case, however, knowing what we know about how derivational affixes are restricted with respect to both their input and their output. Which attaches to *use* first, then: *re-,* or *-able*?

The prefix *re-,* meaning 'do again,' attaches to verbs and creates new words that are also verbs. (Compare with *redo, revisit,* and *rewind.*[1]) The suffix *-able* also attaches to verbs, but it forms words that are adjectives. (Compare with *stoppable, doable,* and *washable.*) When working with problems such as those described in this file, you may find it helpful to anthropomorphize the affixes a bit in your mind. For example, you can think about *re-* as the sort of thing that says, "I am looking for a verb. If you give me a verb, then I will give you another verb," and *-able* as the sort of thing that says, "I am looking for a verb. If you give me a verb, then I will give you an adjective."

---

[1]As important as considering the words that *re-* does form is considering words that it doesn't form. For example, notice that *re-* cannot grammatically combine with adjectives or with nouns:

Adjectives:	*rehappy	*repurple	*replentiful
Nouns:	*rekitten	*rehappiness	*repencil

We learn from examining these two rules that *re-* cannot attach to *usable*, because *usable* is an adjective, but *re-* is "looking for" a verb. However, *re-* is able to attach to the root *use*, because *use* is a verb. Since *reuse* is also a verb, it can then serve as a stem to take *-able*. Thus, the formation of the word *reusable* is a two-step process whereby *re-* and *use* attach first, and then *-able* attaches to the word *reuse*. In this way, the output of one affixation process serves as the input for the next. The restrictions that each affix is subject to can help us determine the sequence of derivation.

Words that are "layered" in this way have a special type of structure characterized as **hierarchical.** This hierarchical structure can be schematically represented by a tree diagram that indicates the steps involved in the formation of the word. The tree for *reusable* appears in (1).

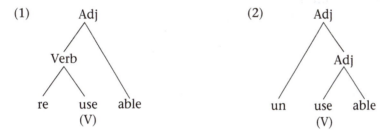

(1) Adj
        Verb
      re   use   able
           (V)

(2) Adj
          Adj
      un   use   able
           (V)

Now consider the word *unusable*. This word also contains three morphemes, so it is tempting to say that they will be put together in the same order as were the morphemes in *reusable*. However, notice that unlike *reuse*, **unuse* is not a word, because in this case, *un-* needs to have its input be an adjective. (Compare with *unhappy, unkind,* and *untrue*.) Fortunately, when *-able* attaches to verbs, it forms adjectives! Once the adjective *useable* (or *usable*) has been formed, the needs of *un-* are met, and it is able to attach in order to form the target word, *unusable*. A tree for this derivation showing the hierarchical structure of *unusable* appears in (2).

Notice that these two trees, that is, the ones in (1) and (2), do not have the same shape. The shape of the tree is particular to the order in which morphemes are combined. Using the tools you have been given, though, it is possible to deduce the hierarchical structures even for very complex words. In (3) there is an example of a word with four morphemes; try to determine for yourself why this is the correct structure for the word *dehumidifier*.

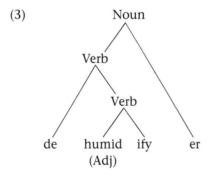

(3) Noun
      Verb
          Verb
      de   humid   ify   er
           (Adj)

4.4.2 Ambiguous Morphemes and Words

Interestingly, some words are **ambiguous;** that is, they can be associated with more than one meaning (see Section 5.5.3). When we examine their internal structure, we find an explanation for this: their structure may be analyzed in more than one way. Consider, for example, the word *unlockable*. This could mean either 'not able to be locked' or 'able to be unlocked.' If we made a list to determine the parts of speech the affix *un-* attaches to, we would discover that there are actually two prefixes that have the form *un-* /ʌn/. The first combines with adjectives to form new adjectives and means 'not.' (Compare with *un-aware, unintelligent,* or *unwise.*) The second prefix *un-* combines with verbs to form new verbs and means 'do the reverse of.' (Compare with *untie, undo,* or *undress.*)

Even though these prefixes sound alike, they are entirely different morphemes. Because of these two different sorts of *un-* in English, *unlockable* may be analyzed in two different ways. First, the suffix *-able* may join with the verb *lock* to form the adjective *lockable,* meaning 'able to be locked'; *un-* may then join with this adjective to form the new adjective *unlockable,* with the meaning 'not able to be locked.' This way of forming *unlockable* is schematized in (4).

In the second *unlockable,* the prefix *un-* joins with the verb *lock* to form the verb *un-lock,* meaning 'do the reverse of lock.' The suffix *-able* then joins with this verb to form the adjective *unlockable,* with the meaning of 'able to be unlocked.' This manner of forming *unlockable* is represented in the tree in (5).

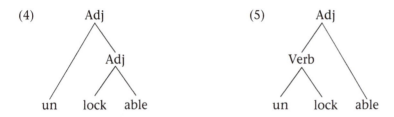

4.4.3   Morphemes That Can Attach to More than One Lexical Category

There are a few prefixes that do not attach exclusively to one lexical category. For example, consider the prefix *pre-. Pre-* attaches to verbs and results in a change of meaning in the words it derives, although the lexical category itself does not change, as the following examples show:

(6)   preexist   preboard (an airplane)
      predetermine   preapprove
      premeditate   prescreen (a movie)

However, there are examples of words with the prefix *pre-* that do not follow the same pattern as those cited above:

(7)   preseason   predawn
      prewar   pregame

In these words, *pre-* attaches to a noun and forms an adjective (*the preseason game, the prewar propaganda, the pregame warm-up*). However, the meaning associated with the prefix is the same as in *preexist, preboard,* etc. (although its function is different). In addition, there are sets of words such as those in (8).

(8)   prefrontal   predental
      preinvasive   prehistoric

In each of these words, *pre-* is attaching to an adjective, forming adjectives, and again the same meaning is associated with the addition of *pre-* as in *preexist, preboard,* etc. Even though it is generally the case that a given affix will be subject to one particular set of conditions on the lexical category that it can attach to and on the lexical category that its resulting derived words will belong to, some morphemes have a much wider range of combinatorial possibilities (historically this may represent an extension from one or two of the productive uses). Such must be the case with *pre-*. Note, however, that what *pre-* combines with and what the combination produces are not totally random or arbitrary. When *pre-* attaches to verbs, it forms only verbs. When it attaches to nouns, it forms only adjectives, and when it attaches to adjectives, it forms only adjectives. So, it is advisable to consider many examples when attempting to determine the generalization about how a given affix combines with stems.

FILE 4.5

Morphological Analysis

4.5.1 The Nature and Goals of Morphological Analysis

When a linguist comes in contact with a new language, one of his or her major tasks is to discover the meaningful units that make up the language. Just as with discovering phonemes and allophones, it is important that the linguist have procedures for discovering these minimal units, since it is impossible to isolate morphemes by intuition.

For example, the Classical Greek word [grapʰɔː] means 'I write,' but if the word is considered in isolation, the linguist has no way of knowing what sound or sequence of sounds corresponds to 'I' and which sequence corresponds to 'write.' In fact, the linguist has no way of knowing even whether the word can be broken down into obvious parts or whether this form was created through alternation or suppletion. It is only by comparing [grapʰɔː] with another form, for instance, [grapʰɛː] 's/he writes,' that one is able to determine what the morphemes of these Greek words are. Looking at these two forms together allows us to hypothesize that [grapʰ] is the part that means 'write.'

Comparison, then, is the best way to begin morphological analysis. But, of course, you will not want to compare just any forms. Comparing a Greek word like [pʰɛːmi] 'to speak' with [grapʰɔː] will not provide much information, since the forms are so dissimilar and seem to have no morpheme in common. What must be compared are partially similar forms, in which it is possible to recognize recurring units. In this way we can identify the morphemes from which words are composed.

Let us consider our Classical Greek example once more. If we compare [grapʰɔː] with [grapʰɛː] 'he writes,' we note similarities between the forms. The sequence [grapʰ-] appears in both forms, [grapʰ-ɛː] and [grapʰ-ɔː], and if we compare these to the English correspondences, we find that the meaning 'write' appears in both 'he writes' and 'I write.' From this, we are justified in concluding that [grapʰ-] means 'write,' since [grapʰ-] and *write* are constants in the Greek and English, respectively. Furthermore, since the final vowels in both Greek forms contrast—and since this contrast is accompanied by a difference in meaning in our English correspondence—we can safely assume that the different vowels in Classical Greek are suffixes that correspond to differences in meaning in our English translation. Therefore we determine that 'I' is marked by [-ɔː] and 'he' is marked by [-ɛː]. In sum, then, the initial step in doing morphological analysis is to compare and contrast partially similar forms.

To give yourself practice, identify and translate the morphemes in the Hungarian data in (1) and (2). ([ɟ] is a voiced palatal stop.) You should be able to identify four distinct Hungarian morphemes: two roots, one prefix, and one suffix.

(1)   [hɔz]   'house'
     [ɛɟhɔz] 'a house'
     [hɔzɔ]   'his/her house'

(2)   [boɾ]   'wine'
     [ɛɟboɾ] 'a wine'
     [boɾɔ]   'his/her wine'

180

Notice that in both the Greek and the Hungarian examples, there have been similarities in both form and meaning between the phonological forms we have considered. In order to perform a successful morphological analysis, both form and meaning similarities are necessary. To demonstrate this point, compare the following English words in (3). (We have not provided glosses because these are words of English.)

(3) work – worker   fast – faster

We notice a similarity in form: the morpheme spelled <er> and pronounced [ɹ] for both [fæstɹ] and [wɪ̩kɹ]. However, if we think about it for a minute, it is apparent that *-er* has two different meanings even though phonetically it looks like the same morpheme. The *-er* in *worker* is the same *-er* that shows up in words like *painter, killer,* and *lover*. In each of these cases, *-er* attaches to verbs to derive a noun and means something like 'one who paints,' 'one who kills,' 'one who loves,' etc. The suffix *-er* in these cases is a derivational suffix known as the agentive morpheme.

The *-er* in *faster,* on the other hand, is the same *-er* that shows up in words like *wider, longer, colder, prettier,* etc. In each of these cases, *-er* attaches to adjective stems to create the comparative form of that adjective. The suffix *-er* in these cases is an inflectional suffix known as the comparative morpheme.

We will want to claim, then, that [ɹ] represents two separate morphemes—[ɹ] as an agent marker, and [ɹ] as a comparative marker—even though they are the same phonetically, i.e., homophonous morphemes. The [ɹ] that is added to verbs to yield nouns and the [ɹ] that is added to adjective stems to yield their comparative forms clearly must be distinct morphemes. This example shows us that it is not sufficient to compare words based on similarity of form alone. There must also be a similarity in meaning (in the case of derivational morphology) or function (in the case of inflectional morphology).

On the flip side, it is also important to recognize that sometimes a similarity in meaning is not matched by an exact similarity in form. Compare the set of words in (4a–e). We notice that each word has a prefix that means 'not.'

(4) a. imprecise   [ɪmpɹəsɑɪs]
     b. inadequate   [ɪnædəkwət]
     c. incomplete   [ɪŋkəmplit]
     d. irresponsible [ɪɹɪspɑnsɪbl̩]
     e. illegible   [ɪlɛdʒɪbl̩]

The problem here is the inverse of the problem in (3). Whereas in (3) we had the same phonetic forms representing two different meanings, in (4) we have five different phonetic forms with the same meaning. Since the phonetic forms of the morpheme meaning 'not' can be predicted on the basis of the phonetic environment, i.e.,

[ɪm] before labials—[p], [b], [m]
[ɪŋ] before velars—[k], [g]
[ɪɹ] before [ɹ]
[ɪl] before [l]
[ɪn] elsewhere (before vowels and other consonants),

we conclude that even though the forms differ phonetically, they belong to the same morpheme since they have the same meaning. We call [ɪm], [ɪŋ], [ɪn], [ɪɹ], and [ɪl] **allomorphs** of the same morpheme. Additional examples of allomorphy in English are the plural morpheme, which is realized as [s], [z], or [əz], depending on the form of the root to which it attaches, and the past tense morpheme, which is realized as [t], [d], or [əd], depending on the form of the root.

4.5.2   Procedure for Performing Morphological Analysis

Now that we have considered several examples of morphological analysis, it is time to spell out exactly what we are trying to do and how we go about doing it. Our goal is this: given a set of data in phonetic representation, perform a morphological analysis of the forms in the data, identifying each morpheme, its meaning, and its type. You should also be able to tell where a morpheme appears with respect to other morphemes in the word. Is it a prefix, suffix, etc.? Does it attach directly to the root, or does it attach after or before another morpheme?

Now it is time to consider the procedure. It can be summed up in three steps.

1. Isolate and compare forms that are partially similar, as we did for Classical Greek [grapʰ-ɛː] and [grapʰ-ɔː].
2. If a single phonetic form has two distinct meanings, it must be analyzed as representing two different morphemes (as in (3)).
3. If the same function and meaning are associated with different phonetic forms, these different forms all represent the same morpheme (i.e., they are allomorphs of the morpheme), and the choice of form in each case may be predictable on the basis of the phonetic environment (as in (4)).

4.5.3   Some Cautionary Notes

People frequently assume that languages are pretty much the same in terms of what each language marks inflectionally. For example, English speakers often assume that all languages mark the plurals of nouns with an ending, or that the subject and the verb agree in person and number in other languages. This is simply not the case.

For example, Tagalog does not usually mark the plural of nouns (in most cases, the number is clear from the context). When it is necessary to be specific, a separate word, *mga*, is used to indicate plural.

(5) [aŋ bata?]   'the child'
     [aŋ mga bata?] 'the children'

When a number is specifically mentioned, no plural marker appears in Tagalog, although the plural marker is obligatory in English (*four dog* is ungrammatical). On the other hand, Tagalog has some markers that English does not. [-ŋ] is a "linker" that links numerals and adjectives to the nouns they modify; English does not use this type of device. Examples of both phenomena can be seen in (6).

(6) [dalawa]   'two'   [dalawaŋ bata?]   'two children'
     [lima]   'five'   [limaŋ bata?]   'five children'

English marks subject-verb agreement (e.g., *I eat* versus *he eats*; see File 5.2), but Tagalog does not. In Tagalog, the same form of the verb is used with all subjects, as in (7).

(7) [kumakain ako]   'eat I'   = 'I eat'
     [kumakain siy]   'eat he' = 'he eats'

Other languages also make distinctions that English doesn't. While English distinguishes only singular and plural verbs, some languages have a dual verb form for when just two people are involved. Consider Sanskrit *juhomi* 'I sacrifice,' *juhuvas* 'we (two) sacrifice,' and *juhumas* 'we (more than two) sacrifice.'

Some languages make another distinction in first-person plural pronouns where English has only *we*. Notice that English *we* in *we are going,* for example, may include everyone in the group the hearer is addressing (i.e., *we* = 'every one of us'), or it may include only some hearers (i.e., *we* = 'I and (s)he,' but not 'you'). Many languages distinguish these two *we*'s: Tagalog has *tayo* (*inclusive,* i.e., 'you and I') and *kami* (*exclusive,* i.e., 'he and I').

Comanche, a Native American language of the Uto-Aztecan family, makes a number of other distinctions that English doesn't. In addition to a singular/dual/plural distinction and an inclusive/exclusive distinction, Comanche also makes a distinction between visible/not visible and near/far. Thus, if you are referring to a thing that is within your view, you use a different form than if the thing is not visible to you. Likewise, a nearby object is designated with a pronoun different from the one used for an object that is far away. Consider the following subject forms:

(8) Elements of the Comanche pronoun system

Singular/Dual/Plural Distinction		***Inclusive/Exclusive Distinction***	
[inɨ]	'you (singular)'	[taa]	'we (inclusive)'
[nikwɨ]	'you (two)'	[nɨnɨ]	'we (exclusive)'
[mɨɨ]	'you (plural)'		

Visible/Not Visible		***Near/Far Distinction***	
[maʔ]	'it (visible)'	[ʔiʔ]	'it (proximate)'
[ʔuʔ]	'it (invisible)'	[ʔoʔ]	'it (remote)'

The lesson to be learned here is that you cannot assume that another language will make distinctions in the same way that English does. For example, while every language has some method of indicating number, not all languages do so in the same way or under the same circumstances. As we've seen, English uses an affix, Tagalog uses a separate word, and Indonesian reduplicates the word to show plurality (see File 4.2). Nor can you assume that the distinctions English makes are the only ones worth making. Languages must be examined carefully on the grounds of their own internal structures.

Finally, although the exercises for File 4.6 will generally involve affixation, do not forget that often in the world's languages, morphological marking will happen through some other process or a combination of processes.

FILE 4.6

....

Practice

File 4.1—Words and Word Formation: The Nature of the Lexicon

Exercises

1. Refer to the drawing at the beginning of this chapter. What does this drawing indicate about the morphological structure of the word *morphology* itself? What do the morphemes that make up the word mean? List five other words containing at least one of these morphemes.

2. The following words are made up of either one or two morphemes. Isolate the morphemes and decide for each if it is free or bound, what kind of affix, if any, is involved (i.e., is it a prefix or a suffix?), and (where applicable) if the affix is inflectional or derivational.

   a. cats
   b. unhappy
   c. rejoin
   d. catsup
   e. milder
   f. hateful
   g. succotash
   h. bicycle
   i. greedy
   j. entrust
   k. signpost
   l. spacious

3. Divide the words below into their component morphemes and give the information about the morphemes as you did in (2). (*Note:* Words may consist of one, two, or more than two morphemes.)

   a. comfortable
   b. Massachusetts
   c. environmentally
   d. reconditioned
   e. unidirectional
   f. senseless
   g. thickeners
   h. nationalization
   i. unspeakably

4. In each group of words that follows two words have the same morphological structure, one has a different suffix from those two, and one has no suffix at all. Your task is to tell which two words have the same suffix, which one has a different suffix, and which has no suffix at all. Having done this, tell the meaning of each suffix. (You may find that they become more difficult as you go along.)

   Example: rider   *-er* is a derivational suffix meaning 'one who. . . .'
             colder *-er* is an inflectional suffix marking the comparative.
             silver There is no suffix.
             smoker This is the same *-er* as in *rider*.

   a. nicer
       painter
       runner
       feather

   b. intolerant
       intelligent
       inflame
       incomplete

   c. friendly
       sadly
       softly
       silly

   d. sons
       lens
       vans
       runs

   e. youngster
       faster
       monster
       gangster

   f. wrestling
       handling
       fling
       duckling

   g. nifty
       ducky
       thrifty
       lucky

   h. given
       maven
       wooden
       taken

184

5. Are the root morphemes in each pair below pronounced the same? Different phonetic shapes of the same stem (or affix, for that matter) are called **allomorphs** (example: in *malign/ malignant*, [məlaɪn]/[məlɪgn] are (root) allomorphs). Identify in IPA any allomorphs that you uncover. (See Section 4.5.1 for more information on this topic.)

Example: malign/malignant: [məlaɪn]/[məlɪgnənt]

   a. autumn/autumnal
   b. hymn/hymnal
   c. damn/damnation
   d. condemn/condemnation
   e. divide/divisible
   f. profane/profanity
   g. serene/serenity
   h. receive/receptive

6. The television show *The Simpsons* coined many new words by using morphology in novel ways. Two examples are *embiggens*, as in "A noble spirit embiggens the smallest man," and *introubleating*, as in "One Springfield man is treating his wife to an extra-special Valentine's Day this year, and introubleating the rest of us." Note that although these are novel words, they are similar to other words of English: *embiggens* is similar to *emboldens*, and *introubleating* is similar to *infuriating*. For each of these two words, perform the following tasks:

   i. Break it up into its component morphemes.
   ii. Provide the meaning of each morpheme and state whether it is free or bound.

Discussion Question

7. Some people describe morphology as the study of how words are built up; others describe it as the study of how words are broken down. What assumptions does each of these two descriptions make about how words are stored in our mental lexicons? Based on what you know so far, is one of these descriptions more or less accurate? Why do you think so? Come back and revisit this question once you have read the entire chapter.

File 4.2—Morphological Processes

Exercises

8. **Bontoc**
   Consider the following data from Bontoc, a Malayo-Polynesian language spoken in the Philippines. These data show an example of derivational morphology in which an adjectival root is turned into a verb. What type of affix is used to form the verb? Describe its placement in the word.

[fikas]	'strong'	[fumikas]	'he is becoming strong'
[kilad]	'red'	[kumilad]	'he is becoming red'
[bato]	'stone'	[bumiato]	'he is becoming stone'
[fusul]	'enemy'	[fumiusul]	'he is becoming an enemy'

9. Imagine that the English suffix *-ful* were instead an infix. Where might it attach in a morpheme like *hope*? Like *pain*? Like *beauty*? (Focus on the pronunciation of the forms, rather than their spelling.) How would you know where to place the infix? Notice that there are a limited number of pronounceable options.

10. For each of the morphological processes explained in the text—affixation, compounding, reduplication, alternation, and suppletion—give an example from English or from your native language that is not given in the text. You will need to provide both the base form and the inflected or derived form for each example.

11. For each of the following words of English, tell what the root word is and the process through which the word was formed. (If you're not sure what the root word is, give what you think is the most basic form of the word.)

   a. bound   f. discover
   b. toenail   g. mama
   c. carries   h. mice
   d. were   i. ladybug
   e. undomesticated   j. rang

12. In Catalan, the form for 'to go' is [əna], and the form for 'I go' is [batʃ]. Which morphological process is this an example of? How do you know?

13. The forms for 'dancer' and 'student' in ASL are shown in (a) and (b).
   i. What part of the **meaning** of 'student' and 'dancer' is similar? (*Hint:* Ask yourself, What is a dancer? What is a student?)
   ii. What part of the **form** of these two signs is similar?
   iii. Which morphological process is responsible for the formation of the signs DANCER and STUDENT? How do you know?

   a. ASL: STUDENT

   © 2006, William Vicars, www.Lifeprint.com. Adapted by permission.

   b. ASL: DANCER

   © 2006, William Vicars, www.Lifeprint.com. Adapted by permission.

14. Refer to image (7) in File 2.7. Explain, as specifically as you can, how the form for the uninflected sign MEET differs from the form of the inflected sign I MEET YOU. What is the simultaneous affix that is used in the sign I MEET YOU?

15. i. In Hebrew, the following pattern is found in the derivation of color terms. (Pay particular attention to the consonants; the vowel change is not as important to this data set.) Which morphological process is this an example of? How do you know?

[lavan]	'white'	[lvanvan]	'whitish'
[kaxol]	'blue'	[kxalxal]	'bluish'
[jaɣok]	'green'	[jɣakɣak]	'greenish'
[ʦahov]	'yellow'	[ʦhavhav]	'yellowish'
[vaɣod]	'pink'	[vɣadɣad]	'pinkish'
[ʃaxoɣ]	'black'	[ʃaxaɣxaɣ]	'blackish'

ii. The Hebrew word for 'red' is [adom]. Based only on the data above, what would you predict the word for 'reddish' to be?

iii. The actual Hebrew word for 'reddish' is [admumi]. Is this word at all similar to what you predicted? If so, how? Can you guess a reason for why the actual word might be different from what you predicted? (Do not attempt to explain why it takes the form that it does; just try to explain why the expected pattern may have failed.)

Discussion Questions

16. i. Look again at the data given in Exercise 15 and consider this new fact: the Hebrew word for the color 'violet' is [sagol]. Based only on the data above, what would you expect that the word [sgalgal] would mean?

ii. The word [sgalgal] actually means 'oval.' Can you think of any examples in English or some other language where you might predict, based on morphological prin-ciples, that a form would mean one thing, but in fact it turns out to mean something else? What do these sorts of cases tell us about morphology and the lexicon of a language?

17. Assume that the English word *raspberry* can be analyzed into *rasp + berry* and *cranberry* into *cran + berry*. Discuss how these two words behave differently from other morphologically complex English words. Is this process more like affixation, or is it more like compounding? How is this process similar to each? How is it different from each?

Activity

18. There are some cases in English where a certain adjective-noun pair has become a compound noun for some speakers but is still two separate words for others. One of these is *cream cheese*. Some speakers put a stress only on the first syllable, while others treat it as two words and give each its own stress.
Construct a survey:

- Choose a number of noun-adjective pairs that are compound nouns for you or one of your classmates. Your goal will be to find out how other people pronounce these: as compounds or as separate words.

- Design questions such that you do not have to say the word yourself (thereby biasing the person responding); for example, "What do you call the white spread that people eat on bagels?"

- Collaborate with others in your class: each of you should ask your set of questions to some number of people (to be specified by your instructor).

- Afterwards, share your findings with your classmates.

File 4.3—Morphological Types of Languages

Discussion Question

19. Often, when people are exposed to languages with properties that are different from those of languages that they already know, their immediate reaction is to think that the new type of language is much more complicated. Of course, this is true regardless of which type of language they speak to begin with. For each of the four types of language presented in File 4.3, list some attributes of that kind of language that would make it easier to learn or to understand the grammar.

Activity

20. With a group of your classmates, make up a fragment of a synthetic language. You should decide whether it will be agglutinative or fusional. Perform the following steps in order to create your language fragment. Be sure to write out the decisions that you make at each step along the way.

    i. First, come up with a name for your language.

    ii. Next, create a small lexicon. It will contain ten words; you can choose to create ten nouns, ten verbs, or five of each. For each of your lexical items, you will need to specify a phonological form (using the IPA) and a meaning (using an English gloss).

    iii. Decide on four morphological functions that you will want to be able to perform: two should be derivational, and two should be inflectional. (Examples: marking nouns for nominal case; marking verbs as past tense, turning nouns into adjectives; turning verbs into nouns, etc.) Don't feel the need to restrict yourself to morphological functions found in English!

    iv. Decide what morphological process your language will use to perform each of these functions. Don't forget to specify how—if at all—these processes will interact with your language's phonology!

    v. Now, write all of the possible derived forms and inflected forms that you can make based on the words of your language and the morphological rules that you have created. For each, tell both the form (using the IPA) and the meaning (using an English gloss).

    vi. Is your language fusional or agglutinative? What evidence shows that this is the case?

File 4.4—The Hierarchical Structure of Derived Words

Exercises

21. All of the words below contain two morphemes: a root and a suffix. First, identify the root in each word and the suffix. Then state the lexical category of the root word and the lexical category of the whole word. (*Hint:* In each list, the lexical categories are the same for all three words.)

a. government	**c.** happiness	**e.** calmest
speaker	rarity	lovelier
contemplation	creativity	sillier
b. fictional	**d.** messy	
childish	bookish	
colorful	mountainous	

22. Isolate the affixes and roots in the following groups of words. Then name the lexical category of the root, and say whether the affixation results in a word belonging to a different lexical category (and if so, which one).

a. spiteful	**b.** unsure	**c.** retake	**d.** stoppable
healthful	untrue	review	fixable
truthful	unhappy	relive	laughable

23. From the examples given for each of the following suffixes, determine: (i) the lexical category of the word whose stem the suffix combines with, and (ii) the lexical category of the words resulting from the addition of the suffix.

   a. -ify: solidify, intensify, purify, clarify, rarefy
   b. -ity: rigidity, stupidity, hostility, intensity, responsibility
   c. -ize: unionize, terrorize, hospitalize, crystallize, magnetize
   d. -ive: repressive, active, disruptive, abusive, explosive
   e. -ion: invention, injection, narration, expression, pollution
   f. -less: nameless, penniless, useless, heartless, mindless

 24. Draw tree diagrams for each of the following words:

a. disappearance	**j.** international	**s.** unmistakable
b. unaffordable	**k.** misunderstandable	**t.** insincerity
c. un-American	**l.** reconstruction	**u.** dysfunctional
d. manliness	**m.** unrespectable	**v.** inconclusive
e. impersonal	**n.** nonrefundable	**w.** premeditatedly
f. irreplaceability	**o.** mismanagement	**x.** overgeneralization
g. oversimplification	**p.** underspecification	**y.** reformer
h. unhappiness	**q.** restatement	**z.** infertility
i. decommission	**r.** premeditation	**aa.** dishonesty

25. Consider the two columns of words below. What do the words in each column have in common? Come up with two more words that go in each column. Do the words in both columns have the same suffix, or do the words on the right have a different suffix from those on the left? Justify your answer.

teacher	stapler
baker	juicer
singer	copier
writer	toaster
fighter	hole-puncher
painter	lighter

26. Consider the English prefix *anti-*. Make a list of words you can think of that begin with *anti-*. Try to come up with at least ten words. (You may use a dictionary if you like.) What lexical categories contain words that can serve as root words for *anti-*? In each case, what are the lexical categories of the output?

27. The made-up words *embiggens* and *introubleating* were introduced in Exercise 6. Draw tree diagrams for these two words.

Activity

28. Make up your own English word that you've never heard before that is composed of at least four morphemes. (If you can't think of a word right now, you are welcome to use *semiunducklike*, as in "A rhinoceros isn't like a duck at all, but a goose is only semiunducklike." However, it's more fun to make your own word!)

    i. Indicate the morphemes that make it up.

    ii. Provide the meaning of each morpheme and state whether it is (1) free or bound; (2) a root, prefix, or suffix; and (3) derivational, inflectional, or neither.

    iii. Provide the meaning of the whole word.

    iv. Draw a tree diagram showing how it was put together.

File 4.5—Morphological Analysis

Exercises

Beginning Exercises

29. Isthmus Zapotec
Examine the following data from Isthmus Zapotec, a language spoken in Mexico. Answer the questions that follow.

a.	[palu]	'stick'	**g.**	[spalube]	'his stick'	**m.**	[spalulu]	'your stick'
b.	[kuːba]	'dough'	**h.**	[skuːbabe]	'his dough'	**n.**	[skuːbalu]	'your dough'
c.	[tapa]	'four'	**i.**	[stapabe]	'his four'	**o.**	[stapalu]	'your four'
d.	[geta]	'tortilla'	**j.**	[sketabe]	'his tortilla'	**p.**	[sketalu]	'your tortilla'
e.	[bere]	'chicken'	**k.**	[sperebe]	'his chicken'	**q.**	[sperelu]	'your chicken'
f.	[doʔo]	'rope'	**l.**	[stoʔobe]	'his rope'	**r.**	[stoʔolu]	'your rope'

    i. Isolate the morphemes that correspond to the following English translations:

        _____   possession (genitive)
        _____   third-person singular
        _____   second-person plural

    ii. List the allomorphs for the following translations:

        _____ _____ 'tortilla' _____ _____ 'rope'
        _____ _____ 'chicken'

    iii. What phonological environment triggers the alternation between these allomorphs?

30. Turkish
Examine the following data from Turkish and answer the questions that follow.

a.	fil	'elephant'	**i.**	kaplan	'tiger'
b.	file	'to an/the elephant'	**j.**	kaplanlar	'tigers'
c.	filden	'from an/the elephant'	**k.**	cambaz	'acrobat'
d.	sirke	'to a/the circus'	**l.**	cambazımız	'our acrobat'
e.	sirkler	'circuses'	**m.**	kaplanın	'of at/the tiger'
f.	sirkin	'of a/the circus'	**n.**	cambazlarım	'my acrobats''
g.	fillerim	'my elephants'	**o.**	kaplanıma	'to my tiger'
h.	sirklerimizin	'of our circuses'	**p.**	cambazdan	'from an/the acrobat'

(cont.)

i. Give the Turkish morpheme that corresponds to each of the following translations; two blanks indicate two allomorphs:

_____ 'elephant' ____ ____ 'to' ____ ____ 'my'
_____ 'circus' ____ ____ 'from' ____ ____ 'our'
_____ 'tiger' ____ ____ 'of' ____ ____ (plural marker)
_____ 'acrobat'

ii. What is the order of morphemes in a Turkish word (in terms of noun stem, plural marker, etc.)?

iii. How would one say 'to my circus' and 'from our tigers' in Turkish?

31. Luiseño
Examine the following data from Luiseño, a Uto-Aztecan language of Southern California, and answer the questions that follow.

a.	[nokaamaj]	'my son'	**m.** [pokaamaj]	'his son'
b.	[ʔoki]	'your house'	**n.** [poki]	'his house'
c.	[potaana]	'his blanket'	**o.** [notaana]	'my blanket'
d.	[ʔohuukapi]	'your pipe'	**p.** [pohuukapi]	'his pipe'
e.	[ʔotaana]	'your blanket'	**q.** [nohuukapi]	'my pipe'
f.	[noki]	'my house'	**r.** [ʔokaamaj]	'your son'
g.	[ʔomkim]	'your (pl.) houses'	**s.** [pompeewum]	'their wives'
h.	[nokaamajum]	'my sons'	**t.** [pomki]	'their house'
i.	[popeew]	'his wife'	**u.** [tʃampeewum]	'our wives'
j.	[ʔopeew]	'your wife'	**v.** [tʃamhuukapim]	'our pipes'
k.	[ʔomtaana]	'your (pl.) blanket'	**w.** [ʔomtaanam]	'your (pl.) blankets'
l.	[tʃamhuukapi]	'our pipe'	**x.** [pomkaamaj]	'their son'

i. Give the Luiseño morpheme that corresponds to each English translation. Note that the plural marker has two allomorphs; list them both.

_____ 'son' _____ 'my' _____ 'their'
_____ 'house' _____ 'his' _____ (plural marker)
_____ 'blanket' _____ 'your (sg.)' _____ 'pipe'
_____ 'wife' _____ 'your (pl.)' _____ 'our'

ii. Are the allomorphs of the plural marker phonologically conditioned?

iii. If so, what are the conditioning environments?

32. Quiché
Some sentences from Quiché, a Native American language spoken in Guatemala, Central America, are given with their English translation in (a)–(h). Analyze the morphemes in these sentences and then fill in the exercises that follow the language data. Note that [x] is a voiceless velar fricative.

	Quiché	*English*
a.	[kiŋsikíx le líbr]	'I read (present tense) the book'
b.	[kusikíx le líbr]	'He reads the book'
c.	[kiŋwetamáx le kém]	'I learn the (art of) weaving'
d.	[kataxín kiŋwetamáx le kém]	'I continually learn the (art of) weaving'
e.	[kataxín kawetamáx le kém]	'You continually learn the (art of) weaving'
f.	[ʃiŋwetamáx]	'I learned (it)'
g.	[ʃuwetamáx le kém]	'He learned the (art of) weaving'
h.	[ʃasikíx le líbr iwír]	'You read the book yesterday'

(cont.)

    i. Fill in the blanks with the corresponding Quiché morphemes:

_____ 'I'   _____ 'learn'   _____ (present tense)
_____ 'he'   _____ 'read'   _____ (past tense)
_____ 'you'   _____ 'the'   _____ 'continually'
_____ 'book'   _____ 'weaving'   _____ 'yesterday'

   ii. What is the order of Quiché morphemes (in terms of subject, verb, object, and tense marker)?

33. American Sign Language
Each of the four signs below includes one affix. The two signs on the left have the same affix. The two signs on the right share a different affix.

a. GRANDMOTHER

c. GRANDFATHER

b. MOTHER

d. FATHER

© 2006, William Vicars, www.Lifeprint.com. Used with permission.

    i. Which phonological parameter differentiates these two affixes: place of articulation, movement, handshape, hand orientation, or non-manual marker?

   ii. Describe the difference in form between the affix in the signs on the left and the affix in the signs on the right.

  iii. Are these two affixes prefixes, suffixes, infixes, or simultaneous affixes?

   iv. What is the meaning of the affix used on the left? What is the meaning of the affix used on the right?

34. Michoacan Aztec
Examine the following words from Michoacan Aztec, a language of Mexico, and answer the questions that follow.

a. [nokali] 'my house' f. [mopelo] 'your dog'
b. [nokalimes] 'my houses' g. [mopelomes] 'your dogs'
c. [mokali] 'your house' h. [ikwahmili] 'his cornfield'
d. [ikali] 'his house' i. [nokwahmili] 'my cornfield'
e. [nopelo] 'my dog' j. [mokwahmili] 'your cornfield'

i. Fill in the blanks with the corresponding Michoacan morphemes:

_____ 'house' _____ 'my'
_____ 'dog' _____ 'your'
_____ 'cornfield' _____ 'his'
_____ (plural marker)

ii. What is the English translation for the Michoacan word [ipelo]?

iii. How would you say 'his cornfields' in Michoacan?

35. Cebuano
The following nouns are from Cebuano, a language of the Philippine Islands. Examine them and answer the questions that follow.

a. [bisaja] 'a Visayan' f. [binisaja] 'the Visayan language'
b. [inglis] 'an Englishman' g. [ininglis] 'the English language'
c. [tagalog] 'a Tagalog person' h. [tinagalog] 'the Tagalog language'
d. [ilokano] 'an Ilocano' i. [inilokano] 'the Ilocano language'
e. [sibwano] 'a Cebuano' j. [sinibwano] 'the Cebuano language'

i. State the rule (in words, precisely) for deriving language names from the names of ethnic groups.

ii. What type of affixation is this?

36. Isleta
Consider the following data from Isleta, a dialect of Southern Tiwa, a Native American language spoken in New Mexico, and answer the questions that follow.

a. [temiban] 'I went' d. [mimiaj] 'he was going'
b. [amiban] 'you went' e. [tewanban] 'I came'
c. [temiwe] 'I am going' f. [tewanhi] 'I will come'

i. List the morphemes corresponding to the following English translations.

_____ 'I' _____ 'go' _____ (present progressive)
_____ 'you' _____ 'come' _____ (past progressive)
_____ 'he' _____ (past) _____ (future)

ii. What sort of affixes are the subject morphemes?

iii. What sort of affixes are the tense morphemes?

iv. What is the order of morphemes in Isleta?

v. How would you say each of the following in Isleta?

- 'He went.'
- 'I will go.'
- 'You were coming.'

37. German
Identify all the plural morphemes and all the different morphological processes that can be involved in the pluralization of nouns in German. Don't worry about trying to describe which plural morpheme goes with which type of word. Just list the morphemes. (Note that the data below are given in normal German orthography, not IPA; vowels <ü> and <ö> are front rounded vowels and <äu> is pronounced [ɔɪ].)

	Singular	*Plural*	*Gloss*
a.	Bild	Bilder	'picture'
b.	Büro	Büros	'office'
c.	Tüte	Tüten	'bag'
d.	Loch	Löcher	'hole'
e.	Uhr	Uhren	'watch'
f.	Rind	Rinder	'bull/cow'
g.	Wagen	Wagen	'vehicle'
h.	Stift	Stifte	'pen'
i.	Haus	Häuser	'house'
j.	Laus	Läuse	'louse'
k.	Hut	Hüte	'hat'
l.	Hütte	Hütten	'hut'
m.	Buch	Bücher	'book'
n.	Dach	Dächer	'roof'
o.	Kind	Kinder	'child'

Intermediate Exercises

 38. Swahili
Examine the following data from Swahili, a language spoken in East Africa, and answer the questions that follow.

a.	[atanipenda]	's/he will like me'	**o.**	[atanipiga]	's/he will beat me'
b.	[atakupenda]	's/he will like you'	**p.**	[atakupiga]	's/he will beat you'
c.	[atampenda]	's/he will like him/her'	**q.**	[atampiga]	's/he will beat him/her'
d.	[atatupenda]	's/he will like us'	**r.**	[ananipiga]	's/he is beating me'
e.	[atawapenda]	's/he will like them'	**s.**	[anakupiga]	's/he is beating you'
f.	[nitakupenda]	'I will like you'	**t.**	[anampiga]	's/he is beating him/her'
g.	[nitampenda]	'I will like him/her'	**u.**	[amekupiga]	's/he has beaten you'
h.	[nitawapenda]	'I will like them'	**v.**	[amenipiga]	's/he has beaten me'
i.	[utanipenda]	'you will like me'	**w.**	[amempiga]	's/he has beaten him/her'
j.	[utampenda]	'you will like him/her'	**x.**	[alinipiga]	's/he beat me'
k.	[tutampenda]	'we will like him/her'	**y.**	[alikupiga]	's/he beat you'
l.	[watampenda]	'they will like him/her'	**z.**	[alimpiga]	's/he beat him/her'
m.	[wametulipa]	'they have paid us'	**aa.**	[atakusumbua]	's/he will annoy you'
n.	[tulikulipa]	'we paid you'	**bb.**	[unamsumbua]	'you are annoying him/her'

i. Give the Swahili morphemes corresponding to the following English translations:

_____	'I'	_____	'we'	_____	(past marker)
_____	'pay'	_____	'like'	_____	(present progressive)
_____	's/he'	_____	'annoy'	_____	(future marker)
_____	'me'	_____	'him/her'	_____	(present perfect)
_____	'beat'	_____	'they'	_____	'you' (if subject)
_____	'us'	_____	'them'	_____	'you' (if object)

(cont.)

   ii. What is the order of morphemes in Swahili (in terms of subject, object, verb, and tense)?

   iii. Give the Swahili word for the following English translations:

- 'I have beaten them.'
- 'They are beating me.'
- 'They have annoyed me.'

- 'You have beaten us.'
- 'We beat them.'
- 'I am paying him/her.'

   iv. Give the English translation for the following Swahili words.

- [atanilipa]
- [utawapiga]
- [walikupenda]
- [nimemsumbua]

39. Sanskrit

Examine the following data from Sanskrit, a classical language of India. Abbreviations are for case (use in the sentence) and number (singular, plural). 'ṣ' is a retroflex.

a.	manas	'mind (nom.sg./stem)'	**l.**	vapuṣe	'wonder (dat.sg.)'
b.	manasi	'mind (loc.sg.)'	**m.**	vapurbhyas	'wonder (dat.pl.)'
c.	manasā	'mind (inst.sg.)'	**n.**	vapuṣas	'wonder (gen.sg.)'
d.	manobhis	'mind (inst.pl.)'	**o.**	vapuṣām	'wonder (gen.pl.)'
e.	manasas	'mind (gen.sg.)'	**p.**	suhavis	'devout (nom.sg./stem)'
f.	manasām	'mind (gen.pl.)'	**q.**	suhaviṣā	'devout (inst.sg.)'
g.	manase	'mind (dat.sg.)'	**r.**	suhavirbhis	'devout (inst.pl.)'
h.	manobhyas	'mind (dat.pl.)'	**s.**	suhaviṣe	'devout (dat.sg.)'
i.	vapus	'wonder (nom.sg./stem)'	**t.**	suhavirbhyas	'devout (dat.pl.)'
j.	vapuṣā	'wonder (inst.sg.)'	**u.**	suhaviṣas	'devout (gen.sg.)'
k.	vapurbhis	'wonder (inst.pl.)'	**v.**	suhaviṣi	'devout (loc.sg.)'

   i. What are the Sanskrit morphemes for the following?

     ___ gen.sg.   ___ gen.pl.   ___ dat.sg.   ___ dat.pl.
     ___ inst.sg.   ___ inst.pl.   ___ loc.sg.

   ii. What are the allomorphs for 'mind', 'wonder', and 'devout'?

   iii. What are the conditioning environments here for the allomorphs?

   iv. Based on the data given here, what morphological type of language is Sanskrit? (See File 4.3.) Briefly explain your answer.

40. Zoque

Examine the following data from Zoque, a language spoken in Mexico, and answer the subsequent questions.

a.	[kenu]	'he looked'	**g.**	[kenpa]	'he looks'
b.	[sihku]	'he laughed'	**h.**	[sikpa]	'he laughs'
c.	[wihtu]	'he walked'	**i.**	[witpa]	'he walks'
d.	[kaʔu]	'he died'	**j.**	[kaʔpa]	'he dies'
e.	[cihcu]	'it tore'	**k.**	[cicpa]	'it tears'
f.	[sohsu]	'it cooked'	**l.**	[sospa]	'it cooks'

   i. What is the Zoque morpheme indicating the present tense?

   ii. For each verb, give the meaning and list the allomorphs of the stem.

(cont.)

     iii. Given any Zoque verb with two stem allomorphs, what morphological category determines the choice of stem? That is, how do you know which stem to use when?

     iv. Describe the relationship between the stem allomorphs in terms of phonological form.

     v. Is there a Zoque morpheme meaning 'he' or 'it'?

41. Serbo-Croatian

Examine the following data from Serbo-Croatian, a Slavic language spoken in Bosnia and Herzegovina, Croatia, Montenegro, and Serbia, and answer the questions below. The data are given in standard Roman orthography.

a.	svirati	'to play' (infinitive)	**o.**	kupovati	'to buy' (infinitive)
b.	diram	'I touch'	**p.**	dirati	'to touch' (infinitive)
c.	gledanje	'the watching'	**q.**	sviranje	'the playing'
d.	gledaju	'they watch'	**r.**	sviraju	'they play'
e.	stanujem	'I live'	**s.**	diraju	'they touch'
f.	stanovati	'to live' (infinitive)	**t.**	nazivanje	'the calling'
g.	kupuju	'they buy'	**u.**	gladovati	'to starve' (infinitive)
h.	kupujem	'I buy'	**v.**	gladovanje	'the starving'
i.	kupovanje	'the buying'	**w.**	gladujem	'I starve'
j.	nazivati	'to call' (infinitive)	**x.**	gladuju	'they starve'
k.	sviram	'I play'	**y.**	diranje	'the touching'
l.	gledam	'I watch'	**z.**	stanovanje	'the living'
m.	gledati	'to watch' (infinitive)	**aa.**	nazivam	'I call'
n.	stanuju	'they live'	**bb.**	nazivaju	'they call'

     i. What is the first-person singular present tense suffix?

     ii. What is the third-person plural present tense suffix?

     iii. What is the infinitival suffix?

     iv. What is the suffix that turns verbal stems into deverbal nouns like *the living* or *the calling*?

     v. Some verbal stems above have exactly the same form regardless of which suffix is added to them (e.g., *sviram, sviraju, svirati, sviranje*), while other verbal stems have one form when you add the first- or third-person present tense suffix to it, and a different form if it occurs with the infinitive or the noun-forming suffix (e.g., *kupujem, kupuju* vs. *kupovati, kupovanje*). If you look at the infinitive form of a verb in Serbo-Croatian, how can you tell whether the stem will stay the same or change when combined with the first- or third-person present tense suffix? Describe as precisely as you can how the form of these stems changes.

     vi. Given the answers you came up with for (i–v), fill in the blanks below.

darovati	'to give a present'	darujem	'I give a present'
_____	'they give a present'	_____	'the giving of a present'
razaram	'I destroy'	_____	'they destroy'
_____	'to destroy'	razaranje	'the destruction'
stvarati	'to create'	_____	'I create'
_____	'they create'	_____	'the creation'
ratuju	'they wage war'	_____	'the waging of a war'
_____	'to wage war'	_____	'I wage war'

42. Hanunoo

Hanunoo is a language spoken in the Philippine Islands. Compare the data from this language horizontally (e.g., (a)-(h)-(o) go together), and answer the questions that follow.

a.	[ʔusa]	'one'	**h.**	[kasʔa]	'once'	**o.**	[ʔusahi]	'make it one'
b.	[duwa]	'two'	**i.**	[kadwa]	'twice'	**p.**	[duwahi]	'make it two'
c.	[tulu]	'three'	**j.**	[katlu]	'three times'	**q.**	[tuluhi]	'make it three'
d.	[ʔupat]	'four'	**k.**	[kapʔat]	'four times'	**r.**	[ʔupati]	'make it four'
e.	[lima]	'five'	**l.**	[kalima]	'five times'	**s.**	[limahi]	'make it five'
f.	[ʔunum]	'six'	**m.**	[kanʔum]	'six times'	**t.**	[ʔunumi]	'make it six'
g.	[pitu]	'seven'	**n.**	[kapitu]	'seven times'	**u.**	[pituhi]	'make it seven'

    i. Two affixes are illustrated in these data. Identify each of them, state what kind of affix each one is, and tell what information or change is associated with each affix.

    ii. Considering the horizontal sets of words, describe the phonological alternations in the stems in each set. (If you have already completed the phonology files, use the relevant terms for phonological processes in your descriptions.)

Advanced Exercises

43. Hungarian

Examine the Hungarian data below and answer the questions that follow. Note that [y] represents a high front rounded vowel.

		Singular	*Plural*
a.	'table'	[ɔstɔl]	[ɔstɔlok]
b.	'worker'	[munkaːʃ]	[munkaːʃok]
c.	'man'	[ɛmbɛr]	[ɛmbɛrɛk]
d.	'white'	[fɛheːr]	[fɛheːrɛk]
e.	'this'	[ɛz]	[ɛzɛk]
f.	'line'	[ʃoɾ]	[ʃoɾok]
g.	'eyeglasses'	[sɛmyvɛg]	[sɛmyvɛgɛk]
h.	'shirt'	[iŋ]	[iŋɛk]
i.	'head'	[fɛy]	[fɛyɛk]
j.	'box'	[doboz]	[dobozok]
k.	'drum'	[dob]	[dobok]
l.	'age'	[kor]	[korok]
m.	'coat'	[kɔbaːt]	[kɔbaːtok]
n.	'flower'	[viraːg]	[viraːgok]

    i. What are the allomorphs of the Hungarian plural marker?

    ii. State the conditioning environment for each allomorph.

44. Popoluca

Examine the following data from Popoluca, a language spoken in Mexico, and answer the questions that follow. (*Note:* 'you' is singular throughout this exercise.)

a.	[ʔiŋkuʔtpa]	'you eat it'	**i.**	[ʔinhokspa]	'you hoe it'
b.	[ʔanhokspa]	'I hoe it'	**j.**	[noːmi]	'boss'
c.	[ʔikuʔt]	'he ate it'	**k.**	[ʔanoːmi]	'my boss'
d.	[ʔimoːja]	'his flower'	**l.**	[ʔikaːma]	'his cornfield'
e.	[moːja]	'flower'	**m.**	[ʔiŋkaːma]	'your cornfield'
f.	[ʔampetpa]	'I sweep it'	**n.**	[ʔamoːja]	'my flower'
g.	[ʔimpet]	'you swept it'	**o.**	[ʔinoːmi]	'your boss'
h.	[ʔantɛk]	'my house'			

(cont.)

i. List all of the Popoluca allomorphs corresponding to the following translations:

_____	'cornfield'	_____	(past tense)
_____	'flower'	_____	(present tense)
_____	'boss'	_____	'I/my'
_____	'house'	_____	'you/your'
_____	'eat'	_____	'he/his'
_____	'sweep'	_____	'hoe'

ii. For those morphemes with more than one allomorph, state the phonetic environments that determine the occurrence of each allomorph.

45. Mongolian

Examine the following Mongolian data. Note that [y] represents a high front rounded vowel, [ø] represents a mid front rounded vowel, and [x] represents a voiceless velar fricative.

		Stem	*Future Imperative*
a.	'enter'	[or-]	[oro:roɪ]
b.	'go'	[jav]	[java:raɪ]
c.	'sit'	[su:-]	[su:ga:raɪ]
d.	'come'	[ir-]	[ire:reɪ]
e.	'do'	[xi:-]	[xi:ge:reɪ]
f.	'come out'	[gar-]	[gara:raɪ]
g.	'take'	[av-]	[ava:raɪ]
h.	'study'	[sur-]	[sura:raɪ]
i.	'finish'	[byte:-]	[byte:ge:reɪ]
j.	'drink'	[y:-]	[y:gø:røɪ]
k.	'find out'	[ol-]	[olo:roɪ]
l.	'conquer'	[jal-]	[jala:raɪ]
m.	'ask'	[asu:-]	[asu:ga:raɪ]
n.	'finish'	[tøgsg-]	[tøgsgø:røɪ]
o.	'beat'	[dev-]	[deve:reɪ]
p.	'give'	[øg-]	[øgø:røɪ]
q.	'say'	[xel-]	[xele:reɪ]
r.	'meet'	[u:lz-]	[u:lza:raɪ]
s.	'become'	[bol-]	[bolo:roɪ]
t.	'write'	[bitʃ-]	[bitʃe:reɪ]
u.	'develop'	[xøgdʒ-]	[xøgdʒø:røɪ]

i. List all of the allomorphs of the Mongolian future imperative marker.

ii. What environments condition the appearance of the different allomorphs?

46. Japanese

Consider the following inflected Japanese verb forms and answer the questions that follow. (X, Y, and Z are used as "dummy" pronouns in the glosses—they are not actually expressed morphologically in the data.)

a. [tabeta] 'X ate Y'
b. [aketa] 'X opened Y'
c. [tabesaseta] 'X made Y eat Z'
d. [akesaseta] 'X made Y open Z'
e. [taberareta] 'X was eaten'
f. [akerareta] 'X was opened'
g. [tabesaserareta] 'X was made to eat Y'
h. [akesaserareta] 'X was made to open Y'
i. [tabesasenai] 'X doesn't/won't make Y eat Z'
j. [tabenai] 'X doesn't/won't eat Y'
k. [tabesaserareru] 'X is/will be made to eat Y'

i. Give the Japanese morphemes for the following English translations:

_____ 'open'
_____ 'eat'
_____ passive marker ('. . . be VERB-ed,' e.g., 'They were opened/eaten')
_____ causative marker ('. . . make X VERB,' e.g., 'Robin makes Tracey laugh')
_____ nonpast marker (present or future tense)
_____ past marker
_____ negative marker

ii. Suppose a Japanese verb form were to include the following sets of morphemes. For each set, indicate the order in which the morphemes would occur in a verb form.

- passive, root, past, causative
- causative, nonpast, root
- root, negative, causative

iii. Give the Japanese verb form that would be used for each of the following English translations. Remember that you don't need to worry about words like *she, him,* and *them.*

- '(She) will make (him) open (them).'
- (He) will be made to open (them).'

iv. In Japanese, [uketa] means '(She) took (a test).' Using this fact along with what you've observed above, how would you say the following in Japanese? Again, don't try to translate the items in parentheses.

- '(She) was made to take (a test).'
- '(She) makes (him) take (a test).'
- '(She) will not take (a test).'

Further Readings

Aronoff, Mark, and Kirsten Fudeman. 2010. *What is morphology?* 2nd edn. Oxford: Wiley-Blackwell.

Haspelmath, Martin, and Andrea D. Sims. 2010. *Understanding morphology.* 2nd edn. New York: Routledge.

Katamba, Francis, and John Stonham. 2006. *Morphology.* 2nd edn. London: Palgrave Macmillan.

Plag, Ingo. 2003. *Word-formation in English.* Cambridge: Cambridge University Press.

CHAPTER
5

······································

Syntax

sentences are made of words

FILE **5.0**

What Is Syntax?

As a component of mental grammar, **syntax** has to do with how sentences and other phrases can be constructed out of smaller phrases and words. As a native speaker of some language, you know which strings of words correspond to sentences in your language, and which don't, because you know what the permissible syntactic combinations of words are in your language. Syntax is also a name for the subfield of linguistics that studies this component of grammar.

The construction of sentences is not a trivial matter. If you take a moment to consider it, you will realize that it isn't possible to take just any bunch of English words, jumble them together in random order, and get an actual sentence of English. Only certain combinations of words actually count as sentences of English—and the same is true of all natural languages.

But how do you know which combinations of words are sentences and which are not? What kinds of factors determine which combinations are possible? How are languages similar and how do they differ with respect to sentence construction? These are the kinds of questions that syntacticians try to answer and that you'll become familiar with in this file.

Contents

FILE 5.1

....

Basic Ideas of Syntax

5.1.1 (Un)Grammaticality

Syntax is the component of grammar that deals with how words and phrases are combined into larger phrases. Words (e.g., *Bob, cake, out*) and phrases (e.g., *out the window, my cake, Bob ate my cake*) are all **linguistic expressions.** A linguistic expression is just a piece of language—it has a certain form (e.g., what it sounds like), a certain meaning, and, most relevantly, some syntactic properties as well. These syntactic properties determine how the expression can combine with other expressions. To rephrase slightly, syntax is broadly concerned with how expressions combine with one another to form larger expressions. Some combinations are successful; others are not. For example, we can all agree that *Sally, Bob,* and *likes* are English expressions. Presumably, we can also agree that (1a) is a sentence of English while (1b) is not.

(1)   a.   Sally likes Bob.
        b.   *Likes Bob Sally.

We can ask, then, why it is that arranging the same three English expressions in one way results in a sentence (see (1a)), while combining them in a different way does not (see (1b)). When a string of words really does form a sentence of some language, we say it is **grammatical** in that language. If some string of words does not form a sentence, we call it **ungrammatical** and mark it with the symbol *, as in (1b) above (see also Section 1.2.3). When a sentence is grammatical, we say that it is syntactically well-formed. If it is ungrammatical, we also refer to it as syntactically ill-formed.

     The native speakers of a given language are uniquely qualified to decide whether a string of words truly forms a sentence of their native language, that is, to make a **grammaticality judgment.** A grammaticality judgment is a reflection of speakers' mental grammar, and not a test of their conscious knowledge of the prescriptive rules (see Files 1.2 and 1.3). So, although the sentence *We are going to quickly wrap up this paragraph and move on to the next file* violates a prescriptive rule ("do not split infinitives!"), we nonetheless consider it grammatical. When making a grammaticality judgment about some string of words, ask yourself whether you could utter the string in question, whether you have ever heard it uttered, and whether you know or can imagine other native speakers of the same language who would utter it. Do not worry about whether the string in question complies with prescriptive rules.

5.1.2 The Relationship between Syntax and Semantics

Along with distinguishing between the prescriptive and the descriptive concept of grammaticality, we also need to distinguish between syntax and semantics, which is concerned with linguistic meaning. These two subject areas are not completely independent of one another. In a way, the purpose of assembling sentences and other phrases is to communicate more complex meanings than we could if we just used individual words. This is because the way in which expressions are syntactically combined with one another contributes to the meaning of the resulting sentence. Consider the following pair of English sentences:

(2)   a. Sally likes Bob.
      b. Bob likes Sally.

Sentence (2a) does not mean the same thing as (2b). However, both of these sentences contain exactly the same expressions (*Bob, Sally,* and *likes*), whose meanings are exactly the same in each of the sentences above. The crucial difference between (2a) and (2b) lies in how these expressions are syntactically combined; it is the different syntactic combinations that produce the different meanings.

In English, we often call the expression that usually occurs immediately to the left of the verb its **subject,** and the one that occurs immediately to the right of the verb (if any) its **object.** One way to explain the syntactic differences between (2a) and (2b) is to say that in (2a), *Bob* is the object of *likes* and *Sally* is the subject of *likes,* while in (2b), these relations are switched: *Sally* is the object of *likes,* while *Bob* is its subject. The different syntactic combinations of *likes, Sally,* and *Bob* in (2) account for their difference in meaning.

The fact that the meaning of a sentence depends on the meanings of the expressions it contains and on the way they are syntactically combined is called the **principle of compositionality** (see also File 6.4). The principle of compositionality underlies the design feature of productivity (see File 1.4). When you know a language, you can produce and understand an infinite number of sentences because you know the meanings of the **lexical expressions** (i.e., words), and you know the consequences that different ways of syntactically combining them will have on the meaning of larger, multi-word **phrasal expressions.** As a result, even though all languages have a finite lexicon, they all allow for the construction of an infinite number of meaningful sentences. In this sense, syntax and semantics are intimately related.

In another sense, however, syntax and semantics are quite independent from one another. First, it is possible to have a grammatical, syntactically well-formed sentence with a bizarre meaning, and, conversely, it is possible to have a non-sentence whose meaning we can understand. Below is a famous sentence, due to Noam Chomsky:

(3)   Colorless green ideas sleep furiously.

This sentence seems to mean something quite strange—colorless things cannot be green, ideas are not the kinds of things that sleep, and it's not clear that sleeping is the kind of activity that can be carried out in a furious manner. However, syntactically speaking, (3) is a perfectly grammatical sentence of English. If you're having trouble appreciating its syntactic well-formedness, compare it with (4).

(4)   *Green sleep colorless furiously ideas.

Sentence (3) may mean something strange, but (4) is just plain (syntactic) garbage!

On the other hand, sometimes a non-sentence can successfully convey a perfectly reasonable meaning. Suppose you have a college friend who is not a native speaker of English and occasionally makes errors. One day your friend comes to you and excitedly exclaims:

(5)   *Me bought dog!

You would probably have no problem figuring out the meaning your friend was trying to express (the fact that she bought a dog), but, at the same time, you would most likely recognize immediately that (5) is not syntactically well-formed in English; you might even repair it to something like (6).

(6) I bought a dog.

Thus, it's possible both for actual sentences to express strange meanings as in (3) and for non-sentences to convey ordinary meanings as in (5).

There is another way in which syntax is independent of semantics: the syntactic properties of expressions cannot be predicted or explained on the basis of an expression's meaning. Consider the following pair of English verbs: *eat* and *devour*. They mean approximately the same thing in that they both refer to the activity of consuming food, but syntactically they behave very differently. Many native English speakers agree with the following pattern of grammaticality judgments:

(7) a. Sally ate an apple.
     b. Sally devoured an apple.

(8) a. Sally ate.
     b. *Sally devoured.

While both *eat* and *devour* can occur with an object (an *apple* in (7a) and (7b)), *eat* does not require one since (8a) is grammatical in English. *Devour*, on the other hand, must occur with an object, since omitting the object results in ungrammaticality as in (8b). So although these two verbs are very similar in meaning, their syntactic properties are different.

Here is another example—both *my* and *mine* intuitively mean the same thing; that is, they describe the relation of possession between the speaker and something else. However, as example (9) shows, their syntactic behavior is different.

(9) a. This dog is mine.   *This is mine dog.
     b. *This dog is my.   This is my dog.

These facts would be puzzling if we assumed that meanings determine the syntactic properties of words. If we acknowledge that words have syntactic properties, distinct and independent from their meanings, the syntactic difference between *mine* and *my* is not surprising at all.

Further, if we assumed that meanings determine the syntactic properties of expressions, we would not expect to see any syntactic differences across languages. However, if you have ever tried to learn a foreign language, it should be clear to you that this is not the case. While different languages have expressions that have the same meanings, these expressions can have vastly different syntactic properties in different languages. Let's examine one point of contrast between English and Serbo-Croatian that has nothing to do with word meanings and everything to do with syntactic properties.

(10) a. Ana has a dog.
     b. Ana   ima   jednog   psa.
        Ana   has   a   dog
        'Ana has a dog.'

(11) a. *Ana has dog.
     b. Ana   ima   psa.
        Ana   has   dog
        'Ana has a dog.'

Sentence (10a) is grammatical in English, and so is its word-for-word translation into Serbo-Croatian in (10b). If we get rid of the English determiner *a,* we no longer have a grammatical sentence of English (see (11a)). However, getting rid of the equivalent determiner *jednog* 'a' from the Serbo-Croatian sentence does not result in ungrammaticality—(11b) is a well-formed sentence of Serbo-Croatian and means the same thing as (10b). What we learn from these examples is that words with equivalent meanings can behave quite differently syntactically in different languages. So, while syntactic combination has consequences for the meanings that sentences express, meanings do not determine the syntactic properties of expressions, and syntactic well-formedness is largely independent of meaning. Since syntactic well-formedness and syntactic properties in general cannot be explained away in terms of other kinds of linguistic properties, we must study them in their own right.

FILE 5.2

....

Syntactic Properties

5.2.1 What Are Syntactic Properties?

If syntax is the study of how expressions combine, but not all combinations of expressions are possible, it is natural to ask what kinds of restrictions exist on these combinations. That is, why are some combinations of expressions syntactically well-formed, but others are not? The short answer is that it has to do with the **syntactic properties** of the expressions that determine their behavior.

In this file, we will see that there are essentially two kinds of syntactic properties. One set of syntactic properties has to do with **word order**—how are expressions allowed to be ordered with respect to one another? The other set of properties has to do with the **co-occurrence** of expressions—if some expression occurs in a sentence, what other expressions can or must co-occur with it in that sentence?

5.2.2 Word Order

Word order is perhaps the most obvious aspect of syntactic well-formedness. In an English sentence, for example, subjects typically precede verbs, while objects follow them, as shown in (1a) and (2a). Deviating from this word order pattern usually results in ungrammaticality, as shown in (1b) and (2b–d).

(1) a. Sally walked.
     b. *Walked Sally.

(2) a. Sally ate an apple.
     b. *Sally an apple ate.
     c. *Ate Sally an apple.
     d. *Ate an apple Sally.

This word order pattern, in which subjects precede verbs which in turn precede objects, is referred to as SVO (an abbreviation of Subject-Verb-Object). About 35% of the world's languages have this word order pattern. The SOV pattern is even more common than SVO; about 44% of languages (e.g., Korean and Turkish) typically show SOV order. About 19% of languages, including Arabic and Irish, have VSO word order. The remaining patterns, VOS, OVS, and OSV, are quite rare. An example sentence from Malagasy, a VOS Austronesian language spoken in Madagascar, is shown in (3).

(3) Manasa   lamba   amin'ny   savony   ny   lehilahy.
     washes *clothes* *with the* *soap*   *the*   *man*
     'The man washes clothes with the soap.'

However, while it may be convenient to label a language as being VOS, SOV, etc., you should keep in mind that such labels can be misleading. For one thing, many languages exhibit different word order patterns in different contexts. In German, for example, main clauses such as (4a) typically have the SVO word order, while subordinate clauses (like the underlined group of expressions in (4b)) exhibit the SOV pattern.

(4) a. Karl   kocht   die   Suppe.
        Karl   cooks   the   soup
        'Karl is cooking the soup.'

     b. Magda   ist   froh,   <u>daß</u>   Karl   die   Suppe   kocht.
        Magda   is   happy   that   Karl   the   soup   cooks
        'Magda is happy that Karl is cooking the soup.'

Even in English, which has a fairly rigid word order, VSO word order can show up in yes/no questions (5a), and OSV word order in so-called **topicalized** sentences (5b).

(5) a. Is Sally a student?
     b. Sally: I know you don't like apples, Polly, so I made you a pecan pie instead of an
                apple pie.
        Polly: Oh, <u>apples, I like</u>. It's pears that I can't stand.

In (5b), the underlined sentence *apples, I like* exhibits the OSV order. Although this sentence requires a special context to be uttered, it is still a possible sentence of English, so it would be misleading to say that English is an SVO language across the board.

Further, some languages have much more flexible word order, so it is not clear that it would be meaningful at all to say that they have a "typical" word order pattern. For example, in some Slavic languages like Russian and Serbo-Croatian, as well as in Dyirbal, an Australian language, all six possible orders of verbs, subjects, and objects result in grammatical sentences.

Word order restrictions go far beyond the relative ordering of verbs, subjects, and objects. In English, for example, expressions such as the demonstrative *that* (part of a larger category called determiners) must precede the noun, as shown in (6), while in Malay, an Austronesian language, they follow the noun, as shown in (7).

(6) a. Sally still hasn't read <u>these books</u>.
     b. *Sally still hasn't read <u>books these</u>.

(7) a. buku-buku   ini
         books   these
         'these books'
     b. *ini buku-buku

Other kinds of expressions can be subject to ordering constraints as well. Prepositions such as *with* in English must come immediately to the left of the noun phrase, as shown in (8).

(8) a. Sally finally met <u>with that person</u>.
     b. *Sally finally met <u>that person with</u>.

In Japanese, however, the expression *to* 'with' must occur immediately to the right of the noun phrase, as shown in (9). For that reason, expressions like *to* are called postpositions, and not prepositions.

(9) a. kono   kodomo   to
      this   *child*   *with*
    'with this child'

    b. *to kono kodomo

Apart from imposing relative ordering constraints between certain kinds of expressions, languages can also have word order restrictions that mandate that a certain expression occur in a specific position in a sentence. For example, Warlpiri, another Australian language, generally allows free ordering of expressions in a sentence. The only word order restriction is that an auxiliary verb (e.g., *will* in English) must occur in the second position in a sentence. It doesn't matter what kind of expression comes right before or right after the auxiliary, and it doesn't matter how the expressions that follow the auxiliary are relatively ordered, so long as the auxiliary is second.

As we have seen, there are many different kinds of word order constraints that languages make use of. However, merely getting expressions in the right order in a sentence doesn't guarantee syntactic well-formedness. There is much more to syntax than just word order.

5.2.3 Co-Occurrence

While the order of expressions is obviously important for syntactic well-formedness, there is another set of syntactic properties that is, in a way, more basic than word order, yet far less obvious. As soon as you decide on using a particular expression in a sentence, this initial choice can dictate the structure of the rest of the sentence. The expression you choose may allow or even require that certain other expressions co-occur with it in a sentence. This section examines these co-occurrence relations between expressions, to which all languages are sensitive.

    a. Arguments. Many expressions have co-occurrence requirements. That is, if they show up in a sentence, certain other expressions are required to occur in that sentence as well. Recall our earlier observation concerning *devoured*:

(10) a.   Sally devoured an apple.
     b. *Sally devoured.

For many native English speakers, an object noun phrase (i.e., *an apple* in (10a)) is required to co-occur with *devoured*. Note that the subject noun phrase is also obligatory, as illustrated in (11), which is not a sentence.

(11) *Devoured an apple.

If the occurrence of some expression X in a sentence necessitates the occurrence of some expression Y, then we say that Y is an **argument** of X. So, *devoured* requires two arguments: an object (*an apple*) and a subject (*Sally*). Alternatively, we say that in (10a), *Sally* and *an apple* are both arguments of *devoured*. Non-subject arguments are specifically called **complements**. Thus, we can also say that in (10a), *an apple* is a complement of *devoured*.

    Even if a language has very flexible word order, it is still sensitive to the co-occurrence requirements of expressions. Consider the following examples from Serbo-Croatian:

(12) a. Marija   voli   muziku.
       Marija   *likes*   *music*
       'Marija likes music.'

     b. Marija muziku voli.
     c. Voli muziku Marija.
     d. Voli Marija muziku.
     e. Muziku voli Marija.
     f. Muziku Marija voli.

(13) a. *Marija voli.
     b. *Voli Marija.

These examples show that in Serbo-Croatian, if *voli* 'likes' occurs in a sentence, an object (in this case *muziku* 'music') has to occur in that sentence as well, since omitting it results in ungrammaticality, as shown in (13). But as long as the object occurs in the sentence, it doesn't matter where it shows up or how it is ordered with respect to the verb and the subject—all six orders are grammatical, as shown in (12).

    Arguments do not have to be noun phrases, like *an apple*. Different kinds of expressions require different kinds of arguments. When we consider complements, we can see that *an apple* is an acceptable complement for *devoured*, but not for *wondered*, since *Sally wondered an apple* is not a sentence. Conversely, *about Bob* is a fine complement for *wondered*, but not for *devoured*—*Sally wondered about Bob* is a sentence of English; however, *Sally devoured about Bob* is not. If a complement is a noun phrase (e.g., *Bob, Sally, an apple*; see File 5.4), then we call it an object.

    Expressions can require multiple complements. Some examples of different kinds of complements of English verbs are given in (14).

(14) a. Sally told <u>Polly</u> <u>she's leaving</u>.
     [*Polly* and *she's leaving* are both complements of *told*]

     b. Sally put <u>the book</u> <u>on the desk</u>.
     [*the book* and *on the desk* are both complements of *put*]

     c. Sally persuaded <u>Bob</u> <u>to go on vacation</u>.
     [*Bob* and *to go on vacation* are both complements of *persuaded*]

    We noted that in English, subjects are also verbal arguments. However, there are languages that allow subjects to be omitted, for example, Italian.

(15) a. Ho   comprato   un   libro.
     have-1sg   *bought*   *a*   *book*
     'I bought a book.'

     b. Io   ho   comprato   un   libro.
     I   *have-1sg*   *bought*   *a*   *book*
     'I bought a book.'

In this example, the auxiliary *ho* 'have' already contains crucial information about the subject, namely, that it has to be the first-person singular 'I.' The subject *io* 'I' can occur, but doesn't have to, in the sentence—(15a) is still a grammatical sentence of Italian.

    It is important to keep in mind that verbs can be very picky about the form of the argument they require. For example, the only possible subject for *rained* in English seems to be *it*, as in the sentence *It rained*. It is not easy to come up with other expressions that could replace *it* in this sentence (excluding poetic usage or other metaphorical extensions). Now consider a verb like *relied*. Its complement can only be some phrase of the form *on x* or *upon x*, for example, *Sally relied <u>on Bob</u>* or *Sally relied <u>on her charm</u>*.

It's not just verbs that can require certain arguments. Other expressions can have their own arguments as well. For example:

(16) a.   Sally came to the party with <u>Bob</u>.
     b.   *Sally came to the party with.
             [*Bob* is an argument of *with*]

(17) a.   Sally is fond <u>of parties</u>.
     b.   *Sally is fond.
             [*of parties* is an argument of *fond*]

(18) a.   Bob invited <u>Polly</u> and <u>Sally</u> to the party.
     b.   *Bob invited Polly and to the party.
     c.   *Bob invited and Sally to the party.
             [*Polly* and *Sally* are both arguments ("conjuncts") of *and*]

For a sentence to be well-formed, all the expressions it contains have to have all and **only** the arguments they need. We emphasize *only* because trying to give expressions more than their share of arguments is as bad as not giving them all the arguments they need. For example, *devoured* needs exactly one subject argument and exactly one complement—both **Sally devoured* and **Sally devoured an apple a pear* are ungrammatical. Similarly, neither **devoured an apple* nor **Sally Tom devoured an apple* is a sentence.

The restriction on the number of arguments that an expression can combine with can also be observed with nouns and determiners. Recall from Section 5.1.2 that, in English, a noun such as *dog* cannot occur by itself. Rather, it has to be preceded by a determiner such as *a*. However, it cannot be preceded by more than one determiner.

(19) a.   Sally has {a/this/my} dog.[1]
     b.   *Sally has dog.
     c.   *Sally has this a dog.
     d.   *Sally has this a my dog.

Finally, we note that languages can differ in terms of co-occurrence restrictions, just as they can differ in terms of word order. For example, in Serbo-Croatian it is possible for multiple determiners to co-occur, as shown in (20).

(20) Marija   sad   ima   tog   mog   psa.
     Marija   *now*   *has*   *this*   *my*   *dog*
     'Marija now has that dog of mine.'

A key goal of this section has been to demonstrate the importance of the co-occurrence requirements of expressions. Many expressions require that certain other expressions—their arguments—occur with them in a sentence. Failing to give expressions the right number and kind of arguments will result in ungrammaticality.

---

[1]"Sally has {a/this/my} dog" is an abbreviation of:
    Sally has a dog.
    Sally has this dog.
    Sally has my dog.
The curly bracket notation, "{a/this/my}," indicates that with respect to the judgment given in the example, each expression within the curly brackets behaves the same. In this case, it would be grammatical for any one of them to occur in the specified position.

b. Adjuncts. While there have to be exactly the right number and type of arguments for each expression in a sentence, there are certain kinds of expressions whose occurrence in a sentence is purely optional. These kinds of expressions are called **adjuncts.** Not only are they optional, but it is also possible to add as many of them as you like without winding up with a non-sentence. Let's consider some examples from English.

(21) a. Sally likes dogs.
    b. Sally likes <u>small</u> dogs.
    c. Sally likes <u>small</u> <u>fluffy</u> dogs.
    d. Sally likes <u>small</u> <u>fluffy</u> <u>brown</u> dogs.

The underlined expressions in (21)—attributive adjectives—don't have to occur in the sentence since (21a) is grammatical. Furthermore, you can in principle add as many of them as you like and the sentence remains grammatical. In addition, they can be freely ordered with respect to one another—that is, *Sally likes fluffy brown dogs* and *Sally likes brown fluffy dogs* are both sentences.

We can make a couple of additional observations about these adjectives. First, while their occurrence is optional, we cannot add them to just any sentence, as (22) and (23) illustrate.

(22) a.   Sally likes Bob.
    b. *Sally likes fluffy Bob.

(23) a.   Sally runs.
    b. *Sally runs small.

In fact, the occurrence of these adjectives in a sentence is dependent on there being some expression like *dogs* in that sentence (i.e., a noun; see File 5.4). So, if you have an attributive adjective like *small* in a sentence, you also have to have a noun like *dogs* in that sentence. This observation should remind you of the definition we gave for arguments: Y is an argument of X if the occurrence of X necessitates the occurrence of Y. We could then say that *dogs* is in a way an argument of *small,* although more commonly we say that *small* is an adjunct of *dogs.*

The point here is that being an argument and being an adjunct are not totally different kinds of co-occurrence relations—they're kind of like mirror images of one another. If X is an adjunct of Y, then Y is an argument of X because the presence of Y in a sentence is necessary for X to occur. However, it is not necessarily true that if Y is an argument of X, then X is Y's adjunct. For example, in *Sally runs, Sally* is an argument of *runs,* but we cannot consider *runs* an adjunct of *Sally.* If *runs* were an adjunct, we would expect it to be possible for multiple expressions like *runs* to occur in a sentence, since one of the defining properties of adjuncts is that we can add as many of them as we like. *Sally runs sleeps* is not a sentence, so *runs* is not an adjunct (and neither is *sleeps,* for that matter). Furthermore, adjuncts are optional, but we cannot get rid of *runs* and still have a sentence—since *Sally* is not a sentence all by itself, *runs* is not optional.

A second observation concerning attributive adjectives has to do with their semantic function (see also File 6.4). In *Sally likes small dogs, small* adds additional information about the meaning of *dogs.* This sentence tells us not that Sally likes dogs in general, but more specifically that she likes dogs that are small. The adjective *small* modifies the meaning of *dogs.* For this reason, adjuncts are sometimes called **modifiers.**

Attributive adjectives are not the only kinds of adjuncts. Other examples of adjunct phrases in English are underlined in the examples that follow. According to the criteria outlined above, they are adjuncts because their occurrence is optional, there can be multiple occurrences of them in a sentence, and they can be ordered freely with respect to one another.

(24) a. Sally went to France.
   b. Sally went to France <u>last year</u>.
   c. Sally went to France <u>last year</u> <u>in July</u>.
   d. Sally went to France <u>last year</u> <u>in July</u> <u>with some friends</u>.
   e. Sally went to France <u>last year</u> <u>in July</u> <u>with some friends</u> <u>to study French</u>.

It is important to point out that the same expression can be an argument in one sentence, but an adjunct in another. This depends on how the expressions in the sentence are syntactically combined. For example, in (24b), *last year* is an adjunct because it can be omitted without loss of grammaticality. However, in the sentence *Last year was the best year of Sally's life*, *last year* is an argument since it is the subject of *was* and cannot be omitted. Here are some other examples of the same expression being used as an argument in one sentence, but as an adjunct in a different sentence.

(25) a. Sally urged Bob <u>to study French</u>.   [argument of *urged*]
   b. Sally went to France <u>to study French</u>.   [adjunct]

(26) a. Sally put the book <u>on the desk</u>.   [argument of *put*]
   b. Sally's cat was sleeping <u>on the desk</u>.   [adjunct]

(27) a. Sally's cat seemed <u>cute</u>.   [argument of *seemed*]
   b. Sally has a <u>cute</u> cat.   [adjunct]

(28) a. Sally behaved <u>very carelessly</u>.   [argument of *behaved*]
   b. Sally did her homework <u>very carelessly</u>.   [adjunct]

Therefore, it is misguided to ask whether an expression X is an argument or an adjunct independent of context; we always have to ask whether X is an argument or an adjunct in some particular sentence.

Table (29) summarizes the main differences between arguments and adjuncts in English and should help you distinguish them from one another. Keep in mind, however, that

(29) Distinguishing arguments and adjuncts

Arguments	**Adjuncts**
Obligatory:	*Optional:*
Sally seemed <u>happy</u>. *Sally seemed.	The cat was sleeping <u>on the table</u>.
	The cat was sleeping.
<u>Sally</u> seemed happy. *seemed happy.	The <u>fluffy</u> cat was sleeping.
	The cat was sleeping.
Cannot have more than required:	*Can have as many as you like:*
Sally seemed <u>cute</u>. *Sally seemed <u>cute</u> <u>happy</u>.	The cat was sleeping. The <u>gray</u> cat was sleeping. The <u>fluffy</u> <u>gray</u> cat was sleeping.
<u>Sally</u> seemed cute. *<u>Sally</u> <u>Bob</u> seemed cute.	Sally left. Sally left <u>yesterday</u>. Sally left <u>yesterday</u> <u>around 3 P.M.</u>
Cannot be freely ordered with respect to one another:	*Can be freely ordered with respect to one another:*
Sally put <u>the book</u> <u>on the table</u>.	The <u>fluffy</u> <u>gray</u> cat was sleeping.
*Sally put <u>on the table</u> <u>the book</u>.	The <u>gray</u> <u>fluffy</u> cat was sleeping.
Sally persuaded <u>Bob</u> <u>to study French</u>.	Sally left <u>yesterday</u> <u>around 3 P.M.</u>
*Sally persuaded <u>to study French</u> <u>Bob</u>.	Sally left <u>around 3 P.M.</u> <u>yesterday</u>.

it may not always be clear whether to count an expression as an argument or as an adjunct. In such cases, you should carefully assess the expression's syntactic behavior with respect to these criteria and see if you can gather more evidence for it being either an argument or an adjunct. Also, remember that different speakers can have different grammaticality judgments (see Section 10.2.5 on syntactic variation), so you and your classmates might arrive at different conclusions about the same expression, and this is perfectly normal.

c. Agreement. We mentioned above that there are often strict requirements regarding the kind of argument that an expression can have. For example, *about Bob* can be a complement of *wondered* but not a complement of *devoured*; the only expression that can be the subject of *rained* is *it*, etc. Another kind of requirement that expressions can have concerns the particular morphological form of their arguments. In this section we discuss how the inflectional morphological form (see Section 4.1.3) of an expression influences its co-occurrence requirements.

Let's begin by considering the examples in (30). Most English speakers would agree with the following judgments:

(30) a.   Sandy likes Bob.
    b.   *{I/you/we/they} likes Bob.[2]
    c.   *Sandy like Bob.
    d.   {I/you/we/they} like Bob.

In (30), we see that *likes* can occur only with a third-person singular subject such as *Sandy*, while *like* occurs with all other kinds of subjects. The only difference between *likes* and *like* is the presence of the inflectional suffix *-s*, but it is precisely that suffix that is responsible for their different co-occurrence requirements.

The inflectional form of an expression can convey information about number, person, gender, and other so-called grammatical features, or some combination of them (e.g., the *-s* in *likes* simultaneously marks person (third) and number (singular)). Distinct expressions in a sentence may be required to have the same value for some grammatical feature, in which case we say that they agree with respect to that feature. Such features are called agreement features, and this phenomenon is called **agreement**. For example, we could say that *likes* agrees with *Sandy* in person and number: they are both third-person singular.

With respect to number in English, demonstratives also show agreement patterns: they have to agree with nouns in number, as shown in (31).

(31) a.   This girl came.
    b.   *This girls came.
    c.   *These girl came.
    d.   These girls came.

In (31a), the demonstrative *this* and the noun *girl* are both singular, and in (31d), *these* and *girls* are both plural (the *-s* in *girls* being the plural inflection). Mixing and matching of expressions that are marked for a different number is not allowed, as indicated by the ungrammaticality of (31b) and (31c).

---

[2]"*{I/you/we/they} likes Bob" is an abbreviation of:

    *I likes Bob.
    *You likes Bob.
    *We likes Bob.
    *They likes Bob.

So in (30b), all the expressions within the curly brackets are unacceptable in the specified position.

English distinguishes only singular and plural number for nouns, but other languages can have different kinds of grammatical number. Inuktitut, a language spoken in northern Canada, morphologically distinguishes between singular, plural, and dual, for groups of two things.

(32) nuvuja   'cloud'
      nuvujak   'two clouds'
      nuvujait   'three or more clouds'

Some languages do not mark grammatical number on nouns at all, for example, Korean. The following Korean sentence could mean either that there is one car or that there are multiple cars on the street, since *chaka* 'car(s)' is not marked for number and neither is the verb *dallinta* 'run'.

(33) kile   chaka   dallinta.
      road   *car*   *run*
      'There is one car running on the road.'
      'There are (multiple) cars running on the road.'

It is important to note that even in languages that do mark number on nouns, grammatical number may not be predictable from the expression's meaning. For example, *scissors* in English is grammatically plural and shows plural agreement (e.g., *These scissors are the best!*), but semantically it refers to a single object. In Serbo-Croatian, *lišće* 'leaves' refers to a plurality of leaves, but syntactically it behaves like a singular noun and has to occur with singular determiners and singular verbs.

Other types of agreement are also observed in languages. For example, in Italian and some other languages, certain verbal forms have to agree with the subject in gender.

(34) a. Lei   è   andata   a   Palermo.
        she *be-3sg*   *go-part.fem.sg.*   *to*   *Palermo*
        'She went to Palermo.'

     b. Lui   è   andato   a   Palermo.
        he   *be-3sg*   *go-part.masc.sg.* *to*   *Palermo*
        'He went to Palermo.'

     c. *Lei è andato a Palermo.

     d. *Lui è andata a Palermo.

In these examples, the form of the verb 'be,' *è*, agrees with the subject in person (third) and number (singular), while the participial form of the verb 'go' agrees with the subject in gender and number. The form *andata* requires a feminine singular subject, while the form *andato* requires a masculine singular subject. Mixing and matching is not allowed, as indicated by the ungrammaticality of (34c) and (34d).

It is worth mentioning that grammatical gender typically has nothing to do with natural gender. Although in the Italian example above, we used *lei* 'she' and *lui* 'he,' which have the expected gender marking (feminine and masculine, respectively), this need not be the case. For example, in German the expression that means 'the girl,' *das Mädchen*, is not feminine in terms of grammatical gender, but neuter. In Serbo-Croatian, if you want to talk about male giraffes, you have to use expressions that have feminine grammatical gender.

In different languages that make use of grammatical gender, the expressions that refer to the same thing may be assigned to a different gender class. Thus, the word that means 'book' is masculine in French (*le livre*), neuter in German (*das Buch*), and feminine in Russian (*kniga*). Therefore, grammatical gender is an arbitrary system of classification. Similar classification systems in other languages are often referred to as noun classes.

In sum, the morphological form of an expression has consequences for its syntactic properties. For that reason, morphology and syntax are often seen as tightly related components of grammar and sometimes even considered and referred to jointly as **morpho-syntax.**

....

Syntactic Constituency

5.3.1 What Are Syntactic Constituents?

Suppose you were asked to break up the sentence *The fluffy cat was sleeping on the desk* into smaller syntactic units. Of course, you'd most likely immediately recognize that each lexical expression (*the, fluffy, cat,* etc.) is a unit in its own right. What about units larger than individual words but smaller than the entire sentence, however? You'd probably consider *on the desk* to be some kind of unit. Similarly, you might intuitively think of *the fluffy cat* as "belonging together." On the other hand, you might have the intuition that *on the* and *cat was* are less likely to be units.

In this file we discuss the idea that certain groups of expressions within a larger phrase can form a syntactic unit—a **syntactic constituent.** The syntactic constituents of a phrasal expression are the smaller expressions out of which the phrase was constructed. You can think of expressions that form a syntactic constituent as being tightly combined together, more tightly than with other expressions in the same sentence. For example, *an apple* in *Sally devoured an apple* is a syntactic constituent. Those two words together function as the complement of *devoured.* Or, *in July* in *Sally went to France in July* is also a syntactic constituent—we can omit both of those words and still have a sentence (*Sally went to France*). However, omitting either one individually results in ungrammaticality (**Sally went to France July*; **Sally went to France in*). Thus, the two words together form a syntactic constituent that functions as an adjunct in *Sally went to France in July.*

It is important to identify the syntactic constituents of a sentence because they reveal the syntactic structure of the sentence; in other words, they show how the sentence was built out of smaller expressions. There are several general constituency tests that can help you determine which groups of expressions form a constituent in some sentence. We will discuss a few of these tests in the following sections.

5.3.2 Answers to Questions

Suppose you're trying to determine whether some string of words in a sentence forms a syntactic constituent or not. One way to do this is to construct a question based on the sentence and see if the string of words you're testing can serve as an answer. If it can, it forms a constituent; if it cannot, then the words in question do not form a constituent. Try to alter the sentence whose constituents you're testing as little as possible. Here are some examples of the application of this test:

(1) Is *on the desk* in *The cat was sleeping on the desk* a constituent? Yes.
    a. Where was the cat sleeping?
    b. <u>On the desk.</u>

(2) Is *sleeping on the desk* in *The cat was sleeping on the desk* a constituent? Yes.
    a. What was the cat doing?
    b. <u>Sleeping on the desk.</u>

(3)   Is *the cat* in *The cat was sleeping on the desk* a constituent? Yes.
       a. Who was sleeping on the desk?
       b. <u>The cat</u>.

Because we can come up with questions based on the sentence *The cat was sleeping on the desk* that can be answered with *on the desk, sleeping on the desk,* and *the cat,* we know that these three strings each form a constituent. However, it's impossible to come up with a question based on that sentence that we could answer with *on the*: **Was cat sleeping desk?* is not even a grammatical question, and we certainly couldn't answer *Where was the cat sleeping?* with *on the*. Consequently, we know that *on the* is not a syntactic constituent.

5.3.3   Clefting

Another constituency test involves constructing a **cleft,** a kind of sentence in which some constituent is displaced (or moved) to the left. It has the general form *It was X that Y,* where X is the displaced constituent and Y is the remainder of the sentence whose constituents you're investigating. If the cleft is grammatical, then the displaced expression is a constituent. If you try to move some expression that does not form a constituent, the cleft will not be grammatical. Here are some examples:

(4)   Is *on the desk* in *The cat was sleeping on the desk* a constituent? Yes.
       It was <u>on the desk</u> that the cat was sleeping.

(5)   Is *the cat* in *The cat was sleeping on the desk* a constituent? Yes.
       It was <u>the cat</u> that was sleeping on the desk.

(6)   Is *on the* in *The cat was sleeping on the desk* a constituent? No.
       *It was <u>on the</u> that the cat was sleeping desk.

Note that the cleft test will not work for all kinds of constituents. We know from the question-answer test that *sleeping on the desk* is a constituent. However, **It was sleeping on the desk that the cat was* is not a grammatical cleft. So, if a cleft is ungrammatical, it doesn't necessarily imply that the displaced expression does not form a constituent. However, if the cleft is grammatical, then you can be pretty sure that the displaced string truly does correspond to a constituent.

5.3.4   Pro-Form Substitution

The final constituency test we will look at is **substitution,** but we note that there are additional tests that can be used, e.g., coordination, deletion, and topicalization. We encourage you to look online for more information if you are interested in how these work.
       The substitution test involves replacing a constituent with a single word (or simple phrase). If you can replace the string of words you are testing with one word and the result is a grammatical sentence, this indicates that the string of words is a single unit or syntactic constituent. The best words to use for this test are **pro-forms.** Pronouns (e.g., *he/him, she/her, it, they/them, one, that*) are the most familiar pro-forms, but there are others as well. For example, there are pro-verbs such as *do (so)* (see (2) above, and Section 5.4.2), *be,* and *have;* and *there, then,* and *such* can substitute for other types of constituents. Look again at our sentence to be tested:

(7)   Is *the cat* in *The cat was sleeping on the desk* a constituent? Yes.
       <u>She</u> was sleeping on the desk.

(8)   Is *on the desk* in *The cat was sleeping on the desk* a constituent? Yes.
       The cat was sleeping <u>there</u>.

(9)   Is *sleeping on the desk* in *The cat was sleeping on the desk* a constituent? Yes.
       The cat was <u>doing so</u>.

(10)   Is *the desk* in *The cat was sleeping on the desk* a constituent? Yes.
       The cat was sleeping on <u>it</u>.

(11)   Is *on the* in *The cat was sleeping on the desk* a constituent? No.
       *The cat was sleeping {<u>it</u>/<u>there</u>/<u>then</u>/<u>such</u>/<u>do so</u>} desk.

(12)   Is *cat was* in *The cat was sleeping on the desk* a constituent? No.
       *The {<u>it</u>/<u>she</u>/<u>there</u>/<u>then</u>/<u>such</u>/<u>do so</u>} sleeping on the desk.

For the strings of words tested in (7)–(10), the fact that they can be replaced with pro-forms indicates that they are constituents, as was also shown by the previous tests. In (11)–(12), by contrast, we are unable to find a pro-form that can substitute for the word strings and still give us a grammatical sentence, which indicates that these strings most likely are not constituents. Pro-form substitution tests will also be used to identify the distributional characteristics of specific types of constituents in the next section (5.4.2).

Constituency tests are a useful tool for discovering the syntactic constituents of a sentence, but they are not perfectly reliable. As already noted, they can give inconsistent results—for example, the question-answer test can show that something is a constituent, while the cleft test suggests otherwise. It is always a good idea to use as many tests as possible before deciding whether some string of words forms a constituent or not.

Discovering which smaller expressions a sentence is built out of is necessary for understanding its syntactic structure. In File 5.5, in which we construct a simple grammar for English, we will return to the notion of syntactic constituency and discuss it in the setting of syntactic rules, which specify how exactly expressions can combine to form larger expressions. We will see that these rules reflect the constituent structure of phrasal expressions.

FILE 5.4

Syntactic Categories

5.4.1 What Are Syntactic Categories?

Thus far, we have used terms like *sentence, noun, noun phrase, attributive adjective,* etc., either relying on your intuitive understanding of them or pointing out particular examples. In this file, we discuss terms like these—names of **syntactic categories**—more explicitly and technically. The notion of syntactic category is similar to but distinct from the traditional notions of parts of speech or lexical categories (see File 4.1).

A syntactic category consists of a set of expressions that have very similar syntactic properties; that is, they have approximately the same word order and co-occurrence requirements. When two expressions have similar syntactic properties, they are usually interchangeable in a sentence; you can substitute them for one another and still have a grammatical sentence. Since such expressions can occur in almost all the same syntactic environments, we say that they have the same **syntactic distribution.**

For example, take any sentence that contains the constituent *the cat.* You can substitute *Fluffy* for *the cat* in all those sentences, and the result will be a grammatical sentence. This indicates that *Fluffy* and *the cat* have the same distribution and, therefore, the same syntactic properties. We can thus conclude that they belong to the same syntactic category. The following examples show that *the cat* and *Fluffy* have the same distribution.

(1) a. Sally likes the cat.   Sally likes Fluffy.
    b. The cat is sleeping.   Fluffy is sleeping.
    c. Sally gave the cat some food.   Sally gave Fluffy some food.
    d. It was the cat that Sally hated. It was Fluffy that Sally hated.
    e. Sally bought it for the cat.   Sally bought it for Fluffy.
    f. The cat's bowl was empty.   Fluffy's bowl was empty.

On the other hand, *Fluffy* and *cat* are not interchangeable, as shown in (2). This indicates that they do not have the same distribution and, therefore, do not belong to the same syntactic category.

(2) a. The cat was sleeping.   *The Fluffy was sleeping.
    b. *Sally gave cat some food.   Sally gave Fluffy some food.
       etc.

But why are syntactic categories important? Suppose one night you're taking a stroll in your neighborhood and you run into a friendly Martian scientist who's working on a descriptive grammar of English. The Martian already knows a lot about English, including many of its syntactic categories. However, she has encountered some new English expressions whose syntactic properties she doesn't know, and she'd like your help. All you would have to do is tell her which syntactic categories the expressions belong to. She would then immediately know the distribution of all of the new expressions: how they can combine with other expressions, how they have to be ordered with respect to other expressions, what their arguments are, etc. If you prefer, substitute "foreign language learner" or "computer" for "Martian scientist" above, and you'll come to appreciate why syntactic categories are important.

In order for syntactic categories to successfully convey detailed syntactic information, they have to be distinguished based on the syntactic properties of the expressions that comprise them. It is important to appreciate the fact that expressions do not belong to a given syntactic category by virtue of their morphological or semantic properties. Rather, it is because of their syntactic properties.

You might have been told at some point in your education that nouns refer to people, places, or things, that verbs are action words, and that adjectives are descriptive words. This is a semantically based classification system; that is, to say that nouns are words that stand for people, places, or things is to make a claim about what nouns are supposed to mean, not about how they behave syntactically. We observed early on in this chapter that semantic properties of expressions do not determine their syntactic properties. Therefore, we cannot successfully assign expressions to syntactic categories by examining their meaning.

For example, *exploded* and *destroyed* are both "action words," but they have different syntactic distributions: *Sally exploded, *Sally destroyed.* On the other hand, it is not clear that *slept* and *vegetated* could be called "action words," even though they have the same distribution as *exploded*: *Sally <u>exploded</u>, Sally <u>vegetated</u>,* and *Sally <u>slept</u>* are all sentences. The expressions *mountains* and *the hill* both refer to "places," but they have somewhat different distributions: first, they have different agreement features (plural vs. singular); and second, *mountains* can combine with determiners, but *the hill* can't (*Sally likes the <u>mountains</u>, *Sally likes the <u>the hill</u>*). Further, we pointed out at the beginning of this chapter that even expressions that mean essentially the same thing can be syntactically different (*my* vs. *mine, ate* vs. *devoured*). The point is that knowing the semantic class that some expression ostensibly belongs to does not help you figure out its syntactic properties.

Additionally, we cannot distinguish syntactic categories based on their morphological properties. For example, verbs comprise a relevant lexical category in English (see File 4.1), so we can say that, morphologically, *sleep, tell, destroy,* and *devour* are all in the same category. However, because these expressions do not all have the same syntactic properties, they do not comprise a useful syntactic category. That is, if the Martian scientist knew that *sleep* and *tell* are verbs, and then you told her that *devour* is also a verb, she would know what kinds of morphemes can combine with *devour*. For example, she would know that *devouring* is a word. Nonetheless, she would not be able to predict the syntactic distribution of *devour* at all, and, as a result, she might go around producing non-sentences like **I'd like to devour now* (cf. *I'd like to sleep now*) or **I'll devour you what I found* (cf. *I'll tell you what I found*).

If you wanted to categorize countries of the world by the size of their population, you would need to take into account how many people live in each country, rather than a country's surface area, its proximity to an ocean, or the level of education of its population. Similarly, if we want to categorize expressions of a language syntactically, we have to take into account their syntactic properties, not their meaning, their morphological properties, or what they sound like. In the following section, we discuss some major syntactic categories in English and the syntactic properties that distinguish them.

As a reminder, the grammar of English (as with any natural language) is very complex. Though we will cover many of its major syntactic categories and grammar rules here and in the next file, our discussion is necessarily quite simplified. We will mention a few specific issues where relevant, and we encourage you to carefully consider how one might account for each new piece of linguistic data you encounter, in this book or elsewhere. Various exercises and discussion questions in File 5.6 have also been provided to help you think through some of these issues.

5.4.2 Syntactic Categories in English

Although you probably have an intuitive understanding of what a sentence is, let's begin with a syntactic test for distinguishing the category **sentence.** This category (abbreviated as S) consists of expressions that can occur in the following syntactic environment:

(3) Sally thinks that _____.

Given this test, *the cat* is not a sentence (**Sally thinks that the cat*). On the other hand, *the cat is cute* is a sentence since we can say *Sally thinks that the cat is cute.*

The syntactic category of **noun phrases,** abbreviated NP, consists of personal pronouns (*he, she, you, it, we,* etc.), proper names, and any other expressions that have the same distribution. The most reliable test that you can use to check whether some constituent is a noun phrase or not is to try to replace it with a pronoun (see Section 5.3.4). If the result is a grammatical sentence, then that constituent is an NP, and if the result is ungrammatical, then it is not. In each of the examples in (4) through (6), the test indicates that the underlined expressions are NPs.

(4) Is *Fluffy* in *Fluffy was sleeping on the desk* an NP? Yes.
    a. <u>Fluffy</u> was sleeping on the desk.
    b. <u>She</u> was sleeping on the desk.

(5) Is *the cat* in *The cat was sleeping on the desk* an NP? Yes.
    a. <u>The cat</u> was sleeping on the desk.
    b. <u>She</u> was sleeping on the desk.

(6) Is *the desk* in *The cat was sleeping on the desk* an NP? Yes.
    a. The cat was sleeping on <u>the desk</u>.
    b. The cat was sleeping on <u>it</u>.

Note, however, that while *the cat* and *the desk* belong to the category NP, *cat* and *desk* do not. The pronoun replacement test indicates that they do not have the same distribution as NPs, as shown in (7) and (8).

(7) Is *cat* in *The cat was sleeping on the desk* an NP? No.
    a. The <u>cat</u> was sleeping on the desk.
    b. *The <u>she</u> was sleeping on the desk.

(8) Is *desk* in *The cat was sleeping on the desk* an NP? No.
    a. The cat was sleeping on the <u>desk</u>.
    b. *The cat was sleeping on the <u>it</u>.

Expressions such as *desk* and *cat* belong to the syntactic category of **nouns,** abbreviated N. As shown in (7) and (8), one way in which Ns and NPs are syntactically different is that Ns can co-occur with **determiners** (abbreviated Det) like *the,* while NPs cannot. The category of nouns consists of those expressions that can combine with a determiner to their left to yield an expression of category NP. For example, we can combine *the* with *cat* and get *the cat,* which, as we have already observed, is an NP.

While this provides a clear distinction for some nouns, there are other expressions for which the situation is more complicated. Nouns like *cat* or *desk* are known as **count nouns,** defined in simple terms as being able to be counted (e.g., *one cat, five cats*); as such, these nouns can also be pluralized (*cats, desks*). As noted above, when these nouns occur in the singular, they must co-occur with a determiner (cf. **Cat is sleeping on desk*). These can be contrasted with **mass nouns,** which cannot be counted and cannot (normally) be pluralized (e.g., *advice/*one advice/*advices*; *gravel/ *one gravel/*gravels*). As is often the case, this distinction is not always clear-cut, since most nouns can function as both types, given the right context (e.g., *He ordered two waters,* though *water* is typically mass, and *After I forgot to put the lid on the blender, I had blueberry all over me,* though *blueberry* is typically count); but we focus on the basic cases here.

Mass nouns, in contrast to count nouns, can occur without a determiner and can be replaced with a pronoun (*Advice can be helpful/It can be helpful*; *The road was covered with gravel/The road was covered with it*). Going by the criteria given above, this would seem to indicate that mass nouns are NPs, like pronouns and proper nouns. In contrast to those categories, however, mass nouns may also co-occur with a determiner (*The advice was helpful*; *The road was covered with the gravel,* versus **The Fluffy* was sleeping*; **The she* was sleeping*). So mass nouns cannot simply fall into the same category as NPs. A similar pattern is seen with plural nouns: they can be replaced by pronouns and do not require the co-occurrence of a determiner in order to form a grammatical sentence (*Cats were sleeping on desks/They were sleeping on them*), but they may co-occur with one (*The cats were sleeping on the desks*). In the very basic grammar we are describing here, there is no simple answer to the question of how to categorize mass nouns and plural nouns. For this reason, we do not include them in most examples and exercises in the rest of this chapter.[1]

English does not have many determiners. In fact, there are so few of them that we could in principle list them all. However, since understanding the syntactic properties of determiners will enable you to figure out which expressions are determiners, we will provide just a partial list in (9).

(9) a. *this, that, these, those*   [demonstrative determiners]
　　 b. *my, your, his, her, our,* etc.   [possessive determiners]
　　 c. *a, some, the, every, all, few, most,* etc.   [quantificational determiners]

A determiner is any expression that can be combined with a noun to its right to form an expression of category NP. Thus, for example, *some* is a determiner because *some cat* is an NP.

In addition to NPs that consist of a determiner and a noun, and single-word NPs (pronouns and proper names), there are also NPs that contain attributive **adjectives** (abbreviated as Adj). For example, the expression *the cute gray cat* has the same distribution as *Fluffy* or *she,* as shown in (10), and consequently we know that it is an NP.

(10) The cute gray cat is sleeping.   Fluffy is sleeping.
　　 Sally likes the cute gray cat.   Sally likes Fluffy.

Expressions like *cute* and *gray* belong to the category adjective, which consists of expressions that can occur between a determiner and a noun in an NP. Note that a noun and

---

[1]We realize, however, that it can be hard to avoid mass nouns and plural nouns in spontaneously constructed examples or examples taken from other sources, since they are very common in everyday language. So while we encourage you to think carefully about how these may best be analyzed (and discussion question 22 in File 5.6 deals with a related issue), we offer two basic suggestions for how one might deal with them. The first option would simply be to say that when they appear in a grammatical sentence without a determiner, then they are acting as NPs and fall into that category; and when they co-occur with a determiner, they are acting as Ns and fall into that category (see Section 5.5.3 on ambiguity). A second option would be to assign them to a separate category or categories with their own set of criteria. Neither of these options is without complications, but these are the sorts of questions and messy data that syntacticians must grapple with.

the adjective-noun sequence have the same syntactic distribution—wherever *cat* can occur, so can *cute cat* or *gray cat,* as shown in the following example.

(11) a. The <u>cat</u> is sleeping.   The <u>gray cat</u> was sleeping.
       b. Sally likes her <u>cat</u>.   Sally likes her <u>gray cat</u>.
       c. The fluffy <u>cat</u> is sleeping.   The fluffy <u>gray cat</u> is sleeping.

We can thus define attributive adjectives as those expressions that can occur immediately to the left of a noun, with the resulting expression having the same distribution as a plain noun.[2]

Now that we know what noun phrases are, we can describe another major syntactic category, namely, the **verb phrase,** abbreviated as VP. The category VP consists of those expressions that, when combined with an NP on their left, will result in a sentence, that is, an expression of category S. The NP that occurs to the left of the VP is referred to as the subject of the sentence. For example:

(12) a. Sally <u>slept</u>.
       b. Sally <u>likes Bob</u>.
       c. Sally <u>gave Bob some money</u>.
       d. Sally <u>traveled to France</u>.
       e. Sally <u>put the book on the desk</u>.
       f. Sally <u>persuaded Bob to study French</u>.

All of the underlined expressions in the sentences in (12) are of category VP, and in each of these sentences, the NP *Sally* is the subject. If some expression is a VP, it will have the same distribution as a verb form like *slept*. It will also have the same distribution as *did so*. Therefore, if it is possible to replace some expression with *slept* or *did so* and still have a grammatical sentence, then the expression in question is of category VP. Take a minute to verify that each underlined expression in (12) can be replaced with *did so* without loss of grammaticality. This should remind you of our earlier observation regarding expressions of category NP: all noun phrases can be replaced in a sentence with a pronoun or a proper name.

Another way to describe a verb phrase syntactically is to say that it consists of a verb (as a morphological category) and any complements it may have.[3] Optionally, a verb phrase can include one or more adjuncts as well. A verb like *slept* requires only a subject argument, so it is a VP all by itself. Traditionally, verbs that require no complements are called **intransitive verbs.** So in the system presented here, intransitive verbs like *slept* are of category VP. Other verbs, such as *liked* or *devoured,* require both an NP complement (an object) and a subject NP argument. Providing these verbs with an NP complement results in a VP. Consider the following example:

(13) Sally liked her cute gray cat.

In (13), *her cute gray cat* is the complement of *liked,* whereas *Sally* is its subject argument. We can confirm that *liked,* together with its complement, is a VP because we can replace

---

[2]We are again ignoring mass nouns and plurals here; if we categorize them as nouns, it will allow them to take adjective adjuncts like other nouns, but unlike *cute cat, cute cats* does not require co-occurrence with a determiner in order to form a grammatical sentence.

[3]To simplify our task here, we do not discuss the syntactic details of verb phrases containing one or more auxiliary verb plus main verb (e.g., <u>*was sleeping*</u> on the desk; <u>*had been working*</u> at home), or verb phrases where the main verb is a form of the "being"-verb (also known as the copula; e.g., *I* <u>*am hungry*</u>; *Sally is* <u>*an engineer*</u>; *The cat* <u>*was cold and wet*</u>; *We* <u>*were at home*</u>) or a verb that patterns like it (but see exercise 29 in File 5.6).

liked her cute gray cat with *slept* or *did so* and still have a sentence. However, we cannot replace *liked* with *did so* or *slept,* which tells us that *liked* itself is not a VP, as shown in (14).

(14) a. Sally liked her cute gray cat.
   b. Sally did so.
   c. Sally slept.
   d. *Sally did so her cute gray cat.
   e. *Sally slept her cute gray cat.

Verbs such as *liked,* which require an NP complement to form a VP, are called **transitive verbs** (abbreviated TV) and form their own syntactic category. Other verbs, such as *gave,* require two NP complements and a subject NP argument, for example, *Sally gave Bob a book.* Combining them with two NP objects results in a VP, which we can verify with *do so* replacement, as shown in (15b). However, neither *gave* by itself (15e), nor *gave* combined with just one of its objects (15c) and (15d), forms a VP. Verbs such as *gave* belong to the syntactic category of **ditransitive verbs,** abbreviated as DTV.[4]

(15) a. Sally gave Bob a book.
   b. Sally did so.
   c. *Sally did so a book.
   d. *Sally did so Bob.
   e. *Sally did so Bob a book.

There are also verbs that require a complement of category S to form a VP, for example, *thought.* We call such verbs **sentential complement verbs,** abbreviated as SV. Example (16) shows that only the combination of a sentential complement verb with its complement sentence is a VP since it is replaceable by *did so* (16b).[5] A sentential complement verb without its complement is not a VP (16c).

(16) a. Sally thought Bob liked her.
   b. Sally did so.
   c. *Sally did so Bob liked her.

Apart from verbs and their complements, recall from our earlier discussion that VPs can optionally contain adjuncts as well. Many expressions that can occur in a verb phrase as adjuncts are of the category **adverb** (abbreviated Adv). For example, the underlined expressions in (17) are all adverbs.[6]

---

[4]Ditransitive verbs in English can take two different structures: the alternative form of *Sally gave <u>Bob</u> <u>a</u> <u>book</u>* is *Sally gave <u>a book</u> <u>to Bob</u>,* where the verb takes an NP and a PP (prepositional phrase; see below) complement instead of two NP complements. For simplicity, we focus here on the type of ditransitive that takes two NP complements. See exercise 28 in File 5.6 for a verb that shares some similarities with the type of ditransitive that takes an NP and a PP complement.

[5]Some of you may have noticed that the word *that* can appear between sentential complement verbs and their S category complement, as in (3) above; for example, *Sally thought (that) Bob liked her; Bob said (that) he liked Sally; I believe (that) I can fly.* As indicated by the parentheses in these examples, in most cases the sentence is equally grammatical with or without the *that* (known as a complementizer). For the sake of simplicity, we set aside this variation and focus on the forms of these sentences without a complementizer.

[6]Adverbs can sometimes occur in other locations within a sentence: *<u>Carefully,</u> Sally wrote the letter; Sally <u>carefully</u> wrote the letter; Sally wrote the letter <u>carefully</u>.* We focus on the sentence-final position here for simplicity. Can you think of a way to account for these other orders?

(17) a. Sally wrote the letter <u>carefully</u>.
    b. Sally walked <u>fast</u>.
    c. Sally put the book on the desk <u>yesterday</u>.
    d. Sally ate her dinner <u>quickly</u>.

Any expression that consists of a VP followed by an adverb has the same distribution as a VP. For example, you can replace a verb and its complements with *did so,* leaving the adverb behind, as in (18b), or you can replace the verb, its complements, and an adverb with *did so,* as in (18c).

(18) a. Sally wrote the letter carefully.
    b. Sally did so carefully.
    c. Sally did so.

Examples like (18) show that VPs with or without adjuncts have the same distribution. From this we can conclude that adverbs combine with a VP to form an expression of category VP, and for this reason they're called **VP adjuncts**. This may remind you of adjectives, which can combine with nouns. Since the resulting expression is also of category N, we call them **N adjuncts**. Thus, both adverbs and attributive adjectives combine with expressions of certain categories (VP and N, respectively), and the resulting expression belongs to that same category. This is true of all adjuncts. However, in contrast to adjuncts, combining an expression with its arguments changes the syntactic category of the resulting expression. For example, *liked* does not have the same distribution as *liked Bob*; *slept* does not have the same distribution as *Sally slept*; etc.

Another kind of VP adjunct is a **prepositional phrase** (PP), which consists of a **preposition** (P) and a noun phrase.

(19) a. Sally wrote the letter <u>with a pen</u>.
    b. Sally walked <u>down the street</u>.
    c. Fluffy slept <u>on the desk</u>.
    d. Sally ate her dinner <u>at the table</u>.

All of the underlined expressions in (19) are called prepositional phrases. Words like *with, down, on, in, over, under, for, from, of,* and *at* are called prepositions. Just like determiners, there are relatively few prepositions in English, and we could in principle list them all. Yet, instead of doing so, we will describe their syntactic properties so that it is always possible to figure out whether a given expression is a preposition based on its syntactic behavior.

Prepositions need an argument of category NP in order to form PPs. Example (19) shows prepositional phrases in the same distribution as adverbs—as VP adjuncts. However, prepositional phrases can also occur as adjuncts inside NPs, whereas adverbs cannot.

(20) a. That bar <u>down the street</u> is my favorite.
    b. Sally likes all cats <u>with long hair</u>.
    c. That cat <u>under the bed</u> is Fluffy.

Inside NPs, PPs occur immediately to the right of the noun, and the resulting expression has the same distribution as a noun. For example, verify for yourself that *bar down the street* has the same distribution as *bar*.

Table (21) summarizes the main syntactic categories in English and their syntactic properties.

(21) Major syntactic categories in English and their properties

Syntactic Category	Relevant Properties	Example
S (sentence)	can occur in *Sally thinks that* _____	Fluffy is cute
NP (noun phrase)	has the same distribution as a personal pronoun or a proper name	she Sally the cat this cute dog that cat under the bed
N (noun)	needs a determiner to its left to form an NP	cat cute dog cat under the bed
Det (determiner)	occurs to the left of the noun to form an NP	the every this
Adj (adjective)	occurs in between a determiner and a noun; can be a noun adjunct, that is, combines with a noun to its right which results in an expression that is also of category N	cute fluffy gray
VP (verb phrase)	consists minimally of a verb and all its complements; combines with an NP to its left which results in a sentence; has the same distribution as *slept* or *did so*	slept wrote the letter quickly liked Bob walked believed she liked that man
TV (transitive verb)	needs an NP complement to form a VP	liked devoured
DTV (ditransitive verb)	needs two NP complements to form a VP	gave sent
SV (sentential complement verb)	needs a sentential complement to form a VP	believed said
Adv (adverb)	can be a VP adjunct, that is, combines with a VP to its left which results in an expression that is also of category VP	fast quickly tomorrow
P (preposition)	combines with an NP to form a PP	at for with
PP (prepositional phrase)	can be a VP or an N adjunct; consists of a preposition and its NP complement	at the table for Sally under the bed

··

Constructing a Grammar

5.5.1 Why Construct Grammars

Syntacticians often try to construct descriptive grammars of natural languages. You can think of such grammars as a linguist's theory of a native speaker's mental grammar. If we focus on syntax alone, such grammars are like a recipe for constructing, in a completely mechanical fashion, all and only the sentences of the natural language that we are trying to describe. This is a complicated task; in fact, there isn't a single complete grammar for any natural language that correctly predicts all and only the sentences of that language.

You can imagine how useful such a grammar would be not only to our Martian scientist friend, but also to foreign language learners. There are also many computational applications for such grammars (see Chapter 16). In this file, we will construct a simple grammar for English. For such a grammar to be useful, it has to assign lexical expressions to syntactic categories, and it has to provide us with recipes for syntactically combining expressions into larger expressions depending on their syntactic categories.

Note that there are many possible ways to construct or model a descriptive grammar. We choose here to use a fairly common system of representing a simplified grammar by means of a lexicon and phrase structure rules, but we intend it only as a way of helping you develop an understanding of the issues involved in grammar construction, with no implication intended that this is the only or best way of constructing a grammar. And while the system as presented here will only cover a fairly small subset of basic English sentences, it has the potential to be expanded to cover other structures, and we encourage you to think about how one might do so any time you come across a sentence that cannot be captured by these rules. (See also the exercises and discussion questions in the next file.)

5.5.2 Parts of the Grammar: The Lexicon and the Rules

In constructing a grammar, we start with a **lexicon,** in which we assign lexical expressions to syntactic categories. This lexicon is, of course, not an actual language user's mental lexicon, but just a representation of lexical expressions and their syntactic properties. To represent in our grammar the fact that *she, Fluffy,* and *Sally* are all of category NP, we write the following **lexical entries:**

(1) NP → she
     NP → Fluffy
     NP → Sally

A lexical entry consists of a syntactic category name followed by an arrow followed by a word. We can abbreviate multiple lexical entries that contain the same category name as follows:

(2) NP → {she, Fluffy, Sally}

Note that there is no real substantive difference between (1) and (2); the latter is just shorthand for (1). Here is a sample lexicon:

(3) NP → {she, Fluffy, Bob, Sally, . . .}
 N → {dog, cat, man, . . .}
 Adj → {fluffy, cute, gray, . . .}
 Det → {the, this, some, . . .}
 VP → {slept, barked, . . .}
 TV → {liked, devoured, . . .}
 DTV → {gave, sent, . . .}
 SV → {thought, said, . . .}
 P → {to, for, with, on, under, . . .}
 Adv → carefully, quickly, yesterday, . . .}

The lexicon simply tells us which syntactic category a given lexical expression belongs to. However, it doesn't tell us how the expressions can combine with one another to form larger expressions. For example, we want our grammar to represent not only the fact that *Sally* is an NP and *slept* a VP, but also the fact that combining an NP and a VP results in a sentence. Similarly, in addition to representing the fact that *dog* is a noun and *this* is a determiner, the grammar needs to state that combining a noun with a determiner results in an NP.

 Phrase structure rules are used to capture patterns of syntactic combination. They are similar in form to lexical entries, except that they contain only names of syntactic categories; they do not contain any actual linguistic forms. We know that if we combine a VP with an NP to its left, we can create a sentence. A phrase structure rule that represents this fact about English appears in (4).

(4) S → NP VP

This phrase structure rule consists of a category name (S), followed by an arrow, followed by a sequence of category names (NP VP). The order in which the categories to the right of the arrow appear represents the relative order in which the expressions of those categories must occur in a sentence. The fact that we find the sequence NP VP to the right of the arrow in (4), as opposed to VP NP, captures the fact that in English, subject NPs occur to the left of verb phrases. For example, since we know that *Fluffy* is an NP, and *slept* is a VP, the phrase structure rule in (4) tells us that *Fluffy slept* is an expression of category S.

 All phrase structure rules allow us to combine expressions to form a larger expression. The expressions that combine via a rule are called the immediate constituents of the resulting expression. For example, the rule in (4) tells us that the immediate constituents of a sentence are an NP and a VP. Immediate constituents are just a special case of the syntactic constituents introduced in File 5.3.

 Once we have a grammar for a language—and we already have a tiny grammar for English since we have some lexical entries and a rule—we can define a syntactic constituent of some expression X to be either an immediate constituent of X or else an immediate constituent of a constituent of X. This definition may seem circular, but it's a perfectly legitimate case of a recursive definition.[1]

 We can conveniently display the way that a sentence is built up from lexical expressions using the phrase structure rules by means of a **phrase structure tree.** For example, the construction of *Fluffy slept* can be represented with the following phrase structure tree:

---

[1]Here's another example of a recursive definition: we can define Sally's descendants to be either her children or the children of her descendants.

(5)

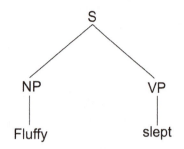

A phrase structure tree is drawn upside down. The leaves of the tree in (5) are *Fluffy* and *slept,* the forms of the lexical expressions that this sentence contains. The lowermost syntactic category names in the tree (NP and VP) represent the syntactic categories of the lexical expressions that occur in the sentence (*Fluffy* is of category NP, and *slept* is of category VP). The root of this tree is labeled with the category name S. The category names that occur immediately below S are NP and VP, in that order. This corresponds to the phrase structure rule in (4) and tells us that the immediate constituents of S are an NP and a VP. When we read the leaves of the tree from left to right, we get *Fluffy slept,* the form of the sentence whose structure is represented in (5).

Not all NPs and VPs consist of single words. We need to add other phrase structure rules to our grammar that will let us construct more complex NPs and VPs, and in turn more complex sentences. We will start with NPs. An NP can consist of a determiner followed by a noun, which is represented in the following phrase structure rule:

(6)   NP → Det N

Nouns can be preceded by adjectives, and, as we observed earlier, the combination of an adjective and a noun is an expression with the same distribution as a noun. The following phrase structure rule captures these facts:

(7)   N → Adj N

Now our grammar predicts that *The fluffy cat slept* is a sentence, since we can construct the phrase structure tree in (8).

(8)

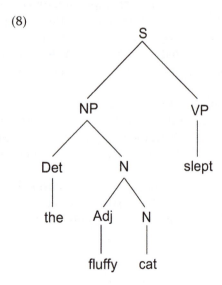

In this tree, as always, the forms of the lexical expressions are the leaves. The syntactic category names that occur right above the leaves represent the syntactic categories of lexical expressions, in accordance with the lexical entries. The tree also shows that the immediate constituents of this sentence are NP and VP (rule 4), that the immediate constituents of NP are Det and N (rule 6), and that the immediate constituents of the higher occurrence of N in the tree are Adj and N (rule 7). Reading the leaves of this entire tree from left to right gives us the string *The fluffy cat slept,* the form of the whole sentence whose structure this tree represents.

Turning our attention now to VPs, we need to add phrase structure rules to our grammar that will allow for the construction of more complex VPs that contain verbs and their complements.

(9)   a. VP → TV NP

     [a VP can consist of a transitive verb followed by an NP]

   b. VP → DTV NP NP

     [a VP can consist of a ditransitive verb followed by a sequence of two NPs]

   c. VP → SV S

     [a VP can consist of a sentential complement verb followed by a sentence]

Our grammar now predicts that *Sally gave Bob this dog* is a sentence, which we can represent by means of the phrase structure tree in (10).

(10)

The rules in (9) allow us to construct VPs that consist of verbs and their complements. However, VPs can also contain adverbs, which the following phrase structure rule captures:

(11) VP → VP Adv

To construct prepositional phrases, we add the following phrase structure rule that allows prepositions to combine with their complement NPs to form PPs.

(12) PP → P NP

Since PPs can be either VP or N adjuncts, we need two more phrase structure rules.

(13) a. N → N PP

      [PPs can be noun adjuncts]

    b. VP → VP PP

      [PPs can be VP adjuncts]

Table (14) lists all the phrase structure rules that we've introduced and describes their purpose.

(14) Phrase structure rules

Phrase Structure Rule	Function
S → NP VP	allows VPs to combine with their subject NP to form a sentence
NP → Det N	allows determiners to combine with a noun to form an NP
N → Adj N	allows attributive adjectives to be noun adjuncts
VP → VP Adv	allows adverbs to be VP adjuncts
VP → TV NP	allows transitive verbs to combine with their object NP to form a VP
VP → DTV NP NP	allows ditransitive verbs to combine with their object NPs to form a VP
VP → SV S	allows sentential complement verbs to combine with their complement S to form a VP
PP → P NP	allows prepositions to combine with their complement NP to form a PP
N → N PP	allows PPs to be noun adjuncts
VP → VP PP	allows PPs to be VP adjuncts

With these phrase structure rules, we can account for a variety of English sentences. We can also show that the same expressions can combine in different ways, resulting in distinct phrases that nevertheless have exactly the same form. This phenomenon, called **ambiguity,** is the focus of the next section.

5.5.3 Ambiguity

We defined a linguistic expression as a piece of language that has a certain form, a certain meaning, and certain syntactic properties. The form is just the sequence of sounds associated with a word or a sequence of words. Linguistic forms can be **ambiguous,** which means that they can correspond to more than one distinct expression. Consider the following example:

(15) a. Sally works at a <u>bank</u>$_1$ downtown.

    b. There is a bike path along the east <u>bank</u>$_2$ of the Olentangy River.

Both underlined expressions in (15) have the same form: [bæŋk]. Yet, we know that they are distinct expressions nonetheless because they mean very different things: *bank*$_1$ refers to a financial institution, and *bank$_2$* to the strip of land next to a river. This means that the word *bank* is ambiguous. Here is another example:

(16) a. They went for a <u>walk$_1$</u>.
     b. They <u>walk$_2$</u> quickly.

Both underlined expressions in (16) have the same form, but they have different syntactic properties. The noun *walk$_1$* is preceded by a determiner *a* with which it forms an NP that is the argument of *for*. On the other hand, *walk$_2$* belongs to the syntactic category VP; its subject argument is *they,* and it is combined with a VP adjunct, the adverb *quickly*.

Distinct expressions can thus share the same form, but nonetheless have different meanings or different syntactic properties. The shared form is said to be ambiguous. In the following sections, we will discuss different types of ambiguity and then show how to use the grammar that we have constructed to analyze a certain kind of ambiguity.

a. Types of Ambiguity. The kind of ambiguity exemplified in (15) and (16), where a single (phonological) word corresponds to distinct expressions that differ in meaning, syntactic properties, or both, is called **lexical ambiguity** or **homophony**. The expressions that correspond to the same single-word form are said to be homophonous. Here are some more examples of homophonous expressions that differ in meaning:

(17) a. Sally is going to have the <u>mole</u> on her back surgically removed.
     b. Sally hates that pesky <u>mole</u> that keeps digging holes in her backyard.

(18) a. We should find some essential readings in syntax and collect them into a <u>reader</u>.
     b. Sally is an avid <u>reader</u> of science fiction.

The following are more examples of homophonous expressions that differ in terms of syntactic properties:

(19) a. We <u>love</u> Fluffy.   *love* is of category transitive verb (TV)
     b. Our <u>love</u> for Fluffy will never die.   *love* is of category noun (N)

(20) a. Sally likes <u>that</u>.   *that* is of category noun phrase (NP)
     b. Sally likes <u>that</u> dog.   *that* is of category determiner (Det)

(21) a. Sally has a <u>fast</u> car.   *fast* is of category adjective (Adj)
     b. Sally walks <u>fast</u>.   *fast* is of category adverb (Adv)

Homophonous expressions can differ in terms of both meaning and syntactic properties, as shown in examples (22) and (23). Try to figure out which syntactic category each of the expressions underlined in the examples below belongs to.

(22) a. I know most people have cats and dogs as pets, but I always wanted to have a <u>duck</u>.
     b. Sandy and Bob are scared of Frisbees—they both just <u>duck</u> if somebody throws one in their general direction.

(23) a. In her <u>present</u> situation, Polly can't afford to move.
     b. Sally got a really cool <u>present</u> from Polly for her birthday.

Strings of words can also be ambiguous. This occurs when two distinct phrasal expressions contain all the same lexical expressions, in exactly the same order, but the way these expressions are combined is different. Consider the string of words in (24).

(24) The cop saw the man with the binoculars.

Remember that sentences are just expressions with a certain form and a certain meaning, whose syntactic category is S. Consequently, the form in (24) actually corresponds to two distinct sentences. The first sentence means that the man whom the cop saw had the binoculars. The second sentence means that the cop used the binoculars to see the man; in other words, the cop was the one with the binoculars.

In this example, the ambiguity arises because the prepositional phase *with the binoculars* can be either a VP adjunct or a noun adjunct. The sentence in which the prepositional phrase is a VP adjunct means that the cop was the one with binoculars. The sentence in which the PP is a noun adjunct and modifies *man* means that the man whom the cop saw had the binoculars. This kind of ambiguity is called **structural ambiguity.** Here is another example of a structurally ambiguous string of words:

(25) Sandy said Tom would be here yesterday.

In (25), *yesterday* could be the adjunct to the VP *would be here yesterday,* or it could be the adjunct to the VP *said Tom would be here yesterday.* In the first case, the resulting sentence means that Sally said that yesterday was the particular day of Tom's arrival. The other sentence means that it was yesterday when Sally said that Tom would be arriving at some point in the future. Note that strings of words can be both lexically and structurally ambiguous. Consider the following example:

(26) I know you like the back of my hand.

On the one hand, the string in (26) could correspond to the sentence in which *like* occurs as a transitive verb, and the sentence *you like the back of my hand* is the complement of *know.* This sentence means something like 'I am aware of the fact that you're a big fan of the back of my hand.' On the other hand, the string in (26) could correspond to a completely different sentence, in which *you* is the object of *know* and *like the back of my hand* is a VP adjunct. In this case, the sentence means something like 'I know you extremely well.' In the second sentence, *like* is not a transitive verb at all, and thus the ambiguity of (26) is partly lexical in character.

Ambiguity is pervasive in language, and it is important to be aware of it as you attempt to determine the syntactic categories of expressions. Now we will show you how the grammar that we have constructed can be used to analyze structurally ambiguous strings of words.

b. Analyzing Structural Ambiguity. We already have the tools to show exactly why some strings of words are structurally ambiguous. Recall the structurally ambiguous string *The cop saw the man with the binoculars.* With our grammar in place, and assuming a straightforward extension of our lexicon, we can show that this string corresponds to two different sentences, depending on whether *with the binoculars* is a VP adjunct or an N adjunct. To show this, the phrase structure rules from (13) are relevant. They are repeated below as (27) for your convenience.

(27) a. N → N PP
     [PPs can be noun adjuncts]

   b. VP → VP PP
     [PPs can be VP adjuncts]

If we make use of the phrase structure rule (27b), which allows PPs to be VP adjuncts, we can construct the phrase structure tree for the sentence that means that the cop had the binoculars and was using them to see the other man, as shown in (28).

(28)

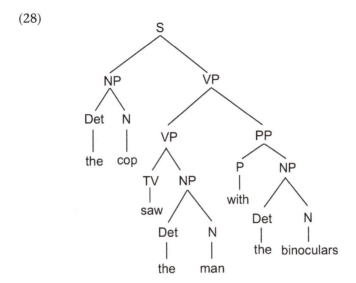

On the other hand, if we use the rule in (27a), which allows PPs to combine with nouns, we get the sentence that means that the man who the cop saw was the one who had the binoculars, as shown in (29).

(29)

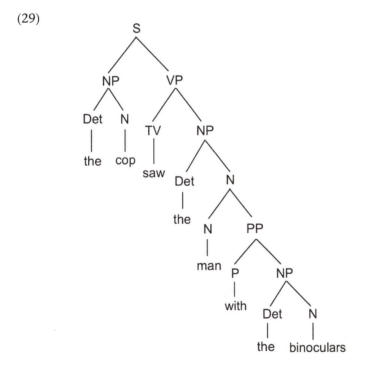

While the grammar we constructed in this file allows us to explain why some strings of words are structurally ambiguous, it is still quite modest in scope. On one hand, it fails to predict that certain sentences of English genuinely are sentences, e.g., *The man who I saw yesterday knows Sally* or *Who do you think won?* On the other hand, it incorrectly predicts that certain non-sentences are sentences, e.g., **Bob likes she*. In the practice section for this chapter, File 5.6, we will ask you to evaluate our grammar and the inventory of the syntactic categories that we have assumed, as well as to extend it to include a larger chunk of English. You will also have an opportunity to try out these tools on other languages.

File 5.1—Basic Ideas of Syntax

Exercises

1. We noted that some sentences can have bizarre meanings but are syntactically well-formed nonetheless, e.g., *Colorless green ideas sleep furiously.* Construct three original sentences of English that all mean something very strange. What does the existence of such sentences tell you about the relationship between syntax and semantics?

2. Look at the following strings of words, and then answer questions (i)–(iv) below.

   a. Sally bought computer.
   b. I explained him how it work.
   c. Bob slept not last night.
   d. This my friend is coming over.

      i. For each string of words above, say whether it is a sentence of English or not.
      ii. Is it possible to understand the intended meaning of the strings of words above that you do not think are syntactically well-formed?
      iii. For each string that does not form a sentence of English, fix it in order to create an actual sentence.
      iv. What does the existence of strings like those in (a)–(d) tell you about the relationship between syntax and semantics?

Activity

3. Take the following twelve words:

   A   Across   And   Boy   Down   Hall   Large   The   The   Threw   Skunk   Walked

      i. Use all of the words in this list. Put the words into an order to create a possible sentence of English. Then do it again. And again. And again. And again. You may find it helpful to write the words down on a sheet of paper and then cut them apart so that you can physically move them into new orders.
      ii. There are 479,001,600 possible ways that these words can be ordered. Are all of them sentences? How do you know? (*Note:* A previous editor of this book, along with her students, managed to create 240 possible grammatical sentences using all and only these words before growing bored and stopping.)
      iii. Now share your five results with the results of several of your classmates. Compare the orders that you and your classmates put the words in. Did you all group them in the same ways?
      iv. If there are differences, what do these differences tell you?
      v. What things are similar among all of your results? What do the similarities tell you?

(cont.)

   vi. Are there certain groups of words that tend to appear together, even in sentences that mean very different things? What are some examples of this? What does this tell you?

   vii. Are there groups of words that seem never to appear together in a particular order? What are some examples of this? What does this tell you?

   viii. Are there certain kinds of words that seem to fit into the same kinds of locations within the sentences? What does this tell you?

   ix. What does this activity tell you about the linguistic properties of discreteness and productivity? (See File 1.4.)

File 5.2—Syntactic Properties

Exercises

4. For each of the following strings of words that do not form sentences of English, say whether they are syntactically ill-formed because of word order, a violation in co-occurrence requirements, or both.

   a. sleeps Sally
   b. Sally is girl
   c. Polly is fond of
   d. is fond of cats Polly
   e. Bob convinced
   f. Sally beer drinks
   g. Polly gave the book Tom
   h. Sally said me that she would be there
   i. bought I this present for
   j. Sally and arrived

5. In each of the following pairs of sentences, the underlined expression is an argument in one sentence, but an adjunct in the other. Figure out in which sentence it is an argument and in which sentence it is an adjunct. Provide evidence for each answer, citing the relevant properties of adjuncts and arguments.

   a. <u>Yesterday</u> was a great day.
      Sally had a great day <u>yesterday</u>.

   b. Polly seemed <u>excited about her new job</u>.
      Bob's roommate, <u>excited about her new job</u>, got up at 6 A.M. on Monday.

   c. The book <u>on the shelf</u> is very dusty.
      Sally put the book <u>on the shelf</u>.

   d. <u>To study French</u> is something Sally always wanted to do.
      Sally went to Paris <u>to study French</u>.

6. Give two pieces of evidence that *his friend* in *Bob bought a birthday present for his friend* is an argument of *for*.

7. Consider the sentence *Sally sent Bob a letter,* and then answer the questions below.
   i. Is *a letter* an argument or an adjunct? Give evidence to support your answer.
   ii. Is *Bob* an argument or an adjunct? Give evidence to support your answer.

8. Consider the sentence *Sally emailed some pictures to Bob.* Are *some pictures* and *to Bob* arguments or adjuncts? Show evidence to support your answer.

9. Consider the sentence *Sally told Bob she was leaving.* Are *Bob* and *she was leaving* arguments or adjuncts? Show evidence to support your answer.

10. Consider the sentence *Sally was scared of Polly.* Is *of Polly* an argument or an adjunct? If it's an argument, which expression is it an argument of?

11. Consider the sentence *I don't want to take a really difficult class.* Is *really* an argument or an adjunct? There is an expression in this sentence that allows *really* to occur in the sentence. If we got rid of this other expression, we would also have to get rid of *really.* Which expression is the occurrence of *really* dependent on?

Discussion Questions

12. We noted that subjects may be omitted in some languages, like Italian. Do you think this implies that in those languages, subjects are not arguments but adjuncts? Can you think of any reason why we still might want to consider subjects to be arguments in those languages, even though they're optional?

13. Examine table (29) in File 5.2, which lists typical properties of adjuncts and arguments. Which of the properties of adjuncts and arguments do you think are common to all languages? Which ones do you think are specific to English or to languages similar to English? Try to be as specific as possible about which properties would be relevant to what kinds of languages. You can draw the evidence for your conclusions from the foreign language examples in this chapter and from any other languages you may be familiar with.

14. Consider the following data:

    a. The girl is sleeping.
    b. *The is sleeping.
    c. *Girl is sleeping.

    These examples show not only that a noun like *girl* cannot occur without some determiner like *the,* but also that a determiner cannot occur without a noun. Carefully think about the definition of an argument. Do you think we should consider the determiner to be an argument of the noun, or should we consider the noun to be an argument of the determiner? Is there any evidence that favors one answer over the other?

File 5.3—Syntactic Constituency

Exercises

15. Consider the sentence *A highly motivated student of mine planned to go to Rome to study Italian.*

    i. Use the cleft test to show that *a highly motivated student* is not a constituent in this sentence.
    ii. Use the question-answer test to show that *to Rome to study Italian* is a constituent.
    iii. Is *to go to Rome to study Italian* a constituent or not? Give evidence from all three tests (clefting, question-answer, and substitution).
    iv. Is *highly motivated student* a constituent or not? Give evidence from all three tests.
    v. Use the substitution test to show that *to Rome* is a constituent.
    vi. Is *planned to go to Rome* a constituent or not? Give evidence from all three tests.
    vii. Is *planned to go to Rome to study Italian* a constituent or not? Give evidence from all three tests.

16. Use the constituency tests to break up each of the following sentences into its syntactic constituents. You don't need to worry about lexical expressions (i.e., individual words). Rather, just determine which phrasal expressions are constituents in each sentence. If the results you get from different constituency tests are inconsistent, use your best judgment in deciding whether something is a constituent or not.

    a. Sandy shot the soldier.
    b. Leslie said it rained.
    c. The girl persuaded Polly to come along.
    d. Sally mailed a card to Polly.
    e. Polly saw Bob with Sally.
    f. Sally put the book on the desk in her study.

File 5.4—Syntactic Categories

Exercises

17. For each pair of expressions below, (i) say whether they have the same syntactic distribution or not, and (ii) give an example supporting your answer. You do not have to say which syntactic category any of the expressions below belong to—just compare their distributions.

    a. Chris   student
    b. Chris   some student
    c. student   bright college student
    d. bright   very bright
    e. seemed   appeared
    f. seemed   appeared happy
    g. seemed happy always seemed happy
    h. loud bar   bar down the street
    i. extremely loud bar the bar
    j. slept all day   liked
    k. quickly   quite
    l. walked   rode the bus

18. For each underlined expression below, say which syntactic category it belongs to and give one piece of evidence supporting your answer.

    a. <u>My</u> sister is a college student.
    b. This girl <u>in my class</u> always wears black.
    c. I like <u>that</u> band.
    d. I like <u>that</u>.
    e. Sally <u>texted</u> Bob last night.
    f. Bob <u>mentioned</u> he would be late.
    g. I got an email <u>from</u> Sally.
    h. Sally sent me a <u>long annoying email</u>.
    i. Sally sent me <u>a long annoying email</u>.
    j. Sally sent me a <u>long</u> annoying email.
    k. Sally <u>rides her bike</u> fast.
    l. Sally <u>rides her bike fast</u>.
    m. <u>The writing of her latest novel</u> took more time than anticipated.

19. Construct your own examples of each of the following:

   a. an NP consisting of a determiner, an adjective, and a noun
   b. an NP consisting of a determiner, a noun, and a PP
   c. a sentence consisting of an NP subject, a transitive verb, an NP object, and an adverb
   d. a VP consisting of an intransitive verb and a prepositional phrase
   e. a VP consisting of a sentential complement verb, its complement sentence, and two VP adjuncts
   f. an expression of category N that consists of two adjectives and a noun
   g. an expression of category N that consists of an adjective, a noun, and a PP
   h. a VP consisting of a ditransitive verb and its two NP complements

20. Compare the distribution of the underlined expressions in each pair below.

   a. <u>Sally</u> called Tom on Saturday.
   <u>Bob and Sally</u> called Tom on Saturday.

   b. Sally called Tom <u>on Saturday</u>.
   Sally called Tom <u>on Saturday and on Sunday</u>.

   c. Sally <u>called Tom on Saturday</u>.
   Sally <u>called Tom on Saturday and emailed him on Sunday</u>.

      i. Do *Sally* and *Bob and Sally* have the same syntactic distribution?
      ii. Do *on Saturday* and *on Saturday and on Sunday* have the same distribution?
      iii. Do *called Tom on Saturday* and *called Tom on Saturday and emailed him on Sunday* have the same distribution?
      iv. What can you conclude, in general, about the syntactic category of expressions of the form *X and Y* compared to the syntactic category of the two conjuncts, *X and Y*?

21. Consider the sentence *Sally sent Bob a very long email,* and then answer the questions below.

      i. Examine the distribution of *very long* and say which syntactic category it belongs to.
      ii. Construct an example to show that *very* is not an adverb.
      iii. Construct an example to show that *very* is not an adjective.
      iv. Come up with two more expressions that have the same distribution as *very*.
      v. Even though *very* is optional in the sentence above, can we consider it an adjunct? Why or why not?

Discussion Questions

22. Consider the following examples, and then answer the questions below:

   a.   This student arrived.
   b.   *This students arrived.
   c.   We saw a student.
   d.   *We saw a students.

What can you conclude about the syntactic distribution of *student* compared to *students*? Do they have the same distribution or not? Do you think they should be considered as belonging to the same syntactic category or not? If you think that *student* and *students* really belong to different syntactic categories, in what way is the inventory of the syntactic categories that we laid out in File 5.4 inadequate? How could we fix it? Explain your answer.

23. Consider example (30) in Section 5.2.3(c) on agreement. What, if anything, does that example show you about the distribution of *likes* compared to *like*? Do you think we should consider *likes* and *like* as belonging to the same syntactic category? Now examine example (31) in the same section. Do you think *this* and *these* belong to the same syntactic category? Can you draw any general conclusions about the relationship between inflectional morphology and syntactic categories?

24. Compare the syntactic distribution of *she* and *her*. Do they have the same distribution or not? Do you think they should be considered as belonging to the same syntactic category or not? How does the syntactic distribution of *Sally* compare to the distribution of *she* on one hand, and the distribution of *her* on the other hand?

25. Consider examples (10) and (11) in Section 5.1.2, which illustrate a syntactic difference between English and Serbo-Croatian. We know that *dog* and *a dog* belong to different syntactic categories in English. What do these examples suggest about the syntactic distribution of *psa* 'dog' and *jednog psa* 'a dog' in Serbo-Croatian? Do they have the same distribution or not? What syntactic category or categories would you assign them to? What, if anything, does this tell you about whether syntactic categories and the syntactic properties associated with them are universal?

26. Consider examples (10) and (11) in Section 5.1.2 and example (20) in Section 5.2.3(a). Based on these examples, and given how we defined noun adjuncts, can you make a case for determiners in Serbo-Croatian being noun adjuncts? Why or why not? What, if anything, does this tell you about whether syntactic categories and the syntactic properties associated with them are universal or language-specific? In addition to the Serbo-Croatian examples, you can bring to bear any other foreign language examples in the text or evidence from foreign languages that you are familiar with.

File 5.5—Constructing a Grammar

Exercises

27. Construct a phrase structure tree for each of the following expressions:

    a. for Bob
    b. liked the gray cat
    c. some fluffy gray dog
    d. the man with Sally
    e. sent the man an email
    f. thought Sally hated Bob
    g. barked yesterday
    h. fell into the pond
    i. drifted slowly under the bridge
    j. this silly picture of Pat
    k. Chris loved Robin passionately
    l. Pat pushed the stubborn horse into the barn
    m. A student from my class claimed the teacher disliked him

28. Consider the sentence *Sally put the book on the desk.*

    i. Show that *on the desk* is an argument of *put,* and not a VP adjunct.
    ii. Show that *put* is not of category VP, TV, DTV, or SV. Then make up the name for the syntactic category that verbs such as *put* belong to.

(cont.)

     iii. Write a phrase structure rule that allows the construction of VPs like *put the book on the desk*. In the phrase structure rule, you will need to refer to the category whose name you made up in part (ii).

     iv. Draw a phrase structure tree for the sentence *Sally put the book on the desk.*

29. Consider the sentence *The student seemed smart,* and then answer the following questions:

     i. Show that *smart* is an argument of *seemed*.

     ii. Show that *seemed* is not of category VP, TV, DTV, or SV. Then make up the name for the syntactic category that verbs such as *seemed* belong to.

     iii. Write a phrase structure rule that allows the construction of VPs like *seemed smart*. In the phrase structure rule, you will need to refer to the category whose name you made up in part (ii).

     iv. Draw a phrase structure tree for the sentence *The student seemed smart.*

30. Consider example (7) in Section 5.2.2, which shows the relative order of determiners and nouns in Malay noun phrases. Suppose that *surat* 'letter' is of category N, *itu* 'that' of category Det, and the whole phrase *surat itu* 'that letter' of category NP. Write a phrase structure rule that allows the construction of NPs out of determiners and nouns in Malay and that reflects their relative order. Then draw a phrase structure tree for the phrase *surat itu* 'that letter.'

31. Consider example (9) in Section 5.2.2 which shows the order of NPs and prepositions in Japanese PPs. Write a lexical entry for each word in the Japanese phrase in that example. Then write a phrase structure rule that allows the construction of PPs out of prepositions and NPs in Japanese. Finally, construct a phrase structure tree for the Japanese phrase *sono hito to* 'with that person.'

32. Since English is an SVO language, our grammar in File 5.5 was set up to predict that objects come after transitive verbs and subject NPs come before VPs, with the following two phrase structure rules:

VP → TV NP
S → NP VP

Change these rules as necessary to make them work for (i) an SOV language, (ii) a VOS language, and (iii) an OVS language.

33. Each of the following forms is lexically ambiguous in terms of syntactic categories. For each one, say what syntactic category each distinct expression corresponds to, and give two examples, each showcasing one of the distinct expressions. The first one is done for you.

     a. dislike
        dislike of category N: Our <u>dislike</u> of Polly was tremendous.
        dislike of category TV: We <u>dislike</u> Polly.
     b. mail
     c. release
     d. hand
     e. some
     f. hard

34. Each of the following strings of words is structurally ambiguous. For each, construct two phrase structure trees to show that the string of words in question corresponds to two distinct sentences.

    a. Polly shot the soldier with a gun.
    b. Sally called her friend from France.
    c. Bob said she ran fast yesterday.

Discussion Questions

35. We observed early on that *ate* can but doesn't have to occur with an object, as both *Sally ate* and *Sally ate an apple* are grammatical. How would you write the lexical entry for *ate* to account for these facts? Do you think that the form *ate* is lexically ambiguous? Why or why not? If you think *ate* is lexically ambiguous, explain how.

36. Currently our grammar predicts that **Bob liked she* is a sentence, although it is not an actual sentence. The grammar also incorrectly predicts that **Her liked Bob* is a sentence, and that **for she* is a PP. This is because the grammar we constructed in File 5.5 assigns both *she* and *her* to the same syntactic category, NP. Discuss how you could modify our grammar to exclude these ungrammatical strings. Would you have to make up new syntactic categories? Which phrase structure rules would you have to change? You may want to work through Exercise 24 first.

37. Currently our grammar incorrectly predicts that **this students, *these student, *a students,* etc., are all syntactically well-formed expressions of category NP. Explain why, given the syntactic categories that we have used, our grammar fails to distinguish between the well-formed *this student* and *these students,* and the ungrammatical **this students* and **these student*. Discuss how you could modify our grammar to exclude these ungrammatical strings. Would you have to make up new syntactic categories? Which phrase structure rules would you have to change?

38. Currently our grammar does not account for subject-verb agreement. That is, it would assign both *like* and *likes* to the syntactic category TV, and then the grammar would incorrectly predict that **We likes* and **She like* are sentences. Discuss how you could modify our grammar to exclude these ungrammatical strings. Would you have to make up new syntactic categories? Which phrase structure rules would you have to change?

39. Phrase structure rules encode both the immediate constituents of phrasal expressions and the linear order among them. The rule S → NP VP, for example, tells us that the immediate constituents of a sentence are NP and VP, and that subject NPs occur to the left of VPs. What about languages with relatively free word order, such as Dyirbal or Serbo-Croatian? Re-examine example (12) from Section 5.2.3(a). Do you think it would be possible to use the kind of grammar that we constructed in File 5.5 to account for Serbo-Croatian sentences? Why or why not? Discuss with your classmates.

Further Readings

Carnie, Andrew. 2013. *Syntax: A generative introduction.* 3rd edn. Oxford: Wiley-Blackwell.
Pollard, Carl, and Ivan A. Sag. 1994. *Head-driven phrase structure grammar.* Chicago: University of Chicago Press.
Tallerman, Maggie. 2013. *Understanding syntax.* 3rd edn. London: Hodder Arnold.

CHAPTER

6

····································

Semantics

KIWI

···

What Is Semantics?

Semantics is a subfield of linguistics that studies linguistic meaning and how expressions convey meanings. It deals with the nature of meaning itself—what exactly are linguistic meanings, and what is their relationship to the language user on the one hand and the external world on the other? Semanticists study not only word meanings, but also how word meanings combine to produce the meanings of larger phrasal expressions. Finally, an important part of the study of natural language meaning involves meaning relations between expressions.

Contents

···

An Overview of Semantics

6.1.1 Lexical and Compositional Semantics

Semantics is the subfield of linguistics that studies meaning in language. We can further subdivide the field into **lexical** and **compositional** semantics. Lexical semantics deals with the meanings of words and other lexical expressions, including the meaning relationships among them. In addition to lexical expressions, phrasal expressions carry meaning. Compositional semantics is concerned with phrasal meanings and how phrasal meanings are assembled.

Every language contains only a finite number of words, with their meanings and other linguistic properties stored in the mental lexicon. However, every language contains an infinite number of sentences and other phrasal expressions, and native speakers of a language can understand the meanings of any of those sentences. Since speakers cannot memorize an infinite number of distinct sentence meanings, they need to figure out the meaning of a sentence based on the meanings of the lexical expressions in it and the way in which these expressions are combined with one another.

Compositional semanticists are interested in how lexical meanings combine to give rise to phrasal meanings, while lexical semanticists focus on meanings of words. In this chapter, we discuss both lexical and compositional semantics, but before we address either, we must first clarify exactly what we mean by *meaning*.

6.1.2 Two Aspects of Linguistic Meaning

There are two aspects of linguistic meaning: **sense** and **reference.** You can think of the sense of an expression as some kind of mental representation of its meaning, or perhaps some kind of concept. Hearing the word *cat* might bring up images of your neighbor's cat, or the thought of pet allergies, or the Latin name for the species. Other things may be packaged into this mental representation—the number of limbs that a typical cat has, the fact that most of them are furry, the fact that they are related to panthers, etc. In short, to know the sense of an expression is to have some mental representation of its meaning.

By virtue of knowing the sense of some expression, you also know its relationship to the world, or its reference. If you have a mental representation of what cats are (four-legged, usually furry, potentially allergy-causing felines, etc.) that is associated with the expression *cat,* you will also be able to pick out those things in the world that are indeed cats. We could show you pictures of different kinds of animals and ask you, "Which of the following animals are cats?" and you would be able to determine that, say, Garfield, Felix, and Fluffy are all cats, but that Fido, Rex, and Fishy the Goldfish are not. To be able to correctly pick out the cats in the pictures is to know the reference of the expression *cat*—in other words, to know what things in the world the expression *cat* refers to. The particular entities in the world to which some expression refers are called its **referents.** So, Garfield, Felix, and Fluffy are among the referents of the expression *cat*. The collection of all the referents of an expression is its reference.

In order to know the reference of some expression, it is necessary to know its sense. However, knowing the sense of some expression does not guarantee that you will invariably be able to pick out its referents. For example, although you probably know the sense expressed by *diamond*, you may not always be able to distinguish real diamonds from fake diamonds—you might think that some fake diamonds are real, and so fail to correctly pick out the referents of *diamond*. Similarly, maybe you have heard the word *lychee* and know that it is some kind of fruit, but are unable to distinguish an actual lychee from a pearl onion. The exact reference of some expressions may be accessible only to experts. It's important to appreciate the fact that in order to know the reference of some expression, you must understand the sense it expresses; however, understanding its sense doesn't guarantee that you'll be able to pick out all of its referents correctly.

Now we will examine a couple of examples to clarify the distinction between sense and reference. Consider the expression *unicorn*. You most likely know the sense of this expression—perhaps the mention of it stirred up the image of a white, four-legged creature with a single horn on its forehead, or anything else your concept of 'unicorn' may include. So the expression *unicorn* definitely has a sense. But what is the relationship of *unicorn* to the world—what is its reference? Unlike *cat*, which refers to many, many different things in the world that are cats, there is no creature in our world that is a unicorn (to the best of our knowledge). Therefore, *unicorn* has no referents—but it has a sense nonetheless.

Similarly, *the queen of the United States* has no referents, but it has a sense. You know that for somebody to be the queen of the United States, she would have to be the highest-ranking member of the reigning royalty, she would have to be female, and, of course, the United States would have to be a monarchy. Precisely because you understand the sense of this expression, and you have some basic knowledge about the world we live in, you know that *the queen of the United States* does not happen to refer to anybody.

Not only is it possible for expressions to have a sense but no referents; it is also possible for multiple distinct expressions with different senses to pick out the same referent. For example, *the most populous country in the world* and *the country that hosted the 2008 Summer Olympics* both refer to China. A person could know that *the most populous country in the world* refers to China without knowing that *the country that hosted the 2008 Summer Olympics* also refers to China. The converse is also possible. This shows that the sense of one of these expressions is not inextricably linked to the sense of the other; that is, they do not have to be packaged into the same mental representation. Consequently, although both expressions *the most populous country in the world* and *the country that hosted the 2008 Summer Olympics* refer to China, the senses associated with those expressions are different.

Sense can also be thought of as the way in which an expression refers to something in the world. For example, while the expressions *Barack Obama* and *the 44th president of the United States* both refer to the individual *Barack Obama*, they do so in different ways. In the first case, Barack Obama is referred to by his name, and in the second case by the uniquely identifying description of his political status.

We cannot do away with either sense or reference but have to consider them together as components of linguistic meaning. The notion of sense underlies the intuition that there is a mental component to linguistic meaning. The notion of reference in turn relates this mental representation to the outside world. If we discounted senses, it would be difficult to talk about the meanings of expressions such as *unicorn* that do not refer to anything. It would also be difficult to accommodate the fact that one and the same thing in the world can be talked about or referred to in many different ways. And if we discounted reference, we would lose the connection between meanings of expressions and what these meanings are **about.** After all, we often use language to communicate information about the world to one another, so there should be some relationship between the meanings of expressions we use to communicate and things in the outside world about which we would like to communicate these meanings.

FILE **6.2**
....

Lexical Semantics:
The Meanings of Words

6.2.1   Dictionary Definitions

When we think about the term *meaning,* we almost always think of word meanings. We are all familiar with looking words up in dictionaries, asking about the meaning of a word, and discussing or even arguing about exactly what a certain word means. The aim of this file is not to discuss what individual words mean, however. Rather, we will endeavor to pin down word meaning (lexical meaning) itself. That is, what exactly does it mean for a word to mean something?

We first consider the commonly held idea that dictionaries are the true source of word meanings. Dictionaries define word meanings in terms of other words and their meanings. This makes them easy to print, easy to access, and easy to memorize. Is it the case, though, that a word's meaning is just what the dictionary says it is? In our culture, where the use of dictionaries is widespread, many people accept dictionaries as authoritative sources for word meanings. Therefore, people may feel that the dictionary definition of a word more accurately represents the word's meaning than does an individual speaker's understanding of the word. But keep in mind that people who write dictionaries arrive at their definitions by studying the ways speakers of the language use words. A new word or definition could not be introduced into a language by way of being printed in a dictionary. Moreover, entries in dictionaries are not fixed and immutable; they change over time and from edition to edition (or year to year, with electronic dictionaries) as people come to use words differently. Dictionaries model usage, not the other way around. There simply is no higher authority on word meaning than the community of native speakers of a language.

6.2.2   Word Senses

Like all other linguistic expressions, words are associated with senses—mental representations of their meaning. In this section, we consider what form these representations might have. How exactly do we store word meanings in our minds?

a. Dictionary-Style Definitions. While dictionaries themselves cannot be the true sources of word meanings, is it possible that speakers' mental representations of word meanings, the senses of words, are much like dictionary entries? Perhaps the nature of a word's meaning is similar to what we might find in some idealized dictionary: a dictionary-style definition that defines words in terms of other words, but that also reflects the way that speakers of a language really use that word. We can envision an imaginary idealized dictionary that changes with the times, lists all the words in a language at a given time, and provides a verbal definition of each according to speakers' use of that word. Would this be an appropriate way to conceptualize word meanings? The answer is that we would still run into problems.

If a word's sense were a dictionary-style definition, then understanding this meaning would involve understanding the meanings of the words used in its definition. But understanding the meanings of these words would have to involve understanding the meanings of the words in their definitions. And understanding these definitions would have to involve understanding the words they use, which, of course, would have to involve understanding even more definitions. The process would be never ending. There would be no starting point: no way to build word meaning out of some more basic understanding. Moreover, circularities would inevitably arise. For instance, one English dictionary defines *divine* as 'being or having the nature of a deity,' but defines *deity* as 'divinity.' Another defines *pride* as 'the quality of state of being proud,' but defines *proud* as 'feeling or showing pride.' Examples like these are especially graphic, but essentially the same problem would hold sooner or later for any dictionary-style definition. Furthermore, don't forget that to understand a definition would require understanding not only the content words, but also such common function words as *the, of, to,* and so on.

We must conclude that dictionaries are written to be of practical aid to people who already speak a language and that they cannot make theoretical claims about the nature of meaning. A dictionary-style entry doesn't explain the meaning of a word or phrase in terms of something more basic—it just gives paraphrases (gives you one lexical item for another). People can and do learn the meanings of some words through dictionary definitions, so it would be unfair to say that such definitions are completely unable to characterize the meanings of words, but it should be clear that dictionary-style definitions can't be all there is to the meanings of the words in a language. In other words, it may be useful for us to define words in terms of other words, but that type of definition cannot be the only way in which meanings are stored in our heads.

b. Mental Image Definitions. What other options are there? One possibility is that a word's meaning is stored in our minds as a **mental image.** Words often do seem to conjure up particular mental images. Reading the words *Mona Lisa,* for example, may well cause an image of Leonardo da Vinci's painting to appear in your mind. You may find that many words have this sort of effect. Imagine that someone asked you, "What does *fingernail* mean?" You would very likely picture a fingernail in your mind while you tried to provide the definition. Your goal would likely be trying to get your conversational partner to wind up with a mental image similar to your own. In some ways, mental image definitions seem more promising than did dictionary-style definitions, because, as the fingernail example shows, mental images are things that we really do have in our heads and that we do use in some way to conceptualize reality.

However, a mental image can't be all there is to a word's meaning any more than a dictionary-style definition could be. One reason is that different people's mental images may be very different from each other without the words' meanings varying very much from individual to individual. For a student, the word *lecture* will probably be associated with an image of one person standing in front of a blackboard, and it may also include things like the backs of the heads of one's fellow students. The image associated with the word *lecture* in the mind of a teacher, however, is more likely to consist of an audience of students sitting in rows facing forward. A lecture as seen from a teacher's perspective is actually quite a bit different from a lecture as seen from a student's perspective. Even so, both the student and the teacher understand the word *lecture* as meaning more or less the same thing, despite the difference in mental images. Likewise, *food* might conjure a different mental image for a pet store owner, a gourmet chef, and your little brother, but presumably all three think that it has roughly the same meaning. It's hard to see how words like *lecture* and *food* could mean essentially the same thing for different people if meanings were just mental images without any other cognitive processing involved.

Consider a similar example: most people's mental image for *mother* is likely to be an image of their own mother—and, of course, different mothers look quite different from one another—but certainly we all mean the same thing when we use the word. This example raises a second concern, though. If you hear the word *mother* in isolation, you may well picture your own mother. But if you hear the word in some context, like "Mother Teresa" or "the elephant's mother," you almost certainly do not picture your own mother! This shows that the mental image you form when you hear *mother* out of the blue is far from being all that the word is able to mean to you. The same is true of almost any word.

Here is a third problem. The default mental image associated with a word tends to be of a typical or ideal example of the kind of thing the word represents: a **prototype.** Often, however, words can be used to signify a wide range of ideas, any one of which may or may not be typical of its kind. For example, try forming a mental image for the word *bird.* Make sure that the image is clear in your mind before reading on.

If you are like most people, your mental image was of a small bird that flies, not of an ostrich or a penguin. Yet ostriches and penguins are birds, and any analysis of the meaning of the word *bird* must take this into account. It may be that the meaning of *bird* should also include some indication of what a typical bird is like, but some provision must be made for atypical birds as well.

A fourth, and much more severe, problem with this theory is that many words, perhaps even most, simply have no clear mental images attached to them. What mental image is associated in your mind, for example, with the word *forget*? How about the word *the* or the word *aspect*? *Reciprocity*? *Useful*? Only certain words seem to have definite images, but no one would want to say that only these words have meanings.

We conclude that, as with dictionary definitions, mental image definitions have some merit, because mental images are associated in some way with the words stored in our heads. But, as with verbal dictionary-style definitions, mental image definitions cannot be all there is to how we store meaning in our minds.

c. Usage-Based Definitions. We have considered and rejected two possibilities for what constitutes the sense of a word, because neither was quite right for the task. In fact, defining the sense of a word is quite difficult. We could simply gloss over the entire issue by saying that sense is some sort of a mental concept, but *concept* itself is rather vague. However, we will leave it as an open question, at this point, as to exactly what lexical sense is: it is a question that linguists, philosophers, and psychologists must continue to investigate.

What we indisputably know when we know a word, though, is when it is suitable to use that word in order to convey a particular meaning or grammatical relationship. If I want to describe a large, soft piece of material draped across a bed for the purpose of keeping people warm while they sleep, I know that I can use the word *blanket.* That doesn't necessarily mean that *blanket* is stored in my mind with the particular set of words just used in the previous sentence ("large soft piece of material . . ."): just that something about a particular set of circumstances tells me whether it is suitable to use that word. Moreover, when somebody else uses a word, I know what the circumstances must be like for them to have used it. This is true for content words like *blanket, bird,* and *reciprocity* as well as for function words like *the, if,* and *to.* Thus, regardless of the form that our mental representations of word meanings take, if we know what a word means, then we know under what conditions it is appropriate to use it.

6.2.3 Word Reference

Whatever the exact nature of word senses may be, another component of a word's meaning is its reference. In this section, we briefly examine certain kinds of reference that words can have.

Proper names present the simplest case. *China* obviously refers to the country China. *Arkansas* refers to the state of Arkansas. *Barack Obama* refers to the individual Barack

Obama. *White House* refers to the thus named building in Washington, DC. In general, proper names refer to specific entities in the world—people, places, etc.

Yet, what do nouns such as *cat* or *woman* refer to? Unlike proper names, they do not refer to some specific thing all by themselves. Suppose somebody asks the following question:

(1) Does Sally have a cat?

They cannot be asking about some specific cat. The expression *cat* in this question cannot be taken to stand for the particular feline that Sally has, since whoever uttered the question doesn't even know whether there is such a feline. In fact, the answer to the question could be *no*. Suppose this question is answered as follows:

(2) No, Sally has never had a cat.

Again, *cat* cannot be referring to a particular cat since the answer explicitly states that there are *no* cats that Sally ever owned.

What is clear from both (1) and (2) is that using the expression *cat* is intended to restrict the attention of the listener to a certain set of things in the world, namely, those things that are cats. If somebody asks *Does Sally have a cat?*, they are inquiring about entities in the world that are cats and whether Sally has one of them. They are not inquiring about entities in the world that are crocodiles or states or notebooks, and whether Sally has any of those. Similarly, if somebody utters (2), they are not trying to state that Sally never had anything, or that Sally never had a computer or a friend, for example.

Thus, common nouns like *cat* do not refer to a specific entity in the world, but rather they focus the attention on all those things in the world that are cats, i.e., the set of all cats. A set is just a collection of things. A set of cats, then, is a collection of precisely those things that are cats. That is the reference of the expression *cat*, and all the individual cats that comprise this set of cats are its referents.

Similarly, the reference of the expression *woman* is the set of all women in the world. The diagram in (3) depicts the reference of the expression *woman* in a simple world that contains very few things. Keep in mind that this diagram is just a visual representation of the reference of the expression *woman*. That is, *woman* does not refer to the collection of figures in the diagram. Instead, *woman* refers to the set of actual individuals in the world who are women.

You may object that an expression like *Sally's cat* does indeed refer to a specific thing, or that *the woman who is married to Barack Obama* refers specifically to Michelle Obama, and not to the set of all women. While this is true, it is not the case that common nouns like *cat* or *woman* in isolation refer to specific individuals. Expressions that contain nouns can have specific referents, but this is a consequence of how noun meanings combine with meanings of other expressions. Put another way, there is something about the combination of *cat* and *Sally's* that produces its specific reference. Similarly, it is the combination of the lexical expressions in *the woman who is married to Barack Obama* that creates the reference to a particular individual. Since the meaning that arises through combinations of expressions is in the domain of compositional, not lexical, semantics, we will return to this general topic in File 6.4.

Just like nouns, intransitive verbs also refer to sets of entities. The reference of an intransitive verb like *swim* is the set of all swimmers in the world. If this seems a little counterintuitive, suppose somebody asks you, *Who swims?* You would probably answer this question by trying to list the swimmers that you can think of, e.g., Sally, Polly, whales, and Sally's dog Fido. You would be trying to identify the set of things in the world that swim. Similarly, the reference of an adjective like *purple* is the set of all purple things in the world.

(3) A visual representation of the set identified by *woman*, relative to all things in the universe

© 2015 by Julia Porter Papke

We have hardly exhausted all of the different kinds of reference that words can have. Nonetheless, we hope to have given you a taste of how words may relate to the things in the world and how we can use diagrams (like the one in (3)) to represent their reference. In the next section, we build on the notion of word reference to discuss different kinds of meaning relations between words.

6.2.4 Meaning Relationships

There are many ways for two words to be related. In previous chapters we have already seen a number of ways: they may be phonologically related (e.g., *night/knight,* which share the same pronunciation), they may be morphologically related (e.g., *lift/lifted,* which both share the same root), or they may be syntactically related (e.g., *write/paint,* which are both transitive verbs). There is yet another way two words can be related, and that is semantically. For instance, the word *pot* is intuitively more closely related semantically to the word *pan* than it is to the word *floor.* The reason, clearly, is that both *pot* and *pan* have meanings that involve being containers used for cooking, while *floor* does not. (We will later reach the conclusion that *pot* and *pan* are sister terms.)

To facilitate our survey of semantic relationships among words, we will focus on their reference. So we will talk about specific things in the world (the reference of proper names) or sets of things in the world (the reference of nouns or adjectives). This will allow us to construct convenient diagrams to represent semantic relationships among words.

a. Hyponymy. One kind of word meaning relation is **hyponymy.** We say that a word X is a **hyponym** of a word Y if the set that is the reference of X is always included in the set that is the reference of Y. When some set X is included in a set Y, we also say that X is a subset of Y.

For example, consider the words *dog* and *poodle.* The reference of *dog* is the set of all things that are dogs, while the reference of *poodle* is the set of all things that are poodles. Suppose that there are exactly three individuals in the world that are poodles, namely, Froofroo, Princess, and Miffy. Of course, all poodles are also dogs. Now in this simple world that we are imagining, in addition to the three poodles, there are also some individuals that are dogs but not poodles, namely, Fido, Spot, and Butch.

Diagram (4) depicts this scenario. The names of the sets that represent the reference of *dog* and *poodle* are in capital letters and underlined. The names of individuals appear inside the sets they belong to. For example, the referents of *poodle* are inside the set that represents the reference of *poodle*.

(4) Visual representation of the hyponymous relation between *poodle* and *dog*

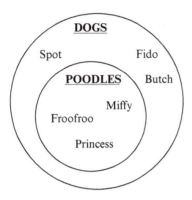

Of course, this diagram is just a visual aid. The referent of *Froofroo* is not a sequence of letters on a piece of paper, but some actual individual. The reference of *poodle* is not a circle with some sequences of letters in it, but a set of actual poodles. For obvious reasons, we cannot put real dogs in this textbook, so a diagram will have to suffice.

What we see in the diagram is that the set of poodles is contained in the set of dogs; i.e., the set that is the reference of *poodle* is a subset of the set that is the reference of *dog*. It represents the fact that all poodles are dogs (so *Miffy* is a member of the set of poodles, but also a member of the set of dogs), but not all dogs are poodles (e.g., *Fido* is a member of the set of dogs, but not a member of the set of poodles). In this case, we say that the word *poodle* is a hyponym of the word *dog*. Conversely, *dog* is a **hypernym** of *poodle*.

Hyponymous relationships stack very well. For example, *poodle* is a hyponym of *dog*, *dog* is a hyponym of *mammal*, *mammal* is a hyponym of *vertebrate*, *vertebrate* is a hyponym of *animal*, etc. We say that two words are **sister terms** if their reference is, intuitively, on the same level in the hierarchy. This means that they are contained in all the same sets, or that they have exactly the same hypernyms. For example, in diagram (4), *Miffy* and *Froofroo* are sister terms because there is no set that Miffy belongs to and Froofroo does not, and vice versa. However, *Fido* and *Miffy* are not sister terms because *Fido* is not in the set of poodles, while *Miffy* is. In diagram (5), *dog* and *cow* are sister terms, while *cow* and *poodle* are not because *dog* is a hypernym of *poodle*, but it is not a hypernym of *cow*.

b. Synonymy. Another kind of semantic relation is **synonymy**. Two words are synonymous if they have exactly the same reference. It may be difficult to come up with pairs of truly synonymous words, but *couch/sofa*, *quick/rapid*, and *groundhog/woodchuck* come close. Anything that is a groundhog is also a woodchuck, and vice versa. The set that is the reference of *groundhog* is exactly the same set as the one that is the reference of *woodchuck*. Of course, the senses of the words in these pairs may differ—it is possible for someone to know what woodchucks are without knowing what groundhogs are, so their senses are not the same thing. Similarly, *quick* and *rapid* may have different senses, but the set of quick things in the world is probably the same as the set of rapid things.

c. Antonymy. A third kind of semantic relation is **antonymy**. The basic notion of antonymy is of being "opposite" in some sense. In order for two words to be antonyms of one another, they must have meanings that are related, yet these meanings must contrast with each other in some significant way.

(5)   Visual representation of sister terms and of nested hyponymous relations

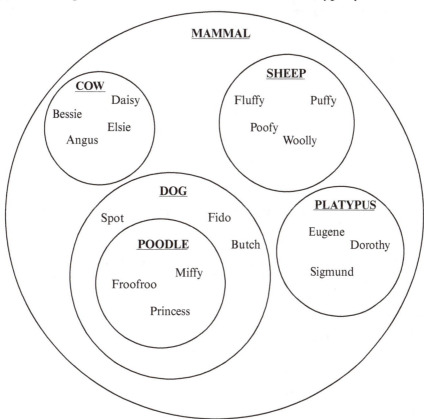

It turns out that the word *opposite* is fairly vague: there are actually several ways for a pair of words to be opposites, and each is distinct from the others. The most straightforward are **complementary** pairs. We can characterize complementary antonymy in terms of word reference. Two words X and Y are complementary antonyms if there is nothing in the world that is a part of both X's reference and Y's reference. Thus, if everything in the world is either in X's reference set or in Y's reference set or in neither of those sets, but crucially not in both sets, and if stating that something is X generally implies that it isn't Y, then X and Y form a complementary pair. (6) gives examples of complementary antonyms.

(6)   Complementary antonyms
      a. married/unmarried
      b. existent/nonexistent
      c. alive/dead
      d. win/lose

For each of these pairs, everything is either one or the other, or else is neither. So, for example, a boulder is neither alive nor dead, but critically, it isn't both.

      The second way a pair of words can be antonyms is by being **gradable** pairs. Gradable antonyms typically represent points on a continuum, so while something can be one or the other but not both, it can also easily be between the two (in contrast to complementary pairs), so saying "not X" does not imply "and therefore Y." For example, water may be hot, cold, or neither, but if you say that the water is not hot, it does not imply that it is cold. It may be warm, lukewarm, cool, chilly, or anywhere else in between. In addition, gradable antonyms tend to be relative, in that they do not represent an absolute value: an old dog has been around many fewer years than an old person, and a large blue whale is a very different size from a large mouse (see also the discussion of relative intersection in Section 6.4.3). Examples of gradable antonyms appear in (7).

(7) Gradable antonyms
     a. wet/dry
     b. easy/hard
     c. old/young
     d. love/hate

The fact that there are often words to describe states in between the two extremes can help in identifying gradable antonyms; for example, *damp* means something like 'between wet and dry,' and *middle-aged* means something like 'between old and young,' but there is no word that means 'between alive and dead' or other complementary pairs. Also, it is possible to ask about the extent of a gradable antonym and to use comparative and superlative endings or phrasing with them. Compare, for example, (8a) and (8b) with (8c) and (8d). It is easy to answer questions like (8a) and (8b) with something like *He is older/ younger than Sally* or *It was the easiest/hardest test I've ever taken,* but it is much stranger to ask or answer a question like (8c) or (8d), and phrases like *less alive* or *more nonexistent* are semantically odd, at best.

(8) a. How old is he?
     b. How hard was the test?
     c. How alive is he?
     d. How nonexistent is that unicorn?

The third kind of antonymy is seen in pairs of words called **reverses,** which are pairs such as those in (9).

(9) Reverses
     a. put together/take apart
     b. expand/contract
     c. ascent/descent

Reverses are pairs of words that suggest some kind of movement, where one word in the pair suggests movement that "undoes" the movement suggested by the other. For example, the descent from a mountain undoes the ascent, and putting something together undoes taking it apart.

Finally, there are **converses.** Converses have to do with two opposing points of view or a change in perspective: for one member of the pair to have reference, the other must as well. Consider the examples in (10).

(10) Converses
     a. lend/borrow
     b. send/receive
     c. employer/employee
     d. over/under

In order for lending to take place, borrowing must take place as well. In order for there to be an employer, there must also necessarily be at least one employee. If an object is over something, then something must be under it. Note how the pairs in (10) thereby differ from the pairs in (9). It is possible, for example, for something to expand without having anything contract.

FILE 6.3

···

Compositional Semantics: The Meanings of Sentences

6.3.1 Propositions and Truth Values

Thinking about what words mean is a critical part of semantics. Having a knowledge of lexical semantics, however, doesn't get us even halfway to being able to perform some of the complex communicative acts that we perform every day. If we could communicate by only using individual words, then our language would lack the sort of productivity that allows us to communicate complex new ideas. Therefore, we must consider not only word meanings but phrase and sentence meanings as well. In this file, we discuss the meanings of sentences, starting with their reference. Once we understand the relationship between sentence meanings and the world—their reference—we will be better equipped to discuss the senses that they express and the meaning relationships between them.

We encountered two types of word reference when we discussed lexical semantics. Some words, like proper names, refer to specific things in the world, while other words, like nouns and intransitive verbs, refer to sets of things in the world. Sentences, however, do not refer to either specific things or sets of things. Consider the following sentence:

(1)   China is the most populous country in the world.

The sentence in (1) is making a specific claim about entities in the world. It doesn't simply refer to China, or to the set of countries, or to the set of very populous countries. Unlike the name *China,* which picks out the entity in the world that is China, or *countries,* which directs our attention to the set of countries in the world, this sentence makes an assertion about certain entities in the world. The claim expressed by a sentence is called a **proposition.**

Note that words in isolation do not express propositions. The expression *China* does not in and of itself make a claim about China. Similarly, the word *countries* does not assert anything about countries or about anything else for that matter. On the other hand, the sentence in (1) does make a claim, namely, that China is the most populous country in the world. We will return to the discussion of propositions themselves—the senses expressed by sentences—shortly. For now, we will focus on the relationship between propositions and the world.

The crucial, in fact defining, characteristic of a proposition is that it can be true or false. The ability to be true or false is the ability to have a **truth value.** We can inquire about the truth value of propositions explicitly. For example, we could ask, *Is it true that China is the most populous country in the world?* Yet it wouldn't make much sense to try to inquire about the truth value of the meanings of nouns or proper names. That is, it would be very strange to ask whether *China* is true or whether *the most populous country in the world* is false. Trying to ask such a question is generally an excellent test for figuring out whether you are dealing with a proposition or not, since, by definition, all propositions have a truth value.

The proposition expressed by the sentence in (1) happens to be true. The proposition expressed by the sentence in (2) also has a truth value, but its truth value happens to be false.

(2)   Luxembourg is the most populous country in the world.

So, having a truth value does not mean being true, but rather being either true or false. To figure out whether a proposition is true or false, we have to evaluate it with respect to the world. In that way, truth values really do represent a relationship between the sense expressed by a sentence (a proposition) and the world. Thus, we consider truth values to be the reference of sentences.

You could think of it this way: when we consider the meaning of the expression *the 44th president of the United States* with respect to the world, we come up with the individual Barack Obama as its reference, and when we consider *cat* with respect to the world, we come up with the set of cats as its reference. Similarly, when we consider the meaning of *China is the most populous country in the world* with respect to the world that we live in, we can determine whether it is true or false. In sum, sentences express propositions and refer to truth values.

What does it mean to understand the proposition expressed by some sentence? Obviously, you must understand the sense of all the words that the sentence contains. You cannot understand the proposition expressed by *China is the most populous country in the world* without having mental representations of the meaning of *China, country, populous*, etc., and knowing how these expressions are syntactically combined to form a sentence. We will return to this discussion in the next file.

Ultimately, though, understanding a proposition must involve being able to determine its reference, in principle. This means understanding what the world would have to be like for the proposition to be true. The conditions that would have to hold in the world in order for some proposition to be true are called **truth conditions.** Thus, understanding the proposition expressed by a sentence means understanding its truth conditions. Consider the following sentence and the proposition it expresses:

(3)   The Queen of England is sleeping.

We all know what the world would have to be like for the proposition expressed by (3) to be true: on [insert current date] at exactly [insert current time] the individual that *the Queen of England* refers to would have to be asleep. However, the majority of us have no idea whether this proposition is actually true or false at any given time. This is not because we don't understand the proposition expressed by this sentence—we do, since we understand under what conditions it would be true—but because we don't have the requisite knowledge about the actual world to determine its reference.

Let's consider a more extreme example. The sentence in (4) expresses a proposition whose truth value nobody definitively knows, although all English speakers understand its truth conditions:

(4)   Sometime in the future, another world war will occur.

It is important to note that just because the truth value of a proposition is unknown does not mean that it doesn't have one. The proposition expressed by (4) indeed has a truth value. However, whether it is actually true or false is not something that we can determine. Notice that we can easily inquire about its truth value. You could, for example, legitimately ask a friend, *Do you think it's true that sometime in the future another world war will occur?* This is how we know that it really does express a proposition.

In sum, in order to know the truth value of a proposition, it is necessary to understand its truth conditions—you cannot begin to figure out whether a proposition is true or false unless you know what the world would have to be like for it to be true. However, since no one has perfect information, it is possible to understand its truth conditions but still not know its reference. This is not entirely unlike the fact that although you may have some mental representation about what *lychee* means, you may nevertheless fail to correctly pick out its referents.

6.3.2 Relationships between Propositions

Now that we know a little bit about propositions, we can investigate different kinds of relationships between them. Consider the following pair of sentences and the propositions that they express:

(5) a. All dogs bark.
     b. Sally's dog barks.

If the proposition expressed by the sentence in (5a) is true, the proposition expressed by (5b) also has to be true. In other words, the truth of (5a) guarantees the truth of (5b). If indeed all dogs in the world bark, and one of those dogs is Sally's pet, then clearly Sally's dog barks too. In this case, we say that the proposition expressed by *All dogs bark* entails the proposition expressed by *Sally's dog barks*. We call this relationship **entailment.**

Note that in reasoning about entailment, we are not concerned with actual truth values of propositions. Rather, we are evaluating their truth conditions. For example, look at the following pair:

(6) a. No dogs bark.
     b. Sally's dog doesn't bark.

In this case, too, (6a) entails (6b), because **if** (6a) were true, (6b) would also have to be true. As we all know, (6a) happens to be false. But its actual truth value is not relevant. What is relevant is that if we lived in a world in which (6a) were true, then (6b) would have to be true as well. Intuitively, the truth conditions for (6a) already include the truth conditions for (6b). Now consider the following pair of sentences:

(7) a. Barack Obama is the 44th president of the United States.
     b. China is the most populous country in the world.

The propositions expressed by both of these sentences happen to be true. However, neither one entails the other. Intuitively, the truth conditions for (7a) have nothing to do with the truth conditions for (7b). It's easy to imagine a world in which (7a) is true but (7b) is false, or vice versa. The truth of (7a) doesn't guarantee the truth of (7b), and the truth of (7b) doesn't guarantee the truth of (7a), so there is no entailment between these two propositions.

Some more examples of entailment follow. In each pair, the proposition expressed by the sentence in (a) entails the one expressed by the sentence in (b).

(8) a. Ian owns a Ford Focus.
     b. Ian owns a car.

(9) a. Ian has a full-time job.
     b. Ian is employed.

(10) a. Ian has visited Spain.
     b. Ian has visited Europe.

Notice that entailment is not necessarily symmetric. For example, if Ian has visited Spain, it has to be true that he has visited Europe. However, if Ian has visited Europe, that doesn't imply that he has visited Spain—perhaps he went to Finland or Ukraine instead. Thus, while (10a) entails (10b), (10b) does not entail (10a). When two propositions entail one another, we refer to their relationship as one of **mutual entailment.** For example, (11a) and (11b) are mutually entailing.

(11) a. Ian has a female sibling.
     b. Ian has a sister.

Propositions can also be **incompatible.** This means that it would be impossible for both of them to be true; that is, the truth conditions for one are incompatible with the truth conditions for the other. The following are some pairs of mutually incompatible propositions:

(12) a. No dogs bark.
     b. All dogs bark.

(13) a. George Washington is alive.
     b. George Washington is dead.

(14) a. Ian has a full-time job.
     b. Ian is not unemployed.

When two propositions are incompatible, it is impossible to imagine a world in which they could both be true.

FILE **6.4**

··

Compositional Semantics: Putting Meanings Together

6.4.1 The Principle of Compositionality

Investigating propositions and their relationships is only one aspect of compositional semantics. Another important set of questions that compositional semantics tries to answer has to do with meaning combinations. Given the meanings of words, how do we arrive at meanings of larger expressions? Clearly, the meanings of phrasal expressions (such as sentences) depend on the meanings of the words they contain. For example, *Sally never had a cat* and *Sally never had a dog* express different propositions, and we could say that this difference boils down to *cat* and *dog* having different meanings. However, it is not just the meanings of words that are relevant for figuring out the meanings of larger expressions that contain them. Consider the following pair of sentences:

(1) a. Sally loves Polly.
     b. Polly loves Sally.

Both of these sentences contain exactly the same words, none of which are ambiguous. However, the sentence in (1a) expresses a different proposition than the sentence in (1b). It is possible for the proposition expressed by (1a) to be true, and the one expressed by (1b) to be false—unrequited love is a real possibility.

What is the source of this difference in meaning between (1a) and (1b) since they both contain exactly the same expressions? It must be the way that these words are syntactically combined. In (1a), *Polly* is the object of *loves,* and *Sally* is its subject. In (1b), the reverse is the case. Thus, the syntactic structure of these two sentences is different, and that has an effect on meaning.

Consider the following structurally ambiguous string of words: *The cop saw the man with the binoculars*. This sequence can be used to express two distinct propositions. It could mean that the cop had the binoculars and was using them to look at the man, or it could mean that the man whom the cop saw was the one who had the binoculars. This difference in meaning arises because the expressions can syntactically combine in two different ways: the PP *with the binoculars* could be a VP adjunct, modifying *saw the man,* or it could be a noun adjunct, modifying *man* (see File 5.5). Therefore, the meaning of a phrasal expression, such as a sentence, depends not only on the meanings of the words it contains, but also on its syntactic structure.

This is precisely what the **principle of compositionality** states: the meaning of a sentence (or any other multi-word expression) is a function of the meanings of the words it contains and the way in which these words are syntactically combined. There has to be some way for speakers to figure out the meanings of sentences based on lexical meanings and syntactic structures, since all languages contain an infinite number of sentences. It is clearly impossible to memorize all distinct sentence meanings. However, the meanings of all words and other lexical expressions are stored in the mental lexicon, and a part of speakers' mental grammar is syntax. Because the meanings of sentences can be computed based on word meanings and syntactic structures, speakers can produce and understand an infinite number of sentences. In this way, the principle of compositionality is related to the design feature of productivity. Crucially, speakers can comprehend the meanings of completely novel sentences, as illustrated by the sentences in (2). While you've most likely never encountered these sentences before, you should have no trouble figuring out what they mean.

(2) a. I stuffed my apron full of cheese and frantically ran away from the dairy snatchers.
     b. It seems unlikely that this book will spontaneously combust while you are reading it, but nonetheless it is theoretically possible that this might happen.
     c. The platypus is enjoying a bubble bath.

The principle of compositionality simply states that the meanings of multi-word expressions are **compositional,** that is, predictable from the meanings of words and their syntactic combination. To appreciate the compositional nature of the meanings of most phrasal expressions, let's look at some examples where compositionality fails. Consider the expression *kicked the bucket* in *Polly kicked the bucket.* This sentence could mean that Polly performed some physical action whereby her foot came into forceful contact with some bucket; this is the compositional meaning of this sentence that we can compute based on the meanings of *Polly, kicked, the,* and *bucket,* along with the syntactic structure of the sentence.

Yet *kick the bucket* also has another, idiomatic meaning, which has nothing to do with forceful physical contact between somebody's foot and a bucket. The non-compositional meaning of *kick the bucket* is 'die,' so *Polly kicked the bucket* could also mean 'Polly died.' Since this meaning is not predictable given the meanings of *kick, the,* and *bucket,* and given their syntactic combination, the entire phrase *kick the bucket* has to be stored in your mental lexicon together with its non-compositional meaning. Thus, even though it's not a single word, *kick the bucket* is a kind of lexical expression. We call such expressions **idioms.**

Whenever the meaning of some multi-word expression is not compositional, it has to be stored in the mental lexicon. Fortunately, in the vast majority of cases, phrasal meanings are compositional. In the remainder of this file, we explore how, exactly, the meanings of words combine into phrasal meanings, which, as you will recall, depends partly on their syntactic combination.

6.4.2   Combining the Meanings of Verb Phrases and Noun Phrases

Recall from Chapter 5 that sentences in English typically consist of a noun phrase (NP) and a verb phrase (VP). As an example, consider the phrase structure tree for the sentence *Sandy runs,* shown in (3). What is the process for computing the meaning of the whole sentence from the meanings of its two constituents, an NP and a VP?

(3)

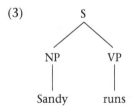

As we discussed in File 6.2, proper names like *Sandy* refer to specific entities in the world, and intransitive verbs like *runs* refer to sets of entities in the world. So *Sandy* refers to some individual Sandy, and *runs* refers to the set of all runners in the world. How can we figure out, based on the reference of *Sandy* and *runs,* what the truth conditions for the proposition *Sandy runs* are? It's quite simple, really: for the proposition expressed by *Sandy runs* to be true, it would have to be the case that Sandy (the referent of *Sandy*) is a member of the set that is the reference of *runs*.

Consider the following scenario. Suppose we live in a very simple world that contains exactly five individuals: Kim, Robin, Lee, Sandy, and Michael. Suppose further that of these five individuals, Robin, Kim, and Lee are runners, but Sandy and Michael are not. In other words, the reference of *runs* in this world is the set that contains the individuals Robin, Kim, and Lee. This situation is depicted in (4).

(4)

In this world, the proposition expressed by *Sandy runs* is false, since Sandy is not in the set that is the reference of runs.

But now suppose that in this simple world in which there are only five individuals, the reference of *runs* is different, so that Sandy, Robin, and Lee are runners while Kim and Michael are not. This situation is depicted in (5).

(5)

In this case, the proposition expressed by *Sandy runs* would be true, since Sandy is in the set that is the reference of *runs*.

Although discussing the details of computing the meanings of multi-word NPs such as *the 44th president of the United States* or multi-word VPs such as *likes Bob a lot* is beyond the scope of this book, we note that many expressions whose syntactic category is NP refer to specific individuals, while expressions whose syntactic category is VP refer to sets of individuals. Thus, *the 44th president of the United States* refers to the individual Barack Obama, and *likes Bob a lot* refers to the set of individuals who like Bob a lot. In many cases, then, the proposition expressed by a sentence is true just in case the referent of the subject NP is a member of the set that is the reference of the VP. For example:

(6) a. Sandy's dog barks.
     <u>truth conditions:</u> true just in case the individual that *Sandy's dog* refers to is in the set of all barkers

   b. The 44th president of the United States eats apples.
     <u>truth conditions:</u> true just in case Barack Obama is in the set of all apple-eaters

6.4.3 Combining the Meanings of Adjectives and Nouns

Computing truth values for simple sentences was a fairly straightforward demonstration of semantic composition. We find a more complex sort of composition when we turn our attention to adjective-noun combinations. While the adjective and the noun syntactically combine the same way in *green sweater, good food,* and *fake money,* we will see that in each of these phrases, their meanings combine differently. How their meanings combine depends primarily on the particular adjective involved.

We'll start out with the simplest form of adjectival combination, **pure intersection.** In the phrase *green sweater,* we have two words, *green* and *sweater,* each of which refers to a set of entities (individuals or objects). The reference of *green* is the set of green entities, and that of *sweater* is the set of entities that are sweaters. To compute the meaning of the phrase, then, we need only collect all the entities that are in the set both of green things and of sweaters. This is illustrated in the following diagram; here, the intersection (the overlapping portions of the two circles) contains the set of entities that are both in the set of green things and in the set of sweaters.

(7)

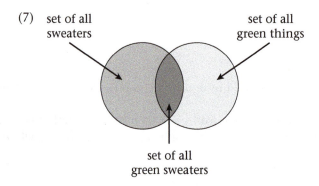

Other phrases that work in the same way are *healthy cow, blue suit, working woman,* etc. Because they produce pure intersections, adjectives like *healthy, blue,* and *working* are called **intersective adjectives.** An important point about these cases of pure intersection is that the two sets can be identified independently. For example, we can decide what is green and what isn't before we even know that we're going to look for sweaters.

Other adjectives do not necessarily combine with nouns according to this pattern; examples of a second kind of semantic combination can be found in the phrases *big whale* or *good beer.* In the case of *big whale,* the problem is that it is not possible to identify a set of big things in absolute terms. Size is always relative: what is big for whales is tiny for mountains; what is big for mice is tiny for whales; what is short for a giraffe is tall for a chicken. While it is possible to find a set of whales independently, the set represented by the adjective *big* can't be just a set identified by the meaning 'big' but rather must be a set identified by 'big-for-a-whale.' Similarly, *tall giraffe* will involve a set of things that are tall-for-a-giraffe, and *loud explosion,* a set of things that are loud-for-an-explosion (compare this with *loud whisper,* which would use a completely different standard for loudness). Such cases we call **relative intersection,** since the reference of the adjective has to be determined relative to the reference of the noun. Examples are shown in (8).

(8)

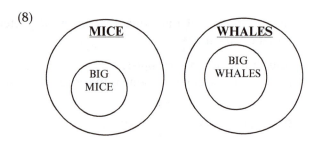

Here, the adjective *big* selects a subset of mice, a subset of whales, and likewise a subset for any other set that we might want to identify big elements of (*big planets, big refrigerators, big feet,* etc.). Therefore, they are called **subsective adjectives.**

Good beer is another case of relative intersection. But *good* is even more relative than *tall* or *loud*. *Tall,* for example, always refers to a scale of vertical distance, and *loud* refers to a scale of volume of sound. We might say that *good* refers to a scale of quality, but what kind of quality? A good beer is probably judged on its taste, but a good ladder on how sturdy and useful it is, and a good record on how pleasurable the music is. *Good beer* could even describe a beer that removes dirt well if we said *That's good beer to wash the walls with.* So *good* apparently refers to anything that fits our purposes well, and these purposes vary with the object and with how that object is used in a given case. In order to use and understand phrases of the form *good + common noun* correctly, we must have more knowledge about the context than in other cases of relative intersection.

Both types of intersection, pure and relative, have in common that these combinations actually refer to some of the objects denoted by the nouns themselves. For *green sweater, tall giraffe,* and *good beer,* we are necessarily talking about sweaters, giraffes, and beer, respectively. But in phrases like *possible solution* and *alleged thief,* this is not the case: *possible solution* does not necessarily refer to a real solution, and *alleged thief* does not necessarily refer to a thief. These are both examples of **non-intersection.** Logically, we can say that the use of intersection-type adjectives entails (or requires) reference to the objects denoted by the nouns, while the use of non-intersection adjectives does not.

Finally, there is a second type of non-intersection adjective (an adjective that does not require reference to objects denoted by the noun). When this kind of adjective combines with a noun, the reference of the resulting expression cannot overlap with the noun's reference. For example, a *fake Picasso* by definition cannot refer to a Picasso. Of course, a fake thing must have some characteristics of the real thing, or the word would not be used at all; in fact a good fake may be like the real thing in every respect except actually being genuine. Adjectives like *fake* we call **anti-intersection adjectives.**

Researchers in compositional semantics concern themselves, among other things, with discovering the sorts of differences examined here and with writing precise rules to describe exactly how different types of expressions combine. It becomes obvious that these rules must actually exist in our minds once one considers that there are an infinite number of sentences in any language and hence an infinite number of meanings to understand and produce.

FILE 6.5

....

Practice

File 6.1—An Overview of Semantics

Exercises

1. Identify each of the following statements as being either mostly about lexical semantics or mostly about compositional semantics:

   a. The phrase *purple books* describes a group of objects (books) that have a certain property (being purple).

   b. The words *couch* and *sofa* mean roughly the same thing.

   c. *Water under the bridge* means something different from *bridge under the water*.

   d. The sentence *John ate a bagel for breakfast* is true just in case an individual by the name of John consumed a round bread product with a hole in the middle for his morning meal.

   e. The opposite of *open* is *shut*.

   f. *Paris* is a word that refers to a particular city in France.

   g. If the sentence *Harold likes checkers and backgammon* is true, then the sentence *Harold likes backgammon* must be true as well.

   h. *Bird* means something like 'warm-blooded, egg-laying animal with feathers, wings, two legs, and a beak.'

   i. When most people hear the word *bird* out of the blue, they are more likely to think of a songbird than a penguin, flamingo, duck, or vulture; however, penguins, flamingos, ducks, and vultures are also kinds of birds.

   j. *Jelly beans that are lemon flavored* has the same meaning as *lemon-flavored jelly beans*.

2. We discussed expressions such as *unicorn* and *the queen of United States* that have no referents.

   i. Come up with three more examples of expressions that have no referents.

   ii. Explain in your own words why the notion of sense is important, taking into account the particular examples you came up with for part (i).

3. We discussed the fact that a single referent can sometimes be picked out by distinct expressions with distinct senses, e.g., *Barack Obama* and *the 44th president of the United States*.

   i. Come up with your own pair of expressions where each expression has a different sense, but where both have the same referent. Say what this referent is. Make up three such pairs of expressions.

   ii. Explain in your own words why examples like the ones you came up with for part (i) require that we distinguish between sense and reference as two different components of linguistic meaning.

Discussion Question

4. The sentence *Barack Obama is the 44th president of the United States* could be informative, i.e., could communicate some new information to somebody who didn't previously know that Barack Obama is the 44th president of the United States. What about *Barack Obama is Barack Obama* or *The 44th president of the United States is the 44th president of the United States?* Are these two sentences as informative as *Barack Obama is the 44th president of the United States?* Why or why not? How do you explain the difference in informativeness given that both *Barack Obama* and *the 44th president of the United States* refer to the same individual?

File 6.2—Lexical Semantics: The Meanings of Words

Exercises

5. For each expression below, specify what its reference is. For example, the reference of *New York City* is the actual city in the state of New York in the United States, the reference of *dog* is the set of all actual dogs in the world, and the reference of *sleep* is the set of all individuals in the world who sleep.

a.	France	**g.**	student
b.	book	**h.**	Massachusetts
c.	red	**i.**	car
d.	Noam Chomsky	**j.**	man
e.	eat	**k.**	movie
f.	fox	**l.**	Statue of Liberty

6. Sort the expressions listed in (a)–(l) in exercise 5 into two groups: one group for the expressions that refer to a particular entity in the world, the other group for the expressions that refer to a set of entities in the world.

7. Explain in your own words why the expression *student,* a noun, cannot have any particular individual in the world as its reference. Give an example sentence to illustrate your point, and explain exactly how your sentence shows that *student* cannot refer to any particular individual.

8. In what way is each of the following pairs of words related? In cases of hyponymy, indicate which word is the hyponym and which word is the hypernym; in cases of antonymy, tell what kind of antonymy it is.

a.	shallow	deep	**f.**	study	studying
b.	apple	banana	**g.**	move	run
c.	suite	sweet	**h.**	sofa	couch
d.	table	furniture	**i.**	green	blue
e.	unmarried	married	**j.**	punch	touch

9. i. Propose a hypernym for each of the following words:

    a. hammer
    b. T-shirt
    c. pink
    d. fish

(cont.)

    ii. Propose a hyponym for each of the following words:

        e. appliance
        f. musical instrument
        g. furniture
        h. fish

10. Come up with your own hierarchical hyponymy relationship for some noun like the one given for *poodle* in File 6.2. It should have at least four hierarchical levels. (For an extra challenge, try to do this exercise with verbs as well!)

11. Consider the verbs *sweat* and *perspire*. Do they have the same sense? If not, how are they different? Do they have the same reference? If not, how are they different? Would you consider them to be synonyms, according to the definition of synonyms in File 6.2? Why or why not?

12. Classify the following pairs of antonyms as complementary, gradable, reverses, or converses:

    a. wide/narrow
    b. smoking/nonsmoking
    c. inflate/deflate
    d. defeat/lose to
    e. good/bad
    f. innocent/guilty
    g. hot/cold
    h. teacher/student
    i. grow/shrink

13. Consider the English prefix *un-* that attaches to verbs to form such verbs as the following:

    unwrap   *undress*   *untangle*
    unlock   *unwind*   *uncoil*

    Which type of antonym does *un-* create? Explain your answer.

14. Consider the English prefix *in-* that attaches to adjectives in order to form such adjectives as the following:

    intolerant   *inhospitable*   *incredible*
    inelegant   *insincere*   *insecure*

    Which type of antonym does *in-* create? Explain your answer.

Discussion Questions

15. In File 6.2, both dictionary-style definitions and mental image definitions are presented as possible ways that word meanings may be stored in our brains. Although neither turns out to be a completely acceptable answer, does one seem to have more merit than the other? Why do you think so?

16. We noted that the reference of intransitive verbs like *swim* is a set of individuals (i.e., exactly those individuals who swim). Consider transitive verbs such as *like* or *hate*. Can we take their reference to be just a set of individuals? What do you think the reference of such verbs is?

File 6.3—Compositional Semantics: The Meanings of Sentences

Exercises

17. For each of the following expressions, determine whether it expresses a proposition or not. Remember, if you are dealing with a proposition, you can question its truth value. For example, we know that *Fido is a dog* expresses a proposition because we can ask *Is it true that Fido is a dog?* Conversely, *a dog* all by itself does not express a proposition because we cannot ask *Is it true that a dog?*

    a. woman   **f.** accidentally
    b. like Bob   **g.** Polly liked
    c. the smallest country in the world   **h.** under the bed
    d. Sally wondered who would be at the party   **i.** Sally likes to sleep
    e. Bob hates Polly   **j.** bring some beer

18. For each of the following sentences, specify its truth conditions, i.e., under what conditions it would be true. For example, *Fluffy is a cat* is true just in case the individual Fluffy really is a cat.

    a. Bob traveled to France.
    b. Barack Obama is the 44th president of the United States.
    c. It will rain tomorrow.
    d. Peru is a country in Europe.
    e. Paris is the capital of France.
    f. The earth is not flat.
    g. The moon is made of green cheese.
    h. Some computers are able to synthesize human voices.
    i. Last week a monkey and an elephant escaped from the zoo, broke into the National Gallery, and stole a valuable painting.
    j. You are currently looking at a copy of the 12th edition of *Language Files*.

19. Try to assign a truth value for each proposition expressed by the sentences in exercise 18. If you cannot determine the truth value for some of them, explain why.

20. Assign truth values to propositions expressed by each of the following sentences:

    a. To have a truth value means to be true.
    b. To have a truth value means to be either true or false.
    c. The reference of a sentence is the proposition expressed by it.
    d. The sense of a sentence is the proposition expressed by it.
    e. The reference of a sentence is some individual in the world.
    f. The reference of a sentence is not a set of individuals in the world.
    g. The reference of a sentence is a truth value.
    h. If you understand the proposition expressed by some sentence, then you know its truth conditions.
    i. If you understand the proposition expressed by some sentence, then you know its truth value.
    j. It's possible to know the truth value of some proposition without knowing its truth conditions.
    k. For every proposition, there is somebody in the world who knows its actual truth value.

21. For each of the following pairs of sentences, tell whether they have the same truth conditions or different truth conditions, and explain how you know.

   a. I ate turkey at Thanksgiving.
       I ate turkey at New Years.

   b. There's a sofa in the living room.
       There's a couch in the living room.

   c. The first president of the United States had dental trouble.
       George Washington had dental trouble.

   d. Susan closed the door.
       The door was closed by Susan.

   e. Penguins live in Antarctica.
       Penguins live on the coldest continent on Earth.

22. Come up with original examples of each of the following:
   a. a pair of sentences where one entails the other, but not the other way around
   b. a pair of mutually entailing sentences
   c. a pair of incompatible sentences

23. For each pair of the following sentences, determine whether one entails the other, whether they are mutually entailing, whether they are incompatible, or none of the above. Explain your answers.

   a. Fifi is a poodle.
       Fifi is a dog.

   b. My last name is Jones.
       My father's last name was Jones.

   c. Bob inherited a car from his grandma.
       Bob owns a car.

   d. Sally lives in Ohio.
       Sally lives in Europe.

   e. Sally lives in Ohio.
       Sally lives in the United States.

   f. Polly speaks Russian.
       Polly is from Russia.

   g. Polly doesn't speak Russian.
       Polly is from Russia.

   h. Bob lives in the capital of Ohio.
       Bob lives in Columbus.

   i. Not all dogs bark.
       Some dogs don't bark.

   j. Sally said she liked Polly.
       Sally said she didn't like Polly.

   k. Polly thinks that Fido is a dog.
       Fido is a dog.

Discussion Questions

24. If two propositions are mutually entailing, what, if anything, do you know about their truth conditions? Explain, using specific examples.

25. Consider a pair of sentences like *The first president of the United States had dental trouble* and *George Washington had dental trouble*. Do they express the same proposition? In other words, do they have exactly the same sense? Why or why not? (*Hint:* Do *George Washington* and *the first president of the United States* have the same reference? Do they have the same sense?)

26. Consider the pair of sentences *Susan closed the door* and *The door was closed by Susan*. Do they always have the same reference? Do you think they have the same sense (i.e., express the same proposition) or not? Why or why not?

File 6.4—Compositional Semantics: Putting Meanings Together

Exercises

27. Each underlined expression below is an idiom. For each of them, explain (i) what its non-compositional, idiomatic meaning is, and (ii) what its compositional meaning is.

    a. <u>The cat is out of the bag</u>.
    b. Sally wouldn't <u>lift a finger</u>.
    c. That's <u>water under the bridge</u>.
    d. <u>A picture is worth a thousand words</u>.
    e. Bob has <u>a chip on his shoulder</u>.
    f. It was Polly's birthday, so <u>I picked up the tab</u>.

28. Consider the following pair of sentences and then answer the questions below:

    a. Sandy likes Bob.
    b. It's not true that Sandy likes Bob.

       i. What is the relationship (e.g., entailment? incompatibility?) between the propositions expressed by these sentences?
       ii. Can you make a generalization about the relationship between the proposition expressed by some sentence X and the proposition expressed by some sentence of the form *It's not true that X*? What is the generalization?
       iii. What can you conclude about the meaning of *it's not true that*?

29. Which of the following are examples of relative intersection, and which are examples of pure intersection?

    a. lavender crayons
    b. huge TVs
    c. old temples
    d. square rugs
    e. fast trains
    f. empty bottles
    g. long streets
    h. sliding doors

Discussion Questions

30. We noted that many VPs refer to sets of entities, while many NPs refer to specific entities, so that for the proposition expressed by some sentence to be true, the individual that the subject NP refers to has to be in the set that is the reference of the VP. For example, *Sally runs* is true just in case the individual picked out by *Sally* is in the set of individuals who run. Consider a sentence like *China is the most populous country in the world*. What is the reference of *the most populous country in the world*: an entity or a set of entities? What are the truth conditions for this sentence? Given examples like *China is the most populous country in the world* or *Barack Obama is the 44th president of the United States,* can you make a generalization about the truth conditions of sentences of the form *X is Y* based on the reference of *X* and *Y*?

31. You should look over question 30 before attempting to answer this one. Now consider sentences like *Sally is a nurse*. Does *a nurse* here refer to an entity or to a set of entities? What are the truth conditions for this sentence? How are they similar to or different from the truth conditions of sentences like *China is the most populous country in the world*? How do you have to revise your generalization about the sentences of the form *X is Y* that you came up with for question 30?

32. Consider the sentence *All dogs bark*. What is the reference of *all dogs*? What is the reference of *bark*? What are the truth conditions for this sentence, given the reference of the subject NP and the VP? What does this sentence assert about the relationship between the reference of *all dogs* and the reference of *bark*? What is the generalization that you can make about the truth conditions of sentences whose general form is *All X Y*?

33. Why is lexical semantics alone not enough to interpret the meaning of a phrase or a sentence? On the other hand, could we work on compositional semantics without having information from the lexical side? Why or why not?

34. The discussion of adjectives given in File 6.4 reveals that there is quite a bit of complexity when it comes to understanding the meanings of adjectives. As if this were not complicated enough, there are many other types of Adjective + Noun combinations besides the four discussed in File 6.4. For example, the adjectives in *An occasional sailor walked by* and *I do a daily six-mile run* function very much like adverbs, as seen by the paraphrases *Occasionally, a sailor walked by* and *Every day I do a six-mile run*. These Adjective + Noun combinations do not follow the same rule of combination as the types discussed in File 6.4. Consider yet another case: in the phrase *a hot cup of coffee,* what is hot is the coffee and not necessarily the cup. Here, the adjective combines with cup, which comes to denote its contents.

Speculate about some of the ways that speakers of a language might go about trying to figure out what kind of intersection (if any) to use to interpret an adjective meaning when that adjective appears in some context.

Further Readings

Hurford, James R.; Brendan Heasley; and Michael B. Smith. 2007. *Semantics: A coursebook.* 2nd edn. Cambridge: Cambridge University Press.

Lyons, John. 1995. *Linguistic semantics: An introduction.* Cambridge: Cambridge University Press.

CHAPTER
7

·····························

Pragmatics

the relevance of context

What Is Pragmatics?

I n Chapter 6, *semantics* was defined as the study of meaning. Given such a definition, it is tempting to suspect that once we understand the semantics of a language, we will automatically understand the meaning of any utterance in that language. In fact, however, identifying the semantic contribution of words and sentences gets us only partway to understanding what an utterance means. Why? The context in which a sentence is uttered may critically affect the meaning that the speaker intends!

Pragmatics is the study of the ways people use language in actual conversations. Pragmaticists study both how context helps to determine whether a particular utterance is appropriate or inappropriate as well as how changes to context alter sentences' meanings.

Contents

....

Language in Context

7.1.1 The Importance of Context

We may often hear someone use a quotation—for example, in defense of a political opinion or a religious viewpoint—only to hear someone else counter, "But that's not really what he (the original speaker) meant! You've taken it completely out of context!" We also become frustrated when something we have said is taken out of context, feeling as though we have been misquoted. We know intrinsically that to ignore the original context of an utterance can misrepresent the speaker's intentions. Experiences like these tell us that context can affect an utterance's meaning. One of the jobs of pragmaticists is to investigate the relationship between context and meaning.

7.1.2 Sentences and Utterances

In order to investigate this relationship, we need a way to talk about language in context. Pragmaticists therefore distinguish between sentences and utterances. A sentence is a phrasal expression that expresses some (complete) idea. Consider a sentence like *There is a platypus in the bathtub*. We know many things about this sentence: it is a sentence of English; it contains seven words; it has a certain syntactic structure; and so on. However, while we are able to describe such properties of a sentence, sentences are abstract entities.

Whenever a sentence is used, though—whenever a person speaks (or signs) it—there has been an **utterance** of the sentence. An utterance is not an abstraction. It is an event, something that happens. Read the sentence *There is a platypus in the bathtub* out loud. Now, ask the next person you see to do the same thing. If you have followed these instructions, then you have just heard two utterances, but there is only one sentence. Likewise, if a theater company puts on a play and performs it ten times, the play will open with the same sentence each time, but there will be ten different utterances.

The distinction between sentences and utterances is so important that it gets marked typographically. Anytime that you see a group of words that look like a sentence and are set in italics, what is being referred to is the sentence: the abstract entity. If you see the same words in quotations, then there is a particular utterance that is being discussed.

Utterances may be described as having many of the same properties as sentences (e.g., language and length). However, utterances have other properties as well: we may talk about the time of an utterance, the place of an utterance, the volume of an utterance, the speaker of an utterance, and so on. It does not make sense to talk about the time or the place of a sentence, though, because a sentence is only an abstract idea; it is not an event, and therefore it does not have a **context**.

7.1.3 How Context Affects Meaning

There are many ways in which context can affect the meaning of an utterance. Consider a simple sentence such as (1) at the top of the next page.

(1)   He is there now.

The above sentence, heard or read out of context, is difficult to interpret, because it includes many **deictic** or "placeholder" words that don't inherently refer to something specific. These words' meanings are always determined by the context in which they are uttered. We know that *he* refers to a male and that *there* refers to a place and that *now* refers to a time, but these vague meanings alone don't give us the precise information that we need to figure out what would be meant by this sentence when uttered in some context. Considering this sentence in isolation, we don't know whom we are talking about, where he is, or when he is there. Sentence (1) could mean that a friend of yours is in class, at the library, or in Europe; it could mean that Elvis Presley is in Las Vegas in the 1970s or that Santa Claus is at the North Pole on Christmas Eve. To determine which meaning was intended by the speaker, one would need to know when the sentence was uttered and what the speaker was talking about.

Deictic elements aren't the only reason that sentences are context dependent though. Any sentence can take on a particular, novel, and distinct meaning relative to a particular context. Consider the example in (2).

(2)   Can you take the trash out?

This sentence seems fairly straightforward, but in fact it could have a range of different meanings. Suppose that your roommate is running late one morning and calls, "Can you take the trash out?" over her shoulder as she leaves. She probably is requesting that you take the trash out. On the other hand, suppose that you have been in a crippling accident and that you are only just beginning to take on simple housework again. If your physical therapist asks you the question in (2), she is not making a request but rather inquiring about your ability to carry out a set of actions. Here's a third case: suppose that your younger sibling is pestering you while you are trying to have a conversation with a friend. Finally, in frustration, you turn to your sibling and say, "Don't you have anything else to do? Can you take the trash out?" Here you might not care whether your sibling takes the trash out at all. Rather, you just want to be left alone! Suppose, on the other hand, that in the same context, instead of saying (2) to your sibling, you have instead turned to your friend and, while pointing at your sibling, asked whether your friend can take the trash out. Now you are suggesting that your sibling **is** the trash, and you want your friend to carry your sibling out of the room! The same simple sentence can thus have at least four very different meanings. With a little creativity, you could come up with many more.

From both of these examples, it is plain to see that we cannot talk about what an utterance of a sentence means without knowing about the context in which it was uttered.

Some people may argue that there are certain default or "out-of-the-blue" interpretations for many sentences. Of course they are correct. For example, for most speakers, the default out-of-the-blue interpretation of (2) is that it is a request. What is important to recognize, however, is that out-of-the-blue is one particular kind of context that affects the meaning of an utterance as much as would any other kind of context.

7.1.4   Types of Context

An utterance's context can be broken up into several components. **Linguistic context** has to do with what preceded a particular utterance in a discourse. It refers to what others have said earlier in the conversation. So, for example, the answer "Yes" means something entirely different when it is an answer to "Do you like green beans?" than when it is an answer to "Is there a computer available in the computer lab?" or "Will you marry me?" The linguistic context of an utterance tells what speakers are talking about: green beans, a platypus,

Santa Claus, or whatever. The linguistic context is made up of all of the sentences that have been uttered in a discourse leading up to the utterance in question.

A second aspect of context is **situational context.** Not surprisingly, an utterance's situational context gives information about the situation in which it is uttered. Situational context allows us to refer to things in the world around us even if they have not been mentioned before in the discourse. If a goat suddenly walked into your classroom, you could say, "It smells," and everyone there would know that you were talking about the goat. No one would wonder whether you meant the fish you had for dinner or your grandmother's perfume. This is true even though no one had mentioned the goat's presence already in the discourse. Likewise, if a friend tells you, "The governor was on TV last night," your friend most likely means the governor of Rhode Island if you are in Rhode Island, the governor of Ohio if you are in Ohio, the governor of Arizona if you are in Arizona, and so on. We apply our situational knowledge to what we hear all the time.

As a third example, a sentence such as *Rachael is very tall* has a different meaning if the Rachael in question is a preschooler, a ten-year-old, or a professional basketball player. In the first case, the speaker might mean that Rachael is three and a half feet tall; in the second or third case, the speaker could not possibly mean this. Why? Because people know that preschoolers tend to be around three feet tall but that basketball players tend to be much taller. Consider a situation in which you are describing your three-year-old niece. If you say to your sister, who has not seen your niece since she was an infant, "Rachael is very tall," your sister will know that you do not mean that Rachael is seven feet tall—or anything resembling that height! This information does not need to have been previously mentioned in the discourse in order for the speakers to use it to understand what others mean. (Refer to File 6.4 for more information about subsective adjectives like *tall*.)

Finally, **social context** includes information about the relationships between the people who are speaking and what their roles are. Social context is what makes it okay for your football coach to tell you to run two laps around the field but makes it unacceptable for you to tell your coach the same thing. Social context lets us know when saying "yes, ma'am" is a sign of respect and when it indicates sarcasm. We use social context to figure out whether the person who says to us "Can you take out the trash?" means 'You must do so right now' or whether she means 'You don't have to, but I'd appreciate it if you did.' (For a more in-depth discussion of the way social context affects language use, refer to Files 10.1 and 11.1.)

Together, these three aspects of context—along with several others—provide critical information about what utterances mean.

7.1.5 Felicity: Appropriateness Relative to a Context

In addition to using context to figure out meaning, speakers also use context to figure out whether an utterance is appropriate in any given setting. Recall that when discussing syntax and other elements of grammar, we may refer to sentences as grammatical or ungrammatical. For example, in the sentences below, (3) is grammatical while (4) is ungrammatical.

(3)   There is a platypus in the bathtub.
(4)   *There is platypus a in bathtub the.

In the same way, when we discuss pragmatics, we refer to utterances as being **felicitous** or **infelicitous.** An utterance that is felicitous is one that is situationally appropriate, one that is appropriate relative to the context in which it is uttered. An utterance that is infelicitous is inappropriate in some way. For example, speaker B's answer in (5) is felicitous, but her responses in (6) and (7) are infelicitous. (Notice that a pound sign # is used to indicate infelicity, just as an asterisk is used to indicate ungrammaticality.)

(5) A: What do you do for a living?
     B: I'm a linguistics professor at Ohio State.

(6) A: What do you do for a living?
     B: #I have a job.

(7) A: What do you do for a living?
     B: #My favorite color is purple, too!

Look more carefully at (6) and (7). What seems to be wrong with these two conversations? In (6), the person answering the question isn't providing enough detail. In (7), she doesn't seem to give an answer that is at all related to the question. There are many different reasons why it might be infelicitous to utter a particular sentence in a particular context; the examples above show only two of these reasons.

It is also important to recognize that an utterance may be called felicitous or infelicitous only relative to a particular context. It is very easy to think of contexts in which the infelicitous sentences in (6) and (7) could be uttered quite acceptably. They aren't felicitous, however, in the context given.[1] In other words, felicity is a property of utterances, not a property of sentences.

In general, the speakers of a language know intuitively whether an utterance is felicitous or infelicitous, just as they know intuitively whether a sentence is grammatical or ungrammatical. Also, as with grammaticality, judgments of felicity may differ from one speaker to another. Nonetheless, there are general guidelines that utterances must follow in order to be deemed felicitous.

The rest of Chapter 7 will be concerned with how to determine whether utterances are felicitous and with how context helps us to figure out the meaning of felicitous utterances.

---

[1]In fact, one could imagine a context in which the entire exchange in (6) was felicitous relative to the rest of a discourse. Suppose, for example, that a thief is discussing his thievery with a business executive. The executive might remark that he thinks thievery is unethical. The thief could then respond that, in spite of the ethical side of things, "Stealing is an excellent way to make sure there's always enough money to go around. What do you do for a living?" At this, the executive could respond indignantly—and perfectly felicitously—"I have a job." However, supposing that a person were asked this question out of the blue, for example, by a seatmate on an airplane, then the answer would be under-informative. The point is that the more you know about the context of an utterance, the better able you are to determine whether it is felicitous.

FILE **7.2**

....

Rules of Conversation

7.2.1   Rules for Conversation

Most social enterprises are governed by rules. A family may have a rule that determines who will set the table on any given night; traffic rules govern who may go first at a four-way stop; board games and sports have rules that outline which plays may be made at any point during the game. The use of language, like other forms of social behavior, is also governed by social rules. Some of these rules are designed to protect people's feelings by showing respect or politeness (e.g., rules governing whether you can use a first name in addressing someone or must use a title and last name). Even more essential are rules designed to protect the integrity of our communication: rules that allow our communication to work.

It is reasonably clear that if people were to decide to tell lies in some random way, so that listeners would have no way of determining when speakers were lying and when they were telling the truth, language would cease to be of much value to us. But there is more to it than that. There are various assumptions—e.g., about the honesty of our conversational partners and their intention to communicate information that is relevant to the speech context—that people bring to conversations. When agreed upon and followed by both speaker and hearer, these assumptions, which emerge naturally within societies, enable effective communication.

In an attempt to capture these facts, the philosopher H. P. Grice (1913–88) formulated the **Cooperative Principle,** which states that the basic assumption underlying conversation is the understanding that what one says is intended to contribute to the purposes of the conversation—that is, that people intend to be cooperative conversational partners. Obviously, what it means to be cooperative will differ depending on the particular context. In a business meeting, one is normally expected to keep one's remarks confined to the topic at hand unless it is changed in some approved way. But some close friends having a few beers at a bar would not be governed by the same sorts of strict expectations of appropriate conversational contributions. Nevertheless, even in a casual context, the conversation will normally have one or more purposes, and each of the participants can be expected by the rest to behave in ways that further these purposes. Thus, even the most casual conversation is unlikely to consist of such random sentences as the following:

(1)   Kim: How are you today?
      Sandy: Oh, Harrisburg is the capital of Pennsylvania.
      Kim: Really? I thought the weather would be warmer.
      Sandy: Well, in my opinion, the soup could use a little more salt.

Grice argued that what prevents such meaningless discourse are what can be described as conversational **maxims,** which are principles guiding the conversational interactions of both speakers and hearers. Following these maxims is an important aspect of ensuring that our utterances are felicitous. In general, felicitous utterances are ones that conform to Grice's maxims.

7.2.2   Introducing Grice's Maxims

Grice divided his maxims into four categories, each of which focuses on a different aspect of the way that utterances are used in cooperative discourse. These categories are quality, relevance, quantity, and manner. Each category contains between one and four maxims. Note that while these are written as "rules" for the speaker to follow, they are broader than that: the speaker follows these in being cooperative, but it is just as important for discourse that the hearer assumes that the speaker is following them. A conversational partner who constantly assumes that the speaker is lying is just as uncooperative as a speaker who always lies.

a. The maxims of quality address our expectations of honesty in conversation. Obviously, effective communication is greatly hindered either if the speaker randomly mixes lies with the truth or if the hearer assumes that anything the speaker says is likely to be a lie. However, it addresses more than just haphazard lying. There are two maxims of quality.

- Do not say what you believe to be false.
- Do not say that for which you lack adequate evidence.

The first maxim of quality is self-evident, as noted above. The second maxim is more interesting, because it is only when we believe we have adequate evidence for some claim that we can have much confidence that we are not saying something false. That is, in order to follow the first maxim, we must also follow the second.

Nevertheless, people can differ strikingly in what they think is good evidence for their views. It is also the case that in different contexts, there are different requirements for how much or what kind of evidence will qualify as "adequate." For example, consider a claim like the one made in (2).

(2)   The venom of the purple-toothed spider isn't strong enough to kill people.

If a biologist specializing in human reactions to venomous bites uttered this at a scientific conference, she would need to have met a certain standard of evidence before she could felicitously incorporate this utterance into her talk. She would need some knowledge of the kinds of chemicals in the venom and human reactions to them; she would also presumably have to know about the history of people who had suffered purple-toothed spider bites and how they had fared. On the other hand, consider a person—not a biologist—who had been bitten by a purple-toothed spider: as a result, he got a painful swelling at the location of the bite but was otherwise unaffected. In chatting with his friends, he might legitimately be able to utter (2) without knowing anything more general about these spider bites; his evidence would be only his personal experience. Thus these two individuals speaking in different contexts have two distinct standards for quality of evidence. Of course, the second individual might be wrong: it might be the case that he was merely very lucky and didn't get very much venom in his body, but a worse bite (or perhaps a bite to a smaller or less healthy person) could cause death. Nonetheless, he has followed Grice's maxims by saying what he does not **believe** to be false and something for which he has adequate evidence based on the situation. If someone asked him, "Are you sure?" he might then consider explaining his evidence or weakening his claim: something like (3).

(3)   Well, when I was bitten by a purple-toothed spider, I didn't die. So at least I know that the venom doesn't always kill people.

Meanwhile, the biologist could likely answer, "Yes; I'm sure," without further qualifications (though at a talk she would be expected to be able to produce evidence for her claim). Even though their levels of certainty differ, both of them would have equal claim to utter (2) given the appropriate context and their stated experience.

b. The maxim of relevance (also called the maxim of relation) is often perceived as being the most obvious. It is also the most simply stated.

- Be relevant.

This maxim has a central role in maintaining the organization of conversation by preventing random topic shifts like those found in (1). To avoid such discourse, we are expected to make contributions that pertain to the subject of the conversation. If someone asks you about your plans for dinner, you should give an answer about that topic rather than telling a story about your trip to the zoo.

From the hearer's perspective, the maxim of relevance helps us to figure out what others mean by their utterances. Our default assumption is that the people we are talking with are cooperative and that they are doing their best to make the conversation work. This assumption allows us to make **inferences.** Consider the following conversation:

(4) Alana: Is Jamie dating anyone these days?
    Sam: Well, she goes to Cleveland every weekend.

If she did not have these assumptions as a part of her linguistic competence, Alana could take Sam's response to be completely unhelpful. However, Alana will assume that Sam intends his contribution to be relevant, so she will likely draw the inference that Jamie is dating someone, in particular, someone who lives in Cleveland. (For a more detailed explanation of inference and implicature, refer to the discussion in File 7.3.)

As with the first maxim of quality, the maxim of relevance seems perfectly obvious, but that doesn't mean that people can't ever change topics. Imagine that two roommates have just arrived back in their dorm on a Friday afternoon; the following is an excerpt from their conversation:

(5) Rachel: We should think of something fun to do this weekend!
    Sarah: Can we talk about something that happened to me in class instead? I want your advice about something.

In (5), Sarah uses the word *instead* to show Rachel that she knows she is supposed to stay on topic and be relevant by discussing weekend plans, but she has something else on her mind, and she asks for permission to go against that maxim. Of course, people don't always point out when they are about to say something irrelevant. We have all had conversations in which we are trying to discuss some particular topic, only to have our conversational partner jump in with an unrelated fact or story. We may or may not be bothered—sometimes we do allow others to go off on tangents—but we are justified in objecting. Someone saying "Wait a minute! You're changing the subject!" acknowledges this jointly held assumption that utterances should be relevant.

c. The maxims of quantity concern how much information it is appropriate for a speaker to give in a discourse. Of course, there are some situations in which more information is needed and others in which less is needed. Notice how the two maxims of quantity are phrased in order to make allowances for these differences.

- Make your contribution as informative as is required.
- Do not make your contribution more informative than is required.

The first of these maxims reflects the fact that we are expected to give all of the information necessary for a given circumstance and to make as strong a claim as is warranted (see the second maxim of quality). The second reflects the expectation that we neither provide too much information nor make a stronger claim than is warranted. Some examples will help to illustrate.

Suppose that you are asked what you are going to do over the weekend. If your German professor asks you in a language conversation drill, it will likely be acceptable to mention only one or two things that you intend to do (and it would be both infelicitous and rude to subject your class to a complete schedule of everything you plan to do). However, if a classmate is trying to schedule a meeting with you, she likely needs to know specific times that you will be available. In this case, if you were to respond with the same short answer, it would be under-informative and therefore infelicitous.

Consider a second example. In this case, the degree of informativeness relates to specificity, or the "strength of the claim." Suppose that someone asks you where you grew up. One could imagine that any of the possible responses given in (6) could be true answers to the question (and thereby follow Grice's maxims of quality and relevance), but it is obvious that some of these answers would be appropriate in certain contexts and not in others. Each response could be too informative, not informative enough, or just right, depending on the circumstances. Try to think of an example of each kind of context.

(6)   a. On the corner of Main Street and Minor Road
      b. In Dayton
      c. In Dayton, Ohio
      d. In Dayton, Ohio, on the corner of Main Street and Minor Road
      e. In Ohio
      f. In the Midwest
      g. In the United States

For more information about making claims with the appropriate strength and how the maxim of quantity is used to calculate certain implicatures, refer to File 7.3.

d. The maxims of manner differ critically from the other three sets of maxims. The maxims of quality, relevance, and quantity all have to do with the information that a speaker is expected to give or not give in a discourse. The maxims of manner, on the other hand, have nothing to do with the information itself; rather, these maxims have to do with expectations about how one goes about giving and interpreting that information in being a cooperative conversational partner.

- Avoid obscurity of expression. (That is, don't use words or phrases that are hard to understand.)
- Avoid ambiguity.
- Be brief.
- Be orderly.

The first maxim, "Avoid obscurity of expression," indicates that speakers should avoid the use of **jargon** (terms restricted primarily to specialized areas of knowledge) or other terms that their listeners cannot reasonably be expected to know and that they should also avoid needlessly complex sentence structures.

The second maxim references the understanding that what we are saying should be clear within the particular context. Speakers should avoid saying things that have more than one meaning (e.g., *He promised to phone at noon*: what happened at noon—the promise or the phone call?) unless their listeners can be expected to know which meaning was intended. While there are many words and phrases that would be ambiguous out of context, the listener is expected to interpret the meaning based on the context. If Polly tells her friend that she's going to the bank to deposit a check and the friend claims to be confused as to whether a financial institution or a river bank is being referred to, it is the friend (the hearer), rather than Polly, who is not following this maxim.

The third maxim, "Be brief," tells us not to expound at length on a topic when a few words will do. The expectation to be brief is different from the expectation to not give too much information. Notice that the speakers in both (7B) and (8B) give exactly the same amount of information, but they do so in different words. Thus, the speaker in (8B) violates a maxim of manner because he is being wordy, but he does not violate a maxim of quantity.

(7) A: What do you do for a living?
    B: I'm a linguistics instructor.

(8) A: What do you do for a living?
    B: #What I do is that I'm an instructor and the subject matter that I teach is linguistics.

The fourth maxim, "Be orderly," comes down to the expectation that what we say should be organized in some intelligent way. So if you have information to convey about several different topics, you should convey all of the information on one topic first, followed by the next, rather than giving one sentence about each in alternation. Often speakers follow this maxim by giving general overview information first and then moving on to specifics. Telling a story in chronological order also is part of following this maxim. For example, consider the strangeness of (9) and (10). The first merely sounds peculiar, while the second is actually hard to follow.

(9) #Leslie read fifty pages and opened her book.

(10) #My mother didn't really want my room to be painted purple. I was worried that I wouldn't get good grades at the new school. When I was a child, my favorite color was purple. I worked very hard in all of my classes to get good grades. My mother told me that if I got good grades, I could paint my room. When I was ten years old, I switched to a new school. I wanted to paint my bedroom a bright color.

Neither (9) nor (10) could be considered felicitous in almost any context: they are so unorderly as to be almost nonsensical.

Thus, we find that although the four maxims of manner do not provide any insight into what information a speaker should share, they are critical with regard to how that information can be clearly understood.

7.2.3 Flouting Maxims

So far, for the most part, we have considered cases in which speakers follow Grice's maxims. Of course, people sometimes violate the maxims: at some point everyone has told a lie, changed the subject, given too much information, or said something confusing. Sometimes people violate the maxims on purpose (e.g., lying in order to intentionally deceive someone), and other times by accident. Strictly speaking, these violations are infelicitous.

But the maxims can also be exploited or flouted in order to communicate indirectly. A speaker **flouts** a maxim when he says something that in its most literal meaning appears to violate a maxim, but the listener is expected to understand the meaning being conveyed due to the shared understanding of the maxims. There are several reasons that one might choose to use the maxims in this way. We sometimes need to avoid saying something directly because doing so could hurt us or someone else. Grice gave an example of a professor who was asked to write a letter of recommendation for a recent PhD graduate who was applying for a teaching position. Suppose that the letter went like this:

(11)

>   Dear Colleague:
>
>   Mr. John J. Jones has asked me to write a letter on his behalf. Let me say that Mr. Jones is unfailingly polite, is neatly dressed at all times, and is always on time for his classes.
>
>   Sincerely yours,
>
>   Harry H. Homer

Do you think Mr. Jones would get the job? Probably not! In this case, the maxim of quantity is being flouted. Professor Homer wanted to convey his negative impression of the candidate without actually saying anything negative about him. The fact that he gives much less information than would normally be expected for this type of letter communicates this message clearly. The recipient of this letter will assume that Professor Homer is intending to be cooperative; the shortness of the letter indicates that he has said all of the relevant positive things he could think of—which is the essence of "damning with faint praise."

The other maxims can also be flouted. For example, if you and a classmate are discussing your professor, and you see your professor rapidly approaching, you may suddenly change the subject by looking pointedly at your classmate and saying, "Oh, really? I didn't know that chocolate originated in Mexico!" In this case, you probably don't want to change the subject to the history of chocolate; rather, you are hoping to prevent your classmate from saying anything untoward! You expect that she will notice your abrupt change in subject and deduce that something is up. You have successfully flouted the maxim of relevance.

It is also possible to flout the maxim of quality. If someone says to you something that you don't believe, you may respond, "Right, and I'm the Queen of England." You don't mean that you are a monarch of the United Kingdom; rather, you mean something like 'What you just said is as obviously false as the idea that I'm the Queen of England.' A sarcastic comment such as this may sound harsh, but it may be perceived (in some contexts) as less hurtful than coming right out and saying, "You're wrong." Flouting the maxim of quality can also allow us to insult people and (usually) get away with it. If your friend is bragging about something mundane, you might say, "That's the most **amazing** thing I've ever heard—please tell me more!" In this case your friend will probably take it as an insult, but not one that he can legitimately take exception to (and utterances like this are often intended to gently poke fun in a friendly way rather than truly be insulting). This conversational inference arises out of the recognition that the insulter is flouting the first maxim of quality—the recognition that the claim is too strong (see the maxims of quantity) for it to likely be true.

The flouting of maxims often plays a particularly large role in humor, but it is an important part of everyday communication; it allows us to draw conclusions and can facilitate efficient communication, as we will discuss further in File 7.3. It is important to remember that when speakers and hearers flout maxims, their intention is to be cooperative conversational partners. But this cooperation requires a higher degree of effort on the part of both speaker and hearer, so it carries the risk of the intended message not getting through. Certainly each of you can think of a situation in which you meant an utterance to be sarcastic or a joke, or meant to imply something, and the person you were speaking to didn't "get it" for whatever reason; this can particularly be a risk when conversing with someone you don't know well, or a child, or someone from a different area or culture who does not share your specific expectations about communication.

7.2.4 Grice's Maxims in a Wider Context

The needs of social harmony, politeness, and linguistic integrity are not always consistent with each other. We have already seen several cases in which politeness keeps us from following pragmatic rules. Recall that we said at the outset that the rules for conversation are **social** rules (i.e., they are not a part of a language's grammar, though they are part of speakers' communicative competence). As such, they are in competition with social rules that come from other aspects of a society, and sometimes, for one reason or another, they lose.

It is said that there are societies in which the failure to answer a stranger's question is considered very impolite and therefore people in this society will give a stranger a wrong or intentionally imprecise answer to a question rather than give no answer. From this we learn that Grice's maxims, being conventions, are very different from natural laws. While their essence may be universal across languages and cultures, the way that they are implemented and the way that they interact with other societal rules will obviously vary between societies.

FILE 7.3

Drawing Conclusions

7.3.1 Drawing Conclusions: Entailment

A crucial part of understanding utterances is being able to draw conclusions from those utterances about the way the world is. However, the conclusions we draw can be based on different kinds of evidence or reasoning. The sorts of reasoning that we use depend largely on the context of the utterance that we are interpreting.

One kind of reasoning commonly used to draw conclusions is based on the concept of **entailment**, which was introduced in File 6.3. For any two sentences X and Y, sentence X entails sentence Y if whenever X is true, Y must be true as well.[1] In the example in (1), the X sentence entails the Y sentence.

(1)   X: Ian eats a large breakfast every day.
      Y: Ian eats a large breakfast on Mondays.

Entailment indicates a commitment from the speaker's point of view. Entailment also does something for the hearer: from the hearer's point of view, entailment allows a conclusion to be drawn very confidently. If you hear and believe X, and X entails Y, then concluding Y is completely safe.

Entailment is a relationship based on literal meaning. Thus, entailments are conclusions that can be drawn irrespective of an utterance's context. But often, if you take only what is literally asserted and entailed by an utterance, that part of the meaning alone is not enough to account for hearers' understanding of the utterance. Speakers routinely intend to convey information in addition to what is entailed by the sentences they utter. Fortunately, hearers also routinely draw conclusions from the utterances they hear, even when the sentence uttered does not entail the conclusion drawn. That is, an utterance's context often helps us to draw conclusions—inferences—that were not entailed by the sentence that was spoken.

7.3.2 Drawing Conclusions: Inference, Implication, and Implicature

In File 7.2, we pointed out that people commonly draw inferences from what others say based on the assumption that speakers are adhering to the Cooperative Principle. It's time now to focus our attention on what is actually happening when a person draws such an inference.

First, consider a situation in which an inference is drawn that does not involve linguistic communication. A meeting between a supervisor and an employee is running longer than the allotted time. The employee doesn't want to say, "Our meeting is running longer than we'd scheduled," because the supervisor might find it rude. Instead, the employee

---

[1]For simplicity's sake, here we discuss entailment as a relationship between sentences. However, it is really a relationship between what sentences assert, i.e., propositions, as explained in File 6.3.

glances at his watch. The employee is **implying** that the meeting is running long: sending the message without saying it directly. The supervisor, if he understands the message, infers that the employee wishes the meeting to end. An **inference** is a conclusion that a person is reasonably entitled to draw based on a set of circumstances.[2]

A person may draw an inference in cases when no one has tried to imply anything at all. If you walk outside and notice that the pavement is wet, you might infer that it had been raining, but you wouldn't want to say that the pavement had implied anything. (There must be someone trying to communicate an idea in order to say that any implying has happened.) In the rest of this file, however, we will be considering only inferences drawn when there is a person trying to send a message, and more specifically, we will consider only cases in which—unlike those above—the message is sent using language. When a speaker implies something using language, we say that her utterance contains an **implicature.** Implicatures are conclusions that are drawn about what people mean based on what we know about how conversation works. There are many different kinds of implicature, and we will consider only a few of them here, namely, those that arise via one of Grice's maxims for cooperative conversation. You should be familiar with Grice's maxims (introduced in File 7.2) before continuing.

7.3.3 Implicature Based on the Maxim of Relevance

If given a suitable context, any maxim can be responsible for helping to generate an implicature. Consider the following sample of discourse between two strangers at a bus stop:

(2) Speaker 1: I'd really like a cup of coffee.
     Speaker 2: There's a place around the corner called Joe's.

Here's a reasonable conclusion Y that we can draw from Speaker 2's utterance of X:

(3) X: There's a place around the corner called Joe's.
     Y: Joe's sells coffee.

It is important to recognize that in (3), X does not entail Y: it is obviously possible for there to be a place around the corner called Joe's that doesn't sell coffee. Thus, the conclusion of Y is an inference: it is based on an implicature rather than an entailment.

How does the implicature arise? Speaker 1 is talking about coffee and looking for information about coffee. If Joe's were a bookstore that didn't serve coffee, then Speaker 2 would be changing the subject, which people usually don't do in the middle of a conversation. Speaker 1 is much more likely to assume that Speaker 2 is following Grice's maxim of relevance: if he wants to interpret Speaker 2's contribution as relevant, he has to "read something into it" that Speaker 2's utterance didn't entail, namely, that Joe's sells coffee. In order to justify conclusion Y, we had to think about pragmatic concepts: people and conversation in context. We say that X **implicates** Y in this situation.

Recall this example from File 7.2:

(4) Alana: Is Jamie dating anyone these days?
     Sam: Well, she goes to Cleveland every weekend.

---

[2]Increasingly, the words *imply* and *infer* are used interchangeably in casual conversation. For the purposes of engaging in linguistic analysis, however, it is important to distinguish between these two actions. Implying is what is done by the person sending the message; inferring is what is done by the person receiving the message.

The implicature from Sam's utterance (again based on the assumption that his contribution is relevant) is that Jamie is dating someone in Cleveland. Sam might instead have said *I believe she may be dating someone because she goes to Cleveland every weekend, and that's not her hometown, and she doesn't have a job there.* Given our set of maxims, though, Sam can say what he does and rely on the listener to figure out what he means without explicitly stating these other steps.

It is important to note that if Sam knew that Jamie went to Cleveland on the weekends to visit her grandmother, then his response would have been either very misleading (if he understood that his utterance had generated an implicature) or at least infelicitous (if he merely thought he was saying something unrelated to the topic at hand).

7.3.4 Implicature Based on the Maxim of Quantity

The conversation in (5) illustrates an implicature that might arise on the assumption that the speaker is obeying the first maxim of quantity: a speaker should give as much information as required.

(5) Mother: Have you done your homework for all of your classes yet?
     Son: I've finished my history homework.

Let us again consider the actual content of what is uttered compared with the conclusion that is likely to be drawn, shown in (6X) and (6Y), respectively.

(6) X: I've finished my history homework.
     Y: I have not finished my homework for my other classes.

Clearly, in this case X does not entail Y. It is very possible for a child to say truthfully that he has finished his history homework and to have also finished the work for his other classes. Rather, the mother is likely to infer Y because her question wasn't looking for information merely about the history homework but rather for information about work for all of her son's classes. She will assume that her son is giving as much of the information as possible that is required to give a complete answer to her question.

Numbers are a particularly common source for the generation of quantity implicatures. Consider the following discourse. What seems to be wrong with it?

(7) Gail: How far can you run without stopping?
     Kim: Ten miles.
     Gail: I guess you can't run a whole marathon without stopping, then.
     Kim: Nonsense, I've done it a number of times.

Notice that what Kim says first must be true if what she says next is true. Certainly, if Kim can run over twenty-six miles without stopping, then she can run ten miles without stopping. However, Gail quite naturally assumed that Kim was obeying the first maxim of quantity with her answer of "ten miles"; Gail therefore inferred that Kim meant 'exactly ten miles, and no more.' If you pay attention, you are likely to be surprised by how often numbers such as 47 are used to implicate 'exactly 47' when the entailed meaning is 'at least 47.' These implicatures are so strong in English that people often view statements like Kim's as lies, even though what Kim says is technically true (following the maxim of quality). The deceptiveness of this statement comes from her clear violation of the maxim of quantity.

7.3.5   Implicature Based on the Maxim of Manner

Recall that one of Grice's maxims of manner tells speakers to be orderly. Keeping this in mind, consider the two stories told in (8) and (9).

(8)   Rebecca took the medication and had an allergic reaction.

(9)   Rebecca had an allergic reaction and took the medication.

Both of these sentences provide exactly the same entailed meaning. However, someone who assumes that the speaker is being cooperative will assume that the speaker is telling the story in an orderly fashion. Thus, someone who hears (8) may infer that Rebecca had an allergic reaction to the medication, whereas someone who hears (9) is more likely to infer that Rebecca took the medication in order to counter her allergic reaction to something else.

Another one of the maxims of manner dictates that speakers be brief. Consider the following utterance:

(10) The man who lives with me is an electrician.

Upon hearing this sentence uttered by a person whom you don't know particularly well, you might infer that the speaker is talking about a house mate (or an apartment mate, or something similar). Of course, as far as entailment is concerned, the speaker could be talking about a husband, son, or brother—all of which might explain their living together—but because "my husband" is shorter than "the man who lives with me," it is likely that the speaker would have used the shorter phrase, were it true.[3] Thus, by using the lengthier expression, the speaker implicates that she does not have one of these other more specific kinds of relationships to the electrician.

7.3.6   Implicature Based on the Maxim of Quality

The second maxim of quality tells us that we can felicitously say only that for which we have adequate evidence. In File 7.2, we pointed out that people often differ in what they think is sufficient evidence for their views. Sometimes, we may draw inferences based on the assumption that we have the same standards for evidence as do our conversational partners. Consider the following conversation:

(11) Sandy: We need someone to make some sort of cake for the picnic.
     Tom: I can make my family's favorite chocolate cake.

Sandy might draw the inference that Tom has made his family's favorite chocolate cake before, because the best evidence that Tom can make this cake would be that he had indeed made it, as spelled out in (12).

(12) X: I can make my family's favorite chocolate cake.
     Y: I have succeeded in making this cake before.

---

[3] Of course, the inference that the speaker is not related to the electrician could also be taken to arise from an implicature based on the maxim of quantity. Can you see why? It is important to recognize that the maxims work together with one another: thus we may infer the content of an implicature for more than one reason!

However, this inference is not entailed by Tom's statement; it is only implicated. Tom could legitimately say that he could make the chocolate cake based on the fact that he had a recipe and had watched it being made many times and thought he knew all he needed to know to make it. Suppose Tom were to make the cake and it turned out very badly. Something like the following conversation might take place:

(13) Sandy: I thought you said you could make this cake!
     Tom: Well, I thought I could.

As Sandy's challenge—which sounds quite felicitous—illustrates, she is justified in being upset that Tom did not have a high enough standard of evidence for saying that he could make the cake. Thus, the inference that she drew was well-founded. Was Tom justified in saying that he could make the cake in the first place? This question is one whose answer will be open to differences of opinion. The point, though, is that we ought to be aware that people may often infer a stronger claim than what has been entailed, based on their assumption about the sort of evidence that might be required in order to felicitously express some proposition.

7.3.7   The Significance of Implicatures to Communication

The system of implicature that has been described in this file is a kind of side effect of Grice's maxims, maxims whose primary purpose is to describe the principles that guide the conversational interactions of both speakers and hearers.

Implicatures are still very useful, however. They allow us to introduce ideas into a discourse with less commitment than we would have to express were we entailing the same propositions. In (4), why would Sam choose to give the answer that he gave instead of saying, "Yes; she's dating someone in Cleveland," or something similar? Whatever his reason, it is clear that he wants Alana to draw her own conclusions. Maybe he isn't certain about Jamie's dating practices and doesn't want to commit for that reason. Perhaps he wishes to be discreet and merely hint at Jamie's dating practices (so that she cannot later accuse him of revealing secrets about her). Implicature gives him a way to communicate the idea he has in mind while still protecting himself from committing to the truth of a proposition that he does not want to commit to.

On the other hand, implicature can serve a function much more fundamental to our conversations than merely protecting noncommittal speakers. One major reason for exploiting the maxims in this way is to make conversation easier. If we were forced to speak only in logically impeccable ways, making sure that what we said entailed every fact that we wanted our hearers to conclude, conversation would proceed at a very slow pace. That is assuming (counterfactually) that most of us have the logical capacity to do this. Communication would become very cumbersome if we could not rely on implicature. We use context and our knowledge about the universe to draw inferences from what we hear because it allows us to use language more effectively.

FILE **7.4**

Speech Acts

7.4.1 An Introduction to Speech Acts

Just as people perform physical acts, such as hitting a baseball, and mental acts, such as imagining hitting a baseball, people also perform another kind of act simply by using language; these are called **speech acts.**

We use language to do an extraordinarily wide range of activities. We use it to convey information, request information, give orders, make requests, make threats, give warnings, make bets, give advice, offer apologies, tell jokes, pay compliments, etc., as the following sentences suggest:

(1) John Jones was at the office yesterday until 6 P.M.
(2) Who ate all the cookies?
(3) Sit down and be quiet.
(4) Please let me know if you'll be attending.
(5) If you do that again, I'll report you.
(6) Watch out—there's a huge pothole there.
(7) Five bucks says that the Buckeyes will beat the Wolverines this year.
(8) You ought to go to class at least once a week.

There can be little doubt that it is our ability to do things with language—to perform speech acts—that makes language useful to us. In fact, with language we can do things that would otherwise be impossible. Consider (7), a bet on the outcome of a football game. If we did not have language, how would this bet be made? We could imagine the speaker taking a five dollar bill and some pictures of football teams and pantomiming some action, but would this action have the force of an actual spoken bet? Probably not. How would the hearer know the specific details intended? In (6), we could warn someone of a pothole by pointing at it, but only if we were in a position to see it. How could we give the advice in (8) without words? It would certainly be difficult.

The following list contains some of the most common speech acts, which we will discuss in this file. Of course, language can be used for all sorts of purposes other than those listed, as well.

(9) Some common speech acts and their functions

Speech Act	Function
assertion	conveys information
question	elicits information
request	(more or less politely) elicits action or information
order	demands action
promise	commits the speaker to an action
threat	commits the speaker to an action that the hearer does not want

7.4.2 Felicity Conditions

In order to be felicitous, each of the kinds of speech acts listed in (9) must be uttered in a certain kind of context. As a rather silly example, consider how infelicitous it would be to request your garbage can to empty itself (assuming a typical garbage can in the early twenty-first century). For a request to be felicitous, it must be directed to a person (or animal or machine) that is capable of doing whatever action was requested. In fact, for any speech act, there is a set of conditions that must hold in order for that speech act to be felicitous. Fittingly, these conditions are called **felicity conditions.** Here are some examples of felicity conditions for two very common speech acts: requests and questions.

(10) Felicity conditions for requests
In order for a speaker to felicitously request a hearer to complete some action, it should be the case that . . .
   a. The speaker believes that the action has not yet been done.
   b. The speaker wants the action to be done (or thinks that the action should be done for some reason).
   c. The speaker believes that the hearer is able to do the action.
   d. The speaker believes that the hearer may be willing to do things of that sort for the speaker.

(11) Felicity conditions for questions
In order for a speaker to felicitously question a hearer about some state of affairs, it should be the case that . . .
   a. The speaker does not know some piece of information about some state of affairs.
   b. The speaker wants to know that information about the state of affairs.
   c. The speaker believes that the hearer may be able to supply the information about the state of affairs that the speaker wants.

Look carefully at the case of requests in (10). The purpose of a request is to get a task accomplished. In light of that goal, these felicity conditions make sense. If any of these conditions were not met, then the goal could not be reached.

To understand when it is appropriate to make a request or to ask a question, then, we need to think about the felicity conditions associated with each of these speech acts. Clearly, the same holds true for other speech acts as well. In order for giving thanks to be felicitous, the thanker must (among other things) appreciate what the thankee has done; in order for an apology to be felicitous, the apologizer must (among other things) want the apologizee to believe that he is contrite; and so on.

When we introduced Grice's maxims in File 7.2, we said that utterances generally had to follow the maxims in order to be felicitous, but that there were exceptions (e.g., flouting). The same is true of felicity conditions: some of the felicity conditions for a speech act may be suspended in certain contexts. For example, in normal conversation we do not ask people questions that we already know the answers to, but there are exceptions: people playing trivia games, lawyers questioning witnesses, teachers giving exams. We recognize these situations to be socially exceptional in one way or another. Playing trivia violates (11b), because in trivia games people don't seriously want the information they seem to ask about; interrogating witnesses violates (11a), because a good lawyer tries to avoid surprises; and asking exam questions violates both (11a) and (11b), because the teacher does know the answers. Exam questions also possibly violate condition (11c) since the point of asking an exam question is to determine whether students can provide an answer. The fact is that we ask questions for a number of different purposes in different social contexts, and to reflect these differences, we can modify the particular felicity conditions. For trivia players we could eliminate felicity condition (11b); for lawyers we could eliminate condition (11a); for teachers we could eliminate all three. However, we have to be careful: for example, we wouldn't want to say that in the case of a teacher asking a question there were no felicity conditions at all; rather, there would be a modified set of felicity conditions including perhaps such items as 'The speaker wants to know whether the hearer is able to supply an answer.'

It will be useful, as we go through the discussion of speech acts in this chapter, to think about them in terms of their felicity conditions. For each type of speech act, think about what the speaker must believe and desire in order for it to be felicitous to use that type of speech act.

7.4.3   Performative Verbs and Performative Speech Acts

Any time that you open your mouth and utter a sentence, you perform a speech act. A special kind of speech act, known as a **performative speech act,** is one in which the particular action named by the verb is accomplished in the performance of the speech act itself. For example, someone can say "I am throwing a ball" without a ball actually being thrown (the throwing action is separate from an assertion about such an action), but someone cannot normally say "I promise to take you to the store later" without actually making such a promise. **Performative verbs** therefore denote purely linguistic actions. Compare (12)–(19) with (1)–(8).

(12) I assert that John Jones was at the office yesterday until 6 P.M.
(13) I ask again: Who ate all the cookies?
(14) I order you to sit down and be quiet.
(15) I request that you please let me know if you'll be attending.
(16) Yes, I'm threatening you: if you do that again, I'll report you.
(17) I'm warning you: there's a huge pothole you need to watch out for.
(18) I bet you five bucks that the Buckeyes will beat the Wolverines this year.
(19) I advise you to go to class at least once a week.

As these sentences illustrate, the speech acts performed by utterances of the sentences in (1)–(8) can also be performed by embedding these sentences as complements of verbs that state the speech act. In (14), for example, we have an order with the performative verb *order,* followed by a specific command.

Certain ceremonies or formal actions require the use of performative verbs, as in (20)–(22).

(20) I hereby pronounce you husband and wife.
(21) I christen this ship the *USS Language.*
(22) We declare the defendant not guilty.

These examples contain a very specialized group of performative verbs in that, by using one, a speaker not only performs a speech act but also changes something about the world: the marriage between two people, the name of a ship, and so on. (Note that when you perform other speech acts, such as giving an order, you do not effect some change on the world in the same way: the other person may or may not do what you have said, so ordering someone to sit down does not accomplish the sitting action. However, the world has been changed in that the person can no longer make a valid claim that he was not told to sit.) These specialized performative verbs often have additional felicity conditions associated with them having to do with the authority of the speaker. For example, if a dentist walked up to two patients in the waiting room and said, "I hereby pronounce you husband

and wife," it would be infelicitous, because the dentist does not have the authority necessary to perform this speech act. Furthermore, the two dental patients would not be married
as a result of the dentist's infelicitous pronouncement. When one of these specialized
speech acts using a performative verb is used infelicitously, then not only is it infelicitous,
but also there is no effect on the world (no marriage, christening, etc.). And like all speech
acts, performatives must fulfill various other felicity conditions in order to be fully felicitous
and effective, as seen with (23) and (24).

(23) I quit!
(24) I promise to drive you to work tomorrow if it rains.

If you yell (23) in a moment of frustration while alone in your office at work, or over
a beer with a friend that evening, you would not be expected to clean out your desk and
begin a new job search the next morning as you would be if you said it to your boss during
a staff meeting. And if your best friend says (24) to you but does not pick you up during the
downpour in the morning, you will consider that a broken promise, but the same will not
be true if your six-year-old brother says it to you. Felicity conditions can also help us in the
task of identifying particular types of speech acts, as we see further below.

7.4.4   Identifying Performative Speech Acts

Not all speech acts containing verbs that can be used performatively are performative
speech acts. Consider the following sentences:

(25) I promise I will help you with your project this week.
(26) John promises he will help you with your project this week.
(27) I will promise to help you with your project this week.

Although all of these sentences use the verb *promise,* only (25) uses it as a performative
verb. Sentence (26) is an assertion about someone else's promise, and (27) is an assertion
about a future promise the speaker will make, so neither of these is a performative speech
act. Why? There are two major requirements for performatives: (i) the subject of the sentence must be first person, *I* or *we,* since these speech acts concern the interaction between
speakers and hearers; and (ii) the verb must be in the present tense, since performative
speech acts, like all actions, take place in the present. Sentences (26) and (27) are therefore
not promises because the subject of the sentence is third-person *John,* and the verb is in the
future tense, respectively.

One test to see whether a verb is being used performatively is the *hereby* test. We take
the word *hereby* and insert it before the potentially performative verb:

(28)   I hereby promise I will help you with your project this week.
(29) #John hereby promises he will help you with your project this week.
(30) #I will hereby promise to help you with your project this week.

If the sentence sounds acceptable with *hereby,* then the verb is being used performatively. If the sentence sounds bad, then the verb is not being used performatively. (Sometimes this test is difficult to use because many such sentences sound awkward. This awk-
wardness may arise because people tend not to utter speech acts using performative verbs
or because *hereby* may sound somewhat archaic.) Note, however, the naturalness of using
hereby in (20) above.

7.4.5 Direct and Indirect Speech Acts

The types of speech acts that we have been considering, including both performative speech acts and the examples in (1)–(8), are called **direct speech acts,** because they perform their functions in a direct and literal manner. That is, the function that the sentence performs in a discourse is evident from its literal meaning. Perhaps the most interesting single fact about speech acts, though, is that we very commonly perform them indirectly, especially when we are trying to be polite (see File 11.4). So far, we have discussed direct speech acts that can be performed in two ways: (a) by making a direct, literal utterance, or (b) by using a performative verb that names the speech act. In addition to these direct speech acts, we can use the felicity conditions to make **indirect speech acts.** Consider the speech acts *question* and *request* once again.

(31) Questions
   A. Direct
      a.   Did John marry Helen?
      b.   I'm asking you whether John married Helen.

   B. Indirect
      a.   I don't know if John married Helen. (cf. (11a))
      b.   I would like to know if John married Helen. (cf. (11b))
      c.   Do you know whether John married Helen? (cf. (11c))

(32) Requests
   A. Direct
      a.   (Please) Take out the garbage.
      b.   I request that you take out the garbage.

   B. Indirect
      a.   The garbage hasn't been taken out yet. (cf. (10a))
      b.   I would like for you to take out the garbage. (cf. (10b))
      c.   Could you take out the garbage? (cf. (10c))
      d.   Would you mind taking out the garbage? (cf. (10d))

There is something up-front about the (31A) questions and the (32A) requests. Sentence (31A.a) taken literally is a request for information about John's marrying Helen. The same is true of (31A.b). Notice, however, that (31B.a) taken literally would not be a question at all. It would be an assertion about the speaker's knowledge, or lack thereof. Sentence (31B.b) would also be an assertion if taken literally. Sentence (31B.c), in contrast, is a question, but a question that literally asks whether the hearer knows something.

As the notes given in connection with sentences (31B) and (32B) suggest, indirect speech acts enjoy a very close connection with the felicity conditions on speech acts. That is, we can perform an indirect speech act in many cases by appealing to a particular one of its felicity conditions. At the same time they are often, although not always, indicative of politeness considerations on behalf of the speaker. So instead of assuming that felicity condition (10d) on requests holds, the speaker might ask if it does, as in *Would you mind taking me to work?* in order to make a polite request.

7.4.6 Identifying Indirect Speech Acts

In an indirect speech act, what the speaker actually means is different from what she or he **literally** says. There are several ways to determine whether an utterance is an indirect speech act. First check to see whether it is a performative speech act, since those are always direct. For example, (31A.b) and (32A.b) both contain performative verbs, and therefore both perform direct speech acts. If the speech act is not performative, it might be indirect.

We can also check to see whether any felicity conditions are violated for the sentence's literal meaning but not for its intended meaning. If any are, then the sentence must be an indirect speech act. For example, if taken literally, (32B.c) would be a question asking whether the hearer is able to take out the garbage. For this to be a felicitous question, felicity conditions (11a) through (11c) must be satisfied. But in many situations (e.g., assuming the hearer is not disabled), (11a) is violated because the speaker clearly knows the answer to this question. On the other hand, for the intended meaning of the speaker requesting the hearer to take out the garbage, felicity conditions (10a) through (10d) are all satisfied. Therefore, this sentence is not a direct speech act of questioning, but an indirect speech act of making a request.

Finally, we can imagine a context in which the utterance is used and consider the way people normally respond to it. Different speech acts arouse different responses. Listeners respond to an assertion by a signal of acknowledgment, such as a nod or a verbal response like *Oh, I see*. People respond to a question by a confirmation or denial or by supplying the information being solicited. People respond to a request or command by either carrying out the action accordingly or refusing with some explanation. If the standard response to an utterance is different from what its literal meaning would arouse, then it is used to perform an indirect speech act. For example, as noted above, the literal interpretation of (32B.c) would be a question. But compare it with something like *Could you lift 200 pounds?* You can respond with a simple *Yes, I could* or *No, I couldn't*, but it is not appropriate, felicitous, or polite to respond to (32B.c) with only this. Instead, people normally respond to such an utterance by actually carrying out the requested action—taking out the garbage, in this case. This shows that while *Could you lift 200 pounds?* is usually a direct speech act of questioning, (32B.c) is usually an indirect speech act of requesting: it has the same effect as (32A.a).

7.4.7 Sentences and Their Relation to Speech Acts

We now turn our attention to the relationship between speech acts and sentences. Remember that speech acts are identified by the speakers' goals. Thus there are many different ways to perform the same speech act, because there are many different sentences that will accomplish the same goal. Not only do we have the choice between speaking directly (with or without performatives) or indirectly, but we can also choose a particular sentence type.

Certain speech acts are so common that many languages have particular **syntactic structures** conventionally used to mark them. Some examples of different types of sentence structures for English are given in (33), along with a basic notation of the order of <u>subject</u> (S), **verb** (V), and *object* (O) as a shorthand for their major syntactic characteristics.

(33)   ***Sentence Type***   ***Examples***
        Declarative   <u>He</u> **is cooking** *the chicken.*
        Interrogative   **Is** <u>he</u> **cooking** *the chicken?*
                      <u>Who</u> **is cooking** *the chicken? What* **is** <u>he</u> **cooking**?
        Imperative   **Cook** *the chicken.*

On the surface, it looks as though declarative sentences, which in English usually follow the basic word order of SV(O), are perfect for making assertions. Interrogative sentences, which usually have a verb form and/or a *wh-* word like *who* or *what* at the beginning of the sentence, are designed for asking questions; and imperative sentences, which usually lack a subject (sometimes referred to as "understood *you*") are made for giving orders. This association is fairly typical and often holds. But don't confuse the **sentence types** (declarative, interrogative, and imperative) with **speech acts** (assertion, question, and request)! They are different, and this association does not always hold.

As with all things related to pragmatics, the key is context. Consider the sentences in table (34). All of these, in an out-of-the-blue context, might be interpreted as serving the function indicated in the table (depending on prosody or other factors). (Note also that in each column, the third declarative sentence is a direct performative speech act.)

(34) Ways to use different sentence forms to complete various speech acts

Type of Sentence	Type of Speech Act		
	Assertion	**Question**	**Order/Request**
Declarative	• Columbus is the capital of Ohio. • I'm telling you that Columbus is the capital of Ohio. • I hereby assert that the capital of Ohio is Columbus.	• I would like to know what the capital of Ohio is. • I've been wondering about which city is the capital of Ohio. • I ask you what the capital of Ohio is.	• It would make me very happy if you would take out the garbage. • I need you to take out the garbage. • I order you to take out the garbage.
Interrogative	• Did you know that Columbus is the capital of Ohio? • May I inform you that Columbus is the capital of Ohio?	• What is the capital of Ohio? • Can you tell me what the capital of Ohio is?	• Will you take out the garbage? • Would you mind terribly if I asked you to take out the garbage?
Imperative	• Remember that Columbus is the capital of Ohio. • Let me tell you that Columbus is the capital of Ohio.	• Tell me what the capital of Ohio is. • Let me ask you what the capital of Ohio is.	• Take out the garbage. • Don't forget to take out the garbage. • Allow me to request that you take out the garbage.

The sentences in table (34) show that any of the three sentence types can be used to perform any of these three speech acts. It is often the case that when declarative sentences are used to make assertions, or interrogative sentences are used to ask questions, or imperative sentences are used to give orders, the resulting sentences are direct speech acts, while other pairings between form and speech act yield indirect speech acts. This generalization does not always hold, however. Note that often within one square of the grid are both a direct and an indirect speech act of the same type that use the same sentence structure. For example, *Columbus is the capital of Ohio* is asserting something directly about Ohio, but *I'm telling you that Columbus is the capital of Ohio* is literally asserting something about what the speaker is saying and only indirectly asserting something about Ohio. Likewise, *Take out the garbage* is a direct request, whereas *Allow me to request that you take out the garbage* literally is a request that the speaker be permitted to make another request! It only indirectly asks the hearer to take out the garbage.

Regardless of how we perform our speech acts, though—directly or indirectly, and using whichever syntax and words that we choose—the take-home message is that there is much that we accomplish by using language.

FILE 7.5

....

Presupposition

7.5.1 Presuppositions of Existence

(1) The Amazon River runs through northern Europe.

Most readers probably have a fairly strong reaction to sentence (1). Some of you may have thought, "Oh, yeah, I knew that," but presumably most of you responded by thinking something like, "No it doesn't! The Amazon River is in South America!" Regardless of which reaction you had, however, none of you responded by thinking, "But there's no such thing as the Amazon River," or wondering whether there's a place called Europe. If you were having a conversation with someone who asserted (1), you would do very well to disagree with that person, but you would be disagreeing about the location of the Amazon River, not its existence. Compare your reaction to (1) with the sort of reaction you might have to (2).

(2) The Bvryzax River runs through northern Europe.

Could you respond to (2) by saying, "No it doesn't!" Indeed, you could not. Why? Because (at least at the time of this publication) there is no river anywhere in the known universe by the name of Bvryzax. In order to say of a river that it does not run through northern Europe, you must believe that the river exists. If you wanted—very rightly—to object to someone's uttering (2), you would have to say something more along the lines of "There's no such thing as the Bvryzax River." Similarly, if a child you know tells you that the monster under her bed has fangs, you would likely not want to say, "No, it doesn't." Responding in that way would merely corroborate the existence of the (perhaps fanged) monster. Rather, you would want to dispute the child's underlying assumption that a monster existed at all.

Both (1) and (2) would be infelicitous in almost any context that you can think of—other than perhaps a work of fiction—but they would be infelicitous for different reasons. An utterance of (1) would be infelicitous because of a violation of Grice's maxim of quality. An utterance of (2) would be infelicitous because it **presupposes** the existence of something that in fact does not exist. A **presupposition** is an underlying assumption that must be satisfied in order for an utterance to make sense or for it to be debatable. Presuppositions appear exceedingly often in the sentences that we hear uttered every day, and most of the time we don't notice their presence at all. However, when they are not satisfied, we are often left not knowing quite how to respond.

What does it mean for a presupposition to be **satisfied**? It means that the participants in the discourse must believe that the presupposed information is true (or at least that they behave as though they believe it) before the sentence containing the presupposition is uttered. Presuppositions can be satisfied either when the information that they contain is considered common knowledge—for example, that there is such a river as the Amazon—or when they contain information that has previously been asserted in the discourse. Either way, the speaker can reasonably assume that all of the participants are aware of it. If a sentence containing a presupposition is uttered in a context where the presupposition is not satisfied, most of the time that utterance is infelicitous.

For example, the claim "The monster under my bed has fangs" presupposes that there is a monster under the speaker's bed. If the presupposition is not satisfied (because not all of the speakers believe it is true), then there is something odd about the utterance: if no such monster exists, then it can neither have fangs nor not have fangs, and if the speakers don't believe the monster exists, they can't felicitously discuss whether it does or not. The new information being presented—the information about fangs—doesn't make sense until after the presupposition of the monster's existence has been dealt with.

One of the most common kinds of presupposition is the variety discussed so far: these are **existence presuppositions.** Whenever someone utters a sentence about a specific thing or person, then the speaker presupposes that that thing or person exists in order to be able to say something about it. (We may sometimes utter sentences that are about things we know don't exist, such as Santa Claus, but we have agreed as a society to continue to behave much of the time as though he did, and this allows us to felicitously make claims about his red suit, reindeer, etc.) To consider another case in which an existence presupposition has not been satisfied, imagine the following discourse between two co-workers who do not know each other very well yet:

(3)   First co-worker: # I'm sorry that I was late to our meeting; I had to take my pet
                                   giraffe to the veterinarian.
      Second co-worker: Wait a minute! You have a pet giraffe?

The second co-worker is right to object to the first co-worker's excuse for being late. Having a pet giraffe is not very common or likely, so the first co-worker really should not have assumed that she could discuss the giraffe in passing without first establishing that it existed. On the other hand, the second co-worker is put in a bit of a difficult situation, because he cannot simply disagree. If he retorts, "No, you didn't have to take your giraffe to the veterinarian," then he has done exactly what he did not want to do, which is to affirm the giraffe's existence. Instead, all he can do is sputter and say, "Wait a minute!" Such is the nature of what infelicity does to conversation. The conversation would have gone much better had the first co-worker said (4) instead.

(4)   I'm sorry that I was late to our meeting. I have a pet giraffe, and it hasn't been feeling
      well, so I had to take it to the veterinarian.

In this case, the second co-worker might believe that the first co-worker is lying, but at least the first co-worker has done her job to establish the existence of something (her giraffe) before beginning to talk about it. Now there is a specific sentence in the first co-worker's utterance ("I have a pet giraffe") that the second co-worker can refute.

7.5.2   Presuppositions and Truth Values

We mentioned above that one of the problems that can arise with sentences containing unsatisfied presuppositions is that we don't seem to be able to tell whether they are true or false. The sentences in (5) presuppose that there is such a place as Disneyland.

(5)   a. Yesterday, Disneyland had over 3,000 visitors.
      b. Yesterday, Disneyland did not have over 3,000 visitors.

Well, in fact there is such a place as Disneyland. Because that is common knowledge, it is almost certain that you, the reader, acknowledged the existence of Disneyland prior to reading (5a). Thus the presupposition was satisfied, and we can move on to answer another question: is (5a) true or false? It is probable that you do not know. (Of course, whether it is true or false will depend largely on which day is denoted by the deictic word *yesterday*.) Whichever day we are talking about, though, either Disneyland did have more than 3,000 visitors, or else it did not. That is, either (5a) is true, or else (5b) is. It is not possible for both (5a) and (5b) to be false.

Now, let's consider the Bvryzax River again. Of course, we see immediately that the sentences in (6) contain a presupposition that is not satisfied: there is no such river as the Bvryzax.

(6) a. #The Bvryzax River reaches a depth of 25 meters.
     b. #The Bvryzax River does not reach a depth of 25 meters.

Is (6a) true? No, it is not. Well, then, following the pattern we saw in (5), if (6a) is not true, then (6b) must be true, right? Well, no; that doesn't seem correct either. Under ordinary circumstances, if you negate a true sentence, then you are left with a false sentence, and if you negate a false sentence, then you are left with a true sentence. In the case of sentences with unsatisfied presuppositions, though, this generalization seems to fall through.

This gives us one way of identifying an unsatisfied presupposition: if a sentence and its logical negation both seem equally untrue, then that sentence likely has an unsatisfied presupposition. There are a number of semantic and pragmatic theories that try to account for how to reconcile this puzzle; for our purposes, we will merely mention it as an intriguing facet of our use of language.

So far we have considered only presuppositions of existence, but there are also many other **presupposition triggers**: words or phrases whose use in a sentence often indicates the presence of a presupposition. We will provide only a small sample here. In each case, notice that if the presupposition is not satisfied, it is not clear whether the sentence containing the presupposition is true or false.

In (7), the presupposition trigger is the phrase *come back*. Think about what *come back* means. In order for a person to come back to a place, he must come to that place after having been there before at some time in the past. But *come back* doesn't mean 'be at a place, leave it, and then come to that place again.' It only has the meaning 'come to that place again.' The part about having been there before is presupposed.

(7) a. Linus <u>came back</u> to the pumpkin patch this October.
     b. Linus did not <u>come back</u> to the pumpkin patch this October.

Therefore, the sentences in (7) presuppose that Linus had previously been in the pumpkin patch. If Linus had never been in the pumpkin patch before, then we cannot felicitously say that he came back, nor can we felicitously say that he did not come back. If Linus had never been to the pumpkin patch before, then (7a) and (7b) would both seem untrue. Moreover, if the speakers in a discourse do not know whether Linus has been to the pumpkin patch before or not, then it would be infelicitous to utter either (7a) or (7b).

Now consider the trigger *stop* in (8) and the trigger *after* in (9). Try not to worry too much about why they these words are triggers. Just think about what must be true in order for a person to felicitously say one of the sentences in (8) or (9).

(8) a. Alan <u>stopped</u> falling asleep during meetings.
     b. Alan did not <u>stop</u> falling asleep during meetings.

(9) a. <u>After</u> the United States added a fifty-fourth state, the US flag design was modified to contain 54 stars.
     b. <u>After</u> the United States added a fifty-fourth state, the US flag design was not modified to contain 54 stars. (Instead, the decision was made to keep the old flag design.)

Could one of the sentences in (8) be uttered if Alan had never fallen asleep during meetings? No; in such a case (8a) and (8b) would both be equally inadequate descriptions of the state of affairs: both would seem untrue. Thus we can conclude that *stop* triggers a presupposition that a person had to previously do whatever it is that he is supposed to have stopped. Therefore, if it were not common knowledge among the participants in a conversation that Alan used to fall asleep in meetings, a speaker could not felicitously utter either (8a) or (8b).

What about the sentences in (9)? Based on what you know about the world, is (9a) true or false? It doesn't seem to be either true or false: we cannot assess what did or didn't happen after the addition of a fifty-fourth state because (as of 2016, at which time the United States has only fifty states) no such addition has taken place. Therefore, (9a) is infelicitous, and (9b) is infelicitous for the same reason.

7.5.3   Prosody as a Presupposition Trigger

We will consider one more kind of presupposition trigger. The prosodic structure of our utterances can also cause certain information to be presupposed. Recall from File 2.5 that we can use **pitch accents** on words in order to make some words more prominent than others. By our choices in where to put these pitch accents, we can force different information to be presupposed. (As in File 2.5, we will use the convention of capitalizing words that are prosodically prominent.)

A particularly clear way of seeing how prosody affects presupposition can be found in sentences containing certain additive words (words like *too, either, also,* and *as well*). Here's an example using *too*: (10a) is felicitous, while (10b) is infelicitous.

(10) a.   Jessica went to Toledo. LAURA went to Toledo, too.
       b.   #Laura went to Fort Wayne. LAURA went to Toledo, too.

The *too* in (10) triggers a presupposition that someone else went to Toledo in addition to Laura, because the prosodically prominent word is *Laura*. Thus its use in (10a) is perfectly acceptable, while it is infelicitous in (10b). The presupposition has not been satisfied: in (10b) we do not know of someone other than Laura who went to Toledo; therefore we aren't allowed to use *too*.

However, the content of the presupposition is dependent entirely on the prosodic structure of the sentence in which *too* appears. To prove this to yourself, consider the pair of sentences in (11).

(11) a.   #Jessica went to Toledo. Laura went to TOLEDO, too.
       b.   Laura went to Fort Wayne. Laura went to TOLEDO, too.

In (11), the presupposition is that Laura went somewhere other than Toledo, because the prosodically prominent word is *Toledo*. When uttered with this prosody, therefore, the sentence is felicitous in context (b), but not in context (a). The explanation for (11) is exactly the inverse of the explanation for (10).

7.5.4   Presupposition Accommodation

So far, we have assumed that the only way for a sentence containing a presupposition to be felicitous is if that presupposition is satisfied at the time that the sentence is uttered. In fact, people use sentences containing presuppositions all the time when the other participants in the conversation would have no way of knowing the presupposed information ahead of time. Consider again the woman who was late for a meeting in (3). She didn't get away with presupposing that she had a pet giraffe. But suppose instead she had said one of the sentences in (12).

(12) a. I'm sorry that I was late to our meeting; I had to take my cat to the veterinarian.
b. I'm sorry that I was late to our meeting; my car broke down.

Both of these sentences also contain existence presuppositions: that the speaker has a pet cat in the first case and that she has a car in the second. Her co-worker is much less likely to object to these presuppositions, however, even if he did not previously know about the car or the cat. The reason is that it is much more plausible that a person might have a car or a cat. The second co-worker **accommodates** the presupposed information, behaving as though he had known it all along and not objecting to its being inserted like this. You can think of accommodation as being sort of like retroactive satisfaction.

Notice, however, that we accommodate only presuppositions that we find plausible. There is no hard-and-fast standard for what is or isn't plausible, but some things (like giraffe ownership) are almost certainly too implausible to pass by without an objection.

There is one more requirement for presupposition accommodation in addition to plausibility. To illustrate, imagine that your roommate (whom you have not seen all day) comes home and exclaims the following:

(13) Roommate: Guess what I did today!
You: What?
Roommate: #I also went to the LIBRARY.

In this case, your roommate's last utterance would be infelicitous because it presupposes that she went somewhere in addition to the library. However, because she hasn't told you where else she has gone, that information is not already common knowledge at the time of utterance. Although you can probably guess that she must have gone many other places during the day (to class, or the store, or a park, or wherever), rendering the presupposition plausible, you cannot access a specific other place that you are certain she went to. Thus the presupposition is inaccessible, so you cannot accommodate it.

These, then, are the two requirements for presupposition accommodation: plausibility and accessibility. By and large, if the content of a presupposition is both plausible and accessible, people will be willing to accommodate it. Suppose that you are sitting indoors in January in Ohio and have not looked out a window recently. If a child were to run up to you and proclaim (14), she would be telling you about her emotional state.

(14) I'm so happy that it's snowing!

Although her sentence is about her being happy, it presupposes that it is snowing, a fact that was not common knowledge before her utterance. Nonetheless, you would likely accommodate the presupposition that it was, indeed, snowing. The presupposition is readily accessible, because it was contained directly in the sentence that the child uttered, and it is plausible, because snow is fairly expected in January in Ohio.

It should not be surprising that this is the note we end on. As a general rule, in order for an utterance to be felicitous, any presuppositions it contains must be satisfied; however, very frequently presuppositions that were not satisfied before the utterance are accommodated afterwards based on elements of the context. Pragmatic rules, principles, and generalizations are all subject to factors that can be determined only from context.

Practice

File 7.1—Language in Context

Exercises

1. Below are descriptions of several possible contexts for the sentence *Do any of you have a watch?*

   i. For each context, paraphrase the message that the speaker seems to be trying to get across by uttering that sentence.

   ii. After doing part (i), write one or two sentences that explain how this exercise as a whole shows the way that context affects the meaning of sentences.

   a. A frantic-looking man runs up to a group of people standing at a bus stop, checks the bus schedule, and then says hurriedly, "Do any of you have a watch?"

   b. A group of preteen girls is comparing jewelry. One girl says, "My jewelry is best, because I have the most." Another says, "Nope. Mine is the best because it all matches." This sort of thing goes on for a while. Finally the last girl pipes up that she thinks she has the best jewelry. "Oh yeah? What makes you so special?" She replies, "Just look at my wrist! Do any of you have a watch?"

   c. A mugger traps a group of people in a dark alley and waves a gun at them while screaming, "Do any of you have a watch?"

   d. Your linguistics instructor left his watch at home this morning, but he will need to monitor his time use in class. He wanders into the department lounge and says to his colleagues, "Do any of you have a watch?"

   e. A woman goes to a masquerade ball and falls in love with one of her dance partners. However, of course, she cannot see his face. She knows only that he wore a very ornate and easily recognizable wristwatch. Now, every time that she approaches a group of eligible-looking men, she begins her conversation with, "Do any of you have a watch?"

   f. A zookeeper is about to let a group of patrons try holding an exotic bird with a known tendency to peck at shiny objects. Before letting anybody hold her, the keeper says, "Do any of you have a watch?"

   g. A Martian has read all about Earth and is very interested in its time-telling devices. On its first trip to our planet, it exits its flying saucer and oozes up to the first group of people it sees. It says excitedly, "Do any of you have a watch?"

2. Identify each of the following as a property that can hold of both sentences and utterances or of utterances only:

a. volume	**d.** location	**g.** length	**j.** pitch
b. truth/falsity	**e.** language	**h.** time	**k.** syntactic structure
c. speaker	**f.** idea expressed	**i.** speed	**l.** number of morphemes

3. In File 7.1, we introduced four possible interpretations of the sentence *Can you take the trash out?* Now, come up with your own context for *Can you take the trash out?* that differs from all of those given so far and that thereby gives it a different meaning from all of those given so far. Describe the context, and then tell what the sentence would mean if uttered in that context.

Example: An author writes a short story and takes it to a publisher. The story contains scenes of a so-called adult nature that the publisher objects to. When the author asks the publisher whether she will publish it, she responds, "Can you take the trash out?" Here, she means: 'If I agree to publish your story, will you remove the objectionable material from it?'

4. For each of the following sentences, construct two different contexts, such that the sentence would mean something different depending on which of the two contexts it was uttered in. (You may specify the situational context, the linguistic context, the social context, or all three.) Then paraphrase what the meaning of the sentence would be in each context that you write.

   a. I seem to have lost my pencil.
   b. There's always a police officer on duty.
   c. I'm supposed to write a five-page paper for my history class.

5. Tell whether each of the following sentences contains any deictic words. For the ones that do, list those words.

   a. They want to go to your concert to see your band perform.
   b. The Ohio State Buckeyes won the NCAA 2014 football championship.
   c. Many authors, such as Mark Twain and Carolyn Keene, chose to write under a pseudonym.
   d. That is so cool; let me see it!
   e. Although there will certainly be another major earthquake in California, no one can predict for sure whether the next big quake will happen tomorrow, next week, or a decade from now.
   f. Hippopotamuses are herbivores.
   g. Is it possible for a technician to come here to help fix the problem, or do I have to take my computer over there?

6. For each of the following questions, write one felicitous response and one infelicitous response. Explain what makes your infelicitous responses infelicitous. Try to have a different reason in each case. (*Hint:* Try answering this question once after reading File 7.1 and a second time after you have read the rest of Chapter 7. What new ways have you learned to make utterances infelicitous?)

   a. What did you do for your birthday?
   b. Which classes do you think you will take next spring?
   c. I'm going to the grocery store. Do you need me to pick anything up for you?

Discussion Questions

7. Think of experiences in which something that you or someone else said was reported out of context. How did this out-of-context report change the meaning of what was said? Why do people often choose to use quotations out of context? What is gained by this practice? What is lost?

8. How would language be different if we had no deictic elements? Could you still communicate as effectively? Could you still communicate as efficiently? Why, or why not?

9. Assuming that you have read File 6.3, discuss the difference between truth conditions and felicity conditions. Are there times that an utterance could be true but infelicitous? Are there times that an utterance could be felicitous but untrue?

Activities

10. Pay attention to the language around you.
  i. Transcribe one utterance that you hear today. Then write down the context of that utterance, being sure to note its linguistic, situational, and social contexts.
  ii. How did knowing the context help you interpret the meaning of that utterance?
  iii. What else might the sentence have meant had it been uttered in a different context?

11. Pay attention to the language being used around you.
  i. Find an example of somebody saying something infelicitous.
  ii. Tell what was said, and describe the context.
  iii. Explain what makes you believe that the utterance was infelicitous for that context.

File 7.2—Rules of Conversation

Exercises

12. Below are descriptions of four university professors. Hopefully you will never have an instructor like any of them, because they are not very pragmatically savvy. Each one is failing to follow one of Grice's maxims in particular. For each professor, tell which category of maxim is being violated.

  a. He's so well-spoken that you can get lulled into thinking that you believe him. Then, after a while, you start to realize that most of what he's saying is just unfounded opinion. He never backs up his statements with anything factual.

  b. Her lectures are really hard to understand. I think that she knows what she's talking about, but she uses all this complicated vocabulary, and she never defines any of the words. Plus, every sentence is about a million words long, and by the time you figure out what it meant, she's giving you another sentence that's even more complicated!

  c. His classes are hard to follow because he goes off on so many tangents. We'll be talking about Russian politics one minute, and then he'll veer off to tell us something about democracy in Ancient Greece. Then he'll get back to the Russian politics only to interrupt himself with a story about what his son did at breakfast this morning.

  d. I feel as though she never gives us thorough answers to our questions. For example, I asked her yesterday why we shiver when we're cold. All she said was "because you're warm-blooded," and then she went on with her lecture. I already knew that people are warm-blooded, but I don't know what that has to do with shivering.

13. In (6) in Section 7.2.2, the following possible answers are given to the question "Where did you grow up?" Suppose that they are all true answers and that the only difference between them is how informative they are. Write a one- or two-sentence linguistic context for each response in which that response would be felicitous.

(cont.)

On the corner of Main Street and Minor Road
   a. In Dayton
   b. In Dayton, Ohio
   c. In Dayton, Ohio, on the corner of Main Street and Minor Road
   d. In Ohio
   e. In the Midwest
   f. In the United States

14. Instead of merely saying "Be brief," Grice's actual statement of the third maxim of manner was "Be brief (avoid unnecessary prolixity)." By phrasing the maxim this way, which two of his maxims of manner did Grice violate?

15. In the discourse below, Sophie fails to follow one of Grice's maxims. Tell which maxim she violates, and explain the violation.

    Josh: What did you do yesterday?
    Sophie: I went to the concert downtown. It was a lot of fun.
    Josh: Who was there?
    Sophie: I saw Jane, David, Susan, and Polly. Oh, and her mother was there.
    Josh: Whose mother?
    Sophie: What? Oh, Susan's, of course!

16. In eighth grade, Chris thought (mistakenly) that it would be funny to prank-call the fire department from a payphone on the wall of the school cafeteria. Based on the following dialogue, answer questions (i)–(iii).

    Fire department operator: Where is the phone that you're calling from?
    Chris: On the wall.

    i. In general, why would an operator at a fire department ask where a caller is calling from?
    ii. Based on the situation (the operator's goals), which maxim does Chris's answer violate?
    iii. Is Chris's answer true? Justify your answer relative to the maxim of quality.

17. Suppose that you ask a friend what he thought of a new movie, and he replies, "Well, the costumes were authentic." His answer does seem to be saying something positive about the movie. Nevertheless, he is guiding you to infer that he probably did not like the movie.

    i. Which maxim is he flouting in order to do this?
    ii. Why might he choose to convey his dislike by flouting that maxim instead of saying directly that he didn't like the movie?

Discussion Questions

18. In Section 7.2.1, we mentioned several components of society in which rules are important. What other social institutions can you think of for which there are preset rules? How is language similar to these institutions? How is it different?

19. **i.** We are taught at a young age not to lie. Nevertheless, there are many times that someone might choose to break Grice's maxim of quality in order to serve a particular purpose. What are some reasons that one might have for doing so?

(cont.)

ii. Considering how many reasons there are to say things that are untrue, and considering how often the maxim of quality must therefore be violated, what evidence do we have that it exists in the first place?

iii. Is there a difference between breaking Grice's maxim of quality and lying? If so, what is the difference? If not, why not? (It is acceptable to argue on behalf of both sides, but be sure that your answer is clear and well-justified.)

Activities

20. Pay attention to the conversation you hear around you. Find two cases of a person flouting one of Grice's maxims and two cases of a person violating one of the maxims (**four** cases total). In each case, explain which maxim is at stake and what effect it has on the conversation when it is broken/flouted. *(If you like, you can intentionally break several maxims in your conversations and write about what happens, but neither the editors of this book nor your instructor can take any responsibility for any effect this activity may have on your social life!)*

21. Comic strips are often a great place to find violations of Grice's maxims.

    i. Locate a comic strip in which the joke or humor value comes from one of the characters violating one of Grice's maxims for cooperativity in conversation. Photocopy or print out the comic, or staple or tape it to a full-sized sheet of paper.

    ii. Tell which maxim is being violated. (Be specific: for example, if it's a maxim of manner, be sure to tell which one is being violated.)

    iii. Explain why what the character says is a violation of that maxim.

    iv. Briefly describe why the violation leads to a humorous reading of the comic strip.

22. Construct your own example of a conversation in which one of Grice's maxims is flouted. Each speaker should have at least several turns in the dialogue in order to establish sufficient context to show the function of the flouting. After you have written your dialogue, tell which maxim is flouted, and to what end.

File 7.3—Drawing Conclusions

Exercises

23. Below is a discourse between Daniel and Amy. They are in the kitchen at their home. Following the discourse is a list of questions. None of the questions is directly answered in the discourse, but all of the answers are implicated by something that either Daniel or Amy says. Answer each question. Then tell which line of the discourse contains the implicature that answers the question and which Gricean maxim you had to appeal to in order to figure out the implicature.

    a. Daniel: Would you like me to make chocolate chip cookies this afternoon?
    b. Amy: Sure. That would be great! Do you have all of the ingredients?
    c. Daniel: Well, I meant to go to the bank this morning, and then I was going to stop at the store on the way home, but I wasn't feeling well, so I didn't go.
    d. Amy: That's too bad. What did you need to buy?
    e. Daniel: Just a few things. Do you know whether we have any eggs?
    f. Amy: After breakfast, there were two left.
    g. Daniel: Then I guess I'll have to borrow some. Are the neighbors home?
    h. Amy: (Looks out the window) I don't see their car out front.

(cont.)

   i. Daniel: That's too bad. Maybe I should make cookies some other day.

      i. What kind of cookies is Daniel planning to make?

      ii. What kind of store had Daniel meant to go to this morning?
         A. shoe store   B. grocery store   C. book store

      iii. What did Amy eat for breakfast this morning?

      iv. How many eggs does Amy think there are in the house?
         A. fewer than two   B. exactly two   C. more than two

      v. How many eggs does the cookie recipe call for?
         A. fewer than two   B. exactly two   C. more than two

      vi. From where does Daniel hope to get eggs now?

      vii. Are Daniel and Amy's neighbors at home?

      viii. Why does Daniel decide not to make cookies today?

      ix. Which of these activities is Daniel most likely to have wanted to do at the bank?
         A. give blood   B. go fishing in the river   C. withdraw cash

      x. How was Daniel feeling this morning?
         A. healthy   B. a little sick   C. extremely ill

24. Two basketball players are close friends. One is a very good player and makes every shot that he attempts. The other is not as good. Their coach has instructed them to try a new and very difficult drill. Both players try the new drill ten times. Of course, the first player puts the ball through the hoop all ten times. Afterwards, the friends get together to discuss how their practice went and have the following conversation:

1st Player: How did you do?
2nd Player: Well, I made it on my fifth try. I bet you did a lot better than me.
1st Player: Well, yeah, but don't feel too bad. I made it on my fourth shot.

    i. Of the ten tries, how many times did the first player make the shot?

    ii. What inference is the first player hoping that the second player will draw, counter to this fact, by saying, "I made it on my fourth shot"?

    iii. Which maxim is the first player using in order to create this implicature?

    iv. Why has the first player chosen to give this answer?

    v. Is the first player violating a maxim of **quality** by saying, "I made it on my fourth shot"?

    vi. Has the first player violated any other maxims? Justify your answer.

Discussion Questions

25. **i.** In Section 7.3.2, the gesture of glancing at a watch is mentioned as a way to imply that a meeting is running late. What are other conventional nonlinguistic signals that are often sent in order to imply various messages? For each signal, what is the intended inference that should be drawn?

    ii. What is the purpose or benefit of having conventionalized these signals?

26. We tend to think of number words as naming exact values—of *forty-seven* meaning 'exactly forty-seven, no more and no less.' However, often we do not use them as though they had these meanings. If a friend asks you "Do you have five bucks I can borrow?", your friend means "Do you have at least five bucks I can borrow?" If you have ten dollars that you would be willing to lend your friend, but he asks about only five of them, you would still answer yes.

(cont.)

     i. In what sorts of contexts do we use the names of numbers to mean 'exactly that amount'?

     ii. In what sorts of contexts do we use the names of numbers to mean 'at least that amount'?

     iii. Can you think of examples of contexts in which the name of a number is used to mean 'at most that amount'?

     iv. When you hear a number word used, what sort of information do you consider in order to figure out whether it is being used with an 'at least,' 'at most,' or 'exactly' meaning?

Activity

27. Construct your own examples of discourse samples that make use of relevance, quantity, or manner implicatures. After writing the discourse, write a short analysis explaining what the implicatures are, why they are used by the speakers in your discourse, and from which maxim they derive.

File 7.4—Speech Acts

Exercises

28. Look at the contexts given for the sentence *Do any of you have a wrist watch?* in Exercise 1. In each case, which speech act is the speaker performing by uttering this sentence (e.g., request, threat, apology, etc.)?

29. Look at your answers to Exercise 4. (If you haven't done that exercise yet, do it now.) For each of your answers, tell whether it was a direct speech act or an indirect speech act.

30. Imagine that you have a child or a younger sibling who wants you to drive him/her to a friend's house.

     i. What speech act would this person need to perform in order to communicate this idea to you?

     ii. Write three sentences that s/he could use to get this point across: make one declarative, one imperative, and one interrogative. Label which is which. Also, label which are direct and which indirect.

31. Take the sentence *It's very warm outside.*

     i. What type of sentence is this?

     ii. Write two contexts for this sentence in which it is used for different purposes.

     iii. In each case, tell the speaker's goal in uttering the sentence; in other words, what is the speech act in question?

     iv. Also, in each case, tell whether the speech act is being performed directly or indirectly.

32. Assume that a speaker wants another person to open the window. This speaker could try to communicate this idea by uttering any of the sentences in (a)–(g) below.

     i. What type of speech act corresponds with the speaker's goal?

     ii. Identify each sentence as a direct or an indirect speech act relative to that goal.

     iii. Identify the type of each sentence.

(cont.)

     a. I see that the window is not yet open.

     b. Can you open the window?

     c. I order you to open the window.

     d. I would appreciate it if you opened the window.

     e. I sure would love to have some fresh air in this room.

     f. Please open the window.

     g. Would you mind opening the window?

33. For each of the following speech acts, write three sentences. (That is, you will write a total of nine sentences: three for each kind of speech act.) First, write two direct speech acts, one with a performative verb and one without; then write an indirect speech act. Be sure to label which is which.

     a. question

     b. request

     c. promise

34. Refer to the table in (34) in Section 7.4.7. Assume that for each column, all of the sentences have the same communicative intention. Which are direct speech acts, and which are indirect speech acts?

35. For each of the following scenarios, tell what kind of speech act seems to be being performed. Then tell whether the utterance is felicitous or infelicitous and why, appealing to the idea of felicity conditions.

     a. A woman sitting next to the ketchup and mustard containers at a table in a restaurant asks the man across the table from her to pass the ketchup.

     b. The bailiff in a courtroom approaches the judge and says, "I find the defendant guilty, your honor."

     c. A girl approaches the school librarian and says, "Excuse me; where can I find a book about butterflies?"

     d. A woman who sees someone wearing a sweater that she admires says, "I really like your sweater."

     e. At the end of a business meeting, an employee says to his supervisor, "You may go now."

     f. A customer walks up to the cashier at a grocery store and says, "The canned vegetables are located in aisle five."

     g. On her way out the door, a woman says to her dog, "I'm going to be home late today. Would you please put dinner in the oven around 6:00?"

     h. A geography teacher says to her fifth-grade class, "The largest mountain range in the eastern half of the United States is the Appalachians."

     i. A man at a bus stop has his hands full of books. One slides off the pile onto the ground, and he says to the person next to him, "Excuse me; could you please pick up that book for me?"

36. Consider the following four scenarios. Each contains a warning, but the warning in each case is infelicitous.

     a. Someone warns an extremely careful and experienced carpenter that his saw is sharp and could cut him.

     b. Two children are taking a walk in the park; one says to the other, "Be careful! There's a daffodil growing in that garden!"

(cont.)

c. A murderer lurking in the shadows yells to his next victim, "Watch out; there's someone here to kill you!" before lunging at her with his knife.

d. A mother living with her child in a neighborhood in New England warns her child, "Be careful; there's an escaped madman running around Vienna!"

> **i.** First, explain what makes each an infelicitous warning.
>
> **ii.** Then, based on what you have observed about these infelicities, write a set of felicity conditions for warnings that would prevent such inappropriate utterances. (For models of what felicity conditions look like, refer to the examples given in Section 7.4.2.)

37. Which of the following sentences contain verbs used performatively? (*Hint:* Exactly five of the underlined verbs are performative.) Explain the difference between the five verbs you chose as performative verbs and the other five verbs that you did not choose.

a. I promise to be there.

b. I suggest that you leave.

c. I convince you that I am right.

d. I warn you not to come any closer.

e. I incite you to be angry.

f. I forbid you to enter this room.

g. I inspire you to write beautiful music.

h. I amuse you with my jokes.

i. I order you to be quiet.

j. I provoke you to punch me.

Activities

38. Choose a short section of a television show or a movie in which there is a lot of dialogue. (Your instructor will tell you how long a segment to choose. It would be best to choose a clip that you have a recording of so that you can watch it multiple times.) List all of the kinds of speech acts that you hear during the clip.

39. Pay attention to language use around you, and keep track of the various speech acts that you hear in various contexts. Choose between two and five kinds of contexts. (Your instructor will tell you how many to choose and how long to spend observing each.) For example, you might choose a conversation between a supervisor and an employee, a group of friends chatting over lunch, two people having an argument, someone explaining an assignment to a classmate, and so on. (It will be **much** easier to complete this activity if you choose conversations in which you are not a participant!)

Create a simple table like the one below that you can fill in. You will fill in the contexts in the left-hand column. Then use tick marks to note how many times you hear each speech act in a given conversation. Don't worry about who utters which; just keep track on a conversation-by-conversation basis. Remember that the form of an utterance doesn't always correspond to the type of speech act that it is! (If you hear an utterance and are not sure of how to categorize it, make a note in the margin of your paper.)

Write a short analysis of what you have observed. Do certain speech acts tend to appear more frequently or less frequently in particular contexts? Offer some hypotheses of why you think this may be so. (Keep in mind that you will be interested in **relative** frequency, that is, how often some kind of speech act appears relative to the other kinds: the actual tally count that you have doesn't give you useful information unless you know how it compares to the others.)

(cont.)

Compare your responses with those of classmates who observed similar kinds of discourse. Are your observations similar to theirs?

CONTEXT	assertion	question	request	order	promise	threat	apology	warning	advice
(fill in . . .)									
(fill in . . .)									

File 7.5—Presupposition

Exercises

40. A classic example of a question that a lawyer might unfairly ask a defendant in a court room is "Have you stopped beating your wife?" Explain, as precisely as possible, why this is a so-called unfair question.

41. List all of the existence presuppositions contained in the following sentences. (Of course, normally when we read nursery rhymes such as these, we are very willing to accommodate the presuppositions that they contain.)

   a. Old Mother Hubbard went to the cupboard to fetch her poor dog a bone.
   b. Little Boy Blue went to blow his horn on account of the sheep were in the meadow and the cows were in the corn.
   c. The black sheep had a bag of wool for his master, a bag of wool for his dame, and a bag of wool for the little boy who lived down the lane.
   d. Jack and Jill went up the hill because they wanted to test Jack's new high-tech anti-fall machine.

42. Pick a book—fiction or nonfiction—of your choosing. Copy out two sentences that contain existence presuppositions and one sentence that contains some other type of presupposition. Then explicitly state the presuppositions.

43. Consider the sentence *Andrea read a book about how ice cream is made, too.* How many different presuppositions could this sentence have if uttered with different prosodies? For each possibility, write a sentence that could go in a discourse before this sentence, and write the given sentence with the appropriate part marked for prosodic prominence. Finally, tell what the presupposition would be. (There are many possible responses for this exercise; try to come up with at least four.)

   Example: Andrea read a book about how pencils are made.
   Andrea read a book about how ICE CREAM is made, too.
   Presupposition: Andrea read a book about how something is made.

Discussion Questions

44. Is each of the following sentences true or false? Why do you think so? (Assume that they are spoken in the early twenty-first century about the present time, such that there is no monarchy in France.) Do you feel the same way about the truth value of all of them?
   a. The king of France is bald.
   b. The king of France had lunch with me yesterday.
   c. I had lunch with the king of France yesterday.

45. Using sentences with presuppositions that have not been satisfied is a strategy often associated with gossips. For example, a gossip might say, "Are you surprised that Jack and Jill are getting married?" In this sentence, the words *surprised that* are a presupposition trigger, so the sentence presupposes that Jack and Jill are getting married without actually coming right out and saying it. Why might a gossip adopt this strategy? Do you believe that it is an effective strategy? Can you think of times that you have heard this strategy used? Describe them.

46. In File 7.5, we mentioned that there are many presupposition triggers other than the ones that we explicitly discussed. Consider the following examples. What are the presuppositions contained in each of the following sentences? What is the presupposition trigger in each case? (Be forewarned that the answers to these questions are not contained in the file; they are an opportunity for further thought and reflection on the topic of presupposition.)

   a. Please take me out to the ball game again.
   b. When we bought our new house, our pet platypus was delighted that it would have its very own bathtub.
   c. That her pet turtle ran away made Emily very sad.
   d. Eli wants more popcorn.
   e. If pigs had wings, where would they fly?
   f. I, too, often have a glass of milk at night.
   g. The elephant will continue to be endangered until we stop destroying its natural habitat.

Activity

47. In casual conversation with your friends, try using sentences that presuppose information that has not yet been asserted in the conversation. (Make sure that it's relevant to whatever you are talking about, though!) How do your friends react? What kinds of presuppositions can you get away with (i.e., which ones do they accommodate?)? What kinds of presuppositions do they call you on or give you weird looks about? Can you make any generalizations? *(As with Activity 20, neither the editors of this book nor your instructor can take any responsibility for any effect this activity may have on your social life!)* How, if at all, do you think your findings would differ if you did this experiment with a group of your professors or with your supervisor at work? Explain.

Further Readings

Grundy, Peter. 2008. *Doing pragmatics*. 3rd edn. London: Hodder Arnold.
Peccei, Jean Stilwell. 1999. *Pragmatics*. New York: Routledge.
Verschueren, Jef. 1999. *Understanding pragmatics*. London: Hodder Arnold.
Yule, George. 1996. *Pragmatics*. Oxford: Oxford University Press.

CHAPTER

8

....

Language Acquisition

FILE **8.0**

What Is Language Acquisition?

Many people believe that language is what sets humans apart from other animals. Languages are highly complex and sophisticated systems. So how do we humans manage to learn such complicated systems? This chapter addresses that question. A predominant theory assumes that part of our ability to acquire language is innate and that children learn language by "inventing" the rules specific to their language.

When acquiring one or more native language(s), all children go through the same stages of language development: they start by babbling, then learn their first words, go through a so-called one-word stage (during which they can utter only one word at a time), enter the two-word stage, and finally learn the more complex structures of their language(s). Language acquisition is not limited to children; many people learn a second language later in life. However, second-language acquisition can differ from first-language acquisition in many respects.

Contents

FILE 8.1

Theories of Language Acquisition

8.1.1 About Language Acquisition

Humans are not born talking. Instead, we typically learn to understand language and to speak during the first few years of our lives, before we even enter kindergarten or grade school. Recall from File 1.2 that language is a communication system consisting of sounds, morphemes, words, and rules for combining all of these. The knowledge of these elements enables people to understand and produce sentences they may never have heard or uttered before. So how does a child acquire this knowledge? If knowing a language were simply a matter of knowing a lot of words, language acquisition would just be a process of figuring out what the words were and memorizing them. Instead, children must acquire a grammar with all its components and rules. How do children learn these rules? For instance, how do they learn that the morpheme *un-* (meaning 'not') attaches to adjectives to form other adjectives having the opposite meanings? How do they learn to compose a sentence from a noun phrase and a verb phrase? Rules, unlike words, are never explicitly stated, so the child cannot just memorize them: he must somehow figure the rules out on his own—a remarkable intellectual feat.

Various theories have arisen that attempt to account for how children acquire language. One theory that has found a lot of support throughout the years is that at least part of the human language ability is **innate.** In the sections that follow, we will first explore the **innateness hypothesis** and the evidence for it.

However, innateness alone does not answer all of the questions about how children acquire the specific language that is spoken around them. Again, there are a number of theories that have been proposed for how additional, more specific knowledge is acquired. We will briefly consider two early ones, **Imitation Theory** and **Reinforcement Theory,** which have been refuted but which remain part of popular belief. It is therefore important to point out why these theories are inadequate. We will then consider three more current theories of language acquisition: the most influential of them is the **Active Construction of a Grammar Theory.** This theory is the one that most linguists believe today. However, there are a number of influential competing theories. Of these, we will introduce **Connectionist Theories** and **Social Interaction Theory.**

8.1.2 The Innateness Hypothesis

A hypothesis underlying many theories of language acquisition asserts that language ability is **innate** in humans. That is, humans are genetically predisposed to acquire and use language (though not any particular language, of course). This theory claims that babies are born with the knowledge that languages have patterns and with the ability to seek out and identify those patterns. Some theorists have even claimed that humans have innate knowledge of some core characteristics common to all languages, such as the concepts of 'noun' and 'verb.' These basic features shared by all languages are called **linguistic universals,** and the theoretically inborn set of structural characteristics shared by all languages is known as **universal grammar.** No one knows exactly what the contents of universal grammar might be, though this is currently an active area of research in linguistics.

The claim that linguistic ability is innate in humans is supported by, for example, the work of biologist Eric Lenneberg. He studied animal behavior and developed a list of characteristics that are typical of innately determined behaviors. Innate behaviors are present in all normal individuals of a species, whereas learned behaviors are not. Walking, for instance, is a behavior for which humans are genetically predisposed (that is, humans learn to walk as a natural part of development, without being explicitly taught), but playing the piano or riding a bicycle must be specifically taught. Is talking like walking, or is it like playing the piano?

To answer this, let's examine Lenneberg's characteristics of biologically controlled behaviors. If language acquisition has each of these characteristics, we can safely assume that it is a genetically triggered behavior.

(1)   Lenneberg's characteristics of biologically controlled behaviors:[1]
    1. The behavior emerges before it is necessary.
    2. Its appearance is not the result of a conscious decision.
    3. Its emergence is not triggered by external events (though the surrounding environment must be sufficiently "rich" for it to develop adequately).
    4. Direct teaching and intensive practice have relatively little effect.
    5. There is a regular sequence of "milestones" as the behavior develops, and these can usually be correlated with age and other aspects of development.
    6. There is likely to be a "critical period" for the acquisition of the behavior.

Consider the first criterion. In what sense is language necessary? From a biological standpoint, language is a behavior that has encouraged the survival and predominance of the human species. Each individual needs the ability to use language in order to take care of other basic needs. But children ordinarily begin to speak a language between the ages of twelve and twenty-four months, long before their parents have stopped providing them with the necessities of life. So language is a behavior that, like walking, emerges well before children have to fend for themselves.

As for the second and third criteria, language is neither the result of a conscious decision nor triggered by external events. Children decide whether or not they want to learn to play baseball or checkers, but they do not make a conscious choice about acquiring a native language; it's just something that all children do. Also, language is not learned as a result of something special triggering the learning. It is not taught the way (for example) piano playing is taught. Think about this: if you grew up hearing brilliantly played piano music, would you automatically pick up that skill the way we all seem to have automatically picked up language? Clearly not. While it is true that a child has to be exposed to language—this is what is meant by the environment being "rich"—it is not the case that a child's caretakers need to make a special effort to teach the child to speak. Other than hearing normal conversation and being spoken to, the child needs no special external stimulus to begin the process of acquiring language.

But doesn't intensive teaching help children learn language? Surprisingly, it does not seem to have much of an effect. Children don't necessarily perceive (or correct!) their mistakes just because an adult points them out (see Section 8.1.4).

Language acquisition also exhibits Lenneberg's fifth characteristic of having a sequence of "milestones" or identifiable stages associated with its development. Specifically, children master linguistic skills in a certain order. You will read about these stages in more detail in subsequent files. Although there is some variability in the milestones and the ages

---

[1]From Aitchison (1976: 60), adapted from Lenneberg (1967).

at which children achieve them, there is a path of developmental stepping stones that all children follow.

Lenneberg further proposes that innate behaviors have a **critical period** associated with their emergence. The term *critical period* describes a period of time in an individual's life during which a behavior—in this case language—must be acquired; that is, the acquisition will fail if it is attempted either before or after the critical period.

The critical period for language acquisition is assumed to extend from birth to approximately the onset of puberty. During this time, a child needs exposure to language in order to develop the brain structures necessary for language acquisition. If a child is not exposed to language at all during this time, then the child will never acquire normal language skills and, in fact, may not acquire language skills at all. If a child has acquired a native language during the critical period and starts learning a second language before the age of twelve, the child will likely achieve native competence in this second language as well. However, if the second language is learned after about age twelve, the child is likely never to acquire complete native competence in the language.

How can we tell whether there really is a critical period for first-language acquisition? To prove this, we would have to show that language skills could not be acquired normally or even at all if the learning began after the critical period had ended. This could be accomplished by depriving a child of linguistic input for the early years of life, but obviously it would be highly unethical to submit a child to such treatment. However, there are least two sources of information available to linguists that support the claims that there is a critical period for first-language acquisition.

First, evidence for the critical period hypothesis comes from children who, owing to unfortunate circumstances, were exposed to little or no language during their early lives. These children were either neglected by their caretakers (**neglected children**) or grew up in the wild, often with animals (**feral children**). When these children were rescued or discovered, researchers attempted to help them acquire language. The success of these attempts depended largely on the age at which the children were discovered. We will consider two such cases, outlined in (2) and (3).

(2) Genie was found in 1970 when she was nearly fourteen years old. She had been abused and isolated since the age of twenty months. When first discovered, Genie was completely silent. Thereafter, her language acquisition was extremely slow, and although she did learn to speak, her speech was abnormal. She was able to memorize many vocabulary items, but her expressions were formulaic, as in *what is X* and *give me X*. She never learned grammar.

(3) Isabelle was discovered in 1937 at the age of six and a half. Her mother was deaf and could not speak. Isabelle's grandfather had kept Isabelle and her mother isolated but had not otherwise mistreated them. Isabelle then began lessons at The Ohio State University, and although her progress was at first slow, it soon accelerated. In two years her intelligence and her language use were completely normal for a child her age.

At first sight, the cases of Genie and Isabelle seem to provide good evidence for the critical period hypothesis: Genie, discovered after the supposed critical period was over, never learned language; Isabelle, discovered before the end of the period, did. But evidence from feral or neglected children is problematic. Such children are usually traumatized or are not socialized before they are rescued or found. So it is possible that it is not the lack of exposure to language but rather a larger trauma that prevents them from acquiring language properly. For example, Genie had been beaten by her father for making noises, so her difficulty with language could have had multiple causes. The case of Isabelle is problematic for the opposite reason: prior to being found, she was locked in a room with her mother, and although her mother could not speak, they developed a rudimentary personal gesture system to communicate. Thus, Isabelle did have some exposure to a communication system during the early years of her life. It is possible that Isabelle acquired language not because she was discovered at an earlier age than Genie, but because she had access to a rudimentary communication system. Likewise, it is possible that Genie didn't learn language not because she was discovered at an older age than was Isabelle, but rather because she had been abused.

Stronger evidence supporting both the innateness of language and the critical period hypothesis for first-language acquisition can be found in instances of deaf children and adults who were initially raised in environments without access to signed language input. One particularly illustrative example is the case of the deaf population of Nicaragua in the late twentieth century. At the end of the 1970s, following Nicaragua's civil war, the country founded a new state school for the deaf. In the late 1970s and early 1980s, deaf children and adults were able to come together in a way that had not been possible earlier in the country's history. Most children and adults arrived at the schools with idiosyncratic and rudimentary homesign gesture systems. **Homesign** gestures are communicative gestures (a form associated with a meaning) that are invented by deaf children and the people with whom they routinely interact in cases where a signed language is not made available. Homesigns may represent the names of individuals such as family members and the names of common activities ('eat') or common objects ('house') that are often referred to. However, a homesign system is not a language: it is an extremely limited lexicon without a grammar. Thus the students arrived at the school with backgrounds that involved social interactions and communication and that were normal in every way except that they did not include exposure to language.

Soon, combining the homesigns that the students brought with them as well as some newly created signs, the children at the school created a pidgin (a type of simplified language—see File 12.3) to communicate with each other. After the pidgin was created by the first students at the school, younger children came and were exposed to the pidgin. Without instruction, and based only on their exposure to the pidgin used by their older peers, these younger children created Idioma de Signos Nicaragense (ISN), which is a full-fledged language with a complex system of grammatical rules.

The creation of ISN has been cited as evidence for the innateness of language, because within two or three generations of students, children created a new and complete language. Because they did not have exposure to any other linguistic system, all of the grammatical principles that were developed in ISN must have arisen through some innate ability in the children to create a complete grammatical system.

However, those students who first came to the school as older children, and who had not acquired any linguistic communication system prior to the time that they enrolled but had otherwise grown up in a caring environment, did not perfectly acquire this new language: in adulthood, their language use still resembles the pidgin, and there are inconsistencies in their use of phonological, morphological, and syntactic principles of the sort that one would not see in a native speaker of the language. This evidence supports the critical period hypothesis because the older children came from backgrounds similar to those of the younger children, yet they were unable to fully acquire language.

Support for a critical period for second-language acquisition involves comparing the acquisition of a second language by children and by teenagers and adults. Teenagers and adults have more difficulty learning languages than do children. People who have learned a language as an adult almost always have a foreign accent, indicating that they have not acquired the phonological rules of the second language perfectly. They may also find syntactic and other rules difficult to master completely. Children, however, can acquire a second (or third) language easily and completely as long as they have sufficient input from those languages. This ability tapers off around the age of puberty. However, the idea of a critical period for second-language acquisition is very controversial. Critics argue that there are (rare) cases of adults learning a second language perfectly. Furthermore, it is possible to learn a second language at any age. Rather than a critical period, there seems to be a steady decline in how well one can learn a second language. Finally, factors such as teaching methods, motivation, identity, dedication, utility, and so on, play a role in how successfully a second language is learned, and these factors may also change with age, confounding studies looking for critical period effects in second-language acquisition.

Another concern related to the critical period hypothesis is that different aspects of language acquisition may behave differently relative to the critical period. For example, many feral or neglected children gain the ability to learn vocabulary and to understand others' speech, but they are not able to learn to use syntax productively. Second-language learners are able to learn large amounts of vocabulary and frequently master the language's syntax, but they rarely master the phonological system. This suggests that a critical period may exist for certain aspects of language (syntax in first-language acquisition and phonology in second-language acquisition), but not for others.

Despite our lack of a complete understanding of the acquisition process, we can conclude that language acquisition shows characteristics of being an innate human behavior.

8.1.3   Imitation Theory

Even if language acquisition is an innate human behavior, the question still remains of how specifically it is acquired by children. The first two theories we will discuss have generally been refuted, but, as is often the case, there is a grain of truth in both that keeps them part of popular belief, even though there is much about the acquisition process that they are incapable of explaining.

We will first consider **Imitation Theory,** which claims that children learn language by listening to the speech around them and reproducing what they hear. According to this theory, language acquisition consists of memorizing the words and sentences of some language. The idea that acquiring a language is a process of learning to imitate the speech of others is at least partly true, of course. Since the connection between the way a word sounds and what it means is largely arbitrary (see File 1.4), children cannot guess what the words of their target language are. They must hear the words used by other speakers and then reproduce or "imitate" them. This theory also helps explain the fact that children learn the language that is spoken around them by parents, caretakers, and others, regardless of what the language of their ancestors may have been. Thus a Korean child, for instance, will speak Korean if raised in a Korean-speaking environment, but Arabic if raised in an Arabic-speaking environment. In other words, a child's genetic makeup has nothing to do with which language the child will acquire.

Unfortunately, however, Imitation Theory explains little else of what we know about language acquisition. Children's speech differs from adult norms: it is full of "errors" of many types. A two-year-old might say *nana* for adult *banana*, a three-year-old might say *Mommy tie shoe,* and a four-year-old might say *hitted* or *goed* rather *hit* or *went.*

The last example clearly cannot be a case of imitation because children would not have heard an adult say *hitted* or *goed.* Rather, it seems that the child who says *hitted* has a rule in her internal grammar that adds *-ed* (pronounced as [d], [t], or [əd]) to a verb to make it past tense. The child has not mastered the exceptions to this rule, such as the use of *hit* rather than *hitted* in the past tense. However, Imitation Theory fails to acknowledge that a child has any sort of internal mental grammar that includes rules for combining words and other elements in systematic ways, so it would incorrectly predict that a child would not produce words like *hitted.*

The most serious fault of Imitation Theory is that it cannot account for how children and adults are able to produce and understand new sentences. If children learned only by imitation, the only way they could understand a sentence is if they had heard it before.

However, we know that there are an infinite number of possible sentences in any language, and speakers (even children) are able to understand and produce completely novel utterances.

8.1.4   Reinforcement Theory

Reinforcement Theory asserts that children learn to speak like adults because they are praised, rewarded, or otherwise reinforced when they use the right forms and are corrected when they use wrong forms. However, the claim that parents and other caretakers frequently correct their children's grammatical mistakes and praise their correct forms is unfounded. Such corrections seldom happen, for although parents often do correct their children, their corrections generally have more to do with the accuracy or truth of a statement than with its grammatical form. Thus, *The dog wants to eat* may receive the response *No, the dog doesn't want to eat* if the dog has just finished its dinner, whereas the sentence *Robin goed to school today* may receive the response *Yes, he did* if Robin did go to school that day.

Reinforcement Theory is also contradicted by the fact that even when adults do try to correct a child's grammar, the attempts usually fail entirely. Consider the following conversation:

(4)   Child: Nobody don't like me.
      Mother: No, say "nobody likes me."
      Child: Nobody don't like me.
                                                (repeated 8 times)
      Mother (now exasperated):   Now listen carefully! Say, "Nobody likes me."
      Child: Oh! Nobody don't likes me.

Notice that although the child does not form negative sentences in the same way the adult does, the child's utterances follow a pattern just as the adult's do. The child's way of forming negative sentences involving *nobody* is completely regular: every such sentence contains *nobody* + a negative auxiliary verb, such as *Nobody can't spell that* or *Nobody won't listen.* If the child produces a variety of such sentences, then he or she must possess a rule that defines this pattern, but the rule is not the same as the one in the adult's grammar. Reinforcement Theory can explain neither where the child's rule came from nor why the child seems impervious to correction. (Incidentally, the conversation sample above is a good example of how direct teaching does not help children to acquire language—recall the criteria for innate behaviors in Section 8.1.2.)

The next three theories are ones that are currently held (and debated) among language acquisition researchers.

8.1.5   Active Construction of a Grammar Theory

The **Active Construction of a Grammar Theory,** the most influential theory of language acquisition, holds that children actually invent the rules of grammar themselves. The theory assumes that the ability to develop rules is innate, but that the actual rules are based on the speech children hear around them; this is their input or data for analysis. Children listen to the language around them and analyze it to determine the patterns that exist. When they think they have discovered a pattern, they hypothesize a rule to account for it. They add this rule to their growing grammar and use it in constructing utterances. For example, a child's early hypothesis about how to form the past tense of verbs will be to add an allomorph of *-ed.* All past tense verbs would then be constructed with this rule, producing forms such as *holded* and *eated* alongside *needed* and *walked.* Notice that at this point the child would have already learned the rules of when the regular past tense ending is pronounced [d], [t], or [əd]. When children discover that there are forms in the language that do not match those produced by this rule, they modify the rule or add another one to produce the additional forms. Eventually, the child has created and edited his or her own grammar to the point where it matches an adult's grammar. At this point, there are no significant discrepancies between the forms produced by the child and those produced by the adults. Clearly, the child has a complete working grammar all along, even before it is essentially adultlike. The child uses this grammar to produce utterances; when those utterances differ from adult speech, they are reflecting the differences in the two grammars.

Within this framework, children's mistakes are expected to occur and to follow nonrandom patterns. This is because the child is forming utterances according to grammatical rules even though the rules are often different from those that adults use. It is important to note also that active reinforcement by adults about a child's mistakes is not enough to help the child "discover" what is wrong with his or her own utterances; the child must make the connection in his or her own time.

8.1.6 Connectionist Theories

Connectionist theories of language acquisition assume that children learn language by creating neural connections in the brain. A child develops such connections through exposure to language and by using language. Through these connections, the child learns associations between words, meanings, sound sequences, and so on. For example, a child may hear the word *bottle* in different circumstances and establish neural connections every time the word is heard. Such connections can be to the word itself, to the initial sound /b/, to the word *milk,* to what the bottle looks like, to the activity of drinking, and so on. Eventually, all of these connections become the child's mental representation of the meaning and the form of the word (see Section 1.4.7). Connections can have different strengths, and language acquisition involves adjusting the strengths of the connections appropriately. The strength of a connection is dependent on input frequency. For example, if a child hears the word *bottle* more frequently in connection with *milk* than with *water,* then the connection between *bottle* and *milk* will be stronger than that between *bottle* and *water.* Thus, instead of developing abstract rules, according to connectionist theories, children exploit statistical information from linguistic input. Such theories assume that the input children receive is indeed rich enough to learn language without an innate mechanism to invent linguistic rules (though note that the ability to make statistical generalizations must be innate).

To get a better feel for how this theory works and how it differs from other theories, let's look at the acquisition of the past tense of verbs again. The Active Construction of a Grammar Theory assumes that children produce words like *goed* or *growed* because they have formed a rule that tells them to add *-ed* to a verb to form the past tense. Connectionist models assume that the child merely exploits statistical information about forming past tenses. Thus, the child says *goed* and *growed* because the existence of forms like *showed, mowed, towed,* and *glowed* makes this pattern statistically likely.

Evidence for the exploitation of statistics as opposed to the development of abstract rules comes from experiments in which, for example, children create the past tense of nonsense verbs. For instance, when asked to complete the phrase "This man is fringing; Yesterday, he ____," many children create nonsense irregular forms such as *frang* or *frought* instead of the nonsense regular form *fringed.* Such data pose a problem for the Active Construction of a Grammar Theory, but the data can be explained in terms of a connectionist model. If children invent rules and then learn exceptions to the rules, they should produce *fringed* as the past tense of *fring* because it is not one of the learned exceptions. However, if children exploit statistical data, they would be expected to sometimes produce irregular forms because of their exposure to words like *sing, ring,* or *bring.*

Of course, it is possible that children both develop rules and also make use of statistical data. That is, it is possible that acquisition of grammatical rules proceeds according to a hybrid model and that children actively construct a grammar by establishing and exploiting neural connections.

8.1.7   Social Interaction Theory

Social Interaction Theory assumes that children acquire language through social interaction, with older children and adults in particular. This approach holds that children prompt their parents to supply them with the appropriate language experience they need. Thus, children and their language environment are seen as a dynamic system: children need their language environment to improve their social and linguistic communication skills, and the appropriate language environment exists because it is cued by the child. Like those who advocate the Active Construction of Grammar Theory, social interactionists believe that children must develop rules and that they have a predisposition to learn language. However, social interaction theorists place a great deal of emphasis on social interaction and the kind of input that children receive, instead of assuming that simply being exposed to language use will suffice. According to this approach, the ways in which older children and adults talk to infants play a crucial role in how a child acquires language. In many Western societies, speech to infants (**child-directed speech**) is slow and high-pitched and contains many repetitions, simplified syntax, exaggerated intonation, and a simple and concrete vocabulary (see File 8.4). Consider the following examples from Berko Gleason and Bernstein Ratner (1998: 385):

(5)   See the birdie? Look at the birdie! What a pretty birdie!

(6)   Has it come to your attention that one of our better-looking feathered friends is perched upon the windowsill?

When pointing out a bird on the windowsill to an infant, adults and older children are likely to say something like (5) in a slow, high-pitched voice with exaggerated intonation. In addition, they are likely to point at the bird. The social aspect of the interaction involves sharing an observation with the child. All of this helps the child to decode what the speech might mean. No adult would normally point out a bird to an infant by uttering something like (6). Social interactionists believe that the way adults speak to children and interact with children is crucial to acquiring language.

Of course, one of the problems with this theory is that children eventually do acquire the ability to utter and understand sentences like those in (6). While child-directed speech may be crucial early on, it is unclear how long a child must be exposed to it. Furthermore, the characteristics of child-directed speech vary from culture to culture, and we do not at this point know what specific aspects of such speech might, in fact, be crucial.

At the same time, this theory is also not completely incompatible with either of the two previous theories. That is, the types of social interactions that infants have may, in fact, be invaluable to language acquisition, which may develop through neural connections and involve the hypothesizing of particular grammatical rules on the part of the child.

FILE 8.2

First-Language Acquisition:
The Acquisition of Speech Sounds
and Phonology

8.2.1 Physiological Prerequisites of Sound Perception and Production

Before children can begin to speak a language, they must first master several tasks related to the form of language: they must be able to identify the sounds (phonemes) of the language they hear; they must learn how to produce each allophone of these phonemes—the variants of the phoneme that depend on the context in which it occurs (see File 3.2); they must decode the larger strings of sounds that they hear into syllables and words; and they must learn to combine the sounds into larger strings themselves. Below, we discuss the basics of how children learn to perceive and produce speech sounds, as well as some of the experimental techniques that researchers use to study child language acquisition.

a. Identifying Sounds. In order to produce spoken language, infants first need to be able to perceive it. In fact, they are able to perceive many distinctions in language much earlier than they are able to produce them. Since we cannot just ask babies about their perception and receive an answer, special methodologies are needed to determine what they can and cannot perceive. One of the most successful techniques used for studying the abilities of infants up to the age of six months is called **High Amplitude Sucking** (HAS). In this technique, infants are given a special pacifier that is connected to a sound-generating system. Each suck on the pacifier generates a noise, and infants learn quickly that their sucking produces the noise. At first, babies suck often because they are interested in hearing the noise. They lose interest, however, in hearing the same noise over again, and their sucking rate slows down. When this happens, the experimenter changes the sound that the pacifier generates. If the infant sucks faster after the change, we infer that he has recognized the change in sound and is sucking faster to hear the interesting new sound. If the infant does not suck faster, we infer that he could not discriminate between the two sounds.

Another important technique is the **Conditioned Head-Turn Procedure** (HT), usually used with infants between five and eighteen months. This procedure has two phases: conditioning and testing. The infant sits on a parent's lap, watching a display and listening to sounds. During the conditioning phase, the infant learns to associate a change in sound with the activation of visual reinforcers. At first, the visual reinforcers are presented at the same time as the change in sound. Then the visual reinforcers are presented shortly after the change. The infant will begin to anticipate the appearance of the visual reinforcers and look for them before they are activated. During the testing phase, if the infant looks to the visual reinforcers immediately after a change in sound, we infer that the infant has perceived the change in sound and can thus discriminate between the two sounds involved. If the infant does not look to the visual reinforcers, we infer that he did not perceive the change and thus cannot discriminate between the two sounds.

HAS and HT have been used in many studies on infants to determine what they can hear and how they process what they hear. DeCasper and Spence (1986), for example, used HAS to show that babies can hear speech in the womb. The researchers wanted to see whether infants whose mothers had read a Dr. Seuss story aloud during the final six weeks of pregnancy would recognize the story after they were born. They therefore tested a group of infants whose mothers had read them the story, along with a control group of infants whose mothers had not. Within a week of birth, the infants were played recordings of a couple of stories, including the Dr. Seuss one. When the infants who had heard the Dr. Seuss story in the womb were played the recording of that particular story, they modified their sucking rate, but the control group showed no such change. DeCasper and Spence concluded that the infants who modified their sucking rate recognized the story as a new stimulus—that is, they heard it as familiar sounds after hearing the unfamiliar sounds of the other stories. The babies who did not change their sucking rate heard unfamiliar sounds throughout the experiment.

Perception studies have also shown that by the age of four months infants can already distinguish between the production of the vowels [ɑ] and [i]. In one experimental paradigm, infants are shown the mouths of two adult faces, one saying [ɑ], the other one saying [i]. Simultaneously, a tape plays one of the two sounds. When the infants hear an [ɑ], they show a preference by looking at the face saying [ɑ]; when they hear an [i], they show a preference by looking at the face producing the [i]. These findings suggest that infants of about four months of age are able not only to distinguish different vowel qualities but also to use visual cues to determine the kind of articulation involved in producing the sounds. In fact, the infants' own coos differ in these two contexts: they are more [ɑ]-like (or [i]-like, respectively), to match the sound heard and the mouth watched.

Not only are babies born with the ability to hear very slight differences between sounds; they can also hear distinctions between sounds that their parents cannot. For example, sounds that English-speaking adults perceive as a /b/ or a /p/ differ in their **voice onset time** (**VOT**; refer to Section 9.4.2). English-speaking adults perceive bilabial stops with a VOT of 20 ms as a /b/, but those with a VOT of 40 ms as a /p/. Six-month-old infants can also perceive this difference. Studies using HAS or HT have shown, however, that the infants can also perceive the difference between a bilabial stop with a VOT of –60 ms (that is, voicing starts 60 ms before the consonant is released) and a VOT of –20 ms. English-speaking adults don't perceive this difference; rather, they hear both sounds as /b/. In contrast, six-month-old infants show an increase in sucking rate when a recording switches from the first to the second sound. Interestingly, however, by the time they are twelve months old, infants living in an English-speaking environment will have lost the ability to perceive the difference between bilabial stops with a VOT of –60 ms and a VOT of –20 ms. Twelve-month-old infants born to Thai-speaking parents, on the other hand, are still able to differentiate between these sounds, as are Thai-speaking adults.

It seems, then, that at six months, infants are able to perceive phonetic distinctions that correspond to phonemes in many languages. Yet by twelve months they are able to distinguish only between sounds that are phonemic (contrastive) in their native language; that is, the particular sounds that can be used in the language to distinguish words. This means that a twelve-month-old with English-speaking parents can no longer differentiate between a bilabial stop with a VOT of –60 and a VOT of –20 because this ability is not important for distinguishing English words. On the other hand, a twelve-month-old child with Thai-speaking parents can tell these sounds apart because the sounds are important for understanding the meaning of words in Thai. It seems that once infants have figured out the important distinctions of their native language(s), they ignore distinctions that are not important.

In addition to being able to distinguish between phonemes of the language they are acquiring, children also need to figure out where one word ends and the next one begins. This is a difficult task because even in relatively slow speech, adults do not pause after every word. In fact, whole phrases or sentences are often uttered as one continuous stream of speech. Some researchers have suggested that children make use of intonational cues (see File 2.5) to help them segment speech. For example, many words in English are stressed on the first syllable. If children born to English-speaking parents take a stressed syllable to indicate the beginning of a word, they would be correct more often than not. A child using this strategy would segment the stream *What a pretty birdie* into *What-a, pretty* and *birdie.* However, this cannot be the only strategy a child uses because not all English words are stressed on the first syllable. Another approach to word segmentation assumes that children make use of statistical cues. For example, if a child hears sentences like *What a pretty birdie. Look! The birdie is flying,* he or she can use the fact that [bɹ] always seems to be followed by [di] to arrive at the conclusion that [bɹdi] is probably a word.

b. Producing Sounds. A child's first vocalizations are present at the very beginning of life. (Everyone knows how adept babies are at crying!) Within a few weeks after birth, a child begins to coo, producing sequences of vowel-like sounds. The child uses these cooing and gurgling noises to indicate contentment and pleasure, or at least this is how most adults interpret these sounds.

Since an infant's tongue is relatively large compared to the size of its vocal tract, the front of the tongue easily makes contact with the roof of the mouth, and a baby is very likely to produce coos that sound vaguely palatal, like the adult phonemes /j/ or /ɲ/. From very early on, the baby "practices" sounds of various kinds. What the baby has to learn are the **articulatory gestures** involved in producing a particular sound (e.g., bringing both lips together to produce a bilabial sound), as well as the timing relationships between these gestures (i.e., starting vocal-fold vibration for voicing a sound, opening the mouth, lowering the velum to allow air passage through the nasal cavity, raising the tongue for an alveolar closure, etc.) (see Files 2.2–2.4). The young child has to practice the execution of the motor programs that underlie speech production. This might seem to be an easy task, but, by analogy, if you were to try patting your right hand on your left knee and rubbing your left hand in circles on your right knee, it would probably take a bit of practice to get the different movements coordinated. Learning to speak is just as hard or harder for infants, since they have to learn to gain control over the muscles in their speech organs and to coordinate the execution of articulatory movements. Therefore, a child's production of speech will generally be slower and more variable than that of an adult.

8.2.2 Babbling

At the age of four to six months or so, children in all cultures begin to **babble,** producing sequences of vowels and consonants if they are acquiring spoken language, or producing hand movements if they are acquiring signed language. Children acquiring signed languages babble by moving their fingers in repetitive rhythmic ways that are very similar to the hand motions that will be needed for making actual signs. Some linguists assume that babies babble to practice the muscle coordination needed to produce language. In the case of spoken languages, this involves the opening and closing movement of the jaw and manipulating other articulators; in the case of signed languages, it involves hand and finger coordination. The following discussion focuses on babbling by children acquiring spoken language. However, apart from the modality, there seems to be no cognitive difference between the babbling of children learning spoken and signed languages.

As mentioned above, a baby's tongue is relatively large compared to the size of its oral cavity. Since the tongue is attached to the lower jaw, as the lower jaw moves up, the tongue moves up with it. For this reason, it is very likely that the infant will produce vaguely palatal sounds like [ɲ] or [j] as the tongue moves up near the hard palate. Since the lower lip is also attached to the jaw, labials such as [b] and [m] occur frequently, too. When the jaw goes down and the tongue lies on the jaw, the infant is very likely to produce the vowel sound [ɑ]. These are, of course, not the only sounds that an infant produces, but they are likely sounds in the very beginning. Also, keep in mind that babbling a certain sequence of sounds is not a conscious process. It is probably accidental if the infant produces a syllable like [ti], since the tongue tip has to contact the alveolar ridge while the mouth is open.

Repeated or **canonical babbling** starts around the age of seven to ten months. The continual repetition of syllables helps the infant practice a sequence of consonant and vowel sounds. For example, a common canonical babble like [mɑmɑmɑmɑ] involves the sequence of a bilabial nasal consonant followed by a low vowel. Since babies breathe mostly through their noses, the velum is open already, and producing an [m] "just" involves closing the lips. However, practicing a sequence consisting of a nasal consonant and a non-nasal vowel also helps practice working on when the velum has to lower and open relative to when the mouth opens for the production of the vowel. Between about ten and twelve months of age, infants begin to produce a variety of speech sounds, even sounds that are not part of the language the child is acquiring natively. At this age, babbling is no longer canonical. Instead of repeating the same syllables as in [mɑmɑmɑmɑ], the infant strings together different syllables as in [bugɑbimo]. This is called **variegated babbling.**

Though babbling is far from being language, it resembles adult language in a number of important respects. For one thing, babbled sequences are not linked to immediate biological needs like food or physical comfort and are thus frequently uttered in isolation for sheer pleasure. Moreover, babbled sequences have many physical characteristics of adult speech. For example, syllables can be identified in a sequence like [gɔŋgɔŋ], and often there is a clear alternation between consonants and vowels. In longer sequences, intonation patterns that might be interpreted in some languages as questions can be discerned. However, the resemblance to adult speech stops here, since there is no evidence for the existence of more abstract structures like sentences or even single words. Only later does the child come to associate word meanings with vocal noises.

Although precisely how babbling relates to language development is not yet clearly understood, psychologists and linguists have suggested that babbling serves at least two functions: as practice for later speech and as a social reward. The first function is intuitively plausible, because the fine motor movements necessary for accurate articulation are exercised extensively during babbling. Indeed, babbling children of about one year of age produce a great variety of sounds, mainly practicing sequences of consonants and vowels.

The second possible function, that children babble for social reward, also seems plausible. Parents often encourage their babies to continue babbling by responding with smiles or speech or nonsense "babbling" of their own, giving the child important experience with the social aspects and rewards of speech. Evidence for the importance of the social factor in babbling comes from the study of severely neglected children, who may begin to babble at approximately the same age as children reared in normal settings but will stop if not encouraged by their parents or caretakers.

It remains to be explained why babbling occurs at more or less the same time in all children, since children receive encouragement for their efforts in unequal doses. According to one hypothesis, children babble because language development involves a process of biological maturation. Thus babbling occurs automatically when the relevant structures in the brain reach a critical level of development. If all children have brains that develop at comparable rates, the universality of babbling is no longer surprising.

Dramatic evidence for this hypothesis comes from some of the children studied by biologist Eric Lenneberg. These children had vocal passages that had become so narrow because of swelling caused by various diseases that they were in danger of choking to death. Breathing could be restored only by constructing an alternative route that bypassed the mouth; this was accomplished by inserting tubes in the trachea (air pipe) through an opening in the neck. Under such conditions, babbling and any other vocalizations are prevented, since air never reaches the vocal cords. Yet Lenneberg observed that when children of babbling age underwent this operation, they produced the babbling sounds typical of their age as soon as the tubing was removed. The behavior of these children demonstrates that babbling is possible when the brain is ready, even if physical limitations prevent any real practice.

8.2.3 Phonological Acquisition

When an eighteen-month-old child attempts to pronounce the word *water,* he or she might say [wɑwɑ], a pronunciation that is quite different from the adult's model. A child's pronunciation of the word *that* may sound like [dæt]. Differences in pronunciations like these may persist for some time, despite drilling by the child's parents or caretakers and even despite the child's own realization that his or her pronunciation does not quite match the adults' pronunciation. All children, regardless of what language they are acquiring natively, make mistakes like these before they have mastered the phonological system of their native language. Yet such errors reveal that they have already learned a great deal, because the errors are systematic, that is, rule-governed, rather than random. In roughly two and a half more years, their speech will resemble that of their parents in all important respects.

It is important to keep in mind that adults analyze the speech of children with reference to their own adult system. Child speech is therefore analyzed as imperfect and full of errors according to the adult's model of grammar. If you listen to young children speak, you will notice that although they try to approximate the forms and pronunciations that they hear around them, many of the sounds they produce do not quite match the adult form. It takes a long time for a child to gain absolute control over the individual movements of the articulators and the timing of these gestures. For example, it is difficult for a young child to produce a consonant sequence like [dɹ] as it occurs in the word *drum.* The child may say something like [dwʌm], which sounds close enough to make an adult understand what is meant, especially if the child is pointing to a drum at the same time.

A major task in the acquisition of phonology involves understanding the word as a link between sound and meaning (see File 1.4). Around the age of eighteen months, children learn and ask for the names of objects in their environment. When children first acquire the concept of a word, their first attempts at production show tremendous variability in pronunciation. Some may be perfect productions; others may be so distorted that they are comprehensible only to the child's closest companions. Some children vary considerably in their pronunciations from one occasion to the next, while others consistently use a "wrong" sound relative to the adult speech model, saying, for example, [wɑɪt] for *right,* [wɛd] for *red,* or [əwɑʊnd] for *around.*

Children initially appear to regard an entire word as if it were a single sound (a sound that can vary somewhat). However, as their vocabulary expands between fifteen and twenty-one months of age, keeping track of a large store of independent sounds becomes very difficult for them to manage. So in order to learn more words, children must begin to break words into a smaller number of simpler units, which are sounds that can be used in different combinations to make up many other words. That is, they arrive at the idea of a word as a sequence of phonemes whose pronunciation is systematic and predictable. In the course of learning a language natively, children must acquire the complete set of phonemes as well as the set of phonological processes found in the language of the adults in their surroundings.

When children learn the phonemes of their native language, they first master sounds that differ maximally from one another. Thus it is no accident that the first meaningful word learned in many languages is often [mɑ] or [pɑ]. When a bilabial stop or nasal is pronounced, the passage of air in the mouth is completely blocked, but the vocal tract is wide open in the low back vowel [ɑ]. Thus, these two sounds are maximally different because one is a consonant (C) and one is a vowel (V). This kind of CV-syllable structure or template appears to be the preferred structure in young children's productions. Only later will they produce consonant clusters, such as [sp] in words like *spill* or [tɹ] as in *tree,* and syllable-final consonants, such as [t] in *cat.* Final consonants are often omitted in children's productions. It is even later before a child will learn to produce longer words or utterances that consist of more than one syllable. Very often, consonants like [l] and [ɹ], which share many properties of vowels and are thus difficult to distinguish from vowels, are mastered last.

Even though children master CV sequences early on, we often find that in longer words, some CV syllables are deleted. In the speech sample in (1), at least one syllable is omitted from every word.

(1) banana [___nænə]   granola [___owə]   potato [___deɪdoʊ]

We might wonder why children leave out the first syllable in these examples and whether this first syllable is in any way different from the other syllables in the word. An answer to this question is that since all of these first syllables are unstressed, they are not very perceptually prominent. In English there is usually one syllable (or vowel) within a word that is somewhat louder and more prominent in relation to the other vowels in that word. This is the vowel with primary stress (see File 2.5).

However, infants may also make use of the stress pattern of a stream of speech to determine where a word ends and the next one begins. This is a big problem for the infant to solve because the baby has only a very limited knowledge of the structure of the language's vocabulary. Babies and young children might begin to master the difficult task of finding the boundaries between words by looking for the most stressed syllable or the most prominent part of the word, since in English the first syllable of a word is often stressed. Such a strategy allows the infant to correctly determine word boundaries more often than not. However, this strategy does not always guarantee the correct result or the correct analysis of where one word begins and where it ends. Consider the word *banana*. This word consists of three syllables: [bə.næ.nə]. The first and the third syllables are not stressed, but the second one is. In this case, a child might unconsciously look for the most stressed syllable and believe it to be the beginning of a word. If the child has already learned that a word can consist of more than one syllable and generalizes that the most stressed syllable is the beginning of the word *banana*, then it makes sense that he or she will incorrectly think that the word is actually [næ.nə].

To summarize, when children acquire the phonological system of their native language, they must master the fine-muscle coordination necessary for producing a rich variety of sounds, learn that combinations of sounds are associated with particular meanings, and eventually realize that their pronunciations of words must consistently match those of adults. Learning a language natively does not result from a conscious learning strategy spontaneously invented by children or from a teaching method devised by adults. Instead, it is a consequence of the human brain's innate capacity for learning language. Children of all backgrounds, provided they have enough input, will learn a language and master the phonological system of their native language. The acquisition of phonology appears to involve a process of biological maturation and is in many aspects like motor development: first the child babbles to practice for later speech, then the articulatory sequences become longer and more complex, and the child is able to pronounce "difficult" consonant clusters. Nevertheless, the adult phonological system is learned only when the child is given models to imitate as well as encouragement.

8.2.4 Language Development from Birth to Twelve Months

The table in (2) provides an overview of infants' language abilities from birth to twelve months of age.

(2) Infants' language abilities, birth to twelve months

Approximate Age	Language and Communicative Developments
1 month	• Cry to express displeasure and make other throaty sounds. • Look at their parents when being talked to.
2–3 months	• Turn their eyes and later their heads to look for sounds and voices. • Cry differently depending on their need and begin to make other noises, like gurgling, squealing, and chuckling. • Smile and make noises in response to familiar faces and voices. • Begin cooing, especially palatal-like sounds like [j], [ɲ].
4–5 months	• Begin to make consonant sounds in addition to their vowel-like cooing, especially sounds like [m], [b]. • Can laugh and begin to try to copy sounds they hear.
6 months	• Respond to sounds by making sounds. • String vowels together in vocalizing and also produce syllables, especially sequences such as [mɑ], [bɑ], [dɑ], [di].[1] • Practice turn-taking and respond to their own name.
7–9 months	• Respond to familiar words and try to copy sounds and gestures. • Begin repeated or canonical babbling, including strings like [mɑmɑmɑ] and [dɑdɑdɑ]. • Begin to use intonational patterns in their babbling. • Understand "no" when directed at them and begin to respond to simple verbal commands.
10–11 months	• Begin variegated babbling, with sequences like [bugɑbimo]. • Understand "bye-bye" and can wave "bye." • *Mama* and *dada* begin to become real words meaningfully associated with mother and father.
12 months	• May say a few words and exclamations in addition to *mama* and *dada*, such as *no, go, bye, uh-oh!* • Can use other simple gestures, such as shaking their head for "no." • Can understand the meanings of several words and recognize objects by name, and can respond to simple requests.

[1]Notice that these sounds are often similar to the words for *mother* and *father* in many languages. While many parents think it is a sign of their child's developing genius that they learn to produce *mommy* and *daddy* as their first words, it is quite likely that the form of these words is simply taken from the first sounds a child can recognizably make!

FILE **8.3**

....

First-Language Acquisition: The Acquisition of Morphology, Syntax, and Word Meaning

8.3.1   The Acquisition of Morphology and Syntax

It is not until about the age of twelve months that a child will begin to consistently produce words of the language he or she is learning. It is at this stage that we can begin to examine the development of syntax and morphology in children's speech.

It is important to note, however, that there is much variation in the age range during which children acquire words, fundamental cognitive concepts, and so on. The fact that a child reaches certain stages more quickly or more slowly than average does not mean that the child is necessarily more or less intelligent or well-developed: it is normal for children to vary in this regard. The ages associated with the different "stages" of language acquisition are only averages. There is also variability in terms of children's behavior. While the term "stage" seems to imply that a child abruptly changes his or her behavior when moving from one stage to the next, this is not actually the case. A child can have behaviors associated with different stages at the same time. Finally, it's important to keep in mind that stages are not specific to children acquiring English: all children tend to go through the same stages no matter what language they are acquiring. The following sections describe some of these stages of language acquisition.

8.3.2   The One-Word Stage

The first stage of morphological acquisition usually involves the child's producing single words in isolation. These first words uttered by a one-year-old child typically name people, objects, pets, and other familiar and important parts of his or her environment. The child's vocabulary soon comes to include verbs and other useful words (including *no,* *gimme,* and *mine*). Often a phrase used by adults will become a single word in the speech of a child, such as *all-gone* and *whasat?* ('what's that?'). The single words produced at this stage are used as more than just labels for objects or events; they may be used for naming, commenting, requesting, inquiring, and so on. This level of development has been called the **holophrastic stage** (a **holophrase** being a one-word sentence). Children at this phase of linguistic development are limited to one word at a time in their production, but they understand and probably intend the meaning of more than a single word. Furthermore, the intonation children use on their one-word utterances may be that of a question, an ordinary or emphatic statement, or demand. If children do consistently use these adult-like sentence intonation patterns (and researchers disagree about whether they do or not), *holophrastic* would seem an especially appropriate name for this phase.

8.3.3   The Two-Word Stage

Between approximately eighteen and twenty-four months of age, children begin to use two-word utterances. At first the utterances may seem to be simply two one-word sentences produced one right after the other. There may be a pause between them, and each word may bear a separate intonation contour. Before long, however, the two words are produced without pausing and with a single intonational pattern.

Children at this stage do not just produce any two words in any order; rather, they adopt a consistent set of word orders that convey an important part of the meaning of their utterances. At this level of development, the structure of utterances is determined by semantic relationships, rather than adult syntactic ones. Word order is used to express these semantic relations; it is not until later that additional syntactic devices are added to the basic word-order rules. Most of the utterances produced by a child at this stage will express a semantic relation like one of the following:

(1) agent + action   baby sleep
    action + object   kick ball
    action + location   sit chair
    entity + location   teddy bed
    possessor + possession   Mommy book
    entity + attribute   block red
    demonstrative + entity   this shoe

Words such as *more* and *'nother* may be used as modifiers of nouns (*more juice, 'nother cup*) to indicate or request recurrence. *Here* and *there* may be used as deictic terms (Section 8.3.5). Some children at this stage of development also use pronouns. For the most part, however, their speech lacks function morphemes and function words, that is, prepositions, auxiliary verbs, determiners, and inflectional affixes (see File 4.1).

Because of the omission of function words (which continues even after the child begins to produce more than two words at a time), the speech of young children is often called **telegraphic.** When you send a telegram or run a classified ad, every word you include costs you money. Therefore, you put in only the words you really need, and not the ones that carry no new information. Children follow the same principle of economy. The words they use and the order in which they use them convey the relevant information; function morphemes are not, strictly speaking, necessary for the child to effectively communicate ideas. Eventually, children do acquire the full set of function morphemes of their language.

8.3.4 Later Stages of Development

Three-word utterances are initially formed by combining or expanding two-word utterances. Two two-word strings with a common element may be combined; for example, *Daddy cookie* and *eat cookie* may be combined to form *Daddy eat cookie*. A two-word utterance may also be expanded from within, when, for example, *throw ball* becomes *throw red ball*. That is, one of the elements of a two-term relation itself becomes a two-term relation.

There is no clear-cut three-word stage of language acquisition, however. Once children are capable of combining more than two words into an utterance, they may use three, four, five, or even more words at a time. These longer utterances are syntactically organized, rather than being just semantically organized sequences of words like those produced in the two-word stage.

Children's speech at this stage is still telegraphic, including only content morphemes and words. Gradually a child will begin to include function morphemes in his or her utterances, but these function morphemes are not acquired randomly. Instead, children acquire them in a remarkably consistent order. For example, in English, the present progressive verbal suffix *-ing* (*she walking*) appears in children's speech well before the past tense marker *-ed* (*she walked*), which in turn is acquired a little before the third-person present tense marker *-s* (*she walks*). Around the time *-ing* appears, so do the prepositions *in* and *on*. Three homophonous morphemes, all phonologically /-z/, are acquired at different times. First, children use the plural morpheme -s (e.g., *shoes*); later they acquire the possessive -'s (*Mommy's*); and finally the third-person present tense morpheme mentioned above is added to verbs. Articles (*a* and *the*) are acquired fairly early, but forms of the (highly irregular) verb *be* appear only at a relatively late stage.

a. Plurals. Recall that the plural morpheme -s is acquired quite early by children—in fact, it is usually one of the very first function morphemes to appear, along with *in, on,* and *-ing.* That does not mean, however, that very young children have complete mastery over the plural system of English.

At first, no plural marker is used at all. Nouns appear only in their singular forms (e.g., *man*). Next, irregular plural forms may appear for a while—that is, a child may say *men* instead of *man,* using the same form adults do. Then the child discovers the morpheme -s and suddenly applies it uniformly to all nouns. In some cases this involves **overgeneralization** of the rule of plural formation; for example, the plural of *man* becomes *mans.* During this stage the child often leaves nouns ending in sibilants (e.g., *nose, house, church,* etc.) in their singular forms. Once children discover the generalization about how the plurals of these nouns are formed, they may go through a brief period during which [-əz] is added to all nouns, giving not only *houses* but also *man-es* or even *mans-es.* This soon passes, however, and the child produces all plurals correctly, except for the irregular ones they haven't encountered yet, of course (such as *oxen* or *sheep* or *cacti*). These are learned gradually and may not be fully acquired by the time the child is five years old. When irregular plurals first appear in a young child's speech, they are simply isolated forms that fit into no pattern. Once they are learned, however, they are exceptions to the child's regular process of plural formation, just as they are for an adult.

b. Negatives. Children also go through a series of stages in learning to produce negative sentences. At first they simply put the word *no* in front of a sentence to negate its meaning, for example, *no baby sleep* or *no I drink milk.* As a matter of fact, this word shows a fairly high occurrence in children's speech, even if children might not initially understand what the word means. Next, they insert a negative word, most often a word like *no, not, can't,* or *don't,* between the subject and the verb of a sentence, resulting in *baby no sleep* or *I no drink milk.* (It is interesting to note that at this stage, *can't, won't,* and *don't* are unanalyzed negative words; that is, the child doesn't parse them as containing two morphemes: an auxiliary verb and a consistent negative marker. The auxiliaries *can, will,* and *do* are not acquired until later; even three-year-olds still tend to have trouble with them.)

The child continues to develop a more adult system of negation, but for a while he or she will use words such as *something* and *somebody* in negated sentences, producing results such as *I don't see something.* Later these words are replaced by *nothing* and *nobody.* Finally, if the child's adult models use the forms *anything* and *anybody,* the child eventually acquires these words.

c. Interrogatives. Very young children can produce questions only by using a rising intonation, rather than by using a particular syntactic structure. The meaning of *Mommy cup?* or *more ride?* would be quite clear when produced with the same question intonation that adults use. Later, at around three years, children begin to use *can, will,* and other auxiliary verbs in yes/no questions, using the appropriate word order. That is, the auxiliary precedes the subject in these questions, as in, for example, *Are you sad?* At this point, however, children still fail to use adult word order in questions that use a *wh-* word (such as *what, who,* or *why*). They follow instead the question word with a sentence in normal declarative word order: *Why you are sad?* Eventually, of course, they learn to invert the subject and the verb in these constructions, as adult speakers do.

The fact that children produce words and sentences like *foots* or *I don't want something* or *Where he is going?* provides clear evidence that they are not merely imitating the adult speakers around them. What we as adults perceive and interpret as "mistakes" are not random but reflect the system of grammar that children are in the process of constructing for themselves.

8.3.5 The Acquisition of Word Meaning

When children hear a word for the first time, they don't know what makes the use of the word appropriate. Consider a preschooler whose teacher chose teams by dividing the class in half and asked each team to sit on a blanket. At home later that day, the student got annoyed because her younger brother kept crawling onto her blanket while she was watching television. "He won't stay way from my team," she complained. With a single exposure to the word *team*, this child formed a definition something like 'a group of people on a blanket'—a reasonable, but incorrect, guess.

Though this trial-and-error process may seem laborious from an adult perspective, consider what every normal child is able to accomplish by using it: children produce their first words at age one, and by age six they have a vocabulary approaching 14,000 words. Simple arithmetic will reveal that children master an average of ten words a day starting from their first birthday. This feat might suggest that children learn the vocabulary of their native language in a more systematic fashion than is apparent from the above example. While it is not possible to speak of particular stages in the acquisition of word meaning like those identified in the acquisition of phonology, morphology, and syntax, linguists have determined that the acquisition of word meaning does follow certain patterns. First of all, the order in which words are learned reflects the intrinsic complexity of the concepts involved. Second, children's initial meanings of words do not deviate randomly from those of adults, but rather they are usually related to and progress toward adult meanings in systematic ways. For example, many nouns are used to refer to sets of objects with something in common (e.g., the adult word *chair* is used appropriately with desk chairs, rocking chairs, easy chairs, and so on, because all of these things can be sat on), but sometimes children may select the wrong unifying characteristic(s), as happens in complexive concepts, overextensions, and underextensions.

a. Complexive Concepts. Sometimes, not only will a child associate a wrong or incomplete set of unifying characteristics with a word, but she will also seem to try out different characteristics each time she uses the word. For example, a child might learn that the word *doggie* refers to dogs and then use it to name other furry things, like soft slippers, and on later occasions, she may use *doggie* to refer to things that move by themselves, like birds, toads, and small toy cars. When a child associates different characteristics with the meaning of a word on successive uses, thereby creating a set of objects that do not have any particular unifying characteristic, we say that she has produced a **complexive concept**. The linguist William Labov reports another example of a complexive concept. His one-year-old son used *oo* to refer to the music produced by his brother's rock and roll band; on later occasions *oo* was applied to the group's jackets, their musical instruments, their cigarettes, and then other people's cigarettes. Note that successive uses of the word tend to pick out objects with similar properties, but the class of objects as a whole has little in common. Complexive concepts serve to form a loose bond between items associated in the child's experience and represent a primitive conception of word meaning.

b. Overextensions. When a child extends the range of a word's meaning beyond that typically used by adults, we say that he has produced an **overextension**. For example, one American-English-speaking child called specks of dirt, dust, small insects, and bread crumbs *fly*; another gave *moon* as the name for cakes, round marks, postmarks, and the letter <O>. A third child overextended the word *ticktock*, using it to refer to clocks, watches, parking meters, and a dial on a set of scales.

At first glance, the set of objects named in overextensions may look as varied and random as those in complexive concepts. In fact, children of age two or so frequently have overextensions and complexive concepts in their speech at the same time. But closer inspection reveals that the concept defined in an overextension does not shift from one occasion to the next. In the above examples, the child's definition of *moon* is applied consistently to pick out any round thing. Likewise, *fly* referred to any small, possibly mobile object. The concept underlying the use of *ticktock* was perhaps more complex, but all of the objects in the child's list contained a dial with small marks.

Usually, the common properties of objects included in the overextension of a word are perceptual features like shape, size, color, or taste. In this respect, the child's strategy for defining a word resembles that of adults, since adults also define words in terms of perceptual features. But if the child's strategy of defining words now resembles that of adults, what misunderstanding is responsible for the overextensions?

Linguist Eve Clark offers one plausible explanation. In her view, the child who uses overgeneralizations has only an incomplete definition of the adult word. The child who calls dogs, cats, slippers, fur coats, and rugs *doggie* has recognized the significance of being furry, but the adult definition mentions more properties; for example, dogs are four-legged. Once the child grasps this property as part of the definition of *dog,* she will no longer overextend the word *doggie* to slippers, rugs, and fur coats. Eventually the child becomes aware of all properties in a definition, which enables her to narrow down the class of objects named by *doggie* to just those observed in adult usage.

c. Underextensions. An **underextension** is the application of a word to a smaller set of objects than is appropriate for mature adult speech. Careful study reveals that, although less commonly noticed than overextensions, underextensions are at least equally frequent in the language of children.

Underextensions also occur among older, school-aged children when they encounter category names like *fruit* or *mammal*. Since most people are unsure of the properties that constitute the definitions of these words, they prefer to think of them in terms of their most ordinary members; thus for many Americans, dogs are the most ordinary mammals and apples are the most ordinary fruits. Children are surprised to learn that whales are mammals, or that olives are fruits, because these deviate so profoundly from the ordinary members of their categories. As a result, children underextend the words *mammal* and *fruit,* failing to apply these labels to the unusual members.

Why do children's first definitions fall into the three classes that we have discussed? Each class represents a different strategy for seeking out the adult definition of a word. Complexive concepts are the most basic and are present in a child's speech for only a short period of time before being replaced by overextensions and underextensions. Psychologists have determined that a child who overgeneralizes a word tries to make the most out of a limited vocabulary. Accordingly, overgeneralizations decrease dramatically after age two, when children experience a rapid vocabulary expansion. The opposite strategy underlies the formation of underextensions: children attempt to be as conservative as possible in their use of language, with the result that they perceive restrictions on the use of words not imposed by adults. By systematically over- and underextending the range of a concept, the child eventually arrives at the adult meaning.

The words discussed so far have been limited to those that denote the members of a set of objects. For example, the word *chair* is used correctly when it is applied to the set that includes objects as different as straight chairs, folding chairs, and rocking chairs. The same skill, identifying members of a set, is required for understanding some types of verbs. For example, all people walk differently, but native speakers of English use the word *walk* correctly when they realize that these minor differences are irrelevant.

But not all words in a language involve the identification of sets. In fact, the mastery of a working vocabulary in any human language requires a wide range of intellectual skills, some easier and some more difficult than those required for grasping the meaning of common nouns and verbs. As an example of a relatively easy concept, consider what is required for understanding proper names: one must simply point out a single individual and attach a label, like *John* or *Daddy*. Because it is easier to associate a label with a single individual than to name a set with common properties, children master the comprehension of proper nouns first, sometimes when they are as young as six to nine months old.

In contrast, a **relational term** like *large* or *small* constitutes a relatively complex concept. (Refer to Section 6.4.3.) The correct use of words like these requires that two things be kept in mind: the absolute size of the object in question and its position on a scale of similar objects. For example, an elephant that is six feet tall at the shoulders may be small as far as elephants go, but a dog of the same height would be huge. Five- and six-year-old children are often unable to make the shift in perspective necessary for using relational words appropriately. In one well-known experiment documenting this conclusion, children were engaged in a pretend tea party with dolls and an adult observer. The adult gave the child an ordinary juice glass and asked the child if it was large or small. Though all of the children in the study agreed that the glass was small from their own perspective, it appeared ridiculously large when placed on the toy table around which the dolls were seated. Nevertheless, the youngest children were still inclined to say that the glass was small when asked about its size with respect to its new context.

Another difficult concept underlies **deictic expressions,** which are words referring to personal, temporal, or spatial aspects of an utterance and whose meaning depends on the context in which the word is used (refer to Section 7.1.3). For example, a speaker may use *here* or *this* to point out objects that may be close to him, while *there* and *that* are appropriate only when the objects are relatively far away. But since there are no absolute distances involved in the correct use of these deictic expressions, children have difficulty determining when the 'close' terms are to be preferred over the 'far' terms. As with relational terms, it is necessary to take into account the size of the object pointed to. Thus a thirty-story building six feet in front of us is close enough to be called *this building,* but an ant removed from us by the same distance is far enough away to be called *that ant.*

Many verbs are conceptually more complex than most nouns. For example, every time someone *gives* something, someone else *takes* it; and every time someone *buys* an item, somebody else *sells* that item. Thus, every event of *giving* or *buying* is also an event of *taking* or *selling,* respectively. However, speakers usually don't talk about such events using both verbs. For example, people will probably say a sentence such as *Peter bought the car from Mike* or *Mike sold the car to Peter,* but not both sentences. So children need to figure out that both sentences refer to the same event without ever hearing both sentences describing the event. Furthermore, many common verbs like *think* or *believe* are abstract, referring to events that cannot be observed. Some researchers believe that verbs' greater conceptual complexity is one of the reasons why verbs are learned later than nouns.

Common and proper nouns, relational terms, deictic expressions and verbs do not exhaust the range of concepts mastered by children, but they do illustrate the variety of tasks involved in acquiring the vocabulary of a first language. Linguists can examine the evidence from the acquisition of word meaning and find support for two fundamental hypotheses: that some concepts are more complex than others and that the acquisition of language requires a considerable exercise of intelligence.

8.3.6 Overview: Language Abilities from Twelve Months to Four Years

The table in (2) provides an overview of children's language abilities from twelve months to four years of age.

(2) Children's language abilities, twelve months to four years

Approximate Age	Language and Communicative Developments
12–18 months	• Continue to increase vocabulary, adding verbs and other useful words, such as *no*, *gimme*, *mine*; can produce 5–50 words. • Can produce only one word at a time, but understand and may intend more than that; use a lot of repetition. • Still babble a lot, but with longer sequences and complex intonational patterns. • Often produce holophrases, such as *all-gone* and *whatsat?*, and may be able to use consistent intonational patterns for questions, statements, or demands.
18–24 months	• Begin to use two-word utterances with a single intonational pattern. • Structure utterances by semantic relationships, such as agent + action *baby sleep*, or possessor + possession *Mommy book*, rather than adult syntax. • May use noun modifiers such as *more* or *'nother*, as well as deictics like *here* and *there*. • Generally do not produce function morphemes and function words. • Can produce 50–100 words and understand several hundred or more.
2 years	• Can produce short sentences and ask and answer simple questions. • Begin to use pronouns, though some are often still confused (e.g., *I* vs. *you*). • Can follow 2-step directions. • Can point to things or pictures when they are named.
3 years	• Understands words like prepositions *in*, *on*, *under*, etc. • Can use some pronouns correctly and begin to use plurals and past tense forms. • Can use hundreds of words, and understand several hundred more. • Can put together 2–3 sentences at a time. • Begin to ask a lot of questions.
4 years	• Can correctly use subject vs. object pronouns and follow other basic rules of grammar. • Can tell stories and use language for many functions. • Can consistently use regular plurals, possessives, and simple past tense forms. • Begin to use some irregular plurals and past tense verb forms. • Utterances are 80–90% intelligible, even to strangers.

FILE 8.4

How Adults Talk to Young Children

8.4.1 Talking to Children

When people talk to one another, their general goal is to get listeners to understand what they are saying, as was illustrated by the communication chain in File 1.2. This goal applies just as much when listeners are young children as when they are adults. The problem is that young children know very little about the structure and function of the language adults use to communicate with each other. As a result, adult speakers often modify their speech to help children understand them. Speech directed at children is called **infant-directed speech** or **child-directed speech**.

How adults talk to children is influenced by three things. First, adults have to make sure that children realize that an utterance is being addressed to them and not to someone else. To do this, adults can use a name, speak in a special tone of voice, or even touch the child to get his attention. Second, once they have the child's attention, they must choose concepts that maximize the child's chances of understanding what is being said. For example, adults are unlikely to discuss philosophy but very likely to talk about what the child is doing, looking at, or playing with at that moment. Third, adults choose a particular style of speaking that they think will be most beneficial to the child. They can talk quickly or slowly, use short sentences or long ones, and so on. Children are thus presented with a specially tailored model of language use, adjusted to fit, as far as possible, what they appear to understand. Each of these three factors will be addressed in turn below.

8.4.2 How Adults Get Children to Pay Attention

Speakers depend on their listeners being cooperative and listening when they are spoken to. But when the listeners are children, adult speakers normally have to work a bit harder to ensure that this happens. They use **attention getters** to tell children which utterances are addressed to them rather than to someone else, and hence which utterances they ought to be listening to. And they use **attention holders** whenever they have more than one thing to say, for example, when telling a story.

Attention getters and attention holders fall into two broad classes. The first consists of names and exclamations. For example, adults often use the child's name at the beginning of an utterance, as in *Ned, there's a car*. Even four-year-olds know that this is an effective way to get a two-year-old's attention. Or, instead of the child's name, adults use exclamations like *Look!* or *Hey!* as a preface to an utterance that they want the child to pay attention to. The second class of attention getters consists of modulations that adults use to distinguish utterances addressed to young children from utterances addressed to other listeners. One of the most noticeable is the high-pitched voice adults use for talking to small children. When the linguist Olga Garnica compared recordings of English-speaking adults talking to two-year-olds, five-year-olds, and adults in the same setting (1977), she found that when talking to children, adults use a wider pitch range: the range of the adults' voices was widest with the youngest children, next widest with the five-year-olds, and narrowest with other adults. These results are consistent with the findings of the psychologist Anne Fernald (1992), who found that in various cultures, speech directed to children is usually higher pitched and shows more pitch excursion (variation) compared to speech addressing adults.

Another modulation adults use is whispering. If children are sitting on their laps or standing right next to them, adults will speak directly into their ears so it is clear they are intended to listen. Garnica observed that all the mothers in her study on occasion whispered to two-year-olds, a few whispered to five-year-olds, but none whispered to adults.

Not all attention getters and attention holders are linguistic. Speakers often rely on gestures as well and may touch a child's shoulder or cheek, for example, as they begin talking. They also use gestures to hold a child's attention and frequently look at and point to objects they name or describe.

8.4.3   What Adults Say to Young Children

Adults both observe and impose the Cooperative Principle (see File 7.2) when they talk to young children. They make what they say relevant, talking about the "here and now" of the child's world. They encourage children to take their turns and contribute to the conversation. And they make sure that children make their contributions truthful by correcting them, if necessary.

a. The "Here and Now." Adults talk to young children mainly about the "here and now." They make running commentaries on what children do, either anticipating their actions—for example, *Build me a tower now,* said just as a child picks up a box of building blocks—or describing what has just happened: *That's right, pick up the blocks,* said just after a child has done so. Adults talk about the objects children show interest in. They name them (*That's a puppy*), describe their properties (*He's very soft and furry*), and talk about relations between objects (*The puppy's in the basket*). In talking about the "here and now," usually whatever is directly under the child's eyes, adults are very selective about the words they use. They seem to be guided by the following assumptions:

(1) • Some words are easier for children to pronounce than others.
     • Some words are more useful for children than others.
     • Some words are hard to understand and best avoided.

Most languages contain "baby talk," words that are considered appropriate in talking only to very young children. For example, adult speakers of English often replace the word for an animal with the word for the sound it makes, as in *meow* and *woofwoof* instead of *cat* and *dog,* or with a diminutive form of the adult word, like *kitty*(-*cat*) or *doggie.* As one would expect, not all types of words have equivalent baby-talk words; instead, the domains in which baby-talk words are found overlap considerably with the domains young children first talk about. They include kinship terms and nicknames (such as *mommy, daddy*); the child's bodily functions and routines (*wee-wee, night-night*); names of animals; games and toys (*peek-a-boo, choo-choo*); and a few general qualities (such as *uh-oh!* for disapproval). Adults appear to use baby-talk words because they seem to be easier for children to pronounce. This assumption may well have some basis in fact, since in many languages, baby-talk words seem to be modeled on the sounds and combinations of sounds that young children tend to produce when trying their first words. At the same time, baby-talk words provide yet another signal that a particular utterance is addressed to a child rather than someone else.

Psychologist Roger Brown (1925–98) has argued that the words parents use in speaking to young children anticipate the nature of the child's world. This seems to be true not only of baby-talk words but also of the other words used in speaking to young children. Adults select the words that seem to have the most immediate relevance to what their children might want to talk about. For instance, they supply words for different kinds of fruit the child might eat, such as *apple* or *orange,* but not the more abstract word *fruit.* They likewise supply the names of animals, but not the word *animal*. In other domains, though, they provide more general words like *tree* rather than the more specific words for different kinds of tree like *oak, ash,* or *birch.* Similarly, they are not likely to point to an Irish wolfhound and say to a one- or two-year-old *That's an Irish wolfhound.* They would be much more likely to say *That's a dog.* Some of the words adults select are very frequent in adult-to-adult speech; others are not. The criterion adults seem to use can be characterized by what Brown called "level of utility": the judgment that one word is more likely to be useful than another in the child's own utterances.

Adults are selective in another way too: they seem to leave out function words and word endings because they think this simplifies what they are saying. (In fact, they do the same thing when talking to non-native speakers.) For example, instead of using pronouns like *he, she,* or *they,* adults often repeat the antecedent noun phrase instead, as in *The boy was running, The boy climbed the tree,* where the second instance of *the boy* would normally be changed to *he*. Where *I* and *you* would be used in adult-to-adult speech, adults often use names instead, as in *Mommy's going to lift Tommy up* for *I'm going to lift you up,* or *Daddy wants to tie Julie's shoe* for *I want to tie your shoe.* Adults often use names in questions addressed to children too, for example, *Does Jenny want to play in the sand today?* addressed to Jenny herself. Adults seem to realize that pronouns are complicated for young children, so they try to avoid them.

b. Taking Turns. From very early on, adults encourage children to take their turns as speaker and listener in conversation. Even when adults talk to very young infants, they thrust **conversational turns** upon them. Adults respond to infants during their very first months of life as though their burps, yawns, and blinks count as turns in conversations. This is illustrated in the following dialogue between a mother and her three-month-old daughter Ann (taken from Snow 1977: 12).

(2) Ann: [smiles]
Mom: Oh, what a nice little smile! Yes, isn't that nice? There. There's a nice little smile.
Ann: [burps]
Mom: What a nice wind as well! Yes, that's better, isn't it? Yes.
Ann: [vocalizes]
Mom: Yes! There's a nice noise.

Whatever the infant does is treated as a conversational turn, even though at this stage the adult carries the entire conversation alone. As infants develop, adults become more demanding about what "counts" as a turn. Yawning or stretching may be enough at three months, but by eight months babbling is what really counts. And by the age of one year or so, only words will do.

Once children begin to use one- and two-word utterances, adults begin to provide both implicit and explicit information about conversational turns. For example, they may provide model dialogues in which the same speaker asks a question and then supplies a possible answer to it.

(3) Adult: Where's the ball?
[picks up ball] THERE'S the ball.
Adult: [looking at picture book with child]
What's the little boy doing?
He's CLIMBING up the TREE.

On other occasions, adults expand on whatever topic the child introduces.

(4)   Child: Dere rabbit.
      Adult: The rabbit likes eating lettuce.
             Do you want to give him some?

By ending with a question, the adult offers the child another turn and in this way deliberately prolongs the conversation. In fact, when necessary, adults also use "prompt" questions to get the child to make a contribution and to take his or her turn as speaker.

(5)   Adult: What did you see?
      Child: [silence]
      Adult: You saw WHAT?

Prompt questions like *You saw what?* or *He went where?* are often more successful in eliciting speech from a child than questions with normal interrogative word order.

   c. Making Corrections. Adults seldom correct what children have to say (see File 8.1), but when they do, they seem to do it mostly to make sure that the child's contribution is true rather than grammatically correct. They may correct children explicitly, as in examples (6) and (7) below, or implicitly, as in (8). In example (9), the child is being corrected with regard to the truth value of the utterances, but the adult also uses the correct form of the verb.

(6)   Child: [points] doggie.
      Adult: No, that's a HORSIE.

(7)   Child: That's the animal farmhouse.
      Adult: No, that's the LIGHTHOUSE.

(8)   Child: [pointing to a picture of bird on nest] Bird house.
      Adult: Yes, the bird's sitting on a NEST.

(9)   Child: Robin goed to school yesterday.
      Adult: No, Robin went to a BIRTHDAY PARTY yesterday.

In each instance, the adult speaker is concerned with the truth of what the child has said, that is, with whether she has used the right words for her listener to be able to work out what she is talking about.

   The other type of correction adults make is of a child's pronunciation. If a child's version of a word sounds quite different from the adult version, a listener may have a hard time understanding what the child is trying to say. Getting children to pronounce recognizable words is a prerequisite for carrying on conversations. What is striking, though, is that adults do not consistently and persistently correct any other "mistakes" that children make when they talk. Grammatical errors tend to go uncorrected as long as what the child says is true and pronounced intelligibly. In correcting children's language, adults seem to be concerned primarily with the ability to communicate with a listener.

8.4.4   How Adults Talk to Children

Just as adults select what they say to young children by restricting it largely to the "here and now," so too do they alter the **way** they say what they say when talking to children. They do this in four ways: they slow down; they use short, simple sentences; they use a higher pitch of voice; and they repeat themselves frequently. Each of these modifications seems to be geared to making sure young children attend to and understand what adults say.

   Speech addressed to two-year-olds is only half the speed of speech addressed to adults. When adults talk to children aged four to six, they go a little faster than with two-year-olds but still speak more slowly than they do to adults. To achieve this slower rate, adults put in more pauses between words, rather than stretch out each word. The higher pitch combined with exaggerated falls and rises in the intonation contour may be acoustically appealing to the infant (Goodluck 1991).

Adults also use very short sentences when talking to young children. Psychologist J. Phillips found that adult utterances to two-year-olds averaged fewer than four words each, while adult utterances to other adults averaged over eight words. These short sentences are generally very simple ones.

There is also a great deal of repetition in adult speech to children. One reason for this repetition is the adults' use of sentence frames like those in the left-hand column in (10).

$$(10) \quad \left\{ \begin{array}{l} \text{Where's} \\ \text{Let's play with} \\ \text{Look at} \\ \text{Here's} \\ \text{That's (a)} \\ \text{Here comes} \end{array} \right\} \quad + \quad \left\{ \begin{array}{l} \text{Mommy} \\ \text{Daddy} \\ \text{(the) birdie} \\ \text{...} \\ \text{...} \\ \text{etc.} \end{array} \right\}$$

These frames mark off the beginnings of words like those in the right-hand column by placing them in familiar slots within a sentence, and one of their main uses besides getting attention seems to be to introduce new vocabulary. Often, these kinds of sentence frames are used by the children too, and we might hear utterances like *Mommy tie shoe* or *Robin want cookie*, where we have a subject followed by a verb followed by an object. Adults also repeat themselves when giving instructions. Repetitions like those in (11) are three times more frequent in speech to two-year-olds than in speech to ten-year-olds.

(11) Adult: Pick up the red one. Find the red one. Not the GREEN one. I want the RED one. Can you find the red one?

These repetitions provide structural information about the kinds of frame the repeated unit (here *the red one*) can be used in. Also, these contrasts are often highlighted by emphasizing the difference in color (indicated by the capitalization). Repetitions also allow children more time to interpret adult utterances, because they don't have to try to remember the whole sentence.

When all of these modifications are put together, it is clear that adults adjust what they say and modify how they say it to make themselves better understood. They first get children to attend; then they select the appropriate words and the way to say them. This suggests that young children are able to best understand short sentences and need to have the beginnings and ends of sentences clearly identified. In addition, the sentences used are about the "here and now," since children rely heavily on the context to guess whenever they don't understand. But as children begin to show signs of understanding more, adults modify the way they talk less and less. The shortest sentences and the slowest rate are reserved for the youngest children; both sentence length and rate of speech increase when adults talk to older children.

8.4.5 How Necessary Is Child-Directed Speech?

The fact that adults systematically modify the speech they address to very young children forces us to ask two questions. First, are the modifications adults make necessary for acquisition? Second, even if they are not necessary, are they at least helpful? It seems that child-directed speech can help children acquire certain aspects of language earlier. For example, Newport and her colleagues (1977) found that mothers who used more yes/no questions in their speech had children who acquired auxiliaries earlier. But is child-directed speech actually **necessary** for language acquisition? Some exposure to language is obviously necessary before children can start to acquire it. But it is quite possible that any kind of spoken language might do. We need to know, for example, whether children could learn language if their only input came from speech they overheard between adults or from what they heard on the radio or television. If they could, it would be clear that child-directed speech is not necessary, even though it might be helpful. On the other hand, if children could not learn from these other sources of information, it would be clear that some child-directed speech is not only helpful but necessary.

Experiments on these topics are difficult if not impossible to devise since it is unethical to deprive children of potentially useful input, but occasionally a real-life situation presents itself in a way that provides a glimpse of the answers to these questions. For example, the hearing children of deaf parents who use only sign language sometimes have little spoken language addressed to them by adults until they enter nursery school. The parents' solution for teaching their children to speak rather than use sign language is to turn on the radio or television as much as possible. Psychologists Jacqueline Sachs and Mary Johnson reported on one such child in 1976. When Jim was approximately three and a half years old, he had only a small spoken language vocabulary, which he had probably picked up from playmates, plus a few words from television jingles. His language was far behind that of other children his age. Although he had overheard a great deal of adult-to-adult speech on television, no adults had spoken to him directly on any regular basis. Once Jim was exposed to an adult who talked to him, his language improved rapidly. Sachs and Johnson concluded that exposure to adult speech intended for other adults does not necessarily help children acquire language.

Exposure to a second language on television constitutes another naturalistic situation in which children regularly hear adults talking to each other. However, psychologist Catherine Snow and her colleagues in the mid-1970s reported that young Dutch children who watched German television every day did not acquire any German (Snow et al. 1976). There are probably at least two reasons why children seem not to acquire language from radio or television. First, none of the speech on the radio can be matched to a situation visible to the child, and even on television people rarely talk about things immediately accessible to view for the audience. Children therefore receive no clues about how to map their own ideas onto words and sentences. Second, the stream of speech must be very hard to segment: they hear rapid speech that cannot easily be linked to familiar situations.

While such evidence may suggest that child-directed speech is necessary for language acquisition, that turns out not to be the case. There are cultures in which adults do not use child-directed speech to talk to infants and children. There are even cultures, for example, the Kaluli of Papua, New Guinea, in which adults do not talk to children at all until they have reached a certain age. Instead the Kaluli "show" their children culturally and socially appropriate language use by having them watch everyday communication routines.

The difference between these cultures, in which children do successfully acquire language, and studies like those of Sachs and Johnson, in which they did not, seems to be related to how immediate the language use is: television and radio speech is too remote to be of any real help to a child. This suggests that one ingredient that might prove necessary for acquisition is the "here and now" nature of the speech children are exposed to, be it through child-directed speech or by being "shown" how to use language in a context that somehow involves the child, even if the child is not being directly addressed.

FILE **8.5**

....

Bilingual Language Acquisition

8.5.1 Scenarios of Bilingual Language Acquisition

In a country like the United States, where the vast majority of people would consider themselves to be monolingual, it may come as a surprise that the majority of people in the world are **bilingual** (speakers of two languages) or **multilingual** (speakers of more than two languages). But when exactly can a person be called bilingual? Definitions of bilingualism are very diverse, ranging from having native-like control of two languages (Bloomfield 1933) to being a fluent speaker of one language and also being able to read a little in another language (Macnamara 1969). Neither of these extreme definitions is satisfactory. We certainly wouldn't want to call a person who speaks English and can read a little French a *bilingual*. One reason is that spoken or signed language is more basic than written language (see File 1.3). Thus, a bilingual should be a person who is able to speak or sign two languages, not just read them. The main problem, however, with both definitions mentioned above bears on the central issue: how well does someone need to know two languages to be called bilingual? Bloomfield's definition excludes too many people: for example, second-language learners who are fluent in their second language but speak with a foreign accent. Macnamara's definition, on the other hand, includes too many people. A better definition lies somewhere in between. For the purposes of this file, we will define being bilingual as being able to hold a conversation with monolingual speakers of two different languages.

There are different ways that a person may become bilingual. Some people learn more than one language from birth (**simultaneous bilingualism**) or begin learning their second language as young children (**sequential bilingualism**). Some children grow up with two or more languages from birth because their parents speak two different languages at home or because their parents speak a language at home that is different from the local language. This is often the case for children when one or two parents are immigrants. Children may also grow up bilingually from birth or early childhood because they grow up in a bilingual or multilingual society, for example, in parts of Belgium or Switzerland, where multiple languages are commonly heard and controlled by most speakers. Finally, children may become bilingual because the language used at school is not their native language. This is the case in many countries where many languages are spoken. Instead of offering instructions in all the languages natively spoken, a neutral language or one that is perceived to be advantageous is chosen as the language of instruction (refer to File 11.3). This is frequently the case in African and Asian countries.

Another way of becoming bilingual is to learn a second language not as a young child but rather later in life. This is called **second-language acquisition** and is the process used, for example, by immigrants who come to a new country as adults and have to learn the local language. Other late learners are often people who learned a second, third, etc., language through formal education and/or travel.

These different ways of becoming bilingual tend to have different characteristics and results; we will discuss each of them in turn below.

8.5.2   Bilingual First-Language Acquisition

When children acquire two languages from birth or from young childhood, we usually talk of bilingual first-language acquisition. Any child who receives sufficient input from two languages will grow up fully bilingual in the sense that Bloomfield meant of having native control over two languages. Research by Barbara Pearson and her colleagues in 1997 suggests that children will become competent speakers of a language only if at least 25% of their input is in that language. In addition, not just any input will do, as was discussed in File 8.4. Children learn language by interacting with speakers of that language. It's not enough, for example, to sit a child in front of a Spanish television program and expect him to learn Spanish. The child will learn Spanish only if he interacts with others in Spanish.

One typical feature of bilingual children's speech is **language mixing** or **code-switching**: using more than one language in a conversation or even within a phrase. Mario, a boy who grew up mostly in the United States and whose parents spoke Spanish to him, frequently used both English and Spanish in the same sentence, as in the following examples (Fantini 1985: 149):

(1)   *Sabes mi* school bus *no tiene un* stop sign.
      "You know, my school bus does not have a stop sign."

      Hoy, yo era line leader *en mi escuela.*
      "Today, I was line leader at school."

      Ponemos cranberries *y* marshmallows *y después se pone el* glitter *con* glue.
      "Let's put cranberries and marshmallows and then we put the glitter on with glue."

The fact that bilingual children mix their languages has led some early researchers to believe that they speak neither of their languages really well. It has even been suggested that mixing in young children shows that their languages are fused into one system. That is, children have not yet figured out that they are using two different languages. However, more recent research has shown that bilingual children can differentiate their languages by the time they are four months old—long before they utter their first words. Laura Bosch and Nuria Sebastián-Gallés (2001) found that four-month-old Spanish-Catalan bilingual infants could distinguish between even these rhythmically similar languages. Since infants can differentiate two rhythmically similar languages like Spanish and Catalan, it is reasonable to hypothesize that four-month-old bilingual infants would also be able to differentiate languages that are rhythmically different (because this would be an easier task). However, more research in this area is needed to confirm this hypothesis.

If bilingual children can differentiate their languages well before they utter their first word, why do they mix languages? Let's take a closer look at Mario's utterances in (1). We can see that Mario does not just randomly mix English and Spanish. Instead, he seems to use some English nouns in what are basically Spanish sentences. Furthermore, all of the English nouns he uses are related either to his school experience in the United States (*school bus, line leader,* etc.) or to typically American items (*cranberries, marshmallows,* etc.). It's then possible that he knows these words only in English or that he uses them more frequently in English. Even if we assume that Mario does not know these words in Spanish, we certainly can't conclude that he's unable to differentiate between Spanish and English.

Alternatively, Mario may mix his languages in the examples above because he knows that the people he is talking to understand both languages. Children are very sensitive to which languages their listeners can understand. If they believe that their listeners speak, say, only Spanish, they would try to stick to Spanish. But if they believe that their listeners know, for instance, English and Spanish, there is no reason for them to make an effort to stick to one language in particular, since many bilingual children grow up in an environment in which adults also frequently code-switch.

Finally, children's language mixing can be a strategy to avoid words that are difficult to pronounce. For example, Werner Leopold (1947) observed that his German-English bilingual daughter Hildegard preferred to use the German *da* [dɑ] instead of English *there* [ðɛɹ], but the English *high* [haɪ] over *hoch* [hox] because they were easier for her to pronounce.

8.5.3 Bilingual vs. Monolingual First-Language Acquisition

Let's go back to the idea that Mario may not know words like *stop sign* or *school bus* in Spanish. Does this mean that his language acquisition is lagging behind monolingual children of his age? Some early researchers have suggested that learning two languages from birth would exceed the limitations of the child's brain. They assumed that bilingual children would lag behind their monolingual peers, and, indeed, studies from that time indicate that bilingual children's language skills are inferior to those of monolingual children.

During the 1980s, however, researchers began reevaluating the earlier studies and found that many of them were methodologically flawed. For example, some studies compared monolinguals' language skills with bilinguals' skills in their non-dominant language. The studies conducted in the 1980s suggested that, on the contrary, growing up bilingually is advantageous. In particular, studies found that bilingual children develop some metalinguistic skills, such as understanding arbitrariness (see File 1.4), earlier than monolingual children.

Current studies on bilingual language acquisition display a more balanced view. On the one hand, bilingual children may lag behind their monolingual peers in certain specific areas, like the vocabulary of one of their two languages (after all, they have to learn twice as much), but they have usually caught up by the time they reach puberty. This doesn't mean that they can't communicate their ideas; instead, it usually just means that there are some concepts that are easier to express in one language than the other. On the other hand, growing up bilingually may have some cognitive advantages, as mentioned above; and, of course, the end result is the ability to communicate fluently in two different languages. Other than that, bilingual children go through the same stages of language acquisition as monolingual children of each of the languages.

It should be mentioned that there are cases of problematic bilingual language acquisition. Sometimes children who grow up bilingually do not become functional bilinguals, usually because they are confronted with a bad attitude toward bilingualism, or one of their languages is not valued in their community and its use is discouraged. Thus, it is not the limitations of a child's brain or capabilities that cause problems in bilingual language acquisition, but rather a negative social environment: any child exposed to two languages in a positive social environment can grow up to be fully bilingual.

8.5.4 Second-Language Acquisition

As mentioned above, not every bilingual speaker acquired both languages during childhood. Many people become bilingual later in life, after already acquiring their native language. This is called **second-language acquisition.** While children exposed to two languages from birth or early childhood will usually grow up mastering both languages as do monolingual native speakers of those languages, people learning a language later in life usually attain different levels of competence. Some people achieve native-like competence in a second language, but the vast majority of second-language learners do not. Speakers may learn the syntax and vocabulary of a second language perfectly (although even this is rare), but few learn the phonological system that well. Thus, most second-language speakers speak with a **foreign accent** (see Section 3.1.3 and File 10.1). It seems that non-native forms, as part of either the morpho-syntax or pronunciation, can become fixed and not change, even after years of instruction. This is called **fossilization.**

There are a number of individual differences that contribute to how well a learner learns a second language. First, the learner's native language plays an important role. A Dutch speaker will have an easier time learning English than, for example, a Chinese speaker, because Dutch and English are closely related languages with similar grammatical and phonological systems, while Chinese and English are not. By the same token, a Burmese speaker will have a much easier time learning Chinese than a Dutch speaker. A speaker's native language also plays a role in second-language acquisition because having learned one language influences the subsequent learning of another language. This is called **transfer.** Transfer can be positive or negative, depending on whether it facilitates or inhibits the learning of the second language. For example, having a native language, regardless of which language it is, facilitates the learning of a second language because we already know much about how language works. In fact, evidence from feral children and deaf children suggests that it's not possible to learn a language later in life without having already learned a native language earlier (see File 8.1).

But a learner's native language can also inhibit learning the second language. For example, we learn the phonological system of our native language early in life. In fact, by the time we are twelve months old, we perceive speech in terms of the phonemic categories of our native language (see File 8.2). This specialization for the sounds of our native language can interfere with learning the phonological system of a second language and is one of the reasons why second-language learners usually have a foreign accent. Let's consider the sounds [p] and [pʰ]. In English, aspirated [pʰ] occurs only syllable-initially (e.g., in *pin, pot,* etc.), whereas unaspirated [p] occurs only after [s] (e.g., in *spin, spot,* etc., as was discussed in File 3.2). Most native speakers of English are not even aware they are using two "different kinds" of /p/ in their speech. In Thai, on the other hand, [p] and [pʰ] are allophones of different phonemes, namely, of the phonemes /p/ and /pʰ/. That is, [p] and [pʰ] are not restricted in their distribution as they are in English. Instead, both [p] and [pʰ] can occur syllable-initially in Thai, as in the words [pai] *to go* and [pʰai] *danger,* for example. Negative transfer occurs when native English speakers learning Thai apply English phonological rules to the Thai words and incorrectly pronounce both *to go* and *danger* as [pʰai]. Negative transfer is not limited to pronunciation; it may affect all levels of second-language acquisition.

A number of other factors influence how successfully a learner will learn a second language. They include the learner's age, working memory, motivation, and context. Motivation plays a particularly large role in the level of fluency second-language learners will achieve. Some learners are perfectly content speaking a second language with a foreign accent and making an occasional mistake here and there. A study by Theo Bongaerts and his colleagues (1997) found that Dutch second-language learners of English who had achieved native competence in English were highly motivated learners and considered not having a foreign accent to be one of their goals.

Finally, the context in which speakers learn a second language and the amount of exposure to the second language also play a role. For example, the highly competent learners in Bongaerts and colleagues' study all learned English in an immersion setting where English was the language of instruction and learners were constantly exposed to native speakers of English. Trying to learn a second language later in life in a situation where you receive forty-five minutes of instruction a day, five days a week, may not result in the same high degree of native-like fluency.

FILE 8.6

....

Practice

File 8.1—Theories of Language Acquisition

Exercises

1. Suppose a friend of yours has a son, George, who is three years old. Your friend has been explaining to you that George has a problem with forming the past tense of verbs, for example, George says "Yesterday I go to the park" and "Last week I swim in the pool." But your friend has a plan: he is going to spend one hour each day with George, having the child imitate the past tense forms of the verbs, and he will give George a piece of candy for each correct imitation.

    i. Which theory/theories of language acquisition does your friend assume?

    ii. Will your friend's plan work? Explain why or why not.

    iii. What suggestions would you give your friend? Explain why, using a relevant theory.

2. For each pair of statements below, indicate which one is true and which one is false. For the true statement, say which theory of language acquisition best accounts for it as well as which theory is the least suited to explain the statement. Explain your answers.

    a. • A Chinese child adopted soon after birth by a Danish family will learn Danish just like other children growing up in Denmark with Danish parents.

    • A Chinese child adopted soon after birth by a Danish family will learn Danish more slowly than other children growing up in Denmark with Danish parents because the child is genetically predisposed to learn Chinese.

    b. • Children say things like *foots* and *both mans* before they master the correct forms *feet* and *both men* because they overuse the rule for regular plural formation.

    • Children never say things like *foots* and *both mans*, because they imitate what adults say and no adult would say this.

3. Consider the following examples of children's speech taken from Clark (1995: 402), and answer the questions:

    [playing with a toy lawnmower] "I'm lawning."
    [pretending to be Superman] "I'm supermanning."
    [realizing his father was teasing] "Daddy, you joked me."
    [of food on his plate] "I'm gonna fork this."

    i. Explain what the children are doing with language. How are these utterances different from the adult norm? What do the children not know about the English language yet? On the other hand, what do the children already demonstrate knowing about English in order to use it so creatively?

    ii. Which theory of language acquisition best accounts for these data? Why?

4. Consider the following exchange taken from Braine (1971: 161). Discuss the effectiveness of the father's strategy in teaching the child. Also think about what the father's and child's respective objectives are. Which theory of language acquisition does this example refute?

Child: Want other one spoon, Daddy.
Father: You mean, you want the other spoon.
Child: Yes, I want other one spoon, please Daddy.
Father: Can you say "the other spoon"?
Child: Other . . . one . . . spoon.
Father: Say "other."
Child: Other.
Father: "Spoon."
Child: Spoon.
Father: "Other spoon."
Child: Other . . . spoon. Now give me other one spoon.

5. Read the following description of a feral child named Victor, and answer the questions below:

Victor was found in France in 1797 when he was twelve or thirteen years old. He had no speech when he was found. However, his hearing was normal and he made some noises. A man named Jean Marc Gaspard-Itard spent five years trying to teach Victor language. When Victor was sixteen, he could name objects. However, he would never use the words to request the objects. He also applied each word to only one object. That is, he would call only a certain shoe a *shoe*, but not other shoes. Victor developed no grammar.

   i. Does Victor's case support the critical period hypothesis? Why or why not?
   ii. What factors other than a critical period could be responsible for Victor's not acquiring normal language skills?

Activity

6. Interview a highly proficient non-native speaker of your native language. How would you rate his or her language skills at each of the following levels of linguistic structure, and how does your non-native speaker rate his or her own skills at these levels? Relate your ratings to the critical period hypothesis for second-language acquisition. You may want to ask the speaker when he or she started to learn the second language.

   a. pronunciation (phonetics and phonology)
   b. grammar (syntax and morphology)
   c. word choice (lexicon)
   d. intonation (phonetics and phonology)
   e. appropriateness (pragmatics)
   f. general comprehension

File 8.2—First-Language Acquisition: The Acquisition of Speech Sounds and Phonology

Exercises

7. For this exercise, go to a video-sharing website (e.g., YouTube, Google Video, etc.), and search for "babbling" and "baby." Choose whatever video you wish (as long as it is of a babbling baby!) and answer the following questions.

(cont.)

    i. Give the URL and/or the exact name of the video so that your instructor can find the video easily.

    ii. Do your best to transcribe in IPA at least five syllables of the baby's babbling.

    iii. What stage of language acquisition is the baby in? (See especially table (2) at the end of File 8.2, but it may also be helpful to also check table (2) at the end of File 8.3.) In particular, what kind of babbling does he or she produce, or could it be more properly described as cooing?

    iv. Based on the stage of language acquisition, how old would you guess the baby is? If the video description includes the baby's age, does that match up with what you would expect?

8. The data below are from a child named Paul at the age of two. They were collected by his father, Timothy Shopen. Consider each set of examples, and answer the questions at the end of each section.

A.

	Adult Word	*Paul*		*Adult Word*	*Paul*
a.	sun	[sʌn]	**d.**	snake	[neɪk]
b.	see	[si]	**e.**	sky	[kɑɪ]
c.	spoon	[pun]	**f.**	stop	[tɑp]

    i. State a principle that describes Paul's pronunciation of these words. That is, how does Paul's pronunciation systematically differ from the adult pronunciation?

B.

	Adult Word	*Paul*		*Adult Word*	*Paul*
g.	bed	[bɛt]	**m.**	bus	[bʌs]
h.	wet	[wɛt]	**n.**	buzz	[bʌs]
i.	egg	[ɛk]	**o.**	man	[mæn]
j.	rake	[ɹeɪk]	**p.**	door	[dɔɹ]
k.	tub	[tʌp]	**q.**	some	[sʌm]
l.	soap	[soʊp]	**r.**	boy	[bɔɪ]

    ii. State another principle describing Paul's pronunciations here. Be sure to word your statement in a way that reflects the fact that (o)–(r) are not affected.

C.

	Adult Word	*Paul*
s.	laugh	[læp]
t.	off	[ɔp]
u.	coffee	[kɔfi]

    iii. State a third principle describing Paul's pronunciation in this section. Based on the principles you have seen so far, suggest how Paul would pronounce the word *love*.

D.

	Adult Word	*Paul*		*Adult Word*	*Paul*
v.	truck	[tʌk]	**aa.**	clay	[keɪ]
w.	brownie	[baʊni]	**bb.**	cute	[kut]
x.	plane	[peɪn]	**cc.**	beautiful	[butəpəl]
y.	broken	[boʊkən]	**dd.**	twig	[tɪk]
z.	crack	[kæk]			

    iv. State a fourth principle describing the new aspects of Paul's pronunciation in these examples.

E.

	Adult Word	*Paul*
ee.	quick	[kwɪk]
ff.	quack	[kwæk]

    v. Do these two words illustrate an exception to the fourth principle? If so, how?

9. The data below are taken from Fasold and Connor-Linton (2006: 233). The data show words pronounced by different children at about the same age. Are there any sounds or sound sequences that seem to be particularly difficult? What patterns are evident in the children's pronunciations?

	Adult Word	Child		Adult Word	Child
a.	bottle	[baba]	**h.**	key	[ti]
b.	butterfly	[bʌfaɪ]	**i.**	duck	[gʌk]
c.	tub	[bʌb]	**j.**	water	[wawa]
d.	baby	[bibi]	**k.**	stop	[tɔp]
e.	tree	[ti]	**l.**	blanket	[bæki]
f.	candy	[kæki]	**m.**	doggie	[gɔgi]
g.	banana	[næna]	**n.**	this	[dɪs]

10. The children below pronounce some words differently than adults do, and differently from one another. Look at the examples of each child's speech and determine how each will pronounce the target phrases that follow.

Child A:

	Adult Word	Child		Adult Word	Child
a.	ghost	[doʊst]	**d.**	gopher	[doʊfəɹ]
b.	dog	[dag]	**e.**	muffin	[mʌfɪn]
c.	cat	[kæt]	**f.**	pig	[pɪg]

Child B:

	Adult Word	Child		Adult Word	Child
a.	ghost	[goʊst]	**d.**	gopher	[goʊf]
b.	dog	[dak]	**e.**	muffin	[mʌf]
c.	cat	[kæt]	**f.**	pig	[pɪk]

Targets:

- Go faster
- Big tummy
- Good baby

File 8.3—First-Language Acquisition: The Acquisition of Morphology, Syntax, and Word Meaning

Exercises

11. For this exercise, go to a video-sharing website (e.g., YouTube, Google Video, etc.), and search for "two year old," "baby," and "talking." Choose whatever video you wish (as long as it is of a talking child that seems to generally be in the two-year-old range and is **at least two minutes long**) and answer the following questions.

   i. Give the URL and/or the exact name of the video so that your instructor can find the video easily.

   ii. Do your best to transcribe (either in normal spelling or IPA) at least five full utterances (e.g., phrases, sentences).

   iii. What stage of language acquisition is the child in? (See especially table (2) at the end of File 8.3.) Is he or she producing two-word utterances, or three words or more? Is the child's speech telegraphic, or does it include function words? Give examples in support of your answers.

(cont.)

iv. Does the child produce any suffixes like *-ing,* or the plural *-s,* or past tense *-ed*? Does the child use any incorrect irregular forms (e.g., *goed, wented, blowed*)? Give examples in support of your answers.

v. Does the child use any words that seem to be overextensions, underextensions, or anything else that does not match up with normal adult usage of a word? Give examples in support of your answers.

12. Consider the examples from children's speech below. Using the linguistic terminology you have learned so far, explain what mistakes the children make. Be as specific as possible. Example 12d is taken from Fasold and Connor-Linton (2006: 233), and examples 12e and 12f from Yule (1996: 159, 160).

a. Mike: What do you want for lunch? Do you want a hotdog?
Calvin: No! I don't like hot! I only want a warm dog!

b. Calvin: That bug had already [baɪtn̩] me.

c. Calvin: I'm so sorry I broked you! Do we need to buy a new mommy?

d. Child calls leaves, grass, moss, green carpet, green towels, spinach, lettuce, and avocado a *leaf.*

e. Child: No the sun shining.

f. Child: Why you waking me up?

13. Read the description of the feral child Victor given in Exercise 5. What mistake does Victor make regarding object names? Do children who were exposed to language from birth make the same mistake? Do children eventually learn the correct referents for these object names? Which stage of the acquisition of lexical items does Victor seem to be stuck in?

14. Each pair of utterances below comes from children at different ages. For each pair, which utterance was most likely said by the older child? Explain your answers.

a. Daddy, go park!
I'm so hungry for go to the park.
b. Why she doesn't liked it?
No wake upping me!
c. More door! More door!
I have another one candy?
d. Now the bad guy show up!
Where go him?
e. This my super awesome bed.
What's name dis?

15. For each word below, explain what a child has to learn about the word in order to use it correctly.

a. cold
b. Susan
c. you
d. bird
e. this

Activity

16. This activity is adapted from Yule (1996: 188–89). Show the following list of expressions to some friends and ask them to guess the meaning:

    a. a snow-car
       a running-stick
       a water-cake
       a finger-brush
       a pony-kid

    Now compare your friends' versions with those of a two-year-old child below (from Clark 1993: 40). What do the examples suggest about the nature of vocabulary acquisition?

    b. [talking about a toy car completely painted white]
       Child: This is a snow-car.
       Parent: Why is this a snow-car?
       Child: 'Cause it's got lots of snow on it. I can't see the windows.

       Child: This is a running stick.
       Parent: A running-stick?
       Child: Yes, because I run with it.

       Child: [in the bath] It's a water-cake.
       Parent: Why do you call it a water-cake?
       Child: I made it in the water.

       Child: I bought you a toothbrush and a finger-brush.
       Parent: What's a finger-brush?
       Child: It's for cleaning your nails.

       Child: [wearing a sun hat] I look like a pony-kid.
       Parent: What's a pony-kid?
       Child: A kid who rides ponies.

File 8.4—How Adults Talk to Young Children

Exercises

17. Read the following "conversations" between three-month-old Ann and her mother (from Snow 1977: 13). Which aspects of how adults talk to young children and what they say to young children can you identify in each "conversation"?

    a. Mom: Oh you are a funny little one, aren't you, hmm?
          [pause]
          Aren't you a funny little one?
          [pause]
          Hmm?

    b. Ann: abaabaa
       Mom: Baba.
          Yes, that's you, what you are.

18. For each pair of sentences, which of the two would an adult most likely say to a young child? Justify your answer.

a. Timmy, see the bird?
Do you see the bird?

b. You are taking a bath now.
Timmy is taking a bath now.

c. Look, the girl is eating. And now she is playing with the ball.
Look, the girl is eating. And now the girl is playing with the ball.

d. That's a birdie.
That's a robin.

e. No, that's a kitty, not a doggy.
No, say *went,* not *goed.*

Discussion Question

19. Many adults use child-directed speech to speak to children, and they seem to be able to use child-directed speech in ways that are helpful to the child. How do you think adults know what to do to be most helpful?

Activity

20. Make a list of all the aspects of how adults talk to children and what they say to children that are discussed in this file. Then observe adults interacting with two children of different ages. Which of the aspects on your list do the adults use? Write down examples. How does the child's age influence the adult speech?

File 8.5—Bilingual Language Acquisition

Discussion Questions

21. Why do you think motivation plays such a big role in the success of second-language acquisition?

22. Do you have any experience trying to learn a second language? How proficient are you? How do you think the factors mentioned in this file affected your proficiency?

Activity

23. Interview a proficient non-native speaker of your language. Find out where and when your speaker learned your native language. Also ask your speaker how motivated he or she was in learning the language. Then listen carefully to your speaker: do you find features in his or her speech that could be attributed to transfer? Think about pronunciation (phonology), grammar (syntax and morphology), word choice (lexicon), intonation, and appropriateness. Does your speaker speak your language at a level that you would expect, considering his or her language-learning background? Why or why not?

Further Readings

Clark, Eve V. 2009. *First language acquisition*. 2nd edn. Cambridge: Cambridge University Press.

Genesee, Fred, and Elena Nicoladis. 2007. Bilingual first language acquisition. *Blackwell handbook of language development,* ed. by Erika Hoff and Marilyn Shatz, 324–42. Oxford: Wiley-Blackwell.

Guasti, Maria Teresa. 2004. *Language acquisition: The growth of grammar*. Cambridge, MA: MIT Press.

Saxton, Matthew. 2010. *Child language acquisition and development*. Thousand Oaks, CA: Sage Publications.

Senghas, Ann, and Marie Coppola. 2001. Children creating language: How Nicaraguan Sign Language acquired a spatial grammar. *Psychological Science* 12(4).323–28.

CHAPTER
9

Psycholinguistics

··

How Do Our Minds Understand and Produce Language?

P revious chapters have examined how languages work, from combining sounds to interpreting utterances in the context of a conversation. But how does your mind actually learn and implement the rules of language? From the hundreds of thousands of words we know, we pick just the right ones and quickly arrange them into grammatical patterns to convey our intended meaning. How are such complex processes carried out so quickly and effortlessly? What can we learn from the mistakes that we make with language? How do we use the patterns of changing air pressure that leave our mouths and hit our ears to make ideas appear in each others' minds? **Psycholinguistics** investigates how the intricate linguistic processes described in the other chapters of this book are actually carried out in our minds as we produce and comprehend language.

Neurolinguistics is the study of language and the physical brain. To discover where and how the brain processes language, we need to know where the language centers of the brain are and how information flows between these areas. Experimental techniques that allow us to see the brain in action play a large role in neurolinguistics, as do studies of patients with language disorders.

Contents

....

Language and the Brain

9.1.1 Why Study the Brain?

Linguists analyze the structure of language and propose models that can account for the linguistic phenomena they observe—sets of phonemes, collections of phonological or morphological rules, guidelines for building syntactic structures, and so on. However, this level of linguistic pursuit is quite abstract and often removed from considerations of the physiology of language: how do we actually create and use language in our brains and minds? By studying how the brain constructs language, we can investigate whether the models that linguists propose to account for specific linguistic phenomena are plausible or even possible models. The areas of linguistics that deal with questions about the brain are **neurolinguistics,** the study of the neural and electrochemical bases of language development and use; and **psycholinguistics,** the study of the acquisition, storage, comprehension, and production of language. Chapter 8 covered language acquisition; the focus of this chapter is language processing, from both a neurolinguistic and a psycholinguistic point of view.

The human brain governs all human activities, including the ability to comprehend and produce language. This file will introduce you to some of the regions and properties of the human brain that are thought to be essential for understanding and using language. Keep in mind as you read that the human brain is an extremely complex organ, and our knowledge of its inner workings is still very limited. There are many aspects of brain function that are understood only poorly and others that we do not understand at all. We present you here with an interesting subset of the facts that have been reliably established at this point and time, facts discovered through numerous elaborate psychological studies and linguistic experiments.

9.1.2 Physical Features of the Brain

The brain is divided into two nearly symmetrical halves, the **right** and **left hemispheres,** each of which is responsible for processing certain kinds of information concerning the world around us. Each hemisphere is further divided into four areas of the brain called **lobes.** The **temporal lobe** is associated with the perception and recognition of auditory stimuli; the **frontal lobe** is concerned with higher thinking and language production; and the **occipital lobe** is associated with many aspects of vision. The **parietal lobe** is least involved in language perception and production.

The two hemispheres are connected by a bundle of nerve fibers called the **corpus callosum.** This bundle of about 200 million nerve fibers is the main (but not only) pathway between the two hemispheres, making it possible for the two hemispheres to communicate with each other and build a single, coherent picture of our environment from the many different kinds of stimuli—visual, tactile, oral, auditory, and olfactory—that we receive.

The brain is covered by a one-quarter-inch thick membrane called the **cortex.** It has been suggested that it is this membrane that makes human beings capable of higher cognitive functions, such as the ability to do math or use language, and that its development was

(1)   Language regions of the brain: the inferior frontal gyrus (IFG), the superior temporal gyrus (STG), the Sylvian parietotemporal area (SPT), and the middle and inferior temporal gyri (MTG/ITG)

IFG (left)
articulatory–based
speech codes

SPT (left)
sensori-motor transformation
auditory-motor mapping

STG (bilateral)
acoustic–phonetic
mapping

MTG/ITG (left)
sound-meaning interface
lexical activation

Figure from "Dorsal and ventral streams: A framework for understanding aspects of the functional anatomy of language," by Gregory Hickok and David Poeppel. *Cognition* 92.67–99. © 2004 by Elsevier B.V. All rights reserved.

one of the primary evolutionary changes that separated us from other animals. In fact, most of the **language centers** of the brain that we will be discussing later in this file are contained in the cortex. This is why even minor damage to the surface of the brain—for example, that caused by a strong blow to the head—can result in language impairment.

As you can see from the image in (1), the cortex is not flat but convoluted with bumps and indentations. The bumps on the surface of the brain are called gyri (singular **gyrus**), and the depressions are called **fissures.** Scientists use certain fissures to demarcate the lobes of the brain. One of the most prominent of these is the **Sylvian Fissure,** the large horizontal fold located in the middle of each hemisphere separating the temporal lobe from the frontal lobe.

Several portions of the cortex are specialized to perform particular functions that play a role in language use. Language is predominantly processed in the left hemisphere (see Section 9.1.4) for 96% of right-handed people and about 73% of left-handed people (Knecht et al. 2000); the description given here assumes left-hemisphere language dominance. Early processing of sound occurs in both left and right hemispheres in the **auditory cortex** in the **superior temporal gyrus (STG).** When navigating around the brain, *superior* and *dorsal* mean "toward the top," while *inferior* and *ventral* mean "toward the bottom." Processing of word meaning and conceptual representations is thought to occur in the **middle** and **inferior temporal gyri (MTG/ITG).** The **Sylvian parietotemporal area (SPT)**— sometimes grouped with the posterior STG and called **Wernicke's area**—is involved in converting auditory and phonological representations into articulatory-motor representations. The **inferior frontal gyrus (IFG)** (also known as **Broca's area**) appears to be responsible for organizing the articulatory patterns of language and directing the **motor cortex,** which controls movement, when we want to talk. This involves the face, jaw, and tongue in the case of spoken language, and the hands, arms, face, and body in the case of signed language. Broca's area also seems to control the use of inflectional morphemes, like the plural and past tense markers, and function words, like determiners and prepositions (see File 4.1), both of which have important functions with respect to the formation of words and sentences.

The final language center we will introduce is the **angular gyrus.** This area, located between the SPT/Wernicke's area and the **visual cortex,** converts visual stimuli into linguistic stimuli (and vice versa). The angular gyrus allows us to match the spoken form of a word with the object it describes, as well as with the written form of the word. This ability is crucial to the human capacity to read and write. Because its role involves converting between visual and linguistic representations of stimuli, the angular gyrus has also been shown to be involved in processing signed languages (Newman et al. 2002).

The brain regions mentioned above have been identified via experimental imaging techniques (see Section 9.7.2) and by studying the brains of people affected with language disorders (see File 9.2). But it is at least as important to understand how these areas are connected to one another. A useful metaphor might be thinking about how the Internet is organized. If you want to understand how the Internet works, knowing where the physical offices of Google and Twitter are located would not be nearly as useful as knowing how information flows between these offices and your computer.

Recent work on the connectivity of brain regions has identified two key pathways along which linguistic information flows (see 2). Rather than regions of gray matter in the cortex, these pathways are composed of bundles of nerve cells called *white matter.* The **arcuate fasciculus** is the primary **dorsal pathway** connecting the STG and SPT, where auditory processing takes place, with the IFG, which is important for speech production. The arcuate fasiculus is important for speech production and syntactic processing, especially for more complex syntactic structures. This pathway is also used when we break down the sounds of words we are hearing—for instance, when we are asked whether there is a /t/ in the word *cat.* The **ventral pathway** connecting the STG and MTG/ITG with the IFG runs instead via the **extreme capsule.** This is the pathway most heavily used to analyze the semantics of incoming speech, and it also aids in syntactic processing.

(2)   Arcuate fasciculus and extreme capsule

Figure adapted from "Dynamic processing in the human language system: Synergy between the arcuate fascicle and extreme capsule," by Tyler Rolheiser, Emmanuel A. Stamatakis, and Lorraine K. Tyler. *The Journal of Neuroscience* 31(47).16949–57. © 2011 by the authors.

9.1.3   The Flow of Linguistic Information

Now that we have identified the relevant physical areas of the brain, let's turn to the question of how these areas of the brain work together to process language. The answer to this question depends on what type of stimulus (auditory, visual, etc.) and what type of language behavior (speaking, reading, understanding, etc.) are involved. For example, to produce a spoken word (see (3)), a person first chooses a word from the mental lexicon. The process of accessing the lexicon activates the MTG/ITG, which then interprets the lexical entry, identifying the meaning of the word, how to pronounce it, and so on. The phonetic information for the entry (how to pronounce it) is sent via the arcuate fasciculus to the IFG (Broca's area). The IFG then determines what combination of the various articulators is necessary to produce each sound in the word and instructs the motor cortex which muscles to move. You may find it useful to compare this process to the steps in the communication chain described in File 1.2.

(3)   Producing a spoken word

MTG/ITG	activated when accessing the lexicon; interprets lexical entry
Arcuate fasciculus	phonetic information sent from MTG/ITG to IFG (Broca's area)
IFG	interprets information received from arcuate fasciculus; transmits articulatory information to motor cortex
Motor cortex	directs movement of muscles for articulation

You can reverse this process to hear and understand a word that has been said to you. First, as shown in (4), the stimulus is brought into the auditory cortex through the ears (or into the visual cortex through the eyes, if you speak a signed language). The MTG/ITG is activated as that auditory stimulus is matched to a word in your mental lexicon. If you have an image or a written form associated with the word, the angular gyrus will activate the visual cortex, and you will have a picture of the item and its spelling available to you.

(4)   Hearing a word

Auditory cortex	processes information perceived by ears
Extreme capsule	semantic information sent from auditory cortex to MTG/ITG
MTG/ITG	interprets auditory stimulus and matches information to a lexical entry

Before reading ahead, can you figure out how you understand a word that you read?

When you are reading a word, the visual information taken in by your eyes is first sent to the visual cortex (see (5)). The angular gyrus then associates the written form of the word with an entry in the mental lexicon, which releases information about the word into the MTG/ITG. This area then interprets the entry and gives you the meaning of the word.

(5)   Reading a word

Visual cortex	processes information perceived by eyes
Angular gyrus	associates written form of word with lexical entry
MTG/ITG	activated during lexical access; makes available the meaning and pronunciation of word

9.1.4   Lateralization and Contralateralization

As mentioned earlier, each of the brain's hemispheres is responsible for different cognitive functions. This specialization is referred to as **lateralization** (*lateral* means "of or related to the side"). For most individuals, the left hemisphere is dominant in the areas of analytic reasoning, temporal ordering, arithmetic, and language processing. The right hemisphere is in charge of processing music, perceiving nonlinguistic sounds, and performing tasks that require visual and spatial skills or pattern recognition. Lateralization happens in early childhood and can be reversed in its initial stages if there is damage to a part of the brain that is crucially involved in an important function. For example, if a very young child whose brain was originally lateralized so that language functions were in the left hemisphere receives severe damage to the language centers, the right hemisphere can develop language centers to compensate for the loss. This ability of the brain to adapt to damage and retrain regions is called **neural plasticity.** Young brains are quite flexible in this regard, though by early adolescence the brain is substantially less able to adapt to traumatic disruption.

There are a number of ways to study the effects of lateralization. Most of them rely on the fact that the connections between the brain and the body are almost completely **contralateral** (*contra* means "opposite," and thus *contralateral* means "on the opposite side"). This means that the right side of the body is controlled by the left hemisphere, while the left side of the body is controlled by the right hemisphere. It is also important to realize that this contralateral connection means that sensory information from the right side of the body is received by the left hemisphere, while sensory information from the left side of the body is received by the right hemisphere. Sensory information can be any data one gathers through hearing, seeing, touching, tasting, or smelling. Many different experiments have provided evidence for contralateralization. One example of this type of experiment, which is rather intrusive, is the anesthetizing of one hemisphere. An anesthetic is injected into the artery of the patient leading to one side of the brain or the other. The patient is then asked to stand with both arms stretched forward from the shoulders. The arm opposite the anesthetized hemisphere slowly goes down as the anesthesia takes effect, providing evidence for contralateralization. If the language hemisphere is anesthetized, the patient also cannot speak at all for a few minutes after the injection, and in the next few minutes after that, the patient appears to be aphasic (unable to perceive or produce fluent language; see File 9.2), providing evidence that the patient's language centers are in that hemisphere.

One experiment that relies on the existence of contralateralization and is designed to test the location of language processing centers is the **dichotic listening task.** The diagram in (6) is a schematic representation of how this kind of task is designed. In this test, two sounds are presented at the same time to a person with normal hearing—one sound in the left ear and one in the right. The sounds may be linguistic (e.g., a person saying a word) or nonlinguistic (e.g., a door slamming). The subject is asked what sound he or she heard in one ear or another. These tests show that responses to the right-ear stimuli are quicker and more accurate when the stimuli are verbal, while responses to the left-ear stimuli are quicker and more accurate when the stimuli are nonverbal. To understand why this is so, note that while some auditory processing is done ipsalaterally (on the same side), most is done contralaterally. Thus, signals presented to the left ear cross to the right hemisphere for basic auditory processing (via the brain stem, not the corpus callosum) and then across the corpus callo-

(6)   A schematic representation of a dichotic listening task

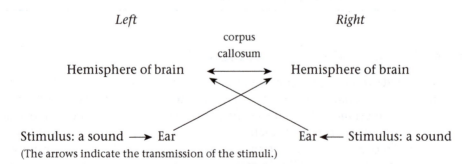

(The arrows indicate the transmission of the stimuli.)

sum back to the left hemisphere, where the language centers are for most people. On the other hand, a linguistic signal presented to the right ear goes directly to the left hemisphere, where it undergoes both basic auditory processing and linguistic processing. We find just the opposite effect with nonlinguistic sounds, where a stimulus presented to the left ear is recognized faster and better than one presented to the right ear. This is because the right hemisphere is more involved in processing nonverbal sounds than the left hemisphere. If a nonverbal stimulus is presented to the right ear, the signal goes to the left hemisphere for auditory processing, and then it must cross the corpus callosum to the right hemisphere in order to be categorized. A nonverbal stimulus presented to the left ear goes directly to the right hemisphere, where it can be processed immediately.

Further evidence for the locations of the language processing centers comes from so-called **split-brain patients.** Normally, the two hemispheres are connected by the corpus callosum, but for certain kinds of severe epilepsy, the corpus callosum used to be surgically severed, preventing the two hemispheres from transmitting information to each other. Since epileptic seizures are caused in part by a patient's motor cortices "overloading" on information sent back and forth between the two hemispheres, this procedure greatly reduced the number and danger of such seizures. This kind of treatment was used in the 1940s and the 1950s, but it is now much rarer because medications have been developed for managing severe epilepsy.

Since the connections from the brain to the rest of the body are contralateral, various experiments can be performed on these split-brain patients in order to identify the cognitive characteristics of the two hemispheres. In one experiment, split-brain patients are blindfolded, and an object is placed in one of their hands. The patients are then asked to name the object. The representation in (7) illustrates how this kind of naming task is designed. If an object is placed in a patient's left hand, the patient usually cannot identify the object verbally. If, however, the object is placed in the patient's right hand, he or she usually can name the object. Can you explain why? When the object is in the patient's left hand, sensory information from holding the object, which in this case is tactile information, reaches the right hemisphere. Since the corpus callosum is severed, the information cannot be transferred to the left hemisphere; because the patient is then unable to name the object despite being able to feel what it is, we conclude that the language centers must be in the left hemisphere. When the object is in the patient's right hand, however, sensory information from holding the object reaches the left hemisphere. In this case, the patient is able to name the object; therefore, the language centers must be in the left hemisphere. The information can be transferred to the language centers because it does not have to cross the corpus callosum to get there. Once it reaches the language centers, the patient can say what the object is.

(7)   A schematic representation of an object-naming task

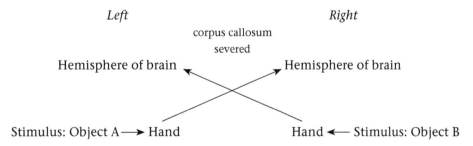

Result: The patient can name object B, but not object A. Therefore, this patient's language centers must be located in the left hemisphere.

(The arrows indicate the transmission of the stimuli.)

Hemispherectomy, an operation in which one hemisphere or part of one hemisphere is removed from the brain, also provides evidence for the location of the language centers. This operation, performed only occasionally on people who experience severe seizures, affects the patient's behavior and ability to think. It has been found that hemispherectomies involving the left hemisphere result in aphasia much more frequently than those involving the right hemisphere. This indicates that the left side of the brain is used to process language in most people, while the right side has much less to do with language processing.

Much of the evidence for the lateralization of the areas of the brain that deal with language processing presented in this file comes from psycholinguistic experiments (e.g., dichotic listening task) and neuro-imaging experiments (see File 9.7). Other evidence, including some of the earliest hints that language processing occurs in specific regions of the brain, comes from examining patients with language disorders. Such cases are discussed in File 9.2.

FILE 9.2

....

Language Disorders

9.2.1 Language Disorders

In the 1860s, physician Pierre Paul Broca observed that damage to the left side of the brain resulted in impaired language ability, while damage to the right side of the brain did not. Since that time, a number of other language disorders have been traced to particular types of brain injuries, helping pin down which regions of the brain are involved in language processing. These conditions, in which patients lose their ability to produce or understand language due to stroke or brain injury, are known as **aphasias.** Other medical conditions that prevent patients from acquiring language normally have also been identified, influencing discussion of how language acquisition works.

9.2.2 Broca's Aphasia

The linguistic skills that are affected as a result of aphasia depend on the exact location of the damage to the brain. Each case of aphasia is unique, since no two individuals have damage to the exact same parts of the brain. However, patients with damage to similar regions of the brain show similar symptoms. Individuals with **Broca's aphasia,** a result of damage to the inferior frontal gyrus (IFG, also known as Broca's area), suffer from an inability to plan the motor sequences used in speech or sign. When they attempt to produce language, they speak or sign haltingly and have a difficult time forming complete words. They also tend to use telegraphic speech. For English, for example, this means that their speech lacks morphological inflection and function words like *to* and *the*. For ASL, this means that their language contains no inflections or classifiers. The examples in (1) and (2) illustrate the speech of two Broca's aphasics, speakers of English and of ASL, respectively.

(1) Speech produced by a Broca's aphasic

    Examiner: Tell me, what did you do before you retired?
    Aphasic: Uh, uh, uh, pub, par, partender, no.
    Examiner: Carpenter?
    Aphasic: [nodding] Carpenter, tuh, tuh, tenty year.

(2) Sign produced by a Broca's aphasic. Examiner's signs are translated into English; aphasic's signs are in CAPITALS; finger-spelled words are hyphenated (from Poizner et al. 1987: 120).

    Examiner: What else happened?
    Aphasic: CAR . . . DRIVE . . . BROTHER . . . DRIVE . . . I . . . S-T-A-D . . . [attempts to gesture stand up]
    Examiner: You stood up?
    Aphasic: YES . . . I . . . DRIVE . . . [attempts to gesture goodbye]
    Examiner: Wave goodbye?

Aphasic:	YES . . . BROTHER . . . DRIVE . . . DUNNO . . . [attempts to wave good-bye]
Examiner:	Your brother was driving?
Aphasic:	YES . . . BACK . . . DRIVE . . . BROTHER . . . MAN . . . MAMA . . . STAY . . . BROTHER . . . DRIVE.

Broca's aphasia seems to result in primarily expressive disorders: it is very difficult for Broca's aphasics to produce speech. The aphasic in (1), for example, produces the word *carpenter* correctly only after several attempts. The aphasic in (2) pauses after almost every word, as indicated by the ellipses. For the most part, Broca's aphasics do not have a problem understanding the speech of others, although they may have some difficulty with unusual or complex syntactic structures. For instance, comprehension is likely to break down when the contributions of function words or inflections are extremely important to the understanding of the message, as in reversible passives such as *The lion was killed by the tiger.* A Broca's aphasic is quite likely to rely on the order of the words in this sentence, understanding it as identical to the active sentence *The lion killed the tiger.*

9.2.3   Wernicke's Aphasia

Individuals with damage to the Sylvian parietotemporal area (SPT) and the posterior superior temporal gyrus (STG), together often known as Wernicke's area, exhibit a much different type of language disorder, called **Wernicke's aphasia,** for Karl Wernike, who studied aphasias in the late nineteenth century. It is very difficult for a patient with this problem to understand the speech of others. This often results in the Wernicke's aphasic misinterpreting what others say and responding in an unexpected way. Moreover, because Wernicke's patients have trouble selecting appropriate words from their mental lexicon, they have a tendency to produce semantically incoherent speech. These two effects result in the type of speech you see in (3).

(3)   A sample of speech produced by a patient with Wernicke's aphasia

Examiner:	Do you like it here in Kansas City?
Aphasic:	Yes, I am.
Examiner:	I'd like to have you tell me something about your problem.
Aphasic:	Yes, I, ugh, can't hill all of my way. I can't talk all of the things I do, and part of the part I can go all right, but I can't tell from the other people. I usually most of my things. I know what can I talk and know what they are, but I can't always come back even though I know they should be in, and I know should something eely I should know what I'm doing. . . .

Wernicke's patients also often speak in **circumlocutions,** or round-about descriptions that people use when they are unable to name the word they want. For example, the patient may say *what you drink* for *water* and *what we smell with* for *nose.* The syntactic order of words is also altered. *I know I can say* may become *I know can I say.* That patients with Wernicke's aphasia are unable to comprehend the speech of others is demonstrated by the fact that they often cannot follow simple instructions, such as "stand up," "turn to your right," and so on. Wernicke's aphasics are the most likely of the aphasic types to experience **anosognosia,** the unawareness of the disturbances in their own language. Patients with anosognosia often seem to believe that their speech is interpretable by others when in fact it is not.

9.2.4 Conduction Aphasia

A third type of language disorder, called **conduction aphasia,** is characterized by an inability to repeat what someone has just said. People with this type of aphasia can understand what is said to them but make characteristic phonological speech errors when speaking spontaneously, especially when attempting to repeat what they are hearing. These aphasics are aware of the errors in their speech and know what words they want to say, but they often pronounce the words incorrectly. After more than one hundred years of attributing conduction aphasia to problems with the arcuate fasciculus, researchers have begun to see evidence that conduction aphasia is due to damage in the STG. Neurologists have even been able to induce conduction aphasia-like symptoms during brain surgery on non-aphasic patients by gently shocking this area of the cortex (Anderson et al. 1999).

9.2.5 Problems with the Angular Gyrus

The last two acquired language disorders we will mention are **alexia** and **agraphia,** which are both caused by damage to the angular gyrus, the part of the brain that converts visual stimuli to auditory stimuli, and vice versa. Alexia is the acquired inability to read and comprehend written words. Patients with alexia were previously able to read, but due to damage to the angular gyrus they can no longer accurately interpret images as linguistic input. Occasionally, this problem is accompanied by the acquired inability to write words, known as agraphia. This disorder is often attributed to the inability of the angular gyrus to relate the phonetic form of a stimulus with a written form in the visual cortex or with the motor controls necessary to write out the word. Interestingly, it is possible to have alexia without agraphia, so that a person can write perfectly well but cannot read what he has just written. Alexia is also sometimes known as acquired dyslexia, but is quite different in cause, effect, and treatment from **developmental dyslexia.** Developmental dyslexia is a type of learning disability that makes it difficult for people to learn to read fluently. There are several different kinds of developmental dyslexia, with different causes resulting in a diverse set of reading difficulties, but it is important to emphasize that dyslexia is **not** a sign of decreased intelligence.

9.2.6 Aphasia in Signers

In Section 9.2.2 you saw that aphasia can occur in users of both spoken and signed languages. You further saw that both the speaker in (1) and the signer in (2) have damage to the same region of the brain (the IFG/Broca's area) and display similar symptoms (both have trouble producing words). These similarities were an important finding, because researchers had previously been unsure about whether signed languages were processed in the same areas of the brain as spoken languages. It had been thought that signed languages were processed in the right hemisphere of the brain because the right hemisphere is responsible for motor control functions in most people, and producing ASL uses the same muscles as, say, picking up a cup. However, this is not the case: users of signed languages with aphasia show damage to the same regions in the left hemisphere of the brain and have the same symptoms as users of spoken languages. A signer with damage to the SPT and the STG (Wernicke's area), for example, would display fluent but meaningless speech, similar to the aphasic in (3).

In hindsight, it makes a lot of sense that signed languages are also processed in the language centers of the brain; after all, they exhibit all the other characteristics of human languages. The idea that they could be processed in the right hemisphere of the brain was possibly guided by a lingering doubt that signed languages were real languages. However, of course, we know that spoken languages are not controlled by the motor control centers of the right hemisphere of the brain, even though the same muscles used to make speech sounds are also used for eating and chewing. Thus, regardless of whether a language user speaks or signs, the muscles he or she uses to do this are controlled by language centers in the left hemisphere of the brain, even though the very same muscles are controlled by the motor control centers of the right hemisphere if he or she is involved in a nonlinguistic motor task.

David Corina and his colleagues (1999) report some interesting data from two signers with brain damage that illustrate the point made above. We all have different facial expressions: we can convey sadness, happiness, anger, fear, surprise, and so on, on our face. These are called **affective facial expressions.** Signed languages, such as ASL, also have particular facial expressions with grammatical functions in the language (see Section 2.7.7). These facial expressions, called **linguistic facial expressions,** or non-manual markers, differ from affective facial expressions in that they do not have to express something about the speaker's emotions, they have a rapid onset and offset, and they may involve the use of individual muscles that generally are not used in affective facial expressions. ASL, for example, requires the use of particular facial expressions in relative clauses, conditionals, some adverbials, and so on. If a relative clause or conditional is signed without the appropriate linguistic facial expression, it is ungrammatical.

Corina and his colleagues investigated the signing of two native ASL speakers with brain damage. Gail had damage to the left IFG (Broca's area), and Sarah had damage to very similar areas in the right hemisphere, in the area responsible for motor control. Examples of how these two women signed are given in (4), (5), and (6) from Corina et al. (1999: 322, 325) and are discussed below. Signs are given in CAPITAL letters, finger-spelled words are hyphenated, and linguistic facial expressions are given above the signs.

(4)   Sign produced by Gail

      ASL: *DIANE, HEARING AUNT, WAIT, PHONE[iterative]
      English translation: 'Diane, hearing aunt, waited for a long time and phoned again
                              and again.'

                              _____rel
      Correct ASL: DIANE, HEARING AUNT, WAIT, PHONE[iterative]
      English translation: 'Diane, who is my hearing aunt, waited for a long time and
                              phoned again and again.'

(5)   Sign produced by Sarah

                                             _____th
      ASL: WOMAN WASH WATER OVERFLOW STUPID SHE STUPID
                              'The woman washed (the dishes), the water flows and she
                              didn't notice it. That's stupid, she's really stupid.'

(6)   Sign produced by Sarah

      ASL: SOMETIMES[Habitual] DEPRESS[Intense], CRY, WHEN I
                              U-P-S-E-T, FIRST STROKE, I CRIED.
      English translation: 'Sometimes I got depressed and I cried. When I first had my
                              stroke, I became very upset about it and cried.

Gail, who has damage to the IFG/Broca's area, is not able to use linguistic facial expressions. The example in (4) illustrates this. The sentence requires the linguistic facial expression for a relative clause, indicated by the *rel* above the sign AUNT in the correct version of the sentence. However, Gail omits the *rel* facial marker, and her sentence is ungrammatical. Despite this, Gail is still able to use affective facial expressions. In fact, she uses more affective facial expressions than many people when she speaks.

Sarah, on the other hand, uses linguistic facial expressions perfectly. An example of this is given in (5), where she correctly uses the linguistic facial expression *th* (which means 'carelessly'). However, she talks about her depression when she first had her stroke (in (6)) without a single affective facial expression. Her face is blank while she tells the story, even though the story is sad and we would expect it to be accompanied by a "sad face," especially because affective facial expressions are particularly prevalent in Deaf culture in the United States. The cases of Gail and Sarah illustrate nicely how the same set of muscles can work for one task but not for another if the tasks are controlled by different parts of the brain. They also provide evidence that linguistic facial expressions are not just muscle movements—they are part of language.

9.2.7 Specific Language Impairment, Williams Syndrome, and the Innateness Hypothesis

Several influential theories of language acquisition posit that our minds are specifically set up to learn and use language (see File 8.1, especially Section 8.1.2). These theories suggest that linguistic processing is done by a dedicated language module in the mind—certain areas and functions that are specific to language and not just the result of a general problem-solving routine applied to linguistic input. If this is true, it might be the case that certain disorders could affect language processing differently than they affect overall problem solving. A disorder that causes all language processing to be poor while general intelligence is still high overall, or, conversely, causes general intelligence to be low but leaves language mostly untouched, would be evidence supporting such a theory. Proponents of theories of innateness have argued that specific language impairment and Williams syndrome are two such disorders.

Specific language impairment (SLI) can be diagnosed when children with otherwise normal cognitive abilities fall significantly behind their peers in language-related tasks. These children perform normally on tests of nonverbal intelligence, receive ample linguistic input in their home environments, and do not have any other disabilities to explain their poor linguistic performance. People with SLI make unusual speech errors like saying *Why the man have two cat?* instead of *Why does the man have two cats?* These errors can occur at many levels of linguistic structure, from speech sounds to words and syntax. SLI seems to have a strong genetic component; if one member of a family has SLI, there's a good chance that others do too. At first glance, this may seem a perfect example of a disorder that targets only the language-processing parts of our brains. However, further research (Tallal 1990) has shown that SLI is not as specific to language as its name implies, since it negatively affects performance in many kinds of tasks that involve quick successions of stimuli. There is also debate as to whether the underlying cause of SLI is a deficit in auditory processing in general or something more tightly tied to language. The case for SLI as a disorder that affects only language is thus not clear-cut.

From the other direction, the rare developmental disorder **Williams syndrome** has been put forth as a case where language processing is relatively spared even when general cognitive development is clearly delayed. This disorder, which is caused by the deletion of about twenty genes on chromosome 7, affects about 1 in 7,500 children. Individuals with Williams syndrome generally exhibit very outgoing social behavior, paired with substantial impairment of visuospatial and mathematical skills. This impairment does not equally affect all cognitive function; while logical reasoning and knowledge of social norms are impaired, individuals with Williams syndrome often show fair to rich vocabulary and oral communication skills. Early descriptions of Williams syndrome patients (Bellugi et al. 1990) pointed to this discrepancy as evidence that language processing relies on specialized brain routines rather than general intelligence functions. However, later studies point out that the claim of "intact language" in Williams syndrome may not stand on sufficient scientific evidence (Brock 2007). Brock argues that the earlier claims about the relative strength of verbal skills in Williams syndrome patients were based on comparisons with the verbal skills of individuals with Down syndrome and with other nonverbal skills that are remarkably delayed in Williams syndrome. In other words, those who said that Williams syndrome spares language were not judging against the correct standards and so have not successfully shown that Williams syndrome patients have normal language abilities. In fact, Stojanovic and colleagues (e.g., Stojanovic 2010) report that individuals with Williams syndrome do not show more advanced language skills than control subjects matched for verbal mental age. When compared to control groups matched for chronological age, Williams syndrome patients showed substantial language deficits (Mervis and John 2008), especially in tests of spatial language (like locative prepositions *in, on, next to*) and relational language (*more/ fewer, before/after*, etc.). As with SLI, debate continues as to whether the language capabilities of those with Williams syndrome support the argument for innateness of language.

All of the language disorders presented in this file present substantial challenges for the people dealing with them. Language is such a fundamental part of our lives that losing all or part of one's linguistic abilities can be quite harrowing, but people with these disorders can and do continue to lead worthwhile, successful lives. As language scientists, we can use the knowledge gained from studying these disorders to develop treatments and to gain a deeper understanding of how our minds actually work to construct language.

·······································

Speech Production

9.3.1 From Thought to Utterance

As described in File 1.2, the communication chain involves both the sending and the receiving of messages. When we send messages using language—that is, when we speak or sign—the brain is involved in planning what we want to say and in instructing the muscles used for speaking or signing. This process of sending messages is called **speech production** and is the focus of this file.

A fair amount of planning is involved in producing an utterance. Refer to the diagram in (1) in File 1.2: steps 1–4 all illustrate the planning stages. First, we need to know what we want to say before we can decide how to say it. That is, we first have an idea or a thought that we then translate into an utterance. However, the nature of our thoughts is different from the nature of our utterances. Our thought process is global or holistic: we think of the complete idea simultaneously. But producing an utterance is linear: we cannot produce all parts of our idea at once. Instead, we produce a sentence one word at a time and, within each word, one sound at a time. (This is true at least of spoken languages. In signed languages, various linguistic elements can be expressed simultaneously. See Files 2.7 and 4.2 for simultaneous aspects of signed-language phonetics and morphology; there are also simultaneous elements of the syntax of signed languages. However, even in signed languages, only some elements are produced simultaneously: there is a linear ordering of various components in any given utterance.)

Imagine that you wanted to express to a friend that you are tired. The idea of being tired is in your thoughts as a whole, in its totality. But when you actually tell your friend that you are tired, that is, when you translate the thought into an utterance, you cannot convey the complete idea simultaneously. Instead, you need to translate your thought into a linear order of words. Suppose that you said to your friend, *I am tired*. In this case, you first convey the information that the message pertains to you, then you express that the message concerns your state of being, and finally you express that this state of being is feeling tired. You cannot convey all the parts of the message at the same time. Note that this linearity is true also at the phonetic level: you don't express the word *tired* in one action; instead, you start with the [t] and then move on to the vowel [ɑɪ] and so on.

9.3.2 Models of Speech Production

Many steps are involved in translating a message from a thought into an utterance. The example above hinted at two of them: when planning an utterance, we need to choose appropriate words and put them in an appropriate order. But much more is involved in producing an utterance. The diagram of the communication chain that was presented in File 1.2 includes some of the other steps, such as putting sounds together with those words. This diagram, however, was an oversimplification of one view of how the chain of events in speech production works. Two of the most prominent models of speech production are discussed below.

Let's first look at Fromkin's model of speech production (1971), one of the earliest models proposing planning stages for speech production.

(1) Fromkin's model of speech production
     1. Meaning is identified.
     2. Syntactic structure is selected.
     3. Intonation contour is generated.
     4. Content words are inserted.
     5. Function words and affixes are inserted.
     6. Phonetic segments are specified.

Fromkin's model suggests that utterance planning progresses from meaning to the selection of a syntactic frame, into which morphemes are inserted, to the choice of allophones. Let's look at an example. To convey *Peter walked down the stairs,* the planning would go through the following stages:

(2) 1. The meaning of the idea of 'Peter walking down the stairs sometime in the past' is identified.
     2. The frame _____ (NP) _____ (V) _____ (Prep) _____ (Det) _____ (NP) is chosen.
     3. An intonation contour appropriate for a statement is chosen.
     4. The content words are inserted into the frame: *Peter* (NP) *walk* (V) _____ (Prep) _____ (Det) *stair* (NP)
     5. Function words and affixes are added to the frame: *Peter* (NP) *walk-ed* (V) *down* (Prep) *the* (Det) *stair-s* (NP)
     6. Phonological rules are applied: for example, the *-ed* in *walked* is pronounced as [t], and the *-s* in *stairs* is pronounced as [z].

Fromkin's model assumes that utterance planning goes through the proposed stages in the order given. Such a model is called **serial** because the different stages of the model form a series or succession. However, other models assume that the different stages involved in planning are all processed simultaneously and influence each other. Such models are called **parallel.**

The model proposed by Levelt (1989) is one of the most influential parallel models. According to this model, three major levels are involved in speech production. The level that corresponds to Fromkin's first stage is called *conceptualization*. Here the concepts of what a speaker wants to express are generated. The second level is called *formulation*. At this level the concepts to be expressed are mapped onto a linguistic form. The formulation level has two sublevels: *grammatical encoding* and *phonological encoding*. At the grammatical encoding level, a syntactic structure and lexical items are selected. Thus, this corresponds to Fromkin's stages 2, 4, and 5. At the phonological encoding level, the phonetic form is specified. This corresponds to Fromkin's stages 3 and 6. The third level is the process of *articulation,* which involves two steps corresponding to grammatical encoding and phonological encoding. Levelt's model is summarized in (3).

(3) Levelt's model of speech production
     • Conceptualization
     • Formulation:
          • Grammatical encoding (selection of syntactic frame and lexical items)
          • Phonological encoding (specification of phonetic form)
     • Articulation

Levelt's model is different from Fromkin's model mainly in that it allows positive feedback to occur in both directions. In other words, later stages of processing can influence earlier stages. This is not possible in Fromkin's model. Slips of the tongue, discussed in the next section, are one source of evidence both for and against each of these kinds of models.

9.3.3 Factors Affecting Speech Production

In fluent speech, native English speakers produce about four syllables per second with very little conscious effort. A number of things affect how quickly we're able to plan and execute speech, including some that might surprise you. As quickly as you can, name the two objects below:

Which one took longer to say? For more than fifty years linguists have known that we access frequent, familiar words more quickly than less frequent, unfamiliar words (Oldfield and Wingfield 1965). *Basket* is about seven times more common than *syringe*, so we're usually faster to name a picture of a basket than a picture of a syringe. Perhaps surprisingly, the length of a word does not have a large effect on how long it takes to begin saying it. Once word frequency is controlled for, it takes about the same amount of time to begin to say *caterpillar* as it does to begin to say *cat*. *Caterpillar* will take longer to physically pronounce, but all of the stages of speech production up to articulation take about the same amount of time regardless of word length (Damian et al. 2010).

When we talk, we often refer to the same objects and use the same words multiple times in a conversation, which leads to faster access for repeated terms. Words also undergo **phonetic reduction** when used multiple times in succession, meaning that they are likely to be pronounced less clearly, with some phonemes shortened or even dropped for successive repetitions. For example, think about how you say *probably* in different contexts. What might be pronounced as [pɹɑbəbli] in careful speech might be reduced to [pɹɑbli] or even [pɹɑli] in casual speech. In conversation, this sort of reduction even happens (to a lesser extent) when the same words are used to refer to different objects, and when different words are used to talk about the same object.

9.3.4 Production Errors: Slips of the Tongue

The previous sections illustrate how much is involved in planning and producing even a simple utterance. This complexity has made speech production difficult to study, especially when you remember that all of these steps occur in the mind, before any actual production has occurred. To learn about the stages involved in speech production, it has proven useful to investigate what happens when something in the production process goes wrong, that is, when we make a **production error** or "slip of the tongue." By *production error* we mean any **inadvertent** flaws in a speaker's use of his or her language. It is important to note that production errors are unintentional: we say something that we did not intend to say. For example, if we say *distactful* because we incorrectly believe that it is an English word, then this error relates to our linguistic competence and our knowledge of English, not to the production process. However, if we say *distactful* when we meant to say *untactful,* then this error relates to the production process, not to our knowledge of English. This is why only inadvertent errors can tell us something about speech production.

Production errors can tell us a lot about the process of speech production because they are very systematic: entire units are moved, added, or omitted during a speech error. These units may be features, sounds, morphemes, and words. The fact that virtually all production errors involve these units provides evidence for the psychological reality of the units and suggests that speakers do indeed organize the speech wave in terms of these units.

a. Types of Production Errors. This section will introduce you to some basic types of speech errors. Examples of all error types are given in (4). **Anticipations** occur when a later unit is substituted for an earlier unit or when a later unit is added earlier in an utterance (4a). **Perseverations** can be seen as the opposite of anticipations: they occur when an earlier unit is substituted for a later unit or when an earlier unit is added later in an utterance (4b). **Addition** and **deletion** errors involve the addition of extra units (out of the blue, so to speak) and the omission of units, respectively ((4c) and (4d)). **Metathesis** is the switching of two units, each taking the place of the other (4e). When a metathesis involves the first sounds of two separate words, the error is called a **spoonerism** (4f) (named after the Reverend Spooner, a renowned chronic sufferer of this type of slip of the tongue). **Shifts** occur when a unit is moved from one location to another (4g). **Substitutions** happen when one unit is replaced with another (4h), while **blends** occur when two words "fuse" into a single item (4i).

(4)	*Intended Utterance*	*Actual Utterance*	*Error Type*
a.	splicing from one tape	splacing from one tape	anticipation
b.	splicing from one tape	splicing from one type	perseveration
c.	spic and span	spic and splan	addition
d.	his immortal soul	his immoral soul	deletion
e.	fill the pool	fool the pill	metathesis
f.	dear old queen	queer old dean	spoonerism
g.	she decides to hit it	she decide to hits it	shift
h.	it's hot in here	it's cold in here	substitution
i.	grizzly/ghastly	grastly	blend

b. What Production Errors Can Tell Us about Speech Production. In most of the examples in (4), the unit involved in the production error is a phone. However, the shift in (4g) and the substitution of *distactful* for *untactful* above involve moving or replacing a morpheme, and the substitution in (4h) involves replacing one word with another. Examples like these provide evidence for the psychological reality of phones, morphemes, and words. That is, phones, morphemes, and words are part of our mental organization of the speech wave. Let's think about how these examples show this: in order to substitute, add, move, or delete a phone, the speaker must think of it as a discrete unit. So the speaker is imposing a structure on the speech signal in his mind, even though this structure does not exist physically. (Remember that we do not produce sounds as discrete units. Rather, in a continuous stream of speech, adjacent sounds are coarticulated, and it is difficult to say where one sound ends and the next one starts.) Because these units can be inadvertently separated by the speaker, we say that the sound unit is psychologically real.

But we can go further than this: production errors also provide evidence that phonetic features (the subparts of sound structure, such as the voicing, place, and manner of articulation of consonants; see File 2.2) are psychologically real and not just a descriptive construct made up by linguists. Consider the production errors in (5), where phonetic features, not whole sounds, are being exchanged.

(5)	*Intended Utterance*	*Actual Utterance*	*Error Type*
a.	clear blue sky	glear plue sky	spoonerism
b.	Cedars of Lebanon	Cedars of Lemadon	metathesis

In (5a), the [k] in *clear* is mistakenly voiced, whereas the [b] in *blue* is mistakenly not voiced. Thus, this is a case of spoonerism involving the feature of voicing. In the second example, air is allowed to resonate in the nasal cavity during the [b] rather than during the [n], resulting in *Lemadon* rather than *Lebanon*. That is, the [b] in *Lebanon* is mistakenly nasalized, whereas the [n] in *Lebanon* is mistakenly not nasalized. The fact that individual articulatory movements can be involved in production errors shows that they too are psychologically real units to the speaker—that is, speakers do mentally organize sounds as being made up of a set of articulatory movements.

Language, of course, involves more than just units of speech. In particular, linguists maintain that there is a complex set of rules that the language user follows when making use of these units. One type of rule whose psychological reality can be confirmed by studying speech errors is **phonotactic constraints.** These constraints tell us which sequences of sounds are possible in a given language. For example, the sequence of sounds [sɹ] doesn't occur at the beginning of a word in English. That speakers of English follow this rule is clear from the slip in (6). Notice that the error looks similar to metatheses of [l] and [ɹ]. But the [s] of *slip* has also been converted to [ʃ]. Since [sɹ], which would be the result of simple metathesis, does not occur word-initially in English (see File 3.1 for more on phonotactic constraints), a further change was made to avoid violating this phonotactic rule. Thus, speakers unconsciously follow these rules, even when making mistakes.

(6) | *Intended Utterance* | *Actual Utterance* | *Error Type* |
|---|---|---|
| F<u>r</u>eudian s<u>l</u>ip | f<u>l</u>eudian sh<u>r</u>ip | metathesis + phonotactics |

The rules that tell us how morphemes are to be pronounced are also obeyed when making speech errors. For example, the morpheme that is used most often to indicate past tense has three different pronunciations, [d], [t], and [əd], depending on the nature of the preceding sound. The reality of the rule governing the distribution of these pronunciations is indicated by the fact that it is followed even when the past tense morpheme is attached to a different word as the result of a production error. Since these rules are always followed, they must be part of our mental organization of the language.

(7) | *Intended Utterance* | *Actual Utterance* | *Error Type* |
|---|---|---|
| a. cook<u>ed</u> a roast ([t]) | roast<u>ed</u> a cook ([əd]) | metathesis |
| b. his team rest<u>ed</u> ([əd]) | his rest team<u>ed</u> ([d]) | metathesis |

These examples also demonstrate the reality of the rules for combining morphemes, since even during a speech error we find only past tense morphemes combined with verbs, plural morphemes combined with nouns, and so on. Because we rarely get nonsensical combinations like "noun + past tense," the rules that tell us how words are built must also be part of our mental organization of language.

Furthermore, speech errors can also give us insights into the organization of words in the **mental lexicon** (see Files 4.1 and 9.5). For example, many errors in the production of speech involve the substitution of one word for another because of some semantic relationship between the words. The errors in (8), and many more like them, reveal that the intended word and the substituted word often share some common semantic feature, and that the retrieval process mistakes one word for another. Thus, these semantic similarities must be recognized and the lexical entries in the brain organized accordingly.

(8) | *Intended Utterance* | *Actual Utterance* | *Error Type* |
|---|---|---|
| a. My thesis is too <u>long</u> | My thesis is too <u>short</u> | substitution |
| b. before the place <u>opens</u> | before the place <u>closes</u> | substitution |
| c. He got hot under the <u>collar</u> | He got hot under the <u>belt</u> | substitution |

A similar type of speech error involves a substitution of one word for another based on phonological, rather than semantic, similarities. Examples of this are given in (9). What happens in these cases is that the speaker's retrieval process inadvertently pulls out a word that sounds like the one he intended to use but that is semantically distinct. This type of error is called a **malapropism.** Malapropisms provide evidence that the mental lexicon is organized in terms of sound as well as meaning.

(9) | *Intended Utterance* | *Actual Utterance* | *Error Type* |
|---|---|---|
| a. spreading like <u>wildfire</u> | spreading like <u>wildflowers</u> | malapropism |
| b. <u>equivalent</u> | <u>equivocal</u> | malapropism |
| c. <u>marinade</u> | <u>serenade</u> | malapropism |
| d. I'm a <u>contortionist</u>! | I'm an <u>extortionist</u>! | malapropism |

9.3.5 Production Errors: Slips of the Hands

So far we have talked only about production errors in spoken languages. But the same phenomena exist in signed languages. In analogy to slips of the tongue, such errors are called "slips of the hands." As in spoken languages, signed production errors are systematic, providing evidence that the parameters proposed to describe sign languages are psychologically real. The errors made in signed languages include all the types of speech errors that we introduced in Section 9.3.4, thus giving more evidence for the fact that signed languages, like spoken languages, have all of the same levels of structure. Just as we have had to make some allowances for the different modalities of signed and spoken languages with respect to the notions of phonetics and phonology, however, we must understand that the units involved in slips of the hands are different from those in slips of the tongue. Where spoken language errors may involve units of sound like phones and features, comparable signed production errors involve the **parameters** that constitute a sign. These parameters (introduced in File 2.7) include place of articulation, movement, handshape, non-manual markers, and hand orientation, as well as considerations such as whether one or two hands are used to produce the sign.

The pictures in (10)–(13) illustrate slips of the hands. Both (10) and (11) are instances of metathesis. In (10), the exchange involves the handshape parameter: the particular shape of the hands in MUST and SEE are exchanged. In (11), there is movement metathesis: TASTE is articulated with the movement for GOOD, and vice versa.

(10) a. Correctly signed phrase:

MUST   SEE

b. Error:

error   error

(11) a. Correctly signed phrase:

TASTE   GOOD

b. Error:

error   error

The error in (12) involves whether the sign is produced with just the dominant hand or with both hands. The error in (12) is an anticipation: the two-handedness of TRY is anticipated, and MUST is inadvertently produced with two hands.

(12) a. Correctly signed phrase:

MUST   TRY

b. Error:

error   TRY

Finally, (13) is a case of perseveration of place of articulation: the sign GIRL is accidentally produced at the forehead, the place of articulation for FATHER.

(13) a. Correctly signed phrase:

FATHER   GIRL

b. Error:

FATHER   error

9.3.6 Learning from Our Mistakes

Production errors and the way we catch ourselves at them can provide evidence for or against different models of speech production. For example, the error in (14a) suggests that Fromkin's stage 5 (insertion of function words and affixes) does indeed come before her proposed stage 6 (specification of phonetic segments). Notice that the error in the example occurred during stage 4: when the content words were inserted, *minister* and *church* were switched. Next, the function words and affixes were added, and *church* received the plural suffix that was intended for *minister*. If the phonetic form of the suffix had already been specified at this point, then the speaker would have pronounced *churches* as [ʧɹʧ] + [z] because the phonetic form of the plural suffix for *minister* (the intended recipient of the plural suffix) is [z]. Notice that even though this example provides evidence for Fromkin's model, it is not incompatible with Levelt's model.

(14) ***Intended Utterance***   ***Actual Utterance***
      a. <u>ministers</u> [mɪnɪstɹz] in our <u>church</u>   <u>churches</u> [ʧɹʧəz] in our <u>minister</u>
      b. <u>sp</u>eech <u>p</u>roduction   <u>pr</u>each <u>s</u>eduction

Let's consider an example that provides evidence for Levelt's parallel model. At first sight, the example in (14b) looks like a type of spoonerism. However, if that were the case, the speaker should have said *preach spoduction*, exchanging [pɹ] with [sp]. The fact that the speaker said *preach seduction* can be explained by the **lexical bias effect,** which refers to the fact that phonological errors give rise to real words more often than chance would predict. Fromkin's model cannot explain this effect since the specification of phonetic segments, the stage at which the error occurred, is the last stage of the model. To explain the error, the content word *seduction* would have to replace *spoduction* after specification of the phonetic segments. However, Fromkin proposes that content words are always inserted **before** phonetic segments are specified. Levelt's model, which allows feedback in both directions, can explain the lexical bias effect: after the phonetic form is specified, feedback from the phonological-encoding level to the grammatical-encoding level causes the selection of the real word *seduction*.

Other explanations for the lexical bias effect that are compatible with both theories rely on the fact that we monitor our own speech. We often catch ourselves just before or just after making a speech error, showing that both Fromkin's and Levelt's theories of speech production need to be supplemented with a feedback mechanism after articulation. When speaking out loud, we listen to what we are saying. Evidence for this comes from studies that show that speakers make more speech errors and correct fewer of their errors when they cannot hear themselves (Postma and Noordanus 1996). An interesting series of experiments by Karen Emmorey and colleagues (Emmorey et al. 2009) investigated how this self-monitoring works for sign language users. Their subjects learned new signs while wearing special glasses that either impaired or completely blocked their vision; errors in these trials were compared to errors when subjects could see normally. Surprisingly, blocking out vision did not affect signers' error rates, leading the researchers to conclude that signers use **proprioception,** our sense of where our body parts are and how they're moving, to determine when speech errors were being made. Proprioception has also been suggested to play a role for oral language users, who may know when their tongues and other articulators are in the wrong places. Klima and Bellugi (1979) remark that the overwhelming majority of sign language production errors they observed resulted in possible signs (as opposed to gestures that could not be grammatical signs), suggesting that sign language constraints that are analogous to phonotactic constraints are also psychologically real.

Monitoring for speech errors also occurs before articulation, as shown by Motley, Camden, and Baars (1982). This study relied on an experimental method called the SLIP

(Spoonerisms of Laboratory-Induced Predisposition) technique to increase the likelihood of producing speech errors. Participants read a series of word pairs that all had similar sounds for the start of each word and then a final pair where the sounds were reversed. An example is in (15). The idea was that this would lead to a spoonerism where the initial sounds would be swapped to match the pattern. Try saying each list out loud:

(15) a. Farm   Smoke   b. Tail   Smoke
        Fern   Smash   Term   Smash
        Fat   Small   Tank   Small
        Smart   Fell   Smart   Tell

Can you guess which list led to more speech errors? Motley et al. found that speakers made more errors in list (b) than list (a). They attributed this to an internal monitoring system that was alerted to the taboo-sounding *fart smell* that would be created by an error in list (15a).

Many of the examples above illustrate that the speech wave, despite its physical continuity, is mentally organized into discrete units and that these units follow specific rules and patterns of formation. We also saw that constraints are never violated, not even by mistake, showing that they are an intrinsic part of language itself; that is, they define for us what language is like. Thus, by studying cases in which an individual's linguistic performance is less than perfect, we can gain more insight into the nature of linguistic competence, the unconscious knowledge that speakers of a language possess. Linguists can then formulate hypotheses about the mental constructs that represent this knowledge. We have seen such hypotheses in the form of two models of speech production.

FILE 9.4

Speech Perception

9.4.1 Receiving Messages

As described in both File 1.2 and File 9.2, the language communication chain involves both sending and receiving messages. This file and the following two files are concerned with how we receive messages, that is, how we perceive and interpret spoken and written language.[1] The process of receiving and interpreting messages is called **speech perception.** Speech perception can be seen as the reverse of speech production: in speech production, we have an idea that we turn into an utterance, whereas in speech perception, we hear or see an utterance and decode the idea it carries.

Our ability to understand linguistic messages is quite remarkable. In a matter of milliseconds, we identify sounds, match them with words in our mental lexicon (see File 9.5), and apply syntactic rules to understand the meaning of the message (see File 9.6). We can do this even in a crowded and noisy bar. We can pick out relevant acoustic information (what someone is telling us) in the presence of other noises such as the person at the next table telling a joke, the waiter dropping a glass of beer, and the music playing in the background.

This file deals with the process of identifying the sounds of speech. This is a difficult task because no sound is ever produced exactly the same way twice. For example, if a person utters the word *bee* ten times, neither the [b] nor the [i] in each production will be physically identical. So how do we match, for example, a [b] with the category /b/ in our head if no [b] is physically the same as another? This is called the **lack-of-invariance** problem. This file introduces a number of speech perception phenomena that help explain how we deal with the lack-of-invariance problem and manage to match highly variable phones to phonological categories in our heads.

9.4.2 Speaker Normalization

Suppose you hear someone say, "Would you pass me that [pɪn]?" You look around, but don't see a pin, though you do see an assortment of writing instruments. This might be confusing unless you are from the southern United States (or if you have read Section 10.3.6), in which case you would recognize that the speaker likely pronounces [ɛ] as [ɪ] before [n]. If you know about this variant pronunciation, or have experience listening to people who use it, you will have no trouble understanding that the speaker intended the word *pen*. Taking accent into account is one example of **speaker normalization,** the way we pay attention to what we know about the person talking when we are trying to understand what she is saying.

The speaker-specific traits we have to consider include the gender and physical size of the person talking. We know that, on average, men are somewhat larger than women, and adults are bigger than children, but it is surprising just how much difference that can make

---

[1]The perception of signed language will not be considered here.

in our voices. The vowel plots in (1) below show average frequencies of the first two formants (see Section 2.6.4) in recordings of certain vowels from speakers in a study by Hillenbrand et al. (1995). The vowel spaces of the adult speakers are outlined in solid lines, and those of the children are outlined in dashed lines. This image illustrates several concepts surrounding the lack of invariance. First, note that the formant values of the vowels hardly ever overlap one another. This means that even for the same phoneme, the actual physical sound can vary quite substantially. Second, the differences between the averaged vowel spaces of the adult male speakers and the adult female speakers mean that the identification of a particular sound will depend on knowing who uttered it. For example, a token of [ʌ] from an adult female sounds physically like an [ɑ] from an adult male; furthermore, an adult male's [ʌ] sounds like a male child's [o]. The overall lower pitch range of adult male speakers also means that there is much less acoustic difference among their vowels than there is for the vowels of adult females and of children. Listeners need to know to compare adult male speakers' vowels to each other rather than to those of adult female speakers or to representations of children's vowels, all because of the lack of invariance.

(1)   Plots of vowel spaces based on averaged measurements of the first two formants for four groups of speakers: 48 adult females, 45 adult males, 19 girls, and 27 boys. Acoustic measurements taken from "Coarse sampling" data file on James Hillenbrand's website (http://homepages.wmich.edu/~hillenbr/voweldata.html). Differences in physical size contribute to substantial differences between speakers; note that even for the same speaker, no two productions are exactly alike.

© 2015 by Kodi Weatherholtz

9.4.3   Categorical Perception

One phenomenon that helps explain how we deal with lack of invariance is **categorical perception,** which occurs when equal-sized physical differences are not equal-sized psychologically. That is, we perceive some continuous physical variables as falling into discrete psychological categories. Differences within categories are compressed, and differences **across** categories are expanded. People come to perceive entities differently after they learn to categorize them. In particular, members of the same category are perceived to be more alike than members of different categories, even if they are equally different. For example, two different kinds of yellow are perceived to be more similar than a yellow and a red, even if the differences in wavelength between the colors in each pair are identical. This is a case of categorical perception.

Many experiments suggest that categorical perception also occurs in language, particularly in consonant perception. Let's look at an example. The sounds [g] and [k] differ only in voicing: [g] is voiced, but [k] is voiceless (see File 2.2). Consider the syllables [gɑ] and [kɑ]. Physically, these sounds differ in their voice onset time (VOT), the time between the opening of the constriction at the end of the stop and the beginning of vocal-fold vibration or voicing in the following vowel, measured in milliseconds (ms). In English, a velar stop with a 0 ms VOT would always be perceived as /g/. In this case, the voicing starts as soon as the stop is released (hence a value of 0 ms for the VOT). However, a velar stop with a 60 ms VOT would always be perceived in English as a /k/. Here the voicing for the /ɑ/ starts 60 ms after the stop is released.

(2) Stimuli for a categorical perception experiment have VOTs of (a) 0 ms, (b) 30 ms, and (c) 60 ms

But what about a velar stop with a 10, 20, 30, 40, or 50 ms VOT? Would it be perceived as a /g/, as a /k/, or as something in between? The answer to this question can be determined by synthesizing velar stops with varying VOTs followed by the same vowel and asking people whether they heard /gɑ/ or /kɑ/. That is, we have a series of syllables of the form [velar stop] + [ɑ]; each velar stop has a different VOT value, ranging from 0 to 60 ms. Figure (2) shows the waveforms and spectrograms of 0 ms (a), 30 ms (b), and 60 ms (c) VOT tokens. Note the difference in frication after the initial release and before the regular pulses of the vowel.

If people listening to this continuum of VOT values were to perceive it as a continuum between /gɑ/ and /kɑ/, we would expect the results of such a task to look like the graph in (3). The larger the VOT, the more /k/-like the sounds would be perceived; we would see a gradual decline in /g/-identification and a gradual increase in /k/-identification as the VOT increases. But if /g/ and /k/ are perceived categorically, we would expect a graph like the one in (4). Sounds within one category (either the /g/ category or the /k/ category) would be perceived as similar or the same, but sounds across category boundaries would be heard as different. In this case we would expect to see a sharp drop in /g/-identifications at the category boundary.

(3)   Schema of continuous perception in an identification task

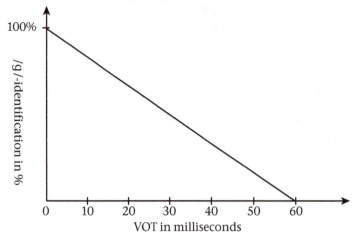

(4)   Schema of categorical perception in an identification task

As already mentioned, consonants are perceived categorically, so (4) and not (3) shows how velar stops with continuously varying VOTs are perceived. The category boundary for speakers of English is at about 30 milliseconds, as shown in (4).

The identification task just described is not enough, however, to prove that consonants are perceived categorically. It is possible that we do perceive the synthesized velar stops as a continuum, but since we have names only for the sounds /g/ and /k/, we pick the sound name that is closest to what we heard: 'g' for everything that sounds similar to a /g/, and 'k' for everything that sounds similar to a /k/. To prove that within-category members are really perceived as the same sound, and across-category members as different sounds, we need to see if listeners can tell the difference between short and long VOT tokens from within the same category. That is, does a 0 ms VOT /g/ sound the same as a 20 ms VOT /g/ for English speakers? If the same physical 20 ms difference matters to perception only when it crosses the boundary (say, from 20 ms VOT to 40 ms, from /g/ to /k/), then we would say we have true categorical perception for this contrast. And this is indeed what discrimination experiments have shown.

Categorical perception occurs as a result of exposure to one's native language. Six-month-old infants of English-speaking parents perceive the difference between two velar stops with 0 and 20 ms of VOT, something that English-speaking adults cannot do (since they hear them both as members of the /g/ category). By the time the infants are twelve months old, they no longer perceive this difference, and they display the same discrimination behavior as English-speaking adults. The difference between 0 and 20 ms VOT never makes a difference in English, but a difference between 20 and 40 ms VOT does, so infants learn to pay attention to only those differences that will be useful to them. This means that exposure to our native language changes the way we perceive consonants, allowing us to deal with the lack-of-invariance problem.

It is important to mention that categorical perception seems to be found in all languages, but that the exact location of the boundaries between different categories differs from language to language. The category boundary between /b/ and /p/ is at about 30 ms, for example, for speakers of English, but at around 0 ms for speakers of Spanish.[2] This means that Spanish speakers perceive a bilabial stop with a VOT of 20 ms as /p/, whereas English speakers perceive the same sound as /b/.

The previous discussion has dealt only with the perception of consonants, because vowels are not perceived categorically. How can we explain this difference between vowels and consonants if categorical perception helps us identify sound categories? It has been suggested that categorical perception is not necessary for vowels because they are usually longer and perceptually more prominent than consonants. Thus, when we hear a vowel, we get enough acoustic information, even in fast speech, to determine the identity of the vowel without having to rely on a mechanism like categorical perception. Consonants, on the other hand, do not always provide enough acoustic information to determine their identity, and we have to rely on categorical perception.

9.4.4 Context and Rate Effects

Knowing now that we perceive consonants categorically may lead us to conclude that making out individual sounds in a stream of speech is a straightforward task despite variability in the acoustic signal. We may hear the sounds [k], [æ], and [t] and understand *cat,* or we may hear [k], [u], and [l] and understand *cool,* both thanks to categorical perception. Now say the phrase *cool cat* to yourself several times. Pay attention to what your tongue feels like during the /k/ at the beginning of each word. Do you feel the difference? Notice that in the previous section we considered two different stops preceding the same vowel [ɑ]. A further complication arises with the [k] in *cat* and the [k] in *cool:* they are acoustically rather different not because of differences in VOT but because the [k] in *cat* is produced farther forward in the mouth than the [k] in *cool.* This is an example of co-articulation, in which the way a phoneme is pronounced is influenced by the surrounding sounds (see Section 2.1.2). Even when we hear the same phoneme, from the same talker, co-articulation means that lack of invariance is still a problem. Luckily, our perceptual system can also handle this: we are able to correctly identify both sounds as the phoneme /k/ by taking the following vowel into account. This means that how we identify an individual sound depends on its context, that is, which sounds occur before and after it. The problem of contextual variation is handled by our perceptual system, but it is one of the major difficulties facing speech synthesis (see File 16.3).

The rate of speech also affects the acoustic properties of a sound. For example, in faster speech, stops have shorter VOTs. This means that a [kɑ] produced twice as fast as another [kɑ] will have a VOT that's approximately half that of the slower production. So if the slower [kɑ] has a VOT of about 40 ms, the faster [kɑ] will have a VOT of about 20 ms. In the previous section we said that a speaker of English will perceive a velar stop with a VOT of 20 ms as a /g/. So how can we tell whether a velar stop with a VOT of 20 ms is a /g/ that is produced comparatively more slowly or a /k/ that is produced faster? The answer is **rate**

---

[2]This means that speakers of Spanish perceive bilabial stops with VOTs greater than 0 ms as /p/, and bilabial stops with VOTs smaller than 0 ms, such as –40 ms, as /b/. A VOT of –40 ms means that the voicing starts 40 ms before the stop is released.

normalization: we are able to take the rate of speech into account when making this decision. Listeners adjust to a person's speaking rate incredibly fast, often within several hundred milliseconds, and decisions about sound categories are then based on this rate adjustment. In fast speech, function words may also undergo substantial phonetic reduction to the point that they are unrecognizable out of context, but listeners taking speech rate into consideration are able to figure out the correct meaning.

9.4.5   The McGurk Effect

The **McGurk effect** (McGurk and MacDonald 1976) is another piece in the puzzle of how we deal with variability. It illustrates that we rely not only on the highly variable acoustic signal but also on visual information to perceive sounds. The McGurk effect occurs when a video showing a person producing one sound is dubbed with a sound-recording of a different sound.

As surprising at it may seem, if you watch a video showing a person producing the syllable [gɑ] with the sounds [bɑ] dubbed over it, you will actually hear [dɑ]! Why would this be the case? The answer is that visual information is integrated with auditory information in the processing of speech. Of particular relevance to our example just above is the fact that [g], [b], and [d] are all voiced stops, differing only in their place of articulation. In addition, [gɑ] and [dɑ] are difficult to distinguish visually because both syllables start with the lips slightly open. Therefore, the visual information is consistent with both [dɑ] and [gɑ], while the auditory information is most consistent with [dɑ] and [bɑ]. The listener perceives [dɑ] because these sounds are most consistent with all the information they are receiving. Notice also that the place of articulation for [dɑ] is at the alveolar ridge, so it is in between the places of articulation for [gɑ] and [bɑ] (see File 2.2). This means that the conflicting visual and auditory information is resolved by a compromise: we hear the sound "in between" the one that is visually presented and the one that is auditorily presented.

The McGurk effect illustrates that, despite considerable variability in the acoustic and visual signals, we are able to combine both types of information to identify speech sounds.

9.4.6   Other Factors Involved in Speech Perception

The previous sections showed that we are able to identify phonological categories despite high variability in the speech signal because our perceptual systems can accommodate many of the contributing factors. There are a number of additional factors that help us categorize sounds, such as our knowledge of phonotactic constraints, the words in our mental lexicon, and the context of an utterance.

As discussed in File 3.1, listeners have unconscious knowledge of the phonotactic constraints of their language. One source of evidence for this knowledge comes from perception errors, also called *slips of the ear*. Specifically, errors of this type always result in possible (though not always actual) words. For example, if we hear the beginning of a word and are not sure whether we heard the sequence [ʃk] or [sk], we can conclude that it was [sk] since English does not allow the consonant cluster [ʃk]. Listeners know what to expect in the way of sequences of sounds; if they did not have this knowledge, we would expect listeners to mistakenly hear words made up of sound sequences that are impossible in their language.

The words in our mental lexicon can also help us identify individual sounds. For example, if we are not sure whether a sound we heard was an /m/ or an /n/, we can determine that it probably was an /m/ if it was preceded by the phones [kɹi] since *cream* is a word of English, but *crean* is not. On the other hand, if the sound was preceded by [kli], we can determine that it was probably an [n] since *clean* is a word of English, but *cleam* is not. Finally, the linguistic context of an utterance can help us identify sounds. For example, the word *heel* is more likely to appear in the context of shoes, whereas the word *peel* is more likely to occur in the context of oranges.

An effect called **phoneme restoration** illustrates how strongly both of these factors influence speech perception. In an experiment by Warren and Warren (1970), participants were played one of the sentences in (5). The * indicates that a sound was replaced with a cough. Interestingly, participants heard the same recording of **eel* as *wheel, heel, peel,* or *meal,* depending on the context that followed. For example, for (5a), they heard *wheel,* while for (5d), they heard *meal.* This means that participants "heard" a sound that was actually not present in the acoustic signal because it fit into the context of the utterance. Furthermore, when they were told that a sound was missing from the utterance and were asked to guess which one it was, listeners were unable to identify the missing sound.

(5) a. It was found that the *eel was on the axle.
  b. It was found that the *eel was on the shoe.
  c. It was found that the *eel was on the orange.
  d. It was found that the *eel was on the table.

FILE 9.5

....

Lexical Access

9.5.1 What Is Lexical Access?

The average college student knows about 50,000 different words (Miller 1996). When we hear a series of phonemes (or see a sign[1]), how do we figure out which word we're hearing? This is the problem of **lexical access.** The words that we know make up our **mental lexicon,** and in order to determine which word we're hearing we need to filter through this imaginary dictionary in our heads to arrive at just the word the speaker intended. This process is incredibly fast, taking only about 250 ms. Lexical access is made even more difficult due to the fact that many words might fit into a sentence at a particular place, some words sound very similar or even identical, and it is often not clear where one word ends and the next begins in the spoken stream of language.

This file will examine how words are arranged and connected in the mental lexicon, how the process of word recognition proceeds, and how our minds deal with lexical ambiguity.

9.5.2 The Mental Lexicon

When trying to determine how many words a person knows, we have to think carefully about what we want to count as different words. *Cheese* and *duck* definitely count as different, but what about *duck* and *ducks*? Should these be listed separately or grouped together? Most people would probably count *ducks* as a morphological variant of *duck,* and indeed this is the strategy that written dictionaries (and the word count given in the previous section) follow. How about all of the variants of *nation* though? We have *nation, nations, national, nationalize, nationalization, international, nationality,* and a host of others. To list each one as its own word would miss the generalization that they have in common the same root word with a few affixes, which are themselves used to build many other words. In fact, we might well want to count *-al, -ize, -ation, inter-,* and *-ity* as "words" themselves. File 4.1 investigates the extent to which root words and affixes exist independently; our concern here is that our minds need to be able to recognize, parse, and recombine these elements.

Several theories have attempted to explain how morphologically complex words are treated by our brains. The **full listing hypothesis** (Butterworth 1983) suggested that every form of a word we have come across gets its own entry in the mental lexicon, with the idea that this would speed up a search because the exact form of the word we need would have an entry. This results in a huge number of words needing to be stored, even for a language like English with relatively little inflectional or derivational morphology. Hankamer (1989)

---

[1]The vast majority of the research summarized here deals exclusively with auditory-oral languages. Research on the perception of signed languages is scarce, but intriguing. There are many similarities, but also some interesting differences, especially surrounding the movement parameter. See Emmorey (2007) for more details.

pointed out that for more morphologically productive languages like Turkish, this could result in literally millions of entries for every verb. In contrast, the **affix-stripping hypothesis** (Taft and Forsters 1975) posits that only root words are stored in the lexicon; morphologically complex words are stripped down in perception and built back up out of the root plus affixes to determine meaning.

Modern theories propose a hybrid of the two, with some morphologically complex words stored as wholes and others accessed via affix stripping (Burani and Thornton 2003, Schreuder and Baayen 1995). One key variable that determines how a word is stored is its frequency—words we hear all the time are more likely to be accessed as wholes, while words that are less common are looked up by their roots and affixes. For example, even though the word *government* can be thought of as *govern + ment,* it is an extremely common word, about 60 times as common as its morphological root *govern.* Since frequency speeds lexical access, relying on the root word *govern* would actually slow down access to *government* (Hay 2001). Lexical access for complex words is thus a race between direct lookup and affix stripping.

9.5.3 Word Recognition

To begin thinking about how we recognize words that are spoken to us, imagine that all of the words in your mental lexicon are in a race. The winner, the word that you will be conscious of hearing, is the one that gets to the finish line first. It is not a fair race though—some words start off closer to the finish line, others farther back. More common words get a head start, as do those that make sense in the context of your current discussion. Syntactic categories can affect a word's starting position too; if you have just heard a preposition, a noun is likely to come next and a verb is unlikely, so all the nouns take a step closer to the finish line and verbs take a step back. Any words that are related to the word you just heard also get a boost. The race begins when we start getting sensory input about the word we are hearing or the sign we are seeing. Those words that match the input best run the fastest, while words that do not match the input stand still or even walk slowly backward. Once a word reaches the finish line, the race is over: we perceive that word, get access to its meaning and associated syntactic content, and all of the words line up again for the next race.

A few key terms are necessary to translate this metaphor into the language of psycholinguistics. First, **resting activation** describes a baseline level of how likely a word is to be recognized (in the metaphor above, the word's starting point in the race). **Spreading activation** flows from words we have just heard to other related words. For example, if we have just heard *car,* activation will spread to *tire,* and it will be a little easier to recognize the word *tire* for hundreds of milliseconds. Spreading activation will even flow out to a second level, meaning that words like *rubber* that are related to *tire* will get a little boost too. Spreading activation is useful because people generally continue talking about the same topic, so words related to the previous word are likely to come up. One of the most important factors that affect word recognition is how frequently a word is encountered in a language. This **frequency effect** describes the additional ease with which a word is recognized because of its more frequent usage. For example, some words (such as *better* or *TV*) occur more often than others (such as *debtor* or *mortgage*), and words that occur more frequently are easier to access. People also recognize a word faster when they have just heard it or read it than when they have not recently encountered it; this phenomenon is known as **repetition priming.** Repetition priming describes the additional ease with which a word is accessed because of its recent occurrence, having primed itself. Finally, the **activation threshold,** like the finish line in the metaphor above, is the amount of activation needed before a word is recognized. Now that we know the terminology, the next two sections will look at two theories of how this lexical access race is actually run.

9.5.4 The Cohort Model

One commonsense theory of word recognition that receives a lot of support from experimental evidence is that as soon as people hear speech, they start narrowing down the possible words that they may be hearing until only one word is left. This is the heart of the **cohort model** (Marslen-Wilson 1984). In this theory, word recognition begins as soon as the first phoneme of the word is identified. We generate the **initial cohort,** a list of all the words we know that begin with this sound. As more sounds are heard, words that do not match the input will be removed from the **cohort**, the list of remaining possible words consistent with the incoming sound string. At some point, possibly even before the end of the spoken word, only one item will be left in the cohort and we will recognize it. The point where this happens is called the **uniqueness point.**

Walking through these predictions with an example will help. Assume that the first sound we hear is /s/. We can rule out words beginning with any other sound, but words like *summer, spring, stone, sister,* and *spine* remain and form the initial cohort. If the next sound is /p/, many other possible words are ruled out, including *summer, stone,* and *sister.* When the next sound we hear is /ɪ/, *spine* is eliminated because it does not match the acoustic evidence. Only *spring* is left from our initial cohort, so we have reached the uniqueness point and can recognize the word, even though we do not have all of the acoustic information yet.

Several experiments have supported this view of word recognition. For example, one obvious prediction of this model is that if the beginning sound of a word is missing, recognition will be much more difficult, perhaps even impossible. As early as 1900, experiments showed that word recognition is impaired much more when the initial sound of a word is mispronounced than when the final sound is mispronounced. This supports the cohort theory: if the end of the word is missing, it can be predicted based on the initial portion, while it is much more difficult to use the end to predict the early part of the word. Supporting evidence also comes from the timing of word recognition. If we measure how long it takes people to recognize a word, we get highly variable results if we measure from the beginning of the word, but consistent results if we start measuring from the uniqueness point. Although this model makes a lot of intuitive sense and has some experimental support, it leaves several questions unanswered.

One problem is that in listening to running speech, people can't always identify where a word starts. In written English, boundaries are clearly marked, but this is often not the case for spoken language. Recent work by Kim (2013) and Kim, Stephens, and Pitt (2012) investigated how strongly people mark word boundaries in phrases like those in (1). If you say these phrases aloud at a normal conversational speaking rate and without context, you may have difficulty identifying where the word boundaries are in the underlined portions.

(1) a. The young girl had <u>acute kidney</u> disease.
     b. The young girl had <u>a cute kitten</u> in her arms.
     c. The people thought <u>ahead</u> to be prepared.
     d. The people thought <u>a head</u> could be buried there.

Kim and colleagues found that people pronounced the ambiguous phrases (*acute/a cute*; *ahead/a head*) almost exactly the same way whether they were intended as one word or two, unless their attention was explicitly drawn to the contrast or they thought they were talking to old or non-native listeners. For a theory like the cohort model, not knowing for certain when a new word begins is a serious problem.

9.5.5 **Neural Network Models**

Another type of model for lexical access is based on **neural networks,** which are computer models that are meant to simulate how the brain might solve particular problems. Specifically, we know that our brains contain incredibly large numbers of nerve cells called **neurons,** each of which sends out signals to its neighbors in response to a limited set of inputs. Neural networks mimic this behavior by having a number of input nodes that activate or inhibit neighboring nodes, which can then activate or inhibit their neighbors, and so on. Neural networks are usually arranged with nodes in several layers, so that early input nodes pass activation up to a middle layer of nodes, and the most activated nodes in the middle layer in turn send activation on up to a final layer of output nodes. The system as a whole links up the input with the output that is most likely given that input. Some models allow the pattern of activation flow to change if the output is deemed incorrect, allowing the neural network to "learn" over multiple trials.

One influential neural network model of lexical access is the **TRACE model** (McClelland and Elman 1986). TRACE has three layers of nodes, representing articulatory features for things like place and manner of articulation (see File 2.2), phonemes, and words. A schematic of TRACE is shown in (2).

(2)   Schematic of the TRACE model

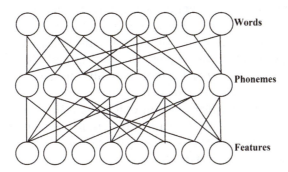

Acoustic input will activate a few of the nodes at the feature level. For example, if we hear someone start to say *Brutus,* the feature nodes for [voiced], [bilabial], and [stop] will be activated. The activated nodes at the feature level will all pass activation to nodes at the phoneme level. In our example, /b/ will be most strongly activated, since it receives support from all three feature nodes. Note that other phonemes will be partially activated: /p/, /d/, /g/, /b/, and /w/ all get support from two nodes, and twelve other phonemes each get activation from one node. This process repeats at the next level: the /b/ node is most activated, so it passes activation up to all words that contain a /b/. Soon, auditory input about the /ɪ/ arrives, a new set of features is activated, and information cascades up to the word level. Words with both a /b/ and an /ɪ/ become the leading contenders, and the process continues until one word reaches its activation threshold.

In the TRACE model, activation can also flow down from the word level to the phoneme level. This allows words that are highly activated to activate a constituent phoneme that may not have had any support from the feature level, a process that could explain the phoneme restoration effect (see Section 9.4.6). Other neural network models, like Shortlist A (Norris 1994), don't have this top-down flow of activation but are still better at compensating for missing information than the cohort model.

Neural network models are an area of ongoing research. Recently, some models, like Shortlist B (Norris and McQueen 2008), have begun to be cast in terms of probability functions rather than spreading activation. In several current neural network models, no single word is declared the winner. Rather, our probability of recognizing each word is proportional to its activation level at each moment of the race. Highly activated words, with supporting evidence from the acoustic signal and linguistic context, are most likely to be perceived. But there is a small chance that our minds will select a less probable competitor instead. However, even the best models only get us up to the point of recognizing the phonological form of the word we are perceiving. What happens when that isn't enough?

9.5.6 Lexical Ambiguity

Sometimes, as in (3), knowing the phonological form of the words we are hearing isn't enough for us to figure out which word the speaker intended.

(3) The judge gave the criminal a very long sentence, but he parsed it just fine.[2]

What happens in word recognition when we get to a **lexical ambiguity** like the word *sentence*? Here, the same phonological string [sɛntɛns] has two possible meanings, and we must figure out which one is applicable. It's probably no surprise that the context plays a big role in helping us select the correct meaning for ambiguous words. In fact, the joke in (3) relies on the context of a judge and a criminal to push your mind toward the 'prison term' meaning of *sentence*. But research reveals that, for a split second, we actually consider all of the possible meanings.

In many painstaking experiments going back at least to the 1970s, researchers have used a wide variety of experimental techniques to show that most of the time, both of the meanings of ambiguous words are at least momentarily considered. The specifics again invoke word frequency—specifically, how frequent one meaning of the ambiguous word is compared to the other. When the frequencies are roughly the same, both meanings are considered. If one meaning is much more frequent than the other, we always consider that option, but we might ignore less frequent meanings if context biases us against them. Interestingly, neurolinguistic studies have shown a consistent pattern whereby the left hemisphere settles on the intended meaning pretty quickly (~200 ms), while the right hemisphere keeps considering both meanings for up to a full second.

---

[2]Sorry! There aren't too many opportunities to use a good linguistics joke.

Sentence Processing

9.6.1 How Do We Put Words Together?

The previous file described how we access words in our mental lexicon and some of the factors that can influence this lexical access. But language is not only about words; it is also about putting words together to form phrases. File 5.5 introduced many of the rules that we follow when we construct sentences and other phrases. However, for any given sentence that we utter or hear, most of us could not explain which rules we use to do so. That is, language users know how to build sentences in their native language(s), but they are not necessarily conscious of the rules that underlie these cognitive processes. Recall that these rules are part of our linguistic **competence** (see File 1.2).

Let's take the sentence *The rock band played all night* as an example. As soon as we hear the word *the*, which can only be a determiner, we expect the next word to be a noun (e.g., *the rock, the platypus*, etc.) or an adjective (e.g., *the loud band, the angry platypus*, etc.). We also expect *the* to be part of a noun phrase and part of the subject of the sentence. Upon hearing *rock*, we update our expectations about what comes next (e.g., *the rock band played, the rock went through the window*, etc.). That is, as we hear a sentence unfold, we assign expressions to syntactic categories (File 5.4) and build a syntactic structure that is updated as a new word comes in. This reconstruction of the syntactic structure of a sentence that is heard or read is called **syntactic parsing**. Just as the word recognition process starts as soon as we hear the first sound of a word (see File 9.4), so also do we start building a syntactic structure as soon as possible. Evidence for this comes from the way we process ambiguous sentences.

9.6.2 Structural Ambiguity

If all linguistic forms were unambiguous and did not correspond to multiple distinct expressions, processing sentences would be a relatively easy task. However, this is not the case. Both **lexical ambiguity** (see File 5.5 and Section 9.5.6) and **structural ambiguity** are constantly present during sentence processing. Structural ambiguity, first introduced in File 5.5, occurs when a string of words has two or more different possible parses resulting from different possible syntactic structures. Below, we consider several different types of structural ambiguity and the problems they cause for sentence processing.

a. Temporary Ambiguity. Let's have a closer look at the example above. We said that the word *the* is unambiguously a determiner. So far, so good. But as soon as we hit the word *rock*, we encounter our first ambiguity. *Rock* could be an adjective, as in *The rock band played*, or a noun, as in *The rock went through the window*. Once we hear *band*, context helps us determine that *rock* is used here as an adjective, since it is unlikely that a rock would have *banned* anything. But now *rock band* is ambiguous, since it could be a complete noun phrase, or it could be used adjectivally to modify a coming noun, as in *The rock band drummer was used to playing loudly*. The ambiguity is finally resolved once we hear *played*: we now know that *band* is a noun, and *played* is not ambiguous. This means that the sentence *The rock band played all night* is ambiguous only temporarily, namely, up until we hear the word *played.* **Temporary ambiguity** is constantly present in everyday conversations. For example, the vast majority of sentences that start with *the* followed by an adjective or noun (e.g., *the good, the tea, the bad, the dream, the small, the dog, the educated, the paper, the slow, the party, the old,* etc.) are temporarily ambiguous in English because many forms are ambiguous between being nouns and being adjectives.

b. The Garden Path Effect. As listeners comprehend temporarily ambiguous sentences, they sometimes momentarily recover a meaning that was not intended by the speaker. These mistakes in syntactic parsing are called **garden path effects** because the syntax of the sentence has led the comprehender "down the garden path" (to a spot where they can go no further and must retrace their steps; think of coming to a dead end in a maze). Garden path sentences are temporarily ambiguous and initially interpreted to have a different syntactic structure than they turn out to have. Let's look at an easy example, given in (1).

(1)   a. While Mary was knitting the scarf fell off her lap.
      b. While Mary was knitting the scarf it fell off her lap.

When we first read *the scarf* in (1a), we are likely to interpret it as the direct object of the verb *knitting.* That is, we interpret the fragment to mean that Mary was knitting the scarf. However, at the verb *fell,* we notice that this parse could not have been correct (because then *fell* would have no subject), and we have to go back and reanalyze the string. In this case, we come to the conclusion that *the scarf* is not the direct object of *knitting* but the subject of the main clause *the scarf fell off her lap.* Such garden path sentences fool us into temporarily entertaining the wrong syntactic structure.

But why are we led down the garden path? The explanation depends on both the syntactic structure of the sentence and the particular lexical items it contains. In (1) we are led down the garden path because *knitting* can be (and often is) transitive. That is, it takes an object: we can knit something, as in (1b), where Mary is actually knitting the scarf. The problem, however, is that *knitting* can also be intransitive (stand alone without a direct object), as in the sentence *Mary fell asleep while she was knitting.* In (1a), the initial assumption is that *knitting* is transitive and that *the scarf* is its direct object; it is only when we come to the verb *fell* that we realize this initial assumption is wrong. This sentence is then a garden path sentence because of this particular property of the verb *knitting.* Compare this to the sentence *While Mary was sneezing the scarf fell off her lap.* Here, we are not led down the garden path because people usually don't sneeze scarves; rather, people just sneeze.

Not all garden path sentences are as easy to recover from as the one above. In fact, for some sentences it can take quite a long time to figure out another structure if our first choice turns out to be incorrect. Some difficult garden path sentences remain **unparsable** for some people. These sentences are grammatical, but their form is so difficult to decipher that some people never figure out the correct structure and meaning. A famous example of a difficult garden path sentence is given in (2).

(2)   The horse raced past the barn fell.

If we interpret the sentence as being about the horse racing past the barn, the sentence seems ungrammatical. This kind of sentence contains a reduced relative clause (that is, a relative clause that lacks the word *that* together with a form of the verb *to be,* in this case, *that was*). Thus, *raced* is not the main clause verb but the verb of the reduced relative clause, and the sentence has the same meaning as *The horse **that was** raced past the barn fell.* Notice that this nonreduced version of (2) is easier to parse. However, both sentences are grammatical and convey the idea of a horse falling while someone was racing it past a barn. To help you understand that *The horse raced past the barn fell* is indeed grammatical, consider the sentence in (3).

(3) The woman driven to the hospital fainted.

This sentence also contains a reduced relative clause and has exactly the same syntactic structure as our difficult garden path sentence. However, people have no trouble identifying (3) as grammatical. If both (2) and (3) have the same syntactic structure, and if (3) is grammatical, then our garden path sentence must also be grammatical. Then why is (2) so much harder to parse than (3)? The answer again lies in the lexical items, in this case the words *raced* and *driven*. First, notice that as a stand-alone sentence, *the horse raced* by itself is fine, but *the woman driven* is ungrammatical. Now consider the simple past and the passive participle forms of *race* and *drive* given in (4).

(4) | **Base Form** | **Simple Past Tense** | **Passive Participle** |
| drive | drove | driven |
| race | raced | raced |

Notice that the simple past and passive participle forms of *race* are identical. This conspires with the fact that a sentence-initial noun phrase such as *the horse* is much more likely to be followed by the verb of the main clause (e.g., *raced* or *drove*) than by a reduced relative clause (e.g., *raced* or *driven*). In conjunction, these facts mean that in the case of (2), we interpret *raced* as the verb of the main clause because this is not only a possible parse but also the more frequently encountered option. In the case of (3), however, we cannot interpret *driven* as the main clause verb. This would be ungrammatical and explains why we have little trouble interpreting *driven* as the verb of a reduced relative clause instead: unlike *raced*, it cannot be the verb of the main clause.

Temporary ambiguities and garden path sentences show that we parse utterances word by word as they are coming in: if we waited until the end of a sentence to begin deciding on a syntactic structure for it, there would be no ambiguities in these utterances since they are compatible with only one syntactic structure.

c. Global Ambiguity. Not all ambiguities are temporary. Some strings of words are **globally ambiguous**; that is, the ambiguity is not resolved by the end of the utterance. Without additional context (such as intonation or preceding/following sentences), there is no way to determine what the intended structure and meaning are. A typical example of a globally ambiguous string of words is given in (5).

(5) The cop saw the man with the binoculars.

The ambiguity lies in how the prepositional phrase *with the binoculars* fits into the rest of the sentence. It could modify the verb phrase *saw the man,* in which case (5) means that the cop used binoculars in order to see the man. This interpretation corresponds to the syntactic structure given in (6a). Intuitively, this structure fits well with the interpretation that the binoculars are used to see the man. Alternatively, *with the binoculars* could modify the noun phrase *the man,* in which case it specifies that the man has binoculars. This is shown in (6b). Strings that are globally ambiguous always have two or more possible syntactic structures, one corresponding to each interpretation. An important question in sentence processing is how people decide which structure a globally ambiguous form has. As with lexical ambiguity, people could consider all possibilities and then decide which one is best, or they could use some strategy to decide which interpretation to consider first and then reconsider if that interpretation does not work out.

In contrast to the way lexical ambiguities are processed (see Section 9.5.6), the garden path phenomenon introduced above suggests that for structural ambiguities, people try one analysis first and consider other possibilities only when the initial analysis does not work out. If people initially considered all the possibilities, they would not be led down the garden path. But what strategies could people use to decide which structure to consider

(6) Two different syntactic structures associated with the same sequence of words
    a.

    b.

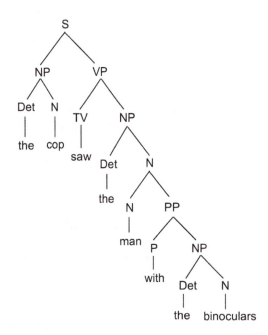

first? Psycholinguists have argued for two different types of theories. **Heuristic models** of parsing suggest that we have certain rules of thumb that we rely on whenever possible in sentence processing. One such strategy, called **late closure,** posits that, if possible, incoming material should be incorporated into the phrase currently being processed. In other words, people attach material to the closest preceding phrase, as long as such an attachment is grammatically possible. In our example, *The cop saw the man with the binoculars,* this means that *with the binoculars* should be preferentially attached to modify *the man* rather than *saw.* If you look at the syntactic trees in (6), you can see that the noun phrase *the man* is "closer" to the prepositional phrase *with the binoculars* than is the verb phrase *saw the man.*

    Constraint-based models of parsing allow nonsyntactic factors like sentence context and real-world knowledge to influence our choices about syntactic structure. If we change (5) to *The cop saw the squirrel with the binoculars,* we would be more likely to interpret it to mean that the cop used the binoculars to see the squirrel than that the squirrel had the binoculars, given that squirrels usually don't have binoculars. On the other hand, if (5) was preceded by the context in (7), we would probably interpret it to mean that the squirrel had the binoculars, despite that fact that this is an unlikely occurrence.

(7) An unusually large squirrel stole a movie star's million-dollar binoculars. The star called the police to report the incident, and a cop was assigned to look for the stolen item. After an hour, the cop saw the squirrel with the binoculars.

Both the choice of lexical items and the preceding context can so strongly favor one interpretation over the other that we may not even notice that a string of words is ambiguous. In fact, naturally occurring conversation is full of ambiguities that are never detected.

Another factor that influences ambiguity resolution is **intonation.** Many ambiguous utterances can be disambiguated via their pattern of pitch changes and pauses, much as punctuation can be used to disambiguate an otherwise ambiguous written sentence. The string in (8a), for example, is ambiguous. It can mean either that Jack and Paul will be invited or else that Mary will be. Alternatively, it can mean that Jack will be invited, and so will either Paul or Mary, but not both of them. Depending on the pronunciation, listeners will favor one interpretation over the other. In particular, (8a) can be said with a **prosodic break** (see File 2.5) after *Paul,* as illustrated in (8b). To see how this works, say the sentence aloud and pause after the word *Paul.* This intonation pattern corresponds to the first interpretation listed above. If people hear it produced this way, they are likely to interpret it to mean that either Jack and Paul will be invited, or else Mary will be invited. On the other hand, if is is produced with a prosodic break after *Jack,* as illustrated in (8c), listeners are more likely to arrive at the interpretation that Jack and either Paul or Mary will be invited.

(8) a. I will invite Jack and Paul or Mary.
    b. [I will invite Jack and Paul] [or Mary.]
    c. [I will invite Jack] [and Paul or Mary.]

The influence of intonation on ambiguity resolution helps explain why we rarely notice ambiguities even though they occur all the time in conversations. Writing, especially informal writing like text messages and email, often lacks disambiguating punctuation and is thus sometimes harder to parse. This is not only the case for global ambiguities. Sentences that might be garden path sentences if they were written do not frequently lead people down the garden path when they are spoken, because a speaker's intonation influences the listener's syntactic parsing process, determining the interpretation that will be chosen before he or she can be misled. For example, if a speaker said the sentence *While Mary was knitting the scarf fell off her lap* with a prosodic break after *knitting,* as in *[While Mary was knitting] [the scarf fell off her lap],* the listener would choose the correct parse to begin with and would not be led down the garden path.

However, it should be mentioned that not all ambiguous forms can be disambiguated through intonation. For example, there are no consistent intonation patterns corresponding to the two interpretations of the sentence *Flying planes can be dangerous,* which can mean 'Planes that are flying can be dangerous' or 'The action of flying a plane can be dangerous.'

In this file we saw that one of the major issues arising in sentence processing is structural ambiguity. Temporary structural ambiguity is constantly present in everyday discourse. Yet we deal with it effortlessly and usually don't even notice the ambiguity. Even when we are led down the garden path, we can usually recover the correct parse rather easily. Globally ambiguous strings aren't any different: we frequently don't notice the ambiguity and are able to decide on a syntactic parse seemingly effortlessly. This is possible because the context of an utterance, common sense, and intonation can help determine the correct parse of an ambiguous string.

....

Experimental Methods in Psycholinguistics

9.7.1 Some General Issues

Other than phonetics, psycholinguistics is probably the area in linguistics that is most experimentally oriented. Files 2.2, 2.3, and 2.6 introduced some of the methods used in experimental phonetics. In this file we introduce selected experimental methods used in the area of psycholinguistics. In particular, we describe some common techniques that are used to investigate particular linguistic phenomena. Some, like fMRI and ERP, introduced below in Section 9.7.2, directly measure brain activity. The methods introduced in later sections are less direct. These allow us to draw conclusions about processing activity by studying participants' behavior: measuring their response times, response types, and so on.

Before talking about methods, however, we should discuss some general issues that arise in experimental research. First, an experiment needs to be well thought through: a researcher needs to find a task or an experimental protocol that will actually address her research question. After selecting a task, the researcher needs to assemble appropriate materials, which, in psycholinguistics, usually consist of words, sentences, and/or pictures presented to subjects either visually or auditorily. In many experiments the materials are designed to trigger some sort of linguistic response in the participants, or the participants are asked to perform a particular task upon being presented with the materials. Two kinds of materials are required. In addition to the experimental stimuli (those words, sentences, and/or pictures that the researcher is interested in), filler items are needed. These are other materials interspersed with the experimental stimuli, used to prevent participants from guessing which aspect of the stimuli the researcher is interested in. Some experiments require one or more **control conditions,** which serve as a baseline against which results from the experimental condition(s) may be compared. Finally, in order to be able to generalize findings, an experimenter should have gathered a large enough number of participants to generate statistically significant data—it's impossible, for example, to draw conclusions about "what speakers of English do" if only three people have been tested.

9.7.2 Measuring Activity in the Brain

Some experimenters are interested in how the brain reacts to certain kinds of linguistic stimuli. To answer this sort of question, psycholinguists select experimental methods that allow them to examine the brain in action. Among these methods are several types of magnetic resonance imaging (MRI), electroencephalography, and magnetoencephalography.

In an MRI, brain activity is investigated by scanning the brain every 1 to 5 seconds with a set of powerful magnets. Depending on the type of MRI, these scans reveal different sorts of information about the structure of the brain. **fMRI** (the f is for "functional") is a technique for determining which physical sensations or activities activate which parts of the brain. As can be seen in the image in (1), it reveals areas of increased blood flow in the brain, which can be related to increased brain activity because active nerve cells consume oxygen, in turn increasing the blood flow to that region. The **dMRI** ("diffusion") looks at

(1) fMRI image highlighting brain regions particularly active in a given task

Image by John Graner via wikicommons

(2) dMRI image showing connections between brain regions

Adapted from image by Aaron G. Filler, via wikicommons. Creative Commons attribution—Share Alike v 3.0 license.

how water flows in the brain, revealing connections between different brain regions, as can be seen in (2), which shows the left and right arcuate fasciculi and part of the corpus callosum. Participants in an MRI experiment cannot move, so the tasks of an MRI study are somewhat restricted. However, participants can be played auditory stimuli, shown visual stimuli, or told to think about something. For example, bilingual participants can be told to think in one of their languages and then in the other to determine whether the same areas of the brain are used for both languages. MRI studies generally provide very good spatial information but, because they are relatively slow, are poorly suited to capturing information about the time course of language processing.

Other experimental methods are used when timing information is critical to answering the research question. Electroencephalography (**EEG**) and magnetoencephalography (**MEG**) detect changes in the electrical or magnetic field given off by the brain. A stimulus is presented to the experimental subject, and researchers look for differences between the responses to target and filler stimuli. Because these responses are a reaction to a particular event (the stimulus), the result is known as an event-related potential, **ERP.** Unlike fMRI, ERP can be used to study the time course of an event, because it detects changes in electrical or magnetic activity in the brain at the millisecond level. MEG can provide high spatial resolution in addition to this temporal resolution, but it is extremely expensive.

ERP analysis refers to certain patterns of electrical or magnetic activity, usually a positive or a negative peak. For example, many studies have found a negative peak around 400 ms after the presentation of an unexpected linguistic stimulus. This is called an N400. Since it occurs after sentences containing unexpected words, it is interpreted as the participant trying to integrate the unexpected word into the sentence context. A positive peak occurring about 600 ms after stimulus presentation, the P600, is strongest in response to agreement violations like *She loves himself* and *I are smart.*

9.7.3 Choosing a Method

One consideration for psycholinguists in selecting their experimental technique is the extent to which the task measures the final result of a process, rather than what happens during the process. Methods that allow us to catch language processing as it is happening are referred to as **online tasks** (*note:* this has nothing to do with the Internet). Methods in which subjects are asked about the results of a completed linguistic process are called **off-**

line tasks. There is not a sharp dividing line between the two; rather, there is a gradient from more offline to more online. One experiment may capture multiple measures, some more online and others more offline.

Another question psycholinguists ask when choosing an experimental method is how natural the task is—that is, whether the task is something a person might do in the normal course of producing or perceiving language in her everyday environment, or whether instead the task is **metalinguistic.** A metalinguistic task is one that requires the person to use explicit knowledge about her language to make judgments about a word or sentence, instead of just using the language as normal. It is somewhat like asking a person to explain exactly how to catch a baseball rather than to just catch one. For this reason, metalinguistic tasks are sometimes dispreferred. Again, this is not an either/or question; some tasks are more natural than others, and some are in between.

The following sections introduce some common tasks that are often used to study language processing. As you read them, consider the extent to which each task is online or offline and natural or metalinguistic. Remember too that this list is far from complete; there are many other topics psycholinguists study and dozens upon dozens of experimental techniques.

9.7.4   Tasks for Lexical Processing

Some common tasks used in the study of lexical processing are lexical decision tasks, naming tasks, and eye-tracking. In **lexical decision experiments,** a participant is asked to identify stimuli as words or nonwords, and the time that it takes the participant to make a decision is measured. Lexical decision experiments have found, for example, that more-frequent words are recognized faster than less-frequent words. **Naming tasks** are similar to lexical decision tasks, but instead of deciding whether a stimulus is a word or not, the participant responds by saying the stimulus aloud. A frequency effect is also found in naming tasks: more-frequent words are produced more quickly than less-frequent words.

Both tasks are often combined with techniques such as **priming.** In priming tasks, participants are presented with one stimulus, the **prime,** right before the stimulus of interest, the **target,** with the idea that having just accessed the prime will affect response times for accessing the target. Priming is often used to study the structure of the mental lexicon. For example, studies have shown that participants are faster to confirm that a stimulus is a word when the prime is semantically related to the target. This means that participants will be faster at confirming that *nurse* is a word when the prime is the semantically related word *doctor* than when the prime is the unrelated word *butter.* From this we can infer that the mental lexicon is partially organized by semantic relatedness. The prime *doctor* partially activated words semantically related to it, such that *nurse* was already partially activated when the target word appeared.

One recent development in the study of online lexical processing is eye-tracking. In eye-tracking experiments, experimenters use special cameras like the glasses in (3) to record all eye movements the participants make during an experiment. Because we usually look at the objects we are thinking about, this method lets researchers study things like the timing of speech perception or how certain aspects of the linguistic input affect what we pay attention to. For example, the participants could be looking at an array of pictures including a caterpillar, a ham, a hamster, a hamburger, a bone, and a bobcat, with the researcher interested in when a listener can distinguish between the three objects all starting with [hæm]. Participants hear an auditory stimulus saying "Now look at the hamster." The eye-tracking device records the point at which the subject looks to the correct object during the auditory stimulus, letting the experimenter know whether listeners are sensitive to the subtle clues that make the [hæm] of *hamster* different from that of *ham* or *hamburger.* Eye-tracking devices have also been used to study sentence processing, as have a number of other methods discussed in the next section.

(3) A student demonstrates use of eye-tracking in a real-world task. One camera in the glasses captures an image of the world in front of her, while another records her eye movement. Combining data from both gives precise information about where she looks.

Photo by Laura Wagner, used with permission.

9.7.5 Tasks for Sentence Processing

As with lexical processing, many different tasks are used to study sentence processing, ranging from the very simple to the very complex. One common task used in the study of sentence processing is an end-of-sentence comprehension task, used to study globally ambiguous forms. The procedure is very easy: participants read ambiguous strings of words and answer a comprehension question after reading each one. For example, to address a question that we addressed in Section 9.6.2, participants might be asked to read *The cop saw the man with the binoculars* and answer the comprehension question *Who had the binoculars?* The answer to this question can tell the researcher how participants interpreted the ambiguous form. This task gives us information only about how a person ends up interpreting an ambiguous string, and participants are often given as much time as they need to answer a comprehension question. As a result, while conscious decision making may be involved in answering the question, that approach cannot tell us what happened during the actual reading and processing. Take, for example, *The cop saw the man with the binoculars*. If in response to the question *Who had the binoculars?* a participant answered that the cop had the binoculars, we would not know whether this was the par-

ticipant's initial interpretation or whether he had originally considered more options before settling on this meaning. It's possible that a participant initially used parsing strategies
such as late closure while reading, but later decided that cops are more likely to have binoculars and therefore changed his interpretation.

To find out what happens during reading itself, a task called **self-paced reading** can be
used. In self-paced reading, participants read a string of words in small chunks, usually one
word at a time. Whenever they have read and understood a word, they push a button to
move on to the next word. For this task, temporarily ambiguous forms are used. Compare
the sentences in (4).

(4)   a. Someone shot the servants of the actress who was standing on the balcony.
      b. Someone shot the servants of the actress who were standing on the balcony.

In (4a), it is the actress who is standing on the balcony, while in (4b), the servants are
standing on the balcony. For these two strings, there is temporary ambiguity up until the
point at which participants read *who,* because whatever follows *who* could modify *the
servants* (i.e., the servants who did something) or *the actress* (i.e., the actress who did something). The choice of *was* or *were* as the next word disambiguates the form: it tells us what
who modifies because rules about verb agreement say that *was* must go with *actress* and
were must go with *servants.* What we are interested in is how long it takes participants to
read the word *was* versus the word *were,* because this will tell us something about how
much processing is required in order to get whichever interpretation the participant is
presented with. To get this information, we measure the time it takes a participant to read
each word (the time between button pushes). If participants thought that *who* modified
servants while they were reading the word *who,* they should take longer to read a following
was than a following *were.* On the other hand, if participants thought that *who* modified
actress while they were reading the word *who,* they should take longer to read a following
were than a following *was.* The reason is that participants would have to change their
analysis if their initial interpretation turned out to be incorrect, and changing the analysis takes time. Thus, unlike the end-of-sentence comprehension task, self-paced reading
allows us to see what happens during processing. Clearly, however, both types of task are
needed to give us a more complete picture of sentence processing.

Practice

File 9.1—Language and the Brain

Exercises

1. Modify each blank diagram of the left hemisphere according to the instructions:

   i. Shade and label the inferior frontal gyrus, the superior temporal gyrus, the middle and inferior temporal gyri, the Sylvian parietotemporal area, the arcuate fasciculus, and the extreme capsule.

(cont.)

ii. Shade and label the areas of the brain and major pathways involved when a word is said aloud.

iii. Shade and label the areas of the brain and major pathways involved when word meaning is accessed.

2. Assume that your brain functions are lateralized in the way that most people's are. Assume you are a subject in a dichotic listening test where you are presented with the following combinations of stimuli. For each pair, which stimulus would you most likely hear more clearly? Explain why you think so.

    a. Left ear: a man saying *cat*
        Right ear: a man saying *dog*

    b. Left ear: a woman coughing
        Right ear: a woman sneezing

    c. Left ear: a door hinge squeaking
        Right ear: a woman saying *horse*

3. A split-brain patient is blindfolded, and a common object is placed in his left hand. Will he be able to say the name of the object? Why or why not? Your answer should include a description of the flow of sensory information from the hand through the brain.

Activity

4. Go to the Links page for Chapter 9 and do the dichotic listening experiments. Based on your responses in the experiment, answer the following questions:

    i. Did the task work for you? In other words, did you hear the word presented either consistently to your right ear or consistently to your left ear?

    ii. Based on your answer, do you think that you process language in the left hemisphere, the right hemisphere, or both hemispheres of the brain? Explain why you think so.

File 9.2—Language Disorders

Exercises

5. Indicate, by putting an "X" on the appropriate lines, which symptoms are found in patients with each type of aphasia.

	Difficulty with Producing Language	*Difficulty with Understanding Language*
Broca's aphasia	_____	_____
Wernicke's aphasia	_____	_____
Conduction aphasia	_____	_____
Alexia	_____	_____
Agraphia	_____	_____

6. A language disorder not mentioned thus far is called *pure word deafness*. In this disorder, patients can hear perfectly fine but cannot interpret what they hear as language. Speech sounds are perceived as hums, whistles, and buzzes, but not as phonemes and words. Given what you know about the areas of the brain involved in language perception, where would you likely look for damage in a patient with pure word deafness? Do you imagine that a similar disorder might exist for signers? Why or why not?

7. A signer with Broca's aphasia has difficulty producing signs. However, the same signer can pick up a cup and even draw pictures. A hearing person, after suffering from a rare virus, lost all motor ability and could not even pick up a cup. However, he was still able to speak fluently. What conclusions do you draw from this for the neurological basis of signs, speech, and general motor control? Explain why.

8. Identify which kind of aphasia the following patients may have. Explain your answers.[1]

    a. Patient: Uh, well this is the . . . the [dodou] of this. This and this and this and this. These things going in there like that. This is [sen] things here. This one here, these two things here. And the other one here, back in this one, this one [gos] look at this one.

        Examiner: Yeah, what's happening there?

        Patient: I can't tell you what that is, but I know what it is, but I don't know where it is. But I don't know what's under. I know it's you couldn't say it's . . . I couldn't say what it is. I couldn't say what that is. This shu- that should be right in here. That's very bad in there. Anyway, this one here, and that, and that's it. This is the getting in here and that's the getting around here, and that, and that's it. This is getting in here and that's the getting around here, this one and one with this one. And this one, and that's it, isn't it? I don't know what else you'd want.

    b. Patient: Wife is dry dishes. Water down! Oh boy! Okay awright. Okay . . . cookie is down . . . fall, and girl, okay, girl . . . boy . . . um . . .

        Examiner: What is the boy doing?

        Patient: Cookie is . . . um . . . catch

        Examiner: Who is getting the cookies?

        Patient: Girl, girl

        Examiner: Who is about to fall down?

        Patient: Boy . . . fall down!

    c. Examiner: Were you in the Coast Guard?

        Patient: No, er, yes, yes . . . ship . . . Massachu . . . chusetts . . . Coast Guard . . . years [raises hands twice with fingers indicating "19"]

        Examiner: Oh, you were in the Coast Guard 19 years?

        Patient: Oh . . . boy . . . right . . . right.

        Examiner: Why are you in the hospital?

        Patient: [points to paralyzed arm] Arm no good. [points to mouth] Speech . . . can't say . . . talk, you see.

        Examiner: What happened to make you lose your speech?

        Patient: Head, fall, Jesus Christ, me no good, str, str . . . oh Jesus . . . stroke.

        Examiner: Could you tell me what you've been doing in the hospital?

        Patient: Yes sure. Me go, er, uh, P.T. nine o'cot, speech . . . two times. . . . read . . . wr . . . ripe, er, rike, er, write . . . practice.

    d. Patient: Boy, I'm sweating. I'm awful nervous, you know, once in a while I get caught up. I can't mention the tarripoi, a month ago, quite a little. I've done a lot well. I impose a lot, while, on the other hand, you know what I mean. I have to run around, looked it over, trebin and all that sort of stuff.

    e. Patient: Well this is . . . mother is away here working out o'here to get her better, but when she's working, the two boys looking in the other part. One their small tile into her time here. She's working another time because she's getting, too.

    f. Examiner: What kind of work have you done?

        Patient: We, the kids, all of us, and I, we were working for a long time in the . . . you know . . . it's kind of space, I mean place rear to the spedwan . . .

    g. Examiner: What kind of work have you done?

        Patient: Me . . . building . . . chairs, no, no cab-in-nets. One, saw . . . then cutting wood . . . working

[1]Part (b) from Avrutin 2001: 87; parts (c) and (d) adapted from Gardner 1975: 61, 68.

File 9.3—Speech Production

Exercises

9. Here is a list of speech errors given in the form *intended production → error*. For each speech error, state what type of error it is (insertion, metathesis, shift, etc.) and which linguistic unit is involved in the error (e.g., phone, morpheme, word, etc.). Is there anything else going on in the error (e.g., phonotactics)? What does each error tell us about the processes involved in speech production?

   a. we have many pets in our house → we have many houses in our pet
   b. brake fluid → blake fruid
   c. an eating marathon → a meeting marathon
   d. speech production → preach seduction
   e. phonological rule → phonological fool
   f. impatient → unpatient
   g. big and fat → pig and vat
   h. Don't drive so fast! → Don't drive so slow!
   i. his immortal soul → his immoral soul
   j. what that adds up to → what that add ups to
   k. Where's the fire extinguisher? → Where's the fire distinguisher?
   l. thin sheets → shin sheets
   m. a no go zone → a no gone [goʊn] zone
   n. also share → alsho share
   o. There's a draft/breeze blowing through the room → There's a dreeze blowing through the room

10. Here is a list of production errors made by signers of ASL. For each speech error, state what type of error it is (e.g., insertion, metathesis, shift, etc.) and which parameter is involved in the error (e.g., place of articulation, movement, handshape, etc.). What does each error tell us about the processes involved in the production of signed languages?

   a. Correctly signed phrase:

RECENT   EAT

Error:

error   error

(cont.)

b. Correctly signed phrase:

FEEL   THAT

Error:

error   THAT

c. Correctly signed phrase:

PLEASE   HELP

Error:

PLEASE   error

Discussion Question

11. Almost all metathesis errors involve switching units from the same phrase. Very few errors involve confusing units between a subordinate clause and a main clause, and even fewer involve units from adjacent sentences. What does this tell us about the way we plan utterances for speech?

Activities

12. Studies of speech errors may involve collecting naturally occurring speech errors or inducing speech errors in an experimental setting. One way to induce speech errors is to have people produce tongue twisters. Start by reading through the tongue twisters in (a) and (b), and answer the questions in (i). Then have a friend read the tongue twisters below out loud. Tell your friend to read them as fast as she can, and record your friend's errors on a piece of paper. Then answer the questions in (ii).

    a. Peter Piper picked a peck of pickled peppers.
    Did Peter Piper pick a peck of pickled peppers?
    If Peter Piper picked a peck of pickled peppers, where's the peck of pickled peppers Peter Piper picked?

    b. One smart fellow; he felt smart.
    Two smart fellows; they felt smart.
    Three smart fellows; they all felt smart.

        i. How do these tongue twisters induce speech errors? Which errors would you expect people to make? Why?

        ii. Which errors did your friend actually make? What type of error are they (e.g., anticipation)? Did you expect this type of error? Why or why not?

13. *Speech jammers* are fun apps that mess up your speech production by introducing a slight delay in the feedback you get about your own speech. Download a speech jammer app (there are many free options), or try the online version at http://www.stutterbox.co.uk/. Attempt to tell a friend a story, and then have them do the same while you listen.

        i. How different was your friend's speech compared to normal? What causes this difference, exactly?

        ii. Did your own speech sound bad to you? Does your friend agree with your rating of your own speech? What might cause you to disagree?

        iii. Experiment with different kinds of utterances—reading aloud, reciting a well-known poem or speech from a play, or singing. Does the interference from the speech jammer affect these in different ways or to different degrees? Why?

File 9.4—Speech Perception

Discussion Question

14. Below are the ASL signs for TWO and THREE. The only difference is the extension of the thumb for THREE. There is no sign in ASL that is produced like TWO but with the thumb only halfway extended. Do you think signers have categorical perception for thumb extension in ASL? Try to design an experiment that would answer this question. What pattern of results would be necessary to claim that categorical perception is present?

(cont.)

2 3

Activity

15. In this activity you will create your own McGurk effect and then answer the questions below. To demonstrate the McGurk effect, you need two other people. The first person will demonstrate the McGurk effect with you. That person should stand behind you and repeatedly produce the syllable [mɑ] while you silently mouth [kɑ]. You may want to practice coordinating your [mɑ]s and [kɑ]s. The second person should watch you but should not be able to see the person standing behind you.

    i. What do you expect the person watching you to hear? Explain why.

    ii. What does the person watching you actually hear? What does he or she hear with closed eyes? How would you explain this?

    iii. Demonstrate the effect again, this time silently mouthing [mɑ] while the person behind you says [kɑ]. Does the effect still work? Why or why not?

    iv. Test the McGurk effect on two other pairs of consonants. Choose a pair of similar consonants and a pair of rather different consonants. For each pair, does the effect still work? Did you expect this? Why or why not?

File 9.5—Lexical Access

Exercises

16. It sometimes happens that we initially misidentify the word that someone says to us, only to recover the correct word a second later. In terms of the race metaphor in Section 9.5.3, this is kind of like what happens when the second-place finisher is promoted to winner due to disqualification of the person who actually crossed the line first. What sort of things could cause a word to get disqualified in speech perception?

17. Say the following sentences out loud at normal speaking rate (that is, relatively fast). What problem do the sentences pose for the cohort model of lexical access?

- This guy looks interesting.
- The sky looks interesting.

18. Look back to the examples of phoneme restoration given in Section 9.4.6 and think about how you might activate the intended word under both the TRACE and cohort models.

    i. Examples like these are very problematic for the cohort model. Why?

    ii. There is a class of phoneme restoration examples that the cohort model can handle just fine. Describe this set of examples and explain why they are not a problem. *Hint:* The word *railroad* could be recognized by the cohort model if the /d/ were missing, but not the /l/—why?

File 9.6—Sentence Processing

Exercises

19. *Bill told Maria he had learned some cool linguistics last week* has an ambiguity based on whether the learning or the telling happened *last week.*

   i. Is this ambiguity lexical or structural?

   ii. Is this ambiguity temporary or global?

   iii. Which meaning of the sentence would be predicted by the late closure strategy?

20. Each of the following strings of words is ambiguous. For each, indicate whether the ambiguity is lexical or structural (draw phrase structure trees if helpful), and paraphrase the two meanings.

   a. The player knew that the ball would be attended by the prince.
   b. The clown caught the thief with the umbrella.
   c. Jill looked for the documents that Julie hid under the table.
   d. We will dispense water to anyone in a sterile plastic bottle.
   e. Tom said that Bill went on a date yesterday.
   f. The mysterious stranger tricked the man with the mask.
   g. Jason mentioned that Susan wanted to go to the movies yesterday.

The following are adapted from news headlines:
   h. We will sell gasoline to anyone in a glass container.
   i. Two sisters reunited after 18 years in checkout counter.
   j. Red tape holds up the new bridge.
   k. Lansing residents can drop off trees.
   l. Stolen painting found by tree.
   m. Enraged cow injures farmer with ax.
   n. Two cars were reported stolen by the Groveton Police.
   o. Kids make nutritious snacks.

21. Each of the following sentences is a garden path sentence. For each sentence, explain how people are led down the garden path. In other words, explain how the sentence is initially parsed and how it needs to be reanalyzed to be parsed correctly. Explain why these sentences lead people down the garden path.

   a. The boat floated downstream sank.
   b. The cotton clothing is made from grows in Mississippi.
   c. The daughter of the king's son admires himself.
   d. The florist sent the flowers was pleased.
   e. They told the boy that the girl met the story.

22. Consider the two strings of words given below. The first one is ungrammatical but easily parsable, whereas the second sentence is difficult to parse (and for some people even unparsable) but grammatical.

Ungrammatical: *The dog ate a bone big.*
Difficult to parse: *The boat floated down the river sank.*

   i. Explain why the first string of words does not form a sentence. For your explanation, you may want to refer to the phrase structure rules for English given in File 5.5.

(cont.)

    ii. Explain why the second sentence is difficult to parse. Explain how the reader initially tries to parse the sentence and why this does not work. What is this kind of sentence called?

    iii. Which of the two strings is harder to understand? Why is it beneficial that we can relatively easily understand at least some non-sentences in our native language?

File 9.7—Experimental Methods in Psycholinguistics

Exercises

23. Assume that your grandfather has had a stroke and is greatly limited in his ability to articulate meaningful speech. How might you determine his comprehension skills? Explain what task you would use and what you could conclude from different potential responses.

24. After completing the activity in Exercise 4, look at the list of reasons the experiment designers say might make the results "messy." (This should appear after you click on "See discussion of experiment.") Explain why each of the points they make might have an effect on your ability to draw conclusions from the experiment.

Further Readings

Banich, Marie T., and Molly Mack (eds.). 2003. *Mind, brain, and language: Multidisciplinary perspectives*. Mahwah, NJ: Lawrence Erlbaum.

Field, John. 2003. *Psycholinguistics: A resource book for students*. New York: Routledge.

Field, John. 2004. *Psycholinguistics: The key concepts*. New York: Routledge.

Sedivy, Julie. 2014. *Language in mind: An introduction to psycholinguistics*. Sunderland, MA: Sinauer Associates.

Traxler, Matthew J. 2011. *Introduction to psycholinguistics: Understanding language science*. Oxford: Wiley-Blackwell.

Wheeldon, Linda. 2000. *Aspects of language production*. Philadelphia: Psychology Press.

CHAPTER
10

Language Variation

·····················

What Is Language Variation?

Most people are aware of the fact that systematic differences exist among languages—for example, that English is different from Spanish, which is different from Arabic, which is different from Russian, and so on. However, many people are probably not aware of the extent to which systematic differences exist **within** languages. **Internal variation** refers to the fact that within a single language, there are different ways of expressing the same meaning. This property is inherent to all human languages and to all speakers of a language. Thus, no two speakers of a language speak exactly the same way, nor does any individual speaker speak the same way all the time.

In this chapter, we will introduce the ways in which languages vary internally and the factors that contribute to **language variation**. For purposes of familiarity, these files will focus primarily on variation in English, but you should keep in mind that variation exists in all languages.

Contents

FILE 10.1

Language Varieties

10.1.1 Languages, Dialects, and Idiolects

The term **language variety** is used by linguists as a cover term to refer to any form of language characterized by systematic features. The term may be used in reference to a distinct language such as French or Italian, in reference to a particular form of a language spoken by a specific group of people, such as Appalachian English or New York English, in reference to the speech of a single person, or even in reference to the way a single person speaks in a particular context. In addition to this cover term, there are more-specific terms that are used to talk about these different types of language varieties. Every native speaker speaks his own **idiolect,** which differs systematically from the idiolects of other native speakers. **Sociolinguistics** is the study of the relationship between these language varieties and social structure as well as the interrelationships among different language varieties.

When a group of speakers of a particular language differs noticeably in its speech from another group, we say that the groups are speaking different dialects. In English, the term *dialect* sometimes carries negative connotations associated with nonstandard varieties. Linguistically speaking, however, a **dialect** is any variety of a language spoken by a group of people that is characterized by systematic differences from other varieties of the same language in terms of **structural** or **lexical** features. In this sense, every person speaks a dialect of her native language. The term *dialect* is also misused by laypeople to refer strictly to differences in pronunciation or sometimes to refer to slang usage. This misuse is easy to understand, because differences in pronunciation or vocabulary are usually accompanied by variation in other areas of the grammar as well and thus correspond to dialectal differences. However, the appropriate term for systematic **phonological** variation (see more in File 10.2) is **accent.** In layperson's terminology, *accent* is often used in reference to "foreign accents" or regionally defined accents such as southern or northern accents. However, here again it must be noted that every person speaks with an accent. This point may be easier to appreciate if you think about accents on a larger scale, such as an "American accent" or an "English accent." Every speaker of English speaks with an accent of some sort.

A group of people speaking the same dialect is called a **speech community.** Speech communities may be defined in terms of a number of **extralinguistic factors** (*extra-* in the sense of 'outside of,' i.e., factors not based in linguistic structure), such as region, socioeconomic status, age, gender, and ethnicity. These factors will be discussed in more detail in Files 10.3 and 10.4. However, it is rarely the case that there exists a speech community in which a "pure" dialect—i.e., purely regional, purely ethnic, etc.—is spoken, because the identification of any speech variety as a pure dialect requires the assumption of **communicative isolation.** Communicative isolation results when a group of speakers forms a coherent speech community relatively isolated from speakers outside of that community. This type of isolation was perhaps once a possibility but is becoming increasingly rare these days owing to social and geographic mobility, mass media, etc. It is far more common that a particular dialect of a speech community is influenced by regional, social, and cultural factors. Thus, in most instances the varieties spoken among members of a speech community are not pure dialects but instead are influenced by the interaction of many different factors.

While these terms may seem simple and convenient, when we consider actual languages, it becomes immediately obvious how difficult it is to make certain distinctions. How do we know, for example, if two or more language varieties are, say, different dialects of the same language or if in fact they are separate, distinct languages? One criterion used to distinguish dialects from languages is **mutual intelligibility.** If speakers of one language variety can understand speakers of another language variety, and vice versa, we say that these varieties are mutually intelligible and therefore they are dialects of the same language. Suppose you are a native of Brooklyn, New York, and you go to visit some friends in Beaumont, Texas. You may notice some differences in the speech of your Beaumont friends (and they in yours), but essentially you will be able to understand each other. Your variety of speech and theirs are mutually intelligible but differ systematically; they are therefore dialects of the same language. If you had never studied Portuguese and traveled to Rio de Janeiro, Brazil, however, you would not be able to understand the speakers of Brazilian Portuguese there. Your variety of speech and theirs are not mutually intelligible; they are therefore different languages.

It is not always this easy, however, to decide whether two language varieties are different dialects of the same language or different languages just on the basis of mutual intelligibility. Other factors, such as cultural, political, geographical, or historical considerations, may cloud the issue. In China, for example, Mandarin is generally spoken in the Northern provinces, and Cantonese in the southern province of Guangdong. Even though these language varieties are not mutually intelligible in spoken form, they are considered by their speakers to be dialects of the same language. Why? One reason is that the varieties share a common writing system (see File 15.2), and are thus mutually intelligible in written form. Another reason is that, politically, the speakers of these two language varieties live in the same country and consider themselves to be part of the same culture.

The opposite situation exists in the American Southwest between Papago and Pima, two Native American languages. These two language varieties are indeed mutually intelligible—there is less linguistic difference between them than there is between Standard American English and Standard British English. However, because the two tribes regard themselves as politically and culturally distinct, they consider their respective languages to be distinct as well. Similarly, in the Balkans, Serbo-Croatian has now split because of political and other reasons into at least four languages that are officially recognized as distinct, yet are mutually intelligible: Bosnian, Croatian, Montenegrin, and Serbian.

Another complication for the criterion of mutual intelligibility is found in a phenomenon known as a **dialect continuum.** This is a situation where, in a large number of geographically contiguous dialects, each dialect is closely related to the next, but the dialects at either end of the continuum (scale) are mutually unintelligible. Thus, dialect A is intelligible to dialect B, which is intelligible to dialect C, which is intelligible to dialect D; but D and A are not mutually intelligible. This situation is found near the border between Holland and Germany, where the dialects on either side of the national border are mutually intelligible, but dialects of Dutch and German that aren't near the border—including the standard dialects of the two languages—are not. Where in this dialect continuum does the language variety being spoken stop being Dutch and become German instead?

Clearly, the criterion of mutual intelligibility does not account for all the facts, and it has further problems. How much of a language does one have to understand to say that that language is mutually intelligible with one's own language? 50%? 80%? 99%? Although the principle of mutual intelligibility is useful in theory, from a practical standpoint, the difference between two dialects and two languages really relates to how native speakers perceive them.

10.1.2 Style and Register

Every speaker speaks a dialect (or more than one dialect) of his language, and, more specifically, every speaker speaks his own idiolect, because no two speakers of a language or dialect speak in exactly the same way. Further, an individual speaker speaks differently in different contexts. In Chapter 7 on pragmatics, we talked about the notion of sentences being infelicitous, or inappropriate in a certain situation. One reason that an utterance may be infelicitous is that, even though it gives the right kind of information, it is inappropriate for the social context. For example, if you were to meet the President of the United States or the Queen of England, you would be ill-advised to say something along the lines of *Oh, hey. How's it going?* This might be a very acceptable way to start a conversation with someone you have just met at a college party, but it is a less acceptable way to greet a country's leader.

Some languages have complex markings in their grammar in order to reflect the social context of a discourse (see File 11.4). In English, though, which does not have such formality markers built explicitly into the lexicon and morphology, speakers distinguish between different **speech styles.** Speech styles may be thought of as systematic variations in speech based on factors such as topic, setting, and addressee. Speech styles can be very different—playful, stilted, strictly formal, etc. Some speech styles are described in terms of degrees of formality. Thus, a speech style may be described as "formal" or "informal," "casual" or "careful." These different levels of speech formality can also be called **registers**—for example, it is appropriate to use a formal register of speech when speaking to the President of the United States.

While we may be aware of making a special effort to modify our language and our manners for certain people or in certain situations, the changes that we make are usually performed effortlessly. If you think about it, you will realize that you probably don't speak to your grandmother exactly the same as you do to your neighbor's two-year-old, nor do you speak to your minister or rabbi as you do to your roommate. However, you usually don't need to plan your speech styles in advance. Automatically adjusting from one speech style to another is known as **style shifting.**

Many people deny even having different speech styles, on the grounds that it would be insincere, a form of playacting, to speak differently to different people. However, "putting on airs" is not the only way to change one's speech style. It isn't even the most common. In reality, adapting one's speech style to the audience is like choosing the right tool for a particular task. You can't eat bouillon with a fork or sirloin steak with a spoon. If you were questioned by your four-year-old cousin about why your begonia needs light, you probably wouldn't explain it in terms of *photosynthesis*. On the other hand, you probably would include that word in your answer to the same sort of question on a botany exam. You may tell your mechanics that one of the wires seems to have come loose from *that funny-looking black thing,* and they may respect the depths of your ignorance by replying to you in similar terms. However, if they talk that way to each other, you may begin to doubt their competence. Thus, common sense makes you choose simple words to speak to a small child and appropriate technical words, if you know them, to speak to an expert about her field.

10.1.3 Jargon and Slang

Technical words, such as *photosynthesis* discussed in the previous section, are called **jargon.** A jargon, also called technical language, is a language variety that differs only in lexical items. Many of us are more or less fluent in a number of different jargons. Every job and every field of study has some technical terms of its own, as does every hobby and sport. Within its own area, technical jargon is clear, expressive, and economical; for outsiders, however, much of it usually remains incomprehensible. Professional jargons are often used to impress people outside the profession. *Rhinitis* sounds a great deal more impressive than "a runny nose." *Rhinoplasty* sounds a lot more serious and professional than "nose job." When the dermatologist says you have *dermatitis,* it sounds like an expert diagnosis; if he were to call it a "rash," you might not be so sure that he knows more about it than you do.

Occasionally a word or an expression of jargon escapes from its original context into general use. In recent years, we have seen this happen with *bottom line* (originally a technical term used in reference to business reports), with *hardware, software,* and *system* (all from computer usage), and with words like *cool* (originally used to refer to a type of jazz). The space program has given us *countdown, A-OK,* and *blast off,* and even people with no interest in baseball know how it feels to *strike out.*

Slang, like jargon, has to do more with stylistic choices in vocabulary than with systematic lexical differences between varieties. Unlike jargon, however, words that are considered "slang" are often less formal than other equivalent words. There are two basic types of slang. The nearly neutral everyday language that most people consider just a little too informal for letters of application and the like is known as **common slang.** This includes words like *fridge* for *refrigerator* or *TV* for *television.* **In-group slang** is the more specialized slang of a particular group at a particular time. In-group slang, like technical language, can be used to keep insiders together and to exclude outsiders. Learning the appropriate in-group slang can thus be a key to entrance into a particular group. In order for the group to preserve its closed status, however, there is often a fairly high turnover and renewal of slang expressions. Some slang is very short-lived, like *twenty-three skidoo!,* but some lasts long enough to become accepted in even the stuffiest circles. *Fan* appeared as a slangy shortening of *fanatic* in the late sixteenth century, and today we have *fan letters, fan clubs, fan magazines,* and *fan (web)sites* for all kinds of things from baseball stars to rock groups. Similarly, the fact that slang often injects a bit of color into otherwise ordinary language means that as the color fades, so to speak, new expressions will be needed. In this way, we see that slang in a sense is the linguistic counterpart of fad behavior; just as hula hoops came and went (and perhaps are coming back again), certain slang expressions have come and gone over the years, some to return again, but others to disappear.

Slang responds to a need in people to be creative in their language use and to show group membership (often unconsciously). These observations liken slang to some feature in the nature of being human and of interacting with humans. For these reasons, slang is found in all languages (even in Ancient Greek of 2,500 years ago, for instance).

10.1.4   Standard Dialects and Notions of Prestige

Contrary to the common view that every language consists of one "correct" dialect from which all other "inferior" or "substandard" dialects depart, all dialects are linguistically equivalent. This misconception has arisen from social stereotypes and biases. It is very important to realize that a person's use of any particular dialect is not a reflection of his or her intelligence or judgment. **Linguistically speaking, no one dialect or language is better, more correct, more systematic, or more logical than any other.** Rather, every language variety is a rule-governed system and an effective means of communication.

The notion of **standard dialect** is very often a complex one and in many ways an idealization. Descriptively speaking, the standard dialect is very often the variety used by political leaders, the media, and speakers from higher socioeconomic classes. It is also generally the variety taught in schools and to non-native speakers in language classes. Every language has at least one standard dialect, which serves as the primary means of communication across dialects. Other dialects can be called **nonstandard dialects** but should not be considered inferior.

In actuality, a language does not have one standard dialect, but instead has many different varieties of what people consider to be the standard. What ties these different notions together is **prestige.** Socially speaking, the standard dialect is the dialect of prestige and power. However, the prestige of any speech variety is wholly dependent upon the prestige of the speakers who use it. In the United States, the prestige group usually corresponds to those in society who enjoy positions of power, wealth, and education. It is the speech of this group, therefore, that becomes the standard, but there is nothing about the variety itself that makes it more prestigious than any other variety.

Consider a case in which the status of a particular linguistic feature has changed over time from standard to nonstandard. Recall from the discussion of prescriptive versus descriptive rules of grammar (File 1.3) that multiple negatives were once commonly used by speakers of standard Old English and Middle English. Take, for example, the multiple-negative construction in (1), from Geoffrey Chaucer's description of the Knight in the General Prologue to the *Canterbury Tales* (from Millward 1989: 158), meaning roughly "he has never in all his life said anything villainous to any creature."

(1) He nevere yet no vileynye ne sayde
     He never yet no villainy not said
     In al his lyf unto no maner wight
     In all his life to no kind of creature

Today, however, the speakers who most commonly employ multiple-negative constructions are typically not members of the higher socioeconomic (i.e., prestige) group. Such constructions are rarely used in public spheres by political leaders or media spokespeople, and English grammar instructors discourage use of these forms in writing or in speech. Thus, multiple negation is today considered a nonstandard feature. This example illustrates a change over time in the **prescriptive standard,** the standard by which people often make judgments of "right" and "wrong" (see File 1.3). It shows that such judgments are not linguistically founded but are instead governed by societal opinion, and most often by the societal evaluation of speakers.

To consider another example of how linguistically arbitrary notions of the standard are, let's look at the following case. Few Standard English speakers use object pronouns in subject position, as in (2).

(2) Kim and me went to the store.

Yet media spokespeople, political leaders, and others of higher socioeconomic status can be observed using subject pronouns in object position as in (3) and (4).

(3) This is a matter between Kim and I.
(4) Give the books to Kim and I.

According to the prescriptive standard, sentences (2), (3), and (4) should all be "corrected" as follows:

(5) Kim and I went to the store.
(6) This is a matter between Kim and me.
(7) Give the money to Kim and me.

However, not only would many standard English speakers not recognize (3) and (4) as violations of a prescriptive rule, but many would argue that intuitively sentences (3) and (4) seem "correct" while (6) and (7) seem "incorrect." This is known as **hypercorrection,** the act of producing nonstandard forms by way of false analogy. This example shows us that even violations of a prescriptive rule (such as sentences (3) and (4) above) can be perceived as standard if they are used by members of the prestige group.

The standard dialect in the United States is called **Standard American English** (**SAE**). As with any standard dialect, SAE is not a well-defined variety but rather an idealization, which even now defies definition because agreement on what exactly constitutes this variety is lacking. SAE is not a single, unitary, homogeneous dialect but instead comprises a number of varieties. When we speak of SAE, we usually have in mind features of grammar rather than pronunciation. In the United States, where class-consciousness is not as strong as in many other cultures, some differences in pronunciation are tolerated. Ideally, SAE is not pronounced with any of the phonological variations characteristic of the regional varieties (discussed in File 10.3). In practice, however, there are varieties of SAE that are spoken with northern accents, southern accents, coastal New England accents, etc. These varieties of SAE, however, are still considered standard by those who speak them and even those who hear them. Often, these SAE dialects are spoken with an accent that is less strong than that of a northern, southern, or coastal New England dialect, but the accent is still there. This is not to say that we do not make evaluations of speech based on accent, though, because we do, but SAE is defined more clearly in terms of grammar than in terms of pronunciation.

In Britain, on the other hand, where class divisions are more clearly defined and social mobility seems to be more restricted, standard pronunciation or Received Pronunciation (RP), also known as BBC English or the Queen's English, takes on the importance of standard grammar and vocabulary. Thus, in Britain both pronunciation and grammar are markers of social status.

All dialects that are not perceived as varieties of the standard are called nonstandard. As we have noted above, however, it is important to understand that nonstandard does not mean "substandard" or "inferior," although this is the perception held by many.

Most nonstandard varieties are stigmatized in the wider community as illogical and unsystematic. It is on this basis that some people justify labeling nonstandard varieties as "bad" or "improper" ways of speaking, as opposed to standard varieties, which are said to be "good" or "proper." Such evaluations are linguistically unfounded. To illustrate, consider the paradigms in (8) showing the use of reflexive pronouns in two varieties of English—one standard, the other nonstandard.

(8) *Standard*   *Nonstandard*
     I like myself   I like myself
     You like yourself   You like yourself
     He likes himself   He likes hisself
     She likes herself   She likes herself
     We like ourselves   We like ourselves
     You like yourselves   You like yourselves
     They like themselves   They like theirselves

Based on these two paradigms, we can develop descriptive rules (see (9)) for the construction of reflexives in these two varieties.

(9) Standard: Add the reflexive suffix *-self* to possessive determiners in the first- and second-person singular, and *-selves* to possessive determiners in the first- and second-person plural.

                    Add the reflexive suffix *-self* to object pronouns in the third-person singular, and *-selves* to object pronouns in the third-person plural.

Nonstandard: Add the reflexive suffix -*self* to possessive determiners in the first-, second-, and third-person singular, and -*selves* to possessive determiners in the first-, second-, and third-person plural.

Given these rules, what is it about the nonstandard variety that makes it any less systematic or less sensible than the standard variety? Nothing. Both varieties are systematic, and both are reasonably constructed. In fact, some may argue that in this instance, the nonstandard variety is more systematic than the standard variety because it consistently uses the same form, the possessive, as the stem for forming the reflexive paradigm. This system, consequently, would be much easier to teach to non-native speakers of English or children learning a first language than the standard system, which must stipulate two separate conditions.

Another misconception about nonstandard varieties is that their speakers are considered "lazy," "uneducated," and "unambitious." Further, speakers of nonstandard varieties may be told that the varieties they speak are "wrong" and "inferior" and that they must learn to speak the varieties taught in school in order to become successful. As a result, children who come from homes where nonstandard varieties are spoken are at an immediate disadvantage in school, where they are forced to make adjustments from the language of their home communities to the standard variety of the school (an adjustment unnecessary for children from homes where standard varieties are spoken). Some make these adjustments and become **bidialectal** speakers, having a mastery of two dialects—one a standard variety, the other a nonstandard variety. Others become only marginally fluent in the standard but retain a mastery of the nonstandard dialect. And still others master the standard and reject the nonstandard dialect altogether.

Which adjustments are made depends on a number of factors. One important factor is the notion of prestige, specifically the distinction between **overt prestige** and **covert prestige.** Overt prestige is the type of prestige discussed above as associated with the "standard dialect"; this is the prestige that is attached to a particular variety by the community at large and that defines how people should speak in order to gain status in the wider community. But there is another type of prestige that exists among members of nonstandard-speaking communities and that defines how people should speak in order to be considered members of those particular communities: covert prestige. In this case, the desire to "belong" to or associate oneself with a particular group often becomes the overriding factor. For example, if you are hanging out with a bunch of old high school friends from back home, you might not want to use the prescriptive standard (which is overtly prestigious) because it does not fit in with how "the guys" are talking and might make you the subject of ridicule ("Listen to so-and-so's educated talk!"). Thus, nonstandard varieties persist, despite their stigmatized status, partially because of covert prestige. In this sense, language becomes a marker of group identification. These ideas will be discussed in more detail in File 10.5, "Language and Identity," and File 11.3, "Language and Power."

FILE 10.2

....

Variation at Different Levels of Linguistic Structure

10.2.1 Variation at All Levels

While we are probably most consciously aware of differences in vocabulary choice or pronunciation, internal variation exists at all the levels of linguistic structure we have discussed in this book: phonetics, phonology, morphology, syntax, and semantics (or the lexicon). If we compare any two language varieties (be they different languages, different dialects, different styles, etc.), we may, and often do, find differences at any of these levels. In this file, we will take each of these levels in turn and look at a few examples of how they may differ between varieties. In addition, we may find differences in the pragmatic conventions of speakers (see File 11.1).

10.2.2 Phonetic Variation

Recall from Chapter 2 that phonetics is the study of how sounds are physically produced, of the acoustics of sound waves, and of the perception of sounds by the brain. Hence, differences at the phonetic level tend to be those where a sound that **functions** the same in the linguistic systems of two varieties has some difference in its physical characteristics. For example, all varieties of American English use the phonemes /t, d, n, s, z/; that is, we can find minimal pairs that make use of these sounds throughout American English. But the phonetics of these sounds are not always the same: some New York City dialects produce these sounds as dental, where the tongue tip touches the top teeth, while most other American English dialects produce them as alveolar, with the tongue touching the alveolar ridge.

Similarly, most dialects of English have a phoneme that functions as an /r/, in words like _really_ or _right_. But, not all /r/s are the same: some English and Scottish dialects have a trilled [r], while most American dialects have a retroflex or bunched approximant [ɹ].

Another source of phonetic variation is simply the fact that every utterance produced is somewhat different. Even if the same person says the same sentence twice in a row, trying to make them as similar as possible, there will be slight phonetic differences in the pronunciations of words, the duration of segments, the tone of voice, and so on. And, of course, these differences are magnified when the utterances are produced by different people.

We frequently find phonetic variation in different styles or registers of speech. For example, you may have been told to "enunciate" clearly when you are speaking in a formal situation like a job interview or when you are speaking to someone who may be hard of hearing. In such situations, you aren't changing the system of sounds you are using (your phonology), but rather you are changing how you pronounce the particular sounds in question (your phonetics). For instance, instead of pronouncing the word _little_ with a flap and a syllabic [l] as in [lɪɾl̩], which is common in casual American speech, you might pronounce it with a [t] and a schwa, as in [lɪtʰəl], to make it "clearer" which phoneme you mean. Similarly, in ASL, the sign for KNOW (shown in (1)) is typically signed in informal situations with the fingers touching the cheekbone. But the "official" version of this sign, the one you might learn in the classroom or use in careful speech, for example, has the fingers touching the temple.

(1)   a. ASL: KNOW (informal)   b. ASL: KNOW (formal)

© 2006, William Vicars, www.Lifeprint.com. Adapted by permission.

10.2.3   Phonological Variation

Phonology deals with the system of sounds in a language, including the way that those sounds are distributed, as discussed in Chapter 3. To see whether two language varieties have differences in their phonologies, we could look at what phonemes speakers use in words that are semantically and historically the "same" words. For instance, we mentioned in Section 2.3.2 that many American dialects have the vowel [ɔ] in the words *caught, dawn,* and *hawk,* which differs from the vowel [ɑ] found in the words *cot, Don,* and *hock.* For these speakers, then, these words are minimal pairs that show the difference between the phonemes [ɔ] and [ɑ]. But in some dialects, all six of these words have the same vowel (usually a vowel closer to [ɑ] than to [ɔ]), so that the words *caught* and *cot* are homophonous. Thus, the phonological systems of the two varieties differ because speakers of the two varieties categorize these words differently.

Similarly, in dialects of southern England (as in American English), words like *flood, but,* and *cup* have the vowel [ʌ], whereas words like *full, good,* and *put* have the vowel [ʊ]. In northern English dialects, however, both sets of words have the vowel [ʊ].

Another way in which language varieties may differ in their phonologies is in terms of what sequences of sounds they allow. For example, Spanish does not allow the sequences /sp/, /st/, or /sk/ to occur at the beginning of a word, while English does (this is why native Spanish speakers often pronounce English words like *student* with an initial vowel, [ɛstudɛnt]—see Section 3.1.3). Another example can be observed in some English dialects, like Standard British English and Boston English, in which sequences of vowel-/r/-consonant or vowel-/r/-word boundary are not permitted; these are called **non-rhotic** varieties. Most other American English dialects are **rhotic** and do permit such sequences. Thus, while a person from Oregon might say the phrase *park the car* as [pʰɑɹk ðə kʰɑɹ], a person from Boston or London might say [pʰɑːk ðə kʰɑː]. Similarly, in some African-American English varieties, sequences of consonant-/r/ or consonant-/l/ are not permitted, especially in unstressed syllables, so that the word *profession* is pronounced [pʰʌfɛʃn̩] in these varieties. Finally, there may be phonological variation between two varieties based on how speakers of the varieties apply phonological rules (see File 3.3). Different varieties can have different phonological rules, or rules that are obligatory in one variety but required in another. For example, in most American English dialects, /t/ and /d/ are realized as [ɾ] in words like *rider* and *butter.* In some British English dialects, however, /t/ and /d/ are realized as [ʔ] in this environment.

10.2.4 Morphological Variation

As discussed in Chapter 4, morphemes are the smallest unit of sound-meaning pairs in a language. While we would classify different pronunciations of the same morpheme as phonetic or phonological variation, we can talk about morphological variation by looking at the distribution of morphemes in two varieties or the use of completely different morphemes for the same function in two varieties.

Although in Standard American English the suffix *-ish* only attaches to some adjectives and nouns—e.g., *reddish, youngish, foolish, childish*—in other varieties of English this suffix has a wider distribution and can also attach to words like adverbs (*now-ish, fast-ish*), additional nouns and proper nouns (*tree-ish, George Clooney-ish, Oprah-ish*), and phrases (*close-to-home-ish*). It can even be used on its own sometimes, acting as a free morpheme: *Are you excited about your trip? Yeah, ish.* In SAE, words like *tree-ish* are usually formed with the suffix *-like* (*tree-like, Oprah-like*), and the meanings of words like *now-ish* are conveyed by phrases, e.g., *about now, kind of fast*, and *pretty close to home*.

Often varieties will use completely different morphemes for the same function; consider the example from File 10.1 of reflexive pronouns. Standard English uses the reflexive pronouns *myself, yourself, himself, ourselves, yourselves*, and *themselves*. Notice that in the first and second person, these pronouns make use of the possessive determiner plus *self* or *selves*, while in the third person, these pronouns are a combination of the object pronoun plus *self* or *selves*. Many dialects of English have made this set of reflexive pronouns more regular by using the possessive determiner in all of them, i.e., *hisself* and *theirselves* instead of *himself* and *themselves*.

Another example of using different morphemes for the same purpose in two different varieties can be seen in the past tense of certain verbs in Appalachian English versus Standard American English. For example, the past tenses of the verbs *climb, eat*, and *heat* in Appalachian English are [klʌm], [ɛt], and [hɛt], respectively, while SAE has [klaɪmd], [eɪt], and [hiɾəd]. Similar variation in past tense forms can be found even within SAE; for example, *dived* and *dove* are both commonly used as the past tense of *dive*, and while *dragged* is generally considered to be the standard past tense of *drag*, the use of *drug* for the past tense is quite widespread among American English dialects. In these cases, the morphological variation comes from the observation that past tenses can be formed by different morphological processes (see File 4.2).

10.2.5 Syntactic Variation

Syntax has to do both with the types of syntactic categories certain words belong to, the syntactic properties of those words and phrases, and the way words are put together to form phrases and sentences (see Chapter 5). We can see variation in all of these properties across language varieties.

For example, in many southern American English varieties, *done* can function as an auxiliary verb, as in *she done already told you*, where Standard American English uses *has*: *she has already told you*. Similarly, in many Appalachian English dialects, *right* can occur before adjectives, as in *a right good meal*, where SAE would use *very*: *a very good meal*. Of course, SAE also has the expressions *done* and *right*, but they function differently: for example, *he has done it* or *the right answer*.

We can also see variation in how words are combined by considering the use of combinations of modals, such as *might could, might would, may can*, and *useta could* in many southern dialects. Such combinations do not occur in Standard English; rather, these meanings, more or less, are expressed by *might be able to, might perhaps, may be able to*, and *used to be able to*.

Another difference in syntactic properties can be found in the use of verbs like *needs* and *wants* in phrases such as *the crops need watered* or *the cat wants petted* in Midwestern American dialects. In these dialects, the verbs are followed by a past participle. In SAE, however, these verbs are followed by "to be" phrases or in some cases by the progressive verb form: *the crops need to be watered/need watering* and *the cat wants to be petted* (see File 5.2).

Finally, we can see differences in how sentences are put together by considering so-called subject "pro-drop" languages, which allow subject noun phrases to be omitted. In Spanish, for instance, it is possible to say either *hablo español* or *yo hablo español* to mean 'I speak Spanish': the latter includes the subject pronoun *yo* meaning 'I' while the former does not. The choice of one version or the other may depend on the context of the conversation or other stylistic considerations (e.g., how easy it is to infer what the "missing" subject is). Other pro-drop languages include Italian, American Sign Language, Japanese, Mandarin, and Polish.

10.2.6 Lexical Variation

Lexical variation refers to differences in the words people use to mean the same thing or to refer to the same object, or differences in what the same word means or refers to.

For example, words for sweet carbonated beverages differ from place to place: *soda* is common in the northeastern and western parts of the United States, while *pop* is common in the Midwest and Northwest, and *coke* is common in the South. And, of course, there are other terms like *soft drink, soda pop, fizzy drinks,* or even *juice* that are used elsewhere.

Another example comes from different varieties of French: in European French, the word for the verb 'to mail' is *poster,* while the Québécois French word is *maller.* Similarly, in Taiwan Sign Language, speakers from Taipei sign the word SHOE by clasping the hands together, while speakers from Tainan sign the same word by touching the fronts of the wrists together, with the hands crossed and in fists.

On the other hand, the same word can also be used to mean different things in different language varieties. For example, *knock up* means 'rouse from sleep by knocking' in British English but 'make pregnant' in American English. Similarly, *to be pissed* is 'to be drunk' in British English but 'to be mad' in American English.

Lexical variation is very common in different styles: the choice of words you use often depends on the register or style you are speaking. So, for example, you might say *I fell on my butt* to a friend but *I fell on my backside* to your grandmother. We also have different words for things like *man* depending on the context: *gentleman* is more formal; *guy* is less formal. Likewise, in French, the standard word for 'man' is *homme,* the more formal word is *monsieur* or *gentilhomme,* and the more casual word is *mec* or *type.*

Although we have focused on lexical variation here, it is worth noting that variation can also occur in how the meanings of larger expressions are compositionally constructed (see File 6.4). This kind of variation is decidedly more complicated, though, and closely interconnected with syntactic and pragmatic variation.

FILE 10.3

Factors Influencing Variation: Regional and Geographic Factors

10.3.1 Why Does Language Vary?

In the previous two files, we have seen that language variation is rampant, and the differences between language varieties can range from major (e.g., distinguishing varieties as separate languages) to minor (e.g., distinguishing two registers of the same dialect spoken by the same person). We have seen examples of the kinds of differences that language varieties can have: phonetic, phonological, morphological, syntactic, and lexical. But, so far, we have not discussed **why** languages vary.

Just as there are many types of variation, so are there many factors that influence variation, and although we can isolate several factors that tend to be particularly influential, it is important to remember that **all** of the factors that will be discussed in the next two files play a role in determining the language variety used by any given person at any given time. For example, think of what you might expect for the language variety of a 13-year-old, African American, middle-class female from Alabama, talking among her school friends. Change any one of those factors, and you might expect to hear something else: What does she sound like on the phone to her grandmother? What does her mother sound like? Her cousin from New York? Her white 85-year-old neighbor originally from Minnesota? How does her 20-year-old brother sound? Her 60-year-old grandmother? Thinking about these variations should help you see how multiple factors work together to determine the language variety used by any given speaker at any given time.

To begin the discussion of these factors, we turn first to the regional and geographic factors that influence variation. These factors typify **regional dialect** variation. A second set, which is equally important, includes attributes such as social class, age, gender, and ethnicity. These factors, which typify **social dialect** variation, are discussed in File 10.4.

10.3.2 Regional and Geographic Variation

One the most obvious reasons for the existence of different language varieties is that languages are spoken in different geographical locations. This type of variation based on geographical boundaries, known as **regional variation,** is responsible, for example, for the differences between American English and British English, or between the Portuguese spoken in Portugal and that spoken in Brazil. It is also the type of variation that we associate with, for example, New York English versus Texan English, or the English spoken in New York City versus that spoken in Saratoga Springs. An example of regional variation in ASL is shown in (1), where two different ASL signs for FOOTBALL are illustrated. The sign on the left is used throughout most of the United States, while the sign on the right is found specifically in Ohio; you can see that it is a completely different sign.

Why does geography play such a large role in determining a dialect? Language varieties tend to be most influenced by the people you are in face-to-face communication with, so people who live close to each other will have considerably more influence on each other's dialects than people who live farther apart; that is, living in close proximity to a group of

(1) FOOTBALL (widespread) and FOOTBALL (Ohio)

Reproduced by permission of Gallaudet University Press, from Shroyer and Shroyer, *Signs across America* (1984), pp. 96, 97.

German speakers will have more of an impact on your speech than living 100 miles from a group of them. So it is often really the patterns of settlement that people fall into, rather than the geography of the region itself, that matters. This means, for example, that there is nothing inherent about southeastern Pennsylvania that makes people who live there more likely to use words like [jɑ] and [neɪ] instead of [jɛs] and [noʊ]; instead, this is because of the large population of German speakers who settled in the area.

This is not to say that physical geography cannot play any role in regional dialects. Being isolated from speakers of other varieties tends to allow a dialect to develop in its own way, through its own innovations that are different from those of other dialects. Regional dialect boundaries therefore often coincide with natural barriers such as rivers, mountains, or swamps. For example, very distinctive varieties of English have developed and have been preserved on Tangier Island off the coast of Virginia and along the Sea Islands of South Carolina, owing in part to the geographic isolation of these areas. Further, the distinctive dialect known as Appalachian English can be attributed at least in part to the isolation imposed by the Appalachian mountain range.

People who study regional dialects, known as **dialectologists,** often rely on fieldwork to determine dialect regions. For example, they may come up with a list of particular characteristics that they know typically vary in the part of a country they are interested in; then they go out and directly ask people in those areas how they say things.

The results of such fieldwork are often plotted on maps, and the boundaries of areas where a particular linguistic form is used are marked by lines called **isoglosses.** When many isoglosses surround the same region or separate the same group of speakers, they are said to be a **bundle of isoglosses,** which indicates that the speech of a particular group is different in a number of ways from that of other groups around it.

The boundaries between dialects are generally marked by bundles of isoglosses. An example of this is shown in (2), where you can see a map of the northeastern United States. The three lines running through northern Pennsylvania represent three isoglosses. The dotted line represents variation between the terms *darning needle* and *dragonfly* to refer to the same insect: speakers north of the line tend to use *darning needle,* while speakers south of the line tend to use *dragonfly.* Similarly, the solid line represents the isogloss between people who say *whiffletree* (to the north) and people who say *swingletree* (to the south),[1] and the dashed line represents the dividing line between those who say *pail* (to the north) and those who say *bucket* (to the south). Although they do not exactly coincide, taken together, this

---

[1]A *whiffletree* (or *swingletree*) is, according to Merriam Webster, "the pivoted swinging bar to which the traces of a harness are fastened and by which a vehicle or implement is drawn."

bundle of isoglosses can be used to mark the dialect boundary between the northern dialect area (to the north) and the midland dialect area (to the south).

(2)   Bundling of three northern isoglosses

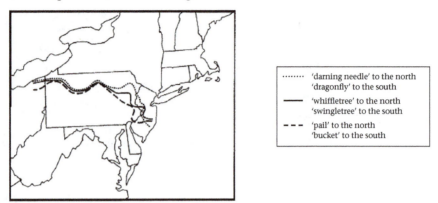

Adapted from the University of Michigan Press from Carver, *American Regional Dialects* (1987), p. 12 (original source *A Word Geography of the Eastern United States*, 1949, fig. 5a).

10.3.3   A Case Study in Regional Variation: The United States

The development of US regional dialects began in part in England, as speakers from various regions of England journeyed across the Atlantic and settled the Eastern seaboard of the United States. These early settlement patterns are reflected in dialectal boundaries still present today. Settlers from the eastern regions of central and southern England settled in eastern New England and the Virginia Tidewater area. Settlers from the New Jersey and Delaware areas came from northern and western parts of England, and Scots-Irish from Ulster settled in parts of western New England, New York, and Appalachia. In time, certain colonial cities such as Boston, Philadelphia, and Charleston acquired prestige as centers of trade and culture. As a result, the dialects spoken in these cities became prestigious and began to exert influence on nearby settlements.

The westward migration reflected the settlement patterns of the Atlantic states to a large extent. People from western New England and upstate New York fanned out while moving west, settling chiefly in the Great Lakes area. Those who came from the Middle Atlantic region (primarily Pennsylvania and Maryland) journeyed west to Ohio, West Virginia, and the Mississippi Valley. Similarly, influence from the southern Atlantic colonies was felt as speakers from this area moved west and settled in the Gulf states. The lines cannot be clearly drawn, however, because the streams of migration often mingled. For example, New Englanders formed a compact community outside their usual area of settlement in Worthington, Ohio. The spread of migration continued to the Rocky Mountain states, essentially following previously established patterns but with greater mingling. And finally, the westward migration reached the west coast, resulting in even greater crossing of dialect lines.

These patterns of Anglo settlement and migration tell only part of the story, however. Contact between English and Native American languages in the seventeenth century contributed significantly to the development of North American English and the dialect regions of the United States. Furthermore, the arrival of other European immigrants resulted in some very distinct regional dialect areas in the United States, including the major influences of French in New Orleans, German in southern Pennsylvania, and Spanish in the Southwest. The arrival of African slaves along the southeast Atlantic seaboard contributed significantly to the development of southern varieties of English. The later migration of African Americans from rural areas such as Mississippi, Alabama, Georgia, and South Carolina to northern cities such as Chicago, Detroit, New York, Philadelphia, and Washington, DC, also had a major impact on the development of the modern American English dialects.

Figure (3) shows the approximate boundaries of the major modern dialect regions that have developed in the United States. The boundary lines on this map do not represent sharp demarcations but are instead compromises between bundles of isoglosses that come together near these lines.

(3)   Approximate major dialect regions of the United States

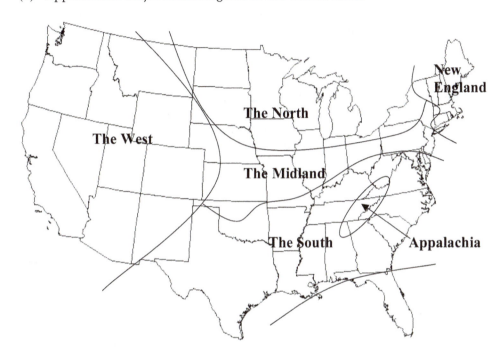

For the most part, the present-day regional dialect areas continue to reflect the initial patterns of dialect formation discussed above. This fact may seem surprising, as you might expect that the impact of television, radio, the Internet, and other forms of broadcast media on US English over the past half-century would lead to more homogeneity among dialects rather than continuing heterogeneity. Although middle-class Euro-American speech across the States is showing some signs of becoming more homogeneous, working-class speech shows little movement in this regard (Kretzschmar 1997, Labov et al. 2006).

There have been a number of explanations for this; the most likely reason is that the settlement of the East Coast, which led to the formation of the initial dialects of the United States, happened considerably earlier than the settlement of other parts of the country. The time lag between initial settlement and later waves of westward migration among settlers led to the formation of strong dialect patterns in original areas, so much so that later immigration groups would have been under considerable pressure to conform to these initial patterns rather than establish different patterns when learning English. As time went on, this pattern of enculturation became entrenched, so that relatively stable patterns continued to be developed.

In the sections that follow, each of the present-day supra-regional dialect areas of the United States, shown in (3) above—the North, New England, the South, Appalachia, the Midland, and the West—will be briefly discussed.[2] Throughout this discussion, it is impor-

---

[2]Much of the description of these dialect areas comes from the *Atlas of North American English* by Labov, Ash, and Boberg (2006); from *American English* by Wolfram and Schilling-Estes (2005); or from papers in *American Voices: How Dialects Differ from Coast to Coast* by Wolfram and Ward (2006). Other references will be cited in the text.

tant to note that the described patterns of speech reflect, for the most part, those of Euro-Americans because of their historical prominence as the majority speech group in the United States. Varieties of other ethnic groups populating these areas, such as African Americans and Hispanic/Latino Americans, are discussed in more detail in Section 10.4.5.

10.3.4 The North

The North is defined in modern-day dialect studies as the portion of the country that includes western Massachusetts; the northern portions of New York, Pennsylvania, Ohio, Indiana, Illinois, Iowa, and South Dakota; and the entire states of Minnesota, Michigan, Wisconsin, and North Dakota.

The most salient phonetic feature that characterizes northern speech is a systematic rotation of the vowel space, affecting the pronunciation of the low and mid vowels. The vowels [æ], [ɑ], and [ɔ] are pronounced higher and closer to the front of the mouth than in other dialects of English, and the vowels [ʌ], [ɛ], and [ɪ] are pronounced farther back and a little lower in the mouth. These patterns are known collectively as the **Northern Cities Shift.** As a result, the northern pronunciations of *bag* and *bat* more closely resemble [bɛg] and [bɛt] rather than the SAE pronunciations [bæg] and [bæt]. At the same time, /ɑ/, the vowel in *lock* and *lot* in other dialects, is pronounced more like [æ], so these words are pronounced [læk] or [læt] in northern varieties. Moreover, [ɛ] is often pronounced further back in the mouth, so that *bet* is more like [bʌt], while *bus* is pronounced as [bɔs] in the North.

Northern speech is also differentiated from other dialects by several morphosyntactic features. One such feature is the use of *with* without an object noun phrase, as in *Do you want to come with?* or *John is coming with.* In other dialects of English, speakers tend to end this type of sentence with an object noun phrase, as in *Do you want to come with me?* Another feature is the use of the *needs VERB+ing* construction, as in *The table needs cleaning,* where speakers of other dialects would say *The table needs to be cleaned.*

There are also a variety of lexical variants specific to the North, as discussed in the Harvard Dialect Survey. For example, Northern speakers often use *by* in sentences where a speaker is describing where he spent his time on an earlier occasion, as in the sentence *I was by Sarah's house yesterday*; speakers of other dialects of English tend to use *at* rather than *by.* In addition, the strip of grass that is found in someone's front yard between the sidewalk and the road is often referred to as either a *parkway* or a *tree lawn,* and the most common term for the gray creature that rolls up into a ball when touched is *roly-poly.* In addition, for many speakers, the generic term for an athletic shoe is *sneaker* (as opposed to *tennis shoe,* which is widely used in other areas), and the most commonly used generic term for a sweetened carbonated beverage is *pop.*

10.3.5 New England

The New England dialect area is defined as the area including western New York (except New York City, which is a distinct speech island), eastern Massachusetts, Connecticut, Vermont, New Hampshire, Rhode Island, and Maine. Interestingly, New England and Northern speakers have historically shared, and still do share, many dialect traits, leading to a high degree of overlap in the features of the two dialect areas. However, there are also some notable differences, which are outlined below.

Turning first to pronunciation, although the characteristics of New England speech are quite similar to those of northern speech, there are two exceptions. The first is that [ɑ], the vowel in words such as *cot, pot,* and *hock,* and [ɔ], the vowel in words such as *caught, thought, hawk,* have merged and are pronounced the same way, so that these words are homophones (see Section 2.3.2). The second is that speakers in most areas within Eastern New England speak non-rhotic varieties (see Section 10.2.3). That is, in words where an /r/ precedes a consonant, either within a word or at the end of the word, it is not pronounced. Thus, the sentence *Park your car* would be pronounced [pʰɑːk jʌ kʰɑː]. Rhoticity is discussed in more detail in File 10.4.

Beyond these phonetic differences, there are also morphosyntactic differences in New England. For instance, speakers throughout much of the area use *so don't I* as a way of showing agreement with another person, whereas speakers of other dialects use *so do I* to express this meaning.

Many of the lexical items used in the New England area also differ from those used in other regions. For example, speakers typically use *on line* to describe a situation where northern speakers would use *in line*, as in the sentence *We were waiting <u>on line</u> at the gate for tickets*. *Berm* or *verge* is used for the generic words that name the strip of grass found in someone's yard, while *pill bug* is used to name the little gray creatures that roll up into balls. Furthermore, many speakers in Eastern New England use *bubbler* as the generic synonym for what Northern speakers would call a *drinking* or *water fountain,* and the generic term usually used for a carbonated beverage is *soda* rather than *pop*.

10.3.6   The South

The Southern dialect area is roughly defined as the area of the country including Texas, Louisiana, Arkansas, Mississippi, Alabama, Georgia, Tennessee, Kentucky, Virginia, southern Ohio, Illinois, Indiana, and Missouri, and most of Oklahoma, West Virginia, and North and South Carolina. (Note that it excludes Florida, which is considered a separate speech island.)

The South has several distinctive pronunciation differences from the other dialect areas. For example, speakers of this dialect tend to follow the front vowels [ɪ] and [ɛ] with glides so that they become diphthongs instead of monophthongs. As a result, one of the features of Southern speech is the pronunciation of [ɛ] as [ɛɪ], so that *led* is pronounced [lɛɪd] and *net* is pronounced [nɛɪt]. Another difference involving [ɛ] is that it is pronounced as [ɪ] when [n] follows, a phenomenon also known as the "pin/pen merger." Hence, *pen,* which is typically pronounced [pɛn] in other dialects, is pronounced as [pɪn]. Another notable characteristic is the pronunciation of /aʊ/ as [æʊ], resulting in *house* as [hæʊs] and *out* as [æʊt] (Thomas 2001). A very well-known characteristic of the southern dialect area is that /aɪ/ is often realized as the monophthong [ɑː], so that *wide* or *my* are pronounced more like [wɑːd] or [mɑː] rather than [waɪd] or [maɪ].

Two morphosyntactic features also distinguish the unique character of southern speech. The first of these is the use of the phrase *fixin' to,* as in *I'm fixin' to clean the gutters,* to signal the intention of completing an action at some point in the near future, where speakers of other dialects would use *getting ready to*. The second is the use of two modals in a verb phrase, also known as a **double modal,** to indicate that a plan has a high degree of tentativeness, as in the sentence *I <u>might could</u> help you clean your house tomorrow.* In other dialects of English, speakers would likely say *I might be able to help you clean your house tomorrow (if something else doesn't come up)* to mean the same thing. Southern speakers often use the double modal as a politeness strategy (see File 11.4) when expressing that the plans are tentative, as it indicates more deference than its SAE equivalent. Although *might could* is the most frequently used double modal, others, such as *might should, might would,* and *useta could* (i.e., *used to could*), are also quite common throughout the South.

Dialect terms that are common in the South include *roly-poly* as the most widespread term for the gray creature that rolls up into a ball when touched (making it similar to the North), while the strip of grass found in someone's front yard between the sidewalk and the road is often referred to either as a *curb strip* or a *devil's strip*. In addition, a widely used term for a cart for groceries is *buggy,* while the most commonly used generic term for a carbonated beverage is *coke.*

10.3.7 Appalachia

Appalachia is the area of the country including the southern Appalachian mountain range, which spans the mid and southern regions of West Virginia, western North and South Carolina and Virginia, northern Georgia, and eastern Tennessee and Kentucky. Settlers to this region included English, Scots-Irish, Pennsylvania Dutch, and French Huguenots, who all contributed to the language varieties that developed in this area. Because of the mountainous barriers, speakers in these areas were for many years severely restricted in their travel outside the Appalachian region. From this isolation developed a culture and a language that are still noticeably distinct from those of the surrounding areas today and that appear to have preserved several linguistic features that no longer exist in surrounding dialects. While linguists disagree on the extent to which the varieties spoken in Appalachia can be considered a single dialect, it is clear that the varieties all share a set of common features that set them apart from other dialects of American English.

Among the most notable phonetic characteristics of Appalachian speech are the pronunciation of words such as *fish* and *push*. In other dialects of English, these words are generally pronounced as [fɪʃ] and [pʊʃ], while in Appalachia, they are pronounced as [fiʃ] and [puʃ] (Brandes and Brewer 1977). In some cases, however, the [ɪ] sound is lowered and pronounced more like [æ], so that *think* is pronounced [θæŋk] (Wolfram and Christian 1976). Another salient difference is how Appalachian speech deals with primary stress. For speakers of this dialect, many words have primary stress (indicated by [´]) on the first syllable of a multisyllabic word, even in cases where most other dialects place the stress elsewhere. Thus, *cigar* is pronounced *cígar* rather than *cigár*, *November* is pronounced *Nóvember* as opposed to *Novémber,* and *insurance* is pronounced *ínsurance* rather than *insúrance* (Brandes and Brewer 1977).

Several morphosyntactic features also mark Appalachian speech as distinctive. First, there is the process known as **a-prefixing.** Appalachian English has preserved the prefix *a-* (which was used commonly in English from the twelfth to seventeenth centuries) in certain verbal constructions, such as *He come a-running to tell me the news* or *The dog was a-cryin' and a-hollerin' when he saw the deer* (Mallinson et al. 2006). Second, Appalachian speech preserves certain irregular verb conjugations in constructing the past tense, where other dialects now use the regular past tense suffix *-ed*. For example, speakers use *clumb* as opposed to *climbed* as the past tense form of *climb*, *het* rather than *heated* as the past tense of *heat,* and *ruck* as opposed to *raked* as the past tense of *rake* (Wolfram and Christian 1976). Third, there is the use of **multiple negation,** where multiple markers are used to negate a sentence. For example, a sentence such as *I had some lunch* is negated as *I didn't have no lunch.* In many other dialects of English, *I had some lunch* is negated as either *I didn't have any lunch* or *I had no lunch,* using only a single negative marker (Brandes and Brewer 1977).[3]

Lexical variation is also quite abundant in Appalachia. Dialect terms that typify Appalachian speech include *jasper,* which is used to describe an outsider or a stranger, and *sigogglin,* which is used to describe something that leans at an angle or is crooked or tilted. Other words that distinguish the area are *poke,* a term used to describe what is usually called a *bag* or *sack* in other dialects of English, and *holler,* a word used to describe a valley surrounded by mountains, while *dope* is used as the generic term for carbonated beverages (Montgomery and Hall 2003).

---

[3]It should be noted that although multiple negation is a salient feature of Appalachian English, it is not exclusive to this dialect. It is also found in African-American English (to be discussed in File 11.4) and in many working-class varieties of English across the United States.

10.3.8 The Midland

In present-day dialect studies, the Midland is defined as the section of the country stretching from the Pittsburgh area in western Pennsylvania to roughly the western edge of Kansas and Oklahoma, although it excludes a large pocket of land surrounding St. Louis (which is considered part of the North instead, since the speech features of the area are more Northern in character). For the sake of simplicity, we included eastern Pennsylvania and New Jersey in the Midland area in the map in (3), but some of the features described in this section are not found in those areas. We will mention some of the specific differences where relevant, referring to the eastern Pennsylvania and New Jersey region as the Mid-Atlantic, which is sometimes considered to be a different dialect area from the Midland.

Although there has been a commonly held popular view that there is "nothing special" about language use in the Midland and that it represents "standard" English, research has shown this stereotype to be untrue. One of the most salient characteristics is the pronunciation of /oʊ/ as [øʊ] (refer to the full IPA chart on the last page of the book), with the nucleus of the vowel produced closer to the front of the mouth and more rounded than in SAE. Thus, Midland speakers produce *boat* as [bøʊt] and *mow* as [møʊ] (Thomas 2001). Another common feature of Midland pronunciation is the tendency to pronounce [l] at the end of a syllable as a vowel or glide, rather than as a consonant with tongue-tip contact on the alveolar ridge: this is known as **/l/-vocalization.** Hence, *belt* is often pronounced as [bɛwt] rather than [bɛlt], and *hill* is often pronounced [hɪw] rather than [hɪl] (Dodsworth 2005).

Yet another feature of the Midland dialect is the pronunciation of the vowels /ɑ/ (in *pot, cot,* or *hock*) and /ɔ/ (in *caught, taught,* or *hawk*) as a **near merger** (this is not true of the Mid-Atlantic area, where these vowels are distinctly different from each other). Although many listeners hear /ɑ/ and /ɔ/ as being the same when produced by Midland speakers, particularly in high-frequency words such as *caught, taught,* or *talk,* recent instrumental phonetic analyses (Durian 2010, Labov et al. 2006) reveal that the vowels are not truly identical in much of the Midwest. Instead, as a near merger, they are produced sometimes the same, but sometimes differently. For instance, many speakers produce *dawn* with [ɑ] rather than [ɔ], but those same speakers may produce *fog* or *law* with [ɔ] rather than [ɑ]. This leads to words like *dawn* and *Don* being **near-homophones.** This feature marks the Midwestern production of [ɑ] and [ɔ] as distinctive from other dialect areas in the United States, such as the West or New England, where full merger of these vowel classes is found in present-day English (Labov et al. 2006).

Many historically Scots-Irish morphosyntactic patterns are prevalent in the Midland dialect. One such feature found to varying degrees throughout the region is the use of *anymore* without a preceding marker of negation (as in SAE *I don't do that anymore*) with a meaning of 'these days' (Murray 1993). Examples are sentences like *It seems to rain every weekend anymore* or *Anymore, I leave early on Fridays.* Other Scots-Irish features are not normally found in the Mid-Atlantic but are common elsewhere in the Midland. One is the use of the phrase *all the further* (or *farther*) where other dialects of American English would use *as far as,* as in the sentence *Johnstown was all the further I could drive* (Thomas 1993). Another feature of Scots roots used by many Midland speakers is the *needs VERB+ed* construction, as in *The table needs washed,* where speakers of many other dialects would say *The table needs to be washed* (Murray et al. 1996).

The Midland is characterized by a variety of dialect terms specific to the area, as described in part by the Harvard Dialect Survey. For instance, the strip of grass that is found in someone's front yard between the sidewalk and the road is typically referred to as either an *easement* or a *tree lawn,* while the most common term for the gray creature that rolls up into a ball when touched is *potato bug.* Outside of the Mid-Atlantic area, sweetened carbonated beverages are typically referred to as *pop,* and many speakers use *sweeper* as a generic synonym for *vacuum cleaner,* while a sweet green pepper is often referred to as a *mango,* particularly among older speakers.

10.3.9　The West

The West as a dialect area is defined as an area stretching from roughly the western sections of Kansas and Nebraska to the western coast of the United States. Geographically, this area includes New Mexico, Colorado, Arizona, Utah, Nevada, Idaho, California, Oregon, and Washington, as well as the western portions of South Dakota and Nebraska. Unlike the other regional dialects, Western speech among Anglo-Americans is less distinctive; there are fewer features that can be specifically discussed as occurring primarily in the West. The reason is that the West was the last dialect area to be extensively settled in the United States, and by the time settlers colonized the area, dialect patterns had become fairly solidified in other areas. Consequently, Western speech can perhaps best be considered a hybrid of the other regional dialects of English.

Generally, Western pronunciation closely resembles that of the Midland patterns previously discussed, with a few notable exceptions. First, the nucleus of /u/ is typically pronounced closer to the front of the mouth than in the Midland (or in other dialect areas for that matter), particularly after alveolar consonants like [t] and [d]. Consequently, where speakers of other dialects produce [u] in words such as *dude* or *new*, many Western speakers produce [ʉ], resulting in *dude* as [dʉd] and *new* as [nʉ] (Ash 2003). However, although /u/ is extensively fronted, /oʊ/ is not, unlike in Midland speech. Also, [ɑ], the vowel in words such as *cot, pot,* and *hock,* and [ɔ], the vowel in words such as *caught, thought, hawk,* are pronounced the same, as in New England speech, rather than as a near merger, as in the Midland. A final difference is the Western pronunciation of /ɪ/. When it occurs in words before [ŋ], speakers tend to pronounce /ɪ/ as [i], so that *thing* is pronounced [θiŋ]. In other contexts, [ɪ] is pronounced as [ɛ], so that *hid* is pronounced [hɛd] rather than [hɪd]. These pronunciation patterns are especially salient in Northern California speech (Eckert 2004).

The morphosyntactic patterns, on the other hand, tend to most closely resemble the patterns previously discussed for the North, although the California youth culture has been responsible for introducing a feature that has become pervasive throughout US (and even global) English: the use of the discourse marker *I'm like*. This marker is used to introduce quoted speech, as in the sentence *I'm like, "No I don't have a crush on Kim."* A related marker is *I'm/he's/she's all*, which also traces its roots to California speech and serves a similar function, as in *I'm all, "No he didn't,"* or *He's all, "Shut your mouth"* (Eckert and Mendoza-Denton 2006).

Dialect terms specific to the West include *lookie lou* to describe a traffic jam caused by drivers slowing down to view an accident and *firefly* as the most common term for the flying bug found in the summertime that lights up at night, according to the Harvard Dialect Survey. In addition, *granola* is often used to describe people who live healthy lifestyles, rather than a name for a breakfast item, as is the common use in other dialect areas. The most widely used generic term for a carbonated beverage is *soda,* making the West akin to Eastern New England (McConchie 2002).

FILE 10.4

Factors Influencing Variation: Social Factors

10.4.1 Social Influences on Language Variation

In File 10.3, we explored the regional and geographic factors that lead to language variation. However, regional variation explains only half of the story. Although regional dialects are particularly salient, there are plenty of language varieties that co-occur within any given regional dialect; in this file, we will explore the factors that lead to this linguistic differentiation within regional dialects. These additional factors are attributes such as socioeconomic class, age, gender, and ethnicity. These are speaker characteristics that are associated with the social groups to which speakers belong, and they reflect what are known as **social dialects** of a language. Each of these social factors is briefly explored below. We will continue to discuss the issue of language as a social phenomenon in File 10.5, where we consider the role language plays in marking certain social characteristics. Here, however, we focus on particular factors that often influence differences among language varieties, and we examine particular examples of this type of variation.

10.4.2 Socioeconomic Variation

One of the social factors that influence language variation is socioeconomic class. We mentioned some issues related to socioeconomic class in File 10.1, when we discussed the notion of "prestige" and the role it plays in deciding which dialect is considered standard: the dialects spoken by people with higher prestige—generally those of a higher socioeconomic status—are considered the standard.

Socioeconomic status affects language varieties for a number of reasons. To a certain extent, people often want to be associated with a particular socioeconomic group (e.g., to express solidarity with those of the same group or to show distance from those of a different group), and language is one way to achieve this (see also File 10.5 on language and identity). Furthermore, socioeconomic status may be associated with particular levels or types of education, and this subsequently affects language use.

One famous study concerning the way socioeconomic status is correlated with language variety was done by William Labov in 1972 in New York City. In New York City speech, non-rhotic speech is a common phonological phenomenon: /ɹ/s at the end of syllables, such as in *four, card, paper, here, there,* and so on, are often not pronounced. Rhotic pronunciation is associated with prestige, or a high socioeconomic status, while non-rhotic pronunciation is associated with low socioeconomic status. Labov tested this claim using salespeople in three department stores also associated with different levels of prestige: Saks (high socioeconomic status), Macy's (moderate socioeconomic status), and S. Klein (low socioeconomic status). He went into the stores and asked salesclerks (who didn't know they were being tested!) a question that would elicit the answer *fourth floor.* This first elicitation represented casual speech; the interviewer then, pretending not to have heard the answer, would lean forward and ask the clerk to repeat the answer. The clerk repeated the answer, but this time in careful speech under emphatic stress.

The results of the study, summarized in (1), showed a clear stratification of rhoticity among the salespeople according to socioeconomic status, as predicted.

(1)   Percentage of [ɹ] in *floor*

	Casual	Careful
Saks	63	64
Macy's	44	61
S. Klein	8	18

The lowest socioeconomic-class store, S. Klein, had the lowest percentage of rhoticity, while the highest socioeconomic-class store, Saks, had the highest percentage of rhoticity. We can also see that careful speech (when salesclerks switched to a more formal register of speech) is similarly associated with a higher percentage of rhoticity.

10.4.3 Age Variation

Another way in which language varieties differ has to do with age: younger speakers may not speak the same way as older speakers. Many times, older speakers will comment on the "degradation" of language, or the "desecration" of language, by the younger generation. From a linguistic point of view, however, the differences between older and younger speech are not "good" or "bad"; they are simply changes that occur naturally, just like any other differences between language varieties.

Some relatively recent changes in English include the use of the word *hopefully* as a sentential adverb (to modify the entire sentence as opposed to just modifying the verb phrase), as in *Hopefully it won't rain tomorrow*; the use of high-rising intonation at the ends of even declarative sentences ("uptalk"); the use of *like* as an interjection (*I, like, didn't know what to do*) or as a quotative (*He was like, "Well, I don't know either"*); the introduction of new words such as *download*; and the loss of older words such as *dungarees* to refer to *jeans*. As these changes occur, younger speakers use the new variants to a much higher degree than older speakers do.

While it is certainly the case that some innovations are adopted by older speakers as well as younger speakers (almost everyone these days uses *hopefully* in the way described above), it is also true that younger speakers often sound distinctly different from the older speakers in their communities. In rare cases the differences between older and younger speakers remain constant, and speakers of a particular age will use a specific linguistic form in successive generations.

10.4.4 Gender Variation

In addition to region, socioeconomic class, and age, another factor that influences language variation is gender.

Gender, as used here, is not a dichotomous category, divided into males versus females, but rather cultural patterns of masculinity and femininity. While there certainly are differences in language varieties that are based on biological sexual differences between males and females (e.g., women's voices on average are of a higher pitch than men's because of differences in the average shape and length of the larynx and vocal folds), these are not the types of differences we mean when we talk about language and gender. Gender can be thought of as a set of ongoing behaviors, so that we are in a sense always "doing gender." To quote Candace West and Don Zimmerman, "'Doing gender' involves a complex of socially guided perceptual, interactional, and micropolitical activities that cast particular pursuits as expressions of masculine and feminine natures" (1991: 13–14). Research in language and gender often tries to explain the role of language in defining, constructing, and reproducing gendered identities, as well as the role of gender in the perception and production of language.

The linking of cultural norms for behavior—including linguistic behavior—with gender is usually arbitrary. This is evidenced by the fact that stereotypes involving language use (e.g., talkativeness, loudness, and silence) are, in different cultures, associated with different genders. For instance, in Malagasy culture (located on Madagascar and other islands in the Indian Ocean), indirect, deferential speech is valued. Malagasy men are often silent in public confrontations, while Malagasy women express anger and criticism through direct, confrontational speech, often to the benefit of their husbands or other male family members (Keenan 1974: 137–39). But there is clearly no direct link between silence and masculinity in all cultures. Many Western cultures value direct, public speech. A number of studies of conversation (see Coates 1993: 115 for a brief overview) have shown that in Western societies, public speech tends to be dominated by men. Although the speech behaviors typical of Malagasy males and females are very different from those of much of Western society, note that in both instances it is the male norms that are more highly valued by the community. (See also Section 11.3.2.)

One pattern that has repeatedly been found, at least in studies of Western cultures, is that women tend to use more prestige (standard) variants than men, and listeners even expect female speech to be more like that of the middle class and male speech to be more like that of the working class. For example, a study in Norwich, England (Trudgill 1974), showed that members of the middle class and women were more likely to use standard verb forms like *running* (with word-final [ɪŋ]), as opposed to nonstandard forms like *runnin'* (with word-final [ɪn]). This is not to say that the use of forms like *running* was limited only to women or only to the middle class, but rather that Norwich women, on average, used these forms more frequently than men. A similar pattern occurred in the speech of working-class adolescents in Sydney, Australia. Boys were more likely than girls to use nonstandard syntactic features such as multiple negation, for example, *they don't say nothing,* and nonstandard past tense forms, for example, *he woke up an' seen something* (Eisikovits 1988: 37–40).

John Edwards (1979) demonstrated the role of gender in perception in a study conducted in Dublin, Ireland, in which adults were asked to listen to recordings of preadolescent children, some of whom were from working-class families and some of whom were from middle-class families. The adults were then asked to identify the gender of each child. The adults had few problems identifying the working-class boys as boys and the middle-class girls as girls, but they did much worse identifying the middle-class boys and the working-class girls, more than doubling their number of errors. To these listeners, the speech of middle-class boys was perceived as feminine, and the speech of working-class girls was perceived as masculine.

A number of different hypotheses have been proposed to explain why this correlation between females and standard language should exist. These explanations are again tied not to anything inherent about being male or female, but rather to the social roles that women and men play. For example, because women have traditionally been considered inferior to men in terms of social status, women may make more of an effort to imitate the prestigious and more standardized language of the social classes above them, in order to be perceived as more prestigious themselves. In addition, it has been suggested that women, being the primary caretakers for children in many societies, may try to expose their children to prestige dialects in order to improve the children's chances of success. In many cases, however, gender influences language simply because certain features of language, such as nonstandard working-class varieties, are associated with masculinity and other features, such as standard varieties, are associated with femininity. Native speakers of American English are generally aware, at some level, of these associations and act accordingly. The linking of cultural norms for behavior—including linguistic behavior—with gender is usually arbitrary.

It is difficult to precisely determine the roles of prestige, economics, age, and so on, in shaping the language of women and men. Eckert and McConnell-Ginet (1992) suggest that limiting the scope of inquiry to isolated factors like these will prove unfruitful. They propose centering language and gender research on **communities of practice.** By their definition, a community of practice is "an aggregate of people who come together around mutual engagement in an endeavor" (p. 464). A community of practice may be a softball team, a family sharing a meal, participants in a linguistics classroom, an election campaign team, the office staff in a workplace, and so on. An individual belongs to any number of overlapping communities of practice, and in each of them she or he will construct a gendered identity differently. For example, an outspoken leader of the local labor union may be quite docile as a student in night school. Focusing on local communities of practice may allow researchers to better understand the complex nature of gender as it is continually being redefined by individual and group behaviors. This, in turn, can enlighten our understanding of the role of gender in the construction of language and the role of language in the construction of gender in the community.

10.4.5   Ethnic Variation

Finally, ethnicity influences variation in multi-ethnic communities. Part of the reason for this is that ethnic groups are often associated with particular languages that represent the group's heritage and culture; pronunciations, words, and constructions from such a language may influence how the group speaks the standard language variety of the country or region they live in. Compounded with this is again the factor of language and identity, which will be discussed more extensively in the next file: members of an ethnic group may want to associate themselves with a particular ethnicity, or distance themselves from other ethnicities and groups, through their use of language. As with any language variety, however, it is important to remember that no variety can be linguistically superior or inferior to any other.

It is also important to note that just as there is nothing inherent about southeastern Pennsylvania that makes speakers in the region use German-influenced language, there is nothing inherent about any ethnic group that causes members of the group to speak one way as opposed to another. There are plenty of people who belong to a particular ethnic group who do not speak a dialect associated with that ethnicity, and there are plenty of people who are not members of a particular ethnicity who nonetheless speak a dialect associated with it. As discussed in the files on language acquisition (Chapter 8), the language a person speaks is not in any way predestined but is instead determined by the language that she is exposed to. In addition, the other factors discussed in this file, as well as regional factors, can lead to further differentiation within ethnic varieties; for example, a younger working-class female Pennsylvania German speaker may use somewhat different phonological and lexical features from those of an older male middle-class speaker of the same ethnic group. Furthermore, no individual speaker of an ethnic variety, or any variety, speaks the same way all the time. Rather, we all vary our speech depending on style and context.

a. African-American English (AAE). There are several varieties of English that have been particularly influenced by ethnicity in the United States and have been the subject of much linguistic study. One of these is African-American English (AAE), which is itself a cover term used by linguists to refer to a continuum of varieties, spoken primarily by and among African Americans. The features of AAE may be very similar to or very different from Standard American English, depending on which end of the continuum you consider. AAE comes from a variety of different sources, although it is clearly a dialect of American English. Because the origins of AAE can be traced to West Africans brought to the southern

United States as part of the slave trade, many of its many features seem to come from southern dialects and others from various West African languages.

There are several phonological features that distinguish AAE from SAE. First, diphthongs are reduced to monophthongs word-finally or before voiced consonants. Through this process, known as monophthongization, words such as *now* and *side,* which are typically pronounced as [naʊ] and [saɪd] in SAE, are pronounced as [naː] and [saːd] in AAE, while other words such as *time* (pronounced as [tʰaɪm] in SAE) are pronounced as [tʰaːm] in AAE. Monophthongization before voiceless consonants, such as *kite* pronounced as [kʰaːt] or *like* as [laːk] also occurs in AAE, but less frequently. These patterns of monophthongization provide some evidence for the dialectal roots of AAE, as they are also found in some varieties of Southern speech (see Section 10.3.6) (Wolfram and Schilling-Estes 2005).

Another phonological feature that is quite prevalent in AAE is word-final consonant cluster reduction, when the following word begins with a consonant. Thus, phrases such as *hand puppet* [hænd pʌpət] and *best day* [bɛst deɪ] are pronounced as [hæn pʌpət] and [bɛs deɪ]. Although this process is also found in other English varieties, AAE differs from SAE in that it is additionally possible to reduce word-final consonant clusters when the following word begins with a vowel. For instance, phrases such as *hand off* [hænd ɔf] and *best ever* [bɛst ɛvɹ̩] are sometimes pronounced [hæn ɔf] and *best ever* [bɛs ɛvɹ̩] in AAE. In past tense forms, the addition of the past tense suffix ([t], [d]) may create a consonant cluster, which would then be reduced in AAE (e.g., *passed* [pʰæst] pronounced as [pʰæs]). The fact that word-final past tense suffixes can be deleted in these environments may give AAE the appearance of lacking a past tense suffix. However, past tense suffixes that do not form consonant clusters are not deleted. Thus, words such as *hated* and *shouted* are pronounced [heɪɾəd] and [ʃaʊɾəd] in AAE, just as they are in SAE (Green 2004).

Besides these phonological processes, AAE is typified by several morphosyntactic processes that distinguish it from SAE. One is the absence of the third-person singular inflectional suffix *-s,* as in *He <u>need</u> to get a book from the shelf,* or *She <u>want</u> us to pass the papers to the front* (Rickford 1999). Another is multiple negation, which is also found in Appalachian speech (as discussed in Section 10.3.7) and thus also provides evidence for AAE's dialectal roots (Wolfram and Schilling-Estes 2005). A third is **copula absence:** the absence of inflected present tense forms of *to be* in sentences where other varieties of English would use an inflected form, as in the sentence *John going to the store.* In SAE, the equivalent sentence is *John <u>is</u> going to the store* (Rickford 1999). Copula absence is possible with all pronominal cases except first-person singular, such that **I going to the store* is ungrammatical. Because copula absence is a feature of some West African languages, this feature provides some evidence of AAE's West African roots. A fourth feature that differentiates AAE from SAE morphosyntactically is the use of **habitual** *be.* Where SAE varieties use adverbials such as *always* or *usually* to express habituality, AAE can employ an uninflected form of *be* to communicate that a state or activity is habitual or repeatable; the use of *be* is all that is needed to indicate this property. Thus, in AAE, a speaker can say *The coffee <u>be</u> cold,* whereas in SAE, a speaker would say *The coffee <u>is always</u> cold* (Green 2004).

b. Chicano English. Another prevalent ethnic dialect in the United States is Chicano English. Chicano English is a cover term for the varieties of English often spoken by second- or third-generation speakers of Mexican descent in the United States. As with AAE, Chicano English is considered a dialect of English, as most of its speakers are native speakers of English. In fact, in many cases, these speakers have little or no fluency in Spanish (Fought 2006). On occasions when Spanish words or phrases are used by these speakers, they are used to symbolically reference Latino and Hispanic cultural heritage and identity. This process is also known as **emblematic language** use. Thus, Chicano English is different from Spanglish (literally, Spanish-English), the mixed-language variety spoken by first- or second-generation speakers of Latino or Hispanic descent who use a mixture of Spanish and English, switching their use between languages in daily speech (Silvia-Corvalán 2004).

Historically, Chicano English traces its roots to varieties of Spanish spoken by immigrant groups from Mexico. Thus, most of the phonological, syntactic, and lexical features that distinguish Chicano English from other dialects of English can be traced to Spanish (Fought 2006). One feature that demonstrates the influence of Spanish is that /oʊ/ is typically pronounced as the monophthong [o] rather than as the diphthong [oʊ], as in most varieties of SAE, although this is not universally true for all varieties of Chicano English (Thomas 2001). Another feature is that /ɪ/, when it precedes [ŋ], as in *going* or *walking*, is pronounced [i], rather than [ɪ] as in SAE (Fought 2006). In addition, [ɑ] and [ɔ] are usually pronounced the same, making the Chicano English pronunciation similar to those found in the New England and Western dialects of English (Thomas 2001). All of these vowel patterns are influenced by the fact that Spanish has only five monophthongal vowels, [i, e, a, o, u], which are never pronounced as diphthongs.

Morphosyntactically, Chicano English is typified by several features that also serve to distinguish it as a unique dialect of English. One feature is the use of past participle verb forms in contexts where SAE speakers would use simple past tense forms, particularly in cases where *have* is normally contracted in SAE. Thus, in Chicano English, a speaker might say *I seen Ramon talking to Sally in her yard,* where speakers of SAE would say *I've seen Ramon talking to Sally in her yard* (Penfield and Ornstein-Galicia 1985). Another feature is the use of embedded question inversion involving *wh-* forms, as in the sentence *I ask myself <u>what would I do</u> without Lucy's help.* In SAE, a speaker would say *I ask myself <u>what I would do</u>* to mean the same thing (Duchnowski 1999). A third feature is the placement of noun phrases that typically occur in the object position of a sentence, but are also the topic of that sentence, at the beginning of the sentence, a process known as **topicalization.** Thus, in Chicano English, a speaker might say *<u>To talk about myself,</u> it's easy for me,* whereas a speaker of SAE would say *It's easy for me <u>to talk about myself.</u>* The use of topicalization appears to be influenced by Spanish, because this is the preferred syntactic structure for these types of sentences in Standard Mexican Spanish (Penfield and Ornstein-Galicia 1985).

In terms of lexical variation, Chicano English makes use of a variety of words found in Standard Mexican Spanish. However, as discussed above, the use of these words is often limited to symbolic contexts, either to reflect cultural heritage or to signify cultural identity. For example, many speakers may refer to their grandfather as *abuelo,* while *ándale* might be used to communicate that someone should move more quickly (Fought 2006). In addition, Chicano English youth in California have been reported to use taboo Spanish words and slang as a way of signaling "toughness" or being "street savvy" (Mendoza-Denton 1997, Cran and MacNeil 2005).

 c. Lumbee English. A third ethnically distinct dialect of American English is that of the Lumbee Indians, the largest Native American group east of the Mississippi River. Although there are members of the Lumbee tribe throughout the United States, today the largest concentration lives in Robeson County, North Carolina (Wolfram 2006). The historical origins of the Lumbee are not known, as records pertaining to their ancestors were never kept, and several major families of Native American tribes, including the Algonquian, Iroquoian, and Siouan, each of which speaks distinct languages, populated the area in colonial times. Most scholars believe that the Lumbee descend from an amalgam of these tribes, and as the Lumbee were reported to be speaking English by the early 1700s, there are no linguistic records by which to trace a historical Lumbee language (Wolfram et al. 2002).

Although the Lumbee have had difficulty tracing their historical roots, they are unified by a common dialect, which is typified by a unique set of linguistic features that, when considered together, mark their speech as distinctive from other varieties of English. One phonetic characteristic of Lumbee speech is the pronunciation of /ɑɪ/ as [ɔɪ]. Hence, *ride* is pronounced [ɹɔɪd] as opposed to [ɹɑɪd], as in SAE, while *time* is pronounced [tʰɔɪm] as opposed to [tʰɑɪm] (Wolfram and Dannenberg 1999). Another characteristic is the pronunciation of *tobacco* as *baccer* and *potato* as *tater,* with a word-final [ɹ] as well as having only two (instead of three) syllables, two features that trace their origins to Appalachian speech (Wolfram 2006).

Lumbee speech is also marked by morphosyntactic features unique to the dialect. One is the use of *weren't* as the first-person past tense form of the verb *to be,* as in the sentence *I weren't over there last night,* where speakers of SAE would use *wasn't* (Wolfram and Dannenberg 1999). Another salient feature of Lumbee English is the use of finite *be* with an *-s* inflection in contexts where speakers of SAE would use *is* or *are,* as in the sentences *John bes playing right now* or *the cats bes playing in the yard.* Like the use of habitual *be* in AAE, *bes* can also be used to indicate a habitual or recurring activity, as in *John bes tired after work* or *The cats bes playing in the yard.* In these sentences, speakers of SAE would use *is* or *are* and the adverbial *usually* or *always,* as in *John is usually tired after work* or *The cats usually are playing in the yard* to mean the same thing (Wolfram 2006).

Beyond these phonetic and syntactic features, Lumbee English is also typified by unique lexical items. For example, the word *ellick* is used as the term to describe what other dialects would call *coffee with cream and sugar,* while *yerker* is used as the term to describe a mischievous child (Wolfram et al. 2002). Other unique terms include *brickhouse* to describe someone who is of high social status, *buddyrow* as a commonly used word for 'friend,' and *toten* as a synonym for the word *ghost* (Wolfram 2006).

FILE 10.5

Language and Identity

10.5.1 Using Language to Mark Identity

Language exists only because people have created it and use it on a daily basis to communicate, and it is therefore a social phenomenon. As was discussed in Chapter 1, and as is further elaborated in Chapter 14 on animal communication, language is a strictly human phenomenon: no other creatures use language as humans do—yet all humans, in all societies, use language. Language therefore sets us apart from the rest of the world and unifies us: it is an indicator of the unique place humans have in the world, a marker of our identity as humans.

At the same time, given the diversity of human languages, language has often also been used as a marker of identity **within** the greater human society, and this use of language is the focus of this file. Because every typically developing human acquires language, and acquiring language depends on the ambient language varieties surrounding the learner (see Chapter 8), language is readily available as a way to show which social groups a person identifies with or dissociates from.

In Files 10.3 and 10.4, we described some of the lines along which languages vary: nationality, ethnicity, age, gender, socioeconomic class, and so on. Throughout those files, we pointed out that there is not usually anything **inherent** about any particular group that might condition the members of that group to speak one way as opposed to some other way. For example, there's nothing about being younger in itself that makes some younger English speakers use more rising intonation than older English speakers—one can easily imagine a world in which the older speakers use more rising intonation and the younger speakers use less, or a world in which older and younger speakers' language is differentiated in some other way entirely. What matters here is that age is one factor that differentiates groups of speakers who identify with each other in some manner, and once these groups are formed, the members of the group may develop particular language characteristics that distinguish their group from other groups. These characteristics are often not consciously developed; they simply happen naturally in the course of language use and are then picked up and propagated by new acquirers of the particular language variety.

10.5.2 Defining "Identity"

The notion of "identity" is obviously a complex one. Most people have more than one group whom they identify with. For example, you may identify yourself in the classroom as a student but at the camp you work at in the summer as an instructor. Or you may identify yourself broadly as an American, but more specifically as someone from northwest Ohio rather than some other part of the country or the state.

To a large degree, your "identity" at any given moment actually depends on the circumstances of the situation—where you are, whom you are talking with, what you are talking about, how you want to be perceived, what you hope to accomplish, who else is present, and so on. Most scholars agree that identity is not a static thing that anyone "possesses" but rather is a dynamic construct that emerges from social interactions. It revolves around establishing the relationship between one individual and the rest of society.

One of the focuses of sociolinguistic research has been to determine both what elements define a person's identity and how identity is established in linguistic interactions. Clearly, identity is not expressed solely through language use—other actions, practices, and characteristics also create a person's identity. It is common, however, to use language to establish or indicate the identity of yourself or of others.

It is important to remember that this use of language is not always conscious or intentional, or even within your control as the speaker. You may use particular lexical items that mark you as coming from a particular region, without even realizing that people from other regions might use different terms. Or the person you are talking to may have ideas about what your pronunciation of a particular word signifies that you do not intend—for example, not pronouncing the /r/s at the end of syllables, in words such as in *four, card, paper,* and so on, might be taken as a sign of your low prestige by a listener from New York but as a sign of your high prestige by a listener from London. The perception of your identity by those listening to you is arguably just as important as **your** perception of it, as identity is rather meaningless in isolation. While you can certainly use your own knowledge of society's associations between particular linguistic phenomena and elements of identity to bolster, downplay, or separate yourself from certain types of identities, you do not have complete control over your linguistic identity.

10.5.3 Signaling Identity

How exactly can particular aspects of identity be signaled through language? You will probably not be surprised to learn that identity can be indicated at every level of linguistic structure, from phonetics to pragmatics.

The most obvious use of language to signal identity is when people overtly state affiliation with or dissociation from a particular group (e.g., *I'm from Ireland,* or *Oh, no, you shouldn't think I'm British*).

Another overt use of language to establish identity that is slightly more subtle than simply stating it is the use of forms that mark a particular identity. For example, when there are different words for male and female versions of the same profession, the use of one or the other signals the speaker's association with a particular gender (*I'm an actor/actress*). In a language such as French where adjectives must agree in gender with the noun they modify, this association is even stronger (*je suis une actrice sportive* 'I am an (fem.) athletic (fem.) actress'). Other speakers also signal their views of someone's identity this way—for example, using the pronoun *he* or *she* indicates that a speaker assumes that the person they are referring to is of a particular gender.

More obliquely, identity can be signaled by making use of linguistic characteristics that society associates with particular social groups. For example, using monophthongal [ɑː] instead of diphthongal [ɑɪ] in words such as *tide* or *I* is associated with the southeast United States. Using *like* as an interjection (*I was, like, going to the store*) is associated with younger speakers. Using *be* to mark habitual action, as in *I always be late to school,* is associated with African-American English. So, using such forms can be taken as a sign of belonging to the associated group.[1]

---

[1] An interesting twist on this is the use of identity to affect language perception. Elizabeth Strand found in a 1999 study that listeners will actually classify phonemes (see File 3.2) differently depending on whether they think they are hearing a man or a woman. Strand synthesized a continuum of fricatives from [s] to [ʃ] and had people categorize each sound on the continuum as one or the other. The listeners heard the sounds while looking at either a male face or a female face—and the categorization of the continuum was different depending on the face!

On a broader level, in societies where multiple languages are used, the choice of one language over another can be used to indicate a certain affiliation or identity. For example, in Canada, both French and English are official languages at the federal level (see File 11.3 for more on official languages). However, most provinces are almost exclusively anglophone (English-speaking), while Quebec is francophone (French-speaking)—New Brunswick is the only officially bilingual province in Canada. Because of various political tensions between Quebec and anglophone Canada (e.g., there has long been an independence movement to separate Quebec from the rest of Canada), the choice of language is sometimes seen as making a political statement. In 1978, Soma Day told of an encounter she had: "I stopped in a garage and struggled to explain that my windshield wipers were *congellé* [frozen over] and I wanted to make them *fonctionner* [function]. The man listened in mild amusement and then said, 'You don't have to speak French to me, Madame. I'm not a separatist'" (reported in Fraser 2006: 144–45). While it has become more socially acceptable for anglophones to speak French in Quebec, the choice of which language to speak when two bilinguals encounter each other is still influenced by a number of factors: "the language the relationship was established in, where the conversation happens, the presence of other people, the nature of the relationship, and a whole series of other factors that can involve shadings of power ('I'll pick the language here'), one-upmanship ('I speak your language better than you speak mine'), exclusion ('I speak my language only with my people—and you're not one of them'), complicity ('We speak this language and they don't'), solidarity ('I'm one of you' or 'You're one of us')—or simply convenience" (Fraser 2006: 144).

It is interesting to note in the above discussion that identity can be marked either by showing the inclusion of the speaker in a particular group or by showing the dissociation of the speaker from a different group. That is, sometimes the usage of linguistic forms directly marks a particular identity (e.g., using habitual *be* might mark the speaker as being African American). But sometimes the usage indicates identity by showing that the speaker is choosing **not** to speak in some other way that might be expected. For example, Elaine Chun's 2001 study showed that some Korean-American men use characteristics of African-American English, not to show that they are African American, but instead to show that they are not Euro-American.

Signaling identity through language can have various consequences. There are plenty of social stereotypes that accompany ideas of identity, so your language use may cause listeners to form ideas about you, your personality, your abilities, and so on. For example, in the United States, British dialects are often considered to be a mark of a more educated person, while speakers of southern US dialects are considered uneducated. Of course, these associations are usually unfounded—someone from Alabama may be more highly educated than someone from Oxford—but they do have consequences for communication and social perception. Thomas Purnell, William Idsardi, and John Baugh did a study in 1999 that showed discrimination by landlords based on the perceived ethnicity of a potential renter, as determined through a telephone conversation. John Baugh, who has fluent command of Standard American English, African-American English, and Chicano English (see Section 10.4.5), called various landlords who had advertised housing for rent. In housing districts that were largely Euro-American in population, when he spoke using either the African-American or the Chicano English dialects, he was often told that the housing was unavailable—and then, using the Standard American English dialect within 30 minutes of the other calls, he was told that it was. This kind of dialect discrimination (which is illegal in the United States) is an unfortunate consequence of the use of language to mark identity; fortunately, John Baugh and his colleagues are working with the US government to fight against it.[2]

---

 [2]To find out more about this study, and to hear recordings of John Baugh, follow the link to his website on the Links page for Chapter 10.

10.5.4 Studying Identity

In the early days of sociolinguistic research, scholars often tried to isolate "essential" elements of speakers' identities. They would determine certain sociological factors that could be defined relatively easily (such as the factors described in Files 10.3 and 10.4: region, age, gender, etc.) and then pick a particular linguistic variable (such as rhoticity, use of *pop* versus *soda,* use of the *needs washed* construction, etc.). Next they would see how the two were correlated (e.g., whether younger speakers use more /ɹ/s at the end of syllables than older speakers do). These studies were extremely valuable at establishing broad characteristics of different types of speech, and the studies formed the foundation of modern sociolinguistic methodology. They are easily replicable and are well-suited to doing statistical analysis. Most of the discussion of sociolinguistics that we have presented has been based on such studies.

At the same time, however, these studies are somewhat limited in determining a person's sociolinguistic identity. First, they make use of sociological factors that are predetermined by the researcher and that may or may not have any actual relevance for a particular speaker's identity. Second, they are tied to the sociological variables that are salient in a society; it is therefore difficult to do meaningful comparative studies across societies. Third, some of these variables are difficult to isolate or establish for a particular person—for example, what do you do about someone who has moved around several times? Someone who is of mixed ethnicity? Someone who grew up with wealthy parents but has since rejected that lifestyle?

While the factors used in such studies clearly do play a role in identity formation (and establishing particular correlations can help determine a person's identity based on her speech patterns), they do not tell the whole story. More recently, researchers have expanded their studies to try to include factors that speakers themselves may identify as being more relevant. For example, does a speaker feel that her involvement in the service organization Habitat for Humanity has created for herself a particular community with which she identifies? Do people involved in Habitat for Humanity have unique speech patterns—for example, the use of certain home-building jargon? Similar groups can be identified for all sorts of communities. One obvious location of such groups is schools—high schoolers often form cliques that distinguish themselves linguistically. Although two speakers could both be 17-year-old, Euro-American, female, middle-class students at the same high school, they may belong to radically different social groups and have different speech patterns that mark those groups. Penelope Eckert's study of Belten High School showed the large linguistic differences between "Jocks" and "Burnouts" (see File 11.5 for a discussion of this study). Jock girls used fairly standard vowel pronunciations, while Burnout girls tended to use more extreme versions of the Northern Cities Shift discussed in File 10.3. The members of the two groups had distinctly different linguistic patterns that reflect their different social groups within a fairly narrowly defined environment.

One problem with many sociolinguistic studies of identity is known as the "observer's paradox." Often, it is impossible to get an accurate picture of what speakers do "naturally" among themselves precisely because observing them makes them change their speech. Knowing that they are being watched, recorded, or studied may make speakers self-conscious, and many will try to speak the way they think the researcher wants them to, rather than how they would normally speak. The perceived identity of the researcher may also play a role in determining the speech of a person being studied: John Rickford and Faye McNair-Knox found in a 1994 study that the same African American participant talked markedly differently when being interviewed by a Euro-American researcher than when being interviewed by an African American researcher. This type of differing language use also points out the ever-changing notion of identity: clearly, the participant was the same person in both situations but projected a different identity each time.

One way of at least partially avoiding the observer's paradox is to use larger databases of speech that have been recorded for other purposes or in such large quantities that speakers seem to forget that they are being recorded. These data can be used for subsequent analysis using techniques known as **discourse analysis** or **conversational analysis** to see how particular identities are established in the course of a conversation. In discourse analysis, the researcher breaks down a conversation between two or more people into its various component parts (e.g., the types of turns that are taken by the participants, the information conveyed, and the linguistic forms at all levels in which it is conveyed). Of course, this kind of study often does not give the researcher the same sort of flexibility as doing a direct interview with someone, because the researcher is reliant on whatever the speakers happened to be talking about.

No matter what technique a researcher uses, there will be advantages and disadvantages. These days, a more complete picture of sociolinguistic identity can be obtained by doing multiple types of studies that complement each other and each bring out a different aspect: for example, starting with a broad ethnographic study of a community and using surveys to begin to study language patterns that naturally occur, and then narrowing down the research with one-on-one interviews and using techniques of discourse analysis that pinpoint particular phenomena.

10.5.5 Martha's Vineyard: A Case Study in Language and Identity

In 1961, William Labov conducted a sociolinguistic study on the island of Martha's Vineyard in Dukes County, Massachusetts, to investigate the impact of social patterns on linguistic variation and change. The linguistic feature chosen for analysis was **centralization** of the diphthongs /ɑɪ/ and /ɑʊ/, as in *why* and *wow*, to [əɪ] and [əʊ], respectively. In a preliminary investigation, Labov discovered that after all phonetic, prosodic, and stylistic motivation had been accounted for, there was still variation in speakers' use of centralized diphthongs. His subsequent study was designed to investigate the motivation underlying this residual variation. Toward this end, Labov set out to test a number of different variables, many of which were introduced in Files 10.3 and 10.4.

Was centralization related to **geography?** The island was, by universal consensus, divided into up-island (strictly rural) and down-island (consisting of the three small towns where 75% of the population lived). United States Census reports were consulted for information on the population distribution of the island.

Was **ethnic group** a factor in centralization? Native Vineyarders fell into four ethnic groups: (1) descendants of old English families, (2) descendants of Portuguese immigrants, (3) a small Native American population, and (4) a miscellaneous group from a number of origins. Another group, not considered in the study, was the summer population.

Were the **economic background** and the current economic situation of the island in any way correlated with linguistic behavior? In comparison to the rest of the state, the Vineyard had higher unemployment, lower average income, and no industry, and thus was heavily dependent on the summer tourist trade. This heavy reliance on tourism was viewed by some islanders as a threat to independence. As a result, many islanders displayed resistance to the summer visitors and took pride in being different from the tourists, the greatest resistance being felt in the rural up-island areas.

The results of the study revealed that, first of all, centralization was a linguistic feature of Martha's Vineyard and thus **regional** in character. That is, residents of the island pronounced /ɑɪ/ and /ɑʊ/ as [əɪ] and [əʊ], while summer tourists and mainland residents did not centralize the diphthongs. But within the island population, some residents centralized, while some did not.

Analysis of centralization by **age** indicated an increase of centralized diphthong use with age, peaking between thirty-one and forty-five years and then decreasing. It was also interesting to note the economic situation of this particular group. Members of this age group seemed to suffer the greatest degree of economic pressure, having chosen to remain on the island while supporting their families, even though employment opportunities were not abundant. Additionally, high school students planning to go to college and then return to the island exhibited greater centralization than those going to college but not planning to return to the island.

With respect to ethnic group, the Portuguese population, which for years had been attempting to enter the mainstream of island life, showed a high degree of centralization. And those of Native American descent, having battled discrimination from the other groups for more than 150 years and also desiring acceptance, also displayed a high incidence of centralization.

Although it is clear that each of these regional and social factors that we might expect to influence linguistic variation does play a role, we can reach a deeper understanding of the effects at work here by thinking about language and identity. Specifically, we can summarize the effects of these different factors on centralization in terms of **group identification.** How closely speakers identified with the island—e.g., wanted to remain, wanted to enter into the mainstream, saw themselves as Vineyarders and were proud of it—was positively correlated with degree of centralization. The use of centralization was not necessarily conscious on the part of these speakers; centralization was, however, associated with being a Martha's Vineyard native, so those who felt especially close to the island tended to increase their use of this linguistic variable. Thus, speakers use and manipulate language to show their own identity. Remember, though, that there are many aspects of a speaker's identity and speakers often desire to signal different identities, or different combinations of identities, at different times and in different contexts.

Practice

File 10.1—Language Varieties

Exercises

1. Suppose that you have a very close relationship with someone whom you plan to marry. How would you introduce your fiancé(e) to the following people under the following circumstances?

    a. your grandmother, at a family dinner
    b. your best friend from high school, at a picnic
    c. the dean of your college, at a reception for a visiting scholar
    d. a group of eight-year-olds in a Saturday morning class you've been working with

    See how many differences you can find in the forms of introduction you can come up with. Then compare your list with a friend's to determine if they differ significantly.

2. The following are some popular myths about slang. See if you can explain what about them is misconceived, especially from the viewpoint established in the discussion on slang in File 10.1.

    a. Slang is bad and degrades the user and the language itself.
    b. Only young people use slang.
    c. There are languages that have no slang.

3. Refer to the cartoon at the beginning of this chapter. Does the difference between the two speakers have to do with dialect or accent? Why?

4. To give you an idea of the richness and variety of slang, we give below a collection of terms for getting or being inebriated. As you look through this list, compare your own current slang usage with that reported here. Which terms are new to you? Can you see how they may have originated? Are there terms here that you know as meaning something else? If so, which ones are they and what do they mean? Why do you suppose there are so many different terms for this activity?

get wasted	loose	hazed	aced
get stiff	fried	z'd	pound a few
snockered	zoned	blasted	catch a cold
crocked	ripped	plastered	pissed
slushed	buzzed	loaded	toasted
stoned	tanked	hammered	tie one on
shit-faced	lubered	blotto	

Discussion Questions

5. An American was hitchhiking in Italy and got picked up by an Italian truck driver. The American spoke no Italian, but was fluent in Spanish. He and the truck driver (who spoke no English or Spanish) had a lively conversation for two hours: the American was speaking Spanish, and the truck driver was speaking Italian. At the end of the trip, the truck driver asked the American which dialect of Italian he was speaking. What does this tell you about the difference between the dialects of Spanish and Italian spoken by these two people as language varieties?

6. Consider the following:

At the turn of the century, the form *ain't* was prestigious among many upper-middle-class English speakers in southern England. Today, however, its use is considered nonstandard or at best appropriate only for casual conversation.

In the United States "dropped *r*'s" in words like *car, father,* and *bark* are perceived as features of nonstandard speech. In Britain, however, "dropped *r*'s" are characteristic of Received Pronunciation and are thus considered part of the prestige dialect.

What do these two examples tell us about standard and nonstandard features? Are they defined on linguistic or social grounds? Explain your answer.

7. Why do you think every language has a standard dialect (at least one)?

8. How might evaluations we make about language as "good" or "bad" help to preserve and perpetuate social stereotypes and biases?

9. Consider which form of the third-person singular pronoun you think should go in the blank: *They've arranged for you and ___ to meet with Dr. Johnson.* Compare your answers with your classmates; do you all agree?

Activities

10. Make up your own list of jargon by examining the terms and expressions that are associated with your major (or hobby or whatever). Compare your list with that of someone else in your major (or hobby or whatever) and with someone not in that group. Does the in-group/out-group designation applied to slang hold here?

11. Look in a thesaurus for all the synonyms of *crazy.* Do they differ in register? If so, rank them from most formal to least formal.

File 10.2—Variation at Different Levels of Linguistic Structure

Exercises

12. Refer to the cartoon at the beginning of this chapter. What level of linguistic structure is involved here?

13. Look at the pictures below of two different variants of the ASL word *about*. What type of variation do these pictures illustrate; that is, what level of linguistic structure is relevant here? Explain your answer.

ABOUT variants in ASL:

Reproduced by permission of Gallaudet University Press, from Shroyer and Shroyer, *Signs across America* (1984), p. 3.

14. For each example below, identify the level of linguistic structure at which the variation exists.

P = Phonetic
Ph = Phonological
M = Morphological
S = Syntactic
L = Lexical

_____ Some Caribbean English dialects do not have the sounds [θ] or [ð]; instead, the sounds [t] and [d], respectively, are substituted, for example, *both* [boʊt], *there* [dɛɹ].

_____ Many dialects of English have multiple negation, as in *I didn't see nobody take no pictures.*

_____ Many American dialects have the mid back lax vowel [ɔ]. However, this vowel is produced very differently in different dialects—some are more rounded, some less so; some are higher or lower than others.

_____ Names differ from place to place to refer to an insect that glows in the dark, including *firefly, lightning bug, glowworm,* and *fire bug.*

_____ Some African-American English dialects do not mark the third-person singular present tense with a suffix, for example, *he kiss, she see, it jump.*

_____ In some Midland dialects of American English, there is no distinction between [ʊ] and [u] before [l] at the end of a word. So the words *full* and *fool*, which are pronounced [fʊl] and [ful], respectively, in many other American English dialects, are homophonous, pronounced (usually) as [fʊl] for both words.

15. Pronunciation
On the next page is a list of words that have different pronunciations in different dialects. Circle the letter corresponding to the pronunciation you use in **relaxed, casual conversation.** If you use more than one, circle all the appropriate letters. If you use an entirely different pronunciation, indicate your pronunciation in the blank at the right. Finally, if you think there is a distinction among the choices between a standard and a nonstandard pronunciation, X out the letter corresponding to the one you consider to be standard.

(cont.)

a. *nucleus:* (a) [nukjələs] (b) [nukliəs]	a	b	_____
b. *washing:* (a) [wɔɹʃɪŋ] (b) [waʃɪŋ]	a	b	_____
c. *fire:* the vowel is (a) [aɪ] (b) [a]	a	b	_____
d. *tomato:* the second vowel is (a) [eɪ] (b) [a]	a	b	_____
e. *where:* begins with (a) [w̥] (b) [w]	a	b	_____
f. *often:* (a) [afn̩] (b) [aftn̩]	a	b	_____
g. *greasy:* (a) [gɹisi] (b) [gɹizi]	a	b	_____
h. *either:* (a) [iðɹ̩] (b) [aɪðɹ̩]	a	b	_____
i. *Columbus:* (a) [kələmbəs] (b) [klʌmbəs]	a	b	_____
j. *police:* stressed on (a) 1st syllable (b) 2nd syllable	a	b	_____

16. **Syntax**

The sentences below, based on a questionnaire used by William Labov, were all produced by some speaker of English. Go through the list of sentences and check, for each sentence, whether you think it is:

- natural for you to use in casual conversation;
- something that some people would use but others wouldn't;
- something that only a nonnative speaker would say.

This exercise is intended to be **descriptive,** not **prescriptive.** The point is not whether you think the sentences are "correct" or "incorrect," "good" or "bad."

	Natural	Some	Non-native
a. The dog is falled asleep.	_____	_____	_____
b. Everyone opened their books.	_____	_____	_____
c. My shirt needs cleaned.	_____	_____	_____
d. Ever since he lost his job, he be sleepin' all day long.	_____	_____	_____
e. You shouldn't ought to put salt in your coffee.	_____	_____	_____
f. You usually go to the one you want, but me never.	_____	_____	_____
g. You can see the cops like they're grabbing kids left and right.	_____	_____	_____
h. He didn't have no book.	_____	_____	_____
i. I want for you to go home.	_____	_____	_____
j. Me and Sally played all afternoon.	_____	_____	_____
k. Noodles, I can't stand in chicken soup.	_____	_____	_____
l. There's nobody can beat her at telling stories.	_____	_____	_____
m. Of whom are you speaking?	_____	_____	_____
n. Them tomato plants won't live.	_____	_____	_____
o. So don't I.	_____	_____	_____

17. Vocabulary

Here are some sentences containing words and idioms that differ from dialect to dialect. Circle the letter corresponding to the expression you use. If you ordinarily use more than one, circle all the appropriate letters. If you use an entirely different word or idiom, write it in the blank at the right.

a. A large open metal container for water is a (a) bucket (b) pail. _____
b. To carry groceries, you put them in a paper (a) bag (b) sack (c) poke. _____
c. Window coverings on rollers are (a) blinds (b) shades (c) roller shades (d) window shades (e) curtains. _____
d. Pepsi-Cola, Coca-Cola, and Seven-Up are all kinds of (a) soda (b) pop (c) coke (d) soft drinks (e) soda pop (f) tonic. _____
e. On summer nights when we were kids, we used to try to catch (a) fireflies (b) lightning bugs (c) fire bugs (d) glow worms. _____
f. If you go to a popular film, you may have to stand (a) on line (b) in line. _____
g. If your living room is messy, before company comes you (a) straighten it up (b) red it up (c) ret it up (d) clean it up. _____
h. If you're talking to a group of friends, you call them (a) you guys (b) you all (c) y'all (d) youse guys (e) you'ns (f) yinz. _____
i. It's now (a) a quarter of 5 (b) a quarter to 5 (c) a quarter 'til 5. _____

Discussion Question

18. Compare your responses in Exercises 15, 16, and 17 with others in the class. What are some of the factors that may influence the choice of one form over the other(s)? (For example, *My shirt needs cleaned* is more typical of Midwestern speech. It is, therefore, influenced by region.

Activity

19. Take the exercises from 15, 16, and 17 above and make photocopies of them. Survey a broad group of people (friends, family, neighbors, co-workers), and collect their answers to these same questions. Can you find any patterns to the responses, based on any of the factors discussed in Files 10.3 and 10.4?

File 10.3—Factors Influencing Variation: Regional and Geographic Factors

Exercise

20. i. Consider the following data illustrating the *pin/pen* merger common in Southern speech patterns. Notice that [ɪ] and [ɛ] are not merged to [ɪ] in all contexts. Identify the phonetic environment that conditions the merger.

Word	*Southern English*	*Standard English*
pin	[pɪn]	[pɪn]
pen	[pɪn]	[pɛn]
lit	[lɪt]	[lɪt]
let	[lɛt]	[lɛt]
Nick	[nɪk]	[nɪk]
neck	[nɛk]	[nɛk]
tin	[tɪn]	[tɪn]
ten	[tɪn]	[tɛn]

(cont.)

ii. Based on your analysis in (i), indicate whether each of the following words would be pronounced with [ɪ] or with [ɛ] in these dialects: *lid, led, kin, Ken, pick, peck, bin, Ben.*

Discussion Questions

21. If you live in the United States, which dialect area does your community fall into? Are the descriptions given for that area accurate for the dialect you hear around you? Which things are inaccurate? Remember, these are rather broad generalizations, and every individual has his own idiolect.

22. If your dialect area was not described in the description of the United States, try to describe it. Although it may be hard to identify characteristics unique to your dialect if you are not familiar with other dialects for comparison purposes, use the descriptions here as a starting point. For example, what do people in your area call a sweetened carbonated beverage? Can you use the morphosyntactic constructions listed for the various dialect areas? Do your pronunciations match any of the ones given?

Activities

23. Go to the Links page for Chapter 10 and find the Harvard Dialect Survey. Go to the maps for the words *merry, marry,* and *Mary* by clicking on question 15. Where do you see the most variation in pronunciation? Why do you think this would be a region of high variation? Explore other maps—do you see similar amounts of high variation for this same area for other questions?

24. Go to the Links page for Chapter 10 and find the British Library Dialect map. Click on one of the samples. Identify as many features (phonetic, morphosyntactic, or lexical) as you can that differ from your own dialect.

25. Go to the Links page for Chapter 10 and find the activity "Where is the speaker from?" Listen to the speech samples and try to place them in the correct regions. How accurate are you? Which samples are easiest to identify? Which are hardest? Why do you think this is? Compare your answers with those of other people in your class. Do you all have trouble with the same speakers? How does your personal background influence your ability to categorize each sample?

File 10.4—Factors Influencing Variation: Social Factors

Exercises

26. Find one example of variation in your community that is not mentioned in this chapter and that seems to be caused by each of the following social factors. Explain your reasoning.

    a. Socioeconomic class
    b. Gender
    c. Age
    d. Ethnicity

27. In Columbus, Ohio, there are two variants of the pronunciation of /stɹ/ clusters at the beginnings of words like *street*: [stɹ] and [ʃtɹ]. David Durian conducted a study in 2004 about the distribution of the two pronunciations and found the following results:

(cont.)

	Gender	
	Male	**Female**
[stɹ]	84%	68%
[ʃtɹ]	16%	32%

	Age (in 15-year groupings)		
	15–30	**35–50**	**55–70**
[stɹ]	61%	71%	91%
[ʃtɹ]	39%	29%	9%

Based on the data above, when both gender and age are considered together as social factors affecting the use of the vernacular pronunciation [ʃtɹ], which gender/age group uses this pronunciation the most? Which gender/age group uses it the least? Based on the explanations provided for age and gender in this file, why do you think these were the patterns of language use Durian observed?

28. As in many dialects of English, there is variation in Norwich, England, in the pronunciation of the ending -ing. Some speakers say [ɪŋ] while others say [ɪn]. In 1974, Peter Trudgill studied this variation and how it was linked to both gender and speech style, collecting the following data:

	Gender	
	Male	**Female**
[ɪŋ]	39%	51%
[ɪn]	61%	49%

	Speech Style		
	Formal	**Informal**	**Casual**
[ɪŋ]	71%	45%	33%
[ɪn]	29%	55%	67%

Based on the data above, when both gender and speech style are considered together as social and linguistic factors affecting the use of the vernacular pronunciation [ɪn], what are the speech style and the gender of the speakers who use this pronunciation the most? What are the speech style and the gender of the speakers who use this pronunciation the least? Based on the explanations provided for gender in File 10.4, as well as speech style in File 10.1, why do you think these were the patterns of language use Trudgill observed?

29. In a study on rhoticity (see discussion in File 10.4) among African American speakers in Detroit, Michigan, in 1969, Walt Wolfram collected the following data:

	Socioeconomic Class			
	Upper-Middle	**Lower-Middle**	**Upper-Working**	**Lower-Working**
non-rhotic	21%	39%	61%	71%
rhotic	79%	61%	39%	29%

Based on the data above, which socioeconomic class group used the non-rhotic pronunciation most often? Which group used it least often? Based on what you learned about overt and covert prestige (Section 10.1.4), speaker orientations to standard and nonstandard speech (Section 10.1.4), and variation based on socioeconomic class (Section 10.4.2), hypothesize a reasonable explanation for why these were the patterns of pronunciation that Wolfram found.

Discussion Questions

30. In Section 10.4.4, the concept of "communities of practice" is discussed in relation to issues involving language variation and gender. However, the concept is one that can be applied to all manner of social and linguistic behaviors of particular groups.

    i. Using the discussion of gender as a starting point, think of other groups whose linguistic behavior defines them as a community of practice.

    ii. Now, choose one of these groups and answer the following questions: what are the social and linguistic characteristics of the group? How does the language use of the group members signal their membership in the group? Are there other social practices that the members of the group engage in that mark their identity as members of the group? What are these practices, and how do they mark membership in the group?

31. What other ethnic groups, besides the ones discussed in Section 10.4.5, can you think of whose use of English may be marked as distinctive, along the lines of the ones discussed in this section? Choose one of these groups and try to determine two or three phonological and lexical features that distinguish the speech of this group. Are there any syntactic features you can think of that mark this group as distinctive? Once you have determined these linguistic factors, try to think of a social or historical explanation that might help us to determine why these linguistic features are particular to this group.

Activity

32. In many regional and social dialects of English, the consonant cluster /stɹ/, as in the words *street, straight,* or *strip,* undergoes a form of allophonic variation in which the cluster-initial /s/ can be pronounced in two different ways, either as [s] or as [ʃ]. Hence, in these dialects, *strip* can be pronounced either with the standard variant, as [stɹɪp], or with the vernacular variant, as [ʃtɹɪp].

However, the story of /stɹ/ is more complicated than this, being sensitive to social variation, such that its use can be affected by each of the social factors discussed in this file (as we saw in Exercise 27). For this activity, your goal is to determine how /stɹ/-cluster variation differs by two of these social factors. For example, you may wish to investigate how people from different parts of the country differ in their use of these variants, as well as how younger speakers versus older speakers vary their use.

In order to collect data, you will need to develop a question that you can use to obtain different /stɹ/ pronunciations from speakers. For example, to get a speaker to say the word *street,* you could ask them for directions to a nearby store that is located on a roadway that contains the word *street* as a part of its name (for instance, *Johnson Street*).

To collect enough data to make meaningful conclusions regarding /stɹ/, we recommend that you collect data from at least ten people, dividing up your informants so that you obtain data from an equal number of people in each of your groups. Then share your data with three other students in your class, so that, combined, you can look at the language use patterns of 40 speakers. Finally, ask yourself the following questions: How does each group's use of /stɹ/ differ from each other? How are the patterns of use the same? Why do you think the patterns of use you observed turned out the way they did?

File 10.5—Language and Identity

Exercises

33. Think about three social groups you belong to (e.g., in your family, at school, at work, as part of hobbies, etc.). Try to list characteristics of your speech that you think might be unique to each setting: for example, are there words, pronunciations, and so on, that you use only in one setting?

34. Explain why vowel centralization in Martha's Vineyard can best be understood in terms of a speaker's group identification rather than a particular isolated variable such as age, region, or ethnicity.

Discussion Question

35. Based on what you have read in this file and your own experiences, why do you think that identity is so changeable or context-dependent? How much control do you think speakers have over how their identity is perceived? What kinds of things can speakers manipulate to affect this perception? Give examples.

Activities

36. Refer to Exercise 33 above. Record yourself in each of the three different social situations you described in the exercise. Listen to the recordings: what elements differ by situation? Play parts of the recordings to someone who knows you well but who wasn't present during any of the recordings. Can he determine which situation each was recorded in? Try playing the same parts to a classmate who is less familiar with you—can she determine the different situations? What cues do you think people use to make these judgments?

37. Search online for dialect quizzes (some examples are the "Yankee or Dixie quiz," the quiz on "What kind of American English do you speak," the *New York Times* dialect quiz," etc.). Many of these quizzes will give you instant feedback on your word and pronunciation choices, labeling you as having a certain identity, usually related to region (e.g., "you are 44% Midwestern"). After taking the quiz, evaluate the label given to your answers. How accurate do you think the response is? Based on what you have read in this file (and other information on language variation), what do you think the percentages signify, if your score is represented that way? In addition to how well it identifies the region you grew up in or live in now, how well do you think it represents your "identity" as a whole? Would you want other people to have this impression of you?

Further Readings

Penfield, Joyce, and Jacob L. Ornstein-Galicia (eds.). 1985. *Chicano English: An ethnic contact dialect.* Amsterdam: John Benjamins.

Rickford, John R. 1999. *African-American Vernacular English.* Oxford: Blackwell.

Shroyer, Edgar H., and Susan P. Shroyer. 1984. *Signs across America: A look at regional differences in American Sign Language.* Washington, DC: Gallaudet University Press.

Talbot, Mary. 2010. *Language and gender.* 2nd edn. Cambridge: Polity Press.

Wolfram, Walt, and Natalie Schilling. 2015. *American English: Dialects and variation.* 3rd edn. Oxford: Wiley-Blackwell.

Wolfram, Walt, and Ben Ward (eds.). 2006. *American voices: How dialects differ from coast to coast.* Oxford: Blackwell.

CHAPTER
11

Language and Culture

....

What Is the Study of "Language and Culture"?

While the focus of much of this textbook has been on the systematic internal structure of language, language is also inextricably tied to human culture. **Linguistic anthropology** is the study of the relationship between language and culture. Language is one of the key characteristics that separate humans from other living creatures; it has shaped our societies into what they are today. In this chapter, we briefly survey some of the ways in which language can both reflect and influence humanity, society, and culture.

Contents

FILE 11.1

Linguistic Anthropology

11.1.1 What Is Linguistic Anthropology?

The American Anthropological Association defines anthropology as "the study of humans, past and present." Since possessing the language faculty is a fundamental part of being human, it may come as no surprise that one of the four traditional branches of anthropology concerns itself with the study of human language. The other three branches are socio-cultural anthropology, which is the study of human culture; archeology, which focuses on past cultures; and physical anthropology, which is concerned with human biology and evolution. **Linguistic anthropology** is the study of how language interacts with and shapes social structure and culture. Indeed, linguistic anthropologists are interested in social organization and cultural meaning as they are reflected in the structure, lexicon, and conventions of a given language. This school of thought is based partly on the idea that speakers use language to represent their natural and social worlds; thus, looking at a certain language is like looking at the world through the lens of the language's speakers, and much can be understood about culture through language. For instance, in English there are a number of metaphors equating time and money, as seen in (1).

(1) Time and money
 - *Spending* time
 - *Wasting* one's time
 - *Investing* time in a project
 - *Budgeting* out one's time

This reflects a system of worth based on currency, as well as a system that values time as a precious resource. A native speaker of English may not even notice this relationship, since this cultural value is so deeply integrated into our linguistic expression of time. As we'll see in File 11.2, time in general is something that can be conceived of differently between cultures.

Drawing this kind of connection between language and culture is part of the study of linguistic anthropology. As we'll see throughout this file, linguistic anthropology uses varied methods to investigate the link between language and culture, which are often viewed as two sides of the same coin.

11.1.2 Kinship Terms

One way cultural values are reflected in language is through kinship terms. For instance, kinship terms in English are organized by gender (*brother* vs. *sister*, *father* vs. *mother*), generation (*daughter, mother, grandmother, great-grandmother, great-great-grandmother*, etc.), and line.g., (direct lineage: *mother, son*, vs. collateral lineage: *aunt, nephew*). There is also an emphasis on blood relation versus relation by marriage, with terms like *step-sibling, half-sibling, mother-in-law*, and so on.

461

The terminology we use to categorize people reflects the cultural ideals we have about social organization. In the case of English, there seems to be an emphasis on precisely *how* one is related (whether directly or collaterally, by marriage or by blood, and how distantly in generational terms). However, it is also significant that most terms are separated by gender, with different names for the same relationship shared by males and females (e.g., *sons* and *daughters* share the same relationship to their mother, the only difference being their gender).

Studying kinship terms in a specific language can help us ascertain what characteristics the speakers value or consider relevant to social organization. In Seneca, an Iroquoian language spoken in New York state and parts of Canada, kinship terms are organized as shown in (2).

(2) Kinship terms in Seneca
     father: [haʔnih]
     father's brother: [haʔnih]
     father's sister: [akeːhak]
     son: [heːawak]
     nephew: [hehsõʔneh]

     mother: [noʔjĕh]
     mother's sister: [noʔjĕh]
     mother's brother: [hakhnoʔsĕh]
     daughter: [khĕawak]
     niece: [khehsõʔneh]

     grandfather: [haksoːt]
     grandfather's brother: [haksoːt]
     grandson: [hejaːteʔ]

     grandmother: [ʔaksoːt]
     grandmother's sister: [ʔaksoːt]
     granddaughter: [khejaːteʔ]

There are some similarities with English kinship terminology in that gender and generation appear to be equally important qualities to capture in Seneca kinship terms as in English. Note, however, that unlike in English, the same words are used for one's mother and her sisters, one's father and his brothers, one's grandmother and her sisters, and one's grandfather and his brothers. This reflects a social relationship whereby one's parent and their same-sex siblings are considered to have the same relationship with each other's children. This differs from English terminology, in which direct versus collateral line.g., is important (thus, one's father's brother—or *uncle*, in English—has a different name from one's father, but the same name as one's mother's brother). In (3), we see that this lack of direct versus collateral distinction is found in words for siblings, too, in which age is identified as the more relevant category than lineage.

(3) Seneca terms for siblings and cousins
     older brother: [hahtsiʔ]
     father's brother's son (older):   [hahtsiʔ]
     mother's sister's son (older):   [hahtsiʔ]

     older sister: [ahtsiʔ]
     mother's sister's daughter (older):   [ahtsiʔ]
     father's brother's daughter (older):   [ahtsiʔ]

younger brother:	[heʔkẽːʔ]
father's brother's son (younger):	[heʔkẽːʔ]
mother's sister's son (older):	[heʔkẽːʔ]
younger sister:	[kheʔkẽːʔ]
mother's sister's daughter (younger):	[kheʔkẽːʔ]
father's brother's daughter (older):	[kheʔkẽːʔ]
other cousin	
(mother's brother's son/daughter,	
or father's sister's son/daughter,	
of any age):	[akjaːʔseːʔ]

In this case, a child of anyone who would be addressed as *mother* or *father* is called *sister* or *brother*. This reveals something not just about social organization, but also about how Seneca speakers conceive of family.

Kaqchikel, a Mayan language spoken in Guatemala, provides an example of another system of kinship organization, seen in (4).

(4) Kinship terms in Kaqchikel

mother:	[teʔeh]
father:	[tataʔah]
son (regardless of speaker's sex):	[akʔwal]
son (female speaker):	[al]
son (male speaker):	[kʔaholaʃel]
daughter (male speaker):	[meʔaleʃel]
grandmother:	[atit]
grandfather:	[mamaʔah]
grandchild (female speaker):	[ij]
grandchild (male speaker):	[mam]
brother (female speaker):	[ʃibʔalon]
sister (male speaker):	[anaʔ]
younger sibling (same sex as speaker):	[tʃaqʔlaxel]
older sibling (same sex as speaker):	[nimalaxel]
youngest sibling (regardless of speaker's sex):	[tʃʔɪp]

As with the English and Seneca kinship terms, gender is at the forefront here. In this case, however, the gender of the speaker himself or herself is important. The speaker uses specific words for 'son,' 'daughter,' 'sister,' 'brother,' and 'grandchild,' depending on whether the speaker is male or female. Interestingly, in the case of siblings, there appears to be an age distinction only if the sibling is the same sex as the speaker. This may reflect a precedence of gender distinction in terms of power relations, followed by an age hierarchy.

11.1.3 Communicative Competence

Researcher Dell Hymes argued that knowing a language means more than just knowing how to produce grammatical utterances (see File 5.1 for grammaticality). For example, in day-to-day interactions in the United States, *What's up?* and *How are you?* are often used as greetings rather than requests for information. Speakers must have this cultural understanding in order to supply the appropriate response. Without this understanding, it would be quite logical to respond to these questions with long descriptions of how the speaker's day went or how the speaker was feeling.

In addition to the common distinction within linguistics between linguistic competence and performance (see File 1.2), Hymes contributed the concept of **communicative competence,** which is the ability to interact and communicate according to cultural norms. Some examples of things one must know to be communicatively competent in a certain language are politeness strategies, speaker roles, turn-taking rules, and greetings.

a. Politeness. What counts as "polite" and what is considered "impolite" are culturally determined. In American English, we use politeness strategies at various levels of grammar, ranging from lexical (*please, thank you*), to morphological (*may* vs. *can*), to pragmatic (use of indirect speech acts rather than direct speech acts; see File 7.4). Part of knowing a language is knowing which politeness strategies to use when, depending on what the context is and who is being addressed. Politeness is discussed in more detail in File 11.4.

b. Speaker Roles. As speakers, we pay close attention to who the other participants in the conversation are. (We also pay attention to others who are not participating but who can hear us.) For instance, we speak differently when chatting with a group of friends than when meeting one-on-one with a teacher. And the teacher probably speaks differently in a one-on-one encounter than he does in front of an entire class of students. Speakers know that interactional expectations change with the setting. Interactional expectations also change with the role that each speaker takes. Different roles have different expectations. Normally, speakers alternate turns relatively frequently, with even the longest turns not lasting more than a few minutes. However, these turn-taking rules are different in a classroom setting, in which the teacher has the liberty of speaking at length without being interrupted and may also select who gets to speak when. Breaking these unspoken rules may make other participants in the interaction uncomfortable, as would be the case if the teacher were interrupted mid-sentence by a student saying, "Glad you got that off your chest. Let's move on." Knowing that such an action would be inappropriate given the context and the student's role in the interaction is part of being communicatively competent.

c. Turn-Taking Rules. As noted above, speakers alternate turns fairly frequently. How long we wait to begin talking after another speaker has finished speaking is another culturally determined aspect of speech, and sensitivity to the length of this pause is part of our communicative competence. In American English, it is not expected that the person addressed will wait longer than 10 to 15 seconds to respond in some manner, even if just to say "I need to think about that for a minute." Most pauses or gaps between speakers are actually much shorter than this. In fact, not responding to someone may be interpreted as anger in American English, as reflected in the common phrase "giving someone the silent treatment." Silence between turns is not viewed this way in all speech communities though. In the case of Western Apache, responding so quickly would be considered disrespectful. A speaker is expected to contemplate fully his or her response before uttering it. Quick responses are considered brash and less thoughtful. Another interesting cultural difference is that Western Apache tend to leave longer pauses between turns with strangers, due to their unpredictability, whereas in English, silence is actually more acceptable with intimate friends than with strangers.

In American English, when speakers take turns, they sometimes indicate the end of their turns by specifically selecting the next speaker (e.g., *I am going to the library later, if you have books that need to be returned, Jane*) or by using more generalized **tag questions** (e.g., *It's kind of hot in here, isn't it?*). Tag questions are utterances beginning with statements that end with a question about the truth of that statement. Because it is expected that if someone asks a question to another speaker, the person addressed will speak next, tag questions are a way of eliciting a response to a general statement.

There are a number of utterances in English that naturally elicit some response, such as *How are you?* (with the response *fine/good/all right*) or *thank you* (with the response *you're welcome/no problem/no worries*). These are called **adjacency pairs,** pairs of adjacent utterances produced by two different speakers in which the first utterance provokes the hearer to respond with the second utterance (or some similar utterance). Indeed, it would seem odd to get no response at all to these utterances, and silence might be interpreted as rude or disrespectful. Questions, requests, offers, and greetings are all examples of adjacency pairs, as shown in (5).

(5)
Part 1 of Adjacency Pair	*Part 2 of Adjacency Pair*	*Speech Act*
a. What time is it?	Three o'clock	Question
b. Can you pass the salt?	Of course	Request
c. Would you like some help?	Yes, please	Offer
d. Hello	Oh, hi!	Greeting

d. Greetings. Greeting sequences frequently occur in the form of adjacency pairs. Some examples of greeting adjacency pairs are shown in (6).

(6)
Part 1 of Adjacency Pair	*Part 2 of Adjacency Pair*	*Language*
a. What's up?	Not much.	English
b. ¿Como estas? 'How are you?'	Bien. 'Good.'	Spanish
c. Ça va? 'How's it going?'	Oui, ça va. 'It's going well.'	French
d. Wawuka? 'Have you woken (well)?'	Nawuka. 'I have woken (well).'	Kasigau (Kenya)
e. Ni chi le ma. 'Have you eaten?'	Hai mei chi. 'Not yet'	Mandarin Chinese

Knowing appropriate greeting sequences in a language and culture represents an important part of one's communicative competence. For instance, while *What's up?* may be an appropriate greeting for friends, it is not the normal greeting one uses with a stranger or authority figure (can you imagine greeting a police officer with a casual, *What's up?*).

While the adjacency pairs in (6) show some variation in greetings between the speakers of different languages, greetings can vary much more than that. In many societies, the linguistic structure and variation of standard greetings is not easily explainable without an understanding of the culture in which they are used. Most speakers of Wolof, a language used in West Africa, have traditionally lived in a caste-stratified society where people are either nobles or non-nobles. Wolof has an elaborate greeting system in which the greeting differs depending on (among other things) what caste the participants are in. The person of lower status (marked as A in (7) below) must go to the person of higher status and begin the greeting sequence; this person (also called the initiator) guides the greeting by giving the first half of each adjacency pair. The greeting begins with a salutation (Sal), followed by a series of questions (Q). A will inquire after B, followed by any member of B's family he wishes, and he can continue to cycle through questions as long as he wants before proceeding to the end of the greeting, praising God (P). B's responses are scripted—he will, for instance, say that a family member is well even if she is dying. Only after the speakers have progressed through all of these stages can they turn to other topics of conversation. An example of a Wolof greeting between two people who are already acquainted is given in (7). Although Wolof society has become more egalitarian in recent times, greetings still reflect a preoccupation with asymmetrical power and status.

(7)   Example of Wolof Greeting (A = noble or high-status person, B = low-status person)[1]

Sal   A: Salaam Maleekum.   May peace be with you.
         B: Maleekum salaam.   May you be at peace.
         A: [B's name]
         B: Naam, [A's name].

Q   A: Na nga def?   How are you?
         B: Maa ngi fii rek.   I am here, only.
         A: Mbaa jàmm nga am?   I hope you have peace?
         B: Jàmm rek, namm.   Peace only, yes.

         A: Ana waa keur gi?   Where is your family?
         B: Nu nga faa.   They're there.
         A: Ana [name of B's family member]?   Where is [name]?
         B: Mu nga fa.   He or she is there.

         A: Mbaa feebaru loo?   I hope you're not sick?
         B: Maa ngiy sant Yalla.   I thank God.
         A: Mbaa ken feebarul?   I hope no one is sick?
         B: Nu ngi sant Yalla.   We thank God.

P   A: Alxamdulilaay.   Thanks be to God.
         B: Tubarkalla.   Blessed be God.
         A: Tubarkalla   Blessed be God.
         B: Tubarkalla.   Blessed be God.

Because communicative competence in this case requires knowing not only the linguistic forms of greeting (which are complex in their own right!) but also the socially stratified rules of greeting, this distinction would be nearly impossible to pin down without an understanding of the culture of Wolof speakers.

Certain types of greetings are also associated with other kinds of social groups. For instance, you might expect the greeting *What's up?* to be uttered by a younger speaker rather than by your grandmother. In the same way, you would not expect a classmate born and raised in Columbus, Ohio, to greet you with *howdy* any more than you would expect him to say *Top of the morning to you.* That is because these greetings have come to be associated with specific social and ethnic groups. Because greetings are closely tied to these social and cultural features, and because they are a frequent and standardized part of many regular conversations, linguists will often study greetings as a means of exploring the communicative competence of speakers. Studying the associations that build over time between greetings (or any other part of language) and social and cultural features represents another aspect of linguistic anthropology, and this idea will be pursued in the following section.

11.1.4 Indexicality

Linguistic anthropologists think of language as a system of **signs**—that is, a system of form-meaning pairs. The form (the sound pattern) of a word is called the **signifier,** and the object or idea to which it refers is called the **referent** (see Chapter 6). Charles Sanders Peirce devised a three-way typology of signs consisting of symbols, icons, and indexes.

A **symbol** is a sign that has an arbitrary relationship between the signifier and its referent and thus relies on convention to signify meaning. An example of a symbolic sign system is language. Different languages have very different words for the same object (e.g., *water,*

---

[1]Adapted from Irvine (1974): 167–91.

eau, vasa). The symbols of a language are expressions (see File 5.1), and the relationship between the form of an expression and its meaning is, in most cases, arbitrary. In fact, arbitrariness is one of the design features of language (see File 1.4).

An **icon,** unlike a symbol, is a sign whose signifier actually resembles or imitates its referent in some direct way. Within language, an onomatopoetic expression has an iconic relationship between its signifier (e.g., *buzz*) and its referent (in this case, the humming buzz of a swarm of bees) (see File 1.4). An example of an iconic relationship between signifier and referent is the subway map in (8), which is meant to resemble the actual train lines from a bird's-eye view (of course, birds can't actually see subways because they're underground!).

(8) Subway map of New York City

Licensed under the Creative Commons Attribution-Share Alike 3.0 Unported license. For this and other maps by the creator, go to http://maps.complutense.org.

An **index** is also a kind of sign, but the relationship between the signifier and its referent is more complicated. The signifier of an index does not resemble its referent, but neither is the relationship between signifier and referent arbitrary. The canonical example of an indexical relationship between signifier and referent is that of smoke and fire. Smoke indexes fire because seeing smoke indicates, or points to, the existence of a fire somewhere. Thus smoke does not resemble fire in any direct way, but the two generally co-occur, so that the presence of smoke means that there is fire nearby. Indeed, the relationship between a signifier and what it indexes is sometimes a causal relationship—in this example, fire causes smoke, so smoke is "symptomatic" of fire.

While symbols and icons may seem familiar, the discussion of **indexicality** is often specific to the socio-cultural study of language. This is because the relationship between the signifier and referent of an index is generally not a direct relationship, but an association that develops over time, such as the association of a specific style of speaking with a certain group of people. For example, if someone said to you, *Dude, that is, like, gnarly,* the image of a West Coast surfer may come to mind. It is not that any of the words used mean 'surfer,' but the speaking style has co-occurred enough with a certain social group (surfers) that it has come to be associated with them in a fairly automatic, subconscious way. Speech styles can index more than one social quality as well, since the phrase *Dude, that is, like, gnarly* probably also brings to mind a younger speaker rather than an older, distinguished college professor, and it may even specifically index a male speaker rather than a female speaker.

In her study of language and gender in Japanese, Elinor Ochs found that certain speaking styles and even grammatical markers indexed masculinity and femininity: "when someone wishes to speak like a woman in Japanese, they may speak gently, using particles such as the sentence-final *wa,* or to speak like a man they may speak coarsely, using the sentence-final particle *ze*" (1993: 151). Because the particle *wa* is associated with more "delicate" speech in Japanese, Ochs argues that using this particle indexes femaleness indirectly through the association of delicate speech and femininity.

Another example of indexicality is found in Martha's Vineyard, where speakers who used high rates of centralized vowel variants were those who most closely self-identified as natives to the island (see File 10.5). Because these vowel variants were used by islanders and not by the tourists who came in summertime, they came to be associated with islander identity and could therefore be used in order to index this identity. Thus, there is a relationship between language variation, which considers what speakers actually say, and indexicality, which considers the associations speakers have between certain forms and certain groups of people.

Language and Thought

11.2.1 What Is Linguistic Relativity?

As most people who have studied another language know, different languages grammatically distinguish different kinds of things (see File 5.2). Some languages mark the grammatical gender of all nouns and adjectives; some languages do not mark gender at all. Some languages have two or three grammatical genders or noun classes; some languages have as many as twenty. Some languages distinguish several tenses grammatically; some have no grammatically marked tenses. Speakers of some languages express spatial relationships in absolute terms (the car is north of the house); some express spatial relationships relatively (the car is to the right of the house). Some languages have counting systems that consist of 'one,' 'two,' and 'many'; some languages have much more elaborate inventories of numbers. Do these differences between languages also indicate differences in the thoughts of their speakers? Does speaking a language without tense markers mean you will think about time differently? Does using politically correct terminology change speakers' perception of women, people with disabilities, and others? Does the grammatical gender of a word influence how we think of it?

In some cases, the answer to this question seems to be yes. A study by Lera Boroditsky (2003) using speakers of German and Spanish showed that the grammatical gender of an inanimate object can influence the way speakers consider it. When asked to describe a key, for which the German word is masculine and the Spanish word is feminine, speakers' descriptions were quite different. German speakers described the key as *hard, heavy, metal, jagged,* or *useful,* while Spanish speakers described the key as *little, lovely, intricate, tiny,* or *shiny.* On the other hand, when shown a picture of a bridge, for which the German word is feminine and the Spanish word is masculine, German speakers called it *pretty, peaceful, elegant, beautiful,* and *fragile,* while Spanish speakers called it *strong, dangerous, sturdy,* and *towering.* Boroditsky argues that the grammatical gender of a word influences how speakers see objects such as keys and bridges.

A prominent debate in linguistics in the past century has been the issue of how language, thought, and culture are interrelated. Simply stated, does language influence thought? Or does language accurately translate "mentalese," the hypothetical system of thoughts represented in the mind prior to any linguistic shape? If so, how do we account for the diversity of linguistic systems? If a language can influence the thoughts of its speakers, how strong is that influence—does the language we speak completely determine our outlook on the world, or does it simply condition its users to think in certain patterns?

The **linguistic relativity** hypothesis argues that the language someone speaks affects how she perceives the world. There are two versions of the linguistic relativity hypothesis. The weak version, called linguistic relativity, simply claims that language affects thought. One way language can influence thought is shown by the example of the words for 'key' and 'bridge' above. The strong version, called **linguistic determinism,** claims that language determines thought; speakers of a language can think of things only in the way that their language expresses them. Linguistic determinism will be discussed in Section 11.2.5.

11.2.2   Early Studies in Linguistic Relativity

The association of language with thought and culture is not new, but its treatment by modern academic social scientists can be traced to anthropologist Franz Boas (1858–1942) in the early twentieth century. Boas noted that language is used to classify our experiences in the world. Although previous ethnologists had focused on word lists, Boas believed that insight into language and culture could be gained only by intensive ethnographic fieldwork in the native language of the group being studied. Because different languages have different ways of classifying the world (e.g., counting systems, tense, spatial relationships), different people will classify the world differently based on the languages they speak. In Boas's view, language could be used to describe or articulate how a person saw the world, but it would not constrain that view.

One of Boas's students, Edward Sapir (1884–1939), took Boas's view one step further, with the idea that linguistic classification is actually the **way** in which people think. That is, his belief was that thoughts about experience are necessarily channeled through and given shape by language; all of human thought is "done" in a particular language, so the language we speak can shape our thoughts and experiences. This theory implies that people have different ways not just of linguistically classifying but of actually thinking about the world. Sapir did not try to extend this line of reasoning to say that language would influence culture: "Culture may be defined as what a society does and thinks. Language is a particular *how* of thought" (Sapir 1949 [1921]: 218).

Benjamin Whorf (1897–1941), a student of Sapir's, also considered the relationship between language, thought, and culture based on his observations about people's use of language and how it seems to influence their thoughts and behaviors. For example, he noticed that workers tended to be careful around full gasoline drums but might smoke or throw cigarette stubs around apparently "empty" gasoline drums, which actually contained a substance more dangerous than gasoline: vapors. He argued that by classifying the drums as "empty," that is, having been emptied of their original contents, the workers thought of the drums as "null and void," that is, that the drums did not in fact contain anything. The mental classification of the drums using a particular meaning of the word influenced the workers' actual perception of the world and then their actions.

Whorf also studied several Native American languages, including Hopi. He claimed to see substantial differences between the structures of English and Hopi. For instance, Whorf argued that English tends to classify the world into discrete objects more than Hopi does. In English, for example, we apply plurality and cardinal numbers to temporal entities as well as to physical entities. Although we say both *ten men* and *ten days,* physically, days and men are quite different. Ten men can be seen all at once, but days are ephemeral or cyclical; you can only see one at a time. The view that time is linear and segmental, Whorf argued, is reinforced by a grammatical system in which past, present, and future are obligatory categories, and this view is tied to the idea that English speakers think of themselves as on a point, the present, moving along the line of time, which extends indefinitely into the past and the future. In Hopi, on the other hand, time is not divided up into units that are used as count nouns; time is expressed adverbially. According to Whorf, in Hopi, which lacks the tense system so common in European languages such as English, ten days are viewed not as a collection of different days but as successive appearances of the same cycle of dawn to dusk—every day contains the potentiality of the future as well as the experiences of the past. The primary distinction indicated by Hopi verbs instead concerns whether the action takes place in the Objective (Manifested) Realm or the Subjective (Unmanifest) Realm.

Whorf argued that these differences in how we talk about time are closely related to how we think of time and how we act. For example, Western society tends to be very concerned with exact dates and records, keeping calendars and diaries that mark time into sequential units. The Hopi that Whorf described, on the other hand, seemed to be unconcerned with this sort of timekeeping; whatever had happened still was, but in an altered form. According to Whorf, the Hopi believed that the present should not be recorded but rather treated as "preparing," and he claimed there is much emphasis on preparation in their culture.

Based on these observations, Whorf developed the principle of linguistic relativity, which is sometimes called the **Whorf hypothesis** or the **Sapir-Whorf hypothesis,** although the two men never formally worked together on this topic. Whorf defined linguistic relativity as follows: "users of markedly different grammars are pointed by their grammars toward different types of observations and different evaluations of externally similar acts of observation, and hence are not equivalent as observers but must arrive at somewhat different views of the world" (1956: 58). Essentially, this means that the language someone speaks affects how he perceives the world.

11.2.3 Criticism of the Early Studies

Linguistic relativity came under scrutiny with the rise of cognitive science and the Universal Grammar (UG) school of thought (see File 8.1), which sought to describe the universals of human cognition and saw linguistic diversity as mere superficialities masking the same fundamental cognitive makeup.

Further, Whorf's studies of the Hopi and their language and culture have been disputed in a number of ways (e.g., see Ekkehart Malotki's 1983 book). First, some scholars have questioned Whorf's analysis of the Hopi worldview of space and time by suggesting that Whorf was simply projecting his ideas about their culture from what he understood of the Hopi grammatical structure. This would make his arguments circular. Second, it has been proposed that while the Hopi may not express time on verbs using tenses, this does not mean that the Hopi do not have ways of locating particular events in time, just as English does. There are certainly other languages that are tenseless (i.e., they do not grammatically mark time on verbs), but this fact is not incompatible with the conceptualization of time in a linear fashion. Third, and perhaps most importantly, Whorf's descriptions of how the Hopi linguistic system categorizes time do not seem to have been completely accurate; for example, time can be expressed using nouns in Hopi, and there are nouns for concepts like 'day,' 'night,' 'month,' and 'year.' Unfortunately, his methods of collecting data were very questionable, and thus any conclusions drawn from his data are equally questionable.

Does this mean that the principle of linguistic relativity is wrong? Not necessarily, but it does mean that we need stronger evidence than Whorf was able to provide. The next section will outline some more contemporary investigations of linguistic relativity.

11.2.4 More Recent Investigation of Linguistic Relativity

Because of these problems, it is generally agreed that Whorf's study did not actually show that language influences thought. Nevertheless, the linguistic relativity hypothesis has been taken up and tested by other scholars. The Whorf hypothesis can be difficult to test because it can be challenging to identify tasks that really are linguistically and culturally neutral, which are desirable features if you are trying to isolate the effects of language and culture upon each other. Nevertheless, many studies have sought to test the nonlinguistic reasoning of speakers of different languages.

a. Color Terms. Several such studies have dealt with colors; these studies are based on the idea that there is a universal color continuum, but that different languages have different ways of dividing this continuum into discrete categories. Although it is acknowledged that many languages may have numerous descriptive terms for many subtle color gradations (e.g., *brick red* vs. *fire engine red* vs. *scarlet*), such studies generally focus on the "basic" color terms of a language. In a 1956 experiment, Eric Lenneberg and John Roberts presented chips of various shades ranging between yellow and orange to English speakers and speakers of Zuñi (a Southwest Native American language). The English speakers, who have two basic color terms for this range (namely, *yellow* and *orange*), were highly consistent in sorting the colors, whereas the Zuñi, who have a single term encompassing yellow and orange, made no consistent choice. These results seem to support the Whorf hypothesis because the fact that English has these color terms resulted in the fact that English speakers could more easily distinguish the colors into two different parts of the spectrum.

A similar experiment by Andre von Wattenwyl and Heinrich Zollinger in 1978, however, found the opposite result. Wattenwyl and Zollinger worked with Q'ueqchi subjects on the blue-green area of the spectrum (for which Q'ueqchi, a Mayan language, has a single term). They showed that speakers tended to form groupings based on criteria apart from their lexicon, separating out blue chips from green chips consistently despite not having terms for these categories. These findings would seem to contradict the Whorf hypothesis, showing that speakers can identify differences in hue even if their language does not code this difference in the lexicon.

One of the most famous studies on the cross-cultural classification of colors into fixed terms, conducted in 1969 by Brent Berlin and Paul Kay, provided strong evidence against the linguistic relativity hypothesis. For each of twenty languages, they listed the basic color words. Then they gave speakers of each language a chart of 329 chips of different colors and asked them to perform two tasks: (a) for each basic color word, circle all those chips that could be called by that word, and (b) for each basic color word, select the best, most typical example of that color. They then calculated the focus of each color word in each language—the best and most central chips for each color. Their findings were as follows:

- About 70% of the chips did not fall within the range of any color word in any language.
- The foci of the color terms for different languages were quite close.
- Universally, every language has at least two color words: black (covering also most dark hues) and white (covering also most light hues).
- If a language has more than two basic color terms, then it follows a hierarchy of color terms:
  - Languages with three color terms have *black, white,* and *red* (the latter having its focus close to English red);
  - Languages with four terms have *black, white, red,* and either *green* or *yellow*;
  - Languages with five terms have *black, white, red,* and both *green* and *yellow*;
  - Languages with six terms have these five plus *blue*;
  - Languages with seven terms have these six plus *brown*;
  - Languages with more than seven terms have these seven plus some of *purple, pink, orange,* or *gray*.

English, according to Berlin and Kay, is an eleven-term language, as are Japanese and Hebrew. Hungarian and Russian have twelve basic terms—Hungarian has the standard eleven with a distinction between *vörös* 'dark red' and *piros* 'light red,' while Russian has the standard eleven with a distinction between *siniy* 'dark blue' and *goluboy* 'light blue.' Shona is a typical three-term language: *citema* covers 'black,' *cicena* 'white,' and *cipswuka* 'red.' Bassa is a typical two-term language. These findings were used to conclude that colors are universal distinctions, and all humans divide the spectrum in different ways, some more elaborately than others. The Berlin-Kay experiment gave strong evidence for a predictable hierarchy of color-coding cross-linguistically.

b. Spatial Relationships. Another area in which the principle of linguistic relativity has been investigated is the study of spatial relationships and the categorization of space in different languages. Some languages, like English, use relative terms such as *left, right, front,* and *back* to indicate the spatial orientation of one object to another: *The chair is to the left of the table,* etc. Not all languages use such terms, however; for example, Tenejapan Tzeltal (a Mayan language spoken in Mexico) uses absolute terms similar to *north, south, east,* and *west* instead. That is, they use a fixed point of reference to locate particular objects (e.g., *the chair is to the north of the table*) rather than using relative reference points that may change based on the location of the speaker.

Various aspects of culture seem to reflect such differences in spatial categorization; for example, in Tzeltal, time "is conceived of as stretching up to the south" (Levinson 1996b: 376), whereas in English, time tends to be conceived of as stretching either from left (past) to right (future) or from behind (past) to in front (future). Perhaps most tellingly, Tzeltal and English speakers respond very differently in experimental tasks that require them to describe objects they see in the world. For example, consider the diagram shown in (1), which sketches the experimental setup used by Stephen Levinson and Penelope Brown to explore the Tzeltal system of spatial reference (e.g., see Levinson 1996a, 1996b, and Brown and Levinson 1993).

(1)   Comparing relative and absolute frames of reference

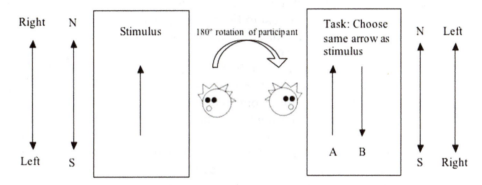

In experiments like this, a participant is first seated at a table as shown on the left side of the diagram; an arrow on the table acts as a stimulus. The participant is asked to look at the arrow and remember which direction it points. The participant is then turned 180°, so that she is facing the opposite direction, as is shown on the right side of the diagram. Two arrows are shown, A and B, pointing in opposite directions. The participant is then asked which one matches the arrow she saw earlier (the stimulus arrow).

Speakers of a language with a relative frame of reference, such as English, consistently choose arrow B, while speakers of a language with an absolute frame of reference, such as Tzeltal, consistently choose arrow A! Levinson and Brown hypothesize that this consistent difference between the groups of speakers is based on the way the languages categorize directions. For English speakers, the stimulus arrow goes from their left to their right; when they are turned around, they still choose an arrow that goes from their left to their right (arrow B). For Tzeltal speakers, on the other hand, the stimulus arrow points from south to north, regardless of which way they are facing; when they are turned around, they still choose an arrow that goes from south to north (arrow A).

This result is particularly compelling given that the tasks can be carried out nonlinguistically; that is, the speakers don't have to say anything in the course of looking at the stimulus, turning around, and indicating which arrow matches the stimulus. Thus, Levinson and Brown have found evidence that the linguistic categories a speaker's language uses can directly affect the speaker's nonlinguistic perception of spatial relationships. Once again, however, while studies like these support the basic principle of linguistic relativity (i.e., that speakers of different languages may have different views of the world), it is difficult to draw conclusions because there is contradictory evidence as well.

11.2.5   Beyond Relativity: Linguistic Determinism and Cultural Anthropology

Since Whorf developed the linguistic relativity hypothesis, it has been interpreted in many different ways. Some have claimed that Whorf said that language actually **determines** thought and culture: that people are in some way confined by their language to be able to understand or think only about concepts that their language can describe. This view, which argues that thought and language are identical and it is not possible to engage in any rational thinking without using language to do so, is called **linguistic determinism,** as noted in Section 11.2.1.

Recently, Peter Gordon (2004) and Daniel Everett (2005) have claimed that evidence for linguistic determinism has been found in the inability of adult speakers of Pirahã, an indigenous language of Brazil, to learn cardinal numbers as we know them in English. While Pirahã speakers could accurately respond to tasks in which they had to count up to two or three objects, and could at least partially count up to ten, their performance with counting numbers or recognizing quantities larger than these was extremely low. Everett points out that this is not a reflection of their natural intelligence or willingness to learn. Rather, it has been attributed to their language's lack of numbers. Pirahã has no word for *one,* but only a word that means 'roughly one' or 'small'; there are also no separate words for *he* as opposed to *they*; etc.

If it is in fact the case that the Pirahã cannot learn to count, this could be interpreted as evidence for linguistic determinism—that the continued use of a particular language system can in fact determine one's ability to categorize the world.[1] Some scientists, however, have questioned the validity of the training techniques or elicitation methods used. Moreover, this example is far outweighed by evidence that speakers can learn new concepts and classifications not present in their native language. Thus, very few people take the idea of linguistic determinism seriously today.

In addition, if linguistic determinism were true, it might be possible to modify social attitudes by forcing changes in language. That language can in fact be changed at all in some ways undermines this entire idea: clearly, introducing new concepts (and subsequently words for them) is quite possible (see Chapter 13 on language change). However, although *underprivileged* or *disadvantaged* have been substituted for *poor,* and *mentally challenged* for *retarded,* social attitudes have not changed much; in time, the substitutions acquire most of the unpleasant connotations of the original term.

If the linguistic relativity hypothesis is true, another possible extension would be the idea that it is possible to interpret a culture simply by looking at the language people speak. Generally, because linguistic anthropologists focus on the relationship between language and culture, they study the details of the language, the culture, and the way in which the two interact. Occasionally, however, anthropologists have tried to describe a culture's worldview by examining only their language and not looking more deeply for additional behavioral, cultural, or cognitive evidence. While most scientists today realize the futility of such attempts, these attempts have added to the debate and the confusion about what linguistic relativity is and whether it should be accepted as true or not.

---

[1]It should be noted that Everett himself believes that linguistic determinism is not quite the right explanation here, and he prefers to appeal to some larger cultural constraint: see Everett (2005).

11.2.6 Is Linguistic Relativity True?

At this point, it seems relatively uncontroversial that language does have some influence on how we think about the world; if you speak a fore.g., language, you have probably noticed times when the classification or description of things is different in one language than in another.

But what exactly is the relation between language and thought? The results of some of the studies discussed in this file, such as the Levinson-Brown experiment on spatial relationships, make it clear that language and thought are not completely separate. While the influence of language on thought and culture may be considered very slight, some influence does seem to be present. Nevertheless, the validity of linguistic relativity remains very much in question, especially if one wants to pin down exactly how much influence language has or can have on thought and culture.

Dan Slobin (1996) has expressed the idea that perhaps we should be concerned not with "language and thought" but with "thinking and speaking." That is, we should accept the fact that in order to speak a particular language, a speaker must use particular language-specific classifications and therefore perhaps take note of different aspects of the world around him. For example, some languages tend to encode the manner of motion in verbs, such as specifying whether someone is *walking, running, climbing, being thrown,* etc., while other languages tend to encode the path or direction of motion in verbs, such as *cross* or *ascend.* Although both path and manner can be expressed in any language, speakers of languages that focus on the manner of movement, such as English, German, and Russian, will almost certainly pay attention to the manner in which movement is performed, but they may or may not think about the path of the movement. Speakers of languages that focus on the path, such as Greek, Hindi, and Spanish, on the other hand, are more likely to pay attention to the path of movement but may not consider the manner of movement while speaking. Thus, Slobin says, we have to learn to "think for speech"—the things we need to think about are influenced by the language we speak. This is essentially a soft view of linguistic relativity. The question remains whether there is some deeper level of nonlinguistic reasoning that all humans share and that remains unaffected by particular languages.

FILE **11.3**

....

Language and Power

11.3.1   The Role of Language in Power Relationships

The idea that words have "power" is not a new one: for example, there are countless ancient legends that revolve around the act of naming someone or something in order to gain power over that person or thing, or the uttering of spells whose words alone have the power to work magic. In the modern world, we can think of the power of words to hold audiences spellbound, to persuade voters to vote a certain way, to educate students in how to become skilled professionals, to convince consumers to purchase particular products, to talk parents into letting their children stay up late, to wound a person's feelings, to calm a child's distress, or to win over a sweetheart's love, among many other extraordinary tasks. Language may have an effect on other humans, and thus it may seem to be powerful, but of course it is really humans' use and interpretation of language that is powerful.

There are many levels at which the use of language can have power. On a small scale, there are various linguistic cues that individuals engaged in the conversation may use or perceive as indicators of power relations: Is one speaker more dominant or subservient? Is one more conciliatory or aggressive? Is one asserting knowledge or ignorance?

On the opposite end of the scale, language can be used to exert power over entire communities or societies. For example, in countries where multiple languages are spoken, the choice of one or two particular languages as the "official" language of politics, government, education, healthcare, and so on, can empower some citizens while excluding or minimizing others.

11.3.2   Power in Conversations

Of course, one of the most obvious ways to use language to express power or subservience is to make a direct statement. By saying, for example, *I am king of the castle,* the speaker has asserted that he is in charge and in a superior position to those around him. But there is more to establishing power or lack thereof than simply the literal meaning of the words spoken: a servant who says clearly and firmly *I bow to your lordship's wishes* may indeed seem more powerful than the lord who responds meekly *Uh, well, yes, um, thank you. . . .*

Just as the association of particular linguistic characteristics with certain social groups is arbitrary, the association of particular linguistic characteristics with the designation of power is also arbitrary. The power relationships expressed by language are defined by those who use language rather than by any inherent properties of the language. In different cultures, stereotypes about various aspects of language use (e.g., talkativeness, loudness, or silence) are associated with different values.

For instance, in Malagasy culture (on Madagascar and other islands in the Indian Ocean), indirect, deferential speech is valued (also discussed in Section 10.4.4). Men, who are dominant in Malagasy culture, are the ones who are chiefly associated with this sort of indirect speech. Malagasy men are stereotypically silent in public confrontations, while it is more socially acceptable for Malagasy women to express anger and criticism through di-

476

rect, confrontational speech, often to the advantage of their husbands or other male family members (Keenan 1974: 137–39). In American society, as well, the "strong, silent type" is valued. But there is clearly no direct link between silence and higher worth in all cultures. Many Western cultures value direct, public speech. A number of studies of conversation (see Coates 1993: 115 for a brief overview) have shown that in Western societies, public speech tends to be dominated by men, where again, it is male norms that are more highly valued by the community. Thus, two different cultures use entirely opposite strategies in order to indicate the relative power of men in the society.

Power in a society is related to a number of different sociological factors (many of which we have discussed previously in Chapter 10 on language variation). For example, William O'Barr and Bowman Atkins found in a 1980 study of speech in a North Carolina courtroom that people who had relatively little power in the courtroom tended to use similar linguistic constructions. "Powerless" language was marked by the use of hedges (e.g., *It's sort of hot; I'd kind of like to go*), polite or complimentary speech (e.g., *Would you please close the door?* vs. *Close the door*), more indirect statements, and so on. Thus, there are particular linguistic characteristics that tend to be used to indicate relative power in particular social settings. Like many other associations, markers of power or powerlessness are culturally determined. The particular markers of subservience found in American courtrooms cannot be taken to be universal markers of subservience or powerlessness.

Power relationships can be established through means that make use of every level of linguistic structure. For example, at the phonetic and phonological levels, a speaker's prosody and volume can influence whether or not he is perceived as powerful in a certain situation. A speaker who speaks with a deliberate, slow tempo and a fairly high volume is often perceived as powerful, while a speaker who talks quickly and has rising intonation at the ends of his sentences may be perceived as powerless. The use of certain morphosyntactic structures (such as those discussed in the preceding paragraph) can likewise signify power or subservience. Word choice and the way that lexical items are used can also play a role. For example, a speaker's use of technical jargon that her audience is unfamiliar with can, in some circumstances, indicate the speaker's attempt to show power relative to a certain topic. What we call people when we talk to or about them—names, titles, nicknames, *sir*, insults, etc.—can also influence whether we and/or they are perceived as powerful. In addition, consider whether, in your speech community, the use of profanity correlates with speakers who have more power or less power in a given situation. Finally, pragmatic factors, such as whether the speaker uses more direct or more indirect speech acts, are involved in the marking of power relationships. And, of course, the message conveyed by the use of any of these strategies will vary between societies and speech communities. The same strategy that establishes dominance in one community may be used to indicate subservience in another.

11.3.3 Power in Society

In the previous section, we saw various ways that individuals' language use can both establish and enforce power differences between individuals. But language is also a powerful tool for establishing more global power relationships: power relationships that are established not between individuals, but rather within and between entire communities. Strategies used to establish these more global sorts of power relationships are based not on particular individual uses of language (e.g., whether a direct or an indirect speech act is used in one instance) but rather on prescriptions of how language may be used at all, or which languages may be used. A rather profound example is found in the fact that the United States (among other countries) guarantees freedom of speech. Under some governments, such liberties may not be guaranteed: thus a government can establish its power over the people it governs by determining when and how they may use language.

Another common (though less extreme) way in which language is used to create power relationships within a society on a large scale is through "official" languages adopted by the governments of particular nations. When a country declares an official language, all official government business must be conducted in that language. This can cause anyone who does not speak that language to be at a disadvantage.

There are many reasons for nations to declare an official language. For instance, many nations have so many languages spoken within their borders that the government must pick one or two to be the official language to avoid the practical difficulties of trying to deal with five, ten, or fifty languages on an official level. On the other hand, a "world language" such as French or English, used over wide areas of the globe, may be chosen as an official language (especially of developing countries), even though it may not be the native language of any speakers in that country. This may be done in order to avoid favoring one of the languages spoken within the country's borders and, in some cases, to make it easier to participate in the world economy. Some countries declare an indigenous language to be official in order to preserve the language's heritage. In Ireland, for example, the indigenous language is Irish, but it is in the process of being replaced by English in general society. Declaring Irish the official language of the country is a way of recognizing the place and importance of this language in the country's past.

Moves like these can clearly have social ramifications, both positive and negative. While declaring one language official may help those who speak it natively or who learn to speak it proficiently to succeed in the worlds of politics and economics, it can seriously hurt those who are not proficient speakers. Citizens who are not comfortable with the official language may be prevented from participating in the political process if ballots are printed only in the official language; they may be physically at risk if public safety messages are monolingual; they may be economically subjugated if they cannot hold jobs without speaking the official language. Sometimes, individuals who dislike a group that does not happen to speak the official language feel that the legality of the "official language" validates their feelings, allowing them to be more open in their contempt for such groups. When a world language like English is chosen over indigenous languages, it can send a message of indigenous inferiority and American or British supremacy, fueling resentment or conflict within a nation.

Issues of multilingualism, nationhood, and language planning are extremely complicated and the subject of much study, debate, and politics. Because language is tied to so many social factors and to people's very identity, these topics often spark strong feelings and opinions. It is therefore important to be well-informed of as many aspects of the issues at hand as possible.

An interesting (and unfortunate) case of how language and choice of language have been used to subjugate a community can be found in the case of how various institutions have instituted policies about the use of signed languages. Recall from Chapter 8 that although all children can acquire language naturally, they will do so only if they have adequate exposure to some particular language. Thus, deaf children will acquire language naturally only if they have exposure to a signed language (because they cannot perceive and interpret spoken language—e.g., through lip reading—without explicit instruction). In and of itself, this fact does not create any problem at all. However, during the course of the history of deaf education in the United States (and in many other countries as well), educators and politicians have used this fact to create a linguistic power differential between deaf and hearing individuals, even within Deaf institutions. Although ASL is one of the most widely used non-English languages in the United States, most hearing people do not perceive the Deaf community as comprising a large part of the overall community.

In 1880, the International Congress of Instructors for the Deaf in Milan, Italy, voted that it was preferable to instruct deaf children to communicate orally by teaching them to read lips, to vocalize, and to speak, rather than to educate them using signed language. In spite of the fact that several Americans voted against it, the oralist approach to deaf education was adopted in most schools for the deaf in America for close to the next century. It was only in the 1970s that a return to signed language once again began to appear in the classroom. During the intervening years, use of signed language was often considered a punishable offense at schools for the deaf—not only in classrooms where English was being used, but also during students' free time. Today, older signers may remember the harsh treatment and punishment that they received for using ASL to communicate at school.

This case is particularly extreme. Whereas a country that declares an official language may require that its citizens use the official language to communicate in court, to vote, or to participate in other official activities, it does not (usually) forbid use of some other language by families around the dinner table! The goal of at least some of the educators who taught using oralist methods, however, was to completely subjugate the culture that went along with signing. This is not to suggest that these people were necessarily uncaring or that they did not value their pupils; rather, they had an educational philosophy that intrinsically required the rejection of the use of signed languages. Regardless of their personal beliefs, however, the effect was to send the message that ASL and, by extension, users of ASL were somehow inferior to English and, by extension, to users of English.

Of course, ASL did not die out in response to these pressures; ASL and Deaf culture both flourish today, and both were propagated throughout the twentieth century in the very schools where their use was forbidden. However, ramifications of the ideology espoused by oralist schools still exist in our society today; many people believe that deaf individuals are somehow less able to function in society or that they cannot communicate as effectively as hearing individuals who use spoken language. This model is one that considers deafness to be pathological—that considers it a disease. Members of the Deaf community, on the other hand, consider deafness to be a cultural phenomenon: it does not inhibit their participation in society at all but rather increases solidarity within the Deaf community. Once again, we are discussing an arbitrary association of a particular aspect of language use—in this case, modality—with a particular role. In some communities, those who use one modality are seen as more powerful, whereas in other communities, those who use the other are seen as more powerful.

It is the case that in order for successful linguistic communication to take place between individuals, the individuals need to have some language in common. Thus, it stands to reason that a country, an international alliance, an organization, a school, or some other group might choose some particular official language. The choice to recognize a language as official is not, in and of itself, a bad thing. However, any language at all (e.g., ASL or Irish) has particular import, cultural value, and communicative significance for the communities of speakers who use it. Thus, recognizing or not recognizing a language as official will inevitably lead to perceptions of how that language does or does not connote power within the society.

Politeness

11.4.1 Politeness across Cultures

In File 7.2, we discussed the idea that conversation has rules that speakers generally follow in order to be cooperative and to move the interaction forward. But Grice's maxims are not the only "rules" at play during an interaction, since a speaker can be chastised not only for being ambiguous or long-winded, but also for being impolite. As discussed in File 11.1, politeness is part of the communicative competence of native speakers, and knowing what is polite in a given context is often as important as knowing the words of a language.

Politeness can be difficult to define, since what is considered polite differs between languages and even within a single language. For instance, in the southern United States it is considered polite to address women as "ma'am," regardless of their age. In contrast, in the northern United States, this term is usually reserved for older, married women and thus can be viewed as extremely impolite if used when speaking to a younger woman. And in the United Kingdom, calling someone "ma'am" simply sounds archaic.

Politeness generally consists of normative or expected linguistic and extralinguistic strategies culturally agreed to be interactionally appropriate for a given situation. The role of politeness is often to avoid conflict, build rapport, and promote cooperative communication despite the sometimes differing goals of participants. As mentioned in File 11.1, part of knowing a language is knowing which politeness strategies to use when. The following sections discuss three types of politeness. As we'll see, though, politeness is culturally defined and, as a result, differs between languages and cultures.

11.4.2 Indirectness

In English-speaking North America, the use of indirect speech acts (see File 7.4) and other such mitigation strategies is normally seen as more polite than speaking directly and bluntly. Compare the examples in (1).

(1) a. Direct: Give me the salt.
    b. Indirect: Are you finished with the salt?
                 Or
                 Would it be possible to pass me the salt?

While the direct speech act in (1a) is clear and unambiguous, speakers often opt for strategies more like those seen in (1b) when making requests. This is because the cultural norm for English is to make requests via implicature rather than directly (see File 7.3).

In contrast, directness is not considered rude in American Sign Language. In fact, two old friends may meet and immediately comment on each other's weight, baldness, or body odor without breaking any cultural taboos. On the other hand, conversational behavior that is common in spoken language can be rude for signers: ASL speakers are accustomed to looking each other directly in the eye throughout a conversation, and purposely breaking eye contact can be quite rude.

11.4.3 Honorifics

Japanese has a different approach to politeness, as seen through their complex system of **honorifics.** Honorifics are grammatical markers of respect and deference that are found in many languages, including Japanese, Korean, and Nahuatl. These markers are used with incredible frequency in Japanese in order to delimit social rank and/or social distance. Deciding which honorific to use when talking to another speaker requires knowledge of that person's age, social position, and role in the specific situation. For instance, younger speakers must always use more polite address forms to their elders. Also, those in a position of power, such as doctors or superiors, will be addressed with more polite forms. Although the Japanese honorific system is far too complicated to discuss here in its entirety, (2) gives some examples of the many forms used in Japanese to indicate social relationships.

(2)

Honorific	*Meaning*	*Used for*
-chan	diminutive, 'cute, little'	children, young women
-san	most common title of respect	friends, strangers, social equals
-sama	'esteemed, admired'	those of higher rank, customers
sensei	elder, 'former-born'	doctors, teachers, authority figures

An example of Japanese honorifics in popular culture is the use of the suffix *-san* by Mr. Miyagi in *The Karate Kid,* in which he refers to his student as "Daniel-san."

11.4.4 The T/V Distinction

A number of European languages, including French, Spanish, and Russian, have a somewhat simpler system of honorifics called the **T/V distinction.** The T/V distinction refers to distinguishing second-person pronouns (e.g., *you*) in terms of social distance or intimacy. Using the 'T' form when talking to someone means that you are familiar or comfortable with her, or of an equal or higher status, while using the 'V' form marks formality, respect, or a power differential between you and the person you are talking to. The 'V' form is also used for strangers. Some examples of the pronouns are given in (3).

(3) T/V forms

	Second-Person 'T'	*Second-Person 'V'*
French:	tu	vous
Italian:	tu	voi/lei
Spanish:	tú/vos	usted
German:	du	Sie
Russian	ty	vy

Think back to your Shakespeare readings from high school English class, and you may remember that English once featured the T/V distinction, with *thee/thou* representing the informal or 'T' form of the second-person pronoun, while *ye/you* was used as the more formal 'V' form of this pronoun. Because English no longer makes this distinction, acquiring T/V forms often causes difficulty for English-speaking students learning French or Spanish, especially since the social expectations in using these pronouns can be quite complex. For instance, referring to a close friend or family member by the 'V' form can be viewed as a sign of respect or as an attempt to distance oneself, depending on context. And using the more intimate 'T' form with a stranger may result in their feeling insulted at not being addressed more respectfully, or, alternatively, it may be taken as a sign of solidarity. It is often the case, too, that there are dialectal differences in expectations for pronoun usage, as is widely reported for varieties of Spanish spoken throughout Europe and Latin America. These potential problems in deciding upon proper, polite usage of T/V pronouns have led to some languages developing verbs that are used to openly discuss use of the 'T' or 'V' form (such as French's *tutoyer* 'to call someone *tu*' and *vouvoyer* 'to call someone *vous*').

11.4.5   Face Theory

One of the most influential approaches to studying politeness has been Penelope Brown and Stephen Levinson's **face theory.** This theory is based on the idea of **face,** or positive self-image, which can be seen in the common English phrase "to lose face," which means to lose public respect or to have one's reputation damaged.

Brown and Levinson (1987) theorized that there are two kinds of face at play at all times: positive face and negative face. Positive face is one's desire to be approved of by others, while negative face is one's desire not to be bothered or have one's independence infringed upon. **Face-Threatening Acts (FTAs)** are speech acts (see File 7.4) such as requests or orders that may threaten one's positive and/or negative face. In order to lessen the blow of FTAs, speakers use a number of politeness strategies: (a) positive politeness, (b) negative politeness, and (c) off-record FTAs. If no politeness or mitigation strategy is used, the actions are called **bald on-record FTAs.** An example of a bald on-record FTA is the demand *Give me a pen!*

Positive politeness is oriented toward positive face wants—that is, in using positive politeness, a speaker is trying to show that he likes his addressee. Positive politeness strategies include appealing to solidarity, friendliness, and in-group reciprocity. An example of positive politeness being used to lessen the blow of an FTA is *Hey, buddy—do me a favor and lend me a pen?* The 'T' in the T/V distinction uses positive politeness.

Negative politeness is oriented toward the hearer's desire to be left alone, with negative politeness strategies expressing the speaker's restraint and avoidance of imposing on the hearer. An example of negative politeness being used to lessen the blow of an FTA is *You wouldn't happen to have a spare pen, would you?* Indirectness is a kind of negative politeness, as is the use of the 'V' form in T/V languages.

Off-record FTA strategies generally consist of indirect speech acts that avoid making any explicit or unequivocal imposition on the hearer. An example of an off-record speech act being used to lessen the blow of an FTA is *I can't believe I forgot to bring a pen.* These politeness strategies for borrowing a pen are shown in (4).

(4)   **Strategy**   ***Example of FTA Using This Strategy***
       Bald-on-record   Give me a pen.
       Positive politeness   Hey, buddy—do me a favor and lend me a pen?
       Negative politeness   You wouldn't happen to have a spare pen, would you?
       Off-record   I can't believe I forgot to bring a pen.

So with all these options, how do we as speakers decide which strategy, or strategies, to use? Brown and Levinson propose that this choice is dependent on three types of social factors:

1. Social distance (symmetric relationship between speaker and hearer)
2. Power (asymmetric relationship between speaker and hearer)
3. Ranking (how much the FTA would impose on the hearer)

Figure (5) illustrates this process, focusing on how the degree of imposition on the hearer influences the speaker's choice of which politeness strategy to use. For example, asking someone who is looking at his watch for the time is not a serious imposition at all, and thus a bald-on-record FTA such as *What time is it?* could be used. By contrast, asking someone to take a week to help you paint your house is a serious imposition, so in that case the speaker would use negative politeness (e.g., *I really hate to bother you, because I know you're busy, but if it's at all possible, would you be able to give me a hand with a project next week?*) or an off-record FTA (e.g., *Painting my house is going to be such a huge job. I have no idea how I'm going to get it all done*), or simply not do the FTA at all and decide to hire someone to do the painting. How do you think social distance and power influence these decisions?

(5)   Politeness strategies for different levels of imposition

Less serious imposition   More serious imposition

← —— →

| Bald-on-record | Positive politeness | Negative politeness | Off-record | Avoid doing the FTA at all |

Brown and Levinson intended their theory to be universal, although, as is probably clear by now, the interpretations of certain politeness strategies differ between cultures. Deciding what politeness strategy to use in any given context is often completely unconscious for native speakers of a language, but it can be very complex for those who are less familiar with the culture.

Ethnography

11.5.1 What Is Ethnography?

A common way of studying language and culture is by performing **fieldwork,** which involves going to the specific communities where a language variety is spoken in order to gather information about the speech community and the language itself. Often the focus of this fieldwork is to document the way language is used in daily communication. One of the methods of achieving this is by writing an **ethnography,** or a description of everyday life in the community. This approach is used within anthropology to better understand different cultures around the world, and within linguistic anthropology to understand the intersection between language and culture. Researchers use ethnographic methods to find and document local knowledge that may not be obvious to an outsider, such as a community's cultural norms and its perspective on social activities, kinship ties, the physical world, and other aspects of everyday life.

An ethnography cannot be written in a day, so researchers often spend months or even years in a community before trusting that they have completed an adequate description. Some linguistic information a researcher may collect in writing an ethnography includes the following:

- How do speakers greet one another or end their interactions?
- What registers/genres are used by different social groups?
- What politeness strategies are generally used, and do they differ based on context and/or speaker roles?
- How do speakers classify animals, colors, kin, and other objects in the physical world? How is this reflected in language use?

There is more than one way to get this information, including formal interviews and participant observation. **Participant observation** consists of systematically observing within a community in order to understand how and why people do the things they do on a daily basis. There are two ways to perform participant observation: passive participation and complete participation.

Passive participation consists of passively watching how everyday life unfolds without partaking in any local activities in order to cause the least disturbance possible to the daily routine of the community being studied. This unintrusive approach has its strengths and weaknesses. To begin with, it can result in more objective observations of the ways people communicate. However, if one of the goals of an ethnography is to get at an insider's perspective and understand how locals perceive and interpret the physical world, this hands-off approach may not answer all the questions the researcher has set out to answer.

Complete participation, in contrast, is a strategy in which the researcher actively participates in the community, attempting to see firsthand how the community functions from the point of view of a local. By becoming part of the community, or "going native," as anthropological researchers call it, the researcher may gain access to information that could not be otherwise gathered. While these native-like interactions can provide important data, there is a danger in this approach as well because a researcher's subjective experience of a community, no matter how immersed the researcher may be, does not necessarily reflect the entire community's overall thoughts, beliefs, and perceptions. There is also the problem of recording—if the researcher is not participating, she is free to write down or record her observations, but if the researcher is actively participating, doing, and talking, she may not have the opportunity to record her observations until later.

Researchers often use a combination of these techniques to juggle both the desire to acquire a native or insider perspective on language and culture and the need to remain as objective as possible in order to accurately describe the community.

11.5.2 Etic and Emic

When ethnographic methods are discussed, the issue of objectivity becomes important. While most researchers agree that it is not possible to be completely objective when collecting data, there is certainly a difference between the outsider's description of an interaction and an insider's perspective on that same interaction. Researcher Kenneth Pike (1912–2000) described this difference as etic versus emic.

Thinking back to Chapters 2 and 3 on phonetics and phonology may help you understand Pike's terminology. In Chapter 3 we learned that when the phonetic difference between two sounds distinguishes meaning (i.e., when changing the sound changes the meaning of the word), this is called a phonemic difference. For instance, a minimal pair such as [kæt] 'cat' and [bæt] 'bat' in English reveals a phonemic distinction between [k] and [b], because changing the sound changes the word. In contrast, the difference between [kæt] 'cat' and [kæʔ] 'cat' shows that [t] and [ʔ] are not phonemic in English because they do not distinguish meaning. It is not the case that the form [kæt] means one thing and the form [kæʔ] means something different; both refer to a feline. Of course, there is a phonetic difference between [t] and [ʔ], even though English speakers do not necessarily notice it. Further, we can study the phonetic details of a language fairly straightforwardly, but in order to study the phonemic distinctions, we need a native speaker of that language to tell us when a change in sound changes the meaning of the word.

Applying this discussion to Pike's terminology, an **etic** (as in phonetic) description is one that describes from an objective, outsider's point of view, not taking into account the local significance of certain actions; for example, *The man raised his hand to about eye level, palm out, fingers extended, and moved it back and forth at the wrist.* In contrast, an **emic** (as in phonemic) description is an insider's description of the events in that the meaning of the actions is taken for granted and described as the viewer sees it, such as *The man waved.* For illustration, below are emic and etic descriptions of a traditional Western wedding:

- *Etic:* Music played as a young woman in a white dress and an older man walked toward a younger man dressed in black. Others sat and watched as a third man in ornate robes talked for some time up front; then the young man in black and the young woman in white gave each other round metallic items which they placed on their fingers. They pressed their lips together while those sitting and watching slapped their hands together, whistled, or made other loud noises.

- *Emic:* As "the wedding march" played, the beautiful bride was escorted down the aisle by her father, who was tearing up at the thought of giving away his daughter. The groom waited at the altar with the priest. The ceremony was brief, as they exchanged vows and rings, were declared husband and wife, and then kissed amid raucous applause from the pews.

While ethnography aims to get at the insider's, or emic, perspective of every interaction, describing situations from an etic point of view can also be helpful to researchers trying to understand local customs, since the etic point of view is in many ways a more accessible perspective to outsiders than the emic perspective.

11.5.3   A Case Study in Ethnography: Jocks and Burnouts at Belten High

In her study of a high school she referred to as "Belten High," which was located in the suburbs of Detroit, Penelope Eckert (2000) used ethnographic methods to understand the relationships between Belten High students in order to find out why certain groups of speakers talked differently from others. In order to gain the confidence and trust of the students so that she would have access to their activities and knowledge but avoid being a distraction, Eckert became a presence at the school. She hung around in the school for two years, tape-recording and interviewing students as well as just being part of the school. She avoided spending time in classrooms in order to avoid being seen as an authority figure, instead spending time with students in the hallway and cafeteria during free periods and before or after school.

Since she was researching a Michigan dialect of English, one of the linguistic variables Eckert focused on was Northern Cities Shift (NCS), which is a chain shift involving vowels in dialects from the northern United States and Canada (see File 10.3). Eckert found that local knowledge about social categories at Detroit area high schools was necessary in order to understand the patterning of NCS vowels among students at Belten High. The two social categories that played the most important roles in this were the Jocks and the Burnouts.

Jocks often—but not always—played sports for the school or participated in other school activities, came from middle-class families, and planned to go to college after high school. Burnouts, in contrast, had a counter–school culture and commonly skipped class. Many Burnouts came from working-class backgrounds and had no plans to continue their education after high school, making it more important for them to have strong ties with friends than with institutional authority figures.

Students showed their membership in either the Jock or the Burnout group by dressing and talking certain ways. For instance, a Burnout could be identified by his bellbottoms, rock T-shirts, and leather jackets. Jocks wore pegged jeans, polos or crewneck sweaters, and varsity letter jackets. Burnouts also tended to smoke and curse more than Jocks, a tendency that Eckert related to their more urban, street-smart identity.

The vowel systems of Burnouts represented more advanced stages of the Northern Cities Shift, while Jocks had more standard vowel pronunciations. Interestingly, Burnout girls tended to have the most advanced NCS vowels, more so even than Burnout boys. In fact, there was more extreme sociolinguistic variation within girls' speech in general at Belten High. Eckert attributed this to the fact that boys had greater access to extralinguistic ways of signaling group membership, by either playing varsity sports (Jocks) or "cruising" in their cars to tougher, more urban sections of town (Burnouts).

Eckert did not stop at describing how social categories and linguistic variation patterned within Belten High—she also drew important parallels between this local distinction of Jocks and Burnouts and larger class issues in Detroit, since Jocks attended more to middle-class ideals, and Burnouts more to working-class sentiments, within the region. None of this would have been obvious to a researcher who did not use ethnographic methods.

Practice

File 11.1—Linguistic Anthropology

Exercises

1. What are some of the competencies that are part of communicative competence?

2. How does cultural competence differ from linguistic competence and from performance?

3. What is an adjacency pair? Make a list of five adjacency pairs in American English not mentioned in the chapter.

4. Refer to the metaphors given in example (1) in File 11.1. What other metaphorical relationships exist in your native language? List at least four metaphors linking two concepts and briefly explain what you think they say about the culture (to get you started, think of metaphors for love, life, work, etc.).

Discussion Questions

5. When and how do you think children acquire communicative competence?

6. What specific rules do we need to know as part of our communicative competence in order to participate in an American English conversation? Give at least four rules. When did we learn each of these things?

7. How does the American English kinship term *cousin* fit into the description of kinship terms discussed in Section 11.1.2? Does it fit the pattern? Why or why not?

Activities

8. Section 11.1.3 gave two examples of greetings in American English: *Hello* and *What's up?* But there are many other acceptable ways to greet someone in American English culture. Make a list of all the greetings you can think of (at least five) in a culture you are familiar with; then consider the following questions for each one:
   i. Who says this?
   ii. In what situation would someone say this?
   iii. Is a response expected?
   iv. If so, what do people say in response?

9. Choose a language and culture and research the kinship terms used in that culture.
   i. How are kinship terms organized in this culture? *(cont.)*

     ii. How is the organization of kinship terms similar to and different from American English?

     iii. How is the organization of kinship terms in this culture similar to and different from Seneca as presented in (2) and (3)?

File 11.2—Language and Thought

Exercises

10. Explain how the words in a language can appear to influence behavior, giving at least one concrete example not found in the textbook.

11. Provide three possible reasons for why adult Pirahã speakers do not seem able to count objects in groups larger than three objects in any of the experiments done. How might experimenters try to tease apart these reasons?

12. Explain why each of the words *tan, ruddy,* and *viridescent* would not be considered basic color terms of English, according to the definition of "basic color term" presented in this file.

Discussion Questions

13. One of the themes of Chapter 10 is the variability of language and how particular language varieties are associated with particular groups. How do you think this relates to the principle of linguistic relativity? For example, do you think that the observation that midwesterners tend to call sweetened carbonated beverages *pop* causes them to have a different worldview from northerners who use the term *soda*? Do you think that your worldview changes depending on what situation you are in (e.g., what register you are using or what identity you are trying to project with your language use)? Explain your answer.

14. What do color terms and direction terms have in common that makes them good candidates for testing the principle of linguistic relativity? Give an example of some other area that might prove to be a fruitful testing ground, and explain how you think it could be used as such.

File 11.3—Language and Power

Discussion Question

15. Based on the material in this file, what are some ways that power relationships can be established in a conversation? Give some concrete examples from your own experience. What cues do you think might be particularly indicative of someone exerting power as opposed to someone acquiescing? Are these cues inherent or socially determined?

Activities

16. You may be surprised to learn that there is no official language in the United States. All official government business in the United States is conducted in English, but no law requires this. English can nevertheless be considered the **national** language of the country, insofar as it is the most widely used. There has been much debate about whether English should be made the official language or not; some states have passed laws making it an official language in that state. Do some research to see which states have English as their official language, which states include other languages, and which states do not have an official language at all. Gather information about why states have made the choices they have and what issues have been raised (e.g., issues dealing with immigration, economics, politics, history, culture, etc.). Set up a debate in your class where half the class argues for making English the official language of the United States and the other half of the class argues against this position.

17. Research the "Deaf President Now" movement that took place at Gallaudet University in 1988. What is Gallaudet University? What was it that the students involved in this movement were trying to accomplish? What originally caused them to become upset? What did they do as a result? What were the consequences of their actions? How does the controversy underlying this story relate to the ideas in File 11.3? How does it relate to the ideas of language and identity introduced in File 10.5?

File 11.4—Politeness

Exercises

18. List ten ways you could get your neighbor to turn down loud music. What type of politeness does each one use?

19. Give two examples of each of the following that you have heard in the last few days, and briefly explain why these are examples of each category:
   a. Bald on-record FTAs.
   b. FTAs done with positive politeness.
   c. FTAs done with negative politeness.
   d. FTAs done off-record.

20. What kind of politeness is a compliment? Why do you think so?

21. As noted in Section 11.4.4, English does use some honorifics (e.g., *your honor, sir*). Make a list of as many honorifics as you can think of. Who uses them and when?

Discussion Questions

22. Rank your answers to Exercise 18 in order of decreasing politeness. What seems to be the strategy that is most polite in American English?

23. As noted in Section 11.4.4, English once had the T/V distinction. Why do think English no longer uses this distinction?

24. Tag questions can be used with imperatives as well as with declarative sentences (e.g., *Tell Angela, will you?*). Do you think these tag questions are more polite or less polite than tag questions with declaratives? Why?

25. What do you think would happen if you began using politeness strategies like Japanese honorifics or the T/V distinction in English? How would people react? Why do you think so?

Activities

26. In groups, come up with three face-threatening acts: one that is very face-threatening, one that is only slightly face-threatening, and one that is in the middle. What politeness strategy would you use for each one? Does this confirm Brown and Levinson's theory?

27. Find an example of an action that is considered very polite in one culture but very rude in another. What does this tell us about politeness?

File 11.5—Ethnography

Exercises

28. Give an etic description and an emic description of each of the following:
  a. How you and a friend greeted one another today.
  b. What you ate, said, and did at lunch today.
  c. How your instructor started class.

29. Explain the difference between passive observation and participant observation, and give an example of each.

Discussion Questions

30. If someone else was going to do an ethnography of a group that you are a member of, what kinds of things would you want them to find? Do you think passive observation or complete observation would be more likely to help the ethnographer see those things?

31. Imagine you were going to do an ethnography. Choose a language, culture, and linguistic feature to look at. How would you get started? What would you try to do first? What do you think would be most difficult?

Further Readings

Ahearn, Laura M. 2012. *Living language: An introduction to linguistic anthropology.* Oxford: Wiley-Blackwell.

Foley, William. 1997. *Anthropological linguistics: An introduction.* Oxford: Blackwell.

Lakoff, Robin T. 1990. *Talking power: The politics of language in our lives.* New York: Basic Books.

Levinson, Stephen C. 2003. *Space in language and cognition: Explorations in cognitive diversity.* Cambridge: Cambridge University Press.

Lucy, John A. 1992. *Language diversity and thought: A reformulation of the linguistic relativity hypothesis.* Cambridge: Cambridge University Press.

Nic Craith, Máiréad. 2006. *Europe and the politics of language: Citizens, migrants and outsiders.* Basingstoke: Palgrave Macmillan.

Watts, Richard J.; Sachiko Ide; and Konrad Ehlich (eds.). 2008. *Politeness in language: Studies in its history, theory and practice.* 2nd edn. Berlin: Mouton de Gruyter.

CHAPTER
12

Language Contact

FILE **12.0**

....

What Is Language Contact?

In **language contact** situations, two or more distinct languages or dialects come into contact with each other either directly through social interaction of the speakers or indirectly through education or literature. Language contact situations differ in the intensity of contact, the kind of contact, and the outcomes of the contact, and such situations often result in changes to one or both of the languages involved. One common outcome is **borrowing,** which usually involves the transfer of lexical items or even structural properties from one language to another. Other outcomes of contact include **language convergence** (where languages in contact become more alike), **language death** (where a language has no more speakers left), and the creation of contact languages such as **bilingual mixed languages, pidgins,** and **creoles.** The prestige and power relationships between speakers of the languages involved in contact situations affect the direction of influence and the outcome of the contact situation.

Contents

12.7   Case Studies in Language Contact
Presents case studies of the contact situations in the Indian village of Kupwar and of Deitsch (Pennsylvania German), spoken in the midwestern United States.

12.8   Practice
Provides exercises, discussion questions, activities, and further readings related to language contact.

FILE 12.1

....

Language Contact

12.1.1　Languages in Contact

Language contact involves the contact of two or more distinct languages either indirectly through the written form and other media, or directly through social contact between speakers. An example of the former is the contact between modern English and many other languages around the world: English is learned as a second language all over the world, frequently without there being any social contact between native speakers of English and the second-language learners. This kind of language contact is becoming more common due to globalization.

The more usual type of contact historically, however, involves direct social contact between speakers, since languages and their speakers do not exist in isolation but rather in social settings. Thus, when we talk about language contact, we are not actually talking about the contact of languages, but rather the contact of people who speak the languages.

Speakers of languages are continually coming into contact with speakers of other languages, creating a variety of contact situations, each with a potentially different result. Such contact may be caused by trade, conquest, migration, or other factors. Two thousand years ago, the expansion of the Roman Empire throughout Europe led to contact between Latin and a variety of local languages, many of which did not survive the contact—that is, they were replaced by Latin, and, as a result, people no longer spoke the local languages. Over one thousand years ago, the version of Latin spoken in the Iberian Peninsula (which was developing into what we now call Spanish and Portuguese) came into contact with Arabic during Arabic rule. In this case, Spanish, Portuguese, and Arabic all survived, but we can identify many influences that they had on each other. In the past century, the arrival of immigrants from Mexico, Cuba, and other Latin American countries to the United States has resulted in close contact between Spanish and American English; we will have to wait and see what the outcome of this contact situation will be.

Contact situations can be described in terms of their influence on the linguistic systems, the social relationships of the speakers in contact, and the linguistic outcome of the contact. We will consider each of these in turn below.

12.1.2　Levels of Borrowing

In language contact situations, the linguistic systems involved are often influenced by **borrowing,** the adoption by one language of linguistic elements from another language. Borrowing can be **lexical** (i.e., the borrowing of words and phrases) or **structural** (i.e., the borrowing of phonological, morphological, or syntactic patterns).

Lexical borrowing is the adoption of individual words into one language from another language. These words are commonly referred to as **loans** or **loanwords.** Examples of borrowings into American English include the words *ballet* and *chaise* from French, *macho* and *taco* from Spanish, *pizza* and *spaghetti* from Italian, *zeitgeist* and *sauerkraut* from German, and *skunk* and *wigwam* from Algonquian. (Borrowings into English will be discussed in more detail in File 12.2.) The pronunciation of such borrowings is adapted to English phonology, illustrating the fact that the effects of borrowing rarely enter the domain of phonological structure. For example, most English speakers pronounce the word *burrito* as [bɹiɾoʊ] (adapted to English phonology) instead of the typical Spanish pronunciation [burito].

Interestingly, there are certain types of words that do not tend to be borrowed between languages. These fall into two main categories: "core" vocabulary and grammatical function words. Core vocabulary consists of the words for basic items that most societies have words for: things like body parts (*head, arm, leg*), familial relations (*mother, sister, uncle*), or basic environmental entities (*sun, moon, water*). These tend not to be borrowed because there is usually no need: if a language exists, it usually already has these words because they are so universal in nature. There is thus no reason for a language to need to adopt equivalent words from another language. On the other hand, words for new kinds of foods or animals (*squash, bratwurst, tequila, vodka, chipmunk, opossum,* etc.), cultural items (*sacrament, sombrero, pajama, mosque, karaoke,* etc.), or political terms (*bailiff, lieutenant, propaganda, democracy, czar,* etc.) are often borrowed because one language had no need for the terms until they were introduced by the other language's culture and society.

Similarly, grammatical function words like *a, the, one, my, you, in, through, by, is,* and so on, do not tend to be borrowed from one language to another because most languages already have such words. Although both core vocabulary and function words are occasionally borrowed, it is much more common for languages to borrow only words for things they do not have than to replace words they already have.

In addition to single lexical items, whole phrases and idiomatic expressions can be borrowed. Examples include English *it goes without saying* from French *il va sans dire,* German *Kettenraucher* from English *chain smoker,* and English *worldview* from German *Weltanschauung.* Phrases such as these, acquired through a word-for-word translation into native morphemes, are called **loan translations** or **calques.**

Phonological borrowing occurs when a language adopts new sounds or phonological rules from a language with which it is in contact. In many cases, this comes about through the borrowing of words. For example, [ʒ] was introduced into English from French via French loanwords like *rouge, leisure, measure,* and *prestige,* rather than being directly borrowed from French as an individual sound. Similarly, educated Muslim speakers of Urdu have borrowed the Arabic sounds [z] and [ʔ]. Phonological borrowing is not limited to sounds, however; for example, phonological rules that convert root-final [k] to [s] in word pairs like *electric/electricity* and [t] to [ʃ] in word pairs like *nominate/nomination* were borrowed into English from French.

Morphological borrowing is the adoption of morphological elements or patterns by one language under the influence of another language. Words are often borrowed along with an attached affix, which then may become part of the morphological system of the language that borrowed it. For example, for many of the words English has borrowed from Latin, the Latin plural form has been maintained. For example, the plural of *colloquium* is *colloquia* for most speakers, not *colloquiums.* Similarly, Albanian has maintained the Turkish form of the plural of words that it has borrowed from Turkish. In some cases, the morpheme becomes productive and is able to be attached to other words. For example, English adopted derivational suffixes *-able/-ible* from French via the borrowing of words such as *incredible.* This affix then became productive and attached to non-French roots, as in words such as *writeable* and *drinkable.*

In syntactic borrowing, ordering requirements of surface elements in one language may be borrowed into another language, replacing the native word order. For example, Romansch, a Romance language spoken in Switzerland, replaced its original noun-before-adjective ordering with an adjective-before-noun ordering under the influence of German. Syntactic borrowing also occurred in Wutun (which belongs to the Chinese language family) which borrowed rigid verb-final word order from Tibetan, as well as the use of postpositions instead of prepositions. And Greek as spoken in Turkey (originally subject-verb-object) has adopted subject-object-verb word order under the influence of Turkish.

12.1.3 Contact Situations

All contact-induced change, including borrowing, is related to certain nonlinguistic characteristics such as **intensity of contact,** which is determined by the duration of the linguistic contact as well as by the level of interaction among the speakers. Intensity of contact is best seen as a continuum ranging from high intensity to low intensity. Long-term contact with a high level of social interaction is considered to be an intense contact situation, whereas contact that has not existed for a long time and allows only limited social interaction of the speakers in contact is characterized as a low-intensity contact situation.

The degree of intensity of the contact is directly related to the nature and degree of contact-induced change. Lexical borrowing requires only a low-intensity contact situation, because single words can be adopted without an in-depth knowledge of the grammatical system of the donor language. However, the adoption of structural elements or rules embedded in the phonology, morphology, or syntax of one language into another requires the existence of at least some speakers who are knowledgeable about both languages. In other words, structural borrowing requires the existence of **bilingualism** (see File 8.5), which requires a relatively intense degree of contact between the groups in order to develop.

Another social factor that influences the effect of contact on the linguistic systems is the **prestige** of the speakers (see Section 10.1.4). If the speakers in the contact situation are equally prestigious, their respective languages are said to be in an **adstratal** relationship. For example, English and Norse in contact in early England were **adstratum languages.** If the speakers are unequal in terms of prestige, the language of the dominant group is called the **superstratum language,** while the language of the less dominant group is called the **substratum language.** In the contact between English and Native American languages, English is the superstratum language and Native American languages are the substratum languages, because of an imbalance in power and prestige. In Germany, the various languages of foreign workers (e.g., Turkish, Serbo-Croatian, Greek, and Italian) are considered to be substratum languages, and German is considered to be the superstratum language. It is important to keep in mind that these classifications of different strata are based only on cultural factors, not on linguistic ones. For example, while Greek may be a substratum language in Germany, it is a superstratum language in Greece.

In both adstratal and substratal/superstratal contact situations, lexical borrowing usually occurs first. However, the direction of the borrowing process usually differs. Adstratum languages function as donor and recipient at the same time, and borrowing takes place in both directions. However, in a situation of unequal prestige or power, the superstratum language is typically the donor language and accepts only a few loanwords from the substratum language(s). To put it simply, adstratal borrowing is primarily bidirectional, while substratal/superstratal borrowing is primarily unidirectional, with words being borrowed from the superstratum language into the substratum language.

Native language (L1) **interference** plays an important role in shaping the result of language contact, especially in contact situations that result from immigration. Many adult immigrants learn the language of their new home (their second language, or L2) through interaction with native speakers, rather than in a school setting. This can be referred to as **second-language acquisition** in a natural setting. In this case, the immigrants' native language influences the way that the second language is learned. This is also called **transfer** or **substrate influence,** since immigrant languages are frequently substratum languages. For example, many Turkish immigrants in Germany do not use locative prepositions in their German. An immigrant may say *Ich gehe Doktor* ('I go doctor') instead of the standard

German *Ich gehe zum Doktor* ('I am going to [the] doctor'). This is a case of native language interference because Turkish does not have any locative prepositions. Instead, Turkish has a locative case (which German does not have) as shown in (1).

(1) The Turkish locative case
     doktor-a   gid-iyor-um
     doctor-LOC   go-PROG-I
     'I am going to the doctor'

Native language influence differs from borrowing because it is native speakers of Turkish who are introducing elements of Turkish into German, rather than native speakers of German borrowing words or patterns from Turkish.

12.1.4 Outcomes of Language Contact

The outcomes of language contact are as varied as the contact situations that produce them If speakers of different adstratal languages enter into an extensive, long-term contact situation, **language convergence** may result. Convergence occurs when two languages become more similar due to contact between them. File 12.7 discusses two cases of language convergence in more detail. When several languages enter into such a linguistic alliance, they form a Sprachbund (a German word meaning 'union of languages'). An example of this is the Balkan Sprachbund of southeastern Europe where Albanian, Macedonian, Greek, Romanian, Bulgarian, and Serbo-Croatian show signs of linguistic convergence as a result of a long-standing linguistic contact.

If there is extensive, long-term contact between languages that have an unequal prestige relationship, **language shift** may result. This is a shift by a group of speakers toward another language, abandoning their native language. If the shifting group is the only group of speakers who used their original language, that language will no longer be spoken once the shift is completed. This is called **language death.** Many Native American languages in the United States have undergone the process of language death through language shift. Language shift can also be observed in Oberwart, a village at the border between Austria and Hungary. After the Second World War, German came to be associated with the prestigious industrial economy, while Hungarian was felt to represent unprestigious "peasantness." The long-standing bilingualism of German and Hungarian, therefore, is giving way to a preference for German monolingualism, especially in the younger generation of Oberwart. Once the shift has been completed, Hungarian will no longer be used in Oberwart. However, this is not a case of language death, since Hungarian, of course, is still widely used in Hungary. Language shift and death will be discussed in greater detail in File 12.6.

Finally, three distinct outcomes of highly intensive language contact situations are the creation of **pidgin languages** (File 12.3), **creole languages** (File 12.4), and **bilingual mixed languages (intertwined languages)**. A pidgin language typically arises in a setting where two or more peoples come together for the purposes of trade. If the traders do not share a common language for communication, they might create a simplified yet distinct language, a pidgin, to facilitate trading. An example of such a trade pidgin is Chinook Jargon, a pidgin spoken by Native American, British, and French traders in the Pacific Northwest in the nineteenth century.

Whereas pidgins are not the primary languages of their users, creole languages arise in situations where the speakers in contact are in need of a common, primary means of communication. This situation characterized plantation settings in the Caribbean and parts of the southern United States in the seventeenth to nineteenth centuries. Here, a large number of Africans speaking a multitude of mutually unintelligible native languages came together with a small number of Europeans. This situation created the need for a common means of communication among the Africans as well as between the Africans and the Europeans. Examples of creoles include English-based Jamaican Creole, Guyanese Creole, Gullah (a creole spoken in the coastal and island regions of South Carolina and Georgia), French-based Haitian Creole, and the Spanish/Portuguese-based creoles Papiamentu (Aruba, etc.) and Palenquero (Colombia).

Bilingual mixed languages occur in contact situations with a high degree of bilingualism among speakers. Examples of intertwined languages are Media Lengua, spoken in Salcedo, Ecuador, by about 1,000 Native American people, as well as Michif spoken in Canada and in the Turtle Mountain Reservation in North Dakota by about 1,000 people altogether. Bilingual mixed languages differ from language convergence in that language convergence occurs when languages mutually become more alike at all levels of language. Bilingual mixed languages develop by combining aspects of one language with aspects of another language. For example, Media Lengua combines Spanish vocabulary (adapted to Quechua phonology) with Quechua grammar, including Quechua morphology. Michif combines Plains Cree and Canadian French, along with some borrowing from other languages. Plains Cree contributes the phonology, lexicon, morphology, and syntax of verb phrases (including their polysynthetic structure; see File 4.3), while Canadian French contributes the phonology, lexicon, morphology, and syntax of noun phrases (including lexical gender and adjective agreement).

FILE 12.2

....

Borrowings into English

12.2.1 Lexical Borrowing

A survey of the 1,000 most frequently used words in English found that only 61.7% had Old English (Germanic) origins. The other 38.3% were **lexical borrowings** from a variety of other languages: 30.9% French, 2.9% Latin, 1.7% Scandinavian, 1.3% mixed, and 0.3% Low German and Dutch. This massive amount of lexical borrowing is the direct result of the vast number of languages with which speakers of English have come into contact over the course of the language's history. Observing the external history of a language can show us why words were borrowed, as well as explain why certain types of words were borrowed.

Speakers of languages are always coming into contact with speakers of other languages, and thus, a single word can be borrowed from one language to another through several intermediate sources. Therefore, it is necessary to distinguish between the immediate source of a borrowed word and the ultimate source of the word. For example, the Greek word πρόβλημα was borrowed into Latin and evolved naturally into the French word *problème*. Centuries later, the French word was borrowed into English as *problem*. While the immediate source of the word was French, its origins lie in Greek. The histories of other words can be even more complicated. For example, the English word *sugar* was borrowed from French, but it had earlier passed through Latin and Arabic, and likely Greek, Persian, and Sanskrit as well. What follows is a brief sketch of the major periods of lexical borrowings (and thus history) of the English language.

12.2.2 Sources of English Words

The languages of the inhabitants of the British Isles were predominantly Celtic upon the withdrawal of Roman troops in the early fifth century C.E., despite four centuries of Roman domination. Shortly thereafter, Germanic tribes entered, defeated the Celts, and took control not only politically, but linguistically as well. The arrival of the Angles, Saxons, and Jutes signified the arrival of Germanic languages (the name *English* comes from the tribe of the Angles), which pushed speakers of the Celtic languages out of the center of Great Britain and into the periphery (Wales and Scotland), where they remain today.

Many words of Scandinavian origin entered the English language during the Norse invasions that took place between the ninth and eleventh centuries C.E. Included in these borrowings are the pronouns *they, them,* and *their,* which are words that are normally rather resistant to borrowing. Other examples of English words that were borrowed from Scandinavian languages are listed in (1).

(1) Borrowings from Scandinavian languages
anger, blight, clumsy, doze, eggs, garden, gate, geyser, law, ski, window

As mentioned in Section 12.2.1, English has borrowed more words from French than from any other language. The Normans invaded England from Northern France and took control at the Battle of Hastings in 1066 C.E. While Normandy and England were united for less than 200 years, the mark Norman French left on the English vocabulary is immense. Some of the many words of French origin in English are listed in (2).

(2) Borrowings from French
     art, beauty, butcher, carpenter, cartoon, catch, cattle, cell, charity, chase, color, company,
     corpse, county, court, design, dinner, dress, enemy, fork, format, govern, grace, grocer, jail,
     judge, jury, lease, mercy, minister, miracle, napkin, painter, paradise, passion, plate, porch,
     power, reign, saint, soldier, suit, supper, table, tailor, troops

In later centuries a number of Parisian French words entered the English language. Some words were even borrowed twice, first from Norman French and later from Parisian French. For example, *chef* and *chief* were both borrowed from French *chef*. Many recent French borrowings can be easily identified as such, for example, *brassiere, fiancé(e), résumé,* and *hors d'oeuvres*. But others, especially the earlier borrowings, look and sound surprisingly English, as the list in (2) shows.

Although England was part of the Roman Empire for over 400 years, English was not strongly influenced by Latin until after the fall of the Empire. Latin words like the ones in (3) entered English during one of two major periods: accompanying Christianity into England (ca. 600 C.E.) and during the Renaissance (sixteenth through seventeenth centuries).

(3) Borrowings from Latin
     abbot, agenda, alibi, animal, bonus, circulate, clerk, colloquium, data, deficit, diet, exit,
     extra, indicate, item, maximum, memento, nominate, penicillin, pope, priest, propaganda,
     radium, spectrum, sponsor, veto, via

Latin was not the only classical language to affect English during the Renaissance. Many words of Greek origin were borrowed as well. Many of the English words of Greek origin listed in (4) passed through Latin due to substantial Greek-Latin contact prior to and during the Roman Empire (e.g., Eng. *stadium* < Lat. *stadium* < Gr. *στάδιον*), but others were borrowed directly from Greek.

(4) Borrowings from Greek
     analysis, angel, bacteriology, botany, catastrophe, climax, comedy, democracy, dialect, dia-
     logue, episode, pediatrics, physiology, physics, philosophy, pneumonia, psychiatry, scene,
     system, theater, tyrant, zoology

As the British began to colonize lands outside of Europe, English came into contact with a greater variety of languages. Many borrowings from Native American languages are plant terms, animal terms, and terms for other items that were new to New World immigrants, as shown in (5).

(5) Borrowings from Native American languages
     caucus, chipmunk, hickory, igloo, kayak, moccasin, moose, muskrat, opossum, pecan, rac-
     coon, sequoia, skunk, teepee, tomahawk, totem, wigwam

English and Spanish did not come into intensive contact in Europe, but rather in America. It is worth noting that many of the Spanish words listed in (6) actually have their origins in Native American languages. The words passed through Spanish before entering English. For example, *condor* was borrowed from Spanish, but it is originally from Quechua, an indigenous language spoken in South America.

(6)   Borrowings from Spanish
      adobe, alligator, armada, cafeteria, canyon, cargo, cockroach, coyote, guerilla, matador, mosquito, mustang, plaza, poncho, potato, renegade, rodeo, sombrero, tornado

Names for items that people consume (be it foods, drinks, or drugs) are frequently borrowed along with the introduction of the item. Examples are *cigar, marijuana, tequila,* and *vanilla* from Spanish; *bratwurst, frankfurter, pretzel,* and *sauerkraut* from German; *chutney* and *basmati* from Hindi; *bagel* and *lox* from Yiddish; *hashish* and *kabob* from Arabic; *yogurt* from Turkish; *sake, sushi,* and *wasabi* from Japanese; *vodka* from Russian; and *whiskey* from Irish. The following are borrowings from a variety of languages that English speakers have come into contact with. Many of the words entered the English language because the item, idea, or concept they represent was imported as well.

(7)   a. Borrowings from Celtic languages (Irish, Welsh, etc.)
         bog, clan, glen, leprechaun, penguin, slogan, shamrock

      b. Borrowings from German
         angst, delicatessen, kindergarten, lager, poke, pumpernickel, noodle, schnitzel

      c. Borrowings from Dutch
         bow, commodore, cruise, dock, freight, leak, lighter, pump, scour, scum, stripe, yacht

      d. Borrowings from Yiddish
         klutz, oy vey, schlep, schmuck

      e. Borrowings from Italian
         alto, attitude, balcony, fiasco, fresco, opera, pasta, piano, replica, soprano, spaghetti, studio, torso, umbrella

      f. Borrowings from South Asian Languages (Sanskrit, Hindi, Tamil, etc.)
         bandanna, bungalow, calico, curry, guru, indigo, jungle, loot, pajama, pundit, thug

      g. Borrowings from Arabic
         emir, gazelle, ghoul, giraffe, harem, lute, minaret, mosque, sultan

      h. Borrowings from Japanese
         anime, bonsai, futon, karaoke, kimono, tempura, typhoon

English is not alone, or even particularly rare, in having a substantial proportion of its lexicon of foreign origin. Any language whose history contains a series of periods of contact with other languages is going to have numerous borrowings from those languages.

....

Pidgin Languages

12.3.1 The Development of Pidgin Languages

Speakers of mutually unintelligible languages who are brought together (perhaps by social, economic, or political forces), and need to communicate with one another, develop various ways of overcoming the barriers to communication. One solution is for all of the speakers to learn one another's languages, but this is not always practical. Another solution is to create **pidgin languages.** These are languages that typically develop in trading centers or in areas under industrialization, where the opportunities for trade and work attract large numbers of people with different native tongues. Thus, the etymology of *pidgin* should come as no surprise: the word *pidgin* is actually a pidginized form of the English word *business.* Pidgin languages develop whenever speakers of different languages do not share a language in common but need to communicate.

Before describing some features of pidgins, we should mention that pidgins are not "grammarless" or "broken" versions of other languages, as is sometimes believed. They do, however, grow and develop over time. In the initial stage of pidgin formation, often called the **prepidgin jargon** stage, there is little or no consistent grammar and rampant variation among speakers. For this reason, people who study pidgin languages talk about pidgins becoming **crystallized,** or establishing grammatical conventions. This is an essential characteristic of pidgins—if there is no established grammar, there is no pidgin.

After crystallizing from a prepidgin jargon, pidgins can develop in different ways. **Prototypical pidgins** are pidgins that emerged rather abruptly in situations where the contact is limited to certain social settings (such as trade). Prototypical pidgins have reduced grammar and vocabulary. Furthermore, they are nobody's native language. **Expanded pidgins,** on the other hand, are not limited to certain social settings. They have larger lexical and structural resources than prototypical pidgins, and they are as linguistically complex as any other language. A pidgin can evolve from a prepidgin jargon to a prototypical pidgin to an expanded pidgin.

12.3.2 Common Features of Pidgins

Many pidgin languages, regardless of their source languages, share certain characteristics. The similarities of pidgin languages (even ones that have formed entirely independently of each other) are sometimes so striking that some researchers have suggested that universal strategies of second-language learning play a role in their formation. Currently debated by researchers is the question of whether the errors people make when learning a foreign language are a result of the strategies adults use in learning second languages or of some innate language learning device. It seems likely that a full account of pidgin formation will have to include an appeal to some sort of language universals.

Some typical features of pidgins are described below. The example here is taken from Cameroonian Pidgin, an expanded pidgin spoken in Cameroon, in West Africa. English supplied much of the vocabulary of this pidgin. For reference, an adapted excerpt from Loreto

Todd's *Some Day Been Dey*, a folktale about a tortoise and a hawk told in Cameroonian Pidgin, is given below, with a loose translation into English. We pick up the tale after the hawk meets the tortoise, explains that she needs food for her children, and invites the tortoise to visit them.

(1) An excerpt from *Some Day Been Dey* by Loreto Todd

    a. [a datwan go gʊd pas mak trɔki ju go kam e]
       "Oh, that would be great, tortoise. You will come, won't you?

    b. [a go glad dat deɪ we ju go kam fɔ ma haʊs]
       "I'll be glad the day when you come to my house."

    c. [i tɔk so i tɔn i bak i go]
       She said this, turned her back, and left.

    d. [i di laf fɔ i bele i tɔk seɪ]
       She was laughing inside. And said:

    e. [ha so trɔki tiŋk seɪ i tu fit go flaɪ ɔp stik i go si]
       "Ha! So Tortoise thinks he too can fly up trees. We'll see."

    [The tortoise notices the hawk's disdain and tricks her into carrying him to her nest, where he eats the hawk's young. She tries to kill him by dropping him from the sky.]

    f. [bɔt trɔki gɛt trɔŋ nkanda nɔtiŋ no fit du i]
       But the tortoise has strong skin. Nothing could hurt him.

    g. [i wikɔp i ʃek i skin muf ɔl dɔs fɔ i skin]
       He got up, shook himself, removed all the dust from his body,

    h. [i go i seɪ a a dɔn du ju wɛl]
       and left, saying: "Oh! I have taught you a good lesson!"

    i. [ɔl dis pipul we dem di praʊd]
       "All these people who are proud!

    j. [dem tiŋk seɪ fɔseka seɪ]
       "They think that because

    k. [a no gɛt wiŋ a no fit du as dem tu di du]
       "I don't have wings, I can't do as they do.

    l. [a no fit flaɪ bɔt mi a dɔn ʃo ju seɪ sens pas ɔl]
       "I can't fly, but I've shown you that intelligence beats everything."

    a. Phonology. Consonant clusters are often reduced in pidgins (see 'strong' [trɔŋ] in (1f) and 'dust' [dɔs] in (1g)). Consonant cluster reduction is an indication that pidgins have a preference for syllable types closer to the CV type.

    b. Morphology. A common feature of pidgin morphology is the absence of affixes. Notice from the Cameroonian example in (1) that 'wings' is [wiŋ] (see (1k)), 'thinks' is [tiŋk] (see (1e)), and 'passes' is [pas] (see (1l)). However, this does not mean that pidgins never have affixes; expanded pidgins can have rather complex morphology. (See (4) below for an example of complex morphology in Tok Pisin.)

    Note also that [i] is the only third-person pronoun in Cameroonian Pidgin, replacing English *he* and *she* (subjective), *him* and *her* (objective), and *his* and *her* (possessive). This simplification avoids the use of case and gender marking.

One other common morphological feature in pidgin languages that is not demonstrated in (1) is the use of reduplication as a simple word formation process (see File 4.2). For example, in Korean Bamboo English (a pidgin developed among Koreans and Americans during the Korean war), reduplication is used (a) to avoid homonymy, as in [san] 'sun' versus [sansan] 'sand,' and (b) for emphasis, as in [takitaki] 'very talkative.'

c. Syntax. The basic word order for pidgins tends to be subject-verb-object (SVO). Like other SVO languages (such as English), pidgins generally use prepositions rather than postpositions (*in the house* rather than *the house in), auxiliaries are usually ordered before main verbs (*must go* rather than *go must), and nouns before relative clauses (*the man who snores* rather than **who snores the man*).

Pidgins show a preference for coordinated sentences (sentences connected by conjunctions such as *and, or*, etc.) over subordinate clauses (sentences connected by conjunctions such as *if, although*, etc.), though subordinate structures do sometimes exist. Articles are generally not used in pidgins, as illustrated by [ɔl dɔs] 'all the dust,' in line (1g). Aspectual distinctions (loosely: the manner of an action) are often marked by auxiliaries in pidgins. Cameroonian Pidgin, for example, classifies actions as to whether they are ongoing, completed, or repeated, as shown in (2).

(2)   Verb aspect in Cameroonian Pidgin

Type of Action	Auxiliary	Example	Gloss	Reference
ongoing:	di	[di laf]	'was laughing'	(1d)
completed:	dɔn	[dɔn du]	'have done'	(1h)
repeated:	di	[di du]	'do (always)'	(1k)

d. Semantics. Pidgins, especially prototypical pidgins, usually have comparatively small vocabularies. To compensate for the lack of variety, however, meanings are extended. Thus [stik] means not only 'stick' but also 'tree' (see (1e)), and [wikɔp] means not only 'wake up' but also 'get up' (see (1g)). Because there are not many words in the vocabulary of the typical pidgin, compounds are more frequent. For example, compounds such as *dog baby* and *cow baby* could be used for 'puppy' and 'calf.'

12.3.3   Sources of Pidgin Lexicon and Grammar

Pidgin languages are usually made up of mixtures of elements from all of the languages in contact. In many cases, the vocabulary of pidgin languages is derived from the superstratum language, though other languages can also supply some of the lexicon. The language that provides most of the vocabulary of a pidgin is also called the **lexifier.** The word order (SVO, SOV, etc.) of pidgins is also frequently derived from the dominant language. The phonology of a pidgin, however, usually reflects the phonological systems of the languages of the other groups in contact and frequently has a strong influence from the substratum language(s). Pidgin syntax is frequently reduced, making it hard to determine which language it is based on. Finally, while pidgins usually have some derivational morphology, they usually do not have any productive inflectional morphology (see File 4.1).

To summarize, pidgin languages usually resemble their substratum languages in phonology and their superstratum languages in vocabulary and word order. Both grammar and lexicon are reduced in prototypical pidgins, often because they emerge so quickly and there is neither adequate instruction nor adequate time for complete mastery of any of the languages involved in the contact situation. We will look at two examples from very different expanded pidgin languages to illustrate some typical characteristics of pidgins.

a. Chinook Jargon. Chinook Jargon was a prototypical pidgin that developed during the second half of the nineteenth century in Canada and the northwestern United

States. It was used as a trade language among several Native American groups and was also learned by Europeans who began to settle in the Northwest. It is presumed that Chinook Jargon predates European settlement, as it shows little European influence in its early form. Its main source of vocabulary was Lower Chinook, and many of the features of Chinook Jargon grammar are derived from other Native American languages that played a role in its formation. Later, vocabulary items from Canadian French and English were borrowed into the language. Today, Chinook Jargon is an expanded pidgin. However, it is an endangered language with fewer than one hundred speakers. Examples of Chinook Jargon vocabulary can be seen in (3).

(3)

Chinook Jargon	**Source**	**Gloss**
ikt	ixt (Chinook)	'one'
mokst	môkst (Chinook)	'two'
man	man (English)	'man'
chuck	ča'úk (Nootka)	'water'

One of the most interesting aspects of Chinook Jargon is its rich and complex consonant inventory, a feature found frequently among the languages whose speakers contributed to its development, but rarely among the languages of the world in general and not at all in other pidgins. Examples of the complexity of Chinook Jargon phonology include its numerous secondary articulations, such as ejective stops and labialized velar consonants; its clusters consisting of two stop consonants; and its rare phonemes, such as lateral obstruents, a velar and post-velar series of stops, and a glottal stop phoneme (see File 2.4).

b. Tok Pisin. Tok Pisin is an expanded pidgin spoken in Papua New Guinea. Most of the words of Tok Pisin are clearly derived from English, as can be seen in (4), which shows that much of the vocabulary of a pidgin is usually derived from the superstratum language.

(4)

Tok Pisin	**English Source**	**Gloss**
dok	dog	'dog'
pik	pig	'pig'
pis	fish	'fish'
pen	paint	'to paint'
penim	paint	'to paint something/someone'
painim	find	'to find something/someone'
lukim	look	'to look at something/someone'
hukim	hook	'to hook something/someone'
nogut	no good	'bad'
man	man	'man'
baimbai	by and by	'soon'
sekan	shake hands	'to make peace'

Notice that most of the words in the above list are not exactly like their English counterparts. They have undergone some phonological and morphological changes from English to Tok Pisin. For example, the word for 'to find' shows [f] changing to [p], and the [d] is deleted in the consonant cluster [nd], both examples of phonological changes. The suffix -*im* [im] found in *penim, painim, lukim,* and *hukim* is a morphological marker that indicates that the verb is transitive. Compare this to the intransitive verb *pen*. Semantic changes are also evident, as in the extension of *shake hands* to the much more general meaning 'to make peace.' These changes from English to Tok Pisin are due at least in part to contributions from the grammar(s) of the substrate language(s). Even though the vocabulary of Tok Pisin derives mostly from English, it shows a significant substratum influence, mainly from Oceanic languages. This is typical for expanded pidgins: they usually begin as prototypical pidgins and then expand their vocabulary and grammar to meet the increasing demands of everyday communication. In this process, speakers draw more and more on the resources of their native languages.

From the perspective of the linguist, it is not always easy to tell which language contributed which words or grammatical features found in a pidgin. While it's true that many words found in a pidgin derive from the superstratum language, and many grammatical features in an expanded pidgin derive from the speakers' native languages, we cannot conclude that a feature is derived from, say, English just because it looks similar to English.

FILE 12.4

Creole Languages

12.4.1 Social Contexts of Creole Formation

Imagine yourself as the son or daughter of first-generation slaves in the New World. Your parents and others like them were kidnapped from their homes, corralled together with other slaves, shipped across vast oceans under inhumane conditions, and forced to work and live in a strange country surrounded by people who didn't speak their language. Your owners divided their slaves into linguistically diverse groups so that you are not with many other slaves who speak the same language. This tactic means that it is difficult for you to organize any sort of resistance. In order to communicate with either the slaveholders or the other slaves, you will have to adopt or develop some new form of communication. It is in plantation settings of this sort that **creole languages** came into being.

Creole languages develop from a pidgin language or prepidgin (or, more precisely, precreole) jargon when it is adopted as the first, or native, language of a group of speakers (for example, by you and the other children of slaves in the hypothetical scenario above). All creoles seem to be languages that were initially non-native to any group of speakers and were adopted as first languages by children in some speech community. This process is called **nativization.**

Various researchers have suggested that the social context found in multilingual plantation settings is unique in human history. On many plantations there was a radical break in linguistic tradition, more severe than simply the coming together of speakers of different languages that typifies the situation in the development of pidgins. Because of this absolute inability to use their native languages to communicate, many adults developed very simplified jargons, as this was the best means of communicating with people from such varied linguistic backgrounds. Children rarely learned the native language of their parents because it was of little or no value to them on the plantation. The only accessible variety of language that had significant usefulness in plantation settings was the jargon that their parents used. Thus, these jargons became the primary language of the adult slaves and eventually the native language of their children. Because of the innate capacity to develop language (see Chapter 8), these children then turned the jargon into a full-fledged new language, known as a creole. So, while some creoles may develop from pidgin languages, others develop straight from precreole jargons.

Another aspect of creoles is that the formation of many creoles involves repeated second-language acquisition, that is, second-language acquisition by successive groups of people. For example, the early contact variety of what is now Haitian Creole was much closer to French dialects than Haitian Creole is today. The subsequent divergence from French is the result of repeated second-language acquisition of the available contact variety by successive waves of African immigrants. This led to greater substrate influence as well as to drastic changes in the structure of Haitian Creole.

12.4.2 Shared Features

The linguistic structure of a creole depends on the varieties that came into contact to form it. In the case that the precreole language was a crystallized or expanded pidgin, the creole bears many of the same features as its predecessor language. For example, the Tok Pisin pidgin introduced in File 12.3 has been nativized into a creole. The differences between nativized (creole) and non-nativized (pidgin) varieties of Tok Pisin are quite subtle. Often, native speakers of Tok Pisin creole will employ the same grammatical devices as second-language speakers of Tok Pisin pidgin, but on a more frequent or consistent basis. Also, native speakers of Tok Pisin creole reduce various phonological elements (e.g., syllables) more than speakers of Tok Pisin pidgin do. On the whole, though, the differences between nativized and non-nativized Tok Pisin are rather small.

However, if the precreole language was a jargon, or if it is a case of repeated second-language acquisition, the creole tends to bear less structural resemblance to the languages that came into contact to form it. Instead, such creoles seem to develop based on more universal principles (be they linguistic, social, or cognitive), as evidenced by the striking structural similarities between creoles that developed from a rather diverse set of input varieties. Derek Bickerton and other scholars have catalogued many of the similarities among such creoles. One of the most striking of these similarities is the inflectional tense, mood, and aspect (TMA) system used with verbs. Bickerton (1983: 121) gives the table shown in (1), slightly modified in its presentation, which illustrates the similarities in TMA systems among these creoles. Note: *anterior* refers to (past) tense, *nonpunctual* refers to aspect (ongoing or habitual action), and *irrealis* refers to mood (future, conditional, and subjunctive).

(1) Comparing tense, mood, and aspect in three creoles

	Hawaiian Creole	**Haitian Creole**	**Sranan**
BASE FORM 'he walked/s'	He walk	Li maché	A waka
ANT(ERIOR) 'he had walked'	He bin walk	Li té maché	A ben waka
IRR(EALIS) 'he will/would walk'	He go walk	L'av(a) maché	A sa waka
NON(PUNCTUAL) 'he is/was walking'	He stay walk	L'ap maché	A e waka
ANT + IRR 'he would have walked'	He bin go walk	Li t'av(a) maché	A ben sa waka
ANT + NON 'he was/had been walking'	He bin stay walk	Li t'ap maché	A ben e waka
IRR + NON 'he will/would be walking'	He go stay walk	L'av ap maché	A sa e waka
ANT + IRR + NON 'he would've been walking'	He bin go stay walk	Li t'av ap maché	A ben sa e waka

The examples in (1) include two English-based creoles (Hawaiian Creole and Sranan) and one French-based creole (Haitian Creole). The substrate languages that contributed to the three languages represented in table (1) are quite different. In Sranan (spoken in Surinam) and Haitian Creole, the substrate was composed of West African languages. In Hawaiian Creole the substrate was composed of languages such as Portuguese and Chinese. But the patterns of TMA marking are the same in all three creoles. Note that in each of them, the anterior element always precedes the irrealis and nonpunctual elements, and the irrealis element always precedes the nonpunctual element. It is important to note that features such as the TMA system, though widespread, are not universal in creoles. Even the most prototypical creoles lack one or more of the features that are common to creoles, so that their grammars, though similar, are not identical. Most creoles that developed from prepidgin creoles, however, show many of the features that have been identified by Bickerton and others.

What is the source of these shared features among creoles with such diverse backgrounds? Bickerton attributes the similarities to innate properties of the human mind. He claims that the similarities among widely scattered creoles provide support for the claim that human beings are linguistically preprogrammed. Bickerton would say that the shared TMA pattern shown in (1) follows from a very specific "bioprogram" in the human mind. Part of this bioprogram includes the TMA categories that human beings will always use automatically unless the patterns of whatever language they are learning are different.

It should be noted, however, that many creolists do not accept the bioprogram hypothesis and have suggested other explanations to account for the similarities, including the common social context of creolization, universal strategies of language learning, universal strategies for reducing language in contact situations, and structural similarities among the substrate and/or superstrate languages that were historically present in these creole contact situations. Most creolists nowadays propose that the similarities among creoles emerged as a result of a special form of second-language acquisition.

FILE 12.5

Societal Multilingualism

12.5.1 Societal Multilingualism

When hearing the term **bilingualism** or **multilingualism,** most people think of an individual's ability to speak two or more languages or dialects (see File 8.5). (We will use the terms *multilingualism* and *multilingual* here for people who speak two, three, four, or more languages or dialects.) However, whole communities or societies can also be multilingual. This is called **societal bilingualism** or **multilingualism** and is particularly common in Africa and Asia, although it occurs in other parts of the world as well.

The term "societal multilingualism" usually refers to a situation in which communities of speakers share two or more languages and use them in everyday life. In India, for example, many people speak their regional language as well as Hindi, the most widely spoken of the country's indigenous official languages. Most educated speakers also speak English, which is also an official language of India. In Kenya, educated people usually speak at least three languages: their tribal (regional) language, Swahili (the national language), and English (the language used in education throughout the country). In many African countries, the language of the former colonizer, usually French or English, is still used either in the government or in education, making the vast majority of educated speakers multilingual. Finally, in the Al-Sayyid Bedouin tribe, most members speak both Al-Sayyid Bedouin Sign Language and Arabic, so this community is bimodally multilingual.

Societal multilingualism is also common among immigrant communities, for example, in Europe and the United States. In these cases, minority-language speakers maintain their language, while using the host language for interaction with its speakers.

Societal multilingualism is sometimes used in a broader sense to refer to the use of two or more languages within the same country. If we equate society with country, we have to conclude that almost all countries in the world, if not all of them, are multilingual. This is the case even for countries we usually associate with only one language, for example, France, where the regional dialects and languages Provençal, Breton, Alsatian, Corsican, Catalan, Basque, and Flemish are spoken in certain regions of the country. In addition, many other languages, such as Armenian, Turkish, and different dialects of Arabic, are spoken mainly in bigger cities by various immigrant groups. When we think about the languages spoken in the United States, English and Spanish come to mind. However, SIL International's *Ethnologue* lists 216 living languages that are spoken in the United States. For example, there are over 800,000 Russian speakers, over 200,000 Armenian speakers, over 1.2 million French speakers, over 150,000 Yiddish speakers, over 1.4 million Tagalog speakers, and over 600,000 Polish speakers in the United States. A number of the languages listed on *Ethnologue*, however, have fewer than 10 speakers left. This is the case for many indigenous (Native American) languages, which are considered **endangered languages** (see File 12.6).

However, equating society with country is problematic: even though there are 216 languages spoken in the United States, the majority of Americans are actually monolingual (making them a minority since the majority of people in the world are multilingual).

510

12.5.2 Code-Switching and Diglossia

In multilingual communities, two common though distinct linguistic phenomena are code-switching and diglossia. **Code-switching** refers to the use of two or more languages or dialects within a single utterance or within a single conversation. Consider the example in (1) from an interview of a nurse in Nairobi (Myers-Scotton 1990: 65). The languages she uses are Swahili (in normal type), English (in italics), and Lwidakho (in bold). The translation is given in (2).

(1)   Interviewer: Unapenda kufanya kazi yako lini? Mchanaau usiku?
         Nurse: *As I told you, I like my job.* Sina ubaguzi wo wote kuhusu wakati ninapofanya kazi. *I enjoy working either during the day* au usiku yote ni sawa kwangu. Hata *family members* w-angu wamezoea mtindo huu. *There is no quarrel at all.* **Obubi bubulaho.** Saa zengine kazi huwa nyingi sana na *there are other times when we just have light duty.* **Valwale vanji,** *more work;* **valwale vadi,** hazi kidogo.

(2)   Interviewer: When do you like to work? Days or nights?
         Nurse: *As I told you, I like my job.* I have no difficulty at all regarding when I do work. *I enjoy working either during the day* or at night, all is OK as far as I'm concerned. Even my *family members* have gotten used to this plan. *There is no quarrel at all.* **There is no badness.** Sometimes there is a lot of work and *there are other times when we just have light duty.* **More patients,** *more work;* **fewer patients,** little work.

The reason the nurse can code-switch extensively in the interview is that she knows that her interviewer also speaks Swahili, English, and Lwidakho. However, she could have chosen to just speak in one language with the interviewer. Such **language choices** are frequently politically, socially, or personally motivated. For example, multilinguals may be more comfortable with one of their languages or insist on speaking only one language to express their cultural identity. However, in the example above, the nurse leaves the language choice open.

Sometimes the choice of language is determined by the social setting. The situation where different languages or dialects are used for different functions is called **diglossia.** One type of diglossia is a situation where a standard or regional dialect is used in ordinary conversation, but a variety learned by formal education is used for most written communication. An example of this is the use of standard Arabic in literature and other writings and the use of local varieties of Arabic in ordinary conversation in the various countries where Arabic is spoken. Frequently, diglossic situations involve one language that is spoken at home or in informal situations and another language that is used for official purposes or in (higher) education. For example, in many African countries, the language of education and instruction is English or French. However, the languages spoken in everyday life, depending on the country and region, are various African languages.

Many of the examples above show that societal multilingualism frequently arises when speakers of different languages are in contact, as in the cases of immigration and colonization. Societal multilingualism is often an outcome of contact if a group of people retain their cultural and language heritage but also learn the language that is dominant in some area of society.

···

Language Endangerment and Language Death

12.6.1 Minority Language Status

Material in other files makes it clear that there are many, many languages around today. Even with the difficulties involved in distinguishing languages from dialects (see File 10.1), and even with our imperfect knowledge of the range of speech forms found in some parts of the world (e.g., Papua New Guinea or various regions in South America), a figure of some 7,000 languages is widely cited and generally accepted as a rough estimate of how many languages there are in the world today. This number is in accord, for instance, with what is known about global ethnic diversity (even if it draws on an overly simplistic equation of language with ethnicity, which is a controversial issue) and with the array of nations, virtually all of which are home to many languages.

A basic observation about these 7,000 or so languages is that not all are equally robust in terms of their number of speakers. In fact, the number of speakers differs greatly from language to language: there are some languages with millions of speakers, some with thousands, some with hundreds, some with tens, and some with just one. Moreover, the number of languages with a small number of speakers is far greater than the number with millions of speakers. In fact, a total of less than 10% of the known languages accounts for more than 90% of the world's speakers. It follows from these numbers that a good many, even most, languages are minority languages within their larger societal context.

The fact that a given language may not just have a small number of speakers, but often has a minority status compared to some other language or languages that it shares territory with, is a key to understanding the phenomena of **language endangerment** and ultimate **language death;** the death of a language is taken to occur when it no longer has any speakers actively using it.

Speakers of minority languages, especially when they are an overt minority immediately and directly confronted by a dominant culture, face particular sorts of pressures that often lead them to give up their language in favor of a language of the majority, or at least of a politically, economically, and socially more dominant group. Among these pressures are the following, some of which are also discussed in File 11.3:

- problems of access to mainstream economic opportunities (e.g., if jobs require skills in the dominant language)
- potential for ridicule, overt discrimination, and prejudice for being different (e.g., being forbidden by law or regulation to speak one's own language)
- lack of instruction in their native language (with the possibility that schools will force the majority language on minority-language-speaking children)
- limited "scope" for using the language (what can be referred to as its "domains of usage")

There are, of course, some positive aspects to maintaining one's language even if it is a minority language. Among these benefits are:

- the potential to maintain one's culture and prevent a sense of rootlessness (to the extent that aspects of the minority culture are tied up with language)
- enhanced pride and self-esteem
- a well-developed self-identity and group membership that allows access to a different culture (see File 10.5)
- cognitive advantages through bilingualism (e.g., added expressiveness, new perspectives afforded by a different worldview, etc.) (see File 8.5).

12.6.2 From Minority Status to Endangerment

For many minority language speakers, the more concrete pressures of access to jobs and stigmatization override the less tangible benefits, and as a result they move toward linguistic assimilation with the more dominant language. In such cases, there is typically a three-generational "drop-off," with the last fully fluent generation giving way to a transitional generation as assimilation sets in, which in turn spawns a generation often more at home—linguistically and culturally—with the dominant language than the traditional one. At that point, especially if this scenario is replicated across all the pockets of speakers of the minority language, or if such minority communities are small to start with, the viability of the minority language as a whole is threatened. In such a case, we talk of the language being endangered, on its way to extinction and, we might say, death.

This sort of scenario is occurring in all corners of the earth, with different dominant languages and cultures being the "heavy," the "killer language," as it were. While many of the European colonial languages, such as English in the United States, Spanish in much of Latin America, or Portuguese in Brazil, have become the dominant language that threatens the viability of indigenous languages in various areas, other languages play the same role elsewhere, including Arabic in northern Africa, varieties of Chinese in parts of China, Thai in northern Thailand, and so on.

Endangerment is really a locally determined phenomenon. For instance, Greek has been a minority language of immigrants within the last century in the United States and Australia but is increasingly losing ground to the more dominant English in each country. However, in Greece itself, where Greek is the socially more powerful language, the Albanian dialect known as Arvanitika is nearing extinction due to pressures on its speakers to function in Greek. In fact, a few of the widespread "killer languages" ("serial killers," some linguists have called them) are themselves threatened in some places. Spanish is giving way to English in parts of the United States, and it is even the case that English is an endangered language in the Bonin Islands, off of Japan, where despite being spoken by Westerners for over 100 years, it is yielding to the local dominant language, Japanese. What cases like these mean is that there is nothing inherent about a particular language itself that makes it a dominant language, nothing intrinsic to English or Spanish, for instance. Rather, endangerment is determined by the particular social circumstances that guide the interaction between two speech communities occupying roughly the same geographical space but differing as to their population numbers and dominance relations as measured by utility in the economic marketplace, cultural dominance, and the like. Languages can, of course, happily co-exist without one threatening the viability of the other. (See Files 12.1 and 12.7 for some discussion of the long-term, more or less peaceful coexistence of languages.)

This process of language loss through language endangerment and language death is quite widespread today, to the point that many scholars are seriously worried about the survival of the rich linguistic diversity that the world has known for millennia, of the particular (and often unique) viewpoints on representing and structuring knowledge about the world that different languages provide, and of the variety of linguistic structure offered by the range of languages that currently exists. It is certainly the case that language endangerment and language death have taken place in the past; one need only see the many names of tribes recorded in ancient histories, for example, that of the fifth-century B.C.E. Greek historian Herodotus, to get a sense of how many peoples were assimilated, linguistically and culturally, in times long past. But the pace at which language extinction is proceeding seems to have accelerated in recent decades, giving a sense of urgency to the current situation.

Many analysts talk about language death when there are no longer any fluent speakers. At such a point, there may well be speakers with some command of the targeted language but not full fluency; such speakers can be referred to as **semi-speakers,** though the more chilling designation *terminal speakers* has also been used. Fluency in a language is a scalar phenomenon, with different degrees possible, and in a language endangerment situation, one finds differing levels of competence with the language on the part of its remaining speakers. Some might have very limited abilities and essentially just barely "pass" as speakers by knowing a few formulaic phrases and appropriate utterances. If all of the more fluent speakers die off—they tend to be the elders in such communities—sometimes all that are left are some speakers who remember a few words and phrases but have no active command of the language. When there are only such "rememberers," the language is effectively dead, though "moribund" might be a fairer characterization.

12.6.3   Can Dying/Dead Languages Be Revived?

Some linguists prefer the term **dormant** language to **dead** or **extinct language,** their thinking being that under the right conditions, languages can be "reawakened" and revived. Although the collective will that is needed to effect such a revival can be daunting and does not happen often, there are some remarkable success stories to point to.

The revival of a form of Biblical Hebrew in the nineteenth and twentieth centuries in what has become the state of Israel is perhaps the most famous case, with modern Israeli Hebrew being a testament to what dedication to such a linguistic cause can do. Although the modern language differs somewhat from Biblical Hebrew, it has become a living language (again). Similarly, dedication is evident in the way that the indigenous New Zealand language Maori has been staging a comeback, as the institution of *te kohanga reo* 'language nests,' a language-immersion experience for young Maori children, seems to have been a successful revival strategy thus far. And, in Ohio, the tireless efforts of one member of the Miami Tribe, Daryl Baldwin, in learning the dormant Miami language as an adult, speaking it with his children, and promoting its use in summer language camps, has created an awareness of the language that would not have seemed possible even twenty years ago.

It must be admitted, however, that the road to renewed viability for any given endangered language is not an easy one. The pressures on speakers referred to above can be overwhelming, and one often finds that speakers "vote with their mouths," as it were, and abandon their heritage language in favor of the locally dominant language.

12.6.4   What Happens to a Language as It Loses Speakers and Dies?

Typically, endangered languages show massive influx of vocabulary and even syntactic structures from the dominant language, but such is not always the case. Languages can die with their native lexicon and native grammatical structures more or less intact. Moreover, borrowing, as seen in Files 12.1 and 12.2, is a phenomenon that even healthy and robust languages engage in. Thus, it is hard to generalize about what a language will look like in an endangered state, but vocabulary loss, loss of some phonological contrasts (e.g., semi-speakers of Arvanitika generally do not distinguish between the trilled /r/ and the tap /ɾ/ found in other healthier dialects), and the decline of native word orders or syntactic combinations are not at all uncommon in seriously threatened languages. Interestingly, new elements can also enter the language at this point, often in the form of sounds from the dominant language that come in with loanwords (as with the voiced velar fricative [γ] found in recent Greek loanwords into Arvanitika).

12.6.5 A Final Word (Or Two)

Two final points are worth making. First, even though the discussion above talks about **language** endangerment and death, the same considerations apply just as readily at the level of **dialect.** That is, there can be endangered dialects just as there are endangered languages, as we saw with the case of Arvanitika discussed above. Some of the once-distinctive dialects of English heard on the Sea Islands on the Atlantic coast of South Carolina and Georgia, for example, have been giving way to more Standard English forms in recent years. Second, even with the loss of languages on a large scale worldwide, there is some replenishing of the stock of the world's languages occurring through ongoing and continual dialect differentiation as well as processes of creolization (see File 12.4). Still, the creation of new languages seems not to be occurring at the same rate as the loss of existing languages. This situation has led many linguists to action with regard to the documentation of poorly described languages that may not survive many more years and to revival efforts such as those described above.

FILE **12.7**

....

Case Studies in Language Contact

12.7.1 Introduction

The following two case studies illustrate some of the different effects that can arise when two or more languages are used regularly in the same locality. In language contact, both linguistic factors and sociohistorical factors can influence the outcomes in particular multilingual communities. Recall the different contact effects mentioned in File 12.1, and note any examples of those effects that you find in the following discussion.

12.7.2 Kupwar

The village of Kupwar, India, with a population of approximately 3,000, is located in the southern Indian district of Maharashtra. This village represents a rather complex example of language contact (Gumperz and Wilson 1971). The residents of this village speak three main languages: Marathi and Urdu, members of the Indo-European language family, and Kannada, a Dravidian language. Speakers of Kannada and Marathi have been in contact in the area for around 600 years, and speakers of Urdu have been in the area for around 400 years. In this village, sociolinguistic factors have contributed to an intricate language contact situation (see File 10.4 for an introduction to some of these factors).

The inhabitants of Kupwar are divided into distinct social groups according to profession, religion, and a strict caste system. A specific language is associated with each social group. Kannada-speaking Jains are the larger of two landowning social classes. Urdu-speaking Muslims constitute the other. Two other social groups pertinent to this discussion are a large Kannada-speaking craftsman class and a class of Marathi-speaking "untouchables." Family interactions are generally monolingual in the native language of that family's social group. Neighborhoods are generally arranged according to language group. Most men in the village are (at least) bilingual, but communication between members of different social groups is customarily carried out in Marathi. Because it is neither the preferred language of the majority of inhabitants nor the language of either of the socially dominant language groups, Marathi has come to be perceived as a socially neutral language. Rules of social interaction require the use of Marathi in mixed social group settings, even by members of the upper social classes, who do not speak it natively. If a Kannada-speaking landowner were to converse in Kannada with a Marathi-speaking farmhand, the landowner would be implicitly including the farmhand in the landowner's higher social group. The strict caste system forbids such acts.

This system of social separation leads the languages spoken in Kupwar to maintain a high degree of autonomy: for example, each of these languages retains its own distinct vocabulary. Owing to the pervasive bilingualism and the intensive and long-standing social contact among the various members of the Kupwar community, however, many other linguistic features have been transferred between the languages. The following examples illustrate both of these features of language contact in Kupwar.

516

a. Possessive Pronouns and Adjectives. The example in (1) demonstrates how Kupwar Kannada follows a Kupwar Marathi pattern. Kannada spoken outside Kupwar has a distinction in form between the words that mean 'yours' and 'your,' *nim-də* and *nim*, respectively. Kannada as spoken in Kupwar has come to follow the pattern seen in Marathi, which has no distinction in form between the words (Urdu follows a pattern similar to that of Marathi). The underlined words in the example in (1) show this pattern.

(1) Non-Kupwar Kannada: ii   məne <u>nim-də</u>   i-du   <u>nim</u>   məne
     Kupwar Kannada: id   məni <u>nim-d</u> eti   id   <u>nim-d</u> məni eti
     Kupwar Marathi: he   ghər <u>tumc-ə</u> haɪ   he   <u>tumc-ə</u> ghər haɪ
     Gloss: *this-one house yours   is   this-one your   house is*
                           'This house is yours.'   'This is your house.'

This example also shows another difference between Kupwar and non-Kupwar varieties of Kannada. Kupwar Kannada follows the Marathi pattern of requiring an explicitly expressed form of the verb 'to be,' *eti* 'is,' while non-Kupwar Kannada does not require an explicit form of 'is.'

b. Verb Formations. In example (2), we see that Kupwar Urdu follows the Kupwar Kannada pattern. Compare the Kupwar and non-Kupwar varieties of Urdu. The forms that mean 'having VERB-ed' represent a verb form called the *past non-finite*, which occurs in both Kannada and Marathi and is similar to an English past participle. Notice the differences between the Kupwar and non-Kupwar Urdu words for 'having cut' and 'having taken.' Kupwar Urdu, like Kupwar Kannada, adds the same morpheme to the end of each verb to mark the past non-finite form. Non-Kupwar Urdu, however, does not have this pattern and shows two different ways of forming past non-finite forms.

(2) Non-Kupwar Urdu: pala   jəra   <u>kat-kər</u>   <u>le</u>   a↓ɪa
     Kupwar Urdu: pala   jəra   <u>kat-kə</u>   <u>le-kə</u>   a↓ɪa
     Kupwar Kannada: təpla   jəra   <u>khod-i</u>   <u>təgond-i</u>   bə↓ɪn
     Gloss: *greens some   having cut   having taken   (I) came*
                        'I cut some greens and brought them.'

From these examples, we can see that two distinct phenomena are occurring. In one respect, these languages are becoming more alike, as patterns of language use are transferred between languages. At the same time, the languages are being kept distinct from each other, in that Kannada uses Kannada words, Urdu uses Urdu words, and so on. The fact that we see both of these patterns happening concurrently is what makes Kupwar a case of such linguistic interest, especially in light of the fact (mentioned in File 12.1) that languages in contact tend to first share lexical items and only later share structural properties.

12.7.3 Deitsch

Also known as Pennsylvania German or Pennsylvania Dutch, Deitsch has a long history of both dialect and language contact. Deitsch emerged in Pennsylvania in the early 1700s as the result of contact between speakers of western varieties of both middle and upper German dialects. There are currently several hundred thousand Deitsch speakers in North America. Most live in the midwestern states, and the vast majority belong to separatist Anabaptist groups, that is, the Amish and the Old Order Mennonites, which are the only communities where children still acquire Deitsch as a first language. All Deitsch speakers are fluent Deitsch-English bilinguals. Schooling is entirely in English, and thus English is the language of literacy, though most speakers also achieve rudimentary literacy in standard German. In spite of their tradition of separation from mainstream society, these groups have always been in contact with English speakers, and the effects of that contact on the Deitsch language are unmistakable.

a. Lexicon. The amount of borrowing of vocabulary from English varies from community to community and is sometimes exaggerated by native speakers. Actual estimates of the percentage of vocabulary borrowed from English range from 8% (Buffington and Barba 1965) to 14% (Enninger and Raith 1988). This percentage appears to be increasing, however, as speakers replace function words, such as *weil* 'because' and even relatively "basic" rural vocabulary, such as *Sai* 'pigs' and *Bauerei* 'farm', with their English counterparts.

English borrowings are often incorporated into Deitsch morphology, as example (3) shows. In this case, the word *bark* is borrowed from English, but it appears with Deitsch infinitive marking.

(3) And   de   Hund   war   an   bark-e[1]
     And   *the* *dog* *was* *on*   *to-bark*
     'and the dog was barking . . .'

Sometimes, however, English morphology is borrowed along with the word, as example (4) shows. Here, *switch, kick,* and *pressure* as well as the suffix *-s* are borrowed from English. Notice also that *pressure* is given masculine grammatical gender through the use of the masculine definite article *der.* Thus, the borrowed word is integrated into the grammatical gender system of Deitsch.

(4) Sel   dat   switch kick-s nei   venn   der   pressure so   veit   drop . . .
     That *there* *switch* *kicks* *in* *when/if* *the* *pressure* *so* *far* *drops . . .*
     'That switch kicks in when/if the pressure drops so far . . .'

b. Lexical Semantics. A number of Deitsch words have changed or extended their meanings so that they match the semantics of the equivalent word in English. Louden (1997) notes that this often occurs as a result of calquing (see File 12.1), in this case word-for-word translations of English phrases into Deitsch. The semantic changes are particularly strong with respect to Deitsch prepositions that are acquiring English idiomatic meanings and in some cases English compound structure. Examples are shown in (5) and (6).

(5) Mir   kenne sie   net   nei-schwetze   fer   gehe.
     We   *can* *them* *not* *into-talk*   *for* *to-go*
     'We can't talk them into going'

(6) Er hot   si   raus-gechecked
     He has *them* *out-checked*
     'He checked them out' (i.e., 'he ogled them')

c. Phonetics. The sound system of Deitsch remains largely unaffected by contact with English, although some new sounds (e.g., /æ/, /t/, and /ʧ/) occur primarily in English loanwords, and in some Pennsylvania communities the trilled or tapped [r] is being replaced by the American retroflex liquid [ɹ].

d. Syntax. The tense and aspect system of Deitsch is based on German. However, due to contact with English, Deitsch has developed a progressive tense, which is not found in German but is found in English. Compare the data in table (7).

---

[1]Example (3) from Fuller (1999: 49). Examples (4) and (6) from Keiser (1999). Example (5) from Louden (1997: 85).

(7)   Comparison of Deitsch, Standard German, and English tense/aspect systems

Tense/Aspect	Deitsch	Standard German	English
Past	*ich hab tschriwwe*	*ich schrieb*	'I wrote'
Present perfect	*ich hab tschriwwe ghatt*	*ich habe geschrieben*	'I have written'
Past progressive	*ich war an schreiwe*	—	'I was writing'
Present	*ich schreib*	*ich schreibe*	'I write'
Present progressive	*ich bin an schreiwe*	—	'I am writing'
Future	*ich zell/figger schreiwe*	*ich werde schreiben*	'I will/am going to write'
Future perfect	*ich zell/figger tschriwwe hawwe*	*ich werde geschrieben haben*	'I will/am going to have written'

The Deitsch progressive tense is modeled on the (Standard) German forms *ich war am Schreiben* ('I was writing') and *ich bin am Schreiben* ('I am writing'). These forms are very similar to a progressive tense since they have the same meaning as that expressed by a progressive tense. However, the Standard German forms are nominalizations. Thus, Deitsch developed a progressive tense in order to better match the English tense/aspect system, but the specific content of the progressive tense is based on German. Many of the changes that Deitsch has undergone in contact with English are changes that make it easier for speakers to switch back and forth between Deitsch and English.

12.7.4   Conclusion

The Kupwar and Deitsch cases show how language varieties can converge on similar patterns of meaning and structure when they remain in contact for an extended period. This can result in particular regional varieties (dialects) that are in some ways more like the neighboring variety of a different language than they are like other varieties of the same language. The development of convergent varieties allows speakers to switch from one language to another more directly, and it may be that the similarity of expression also allows children to acquire the multiple local languages more readily than they might learn two totally different (non-convergent) language varieties.

Practice

File 12.1—Language Contact

Exercises

1. Find ten words that English has recently borrowed from another language. One way to find lists of words that have recently been created or borrowed is by searching online for the word "neologisms."

    i. What language were the words you found borrowed from? Why do you think these words were borrowed?

    ii. Do you think the words are just a fad, or do you think they will become widely used?

    iii. Was it easy to find ten borrowed words? If not, describe how else English creates new words.

2. Go to the Links page for Chapter 12 and choose a language from the list. Find ten words that were recently borrowed from English into that language. Why do you think these words were borrowed? What topic do the words relate to?

3. If a group of English speakers came into contact with a group of speakers of language X, what words would you expect them to borrow from language X? Why? What words would you not expect them to borrow from language X? Why?

4. How can you identify whether a language is an adstratum language, a substratum language, or a superstratum language?

5. What is the difference between borrowing and native language influence?

Discussion Question

6. What languages are in contact in the area or in the country where you live? Are they in an adstratal or a substratal/superstratal relationship? Is there evidence of borrowing between the languages? How intense is the language contact? Are there bilingual speakers? What do you predict for the future development of the languages in contact?

File 12.2—Borrowings into English

Exercises

7. Consider what you know about the history of the speakers of a language other than English. What languages might you expect that language to have borrowed words from? Why?

8. The following is from the *Oxford English Dictionary's* (*OED's*)[1] etymological entry for *chocolate*:

> < French *chocolat,* Spanish *chocolate,* < Mexican *chocolatl* 'an article of food made of equal parts of the seeds of cacao and those of the tree called pochotl' [*Bombax ceiba*] Siméon *Dict. de langue Nahuatl.*

Dissect this definition. Show the history of this word, from its origins to the point in which it was borrowed into English. State the language of origin, as well as any intermediate languages.

9. The following is the *OED's* etymological entry for *apricot*:

> originally < Portuguese *albricoque* or Spanish *albaricoque,* but subseq. assimilated to the cognate French *abricot* (*t* mute). Compare also Italian *albercocca, albicocca,* Old Spanish *albarcoque,* < Spanish Arabic *al-borcoq(ue* (P. de Alcala) for Arabic *al-burqūq, -barqūq,* i.e. *al* the + *barqūq,* < Greek πραικόκιον (Dioscorides, *c*100; later Greek πρεκόκκια and βερικόκκια plural), probably < Latin *praecoquum,* variant of *praecox,* plural *praecocia,* 'early-ripe, ripe in summer,' an epithet and, in later writers, appellation of this fruit, originally called *prūnum* or *mālum Armeniacum.* Thus Pallad. (*c*350): 'armenia vel præcoqua.' The change in English < *abr-* to *apr-* was perhaps due to false etymology; Minsheu 1617 explained the name, quasi, 'in *aprīco coctus*' ripened in a sunny place: compare the spelling *abricoct.*

Dissect this rather densely worded definition. Show the history of this word, from its origins to the point in which it was borrowed into English. State the language of origin, as well as any intermediate languages.

Discussion Question

10. Many speakers of languages that borrow freely from English feel that their language is threatened by this "infiltration" of English words. The French even have an agency, the Académie Française, which tries to limit the borrowing of foreign words and promote the use of French words. Do you think that extensive borrowing is a threat to a language? Why or why not?

Activities

11. Using a good etymological dictionary, such as the *OED*, list the language that English **most recently borrowed** each of the following words from. (*Hint:* Look for the first language listed after a./ad., which stands for 'adapted from,' or "<")

   a. brandy   **d.** dinner   **g.** jaguar   **j.** sauna
   b. elephant **e.** jungle   **h.** tycoon   **k.** parka
   c. yam   **f.** ballot   **i.** robot   **1.** shampoo

12. Using a good etymological dictionary, such as the *OED*, list the language that each of the following words **originally** descends from. (In this case, you will have to read the whole entry.)

   a. tea   **c.** hurricane
   b. coach   **d.** admiral

---

[1]There is a link to the *OED* on the Links pages for Chapter 12.

13. Using a good etymological dictionary, such as the *OED,* answer the following questions about the English word *hippopotamus:*

    i. The word *hippopotamus* was adopted from Latin, but its origins lie in another language. What language does this word originally come from?

    ii. The *OED* entry shows how this word can be broken down into constituent parts. What morphological process is responsible for the formation of this word? What parts can this word can be broken down into? What do these words mean in English? (To answer these questions, you may want to refer to File 4.2.)

14. English has established itself as the current international language of commerce and scholarship. Many languages are currently borrowing words from English, especially in the areas of technology, computers, telecommunications, sports, and business. Pick two of these areas and write down ten words related to each. Then pick two foreign languages and find an online dictionary. Translate your words into your chosen languages and answer the following questions:

    i. Which of the words translated into each language seem to be borrowings from English? How, if at all, do they differ from the original English words (e.g., spelling and structure)?

    ii. Which of the languages you chose seems to borrow more from English? Which words of which topic are more widely borrowed?

    iii. Do some of the English words have more than one equivalent in the foreign languages you picked? Do all the translations seem to be borrowings, or do some seem to be native? Do you think speakers would prefer a native word or a borrowed word? Why?

File 12.3—Pidgin Languages

Exercises

15. How are creoles formed? How is this different from the way most children learn language? (See Chapter 8.)

16. The following data are taken from Tok Pisin, an English-based expanded pidgin. Which of the common features of pidgins mentioned in File 12.3 are found in these examples? Consider phonology, morphology, syntax, and semantics.

    a. kapa   bilong   pinga i waitpela
       lid/cap   belong   finger white
       'The fingernail is white/The fingernails are white'

    b. jumi   save   tok   pisin
       we   can   talk   pidgin
       'We can speak Tok Pisin'

    c. mi   laik   baim   sampela pis
       I   like   buy   some   fish
       'I want/would like to buy some fish'

    d. mi   dringim   liklik hap   wara
       *I   drink-*TRANS   *little   bit   water*
       'I drink a little water'

17. The following words are from Tok Pisin, an English-based expanded pidgin. Which English words are the Tok Pisin words derived from? In other words, how would they be translated literally into English? (*Hint:* Try saying the Tok Pisin words aloud.)

Tok Pisin	*English Translation*
a. taim bilong kol	'winter'
b. taim bilong san	'summer'
c. man bilong wokim gaden	'farmer'
d. kamap	'arrive'
e. tasol	'only'
f. haus sik	'hospital'
g. haus mani	'bank'
h. olgeta	'all'
i. sapos	'if'
j. solwara	'ocean'
k. kukim long paia	'barbeque'
l. handet yia	'century'
m. hamas krismas yu gat	'How old are you?'
n. hangre long dring	'thirsty'
o. pinga bilong fut	'toe'

18. Consider the Russenorsk, Norwegian, and Russian data below and answer the questions. Russenorsk is a pidgin derived through contact of Norwegian and Russian. (Data are adapted from Jahr 1996 and Broch and Jahr 1984.)

   i. Based on the example sentences given, which Russenorsk elements do you think derive from Russian and which from Norwegian?

   ii. Why do you think the Russenorsk phrase for *I shall die soon* is *I'll sleep on the church soon*?

   iii. Why do you think the Russenorsk word for *captain* is *principal*?

   a. Russenorsk: Moja kopom fiska
   Norwegian: jeg kjøper fish
   Russian: Ja pokupaju rybu
   Translation: 'I buy fish'

   b. Russenorsk: stari gammel, snart på kjæka slipom
   Norwegian: jeg er gammel, jeg skal dør snart
   Russian: Ja staryj. Ja skoro umru
   Translation: 'I'm old, I shall die soon'
   (literally: 'I'm old, I'll sleep on the church soon')

   c. Russenorsk: Moja vil spraek på principal
   Norwegian: Jeg vil taler med kapteinen
   Russian: Jaču pogovorit's kapitanom
   Translation: 'I want to speak with the captain.'

19. Consider the following pidgin texts from New South Wales in southeastern Australia (from *The present state of Australia,* 2nd edn., by Robert Dawson. London: Smith, Elder and Co., 1831). The texts are from 1826. Which aspects of the texts are similar to and which are different from today's English? How much can you understand?

He . . . declar[ed] that all the harbour and country adjoining belonged to him. "I tumble down pickaninny here. . . . Belonging to me all about, massa; pose you tit down here, I gib it to you." (p.12)

(cont.)

"You no pear, massa, black pellow no hit me." (p. 65)

"Nebber mind, you gib it letter, masa dat go plenty toon to-night—den take it boat when urokah jump up tomorrow." (p. 256)

"I know you, massa—I been tee you Port Tebid good while ago." (p. 258)

File 12.4—Creole Languages

Exercises

20. Consider the Belize Creole text below. It is the beginning of a story involving Anansi and Tiger. Which aspects of the text are similar to and which are different from English? How much of the text can you understand? (*Hint:* Try to read the text as if it were written in IPA, and listen to the recording online.)

> Wans apan a taim dier waz bra hanasi an bra taiga. So nou, ina kriol yu want a tel yu? Ina kriol? So nou de . . . wa maami tri mi de klos di haus. So nou . . . wan de . . . bra hanansi, yu no hou him triki aredi . . . i tel bra taiga mek dem go pik . . . maami. So nou bra taiga se "oke den les go," so . . . den gaan.

21. Consider the Hawaiian Creole English text below (*Hawai'i Tribune Herald* 1946). Which aspects of the text are similar to and which are different from English? How much of the text can you understand?

> Hukilepo, get many peoples on dees islan who stay tink me I outa be een som pupule hospeetal. But me I goin tell you something . . . One keiki been tell da udder one fo go buy ice cream fo dey eat up on top da bus. Den da udder one newa like go so he been say, "Poho money." Wasamala wid heem, he no can say "Me I stay broke?"

Discussion Questions

22. What is the difference between an expanded pidgin and a creole?

23. Discuss Bickerton's claim that the similarities found in the TMA marking of many creoles is due to a "bioprogram" in the human mind. Is his argument convincing? Why or why not?

File 12.5—Societal Multilingualism

Exercises

24. Consider the following dialogue that took place in Quebec (Heller 1982: 133). French is marked by *italics*. What do you think is going on in the dialogue? What does this tell you about language choice or language abilities?

Man:	Could you tell me where the French test is?
Receptionist:	*Pardon?* (Pardon?)
Man:	Could you tell me where the French test is?
Receptionist:	*En français?* (In French?)
Man:	I have the right to be addressed in English by the government of Quebec.
Receptionist:	*Qu'est-ce qu'il dit?* (What's he saying?)

25. Consider the following dialogue in Spanish and Galician (adapted from Auer 1995: 128). Spanish is marked by *italics*. What do you think is going on in the dialogue? What does this tell you about language choice or language abilities?

A: *Y, qué tal el nivel de la Universidad? Es alto no?*
R: *Si.*
A: *Y qué haces? Filología inglesa? O . . .*
R: Nom, e, lingüística . . . pero estou interessado no galego.
A: Ai, no galego. *Bueno y fuiste becado, becado para allá? O, o . . .*
R: Eh? Si, bueno ali estou tamém trabalhando na universidade e . . . despois derom-me umha beca pra vir aqui a Galiza.
R: Ai, pra vir a Galícia.

English Translation:
A: *And what about the standards of the universities? They are high, aren't they?*
R: *Yes.*
A: *And what what are you studying? English Philology? Or . . .*
R: No, uh, linguistics . . . but I'm interested in Galician.
A: Oh, in Galician. *So you went there with a scholarship? Or, or . . .*
R: Uh? Yes, well, there I'm also working at the university and . . . later they gave me a grant to come here to Galiza.
R: Oh, to come to Galicia.

Activity

26. Find an example of a multilingual society. Who uses which language(s)? In what context(s) and for what purpose(s) is each language used? How stable do you think these conventions are?

File 12.6—Language Endangerment and Language Death

Discussion Questions

27. Files 12.1 and 12.6 mention that many Native American languages in the United States have undergone the process of language death; that is, they are no longer spoken. In many regions of the world, there is an effort to prevent endangered languages from dying out or even to revive dormant languages. Do you think this is a worthwhile effort? Why? For your discussion, consider the following comments from people of the Miami tribe below:

Person: Rosa Boington Beck (1969)
Comment: But they never allowed them to talk Indian. They couldn't talk their Indian language out there. Everything had to be English. And sometimes I think that was kind of bad because it got them away from their Indian language, their own tongue you know. I think we ought to kind of had some of that left to us. But they didn't. They took it away from us.

Person: Daryl Baldwin (2003)
Comment: Because the language reflects traditional beliefs and values, it begins to bring many community elements back together. The language is truly the glue that holds us together in our thoughts and in our hearts.

Person: Scott Shoemaker (Harrison 1999)
Comment: The language is part of who we are. When you speak Miami, you think Miami. By learning the language, you learn about our ancestors' views of the world and their place in it.

(cont.)

Person: A writer for the tribal newspaper (2002)

Comment: Sometimes we [the Oklahoma tribal community] question, "Does anyone speak Miami?" Then we all point with confidence, at Daryl Baldwin, his family and those members who return year after year to the summer language program, and say 'Yes—we have members who speak Miami.'

28. Consider a minority language or minority dialect that is spoken in the area where you live. Do you think this language or dialect is endangered? Why? For your answer, think about the number of speakers the minority language or dialect has, what the prestige and power situation is, how much pressure to assimilate to the majority language exists, and so on.

File 12.7—Case Studies in Language Contact

Discussion Question

29. Both of the case studies given in this file had characteristics that are atypical of language contact situations (e.g., the lack of lexical borrowing among the languages in Kupwar, the borrowing of English basic vocabulary and morphology into Deitsch). Explain why these are atypical, and then give reasons why they might be happening in these particular contact situations.

Activity

30. Interview someone who speaks a language at home other than the majority language. Find out the following information from your language informant:

   i. How well do your informant and his or her family speak the minority and majority languages? This may differ for different members of the family.

   ii. Do you think the languages of your informant are in an adstratal or a substratal/superstratal relationship? Why do you think so?

  iii. Is the way your informant and his or her family speak the majority language affected by the language of the home? Consider pronunciation, grammar, vocabulary, and usage. How can you explain these effects? Consider the speakers' proficiency and the contact situation (adstratal versus substratal/superstratal).

  iv. Is the way your informant and his or her family speak the language of the home affected by the majority language? Again, consider pronunciation, grammar, vocabulary, and usage. How can you explain these effects? Consider the speakers' proficiency and the contact situation (adstratal versus substratal/superstratal).

Further Readings

Harrison, K. David. 2007. *When languages die: The extinction of the world's languages and the erosion of human knowledge.* Oxford: Oxford University Press.

Kastovsky, Dieter, and Arthur Mettinger. 2003. *Language contact in the history of English.* 2nd edn. New York: Peter Lang.

Thomason, Sarah G. 2001. *Language contact: An introduction.* Washington, DC: Georgetown University Press.

Tsunoda, Tasaku. 2006. *Language endangerment and language revitalization: An introduction.* Berlin: Mouton de Gruyter.

Velupillai, Viveka. 2015. *Pidgins, creoles and mixed languages: An introduction.* Amsterdam: John Benjamins.

Winford, Donald. 2003. *An introduction to contact linguistics.* Malden, MA: Wiley-Blackwell.

CHAPTER
13

Language Change

FILE 13.0

···

What Is Language Change?

All languages change through time, but how they change, what drives these changes, and what kinds of changes we can expect may not be obvious. By comparing different languages, different dialects of the same language, or different historical stages of the same language, we can discover the history of languages and language groups or **families.** We can also make hypotheses about the grammar, vocabulary, and pronunciation of a language long dead. This chapter considers the ways in which languages change and some of the factors that influence those changes.

Contents

FILE **13.1**
....

Introducing Language Change

13.1.1 Synchronic vs. Diachronic Linguistics

One of the biggest successes of linguistics has been the scientific investigation and understanding of language change for what it really is: an inescapable fact about natural human languages and not the result of moral corruption or intellectual deterioration of communities of speakers, as traditionally thought by many language "authorities." All languages change except for the ones that do not have any native speakers left (i.e., dead languages), such as Latin, Sanskrit, and Attic Greek—and when these languages did have native speakers, they changed, too.

When linguists describe the current phonological processes of a particular language, isolate that language's morphemes, or discover that language's syntactic rules, they analyze that language **synchronically**; that is, they analyze that language at a particular point in time.

Languages, however, are not static; they are constantly changing entities. For example, consider the English word *know*. Why is it spelled with a <k> at the beginning? Was this letter ever pronounced? If it was pronounced at some earlier stage of the language, when and why was it "dropped"? The <k> in English words like *know* is a linguistic fossil reflecting in its spelling an earlier stage of the pronunciation of the language, as we will see in the following files. Although most of what has been presented in this book so far has been synchronic linguistics, linguists can also study language development through time, providing **diachronic** ('across-time') analyses.

If it seems odd that languages would change, consider the ways in which languages are tied to other social factors. For example, think about the numerous types of variation that were discussed in Chapter 10: a single language may have different varieties tied to the regions, ages, genders, ethnicities, or social classes of its speakers. This variation contributes to language change in at least two ways. First, if any of those external factors changes, the language may change in tandem. Second, the large amount of variation present in a language means that there are more choices, as it were, for speakers to select from in forming an utterance. Speakers and hearers thus may not use or encounter the same linguistic structures every time they use language. This variation gives language the capacity for change, because its users must be flexible anyway.

Historical linguistics is concerned with language change. Historical linguists are interested in what kinds of changes occur and why, and, equally important, what kinds of changes don't occur and why not. They attempt to determine the changes that have occurred in a language's history and how languages relate to one another historically.

Historical linguistics as we know it began in the late eighteenth century, when Western European scholars began to notice some linguistic characteristics that were shared among ancient European and Asian languages, such as Latin, Greek, Gothic, Old Persian, and Sanskrit. These similarities led linguists to believe that these languages, and their modern descendants, must have evolved from a single ancestor language called **Proto-Indo-European (PIE)**. Thus, these languages form a single language **family**. Since then, we have discovered many other language families (see File 13.2).

13.1.2 How Does Language Change?

To see how English has changed over time, compare the following versions ((1) through (4)) of the Lord's Prayer from four major periods in the history of English. These passages are written in the standard spelling of the times they come from. While we know that spelling is not necessarily a good transcription system (see File 2.1), the writings here do give a fairly accurate sense of some of the changes that have occurred in English. (*Note:* The symbol <þ>, called *thorn*, is an Old English symbol for the voiceless interdental fricative [θ], as in *three*; <ð>, called *edh* (or *eth*), is the more familiar symbol for the voiced interdental fricative [ð], as in *then*.)

(1) **Old English** (text ca. 1100)
Fæder ure þu þe eart on heofonum, si þin nama gehalgod. Tobecume þin rice. Gewurþe þin willa on eorðan swa swa on heofonum. Urne gedæghwamlican hlaf syle us to dæg. And forgyf us ure gyltas, swa swa we forgyfað urum gyltedum. And ne gelæd þu us on costnunge ac alys us of yfele. Soþlice.

(2) **Middle English** (text ca. 1400)
Oure fadir that art in heuenes halowid be thi name, thi kyngdom come to, be thi wille don in erthe es in heuene, yeue to us this day oure bread ouir other substance, & foryeue to us oure dettis, as we forgeuen to oure dettouris, & lede us not in to temptacion: but delyuer us from yuel, amen.

(3) **Early Modern English** (text 1611)
Our father which art in heaven, hallowed be thy Name. Thy kingdome come. Thy will be done, in earth, as it is in heaven. Giue vs this day our dayly bread. And forgiue vs our debts, as we forgiue our debters. And leade vs not into temptation, but deliuer vs from euill. Amen.

(4) **Contemporary English** (text 1994)
Our Father, who is in heaven, may your name be kept holy. May your kingdom come into being. May your will be followed on earth, just as it is in heaven. Give us this day our food for the day. And forgive us our offenses, just as we forgive those who have offended us. And do not bring us to the test, but free us from evil. Amen.

As we can see, languages change in all aspects of the grammar: the phonology, morphology, syntax, and semantics. Subsequent files will describe the various types of language change in detail.

13.1.3 Why Does a Language Change?

If, as discussed above, languages such as Latin, Greek, English, and Sanskrit did in fact share a common ancestor, a reasonable question to ask is, why are they different languages? One of the causes of language change is the loss of homogeneity due to geographical division. No two people speak exactly the same way, let alone two groups of people (see File 10.1). This intrinsic variation between speakers is compounded by other external factors such as geographical or social barriers. As groups of people who had once spoken the same language spread out through Europe, they lost communication with each other, so that the language of each group went its own way, underwent its own changes, and thus came to differ from the others.

Another major cause of language change is language contact (see Chapter 12), with the effect that languages in contact with each other begin to show similarities. American English has borrowed many Spanish words from Spanish-speaking communities in California and the Southwest, for example, as well as from contact with Mexican and Cuban immigrants. Language contact does not, of course, explain why Proto-Indo-European subdivided as it did, but it does help to explain a number of shared characteristics—especially lexical items—among the world's languages. Language contact, like any other explanation for language change, does not provide a complete explanation, only a partial one.

At times, linguists cannot find any particular cause that would motivate a language to change in a particular direction. Language change, then, may simply just happen.

13.1.4 Is Language Change Bad?

Often people view such change as a bad thing, so they try to resist it. Jonathan Swift, the late-seventeenth-century satirist who wrote *Gulliver's Travels*, supported the movement among English grammarians to stipulate prescriptive rules that would have the effect of regulating current language usage as well as change. These grammarians based their rules on classical Latin from the first century B.C.E, viewing it as the perfect, model language, since it did not change. Even today, when we don't look to a language such as Latin as a model, some people consciously resist linguistic change. Consider the word *comprise*. Traditionally, the whole comprises, that is, 'takes in' or 'encompasses,' its parts as in:

(5)   A chess set comprises thirty-two pieces.

Increasingly, however, people say:

(6)   A chess set is comprised of thirty-two pieces.

in which the parts now comprise, that is, 'make up' or 'constitute,' the whole. Strict prescriptive grammarians regard this second utterance as ungrammatical because it is a change from the older use. Despite these social views toward change, linguists regard change as neither good nor bad; descriptively speaking, it is simply a fact of language.

As Chaucer wrote in the fourteenth century:

(7)   Ye knowe ek that in forme of speche is chaunge
       Withinne a thousand yeer, and wordes tho
       That hadden pris now wonder nyce and straunge
       Us thinketh hem, and yet thei spake hem so.
       And spedde as wele in love, as men now do.
       —Geoffrey Chaucer, *Troilus and Criseyde,* ca. 1385

       You know that even forms of speech can change
       Within a thousand years, and words we know
       Were useful once, seem to us wondrous strange—
       Foolish or forced—and yet men spoke them so.
       And they spoke of love as well as men now do.

Language Relatedness

13.2.1 Similarities across Languages

If you look at two different languages, you often find similarities between them in addition to the numerous differences. Why might this be the case? As it turns out, there are a number of reasons for two languages to have certain elements in common.

One reason is so basic that it seems rather obvious: languages are spoken by humans, and humans are anatomically similar. So the fact that many languages around the world make use of many of the same sounds in their phonological inventories is at least in part due to the similarity of the apparatus we all use to make those sounds. The sounds [p] and [a] occur in most languages of the world because they are some of the most basic sounds a human can make. The fact that these sounds recur does not tell us anything about the history of the languages with respect to each other (but see File 3.4 for more on implicational hierarchies in the sound systems of the world's languages).

Another reason two languages might look similar is that they have completely coincidentally hit upon similar ways of expressing the same meaning. In File 1.4, we said that language is arbitrary: that is, the sounds or gestures used to express particular thoughts are independent of the meanings of those thoughts. Though it is therefore quite rare that two languages would independently end up with words for the same concept that are similar phonetically, it does occasionally happen. For example, the Modern Greek word for *eye* is [mati], and the Malay word for *eye* is [mata]. These similarities are purely coincidental and independent: the two languages are not related to each other in any way, nor has there been any contact between them.

Yet another reason for two languages to have similar words for the same concepts is that, occasionally, language is **not** arbitrary; that is, there is an iconic connection between the form of the word and the meaning. This is the case with many onomatopoetic words: for example, the words in English, Arabic, and Mandarin for a clock ticking are [tıktɑk], [tıktık], and [tiʔtaʔ], respectively (see File 1.4). This is not coincidence; it is a consequence of the fact that clocks make a particular sound when they tick, and this sound is mimicked by speakers of each language.

In addition, languages may be similar to each other because of language contact, which was discussed in some detail in File 12.1. When two languages are in contact with each other, it is quite common for one language to borrow words from the other language. So, for example, Spanish has borrowed the words *alcalde* 'mayor' and *naranja* 'orange' from Arabic, and Taiwan Sign Language borrowed the "thumbs-up" sign meaning 'good' from British Sign Language. It is important to note that Spanish and Arabic are not related, and neither are Taiwan and British Sign Languages. These languages simply share some of the same vocabulary because they were in contact with each other.

The final main reason that languages can be similar to each other is that they may in fact be "genetically related" to each other.[1] That is, at one point, the two languages were the

---

[1]Note that this is not "genetically related" in the biological sense, but rather in the sense of "having to do with common origins."

same language—but over time, the language split into two different varieties, and each variety underwent enough changes that they can now be considered separate languages. This is known as the **relatedness hypothesis.**

It is important to realize, however, that there are many reasons that languages might be similar to each other, and you should never assume that just because two languages share some similar words, they must be related.

How, then, might we determine whether two languages are in fact related or simply similar for other reasons? First, we would want to see that there are a large number of correlations between form and meaning across the two languages. When the correlations are not confined to a few words and occur across the entire vocabulary, we minimize the chances of coincidence or onomatopoeia misleading our thinking. For example, if we looked at the Latin and the Basque words for 'peace,' shown in (1), we might think that they are similar.

(1) Latin: [paːkɛm]
     Basque: [bake]
              'peace'

Both words start with a bilabial stop, followed by the vowel [a] and a voiceless velar stop, and they mean the same thing. Also, there is not any obvious use of onomatopoeia here: what is the sound of 'peace,' after all? Could the languages be related?

To find out, we would first try to gather other words in the two languages to see whether these similarities are widespread. What do the data in (2) tell you?

(2) Latin: [uːnus]   [treːs]   [aʊrɪs]   [soror]
     Basque: [bat]   [iɾu]   [belari]   [aispa]
              'one'   'three'   'ear'   'sister'

Based on the words in (2), we would not be tempted to think that Latin and Basque are related. As it turns out, there are far more words that seem to be dissimilar than similar in the two languages, which indicates that they are not genetically related—the similarity between the two words for 'peace' in (1) must be due either to borrowing or to coincidence.

Another good indicator of whether two languages are related is the type of words that correlate across the two languages. That is, even finding a lot of words that seem to have similar form-meaning mappings still doesn't mean that the two languages are necessarily related. Sometimes, one language borrows so heavily from another language that their vocabularies overlap to a high degree.

Fortunately for linguists, some words tend not to be borrowed, as was discussed in File 12.1. In that file, we explained how both core vocabulary items and grammatical function words usually are not borrowed, because languages tend to already have them, and so there is no need to borrow terms from another language. So even though core vocabulary or function words can sometimes be borrowed, most borrowings are words for things that a culture does not already have.

This fact about borrowings is useful for linguists because it can help tease apart languages that are actually related from languages that have simply been in intensive contact with each other. When two languages share many form-meaning mappings across their vocabularies, particularly in the areas of core vocabulary and grammatical function words, it is generally the case that the two languages are genetically related to each other—that is, derived from a common source. In addition, we can be more confident that languages are related if the differences between them, especially in the words with similar forms and meanings (called **cognates**), are systematic and seem to be the result of language change, as discussed in the rest of this chapter. The rest of this file discusses some of the ways that language relatedness can be modeled, given what linguists have discovered about the language families of the world. We will discuss more about discovering **how** languages are related in File 13.7.

13.2.2 Models of Language Relatedness

The notion that similar languages are related and descended from an earlier, common language (a **protolanguage**) goes back to the late eighteenth century when Sir William Jones suggested that the linguistic similarities of Sanskrit (an important ancient language of India) to Ancient Greek and Latin could best be accounted for by assuming that all three were descended from a common ancestral language. This language was called Proto-Indo-European.

Jones's suggestion was developed in the nineteenth century and gradually came under the influence of Darwin's theory of the evolution of species. Scholars at the time considered language and linguistic development to be analogous in many ways to biological phenomena. Thus, it was suggested that languages, like other living organisms, had "family trees" and "ancestors." A "genealogical tree" for the Indo-European family of languages appears in (3).

(3)   Indo-European family tree

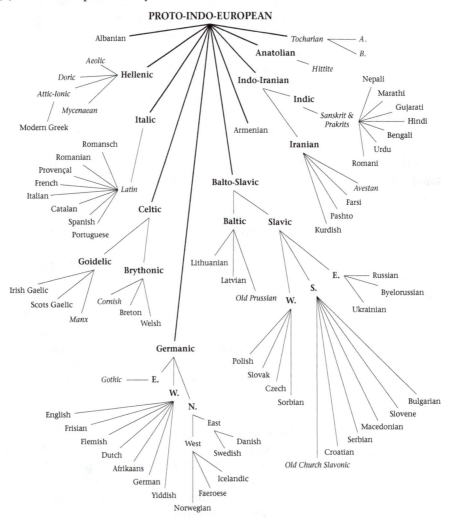

Languages that are no longer spoken are italicized (*Cornish*), and significant subbranches are in boldface (**Baltic**).

The **family tree theory,** as formulated by August Schleicher in 1871, assumes that speech sounds change in regular, recognizable ways (the **regularity hypothesis**; see Section 13.3.3), and that because of this, phonological similarities among languages may be due to a genetic relationship among those languages.

In keeping with the analogy of language relationships to human families, the theory makes use of the terms *mother* (or *parent*), *daughter,* and *sister* languages. In the family tree of Proto-Indo-European, for example, French and Spanish are sisters, and both are daughters of Latin, Germanic is the mother of English, and so on. The model clearly shows the direction of change and the relations among languages, the older stages of the languages being located fewer nodes from the top of the tree and direct descendants being linked to their ancestors through the straight lines or "branches."

Of course, family tree models can be created for any group of related languages, not just Indo-European languages. Current linguistic research has traced most of the world's languages back to a certain number of language families that are essentially independent of each other. According to SIL International's publication *Ethnologue,* there are 141 language families (e.g., Indo-European, Sino-Tibetan, Niger-Congo, Uralic, etc.) along with 137 signed languages, 88 creoles, 13 pidgins, 21 mixed languages, 75 language "isolates" that do not seem to be related to anything, and 51 unclassified languages. As you can see in the tree model for Indo-European in (3), most families can be broken down into smaller subbranches of even more closely related languages. These relationships may be somewhat familiar to you because we have made reference to them throughout the book when presenting data from various languages. For example, in the phonology exercises, we might tell you that Russian is an Indo-European language (the family) of the Slavic branch (the smaller branch of the main family), or that Bukusu is a Niger-Congo language of the Bantu branch. To illustrate another language family, (4) gives the family tree of the Uralic family. Most of the Uralic languages are spoken in northern and eastern Europe: in Finland, Sweden, Estonia, Russia, and Hungary. Although many are in close contact with Indo-European languages such as Swedish or Russian, the Uralic languages seem to be unrelated to the Indo-European languages.

However, there is a disadvantage to this model in that the structure of the family tree may lead to two misconceptions about language change: first, that each language forms a uniform speech community without internal variation and without contact with its neighbor languages, and second, that the split of a parent language into its daughter languages is a sudden or abrupt occurrence, happening without intermediate stages.

These two views are not supported by the linguistic evidence we have from modern languages. No language is uniform or isolated from others. Rather, a language is always made up of dialects that are still recognized as belonging to the same language (see Chapter 10 on language variation), and a language always shares similarities with other languages in its family, even those belonging to a different subgroup. Furthermore, studies of modern language change have shown that languages do not split apart abruptly, but rather drift apart very gradually, starting as dialects and ending up as separate languages only after years of accumulated change. In fact, the dividing point between two "dialects" and two "languages" is usually impossible to locate exactly and is often obscured by nonlinguistic (e.g., political, social, or geographic) factors. In addition, languages often become more similar due to language contact. In some cases, this is as simple as speakers borrowing words from speakers of another language, but in other cases the changes caused by language contact are more profound (see File 12.1 for the outcomes of language contact). Thus, there are a number of changes that can spread across the branches depicted in tree diagrams or that don't map neatly onto single, separate lines.

(4)   Uralic family tree

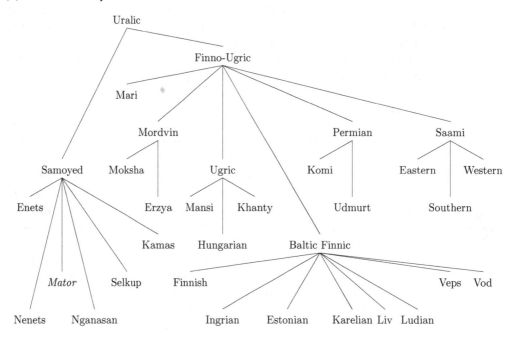

To supplement the family tree model and help overcome these difficulties, Johannes Schmidt in 1872 proposed the **wave theory,** which represents language relationships in a different manner. This theory recognizes the gradual spread of change throughout a dialect, language, or group of languages, much as a wave expands on the surface of a pond from the point where a pebble (representing the source of the sound change) has been tossed in. Dialects are formed by the spread of different changes from different starting points and at different rates; some changes reinforce the area of existing changes while others only partially overlap or affect only a certain area, much as the waves formed by a scattering of pebbles thrown into a pond may partially overlap. These changes can either bring branches of language families closer together or push them farther apart.

The diagram in (5) illustrates how part of the same Indo-European family shown in the tree diagram in (3) might be modeled as a wave diagram. In (5), the traditional genetic subgroups of languages that you might find on a tree diagram are enclosed in solid lines, while "diffusion" groups (those that have become more similar over time through the sharing of particular historical changes, despite being considered separate genetic subgroups at the time of their mutual influences) are enclosed in dashed lines, cutting across the traditional categories of the family tree. These groupings show similarities between languages that are on separate branches in (3). By looking at ever-smaller linguistic changes, one can also show the languages within each group and the dialects within each language, indicating clearly how variable languages can be. In this way, the wave diagram avoids the two faults of the family tree model, though it in turn suffers from disadvantages relating to problems in analyzing the genetic history of the languages involved.

(5)   Indo-European wave diagram

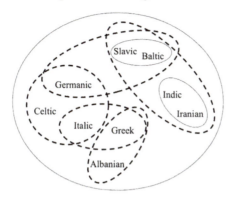

In fact, neither the family tree model nor the wave model presents an entirely adequate or accurate account of language change or the relatedness of languages, although each model accurately presents certain aspects of language relatedness and therefore provides a useful framework for the discussion of language change. It is important to remember, however, that languages can show linguistic similarities without necessarily being related. The similarities may be the result of borrowing in situations of language contact, language drift (i.e., independent but identical changes in distinct dialects or languages), similarities in types of morphological structures, syntactic similarities, or other reasons.

FILE 13.3

····················

Sound Change

13.3.1 What Is Sound Change?

Sound change is the most widely studied aspect of language change. There are a number of reasons why this is so. First, the study of how the sounds of languages change has a long tradition behind it, more so than any other area of historical linguistics. As a result we are more informed about this particular area of language change than other areas. Second, it is often impossible to understand changes in other areas of the language system without studying sound change, because sound change does not affect just the system of sounds of a language but may also affect a language's morphology, syntax, and semantics.[1] Third, the study of sound change has provided a basis for the study of language relationships and the reconstruction of parent (proto-) languages, which will be discussed in File 13.7.

Sound change is an alteration in the phonetics (Chapter 2) of a sound as a result of a phonological process (Chapter 3). If a phonological process is introduced into a language where it did not formerly occur, it may result in a sound change. For example, at an early period in the history of English the voiceless velar stop [k] occurred before the long front vowel [iː] in words like *cidan* 'chide' [kiːdan]. Later in the Old English period the velar consonant [k] was palatalized to [ʧ] before the front vowel [iː]. The introduction of the phonological process of palatalization resulted in the sound change [k] > [ʧ] before [iː] in Old English.[2] The phonetic shape of [k] (the voiceless velar stop) was altered to [ʧ] (a voiceless post-alveolar affricate) as a result of the phonological process of palatalization.

At this point, it is necessary to make the distinction between the introduction of a phonological process and sound change clearly understood. The introduction of a phonological process into a language alone cannot be considered sound change. While it is a necessary first step in the process of sound change, the introduction of a phonological process at first changes the structure of a word in certain specific speech contexts. For example, the basic pronunciation of the word *accidentally* is [æksɪdɛntəli], and this pronunciation occurs most often in formal speech situations, for example, when talking with business associates. When we speak with close friends in a casual situation, however, we may allow the phonological process that deletes schwa [ə] before the liquids [ɹ] and [l] to apply and pronounce the word as [æksɪdɛntli]. But we cannot assume that there has been a sound change

---

[1]For example, nouns in Latin were morphologically marked to indicate their grammatical roles (subject, object, etc.). This marking allowed Latin to have relatively free word order, because each word's role was marked, regardless of where it appeared in the sentence. However, many of the markers of grammatical roles eventually disappeared through sound changes. As a result, the nouns themselves did not have any overt indication of their grammatical roles anymore. This meant that Latin had to develop another way of indicating the roles; instead of having morphemes marking them, word order was used. So, for example, the subject always came first, the verb second, and the object third, an order that had not been required before. In this way, sound changes led to morphological and then syntactic changes!

[2]*Note:* As you may have already noticed, when writing sound change rules, it is traditional to use a "greater than" sign, >, pointing from the earlier sound to its later outcome.

538

of [ə] > Ø before liquids on the basis that a phonological process has been applied in casual speech. For sound change to occur, the basic form of a word must be permanently altered in all contexts In the example above, speakers would have to choose the variant pronunciation of *accidentally* [æksɪdɛntli] in all speech situations and abandon the pronunciation [æksɪdɛntəli] altogether. Thus sound change is closely related to, and stems from, phonetic and phonological variation. We can say that the change has occurred when speakers no longer have a choice between variants, because one of them has taken over.

Obviously this has not happened (yet!) in the case of *accidentally*, though it did happen in the Old English example discussed above. Recall that the introduction of palatalization resulted in alternate pronunciations for the word *cidan* 'chide' [kiːdan] and [ʧiːdan]. When the pronunciation [ʧiːdan] was first introduced into Old English, it was no doubt tied to certain speech situations, much as the pronunciation [æksɪdɛntli] is in Modern English. Gradually, however, over a considerable period of time, the pronunciation [ʧiːdan] was adopted by Old English speakers and the pronunciation [kiːdan] was abandoned. In this way the basic form of the word was permanently altered in Old English to [ʧiːdan]. Thus the introduction of the palatalization process resulted ultimately in the sound change [k] > [ʧ] before [iː].

13.3.2 Phonetic vs. Phonological Change

When we speak of sound change, it is often helpful to make a distinction between **phonetic** and **phonological** change. Phonetic change refers to a change in pronunciation of an allophone that has no effect on the phonological system of the language. For example, over the course of time, the English phoneme /r/ has undergone several changes. Early in the history of English the unrestricted ("elsewhere") allophone of the phoneme /r/ was pronounced as a trill, [r] (as it still is in Scottish English). At present, however, in American English at least, the unrestricted allophone of /r/ is pronounced as an alveolar retroflex liquid [ɹ]. This is a phonetic change because it affects only the **pronunciation** of words with /r/: all of them still have the phoneme /r/ in the same phonological distribution. That is, it is not the case that one dialect has developed a phonemic contrast between, for example, /ɹ/ and /r/; all of the dialects have the same phonemes but with different phonetic realizations.

A phonological change, on the other hand, changes the phonological system in some way, by the addition or loss of a phoneme or by a change in the distribution of allophones. In the Middle English period, voiceless stops were not aspirated in initial position. There was only one allophone for each of the three stop phonemes: /p/-[p], /t/-[t], /k/-[k]. Then these sounds underwent a sound change whereby stop consonants became aspirated initially before a stressed vowel. There are two aspects of this sound change. First, there is a phonetic change regarding the pronunciation of the voiceless stops in this position. But there is also a phonological change: the addition of a new allophone to each phoneme; /p/ has the allophones [p] and [pʰ], /t/ has the allophones [t] and [tʰ], and /k/ has the allophones [k] and [kʰ].

In addition, sound change can change the phonological system of a language more profoundly by the addition or loss of a phoneme. In Old English the phoneme /f/ had one allophone, [f], until about 700 C.E., and there was no separate phoneme /v/. Then a change occurred whereby [f] was voiced when it occurred between voiced sounds, for example, Old English *wives* [wiːvas]. At this time the sound change merely created an additional allophone for the phoneme /f/, namely, [v]. Later borrowings from French into English, however, in addition to other changes, created situations in which the two sounds came into contrast with one another, e.g., *safe* [seɪf] and *save* [seɪv]. As a result, we must now consider these two sounds to be members of separate phonemes—/f/-[f] and /v/-[v], respectively. Thus, the original sound change [f] > [v] ultimately led to the creation of a new phoneme, /v/.

13.3.3 The Regularity of Sound Change

One of the most fascinating aspects of sound change that emerges after studying a particular change over a long enough period of time is that it will almost always turn out to be completely regular; that is, every instance of the sound in question will undergo the change. Thus, in our Old English example we would say that the sound change [k] > [tʃ] before [iː] is **regular** because in every Old English word that contained [k] before [iː], the [k] changed to [tʃ]; the change was not isolated to the word for 'chide.'

Sound change does not spread to all possible words instantaneously, nor does every speaker in a community pick up a sound change overnight. The acceptance of sound change in a community is a gradual process, spreading, often rapidly, from word to word, or word-class to word-class, and from one speaker to the next until all possible words and speakers are affected. You may recall, from the language variation files in Chapter 10, that a particular pronunciation may be associated with one group or another in a speech community, and that this may be correlated with region, social class, age, ethnicity, and so on. One way to conceive of the dynamic spread of sound change is as spread across socially based varieties.

Though sound change spreads gradually, the ultimate regularity of sound change can be verified quite easily. In Old English, for example, the ancestor of our Modern English word *house* was spelled *hus* and pronounced [huːs]. If we compare these two words, we observe a change in the quality of the vowel. In Old English, the vowel was the long high back rounded vowel [uː], while in Modern English the vowel is a diphthong, [aʊ]. What is important is that this is not the only example of the sound change [uː] > [aʊ] in the history of English. In fact we can find any number of Old English words with [uː] that are pronounced with the diphthong [aʊ] in Modern English, for example, Old English *mus* [muːs] > Modern English *mouse* [maʊs]; Old English *lus* [luːs] > Modern English *louse* [laʊs]; Old English *ut* [uːt] > Modern English *out* [aʊt]; and so on. This change is only one of many regular sound changes in the history of English.

It is possible, although rare, that a sound change will not be regular, even after a long time has passed, because it did not finish spreading. A change might spread through some or many words, word classes, or social varieties and then stop before spreading to all of them. This usually occurs for social reasons and is fairly rare; sound change is overwhelmingly regular. In fact, it is the assumption that sound change is regular that has allowed historical linguists to reconstruct ancestor languages and language families, as is discussed in File 13.7.

There are, however, some types of sound change that are not always regular. Dissimilation, insertion, and metathesis, discussed in the following section, are only sometimes regular.

13.3.4 Types of Sound Change

The development of Old English [uː] is an example of **unconditioned sound change.** That is, every instance of [uː], no matter where it occurred in a word or what sounds were next to it, became [aʊ].

More often than not, however, sounds are influenced by the sounds that occur around them. When a sound changes because of the influence of a neighboring sound, the change is called a **conditioned sound change.** We have already considered a good example of a conditioned sound change from the history of English, namely, the palatalization of [k] before the front vowel [iː]. Notice that the only voiceless velar stops that were palatalized were those occurring before the vowel [iː]; all other velar stops remain nonpalatal. Evidence of this is Old English *ku* [kuː], corresponding to Modern English *cow* [kaʊ]. In this case, although the vowel changed by the [uː] > [aʊ] change just discussed, the consonant was not palatalized because it did not occur before [iː]. Only [k] conditioned by a following [iː] underwent the change.[3]

One of the ways to determine whether a sound change is conditioned or not is to see if it applies only when a sound appears in particular environments (conditioned) or if it applies wherever that sound appears (unconditioned). For example, if you can write a rule to describe the sound change in the form that we saw in File 3.3 on phonological rules, X > Y / C __ D, then the sound change must be conditioned: X becomes Y only when it comes after C and before D. If, on the other hand, your rule simply looks like X > Y, then you have an unconditioned sound change.

Below we discuss several types of sound changes that are particularly common in the world's languages. For each type, we give an example or two of changes that have happened in English. Note that the first two, assimilation and dissimilation, are by definition conditioned sound changes: they both involve sounds becoming more like or less like the sounds that are near them. The other changes can occur as either conditioned changes or unconditioned changes; for each example we give, we indicate whether it is conditioned or not. Some of the terms may be familiar from Chapter 3; see File 3.3 in particular. Keep in mind the difference between a phonological rule and a sound change, though.

a. Assimilation refers to a situation in which one sound becomes more like another sound. In Old English, voiceless fricatives became voiced when they occurred between voiced sounds; for example, the Old English word for 'wolves,' *wulfas* [wulfas], came to be pronounced [wulvas] in Middle English. That is, the voiceless fricative assimilated to the surrounding sounds by becoming voiced. This is how modern English comes to have an alternation between [f] and [v] in the singular *wolf* versus the plural *wolves*.

b. Dissimilation refers to a situation in which two similar sounds become less like one another. The English word *fifth* [fɪfθ], which ends with two consecutive voiceless fricatives [f] and [θ], has undergone a dissimilating sound change in some varieties whereby the second fricative has been replaced by a voiceless stop [t], giving the pronunciation [fɪft].

It is interesting (and important) to observe that in varieties where this change occurred, we talk about a **diachronic** sound change ([θ] > [t] / [f] __ #), but if we compare a changed variety to a variety of English that has not undergone this change, we can see **synchronic** variation within English ([fɪfθ] in some varieties, [fɪft] in others). Consider this distinction with respect to the other examples as well. It is important to note that this change is not (yet) regular.

c. Deletion occurs when a sound is no longer pronounced. At the end of the Middle English period unstressed word-final [ə] was deleted, for example, Middle English *nose* [nɔːzə] > Modern English *nose* [noʊz]. In this case, spelling has remained the same, yet a sound change has taken place. This is an example of a conditioned sound change because only word-final [ə] was deleted, not [ə] in all environments.

d. Insertion is the opposite of deletion and occurs when a sound is added to the pronunciation of a word. In a considerable number of Modern English varieties, the word *athlete* is pronounced [æθəlit]. In this word a sound change has taken place, inserting [ə] between the consonants of a cluster that was perceived to be difficult to pronounce. The older form of the word, still common in varieties that have not undergone this change, is [æθlit]. This, too, is an example of a conditioned sound change: [ə] is inserted only between [θ] and [l], not in between every two segments.

e. Monophthongization refers to a change from a diphthong (a complex vowel sound consisting of two vowel sounds) to a simple vowel sound, a monophthong. A good example

---

[3]It is important to focus on the phonetics here, as in all discussions of sound change, rather than the spelling, because even though the spelling has changed from <k> to <c>, this does not necessarily imply a change in pronunciation.

of unconditioned monophthongization occurred at the beginning of the Modern English period. In Middle English the diphthong [aʊ] occurred in words such as *law, taught, laundry, claw, daughter,* and so forth. In Modern English this diphthong became a simple vowel [ɔ] (or [ɑ]; see File 2.3); this change is apparent in the modern pronunciations for these words: *law* [lɔ], *taught* [tɔt], *laundry* [lɔndɹi], *claw* [klɔ], *daughter* [dɔɾɹ]. This is an unconditioned change because **all** instances of Middle English [aʊ] have changed to [ɔ] (or [ɑ]).

f. Diphthongization is the opposite of monophthongization; it refers to a change from a simple vowel sound to a complex one. In the Middle English period the long high front vowel [iː] became a diphthong [aɪ]; for example, Middle English *is* [iːs] became Modern English *ice* [aɪs]. This is parallel in many ways to the diphthongizing change discussed earlier of [uː] > [aʊ], seen in Old English *hus* [huːs] > Modern English *house* [haʊs]. This, too, was an unconditioned sound change, as all instances of [iː] were affected.

g. Metathesis refers to a change in the order of sounds. For example, the Old English words *hros, frist, thridde,* and *bridd* became Modern English *horse, first, third,* and *bird,* respectively: in these words, a consonant-/r/-vowel-consonant sequence changed to a consonant-vowel-/r/-consonant sequence, with the vowel and /r/ sounds switching places. This is a conditioned sound change; it is not just any /r/-vowel sequence that metathesized, but rather only those both preceded and followed by a consonant. So, for example, *rude* and *brew* did not undergo this change.

h. Raising and **lowering** refer to changes in the height of the tongue in the production of vowels. At the beginning of the Middle English period the word *noon* was pronounced [noːn], with a long mid back round vowel. By the end of the Middle English period, however, the word was pronounced [nuːn], with the tongue height raised from mid to high. Thus the sound change [oː] > [uː] is called *raising*. Though raising is often conditioned by surrounding segments, such as neighboring higher or lower vowels, this particular change was unconditioned in English.

i. Backing and **fronting** refer to alterations in the frontness or backness of the tongue in the production of vowels. At the beginning of the Modern English period there was an unconditioned sound change whereby the back vowel [ɑ] became the front vowel [æ], for example, in words like *calf, path, glass, past, ask.*

Morphological Change

13.4.1 What Is Morphological Change?

Consider the early modern past tense of the verb *climb*. As recently as several hundred years ago, the usual past tense of this verb was *clomb* ([klom]). In Modern English, on the other hand, the past tense is *climbed* ([klɑɪmd]). Thus, over the course of the past few centuries, *climbed* has replaced *clomb* as the past tense of *climb*. This is an example of morphological change, where the morphological structure of the word has changed. Other morphological changes can include the introduction of new words or morphological processes.

As with sound change, the new forms introduced by morphological changes and new word formation processes do not necessarily take hold instantaneously. Most often, there is a period of competition between the old form and the new one. This helps to explain some of the fluctuation evident in Modern English past tense formations, for example, in which some people say *fit* and others say *fitted*, or some say *lit* and others say *lighted*, and so on. Thus the processes of morphological change are often at the heart of synchronic variation, which is evident in all languages.

Unlike sound change, however, morphological change does not necessarily apply regularly in the system: changes can apply to individual words or end up not being accepted by speakers. One particularly interesting aspect of word formation is that it is sometimes rather analogous to fads and fashion in that new items are introduced in particular groups or communities, and these may or may not spread and become popular in the wider population of consumers (in this case, language users). For example, there was a time in recent American popular usage when the suffix *-age* (as in established lexical items like *mileage* and *roughage*) was applied productively to roots from several part-of-speech classes to form new nouns meaning 'some unspecified amount of (root),' for example, *beerage* 'some amount of beer,' *spoilage* 'some amount of spoiled material,' *tun(e)age* 'some amount of music (tunes),' and so on. These words are/were acceptable on a socially and perhaps regionally limited basis; that is, they are not equally known to or used by all speakers of English.

13.4.2 Proportional Analogy and Paradigm Leveling

It should not have escaped your notice that the new form of the past tense of *climb* discussed above is exactly what would be expected as the regular past tense of an English verb, that is, [-d] after a voiced consonant (compare *rhyme* [ɹɑɪm] : *rhymed* [ɹɑɪm-d]). In terms of the formation of the past tense, *clomb* is an irregularity because past tense in English is not generally formed by altering the vowel of the base. Thus, it appears that the irregular past tense form (*clomb*) has given way to a past tense form made with the productive, regular past tense morpheme, *-ed*. In a sense, then, we can talk about the change as being one that brought *climb* more in line with the majority of verbs of English, and that these verbs—and in particular the productive pattern of forming the past tense with these verbs—exerted some influence on *climb*.

This example provides us with some insight into the nature of morphological change: it often involves the influence of one form or group of forms over another. This influence of one form or set of forms over another is called **analogy** (or **analogical change**). In the case of *clomb → climbed,* the influence of the regular past tense forms led to the change. This type of morphological change can often be schematized as a four-part proportion, as in (1).

(1)   a   :   b   ::   c   :   X
       Read: "*a*   is to   *b*   as   *c*   is to   *X*"

The proportion is complete when you "solve for X" and find something that bears the same relationship to *c* that *b* bears to *a*. This four-part proportion applied to the past tense of *climb* gives the following:

(2)   rhyme   :   rhym + ed   ::   climb   :   X = climb + ed

You don't have to be a mathematician to solve for X and get *climbed*. The word *rhyme* was chosen here only as an example; it is perhaps more accurate to state the proportion in terms of a general pattern that is extended to another verb.

(3)   VERB   :   VERB + ed   ::   climb   :   climb + ed
      (present)   (past)   (present)   (past)

Since this type of morphological change can be schematized as a four-part proportion, it is generally known as **proportional analogy.**

As with *clomb → climbed,* analogical change generally introduces regularity into a system, often by reducing the number of allomorphs. For example, in the early stages of Latin, the **paradigm** (a set of inflectionally related forms) for the word for 'honor' included the following forms:

(4)   Nominative   honos
      Genitive   honos-is
      Accusative   honos-em

This paradigm was perfectly regular in that there was just a single form of the stem *honos-* to which the inflectional endings were added. Somewhat later in the development of Latin, a sound change took place by which [s] became [r] between vowels (likely with an intermediate stage of [z]); this was regular and affected all instances of intervocalic [s] in that language. The effect on the paradigm of the word for 'honor' was to create two different forms of the stem: *honos-* in the nominative and *honor-* in the other cases (because the [s] was intervocalic in those but final in the nominative).

(5)   Nominative   honos
      Genitive   honor-is
      Accusative   honor-em

The resulting paradigm was thus irregular in its having two stem shapes. Later on in Latin, a further change took place creating a regular paradigm once more: the nominative took the form *honor,* giving:

(6)   Nominative   honor
      Genitive   honor-is
      Accusative   honor-em

This last change was not a widespread one, and there are many instances of final [s] in Latin that did not change to [r] (e.g., *genus* 'kind,' *navis* 'ship,' etc.). This change is therefore different from sound change; only one word paradigm was affected.

Note that this morphological change has a result similar to that in the first example, namely, introducing regularity. This change introduced regularity into a paradigm that had been disturbed by sound change. This type of analogical change, which takes place within a paradigm, is often called **paradigm leveling.** The motivation is the same as with the form-class type of analogy (proportional analogy) seen with *clomb → climbed*; that is, it eliminates irregularity among morphologically related forms.

The two analogical changes discussed above involve the elimination of irregularities in the morphological subsystem of a language. While regularity is perhaps the most notable result of analogical change, it is not, however, the only outcome. There are other analogical changes that have little, if anything, to do with regularization. We turn now to a brief discussion of these changes.

13.4.3 Back Formation and Folk Etymology

The process of **back formation** can be illustrated by the following examples:

(7) a. work + er   :   work   ::   burglar   :   X = burgle
       (agent noun)   (verb)   (agent noun)   (verb)

    b. operat + ion   :   operate   ::   orientation   :   X = orientate
       (noun)   (verb)   (noun)   (verb)

As you may have noticed, the process of back formation appears to be similar to the process of proportional analogy. However, the fundamental difference becomes apparent upon closer inspection. Back formation involves the creation of a new stem form (e.g., *burgle*), whereas proportional analogy involves the creation of a new inflected or derived form.

Another difference between back formation and proportional analogy is the fact that back formation is often preceded by reanalysis. The first example of back formation cited above is a case in point. English speakers borrowed *burglar* from Norman French speakers as a monomorphemic word; at this time there was no word *burgle* in English. But *burglar* was reanalyzed by English speakers as consisting of a verb *burgle* plus an affix *-er* because its phonological structure and its meaning resembled the set of English words that had been formed by such a process, for example, *worker, runner,* and so on. As a result, the identification of *burglar* with this pattern of word formation, namely, verb + *-er* → agent noun, resulted in the creation of a new verb, *burgle.*

As we saw from the preceding discussion, the primary motivation for the back formation of *burgle* from *burglar* was the common derivational process verb + *-er* → agent noun. Interestingly, the influence of productive inflectional processes can also result in back formations. Consider the case of Modern English *cherry—cherries*. This word was borrowed from Norman French *cherise*. Note, however, that this word was a singular, not a plural, noun for French speakers. But to English speakers this noun sounded like a plural since it appeared to follow the regular pattern for the formation of plural nouns. As a result, the word *cherise* was reanalyzed as a plural, and a new singular noun was back-formed, namely, *cherry.*

As a final example of analogical change, we consider the process known as **folk etymology.** As we saw from the example of back formation discussed above, reanalysis played an important role as a motivating factor for the creation of the verb *burgle.* Similarly, the driving force behind the process of folk etymology is also reanalysis. In the case of folk etymology, however, obscure morphemes are reanalyzed in terms of more familiar morphemes. As an example of folk etymology consider the following case taken from an article in a university student newspaper. In this article the author referred to a variety of snake known as the garter snake as a "garden snake." In this example, the word *garden* has been substituted for the word *garter*. There were probably a number of reasons for the reanalysis of *garter* as *garden*. Foremost among them was undoubtedly the fact that the two words are very similar phonologically, differing significantly only in the manner of articulation of the final consonant. Moreover, from the point of view of semantics it is not very clear to most English speakers why the word *garter* should be used to describe the stripes that are found on most varieties of garter snakes, particularly since the noun *garter* refers most commonly to an elasticized band worn around the leg to support hose. The final factor contributing to this reanalysis was undoubtedly the fact that, at least in urban areas, garter snakes are commonly found in and around gardens.

The case of folk etymology just discussed illustrates an important point about this analogical process: it occurs most often in cases where the morphological makeup of a word is obscure to speakers. There are a variety of reasons for morphological obscurity. One reason is illustrated by the Old English word *brydeguma*, Modern English *bridegroom*. The morphological makeup of this word ('bride-man' in Old English) was obscured by the fact that *guma* 'man' ceased to exist as an independent word in English. In order to make this word more accessible in terms of its structure, English speakers substituted the word *groom*. Note again that, as was the case with the substitution of *garden* for *garter*, the substitution of *groom* is motivated by phonological similarity (*guma* and *groom* sound a lot alike) and a semantic relationship (a *groom* is also a man, more specifically a serving-man or a man who attends to others). Further examples of folk etymology are given in (8).

(8)	*Folk Etymology*		*Source Phrase or Word*
	sick-as-hell anemia	<	sickle-cell anemia
	old-timer's disease	<	Alzheimer's Disease
	nephew-tism	<	nepotism
	sparrow-grass	<	asparagus
	chaise lounge	<	chaise longue

Proportional analogy and paradigm leveling are characterized by the elimination of irregularities from the morphological subsystem of a language. Back formation and folk etymology, on the other hand, involve the reanalysis of unfamiliar morphemes in ways that make them more accessible to speakers. Nevertheless, the four varieties of analogical change that we have discussed are characterized by the fact that they involve the influence of one particular form or set of forms over another.

13.4.4   Adding New Words to a Language

One other way that languages can change morphologically is by the addition of new words to their vocabularies. Of course, words are often borrowed from other languages (see File 12.2 for borrowings in English), but there are also other ways in which new words come into a language, and many of these processes occur not only in English but also in many of the world's languages. Here we will look at some of these new-word formation processes. Processes of derivational morphology discussed in Chapter 4 are also relevant here.

a. Acronyms are formed by taking the initial sounds (or letters) of the words of a phrase and uniting them into a combination that is itself pronounceable as a separate word. Thus *NATO* is an acronym for **N**orth **A**tlantic **T**reaty **O**rganization, *laser* for **l**ight **a**mplification through the **s**timulated **e**mission of **r**adiation, and *radar* for **ra**dio **d**etection **a**nd **r**anging.

Notice that the initials used are not always one per word, and function words are often skipped altogether in the creation of acronyms.

b. Blends are combinations of the parts of two words, usually (but not necessarily) the beginning of one word and the end of another: *smog* from *smoke* and *fog*, *brunch* from *breakfast* and *lunch*, and *chortle* from *chuckle* and *snort*. An important point here is that neither piece used in the formation of a blend should be a morpheme in its own right; for example, the pieces of *brunch* are *br-* + *-unch*, but neither piece is meaningful on its own in English.

c. Clipping is a way of shortening words without paying attention to the derivational morphology of the word (or related words). *Exam* has been clipped from *examination, dorm* from *dormitory*, and both *taxi* and *cab* from *taxi cab* (itself a clipping from *taximeter cabriolet*). Be careful to distinguish clipping from the pieces used in blending.

d. Coinages are words that are created without using any of the methods described above and without employing any other word or word parts already in existence; that is, they are created out of thin air. Such brand names as *Kodak* and *Exxon* were made up without reference to any other existing word or morpheme, as were the words *pooch* and *snob*.

e. Conversions are new words created simply by shifting the part of speech of a word to another part of speech without changing the form of the word. *Laugh, run, buy,* and *steal* started out as verbs but can now also be used as nouns, while *position, process,* and *contrast* are nouns from which verbs have been formed. This process is sometimes also called **functional shift**.

f. Eponyms are words (often places, inventions, activities, etc.) that are named for persons somehow connected with them; for instance, *Washington, DC* (for *George Washington*, and *District of Columbia* for *Christopher Columbus*), German *Kaiser* and Russian *tsar* (for *Julius Caesar*), and the units of measurement *ohm* and *watt* (for *Georg Simon Ohm* and *James Watt*, respectively).

FILE 13.5

Syntactic Change

13.5.1 Defining Syntactic Change

As noted in File 13.1, linguistic change is not restricted to one particular component of a language. Thus, in the same way that the sounds and words and meanings of a language are subject to change, so too are the patterns into which meaningful elements—words and morphemes—fit in order to form sentences. That is to say, change can be found in the syntactic component of a language, the domain of a grammar concerned with the organization of words and morphemes into phrases and sentences.

In syntactic change, therefore, the primary data that historical linguists deal with are changes in the variety of elements that go into the syntactic structuring of a sentence. These include (but are not restricted to) changes in word order, changes in the use of morphemes that indicate relations among words in a sentence (e.g., agreement markings on a verb caused by the occurrence of a particular noun or on an adjective caused by the noun it modifies), and changes in the arguments of words (e.g., the adjective *worthy* requires the preposition *of*, as in *worthy of consideration*; the verb *believe* can occur with a *that*-clause following it; etc.; see File 5.2). All of these aspects of sentence structure are subject to change diachronically.

The examples given below are drawn from the history of English, but they can be taken as illustrative of change in the syntactic component of any language. Moreover, they are representative of the nature of syntactic change in general and show ways in which syntactic change differs from sound change (discussed in File 13.3). Perhaps the most striking characteristic of sound change is that it is regular in that it affects all possible candidates for a particular change; for example, all instances of Old English [uː] became Modern (American) English [ɑʊ], and no examples of the older pronunciation remain. With syntactic change, however, while new patterns are produced that the language generally adheres to, exceptions nonetheless can occur; for example, even though word order in commands changed, the interjectional commands *mind you* and *believe you me* retain the older order with the pronoun after the verb, and so does the (consciously) archaic expression *hear ye, hear ye*. Moreover, unlike sound change and more like morphological change, syntactic changes are often specific to the syntactic properties of particular words.

13.5.2 Changes in Word Order

One example of syntactic change is that in earlier stages of English, it was quite usual (though not obligatory) for a possessive determiner to follow the noun it modified, in the opposite order from what the rule is today. Thus, where currently we say *our father*, in Old English the phrase was usually *fæder ure*. One way of describing this change is to say that the generalization about the placement of words in such a noun phrase has changed. Thus one of the two possible structures for a noun phrase in Old English was:

(1) NP → N + Det

That structure, however, is not a part of the grammar of Modern English; instead, the modern phrase structure rule for a noun phrase has (2) as one of its possibilities.

(2) NP → Det + N

Similarly, in earlier stages of English, in an imperative (command) sentence, the pronoun *you,* if expressed at all, could appear either before or after the verb, while today, such a pronoun regularly precedes the verb (so that *You go!* is acceptable while **Go you!* is not).

Another very dramatic syntactic change in English has been the positioning of main verbs in questions and negative statements. In Modern English, if a statement lacks an auxiliary verb (a verb such as *will, can,* or *have*), then the word *do* must be used in forming a question or a negative sentence. Compare (3) and (4) with (5).

(3) Sentence: she   will   go
    Question: **will**   she   go?
    Negative: she   will   **not**   go.

(4) Sentence: he   has   gone.
    Question: **has**   he   gone?
    Negative: he   has   **not**   gone.

(5) Sentence: they   went.
    Question: **did**   they   go?
    Negative: they   did   **not**   go.

There is no *did* in *they went;* it is inserted in the question and the negative.

But as the examples in (6) from Shakespeare's *Othello* show, in Early Modern English the main verb appears before the subject of the sentence in the question, and before *not* in the negative.

(6) a. O heaven! **How got she out?** O treason of the blood! (Act 1, Scene 1)
       cf. How did she get out?

    b. Fathers, from hence **trust not your daughters' minds**
       By what you see them act. (Act 1, Scene 1)
       cf. Do not trust your daughters' minds.

    c. But though **they jump not** on a just account,—
       (Act 1, Scene 3)
       cf. They do not jump.

13.5.3 Changes in Co-Occurrence

The change of *fæder ure* to *our father* shows another type of syntactic change in addition to the change in word order. In Modern English, a noun phrase such as *our father* has the same form regardless of whether it is a subject or an object, as in (7). Rather, it is the position in the sentence that tells us whether it is the subject or the object.

(7) (subject)   <u>Our father</u> drinks a lot of coffee.
    (object)   We love <u>our father</u>.

In Old English, however, such a difference in grammatical function of a noun phrase was signaled by changes in the form of a noun phrase:

(8) (subject)   fæder ure
    (object)   fæder urne

Thus the passage from Old English to Modern English has seen a change in the way that grammatical function—a matter of sentence structure—is marked (from a "case-marking" morphological system to a syntactic system based on word order).

Similarly, adjectives in Old English regularly agreed with the noun they modified in gender (masculine/feminine/neuter), number (singular/plural), and case (e.g., subject/object, etc.); in Modern English, the only remnants of Old English number agreement with adjectives are to be found with the modern determiners *this/that* (with singular nouns) and *these/those* (with plural nouns).

Finally, as an example of a syntactic change involving co-occurrence requirements, we can consider the adjective *worthy*. In earlier stages of English, this adjective regularly occurred with a *that*-clause following it, as in:

(9) ic   ne   eom wyrðe   þæt   ic   þin   sunu beo genemned
    I   not am   worthy that I   your son   be   called

which literally is 'I am not worthy that I be called your son'; the Modern English equivalent of this sentence, though, is *I am not worthy to be called your son,* indicating that the co-occurrence requirement of *worthy* has changed from permitting a following *that*-clause to allowing only infinitival clauses (clauses with *to* plus a verb).

13.5.4 Causes of Syntactic Change

A few words on the causes of syntactic change are in order. As with all other language change, there are both language-internal and language-external causes of syntactic change. Thus, word-order changes in specific syntactic environments and phrases, for example, the noun + determiner discussed above, are often linked (correlated) with other changes in word order (e.g., involving the placement of an object with respect to the verb, a relative clause with respect to the noun it modifies, a noun with respect to a prepositional element, etc.). That is, there is often a system-wide change in the ordering of elements that is realized in different ways in different syntactic environments (see Chapter 5). At the same time, though, such system-internal factors are only one side of the story. Innovative syntactic patterns often compete with older patterns for some time, and external, that is, social, factors often play a role in deciding the competition.

An example is the case-marking distinction involving *who* versus *whom* in Modern English, where the use of one as opposed to the other in a sentence such as *Tell me who/whom you saw yesterday* is tied to such socially relevant factors as speakers' educational level, their attitudes toward education, the impression they wish to convey, and the like.

FILE 13.6

....

Semantic Change

13.6.1 Changing the Meanings of Words

The semantic system of a language (see Chapter 6), like all other aspects of its grammar, is subject to change over time. As a result, the meanings of words do not always remain constant from one stage of the language to the next. If we think of the meaning of a word as being determined by the set of contexts in which the word can be used, we can characterize semantic change as a shift in the set of appropriate contexts for that word's use. Alternatively, we could view semantic change as a change in the set of **referents** for a word, that is, as a change in the set of objects the word refers to. Since these views are simply two aspects of what we call meaning, these two characterizations of semantic change are more or less equivalent.

The motivating factors behind semantic change are not well understood. Such changes sometimes result from language contact or accompany technological innovations or migrations to new geographic regions. In each of these cases the introduction of a new object or concept into the culture may initiate a change in the meaning of a word for a related object or concept, though this does not always occur. Semantic changes can also result from changes in the relative status of the set referred to by the word; that is, the word will take on new aspects of meaning to reflect this difference in social status. Sometimes changes result from a change in the status of the word itself, as is often the case with taboo words. It is, however, frequently the case that the sources of particular changes are not at all obvious; they appear to be spontaneous and unmotivated (though this may simply be due to our own lack of understanding).

Whatever the underlying source, only certain types of changes seem to occur with any frequency. Some of the most common types include extensions, reductions, elevations, and degradations.

13.6.2 Semantic Extensions

Extensions in meaning occur when the set of appropriate contexts or referents for a word increases. Extensions are frequently the result of generalizing from the specific case to the class of which the specific case is a member. An example of this type would be the change in meaning of the Old English (OE) word *docga,* modern-day *dog.* In OE *docga* referred to a particular breed of dog, while in modern usage it refers to the class of dogs as a whole. Thus the set of contexts in which the word may be used has been extended from the specific case (a particular breed of dog) to the general class (all dogs, dogs in general). A similar type of change has affected the Modern English word *bird.* Though it once referred to a particular species of bird, it now is used for the general class.

A contemporary example of this type of change would be the shift in meaning undergone by the recently formed verb *nuke.* This verb was based on the noun *nuke,* a shortening (clipping; see Section 13.4.4) of *nuclear weapon* and originally meant 'to drop a nuclear bomb on something.' In some varieties, this verb has been extended to mean simply 'to damage' or 'to destroy,' as in *Robin nuked his Porsche last night.* Thus the meaning of *nuke,* for these speakers at least, has gone from referring to a particular type of damage or destruction to damage or destruction in general.

Semantic extensions are particularly common with proper names and brand names. Thus the name *Benedict Arnold* has come to be synonymous with the word *traitor.* Similarly, the name of the fictional character *Scrooge* can be used to refer to anyone with miserly traits. Examples of the semantic extension of brand names are equally easy to find: *Jell-O* is often used to refer to any flavored gelatin, regardless of brand. *Kleenex* is used for any facial tissue, and *Xerox* for any photocopy. In some parts of the United States *Coke* can be used for any carbonated beverage, not just one particular brand (as a sign of its generality, it may even appear without the capital <C>, as <coke>). In each of these cases the meaning of the word has been generalized to include a less specific group of items in its set of referents.

In the examples discussed thus far, the relationship between the original meaning of the word and the extended meaning of the word has been quite straightforward: the name of a particular traitor has been generalized to any traitor, the name of a particular type of photocopy has been generalized to any photocopy, and so on. This needn't always be the case, however. The meanings of words often become less narrow as a result of what is referred to as **metaphorical extension.** Thus, the meaning of a word is extended to include an object or a concept that is like the original referent in some metaphorical sense rather than a literal sense. A classic example of this type is the word *broadcast,* which originally meant 'to scatter seed over a field.' In its most common present-day usage, however, *broadcast* refers to the transmission of some sort of program or information via a media outlet of some type—a metaphorical extension of its original sense. Another classic example of metaphorical extension is the application of preexisting nautical terms (such as *ship, navigate, dock, hull, hatch, crew,* etc.) to the relatively new realm of space exploration. Again, notice that space exploration is not like ocean navigation in a literal sense, since very different actions and physical properties are involved. Rather, the comparison between the two realms is a metaphorical one. Another example that we've seen in this text is the use of *phoneme* to apply to a minimal unit of form in signed languages. When the term was first used, it was clearly related to minimal units of sound, but because the linguistic concept of the phoneme is present in signed languages, the term has been extended.

We can also find cases of metaphorical extension in progress in the language around us, particularly if we consider creative uses of slang terms. Consider the use of the verb *nuke,* discussed above, to refer to microwave cooking. In this case, the metaphor hinges on the idea that microwave radiation is released during nuclear explosions. Thus, a parallel is being drawn between cooking in a microwave and bombing your food, though literally the two actions are quite different. Notice that this use of *nuke* is not (yet) accepted by all speakers.

13.6.3 Semantic Reductions

Reductions occur when the set of appropriate contexts or referents for a word decreases. Historically speaking, this is relatively less common than extensions of meaning, though it still occurs fairly frequently. An example of a semantic reduction would be the Old English word *hund,* modern-day *hound.* While this word originally referred to dogs in general, its meaning has now been restricted, for the most part, to a few particular breeds of dog. Thus its usage has become less general over time. Similarly, the word *worm* once was used for any crawling creature but is now restricted to a particular type of crawling creature.

Other examples of semantic reduction include the Modern English words *skyline* and *girl.* *Skyline* originally referred to the horizon in general. It has since been restricted to particular types of horizons—ones in which the outlines of hills, buildings, or other structures appear. In Middle English the word corresponding to modern-day *girl* referred to young people of either sex. A semantic reduction has resulted in its current, more specific meaning.

13.6.4   Semantic Elevations

Semantic **elevations** occur when a word takes on somewhat grander or more positive connotations over time. For example, the word *knight* (OE *cniht* or *cneoht*) originally meant 'youth' or 'military follower'—referring to relatively powerless and unimportant people. The meaning of *knight* has since been elevated to refer to people of a somewhat more romantic and impressive status. Similarly, the word *chivalrous* was at one time synonymous with *warlike*; it now refers to more refined properties such as fairness, generosity, and honor. A particularly good example of this type is the shift in meaning undergone by the word *squire*. The Middle English (ME) equivalent of *squire* was used to refer to a knight's attendant, the person who held his shield and armor for him. In Modern English, however, a squire is a country gentleman or large landowner. Thus the meaning of *squire* has changed rather drastically over time, acquiring a socially more positive meaning.

13.6.5   Semantic Degradations

Semantic **degradations** are the opposite of semantic elevations; they occur when a word acquires a more pejorative meaning over time. Examples of words whose meanings have been degraded include *lust, wench,* and *silly*. In OE *lust* simply meant 'pleasure,' making its current association with sinfulness a degradation of the original meaning. Similarly, the ME word *wenche(l)* meant 'female child' and later 'female servant.' It then came to mean 'lewd female' or 'woman of a low social class.' The word *silly* is a particularly interesting example of semantic degradation because the social force of the word has almost completely reversed. Whereas in ME *silly* meant something akin to 'happy, blessed, innocent,' it now means 'foolish, inane, absurd.' Thus the connotations of *silly* have gone from strongly positive to strongly negative in a matter of a few centuries.

13.6.6   Interactions of Semantic Changes

It is interesting to note that semantic changes in one word of a language are often accompanied by (or result in) semantic changes in another word. Note, for instance, the opposite changes undergone by OE *hund* and *docga*, discussed above. As *hund* became more specific in meaning, *docga* became more general. Thus, the semantic system as a whole remains in balance despite changes to individual elements within the system.

A somewhat more elaborate example of the same principle involves the OE words *mete, flæsc,* and *foda*. In OE, *mete,* modern-day *meat,* referred to food in general while *flæsc,* now *flesh,* referred to any type of animal tissue. Since then, the meaning of *meat* has been restricted to the flesh of animals and the meaning of *flesh* largely to human tissue. *Foda,* which was the OE word for 'animal fodder,' became modern-day *food,* and its meaning was generalized to include all forms of nourishment. Thus the semantic hole left by the change in referent for *meat* has been filled by the word *food*.

....

Internal Reconstruction and Comparative Reconstruction

13.7.1 Reconstruction

One of the goals of historical linguistics is to document and examine how languages change over time. In order to do this, linguists must know both what languages today look like and how they used to look. Unfortunately, of course, we do not have a time machine that would allow us to go back in time to study earlier states of languages directly. Therefore, linguists have come up with a number of ways of looking at older states of language.

The most useful tools for a historical linguist are direct samples of older language: recordings of speakers from the late nineteenth century, for example, or transcripts of speech from eras before sound-recording was possible. In the absence of such transcripts, other early written descriptions of a language, or documents in the language, can help linguists see how a given language used to be. But even when few (or no) written sources exist, linguists can often determine both how a single language used to look and how several languages might have derived from a common source historically. These tasks are accomplished using methods of **reconstruction.** There are two primary methods of reconstruction: internal reconstruction and comparative reconstruction. **Internal reconstruction** involves the analysis of data from a single language in order to make hypotheses about that language's history. **Comparative reconstruction** involves the systematic comparison of multiple related languages in order to make hypotheses about the common protolanguage they descended from. We will consider each in turn in the sections that follow.

13.7.2 Internal Reconstruction

As we have seen from our survey of sound changes that have occurred in the history of English, one of the effects of conditioned sound change is the creation of alternate pronunciations for the same morpheme, which is usually called morphological **alternation.** For example, early in the history of English, fricatives became voiced intervocalically. As a result, the plural form of the word *wife* changed from [wiːfas] to [wiːvas]. In the singular form [wiːf], however, the fricative [f] did not become voiced because it did not occur intervocalically. The net result of this sound change was to create alternate pronunciations for the different forms of the stem of 'wife': [wiːf] in the singular but [wiːv] in the plural. The alternation, which we can consider to be the "trace" of the completed sound change, is still evident in Modern English today, as is evident in the forms *wife/wives.*

When morphological alternations are created by sound change, we can often examine the phonetic context of the alternate pronunciations and infer what sound change(s) caused the alternations in the first place. This type of analysis, whereby the linguist examines data available from one language and one language only and makes hypotheses about that language's history, is what we mean by **internal reconstruction.** Using the internal reconstruction method, a linguist may learn much about a language's history, even if for some reason there are no known related languages to compare it with. This is not unlike seeing puddles in the street and reasoning that it rained, or seeing glass shards and reasoning that a glass or a window has been broken. In each case we are hypothesizing about what happened to cause what we see as the current state of things.

English can provide us with a very straightforward example of the recovery of an earlier sound change via morphological alternation. In English the voiced velar stop [g] is not pronounced when it precedes a word-final nasal, for example, *sign* [sɑɪn], but it is pronounced in related words if this nasal is not word-final, for example, *signal* [sɪgnəl]. As a result, morphological alternations occur between morphemes with and without the voiced velar stop, for example, *dignity* [dɪgnəɾi], *deign* [deɪn]; *paradigmatic* [pɛɹədɪgmæɹɪk], *paradigm* [pɛɹədɑɪm]. On the basis of these alternations we can make some inferences about the history of English. Specifically, we can assume that at an earlier period the morphological alternation did not exist—that there was only one pronunciation for morphemes that had the sound sequence [gn] or [gm], and that at some point there was a sound change whereby voiced velar stops were lost when they occurred before a word-final nasal.

Sometimes, however, it is impossible to detect the sound change(s) that have created the morphological alternations that exist in a language. This is usually the case when later sound changes take place that obscure the original cause of the alternate pronunciations. Consider the following example from the history of English. At present in English the past tense of the verb *sleep* is [slɛpt] and not [slipt] as we might expect. It is only natural to wonder why the word *sleep* has forms with alternate pronunciations [slɛp] and [slip]. Unfortunately we can arrive at no satisfactory answer just by considering the evidence that exists in Modern English. We cannot say that the alternation is due to the fact that the vowel is followed by two consonants in the past tense form, because other verbs that form the past tense in a similar manner do not have alternate pronunciations, for example, *freak* [fɹik], *freaked* [fɹikt] and *peak* [pik], *peaked* [pikt]. Since we have words that form the past tense regularly and words that have an alternate pronunciation in the past tense and we can determine nothing from the phonetic contexts, it is impossible to attempt internal reconstruction in the way we did with *sign* and *signal*. In cases such as this, internal construction does not give us the answer.

Although internal reconstruction is most often used to discover sound changes using morphophonemic alternations in the synchronic state of the language, it can also be used to recover other kinds of language change. We can hypothesize about structure at earlier stages of the language by comparing variants and patterns in the current state of the language.

Even though there are limits to what internal reconstruction can reliably tell us about the history of a language, it can be very useful when working on languages for which evidence of related languages or previous stages of the language is not available.

13.7.3 Comparative Reconstruction

Unlike internal reconstruction, comparative reconstruction relies on the existence of multiple related languages; these are compared in order to establish what language the related languages descended from and how closely related they are.

In order to use the **comparative method** of reconstruction, you must start out with related languages, using the techniques discussed in File 13.2 on language relatedness. Otherwise, you would be "reconstructing" a system that would not represent any actually occurring language. By working with related languages, you know that you can at least theoretically reconstruct an actual source language from which the languages you are working with have descended.

Another key to using the comparative method successfully is the assumption (discussed in File 13.3) that sound change is regular; that is, all the sounds in a given environment will undergo the same change, and when a language undergoes a certain sound change, that change will (eventually) be reflected systematically throughout the vocabulary of that language. For example, a language might undergo an unconditioned sound change of [p] to [f], in which every [p] in every word is replaced by [f]. Or, for example, a language might undergo a conditioned sound change of [p] to [f] in some specific phonetic environment, such as between vowels, in which case every word with a [p] between two vowels would develop an [f] in place of the intervocalic [p]. A sound change may be conditioned by phonetic environment (e.g., it occurs only when the sound in question is between two vowels, or before a certain other sound, or after a certain sound, or at the beginning of a word, or at the end of a word, etc.), but nothing other than the phonetic environment ever limits a sound change. A sound change never randomly affects some words but not other phonetically similar words, never occurs just in words with a certain kind of meaning, and so on. That is what is meant by the regularity of sound change.

These two tendencies make it possible for linguists to establish language relationships. The arbitrary relationship between a word's form and meaning is important because it makes it highly unlikely that unrelated languages will share large numbers of words of similar form and meaning. The regularity of sound change is important because it means that two (or more) languages that are related will show regular **sound correspondences**. Let us consider an example to illustrate what we mean. Consider the forms in (1).

(1) | **English** | **German** | **Dutch** | **Swedish** | **Gloss** |
|---|---|---|---|---|
| [mæn] | [man] | [man] | [man] | 'man' |
| [hænd] | [hant] | [hant] | [hand] | 'hand' |

If we compare the vowel sounds in all four languages, we can establish the following sound correspondence in the word meaning 'man': [æ] in English corresponds to [a] in German, Swedish, and Dutch. In order for this sound correspondence to be regular, it must occur in other **cognates,** words that have similar forms and meanings and that are descended from the same source. And, of course, it does, as a comparison of the words meaning 'hand' confirms.[1] Note that since this correspondence (æ—a—a—a) occurs regularly (is not unique to the word for 'man'), we have eliminated the possibility of being misled by chance similarity between words with similar form and meaning in unrelated languages.

Although comparative reconstruction is most often used to discover sound changes and reconstruct the phonetic form of words, it can also be used to recover other kinds of language change. We can hypothesize about structure at earlier stages of the language by comparing variants and patterns in two (or more) languages that are related.

The task of the comparative linguist does not end with the discussion of correspondences between languages or with the assumption that these correspondences indicate that the languages in question are related. The linguist is also interested in discovering how languages that are related developed from the protolanguage into their present forms; in other words, the linguist is interested in linguistic history.

In order to discover how languages have developed from a protolanguage, the protolanguage itself must be recoverable. And in some cases it is. For the Romance languages (French, Spanish, Portuguese, Romanian, etc.) the protolanguage (Vulgar Latin) is attested by numerous written records, for example, manuscripts, public inscriptions, funerary inscriptions, graffiti, and so on. As a result it is possible to trace the development of the various Romance languages from their parent with considerable accuracy.

In other cases, however, written records for the protolanguage do not exist. But this does not mean that we cannot gather any information about the protolanguage; in these cases it is possible to infer what the protolanguage looked like by comparing the forms and grammars of the related languages. For example, some words in Proto-Indo-European can be reconstructed on the basis of words in the daughter languages. The lists in (2) and (3)

---

[1]Actually, we would want to see many more than just two words with the same correspondences, but these serve as an example.

contain sets of words having the same meaning from six Indo-European languages. The asterisk (*) means that the word is a **reconstructed form,** or a **protoform,** not one that we have ever seen attested by people who spoke the language.[2]

(2)		*'father'*	*'mother'*	*'brother'*
	Proto-Indo-European	*[pəteːr]	*[maːteːr]	*[bʰraːteːr]
	English	[fɑðɹ̩]	[mʌðɹ̩]	[bɹʌðɹ̩]
	Greek	[patɛːr]	[mɛːteːr]	[pʰraːteːr]
	Latin	[patɛr]	[maːter]	[fraːter]
	Old Church Slavonic	—[3]	[mati]	[bratrə]
	Old Irish	[aθɪr]	[maːθɪr]	[braːθɪr]
	Sanskrit	[pɪtər-]	[maːtər-]	[bʰraːtər-]

(3)		*'mead'*	*'is'*	*'I bear'*
	Proto-Indo-European	*[medʰu]	*[esti]	*[bʰer-]
	English	[mid]	[ɪz]	[bɛɹ]
	Greek	[mɛtʰu]	[esti]	[pʰɛrɔː]
	Latin	—	[ɛst]	[fɛroː]
	Old Church Slavonic	[mɛdə]	[jɛstə]	[berõ]
	Old Irish	[mið]	[is]	[biru]
	Sanskrit	[mədʰu]	[əstɪ]	[bʰəraːmɪ]

Since inferences are made by comparing words of similar form and meaning in the languages we assume to be related, the method is called the *comparative method*. Note that the comparative method is itself possible because of the regularity of sound change. If two or more languages show regular correspondences between themselves in words where the meanings are the same or similar, it means that these words have descended from a common source.

As a small preliminary example of how the comparative method works, let us return to our English-German-Dutch-Swedish example from (1). We note that the first consonant in the first word is an [m] and that the final consonant is an [n] in all four languages. Thus we can safely assume that the protolanguage had an initial *[m] and a final *[n] in the word meaning 'man,' so that at this point we can reconstruct *[m__n] in our protolanguage. With respect to the vowel sound there is some uncertainty because there is variation in the sound: English has [æ], while German, Dutch, and Swedish have [a]. However, since there are more [a] outcomes in the daughter languages than [æ] outcomes, assuming that [a] is the sound that the protolanguage possessed and that English alone has changed *[a] > [æ] allows for a simpler solution overall, with fewer changes needing to be posited. Thus we reconstruct the protoform for 'man' as *[man], and the sound change *[a] > [æ] ("*[a] changes to [æ]") for English.

13.7.4 Comparative Method Procedure

The goal of the comparative method is to reconstruct the protoforms of the protolanguage from the comparison of languages that are assumed to be related. Once the protolanguage forms have been reconstructed, it is possible to determine the changes by which the daughter languages have become distinct by comparing the protoforms with the forms present in the daughter languages.

---

[2]Note that this is the same symbol that we use for marking ungrammaticality. Generally you can tell from context which meaning is intended.

[3]There was an OCS word for 'father' [otətsə], but it derives from a different root.

a. Compile Cognate Sets, Eliminate Borrowings. The first step is to gather and organize data from the languages in question, forming cognate sets. A cognate of a word is another word that has descended from the same source; consequently, cognates are very similar in form and are usually identical or similar in meaning. As an example of a cognate set, consider the words for 'keel' in four Austronesian languages (specifically, the Polynesian branch of Austronesian).

(4)
Samoan	*Māori*	*Fijian*	*Hawaiian*	
[taʔele]	[takere]	[takele]	[kaʔele]	'keel'

Because of their semantic identity and phonetic similarity, these four words form a cognate set.

While gathering cognates, you should make sure that "suspicious-looking" forms are eliminated. Sometimes among the cognate sets you are compiling for some group of languages, there will be a cognate set with an "oddball," a form that is phonetically so different from the other members of the cognate set that it is improbable that it derived from the same source. The "oddball" may have been borrowed from some other possibly genetically unrelated language. The original form, which fit the cognate set, was probably dropped in favor of the borrowed form. When you come across one of these borrowed forms, simply ignore it for the purposes of the comparative method.

b. Determine Sound Correspondences. Next determine the sound correspondences that exist between sounds in the same positions in the words in each cognate set. The sound correspondences for our cognate set in step (a) are given in (5).

(5)
Position	*Samoan*	*Māori*	*Fijian*	*Hawaiian*
1.	[t]	[t]	[t]	[k]
2.	[a]	[a]	[a]	[a]
3.	[ʔ]	[k]	[k]	[ʔ]
4.	[e]	[e]	[e]	[e]
5.	[l]	[r]	[l]	[l]
6.	[e]	[e]	[e]	[e]

c. Reconstruct a Sound for Each Position. Given these sound correspondences, you must try to determine the earlier protoform from which the cognates have descended, following these steps **in this order:**

(i) *Total Correspondence.* If all the languages exhibit the same sound in some position in a cognate set, reconstruct that sound. In our example, in positions 2, 4, and 6, each of the languages has the same vowel, so we construct [a] for position 2, [e] for position 4, and [e] for position 6. Leaving blanks for positions that do not have total correspondence, we can collapse and write this information as *[_a_e_e].

(ii) *Most Natural Development.* For each of the remaining positions, if possible, reconstruct the sound that would have undergone the most **natural** sound change. Years of study in phonetics and historical linguistics have shown that certain types of sound changes are very common, while others almost never happen. For example, in a position between vowels, the change of a stop to a fricative at the same point of articulation is a very common change, while the reverse is much less common. Thus, if one cognate contains a stop between vowels and the other contains a fricative, the stop should be reconstructed. For each of the common sound changes listed in (6), it should be understood that the reverse direction of change is rare.

(6) Common sound changes
- Voiceless sounds become voiced between vowels and before voiced consonants.
- Stops become fricatives between vowels.
- Consonants become palatalized before non-low front vowels.
- Consonants become voiceless at the ends of words.
- Difficult consonant clusters are simplified.
- Difficult consonants are made easier (for example, voiced aspirated stops might become plain voiced stops).
- Oral vowels become nasalized before nasals.
- Fricatives other than [h] become [h], and (voiceless) stops other than [ʔ] become [ʔ].
- [h] deletes between vowels.
- Clusters of vowels are broken up by consonants.

In our Austronesian words for 'keel,' for example, we have a choice between [k] and [ʔ] in position 3. Because we know that stops other than [ʔ] often become [ʔ], we reconstruct [k] so that *[k] > [ʔ] in Samoan and Hawaiian. So at this point, we have constructed *[_ake_e].

(iii) *Occam's Razor.* This technical term refers to a guideline for evaluating competing analyses: given any pair of possible analyses, prefer the one that is simpler overall. In the case of historical linguistics, this translates into preferring a solution that requires the positing of fewer changes over one that covers the same facts but requires more changes to do so. (*Occam's Razor* is named for the medieval English philosopher William of Occam, who proposed the principle, and "razor" refers here to the way the guideline encourages the "cutting out" of extra complications.) We have already applied this principle in the English-German-Dutch-Swedish example above when it was suggested that a single change *[a] > [æ] for English was a simpler solution than having three instances of a change *[æ] > [a].

So for position 1 in our example, where we have a choice between [t] and [k], we reconstruct *[t], because this would involve a single change *[t] > [k] for Hawaiian. To choose *[k] would require us to posit three instances of the change *[k] > [t], separately in Samoan, Fijian, and Māori. Similarly, for position 5, we reconstruct *[l], since this will involve only a single change *[l] > [r] in Māori, rather than three instances of the change in the other direction in the other three languages. Using the comparative method, then, we have determined that the pronunciation of the word meaning 'keel' in the protolanguage from which Samoan, Māori, Fijian, and Hawaiian descended was most probably *[takele].

d. Check for Regularity of Sound Change. Although the procedure outlined in steps (a) through (c) can be used to reconstruct a protoform for each cognate set individually, you must check to see whether your results are consistent across the whole collection of cognate sets. We know that sound change is regular, and therefore we should be able to give for each daughter language (Samoan, Māori, Fijian, and Hawaiian in our example) a list of sound changes that applied regularly to all words in the protolanguage, resulting in the respective daughter languages. If you cannot formulate the sound changes, you must minimally modify the choices you made in step (c) so that your results conform to the regularity hypothesis.

In order to demonstrate this situation, we need to add another cognate set to our data, as shown in (7).

(7)

Samoan	*Māori*	*Fijian*	*Hawaiian*	
[taʔele]	[takere]	[takele]	[kaʔele]	'keel'
[tapu]	[tapu]	[tabu]	[kapu]	'taboo'

Confirm that steps (a) through (c) produce *[tɑpu] for the word meaning 'taboo.' We see that they do, with the further addition that *[p] > [b] (intervocalically) in Fijian, and that the sound changes listed in (8) apply regularly to both reconstructed forms, giving the correct forms in Samoan, Māori, Fijian, and Hawaiian.

(8) a. Derivation of 'keel'

	Samoan	*Māori*	*Fijian*	*Hawaiian*
Protoform:	*[takele]	*[takele]	*[takele]	*[takele]
Sound changes:	*[k] > [ʔ]	none	none	*[k] > [ʔ]
	none	none	none	*[t] > [k]
	none	*[l] > [r]	none	none
Cognate set:	[taʔele]	[takere]	[takele]	[kaʔele]

b. Derivation of 'taboo'

	Samoan	*Māori*	*Fijian*	*Hawaiian*
Protoform:	*[tapu]	*[tapu]	*[tapu]	*[tapu]
Sound changes:	none	none	none	*[t] > [k]
	none	none	*[p] > [b]	none
Cognate set:	[tapu]	[tapu]	[tabu]	[kapu]

This example was fairly straightforward, but comparative reconstruction can be challenging when more sound changes take place between the reconstructed form and the cognate set. In some cases, when multiple changes affect the same sound, or one change provides the conditioning environment for another, the order in which the changes take place is very important, as with the phonological rules discussed in File 3.3.

Another clue that you may find helpful in doing comparative reconstruction is to find a pair of words that is the same (homophonous) in language A but different in language B. When such a situation arises, you may be fairly confident in reconstructing the protoforms as they appear in B (or at least as being different from one another, unlike in A). This reconstruction follows from the fact that if you were to reconstruct both the forms as they appear in A (i.e., as identical to each other), there would be no way that they would subsequently differentiate themselves in B: no sound change can apply to only one of two homophones. This is illustrated by the data in (9) from languages in the Gbe branch of the Niger-Congo family.

(9) **Gen** **Fon** **Gloss**
    [tó]   [tó]   'ear'
    [tó]   [só]   'pound'

Given the data in (9), we would have to reconstruct the protoforms *[tó] 'ear' and *[só] 'pound,' and hypothesize a sound change *[s] > [t] in Gen. If we had instead reconstructed both forms as *[tó], as they occur in Gen, it would be impossible, given the regularity of sound change, to write a rule by which one of them (but not both) changes to [só] in Fon.

The flowchart in (10) should help you work through a set of data to reconstruct earlier forms of words that are related in several languages. The rectangular boxes ask you to do something or give you some information that your working through the flowchart has revealed. The diamond-shaped boxes pose a question. Try reading through the flowchart before you attempt to solve a reconstruction problem like those found in File 13.8; it may help you understand how the whole process works.

(10) Flowchart for reconstructing word forms using the comparative method

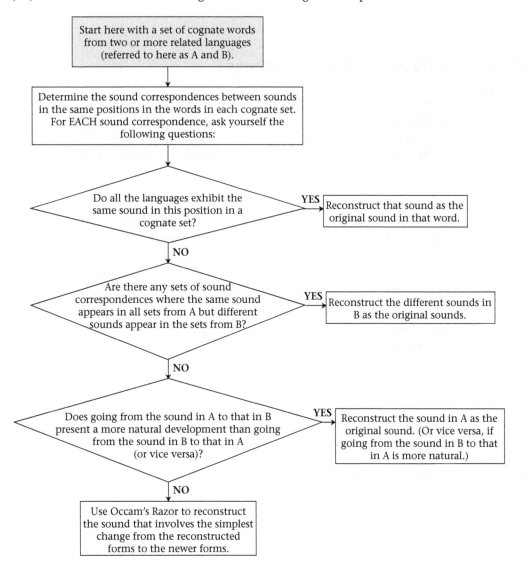

Practice

File 13.1—Introducing Language Change

Exercises

1. Looking at the versions of the Lord's Prayer given in (1)–(4) in File 13.1, identify at least one of each of the following types of change in the transformation of English between Old English and Modern English: sound change, morphological change, syntactic change, semantic change.

2. Looking at the excerpt of Chaucer's *Troilus and Criseyde* given in (7) in File 13.1, identify at least one of each of the following types of change in the transformation of English between Middle English and Contemporary English: sound change, morphological change, syntactic change, semantic change.

Discussion Question

3. Why do you think that we said that the passages in (1)–(4) in File 13.1 give a reasonably good impression of the language as it was spoken at various stages, even though they are not written in the IPA?

Activity

4. Find a passage from an older English text like *Canterbury Tales* by Chaucer or one of Shakespeare's plays. Rewrite it in Modern English. What kinds of changes do you have to make?

File 13.2—Language Relatedness

Exercises

5. For each of the following Indo-European branches, list two modern languages that are members of each branch:

   a. Celtic   **c.** Indic
   b. Baltic   **d.** Iranian

6. Consider the following data:

Language A	Language B	Language C	Language D	Gloss
due	bi	dó	doi	'two'
naso	sudur	srón	nas	'nose'
fratello	anaia	bráthair	frate	'brother'
padre	aita	athair	tată	'father'
sette	zazpi	seacht	sapte	'seven'

(cont.)

| orecchio | belarri | cluas | ureche | 'ear' |
| dieci | hamar | deich | zece | 'ten' |

   i. Which two languages seem to be very closely related? How can you tell?

   ii. What language seems to be at least distantly related to the two languages you identified in (i)? How can you tell?

   iii. Which language is not related to the others? How can you tell?

Discussion Questions

7. Go to the Links page for Chapter 13, click on "Ethnologue," and go to the "Language Family Index." You will see that there are languages that do not have a familial classification. Why do you think researchers have not been able to affiliate these languages with other groups? (There may be multiple reasons!) Do you think we are likely to be able to determine their affiliations in the future? Why or why not?

8. The words meaning 'city' in Hungarian (*varós*) and Romanian (*oraş*) are related. Given **only** this information, can we assume that Hungarian and Romanian are closely genetically related? Could there be other reasons for this similarity? What do you think caused this similarity?

9. How do we know there was a proto-Germanic even though we do not have written records of it (i.e., we don't have anything like Latin, as we have with French, Spanish, Italian, etc.)?

10. How are the family tree model and the wave model similar? How are they different? What kinds of relationships are presented most clearly in each one? In what situations do you think you might want to use one instead of the other?

Activities

11. Go to the Links page for Chapter 13, click on "Ethnologue," and go to the "Language Family Index." Choose a language family and draw a family tree to show how the languages in that family are related.

12. Investigate the relatedness of Taiwan Sign Language and Japanese Sign Language. Given the criteria for language relatedness described in File 13.2, do you think these languages are related or not?

File 13.3—Sound Change

Exercises

13. Why do we spell the words *knife* and *knight* with a <k> when they are pronounced with an initial alveolar nasal?

14. i. Based **only** on the data below, what seems to be the outcome of word-initial Latin [k] in Italian?

Latin		*Italian*	*Gloss*
[keno]	>	[tʃeno]	'I dine'
[kentum]	>	[tʃɛnto]	'hundred'
[kirkus]	>	[tʃirko]	'circus'
[kivilis]	>	[tʃivile]	'civil'

(cont.)

ii. Now look at the additional data below. Do these data make you revise your answer? Why? According to these two sets of data, what are the outcomes of word-initial Latin [k] in Italian? Explain your answer and be as specific as possible: describe the different environments required for each outcome.

Latin		Italian	Gloss
[kampus]	>	[kampo]	'field'
[kontra]	>	[kontra]	'against'
[kuriositas]	>	[kuriosita]	'curiosity'
[kredo]	>	[kredo]	'I know'

15. For each word specify the sound change(s) between Proto-Quechua and one of its daughter languages, Tena. Then, after considering all the data, say whether each sound change is conditioned or unconditioned and, further, what type of conditioned or unconditioned change each sound change is.

Proto-Quechua	Tena	Gloss
[tʃumpi]	[tʃumbi]	'belt'
[timpu]	[timbu]	'boil'
[nutku]	[nuktu]	'brains'
[akla]	[agla]	'choose'
[wakli]	[wagli]	'damage'
[utka]	[ukta]	'fast'
[kunka]	[kunga]	'neck'
[ljantu]	[ljandu]	'shade'
[mutki]	[mukti]	'smell'
[pukju]	[pugju]	'spring'
[inti]	[indi]	'sun'
[sanku]	[sangu]	'thick'
[hampatu]	[hambatu]	'toad'

16. Specify the changes between Proto-Slavic and one of its daughter languages, Bulgarian. Classify the changes as conditioned or unconditioned. Then say what type of conditioned or unconditioned change each sound change is. Note that the order of the changes is important; that is, if the changes had occurred in different orders, they would have given different results. The order of changes that gives exactly the results we see in Bulgarian is the best hypothesis about the actual relative chronological ordering of the changes, that is, how they unfolded in time with respect to one another. Give the correct order of the changes you have identified, and point out at least one wrong result that a different order of changes would produce.

Proto-Slavic	Bulgarian	Gloss
[gladuka]	[glatkə]	'smooth'
[kratuka]	[kratkə]	'short'
[blizuka]	[bliskə]	'near'
[ʒeʒika]	[ʒeʃkə]	'scorching'
[lovuka]	[lofkə]	'adroit'

17. Determine the sound changes that took place in the development of Marathi from Old Indic. Classify the sound changes as conditioned or unconditioned. Then specify what type of sound change each one is. [c] is a voiceless palatal stop, [ʈ] a voiceless retroflex stop, and [ɖ] a voiced retroflex stop.

(cont.)

Old Indic	Marathi	Gloss
[aŋka]	[aŋka]	'hook'
[arka]	[akka]	'sun'
[bʰakti]	[bʰatti]	'devotion'
[catwaːri]	[cattaːri]	'four'
[kalpa]	[kappa]	'rule'
[kardama]	[kaddama]	'mud'
[kaʈaka]	[kaɖaː]	'bracelet'
[mudgara]	[muggara]	'mallet'
[pitaː]	[piaː]	'father'
[rudra]	[rudda]	'terrible'
[sapatniː]	[savattiː]	'co-wife'
[supta]	[sutta]	'asleep'
[ʃabda]	[sadda]	'sound'
[ʃata]	[saː]	'hundred'
[vikrama]	[vikkama]	'strength'
[viʈapa]	[viʈava]	'branch'

Discussion Questions

18. Based on what you know about the outcome of sound change, do you think it is possible for two homonyms (like *pair* and *pear*) to be pronounced differently in the future just because of a sound change? Why or why not?

19. Just as signed languages can metaphorically be thought of as having phonetics and phonology, so can they metaphorically undergo sound change—and, in fact, they can undergo both phonetic and phonological change.

    One example of sound change in American Sign Language is the tendency for signs that were originally made with both hands in the same shape, where the same motion was made on either side of the signer, to now be signed with just one hand. Many signs for the names of animals are like this: DEER, RABBIT, COW, and so on, as illustrated in (a) and (b).

    a. ASL: COW (older)

    b. ASL: COW (newer)

(*cont.*)

Another example of a sound change is shown in (c) and (d). In this case, the difference in the signs is which handshape is being used. The older sign for DECIDE used an F-handshape, while the newer one uses a D-handshape.

c. ASL: DECIDE (older)

d. ASL: DECIDE (newer)

Based on this information, answer the following questions for each set of photos:

i. Why is this change considered to be analogous to sound change (as opposed to, for example, morphological change or semantic change)?

ii. What type of sound change is this an example of, given the list in Section 13.3.4? Why? If you don't think that the sound change type is given on the list, explain why, tell what kind of change you think it is, and say which type of change you think it is most analogous to.

iii. Would you consider this to be a phonetic or a phonological change? Why?

File 13.4—Morphological Change

Exercises

20. Historically, the past tense of the verb *dive* is formed by the regular pattern of past tense word formation, that is, verb + *-ed* → [past tense] (*dived*). However, in a number of American English dialects *dived* has been replaced by *dove* [doʊv]. It is normally assumed that *dove* replaced *dived* as the result of the pattern *drive* [present tense] : *drove* [past tense]. Would you consider the replacement of *dived* by *dove* to be an example of proportional analogy? What does this tell us about the notions of productivity/regularity and analogical change?

21. Try to come up with other aspects of English morphology that currently show some degree of fluctuation and variation (e.g., *saw* versus *seen* as the past tense form of *see*). To what extent are analogical processes at work in causing these fluctuations?

Discussion Questions

22. Consider verbs that have "irregular" past tenses (e.g., *run–ran, give–gave, win–won*, etc.). If the past tense of these verbs changed, what would you expect the new form to be? Why? Do you hear these forms in Modern English?

23. Consider the statement (sometimes called "Sturtevant's Paradox") that "sound change is regular but produces irregularity; analogy is irregular but produces regularity." What do you think this means? Do you think it's true? Why or why not?

Activity

24. For each of the following words, give the word or phrase from which it is derived and indicate the morphological process by which it was changed. You may need to use the *Oxford English Dictionary* or some other etymological reference.

    a. blues   **e.** sitcom
    b. brash   **f.** recap
    c. op-ed   **g.** electrocute
    d. ramshackle   **h.** frazzle

File 13.5—Syntactic Change

Exercises

25. Here are a few lines from Geoffrey Chaucer's *Canterbury Tales*, written in Middle English. Identify and discuss the difference(s) between the Middle English syntax and the Modern English syntax, and give a brief description.

    a. Whan that Aprill with his shoures soote
       When April with its sweet-smelling showers

    b. Thanne longen folk to goon on pilgrimages,
       Then folk long to go on pilgrimages,

    c. The hooly blisful martir for to seke,
       To seek the holy blessed martyr,

26. How would the following sentences of Shakespeare appear in Modern English? Explain what the difference is in each case (from *All's Well That Ends Well*, Act 1, Scene 1).

    a. How called you the man you speak of, madam?
    b. Virginity being blown down, man will quicklier be blown up.
    c. I will return perfect courtier; in the which, my instruction shall serve to naturalize thee . . .

File 13.6—Semantic Change

Discussion Questions

27. Why do you think curse words often lose their "taboo" status?

28. Think about terms you use to talk about computers and actions on computers (e.g., "surf the Internet").

   i. How many of these are old words that have been put to new use, and how many are totally new words? Why do you think this would be the case?

   ii. For those old words that have been put to new use, what kind of semantic change (extension, reduction, elevation, or degradation) has occurred? Why do you think this would be the case?

29. In ASL, many signs have become less iconic over time; that is, the signs are less transparently related to what they mean. This is especially the case for a number of compound words. For example, the sign for HOME at one point was a compound of the signs for EAT (an O-hand at the mouth) and BED (a flat hand against the cheek); now it is a series of two touches of the O-handshape on the cheek. Do you think this change in form has affected the meaning of the word in any way? Why? What design feature of language (see File 1.4) is this evidence for?

Activities

30. In the following somewhat nonsensical paragraph, the meanings of the italicized words are quite different now from what they were at earlier stages of English. For these words, using an earlier meaning instead of the current one will give a logical interpretation to the paragraph. For each italicized word, (i) determine which earlier meaning makes sense here, and (ii) identify the type of semantic change the word has undergone. You can find the earlier meanings, which may come from different time periods, in the *Oxford English Dictionary,* the Online Etymological Dictionary (http://www.etymonline.com/), or other sufficiently detailed sources.

> He was a happy and *sad girl* who lived in a *town* 40 miles from the closest neighbor. His unmarried sister, a *wife* who was a vegetarian member of the Women's Christian Temperance Union, ate *meat* and drank *liquor* three times a day. She was so fond of oatmeal bread made from *corn* her brother grew, that one night, when it was dark and *wan* out, she *starved* from overeating. He fed nuts to the *deer* who lived in the branches of an *apple* tree that bore pears. He was a *silly* and wise *boor,* a *knave* and a *villain,* and everyone liked him. Moreover, he was a *lewd* man whom the general *censure* held to be a model of chastity.[1]

31. Particularly interesting cases of semantic change are ones in which the meaning of a word appears to have been reversed through time. For example, the English word *black* is closely related to Slavic words meaning 'white.' *Black* is actually derived from a Germanic past participle meaning 'to have blazed' or 'to have burned.' Given these facts, can you think of a plausible explanation for the present-day meaning of *black*? Using a good etymological dictionary (such as the *Oxford English Dictionary*) for reference, list some Modern English words that are related to *black*. Try to determine the types of semantic change these words must have undergone to arrive at their present-day meanings.

---

[1]Paragraph republished with permission of Cengage Learning SO from *Problems in the origins and development of the English language,* by John Algeo, 3rd edn. New York: Narcourt, Brace, and World, 1982, pp. 245–46. Permission conveyed through Copyright Clearance Center, Inc.

32. Using the *Oxford English Dictionary* or some other etymological reference, find the earlier meanings of each of the following words. What kind of semantic change (extension, reduction, elevation, or degradation) has occurred in each case?

a. cynic	**c.** anecdote	**e.** parakeet	**g.** captivated
b. hacker	**d.** grotesque	**f.** leer	**h.** paisley

33. Do some research using the *Oxford English Dictionary* or some other etymological reference to find words that used to be curse words but that have lost their taboo nature (e.g., *poppycock*). Consider current taboo words: where have they come from?

File 13.7—Internal Reconstruction and Comparative Reconstruction

The following directions pertain to all of the reconstruction exercises contained in this file:

   i. Set up the sound correspondences for each cognate set, and reconstruct the earlier form for the word from which the cognates have descended.

   ii. Establish the sound changes that have affected each language. Note that in some cases, the ordering of the changes is important.

Exercises

34. Middle Chinese

For this exercise, we have simplified the Chinese data somewhat. [tɕ] and [dʑ] are the voiceless and voiced alveolo-palatal affricates, respectively.

	Mandarin (Beijing)	*Hakka (Huizhou)*	*Gloss*
a.	[tɕin]	[kim]	'zither'
b.	[la]	[lat]	'spicy hot'
c.	[mɔ]	[mɔk]	'lonesome'
d.	[lan]	[lam]	'basket'
e.	[dʑi]	[gip]	'worry'
f.	[lan]	[lan]	'lazy'
g.	[pa]	[pa]	'fear'

35. Proto-Peninsular Spanish

	Castilian	*Andalusian*	*Gloss*
a.	[majo]	[majo]	'May'
b.	[kaʎe]	[kaje]	'street'
c.	[poʎo]	[pojo]	'chicken'
d.	[pojo]	[pojo]	'stone bench'
e.	[dos]	[dos]	'two'
f.	[dieθ]	[dies]	'ten'
g.	[θiŋko]	[siŋko]	'five'
h.	[si]	[si]	'yes'
i.	[kasa]	[kasa]	'house'
j.	[kaθa]	[kasa]	'a hunt'
k.	[θiβiliθaθion]	[siβilisasion]	'civilization'

[ʎ] represents a palatal lateral.

[β] represents a voiced bilabial fricative.

36. Proto-Numic

	Yerington Paviotso	*Northfork Monachi*	*Gloss*
a.	[mupi]	[mupi]	'nose'
b.	[tama]	[tawa]	'tooth'
c.	[piwɪ]	[piwɪ]	'heart'
d.	[soŋo]	[sono]	'lungs'
e.	[sawaʔpono]	[sawaʔpono]	'proper name (fem.)'
f.	[nɪwɪ]	[nɪwɪ]	'liver'
g.	[tamano]	[tawano]	'springtime'
h.	[pahwa]	[pahwa]	'aunt'
i.	[kuma]	[kuwa]	'husband'
j.	[wowaʔa]	[wowaʔa]	'Indians to the West'
k.	[mɪhɪ]	[mɪhɪ]	'porcupine'
l.	[noto]	[noto]	'throat'
m.	[tapa]	[tape]	'sun'
n.	[ʔatapɪ]	[ʔatapɪ]	'jaw'
o.	[papiʔi]	[papiʔi]	'older brother'
p.	[patɪ]	[petɪ]	'daughter'
q.	[nana]	[nana]	'man'
r.	[ʔati]	[ʔeti]	'bow, gun'

37. Proto-Uto-Aztecan

	Shoshone	*Ute*	*Northern Paiute*	*Gloss*
a.	[tuhu]	[tuu]	[tuhu]	'black'
b.	[nika]	[n̥ika]	[nika]	'dance'
c.	[kasa]	[kạsi]	[kasa]	'feather'
d.	[tuku]	[tụku]	[tuku]	'flesh'
e.	[juhu]	[juu]	[juhu]	'grease'
f.	[pida]	[pida]	[pita]	'arm'
g.	[kadi]	[kadi]	[kati]	'sit'
h.	[kwasi]	[kwạsi]	[kwasi]	'tail'
i.	[kwida]	—	[kwita]	'excrement'

38. Proto-Western Turkic

	Turkish	*Azerbaijani*	*Crimean Tartar*	*Kazan Tartar*	*Gloss*
a.	[burun]	[burun]	[burun]	[bɪrɪn]	'nose'
b.	[kabuk]	[gabɪx]	—	[kabɪk]	'bark'
c.	[bojun]	[bojun]	[mojun]	[mujɪn]	'neck'
d.	[toprak]	[torpax]	[toprak]	[tufrak]	'earth'
e.	[kujruk]	[gujruk]	[kujruk]	[kɪjrɪk]	'tail'
f.	[japrak]	[jarpak]	[ʤaprak]	[jafrak]	'leaf'

Discussion Question

39. We have seen that the regularity of sound change provides one of the bases for the comparative method. How might the workings of analogical change pose problems for the comparative method?

Further Readings

Campbell, Lyle. 2013. *Historical linguistics: An introduction.* 3rd edn. Cambridge, MA: MIT Press.

Campbell, Lyle, and Mauricio J. Mixco. 2007. *A glossary of historical linguistics.* Edinburgh: Edinburgh University Press.

Crowley, Terry, and Claire Bowern. 2010. *An introduction to historical linguistics.* 4th edn. Oxford: Oxford University Press.

Fortson, Benjamin W., IV. 2009. *Indo-European language and culture: An introduction.* 2nd edn. Oxford: Blackwell.

Hock, Hans Henrich, and Brian D. Joseph. 2009. *Language history, language change, and language relationship.* 2nd rev. edn. Berlin: Mouton de Gruyter.

Millward, C. M., and Mary Hayes. 2011. *A biography of the English language.* 3rd edn. Boston: Wadsworth, Cengage Learning.

Animal Communication

....

How Do Animals Communicate?

H umans are not the only creatures that communicate: in fact, almost all creatures have some sort of communication system, sometimes a very elaborate system. Are these systems comparable to human language? From what we know about how animals communicate in the wild, it seems that no other animal uses a system that we can call "language." Human language has a number of characteristics that set it apart from other communication systems. For example, dogs cannot talk about what will happen tomorrow or about the climate on another continent. Nevertheless, animal communication systems are interesting to study in their own right in order to understand how animals naturally communicate in the wild.

Another question that has interested many researchers is whether humans can teach animals to use language. A number of studies have been conducted to teach language to a variety of animals. The success of these attempts is still debated, but we can say that so far no animal has been taught human language to the same extent and degree of sophistication that a human child acquires it naturally without instruction.

Contents

FILE 14.1

....

Communication and Language

14.1.1 Design Features Revisited

The previous chapters have provided an introduction to various aspects of how humans use language to communicate. However, we are not the only species that communicates; most animals have some sort of communication system. All varieties of birds make short calls or sing songs, cats meow to be fed or let outside, dogs bark to announce the arrival of strangers or growl and bare their teeth to indicate their intent to attack, and so on. The fact that other animals send and receive messages is in evidence all around us. But can we call the communication systems of animals "language"?

Most people assume that only humans use "language"—it is something that sets us apart from all other creatures. But is it possible that when we examine animal communication systems, we will discover that our assumption that only humans use language was wrong? The task of comparing human communication with various animal communication systems is not an easy one. First, we need a suitable way to identify "language" on which to base our comparisons. Unfortunately, no definition seems to adequately define "language" or to be agreeable to everyone. One approach to getting around this problem, suggested by the linguist Charles Hockett, is that we identify the requisite descriptive characteristics of language rather than attempt to define its fundamental nature. Hockett identified nine **design features**, introduced in File 1.4. Human language has all of these design features, but as far as we know, no animal communication system does. Therefore, if we define *language* as a communication system that possesses all nine of these features, we are correct in saying that only humans use language. The following sections discuss Hockett's design features with respect to animal communication systems.

14.1.2 Design Features Shared by All Communication Systems

All communication systems have the following features in common:

Mode of communication refers to how a message is transmitted. Different animals transmit messages via different media. Many animals—for example, birds, whales, frogs, rattlesnakes, and crickets—use their bodies to produce sound to communicate. In addition to the sounds we are familiar with, such as dogs barking and birds singing, some animals produce sounds that are not audible to humans. Elephants use infrasound—very low pitched sounds (less than 20 Hz)—to send messages. These sounds can travel several miles and allow elephants to communicate over long distances. Bats and whistling moths, on the other hand, use ultrasound—very high pitched sounds (over 20,000 Hz)—to communicate. Such sounds do not travel very far, but not much energy is needed to produce them. Other animals use objects to produce the sounds they use for communication. Kangaroos, hares, and rabbits thump their hind legs on the ground as a warning signal, while the death-watch beetle bangs its head against wood to communicate.

Some animals communicate using visual cues. For example, dogs and apes use certain facial expressions and body postures to express submission, threat, playing, desire, and so on. Female rabbits use the white of their tail as a flag to lead their young to the safety of their burrows. Fireflies find mates by producing light, male spiders use elaborate gestures to inform a female that they are healthy and capable of mating, and fiddler crabs wave their claws to communicate.

Animals may also use touch to communicate. Monkeys hug, big cats and rhinos nuzzle each other, and bees use touch to communicate the location of a food source.

Other animals use odor to communicate. The best-known example of this kind of chemical communication is the pheromones used by many insects to attract mates. In addition, ants use scent trails in order to communicate which path other ants in the colony should travel along.

Some fish and amphibians use electrical signals to communicate. These are often used to identify mates, broadcast territoriality, and regulate schooling behavior. Unlike sound, electrical signals don't get distorted when passing through different materials, for example, murky water.

Semanticity and **Pragmatic Function,** respectively, refer to the fact that signals in all communication systems have meaning and that all communication systems serve some useful purpose. The previous paragraphs have already mentioned many of the meanings conveyed by their animal communication systems. Since survival is the key function of animal communication systems, meaning of signals usually has to do with eating, mating, and other vital behaviors, such as deciding to fight or flee. In all of the previously mentioned examples, such as bees communicating the location of a food source and dogs and apes communicating submission or threat, the messages being communicated have clear purposes: helping others find food, and warning others of danger. In some cases, these pragmatic functions are clearer than those commonly expressed in human language!

14.1.3   Design Features Exhibited by Some Animal Communication Systems

Some, but not all, animal communication systems exhibit the following features:

Interchangeability refers to the ability to both send and receive messages. For example, every elephant can use infrasound to send messages and can also receive messages sent this way from other elephants. But not all animals can both send and receive signals. For example, the silkworm moth's chemical communication system does not display interchangeability with respect to mating. When the female is ready to mate, she secretes a chemical that males can trace back to her. The males themselves cannot secrete this chemical; they can only be receivers. On the other hand, for whistling moths, it is the males that send the signal (in this case to communicate messages about territory). Male whistling moths have a rough edge on their wings that they can rub together to make a sound; both males and females can hear and react to these sounds, but only males can produce them.

Cultural transmission refers to the notion that at least some part of a communication system is learned through interaction with other users. In most organisms, the actual signal code itself is innate, or genetically programmed, so an animal or insect can no more learn a new signal code than it can grow an extra eye. For example, fireflies are not taught how to produce or interpret their light displays; they are born with these abilities and perform them naturally and instinctively at the appropriate time. Likewise, cowbirds lay their eggs in other birds' nests and therefore are not raised around adult cowbirds. However, they nevertheless grow up to produce cowbird calls and not the calls of the birds raising them. This means that their calls are fully innate.

However, for some animals, aspects of their communication systems seem to be learned. For example, regional dialectal variation (see File 10.3) has been discovered in a number of bird species' songs, in killer whales' communication, and also in chimpanzee gestures. Dialectal variation indicates that there has been cultural transmission in these cases because the birds learn their dialect from hearing other birds singing, killer whales learn from hearing the clicking and whistling of other killer whales, and chimpanzees learn from seeing other chimpanzees using the specific gestures. These behaviors are not genetically encoded: if a young killer whale is raised in a pod of whales it is not related to, it will learn the communication system of the pod it is living with, not the communication system of its mother's pod.

In some cases, the division between what is culturally transmitted and what is not is less clear. In experiments with finches, juvenile finches that were isolated until adulthood were able to make simple calls, indicating that finch calls are somewhat innate, but their calls were not as complex as those of finches raised in groups. These experiments suggest that finches have a critical period for song acquisition, indicating that some aspects of finch call making are transmitted culturally (see File 8.1 for critical periods in humans). Those finches that were not exposed to calls early in life exhibited the aspects of calls that are innate but did not exhibit the aspects of calls that are culturally transmitted.

Arbitrariness means that the form of a symbol is not inherently or directly related to its meaning or function. Since most animal systems use iconic signals that in some way directly represent their meaning, most animal signals are not arbitrary. For example, when a dog bares its teeth to indicate it is ready to attack, the signal (bared teeth) is directly related to its meaning ('I will bite you'). Likewise, a dog may roll over and show its belly in order to indicate submission; this is an iconic way for the dog to indicate that it is making itself vulnerable. Many animals, including several species of snake, lizard, and frog, will stand up taller, puff out their features, or otherwise make themselves look larger in order to signify that they are making a threat; since larger individuals are often better able to win in a physical confrontation, using size to indicate threat is also iconic.

However, not all of the signals animals use are iconic. For example, the dorsal region of the male western fence lizard turns different shades of blue to indicate territoriality. A darker blue indicates territorial ownership and the lizard's willingness to fight to keep its territory. A lighter blue indicates that the lizard does not consider a territory its own. It is used when walking across another male's territory to indicate that the lizard is not challenging the other's territorial ownership. Here, the color blue does not iconically represent owning a territory. However, western fence lizards also use iconic signals to communicate; they make themselves look bigger (by turning sideways) to indicate threat. Another example of arbitrariness in animal communication is the variety of alarm calls of primates, which will be discussed in the next file. Thus, animal communication systems can include both iconic and arbitrary signals.

Discreteness refers to the property of being able to construct complex messages that are built up out of smaller discrete parts. The messages in most animal communication systems that we are familiar with do not have this property. Each message is an indivisible unit. However, limited discreteness can be found in some communication systems. One example is the way in which bees' dances are built up of smaller parts: the dance pattern, the direction, and the vivacity of the dance, each of which contributes different information to the message. The bees' dance will be described in detail in the next file.

14.1.4 Design Features Not Found in Animal Communication Systems

Only human language exhibits the following features:

Displacement refers to the ability to communicate about things that are not present in space or time. No animal communication system appears to display this feature. However, there is some debate as to whether bees (see File 14.2) and some apes exhibit it to a limited degree. For example, Menzel and his colleagues (2002) studied spatial memory in bonobos. They used road signs with arbitrary symbols (**lexigrams**) that described where in a forest food was hidden. The bonobo Kanzi could use the information on the sign to find the hidden food, even though it could not be seen from the location of the road sign. Thus, even though the food was not present in his visible space, Kanzi used information on the sign to determine its location.

This does seem to suggest that bonobos can understand messages about things not present in their immediate environment. This is based on interpreting the road signs' messages as something like *There's a food source hidden at this location,* though. This translation assumes a message **about** a distant, invisible object. But the message can be represented differently—and more simply—as *Perform this behavior now,* that is, *Go to this location now.* This is no different from most messages sent in animal systems and does not involve communicating about things that are not present. Thus, we don't know whether Kanzi understands the signs in terms of food being hidden somewhere, which would indicate displacement, or in terms of an order to perform a certain behavior. In other words, we don't know if Kanzi interprets the messages as representing objects that are not present or as an instruction to go somewhere. Thus, it is unclear whether bonobos exhibit limited displacement, or whether they do not possess this feature to any degree.

Productivity refers to the property of a language that allows for the rule-based expression of an infinite number of messages, including the expression of novel ideas. In practical terms, it refers to the ability of an individual to produce and understand messages that the individual has not been exposed to before by applying rules and combining discrete components of the language in new ways.

In all animal communication systems, the number of signals is fixed. Even though the signals in some animal communication systems are complex, there is no mechanism for systematically combining discrete units in new ways to create new signals. For example, some species of birds and whales have songs composed of different units that are combined in various ways. However, it seems that regardless of the order in which the units appear, the song still has the same meaning. That is, while these birds and whales do use different combinations of discrete units, they do not seem to use the different combinations of units to create signals with novel meanings or to convey novel ideas. These nonproductive systems are thus called *closed communication systems.*

14.1.5   What the Design Features Show Us about Animal Communication

In the comparison of human language with animal communication systems, a debate has arisen over whether human language and other systems differ **qualitatively** or **quantitatively.** If there were merely a quantitative difference, then we would expect to find an animal communication system that possesses all nine of these features, but with some expressed to a lesser degree than in human language. If, on the other hand, human language and other communication systems differ qualitatively, we would not expect to find an animal communication system that possesses each and every design feature. However, it is sometimes difficult to decide whether an animal communication system displays a feature to a certain extent or not at all, as the displacement example above shows.

At any rate, no animal communication system has been identified to date that has all nine design features. If we agree that a communication system must have all of the design features to be considered a language, we must conclude that animal communication systems are not language.

FILE 14.2

··

Animal Communication in the Wild

14.2.1 Bee Communication

In File 14.1 we claimed that no animal communication system is qualitatively the same as human language because no animal system with which we are familiar possesses all of Hockett's design features. In this file we will investigate three animal communication systems in a little more detail: that of an Italian species of honeybee (*Apis mellifera ligustica*), that of the European robin (*Erithacus rubecula*) and other bird species, and that of the rhesus monkey (*Macaca mulatta*). These investigations will describe how these species communicate in the wild and will provide further support for the claim that, although enormously complex, animal systems are quite different from human language.

We will begin by discussing honey bees. When a forager bee returns to the hive, if it has located a source of food, it does a dance that communicates certain information about that food source to other members of the colony. The dancing behavior may assume one of three possible patterns: round, sickle, and tail-wagging. The choice of dance pattern is determined by the distance of the food source from the hive. The round dance indicates locations near the hive, within 20 feet or so. The sickle dance indicates locations at an intermediate distance from the hive, approximately 20 to 60 feet. The tail-wagging dance is for distances that exceed 60 feet or so.

In all the dances, the bee alights on a wall of the hive and moves through the appropriate pattern. For the round dance, the bee's motion depicts a circle. The only semantic information imparted by the round dance other than the approximate distance from the hive to the food source is the quality of the food source. This is indicated by the number of repetitions of the basic pattern that the bee executes and the vivacity with which it performs the dance. This feature is true of all three patterns. To perform the sickle dance, the bee traces out a sickle-shaped figure eight on the wall. The angle formed by the open end of the sickle intersecting with an imaginary vertical line down the wall of the hive is the same angle as the angle of the food source from the sun. Thus, the shape of the sickle dance imparts information about the approximate distance, direction, and quality (see (1)).

(1) The sickle dance. In this case the food source is 20 to 60 feet from the hive.

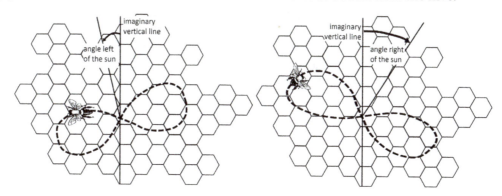

579

In the tail-wagging dance, shown in (2), the bee's movement again describes a circle, but this time the circle is interrupted when the bee cuts across the circle doing a tail-wagging action. The tail-wagging dance imparts all the information of the sickle dance (in this case it is the angle between a vertical line and the tail-wagging path that communicates the angle to the sun), with one important addition. The number of repetitions per minute of the basic pattern of the dance indicates the precise distance: the slower the repetition rate, the greater the distance.

(2)   The tail-wagging dance. The number of times per minute the bee dances a complete pattern (1–2–3–1–4–5) indicates the distance of the food source.

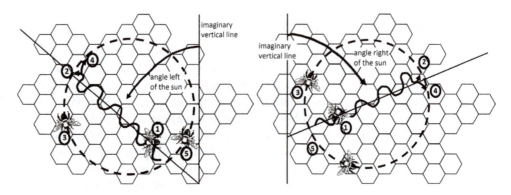

The bees' dance is an effective system of communication that is capable, in principle, of infinitely many different messages. In this sense the bees' dances are infinitely variable, like human language. But unlike human language, the communication system of the bees has limited semantic value; the topics that bees can communicate about are limited. For example, an experimenter forced a bee to walk to a food source. When the bee returned to the hive, it indicated a distance 25 times farther away than the food source actually was. The bee had no way of communicating the special circumstances or taking them into account in its message. This absence of **creativity** makes the bees' dance qualitatively different from human language.

In the previous file, we discussed the design feature of arbitrariness. Does the bees' dance exhibit this feature? What are the forms of the signs, and to what meanings do they correspond? Are the relationships arbitrary or non-arbitrary? In the tail-wagging dance, one form is the vivacity of the dance, with a corresponding meaning 'quality of food source.' The relationship is arbitrary, for there is nothing inherent about vivacity that indicates good or bad quality. Because the relationship is arbitrary, there is no *a priori* way of telling what the form means.

What about distance? The question here is more complicated. Remember that the slower the repetition rate, the greater the distance. On the surface this relationship may seem arbitrary, but consider it this way: the longer it takes to complete the basic pattern, the longer it will take a bee to fly to the source. Thus, we see that this sign is in some sense non-arbitrary. Similarly, the direction-determining aspect of the dance is obviously non-arbitrary, since the angle of the dance mirrors the angle to the food source. Therefore, we see that bee dances have both arbitrary and iconic (non-arbitrary) components.

14.2.2 Bird Communication

Birds communicate using both calls and songs. Calls are typically short, simple sounds that may warn of predators, express aggression, coordinate flight activity, or accompany feeding or nesting behavior. Flight calls, for example, are typically short sounds, and their place of origin is easy to pinpoint: they allow the bird flock to stay together more easily. Sounds warning of predators, on the other hand, are typically thin, high-pitched, and difficult to locate. They allow birds to warn other members of the group of predators without giving away their location. We can see that these bird calls are not completely arbitrary; rather, the calls are functionally related to the meaning they convey: the calls that imply the meaning 'locate me' are easy to locate, whereas the calls that imply the meaning 'I don't want to be found' are difficult to locate.

Bird song is different from bird calls. In most species, only males sing, often to delimit their territory or attract a mate. Unlike calls, songs are largely seasonal. But, like calls, the songs of certain species of birds have definite meanings. One song may mean 'let's build a nest together,' while another song may mean 'go get some worms for the babies.' But the bird cannot make up a new song to cope with a new situation.

Scientists who have studied the songs of the European robin found that the songs are very complicated indeed. But, interestingly, the complications have little effect on the message that is being conveyed. Scientists studied the song that signaled the robin's possession of a certain territory. They found that rival robins paid attention only to the rate of alternation between high-pitched and low-pitched notes, but that which of the two tones came first didn't matter at all. A higher rate of alternation shows a greater intention to defend the territory. Thus, a robin's message varies only to the extent of expressing how strongly the robin feels about his possession and how much he is prepared to defend it and start a family in that territory. This means that the robin is creative in his ability to sing the same message in many different ways, but not creative in his ability to use the same units of the system to express many different tunes, each with a different meaning. In other words, there is evidence that certain birds combine parts of their songs in different orders, but there is no evidence that different meanings are associated with this recombination.

Similar patterns are seen in the songs of other songbirds, for example, the branded wren (*Thryothorus pleurostictus*). If we look more closely at the ways the songs can vary, some interesting patterns emerge. There are particular chunks or phrases that are the basis for song construction (rather than, for example, individual notes, as in human music). Let's suppose that the bird has four kinds of phrases, and we'll term them A, B, C, and D. Again, like that of the robin, the song of the branded wren does not change its meaning depending on how it is being sung. The components A, B, C, D, and so on do not carry any meaning on their own (i.e., the song of the branded wren does not show discreteness). Unlike human language, there is no compositionality (see File 6.4). A possible form of a typical song is shown in (3).

(3) ABABABCCCCD
     ABABABABABABCCD
     ABCCCD

There are simple rules governing the constructions of these songs: start with A, go to B, and alternate between A and B as many times as you like; then go to C, and repeat that at least twice, before finishing with D. This rule-based system for the combination of symbols is very similar to syntax in human language (see Chapter 5). However, it is nowhere near as complex as the syntax of a human language—no human language works with rules this simple. The memory load for these rules is very low—for example, if a bird is singing A, it knows that the next phrase must be B, no matter what. Similar syntax-like structures can be found in the calls of gibbons, diana monkeys, and whales. The syntax of human languages cannot be explained with such a simple model: we can rarely predict what word will come next based only on the current word.

14.2.3   Primate Communication

Many species of animals have communication systems that are much more complex than one might imagine, but they still appear to be very different from human language. Studies of non-human primates such as the vervet and rhesus monkeys, studied both in the wild and in captivity, have revealed elaborate systems of vocal and facial communication that are almost invariably triggered by proximal external stimuli, such as the presence of predators or food sources. Vervet monkeys have been observed to use a variety of alarm calls to warn each other of different kinds of predators. A vervet monkey that emits a loud bark communicates to the rest of the group that a leopard has been spotted. This type of alarm call sends everybody up into the trees. A short, interrupted, usually two-part, cough-like sound means that an eagle is in the vicinity, and monkeys immediately look up and then hurry to take cover under thick bushes. If a snake has been seen by a member of the troupe, he or she will make a soft whirring noise that immediately prompts everybody to stand up and look around the grass cautiously.

Other types of vervet monkey calls deal with social hierarchy arguments, mating rituals, and territorial disputes between different groups of monkeys. This limited "vocabulary" of monkey calls is rigid and fixed. There have been some claims that some "cheating" monkeys might emit an alarm call in the absence of a predator in order to monopolize a food source by sending everybody else to seek shelter. Such reports indicate that the monkeys are able to use their limited array of calls for different purposes (either to give a genuine warning, or just to clear the area for selfish reasons). These instances of "cheating" indicate that the monkeys are aware of the behavioral effects that their calls have on other members of the troupe. However, these cases do not represent novel utterances or new signals. In fact, if we were to provide the gloss of 'Hey, everybody go climb a tree' instead of 'Hey, everybody, there's a leopard,' then it would be totally reasonable to expect the same call to be used in two different sets of circumstances. Most animal communication systems do not have the sophistication to use the same signal for different purposes in this way, but even a double usage like this doesn't come close to mirroring the complexity of human language.

A recent study of rhesus monkey calls has also revealed a human-like ability to enhance the auditory perception of vocal signals with visual cues. In (4), we can see two different types of rhesus monkey calls and the accompanying facial expressions. The picture on the left represents a cooing call, and the picture on the right a threat call. Cooing calls are long tonal sounds, and threat calls are short and pulsating, cough-like sounds. The study revealed that rhesus monkeys are able to recognize the correspondence between the particular call and the appropriate facial expression. This is a very human-like ability.

The great apes (gorillas, chimpanzees, bonobos, and orangutans) also communicate with facial expressions, gestures, and calls to express anger, dominance, fear, danger, acceptance in a group, and the like. These are also human-like behaviors. However, as complex and human-like as these systems may seem, they lack displacement and productivity: apes do not communicate about things that are not physically present, nor can they combine their independent gestures or calls in novel ways to create new meanings.

(4) Facial expressions, waveforms, and spectrograms of rhesus monkeys' cooing (left) and threat (right) calls

Reproduced by permission by © 2003 Nature Publishing Group, "Neuroperception: Facial Expressions Linked to Monkey Calls" by Asif A. Ghazanfar & Nikos K. Logothetis et al. *Nature*, Vol. 423, pp. 937–38.

14.2.4 Concluding Remarks

The philosopher and mathematician René Descartes pointed out more than three hundred years ago, in his "Discourse on Method," that the communication systems of animals are qualitatively different from the language used by humans:

> It is a very remarkable fact that there are none [among people] so depraved and stupid, without even excepting idiots, that they cannot arrange different words together, forming of them a statement by which they make known their thoughts; while, on the other hand, there is no other animal, however perfect and fortunately circumstanced it may be, which can do the same.

Descartes went on to state that one of the major differences between humans and animals is that human use of language is not just an immediate response to external, or even internal, emotional stimuli, as are the grunts and gestures of animals.

All the studies of animal communication systems provide evidence for Descartes's distinction between the fixed stimulus-bound messages of animals and the creative linguistic ability possessed by humans. Even though animal communication systems are not like human languages, they are nevertheless frequently very complex, interesting to study, and different from human languages in fascinating ways.

FILE **14.3**

....

Can Animals Be Taught Language?

14.3.1 Attempts to Teach Animals Language

The previous file discussed how animals communicate in the wild. As far as we know, no naturally occurring animal communication system is either qualitatively or quantitatively equivalent to human language. But just because animals do not use or acquire language naturally does not necessarily mean that they cannot be taught. This file describes attempts to teach animals language.

14.3.2 Primate Studies

The great apes (gorillas, chimpanzees, bonobos, and orangutans) are very intelligent creatures and *Homo sapiens'* nearest relatives in the animal kingdom. Chimpanzees, for example, share close to 99% of their genetic material with human beings. This biological similarity of ape and human, as well as the apes' intelligence, has prompted some scientists to wonder if language could be taught to apes, even though they do not use language naturally (see File 14.2). Many such projects have been conducted, most in the past fifty years or so. The ape used most often has been the chimpanzee, primarily because they are more easily available than other primates. They are also considered to be one of the most intelligent of the great apes. Orangutans, gorillas, and bonobos have also been used in some studies.

These experiments have generated both exuberance and disappointment, and a rigorous debate about the interpretation of their results continues to the present day. On the one hand, there are still some scientists who maintain that they have indeed taught an ape to use human language. On the other hand, many scientists dispute this claim and have proposed alternative explanations for the behaviors other researchers assumed could only have been language use.

a. Early Projects. The first prominent experiment conducted on the linguistic capacity of great apes in the United States took place in the 1930s. W. N. and L. A. Kellogg wanted to raise a baby chimpanzee in a human environment to determine whether the chimp would acquire language on its own, just as a human child does, merely by being exposed to it. They decided not to give any training or "forcible teaching" to Gua, the chimp they acquired at seven and a half months, other than that which would be given a human infant. Gua was raised alongside the Kelloggs' newborn son, Donald, and the development of the chimp was compared to the boy's. W. Kellogg stated that his intent was to determine how much of human language ability derived from heredity and how much from education. He reasoned, a bit naively in retrospect, that what the chimp could not learn would be those aspects of language that a human inherently knows. Kellogg admitted one violation of this program when, at one point, he attempted to mold Gua's lips in an effort to teach her to say *papa*. This effort, lasting several months, proved unsuccessful.

In the 1950s, Keith and Cathy Hayes decided to raise Viki, a female chimp, also as much like a human child as possible, believing that with a proper upbringing, a chimp could learn language. The Hayeses believed that they could teach Viki to speak, even though doubt was emerging at the time about whether the chimpanzee's vocal anatomy could even produce human speech sounds. The Hayeses, however, believed that the vocal tract of the chimp was similar enough to a human's for it to be able to articulate human sounds, and they had no aversion to "training." Their program included first teaching Viki to vocalize on demand (this took five weeks) and then shaping her lips with their hands into various configurations that yielded consonant sounds. After three years, Viki could "speak" three words—*cup, mama,* and *papa*—although they were accompanied by a "heavy chimp accent": it sounded as if Viki were whispering. The Hayeses reported that Viki could "understand" many words, but they offered no experimental proof of this. The Kelloggs' and Hayeses' experiments were not viewed by scientists as successful attempts to teach language to apes. Three words are not very many when one is trying to prove human language capability.

Allen and Beatrice Gardner believed, contrary to the Hayeses, that chimps were not capable of producing human speech sounds, so they felt that trying to teach a chimp to speak was fruitless. Since chimps are manually dexterous and use gestures to communicate naturally, the Gardners decided to teach American Sign Language (ASL) to a chimp they named Washoe. Their methods were quite different from those used with Gua and Viki. Washoe was not raised as a human infant but was brought up with minimal confinement in a stimulating atmosphere. Spoken English was not allowed in her presence because the Gardners feared she would come to understand spoken language first and not be motivated to learn ASL. Like Viki, Washoe also received deliberate training. Objects were presented to her, and the trainers molded Washoe's hands into the shapes for their signs. Eventually, in order to be rewarded, she had to produce the signs herself and to produce them with greater and greater accuracy.

The experiment was considered at the time to be a great success. By the time Washoe was five years old, she had learned 132 signs; by the end of her life in 2007, she had learned over 250, not all of them in a training environment. More important, she supposedly exhibited some amount of productivity in her communication by inventing her own novel combinations such as *dirty Roger,* where *dirty* was used as an expletive, and *water bird,* upon seeing a swan on a lake. There is some debate as to whether combinations such as *water bird* are compositional (see File 6.4) or whether Washoe was commenting on two separate things: she saw some *water* and she saw a *bird.* If the latter were true, the example would not show that Washoe had developed productivity in her language use.

Even more impressive, Washoe taught signs to her adopted son. Loulis was adopted by Washoe when he was 10 months old, and she taught him to sign in the same way she was taught: by molding his hands to make the signs. She taught him about 40 signs. This makes Loulis the first non-human to learn parts of a human language from a non-human! The Gardners and others, such as Robert Fouts, have continued the project with Loulis and other chimpanzees: Tatu, Dar, and Moja.

The Gardners' insight about the vocal limitations of the chimp has been noted by every researcher since. Consequently, subsequent endeavors have all involved simplified versions of either a signed language or visual signs such as **lexigrams,** symbols composed of geometric shapes used to represent words.

Anne and David Premack began in 1966 to work with a chimpanzee named Sarah. Like the Gardners, David Premack decided to try to find and use the best possible training procedure rather than raising Sarah as a child. The "language" used was also atypical. Instead of a simplified version of ASL, Premack used differently shaped and colored plastic chips. He arbitrarily associated an English word with each chip. Communication between the trainers and Sarah involved placing these chips on the "language board." Sarah was taught how to do one type of "sentence" at a time. Typically, her task was to choose an appropriate chip from a choice of two or to carry out a task indicated on the language board.

Premack intended to teach Sarah the names of objects as well as the names of categories of objects. He originally claimed to have taught her 130 symbols, including category names such as *color* and concepts such as *same* and *different*. Premack also claimed that Sarah learned the word *insert*. As proof of this, Premack offered the observation that in one task, when Sarah saw *Sarah banana pail insert* on her language board, she correctly executed the task.

Duane Rumbaugh wanted to design an ape language experiment with as much of the training taken out of the hands of human trainers as possible. He reasoned that if the training were automated, one could avoid cueing the animal, and the training could be more efficient and constant. So he and his associates designed a computer that would do the training. The computer could execute certain commands, such as dispensing food or displaying slides in response to an operator giving proper commands. Commands were given by lighting up symbols of an invented "language." Like the Premacks with Sarah, Rumbaugh used lexigrams—in this case they were various combinations of nine different geometric figures, such as a big circle, a little circle, and a large *X*—as the language the operator of the machine would use. This operator was, of course, a chimp; her name was Lana. Lana did learn to use the keyboard quite well and managed to make the computer execute various commands, and Rumbaugh thought that he had succeeded in teaching a chimp some human language.

In 1972 Francine Patterson began to teach ASL to a gorilla named Koko. This project has been one of the longest lasting of its kind, and Patterson has made some of the most dramatic claims for such a project's success. According to Patterson, Koko knows several hundred signs and has invented many of her own combinations, such as *finger bracelet* for 'ring.' Koko also supposedly uses her signs to insult people and things she doesn't like. After being reprimanded one day, for example, Koko called Patterson a *dirty toilet devil*. In addition, Koko is reported to understand spoken English. The evidence given by Patterson to support this claim is that Koko occasionally rhymes, putting together such signs as *bear* and *hair* even though the signs themselves have no visual similarity to each other. Koko also substitutes homophones for words when she cannot think of the sign, such as *eye* for *I* or *know* for *no*. Although Koko has exhibited a remarkable grasp of many linguistic properties, she does not yet seem to have displayed the abilities necessary to justify Patterson's claim that "Koko is the first of her species to have acquired human language."

b. Criticisms of the Early Projects. The results and conclusions of these projects have been critically questioned; the first to do so was a researcher named Herbert Terrace. His criticism was based on a critical review of his own project to teach a chimpanzee the use of grammar. He then critically reviewed other projects and found similar shortcomings.

In the late 1970s, Terrace began his project, which was similar to that of the Gardners, with a chimpanzee he humorously named Nim Chimpsky (hoping that when Nim learned language, the joke would be on Noam Chomsky, the noted linguist who claimed such a thing was impossible). Terrace's goal was to prove that a chimp could acquire and display some use of grammar. Terrace believed, as did most researchers at the time, that the evidence of human language capability was the use of grammar and not just the use of signs. By the time Nim was four years old, he had acquired 125 signs based on ASL and had combined them in various ways, and Terrace felt that Nim had acquired human language abilities as well.

This project was the first to videotape all interactions between chimp and trainer, however, and it was on reviewing these tapes that Terrace decided he must reverse his claim and instead acknowledge that the ape's use of signs was very different from human language. He noted that there were many dissimilarities between Nim's and a human child's acquisition of "language." Nim, for example, almost never initiated signing. Upon reviewing the tapes, Terrace found that only 12% of Nim's signs were spontaneous, and a full 40% were mere repetitions of what the trainer had just signed. This subtle interaction was never noticed by the trainer at the time. In addition, Nim's spontaneous signing was invariably a request for food or social reward; he never made unsolicited statements or asked questions. Quite unlike a human child, he did not display turn-taking behavior and was more likely to interrupt his trainer's signing than not. There was also no evidence that Nim knew any grammar. His combinations had variable word order, and, more importantly, Nim rarely went beyond two-word combinations. Even when he did, the additional signs added no new information. For example, Nim's longest utterance was *give orange me give eat orange me eat orange give me eat orange give me you.*

Terrace called into question the results of all previous experiments. He reviewed tapes of Washoe and Koko and concluded that they too had been cued by their trainers. He and others leveled even more serious criticisms of the Premack project, arguing that the training procedure taught problem solving rather than language and that Premack's conclusions were not well founded, given his experimental design and his results. Consider Premack's claim that Sarah learned the word *insert* because she could correctly insert a banana into a pail when seeing *Sarah banana pail insert* on her language board. When the word *insert* was tested against the word *give,* however, Sarah could not distinguish the two. Premack likewise claimed that Sarah knew the prepositions *on* and *in* but never administered a test where Sarah would have to distinguish one from the other. Following instructions did not necessarily involve Sarah's understanding a sentence on the language board, but rather her recognizing, for example, a banana chip and a pail chip and imitating what she had been trained to do in the first stage of the test—in this case, to insert the banana into the pail. (A banana couldn't go *on* an upright pail!)

c. More Recent Projects. Terrace's revelations had a great effect on the field of animal language studies. Funding for projects was thereafter hard to come by, and many scientists responded with new cynicism to any and all claims of animal language researchers. Researcher Sue Savage-Rumbaugh maintains that both the initial easy acceptance of claims in this field and the post-Terrace cynicism are too extreme.

She has begun another project with several apes, but the focus of her work is quite different. She believes that looking for evidence of grammatical capabilities in apes as Terrace did was far too premature. She considers a more fundamental question: when apes use a sign, do they know what it **means**? This question is by no means easy to answer, and it is surprising in hindsight that the early researchers took it for granted that when an ape produced a sign, it was using it in the same way humans do: as a symbol with a mental representation as part of the meaning. A symbol is an arbitrary relationship between a form (the sound pattern or gesture) and its meaning (see Section 11.1.4). One aspect of meaning is the sense, or mental representation (see File 6.1). Mental representations have an existence separate from their referents and can be manipulated independently of them. Thus we can think and talk about things that are not present; in fact, we can talk about things that don't even exist (e.g., unicorns).

Note that this approach represents a departure from the attempt to assess animal language capabilities in terms of the descriptive "design features," such as productivity and displacement, as discussed in File 14.1, by assessing **how** linguistic expressions are used. The use of a mental representation as part of a symbol is a separate characteristic that distinguishes human language from the natural animal communication systems discussed in Files 14.1 and 14.2.

No one disputes that humans use their words in this way. Furthermore, no one disputes that, in many cases, animals have been able to associate a phonological or visual form of a sign with a referent. But how are we to know whether an ape, when it uses a sign in the same way we might, really has a mental representation for it? Savage-Rumbaugh has suggested that in all previous experiments, apes were not using their signs symbolically. She argues that apes had merely learned to associate certain behaviors (making or seeing a particular sign) with certain consequences (e.g., getting something to eat)—similar to a dog that, upon hearing the word *walk,* knows it's going to get to go for a walk. This is an extremely subtle distinction for humans to perceive, since the use of symbols comes naturally to us. We interpret other creatures' signals to us in the same way we interpret those from each other, but that doesn't necessarily mean they're intended in the same way. For this reason, Savage-Rumbaugh has pointed out the necessity of proper experiments that prove that an ape has truly acquired a word in the same way a human has. She has criticized the claims made about previous projects either because they were not based on testing with proper controls or because use of symbols had not been tested at all. In addition, Savage-Rumbaugh reasoned that because apes had not learned to use symbols given the training techniques used previously (which had assumed that the symbol aspect of sign use would come naturally), apes must specifically and intentionally be taught to use symbols first, before tests could be informatively administered.

How could Savage-Rumbaugh determine whether such instruction was successful? How can one find evidence of a mental phenomenon? One must still look for it in the behavior of the animal or in the "processes of the exchange" with the trainer, but one must be more discriminating about what counts as evidence. Savage-Rumbaugh and her colleagues have worked extensively with two male chimpanzees, Sherman and Austin, attempting to teach them language skills with the computer and the lexigrams used with Lana. They have found that use of symbols by humans is not a single holistic phenomenon but rather a complex of independent abilities and behaviors. For example, the ability to produce a symbol was found to be composed of at least three separate abilities. Using the association of a lexigram and an object to request the object is only one of these (and a display of this ability does not prove that the user has a mental representation for the symbol). Naming is a second relevant behavior, which involves providing the lexigram associated with an object without the expectation of consuming or receiving that object. The third ability involved in symbol use is called *comprehension of the symbol.* It involves linking the symbol to its referent. One might find it difficult to separate these three, but they each had to be taught separately to the chimpanzee, and the presence of one ability could not be assumed because of the presence of another.

Savage-Rumbaugh also points out the extreme importance of a fourth aspect of symbol use and human communication that had previously been overlooked: the role of the receiver or listener. This in itself was also found to comprise its own complex of skills and behaviors, each of which had to be taught separately to Sherman and Austin. Savage-Rumbaugh claims to have been successful at teaching the chimps these skills as well as the links between them (the coordination that occurs naturally in humans).

Furthermore, she has acknowledged Terrace's criticisms of other projects but maintains that Sherman and Austin do not evidence Nim's shortcomings. She maintains that they take turns, their utterances are not imitations of their trainers, and they produce messages not only when they are elicited, but at other times as well.

This project certainly has made real progress both in clarifying what human language skills are and in investigating our ability to teach them to apes. Criticisms have been leveled, of course. Some suggest that, again, the apes have been skillfully trained but still neither comprehend what they are saying nor use their signs symbolically. After all, it is perhaps impossible to know whether another creature has a mental representation for a word. Savage-Rumbaugh might respond that this criticism is a reflection of a cynical attitude rather than scientific considerations. However, given past experience and the tendency to overinterpret results and behaviors, there is a need to scrutinize the claims in this field.

Savage-Rumbaugh's most recently begun project must be mentioned. She has started to work with another species of ape, the bonobo, *Pan paniscus,* which she claims is more intelligent than the common chimpanzee, *Pan troglodytes,* which she had used in all of her other projects. She claims that the bonobo she has been working with, Kanzi, has learned to comprehend spoken English just by being exposed to it and has spontaneously begun to use the keyboard with lexigrams to make requests and comment on his environment. Savage-Rumbaugh reports both anecdotal observations and the results of tests that might substantiate these astonishing claims. Again, these newest claims are difficult to accept without further confirmation based on carefully controlled experimentation and the objective scrutiny that was advocated at the inception of the Sherman and Austin project.

While there are still some ways in which Kanzi's acquisition and use of English and lexigrams differ from the language acquisition of a human child, Savage-Rumbagh's work with Kanzi is the closest we have come to teaching a primate human language.

14.3.3 Non-Primate Studies

Primates have long been the focus of investigations into the linguistic capacity of animals, primarily because of their intelligence. However, attempts have also been made to teach small parts of language to non-primates.

a. Domestic Animals. Humans have always had close relations with domestic animals, and many people anecdotally claim that their pet can understand what is being said to them. Is this simply because of a confirmation bias or an emotional connection, or is there some truth to this claim? To what extent can domestic animals understand human language?

Wilhelm von Osten was a German math teacher and amateur horse trainer in the early 1900s. He owned a horse called "Clever Hans" who was claimed to be able to understand simple arithmetical questions and answer by tapping his hoof. For example, Wilhelm would ask, "Hans, what is ten minus three?" The horse would then tap his hoof seven times. However, investigation by the psychologist Oskar Pfungst revealed that Hans was actually paying attention to the subconscious body language cues of his owner Wilhelm, who knew the answer. So Hans was not so clever after all—he was simply a keen observer of humans. This result highlights the importance of testing animals in a neutral environment, away from potential factors that may cue them to the answer.

Domestic dogs are well-known for their language ability, and many people train their dogs to respond to commands—for example, "sit," "fetch," and "beg." Herding dogs that work with farmers can learn many commands to help move herds of livestock. Is there a limit to this ability? A border collie named Chaser, working with her owner, psychology professor Dr. John Pilley, might be the smartest dog ever tested. Chaser can accurately retrieve over 1,000 toys by name and has been shown to associate names she's never heard before with new toys by a process of elimination. Chaser also seems to understand the idea of categories, having learned that many round toys, each with a specific name, can also be called "balls." Chaser's understanding goes beyond a simple mapping of word to behavior, as she also can carry out novel two-word commands like "paw elephant" and "nose dice," combining a verb and noun in the appropriate way. While still controversial, this may show that Chaser is using words symbolically. However, dogs' natural use of barks do not meet the test of the design features described in File 14.1, so we do not say that even the smartest dogs use language.

b. Alex the Parrot. Irene Pepperberg, an animal psychologist, bought an African grey parrot from a pet store in 1977 and attempted to teach him to speak. She named the parrot "Alex," which was an acronym for "Avian Learning Experiment."

Alex was trained with the "model-rival" technique, in which two trainers work with the animal. One trainer gives instructions, while the other trainer models correct and incorrect responses. This way, the second trainer is competing with the animal for the attention of the first trainer. The trainers then swap roles and repeat the process. After observing, the animal then tries to model the correct behavior for the trainers. The following is an excerpt of a training session using the model-rival technique. Irene (I) Pepperberg is the principal trainer, with Kimberly (K) Goodrich assisting as secondary trainer. In the excerpt in (1), Alex (A) is being taught to differentiate colors and shapes.[1]

(1) I: Kim, what color? (Holds up a green triangular piece of wood.)
     K: Green three-corner wood.
     I: (Briefly removes object from sight, turns body slightly away) No! Listen! I just want to know color! (Faces back toward K; re-presents object) What *color*?
     K: Green wood.
     I: (Hands over exemplar) That's right, the color is *green*; green wood.
     K: OK, Alex, now you tell me, what shape?
     A: No.
     K: OK, Irene, *you* tell me what shape.
     I: Three-corner wood.
     K: That's right, you listened! The shape is three-corner; it's *three-corner* wood (Hands over exemplar).
     I: Alex, here's your chance. What color?
     A: Wood.
     I: That's right, wood; what *color* wood?
     A: Green wood.
     I: Good parrot! Here you go (Hands over exemplar). The color is green.

Alex was trained to identify four different shapes, five different colors, and three different materials. In a test where he was presented with both novel and familiar items, he displayed at least 80% accuracy in description. Alex was also able to respond to questions like "What is the same?" and "What is different?" between two objects, and other second-order logical tasks. Pepperberg claims that this evidence supports the idea that Alex had well-defined mental categories and conceptual representations. However, she did not claim that Alex knew language; instead, she called it "complex two-way communication."

In light of Terrace's criticisms of primate language studies mentioned above, Pepperberg's work came under heavy scrutiny. How do we know that Alex wasn't just a very sophisticated mimic, learning what sound to make to correspond to a given object in order to get some food? Were Pepperberg's experiments really testing for language ability, or were they more related to the cognitive abilities of grey parrots? To what extent can we call Alex's utterances "language"? The same questions Savage-Rumbaugh asked of the apes can be asked of Alex: what kinds of mental representations does Alex have, and can we ascribe "meaning" to them?

Although grey parrots normally live for 50 years, Alex died unexpectedly at the age of 31 in 2007. Pepperberg continues to work with grey parrots; but none yet approach Alex's ability. The demonstration of Alex-like ability in other parrots will be the real test of the validity of her findings.

---

[1]With kind permission from Springer Science+Business Media: *Animal Learning & Behavior*, "Cognition in the African Grey parrot: Preliminary evidence for auditory/vocal comprehension of the class concept," volume 11, 1983, page 181, by Irene M. Pepperberg, Table 1.

FILE **14.4**

....

Practice

File 14.1—Communication and Language

Exercises

1. The file mentions that when a dog bares its teeth, it indicates that it is ready to attack. Compare this with humans baring their teeth when they are smiling. What does it mean when we smile? Does it mean that we are ready to attack? Is this arbitrary or iconic? How do dogs probably interpret smiling in a person they don't know?

2. Many people insist that their dogs, cats, or other pets are able to understand what they want and to communicate with them. There is no doubt that our pets are often able to meld very well into our lives. There is also no doubt that often there is at least some level of communication between people and their pets. Based on what you have read in File 14.1, however, how would you refute a person's claim that her dog or cat "knows exactly what I mean when I talk to him"?

3. Refer to the communication chain diagram in File 1.2. Although all animal communication systems have a mode of communication, semanticity, and a pragmatic function, all three of these are not required to make the communication chain work. Which are, and which aren't? Explain your answers.

4. A wolf is able to express subtle gradations of emotion by different positions of the ears, the lips, and the tail. There are eleven postures of the tail that express such emotions as self-confidence, confident threat, lack of tension, uncertain threat, depression, defensiveness, active submission, and complete submission. This system seems to be complex. Suppose there were a thousand different emotions that the wolf could express in this way. Would you then say that a wolf had a language similar to a human's? Why or why not?

Discussion Questions

5. In File 14.1, many modes of communication are introduced. What are some reasons that a certain mode of communication might be well-suited to some species but not to others?

6. Think about the following situation: two male crayfish fight with each other. One of them wins, and a female crayfish chooses the winner as her mate. Who is communicating with whom in this situation? Are the males communicating with each other? Or are they using the other in order to communicate with the female? Explain your answer.

7. The male Túngara Frog (*Physalaemus pustulosus*), native to Central America, gives a call during the mating season described onomatopoeically as a "whine-chuck." The call serves to attract females and discourage nearby males from approaching, but it also reveals the frog's location to the predatory fringe-lipped bat (*Trachops cirrhosus*). To what extent can we say that the male frog intends for any of these consequences to happen?

File 14.2—Animal Communication in the Wild

Exercises

8. Consider the bee communication system described in File 14.2 and answer the questions. Be sure to discuss all nine design features.

  i. Which design features does the system display? Please explain.

  ii. Which design features does the system clearly not display? Please explain.

  iii. For which design features does the file not provide you with enough evidence or information to decide whether the feature is present in the communication system or not? What would you need to know about the system to make a decision? What would the system have to be like in order for the feature to be present?

9. Consider the bird communication systems described in File 14.2, and answer parts (i) and (ii) from Exercise 8.

10. Consider the primate communication systems described in File 14.2, and answer parts (i) and (ii) from Exercise 8.

Activities

11. Male humpback whales (*Megaptera novaeangliae*) make low-frequency vocalizations often referred to as songs (female whales do not sing, as far as we know). The purpose of the songs is not entirely clear, but they could be for foraging, mating and parental behavior, long-range contact, assembly, sexual advertisement (male-male or male-female), greeting, spacing, threat, individual identification, and/or sensing of the environment. Under optimal conditions, these songs can be heard hundreds of kilometers away.

The songs consist of a series of notes organized into tunes, for example, a slowly rising intonation followed by several sharp drops. The tunes are repeated and organized hierarchically, so that each song as a whole is a palindrome (it reads the same backwards as it does forwards). For instance, if we have tunes A, B, and C, a possible song is A B C B A, or C A B A C. This recursive organization is reminiscent of syntactic structure in human language (see Chapter 5).

Which of Hockett's design features of language are present in humpback whale songs, and which are not? For each feature, explain your reasoning in a sentence or two.

12. Use the Internet, an encyclopedia, an animal behavior text, or other resource to investigate a natural animal communication system other than the ones described in File 14.2. Describe this system relative to the design features outlined in File 14.1.

File 14.3—Can Animals Be Taught Language?

Exercise

13. There are transcripts of several "chats" with Koko the Gorilla available online. Pick a chat from the links on the Links page for Chapter 14 and answer the questions below.

   i. What is Koko's longest utterance in the chat? What is Koko's average length of utterance; that is, how many words on average do Koko's utterances have? (You can estimate this.)

   ii. About what percentage of the time did you understand Koko's utterances without any help from Dr. Patterson? About what percentage of the time did you need her to interpret for Koko?

   iii. How relevant were Koko's utterances?

   iv. Did Koko interrupt other speakers frequently or rarely?

   v. What are the main topics that Koko talks about? What, if anything, does this reveal about her language use?

   vi. Does Koko ever seem to repeat or imitate Dr. Patterson's signs? About how frequently does she do so?

   vii. Do you find evidence that Koko really knows the meaning of the signs she uses? If so, what kinds of evidence do you find? Please give specific examples.

   viii. Compare your answers to (i)–(vii) with the sorts of responses you would give after reading the transcript of a conversation between humans. Based on this comparison, do you think Koko can really use language? Justify your answer. Explain both the things she does that do seem to model language use and the ways in which her behavior is dissimilar from human language use.

Discussion Questions

14. Imagine that you wanted to teach language to an animal other than a primate or a parrot. Consider how you would go about doing this, and then answer the questions below.

   i. Which animal would you choose and why?

   ii. What mode of communication would you choose to teach this animal? Why?

   iii. If you tried to teach the animal symbols and a simple syntax, how would you test whether it had learned to combine the symbols to form different messages?

   iv. Do you think the animal would be better at comprehending or producing both symbols and simple syntax? Why do you think so?

15. In File 14.3, a distinction is often drawn between teaching an animal language and teaching an animal to use language. However, the distinction between these two terms is never clearly defined. Based not only on what you have read in File 14.3 but also on your studies of language and linguistics throughout the book so far, what would you say the difference is between teaching an animal language and merely teaching an animal to use language?

16. Throughout this book, we have presented both signed and spoken modalities of human language. Both are equally authentic and natural modes of human communication. Presumably, then, the choice of whether to train an ape using one or the other of these two types of language is not particularly relevant to whether we conclude that it has, in fact, learned language. Now consider the case of lexigrams. Does using lexigrams to communicate have any less authenticity than either speech or signing? Why do you think so?

17. Suppose that animals can master some aspects of productivity (such as Koko creating the word *finger-bracelet* for 'ring' and Washoe using *water bird* for 'swan.' If they have the cognitive capacity to put discrete units together in new ways, why do you think we haven't found examples of productivity in apes' natural communication systems?

18.   **i.** Savage-Rumbaugh claims that if we are able to teach an ape to use symbols (using her three-part definition), it will be a more important indication of its ability to use language than would use of grammar. Do you agree?

    ii. Suppose that we were able to teach a hypothetical animal—let's say a super-intelligent mutant guinea pig—to productively put together complex grammatical utterances using consistent word order, function words, and so on, but that the guinea pig was unable to use signs symbolically. Would you say that the guinea pig had a better command of language or a worse command of language than a bonobo that understood the symbolism of language but that did not have a grasp of a grammatical system?

19. Researchers have by and large concluded that—even if apes can be taught to use elements of human language—they cannot acquire human language naturally in the way that human children do. Imagine that on some alien planet we were to discover a new species of animal. Further imagine that these animals never learned language naturally (either growing up in communities with each other or growing up in a home with humans as a human child would) but that following instruction, the aliens mastered language use completely. That is, they exhibited language use encompassing all of the design features and full use of symbols: they could hold conversations, write speeches, tell jokes, and so on. How would you describe the linguistic abilities of these aliens? Would you say that their linguistic abilities (after training) were as genuine as those of humans, or would you say that they were still lacking in some way? Why would you make this judgment?

20. The work that Terrace did and his interpretation of his results shed doubt on the entire enterprise of trying to teach human language to animals. As a result, there was a loss of grant funding for this sort of work. Such responses are very common in the scientific community: those who fund grants have only so much money to give, and understandably they generally try to underwrite projects that have a high level of support within the community. Suppose, though, that there was an unlimited amount of monetary funding. Do you think, following pronouncements such as Terrace's, that it would be appropriate to reduce the amount of effort put into researching a particular concept?

Further Readings

Candland, Douglas Keith. 1993. *Feral children and clever animals: Reflections on human nature.* Oxford: Oxford University Press.

Hauser, Marc D., and Mark Konishi (eds.). 2003. *The design of animal communication.* Cambridge, MA: MIT Press.

Hillix, William A., and Duane M. Rumbaugh. 2004. *Animal bodies, human minds: Ape, dolphin, and parrot language skills.* New York: Springer.

Pepperberg, Irene Maxine. 1999. *The Alex studies: Cognitive and communicative abilities of grey parrots.* Cambridge, MA: Harvard University Press.

Savage-Rumbaugh, Sue, and Roger Lewin. 1994. *Kanzi: The ape at the brink of the human mind.* New York: John Wiley and Sons.

Wise, Steven M. 2002. *Drawing the line: Science and the case for animal rights.* Cambridge, MA: Perseus Books.

CHAPTER
15

Writing Systems

FILE 15.0

....

What Is Writing?

We made the point in Chapter 1 that the primary form of linguistic expression is either vocal or manual (spoken or signed) rather than written. Knowing a language requires knowing how to speak it, but not how to read or write it; in fact, most of the languages that exist today or have existed in the past have not had a writing system. The majority of this book therefore has focused exclusively on the structure of spoken language itself, and not on how it is written. (Ironically, of course, we have had to rely on written language in order to create this book!)

At the same time, however, writing is an interesting topic, and it is clearly related to the study of language: even though language does not depend on writing, writing does depend on language. While the actual noun *writing* may refer to various things (like a person's style of handwriting or an author's technique of writing), the type of **writing** we are referring to here is "the use of graphic marks to represent specific linguistic utterances" (Rogers 2005: 2). Hence, writing is a system that is used to record language.

Contents

FILE **15.1**
....

Writing, Language, and Culture

15.1.1 What Is Writing?

When we write something down, such as when we write a note to ourselves to remember something, or write a letter to Aunt Anne in another state, or write a blog post on the Internet, we are recording a particular utterance or idea for a particular audience. Writing allows us to communicate with others beyond the capability of spoken language.

Writing is not, however, the only kind of visual, permanent communication. There are many kinds of nonlinguistic communication, many of them visual and permanent—for example, art, traffic signs, and warning signs. A painting can often communicate ideas of peace, fear, happiness, nobility, or cruelty, but these are vague ideas rather than specific ones. We could use any of several utterances of language to describe a painting, but we cannot say that any of these utterances are specifically communicated by the picture. Language, and the writing that encodes it, allow us to communicate very specific ideas accurately and efficiently.

Some images, however, are fairly specific. In some cases, such as traffic signs, they may be used to avoid disadvantaging those who cannot read or do not speak a particular language. Such images are part of our everyday lives. These are not writing either, though, because language includes many things that cannot be represented by such pictures. It is hard to imagine an image that could say such an ordinary thing as "What's for dinner?" More importantly, however, these images have no systematic structure.

Systematic structure is a vitally important aspect of writing. The elements of writing, called **graphs** or **graphemes,** do not just occur randomly. There are conventions for relating parts of spoken language to parts of the writing and parts of the writing to one another. One of these conventions is the direction of writing, which is independent from the language itself. The English writing system is written left-to-right in rows starting at the top left corner of the page. Arabic orthography is also written in rows beginning at the top of the page, but each row is written right to left. Chinese writing may be done in rows from left to right like English, or, more traditionally, it may be written in columns from top to bottom, starting at the top right corner of the page.[1] Some writing systems have nonlinear elements that appear above or below the line of writing. Other structural details of a writing system include conventions for spacing between words or syllables, punctuation, and capital letters. Writing systems, then, are systematic ways of recording language by means of visual, permanent marks.

---

[1]Can you imagine switching to reading English vertically from right to left? Try it below:

h	s	t	d
a	e	h	o
r	e	i	e
d	m	s	s

15.1.2 Writing and Language

Writing is obligatorily connected to language. It is dependent on language by definition—if writing is used to represent linguistic utterances and to record language, it cannot exist without language. Although the kinds of images and symbols discussed above can be "translated" into many languages and are therefore independent of language, no writing system can exist independent of the language it is recording.

But writing is not language. Writing is distinct from language in many ways (see File 1.3). Knowing a language requires knowing how to speak it, but not how to write it, and many languages have no written form at all. Writing is not acquired in the way language is, but must be taught. Spoken language encodes thought into a physically transmittable form, while writing, in turn, encodes spoken language into a physically preservable form. Spoken language is, on the one hand, usually more fleeting than writing (once an utterance has been said, we rely on memory to preserve it if it has not been recorded) but, on the other hand, less changeable (once you have said something, you can't "take it back").

If writing is separate from language, how does it relate to language? There are many types of writing systems, but all writing systems relate to language in terms of sound, meaning, or a combination of the two. These types of writing systems will be discussed in File 15.2.

It is important to remember that writing systems are largely arbitrary, just as spoken language is arbitrary (see File 1.4 for the meaning of *arbitrary* with respect to language) and that they are used successfully only because of social conventions. Any language could be written using some other writing system, and there is no inherent correspondence between graphemes and their associated sound or meaning. For example, Serbian and Croatian are very closely related (see File 10.1), but Serbian is typically written using the Cyrillic alphabet, and Croatian is typically written using the Roman alphabet. This arbitrariness is particularly clear when you consider the case of Cherokee, an Iroquois language spoken in North Carolina and Oklahoma. A man named Sequoyah developed a phonographic writing system for Cherokee in the nineteenth century, making use of Roman letters he had seen in English texts as well as new characters of his own design. Interestingly, however, the system he developed was syllabic, so each character represented a consonant-vowel sequence, and because he was most likely illiterate in English, the Roman letters do not represent anything remotely like the sounds they represent in English! For example, the symbol <K> represents the sounds [tso] and [tsʰo], while the symbol <J> represents the sounds [ku] and [kʰu]. It is important to remember that there is a convention mapping the written graphemes to spoken sounds and words: the mapping itself must be learned explicitly for each language.

15.1.3 Writing and Culture

Writing has had a profound impact on human culture. Writing allows us to encode thoughts in a way that can be preserved over space and time, and therefore shared with many more people than spoken language alone allows. It allows much more complex calculation than could be done just by using spoken language and memory, and it is much more suited to revision and refinement: that is, you can go back and change or edit a written document before it is shared in a way that you can't do for utterances that have been spoken. Writing also allows us to supplement our own memory. We can read and have access to much longer written texts, and many more written texts, than we can memorize. We can keep long-term records of weather and growth. Because of this, we can create a much more complex society using writing than would be possible without it.

Of course, the effects of writing on culture have not always been viewed positively, and languages that are only spoken are not in any way inferior to ones that have a writing system. Indeed, when writing systems (and later printing) were introduced, many people worried about their potentially negative impact on the human mind (much as some people worry today about the influence of calculators, computers, and smartphones on our ability to think for ourselves). Similarly, concerns have been raised that "textspeak" is ruining the verbal abilities of young people. Walter Ong, in his book comparing oral and literate cultures, describes some of the complaints against writing systems:

> Writing, Plato has Socrates say in the *Phaedrus,* is inhuman, pretending to establish outside the mind what in reality can only be in the mind. It is a thing, a manufactured product. . . . Secondly, Plato's Socrates urges, writing destroys memory. Those who use writing will become forgetful, relying on an external resource for what they lack in internal resources. Writing weakens the mind. . . . Thirdly, a written text is basically unresponsive. If you ask a person to explain his or her statement, you can get an explanation; if you ask a text, you get back nothing except the same, often stupid, words which called for your question in the first place. (1982: 79)

So while writing has indubitably caused a massive transformation in the structure of human communication and culture, it is clear that this transformation can be seen in both positive and negative lights. There have been many discussions on the effect of writing systems on culture (it has been called "one of the most significant cultural accomplishments of human beings" (Rogers 2005: 1)), some of which are listed in File 15.4 under Further Readings.

Although writing has influenced the cultures in which it is used, it is also important to note that culture influences writing. In practice, it is not always the case that writing records the spoken language. Writing is always done in a social and cultural context. In northwestern Scotland, for example, speakers of Scots Gaelic do almost all of their writing in English. In many Arabic-speaking countries, the form of Arabic that speakers use in spoken language is quite different from the form of Arabic that they use in writing. Although it is possible to write a spoken Arabic dialect, this is rarely done, and many Arabic speakers are uncomfortable with it. Even in English, the written form of the language usually differs from the spoken form of the language. In fact, some consider writing to be a separate dialect. In addition, as we shall see in the following section, many cultures and societies have multiple writing systems.

15.1.4 Functional Writing Systems

In any advanced literate society, we can find a variety of different writing systems. In some cases, there are different writing systems for different languages. In addition, though, there are different ways of writing one and the same language. These different writing systems are generally used by different people, in different contexts, and for different purposes and audiences. Writing systems can function as dialects or identity markers (see Chapter 10), and it is of sociolinguistic interest to ask, "Who is using which writing system for what purpose and audience?" For instance, executives may not be able to decipher the shorthand their administrative assistants use, and many groups of friends have written abbreviations of phrases, names, and in-group activities.

John Mouton divides writing systems into five classes based on their functionality and the answers to the questions above: pedographies, technographies, shorthands, cryptographies, and orthographies.

a. Orthographies include the vast majority of writing systems. They are the most elaborate, the most versatile, and the most numerous. They are used for all purposes not provided for by the other four types and are sometimes used for those purposes as well. Many languages have multiple orthographies used by different people in different contexts.

b. Pedographies are writing systems designed for learners, whether of their first or second language, as a stepping-stone to the standard orthography of the language. Many of the standard orthographies of languages are not learner-friendly, and it was common in the early twentieth century to begin reading with a pedography and only later switch to the standard orthography. For example, languages whose orthographies do not write the vowels (called abjads) are often written with vowels inserted by and for language learners.

c. Technographies are scientific tools designed and used by a specialized field. Within linguistics, the most obvious example of a technography is the IPA, introduced in Chapter 2. In addition to the IPA and other phonetic transcription systems, there are additional writing systems used for phonetic fieldwork and some kinds of linguistic analysis. Outside linguistics, technographies are used for chemical notation, computer coding, and cartography.

d. Shorthands are designed so that they can be written faster than traditional orthographies—fast enough to record speech verbatim, either by hand or while typing. Shorthands were also used in inscriptions in Ancient Greece, to record the speeches of Cicero in Rome, and to record criminal confessions in imperial China. Knowledge of shorthand was once absolutely crucial for secretaries and reporters, and although its use and importance have lessened with the increase of convenient sound-recording devices, it is still frequently used for court reporting, press reporting, and some commercial and professional correspondence, and by some professional writers. An example of shorthand is given in (1).

(1)　The Lord's Prayer in Pitman's Shorthand

e. Cryptographies, or codes, are designed to conceal information. They are used, for example, in diplomatic and military communications and in some industrial and commercial activities. Codes and code-breaking are discussed at length in File 17.5.

15.1.5　Computer-Mediated Communication

Although the functions and forms of writing systems have varied endlessly over the millennia, they have almost always been written on physical media (books, letters, etc.), which has put constraints on their usage. Recently, however, the massive spread of digital communication has created a new field for written language, with new uses, new features, and possibly new consequences. The presence of written systems on the Internet, in text messaging (or texting), and other digital media has led to the usage of writing systems for new forms of communication. Most previous written communication was **asynchronous**: communications were not conducted in real time. However, forms of digital communication such as instant messaging come much closer to being **synchronous,** where both sides of the conversation occur simultaneously.

So, is **computer-mediated communication** (or CMC) more like speech than it is like traditional writing? Unfortunately, this is not a simple question to answer; communication in email is different from communication in online chats, which is different from communication on blogs and social media websites, which is different from texting. David Crystal examined seven features of spoken and written communication in various forms of

CMC and concluded that although online communication is closer to writing, it "selectively and adaptively displays properties of both" writing and speech (2006: 51).

This structural uniqueness of digital communication has already led to textual innovations. CMC's usage in real-time conversation has facilitated the shortening of commonly used words and expressions and the development of acronyms such as *brb* for *be right back*. Engaging in communication without being able to see others' body language or hear their prosodic features has also led to the creation of emoticons and emoji, which are ideographs that indicate the mood of the speaker and serve various other pragmatic and communicative functions. Finally, the informal nature of many forms of digital communication has led to decreased usage of capitalization, punctuation, and other traditional features of many writing systems.

But are these developments in CMC leading to permanent changes in written language? In both British and American English, concerns have been raised in recent years that "textspeak" and "IM language" are producing a generation of children who lack basic skills in more traditional orthographies. Some have claimed that digital communication is the harbinger of a return to destandardized, pre-Modern English forms of writing.

Yet there is just as much evidence to counter this claim as there is to support it. Abbreviated words and sentences have long been common in telegraphy, and textual codes for emotion have existed since the nineteenth century, both without long-term consequences on writing as a whole. As the use of digital communication continues to expand and diversify, it remains to be seen what changes it will undergo and what, if any, effect it will have on other forms of communication.

FILE 15.2

Types of Writing Systems

15.2.1 Classifying Writing Systems

Since writing represents language, and spoken language consists of arbitrary relationships between particular sounds (or gestures[1]) and particular meanings, there are at least three ways in which a writing system may approach the language it represents: from the **meaning** side, the **sound** side, or simultaneously from both the meaning and the sound sides.

Example (1) helps you visualize the (somewhat simplified) relationship between the spoken language and its writing system. In (1a), we illustrate how English writes the word *box* with symbols that represent only the sounds of the language, without any regard to the meaning. In (1b), we illustrate how Mandarin Chinese writes the word for 'box' with symbols that represent both the sound and the meaning of the word. Finally, in (1c), we illustrate how Mandarin writes the word for 'meaning' or 'intention' with symbols that represent only the meaning of the word, without any regard to the sound.

(1)   Visualizing the relationship between the spoken language and its writing system

      a. English

      b. Mandarin Chinese

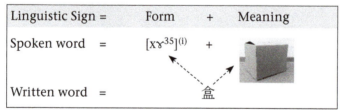

---

[1]We should note that most signed languages do not have their own writing systems, instead often relying on the writing system and language used by the dominant spoken language in a country. Most dictionaries and references represent signed languages pictorially, with pictures of the hands and arrows representing movement, as we have done throughout this book. There are some writing systems for signed languages, which often represent the various phonetic components of the signs (e.g., handshape, orientation, and movement) (see, for example, Martin 2000). Because of the current limited use of written forms of signed languages, we will not go into any detail about them here.

c. Mandarin Chinese

Linguistic Sign =	Form	+	Meaning
Spoken word　=	[ji⁵¹]	+	'meaning, intention'
Written word　=	意		

Spoken word $=$ $[ji^{51}]$ $+$ 'meaning, intention'

Written word $=$ 意

----▸ indicates the written form's approximation of form and/or meaning.
(i) The numbers after the segments are Chao-type tone numbers, with '5' denoting the highest pitch in the pitch range, and '1' the lowest (see Section 2.5.4).

In English, we use the letters <box> to represent the sounds [bɑks], which is how we pronounce the word *box*. These sounds and letters have nothing to do with the meaning of the word as a type of 'container'—for example, the same set of sounds and letters could be (and in fact is!) used to mean 'to spar with someone using fists.' In Mandarin Chinese, the written form 盒 represents both the sound and the meaning of the word. The upper half of the written form, pronounced as [xɤ³⁵], indicates the pronunciation; the lower half indicates that the meaning of the word is 'container.' By contrast, the written form 意 of the Mandarin word for 'meaning, intention' does not give any indication as to its pronunciation. Instead, it is a combination of two characters: the character for 'voice' (音, [jin⁵⁵]) and the character for 'heart' (心, [ɕin⁵⁵]), which together mean 'the voice of the heart,' from which comes 'meaning, intention' (when the character was created, the bottom part was actually not 心, but 口 'sound,' so the character's original meaning was 'the voice/sound of the mouth').

In English, our standard writing system is based primarily on sound correspondences, although you do sometimes see writing incorporated with images representing meaning in advertising or illustrations, as in (2).

(2)　Example of symbols representing both sound and meaning in English

In Chinese, the writing system is a combination of sound- and meaning-based representations. Some written forms, like the Mandarin word for 'box' above, represent both in the same word; others may represent either the sound in isolation or the meaning in isolation, like the Mandarin word for 'meaning, intention'.

We can classify writing systems along these lines, depending on whether they represent sounds, meanings, or both. In reality, there are no entire writing systems based exclusively on sound or on meaning. All writing systems include elements based on both sound and meaning, and thus they include some variation as to the level of linguistic structure that they relate to. We can, however, talk about whether the graphemes of some writing system represent predominately the sound or the meaning.

Systems that rely predominantly on the representation of sound can be considered **phonographic** systems, where the *phono-* prefix relates to the notion of speech sounds. These systems may be like English, where each symbol approximately represents a single sound (**alphabetic** or **phonemic** writing systems), or like Cherokee, where each symbol approximately represents a consonant plus vowel combination (**syllabic** writing systems). On the other hand, systems like Mandarin Chinese, discussed above, can be considered **morphographic** systems, where the *morpho-* prefix relates to the notion of the *morpheme*. Such systems are sometimes referred to as **logographic,** where the prefix *logo-* means 'word,' but since we know that words may be made up of smaller sound-meaning pairs (see Chapter 4), and such writing systems usually represent these smaller units, it is more accurate to call these systems *morphographic.*

When you look at a written text, you may also see symbols on the page that do not (at least directly) represent either sound or meaning; these symbols include spaces between words, indentation at the start of paragraphs, and commas, periods, exclamation points, and other punctuation. Such symbols are used to visually mark the structure of the written language and may or may not correspond to aspects of the spoken language. For example, when we speak, we do not usually pause between all words; adding spaces between written words gives the reader an aid in word segmentation that a listener does not have (see File 9.4). On the other hand, we do often place commas at natural spoken intonation breaks, and question marks may correspond to a particular type of question intonation (see Section 2.5.3). Different writing systems have different conventions for what elements are marked; for example, most Chinese texts do not mark the boundaries between words, while in Tibetan, every syllable boundary is marked with a raised dot.

In the rest of this file, we will take a closer look at both morphographic and phonographic writing systems.

15.2.2 Morphographic Writing Systems

Morphographic writing systems rely predominately on a correspondence between a written grapheme and a particular morpheme, primarily the meaning of that morpheme. The symbols themselves may or may not tell the reader anything about how the morpheme is pronounced: the reader just has to know. While this may at first seem a bit strange to someone who only reads a language like English, which uses a phonographic writing system, it may be easier to understand once you realize that we do, in fact, have some morphographic characters in English. For example, the symbol <2> is morphographic; it represents the meaning 'two.' It is pronounced with the phonemes /tu/, but the grapheme itself does not tell us this. The same character is used with the same meaning but different pronunciations in different languages (e.g., in Spanish, <2> is pronounced [dos], and in German, [tsvai]). It is simply a character that has a particular meaning associated with it but that says nothing about its pronunciation. Similarly, <&> and <%> are morphographic characters—they relate to language primarily at the level of meaning, not sound. Although we know that <&> is pronounced [ænd], we cannot use this grapheme to stand for [ænd] in other words; for example, we do not write *land* <l&>.

An example from a highly morphographic system, traditional Chinese characters, is given in (3a), in which each character stands for a word as a whole; another example from Chinese is given in (3b), in which each character stands for a morpheme that makes up a longer word.

(3) Chinese morphographs

    a. 與　　狼　　共　　舞
       with　　wolf(s)　　together　　dance　　'Dancing with Wolves'
       (The Chinese translation of a movie name)

    b. 發　　展
       expand　extend　　　　　　　　　'to develop'
       (A longer word in Chinese)

Traditionally, people have often thought that morphographic writing systems used symbols stylized from earlier **pictograms** (i.e., pictures drawn to express ideas) that do not convey any information about the sound of the word at all. In a dichotomous categorization of writing systems (i.e., sound-based versus meaning-based), these morphographic systems are thus categorized as meaning-based. This view, however, is true only of the earliest stage in the historical development of the morphographic writing systems. As these systems develop, a very large proportion of the morphographs come to represent the sound, as well as the meaning, of the words. Morphographic writing systems often have many more graphemes than phonographic writing systems.

Let us use the Chinese writing system as an example. In early Chinese writing the concepts of 'above' and 'below' were represented by drawing a shorter line above or below a longer horizontal line (see (4)).

(4) Examples of morphographs in early Chinese: 'above' is on the left; 'below' is on the right.

Note that these two morphographs do not indicate the pronunciation of the two words. It did not take long for people to realize that representing concepts solely in this way was insufficient. Hence, morphographs began to be borrowed based on their phonemic value alone to represent concepts that did not formerly have a written representation and concepts that were not easily expressed otherwise. For example, the Chinese character 來 was developed from a pictogram of wheat to represent the idea 'wheat.' Later on, this character 來, meaning 'wheat,' was borrowed to represent the concept 'come,' simply because these two concepts shared the same pronunciation (*[ləg][2] in early Chinese). This method is known as the **rebus principle**: borrowing a symbol only for the phonemic value that it encodes. To help illustrate, try to read the picture on the left (an eye) and then the picture on the right (a sea):

(5) Illustrating the rebus principle in English

As you say [ɑɪ si], you probably don't mean 'eye sea' (which doesn't make much sense), but rather 'I see.' By the same token, the character 來 is like the pictures of *eye* and *sea*. That is, you look at the character 來 and say it out loud, and you mean 'come,' not 'wheat.'

As a matter of fact, combining a phonetic and a semantic component to create new characters to represent ideas has been extremely productive in the historical development of the Chinese writing system. The majority of Chinese characters have been created this way. (Statistics show that 81.2% of the Chinese characters in 100 C.E. in the Han dynasty (Norman 1988: 267) and 90% of the Chinese characters today (DeFrancis 1984) have both a phonetic and a semantic component.) For instance, the character 來 above has become the phonetic component of other words, while the semantic component of these words is indicated by the non-來 part (or the radical) of the characters as shown in (6a); more examples are given in (6b).

---

[2]The asterisk * indicates that the pronunciation is a historical reconstruction for early Chinese. Details about historical reconstruction can be found in File 13.7.

(6) Combining a phonetic component and a semantic component to create new characters to represent concepts in Chinese.

a. Examples using 來 'wheat (in early Chinese)/come' as the phonetic component (pronunciations given in present-day Mandarin Chinese)

Meaning Component		Phonetic Component		Written Form and Pronunciation	Word Meaning
木 'wood'	+	來 [lai³⁵]	→	棶 [lai³⁵]	'large-leaved dogwood'
金 'gold'	+	來 [lai³⁵]	→	鎀 [lai³⁵]	'rhenium'
山 'mountain'	+	來 [lai³⁵]	→	崍 [lai³⁵]	'Qionglai' (name of a mountain)
水 'water'	+	來 [lai³⁵]	→	淶 [lai³⁵]	'Laishui' (name of a river in the north of China)
目 'eye'	+	來 [lai³⁵]	→	睞 [lai⁵¹]	'to squint'

b. Examples using 馬 'horse' as the phonetic component (pronunciations given in present-day Mandarin Chinese)

Meaning Component		Phonetic Component		Written Form and Pronunciation	Word Meaning
口 'mouth'	+	馬 [ma²¹⁴]	→	嗎 [ma⁰]	question particle
口 'mouth'	+	馬 [ma²¹⁴]	→	罵 [ma⁵¹]	'to scold'
女 'woman'	+	馬 [ma²¹⁴]	→	媽 [ma⁵⁵]	'mother'
虫 'insect'	+	馬 [ma²¹⁴]	→	螞 [ma²¹⁴]	'ant/leech/locust'
玉 'jade'	+	馬 [ma²¹⁴]	→	瑪 [ma²¹⁴]	'agate'

As you can see from these examples, the traditional view that the morphographic writing system of Chinese, and that of other languages such as Egyptian, is solely meaning-based is not accurate. Perhaps a better way to characterize a given writing system is to evaluate it on a continuum where purely sound-based and purely meaning-based are two extremes. For a writing system such as Chinese, in which a large proportion of the morphographs represent **both** the sound and the meaning of the words, it is obvious that placing it at the meaning-based extreme of the continuum is not appropriate. When compared to the phonographic systems of the next section, however, it is clear that the meaning-based component of these systems is much more distinct and significant than the meaning-based component of phonographic systems.

Morphographic writing systems have been developed independently in separate parts of the world and are the oldest type of writing. Besides the Chinese writing system, the hieroglyphic writing of ancient Egypt and the cuneiform writing of ancient Mesopotamia were based solely on meaning in their earliest forms, although they too each became modified to include sound-based elements as they were utilized by succeeding generations. Both of these latter writing systems were invented at least 5,000 years ago, like the Chinese system, and survived for thousands of years.

15.2.3 Phonographic Writing Systems

Phonographic systems, by contrast, are more heavily weighted toward the sound-based end of the continuum. Again, however, this classification must be taken only loosely, for it is not the case that there is a one-to-one correspondence between graphemes and sounds in many phonographic systems (as was mentioned in File 2.1 in the context of discussing phonetic transcription systems). For example, you probably think of English writing as a phonographic system, especially if you were taught to "sound words out" when you came across an unfamiliar word in reading. If you think about it, however, you will see that even in a phonographic system like English, there is a heavy reliance on knowledge of the morphemes themselves in order to actually read a text. For example, the grapheme sequences <through> and <though> are pronounced as [θɹu] and [ðoʊ], respectively: although they differ in writing by only a single grapheme, they do not, in fact, share a single phoneme! You can think of these sequences as being (arbitrary) graphic representations of the whole morphemes—while these sequences are obviously historically derived from more direct sound representations of the words, they have become dependent on the reader's knowledge of the meanings to be recognizable (see File 13.3 on sound change). This is exactly analogous to the development of meaning-based pictograms into sound- and meaning-based characters that we saw in the section on morphographic writing above. Some writing systems, such as Spanish writing and Finnish writing, are closer to a purely phonographic writing system, but still have some meaning-based elements.

Although the graphemes of a morphographic writing system represent the morphemes of a language fairly straightforwardly, phonographic writing systems can represent the sounds of a language in a variety of ways. As a basic distinction, the graphemes of phonographic writing systems can represent individual sounds or syllables.

a. Syllabic Writing Systems. One type of phonographic writing system uses characters to represent particular sequences of sounds. Because each character is usually a syllable, such systems are often called *syllabic writing systems,* and the total set of characters that are used for a given language is often referred to as a **syllabary**. This nomenclature can be somewhat misleading in that it is not always the case that every possible syllable in the language is represented with a separate character; some syllables may have to be written using multiple characters, with the understanding that some characters are pronounced as extra sounds in a syllable rather than as separate syllables in their own right.[3]

Syllabaries have been used for languages such as Ancient Persian, Japanese, and Cherokee. Japanese is particularly interesting because it actually uses three separate writing systems, two phonographic syllabaries (called "hiragana" and "katakana," but known collectively as "kana") and one morphographic system (called "kanji"), which consists of borrowed morphographic characters from Chinese. Although any word can be written using characters from the syllabaries, there are systematic ways of using the three writing systems. As a rough generalization, traditional Japanese writing normally uses a combination of syllabic symbols from the hiragana for function morphemes, and morphographic characters from kanji for content morphemes (see File 4.1). Katakana characters are normally used for Western loanwords, for onomatopoetic words, and for emphasis. Some examples of the kana symbols are given in (7).

---

[3]A more accurate term for these writing systems is *moraic;* each character represents a *mora,* a unit of timing somewhat similar to a syllable. We will not try to address the differences between syllables and moras in this book.

(7) Examples of some of the corresponding syllables in hiragana and katakana

Hiragana					Katakana				
だ	ぢ	づ	で	ど	ダ	ヂ	ヅ	デ	ド
[da]	[ʤi]	[ʣu]	[de]	[do]	[da]	[ʤi]	[ʣu]	[de]	[do]
わ			を	ん	ワ			ヲ	ン
[wa]			[wo]	[n][4]	[wa]			[wo]	[n]

The examples in (8) show the representations for the word 'telephone' in hiragana, katakana, and kanji. In each of the kana, the first two symbols represent [de] and [n], and the third represents [wa]. In the kanji, the two symbols are Chinese characters that stand for the morphemes meaning 'electricity' and 'words,' respectively.

(8) The word 'telephone' written in Japanese using hiragana, katakana, and kanji

Hiragana	Katakana	Kanji
でんわ	デンワ	電話
[den wa]	[den wa]	[den wa]

b. Phonemic Writing Systems (Alphabets, Abjads, and Abugidas). The other main type of phonographic writing system uses characters that represent individual sounds or segments, that is, letters that represent phonemes. Each of the syllables that make up the words of a language is, in turn, composed of one or more speech sounds and therefore one or more letters. Since there are just a limited number of speech sounds used by any given language, there are fewer unique speech sounds than unique syllables in a language. Therefore, it stands to reason that a phonemic writing system requires fewer characters than a syllabic writing system.

Not all phonemic writing systems represent all of the phonemes used in the spoken language. Systems that do represent all the sounds, both consonants and vowels, are said to use an **alphabet**. Systems that represent only the consonants but not the vowels are called **abjads**. Finally, systems that represent the consonants with full graphemes and the vowels with extra marks (called **diacritics**) on the consonants are called **abugidas**. There are no systems where only the vowels are represented without the consonants.

(i) Abugidas. Examples of abugidas include: Devanāgarī, the script used to write Sanskrit, Hindi, Marathi, and Nepali; Gujarātī, the script used to write Gujarātī and Kacchi; and Bengali, the script used to write Assamese and Bengali. These languages are all Indo-Aryan languages spoken in South Asia, and they all use scripts that are descended from the ancient Brāhmī script. In these systems, all consonant graphemes automatically have a following vowel sound (usually a short [a] or [ə]), unless another vowel symbol is used. So the symbol क all by itself is pronounced as the syllable [ka]. If a different vowel is necessary, then the symbol is marked in a specific way, as shown in (9). The vowels are each marked the same way regardless of the consonant they are associated with.

(9) Syllables in Devanāgarī starting with [k]

क	का	कि	की	कु	कू	के	कै	को	कौ	कृ
[ka]	[kaː]	[ki]	[kiː]	[ku]	[kuː]	[ke]	[kai]	[ko]	[kau]	[kr̩]

---

[4]Note that this [n] and the one for Katakana is used only for the final [n] of a syllable.

Vowels in initial position have distinct forms. The vowel symbols in (10) are used only in initial position; otherwise, vowels are marked on the preceding consonant.

(10) Initial vowel symbols in Devanāgarī

अ   आ   इ   ई   उ   ऊ   ए   ओ

[a]   [aː]   [i]   [iː]   [u]   [uː]   [e]   [o]

In (11), you can see how a Devanāgarī word is built up from various symbols. Devanāgarī is (mostly) written from left to right.

(11) Writing the word [gadʒena] 'elephant' in Devanāgarī

ग   जे   न   गजेन

[ga]   [dʒe]   [na]   [gadʒena]

(ii) Abjads. The Arabic and Hebrew writing systems are traditionally considered examples of abjads. An example is shown in the Hebrew words in (12). (Note that Hebrew is written from right to left.) It might at first seem that writing without vowels would be very difficult to read, but one's knowledge of the language usually allows one to "fill in" the vowels by observing the overall context of a sentence. This is illustrated by the following example from English, in which only the consonants are written: *Ths sntnc s wrttn wth th vwl smbls lft t.*[5]

(12) Some Hebrew words

Hebrew Orthography and Letter-by-Letter IPA	Full IPA Transcription of the Pronunciation	English Gloss
גמל l m g	[gamal]	'camel'
מברשת t ʃ ɣ v m	[mivɣɛʃɛt]	'brush'
סלם m l s	[sulam]	'ladder'
מדפסת t s p d m	[madpɛsɛt]	'printer'

As you might expect, however, writing only the consonants of words can create ambiguities. Thus, both the Arabic and the Hebrew writing systems do also have diacritics for the vowels, which are sometimes inserted to make the pronunciation of the words more explicit. In (13), the Hebrew word 'ladder' from (12) is repeated, but using vowel diacritics to indicate the full pronunciation. Because it is an abjad, however, these vowel diacritics are not necessary. In Devanāgarī, which is an abugida, the vowel symbols are required.

(13) The word 'ladder' in Hebrew containing vowel diacritics

סֻלָם   [sulam]   'ladder'

m l s
   a u

---

[5]For comparison, try reading the same sentence with only the vowels: *i eee i ie i e oe yo e ou.* The difficulty in reading just the vowels explains why no such writing systems exist!

(iii) Alphabets. Finally, there are several different alphabets used throughout the world today. The most familiar alphabet is probably the Roman (Latin) alphabet used to write such diverse languages as English, Swahili, Finnish, and Turkish. Each of these languages uses a slightly different version of the Roman alphabet, and each has a slightly different way of relating the letters of the alphabet to the sounds of the language. The Roman alphabet is a variant of an early Greek alphabet used by Greek colonists south of Rome and by the Etruscans. Later on, this Greek alphabet was adapted by Slavic speakers to form the Cyrillic alphabet. A list of the symbols of the Cyrillic alphabet used to write Russian is provided in (14). Slightly different versions of the Cyrillic alphabet are used to write other Slavic languages such as Serbian, Bulgarian, and Ukrainian (some Slavic languages, such as Polish and Czech, use the Roman alphabet). The Cyrillic alphabet is also used to write some non-Slavic languages of the former Soviet Union (e.g., Moldovan, a Romance language, and Uzbek, a Turkic language).

(14) The Cyrillic alphabet used for Russian (both capital and lowercase letters are given)

Аа	[a]	Кк	[k]	Хх	[x]
Бб	[b]	Лл	[l]	Цц	[ts]
Вв	[v]	Мм	[m]	Чч	[tʃ]
Гг	[g]	Нн	[n]	Шш	[ʃ]
Дд	[d]	Оо	[o]	Щщ	[ʃʲ]
Ее	[je]	Пп	[p]	Ъъ	"hard sign"
Ёё	[jo]	Рр	[r]	Ыы	[ɨ]
Жж	[ʒ]	Сс	[s]	Ьь	"soft sign"
Зз	[z]	Тт	[t]	Ээ	[ɛ]
Ии	[i]	Уу	[u]	Юю	[ju]
Йй	[j]	Фф	[f]	Яя	[ja]

In the Cyrillic alphabet, notice that the "hard sign" and the "soft sign" usually have no pronunciation of their own. Instead of being symbols for separate phonemes, they indicate something about the preceding consonant. The "soft sign" indicates that the preceding consonant is unpredictably palatalized (see Section 3.3.3 for a discussion of palatalization), and it appears at the syllable boundary after the palatalized consonant (see (15) for examples). Another way to mark palatalization is to use a different vowel sign; notice that there are four vowel symbols in (14) that represent [jV] (where V is any vowel). Generally, a sequence of a palatalized consonant plus a vowel is written with a consonant and one of these special vowel symbols, though there are cases where both the consonant **and** the vowel are marked with palatalization, in which case the consonant is palatalized and then followed by a palatal glide (see (15) for examples).

The "hard sign" is used to mark that a consonant is not palatalized in a context where you might expect it to be. The default assumption, however, is that a consonant is not palatalized unless it is followed by a soft sign or is inherently palatal, so the hard sign is used much less often than the soft sign. The hard and soft signs are somewhat analogous to the "silent <e>" in English orthography; the grapheme itself has no sound, but it tells us something about the pronunciation of the preceding vowel. (Compare *bit* and *bite*.)

(15) Examples of Russian orthography

	Russian Orthography	**Phonemic IPA Transcription**	**English Gloss**
No palatalization	дом<u>а</u>	/do<u>ma</u>/	'at home'
	лу<u>чш</u>е	/lu<u>tʃʃ</u>e/	'better, rather'
Palatalization marked on the consonant (with the soft sign)	се<u>мь</u>	/sʲe<u>mʲ</u>/	'seven'
	бо<u>ль</u>ше	/bol^jʃe/	'more'
Palatalization marked on the vowel (using a special vowel symbol)	се<u>мя</u>	/sʲem^j<u>a</u>/	'seed'
	л<u>ю</u>бовь	/lʲ<u>u</u>bovʲ/	'love'
Palatalization marked on both the consonant and the vowel	се<u>мья</u>	/sʲem^j<u>ja</u>/	'family'
	ко<u>ль</u>е	/kol^j<u>je</u>/	'necklace'

In conclusion, we have seen that there are many different types of writing systems, each making use of different linguistic properties of the language they are representing. Although each writing system has its own conventions for relating the sounds and morphemes of the language to the graphemes of the orthography, the common thread that unites them is their ability to transfer fleeting spoken language into a more tangible and permanent form.

FILE 15.3

The Historical Evolution of Writing Systems

15.3.1 The Creation of Writing Systems

Writing systems can be created in three ways. First, writing can be developed and invented as a completely new phenomenon. This has happened only rarely, but it has happened at least three times that we know of. The earliest writing system was developed by the Sumerians about 5000 years ago. The Chinese and the Maya also invented writing systems without knowledge of other existing writing systems.

Second, a new script can be created for a language, usually for a language that does not already have a writing system. This is also rather rare, but new writing systems have been created for the Cherokee language (see File 15.1) and for other Native American languages. Many people who construct languages, such as J.R.R. Tolkien, create new orthographies for their created languages.

Finally, a writing system can be borrowed (see Chapter 12) from one language or culture to another. Almost all of the writing systems we see today have been borrowed and adapted at least once. For example, several Asian cultures have borrowed the Chinese writing system and adapted it. Similarly, many modern languages use some version of the Roman alphabet. Even when a writing system is borrowed, though, it is often not borrowed completely or perfectly; there are often differences in the newly borrowed writing system, both in the appearance of the graphemes and in the relationship between the graphemes and the language they encode. Although borrowing writing systems is quite common, very few languages use completely identical writing systems. We will discuss this borrowing and adaptation in Section 15.3.3.

15.3.2 Early Writing Systems

Morphographic writing systems were developed first. The first characters developed for such systems were simple **pictograms,** which are merely stylized drawings of concrete objects and are usually iconic. As an example, the Ancient Mesopotamian, Ancient Egyptian, and Ancient Chinese writing systems used the pictograms in (1).

Such pictograms, like the traffic signs and pictures discussed in File 15.1, are technically not writing because they do not represent language. Rather, they are visual representations of objects. A refinement that was soon made in each of these ancient writing systems, however, was the semantic extension of the original pictograms. This means that the original pictograms came to be used not just to refer to the concrete objects they originally pictured but also to refer to activities and abstract concepts associated with those objects. For instance, the Ancient Egyptian hieroglyphs in (2) were used to refer to activities or concepts that were not directly picturable. At the point where such semantic extension has taken place, the characters of a writing system are considered morphograms, rather than pictograms, because they are used to represent all types of words—abstract nouns, verbs, adjectives, etc.—as well as concrete nouns.

(1) Comparison of some pictograms

	Sumerian	**Egyptian**	**Chinese**
'man'			
'ox'			
'star'			
'sun'			
'water'			
'road'			

(2) Semantic extension of some Egyptian hieroglyphs

	Original Significance	**Extension**
	'knife'	'to cut, slay'
	'fire'	'to cook, burn'
	'sail'	'wind, air'
	'man with arms down'	'submission'
	'man with arms raised'	'to pray, praise'
	'men grasping hands'	'friendship'

It is thought that phonographic writing systems were developed from morphographic writing systems. John DeFrancis has argued that a truly morphographic writing system is impossible and that some relation to sound must be present in the writing system for it to truly be writing. Although at first morphographic characters represented the meaning of entire words, as time went on the conventional symbols used as morphograms came to be associated more closely with the pronunciations of the words they represented—this is known as phonological extension. This meant that in the minds of their users, the symbols began to represent sequences of sounds. Consequently, people used the symbols to write sequences of sounds, or syllables, rather than whole words, abstracting away from the meaning that these symbols originally represented. For example, the Egyptians used the hieroglyphs in (3) to represent syllables.

(3)   Sound associations of some Egyptian hieroglyphs

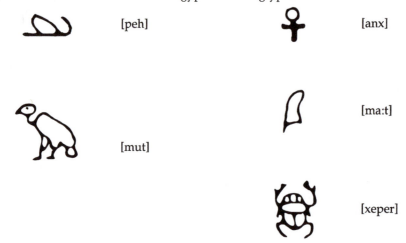

Also, some morphographic characters were used to refer to sequences of sounds in an abbreviated fashion. That is, they came to represent the first sound of the phonological form of the word they originally stood for. For example, the Egyptians originally used the symbol in (4) to represent an owl, the word for which was pronounced something like [mulok].

(4)   Egyptian symbol for *owl* [mulok]

Eventually this hieroglyphic character came to indicate the sound [m]. There were similar developments in other originally morphographic writing systems, including the Mesopotamian cuneiform system and the Chinese systems.

15.3.3   The Development of the Greek and Roman Alphabets (and Other Writing Systems)

The Semitic tribes living in the Sinai developed a system of writing based on the Egyptian usage of symbols to represent the first sound in the phonological form of the word represented by the character. This eventually gave rise to the abjads used by the Hebrews and the Arabs. For example, in the Semitic writing system, the character in (5a) represented an ox's head, and the character in (5b) represented a house.

(5)   Semitic symbols for (a) 'ox' [ʔalef] and (b) 'house' [bet]
   a. X
   b. ϑ

The Semitic words for these objects were something like [ʔalef] and [bet], respectively. Therefore, the Semites used the first symbol to write the glottal stop consonant [ʔ], which was the first sound in the word for 'ox,' and the second to write the bilabial stop consonant [b], which began the word for 'house.' (All the characters in this alphabet were called by the names of the objects that they originally represented.)

The Phoenicians, who used the Semitic abjad, taught it to the Greeks, who adapted it for use in writing the words of their own language. Since Ancient Greek did not have some of the consonants used in the pronunciation of Semitic languages, the Greeks began employing some of the borrowed characters to write the vowel sounds of their language. For example, since the glottal stop [ʔ] was not used in the pronunciation of any Greek words, the symbol came to represent the vowel [a] at the beginning of the borrowed word [ʔalef], which the Greeks pronounced [alpʰa] (which later became [alfa]). The Greeks borrowed all the names for the Phoenician characters along with the characters, adapting the pronunciation of each to Greek phonological patterns. They referred to the whole list of symbols by the Greek version of the names of the first two symbols in the list, namely, [alfa] and [beta], which is the source of the term *alphabet*. The Greek alphabet is shown in (6), along with the pronunciations of all the letters in Modern Greek.

(6) The Greek alphabet

Greek Letters (Capital, Lowercase)	IPA Value	Greek Pronunciation of Letter Name	Greek Letters (Capital, Lowercase)	IPA Value	Greek Pronunciation of Letter Name
Α α	[a]	[alfa]	N ν	[n]	[ni]
Β β	[v]	[vita]	Ξ ξ	[ks]	[ksi]
Γ γ	[ɣ]	[ɣama]	O o	[o]	[omikran]
Δ δ	[ð]	[ðelta]	Π π	[p]	[pi]
Ε ε	[ɛ]	[epsilan]	P ρ	[r]	[ro]
Z ζ	[z]	[zita]	Σ σ ς	[s]	[siɣma]
H η	[i]	[ita]	T τ	[t]	[taf]
Θ θ	[θ]	[θita]	Y υ	[i]	[ɪpsilan]
I ι	[i]	[aɪota]	Φ φ	[f]	[fi]
K κ	[k]	[kapa]	X χ	[x]	[çi]
Λ λ	[l]	[lamða]	Ψ ψ	[ps]	[psi]
M μ	[m]	[mi]	Ω ω	[o]	[omeɣa]

Notice that, like the Roman alphabet for English, there is not a one-to-one correspondence between sounds and graphemes in the Greek alphabet. For example, the sound [i] can be represented with the letters <η>, <ι>, or <υ>, depending on the word. As in English, many of these discrepancies are due to historical sound change (see File 13.3); that is, these symbols did not all always stand for the sound [i].

Also interesting in the Greek alphabet is the use of two separate lowercase characters for the sound [s], both of which are called [siɣma]: <σ> and <ς>. The use of one or the other of these two characters is completely predictable: the first, <σ>, is used at the beginnings or in the middle of words, while the second, <ς>, is used at the ends of words. You can think of these as **allographs** of a single grapheme, just as we have allophones of phonemes (Chapter 3) and allomorphs of morphemes (Chapter 4). While this may seem unusual at first, we see the same phenomenon in any language that uses capital and lowercase letters.

Capital letters in English, for example, appear only at the beginnings of sentences, at the beginnings of proper nouns, in acronyms, and in a few other specialized places. Lowercase letters appear everywhere else. Thus, these two types of letters are also in complementary distribution and therefore allographic. Note that having capital and lowercase letters is not a requirement of alphabets or other phonographic writing systems: for example, Aramaic does not make this kind of distinction.

The Greek alphabet was adapted by the Romans. Thus, the alphabet we use today is referred to as the "Roman" alphabet, brought to England in the early Middle Ages. The Cyrillic alphabet seen in the previous file was based on the Greek alphabet as well (see if you can figure out which characters in the Cyrillic alphabet in Section 15.2.3 correspond to the Greek letters shown in (6)). In fact, nearly all the alphabetic writing systems of the world can be traced directly or indirectly to the writing system of the Phoenicians.

There have been many attempts over the last few hundred years to change or reform English orthography to make it a more closely phonographic system. Those who support spelling reform have argued that many letters are redundant and that a purely phonographic system would be easier for children and immigrants to learn to read. Opponents of spelling reform point out that the current spelling system shows morphological relationships that would be lost if the writing system was based only on sound; this is a way in which the English writing system is partially morphographic. Some proposals for orthographic change have consisted of changing the standard orthography of words given our current alphabet of 26 letters. Others have included adding letters or diacritics to account for the fact that, as we saw in Chapter 2, English has more than 26 sounds. Some of the English spelling reforms have been more popular than others, but none have been very successful. Spelling reform has been successful in other writing systems, though. Greek orthography was reformed in 1982, primarily in its use of diacritics, but also in spelling.

We should note that not all phonographic writing systems are direct descendants of a particular morphographic system. For example, the Cherokee syllabary mentioned in File 15.1 was designed as a new writing system for the Cherokee language by Sequoyah. While Sequoyah did use some characters that he had seen used for English writing, which ultimately can be traced back to pictograms like those in (5a) and (5b) above, it would not really be fair to say that the Cherokee syllabary itself derived from these symbols. Sequoyah is generally believed to have been illiterate in English and certainly did not attach the same sound correspondences to the symbols that English speakers do, and, of course, he was creating a syllabary instead of an alphabet.

15.3.4   Deciphering Ancient Languages

Archeologists sometimes find inscriptions written using writing systems that they do not know. Obviously, it would be helpful to find out what these texts mean. Between roughly 400 C.E. and the 1820s, nobody was able to read Egyptian hieroglyphics. They were eventually deciphered by Jean-François Champollion, using techniques that are in some ways similar to those used by cryptologists (see File 17.5). Usually, you need linguistic sophistication to find your way in. Champollion's success came from two main sources. First, he had access to the Rosetta Stone (a stone with three versions of the same text, one of them in ancient Egyptian hieroglyphics, another in Egyptian Demotic script, and the third in Ancient Greek). Second, he guessed that the ancient Egyptian language of the hieroglyphics was closely related to Coptic, a language that he knew. These clues were enough to get a start on decipherment and led to a wonderful flowering of knowledge about ancient Egypt.

Another hugely impressive decipherment was the work done by Michael Ventris on a writing system called Linear B. This was a script found on clay tablets from a Minoan palace. The decipherment is a fantastic accomplishment that required not only organized and deep analytical work but also the inspired guess that the language on the tablets might be a preclassical dialect of the Greek language. Unfortunately, the text that Ventris uncovered turns out to be a rather dull list of commercial transactions and does not really advance our knowledge of ancient civilizations.

There are still scripts and writing systems that have resisted decipherment. In some cases (such as the so-called Indus script) there is even doubt whether the inscriptions that have been found really are writing systems at all; in others (e.g., Etruscan) there is just too little available text to make progress. In others (for example, the Easter Island script called Rongorongo), a decipherment has been claimed, but not everyone believes that it is correct. This area is a fascinating blend of linguistics, history, and archeology.

File 15.1—Writing, Language, and Culture

Exercise

1. **i.** How does writing relate to language?
   ii. How does writing relate to culture?

Discussion Questions

2. "Email writings and instant messaging can be equated with speech because people often use contractions like *I'm, won't, isn't* or spellings like *c ya* or *where r u* that reflect the spoken form." Do you agree with this statement? Why or why not?

3. Do you think emoji can be considered to be a new written language? Why or why not?

Activities

4. Find an example (there are some on the Links page for Chapter 15) of a pedography, a shorthand, and a cryptography. How are they similar to and different from Standard English orthography? How are they similar to and different from the IPA (as an example of a technography)?

5. Collect a small amount of writing from Computer-Mediated Communication (e.g., instant messages, texting). What differences do you see between this orthography and Standard English orthography? Compare your results with those of your classmates.

File 15.2—Types of Writing Systems

Exercises

6. Consider the symbol <$>. Is it morphographic or phonographic? What sounds does it represent? What meaning does it represent?

7. The following texts all express the English words *itsy bitsy teeny weeny yellow polka dot bikini* but are written in three different (made-up) left-to-right scripts. Identify what kind of writing system (morphographic, syllabic, alphabet, abjad, abugida) each script is. Explain how you made each of your decisions.

   a. τσ βτσ τν ων φλ πλκ δτ βκν

   b. ȣ× ⌘× ◆⊡ ◆⊡ ♌ℭ ■○ ♎ ♍✷⊡

   c. ℭ ○ ≈ ℵ □ ◎ ✠ ✑

8. Given that the symbol 巴 is pronounced as [pa] (tone omitted) in Chinese, take a look at the words (a) through (h) and try to answer the following questions.

a. 芭   **c.** 笆   **e.** 钯   **g.** 爸

b. 吧   **d.** 疤   **f.** 靶   **h.** 耙

   i. If the words in (a)–(h) follow the same model as those in (6a) and (6b) in Section 15.2.2, how do you think these words are pronounced? (You can omit the tones of the words.)

  ii. Do you think the eight words all share the same meaning?

 iii. Given that 父 means 'father,' which one of the eight words is most likely to represent the word 'dad' in Chinese?

  iv. For the word in (g), draw a table like those in (1) in Section 15.2.1 to demonstrate the relationship between the spoken language and its writing system.

9. Write the following Devanāgarī words in the Devanāgarī script. You will need to make use of the following symbols as well as those given in the text of Section 15.2.3.

ज	त	द	ध	न	प	भ	म
[ʤa]	[ta]	[da]	[dʰa]	[na]	[pa]	[bʰa]	[ma]

य	ल	र	व	स	श	ह	ग
[ja]	[la]	[ra]	[va]	[sa]	[ʃa]	[ha]	[ga]

a. [vadaːmi]   'I speak'
b. [aːjudʰaːni]   'weapons'
c. [nalena]   'by Nala'
d. [kr̩tamauna]   'silent'
e. [dʰaːvasi]   'you run'
f. [edʰate]   'he prospers'
g. [devanaːgariː]   'Devanāgarī'

10. The following words are names of Greek gods and goddesses, written in Greek in the Greek alphabet. Using the table in Section 15.3.3, what are the names written in English in the Roman alphabet?

a. Ζευς   **c.** Ποσειδωνας   **e.** Αρης

b. Αφροδιτη   **d.** Αθηνα

Discussion Questions

11. Suppose that English orthography was a purely phonographic system where each sound was always spelled the same way (i.e., there would be no homophones with different spellings like *cite* and *site* and *sight*). Would this make it easier to read? To write? Why or why not?

12. Suppose that English orthography was a purely morphographic system (i.e., there would be no words that were spelled the same but had different meanings like *free* 'not enslaved' and *free* 'does not cost money'). Would this make English easier to read? To write? Why or why not?

13. Estimate the number of characters you think a typical morphographic writing system would have to have. How about a typical syllabic writing system? An alphabetic writing system? How did you arrive at these figures?

14. **i.** How do you think new words are written in each of the following types of writing systems?

    a. morphographic
    b. syllabic
    c. phonemic

    ii. Do you think that the people who use these systems reach a consensus on the writing of new words with the same ease for each type of system? Why or why not?

15. You have been hired to develop a syllabic writing system for a language that contains only the following words: *hi, who, hay, die, do, day, cry, crew, crude, creed, creep, crudely, cruel, cruelly, creepy, daily, daylily*. You can assume that these words are pronounced as they are in your dialect of English. How many syllable types will be represented in your syllabary, and what will they be? If you were to try to expand the syllabary to be able to write all of English, what problems would you run into? How many characters do you think you would need?

File 15.3—The Historical Evolution of Writing Systems

Exercise

16. Describe five differences between the Roman alphabet used to write English and the Greek alphabet. Why do you think those differences arose?

Discussion Questions

17. Based on the phonetic values of the symbols given for the Cyrillic (in (14) in Section 15.2.3) and the Greek writing systems (in (6) in Section 15.3.3), can you think of English words that could not be written with one or the other system? If we were forced to use these systems instead of the Roman alphabet, what do you think people would do to solve the problem?

18. Explain why <σ> and <ç> are not contrastive in the Greek writing system. What sort of evidence would you need to show that they **were** contrastive?

Activities

19. **i.** What do you think you need to know (or guess) about an unknown script in order to decipher it?

    ii. Go to the Links page for Chapter 15 and choose one of the discussions of a deciphered writing system. How did those deciphering the writing system figure out the things you thought they needed to know? Was there anything else they needed to know that you did not think of in (i)?

20. Trace the history of a writing system other than the Roman, Greek, and Cyrillic alphabets. When and where was it created? How many times was it borrowed or adapted for other languages and cultures?

Further Readings

Baron, Naomi S. 2008. *Always on: Language in an online and mobile world.* Oxford: Oxford University Press.

Coulmas, Florian. 1989. *The writing systems of the world.* Oxford: Blackwell.

Crystal, David. 2006. *Language and the Internet.* 2nd edn. Cambridge: Cambridge University Press.

DeFrancis, John. 1989. *Visible speech: The diverse oneness of writing systems.* Honolulu: The University of Hawai'i Press.

Ong, Walter J. 2012. *Orality and literacy: The technologizing of the word. 30th anniversary edition.* London: Routledge.

Robinson, Andrew. 2007. *The story of writing: Alphabets, hieroglyphs, & pictograms.* 2nd edn. New York: Thames & Hudson.

Rogers, Henry. 2005. *Writing systems: A linguistic approach.* Malden, MA: Blackwell.

CHAPTER
16

Language and Computers

FILE 16.0

What Is Computational Linguistics?

Both computers and people can be considered information processing systems. A number of the processing tasks that humans carry out with language can be automated to some degree on a computer: recognizing words in speech, pronouncing these words, translating from one language to another, and so on. Language processing in humans is, as we have seen, incredibly complex (Chapter 9), so it isn't currently possible to give machines the full conversational skills of a human being. However, programming a computer to work with language—written or spoken—can nonetheless be viewed as creating a (limited) model of language processing. Computers are therefore ideal for testing linguists' theories about language processing, because programming a computer requires explicitly specifying all details of an operation. By programming a computer according to our current understanding of various linguistic phenomena and then observing how well the computer's behavior mirrors human behavior, we can get a better idea of how good our models of those linguistic phenomena are.

Of course, there are also many practical applications to giving computers language processing ability, and we benefit from advances in the field of computational linguistics in our everyday interactions with technology.

Contents

FILE 16.1

....

Speech Synthesis

16.1.1 Synthesized Speech

Speech synthesis is the use of a machine, usually a computer, to produce human-like speech. Artificial speech can be produced in several ways: by playing prerecorded utterances and phrases, called **canned speech**; by piecing together smaller recorded units of speech into new utterances; or by creating speech "from scratch," which is called **synthesized speech.** Not too many years ago, talking machines were found only in science fiction stories. Now they are found in many items in our daily lives, such as cars, elevators, GPS devices, telephone customer service centers, automated grocery checkout lanes, and, of course, smartphones. In fact, you probably grew up playing with toys that talk. Many commercial machines that talk use canned speech, which is of little interest to linguists because the use of canned speech does not require language processing: it comes preprocessed. On the other hand, machines that talk using synthesized speech are of the utmost interest to linguists because synthesizing speech provides an opportunity to test our understanding of language and to apply knowledge that has been gained through linguistic investigation. Comparing synthesized speech with speech produced by people is a very rigorous test of how thorough our knowledge of language and speech is.

Synthesized speech should be intelligible and sound natural. **Intelligibility** refers to how well listeners can recognize and understand the individual sounds or words generated by the synthesis system. **Naturalness** refers to how much the synthesized speech sounds like the speech of an actual person. Speech that does not sound natural is usually reported to sound "robotic" and unpleasant. Usually, as a synthesized speech sample gets longer, it becomes less natural sounding. Linguists and computer scientists who work on speech synthesis use a variety of tests, often pertaining to speech perception, to achieve the highest levels of intelligibility and naturalness.

16.1.2 The Earliest Synthesis Machines

The very first speech synthesizers were mechanical. In 1779, Russian scientist Christian Gottlieb Kratzenstein built five acoustic resonators that could produce the five vowels [a], [e], [i], [o], [u]. In 1791, Hungarian Wolfgang Von Kemplen constructed a machine that could produce both consonants and vowel sounds. The earliest electronic speech synthesizer seems to have been made in the early 1920s by J. Q. Stewart, who put together circuitry that gave vowel-like formants to the sound generated by a buzzer (see File 2.6 for an explanation of formants). The 1930s saw the appearance of the "Voder," a device something like an electronic organ. An operator could change the pitch of the voice-source by pushing a pedal while turning various frequencies on and off with the buttons on a keyboard. The output of this machine, if the operator was a virtuoso, was marginally intelligible.

The 1950s saw the advent and extensive use of the "Pattern Playback" machine in research on speech perception. This machine took spectrograms (a kind of visual representation of sound waves; see File 2.6) as its input, which a researcher painted on a clear piece of plastic. The machine "read" these spectrograms by shining light through the plastic and producing the sounds indicated by the images. Literally hundreds of experiments were performed using pattern playback machines, forming the basis of much of the present research on speech perception. The ghostly sounds that this machine emitted were estimated to be between 85% and 95% intelligible, depending on how good the painted spectrograms were.

Later electronic speech synthesizers differed crucially from these early ones in one primary respect. Whereas the early ones took a tremendously rich and complicated description of the sound to be produced as input, later machines were designed to take into account only the types of sounds humans emit as speech. By greatly limiting the types of sounds the machines produced, the amount of information the machines needed to produce the appropriate sound was reduced.

16.1.3 Articulatory Synthesis

The earliest speech synthesizers were designed only to mimic the sounds of human speech, regardless of the process through which those sounds were produced. **Articulatory synthesis,** on the other hand, is a synthesis technique that generates speech "from scratch" based on computational models of the shape of the human vocal tract and the articulation processes. Most articulatory synthesis systems have not been very successful, because there are too many as-yet-unanswered questions about the vocal tract and articulation processes. For a long time, however, articulatory synthesis was thought of as the most promising way to synthesize speech because it most closely models the way humans produce sounds.

Early synthesizers of this kind included OVE (Orator Verbis Electris) and PAT (Parametric Artificial Talker), developed in the 1950s and 1960s. They were made of circuitry that imitated various aspects of sounds produced in the vocal tract. Both machines were based on the **source-filter theory** of speech production, which claims that there are two independent parts to the production of speech sounds.

The first part consists of some mechanism that creates a basic sound and is therefore called the **source.** The second part, called the **filter,** shapes the sound created by the source into the different sounds we recognize as speech sounds, such as the vowels [i] and [u] or the consonants [l], [s], or [t]. For example, in human speech, the sound [i] is produced by combining a periodic sound wave created by air flowing through the vibrating vocal folds (the source) with a particular oral tract configuration that involves the tongue being in a high front position (the filter). See Chapter 2 for a description of how vowels and consonants are made by human speakers.

Both OVE and PAT were designed to directly mimic human speech production by having some source that produced a basic sound similar to those produced by humans and by having some method of filtering this basic sound into the particular speech sounds needed. Using this technique, the OVE II was the first synthesizer that could produce an utterance that was indistinguishable from that of a real male speaker, though this production involved a long series of manipulations and settings by a human guide.

However, speech generated in this manner, "from scratch," rarely sounds natural. The main problems involve the accurate production of voicing, frication, intonation, sentence stress, and timing. For example, the characteristics of voicing are extremely complex and change continuously, depending on the thickness and consistency of the vocal folds, how close the speaker places the vocal folds to one another during voicing, and how much air is being pumped through the larynx. Other aspects of speech are equally complex and therefore difficult to generate from scratch.

16.1.4 Concatenative Synthesis

Concatenative synthesis is the most commonly used speech synthesis technology today because it generates very natural sounding speech. Unlike the systems introduced in the previous section, concatenative synthesis uses recorded speech, which eliminates the major problems that articulatory synthesis faced. Most commercial speech synthesis systems now start by recording speech, and then they manipulate the speech samples. Since high-quality sound recordings are extremely bulky (even if only small sound segments are stored), a synthesizer may need a lot of storage space. Thus, only recently—with the advent of computer technology that allows affordable storage of large amounts of data—has it become practical to use recorded data for speech synthesis.

Concatenative synthesis works by first stringing together (concatenating) pieces of recorded speech and then smoothing the boundaries between them. One kind of concatenative synthesis is called **unit selection synthesis.** The units, as discussed below, vary in size depending on the application.

The basic idea of unit selection synthesis is to take large samples of speech and build a database of smaller units from these speech samples. These units are then concatenated to create words or sentences that were not originally recorded. The process begins by recording real speech, usually predetermined sentences, in a quiet environment. The recorded sentences are segmented into smaller units, which may be individual sounds, diphones (discussed below), syllables, morphemes, words, phrases, or some combination of these units. There will often be many samples of the same sound unit recorded in differing contexts, for example, at the beginning of a sentence and at the end of a sentence. After segmentation, each unit receives an index label that includes information about its pitch, duration, neighboring sounds, and other relevant data. When generating speech, the system uses a complex algorithm to choose the best units from the database, matching the sound and context of the new utterance as well as it can to the sound-context pairs available in the database. Unit selection synthesis is successful at creating natural sounding speech because it uses a large number of well-indexed units extracted from natural speech. In other words, it sounds like human speech because it is derived from human speech.

The question remains as to what type of speech segments to use for the best-sounding synthesis. On the one hand, large segments of recorded speech, such as complete sentences, will sound the most natural when played back in full. However, most applications will require too many distinct sentences for this to be practical. Segmenting speech at the word level is useful for many applications in which the same words are often repeated. If enough words are present in the database, a very large number of sentences can be produced by concatenating the words in various arrangements. By including words that have been recorded multiple times, with intonation for both declarative and interrogative sentences, the system can be quite expressive. However, only words that have been recorded will ever be produced. To solve this problem and allow for new words to be pronounced, speech can be segmented at the level of the phoneme (see Chapter 3). When a new word is requested, the system will go through steps to find the appropriate allophones, concatenate them, and pronounce the word.

Even more successful than phoneme synthesis is **diphone synthesis. Diphones** are pairs of adjacent sounds: the end of one phone attached to the beginning of the next phone. The image in (1) represents all of the diphones in a stream of speech with four adjacent sounds. Connecting phones in the middle, as happens when we string together two diphones, is usually more successful than stringing together two different sounds. The resulting synthesized speech sounds more natural, because it accounts for effects of coarticulation (where overlapping sounds affect each other).

(1) | Sound 1 | Sound 2 | Sound 3 | Sound 4 |
      | Diphone 1 | Diphone 2 | Diphone 3 | Diphone 4 | Diphone 5 |

Concatenative synthesis is especially successful when applied to one particular domain, or topic, such as travel information or weather reports. **Domain-specific synthesis** systems create utterances from prerecorded words and phrases that closely match the words and phrases that will be synthesized. At the generation step, large segments such as words or phrases may be chosen from the database, increasing the naturalness of the speech. Generating new utterances is also possible using smaller segments, such as diphones, collected from the same recordings. If the vocabulary and sentence structure of the generated speech remain close to those of the speech that was recorded, the result will be very natural sounding.

Why is it important to choose sounds or words with their immediate context in mind? Two main reasons are the duration of sounds and the intonation of words and phrases. Certain sounds, especially vowels, vary in duration depending on where in a word they occur. The duration and intonation of full words depend on where in a sentence or phrase they occur. This is illustrated below with the word *Tom* in different contexts.

(2)   Hi, I'm Tom.
      Are you Tom?
      Tom! Please stop crying!
      Tom went to the store.
      Sam, Tom, and Sue went to the store.
      Sam, Sue, and Tom went to the store.

If you read the examples aloud, you will see how the intonation of *Tom* differs in each sentence. You may notice that the duration of the vowel changes, too. So if we want to generate the word *Tom* as the subject of a declarative sentence, it will be best if we can choose a speech sample of *Tom* where it was recorded serving the same grammatical function. The same holds true for smaller and larger sound segments.

16.1.5   Text-To-Speech Synthesis

Many speech synthesizers accept symbolic input, for instance, a phrase written in IPA or some other phonetic alphabet. Using the IPA can tell a speech synthesizer exactly which phonemes or diphones to select. However, it is more convenient for us to use ordinary written language to tell the synthesizer what words or phrases to generate. In **Text-To-Speech Synthesis** (TTS), speech is generated directly from text entered with normal orthography (spelling). For the following discussion, assume that we are using a concatenative synthesis system and diphone segments to produce the speech. If the system is given a phrase to produce, it must decide which series of diphones will best represent that phrase.

If the system will be required to pronounce only a limited number of words, and that number is relatively small, then simple word-to-pronunciation rules can be stored in the system. That is, the computer is told, for each sequence of letters, which sequence of sounds should be produced. If only one pronunciation per word is stored, then each word will always be pronounced the same way, using the same diphone segments from the database. If more than one pronunciation is stored for a given word, then the system might decide which pronunciation to use based on the context of that word in a phrase.

If the vocabulary is quite large, or even unlimited, then there must be rules that describe how to pronounce words in general based on how they are spelled. For some words, and in some languages, this is easy, because certain words are "spelled the way they sound," with one letter representing each sound. In English, however, there are sounds that are represented by multiple letters, and many letters represent more than one sound (see File 2.1). These inconsistencies mean that spelling-to-sound rules are often inadequate. As a result, systems that use spelling-to-sound rules usually include an **exceptions dictionary,** which lists the correct pronunciation of words that do not follow the rules.

Having taken care of spelling inconsistencies, what can be done about **heteronyms?** These are words that can be pronounced in two or more ways, although they are spelled only one way. For instance, there are many words like *record* that can be used as a verb or a noun and have different pronunciations based on their usage, as illustrated in (3).

(3)   We may record this call for quality assurance.
My mom doesn't know about technology. She calls a CD a record.

In the first case, where *record* is a transitive verb, the first vowel is [ə] and the stress is on the second syllable. In the second case, where *record* is a noun, the first vowel is [ɛ] and takes the stress. This is a common type of alternation in English, and there are many others. So a good, wide-domain TTS system must be able to detect the syntactic structure of a sentence, and thereby the grammatical role of each word, in order to pronounce the words correctly.

In summary, a TTS system will carry out some combination of the following steps to convert a word from normal spelling representation to a pronounceable representation: look up the word in a complete pronunciation dictionary; look up the word in an exceptions dictionary; use spelling-to-sound rules to generate a pronunciation; and detect the grammatical role of the word to choose an appropriate pronunciation from a set. A further necessity of a TTS system, not explored here, is assigning and adjusting for the intonation of individual words and phrases.

16.1.6   Applications of Speech Synthesis

One research application of speech synthesis is testing our knowledge about speech production and recognition. For instance, when investigating phonemic contrasts, a researcher can synthesize the relevant phones and manipulate various acoustic characteristics. Native speakers can then be tested to see which synthesized sounds are perceived as one phoneme and which are perceived as the other, allowing the researcher to test hypotheses about which acoustic properties are most relevant for phonemic categorization (see File 9.4). While we have begun to tap the research value of speech synthesis, many other research applications are yet to be explored.

Commercial applications of speech synthesis are found in many aspects of daily life. Various systems and programs designed to help teach children to read or adults to learn a foreign language are available. Telephone customer service centers often use synthesized speech either for complete interactions or to direct a customer to the appropriate service representative. Public transportation systems use synthesized speech to announce upcoming stops and other information. Navigation systems, video games, smartphones, and computer programs that make use of concatenative synthesis and/or playback of prerecorded phrases and sentences are only some of the other common applications.

Perhaps more important, though not as well funded, are uses of synthesis in various devices to aid the physically handicapped. One such use is for the vocally handicapped. The American Speech and Hearing Association estimates that there are around 1.5 million nonspeaking people in the United States alone (not including those deaf individuals who are in principle able to speak): people who have lost the use of their larynx through injury or disease, for instance. Modern speaking aids allow many people to communicate vocally who would not otherwise be able to do so.

A similar application is reading aids. The number of people in the United States who cannot read normal newspaper print, even with corrective glasses, is about as high as the number of vocally impaired. For this segment of the population, machines and computer programs that read printed text aloud are of great use, as are talking clocks, thermometers, calculators, and other commonplace objects.

....

Automatic Speech Recognition

16.2.1   The Nature of Speech Recognition

Talking to computers has been a standard of science fiction for many decades. Many of the linguistic and engineering challenges involved in machines' understanding of speech remain to be solved, but the dream of having computers understand what we say is daily becoming more and more a reality. True speech understanding entails many different levels of linguistic processing, so **automatic speech recognition** is usually defined more narrowly as the conversion of an acoustic speech waveform into text. Put another way, automatic speech recognition is the process through which a computer takes sounds of speech and converts them into words of some particular language. Dealing with the meaning of those words, once recognized, is usually handled by other computer programs (see File 16.3).

Although today's speech recognition systems still cannot perform as well as many of the computers of science fiction, current technology is used in many applications. For example, automatic speech recognition is used in entering or requesting information verbally from automated telephone customer service systems, in dictating documents or email, and in interacting with cell phones, smartphones, tablets, and computers through voice commands. This field has advanced rapidly in recent years, and in this file we will look at the basic components of speech recognition systems and the challenges they face.

16.2.2   The Noisy Channel Model

The basic architecture for speech recognition software is built on a view of language processing called the **noisy channel model.** The insight guiding this model involves treating speech input as if it has been passed through a communication channel that garbles the speech waveform, producing a "noisy" or distorted version of the original words spoken. By modeling the distortion, its effects can be removed, and the original signal can be reconstructed.

In speech recognition, **noise** refers to variations in pronunciation that distort words' canonical form. For example, the canonical pronunciations of *did* and *you* are [dɪd] and [ju], but in an utterance like "Did you go yet?" those two words may be pronounced something like [dɪdʒu] (e.g., [dɪdʒugoʊjɛt]). Other sources of noise include acoustic variation introduced by the microphone or telephone network that the computer program gets its information from. Accounting for this variability makes it possible to decode a noisy utterance and retrieve the original intended phonemes.

In practical terms, speech recognizers solve the noisy channel problem by comparing an input speech waveform to a huge number of potential sentences and choosing the one that is most likely to have generated the input signal. Speech is highly variable, and uncertainty is an inherent part of the comparison process. Therefore, speech recognizers rely on a number of components designed to handle specific portions of the recognition process. These components work together to provide the best guess at what a person originally said and produce the final recognized text.

16.2.3   Components of an Automatic Speech Recognition System

A typical speech recognition system consists of several components, each layered on top of the previous. Here is a brief overview of the four main components. At the base is a signal-processing component responsible for converting a speech waveform into a numeric representation that can be used for further processing. An acoustic model provides a way to map energy in the speech waveform onto phonemes. Pronunciation and language models describe the sound and word sequences that the recognizer is likely to encounter. We will now go through each component in more detail.

a. Signal Processing. The first step in the speech recognition process involves recording the speech waveform with a microphone and storing it in a manner that is suitable for further processing by a computer. Measurements of the speech signal are taken every 10 to 20 milliseconds, and these measurements are transformed into a digital representation of acoustic features that expresses information about the amount of energy present at different frequencies. One purpose of this acoustic feature extraction is to separate two kinds of information in the waveform: information about vocal tract characteristics (e.g., pitch, speaker identity, etc.) and information that corresponds to phonetic segments (e.g., the acoustic differences that distinguish [p] from [b]). This portion of the speech recognition process can be seen as an application of the source-filter theory of speech production (see Section 16.1.3). The output of the signal-processing stage is a compact, numeric representation of the energy values in the original speech waveform.

b. Acoustic Modeling. The second step in converting an acoustic waveform into words is mapping the energy values extracted during the signal-processing stage onto symbols for phones. In order to carry out this conversion, the computer needs access to a model of the energy levels of different phones. An acoustic model of phones is typically created by automatically aligning a large set of audio-recordings of speech with phonetic transcriptions that have been prepared for this purpose. The resulting data set—the mapping between segments of sound in the recording and symbols in the transcription—is used to compute how often particular energy values are associated with each phone. Because speech is so variable, similar energy values may be associated with more than one phone. Instead of relying on only one possible association from energy values to phones, speech recognition systems use a probabilistic calculation of the most likely mapping from a set of acoustic measurements to a phone label. This approach allows for some flexibility in dealing with uncertain energy measurements.

Because energy measurements are taken at such short time intervals, it is also useful to break sound segments down into smaller parts and map the energy values onto those smaller parts instead of taking the phoneme as a whole. Most speech recognition systems break phones down into three parts: an onset (beginning), a middle, and an offset (end). Treating portions of a phone separately makes it possible to map them onto the acoustic measurements more accurately. The energy values in the onset and offset of a phone vary due to co-articulation effects from preceding or following phones, while the energy in the middle portion is relatively stable, regardless of the environment in which the phone is produced.

c. Pronunciation Modeling. Because of the inherent uncertainty in identifying individual phones, speech recognizers rely on knowledge of which sequences of phones are most likely in some given language. This knowledge can be used to filter out unlikely sound sequences. For example, [n] and [ŋ] are relatively similar in terms of their energy characteristics, and a speech recognizer may tend to confuse them. However, no English words start with [ŋ], while many words start with [n]. Knowledge of this sort can help a speech recognizer assign the correct label even when the acoustic information is not sufficiently reliable.

Building a pronunciation model is fairly straightforward and mainly involves using a pronunciation dictionary to obtain the phonetic sequences that correspond to orthographic words. Alternate pronunciations may be given in cases where such information would be considered helpful. For example, in giving phone numbers it is possible to pronounce the digit <0> as [ziɹoʊ] or [oʊ], and having both pronunciations in the pronunciation model will improve recognition accuracy.

d. Language Modeling. Like acoustic modeling and pronunciation modeling, language modeling involves calculating the probability of sequences. In the case of language modeling, we are interested in calculating the probability of word sequences. For example, a language model may tell us that people are more likely to say *drive a car* than to say *drive a call,* and this information can be used by a speech recognizer to make choices about words.

Most speech recognizers use the probability of sequences of one, two, or three consecutively occurring words (called *unigram, bigram,* and *trigram sequences,* respectively). Calculating probable word sequences involves little more than counting how often each sequence occurs in a corpus (a collection of language samples; see File 16.5). Calculating unigram probabilities simply requires counting how often each word occurs in a corpus and then dividing by the total number of words. More frequent words have a higher unigram probability. A similar calculation is performed to calculate bigram and trigram probabilities.

A language model can be calculated from any text, but it is most helpful to derive the model from text that represents the kinds of things people using the speech recognizer are likely to say. For example, knowing the probability of word sequences from the works of Shakespeare will not help a speech recognizer used for transcribing medical documents. In this case, it is better to calculate probable word sequences from similar medical documents.

e. Putting It All Together. In order to actually perform speech recognition, the output of each of the modules described above is composed in order to complete the mapping from an acoustic speech waveform to a string of recognized words. First, an input speech waveform is recorded by a microphone and converted to a sequence of acoustic features (signal processing). These acoustic features are combined with the acoustic model to generate the likelihood of individual phones (acoustic modeling). Next, the pronunciation model is applied to the proposed phonetic sequences to filter out the ones that do not correspond to actual words (pronunciation modeling). Finally, the language model is applied to this large set of possible words to filter out unlikely combinations and choose the sequence that is most likely to make sense (language modeling). Integrating these components provides an efficient way to examine many possible sound and word combinations at the same time and minimize the effort spent considering unlikely sentences.

16.2.4   Types of Speech Recognition Systems

Speech recognition systems can be categorized according to several parameters. In some cases, such as data entry or dictation, the recognized words may be the final product of the recognizer. In other cases, recognizing the words spoken may be the first step in some further natural language processing. For example, natural language dialogue systems require speech recognition as a first step toward extracting the meaning of what a user says. In such systems, recognized words must be mapped onto a recognition grammar that specifies what commands the computer should carry out in response to user input. Some of the other parameters that characterize speech recognition systems are given below.

a. Speaking Mode. A speech recognition system may accept only isolated word input or continuous speech input. Isolated word systems limit user response to single-word answers (e.g., cell phones that map names to phone numbers) or require the user to pause after each word. Continuous speech systems allow freer input and are designed to recognize running speech. Recognition accuracy is usually higher for isolated word systems, because the task is more constrained and there is less potential for ambiguity.

b. Vocabulary Size. Speech recognizers may have small (fewer than 100 words) or large (more than 20,000 words) vocabularies. Generally, recognition accuracy is higher for small vocabulary systems. A large vocabulary system that allows continuous speech input will face a more difficult recognition task because at any given point, many words are potential recognition candidates.

c. Speaker Enrollment. A speech recognition system may be speaker-dependent or speaker-independent. A speaker-dependent system requires that a user train the system to recognize only his voice, whereas a speaker-independent system does not require such training. Recognition accuracy is generally higher for speaker-dependent systems, since there is less variability in an individual's speech than in the speech of a larger population. Typically, dictation software enrolls its users so as to provide higher-quality output for a single speaker, whereas a system providing flight information via the telephone to anyone who calls cannot use speaker enrollment since new people call the system every day.

16.2.5 Problems in Speech Recognition

The main difficulties for speech recognition revolve around the tremendous variability associated with the acoustic signal. This variability comes from several sources. At the acoustic level, any change in the physical environment—such as changing the position of the microphone, echoes, background noise, or using a different microphone—can have substantial effect on the acoustic signal. Whereas people accommodate these differences largely without even noticing, they are more difficult for speech recognition systems.

Phonetic variability (both among different speakers and even within the same person's speech) is another challenge for automatic speech recognition. For example, the phoneme /t/ is usually pronounced quite differently in words such as *tool, tree, still, butter,* and *button,* and these differences have to be accounted for explicitly in a speech recognizer. Sociophonetic pronunciation differences (e.g., File 10.2) and foreign accents (File 3.1) account for another source of variability that is difficult for speech recognizers to deal with.

Differences in vocal tract size and shape also affect the acoustics of the speech signal. For example, the energy characteristics of a vowel produced by a woman are somewhat different from the typical energy characteristics of the same vowel spoken by a man, and speech recognizers must have a way of adjusting to these differences. Within-speaker variability, such as differences in voice quality that arise from having a cold or being tired, or speaking rate and changes in speaking style (e.g., carefully enunciated versus casual speech), also impacts recognition accuracy.

16.2.6 Future Directions

In addition to research aimed at continually improving speech recognition accuracy, researchers are also looking at ways to extend the capabilities of speech recognition systems. For example, one area of research involves detecting emotion in people's speech, since tone of voice conveys a lot of useful information. A related area of research concerns detecting which words are emphasized, since they are usually more likely to contain new topical information than words that are not. Other researchers are working on using knowledge of grammar to aid the recognition process. For example, knowing that a noun is more likely to follow a determiner (e.g., *the* Det *computer* N) than a verb can eliminate some types of recognition errors. Similarly, using semantic knowledge to guide the recognition process can help a system focus on words that make sense in the context of what it has already recognized.

....

Communicating with Computers

16.3.1 Interacting with Computers Using Natural Language

Computers are tools that humans use for various tasks. However, the way we use computers often differs in an important way from the way we use other tools such as a hammer or a backhoe: someone who uses a computer interacts with the computer. When this interaction involves giving and receiving information, it makes sense to talk about *communicating* with a computer.

For humans, natural language is the most familiar, convenient, and efficient method of communication in most situations. Therefore, it is clearly desirable for people to be able to use natural language to interact with computers. However, as is the case for many tasks, what is effortless for people can be extremely difficult for computers. Computers have been around for over 70 years, but systems allowing effective natural language communication with them are relatively new. As with other topics in this chapter, this field has advanced rapidly in recent years, but this file will discuss the history and basic components of such systems and some of the issues and difficulties that arise in developing them.

16.3.2 Interactive Text-Based Systems

One of the first computer programs that could carry on a conversation using a natural language (in this case, English) was a program called ELIZA, which was created in 1966 by Joseph Weizenbaum and was designed to carry on dialogue parodying a psychotherapy session. ELIZA is text based, meaning that the user types input in using a keyboard and ELIZA responds on the screen. Here is a sample conversation with ELIZA:

(1)   1. User: I am stressed.
       2. ELIZA: How long have you been stressed?
       3. User: Since I started writing this chapter.
       4. ELIZA: Can you elaborate on that?
       5. User: I can't stop thinking about human-computer interaction.
       6. ELIZA: Have you tried?
       7. User: No I guess not really.
       8. ELIZA: You are being a bit negative.
       9. User: Well what can I do to change my attitude?
      10. ELIZA: Why do you say your attitude?
      11. User: Because you said I was being negative.

ELIZA may appear to understand the user, but, in fact, the program works by simply looking for basic patterns in the user input and constructing responses in response to those patterns. Here is an example of one of ELIZA's strategies in action:

(2) User: I was once the captain of a ship.
ELIZA: Why do you tell me you were once the captain of a ship just now?
User: I was never good at soccer.
ELIZA: Why do you tell me you were never good at soccer just now?

All ELIZA has to do to generate the responses in (2) is to look for the pattern *I was* [OTHER-WORDS] in what the user types and respond with *Why do you tell me you were* [OTHER-WORDS] *just now,* copying the [OTHER-WORDS] part verbatim from the input to the reply. The program need not know anything about ships or soccer, or even recognize these words. This technique is called **word spotting**: the program focuses on words it knows, like *I was,* and ignores ones it doesn't. Another example of ELIZA's word-spotting strategies occurs in lines 7–8 in example (1); the reply *You are being a bit negative* is triggered by spotting the negative words *no* and *not* in the input.

Clearly, communication with ELIZA barely counts as communication at all. Intuitively, the strategies she uses seem like a kind of cheating. But the really deficient aspect of interaction with ELIZA is that a user can't get any useful behavior or information by talking to her.

More useful programs have been created in recent years that use the same simple pattern-matching strategies, often in addition to more advanced natural language processing systems, to engage in productive communication. For example, companies may use automated online assistants to answer customer questions and direct readers to further relevant information on their websites. Programs like this perform better when their use is restricted to a **limited domain,** such as typical banking services. Other systems we will see below use similar restrictions; for example, a flight booking system will generally only know words likely to come up in conversations about booking flights.

16.3.3 Spoken-Language Dialogue Systems

The examples presented above involve interaction with a computer via typed text. A more challenging task is the development of **spoken-language dialogue systems**. These are to be distinguished from other computer applications involving speech, such as the Text-To-Speech programs discussed in File 16.1, or interactive systems that produce but do not understand speech, such as touch-tone telephone services that present options verbally but require the user to answer by pressing buttons. A spoken-language dialogue system will make use of strategies used by both of these less complex types of systems, but it will require other strategies as well.

Spoken-language dialogue systems differ from one another in their degree of sophistication. For instance, some can correctly handle only **isolated speech,** in which the user speaks the input clearly and without extraneous words (e.g., *yes*). Other more complex systems can deal with **continuous speech,** in which the input can be more like normal speech (e.g., *well, yes, I guess so*). Systems also differ as to whether or not they are confused by **barge-in,** where the impatient user interrupts and talks over the computer.

The advantages of having spoken-language dialogue systems are clear. For example, they allow hands-free usage of technology (e.g., using cell phones and navigation systems while driving), provide options for faster and easier searching (e.g., in comparison to typing on a smartphone or tablet keyboard), and offer companies ways to cut customer service costs.

While spoken-language dialogue systems are now very common in smartphones and tablets, most earlier applications operated over telephone lines, and these systems continue to play a large role in telephone-based customer service. Customers can access services by phone, for example, placing orders, requesting or canceling a service, or checking an account status, in addition to inquiring about train and flight timetables and reserving tickets.

An example from the CMU Darpa Communicator, an earlier automated telephone-based dialogue system for booking flight information, is given in (3).

(3) System: Hello. Welcome to the Carnegie Mellon Communicator. Are you a registered user?

User: Hi, this is Alex Rudnicky. I'd like to fly to Charleston, please.

System: Hello, Dr. Rudnicky, I'm glad to hear from you again. You can ask me for help at any time. You can fly to Charleston in South Carolina or Charleston in West Virginia.

User: South Carolina.

System: A flight to Charleston. Departing Pittsburgh on what day?

User: On the fifteenth.

System: I'm sorry. I must have misheard the date . . . a flight on Tuesday, February fifteenth. Okay what day would you be traveling?

User: On March fifteenth.

System: Traveling on Wednesday, March fifteenth. One Moment Please . . . Let's see . . . flights from Pittsburgh to Charleston . . . if you'll just hold on, this shouldn't take too long . . . Gosh, the network has been slow all day . . . I'm glad you called, though . . . I'm not sure how long this will take . . . This has been a long day, but I'm glad you called . . . hummmmm . . . this is taking longer than usual . . . I wonder if something is wrong . . . I'll bet the network is down again! I have a nonstop on US Airways departing Pittsburgh at eleven thirty five A.M., arrives Charleston at one thirty five P.M.

User: How 'bout something later?

System: The flight after that departs Pittsburgh at two ten P.M. arriving in Charleston at four ten P.M. Is that Okay?

User: Okay, that's fine.

System: Will you return to Pittsburgh from Charleston?

User: Yes, on Saturday.

System: Traveling on Saturday, March eighteenth. Okay I have a nonstop on US Airways departing Charleston at eleven oh five A.M. arrive Pittsburgh at one thirteen P.M. Do you want to take that?

User: That's perfect. I'll take it.

System: Do you need any hotel or car reservations?

User: Yes, I'll need a car.

System: No hotels. Do you need a car in Charleston?

User: Yes, please.

System: I've made a request for a car with Avis in Charleston. Do you want a summary of your trip?

User: Yes, please.

System: Your first flight is a US Airways flight 4072 leaving Pittsburgh at two ten P.M. on Wednesday, March fifteenth, arriving in Charleston at four ten P.M. Then, the next flight is a US Airways flight 4120 leaving Charleston at eleven oh five A.M. on Saturday, March eighteenth, arriving in Pittsburgh at one thirteen P.M. I've made no hotel reservations for your trip. I've requested a rental car in Charleston. Are you satisfied with this itinerary?

User: Yes.

System: Mail sent to air@cs.cmu.edu. Thank you for using the Carnegie Mellon Communicator. Please tell me any comments. When you're finished, just hang up.

16.3.4 Components of a Spoken-Language Dialogue System

Take a closer look at the dialogue example in (3). What are the different components that must be present to allow such a dialogue to take place?

a. Automatic Speech Recognition. For computer programs that use a spoken interface (rather than a written interface), speech recognition is a necessary first step. As described in File 16.2, speech recognition involves the use of computers to transform spoken language into written (or computer-understandable) language. One system of speech recognition uses sound templates (or sound patterns) of individual words, which are matched to the incoming words through a microphone. For a very simple dialogue system in which the user will say a limited number of utterances, this strategy may suffice. This process is slow and limited, however, and may produce errors if a user's speech is not sufficiently similar to the templates stored in the system.

A more linguistic approach to speech recognition involves combining all the levels of linguistic knowledge (e.g., phonology, syntax, semantics, pragmatics) in order to allow speaker-independent understanding of continuous speech. In this case, speech recognition systems make use of acoustic cues to help figure out what sounds are being spoken. The sound waves themselves often don't contain enough information to determine what the words are. As a classic example, the phrase *How to recognize speech,* when spoken rapidly, sounds almost exactly like *How to wreck a nice beach.* Deciding which of the two possibilities is right generally requires further information, for example, what the topic of conversation is. The other parts of a spoken-language dialogue system can provide such information to help make such decisions. For instance, if the computer has just asked *What is your customer number?*, the dialogue management component (see below) should expect the reply to contain words for numbers. This can help the speech recognizer decide that a sequence of sounds that could be understood as *tooth reef oar* should actually be understood as *two three four.*

b. Language Processing and Understanding. For some tasks, it is sufficient to use simple techniques such as word spotting and pattern matching to process the user's input and use that simple input to accomplish a given task. Other tasks require that the computer reach more of an "understanding" of what the user says. This is true when the system asks the user an open-ended question such as *What seems to be the problem?* or *What can I do for you today?* When there is potential for a wide range of answers, the system must decipher not only the individual words, but also the intention of the speaker. Often a deep analysis of the input is required, including building syntax trees (see File 5.5) to figure out the input's structure. Analyzing sentences syntactically is known as **parsing,** which is a difficult and sometimes slow process. Syntactic rules alone are not sufficient to guide the parsing process. Semantics, pragmatics, context, and world knowledge must play a role as well. This is why limited-domain applications are often more successful than very broad applications; when the context of an utterance is known, it is easier to deduce the meaning of that utterance.

c. Dialogue Management. An important part of carrying on a conversation is keeping track of the context and what the topic of conversation is. Since a system such as a flight reservation application is really working together with the user toward the common goal of booking a flight, it needs to understand the **intentional structure** of the conversation. For instance, in (3), the main intention is to schedule a travel itinerary, but this goal can be achieved only by accomplishing certain subtasks. Thus, in (3), the subtask of determining the desired departure and arrival cities is undertaken first, followed by the task of determining the day and time of travel. The need to structure conversation in this way may seem so obvious as to be hardly worth mentioning; however, the computer needs to be told how to complete each step. The system needs this information in order to know how to interpret the user's input, how to reply to the user's input, and what kinds of questions it needs to ask of the user. A large part of the system design process is devoted to how the dialogue should "flow," which depends on the subgoals of the dialogue.

The dialogue management component may also be responsible for dealing with **error recovery,** that is, getting the conversation back on track after a misunderstanding, for example, one caused by a speech recognition problem. For example, the system in (3) simply asked for clarification (*I'm sorry. I must have misheard the date . . . Okay what day would you be traveling?*) when it was unable to make out what the user said.

d. Text Generation. Text generation involves the use of computers to respond to humans using natural language (whether it be written or synthesized into speech) by creating sentences that convey the relevant information. Just as was the case with text understanding, syntactic rules alone are not sufficient to generate meaningful text. A text generation program must know what real-world knowledge is relevant before it decides on such things as the type of sentence it should generate (e.g., question, statement), or what tenses, order, and types of words it should use.

Sometimes the system's replies need to be more than canned answers. Often, a system retrieves an answer to a user's question from a database and needs to explain that answer to the user. The answer will probably be in an internal computer language that the user cannot understand, so it is necessary for the computer to translate from this answer to a suitable sentence of natural language. For example, an answer from a database containing flight information may look like this in a system's internal language:

(4)	DEP_AIRPORT	ARR_AIRPORT	AIRLINE	DEP_TIME	ARR_TIME
	CMH	JFK	American	11:45am	14:30pm

This table cannot be read to the user the way it is. Rather, the information needs to be put into a sentence like *There is an American Airlines flight leaving Port Columbus at 11:45 A.M. and arriving at JFK at 2:30 P.M.* This is often accomplished via a template that looks something like this: "There is a/an AIRLINE flight leaving DEP_AIRPORT at DEP_TIME and arriving at ARR_AIRPORT at ARR_TIME." A system may have several different templates to express the same information in order to not sound repetitive or to stress some information over other information. More complex systems use syntactic trees rather than templates to construct sentences, in a process analogous to parsing.

e. Speech Synthesis. Finally, if the computer program is one that interacts in spoken language rather than written language, the words that make up the generated text must be converted into a sequence of sounds. This process is discussed in greater detail in File 16.1.

16.3.5   Evaluation of Interactive Systems

Especially for commercial systems, the ultimate test of success is customer satisfaction. The best way to measure satisfaction is to have people who do not know anything about the application try to use it. Data can be recorded on how often the users get the results they need (e.g., the right flight information in a timetable system), how long it takes to do so, how many times the system misunderstands the input, and so on. The users can also answer questionnaires about their experiences that can be used to guide improvements. Experiments that test spoken-language dialogue systems are important for commercial applications, because satisfaction can be affected by unexpected factors, such as whether users tend to have a preference for a male or a female voice. Such factors have no bearing on linguistic principles at work in the system per se, but they do have a profound effect on how useful the software eventually turns out to be.

However, interactive systems can become large and complex, and this creates a problem for testing. The system needs to be functional before it can be tested in realistic situations, but the information gained from such testing is much more useful if it is available early on to guide development. Once an application is up and running, many aspects of it can be hard to change. A common solution is the use of **Wizard of Oz simulations,** in which the users think they are interacting with the actual computer system, but in fact (in the manner of the wizard from Frank Baum's book), a hidden human controller simulates some aspects of the system. For example, the system developers may be interested in testing whether users prefer to have some kinds of information repeated twice. The experiment can be set up so that the "wizard" can hear the user and then choose a response that a Text-To-Speech component speaks aloud back to the user. In this way, both confirmation options can be tried, and the developer gains feedback about the human-computer interaction without fully building the system. Then the results of the experiments can be built into the final version of the program.

·······················

Machine Translation

16.4.1 What Is Machine Translation?

The existence of a large number of diverse languages and cultures makes for a much more interesting world, but at the same time it poses a problem when texts in one language need to be read in another. The task of converting the contents of a text written in one language (the **source language**) into a text in another language (the **target language**) is referred to as **translation**.

The need for translation may arise not only in the case of literary works but also in the world of international business, where all kinds of reports, legal documents, instruction manuals, technical documents, and correspondence must be routinely, rapidly, and accurately translated. **Machine Translation** (MT)—the use of computers to carry out translation—has recently emerged as a viable alternative to human translators for such business and technical translating needs. Two main factors make MT an attractive alternative. First, with increasing globalization, the volume of business-oriented translation has increased so much in recent years that often there aren't enough translators to meet the demand. Second, and perhaps more pressing, human translators can be extremely expensive. For example, a translation into English of a Japanese technical document of moderate difficulty could cost up to 20 cents a word, so that a standard double-spaced page containing 300 words would cost $60.

From the user's point of view, speed, accuracy, and cost of translation are the main issues, and MT's goal is to optimize these elements: to provide accurate translations at high speed and a very low cost. Although many commercial MT systems exist today—some of them fairly successful—the fact remains that not enough is known about language and the process of translation to enable a computer to duplicate the efforts of a human being. In this file, we consider what the process of translation involves and how computers are made to approximate this process.

16.4.2 The Translation Problem

Suppose that you are a translator and that you work with Japanese and English. Given a sentence in Japanese, how would you proceed? First, you must understand the content of the text. To do this, you would have to consult a physical or mental dictionary to assign meanings to the words, and you would have to parse the structure correctly, assigning meaning to the whole sentence. Your decisions about the meanings you assign to each word and the correct parse will depend on common sense and on several syntactic, semantic, and pragmatic factors. Once you have understood the sentence, your next step would be to create a sentence in English that is equivalent in meaning. Again, you would look up English equivalents of the Japanese words in a physical or mental dictionary and construct a grammatical English sentence using those words. This process sounds so deceptively simple that many scientists and philosophers were fooled into believing it could be easily mechanized.

To appreciate the difficulty involved in translation, let us consider a simple example: your job is to translate into English a sentence from a car repair manual written in Japanese. Suppose that the Japanese text instructs the reader to remove the front wheels. As it happens, Japanese does not have a plural marker to refer to more than one wheel, like the -*s* in *wheels*. The Japanese text may say either something like 'remove both front wheel,' or it may just say something like 'remove front wheel.' In the former case, there will be no problem in translating the sentence into English with the plural *wheels* because the word for 'both' is present in the Japanese version. But in the latter case, only the context can tell the translator whether the instruction is to remove a single front wheel or both front wheels. This would involve extralinguistic knowledge about the particular procedure: does it require the removal of both the front wheels or not? This sort of knowledge is extremely difficult, some say impossible, to encode in an MT system.

Another simple example is the problem of lexical ambiguity. In German, there are two words that correspond to English *wall*, with *Mauer* referring to an external wall and *Wand* referring to an internal wall. A human translator translating from English to German would know which one to use from the context, but encoding this information into an MT system is not an easy task. In a real translation, such problems (and many others) appear so frequently that mechanizing translation appears to require simulating general human intelligence in addition to knowledge of language.

Perhaps the first person to try to automate the translation process was a Russian named Petr Smirnov-Troyanskii. In 1933 he developed a three-step process: (1) analysis of the source language, (2) the conversion of source language sequences into target language sequences, and (3) the synthesis of these target language sequences into a normal target language form. These three stages form the conceptual basis of most MT systems today, with conversion, the second stage, receiving the focus of attention.

In the United States, the first steps toward building MT systems culminated in a public demonstration at Georgetown University in 1954. Although this MT system was very modest in scope, it sparked a great deal of interest, and large-scale funding became available for MT research. Over the following decade, however, it soon became apparent that the main aim of achieving **fully automatic high-quality translation** (FAHQT) was far from being achieved. Growing criticism of the MT effort resulted in government sponsors of MT research forming the Automatic Language Processing Advisory Committee (ALPAC) in 1964. This committee came to the strong conclusion that useful MT had no "immediate or predictable prospect." The ALPAC report turned out to be very influential, and funding for MT research in the United States was effectively cut off for subsequent years, although research continued in other countries. It wasn't until 1985 that MT was revived in the United States, this revival being due largely to successful efforts in Japan and Europe, improvements in computer technology and developments in linguistics, and more realistic expectations about the goals of MT: instead of aiming for FAHQT, the emphasis shifted to machine-aided human translation and human-aided machine translation.

16.4.3 MT System Design

In developing an MT system, several design decisions need to be made at the start that will determine the details of the final working system. The design decisions discussed below do not constitute a complete list; other factors, like the choice of a linguistic theory or framework and certain computational decisions, also play an important role (see the Further Readings in File 16.6).

First, the designers need to decide whether the system will be fully or partly automatic. A fully automatic system would, in principle, not require any human intervention in the translation process: given a source language text, the MT system would output an accurate translation in the target language. However, as the discussion above shows, this is rarely a realistic goal. Partial automation is a more practical approach, and one that most systems use. In partial automation, the source language text can first be **pre-edited** by a person so as to "prime" it for the MT system. Typically, pre-editing involves rewriting the source language text into a **controlled language,** which has fewer ambiguities and simpler syntactic patterns, or marking the source language text to indicate word boundaries, proper names, plurals, and so on. Pre-editing can be performed by anyone fluent in the source language; it does not need to be performed by a bilingual or a translator. Thus, this sort of design can be cost- and resource-effective.

A system can also be designed to be **interactive,** so that it turns to a person to resolve ambiguities (such as the singular-plural problem discussed above). Finally, the output of the system can be **post-edited.** Here, a person revises the machine's output, either correcting errors due to ambiguities in the source text (e.g., converting wrong instances of singular nouns to plurals) or converting the translated text into an idiomatic version of the target language. While these two tasks must be carried out by a bilingual, they are less time-intensive than translating a document from scratch.

Another major consideration is the proposed application of the system. Will the system serve to translate texts in a particular technical or business field, or will it be for general use? Generally, the more limited the type of document, the easier it is to design the system, since a more restricted field allows the use of a smaller lexicon and less variation in syntactic patterns.

A third consideration is whether to build a **multilingual** system, involving more than one language pair, or a **bilingual** one, which deals with only one language pair. Bilingual systems may be bi-directional, carrying out translation in either direction for the language pair chosen (e.g., Japanese to English, or English to Japanese), or unidirectional (e.g., Japanese to English only). A real-life example of a multilingual system was the European Commission's Eurotra project, which aimed to translate nine languages in all directions—that is, 72 language pairs! (It never succeeded in this goal, however.)

Another consideration is which translation approach to adopt. MT systems in operation today use one of three strategies. The oldest one (1950s to early 1960s) is known as **direct translation.** In this approach, the MT system is designed for bilingual, unidirectional translation; every word is translated, and then some reordering is performed based on morphological and syntactic rules of the target language in order to produce the finished text. The English sentence *He bought two white houses,* for example, would be translated into Spanish as shown in (1).

(1)   Direct translation

Source language text:	He	bought	two	white	houses
Breakdown in source language:	He	buy	two	white	house
Dictionary look-up:	El	comprar	dos	blanco	casa
Adaptation to target language:	El	compró	dos	casas	blancas

As you can see, the translation in (1) required that the translation software know words of English and Spanish, rules about word order (such as whether adjectives come before or after nouns), and rules about agreement and morphology (such as how to mark the past tense). The example in (1) suggests that direct translation is fairly effective, and in some cases it can be. However, direct translation does not include any attempt at parsing or semantic analysis. The result is, predictably, unsatisfactory, as shown in the Russian-to-English examples in (2) and (3).

(2)   Vcera my tselyi cas katalis' na lodke.
      Yesterday we the entire hour rolled themselves on a boat.
      Intended: Yesterday we went out boating for a whole hour.

(3)   Ona navarila scei na nescol'ko dnei.
      It welded on cabbage soups on several days.
      Intended: She cooked enough cabbage soup for several days.

As computer science and linguistic theory developed, an improved method was proposed whereby the source language text is first translated into an intermediate abstract representation that contains sufficient information in it to allow the creation of a target language text. This is referred to as the **interlingua** method. This method is an improvement over the direct method because it allows the creation of multilingual systems with relative ease: for every language, we only need to have a method for analyzing the language into an intermediate representation and a way to generate the language from this intermediate representation; the intermediate representation is common to all the language pairs, as the representation in (4) illustrates.

(4) Interlingua method

```
Language 1 ⟍                                ⟋→ Language 1
Language 2 —————→ interlingua ————→ Language 2
Language 3 ⟋                                ⟍→ Language 3
etc.                                              etc.
```

However, with this method the problem is that creating a common intermediate representation, or interlingua, is a very difficult task, even for related languages such as English and German. In spite of the emergence of sophisticated syntactic and semantic theories of natural language over the last 50 years or so, we simply do not yet know enough about language to create an interlingua for MT systems.

In response to the difficulties encountered in attempts to create language-independent intermediate representations, one solution is to have language-dependent ones. Such a strategy is called the **transfer** method. In this case, the source text is analyzed to produce a source-language intermediate representation, which is then transferred to a target-language intermediate representation, and then the target-language text is generated. Although the transfer method involves more steps, it is more effective than the interlingua method because language-dependent intermediate representations are easier to create. Because the system is automated, the extra steps increase the time to produce a translation by only a small amount.

A central issue in designing MT systems has been the lack of an adequate theory of translation, which in turn rests on the development of satisfactory linguistic theories. But some MT researchers dispute the central role of linguistics in MT systems, and alternative strategies range from example-based MT (the use of large amounts of pretranslated parallel texts of the source and target languages) to statistics-based MT (e.g., using probability to determine the likelihood that a word in the source language corresponds to a word or words in the target language). The trend most recently, however, has been toward hybrid or mixed systems, that is, systems that are based on more than one principle (linguistics, examples, statistics).

MT systems still have a long way to go, but there have been some success stories. One such case was the Canadian METEO system for translating English-language weather reports into French. In Canada, a bilingual country, weather bulletins must be produced in both languages, but translating weather bulletins is an extremely boring and repetitive job. The METEO system was installed in 1976 and was used until 2001; its successor was translating more than 5 million words a year as of 2015 (Macklovitch 2015: 269). Much of this success is because the range of expressions found in weather reports is very limited; this illustrates the fact, mentioned earlier, that restricted types of documents are easier for designing MT systems. As we continue to learn more about language and develop more complete theories of how language works, we will be able to develop machine translation software that is increasingly reliable and easy to use.

FILE 16.5

....

Corpus Linguistics

16.5.1 What Is a Corpus?

So far in this chapter, we have discussed ways that we can apply our knowledge of various structural components of language—for example, phonetics, syntax, and semantics—in order to create machines that are able to produce or interpret human language in some way. We have seen that these applications have a wide variety of uses. However, there is a second side to computational linguistics: using computer programs to help us analyze language. Computers have the ability to process a large amount of data in a relatively short period of time, so we can use computers to find patterns in linguistic data much more rapidly than we could if we had to examine those data manually. Using computers therefore allows us to test hypotheses about language and linguistic rules more quickly. Using computers to analyze linguistic data has also made it more practical to think about linguistic rules in a new way.

Traditionally, linguists have tried to describe and analyze linguistic rules as though, for any linguistic form, either that rule has been followed or else it has not been followed. This approach would say, for example, that in syntax, sentences are either grammatical or not; in morphology, words are either well-formed or not; and in pragmatics, utterances are either felicitous or not. According to this traditional view, "proper" linguistic description is a matter of being able to discern and then state the rules that distinguish the set of well-formed linguistic forms from the set that is not. Recently, some linguistic investigation has begun to depart from this binary "acceptable-or-unacceptable" tradition. Of late, the statistical properties of language have received more and more attention for the insights they may bring to theoretical issues, especially in phonology and syntax. Psycholinguists have also long been interested in the effects that frequency (of words, phonemes, etc.) has on human language processing. Finally, computational applications such as **natural language processing** (NLP) and speech recognition have placed more emphasis on incorporating statistical models of language into theoretical frameworks.

The central insight here is that certain types of linguistic forms (phones, syllables, words, phrases, or sentences) appear more frequently than others. Thus, instead of saying that a certain construction is "acceptable" or "unacceptable," we may want to say that it is "relatively common" or "relatively rare." However, this insight by itself is of quite limited use without some idea of just how frequent particular linguistic phenomena are. How might these frequencies be calculated? Ideally, we might follow around an individual for his entire life and record all the language he ever experiences—but obviously, this is impractical. An approximation to this is to gather up a more or less representative sample of language (either spoken or written) and use statistics over this sample as estimates for the language as a whole. A collected body of text is called a **corpus** (plural *corpora*), from the Latin word for 'body.' A linguistic corpus is a collection of linguistic materials (written, spoken, or some combination) appropriate for specific purposes of research, such as data analysis, training, and testing. **Corpus linguistics** involves the design and the annotation of corpus materials that are required for specific purposes.

644

16.5.2 Kinds of Corpora

Because different kinds of corpora are more or less appropriate for different tasks, one must differentiate various types of corpora, based on what the source material is and on what kinds of extralinguistic information are added.

a. Source of the Corpus. Corpora can be composed from spoken, signed, or written language. As written documents are comparatively easy to obtain and store electronically, the vast majority of corpora are composed of written texts. Often, then, we find corpora composed entirely of news texts like the *Wall Street Journal* or composed of various books, stories, technical reports, and other written varieties of language. However, because many linguists are interested in how people speak (see File 1.3 on speech and writing), there is a great demand for corpora composed of speech. Corpora may also be composed from a combination of speech and writing. The British National Corpus, for example, contains about 90% written text and 10% spoken—the larger portion of written text due to the fact that it is much easier to obtain.

In addition, corpora can be classified by the genre of the source material. Because news text is very common and easy to obtain, it is often used as the source for corpora. For example, one English corpus consists of *Wall Street Journal* text from the early 1990s; one Chinese corpus consists of texts collected from newspapers in mainland China, Hong Kong, and Taiwan, also from the early 1990s. Most very large corpora are of this type, particularly in less commonly studied languages.

Of course, news text does not provide a very broad picture of how language is used, so some efforts have focused on creating **balanced corpora,** corpora that try to remain balanced among different genres. An early example was the Brown corpus, which contains newspaper stories, but also scientific papers, Western stories, and so on. Although such corpora can be quite small (the Brown corpus contains only 1 million words), they are often more useful for accurate pictures of the relative frequencies of words than news-heavy corpora. Technological advances have made size less of a concern, however: the Corpus of Contemporary American English (COCA), which contained more than 520 million words as of 2016 (covering 1990–2015), is a regularly updated balanced corpus equally divided among spoken texts, fiction, popular magazines, newspapers, and academic texts.

Most of these corpora tend to capture language in one particular time or place. In many cases they are frozen, meaning that once a specified amount of texts has been collected and annotated, the corpus is complete; this is called a **reference corpus.** Another possibility is to have a **monitor corpus**: as new texts continue to be written or spoken, a monitor corpus continues to grow, gathering more and more data.

We can also find corpora in many languages. Usually, this means that we find the same text written in two or more languages. The Hansard corpus, for example, contains French and English versions of the same Canadian parliamentary sessions. There are also several corpora, such as the MULTEXT corpus, which contain more than two languages. The MULTEXT-East corpus, for example, has George Orwell's book *1984* written in English and in 13 other languages.

Although a corpus could theoretically contain multiple unaligned texts in different languages, texts that contain the same sentences written in different languages are more useful data for applications such as machine translation. Such texts are commonly called **bi-texts.** A corpus containing bi-texts is called a **parallel corpus.** It is useful for a machine translation system to see the same thing written in two different languages because it can use this information to learn what words and syntactic patterns correspond to each other in each language. In German and English bi-texts, for example, the machine translation system can use the information that every time *I* occurs in the English text, *ich* occurs in the German text. However, matching the corresponding parts of the corpus accurately (known as *aligning the corpus*) is a nontrivial task that has only recently become practical to perform automatically.

b. Levels of Annotation. Linguistics is generally divided into several subfields, all studying a particular aspect of language (see the topics covered in the table of contents in this book). Likewise, corpora can be made to show different kinds of linguistically relevant information, called **representations**. For example, the word *chair* is a third-person singular noun. Each representation receives a label called **annotation**. For example, the fact that *chair* is a third-person singular noun can be labeled as "chair_3SN." One of the most common annotations is lexical category. Each word in the corpus is given a lexical category label (e.g., noun, verb, adjective, etc.). But we can have other labels, such as a word's function in the sentence (e.g., subject or direct object), the phonetic transcription, or the word's root (e.g., *dog* is the root of *dogs*). Additionally, more complicated annotation, such as the syntactic tree structure of a sentence, can be included in a corpus. Often, this kind of representation builds off of lexical category annotation. These corpora usually require many years to develop, and they also require a way to encode the more complicated annotations.

Additional kinds of annotation are possible for spoken corpora. Most spoken corpora include at least a transcription of the audio- and/or visual-recording, typically a word-by-word transcription in standard spelling. An example is the British National Corpus, which uses standard spelling and also renders words like *gotta, um,* and so forth.

Some spoken corpora use phonetic transcription to render spoken words or use both regular spelling and phonetic transcription alongside speech. Phonetic transcription provides information on which segments (or phones) were actually uttered. A variety of phonetic encodings are possible here, depending on the needs of the end-users (often programs as well as people), who may require input using limited characters, one-letter-per-sound, or other constraints. For example, *gotta go* could be written as [gɑɾə goʊ] (IPA), [gA4@ goU] (Sampa encoding), or [g aa dx ax g ow] (DARPA encoding).

Recently, information about suprasegmentals (prosodic elements), such as intonation and phrasing, has been transcribed as well. In a number of corpora, the ToBI (for **To**nes and **B**reak **I**ndices) system for prosodic transcription is used.

Syntactic, phonetic, and especially prosodic annotation are rare because they are time-intensive and they require a person trained in syntax, phonetic transcription, or prosodic transcription, respectively. The Corpus of Spoken Dutch (Corpus Gesproken Nederlands), for example, contains syntactic, phonetic, and prosodic annotation. It was constructed between 1998 and 2004. All of the almost 9 million spoken words were transcribed using standard Dutch spelling. About 1 million words received additional phonetic annotation, and the same number of words received additional syntactic annotation. Fewer than 250,000 words were transcribed prosodically. These numbers illustrate how difficult and time-consuming corpus annotation is.

Most corpus annotation is done first with a specially designed computer program and then is carefully hand-checked afterwards. Improving the quality of both of these steps is crucial to getting accurate data for other applications and has become an interesting natural-language processing task in its own right.

FILE **16.6**

·······················

Practice

File 16.1—Speech Synthesis

Exercise

1. File 16.1 mentions that TTS systems use spelling-to-sound rules to generate the pronunciation for some words. This process is used for words that have rule-governed pronunciation. For example, <ou> is usually pronounced [ɑʊ] as in *mouse*. However, <ou> in *bought* is pronounced [ɔ]. The rule a TTS system uses to account for *bought* is something like "pronounce <ou> as [ɔ] if it is followed by <ght>."

   i. Write pronunciation rules that would allow the TTS system to produce the words in parts (a)–(e) correctly. Focus on the letter <c> in part (a) and on the vowels in parts (b)–(e).

   ii. Some of the words are irregular and cannot be pronounced correctly using spelling-to-sound rules. Which are they, and how would a TTS system pronounce them, according to the rules that you gave for part (i)? How can you make the TTS system pronounce them correctly?

   a. call, cab, cake, cone, cob, cinder, city, cell, cent, cello
   b. zoo, boo, moon, spoon, food, room, good, stood, book
   c. tough, rough, plough, enough, cough, bough
   d. mould, could, would, should
   e. bone, home, rode, stove, dove, love, done, move

Activities

2. Go to the Links page for Chapter 16 and choose one of the links given for this activity.

   i. Try to construct input that the speech synthesizer cannot say correctly. You may type in words, full sentences, even song lyrics if you like. Describe how the system mispronounces it, and venture a guess as to why the system may have a problem with the input you chose.

   ii. For the input that the speech synthesizer did say correctly, were there any instances that impressed you? If so, explain why you were impressed. If not, say why you were not impressed even though the output was correct.

   iii. Repeat (i) and (ii) using a different speech synthesizer. How do the two systems compare? Which system do you think is better? Why?

3. RUTH (Rutgers University Talking Head) is an animated talking face. Go to the Links page for Chapter 16 and view some of the sample animations created with RUTH. Then answer questions (i)–(iv).

   i. Did RUTH's speech sound natural? Was it intelligible? Based on your judgment of how natural and intelligible RUTH sounds, what kind of speech synthesis system might RUTH be using? Justify your answer.

   ii. In order for us to see and hear RUTH, natural-looking head and eye movements, facial expressions, and lip movements need to be simulated. How natural does RUTH look? Which movements or expressions look unnatural? How so?

   iii. Simulating appropriate lip movements to accompany speech is called *visual speech synthesis*. Appropriate lip movements are important because, if done correctly, they aid the perception of synthesized speech (which can sometimes be hard to understand). Listen to the animation again, this time without looking at RUTH. Do you think that RUTH's lip movements help you understand the system's speech?

   iv. A problem of visual speech synthesis is co-articulation. If you wanted to synthesize lip movements, how would you deal with the problem of co-articulation? What are the advantages or disadvantages of your approach?

File 16.2—Automatic Speech Recognition

Activity

4. Experiment with an automatic speech recognition system you have access to on your smartphone, computer, etc. (e.g., OK Google, Siri, Cortana). How accurate it is? Are there particular sounds or words that it has problems with? Do some accents or variant pronunciations cause it to be less accurate?

File 16.3—Communicating with Computers

Exercise

5. Not only can we communicate with computers, but we can also use the computer to communicate with other people, for example, via email. A common problem for email users is spam (unwanted, unsolicited emails). Many people use a spam filter to redirect or throw away unwanted messages.

   i. Explain how spelling the word *Viagra* as <V!2AGGRA> might let it pass through a spam filter.

   ii. How might you design a spam filter that would not allow words like <V!2AGGRA> to pass through?

   iii. What are some examples of spam messages that have gotten past your spam filter into your email inbox, and what are some examples of legitimate messages that were incorrectly categorized as spam? What particular characteristics of those messages do you think contributed to these problems?

Activities

6. Try out ELIZA by going to the Links page for Chapter 16 and clicking on ELIZA. Then answer questions (i) and (ii):

   i. Try to figure out some of the strategies ELIZA uses to formulate replies to your input. What information does ELIZA need to extract from your input to do this? What parts can ELIZA just copy verbatim?   *(cont.)*

ii. Sometimes ELIZA's strategies don't work. For instance, one strategy for replying to a question is simply to say *Does that question interest you?*

> User: When will the Yankees win the pennant?
> ELIZA: Does that question interest you?

ELIZA assumes that this is a question because it begins with the question word *when*. However, it is possible to trick ELIZA by using declarative sentences with *when*:

> User: When I sneeze, I see stars.
> ELIZA: Does that question interest you?

Here ELIZA's response is not appropriate because the user's input was not a question. Find other examples of inappropriate responses that Eliza gives to various input, and try to explain what ELIZA's strategy is and how it fails.

7. Listen to the dialogue given in Example (3) of File 16.3 by going to the Links page for Chapter 16 and clicking on "Idom." Then answer questions (i)–(iv).

   i. How natural and intelligible is the system's speech? How well does the conversation "flow"? Give examples.

   ii. What features of the system are intended to make it appear like a real person? Give examples.

   iii. Listen to how the system pronounces the email address at the end of the dialogue. How is it different from the rest of the speech? What does this tell you about the kind of speech synthesis the system might be using?

   iv. How well does the system understand the user's speech? Do you think the user has to speak more clearly than he usually would?

File 16.4—Machine Translation

Activity

8. Go to the Links page for Chapter 16 and choose one of the free online MT systems.

   i. Use the system to translate some English text into a foreign language, and then translate it back into English. Does the result differ from the original? How?

   ii. Find a web page that is written in one of the languages that the system can translate from, preferably a language that you don't know. To find such a web page, you can use a search engine and set the search language to, for example, *Spanish*. Then search for any word or topic you like, such as *computer* or *rock* or the name of a famous person.

   iii. Now, use the MT system to translate (part of) the web page you found in (ii) into English. Is the translation comprehensible? Is the English text good enough to publish? Is it at least good enough so that you can understand what the page is about and follow the discussion?

   iv. Repeat exercises (i) and (ii) using a different MT system. How do the two systems compare with each other? Which system do you think is better? Why?

File 16.5—Corpus Linguistics

Exercise

9. Imagine you are given a corpus of English literary texts. Your professor has asked you to develop a way to do the following four things automatically. In which order would you want them to be done? Why?

(cont.)

    a. Find the subjects, direct objects, and indirect objects (if applicable) in each sentence.

    b. Build a syntactic tree for each sentence, so as to show which words combine to form noun phrases, prepositional phrases, verb phrases, sentences, and so on.

    c. Give a part-of-speech tag to each word in each sentence.

    d. Produce the root for each word in the corpus.

Discussion Questions

10. Imagine you have collected fifteen hours of spoken dialogue for linguistic research. It is up to you to transcribe the speech you recorded.

    i. What advantages/disadvantages are there to using phonetic transcription to transcribe a spoken corpus? For example, if a person wanted to search for a particular word, would the word be easier to find in a phonetically transcribed corpus or in a corpus transcribed using English spelling? What kinds of research might IPA transcriptions be useful for?

    ii. Think about other ways that your corpus could be transcribed. Propose a different way to transcribe your corpus.

    iii. What advantages does your transcription system have, and what kinds of research would it be useful for?

11. A portion of the British National Corpus (BNC), the BNC-Sampler, contains 50% written and 50% spoken language. Why would the corpus designers choose an even split between spoken and written language? Is it a fair, or balanced, representation of language use overall? Would a corpus that contained 90% spoken language or 90% written language be more representative of language use? Why do you think so?

Activity

12. Go to the Links page for Chapter 16 and search the British National Corpus. Then answer questions (i)–(ii).

    i. Find out which are the most frequent color terms in the English language: select at least ten color terms, and check the BNC for the terms' frequencies. Which are the color terms used most frequently in the corpus? Do you think the BNC accurately captures which color terms are frequently used in English? Why or why not?

    ii. The word *tie* can be a noun or a verb. Find out whether it is used more frequently as a noun or as a verb: search the BNC for the word *tie* and examine the first fifty entries. (*Note:* This activity assumes that the first fifty entries are representative of the remaining entries.) How many times is *tie* used as a verb, and how many times is it used as a noun? When used as a verb, does *tie* always mean the same thing? Similarly, when used as a noun, does *tie* always mean the same thing? Why does searching just for *tie* not give you a complete picture of the relative frequencies with which *tie* is used as a verb or a noun? Which words would you have to include in your search to get a more accurate picture?

Further Readings

Dickinson, Markus; Chris Brew; and Detmar Meurers. 2013. *Language and computers.* Oxford: Wiley-Blackwell.

Jurafsky, Daniel, and James H. Martin. 2008. *Speech and language processing: An introduction to natural language processing, computational linguistics, and speech recognition.* 2nd edn. Upper Saddle River, NJ: Prentice-Hall.

Stork, David G. (ed.). 1997. *HAL's legacy: 2001's computer as dream and reality.* Cambridge, MA: MIT Press.

CHAPTER
17

Practical Applications

....

What Can You Do with Linguistics?

The past sixteen chapters have presented an introduction to the study of language and linguistics. You may now be wondering about ways in which linguistics is applied. The late actor and comedian Robin Williams, in speaking about his children, once quipped "I want to introduce . . . Zachary, the linguist. He does very good. He's going to open a Syntax Repair Shop." Presumably this is not actually what Zachary will end up doing, as there's no such thing as a Syntax Repair Shop. There are, however, plenty of real applications of the study of linguistics. A few of these, though by no means all, will be described in the files that follow. A list of links to useful resources associated with each of the applications discussed here is available on the Links page for Chapter 17.

Contents

FILE **17.1**
....
Language Education

17.1.1 Job Description

Under normal circumstances, infants and young children seem to effortlessly acquire one or more native languages. However, later in life, language acquisition becomes more difficult for most people. Additionally, many people learn a second language in a classroom environment, rather than by being completely immersed in the language. This file focuses on teaching a foreign language to teenagers and adults.

Language teachers work in a variety of different settings: at middle and high schools, at immersion schools, at universities, at special language schools and institutes, as teachers in a foreign country, or as private teachers and tutors. In a school or university setting, language teachers usually teach students who all have the same linguistic background, but at language schools and institutes or as private instructors, they may teach students with a variety of different native languages. Depending on the setting and goal of the course(s), a teacher may teach several different classes or teach the same students for several hours every day.

Several factors determine how a teacher will teach a class. Sometimes the company or institution employing the teacher has certain requirements (for example, that all classes be taught using only the foreign language). A second factor is the level of the class: in introductory-level classes, the teacher may focus on teaching vocabulary and grammar, but there might be a different focus in advanced classes. When talking to beginning students, the teacher will have to use simple grammar and basic vocabulary. In more advanced classes, many students already have a good command of the grammar and a sufficiently large vocabulary base. Here the teacher may focus more on class discussions or reading literature. Finally, the goal of the class influences the way it is taught. Sometimes classes are intended to teach students only one aspect of a foreign language, for example, pronunciation classes or classes that teach reading scholarly literature in a foreign language. The goal of the majority of classes, however, is to teach students how to communicate in the foreign language. In many classes, all four language-related skills are taught: speaking, listening, reading, and writing.

The most common teaching methodology today is probably the **communicative approach.** This approach focuses on speaking and listening skills. In this teaching methodology, getting the message across is considered more important than having perfect grammar. Typical activities include role playing, games, and information gap activities. In information gap activities, students receive only partial information about a certain topic or task and have to talk to other students to get the missing information. Classes taught using the communicative approach are usually student-centered: Instead of having the teacher lecture while the students absorb, the teacher functions more as a guide or coach. He or she introduces grammar and activities and is available for questions. However, the students are expected to do much of the speaking. Every teaching methodology is based on a different philosophy as to how languages are acquired. The communicative approach is based on the belief that people learn languages through interaction with other speakers.

Apart from choosing a particular teaching methodology (or having one chosen by a company or an institution), a language teacher must be able to adapt to different learning styles and temperaments. This is especially important in a classroom setting that is not lecture-oriented, one in which students get actively involved.

The preceding discussion has focused on the time teachers spend in the classroom. However, much time is spent preparing classes (choosing or developing activities that ideally develop all four language-related skills—speaking, listening, reading, and writing—and adapt to different learning styles, deciding how to introduce new grammar and vocabulary, using the frequently limited amount of time effectively, etc.), writing quizzes and exams, and grading.

17.1.2 Jobs Available and Job Qualifications

Of course, the most important qualification for a language teacher is the ability to speak the language he or she wants to teach. It can be the teacher's native language or a second or foreign language. A number of language schools, however, accept only native speakers of a language as instructors of that language.

There are also a number of degrees that often help and are sometimes required for certain teaching positions. In particular, a degree in a foreign language, applied linguistics, English as a second language (ESL), or education is desirable. For most full-time language education jobs, one of these degrees is needed. For example, some states in the United States require a master's in education to teach foreign languages at the middle or high school levels, and many language schools offering ESL classes expect certification in ESL.

However, language teaching is also something that can be done as a part-time job, freelance, or for just a couple of hours each week. There are many opportunities, such as offering private lessons, tutoring, or teaching in continuing education programs. In these cases, a degree is often not required, especially if the instructor is a native speaker of the language being taught.

17.1.3 Language Education and Linguistics

A degree in linguistics is not necessary to teach foreign languages. However, knowledge of the linguistic principles of the language you want to teach is very helpful. For example, if you were teaching English pronunciation, it would be useful to be able to inform your students (usually using layman's terminology) that the regular plural morpheme has three different pronunciations: [s] as in [kæts] *cats,* [z] as in [dɑgz] *dogs,* and [əz] as in [bɹɪdʒəz] *bridges.* Most students will probably figure out that the plural morpheme in *bridges* sounds different from the one in *dogs,* but many may not realize that the plural morphemes in *cats* and *dogs* are also pronounced differently. And it is up to the language teacher to point out such distinctions and to explain the rules that govern the differences in pronunciation. Understanding that these differences are rule-governed and being able to teach your students the rule makes their task of learning the language much easier than it would be if they simply had to memorize lists of words that used different pronunciations of the morpheme.

Apart from structural issues that are directly related to the language you are teaching, there are some more general areas of linguistic knowledge that can be helpful in teaching a language. For example, knowledge of theories of second-language acquisition and characteristics of foreign language learners (see File 8.5) will help you understand why your students make the mistakes they make and how your teaching can most effectively handle this. Knowledge of sociolinguistics, especially variation, will also help you prepare students to communicate with native speakers of the language. For example, students need to be aware that there is variation and that, even after years of learning a language, they may come across a speaker they cannot understand. This is especially important for languages such as German, English, or Italian, where there is so much dialectal variation that not even native speakers of the language can understand all of the dialects. Finally, a background in linguistics helps bridge the gap between the largely prescriptive rules that are commonly taught in the classroom and the linguistic reality of the language.

······································

Speech-Language Pathology and Audiology

17.2.1   Job Description

Throughout this book, we have described the study of language, from the physical properties of speech sounds to the ways in which they are organized meaningfully into words and used in context. The ability to understand and use language is important for successful interpersonal communication.

Some people, however, have a difficult time understanding or producing language and find it challenging to communicate with others. According to the American Speech-Language Hearing Association, between 6 and 8 million people in the United States were diagnosed with some form of language impairment in 2006. **Speech-language pathologists** (SLPs) are professionals who are trained to diagnose speech and language problems and to help individuals become more effective communicators.

SLPs work with people who have difficulty with a wide range of language-related tasks, both physical and cognitive. These difficulties may be receptive (involving the comprehension of language), expressive (involving the production and articulation of language and speech), and/or pragmatic (involving the social aspects of language). SLPs work with both children and adults and with both those who were born with communication disorders and those who have acquired difficulty using speech and language as a result of illness or injury. They may also offer services for people who don't have any particular communication disorder, but who want to become more effective speakers by changing their pronunciation, vocabulary, or presentation style.

A variety of speech impairments, stemming from a variety of causes, can be treated by SLPs. A problem with articulation, for example, might arise from a congenital disorder, such as cerebral palsy and cleft lip and/or palate, from a neurodegenerative disorder, such as muscular dystrophy, amyotrophic lateral disease (ALS), or Parkinson's disease. It could also arise from a developmental disorder, such as autism, or from trauma to the brain associated with a stroke or an accident. An SLP, therefore, must be well trained in all aspects of the study of language, from the theories we have introduced in this book to the physical, anatomical, and neurological foundations of language you might expect to read about in a biology text.

SLPs make use of a number of techniques to help the people they work with, including skills development in one or more areas of language. Their approach to these areas may be spoken, written, signed, or augmented—that is, assisted by a computer or other device—or a combination of all four.

Audiologists are similar to speech-language pathologists in that they work with people who have difficulty with language, but audiologists specialize in issues related to hearing, including the evaluation of normal and impaired hearing, hearing aid and assistive-listening technology, and the prevention of hearing loss. While some individuals are born with hearing impairment, many hearing problems are acquired as a result of accidents, illness, and noise exposure. Audiologists work closely with SLPs in order to provide rehabilitation services to individuals whose communication skills are impaired as a result of hearing loss.

Speech-language pathologists and audiologists may work in a variety of settings such as schools, hospitals, community clinics, corporations and businesses, colleges and universities, or private practices. When a person comes to an SLP or an audiologist for help, the first step is to determine whether there is evidence of a speech, language, or hearing problem by conducting a thorough evaluation. If results from the assessment show that the individual is functioning at a level below what is expected for a person of his or her age or potential, then therapy services may be recommended. The type and duration of speech-language therapy or audiological rehabilitation that is prescribed will depend on the nature of the problem and the characteristics of the patient. It is the responsibility of the treating SLP or audiologist to monitor the individual's progress to determine the effectiveness of the treatment.

17.2.2 Job Qualifications

Prospective candidates to the field of speech-language pathology or audiology might complete an undergraduate degree in speech and hearing science, communication sciences and disorders, psychology, linguistics, education, biology, English, or other fields. However, graduate training in speech and hearing science, communication sciences and disorders, or an equivalent program at an accredited postsecondary institution is required in order to become a licensed speech-language pathologist or audiologist in the United States. Clinical certification in speech-language pathology or audiology requires focused clinical training during graduate school, successful completion of a national (praxis) examination, and a supervised clinical experience (Clinical Fellowship Year) after graduation. In addition to national certification through the American Speech-Language Hearing Association, a state license is also required. Additional certification may be necessary depending on the desired area of clinical focus. For example, school certification is necessary for public school employment, and a PhD is generally required for advanced research and teaching.

Forensic Linguistics

17.3.1 Legal Applications of Linguistics

One field in which there are many distinct applications for linguistic analysis is law. Although in general the legal professions—unlike several others discussed in this chapter—do not require explicit training in language or in linguistic analysis, an awareness of linguistic principles can nonetheless inform the work of many such professionals. Writing law and interpreting law, particularly by determining whether a law has been followed in any particular case, are instances of linguistic analysis. Linguists are sometimes called upon to help inform the legal system of what the law actually says.

A critical component in the education of anyone who practices law is learning to use and interpret language according to pragmatic principles that differ rather markedly from those of standard language use in our society. The specialized language that is used, for example, in the preparation of contracts or wills adheres to conventions that are specific to those domains. Not only is there specialized vocabulary, as there is in any field, but there is also an attempt to avoid the use of the ambiguous language and implicature that pervade normal language use (see Chapter 7). Therefore, a background in linguistic analysis and a familiarity with thinking critically about language can benefit anyone in one of the legal professions.

One domain of language use that has received a lot of media attention—both through the many celebrity trials that have been in the news in recent years and through the large proliferation of court-themed television series—is the courtroom. Issues of language and power (see File 11.3) emerge in how lawyers examine various witnesses. Although witnesses will likely be given much freedom to tell their story by the lawyer who has originally called them to the stand, they will not meet with such freedom on cross-examination. This allows the cross-examining lawyer to choose how the story will be told, potentially using presuppositions in order to get witnesses to agree to his version of the story. Thus, attorneys in the courtroom must be keenly aware of how they and their adversaries use language, how those on the witness stand use language, and, of course, how the language used may affect the judge or jury.

In addition, there is a particular field of applied linguistics—forensic linguistics—in which the formal study of language is directly applied to matters of law and law enforcement. This is discussed in the rest of this file.

17.3.2 Forensic Linguistics

Forensic linguistics is the application of linguistic analysis in judicial and law enforcement settings. A forensic linguist studies linguistic evidence from a legal investigation, looking for patterns in the evidence that may shed light on how a crime was committed, and/or by whom. In this sense, forensic linguistics is similar to other types of forensic investigation: in each case, the goal is to use the information available in order to determine what is not immediately evident. Forensic linguists study any instance in which a particular use of language may shed light on an investigation.

Evidence may include interviews conducted by law enforcement officers with witnesses or with suspects. Evidence may also include writing samples, if the authorship of texts is part of the investigation. In other cases, forensic linguists may study recordings made at the crime scenes themselves (for example, from surveillance equipment) or recordings of suspects in other situations. These recordings may be recovered from investigative work—voicemail recordings, for example—or they may be garnered in sting investigations, investigations in which law enforcement officers set up recording equipment with the specific intent of capturing a suspect incriminating himself. In general, an audio-recording is preferred, although in some cases a written transcript must suffice.

Once a recording is obtained, from whatever source, a forensic linguist may engage in different kinds of analysis depending on the goal. In some cases, it may be the linguist's responsibility to determine who the speakers are, for example, by using phonological clues. In other cases, the linguist's job will be to analyze a conversation in order to determine what the language use reveals about how a crime may have been committed. In these cases, the linguist will carefully investigate the turns in the conversation to determine who says what and in what context. Useful information may be derived from such details as who in a conversation talks more, who is responsible for controlling the topic of conversation, how often the topic of conversation changes, whether the speakers interrupt each other, whether they seem to understand each other, and so on. This may be important in determining the extent to which someone was involved in a crime. In order to do this, a forensic linguist needs to be familiar with issues of semantics and pragmatics as well as with sociolinguistic concerns. After analyzing the collected evidence, a forensic linguist may then be called as an expert witness in the courtroom to discuss how certain conclusions were reached.

Although an important part of forensic linguistics is to help determine whether or how a crime was committed, forensic linguists are also involved in helping to ensure that justice is carried out properly. For example, in cases where a suspect is a non-native English speaker, it is important to ensure that he is successfully made aware of his rights, even though he may not understand English. Likewise, if a translator is used in any interrogation, it is important to make sure that the nuances and implicatures used by each party are understood by the other parties. These are processes that a forensic linguist may be asked to evaluate in order to ascertain whether they were satisfactorily accomplished. Forensic linguists may also be called upon to determine whether an interrogation that led to an arrest was conducted fairly from a linguistic perspective, for example, whether questions used presuppositions that compelled suspects to inadvertently make claims they did not intend, or whether investigators drew too strong an implicature from something that a suspect may have said.

Although it often falls to trained forensic linguists to do the sort of analysis outlined above, in fact, anyone involved in law enforcement needs to be aware of many principles of linguistics in order to ensure that sting investigations are designed to be maximally effective and that they are conducted properly, that interviews are conducted fairly, and that any communication with witnesses or suspects does not obstruct justice in any way.

17.3.3 Jobs Available and Job Qualifications

As you have seen from the preceding sections, there are many avenues that lead to careers in which an understanding of both linguistics and law will prove beneficial. These include law enforcement—itself a diverse field with many jobs, each with its own set of qualifications—and those who practice law: lawyers and judges. To practice law requires a law degree, generally three years of postgraduate education. Forensic linguists, like other linguists (see File 17.6), need a strong background in academic linguistics, but they also need a background in criminology, forensic science, or some related field. The exact degrees required—both what level of degree is required and in which fields—will be determined by the organization that employs the linguist.

Of course, even if you do not pursue one of these careers, it is almost certain that, in your endeavors to be a law-abiding citizen, at some point in your life you will have contracts that you will be expected to uphold. You will have to interpret what is required of you to submit your income taxes, and you may be called upon to be a juror and evaluate criminal proceedings in which there may be linguistic evidence presented. Thus, recognizing the importance that language can play in legal proceedings is important for everyone.

FILE 17.4

Language in Advertising

17.4.1 Language and the Goals of Advertising

Advertising is a business in which language is used to persuade people to do things: to buy a particular product, to watch a certain television show, to donate to a given cause, to engage in a certain practice (such as getting a vaccine or not smoking), to go to some community function, to vote for someone, or to hold certain beliefs (for example, that a corporation is trustworthy or that a political philosophy is a good one). Each of these specific goals of advertising is very different from the others, yet advertisers use strikingly similar techniques to achieve each one. Depending on the medium—television, radio, billboard, newspaper, the Internet, and so on—an advertiser may or may not have tools such as images, video, or sound available. However, in almost every single advertising campaign, at one level or another, language is used to convey a message. That means that advertisers must be very savvy users of language, regardless of whether they have any formal training in linguistics or language analysis.

On the one hand, understanding something of the language used in advertising is useful for those who consider careers in marketing and advertisement or for those who may need to hire a marketing company to produce an advertisement. On the other hand, having a basic understanding of the language in advertising is useful to the average consumer as well, as it can help us to discern the ways in which advertisers are trying to communicate with us and to disentangle any informative content that an advertisement may contain from the (often misleading) packaging that it comes in.

Successful advertisers must do at least three things. First, they must establish the trust of their audience so that the audience is compelled to pay attention to the content of the advertisement. Second, they must convey some message about what is being advertised. Finally, they must convince their audience to act in some way: to buy the target product, to vote for the target politician, or to do whatever else the advertiser has set as the goal. Language can be used to accomplish all three of these tasks, and often it takes rather subtle linguistic analysis—especially in the domain of pragmatics—in order to discern how the language of advertisements is used to manipulate its audiences. In this file, we'll discuss some of the ways in which the first two of these things, establishing trust and conveying a message, are done in American advertising.

17.4.2 Using Language to Establish Trust

Trust is obviously a critical part of almost any advertising campaign: if consumers believe that a company is not trustworthy for some reason, then the advertiser is much less likely to attain its goal. Advertisers use many strategies to establish consumer trust. In some cases, an advertiser may address the issue of trust outright. For example, McCormick, a company that sells spices and seasonings, has as its slogan *McCormick: the taste you trust.* In a commercial during an Ohio political campaign, a woman says to a particular senatorial candidate, *I just don't trust you,* suggesting that the candidate in question is not trustworthy (and thereby that the other candidate is more trustworthy). Both of these campaigns chose to explicitly connect the idea of trust to what they were advertising.

More often, though, the trustworthiness of a product or company is addressed indirectly, through an **implicature** (see File 7.3). One common strategy is to announce how long a company has been in business: a simple Internet search for the phrase *in business since* results in over 13 million hits. This information is generally given at the very end of a commercial, following information about a product or service that the company offers. Recall that a fundamental principle of pragmatics is that people are expected to be cooperative when they communicate and that part of being cooperative is making all contributions relevant to the topic at hand. At face value, the age of a company doesn't seem to be relevant at all, because the age of a company does not directly affect the quality of a product or service it provides. Therefore, there must be an implicature that we are supposed to derive from claims about the company's longevity. Based on the maxim of relevance, we infer that such claims are intended to mean that a company does something well enough to stay in business for an extended period of time.

At some level, though, trust is about more than saying that a product or company is trustworthy. Trust is also about forging a relationship between the audience and the advertiser or the product. One tool that advertisers often use in order to establish such a relationship is presupposition. Recall (from File 7.5) that a **presupposition** is an underlying assumption implicit in an utterance. Under ordinary circumstances, presuppositions are felicitous only when all participants in a discourse are familiar with the content of what is presupposed. Thus, by using a presupposition, an advertiser can create a feeling of common ground between itself and a consumer. In (1)–(4), the presupposition triggers have been underlined in order to call attention to what the advertiser is presupposing.

Consider the following example, a line that has appeared in commercials for the Midwest-based superstore Meijer:

(1)   We're cutting prices <u>again</u>.
      (presupposes that prices have been cut before)

In (1), the presupposition trigger is the word *again*: it triggers the presupposition that prices have been cut before. Had the advertiser instead come right out and stated the presupposed content explicitly—*We have cut prices before, and we are cutting them again*—the content would have been much the same, but the effect would have been different. By choosing to presuppose the information that prices have been cut before, the advertiser suggests that there is a shared understanding between the advertiser and people watching the commercial that the viewers should have familiarity with previous price cuts. The advertiser expects viewers to know (implicitly) that a presupposition suggests that everyone is familiar with the presupposed content, and therefore hopes that viewers may accommodate the presupposition and think *Oh, yes, I suppose prices have been cut before, and that's the sort of thing that most people are aware of, so I should be aware of that too*. Thus, the advertiser has ingeniously suggested not only that Meijer has cut prices before, but also that it does so with such regularity that the average consumer is generally familiar with this process. Any time an advertiser uses a presupposition rather than an entailment to share information about a product, the advertiser is suggesting that the information should be considered general knowledge, and it is welcoming the consumer into the sphere of people who have this knowledge.

In other cases, presuppositions are more personal, presupposing information not about what is being advertised, but rather about the consumer! The following is a sample line that could have come from any number of advertisements that air every season. The words *don't forget* are a mainstay in the vocabularies of many advertisers.

(2) Don't <u>forget</u> to come check out our super end-of-season close-out sale!
(presupposes that you already intended to do so)

In (2), the advertiser might instead have said *Come check out our sale,* but if they did, consumers would recognize that they were being told to do something that they might not otherwise have intended to do. The wording in (2) is much gentler: it doesn't seem to be telling people to do something because the advertiser asked them to; rather it seems to be suggesting that they do something they intended to do anyway. Most people don't like to be told what to do, but they do like to be reminded of things that they might have forgotten. Lines like those in (2) establish the advertiser as helpful rather than bossy. This is an artful way of ingratiating the consumer to the advertiser. Other advertisements contain lines such as (3).

(3) Let <u>them</u> <u>know that</u> you love <u>them</u>.
(presupposes first that *them* refers to someone, and second that you love them; in other words, presupposes that you love someone)

The line in (3) is from a December holiday-time commercial: the advertiser is assuming that many television viewers will be in the process of buying holiday presents for loved ones. The advertisement takes advantage of this fact by presupposing that viewers have loved ones. Consider how an advertiser might have gotten around this presupposition. The advertisement could have said *If there are people that you love, then let them know that you love them.* But this phrasing would have seemed unusual at best and offensive at worst (by suggesting that perhaps a viewer did not have any loved ones). By instead presupposing that viewers of an advertisement have loved ones, the advertisers suggest that they know those viewers and are not strangers, thereby establishing a feeling of trust based on familiarity.

Some commercials take their use of presupposed material yet one step further, using a presupposition to single out members of a particular target audience. Consider (4) below.

(4) Trying to <u>quit</u> smoking <u>again</u>?
(presupposes both that you smoke and that you have tried to quit before)

Unlike in (3), where the advertiser assumed that almost all viewers would have some loved one or other, in (4) the advertiser certainly does not assume that anywhere close to all of the viewers are smokers who have tried to quit in the past, but nonetheless only that group of people is being addressed. The advertiser certainly could have asked three questions instead of one: *Do you smoke? Have you tried to quit before? If so, are you trying again?* In so doing, the advertiser would gradually narrow down the target audience, involving every viewer in the process. But this is not the advertiser's goal. In this case, the advertiser wants to specifically target smokers who are trying to quit again, so the advertisement jumps right in to talk only to those people. By using presuppositions like those in (4), the advertiser hopes to establish a feeling of camaraderie with the target audience, to make a prospective client have the feeling *Wow; they are talking directly to me.* Using a presupposition thus also allows advertisers to make individuals feel singled out or special. Making people feel as though the advertiser knows them or understands them or their situation is yet one more way to establish a feeling of familiarity and trust.

17.4.3 Using Language to Convey a Message of Superiority

An advertiser's job isn't finished after establishing a relationship with the viewer. Ordinarily, the advertiser also wants to send a message about the superiority of whatever is being advertised. These claims can't be just blindly invented; advertisements are bound by law to be accurate. On the other hand, as discussed in Chapter 7, the study of pragmatics has made clear that the same sentences can have very different meanings under different circumstances. The question, then, is to how to determine the accuracy of a message in advertising: should advertisers be responsible only for what their claims entail, or should they also be responsible for what they implicate? Usually, advertisers are held legally responsible only for the entailments. Much of the art of advertising, then, revolves around formulating claims that implicate a lot but entail little. Below we will investigate some of the more common techniques for accomplishing this goal.

One way to implicate a lot and entail little is to qualify very strong claims with adverbs or with modal auxiliaries (e.g., *can, could, might,* etc.) as happens in (5)–(9), where the qualifying word or words are underlined. In each of these cases, the maxim of quantity will encourage the audience of the advertisements to infer that a stronger claim is intended than the one that is actually entailed.

(5)   Leaves dishes <u>virtually</u> spot free. (Cascade)

(6)   Get <u>up to</u> ten times stronger hair. (Pantene ProV)

Upon hearing an advertisement that a dishwashing product leaves dishes *virtually spot free,* a potential consumer may think that there will be no spots at all, but of course there is no way to measure what is meant by *virtually. Virtually* is a favorite word among advertisers; other advertisements may claim that a product will leave clothing *virtually static free* or that you will wait in line for *virtually no time at all,* but such claims do not tell how many spots, how much static, or how long a wait should be expected. Similarly, after hearing (6), a prospective consumer might expect that using the particular Pantene conditioner will leave her hair *ten times stronger,* or at least close to it, but in this case the qualifying term is *up to.* Amazingly, (6) is true even if no one who uses the shampoo gets stronger hair: it is true so long as no one has hair that becomes more than ten times stronger! Pantene has been subjected to legal questioning as a result of this claim, but there is no guarantee that similar claims won't be made in the future. The following three claims use modal verbs as qualifiers:

(7)   If you choose to finance or lease your new GMAC vehicle someplace other than GMAC, you <u>might</u> find yourself waiting in line instead of coming out hugging one. (GMAC)

(8)   There's another way for new homeowners to save money: the Allstate New House Discount. It <u>could</u> save you <u>up to</u> 15% on Allstate homeowners insurance. (Allstate)

(9)   Vesicare <u>may</u> <u>help</u> effectively <u>manage</u> leakage. (Vesicare)

An observant consumer will notice that in (7) and (8), neither a short line nor savings on insurance is guaranteed. (Note that the words *up to* appear in (8) as well.) Finally, (9) contains two qualifiers. It is taken from an advertisement for a drug to treat people with an overactive bladder. These people presumably want to have no leakage at all; however, the commercial doesn't say that Vesicare will eliminate leakage, but rather only that it may be "managed" and, moreover, that Vesicare can only "help" to manage it. The term *managed* is not defined. In any case, the advertisement also does not guarantee that the drug will help to manage leakage (whatever that means)—only that it may.

One of advertisers' favorite ways of implicating a lot while entailing little is to leave out the *than* clause or prepositional phrase in a comparative construction. For example,

Campbell's Soup has advertised that its soups had *one-third less salt*. The appropriate question to ask here is *One-third less salt than what?* Nowhere in the commercial is this question answered; the claim is always just *one-third less salt*. By the maxim of relevance, the audience is inclined to fill out the comparative with the most likely choices, such as *one-third less salt than it used to have* or *one-third less salt than its competitors' soups*. However, neither of these claims is entailed by Campbell's claim. All that is entailed is that their soup has one-third less salt than something. That something could be anything, including the Great Salt Lake. If you think that bringing up the Great Salt Lake is going overboard just a bit, the following should change your mind:

(10) When the Ford Motor Company advertised that the Ford LTD was 700% quieter, one might have presumed that the model was 700% quieter than some competing car or, at least, 700% quieter than some other model of Ford. But when the Federal Trade Commission demanded substantiation of the claim, the Ford Company "revealed that they meant the inside of the Ford was 700% quieter than the outside." (Bolinger 1980)

These open-ended comparatives are plentiful in the world of advertising. Here are a few more examples.

(11) a. <u>More</u> people sleep on Sealy Posturpedic.
b. Maytags are built to last <u>longer</u> and need <u>fewer</u> repairs.
c. <u>More</u> people are switching from ordinary dandruff shampoo to Selsun Blue.
d. Complete cat care for <u>more</u> years of healthy, contented purrs. (Iams)

A third favorite technique of advertisers is to make use of idiomatic language. An idiom is ambiguous between its literal compositional reading and a more idiomatic reading, and the audience tends to lean toward the stronger of the two—that is, the reading that makes the stronger claim—because the weaker claim (the literal meaning) would be irrelevant given that the advertiser is attempting to persuade the listener to buy something. For example, Mercedes-Benz has claimed that its cars are *engineered like no other car in the world*. On the idiomatic reading, Mercedes are engineered *better* than any other car in the world, but on the literal meaning, they're only engineered *differently* from any other car in the world. Every car can make that claim. Kenmore has claimed, *In one out of two American homes you'll find Kenmore appliances*. The most natural reading is that 50% of American homes have Kenmore appliances. But there is another reading, by which there are two American homes in particular, one with Kenmore appliances and another without.

There are many similar methods that advertisers employ to achieve similar results, and paying a little attention to the language of advertising should help you to extend this list of tactics considerably. Here are a couple to get you started. Be on the lookout for rhetorical questions (in which the advertiser merely implicates that the answer is *yes*). Likewise, watch for advertisers giving information that does not directly correlate to the quality of a product in any clear way or, worse, information that does not relate to the product at all. In such cases, an advertiser is almost always trying to use the maxim of relevance to implicate superiority without grounds for doing so. For example, if a particular Iams cat food contains more chicken, egg, and tuna than its competitors, does that necessarily make it a better cat food? Likewise, if Exxon tells its audience that it engages in environmental research, that doesn't mean that the gasoline it is advertising is any more environmentally friendly than that of its competitors.

We began this file by noting that people in the advertising industry must be savvy users of language in order to sell their products. After all, in many cases the products in competition with each other are very similar, so in order to suggest that one is superior to all of the others without saying something untrue requires the use of implicature. Even in cases such as political races in which the competitors may be quite different from one another, an advertisement should appeal to as many potential voters as possible, so the choice may be made not to emphasize particular substantive differences, but rather to use turns of language in order to make one candidate seem better than another.

17.4.4 Job Qualifications

Jobs in advertising often require a degree in advertising, economics, writing, statistics, graphic design, communication, or some related field. The specific degree required is largely dependent on the particular aspect of advertising you want to do. If you want to be in copywriting or content development, a degree in writing or a related field is often needed. Specific requirements, concerning both what level of degree is required and in which field(s), are determined by the company or organization.

FILE 17.5

Codes and Code-Breaking

17.5.1 Code-Breaking

Government agencies involved in codes and code-breaking are among the largest employers of linguists and mathematicians. This is because code-making and code-breaking are all about the discovery and exploitation of patterns in language and communication. Mathematicians are experts in the abstract study of patterns, while linguists are needed because the patterns are not completely abstract, but crucially involve the use of language. It is also helpful for code-breakers to have good foreign language skills since the secret messages might not be in English, but the analytical skills that you learn in linguistics classes are even more important. The science of codes and ciphers is called **cryptology.** The task of a cryptologist is to understand the strengths and weaknesses of existing codes and ciphers and to provide advice to potential users on how to make effective use of these systems for secure communication.

17.5.2 Alice, Bob, and Eve

Codes exist because companies, governments, and private individuals want to create secret messages that can be read only by the intended recipients. The original text is called the **plaintext,** and the encoded text is the **ciphertext.** There is a convention in cryptology that the message sender is called **Alice,** the intended recipient is called **Bob,** and both are trying to conceal the message from an unauthorized eavesdropper who is called **Eve.** There are many ways for Alice and Bob to do this, ranging from simple protocols that can be understood in ten minutes and executed by hand to methods whose design relies on mathematics so advanced that they are virtually impossible to use without the help of fast digital computers.

Almost all practical codes, whether simple or complex, rely on the idea that Alice and Bob have a shared secret, which Eve does not know. In cryptology, we call this shared secret a **key,** because it can be used to unlock the message. Unless Eve knows the key, or can work it out, the message will be incomprehensible. It is easy for Bob to decode the message, because he knows the secret. In cryptology, we usually assume that Eve knows all about the code system that Alice and Bob are using, but that she does not have access to the shared key. The difference between **decryption** and **decipherment** is that in decipherment you know the key, whereas in decryption you do not. Decipherment is what Bob does; decryption is what Eve tries to do. The key can be simple or complex, short or long. Long complex keys are preferable for secrecy, but hard to use in practice. It is much easier to memorize a short English word as your key than a 1,024-character string of random-looking gibberish. Several common types of keys are described in Section 17.5.5.

17.5.3 The Limits of Secrecy

In 1948 Claude Shannon, a cryptologist from Bell Laboratories, found a mathematical proof that perfect secrecy is possible even if Eve has unlimited time and computer power.

Unfortunately this result, while striking, comes with a catch. The catch is that Alice and Bob need to share a key that is at least as long as the total amount of text that they plan to transmit. This is because for perfect secrecy, the key needs to be completely random. If there is any non-random patterning in the key, Eve might be able to exploit the non-randomness and gain access to the message. This means that every letter needs to be encoded in a different way and that the key needs to include decoding information for every single letter, making the key at least as long as the message itself. Alice and Bob now face the problem of sharing a long key in a secure way. This is known as the **key distribution problem.**

Soviet embassies used a variant of Shannon's scheme called the **one-time pad** to communicate with their embassies during the Cold War. This is very secure, but it requires Alice to make two identical copies of a pad of completely random numbers and to send one copy to Bob ahead of time. This is no great problem for embassies, since they can arrange regular deliveries of one-time pads via the diplomatic bag (a couriered delivery to and from the embassy's home country that has diplomatic immunity from search or seizure) and then use the pads to send urgent messages. Modern computer-based systems have even more clever ways of getting around this problem. If you need to work by hand and are not on the staff of an embassy, however, the practical difficulties of ensuring that both partners in the conversation have the same one-time pad are usually prohibitive. In any case, if you are a spy working in hostile territory, you are unlikely to be keen on being caught in possession of anything as incriminating as a one-time pad.

So because the one-time pad is impractical, there is always some chance that Eve will manage to recover the message, because without it, perfect secrecy cannot be obtained. But Alice and Bob can do a lot to make her task harder. Instead of insisting on absolute secrecy, cryptologists aim to design code systems that will resist Eve's efforts for long enough that the information that she eventually uncovers will be so old that it will be of little practical value. If your goal is to win a baseball game by eavesdropping on the coded signals that the catcher is using to communicate with the pitcher, you want to break the code well before the game is over, and you want to make sure that the other team does not suspect that you have broken the code, since it would be easy for them to change it if they did suspect.

17.5.4 Traffic Analysis

Sometimes you can gain useful information simply by looking at the pattern of who sends messages to whom. This is called **traffic analysis.** Suppose that you are an intelligence analyst working on criminal investigations, and you notice somebody who suddenly starts to get a lot of text messages from notorious drug traffickers. What does this mean? It could be that we are dealing with the planning phase of a smuggling operation, or that a law enforcement agent is setting up a sting, or that a journalist is researching an article on organized crime. None of these may be exactly what you are looking for, but it is clear that the traffic patterns are telling you something.

Traffic analysis is fairly easy to do, does not rely on the ability to actually break the code, and can yield useful information. It was used heavily throughout the twentieth century, and it is still important today, particularly because it is easier to automate than the process of decoding and interpreting the actual messages themselves is. Indeed, now that we have the Internet, it is likely that traffic analysis is going to be essential even if no codes are involved, simply because there are too many messages for anyone to read. Linguists who have studied social networks or communities of practice (see Section 10.4.4) are well placed to help out with traffic analysis, since they have highly relevant experience of thinking clearly about how to make sense of patterns of communication.

17.5.5 Codes and Ciphers

We have been using the terms *code* and *cipher* interchangeably up to now. In cryptology, these are actually different things. A **code** is a cryptographic system that replaces each word in the plaintext with a suitable chosen word, number, or symbol. So a code using numbers might encode a couple of typical military messages as in (1).

(1) Admiral   Nimitz   will   inspect   the   fleet
     41   35   **76** **213**   **5** 19

     Colonel   Sanders will   inspect   the   cooks
     43   432   **76** **213**   **5** 221

To be effective, a numerical code like this one has to be written down in a shared codebook. In the twentieth century, navies made especially heavy use of codes. The users worked hard to keep the codebook safe and to make sure that everyone had a current version, and code-breakers worked hard to capture the book.

Capturing the codebook is not the only approach that code-breakers could take; they can also try to reconstruct it. To do this, they would collect a large volume of coded messages, cross-reference them, and look for repeating patterns. For example, the sequence 76 213 5 turns up in both of the example messages in (1). You do not initially know what it stands for, but once you have seen enough messages and noticed enough connections between messages and real-world events, you may be able to begin to work things out. Allied code-breakers stationed in Australia during the Second World War did a lot of this type of work on codes used by the Japanese navy. This approach is related to the ones that were used by archeologists and linguists to decipher Egyptian hieroglyphs (see File 15.3).

A **cipher** differs from a code because it works letter-by-letter rather than word-by-word. Some common ciphers are described below. Ciphers do not require a codebook. In the twentieth century, armies and air forces tended to use ciphers rather than codes, because it would have been hard for them to distribute a codebook or to keep it safe once it had been distributed.

a. Shift Ciphers. The simplest kind of cipher is a **shift cipher**. In a shift cipher, the ciphertext is created by replacing the letters of the plaintext with a corresponding letter from an alphabet that has been shifted some number of places away from its normal position. For example, if the plaintext is SEND MORE TROOPS and we are using a one-letter shift, then the ciphertext (i.e., the message that you, the staff officer, might have received from your field commander) will be TFOE NPSF USPPQT. The correspondence between the plaintext alphabet and the ciphertext alphabet is shown in (2). Notice that the ciphertext equivalent for Z is A, because the ciphertext wraps around from Z to A when we run out of letters.

(2) Plaintext: A B C D E F G H I J K L M N O P Q R S T U V W X Y Z
     Ciphertext: B C D E F G H I J K L M N O P Q R S T U V W X Y Z A

Consider the ciphertext CPZPAPUNHBUAZJHUILHWYVISLT. For decryption, what we need to do is systematically explore different shifted alphabets until we find one that makes this look like English. Fortunately, there is a good way of doing this systematically. What you do is write the alphabet downwards, in columns, starting with the ciphertext letter. When you get to Z, wrap around back to A, as shown in (3). Then look for the horizontal line in (3) that makes this into good English words. This method for solving shift ciphers is called the **tabular method.**

(3)
```
C P Z P A P U N H B U A Z J H U I L H W Y V I S L T
D Q A Q B Q V O I C V B A K I V J M I X Z W J T M U
E R B R C R W P J D W C B L J W K N J Y A X K U N V
F S C S D S X Q K E X D C M K X L O K Z B Y L V O W
G T D T E T Y R L F Y E D N L Y M P L A C Z M W P X
H U E U F U Z S M G Z F E O M Z N Q M B D A N X Q Y
I V F V G V A T N H A G F P N A O R N C E B O Y R Z
J W G W H W B U O I B H G Q O B P S O D F C P Z S A
K X H X I X C V P J C I H R P C Q T P E G D Q A T B
L Y I Y J Y D W Q K D J I S Q D R U Q F H E R B U C
M Z J Z K Z E X R L E K J T R E S V R G I F S C V D
N A K A L A F Y S M F L K U S F T W S H J G T D W E
O B L B M B G Z T N G M L V T G U X T I K H U E X F
P C M C N C H A U O H N M W U H V Y U J L I V F Y G
Q D N D O D I B V P I O N X V I W Z V K M J W G Z H
R E O E P E J C W Q J P O Y W J X A W L N K X H A I
S F P F Q F K D X R K Q P Z X K Y B X M O L Y I B J
T G Q G R G L E Y S L R Q A Y L Z C Y N P M Z J C K
U H R H S H M F Z T M S R B Z M A D Z O Q N A K D L
```
V I S I T I N G A U N T S C A N B E A P R O B L E M
```
W J T J U J O H B V O U T D B O C F B Q S P C M F N
X K U K V K P I C W P V U E C P D G C R T Q D N G O
Y L V L W L Q J D X Q W V F D Q E H D S U R E O H P
Z M W M X M R K E Y R X W G E R F I E T V S F P I Q
A N X N Y N S L F Z S Y X H F S G J F U W T G Q J R
B O Y O Z O T M G A T Z Y I G T H K G V X U H R K S
```

Notice that even in the tabular method there is room for human judgment, because the analyst still has to use knowledge of language, and of the language being used, in order to spot the correct row. This is not necessarily a trivial matter. One twist on a shift cipher is to write the message backwards. In that case, none of the lines would look like English at first glance.

b. Monoalphabetic ciphers. A shift cipher is a simple kind of monoalphabetic cipher. In a monoalphabetic substitution, each letter always translates to the same letter in the ciphertext, but now the letters can occur in any order. We're now going to practice frequency analysis, which is a way of solving these ciphers. This method is overkill if you are sure that you are dealing with a shift cipher, but it is worthwhile because it generalizes beyond shift ciphers to any monoalphabetic substitution.

The basic idea of frequency analysis is to use the fact that some letters are more common than others. For example, the most common letter of English is <e>, while <x>, <j>, <q>, and <z> are among the least common. The full letter-frequency breakdown for one nineteenth-century novel is shown in (4).

(4)

338,214	e	166,934	h	74,504	m	42,504	b	3,247	q
232,105	t	166,751	s	63,418	c	41,363	p	1,150	z
210,111	a	164,166	r	63,186	w	29,056	v		
207,579	o	112,708	d	62,045	f	16,295	k		
191,572	n	105,007	l	60,424	y	4,532	x		
182,630	i	77,320	u	51,694	g	4,179	j		

If a ciphertext is based on a monoalphabetic substitution, then there will be some letter that stands for <e>, and this letter is likely (but not completely certain) to occur frequently in the ciphertext. An enciphered version of an English short story (Conan Doyle's "A Case of Identity," from *The Adventures of Sherlock Holmes*) starts off like this:

(5) "ub zijn piqqcd." ajrz aminqcsg mcquia ja di ajf ch irfmin arzi cp fmi prni rh mra qczkrhka jf vjgin afniif, "qrpi ra rhprhrfiqb afnjhkin fmjh jhbfmrhk dmrsm fmi urhz cp ujh scyqz rhoihf. Di dcyqz hcf zjni fc schsiroi fmi fmrhka dmrsm jni nijqqb uini scuuchtqjsia cp ixrafihsi. rp di scyqz pqb cyf cp fmjf drhzcd mjhz rh mjhz, mcoin coin fmra knijf srfb, kihfqb niucoi fmi nccpa, jhz tiit rh jf fmi wyiin fmrhka dmrsm jni kcrhk ch, fmi afnjhki scrhsrzihsia, fmi tqjhhrhka, fmi sncaa-tyntcaia, fmi dchz-inpyq

You can make a frequency table from the whole of this story (our ciphertext) and line this up with the frequency table from the novel in (4). In other words, we guess that the most common letter in the ciphertext, which is <i>, corresponds to plaintext <e>, because <e> is almost always the most common letter in English. The frequency tables are shown in (6), and a more compact version of the letter correspondences is shown in (7).

(6)

Ciphertext		Plaintext		Ciphertext		Plaintext	
i	3657	e	338214	d	767	c	63418
f	2770	t	232105	s	687	w	63186
j	2364	a	210111	p	644	f	62045
c	2160	o	207579	b	600	y	60424
r	2050	n	191572	k	528	g	51694
h	1978	i	182630	t	430	b	42504
m	1955	h	166934	v	416	p	41363
a	1850	s	166751	o	324	v	29056
n	1685	r	164166	g	245	k	16295
z	1191	d	112708	x	32	x	4532
q	1163	l	105007	w	31	j	4179
y	869	u	77320	l	27	q	3247
u	828	m	74504	e	13	z	1150

(7) a b c d e f g h i j k l m n o p q r s t u v w x y z
    s y o c z t k i e a g q h r v f l n w b m p j x u d

Using the letter correspondence established above, we get the text in (8), which is not bad, but not perfect either. Not all the letters in (8) are in just the right place, but most of them are pretty close.

(8) "my dear felloc." sand sherlowk holmes as ce sat oi enther snde of the fnre ni hns lodgnigs at paker street, "lnfe ns nifnintely straiger thai aiythnig chnwh the mnid of mai would niveit. ce could iot dare to woiwenve the thnigs chnwh are really mere wommoiblawes of exnsteiwe. nf ce would fly out of that cnidoc haid ni haid, hover over thns great wnty, geitly . . .

It is pretty easy to see that what should be the plaintext letters <i> and <n> are wrong. We have ciphertext <h> matched with plaintext <i>, and ciphertext <r> matched with plaintext <n>. Let's change this: for example, the third letter in the fourth word should be plaintext <i>, so we can match ciphertext <r> with <i>. The equivalences for <c> and <w> also seem wrong. So let's change that too and try a different part of the text as a check, which is shown in (9).

(9) . . . if we could fly out of that window hand in hand, hover over this great city, gently remove the roofs, and beeb in at the jueer things which are going on, the strange coincidences, the blannings, the cross-burboses,

Now it looks as if <p> has been confused with <b> and <q> confused with <j>. Fix that and you have the original text from Conan Doyle's *Sherlock Holmes*. We have now solved the cipher.

What have we learned, and how can we use what we have learned to guide us in studying language? The shift cipher was easy, because there were only a few possibilities to consider and an easy way to organize the process of exploring the possibilities. Many practical problems are like this: it is not hard to systematically try out all the possibilities, and once you have done that, the solution is obvious. But this isn't the case for general monoalphabetic ciphers, because the number of possibilities is too great to explore by hand (although not too great to explore with the help of a computer).

So, rather than trying all the possibilities, we looked for a **heuristic** (a solution that is likely but not certain to work) that would get us close to the correct solution. The heuristic that we used was the following: *Probably the pattern of letter frequencies in the transmitted text will be close to what we have seen before.* As we saw, simply applying the standard letter frequencies produced text that was nearly English. If you have programming skills, it is fairly easy to write a program that counts the number of each letter in the ciphertext and then matches it to the known frequencies of the letters of English. Once we had that, we were able to make sensible guesses about small changes that would make the text even more like English, and eventually the correct text emerged. Methods based on heuristics are often effective when it is too time-consuming to try all the possibilities.

In this example, we had it easy in comparison to real code-breakers because we kept the word breaks. This can be a big help, so real codes will be written with no gaps between the words. In Renaissance Italy this was not so well known. Among other things, this made it possible for a code-breaker to get big hints by looking at the ends of words. In Italian, almost all words end in vowels, so the symbols that appear regularly at the ends of words are highly likely to be vowels.

c. Polyalphabetic ciphers. We have seen that monoalphabetic ciphers are vulnerable to frequency analysis. It is too easy to break them by finding the letters that correspond to E, T, A and the other high-frequency letters and then filling in the gaps. To do better, we would like a cipher that produces a much more even distribution of ciphertext letters. In addition, as we solved the monoalphabetic cipher, we relied on the assumption that each ciphertext letter corresponds to one and exactly one plaintext letter. This is a second weakness of a monoalphabetic system. The Vigenère cipher, an example of a polyalphabetic cipher, removes both of these vulnerabilities. The core idea of the Vigenère is to use several different alphabets rather than just one. The first step is to lay out a table containing all the shift ciphers, as shown in (10).

(10) A B C D E F G H I J K L M N O P Q R S T U V W X Y Z
     B C D E F G H I J K L M N O P Q R S T U V W X Y Z A
     C D E F G H I J K L M N O P Q R S T U V W X Y Z A B

     . . .

     Z A B C D E F G H I J K L M N O P Q R S T U V W X Y

The Vigenère cipher uses a keyword. Let's say that the keyword is BUCKEYE. This means that we are going to use the rows of the Vigenère table corresponding to B, C, E, K, U, and Y, so the table we need is shown in (11).

```
(11) a b c d e f g h i j k l m n o p q r s t u v w x y z
     B C D E F G H I J K L M N O P Q R S T U V W X Y Z A
     C D E F G H I J K L M N O P Q R S T U V W X Y Z A B
     E F G H I J K L M N O P Q R S T U V W X Y Z A B C D
     K L M N O P Q R S T U V W X Y Z A B C D E F G H I J
     U V W X Y Z A B C D E F G H I J K L M N O P Q R S T
     Y Z A B C D E F G H I J K L M N O P Q R S T U V W X
```

Let the plaintext be *time and change will surely show.* To produce the ciphertext, we start by using the first letter of the keyword, which is <B>, and the first letter of the message, which is <t>. We look up <t> in the top row of the table, and then go down until we reach the <B> alphabet, finding the letter <U> as the first character of the ciphertext. Next, we use the second letter of the key, which is <U>, to encode the <i> of *time.* We find <i> in the top row, read down the column, and get <C>. Next, we use the <C> of the keyword to encode <m> and get <O>, followed by the <K> to encode <e> and get <O> again. Continuing this, recycling the keyword as necessary, gives the result in (12).

```
(12) B U C K E Y E B U C K E Y E B U C K E Y E B U C K E Y
     t i m e a n d c h a n g e w i l l s u r e l y s h o w
     U C O O E L H D B C X K C A J F N C Y P I M S U R S U
```

If you know the keyword, decoding a Vigenère is the obvious reverse process. Using the current keyword letter, look up the ciphertext in the relevant row of the body of the table and then read up till you get to the plaintext at the top. Provided you have the same keyword as the sender, you will get back the original plaintext.

But if you are the eavesdropper and do not know the keyword, how do you proceed? The main weakness of Vigenère is that the key repeats. Because the keyword is 7 letters long, the 8th character of the message will be encoded using the same shifted alphabet as the first, the 9th same as the second, and so on. In the specific case of BUCKEYE there is actually an extra repeat because of the two E's in the keyword, but the main repeating pattern is caused by the need to recycle the 7-letter keyword.[1]

17.5.6 Enigma

During the Second World War, a polyalphabetic cipher called the Enigma was used by the Axis forces to communicate secretly. The basic idea is to use a system a lot like the Vigenère cipher, but with a very long key generated by an electromechanical device. This device, the Enigma, was a modified teletype machine with a typewriter keyboard. As the cipher clerk typed, the message passed through a series of plugs and rotors, and each letter was converted into a different letter. When the message was received, the cipher clerk at the other end typed the encoded letter into his machine, whereupon the original letter would light up.

This was possible because the sender and the receiver had a shared secret: at the beginning of transmission, both machines would be set to the same settings of the rotors and the plug board. As the message was received, the rotors of the two machines moved in lockstep, always staying synchronized. In comparison to a monoalphabetic cipher, this is a very secure system because the code keeps changing as the rotors move and thus standard tricks like frequency analysis are of little use. Fortunately for the Allied war effort, Enigma did still

---

[1]A link to an explanation of one way to break the Vigenère cipher is on the Links page for Chapter 17.

have weaknesses, and its German users made a number of mistakes that allowed experts working at a secret code-breaking establishment in Bletchley Park, England, to crack the code. In the process, the staff at Bletchley Park, led by an astonishingly talented mathematician, Alan Turing, created a number of electromechanical and electronic machines that later played an important role in the development of the digital computer. Similar work by American code-breakers in the Pacific made it possible for US commanders to gain advance knowledge of Japanese plans, including crucial information leading to the American naval victory at Midway. Overall, the information that was obtained from code-breaking does seem to have significantly shortened the war, and perhaps even changed its outcome.

In addition to the mathematicians, there were linguists, translators, chess champions, and many others who turned out to have the peculiar combination of pattern recognition skills that was required by the work. Indeed, one of the things that recruiters looked for was an unusual ability to solve cryptic crosswords. There is little doubt that code-breaking is one of the areas in which careful study of language and persistent attention to detail has changed the world. This kind of work is now carried on by the National Security Agency and other government agencies.

17.5.7   Job Qualifications

Those wishing to work in cryptology may find it useful to complete an undergraduate degree in mathematics, computer science, statistics, (computational) linguistics, or other fields. However, many positions require graduate training in cryptology as part of a degree in mathematics, computer science, computational linguistics, or a related field.

FILE 17.6

Being a Linguist

17.6.1 Job Description

In the course of this book, we have introduced many of the ways in which language can be studied and have presented evidence from linguists about many different aspects of language. But from a practical standpoint, you may be wondering, what **is** a linguist? Where do linguists work? How did they get into their fields? What do they do on a daily basis? How could I become a linguist? While there are, of course, many different answers to these questions, this file will give you some idea of the possibilities that are out there.

Although someone who has been trained to be a linguist could be hired almost anywhere, there are two main fields that most linguists enter: academia and industry. In academia, you will find linguists in many different university departments, including actual linguistics departments, anthropology, cognitive science, computer science, philosophy, psychology, sociology, speech and hearing, and language departments. Linguists in university settings, like other academics, are generally expected to do their own research, teach classes in their areas, and contribute service to the university.

Most linguists have a particular area of linguistic research that they focus on, but this could take many different forms: some linguists choose to study a particular language or language family (e.g., they could be a specialist in Bantu linguistics of all sorts); others choose a particular subfield of linguistics (e.g., they could be a syntactician, looking at the syntax of many different languages); and still others choose a particular aspect of language or language's interface with other phenomena (e.g., they could be a psycholinguist and focus on how humans process language). A linguist's area (or areas) of specialization will determine the types of research he or she does. Sociolinguists, for example, study how language interacts with society—thus many sociolinguistic studies have involved doing interviews with native speakers of a language in order to learn about both usage patterns and ideas about language and society. On the other hand, a theoretical linguist might be interested in developing theoretical mathematical models of how language works, rather than doing fieldwork to collect new language data. Regardless of the particular focus of research, all linguists rely on already existing research and theories as well as collaboration with other researchers—so a lot of time is spent reading, writing, and discussing ideas and new lines of research.

In industrial settings, linguists may also be involved with a wide variety of linguistic areas, but the research they do is usually geared toward advancing a particular project that the company they work for has in mind, rather than doing research for its own sake. A computational linguist with training in phonetics, for example, might work at a communications company such as Nuance Communications to help improve automated speech recognition or computerized dialogue systems in particular types of software. A specialist in child language acquisition might be employed at a company that produces children's toys, such as LeapFrog or The Learning Journey, to help the company develop age-appropriate educational games and toys. Or a semanticist might find a job working with a company that comes up with new names for products that convey particular ideas to their target audience, such as Brand Institute or NameBase.

17.6.2 Job Qualifications

The job qualifications for a linguist will vary depending on the type of job they are being hired for. Most academic linguists are required to have a PhD in linguistics or a closely related subfield; earning a PhD involves going to graduate school for about five years after finishing an undergraduate degree. Although having an undergraduate degree in a field related to language study may help prospective graduate students know what they want to study or find the graduate school that will most closely suit their needs, it is usually not necessary to have an undergraduate degree in linguistics or a particular language in order to be accepted into a linguistics graduate program.

To work in industry as a linguist, the requirements are much more varied. Some companies are simply looking for someone with a bachelor's or master's degree in general linguistics, with enough knowledge of language to be employed in a language-related area of the company (perhaps with additional training by the company). On the other hand, some companies are looking for a linguist with advanced PhD-level training in a particular field to work on highly specialized projects.

Practice

File 17.1—Language Education

Exercise

1. Imagine that you were teaching your native language to someone who doesn't speak it. Choose one grammatical characteristic of your language and describe how you would teach it. For example, how would you teach someone the past tense of English? Think about how you would explain the characteristic you chose, what activities you could do with your student, and what exercises you would give him or her as a homework assignment. (*Hint:* There are many teaching resources available online.)

Discussion Question

2. Do you think it would be easier to teach a group of students who all have the same linguistic background or a group of students with different linguistic backgrounds? Why?

Activity

3. Interview a foreign language instructor at your school about his or her job. Your interview may include the following questions:

   a. What is the instructor's educational background?
   b. What classes is the instructor teaching?
   c. What skills are emphasized in the classes?
   d. What teaching methodology does the instructor use? Why?
   e. What preparation work is involved in teaching the classes?
   f. How does the instructor deal with different learning styles?
   g. Does the instructor have exercises or activities that work particularly well? Why does the instructor think they work so well?

File 17.2—Speech-Language Pathology and Audiology

Discussion Questions

4. Some speech-language pathologists teach children how to articulate sounds. How might an SLP explain how to produce [s], [ʃ], [z], and [ʒ] to a child who is having difficulty with these sounds? What kinds of activities might the SLP use to practice these sounds with the child?

5. Some speech-language pathologists make use of "oral motor" exercises as part of their treatment plans for patients. Such exercises are designed to work on developing oral muscle coordination and strength in a nonspeech environment. For example, they might have a patient suck a very thick milkshake through a narrow straw or blow bubbles. Based on your

knowledge of language and the types of disorders SLPs treat, what types of disorder do you think these exercises might be useful for? How effective do you think they are?

Activity

6. Find a practicing speech-language pathologist or audiologist. Interview him or her to find out what type of work they are doing. What sorts of patients do they see? What kinds of problems do they treat? What techniques do they use in treating them? Compare your answers with those of your classmates to get a sense of the diversity of jobs that speech-language pathologists and audiologists do.

File 17.3—Forensic Linguistics

Discussion Questions

7. Why would forensic linguists prefer to have access to an audio recording of any evidence they may have to examine, rather than a written transcript? (There are many reasons, so consider this question carefully: think about various levels of linguistic analysis that you have learned about during your study of linguistics.)

8. One intersection between the domains of language and the law that was not mentioned in this file is that of language crimes: cases in which specific kinds of language use are illegal. These cases include slander (using language to negatively affect someone's image), perjury (using language to mislead while under oath), and placing a bomb threat (using language to suggest that there is an explosive device somewhere that it could cause a public threat—even if, in fact, there is no bomb).

i. Why, do you believe, is each of these uses of language illegal in the United States?

ii. In File 11.3, we discussed the fact that in America there is a guarantee to freedom of speech. Do you believe that declaring certain kinds of language use to be crimes undermines that? Why or why not?

iii. What does the fact that these uses of language have been declared crimes tell us about the power that people perceive language to have? What does it tell us about speech acts and the sorts of actions that can be done using language?

Activities

9. A particularly famous legal case in which linguistic analysis played a large part was the impeachment trial of President Bill Clinton. Investigate the role that language analysis played. You should find information that you can connect to what you have learned about various ideas of word meanings, descriptivism versus prescriptivism, entailment, and implicature.

10. Obtain a copy of a will or a contract that has been drawn up by a lawyer. (Examples are often available online.)

i. Read the document and make note of places in which you believe that language is being used in a particular way that does not sound like "normal" discourse. Why do you believe that these particular words or constructions were used in writing the will or contract?

ii. Speak with a lawyer whose duties include drawing up such documents, and determine whether your guesses were correct. Ask about what other specific uses of language—both words and constructions—are specifically chosen in writing wills and legal contracts.

11. Find out whether there are any forensic linguists practicing in your area. Set up an interview, or invite them to come to your class to discuss what they do. What sort of training did they receive? What other sorts of people (in law enforcement and in forensic investigation) do they work with, and how do they interact with these people? What kinds of cases have they investigated using language analysis? What sorts of cases have they testified in and to what end? What sorts of linguistic analysis do they perform?

File 17.4—Language in Advertising

Exercises

12. The following advertising claims contain implicatures that are not entailed. Identify what these implicatures are. Explain why they are not entailments, and tell which Gricean maxims cause them to arise.

   a. "People from Ford prefer Chevy trucks." (*Ford* refers to Ford County.)

   b. "Interesting fact about what he took. Its decongestant lasts only 4 hours per dose, and it contains aspirin, which can upset your stomach. Contac lasts up to twelve hours per dose and does not contain aspirin." (*Hint:* What is entailed/implied about how long Contac lasts and whether or not it upsets your stomach?)

   c. "STP reduced engine lifter wear up to 68%." (Fine print at bottom of screen: "Results vary by type of car, oil, and driving.")

   d. "Isn't it time you got your health on the right course? Now you can cut back on cholesterol, cut back on sodium, cut back on fat, and still love the food you eat because now there's new Right Course from Stouffer's."

   e. No other pain reliever has been proven more effective against headaches than _____. (*Hint:* What has or has not been proven?)

   f. This calling plan can save you up to 15% over Midwestern Telephone.

   g. I'm concerned about my heart. Plenty of supplements contain selenium but only _____ has garlic.

   h. Presidential candidate John Smith is serious about air quality. He was governor of _____, one of the first states to pass legislation cracking down on coal-burning plants.

13. Several commercials for the Icy Hot Back Patch conclude, "Count on it." What does this line aim to communicate? Why do advertisers wish to communicate that message?

14. One advertiser that has had distinctive and well-known slogans for decades is McDonald's. Consider the four McDonald's slogans below:

   a. 1993: Do You Believe in Magic?

   b. 1997: Did Somebody Say McDonald's?

   c. 2000: We Love to See You Smile

   d. 2003: i'm lovin' it

   i. For each, tell what implicature(s) the advertiser was trying to convey.

   ii. What is a slogan? Why are slogans particularly useful in advertising campaigns?

Discussion Question

15. Do you think advertisers should be responsible for the truth only of what their advertisements entail, or should they also be responsible for the truth of implicatures? If both, who should be responsible for determining what a given advertisement implicates, and how should it be determined?

Activities

16. Look at the advertising section in a newspaper, watch a few commercial breaks on television, or look for ads or commercials online. Find examples of each the following. For each, record what was said, show how the implicated content is different from the entailed content, and explain the linguistic trick that the advertiser is using in order to persuade its audience to act in a certain way.

    a. A presupposition designed to establish camaraderie between the advertiser and consumer.

    b. A description using a comparative and lacking a *than* expression.

    c. An example of a word or phrase that qualifies a claim.

    d. A case in which a product is described as being "different" or "unique" in order to implicate that it is superior.

    e. An implicature that makes use of seemingly irrelevant information.

    f. An implicature indicating that purchasing or using a product will lead to some desired end.

17. Write an advertisement for something of your choosing. You may choose to write it as though it were going to be a printed advertisement or a commercial for the radio or television. Write the commercial three ways:

    i. First, write an advertisement that employs several of the tools described in this file, including both presuppositions and implicatures.

    ii. Second, rewrite your advertisement so that it has no presuppositions or so that all of the presuppositions are satisfied at the time of utterance.

    iii. Third, rewrite your advertisement so that all of the information that you can truthfully convey is entailed rather than implicated.

    iv. Which of the three versions do you think seems the most natural? Which seems most like the sort of advertisement you might come in contact with in the real world? Which do you think would do the best job at accomplishing its goal?

File 17.5—Codes and Code-Breaking

Exercises

18. i. Use the alphabets shown in (2) in File 17.5 to encipher the following plaintext: NO TROOPS AVAILABLE. Write down the ciphertext letters that you would send back to the field commander.

    ii. Use the same alphabets to decipher the following ciphertext from your field commander: XF XJMM EP PVS CFTU. What is the plaintext?

19. Julius Caesar used a shift cipher like the one introduced in (2) in File 17.5, but his had a shift of 3 letters rather than 1. (For shift ciphers the key is always a number, but for other ciphers the key might be a word or a sentence.) Make an alphabet table like the one given in (2) in File 17.5, but for Caesar's cipher.

    i. Use your table to encipher the following plaintext: THE BRITONS ARE REVOLTING.

    ii. Use your table to decipher JLYH WKHP D FXS RI WHD.

20. Decrypt the following message using the tabular method:

    HXDBXUENMCQNLXMN

21.　**i.** How does a polyalphabetic cipher differ from a monoalphabetic cipher?

　　ii. What impact do you think this has on ease of decipherment? Ease of decryption?

　　iii. In what situations might you choose to use a monoalphabetic cipher? In what situations might you choose to use a polyalphabetic cipher? Why?

Discussion Questions

22. **a.** How many different shift ciphers are there? (*Hint:* What does a shift of 26 do?)

　　b. Exactly how many possible monoalphabetic ciphers are there? Another way to think of this problem is to ask how many different orders are possible for the 26 letters of the English alphabet. Do you agree that there are too many possibilities to explore by hand?

23. One of the "codes" used by the US Marines during World War II that was never deciphered is Navajo, a Na-Dene language spoken today in areas of Arizona, New Mexico, Utah, and Colorado. At the time Navajo had no alphabet and was spoken by fewer than 30 non-Navajos. Why do you think Navajo "code" was never deciphered? To answer the question, think about how using a language not known to Eve is different from using encoded English.

File 17.6—Being a Linguist

Exercise

24. Choose a topic that was covered in this book that you find particularly interesting (e.g., phonetics, syntax, historical linguistics, etc.). Think of a question that you are curious about related to that field (e.g., Does Yeli Dnye have agglutinating morphology? Are all productions of [l] the same in American English?). Describe how you might go about investigating the answer(s) to this question.

Activity

25. Find a professor at your institution who describes himself or herself as a linguist (remember, even if you do not have a linguistics department, linguists may be found in language departments, psychology departments, etc.). Interview him or her to find out what type of research he or she is doing. How does this research tie in to the concepts you have learned about from this book?

Further Readings

Conley, John M., and William M. O'Barr. 2005. *Just words: Law, language, and power.* 2nd edn. Chicago: University of Chicago Press.

Macaulay, Monica. 2011. *Surviving linguistics: A guide for graduate students.* 2nd edn. Somerville, MA: Cascadilla Press.

Oaks, Dallin D. 1998. *Linguistics at work: A reader of applications.* Fort Worth: Harcourt Brace College Publishers.

Olsson, John. 2008. *Forensic linguistics: An introduction to language, crime and the law.* 2nd edn. New York: Continuum International Publishing Group.

Olsson, John. 2009. *Wordcrime: Solving crime through forensic linguistics.* New York: Continuum International Publishing Group.

Sedivy, Julie, and Greg Carlson. 2011. *Sold on language: How advertisers talk to you and what this says about you.* Chichester: John Wiley & Sons.

Shuy, Roger W. 2006. *Linguistics in the courtroom: A practical guide.* Oxford: Oxford University Press.

Singh, Simon. 1999. *The code book: The science of secrecy from Ancient Egypt to quantum cryptography.* New York: Anchor Books.

Solan, Lawrence M. 1993. *The language of judges.* (Language and Legal Discourse series.) Chicago: University of Chicago Press.

Stephenson, Neal. 2002. *Cryptonomicon.* New York: Harper Perennial. (This is a fictional but informative and accurate account of British and American work on code-breaking in World War II.)

APPENDIX

··

Answers to Example Exercises

File 3.6   Exercise 22—Phonology Exercise on Mokilese

Since there are no minimal pairs in the data where [i] and [i̥] are the only different sounds between the pair, and none where [u] and [u̥] are the only different sounds, we proceed to look for complementary distribution. To examine the environments more easily, we can list the sounds that surround the sounds in question.

(1) [i̥]   [i]   [u̥]   [u]
     p_s   l_ŋ   t_p   #_d
     p_ʧ   p_l   p_k   d_k
     s_k   k_#   s_p   l_ʤ
             r_k   k_r

If these allophones are in complementary distribution, the environment that precedes them cannot be the conditioning environment on its own. For the pair [i̥] and [i], while [i̥] appears only after voiceless consonants ([p] and [s] in the examples given here), [i] also appears after voiceless consonants ([p] and [k] here), in addition to after the voiced [l] and [r]. Similarly, for the pair [u̥] and [u], [u̥] appears only after voiceless consonants ([t], [p], and [s] here), but [u] also appears after a voiceless consonant ([k] here), in addition to after the voiced consonants [d] and [l] at the beginning of a word. So while a generalization can be made about the sounds preceding both of the voiceless vowels (i.e., [i̥] and [u̥] occur only after voiceless consonants), because the voiced vowels [i] and [u] can also occur after voiceless consonants, we cannot use the preceding environment on its own to predict which allophone will occur.

We run into a similar situation in looking at the environments following the vowels. For the pair [i̥] and [i], [i̥] appears only before voiceless consonants ([s], [ʧ], and [k] here), but [i] also appears before a voiceless consonant ([k] here), in addition to before the voiced [ŋ] and [l] and at the end of the word. Similarly, for [u̥] and [u], [u̥] appears only before voiceless consonants ([p] and [k] here), but [u] also appears before a voiceless consonant ([k] here), in addition to before the voiced [d] and [r]. So while we can make the generalization that the voiceless vowels [i̥] and [u̥] occur only before voiceless consonants, because the voiced vowels [i] and [u] can also occur before voiceless consonants, we cannot use the following environment on its own to predict which allophone will occur.

You should have noticed by now, though, that the generalizations we can make about the environments preceding and following the voiceless vowels [i̥] and [u̥] are similar: they occur only after voiceless consonants, and they occur only before voiceless consonants, which means that they occur only **between voiceless consonants.** We are not able to make similar generalizations based on natural classes about the voiced [i] and [u], since they occur after voiced and voiceless consonants, before voiced and voiceless consonants, and at the beginnings and ends of words. So our next step is to check whether [i] and [u] ever occur between voiceless consonants. In this case, we see that they do not: they can have a voiceless consonant on one side, but never on both sides. This means that [i̥] and [i] never appear in the same environment, which means they are in complementary distribution and thus allophones of a single phoneme, and the same is true for [u̥] and [u]. We can thus state a rule that accounts for the distribution of these sounds:

(2) [i] and [u] become voiceless between voiceless consonants

We can assume that /i/ and /u/ are the "basic" sounds because they are the ones that appear in a non-natural set of environments. (It would be difficult to write a rule saying that /i̥/ and /u̥/ turn into [i] and [u] any time one of the sounds on either side of it are anything other than a voiceless segment.) Note that we cannot say that all vowels become voiceless between voiceless consonants as the word [masak] illustrates. However, we could make our rule more general by noting that [i] and [u] are both high vowels. Thus our rule becomes:

(3) High vowels become voiceless between voiceless consonants.

File 4.6   Exercise 24(a)—Morphology Exercise on Hierarchical Structure

Draw a tree diagram for the word *disappearance.*

The tree diagram is a representation of the structure of the word, so before you can draw a tree, you must determine what this structure is. That is, you must determine how many morphemes there are in the word and in what order they attach to one another. The word *disappearance* can be broken down into three morphemes, *dis-* (meaning roughly 'not'), *appear,* and *-ance* (a derivational affix that changes a verb into a noun).

We must next determine whether *dis-* or *-ance* attaches first to *appear.* This can be done by listing and then analyzing words that have the prefix *dis-* and other words that have the suffix *-ance.* For example,

(4) a. disconnect   b. appearance
        disagree   endurance
        disbelieve   grievance
        disappear   acceptance
        disassociate   interference

When drawing up such lists, remember to keep a couple of things in mind. First of all, choose words with only two morphemes (the one in question and one other). Second, the other morpheme should belong unambiguously to one lexical category. For example, words such as *disquiet* might be excluded, since *quiet* could be either an adjective or a verb. Third, make sure that the words you include have the morpheme in question. For example, the word *distant* has /dɪs/ in it, but this *dis* is not the same as that in *disappearance* since it cannot be analyzed as being a separate morpheme in this word.

Now, we can determine the types of words that *dis-* and *-ance* attach to. *Connect, embark, believe, appear,* and *associate* are all verbs, so *dis-* must attach to verbs. Furthermore, since *disconnect, disagree,* and so on, are all verbs as well, *dis-* does not change the part of speech. *Endure, grieve, accept,* and *interfere* are all verbs, so *-ance* attaches to verbs as well. *Appearance, endurance,* and so on, are all nouns, so *-ance* changes verbs into nouns.

Let's see how we can use these facts to determine the structure of *disappearance*. Let's consider all possible combinations (there are two in this case):

(5) a. appear + ance   b. dis + appear
         dis + appearance   disappear + ance

In (5a), *-ance* connects first to *appear*, then *dis-* connects to *appearance*. But this arrangement would violate the rules that govern how the affixes may attach. When *-ance* attaches to *appear*, it forms a noun. To say that *dis-* then connects to *appearance* violates the rule that *dis-* connects only to verbs. The arrangement in (5b), on the other hand, involves no violations of these rules. Therefore, we know that *dis-* must first attach to *appear* and then *-ance* attaches to *disappear*.

The tree representing this structure is given below.

(6)

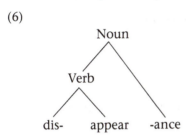

File 4.6   Exercise 29—Morphology Exercise on Isthmus Zapotec

   i. The morpheme indicating possession is [s], the one indicating third-person singular is [be], and the one indicating second-person is [lu].
   ii. The allomorphs for 'tortilla' are [geta] and [keta], for 'chicken' they are [bere] and [pere], and for 'rope' they are [doʔo] and [toʔo].
   iii. The allomorphs that begin with a voiceless consonant are conditioned by a preceding voiceless consonant. The allomorphs that begin with a voiced consonant are conditioned by a preceding voiced consonant.

File 7.6   Exercise 13—Pragmatics Exercise on the Maxim of Quantity

This exercise asks you to construct a linguistic context for the question *Where did you grow up?* such that the answer *On the corner of Main Street and Minor Road* would be felicitous. In order to do this, you must think of a situation in which an answer with this level of specificity would be appropriate.

A sample solution is the following:

(7) "Oh, you grew up in Dayton? I used to live there, near where 70 and 75 meet. Where did you grow up?"

This linguistic environment establishes that both speakers know that the city they are talking about is Dayton and that the person asking the question has a basic understanding of the layout of Dayton. Therefore, it is appropriate for the person answering the question just to specify the street intersection in question without giving other additional information.

File 13.8   Exercise 34—Reconstruction Exercise on Middle Chinese

i. Protoforms:

Protolanguage	*Gloss*
*[kim]	'zither'
*[lat]	'spicy hot'
*[mɔk]	'lonesome'
*[lam]	'basket'
*[gip]	'worry'
*[lan]	'lazy'
*[pa]	'fear'

ii. Rules:

Mandarin	*Hakka*
*velar stops > alveolo-palatal affricates / before [i]	none
*m > n / at the ends of words	none
*voiceless stops > Ø / at the ends of words	none

Explanation:

Total correspondence allows us to reconstruct the following sounds:

Protolanguage	*Gloss*
*[_i_]	'zither'
*[la_]	'spicy hot'
*[mɔ_]	'lonesome'
*[la_]	'basket'
*[_i_]	'worry'
*[lan]	'lazy'
*[pa]	'fear'

Position 1 in the 'zither' cognate set exhibits a [tɕ]-[k] alternation. Since [tɕ] is palatal and we know that it is very natural for "consonants to become palatalized before front vowels," we need to know if there is a front vowel in position 2. There is, so we reconstruct *[k] because doing so results in the most natural development. In the cognate set for 'worry,' we have a very similar choice. By the same reasoning we reconstruct *[g]. *[tɕ, dʑ] and *[k, g] are the natural classes of alveolo-palatal affricates and velar stops, respectively. Therefore we can group these two sound changes together and use a single rule—making use of natural classes—to describe the change for both alternations.

In position 3 in the 'zither' cognate set, there is an [m]-[n] alternation. Neither direction of change is more natural. In such a case, we need to look at the other cognate sets. In the cognate set for 'lazy,' both languages have a word-final [n]. This information resolves the [m]-[n] alternation dilemma because sound change is regular. We must reconstruct *[m], because if we reconstructed *[n], then in Hakka we cannot account for a word-final [n] in [lan] 'lazy' and a word-final [m] in [kim] 'zither' with a regular sound change. This is particularly clear if we compare 'lazy' to 'basket.' Because 'lazy' must end in an [n] due to total correspondence, 'basket' cannot; if it did, one protoform *[lan] would have changed while the other one did not—an impossible situation! Of course, the change of *[m] to [n] in Mandarin occurs only word-finally (because [mɔ] 'lonesome' begins with [m]). We also need to put that condition on the rule.

In cognate sets 2, 3, and 5, there are [t]-Ø, [k]-Ø, and [p]-Ø alternations, respectively. [t,k,p] is a natural class (voiceless stops). Once again, we must reconstruct the voiceless stops and delete them in Mandarin in order to be able to posit regular sound changes. If we chose not to reconstruct the stops, we would have trouble predicting which stop would be added to the end of a word in Hakka. Worse yet, there would be no explanation for why there is no voiceless stop at the end of [pa] 'fear' in Hakka. This sound change too is limited to the ends of words, as the word-initial [p] in Mandarin [pa] 'fear' does not delete.

GLOSSARY

....

Note: Numbers in parentheses after headwords indicate the number of the file or section where the term is first introduced. See the index for a complete listing of references in the text.

A

Abjad (15.2.3)   A **phonemic writing system** that represents only consonants and not vowels. (See also **Abugida** and **Alphabet**.)

Abugida (15.2.3)   A **phonemic writing system** that represents consonants with full graphemes and vowels with **diacritics**. (See also **Abjad** and **Alphabet**.)

Accent (10.1.1)   Systematic phonological variation inherent in any person's speech.

Accommodation (7.5.4)   See **Presupposition Accommodation**.

Acoustic Modeling (16.2.3)   In **automatic speech recognition**, the mapping of energy values extracted from recorded speech onto symbols for phones.

Acoustic Phonetics (2.0)   Subfield of phonetics that is concerned with the physical characteristics of the sounds of speech. (See also **Articulatory Phonetics** and **Auditory Phonetics**.)

Acronym (13.4.4)   An abbreviation formed by taking the initial sounds (or letters) of the words of a phrase and uniting them to form a pronounceable word.

Activation Threshold (9.5.3)   The amount of activation needed before a word is recognized in **lexical access**.

Active Construction of a Grammar Theory (8.1.1; 8.1.5)   Theory of **language acquisition** that says that children acquire a language by inventing rules of grammar based on the speech around them. (See also **Reinforcement Theory, Imitation Theory, Connectionist Theory,** and **Social Interaction Theory**.)

Addition (9.3.4)   **Production error** involving the addition of extra units (out of the blue). (See also **Deletion**.)

Adjacency Pairs (11.1.3)   Pairs of adjacent **utterances** produced by two different speakers, in which the first utterance provokes or requires the hearer to respond with the second utterance.

Adjective (Adj) (4.1.2; 5.4.2)   The name of a **lexical category** and a **syntactic category**. Morphologically, the category consists of words to which the comparative suffix *-er* or the suffix *-ness* can be added. Syntactically, the category consists of those expressions that can be **noun adjuncts** or occur in between a **determiner** and a **noun**.

Adjunct (5.2.3)   A **linguistic expression** whose occurrence in a sentence is optional; also called modifier. (See also **Verb Phrase Adjunct** and **Noun Adjunct**.)

Adstratum or **Adstratal Language** (12.1.3)   One of two or more languages in contact that mutually influence one another, owing to relatively equal degrees of power and **prestige** associated with the groups of speakers. (See also **Substratum** and **Superstratum**.)

Adverb (Adv) (4.1.2; 5.4.2)   The name of a **lexical category** and a **syntactic category** that consists of expressions such as *quickly, well, furiously,* etc. Syntactically, adverbs can be **verb phrase adjuncts**.

Affective Facial Expression (9.2.6)   Facial expression that conveys an emotion such as sadness, happiness, anger, fear, surprise, and so on. (See also **Linguistic Facial Expression**.)

Affix (4.1.2)   **Bound morpheme** that attaches to a **stem**. (See also **Prefix, Infix,** and **Suffix**.)

Affixation (4.2.2)   Process of forming words by adding **affixes** to **morphemes**.

Affix-Stripping Hypothesis (9.5.2)   Hypothesis that each **morpheme** is stored individually in the **mental lexicon**.

Affricate (2.2.5)   Sound produced by complete obstruction of the airflow followed by a slight release of the obstruction, allowing **frication**. An affricate can be thought of as a combination of a **stop** and a **fricative**.

Agglutinating (Language) (4.3.4)   A type of **synthetic language** in which the relationships between words in a sentence are indicated primarily by **bound morphemes**. In agglutinating languages, morphemes are joined together loosely so that it is easy to determine where the boundaries between morphemes are. (See also **Polysynthetic Language** and **Fusional Language**.)

Agglutination (4.3.4)   The putting together of **morphemes**. (See also **Agglutinating Language**.)

Agraphia (9.2.5)   Language disorder caused by damage to the **angular gyrus**; characterized by an acquired inability to write words. Often accompanied by **alexia**.

Agreement (5.2.3)   The phenomenon by which certain expressions in a sentence (e.g., a verb and its subject) must be inflectionally marked for the same person, number, gender, etc.

Airstream Mechanism (2.2.2; 2.4.6)   Any of the various ways to produce a stream of moving air through the vocal tract for the production of speech sounds. Some major mechanisms are pulmonic, glottalic, and velar; each may be produced with an egressive or an ingressive airstream. (See also **Pulmonic Egressive Airstream Mechanism**.)

Alexia (9.2.5)   Language disorder caused by damage to the **angular gyrus**; characterized by an acquired inability to read and comprehend written words. Often accompanied by **agraphia**.

Alice (17.5.2)   In **cryptology**, the sender of a message. (See also **Bob** and **Eve**.)

Allograph (15.3.3)   One of a set of nondistinctive ways of writing a particular **grapheme**; the distribution of allographs in a writing system is predictable.

Allomorph (4.5.1)   One of a set of nondistinctive realizations of a particular **morpheme** that have the same function and are phonetically similar.

Allophone (3.2.2)   One of a set of **noncontrastive** realizations of the same **phoneme**; an actual phonetic segment. (See also **Basic Allophone** and **Restricted Allophone**.)

Alphabet (15.2.3)   A **phonemic writing system** that represents both vowels and consonants with full graphemes. (See also **Abjad** and **Abugida**.)

Alphabetic Writing System (15.2.1)   See **Phonemic Writing System**.

Alternation (4.2.6; 13.7.2)   The morphological process that uses morpheme-internal modifications to make new words or morphological distinctions.

Alveolar (Speech Sound) (2.2.4)   Sound produced by raising the front of the tongue toward the front of the upper **alveolar ridge**.

Alveolar Ridge (2.2.4)   A bony ridge of the upper or lower jaw that contains the sockets for the teeth. In phonetics, usually refers specifically to the upper alveolar ridge.

Ambiguity (4.4.2; 5.5.3)   The phenomenon by which a single linguistic form (e.g., a word or a string of words) can be the form of more than one distinct **linguistic expression**. The form that is shared by more than one expression is said to be ambiguous. (See also **Lexical Ambiguity** and **Structural Ambiguity**.)

Analogy or **Analogical Change** (13.4.2)   A type of historical change in a grammar that involves the influence of one form or group of forms on another, causing one group of forms to become more like the other.

Analytic (Language) (4.3.1; 4.3.2)   Type of language in which most words consist of one morpheme and sentences are composed of sequences of these free morphemes. Grammatical relationships are often indicated by word order. Examples are Chinese and Vietnamese. (Also known as an isolating language.)

Angular Gyrus (9.1.2)   Language center of the brain located between the **Sylvian parietotemporal area (SPT)** and the posterior parts of the **superior temporal gyrus (STG)** (i.e., Wernicke's area) and the **visual cortex**, responsible for converting visual stimuli to linguistic stimuli, and vice versa.

Annotation (16.5.2)   Labeling of linguistically relevant information (e.g., in a **corpus**) such as **lexical category**, **syntactic category**, phonetic representation, etc.

Anosognosia (9.2.3)   Any **aphasia** in which the aphasic is unaware that he has aphasia. Frequent in Wernicke's aphasics who often seem to believe their speech is interpretable by others when in fact it is not. (See also **Wernicke's Aphasia**.)

Anticipation (9.3.4)   **Production error** in which a later unit is substituted for an earlier unit or in which a later unit is added earlier in an utterance. (See also **Perseveration**.)

Anti-Intersection Adjective (6.4.3)   An adjective whose **referents** are not in the set referred to by the noun that it modifies.

Antonymy or **Antonym** (6.2.4)   A meaning relationship between words where their meanings are in some sense opposite. (See also **Gradable Antonyms**, **Complementary Antonyms**, **Converses**, and **Reverses**.)

Aphasia (9.2.1)   Acquired inability to perceive, process, or produce language because of physical damage to the brain. (See also **Broca's Aphasia**, **Conduction Aphasia**, and **Wernicke's Aphasia**.)

Applied Linguistics (17.2.1)   The application of the methods and results of linguistic research to such areas as language teaching, national language policies, lexicography, translation, and language in politics, advertising, classrooms, and courts.

Approximant (2.2.5)   Consonant sound produced by constriction of the vocal tract that is not narrow enough to block the vocal tract or cause turbulence; can be subdivided into **liquids** and **glides**.

a-Prefixing (10.3.7)   The process of attaching the prefix *a-* to the beginning of certain verbs in English, as in *a-running*.

Arbitrariness (*adj:* arbitrary) (1.4.7; 14.1.3)   In relation to language, refers to the fact that a word's meaning is not predictable from its linguistic form, nor is its form dictated by its meaning. (See also **Design Features** and **Nonarbitrariness**.)

Arcuate Fasciculus (9.1.2)   A bundle of nerve fibers in the brain connecting the **Sylvian parietotempo-**

ral area (SPT) with the **inferior frontal gyrus (IFG)**; primarily responsible for sharing of phonetic and phonological information between these centers. (See also **Dorsal Pathway**.)

Argument (5.2.3)   A **linguistic expression** that must occur in a sentence if some other expression occurs in that sentence as well. If the occurrence of an expression X in a sentence requires the occurrence of an expression Y in that sentence, we say that Y is an argument of X. (See also **Adjunct** and **Complement**.)

Articulation (2.2.1)   The motion or positioning of some part of the **vocal tract** (often, but not always, a muscular part such as the tongue or lips) with respect to some other surface of the vocal tract in the production of a speech sound.

Articulatory Description (2.2.1)   For an **auditory-vocal language**, the description of the motion or positioning of the parts of the vocal tract that are responsible for the production of a speech sound. (See also **Place of Articulation**, **Manner of Articulation**, **Voicing**, **Height**, **Frontness**, **Rounding**, **Tense**, and **Lax**.) For a **visual-gestural language**, the description of the motions or positioning of the hands, arms, and relevant facial expressions. (See also **Location**, **Movement**, **Handshape**, **Orientation**, and **Non-Manual Marker**.)

Articulatory Gesture (2.2.1; 8.2.1)   A movement of a speech organ in the production of speech, for example, the movement of the **velum** for the production of a nasal consonant.

Articulatory Phonetics (2.0)   Subfield of phonetics concerned with the production of speech sounds. (See also **Acoustic Phonetics** and **Auditory Phonetics**.)

Articulatory Synthesis (16.1.3)   Generating speech "from scratch" based on computational models of the shape of the human vocal tract and natural articulation processes.

Aspiration (2.6.5)   A puff of air that follows the release of a consonant when there is a delay in the onset of **voicing**. Symbolized by a superscript <h> (e.g., [pʰ]).

Assimilation (3.3.3; 13.3.4)   A process by which a sound becomes more like a nearby sound in terms of some feature(s).

Asynchronous (Communication) (15.1.5)   Communication not conducted in real time. (See also **Synchronous**.)

Attention Getter (8.4.2)   Word or phrase used to initiate an address to children.

Attention Holder (8.4.2)   A tactic used to maintain children's attention for extended amounts of time.

Audiologist (17.2.1)   A professional who specializes in issues related to hearing, including the evaluation of normal and impaired hearing, hearing aid and assistive-listening technology, and the prevention of hearing loss. (See also **Speech-Language Pathologist**.)

Auditory Cortex (9.1.2)   Language center of the brain located in the **superior temporal gyrus (STG)** next to the **Sylvian fissure**; responsible for receiving and identifying auditory signals and converting them into a form interpretable by other language centers of the brain.

Auditory Phonetics (2.0)   Subfield of phonetics concerned with the perception of speech sounds. (See also **Acoustic Phonetics** and **Articulatory Phonetics**.)

Auditory-Vocal Language (1.5.1)   Language with a spoken **modality** (produced with the voice and interpreted auditorially); also called aural-oral. (See also **Visual-Gestural Language**.)

Aural-Oral Language (1.5.1)   See **Auditory-Vocal Language**.

Automatic Speech Recognition (16.2.1)   The conversion of an acoustic speech waveform into text. The steps involved are **acoustic modeling**, **pronunciation modeling**, and **language modeling**.

B

Babbling (*verb:* **Babble**) (8.2.2)   A phase in child language acquisition during which the child produces meaningless sequences of consonants and vowels. Generally begins around the age of six months.

Back (Vowel) (2.3.3)   An articulation for which the highest point of the tongue is held at the back of the oral cavity.

Back Formation (13.4.3)   Word formation process in which a new stem form is created from an apparently similar derived or inflected form.

Backing (13.3.4)   A type of sound change in which a **front** sound becomes a **back** sound. (See also **Fronting**.)

Balanced Corpus (16.5.2)   A **corpus** that tries to remain balanced between different genres by including articles from different sections in the newspaper, scientific papers, and other diverse sources.

Bald On-Record FTA (11.4.5)   In **face theory**, a case in which no politeness strategy is used.

Barge-In (16.3.3)   The act of users interrupting and talking over the computer, which may confuse some **spoken language dialogue systems**.

Basic Allophone (3.5.2)   The **allophone** of a **phoneme** that is used when none of the change-inducing conditions are fulfilled. Of a set of allophones, it is generally least limited in where it can occur; also termed the elsewhere allophone. (See also **Restricted Allophone**.)

Bidialectal (10.1.4)   Having mastery of two dialects.

Bilabial (Speech Sound) (2.2.4)   Sound produced by bringing both lips together.

Bilingual (*noun:* **Bilingualism**) (8.5.1; 12.1.3; 12.5.1; 16.4.3)   State of commanding two languages; having **linguistic competence** in two languages. In **machine translation**, a system that can translate between only one language pair.

Bilingual Mixed Language (12.1.4)   Language in which different aspects of linguistic structure derive from different languages, resulting from a high degree of bilingualism among speakers. (Also called an intertwined language.)

Bi-Text (16.5.2)   Text that contains the same material written in different languages.

Blend (9.3.4; 13.4.4)   In **speech production**, a production error in which two words "fuse" into a single item. In language change, a new word created by combining the parts of two different words, usually the beginning of one word and the end of another.

Bob (17.5.2)   In **cryptology**, the intended recipient of a message. (See also **Alice** and **Eve**.)

Borrowing (12.1.2)   Process by which one language adopts words, phrases, or grammatical structures from another language.

Bound Morpheme (4.1.5)   Morpheme that always attaches to other morphemes, never existing as a word itself. (See also **Affix** and **Free Morpheme**.)

Bound Root (4.1.5)   Morpheme that has some associated basic meaning but that is unable to stand alone as a word in its own right.

Broca's Aphasia (9.2.2)   Inability to plan the motor sequences used in speech or sign owing to damage to the **inferior frontal gyrus (IFG)**.

Broca's Area (9.1.2)   See **Inferior Frontal Gyrus (IFG)**. (See also **Broca's Aphasia**.)

Bundle of Isoglosses (10.3.2)   A set of **isoglosses** surrounding the same geographic region or distinguishing the same group of speakers, marking a particular **language variety**.

C

Calque (12.1.2)   See **Loan Translation**.

Canned Speech (16.1.1)   Prerecorded phrases and sentences.

Canonical Babbling (8.2.2)   The continuous repetition of sequences of vowels and consonants like [mamama] by infants; also called repeated babbling. (See also **Variegated Babbling**.)

Categorical Perception (9.4.3)   Phenomenon by which people perceive entities differently after learning to categorize them: differences within categories are compressed, and differences across categories are expanded.

Centralization (10.5.5)   Process by which a speaker's pronunciation of a vowel approaches that of the central vowels [ə] or [ʌ].

Child-Directed Speech (8.1.7; 8.4.1)   Speech used by parents or caregivers when communicating with young children or infants. In many Western societies, child-directed speech is slow and high-pitched and has many repetitions, simplified syntax, exaggerated intonation, and a simple and concrete vocabulary.

Cipher (17.5.5)   A cryptographic system in which symbols are substituted for individual characters of the original **plaintext**. (See also **Shift Cipher**, **Monoalphabetic Cipher**, and **Polyalphabetic Cipher**.)

Ciphertext (17.5.2)   In **cryptology**, the encoded text. (See also **Plaintext**.)

Circumlocution (9.2.3)   Descriptions of a word's meaning, used when a speaker is unable to name the intended word.

Clear [l] (2.4.6)   An [l] produced with the tongue body down and the tongue-tip up, as in *Lee* [li] in English. (See also **Dark [l]**.)

Cleft (5.3.3)   A type of sentence that has the general form *It is/was X that Y*, e.g., *It was Sally that I wanted to meet*. Can be used as a constituency test.

Clipping (13.4.4)   Process of creating new words by shortening a longer word.

Closed Lexical Category (4.1.2)   **Lexical category** in which the members are fairly rigidly established and additions are made very rarely and only over long periods of time. (See also **Function Word** and **Open Lexical Category**.)

Co-Articulation (2.1.2)   The adjustment of articulation of a segment due to the influence of a neighboring sound(s).

Coda (2.1.3)   In a **syllable**, any consonant(s) that occur in the **rhyme**, after the **nucleus**.

Code (1.5.2; 17.5.5)   A way of representing a language by replacing units of the language (morphemes, words, or written characters) with different symbols, yet preserving the structure of the original language. In **cryptology**, a system that replaces each entire word in **plaintext** with a suitable chosen word, number, or symbol. (See also **Cipher**.)

Code-Switching (8.5.2; 12.5.2)   Using words or structural elements from more than one language within the same conversation (or even within a single sentence or phrase).

Cognate (13.2.1; 13.7.3)   One of two or more words that descend from the same source. Usually similar in both form and meaning.

Cohort (9.5.4)   In the **cohort model** of lexical access, the cohort is the set of all the words that remain on the "list of possible words" as the auditory input progresses.

Cohort Model (9.5.4)   Model of lexical access in which possible words in the **mental lexicon** are identified based on the initial sounds of the word; impossible words are eliminated as the auditory input progresses. A word is accessed once all other competitor words are eliminated.

Coinage (13.4.4)   Process of creating new words without employing any other word or word part already in existence. Words are created "out of thin air."

Common Slang (10.1.3)   A type of **slang** that is fairly neutral and is simply informal, everyday language. (See also **In-Group Slang**.)

Communication Chain (1.2.2)   The process through which information is communicated, consisting of an information source, transmitter, signal, receiver, and destination.

Communicative Approach (17.1.1)   Foreign language teaching methodology that focuses on developing students' speaking and listening skills.

Communicative Competence (11.1.3)   The ability to interact and communicate according to cultural norms.

Communicative Isolation (10.1.1)   Situation in which a group of speakers forms a coherent speech community relatively isolated from speakers outside that community.

Community of Practice (10.4.4)   A group of people who come together to share some activity or lifestyle.

Comparative Method (13.7.3) or **Comparative Reconstruction** (13.7.1)   A technique that compares words of similar form and meaning in languages that are assumed to be related, in order to establish historical relationships among them. (See also **Internal Reconstruction.**)

Competence (1.2.1; 9.6.1)   See **Linguistic Competence.**

Complement (5.2.3)   A non-subject **argument** of some expression.

Complementary Antonyms (6.2.4)   Pair of **antonyms** such that everything must be described by the first word, the second word, or neither; and such that saying of something that it is not a member of the set denoted by the first word implicates that it is in the set denoted by the second word. (See also **Gradable Antonyms, Converses,** and **Reverses.**)

Complementary Distribution (3.2.3)   The occurrence of sounds in a language such that they are never found in the same phonetic environment. Sounds that are in complementary distribution are **allophones** of the same **phoneme.**

Complete Participation (11.5.1)   A type of **participant observation** in which the researcher actively participates in the community. (See also **Passive Participation.**)

Complexive Concept (8.3.5)   A term used in the study of child language acquisition. A group of items (abstract or concrete) that a child refers to with a single word for which it is not possible to single out any one unifying property.

Compositional Meaning (6.4.1)   The meaning of a **phrasal expression** that is predictable from the meanings of smaller expressions it contains and how they are syntactically combined. (See also **Principle of Compositionality** and **Idiom.**)

Compositional Semantics (6.1.1)   A subfield of **semantics** that studies the meanings of **phrasal expressions** and how those meanings arise given the meanings of the **lexical expressions** they con-

tain and how they are syntactically combined. (See also **Principle of Compositionality.**)

Compositionality (5.1.2; 6.4.1)   See **Principle of Compositionality.**

Compounding (4.2.4)   Process of forming words by combining two or more independent words.

Compression (2.6.2)   Physical phenomenon resulting in a higher concentration of air molecules within a given space. (See also **Rarefaction.**)

Computer-Mediated Communication (CMC) (15.1.5)   Digital forms of communication such as instant messaging and texting.

Concatenative Synthesis (16.1.4)   In speech synthesis, stringing together (concatenating) and then smoothing pieces of recorded speech.

Conditioned Head-Turn Procedure (HT) (8.2.1)   Experimental technique usually used with infants between five and eighteen months with two phases: conditioning and testing. During the conditioning phase, the infant learns to associate a change in sound with the activation of visual reinforcers, first presented at the same time and then in succession, such that the infant begins to anticipate the appearance of the visual reinforcers and look at them before they are activated. During the testing phase, when the infant looks to the visual reinforcers immediately after a change in sound, it suggests that the infant has perceived the change in sound, thereby demonstrating the ability to discriminate between the two sounds involved.

Conditioned Sound Change (13.3.4)   Sound change that occurs under the influence of nearby sounds.

Conditioning Environment (3.3.1)   Neighboring sounds of a given sound that cause it to undergo a change.

Conduction Aphasia (9.2.4)   Type of **aphasia** thought to be caused by damage in the **superior temporal gyrus (STG).** Patients are able to comprehend the speech of others, but make characteristic phonological errors in their own speech, especially when trying to repeat back the speech of others.

Conjunction (Conj) (4.1.2)   A **lexical category** that consists of **function words** such as *and, but, however,* etc.

Connectionist Theory (8.1.1; 8.1.6)   Theory of **language acquisition** that claims that children learn language through neural connections in the brain. A child develops such connections through exposure to language and by using language. (See also **Imitation Theory, Reinforcement Theory, Active Construction of a Grammar Theory,** and **Social Interaction Theory.**)

Consonant (2.1.3)   Speech sound produced with a constriction somewhere in the **vocal tract** that impedes airflow. (See also **Vowel.**)

Constituent (5.3.1)   See **Syntactic Constituent.**

Constraint-Based Models (9.6.2)   Models of sentence parsing in which context, frequency, and specific lexical information can influence decisions about **structural ambiguities.**

Constructed Language (1.4.11)   A language that has been designed by an individual or a group of individuals for some particular purpose, such as use in a fictional world or for international communication, but that did not originate as the native language of any speech community. (See also **Natural Language.**)

Contact (12.0)   See **Language Contact.**

Contact Situation (12.1.1)   Social situation in which speakers of distinct language varieties are brought together by social and/or economic factors such as settlement, trade, or relocation.

Content Morpheme (4.1.5)   Morpheme that carries semantic content (as opposed to merely performing a grammatical function). (See also **Function Morpheme.**)

Content Word (4.1.5)   A word whose primary purpose is to contribute semantic content to the **phrase** in which it occurs. All free **content morphemes** are content words.

Context (7.1.2)   The set of circumstances in which an utterance is uttered. (See also **Linguistic Context, Social Context,** and **Situational Context.**)

Continuous Speech (2.1.4; 16.3.3)   See **Running Speech.**

Contralaterality (*adj:* **Contralateral**) (9.1.4)   Property of the brain such that one side of the body is controlled by the opposite hemisphere of the brain: the left hemisphere controls the right side of the body, and the right hemisphere controls the left side of the body.

Contrastive (3.2.2)   A term used to describe two sounds that can be used to differentiate words in a language. (See also **Noncontrastive.**)

Contrastive Distribution (3.2.3)   The occurrence of sounds in a language such that their use distinguishes between the meanings of the words in which they appear, indicating that those sounds are **phonemes** of the language in question. Sounds that are in contrastive distribution are **allophones** of different phonemes. (See also **Overlapping Distribution.**)

Control Condition (9.7.1)   Experimental condition that serves as a baseline against which results from the target condition(s) may be compared.

Controlled Language (16.4.3)   In **machine translation,** a subset of natural languages that have been edited for ease of processing by a machine so as to have fewer ambiguities and simpler syntactic patterns.

Conventionalized (*noun:* **Convention**) (1.4.7)   Something that is established, commonly agreed upon, or operating in a certain way according to common practice. When an **arbitrary** relationship of a linguistic sign and its meaning is conventionalized, the **linguistic sign** bears a constant relationship only because people consis-

tently use that linguistic sign to convey that meaning.

Conversational Analysis (10.5.4)   See **Discourse Analysis.**

Conversational Turn (8.4.3)   The contribution to a conversation made by one speaker from the time that she takes the floor from another speaker to the time that she passes the floor on to another speaker.

Converses (6.2.4)   **Antonyms** in which the first word of the pair suggests a point of view opposite to that of the second word. (See also **Complementary Antonyms, Gradable Antonyms,** and **Reverses.**)

Conversion (13.4.4)   A word created by shifting the **lexical category** of a word to a different category without changing the form of the word.

Cooperative Principle (7.2.1)   Principle formulated by the philosopher H. P. Grice, stating that underlying a conversation is the understanding that what one says is intended to contribute to the purposes of the conversation. (See also **Gricean Maxims.**)

Co-Occurrence (5.2.1)   The set of **syntactic properties** that determines which expressions may or have to co-occur with some other expressions in a sentence. (See also **Argument, Adjunct,** and **Word Order.**)

Copula Absence (10.4.5)   The absence of inflected present-tense forms of the verb *to be* in sentences for which **Standard American English** would use an inflected form.

Corpus (*plural:* **Corpora**) (16.5.1)   A collected body of text (or, less frequently, of recorded speech with or without a transcription).

Corpus Callosum (9.1.2)   Bundle of nerve fibers in the brain that is the major connection between the two hemispheres; partially severed in **split-brain patients.**

Corpus Linguistics (16.5.1)   Subfield of linguistics involving the design and annotation of **corpus** materials that are required for specific purposes.

Correspondence (13.7.3)   See **Sound Correspondence.**

Cortex (9.1.2)   Outer surface of the brain responsible for many of the brain's cognitive abilities or functions.

Count Noun (5.4.2)   In simple terms, a **noun** that can be counted and pluralized. (See also **Mass Noun.**)

Covert Prestige (10.1.4)   Type of **prestige** that exists among members of nonstandard speech communities that defines how people should speak in order to be considered members of those particular communities. (See also **Overt Prestige.**)

Creole (Language) (12.1.4; 12.4.1)   A language that developed from contact between speakers of different languages and that serves as the primary means of communication for a particular group of speakers.

Critical Period (8.1.2)   Age span, usually described as lasting from birth to the onset of puberty, during which children must have exposure to language and must build the critical brain structures necessary in order to gain native speaker competence in a language.

Cryptography (15.1.4)   A writing system designed to conceal information, also called a **code**. (See also **Orthography, Pedography, Shorthand,** and **Technography.**)

Cryptology (17.5.1)   The science of making and breaking **codes** and **ciphers**.

Crystallization (*verb:* **Crystallize**) (12.3.1)   The process through which a **pidgin** establishes regular grammatical **conventions**.

Cultural Transmission (1.4.6; 14.1.3)   Property of a communication system referring to the fact that at least some aspects of it are learned through interaction with other users of the system. (See also **Design Features.**)

D

Dark [l] (2.4.6)   An [l] produced with the tongue body up, moving toward the velum, and the tongue-tip down. The dark [l] is more accurately described as **velarized** and is transcribed as [ɫ]. (See also **Clear [l].**)

Dead Language (12.6.3)   A language that does not have any speakers; also called extinct language. (See also **Dormant Language.**)

Decipherment (17.5.2)   In **cryptology,** decoding a message knowing the **key**. This is what **Bob** does. (See also **Decryption.**)

Declarative (7.4.7)   A kind of sentence that makes a claim or an assertion, that is, expresses a proposition. (See also **Imperative** and **Interrogative.**)

Decryption (17.5.2)   In **cryptology,** decoding a message without knowing the **key**. This is what **Eve** tries to do with an encoded message. (See also **Decipherment.**)

Degradation (13.6.5)   Semantic change by which a word acquires a more pejorative meaning over time. (See also **Elevation.**)

Deictic (Expression) (7.1.3; 8.3.5)   Word or expression that takes its meaning relative to the time, place, and speaker of the utterance.

Deletion (3.3.3; 9.3.4; 13.3.4)   In phonology, a process by which a sound present in the phonemic form (i.e., underlying form) is removed from the phonetic form in certain environments. (See also **Insertion.**) In **speech production,** a production error involving the inadvertent omission of units. (See also **Addition.**)

Dental (Speech Sound) (2.2.6)   Sound produced by raising the front of the tongue toward the teeth.

Derivation (4.1.2)   A morphological process that changes a word's **lexical category** or its meaning in some predictable way.

Descriptive Grammar (1.2.5)   Objective description of a speaker's or a group of speakers' knowledge of a language (**competence**) based on their use of the language (**performance**). (See also **Prescriptive Grammar.**)

Design Features (of Language) (1.4.1; 14.1.1)   A set of nine descriptive characteristics of language, first introduced by the linguist Charles Hockett. Each design feature is a condition necessary for a communication system to be considered language. (See also **Mode of Communication, Semanticity, Pragmatic Function, Interchangeability, Cultural Transmission, Arbitrariness, Discreteness, Displacement,** and **Productivity.**)

Determiner (Det) (4.1.2; 5.4.2)   The name of a **lexical category** and a **syntactic category** that consists of expressions such as *the, a, this, all,* etc. Syntactically, consists of those expressions that when combined with an expression of category **noun** to their right result in an expression of category **noun phrase.**

Developmental Dyslexia (9.2.5)   A type of learning disability that affects a person's ability to learn to read.

Diachronic Analysis (13.1.1)   Analysis of language change through time (from the Greek *dia* = 'across'; *chronos* = 'time'). (See also **Synchronic Analysis.**)

Diacritic (15.2.3)   An extra mark on a written symbol, representing either some other characteristic of its pronunciation (in a phonetic transcription system) or a vowel (in an **abugida**).

Dialect (10.1.1)   A variety of a language defined by both geographical factors and social factors, such as class, religion, and ethnicity.

Dialect Continuum (10.1.1)   Situation in which a large number of contiguous dialects exist, each mutually intelligible with the next, but with the dialects at either end of the continuum not being mutually intelligible.

Dialectologist (10.3.2)   A person who studies **Regional Dialects** and **Regional Variation.**

Dichotic Listening Task (9.1.4)   Experiment that presents two different sounds (speech and/or non-speech) simultaneously, one in each ear. Participants indicate which sound they have heard.

Diglossia (12.5.2)   A situation in which two distinct languages or dialects are used for different functions within one society.

Diphone (16.1.4)   Pair of adjacent speech sounds. (See also **Diphone Synthesis.**)

Diphone Synthesis (16.1.4)   In speech synthesis, a kind of **concatenative synthesis** that uses **diphones** to synthesize speech.

Diphthong (2.1.3; 2.3.6)   A complex vowel, composed of a sequence of two different configurations of the vocal organs. (See also **Monophthong.**)

Diphthongization (13.3.4)   Change of a simple vowel sound to a complex one. Process by which a **monophthong** becomes a **diphthong.**

Direct Speech Act (7.4.5)   Utterance that performs

its function in a direct and literal manner. (See also **Indirect Speech Act** and **Performative Speech Act**.)

Direct Translation (16.4.3) The oldest approach (1950s to early 1960s) to **machine translation,** employing word-for-word unidirectional translation between two languages.

Discourse Analysis (10.5.4) The study of the use of language in a discourse or conversation. Discourse analysts examine the structure of the information flow of speech, the interdependencies of sentences in speech, and other aspects of language use.

Discreteness (1.4.8; 14.1.3) The property of communication systems by which complex messages may be built up out of smaller parts. (See also **Design Features**.)

Displacement (1.4.9; 14.1.4) The property of some communication systems that allows them to be used to communicate about things, actions, and ideas that are not present at the place or time where communication is taking place. (See also **Design Features**.)

Dissimilation (3.3.3; 13.3.4) Process by which two nearby sounds become less alike with respect to some feature.

Distribution (3.2.3; 3.5.2) The set of phonetic environments in which a sound occurs. (See also **Overlapping Distribution, Complementary Distribution,** and **Contrastive Distribution**.)

Ditransitive Verb (5.4.2) The name of a **syntactic category** that consists of those expressions that if combined with two expressions of category **noun phrase** to their right result in a **verb phrase**. A **verb** that needs two noun phrase **complements**.

dMRI (diffusion Magnetic Resonance Imaging) (9.7.2) A neuro-imaging technique that monitors the flow of water through particular brain regions to see how different regions are connected. (See also **fMRI**.)

Domain-Specific Synthesis (16.1.4) In speech synthesis, a kind of **concatenative synthesis** for use in one particular area of application only. Utterances are created from prerecorded words and phrases that closely match the words and phrases that will be synthesized. New utterances can also be created using smaller segments, such as **diphones,** collected from the same recordings. (See also **Limited Domain**.)

Dormant Language (12.6.3) A term used to label **dead languages** by people who believe they may be revived.

Dorsal Pathway (9.1.2) Connects the **Sylvian parietotemporal area (SPT)** with the **inferior frontal gyrus (IFG)** via the **arcuate fasciculus**. Primarily used to pass phonetic and phonological detail.

Double Modal (10.3.6) The use of two modals in a single verb phrase, as in *might could* or *might should*.

Dynamic Palatography (2.2.6) Experimental method that tracks the contacts and contact patterns between the tongue and the **hard palate** over time.

E

EEG (Electroencephalography) (9.7.2) An experimental technique that uses a network of electrodes on the scalp to detect small changes in electrical activity from the brain, usually in response to some experimental stimuli.

Ejective (2.4.6) Consonant sound produced by compressing air in the mouth or pharynx while the **glottis** remains closed, and then releasing. It is also called a glottalic or glottalized sound and is transcribed with an apostrophe following the segment involved, for example, [p'].

Elevation (13.6.4) Semantic change by which words take on a grander or more positive connotation over time. (See also **Degradation**.)

Emblematic Language (10.4.5) A particular language variety used to refer symbolically to a particular cultural heritage or identity.

Emic (11.5.2) A description from an insider's point of view, in which the meaning of the action is taken for granted and described as the viewer sees it. (See also **Etic**.)

Endangered Language (12.6.1) A language that has very few speakers left. (See also **Language Death**.)

Entailment (*verb:* Entail) (6.3.2; 7.3.1) A relationship between **propositions** where a proposition p is said to entail another proposition q just in case if p is true, q has to be true as well.

Eponym (13.4.4) A word (such as a place name, an invention, or an activity) that is based on the name of a person or people somehow connected with the word.

ERP (Event-Related Potentials) (9.7.2) Consistent changes in the brain's electrical or magnetic fields that occur in reaction to particular stimuli of interest to the experimenter. ERPs are generally detected via **EEG** or **MEG** tests.

Error Recovery (16.3.4) A function of the dialogue management component in a **spoken language dialogue system** that gets the conversation in question back on track after a misunderstanding, for example, one caused by a speech recognition problem.

Ethnography (11.5.1) A description of everyday life and speech in a community. (See also **Fieldwork** and **Participant Observation**.)

Etic (11.5.2) A description from an objective, outsider's point of view, not taking into account the local significance of certain actions. (See also **Emic**.)

Eve (17.5.2) In **cryptology,** an eavesdropper from whom **Alice** and **Bob** are trying to conceal a message.

Exceptions Dictionary (16.1.5) In **text-to-speech synthesis,** a dictionary that lists the correct pronunciation of words that do not follow a language's standard rules for pronunciation.

Existence Presupposition (7.5.1) The **presupposition** that an item referred to in discourse exists.

Expanded Pidgin (12.3.1) **Pidgin** whose use is not

limited to certain social settings. An expanded pidgin is a full language, unlike a **prototypical pidgin**.

Expression (5.1.1)   See **Linguistic Expression**.

Extension (13.6.2)   In language change, a diachronic semantic change by which the set of appropriate contexts or **referents** for a word increases. (See also **Metaphorical Extension** and **Reduction**.)

Extinct Language (12.6.3)   See **Dead Language**.

Extralinguistic Factor (10.1.1)   A factor influencing language variation not based in linguistic structure, such as region, socioeconomic status, ethnicity, and so on.

Extreme Capsule (9.1.2)   Bundle of nerve fibers in the brain connecting the **Sylvian parietotemporal area (SPT)** with the **inferior temporal gyrus (ITG)**. Primarily used to pass semantic information. (See also **Ventral Pathway**.)

Eye-Tracking (9.7.4)   Experimental protocol in which participants' eye movements (where the eyes are looking at any given time) are recorded, allowing researchers to draw conclusions about processing.

F

Face (11.4.5)   Positive self-image. (See also **Face Theory**.)

Face Theory (11.4.5)   Theory of politeness based on **face**; different politeness strategies are used in different situations. (See also **Positive Politeness**, **Negative Politeness**, and **Face-Threatening Acts**.)

Face-Threatening Acts (11.4.5)   Speech acts such as requests or orders that may threaten one's positive or negative face.

Family (13.0)   See **Language Family**.

Family Tree Theory (13.2.2)   Theory formulated by August Schleicher that says that languages change in regular, recognizable ways and that similarities among languages are due to a "genetic" relationship among them.

Felicitous (7.1.5)   Describes an utterance that is appropriate for the context in which it is uttered. (See also **Felicity Conditions** and **Infelicitous**.)

Felicity Conditions (7.4.2)   The circumstances required to render a particular variety of **speech act** felicitous. (See also **Felicitous** and **Infelicitous**.)

Feral Child (8.1.2)   Child who grew up in the wild without care by human adults, often with animals.

Fieldwork (11.5.1)   The act of going to the specific communities where a language variety is spoken in order to gather information about the speech community and the language variety itself.

Filter (16.1.3)   In **speech synthesis**, the mechanism through which a basic sound from the **source** is shaped to create particular speech sounds. (See also **Source-Filter Theory**.)

First-Language (L1) Acquisition (8.0)   The process by which children acquire the lexicon and grammatical rules of their native language. (In the case of native bilinguals, both languages are acquired as first languages.) (See also **Second-Language (L2) Acquisition**.)

Fissure (9.1.2)   Depression in the **cortex** of the brain's hemispheres that serves as a physical boundary for the identification of different sections of the brain. (See also **Gyrus**.)

Flap (2.2.5)   A sound produced by bringing two articulators together very quickly.

Flout (a **Gricean Maxim**) (7.2.3)   To say something that in its most literal meaning appears to violate one of the **Gricean maxims**, but with the specific intention of conveying a different meaning based on a shared understanding of the maxims and the **cooperative principle**.

fMRI (functional Magnetic Resonance Imaging) (9.7.2)   A neuro-imaging technique that monitors blood oxygenation levels in different parts of the brain to determine which brain regions are used for a particular task.

Folk Etymology (13.4.3)   The reanalysis of a word or phrase (usually an unfamiliar one) into a word or phrase composed of more commonly known words.

Foreign Accent (8.5.4)   An **accent** that is marked by the phonology of another language or other languages that are more familiar to the speaker.

Forensic Linguistics (17.3.2)   Application of linguistic evidence in judicial and law enforcement settings.

Form (1.4.7)   The structure or shape of any particular linguistic item, from individual segments to strings of words.

Formal Language (1.4.11)   A communication system, such as one of the many systems of logical notation or most computer languages, that has both semantic and syntactic rules and that encodes ideas with symbols that represent particular meanings, but that could never be the native language of a human.

Formant (2.6.4)   Resonant frequency that amplifies some groups of harmonics above others; appears as a dark band on a **spectrogram**.

Formation (4.2.1)   See **Word Formation Process**.

Fossilization (8.5.4)   Process through which forms from a speaker's non-native language usage become fixed (generally in a way that would be considered ungrammatical by a native speaker) and do not change, even after years of instruction.

Free Morpheme (4.1.5)   A **morpheme** that can stand alone as a word. (See also **Bound Morpheme**.)

Free Variation (3.2.4)   Term used to refer to two sounds that occur in overlapping environments but cause no distinction in the meaning of their respective words.

Frequency Effect (9.5.3)   Additional ease with which a word is accessed owing to its repeated occurrence in the discourse or context.

Frication (2.2.5)   A turbulent, hissing mouth noise that is produced by forming a nearly complete obstruction of the vocal tract. The opening through which the air escapes is very small, and as a result a turbulent noise is produced. (See also **Fricative**.)

Fricative (2.2.5)   Sound made by forming a nearly complete obstruction of the airstream so that when air passes through the small passage, turbulent airflow (i.e., **frication**) is produced.

Front (Vowel) (2.3.3)   An articulation where the highest point of the tongue is held in the front of the oral cavity.

Frontal Lobe (9.1.2)   Area of the brain concerned with higher thinking and language production.

Fronting (13.3.4)   A type of sound change in which a **back** sound becomes a **front** sound. (See also **Backing**.)

Frontness (2.3.3)   A property of the production of vowels having to do with how advanced or retracted the body of the tongue is. (Sometimes called backness; also called tongue advancement.)

Full Listing Hypothesis (9.5.2)   Hypothesis that every word is stored as a separate entry in the mental **lexicon**.

Fully Automatic High-Quality Translation (FAHQT) (16.4.2)   Very accurate machine translation that is performed completely automatically, without any guidance from human users.

Function Morpheme (4.1.5)   Morpheme that provides information about the grammatical relationships between words in a sentence. (See also **Content Morpheme**.)

Function Word (4.1.5)   A word that has little semantic content and whose primary purpose is to indicate grammatical relationships between other words within a **phrase**. (See also **Content Word**.)

Functional Shift (13.4.4)   See **Conversion**.

Fundamental Frequency (2.6.3)   The rate at which the vocal folds vibrate during voicing. The frequency of repetition of a periodic wave. Closely related to pitch.

Fusional (Language) (4.3.5)   A type of **synthetic language** in which the relationships between the words in a sentence are indicated by **bound morphemes** that are difficult to separate from the stem. (See also **Polysynthetic Language** and **Agglutinating Language**.)

G

Garden Path Effect (9.6.2)   Phenomenon by which people are fooled into thinking a sentence has a different structure than it actually does because of a temporary **ambiguity**.

Glide (2.2.5)   Sound produced with only a slight closure of the articulators and that requires some movement (or "gliding") of the articulators during production. (See also **Approximant**.)

Global Ambiguity (9.6.2).   A type of **structural ambiguity** that isn't resolved by the end of the utterance.

Glottal (Speech Sound) (2.2.4)   Sounds produced at the **larynx**.

Glottalization (2.4.6)   The production of a speech sound with creaky voice or with a simultaneous glottal stop. (See also **Ejective**.)

Glottis (2.2.3)   The space between the **vocal folds**. (See also **Voicing** and **Larynx**.)

Gradable Antonyms (6.2.4)   Words that are **antonyms** and denote opposite ends of a scale. (Also known as gradable pairs and as scalar antonyms. See also **Complementary Antonyms, Converses,** and **Reverses**.)

Grammar (1.2.4, 1.3.3)   A system of linguistic elements and rules. (See also **Descriptive Grammar, Prescriptive Grammar,** and **Mental Grammar**.)

Grammatical (1.2.3; 5.1.1)   A term used to describe a sentence that is in accordance with the descriptive grammatical rules of some language, especially syntactic rules. When some **phrasal expression** is constructed in accordance with the syntactic rules of a language, we say it is grammatical or syntactically well-formed. (See also **Ungrammatical**.)

Grammaticality Judgment (5.1.1)   An instance of a native speaker of some language deciding whether some string of words corresponds to a syntactically well-formed or **grammatical** phrasal expression in their native language.

Grapheme or **Graph** (15.1.1)   An individual symbol used for writing; may represent a segment, a syllable, a morpheme, or some other unit of linguistic structure.

Gricean Maxim (7.2.1)   One of a set of principles guiding the conversational interactions of both speakers and hearers in accordance with the **cooperative principle**.

Gyrus (*plural:* **Gyri**) (9.1.2)   Protrusion in the **cortex** of the brain's hemispheres that serves as a physical landmark for the identification of different sections of the brain. (See also **Fissure**.)

H

Habitual *be* (10.4.5)   The use of an uninflected form of the verb *to be* to indicate that a state or activity is habitual.

Handshape (2.7.5)   The configuration of the hands and fingers in a sign; one of the **parameters** of visual-gestural languages.

Hard Palate (2.2.4)   Bony portion of the roof of the mouth, extending from the front of the upper **alveolar ridge** to the **velum**. (Also called the palate.)

Harmonic (2.6.3)   Overtone of the **fundamental frequency** of the vocal tract; multiple of the fundamental frequency.

Height (2.3.2)   A property of the production of vowels having to do with how high or low the body of the tongue is.

Hemispherectomy (9.1.4)   An operation in which one **hemisphere** or part of one hemisphere is surgically removed from the brain.

Heteronymy or **Heteronym** (16.1.5)   The phenomenon where two or more distinct words are spelled the same way but pronounced differently.

Heuristic (17.5.5)   A solution that is likely but not certain to work; used when an exhaustive search is impossible or prohibitive.

Heuristic Model (9.6.2)   Model of sentence parsing in which we rely on a few universal rules of thumb, such as **late closure**, to resolve **structural ambiguities**.

Hierarchical Structure (4.4.1)   The dominance relationship among morphemes in a word or among constituents in a phrase.

High (Vowel) (2.3.2)   An articulation in which the tongue is held at a relatively high (i.e., neither **low** nor **mid**) area of the oral cavity.

High Amplitude Sucking (HAS) (8.2.1)   Experimental technique used to study sound discrimination in infants from birth to about six months. Infants are given a special pacifier that is connected to a sound-generating system. Each suck on the pacifier generates a noise, and infants' sucking behavior is used to draw conclusions about discrimination abilities.

Historical Linguistics (13.1.1)   The study of how languages change through time; the study of how languages are historically related to one another.

Holophrase (8.3.2)   A one-word sentence.

Holophrastic Stage (8.3.2)   See **One-Word Stage**.

Homesign (System) (8.1.2)   A rudimentary visual-gestural communication system (not a language) that is developed and used by deaf children and their families when a signed language is not made available for their communication.

Homophony (*adj:* **Homophonous**) (4.1.4; 5.5.3)   The phenomenon by which two or more distinct **morphemes** or nonphrasal **linguistic expressions** happen to have the same form, i.e., sound the same. (See also **Lexical Ambiguity**.)

Honorific (11.4.3)   **Politeness** strategy; grammatical marker of respect and deference.

Hypercorrection (10.1.4)   The act of producing nonstandard forms by way of false analogy to standard forms.

Hypernym (6.2.4)   See **Hyponymy**.

Hyponymy or **Hyponym** (6.2.4)   A meaning relationship between words where the **reference** of some word X is included in the reference of some other word Y. X is then said to be a hyponym of Y, and conversely, Y is said to be a **hypernym** of X. (See also **Sister Terms**.)

I

Icon (11.1.4)   A **linguistic sign** whose **signifier** actually resembles or imitates its **referent** in some direct way.

Iconicity (*adj:* **Iconic**) (1.4.7)   Relationship between **form** and meaning such that the form of a word bears a resemblance to its meaning. (See also **Arbitrary** and **Onomatopoeia**.)

Idiolect (10.1.1)   The language variety of an individual speaker.

Idiom (6.4.1)   A multi-word **lexical expression** whose meaning is not **compositional**.

Imitation Theory (8.1.1; 8.1.3)   Theory of **language acquisition** that claims that children acquire language by listening to the speech around them and reproducing what they hear. (See also **Active Construction of a Grammar Theory, Reinforcement Theory, Connectionist Theory,** and **Social Interaction Theory**.)

Imperative (7.4.7)   A kind of sentence that expresses a command. In English, imperative sentences begin with a bare verb stem and do not have an explicitly named subject. (See also **Declarative** and **Interrogative**.)

Implication (*verb:* **Imply**) (7.3.2)   An idea that is communicated indirectly (either through language or otherwise) but that is not **entailed**.

Implicational Law (3.4.2)   Observation about language universals that takes the form of an implication (e.g., if A then B, meaning that if a language has feature A, then we can expect it to have feature B).

Implicature (*verb:* **Implicate**) (7.3.2; 17.4.2)   An idea that is communicated based on the way that language is used and on what speakers know about language use rather than on what is directly entailed.

Impressionistic Phonetic Transcription (2.1.1)   A method of writing down speech sounds with the intent of capturing how they are pronounced (e.g., by using a phonetic alphabet). Usually based simply on how the sounds are perceived when heard without any special analysis.

Incompatibility (6.3.2)   The relationship between two **propositions** where it is impossible for both of them to be true simultaneously.

Incorporation (4.3.6)   Morphological process by which several distinct semantic components are combined into a single word in a **polysynthetic language**.

Index (11.1.4)   A **linguistic sign** where the relationship between the **signifier** and its meaning is neither arbitrary nor iconic (e.g., smoke and fire). (See also **Icon** and **Symbol**.)

Indexicality (11.1.4)   The study of the associations speakers have between certain **forms** (**indexes**) and certain groups of people.

Indirect Speech Act (7.4.5)   Utterance that performs its function in an indirect and nonliteral manner. (See also **Direct Speech Act**.)

Individual Bilingualism (12.5.1)   The ability of a person to speak more than one language.

Infant-Directed Speech (8.4.1)   See **Child-Directed Speech**.

Infelicitous (7.1.5)   Describes an utterance that is not appropriate for the context in which it is uttered. Infelicity can result from a violation of one of the

Gricean maxims, from the lack of fulfillment of some **felicity condition,** from an unsatisfied **presupposition,** or from some other source. An infelicitous utterance is marked with a pound sign. (See also **Felicitous.**)

Inference (*verb:* **Infer**) (7.2.2; 7.3.2)   A conclusion that is drawn from an **implication** or an **implicature.**

Inferior Frontal Gyrus (IFG) (9.1.2)   Lower portion of the **frontal lobe;** the left IFG organizes articulatory representations of language and coordinates motor commands for speech. Also known as **Broca's area.**

Inferior Temporal Gyrus (ITG) (9.1.2)   Lower portion of the **temporal lobe;** the left ITG is involved in processing word meaning.

Infix (4.2.2)   A type of **bound morpheme** that is inserted into the middle of the stem. (See also **Affix, Prefix,** and **Suffix.**)

Inflection (4.1.3)   A morphological process whereby the form of a word is modified to indicate some grammatically relevant information, such as person, number, tense, gender, etc. (See also **Derivation.**)

In-Group Slang (10.1.3)   A type of **slang** that is associated with a particular group at a particular time. (See also **Common Slang.**)

Initial Cohort (9.5.4)   In the **cohort model** of lexical access, the words that are activated as possible candidates when the first sound of a word is perceived.

Innate (8.1.1; 8.1.2)   Determined by factors present from birth. (See also **Innateness Hypothesis.**)

Innateness Hypothesis (8.1.1; 8.1.2)   A hypothesis that humans are genetically predisposed to learn and use language.

Input (4.4.1)   The linguistic **form** before the application of a rule or a set of rules. (See also **Output.**)

Insertion (3.3.3; 13.3.4)   Phonological process by which a segment not present in the phonemic (or underlying) form is added in the phonetic form. (See also **Deletion.**)

Intelligible (*noun:* **Intelligibility**) (16.1.1)   Capable of being understood. (See also **Mutual Intelligibility.**) In **speech synthesis,** how well listeners can make out the individual sounds or words generated by the synthesis system.

Intensity of Contact (12.1.3)   Level of contact between speakers of different languages, determined by the duration of the linguistic contact and the amount of interaction among the speakers.

Intentional Structure (16.3.4)   The organization of discourse segments' purposes and their interrelationships.

Interactive (16.4.3)   Computer systems that interact with a human user to obtain data and to give results or information.

Interchangeability (1.4.5; 14.1.3)   The property of a communication system by which all individuals have the ability to both transmit and review messages (as opposed to systems where some individuals can only send messages and others can only receive messages). (See also **Design Features.**)

Interdental (Speech Sound) (2.2.4)   Sound produced by positioning the tip of the tongue between the upper and lower teeth.

Interlingua (16.4.3)   In **machine translation,** a language-independent "intermediate" language constructed to represent important linguistic properties (such as syntactic and semantic properties) that are necessary for the automatic translation from a **source language** into the **target language**(s). (See also **Transfer Method.**)

Internal Reconstruction (13.7.2)   Method of analysis used to hypothesize about a language's history by comparing forms that are assumed to be related within a single language. (See also **Comparative Method.**)

Internal Variation (10.0)   The property (of languages) of having more than one way of expressing the same meaning. (See also **Language Variation.**)

Interrogative (7.4.7)   A kind of sentence that expresses a question. In English, interrogative sentences have an auxiliary verb that precedes the subject. (See also **Imperative** and **Declarative.**)

Intersective Adjective (6.4.3)   An adjective whose reference is determined independently from the reference of the noun that it modifies.

Intertwined Language (12.1.4)   See **Bilingual Mixed Language.**

Intonation (2.5.3; 9.6.2)   Commonly refers to the pattern of pitch movements across a stretch of speech such as a sentence. The meaning of a sentence can depend in part on the intonation contour of the sentence. (See also **Pitch Accent** and **Phrase Tone.**)

Intransitive Verb (5.4.2)   The name for the set of **lexical expressions** whose syntactic category is **verb phrase.**

Isogloss (10.3.2)   A line drawn on a dialect map marking the boundary of an area where a particular linguistic feature is found.

Isolated Speech (16.3.3)   With regard to speech recognition software, clear speech input without extraneous words.

Isolating (Language) (4.3.2)   See **Analytic Language.**

J

Jargon (7.2.2; 10.1.3)   Speech usually associated with or used within a particular occupation, hobby, or sport. (Also known as technical language.) (In **contact situations,** see **Prepidgin Jargon.**)

K

Key (17.5.2)   In **cryptology,** the secret or code that can decode the message.

Key Distribution Problem (17.5.3)   The problem of safely delivering the **key** that allows deciphering an encoded message to the intended receiver of the message.

L

/l/-Vocalization (10.3.8) The process of pronouncing syllable-final /l/ as a vowel or a **glide.**

Labial (3.3.2) A member of a **natural class** of sounds produced with the lips; includes both **bilabial** and **labiodental** sounds.

Labiodental (Speech Sound) (2.2.4) Sound produced by making contact between the lower lip and the upper teeth.

Lack of Invariance (9.4.1) Problem in speech perception because no sound is ever produced exactly the same way twice.

Language (1.0) An abstract cognitive system that uniquely allows humans to produce and comprehend meaningful utterances. (See also **Natural Language, Constructed Language,** and **Formal Language.**)

Language Acquisition (1.2.4, 8.0) See **First-Language Acquisition** and **Second-Language Acquisition.**

Language Center (9.1.2) Parts of the **cortex** of the brain that are used in the production and comprehension of language.

Language Choice (12.5.2) A bilingual or multilingual person's decision—often politically, socially, or personally motivated—to speak a certain language in a certain situation.

Language Contact (12.0) Situation in which groups of speakers of different languages come into contact with one another.

Language Convergence (12.0; 12.1.4) The process by which two or more languages in contact become increasingly similar in both grammar and lexicon.

Language Death (12.0; 12.1.4; 12.6.1) The complete demise of a language; a dead language no longer has any speakers. (See also **Endangered Language.**)

Language Endangerment (12.6.1) See **Endangered Language.**

Language Family (13.0) A group of related languages, in the sense that they come from common origins.

Language Mixing (8.5.2) See **Code-Switching.**

Language Modeling (16.2.3) In **automatic speech recognition,** filtering out unlikely word sequences.

Language Shift (12.0; 12.1.4) The process by which a group of speakers abandons their native language in favor of another language.

Language Variation (1.2.4, 10.0) The property of languages having different ways to express the same meanings in different contexts according to factors such as geography, social class, gender, etc.

Language Variety (10.1.1) Any form of language characterized by systematic features. Varieties can range from **idiolects** to **dialects** to distinct **languages.**

Larynx (2.2.2) Cartilage and muscle located at the top of the trachea, containing the vocal folds and the **glottis;** commonly referred to as the voice box.

Late Closure (9.6.2) Proposed universal parsing principle according to which incoming material is incorporated into the phrase currently being processed if possible. (See also **Syntactic Parsing.**)

Lateralization (9.1.4) Specialization of the brain **hemispheres** for different cognitive functions.

Lax (Vowel) (2.3.5) Vowel sound that has a less peripheral position in the vowel space. (See also **Tense.**)

Left Hemisphere (9.1.2) The left side of the brain; the location of many language-controlling parts of the brain for most people; receives and controls nerve input from the right half of the body. (See also **Right Hemisphere.**)

Length (2.5.2) The duration of a segment. (See also **Suprasegmental Features.**)

Lexical Access (9.5.1) Process by which we determine which word we are hearing.

Lexical Ambiguity (5.5.3; 9.5.6) The phenomenon where a single word is the form of two or more distinct **linguistic expressions** that differ in meaning or syntactic properties. (See also **Homophony, Structural Ambiguity,** and **Global Ambiguity.**)

Lexical Bias Effect (9.3.6) Describes the fact that phonological errors give rise to real words more often than chance would predict.

Lexical Borrowing (12.1.2; 12.2.1) Process of adopting words or phrases from another language. (See also **Borrowing.**)

Lexical Category (4.1.2) Class of words grouped together based on morphological properties. Traditionally known as part of speech. (See also **Syntactic Category.**)

Lexical Decision (9.7.4) An experimental protocol in which a participant is asked to identify stimuli as words or nonwords and the decision time is measured.

Lexical Entry (5.5.2) A representation of a **lexical expression** and its linguistic properties within a descriptive grammar of some language. A collection of lexical entries constitutes the **lexicon.** A lexical entry has the form f → X, where f is the **form** of some particular lexical expression, and X is its **syntactic category.**

Lexical Expression (5.1.2; 6.4.1) A **linguistic expression** that has to be listed in the mental **lexicon,** e.g., single-word expressions and **idioms.**

Lexical Processing (9.5.1) The task of recognizing single whole words.

Lexical Semantics (6.1.1) A subfield of **semantics** that studies meanings of **lexical expressions.** (See also **Compositional Semantics.**)

Lexicon (1.2.4; 4.1.1; 5.5.2; 6.1.1; 9.3.4; 9.5.1) A mental repository of linguistic information about words and other **lexical expressions,** including their form and meaning and their morphological and syntactic properties. As a part of a descriptive, not mental, grammar, the lexicon is the representation of the mental lexicon, consisting of **lexical entries** that capture the relevant properties of lexical expressions (e.g., their **form** and **syntactic category**).

Lexifier (12.3.3)   The language that provides most of the vocabulary of a **pidgin**. (See also **Superstratum Language**.)

Lexigram (14.3.2)   Visual symbols used as part of a system for communication between humans and trained animals (generally apes). Lexigram communication shares several properties of language but is not as complex.

Limited Domain (16.3.2)   A restricted scope of application.

Linguist (1.1.4)   Someone who studies the structure of language and its use.

Linguistic Anthropology (11.0; 11.1.1)   The study of how language interacts with social structure and culture.

Linguistic Competence (1.2.1; 9.3.4; 9.6.1)   What we know when we know a language; the unconscious knowledge that a speaker has about her or his native language. (See also **Linguistic Performance**.)

Linguistic Context (7.1.4)   The linguistic environment in which an **utterance** is uttered: specifically, the discourse that has immediately preceded the utterance in question. (See also **Context, Social Context,** and **Situational Context**.)

Linguistic Determinism (11.2.1; 11.2.5)   A stronger version of the principle of **linguistic relativity** that claims that a society is in some way confined by its language, that language actually determines thought and culture.

Linguistic Expression (5.1.1)   A piece of language with a **form**, a meaning, and **syntactic properties**. (See also **Lexical Expression** and **Phrasal Expression**.)

Linguistic Facial Expression (2.7.7; 9.2.6)   See **Non-Manual Marker**.

Linguistic Performance (1.2.1)   The observable use of language. The actualization of one's **linguistic competence**.

Linguistic Relativity (11.2.1)   The hypothesis that the worldview of a speech community is influenced by the structure of its language. (See also **Linguistic Determinism**.)

Linguistic Sign (1.4.7)   The combination of a linguistic **form** and meaning. (See also **Linguistic Expression**.)

Linguistic Universal (8.1.2)   Property believed to be held in common by all **natural languages**.

Linguistics (1.1.4)   The scientific study of language.

Liquid (2.2.5)   Sound produced with slightly more constriction than a **glide**, and in which the quality changes (is "liquid") depending on where it occurs in a word. (See also **Approximant**.)

Loan Translation (12.1.2)   A **borrowing** of a phrase into a language by way of a word-for-word translation into native morphemes. (Also called a **calque**.)

Loanword (12.1.2)   Word borrowed from one language into another. (See also **Borrowing**.)

Lobe (9.1.2)   An area in a hemisphere of the brain. (See also **Temporal Lobe, Frontal Lobe, Occipital Lobe,** and **Parietal Lobe**.)

Location (2.7.3)   Where a sign takes place; one of the **parameters** of visual-gestural languages.

Logographic Writing System (15.2.1)   See **Morphographic Writing System**.

Low (Vowel) (2.3.2)   An articulation where the tongue is held at a relatively low (i.e., neither **high** nor **mid**) area of the oral cavity.

Lowering (13.3.4)   A type of sound change in which a **high** or **mid** vowel becomes a lower vowel. (See also **Raising**.)

M

Machine Translation (MT) (16.4.1)   Use of computers to translate from one language to another.

Malapropism (9.3.4)   **Performance error** by which a speaker uses a semantically incorrect word in place of a phonetically similar word.

Manner of Articulation (2.2.5)   Term used to refer to how the airstream is modified by the articulators in the vocal tract to produce a **consonant**.

Mass Noun (5.4.2)   In simple terms, a **noun** that cannot be counted and cannot (normally) be pluralized. (See also **Count Noun**.)

Maxim (for Cooperative Conversation) (7.2.1)   See **Gricean Maxims**.

McGurk Effect (9.4.5)   Effect illustrating that we rely not only on an acoustic signal in the perception of speech but also on visual information. Occurs when a video showing a person producing one sound is dubbed with a sound-recording of the production of a different sound, and an observer's perception of the sound is affected by both kinds of input.

MEG (Magnetoencephalography) (9.7.2)   An experimental technique that uses extremely sensitive magnets to detect small changes in magnetic fields generated by the brain, usually in response to some experimental stimuli.

Mental Grammar (1.2.4)   The mental representation of **grammar**. The knowledge that a speaker has about the linguistic units and rules of his native language.

Mental Image Definition (6.2.2)   A conception of a word's **sense** as a picture in the mind of the language user that represents its meaning.

Mental Lexicon (1.2.4; 4.1.1; 9.3.4; 9.5.1)   See **Lexicon**.

Metalinguistic Task (9.7.3)   Any experimental method that requires the person to use explicit knowledge about her language to make judgments about a word or sentence, instead of just using the language.

Metaphorical Extension (13.6.2) An expansion of the meaning of a word to include an object or concept that is like the original **referent** in some metaphorical sense rather than a literal sense. (See also **Extension**.)

Metathesis (3.3.3; 9.3.4; 13.3.4) Switching of the order of two sounds, each taking the place of the other.

Mid (Vowel) (2.3.2) An articulation in which the tongue is held at a relatively middle (i.e., neither **high** nor **low**) area of the oral cavity.

Middle Temporal Gyrus (MTG) (9.1.2) Middle portion of the **temporal lobe**; the left MTG is involved in processing word meaning.

Minimal Pair (3.2.3) Two words that differ only by a single sound in the same position and that have different meanings.

Minority Language (12.6.1) A language that is spoken by a minority of the population in a territory. (See also **Endangered Language**.)

Modality (1.4.2; 1.5.1) See **Mode of Communication**. (See also **Auditory-Vocal Language** and **Visual-Gestural Language**.)

Mode of Communication (1.4.2; 14.1.2) Means through which a message is transmitted for any given communication system. (See also **Design Features**.)

Modifier (5.2.3) See **Adjunct**.

Monitor Corpus (16.5.2) A **corpus** that is continually growing. As new texts continue to be written or spoken, the corpus continues to grow, gathering more and more data. (See also **Reference Corpus**.)

Monoalphabetic Cipher (17.5.5) A **cipher** in which the letters of the **plaintext** are each replaced with a randomly selected corresponding letter from a character set, such that each letter of the plaintext always translates to the same letter in the ciphertext. (See also **Polyalphabetic Cipher**.)

Monophthong (2.1.3) A simple vowel, composed of a single configuration of the vocal organs. (See also **Diphthong**.)

Monophthongization (13.3.4) Vowel change from a **diphthong** (a complex vowel) to a **monophthong** (a simple vowel). (See also **Diphthongization**.)

Monosyllabic (2.1.3) Consisting of only one syllable.

Morpheme (4.1.4) Smallest linguistic unit that has a meaning or grammatical function.

Morphographic Writing System (15.2.1) A writing system that relies predominantly on the representation of the meanings of words. Each symbol usually represents a **morpheme**. Sometimes referred to as logographic. (See also **Phonographic Writing System**.)

Morphology (1.2.3; 4.0) The study of how words are constructed out of **morphemes**.

Morphosyntax (5.2.3) The name for **syntax** and **morphology** considered jointly as a single component of **grammar**.

Motor Cortex (9.1.2) Posterior portion of the **frontal lobe**; responsible for signaling voluntary muscle movements.

Movement (2.7.4) Whether the hands move during a sign, and, if so, the path or type of that motion; one of the **parameters** of visual-gestural languages.

Multilingual (*noun:* **Multilingualism**) (8.5.1; 12.5.1; 16.4.3) The state of commanding three or more languages; having **linguistic competence** in three or more languages. In **machine translation**, a system that can translate between more than two languages.

Multiple Negation (10.3.7) The process of using more than one marker of negation when only one such marker would be used in **Standard American English**.

Mutual Entailment (6.3.2) The relationship between two **propositions** where they **entail** one another.

Mutual Intelligibility (10.1.1) Situation in which speakers of different language varieties are able to understand and communicate with one another. (See also **Intelligibility**.)

N

Naming Task (9.7.3) A task in which a participant responds to a stimulus by saying the word for the stimulus aloud while an experimenter measures the response time.

Nasal (Speech Sound) or **Nasal Stop** (2.2.5) Sound produced by making a complete obstruction of the airflow in the oral cavity and lowering the velum to allow air to pass through the nasal cavity, unlike **oral stops**.

Nasalized (Vowel) (2.4.2) Vowel produced while lowering the velum to allow air to pass through the nasal cavity.

Native Language (L1) Interference (12.1.3) The process of carrying over features from one's native language into another language, usually in **language contact** or **second-language acquisition** situations.

Nativization (12.4.1) Process by which some variety of speech that was no one's native language is learned by children in a speech community as their first language.

Natural Class (3.3.2) Group of sounds in a language that satisfy a given description to the exclusion of other sounds in that language.

Natural Language (1.4.11) A language that has evolved naturally in a **speech community**.

Natural Language Processing (NLP) (16.5.1) The ability of computers to analyze, parse, interpret, and generate **natural language** (thereby allowing humans to interact with computers using natural language instead of formal computer languages).

Naturalness (16.1.1) In **speech synthesis**, how much the synthesized speech sounds like the speech of an actual person.

Near-Homophones (10.3.8)   Words that are sometimes pronounced the same, but sometimes are pronounced differently; often the result of a **near merger.**

Near Merger (10.3.8)   When two sounds have become so phonetically close to one other that observers claim they are merged and even their speakers have trouble perceiving the distinction.

Near-Minimal Pair (3.5.3)   Similar to a **minimal pair,** but whereas the words in a minimal pair are identical apart from the **contrastive** sounds, the words in a near-minimal pair are only **almost** identical, apart from the contrastive sounds.

Negative Politeness (11.4.5)   In **face theory,** a politeness strategy to accommodate one's desire not to be bothered or to have one's independence infringed on. (See also **Positive Politeness.**)

Neglected Child (8.1.2)   A child who is neglected by caretakers, often resulting in significantly lower exposure to language as a child.

Neural Networks (9.5.5)   Computer models that simulate brain functions via many simple units and the connections between these units.

Neural Plasticity (9.1.4)   The ability of the brain to adapt to damage in one region by reassigning processing functions to another region.

Neurolinguistics (9.0; 9.1.1)   The study of the neural and electrochemical bases of language development and use.

Neuron (9.5.5)   A nerve cell.

Noise (1.2.2)   Interference in the **communication chain.**

Noisy Channel Model (16.2.2)   In **automatic speech recognition,** modeling variations in pronunciation that distort the words' canonical form. By modeling the distortion, its effects can be removed and the original signal reconstructed.

Nonarbitrariness (1.4.7)   Direct correspondence between the physical properties of a **form** and the meaning that the form refers to. (See also **Arbitrariness.**)

Noncontrastive (3.2.2)   A term used to describe two sounds that are not used to differentiate words in a language. (See also **Contrastive.**)

Non-Intersection Adjective (6.4.3)   An adjective whose reference is a subset of the set that the noun it modifies refers to, but that does not, in and of itself, refer to any particular set of things.

Non-Manual Marker (2.7.7)   Any gesture(s), such as facial expressions or head movements, made during a sign that are not made with the hands; one of the **parameters** of visual-gestural languages; also called linguistic facial expression.

Non-Rhotic (10.2.3)   A language variety in which sequences of vowel-/r/-consonant or vowel-/r/-word boundary are not permitted to occur. (See also **Rhotic.**)

Nonstandard Dialect (10.1.4)   Any variety of a language not considered to be representative of the prestige or standard variety. (See also **Standard Dialect.**)

Northern Cities Shift (10.3.4)   The systematic rotation of the vowel space found in speakers in the northern region of the United States.

Noun (N) (4.1.2; 5.4.2)   The name of a **lexical category** and a **syntactic category.** Morphologically, consists of words to which the plural suffix *-s* or the suffix *-like* can be added. Syntactically, consists of expressions that can combine with **determiners** to their left, the resulting expression being of category **noun phrase.**

Noun Adjunct (5.4.2)   A kind of **adjunct** that combines with an expression of syntactic category **noun** with the resulting expression also being of category noun.

Noun Phrase (NP) (5.4.2)   The name of a **syntactic category** that consists of proper names, pronouns, and all other expressions with the same **syntactic distribution.**

Nucleus (2.1.3)   The core element of a **syllable,** carrying **stress, length,** and pitch (**tone**). It usually consists of a vowel or a **syllabic consonant.**

O

Object (5.1.2)   A **noun phrase** that usually occurs immediately to the right of the verb in English. A noun phrase **complement.**

Obligatory Rule (3.3.5)   Phonological, morphological, or syntactic **rule** that applies in the speech of all speakers of a language or dialect, regardless of style or rate of speech. (See also **Optional Rule.**)

Obstruent (3.3.2)   A **natural class** of sounds produced with an obstruction of the airflow in the oral cavity while the nasal cavity is closed off. Includes **oral stops, fricatives,** and **affricates.** (See also **Sonorant.**)

Occipital Lobe (9.1.2)   Area of the brain associated with many aspects of vision.

Offline Task (9.7.3)   Any task that measures the final result of a process but not what happens during the process. (See also **Online Task.**)

Off-Record FTA (11.4.5)   **Indirect speech acts** that avoid making any explicit imposition on the hearer (See also **Face-Threatening Act** and **Bald On-Record FTA.**)

One-Time Pad (17.5.3)   A very secure method to send encoded messages. **Alice** makes two identical copies of a pad of completely random numbers and sends one copy to **Bob** ahead of time. The pad is then used at a later time to encode and decipher a message.

One-Word Stage (8.3.2)   Stage in **first-language acquisition** during which children can produce only one word at a time. (Also called the **holophrastic stage.**)

Online Task (9.7.3)   Any task that is designed to reveal what happens during a process and when during the process it happens. (See also **Offline Task.**)

Onomatopoeia (*adj:* **Onomotopoetic**) (1.4.7)   Iconic use of words that are imitative of sounds occurring in nature or that have meanings that are associated with such sounds.

Onset (2.1.3)   In a **syllable**, any consonant(s) that occurs before the **rhyme**.

Open Lexical Category (4.1.2)   **Lexical category** into which new members are often introduced. (See also **Content Word** and **Closed Lexical Category**.)

Optional Rule (3.2.5)   Phonological, morphological, or syntactic **rule** that may or may not apply in an individual's speech. (See also **Obligatory Rule**.)

Oral Stop (2.2.5)   A **stop** made with the **velum** raised so that no air escapes through the nose (unlike a **nasal stop**).

Orientation (2.7.6)   The direction that the hand or hands are facing during a sign; may also include whether there is contact between the hands and how that contact takes place. One of the **parameters** of visual-gestural languages.

Orthography (15.1.4)   Writing systems used for most purposes. (See also **Pedography, Cryptography, Shorthand,** and **Technography**.)

Output (4.4.1)   The linguistic form obtained after an application of a rule or a set of rules. (See also **Input**.)

Overextension (8.3.5)   In the study of child language acquisition, a relationship between child and adult perception of word meaning: the child's application of a given word has a wider range than the application of the same word in adult language. (See also **Underextension**.)

Overgeneralization (8.3.4)   In the study of child language acquisition, a relationship between child and adult application of rules relative to certain contexts: a process in which children extend the application of linguistic rules to contexts beyond those in the adult language.

Overlapping Distribution (3.2.4)   The occurrence of sounds in the same phonetic environments. (See also **Contrastive Distribution** and **Free Variation**.)

Overt Prestige (10.1.4)   Type of **prestige** attached to a particular variety of language by the community at large that defines how people should speak in order to gain status in the wider community. (See also **Covert Prestige**.)

P

Palatal (Speech Sound) (2.2.4)   Sound made by raising the body of the tongue toward the hard part of the roof of the mouth (i.e., the **hard palate**).

Palatalization (3.3.3)   A process wherein a sound takes on a **palatal** place of articulation, usually in **assimilation** to **high** or **mid** front vowels like [i] or [e].

Palatalized (2.4.6)   A term used to describe the articulation of a sound that involves the tongue moving toward the **hard palate**.

Palatography (2.1.1; 2.2.6)   Experimental method that shows the contact between the tongue and the roof of the mouth. Can be **static** or **dynamic**.

Paradigm (13.4.2)   A set of grammatically (i.e., inflectionally) related forms all stemming from a common **root**.

Paradigm Leveling (13.4.2)   A type of morphological change in which irregular members of a **paradigm** become regular through **analogy**.

Parallel (9.3.2)   Pertains to a model of speech processing in which different stages are all processed simultaneously and influence each other. (See also **Serial**.)

Parallel Corpus (16.5.2)   A **corpus** including texts that contain the same sentences written in different languages.

Parameter (2.7.2; 9.3.5)   In signed languages, aspects of articulation that describe **primes**.

Parietal Lobe (9.1.2)   Area of the brain that is least involved in language perception and production.

Parsing (9.6.1; 16.3.4)   See **Syntactic Parsing**.

Part of Speech (4.1.2)   See **Lexical Category**.

Partial Reduplication (4.2.5)   Morphological **reduplication** in which only part of a morpheme is reduplicated. (See also **Total Reduplication**.)

Participant Observation (11.5.1)   A type of **fieldwork** that consists of systematically observing within a community in order to understand how and why people do the things they do on a daily basis. (See also **Passive Participation** and **Complete Participation**.)

Passive Participation (11.5.1)   A type of **participant observation** in which the researcher passively watches everyday life in the community without actively taking part. (See also **Complete Participation**.)

Pedography (15.1.4)   Writing system designed for learners as a stepping stone to the standard **orthography** of the language. (See also **Cryptography, Shorthand,** and **Technography**.)

Performance (1.2.1)   See **Linguistic Performance**.

Performance Error (1.2.1)   Errors in language production or comprehension, including hesitations and slips of the tongue. (See also **Linguistic Performance**.)

Performative Speech Act (7.4.3)   A **speech act** that employs a **performative verb**, in which the particular action named by the verb is accomplished in the performance of the speech act itself.

Performative Verb (7.4.3)   A verb that denotes a purely linguistic action; a verb that is used to perform the act that it names. (See also **Performative Speech Act**.)

Periodic Wave (2.6.2)   Sound wave that repeats itself at regular intervals.

Perseveration (9.3.4)   **Production error** in which an earlier unit is substituted for a later unit or in which an earlier unit is added later in an utterance. (See also **Anticipation**.)

Pharynx (2.4.5)   The part of the oral tract above the

larynx but behind the **uvula**. Commonly referred to as the throat.

Phone (2.1.2)   A speech sound. Phones are written in square brackets, for example, [t].

Phoneme (3.2.2)   A class of speech sounds identified by a native speaker as the same sound; a mental entity (or category) related to various **allophones** by **phonological rules**. Phonemes are written between slashes, for example, /t/.

Phoneme Restoration (9.4.6)   Hearing a sound that was not actually produced, because the sound fits in the context of the utterance.

Phonemic Writing System (15.2.1)   A **phonographic writing system** in which each symbol represents a single **segment** like a consonant or a vowel; also known as an alphabetic writing system. (See also **Alphabet, Abugida,** and **Abjad.**)

Phonetic Environment (3.2.3)   The sounds that come before and after a particular sound in a word.

Phonetic Inventory (3.1.1)   The set of sounds that are produced as part of the grammar of a language.

Phonetic Reduction (9.3.3)   Process by which the phonetic detail of words is reduced, with some phonemes shortened or dropped entirely; more common when words are repeated or are highly predictable from context.

Phonetic Sound Change (13.3.2)   Change in the pronunciation of **allophones** that has no effect on the phonological inventory or distribution of a language.

Phonetics (1.2.3; 2.0)   The study of the minimal units of language (e.g., the sounds of spoken language). (See also **Articulatory Phonetics, Acoustic Phonetics,** and **Auditory Phonetics.**)

Phonographic Writing System (15.2.1)   A writing system that relies predominantly on the representation of the sounds of words. (See also **Phonemic, Syllabic,** and **Morphographic Writing Systems.**)

Phonological Rule (3.3.1)   The description of a relationship between a **phoneme** and its **allophones** and the conditioning environment in which the allophone appears. (See also **Rule.**)

Phonological Sound Change (13.3.2)   Change in the phonological system, by either the addition or loss of a **phoneme** or by a change in the distribution of **allophones.**

Phonology (1.2.3; 3.0)   The study of the sound system of a language, how the particular sounds contrast in each language to form an integrated system for encoding information, and how such systems differ from one language to another.

Phonotactic Constraint (3.1.1; 9.3.4)   Restriction on possible combinations of sounds, often in particular environments. (See also **Sound Substitution.**)

Phrasal Expression (5.1.2)   A **linguistic expression** that results from the syntactic combination of smaller expressions. A multi-word linguistic expression. A **sentence** is a special kind of phrasal expression.

Phrase (5.1.2)   See **Phrasal Expression.**

Phrase Structure Rule (5.5.2)   A recipe for syntactically combining expressions of certain syntactic categories. Along with the **lexicon**, phrase structure rules are a part of a **descriptive grammar** of some language. Phrase structure rules have the general form $X \rightarrow Y_1 \ldots Y_n$ where X is a **syntactic category** and $Y_1 \ldots Y_n$ is a sequence of syntactic categories. The categories to the right of the arrow $Y_1 \ldots Y_n$ correspond to the immediate **syntactic constituents** of the expression whose category is X.

Phrase Structure Tree (5.5.2)   A visual representation of how **phrases** are constructed within a descriptive grammar, given the **lexicon** and the **phrase structure rules.**

Phrase Tone (2.5.3)   A change in fundamental frequency at the end of a phrase, for example, to indicate a question or statement or to group words into a linguistic unit. (See also **Pitch Accent** and **Intonation.**)

Pictogram (15.2.2; 15.2.3)   Stylized drawing of concrete objects used as characters in certain writing systems to represent the idea of the object iconically.

Pidgin (Language) (12.1.4; 12.3.1)   A simplified language that develops in **contact situations** in which speakers previously shared no common language. (See also **Prototypical Pidgin** and **Expanded Pidgin.**)

Pitch Accent (2.5.3, 7.5.3)   A change in **fundamental frequency** used to put prominence on a particular word in an utterance. (See also **Phrase Tone** and **Intonation.**)

Place of Articulation (2.2.4)   The place in the vocal tract where the constriction for the production of a **consonant** is made.

Plaintext (17.5.2)   In **cryptology**, the original, non-encoded text. (See also **Ciphertext.**)

Politeness (11.4.1)   Expected or normative linguistic and extralinguistic strategies culturally agreed upon to be appropriate for a given situation. (See also **Honorifics, T/V Distinction, Face Theory, Positive Politeness,** and **Negative Politeness.**)

Polyalphabetic Cipher (17.5.5)   A **cipher** in which the characters of the **plaintext** are substituted from multiple substitution alphabets. (See also **Monoalphabetic Cipher.**)

Polysynthetic (Language) (4.3.6)   A type of language that attaches several **affixes** to a **stem** to indicate grammatical relationships. (See also **Agglutinating Language** and **Fusional Language.**)

Positive Politeness (11.4.5)   In **face theory**, a politeness strategy to accommodate one's desire to be approved of by others. (See also **Negative Politeness.**)

Post-Alveolar (2.2.4)   Sound produced by raising the tongue toward the front part of the **hard palate**, just behind the **alveolar ridge**.

Post-Editing (16.4.3) In partially automated **machine translation,** the process of revising the machine's output, either correcting errors due to ambiguities or converting the translated text into a more idiomatic version of the target language. (See also **Pre-Editing.**)

Pragmatic Function (1.4.4; 14.1.2) The useful purpose of any given communication system. (See also **Design Features.**)

Pragmatics (1.2.3; 7.0) The study of how **context** affects language use: both whether or not a particular **utterance** is **felicitous** in a given context and how the context affects that utterance's meaning or interpretation.

Pre-Editing (16.4.3) In partially automated **machine translation,** the process of rewriting the source text in simpler, less ambiguous language or marking the text to indicate word boundaries, proper names, plurals, and other features that will need to be addressed during the translation process. (See also **Post-Editing.**)

Prefix (4.1.4; 4.2.2) **Affix** that attaches to the beginning of a **stem.** (See also **Suffix.**)

Prepidgin Jargon (12.3.1) An extremely rudimentary and variable type of language formed in the earlier stages of **contact situations.**

Preposition (P) (4.1.2; 5.4.2) The name of a **lexical category** and a **syntactic category** that consists of expressions such as *of, in, for, with,* etc. Syntactically, this category consists of those expressions that when combined with an expression of category **noun phrase** to their right result in an expression of category **prepositional phrase.**

Prepositional Phrase (PP) (5.4.2) The name of a **syntactic category** that consists of those expressions that contain a **preposition** and a **noun phrase.** Can be **verb phrase adjuncts** or **noun adjuncts.**

Prescriptive Grammar (1.3.3) A set of rules designed to give instructions regarding the socially embedded notion of the "correct" or "proper" way to speak or write. (See also **Descriptive Grammar.**)

Prescriptive Standard (10.1.4) The standard by which a society makes judgments of "right" or "wrong."

Prestige (*adj:* **Prestigious**) (10.1.4; 12.1.3) Having high standing or respect in a community. Can be **overt** or **covert.**

Presupposition (7.5.1, 17.4.2) An underlying assumption that a speaker believes (and that the speaker behaves as though other participants in the discourse believe) prior to making an utterance. In order for an utterance to make sense or for it to be debatable, any presuppositions must be either **satisfied** or accommodated. (See also **Presupposition Accommodation.**)

Presupposition Accommodation (7.5.4) The process by which participants in a discourse decide to accept (and not question) information that is presupposed by a sentence uttered in the discourse,

even though the **presupposition** was not **satisfied** prior to the utterance.

Presupposition Trigger (7.5.2) A word or phrase that typically indicates that a sentence has a **presupposition;** a word or phrase whose meaning generates presuppositions.

Prime (2.7.2; 9.7.3) With regard to **visual-gestural languages,** a fundamental element, equivalent in many ways to a **phoneme** in an **auditory-vocal language,** with the exception that primes are produced simultaneously, whereas phonemes can be produced only sequentially. (See also **Location, Movement, Handshape, Orientation,** and **Non-Manual Marker.**) In language processing, the stimulus presented in a **priming** task right before the stimulus of interest. (See also **Target.**)

Priming (9.7.3) Any experimental task in which participants are presented with a stimulus right before the stimulus of interest in order to see how or whether presentation of the earlier stimulus affects response to the stimulus of interest. (See also **Prime** and **Target.**)

Principle of Compositionality (5.1.2; 6.4.1) The notion that the meaning of a **phrasal expression** is predictable from the meanings of the expressions it contains and how they were syntactically combined.

Production Error (9.3.4) Inadvertent flaws in a speaker's use of his or her language: "slips of the tongue" or "slips of the hands."

Productive (1.4.10; 4.1.5) Describes a **morpheme** or **rule** (such as a morphological rule stating under what circumstances an affix may be added to a stem) that can be used to produce novel grammatical forms.

Productivity (1.4.10;14.1.4) The capacity of a communication system (unique to human language) for novel messages built out of discrete units to be produced and understood. (See also **Design Features.**)

Pro-form (5.3.4) A word (e.g., a **pronoun**) that can replace a **syntactic constituent.** (See also **Substitution.**)

Pronoun (4.1.2) The name of a **lexical category** that consists of words such as *I, she, us,* etc. Syntactically, pronouns belong to the category **noun phrase.**

Pronunciation Modeling (16.2.3) In **automatic speech recognition,** the filtering out of unlikely phoneme sequences.

Proportional Analogy (13.4.2) A type of morphological change caused by the influence of one pair of morphologically related words on another. (See also **Analogical Change.**)

Proposition (6.3.1) The **sense** expressed by a sentence. Characteristically, propositions can be true or false, i.e., have **truth values.**

Proprioception (9.3.6) Our sense of where our body parts are and how they are moving.

Prosodic Break (9.6.2)   **Intonational** cues in the speech continuum that cause the parser to divide the continuum into discrete units.

Protoform (13.7.3)   A **reconstructed form** of a word.

Proto-Indo-European (PIE) (13.1.1)   The single ancestor of most of today's languages of Europe and India.

Protolanguage (13.2.2)   An earlier common ancestor of similar languages.

Prototype (6.2.2)   For any given set, a member that exhibits the typical qualities of the members of that set.

Prototypical Pidgin (12.3.1)   **Pidgin** that emerges rather abruptly in **contact situations** in which the contact is limited to particular social settings (such as trade). A prototypical pidgin has a reduced linguistic structure but may evolve into an **expanded pidgin.**

Psycholinguistics (9.0; 9.1.1)   The study of how the human mind processes language in the perception, production, storage, and acquisition of language.

Pulmonic Egressive Airstream Mechanism (2.2.2)   **Airstream mechanism** that produces speech sounds by modifying the stream of air forced out of the lungs and passed through the oral and/or nasal cavities.

Pure Intersection (6.4.3)   The relationship between the reference of an adjective and a noun it modifies such that each picks out a particular group of things, and the reference of the resulting phrase is all of the things that are in both the reference set of the adjective and the reference set of the noun.

R

Raising (13.3.4)   A type of sound change in which a **low** or **mid** vowel becomes a higher vowel. (See also **Lowering**.)

Rarefaction (2.6.2)   Physical phenomenon by which air molecules become less concentrated within a given space (i.e., pressure decreases). (See also **Compression**.)

Rate Normalization (9.4.4)   The modification of our expectations or judgments about linguistic input to account for what we know about the speech rate.

Rebus Principle (15.2.2)   A principle found in some writing systems whereby a picture of a particular object is used to represent the sounds (but not the meaning) of the name of that object.

Reconstructed Form (13.7.3)   Hypothetical word form recreated through **reconstruction**.

Reconstruction (*verb:* **Reconstruct**) (13.7.1)   The process of recreating earlier forms of a language or a protolanguage through either the **comparative method** or **internal reconstruction**.

Reduction (13.6.3)   Semantic change by which the set of appropriate contexts or **referents** for a word decreases. (See also **Extension**.)

Reduplicant (4.2.5)   The morpheme or part of a morpheme that is repeated in **reduplication**.

Reduplication (4.2.5)   Process of forming new words by doubling either an entire word (**total reduplication**) or part of a word (**partial reduplication**).

Reference (6.1.2)   A component of linguistic meaning that relates the **sense** of some expression to entities in the outside world. The collection of all the **referents** of an expression.

Reference Corpus (16.5.2)   A **corpus** that captures language in one particular time or place. That is, once a specified amount of texts have been collected and annotated, the corpus is complete. (See also **Monitor Corpus**.)

Referent (6.1.2; 11.1.4)   An actual entity or an individual in the world to which some expression refers.

Regional Dialect (10.3.1)   Variety of language defined by region or geography.

Regional Variation (10.3.2)   **Internal variation** of a language based on region or geography.

Register (10.1.2)   See **Speech Style**.

Regular (13.3.3)   A change or rule that applies in every possible word.

Regularity Hypothesis (13.2.2)   The assumption that speech sounds change in **regular**, recognizable ways.

Reinforcement Theory (8.1.1; 8.1.4)   Theory of **language acquisition** that says that children learn to speak like adults because they are praised, rewarded, or otherwise reinforced when they use the right forms and are corrected when they use the wrong ones. (See also **Active Construction of a Grammar Theory**, **Connectionist Theory**, **Social Interaction Theory**, and **Imitation Theory**.)

Relatedness Hypothesis (13.2.1)   The hypothesis that similarities among certain languages may be due to a genetic relationship among them, that is, due to their coming from common origins.

Relational Term (8.3.5)   See **Relative Intersection**.

Relative Intersection (6.4.3)   Type of relationship between adjective and noun reference where the reference of the adjective is determined relative to the noun reference. (See also **Subsective Adjective** and **Non-Intersection Adjective**.)

Repeated Babbling (8.2.2)   See **Canonical Babbling**.

Repetition Priming (9.5.3)   A type of priming in which a word is accessed more easily because of its recent occurrence, having primed itself.

Representation (16.5.2)   A symbolic presentation of elements of linguistic structure, as, for example, a **phrase structure tree** or another presentation of linguistically relevant information, for example, the tags in a **corpus**.

Resting Activation (9.5.3)   Baseline level of how likely it is that a word or a phoneme will be recognized.

Restricted Allophone (3.5.2)   An **allophone** of a **phoneme** that appears in a more limited set of phonetic environments. (See also **Basic Allophone**.)

Retroflex (2.2.5)   Sound produced by curling the tip

of the tongue back behind the **alveolar ridge**, usually to the top of the mouth.

Reverses (6.2.4)   **Antonyms** in which one word in the pair suggests movement that "undoes" the movement suggested by the other. (See also **Complementary Antonyms, Gradable Antonyms,** and **Converses.**)

Rhotic (10.2.3)   A language variety in which sequences of vowel-/r/-consonant or vowel-/r/-word boundary are permitted to occur.

Rhyme (2.1.3)   In a syllable, the vowel and any consonants that follow it. (See also **Onset.**)

Right Hemisphere (9.1.2)   The right half of the brain, which is in charge of processing music, perceiving nonlinguistic sounds, and performing tasks that require visual and spatial skills or pattern recognition; receives and controls nerve input from the left half of the body. (See also **Left Hemisphere.**)

Root (4.1.2)   The **free morpheme** or **bound root** in a word that contributes most semantic content to the word, and to which **affixes** can attach.

Rounded (Vowel) (2.3.4)   An articulation in which the lips are pursed or rounded. (See also **Rounding** and **Unrounded.**)

Rounding (2.3.1)   A property of the production of vowels having to do with whether the lips are **rounded** or not.

Rule (1.2.4)   A formal statement of an observed generalization about patterns in language. (See also **Phonological Rule** and **Phrase Structure Rule.**)

Running Speech (2.1.4; 16.3.3)   The usual form of spoken language, with all the words and phrases run together, without pauses in between them. Sometimes called continuous speech.

S

SAE (10.1.4)   See **Standard American English.**

Sagittal Section (2.2.4)   A cross section of the human head, designed to show a side view of the vocal anatomy.

Sapir-Whorf Hypothesis (11.2.2)   See **Linguistic Relativity.**

Satisfaction (of a Presupposition) (7.5.1)   Describes a state of affairs in which the content of a **presupposition** is known and agreed upon by the participants in a discourse prior to the utterance of the sentence that contains the presupposition.

Satisfied (7.5.1)   Of a **presupposition**, being such that the participants in a discourse know and believe the contents of the presupposition prior to the utterance of a sentence containing it.

Scalar Antonyms (6.2.4)   See **Gradable Antonyms.**

Second-Language (L2) Acquisition (8.5.1; 8.5.4; 12.1.3)   Acquisition of a second language as a teenager or adult (after the **critical period**). (See also **First-Language (L1) Acquisition.**)

Segment (2.1.3)   The individual units of the speech stream; segments can be further subdivided into **consonants** and **vowels.**

Self-Paced Reading (9.7.5)   An experimental protocol in which participants read a sentence in small chunks, usually one word at a time, and push a button to move on to the next word or chunk of words.

Segmental Feature (2.2.1)   A phonetic characteristic of speech sounds, such as **voicing, place of articulation, rounding,** etc. (See also **Suprasegmental Feature.**)

Semanticity (1.4.3; 14.1.2)   Property of having signals that convey a meaning, shared by all communication systems. (See also **Design Features.**)

Semantics (1.2.3; 6.0; 6.1.1)   The study of linguistic meaning. (See also **Lexical Semantics** and **Compositional Semantics.**)

Semi-Speaker (12.6.2)   A person who does not speak a language fluently.

Semivowel (2.6.7)   See **Glide.**

Sense (6.1.2)   A mental representation of an expression's meaning. (See also **Reference.**)

Sentence (5.4.2)   A syntactic category that consists of all **phrasal expressions** that can grammatically occur in *Sally thinks that _____*.

Sentential Complement Verb (5.4.2)   The name of a **syntactic category** that consists of those expressions that if combined with a **sentence** to their right result in a **verb phrase**; a **verb** that needs a sentence as its **complement.**

Sequential Bilingualism (8.5.1)   Bilingualism in which the second language is acquired as a young child. (See also **Simultaneous Bilingualism.**)

Serial (9.3.2)   Pertains to a model of speech processing in which different stages of the model form a series or succession, each influencing only those that follow. (See also **Parallel.**)

Shift (9.3.4)   In speech production, a production error in which a linguistic unit is moved from one location to another.

Shift Cipher (17.5.5)   A **cipher** in which the letters of the **plaintext** are replaced with a corresponding letter from an alphabet that has been shifted some number of places away from its normal order.

Shorthand (15.1.4)   Writing system designed to be written more quickly than traditional **orthographies**—fast enough to record speech verbatim. (See also **Cryptography, Pedography,** and **Technography.**)

Sibilant (3.3.2)   A member of the **natural class** of sounds that are characterized by a high-pitched hissing quality.

Sign (1.4.7; 1.5.1; 11.1.4)   See **Linguistic Sign** or **Visual-Gestural Language.**

Sign Language or **Signed Language** (1.5.1)   See **Visual-Gestural Language.**

Signifier (11.1.4)   The **form** of a word (as part of a linguistic sign).

Simultaneous Affix (4.2.3)   An **affix** that is articulated at the same time as some other affix or affixes in a word's **stem**; exists only in **visual-gestural languages**.

Simultaneous Bilingualism (8.5.1)   Bilingualism in which both languages are acquired from infancy. (See also **Sequential Bilingualism**.)

Sister Terms (6.2.4)   Words that, in terms of their **reference**, are at the same level in the hierarchy, i.e., have exactly the same **hypernyms**.

Situational Context (7.1.4)   The aspect of an utterance's **context** that includes such information as where the speakers are, who is speaking, what is going on around them, and what is going on in the world that all speakers can reasonably be expected to be aware of. (See also **Linguistic Context** and **Social Context**.)

Slang (10.1.3)   Words or expressions used in informal settings, often to indicate membership in a particular social group. (See also **Common Slang** and **In-Group Slang**.)

Social Context (7.1.4)   The aspect of an utterance's **context** that includes information about the social relationships between participants in the discourse, what their status is relative to each other, and so on. (See also **Linguistic Context** and **Situational Context**.)

Social Dialect (10.3.1; 10.4.1)   Variety of a language defined by social factors such as age, religion, ethnicity, or socioeconomic status.

Social Interaction Theory (8.1.1; 8.1.7)   Theory of **language acquisition** that claims that children acquire language through social interaction—in particular with older children and adults—and prompt their caregivers to supply them with the appropriate language experience they need. (See also **Imitation Theory**, **Reinforcement Theory**, **Active Construction of a Grammar Theory**, and **Connectionist Theory**.)

Societal Bilingualism (12.5.1)   Phenomenon in which **bilingualism** is the norm for a group of people.

Societal Multilingualism (12.5.1)   Phenomenon in which **multilingualism** is the norm for a group of people.

Sociolinguistics (10.1.1)   The study of the interrelationships of language and social structure, of linguistic variation, and of attitudes toward language.

Sonorant (3.3.2)   Sound (usually voiced) produced with a relatively open passage of airflow. **Nasals, liquids, glides**, and **vowels** are all sonorants. (See also **Obstruent**.)

Sound Correspondence (13.7.3)   Sounds that occur in similar positions in words that are believed to be related. (See also **Reconstruction**.)

Sound Spectrograph (2.1.1)   Equipment that generates **spectrograms** from speech input.

Sound Substitution (3.1.3)   A process whereby sounds that already exist in a language are used to replace sounds that do not exist in the language

when borrowing or when a speaker is trying to pronounce a foreign word. (See also **Phonotactic Constraint**.)

Sound Symbolism (1.4.7)   Phenomenon by which certain sounds are evocative of a particular meaning.

Source (16.1.3)   In **speech synthesis**, the mechanism that creates a basic sound. (See also **Source-Filter Theory**.)

Source Language (SL) (16.4.1)   In translation and interpretation, the language that is going to be translated into the **target language(s)**.

Source-Filter Theory (16.1.3)   Theory of speech production claiming that there are two elements in the production of speech sounds: the **source** and the **filter**.

Speaker Normalization (9.4.2)   The modification of our expectations or judgments about linguistic input to account for what we know about the speaker.

Specific Language Impairment (SLI) (9.2.7)   A disorder that affects the way people process language and other quickly changing stimuli.

Spectrogram (2.2.3; 2.6.4)   A three-dimensional representation of sound in which the vertical axis represents frequency, the horizontal axis represents time, and the darkness of shading represents amplitude.

Speech (1.5.1)   **Utterances** of any language—both **auditory-vocal languages** and **visual-gestural languages**. (May sometimes be used to refer specifically to utterances of auditory-vocal languages; however, this is not the most commonly intended meaning of the term and applies in this book only when auditory-vocal languages and visual-gestural languages are being directly contrasted with one another.)

Speech Act (7.4.1)   Actions that are performed only through using language: a term that describes the use of speech emphasizing the speaker's intention or goal in producing an utterance. (See also **Direct Speech Act**, **Indirect Speech Act**, and **Performative Speech Act**.)

Speech Communication Chain (1.2.2)   See **Communication Chain**.

Speech Community (10.1.1)   A group of people speaking the same **dialect**, usually defined by factors such as geographical distribution, age, gender, and socioeconomic status.

Speech-Language Pathologist (SLP) (17.2.1)   A professional who is trained to diagnose speech and language problems and to help individuals become more effective communicators. (See also **Audiologist**.)

Speech Perception (9.4.1)   The processes involved in understanding speech and sign. (See also **Speech Production**.)

Speech Production (9.3.1)   The processes involved in producing speech and sign. (See also **Speech Perception**.)

Speech Recognition (16.2.1)   See **Automatic Speech Recognition.**

Speech Style (10.1.2)   Way of speaking marked by degrees of formality (i.e., formal versus informal, casual versus careful). (Also called register.)

Speech Synthesis (16.1.1)   The use of computers and sound-generating devices for the creation of speech sounds that approximate the acoustic characteristics of human speech.

Split-Brain Patient (9.1.4)   Individual whose **corpus callosum** has been surgically disconnected (a procedure once commonly used in the treatment of severe epilepsy).

Spoken Language (1.5.1)   See **Auditory-Vocal Language.**

Spoken Language Dialogue System (16.3.3)   System that allows interaction with a computer via speech.

Spoonerism (9.3.4)   **Production error** in which the first sounds of two separate words are switched. (See also **Metathesis.**)

Spreading Activation (9.5.3)   Activation that flows from words just accessed to other related words, raising (or sometimes inhibiting) the resting activation of those related words.

Standard American English (SAE) (10.1.4)   The **standard dialect** of English spoken in the United States.

Standard Dialect (10.1.4)   The variety of a language that is used by political leaders, the media, and speakers of higher socioeconomic classes and that is taught in schools; the variety of a languages associated with (overt) **prestige**. (See also **Nonstandard Dialect.**)

Static Palatography (2.2.6)   Experimental method that displays the contact resulting from a single articulatory gesture between the tongue and the **hard palate.**

Stem (4.1.2)   The base, consisting of one or more morphemes, to which some affix is added. The stem always includes the **root** and may also include one or more **affixes.**

Stop (2.2.5)   Sound produced by completely obstructing the airstream in the oral cavity and then quickly releasing the constriction to allow the air to escape. Also called an **oral stop** when made with the **velum** raised so that no air escapes through the nose. (See also **Nasal Stop.**)

Strengthening (3.3.3)   A process through which sounds are made "stronger" according to some criterion. (See also **Weakening.**)

Stress (2.5.5)   A property of syllables; a stressed syllable is more prominent than an unstressed one, due to having greater loudness, longer duration, different pitch, or full vowels.

Structural Ambiguity (5.5.3; 9.6.2)   The phenomenon where a single string of words (or morphemes) is the form of more than one distinct **phrasal expression** (or word). Arises because the same expressions can combine differently syntactically, resulting in distinct phrases that happen to have the same form. (See also **Lexical Ambiguity.**)

Structural Borrowing (12.1.2)   Process of adopting grammatical structures from another language. (See also **Borrowing.**)

Style Shifting (10.1.2)   Process of automatically adjusting from one **speech style** to another.

Subglottal System (2.2.2)   The part of the respiratory system located below the **larynx.**

Subject (5.1.2)   An expression, typically a **noun phrase**, that occurs to the left of the **verb phrase** in an English sentence.

Subsective Adjective (6.4.3)   An adjective whose reference is included in the set of things that the noun it modifies refers to.

Substitution (5.3.4; 9.3.4)   In syntax, a constituency test that involves replacing a constituent with a single word (or simple phrase), such as a **pro-form.** In language processing, a production error in which one unit is replaced with another.

Substrate Influence (12.1.3)   See **Native Language (L1) Interference.**

Substratum or **Substratal Language** (12.1.3)   In a contact situation, the native language of speakers of a politically and economically non-dominant group. (See also **Adstratum** and **Superstratum.**)

Suffix (4.1.4; 4.2.2)   **Affix** that attaches to the end of a **stem.** (See also **Prefix.**)

Superior Temporal Gyrus (STG) (9.1.2)   Upper portion of the **temporal lobe**; the left STG is involved in sound processing and mapping physical sounds to linguistic phones.

Superstratum or **Superstratal Language** (12.1.3)   The **target language** in a language contact situation; the language associated with the politically and economically dominant group. (See also **Adstratum** and **Substratum.**)

Suppletion (*adj:* **Suppletive**) (4.2.7)   A morphological process between forms of a word wherein one form cannot be phonologically or morphologically derived from the other.

Suprasegmental (Feature) (2.1.3; 2.5.1)   A phonetic characteristic of speech sounds, such as **length, intonation, tone,** or **stress,** that "rides on top of" segmental features. Must usually be identified by comparison to the same feature on other sounds or strings of sounds. (See also **Segmental Feature.**)

Syllabary (15.2.3)   The set of characters used in a given **syllabic writing system.**

Syllabic Consonant (2.2.5)   A consonant that is the **nucleus** of a **syllable** and takes on the function of the vowel in that syllable.

Syllabic Writing System (15.2.1)   A **phonographic writing system** in which each symbol represents roughly one syllable of the language. (See also **Phonemic Writing System.**)

Syllable (2.1.3)   A unit of speech, made up of an **onset** and **rhyme.**

Sylvian Fissure (9.1.2)   A large horizontal fold

located in the middle of each **hemisphere** of the brain that separates the **temporal lobe** from the **frontal lobe** of the brain.

Sylvian Parietotemporal Area (SPT) (9.1.2)   Brain region at the juncture of the **parietal** and **temporal lobes**; the left SPT is involved in converting phonological representations into motor representations.

Symbol (11.1.4)   A **linguistic sign** that has an arbitrary relationship between the **signifier** and its meaning.

Synchronic Analysis (13.1.1)   Analysis of a language at a particular point in time. (See also **Diachronic Analysis**.)

Synchronous (Communication) (15.1.5)   Communication in which both sides of the conversation occur simultaneously. (See also **Asynchronous**.)

Synonymy or **Synonym** (6.2.4)   A meaning relationship between words where their **reference** is exactly the same. For example, *couch* and *sofa* are synonyms.

Syntactic Category (5.4.1)   A group of expressions that have very similar **syntactic properties**. All expressions that belong to the same syntactic category have more or less the same **syntactic distribution**.

Syntactic Constituent (5.3.1)   A group of **linguistic expressions** that function as a syntactic unit within some larger expression; the smaller expressions out of which some larger phrasal expression was constructed in accordance with the **phrase structure rules**.

Syntactic Distribution (5.4.1)   Refers to the set of syntactic environments in which an expression can occur. If two expressions are interchangeable in all syntactic environments, we say that they have the same syntactic distribution and therefore belong to the same **syntactic category**.

Syntactic Parsing (9.6.1)   The analysis (by a human or computer) of the syntactic structure of a sentence; the reconstruction of the syntactic structure from a string of words.

Syntactic Properties (5.2.1)   Properties of **linguistic expressions** that dictate how they can syntactically combine with other expressions, namely, **word order** and **co-occurrence** properties.

Syntax (1.2.3; 5.0)   A component of mental grammar that deals with constructing **phrasal expressions** out of smaller expressions. Also a name for the subfield of linguistics that studies how expressions can combine to form larger expressions.

Synthesized Speech (16.1.1)   Speech generated by concatenating small speech units or artificially generating speech.

Synthetic (Language) (4.3.1; 4.3.3)   Language in which **affixes** are attached to other morphemes, so that a word may be made up of several meaningful elements. (See also **Agglutinating Language, Polysynthetic Language**, and **Fusional Language**.)

T

Tabular Method (17.5.5)   A method for solving **shift ciphers**.

Tag Questions (11.1.3)   **Utterances** that begin with statements and end with a question about the truth of that statement (e.g., *It's kind of late, isn't it?*).

Target (9.7.3)   In **priming** tasks, the stimulus of interest that follows the **prime**.

Target Language (TL) (16.4.1)   In translation and interpretation, the language that some text is translated into. (See also **Source Language**.) In contact situations, the language associated with the politically and economically dominant group. (See also **Superstratum Language**.)

Technography (15.1.4)   A writing system designed as a scientific tool for a specialized field (e.g., the IPA). (See also **Cryptography, Orthography, Pedography**, and **Shorthand**.)

Telegraphic Stage (8.3.3)   A phase during child language acquisition in which children use utterances composed primarily of **content words**.

Telegraphic Utterances (8.3.3)   Utterances containing primarily **content words** (in the style of a telegram with many function words and function morphemes left out).

Temporal Lobe (9.1.2)   Area in the brain associated with the perception and recognition of auditory stimuli.

Temporary Ambiguity (9.6.2)   **Structural ambiguity** that is present up until some point during the processing of a sentence but that is resolved by the end of the sentence (because, in fact, only one of the original parses is consistent with the entire sequence of words).

Tense (Vowel) (2.3.5)   Vowel sound that has a more peripheral position in the vowel space. (See also **Lax**.)

Text-To-Speech Synthesis (TTS) (16.1.5)   In **speech synthesis**, generating speech directly from text entered with normal orthography.

Tone (2.5.4)   Pitch at which the **syllable** of a word is pronounced; can make a difference in meaning. (See also **Tone Language** and **Suprasegmental Feature**.)

Tone Language (2.5.4)   Language that uses pitch contrast on syllables to signal a difference in word meaning.

Topicalization (5.2.2, 10.4.5)   A syntactic process by which (in English) a **syntactic constituent** occurs at the beginning of a sentence in order to highlight the topic under discussion.

Total Reduplication (4.2.5)   Reduplication in which an entire morpheme is repeated. (See also **Partial Reduplication**.)

TRACE model (9.5.3)   An influential **neural network** model of **lexical access**. Three layers of nodes represent features, phonemes, and words; activation flows upward from one layer to the next and may flow back from words to phonemes.

Trachea (2.2.3)   The windpipe; the tube between the **larynx** and the lungs through which air travels.

Traffic Analysis (17.5.4)   The study of the pattern of who sends messages to whom.

Transfer (12.1.3)   The influence of one's native language on the learning of subsequent languages (which can facilitate or inhibit the learning of the second language). (See also **Native Language (L1) Interference.**)

Transfer Method (16.4.3)   In **machine translation**, a strategy to have language-dependent "intermediate" languages that represent important linguistic properties (such as syntactic and semantic properties) that are necessary for the automatic translation from a **source language** into the **target language**(s). (See also **Interlingua.**)

Transitive Verb (TV) (5.4.2)   The name of a **syntactic category** that consists of those expressions that if combined with an expression of category **noun phrase** to their right result in a **verb phrase**; a **verb** that needs a noun phrase **complement**.

Translation (16.4.1)   The work or the process of rendering one language into another.

Trigger (7.5.2)   See **Presupposition Trigger.**

Trill (2.4.6)   A sound produced by bringing two articulators together in a series of quick taps.

Truth Conditions (6.3.1)   The set of conditions that would have to hold in the world in order for the **proposition** expressed by some sentence to be true.

Truth Value (6.3.1)   Either true or false. The **reference** of a sentence.

T/V Distinction (11.4.4)   **Politeness** strategy in which second-person pronouns are distinguished in terms of social distance or intimacy. (See also **Honorific.**)

Two-Word Stage (8.3.3)   Stage in first-language acquisition at which children produce two-word utterances in addition to one-word utterances.

U

Unconditioned Sound Change (13.3.4)   Sound change that occurs without influence from neighboring sounds.

Underextension (8.3.5)   Application of a word to a smaller set of objects than is appropriate for mature adult speech or the usual definition of the word. (See also **Overextension.**)

Underlying Form (3.3.1)   The phonemic form of a word or morpheme before **phonological rules** are applied.

Ungrammatical (1.2.3; 5.1.1)   Not in accordance with the descriptive grammatical rules of some language, especially syntactic rules. When some **phrasal expression** is not constructed in accordance with the syntactic rules of a language, we say it is ungrammatical or syntactically ill-formed. (See also **Grammatical.**)

Uniqueness Point (9.5.4)   Point in the articulation of a word at which the word can be uniquely identified relative to all other words in the language that may begin with the same sound or sequence of sounds.

Unit Selection Synthesis (16.1.4)   A kind of **concatenative synthesis** that uses large samples of speech and builds a database of smaller units from these speech samples, which are then put together in order to synthesize speech.

Universal Grammar (8.1.2)   The theory that posits a set of grammatical characteristics shared by all **natural languages**. Also, the name of this set of shared characteristics. (See also **Linguistic Universal.**)

Unparsable (9.6.2)   Describes a phrase or sentence that is grammatical, yet for which a person is unable to determine the syntactic structure, often due to the **garden path effect**. (See also **Syntactic Parsing.**)

Unrounded (Vowel) (2.3.4)   An articulation in which the lips are spread or not rounded. (See also **Rounded.**)

Usage-Based Definition (6.2.2)   A characterization of a word's **sense** based on the way that the word is used by speakers of a language.

Utterance (7.1.2)   A speech event: a particular occurrence of a person speaking or signing. Also, the content—words, phrases, or sentences—of what is said. Utterances are represented by the use of quotation marks.

Uvula (2.4.5)   The small fleshy mass that hangs down at the back of the throat; used to produce uvular consonants.

V

Variation (1.2.4; 10.0)   See **Language Variation.**

Variegated Babbling (8.2.2)   Production of meaningless consonant-vowel sequences by infants. (See also **Canonical Babbling.**)

Variety (10.1.1)   See **Language Variety.**

Velar (Speech Sound) (2.2.4)   Sound produced by raising the back of the tongue toward the **velum.**

Velarized (2.4.6)   A term describing a secondary articulation of a speech sound that is produced with the tongue body moving toward the **velum.** For example, the [l] in the English word *eel* [il] is velarized. (See also **Dark [l].**)

Velum (2.2.4)   Soft part of the roof of the mouth behind the **hard palate**, also known as the soft palate. When the velum is raised, the passage between the **pharynx** (throat) and the nasal cavity is closed. When it is lowered, air escapes from the nose, and a **nasal** sound is produced.

Ventral Pathway (9.1.2)   Connects the **Sylvian parietotemporal area (SPT)** with the **inferior temporal gyrus (ITG)** via the **extreme capsule**. Primarily used to pass semantic information.

Verb (V) (4.1.2)   The name of a **lexical category** that consists of all words to which, for example, *-ing* or *-able* can be suffixed. Not a **syntactic category.**

Verb Phrase (VP) (5.4.2)   The name of a **syntactic category** that consists of all expressions that, if combined with a **noun phrase** to their left, result in a **sentence.**

Verb Phrase Adjunct (5.4.2)   A kind of **adjunct** that combines with an expression of syntactic category **verb phrase** with the resulting expression also being of category verb phrase.

Visual Cortex (9.1.2)   Area of the brain located in the posterior **occipital lobe** of each hemisphere; responsible for receiving and interpreting visual stimuli.

Visual-Gestural Language (1.5.1)   Language with a signed **modality** (produced with gestures of the hands, arms, and face and interpreted visually). (See also **Auditory-Vocal Language.**)

Vocal Folds (2.2.3)   Folds of muscle in the **larynx** responsible for creating **voiced** sounds when they vibrate. (See also **Glottis** and **Voicing.**)

Vocal Tract (2.2.2)   The entire air passage above the **larynx,** consisting of the **pharynx,** oral cavity, and nasal cavity.

Vocalization (10.3.8)   The process of pronouncing a nonvowel as a vowel.

Voice Bar (2.6.5)   The dark band at the bottom of a **spectrogram** that indicates that a sound is **voiced.**

Voice Onset Time (VOT) (8.2.1; 9.4.3)   The length of time between the release of a consonant and the onset of voicing, that is, when the vocal folds start vibrating.

Voiced (2.2.3)   Sound made with the vocal folds vibrating.

Voiceless (2.2.3)   Sound made without the vocal folds vibrating.

Voicing (2.2.3)   Vibration of the approximated vocal folds caused by air passing through them. When the vocal folds vibrate, a **voiced** sound is produced; when the vocal folds do not vibrate, a **voiceless** sound is produced.

Vowel (2.1.3)   Speech sound produced with at most only a slight narrowing somewhere in the **vocal tract,** allowing air to flow freely through the oral cavity. (See also **Consonant.**)

Vowel Harmony (3.3.3)   Long-distance **assimilation** between vowels.

Vowel Space (2.3.5)   Range of possible vowel sounds of a language from the high front vowel to the high back vowel. Languages and dialects choose a subset of possibilities in the vowel space but do not exploit all possibilities.

W

Wave Theory (13.2.2)   The theory describing the gradual spread of change throughout a dialect, language, or group of languages, similar to a wave expanding on the surface of a pond from the point where a pebble (i.e., the source of the change) has been tossed in.

Weakening (3.3.3)   A process through which sounds are made "weaker" according to some criterion. (See also **Strengthening.**)

Wernicke's Aphasia (9.2.3)   A speech disorder commonly associated with damage to the **Sylvian parietotemporal (SPT) area** and posterior parts of the **superior temporal gyrus (STG)** (i.e., Wernicke's area) that involves the inability to understand linguistic input.

Wernicke's Area (9.1.2)   Older term for the **Sylvian parietotemporal (SPT) area** and posterior parts of the **superior temporal gyrus (STG).**

Whorf Hypothesis (11.2.2)   See **Linguistic Relativity.**

Williams Syndrome (9.2.7)   A disorder due to deletion of genes on chromosome 7 that substantially impairs cognitive function but has been argued to leave language processing relatively intact.

Wizard of Oz Simulations (16.3.5)   A technique used for **spoken language dialogue system** development in which participants are told that they will interact with a computer system through a natural language interface, but in fact they interact with a human operator (i.e., the "wizard"). This allows testing aspects of how humans will interact with a dialogue system before the system is developed.

Word Formation Process (4.2.1)   The combination of **morphemes** according to rules of the language in question to make new words or forms of words.

Word Order (5.2.1)   The linear order in which words can occur in some **phrasal expression.** Also, the set of **syntactic properties** of expressions that dictates how they can be ordered with respect to other expressions. (See also **Co-Occurrence.**)

Word Spotting (16.3.2)   In interactive computer systems, a technique in which the computer program focuses on words it knows and ignores ones it doesn't know.

Writing (1.3.2; 15.0)   Creating visual symbols on a surface to record linguistic forms; the representation of language in a physical medium other than sound.

X

X-Ray Photography (2.1.1; 2.3.7)   X-rays used in conjunction with sound film. The use of this technique can reveal the details of the functioning of the vocal apparatus. The entirety of how a sound is produced is revealed and can actually be seen as it happens.

SELECTED BIBLIOGRAPHY

Aitchison, Jean. 1976. *The articulate mammal: An introduction to psycholinguistics.* London: Hutchinson and Co.

Akmajian, Adrian; Richard A. Demers; Ann K. Farmer; and Robert M. Harnish. 2010. *Linguistics: An introduction to language and communication.* 6th edn. Cambridge, MA: MIT Press.

Anderson, Jeffrey M.; R. Gilmore; S. Roper; B. Crosson; R. M. Bauer; S. Nadeau; D. Q. Beversdorf; J. Cibula; M. Rogish III; S. Kortencamp; J. D. Hughes; L. J. Gonzalez Rothi; and K. M. Heilman. 1999. Conduction aphasia and the arcuate fasciculus: A reexamination of the Wernicke–Geschwind model. *Brain and Language* 70.1–12.

Aronoff, Mark, and Kirsten Fudeman. 2010. *What is morphology?* 2nd edn. Oxford: Wiley-Blackwell.

Aronoff, Mark; Irit Meir; and Wendy Sandler. 2005. The paradox of sign language morphology. *Language* 81.302–44.

Aronoff, Mark, and Janie Rees-Miller. 2003. *The handbook of linguistics.* Oxford: Blackwell.

Ash, Sharon. 2003. A national survey of North American dialects. *Needed research in American dialects* (Publication of the American Dialect Society 88), ed. by Dennis Preston, 57–73. Durham, NC: American Dialect Society, Duke University Press.

Auer, Peter. 1995. The pragmatics of code-switching: A sequential approach. *One speaker, two languages: Cross-disciplinary perspectives on code-switching,* ed. by Lesley Milroy and Pieter Muysken, 115–35. Cambridge: Cambridge University Press.

Avrutin, Sergey. 2001. Linguistics and agrammatism. *GLOT International* 5.87–97.

Baker, Charlotte, and Dennis Cokely. 1980. *American Sign Language: A teacher's resource text on grammar and culture.* Silver Spring, MD: T. J. Publishers.

Baldwin, Daryl. 2003. Miami language reclamation: From ground zero. (Speaker series 24.) Minneapolis: Center for Writing, University of Minnesota. Online: http://writing.umn.edu/lrs/assets/pdf/speakerpubs/baldwin.pdf.

Baron, Naomi S. 2008. *Always on: Language in an online and mobile world.* Oxford: Oxford University Press.

Beck, R. B. 1969. Ethnographic interview by Peggy Dycus. Miami, OK: Miami Tribal Library.

Bellugi, Ursula; Amy Bihrle; Terry Jernigan; Doris Trauner; and Sally Doherty. 1990. Neuropsychological, neurological, and neuroanatomical profile of Williams syndrome. *American Journal of Medical Genetics* 37(S6).115–25.

Benson, Larry D. (ed.). 1987. *The Riverside Chaucer.* 3rd edn. Boston: Houghton Mifflin.

Berko Gleason, Jean. 2005. *The development of language.* 6th edn. Boston: Pearson.

Berko Gleason, Jean, and Nan Bernstein Ratner (eds.). 1998. *Psycholinguistics.* 2nd edn. Fort Worth: Harcourt Brace College Publishers.

Berlin, Brent, and Paul Kay. 1969. *Basic color terms: Their universality and evolution.* Berkeley: University of California Press.

Bickerton, Derek. 1983. Creole languages. *Scientific American* 249(1).116–22.

Bloomfield, Leonard. 1933. *Language.* New York: Holt, Rinehart and Winston.

Bolinger, Dwight L. 1980. *Language, the loaded weapon: The use and abuse of language today.* London: Longman.

Bongaerts, Theo; Chantal van Summeren; Brigitte Planken; and Erik Schils. 1997. Age and ultimate attainment in the pronunciation of a foreign language. *Studies in Second Language Acquisition* 19.447–65.

Bonvillain, Nancy. 2013. *Language, culture, and communication: The meaning of messages.* 7th edn. Boston: Pearson.

Boroditsky, Lera. 2003. Linguistic relativity. *Encyclopedia of cognitive science,* ed. by Lynn Nadel, 917–22. London: Macmillan.

Bosch, Laura, and Nuria Sebastián-Gallés. 2001. Evidence of early language discrimination abilities in infants from bilingual environments. *Infancy* 2(1).29–49.

Braine, M. D. S. 1971. The acquisition of language in infant and child. *The learning of language,* ed. by Carroll E. Reed, 7–95. New York: Appleton-Century-Crofts.

Brandes, Paul D., and Jeutonne Brewer. 1977. *Dialect clash in America: Issues and answers.* Metuchen, NJ: Scarecrow Press.

Brentari, Diane. 2002. Modality differences in sign language phonology and morphophonemics. *Modality and structure in signed and spoken languages,* ed. by Richard P. Meier, Kearsy Cormier, and David Quinto-Pozos, 35–64. Cambridge: Cambridge University Press.

Broch, Ingvild, and Ernst Håkon Jahr. 1984. Russenorsk: A new look at the Russo-Norwegian pidgin in northern Norway. *Scandinavian language contacts,* ed. by P. Sture Ureland and Iain Clarkson, 21–65. Cambridge: Cambridge University Press.

Brock, Jon. 2007. Language abilities in Williams syndrome: A critical review. *Development and Psychopathology* 19(1).97–127.

Brown, Penelope, and Stephen C. Levinson. 1987. *Politeness: Some universals in language usage.* Cambridge: Cambridge University Press.

Brown, Penelope, and Stephen C. Levinson. 1993. *Linguistic and nonlinguistic coding of spatial arrays: Explorations in Mayan cognition.* (Cognitive Anthropology Research Group Working Papers 24.) Nijmegen: Max Planck Institute for Psycholinguistics.

Brown, Roger. 1973. *A first language: The early stages.* Cambridge, MA: Harvard University Press.

Buffington, Albert F., and Preston A. Barba. 1965. *A Pennsylvania German grammar.* Allentown, PA: Schlechter.

Burani, Cristina, and Anna M. Thornton. 2003. The interplay of root, suffix and whole-word frequency in processing derived words. *Morphological structure in language processing,* ed. by R. Harald Baayen and Robert Schreuder, 157–207. Berlin: Mouton de Gruyter.

Butterworth, B. 1983. Lexical representation. *Language production, vol. 2: Development, writing and other language processes,* ed. by B. Butterworth, 257–94. London: Academic Press.

Campbell, Lyle. 2013. *Historical linguistics: An introduction.* 3rd edn. Cambridge, MA: MIT Press.

Carroll, David W. 2004. *Psychology of language.* 4th edn. Belmont, CA: Wadsworth/Thomson Learning.

Carver, Craig M. 1987. *American regional dialects: A word geography.* Ann Arbor: University of Michigan Press.

Chun, Elaine W. 2001. The construction of white, black, and Korean American identities through African American Vernacular English. *Journal of Linguistic Anthropology* 11(1).52–64.

Clark, Eve V. 1993. *The lexicon in acquisition.* Cambridge: Cambridge University Press.

Clark, Eve V. 1995. Later lexical development and word formation. *The handbook of child language,* ed. by Paul Fletcher and Brian MacWhinney, 393–412. Oxford: Blackwell.

Clark, Eve V. 2009. *First language acquisition.* 2nd edn. Cambridge: Cambridge University Press.

Clark, Ross. 1983. Social contexts of early South Pacific pidgins. *The social contexts of creolization,* ed. by Ellen Woolford and William Washabaugh, 10–27. Ann Arbor, MI: Karoma.

Coates, Jennifer. 1993. *Women, men, and language.* 2nd edn. New York: Longman.

Comrie, Bernard. 1989. *Linguistic universals and linguistic typology.* 2nd edn. Chicago: University of Chicago Press.

Corina, David P.; Ursula Bellugi; and Judy Reilly. 1999. Neuropsychological studies of linguistic and affective facial expressions in deaf signers. *Language and Speech* 42(2–3).307–31.

Costello, Elaine. 1995. *Signing: How to speak with your hands.* Revised and updated edn. New York: Bantam Books.

Coulmas, Florian. 1989. *The writing systems of the world.* Oxford: Blackwell.

Cowan, William, and Jaromira Rakušan. 1998. *Source book for linguistics.* 3rd revised edn. Amsterdam: John Benjamins.

Cran, William, and Robert MacNeil. 2005. *Do you speak American?* A MacNeil/Lehrer & Paladin InVision Production, with Thirteen/WNET New York, in association with KLRU Austin, Texas. Companion website: http://www.pbs.org/speak/.

Crowley, Terry, and Claire Bowern. 2010. *An introduction to historical linguistics.* 4th edn. Oxford: Oxford University Press.

Crystal, David. 2006. *Language and the Internet.* 2nd edn. Cambridge: Cambridge University Press.

Crystal, David. 2010. *The Cambridge encyclopedia of language.* 3rd edn. Cambridge: Cambridge University Press.

Damian, Markus F.; Jeffrey S. Bowers; Hans Stadthagen-Gonzalez; and Katharina Spalek. 2010. Does word length affect speech onset latencies when producing single words? *Journal of Experimental Psychology: Learning, Memory, and Cognition* 36.892–905.

Daniels, Peter T., and William Bright. 1996. *The world's writing systems.* Oxford: Oxford University Press.

DeCasper, Anthony J., and Melanie J. Spence. 1986. Prenatal maternal speech influences newborns' perception of speech sounds. *Infant Behavior and Development* 9.133–50.

DeFrancis, John. 1984. *The Chinese language: Fact and fantasy.* Honolulu: University of Hawai'i Press.

DeFrancis, John. 1989. *Visible speech: The diverse oneness of writing systems.* Honolulu: University of Hawai'i Press.

Descartes, René. 2006. *A discourse on the method.* Trans. by Ian Maclean. (Oxford World's Classics.) Oxford: Oxford University Press.

Dickinson, Markus; Chris Brew; and Detmar Meurers. 2013. *Language and computers.* Oxford: Wiley-Blackwell.

Dodsworth, Robin. 2005. Attribute networking: A technique for modeling social perceptions. *The Journal of Sociolinguistics* 9(2).225–53.

Doyle, Arthur Conan, and Christopher Morley. 1930. *The complete Sherlock Holmes.* Garden City, NY: Doubleday.

Duchnowski, Dawn. 1999. Chicano English: Language issues and their relationship to culture. *Virtual International Classroom.* Online: http://courses.wcsu.edu/valkommen/dawn.htm.

Duranti, Alessandro. 1997. *Linguistic anthropology.* Cambridge: Cambridge University Press.

Durian, David. 2004. The social stratification of word-initial (str) in Columbus, OH shopping malls. Columbus: The Ohio State University, Ms. Online: http://www.ling.ohio-state.edu/~ddurian/strss-cds.pdf.

Durian, David. 2010. *A new perspective on vowel variation across the 20th century in Columbus, OH.* Columbus: The Ohio State University dissertation.

Early 1900s statistical records tell story. 2002. *Aatotankiki Myaamiaki (The quarterly newspaper of the Miami Nation).*

Eckert, Penelope. 2000. *Linguistic variation as social practice: The linguistic construction of identity in Belten High.* Oxford: Blackwell.

Eckert, Penelope. 2004. Vowel shifts in Northern California and the Detroit suburbs. Online: http://www.stanford.edu/~eckert/vowels.html.

Eckert, Penelope, and Sally McConnell-Ginet. 1992. Think practically and look locally: Language and gender as community based practice. *Annual Review of Anthropology* 21.461–90.

Eckert, Penelope, and Norma Mendoza-Denton. 2006. Getting real in the Golden State (California). *American voices: How dialects differ from coast to coast,* ed. by Walt Wolfram and Ben Ward, 139–43. Oxford: Blackwell.

Edwards, John R. 1979. *Language and disadvantage.* London: Edward Arnold.

Eisikovits, Edina. 1988. Girl-talk/boy-talk: Sex differences in adolescent speech. *Australian English: The language of a new society,* ed. by Peter Collins and David Blair, 35–54. St. Lucia: University of Queensland Press.

Emmorey, Karen. 2007. The psycholinguistics of signed and spoken languages: How biology affects processing. *The Oxford handbook of psycholinguistics,* ed. by M. Gareth Gaskell, 703–21. Oxford: Oxford University Press.

Emmorey, Karen; Rain Bosworth; and Tanya Kraljic. 2009. Visual feedback and self-monitoring of sign language. *Journal of Memory and Language* 61.398–411.

Enninger, Werner, and Joachim Raith. 1988. Varieties, variation, and convergence in the linguistic repertoire of the Old Order Amish in Kent County, Delaware. *Variation and convergence: Studies in social dialectology,* ed. by Peter Auer and Aldo di Luizo, 259–92. Berlin: Mouton de Gruyter.

Everett, David L. 2005. Cultural constraints on grammar and cognition in Pirahã: Another look at the design features of human language. *Current Anthropology* 46(4).621–46.

Fantini, Alvino E. 1985. *Language acquisition of a bilingual child: A sociolinguistic perspective (to age ten).* Clevedon: Multilingual Matters.

Fasold, Ralph W., and Jeff Connor-Linton. 2006. *An introduction to language and linguistics.* Cambridge: Cambridge University Press.

Fernald, Anne. 1992. Human maternal vocalizations to infants as biologically relevant signals: An evolutionary perspective. *The adapted mind: Evolutionary psychology and the generation of culture,* ed. by Jerome H. Barkow, Leda Cosmides, and John Tooby, 391–428. Oxford: Oxford University Press.

Fortson, Benjamin W., IV. 2009. *Indo-European language and culture: An introduction.* 2nd edn. Oxford: Blackwell.

Fought, Carmen. 2006. Talkin' with mi gente (Chicano English). *American voices: How dialects differ from coast to coast,* ed. by Walt Wolfram and Ben Ward, 233–37. Oxford: Blackwell.

Fraser, Graham. 2006. *Sorry, I don't speak French: Confronting the Canadian crisis that won't go away.* Toronto: McClelland and Stewart.

Frazier, Lyn. 1987. Sentence processing: A tutorial review. *Attention and performance XII: The psychology of reading,* ed. by Max Coltheart, 559–86. East Sussex: Lawrence Erlbaum.

Fromkin, Victoria A. 1971. The non-anomalous nature of anomalous utterances. *Language* 47.27–52.

Fromkin, Victoria A. 1988. Sign languages: Evidence for language universals and the linguistic capacity of the brain. *Sign Language Studies* 59(Summer).115–27.

Fromkin, Victoria, and Robert Rodman. 1978. *An introduction to language.* 2nd edn. Fort Worth: Harcourt Collins. [10th edn., by Victoria Fromkin, Robert Rodman, and Nina Hyams, published 2014. Boston: Wadsworth, Cengage Learning.]

Fuller, Janet M. 1999. The role of English in Pennsylvania German development: Best supporting actress? *American Speech* 74(1).38–55.

Gal, Susan. 1978. Variation and change in patterns of speaking: Language shift in Austria. *Linguistic variation: Models and methods,* ed. by David Sankoff, 227–38. New York: Academic Press.

Gardner, Howard. 1975. *The shattered mind.* New York: Knopf.

Garnica, Olga K. 1977. Some prosodic and paralinguistic features of speech to young children. *Talking to children: Language input and acquisition,* ed. by Catherine E. Snow and Charles A. Ferguson, 63–88. Cambridge: Cambridge University Press.

Geschwind, Norman. 1979. Specializations of the human brain. *Scientific American* 241(3).180–99.

Ghazanfar, Asif A., and Nikos K. Logothetis. 2003. Neuroperception: Facial expressions linked to monkey calls. *Nature* 423(6943).937–38.

Giddens, Anthony. 2009. *Sociology.* 6th edn. Cambridge: Polity.

Goodluck, Helen. 1991. *Language acquisition: A linguistic introduction.* Malden, MA: Blackwell.

Gordon, Peter. 2004. Numerical cognition without words: Evidence from Amazonia. *Science* 306(5695).496–99.

Green, Lisa. 2004. African American English. *Language in the USA,* ed. by Edward Finegan and John R. Rickford, 76–91. Cambridge: Cambridge University Press.

Grenoble, Lenore A., and Lindsay J. Whaley. 2005. *Saving languages: An introduction to language revitalization.* Cambridge: Cambridge University Press.

Grice, H. Paul. 1989 [1975]. *Studies in the way of words.* Cambridge, MA: Harvard University Press.

Groce, Nora Ellen. 1985. *Everyone here spoke sign language: Hereditary deafness on Martha's Vineyard.* Cambridge, MA: Harvard University Press.

Grosjean, François. 1979. A study in timing in a manual and a spoken language: American Sign Language and English. *Journal of Psycholinguistic Research* 8.379–405.

Grundy, Peter. 2008. *Doing pragmatics.* 3rd edn. London: Hodder Arnold.

Gumperz, John J., and Robert Wilson. 1971. Convergence and creolization: A case from the Indo-Aryan/Dravidian border in India. *Pidginization and creolization of languages,* ed. by Dell H. Hymes, 151–67. Cambridge: Cambridge University Press.

Hall, Kira, and Mary Bucholtz (eds.). 1995. *Gender articulated: Language and the socially constructed self.* New York: Routledge.

Hankamer, Jorge. 1989. Morphological parsing and the lexicon. *Lexical representation and process,* ed. by William Marslen-Wilson, 392–408. Cambridge, MA: MIT Press.

Harrison, J. 1999. Research rescues language of the Miami. *Indianapolis Star,* November 27.

Harvard dialect survey. 2002. Available online: www4.uwm.edu/FLL/linguistics/dialect/index.html.

Haspelmath, Martin, and Andrea D. Sims. 2010. *Understanding morphology.* 2nd edn. New York: Routledge.

Hauser, Marc D., and Mark Konishi (eds.). 2003. *The design of animal communication.* Cambridge, MA: MIT Press.

Haviland, William; Robert Gordon; and Luis Vivanco. 2005. *Talking about people: Readings in contemporary anthropology.* 4th edn. Columbus, OH: McGraw-Hill.

Hawaii Tribune Herald, November 2, 1946.

Hay, Jennifer B. 2001. Lexical frequency in morphology: Is everything relative? *Linguistics* 39.1041–70.

Hayes, Bruce. 2009. *Introductory phonology.* Oxford: Wiley-Blackwell.

Heller, Monica S. 1982. Negotiations of language choice in Montreal. *Language and social identity,* ed. by John J. Gumperz, 108–18. Cambridge: Cambridge University Press.

Hickok, Gregory, and David Poeppel. 2004. Dorsal and ventral streams: A framework for understanding aspects of the functional anatomy of language. *Cognition* 92.67–99.

Hillix, William A., and Duane M. Rumbaugh. 2004. *Animal bodies, human minds: Ape, dolphin, and parrot language skills.* New York: Springer.

Hock, Hans Henrich. 1991. *Principles of historical linguistics.* 2nd edn. Berlin: Mouton de Gruyter.

Hock, Hans Henrich, and Brian D. Joseph. 2009. *Language history, language change, and language relationship*. 2nd rev. edn. Berlin: Mouton de Gruyter.

Hockett, Charles F. 1966. The problem of universals in language. *Universals of language,* ed. by Joseph H. Greenberg, 1–29. Cambridge, MA: MIT Press.

Hoffmann, Charlotte. 1998. *An introduction to bilingualism*. London: Longman.

Hopkins, C. D. 1999. Design features for electric communication. *The Journal of Experimental Biology* 202.1217–28.

Humphries, Tom; Poorna Kushalnagar; Gaurav Mathur; Donna Jo Napoli; Carol Padden; and Christian Rathmann. 2014. Ensuring language acquisition for deaf children: What linguists can do. *Language* 90(2).e31–e52.

Hurford, James R.; Brendan Heasley; and Michael B. Smith. 2007. *Semantics: A coursebook*. 2nd edn. Cambridge: Cambridge University Press.

Irvine, Judith T. 1974. Strategies of status manipulation in the Wolof greeting. *Explorations in the ethnography of speaking,* ed. by Richard Bauman and Joel Sherzer, 167–91. Cambridge: Cambridge University Press.

Jahr, Ernst Håkon. 1996. On the pidgin status of Russenorsk. *Language contact in the Arctic: Northern pidgins and contact languages,* ed. by Ernst Håkon Jahr and Ingvild Broch, 107–22. Berlin: Mouton de Gruyter.

Jay, Timothy B. 2003. *The psychology of language*. Upper Saddle River, NJ: Prentice Hall.

Jeffers, Robert J., and Ilse Lehiste. 1979. *Principles and methods for historical linguistics*. Cambridge, MA: MIT Press.

Johnson, Keith. 2012. *Acoustic and auditory phonetics*. 3rd edn. Malden, MA: Wiley-Blackwell.

Jurafsky, Daniel, and James H. Martin. 2008. *Speech and language processing: An introduction to natural language processing, computational linguistics, and speech recognition*. 2nd edn. Upper Saddle River, NJ: Prentice Hall.

Kathol, Andreas. 2000. *Linear syntax*. Oxford: Oxford University Press.

Keenan, Elinor. 1974. Norm-makers and norm-breakers: Uses of speech by men and women in a Malagasy community. *Explorations in the ethnography of speaking,* ed. by Richard Bauman and Joel Sherzer, 125–43. Cambridge: Cambridge University Press.

Keesing, Roger M. 1988. *Melanesian Pidgin and the oceanic substrate*. Stanford, CA: Stanford University Press.

Keiser, Steve Hartman. 1999. Language contact phenomena in Pennsylvania German: A literature review. Columbus: The Ohio State University, Ms.

Kim, Dahee. 2013. *The production and perception of signal-based cues to word boundaries*. Columbus: The Ohio State University dissertation.

Kim, Dahee; Joseph D. W. Stephens; and Mark A. Pitt. 2012. How does context play a part in splitting words apart? Production and perception of word boundaries in casual speech. *Journal of Memory and Language* 66.509–29.

Klatt, Dennis H. 1987. Review of text-to-speech conversion for English. *Journal of the Acoustical Society of America* 82(3).737–93.

Klima, Edward S., and Ursula Bellugi. 1979. *The signs of language*. Cambridge, MA: Harvard University Press.

Knecht, Stefan; Bianca Dräger; Michael Deppe; Linus Bobe; Hubertus Lohmann; Agnes Flöel; E.-Bernd Ringelstein; and Henning Henningsen. 2000. Handedness and hemispheric language dominance in healthy humans. *Brain* 123(12).2512–18.

Kretzschmar, William A., Jr. 1997. American English for the 21st century. *Englishes around the world: Studies in honour of Manfred Görlach. Vol. 1: General studies, British Isles, North America,* ed. by Edgar W. Schneider, 307–24. Amsterdam: John Benjamins.

Labov, William. 1972. *Sociolinguistic patterns*. Philadelphia: University of Pennsylvania Press.

Labov, William. 1990. The intersection of sex and social class in the course of linguistic change. *Language Variation and Change* 2.205–54.

Labov, William. 2006. *The social stratification of English in New York City*. 2nd edn. Cambridge: Cambridge University Press.

Labov, William; Sharon Ash; and Charles Boberg (eds.). 2006. *Atlas of North American English: Phonetics, phonology, and sound change*. Berlin: Mouton de Gruyter.

Ladefoged, Peter. 1996. *Elements of acoustic phonetics*. 2nd edn. Chicago: University of Chicago Press.

Ladefoged, Peter, and Sandra Ferrari Disner. 2012. *Vowels and consonants: An introduction to the sounds of languages*. 3rd edn. Malden, MA: Wiley-Blackwell.

Ladefoged, Peter, and Keith Johnson. 2015. *A course in phonetics.* 7th edn. Stamford, CT: Cengage Learning.

Ladefoged, Peter, and Ian Maddieson. 1996. *The sounds of the world's languages.* Oxford: Blackwell.

Lakoff, Robin T. 1990. *Talking power: The politics of language in our lives.* New York: Basic Books.

Lane, Harlan; Robert Hoffmeister; and Ben Bahan. 1996. *A journey into the DEAF-WORLD.* San Diego: DawnSign.

Lenneberg, Eric H. 1967. *Biological foundations of language.* New York: John Wiley & Sons.

Lenneberg, Eric H., and John M. Roberts. 1956. The language of experience: A study in methodology. *International Journal of American Linguistics* 22, Memoir 13.

Leopold, Werner F. 1947. *Speech development of a bilingual child: A linguist's record. Vol. II: Sound-learning in the first two years.* Evanston, IL: Northwestern University Press.

Levelt, Willem J. M. 1989. *Speaking: From intention to articulation.* Cambridge, MA: MIT Press.

Levinson, Stephen C. 1996a. Frames of reference and Molyneux's question: Crosslinguistic evidence. *Language and space,* ed. by Paul Bloom, Mary A. Peterson, Lynn Nadel, and Merrill F. Garrett, 109–69. Cambridge, MA: MIT Press.

Levinson, Stephen C. 1996b. Language and space. *Annual Review of Anthropology* 25.353–82.

Lewis, M. Paul; Gary F. Simons; and Charles D. Fennig (eds.). 2015. *Ethnologue: Languages of the world.* 18th edn. Dallas, TX: SIL International. Online version: http://www.ethnologue.com/.

Lieberman, Philip, and Sheila E. Blumstein. 1988. *Speech physiology, speech perception, and acoustic phonetics.* (Cambridge studies in speech science and communication.) Cambridge: Cambridge University Press.

Louden, Mark. 1997. Linguistic structure and sociolinguistic identity in Pennsylvania German society. *Language and lives: Essays in honor of Werner Enninger,* ed. by James R. Dow and Michele Wolff, 79–92. New York: Peter Lang.

Lowth, Robert. 1762. *A short introduction to English grammar, with critical notes.* London: Printed by J. Hughs for A. Millar and R. and J. Dodsley.

Lucas, Ceil; Robert Bayley; Ruth Reed; and Alyssa Wulf. 2001. Lexical variation in African American and white signing. *American Speech* 76(4).339–60.

Lucy, John A. 1992. *Language diversity and thought: A reformulation of the linguistic relativity hypothesis.* Cambridge: Cambridge University Press.

Lyons, John. 1995. *Linguistic semantics: An introduction.* Cambridge: Cambridge University Press.

Macaulay, Monica. 2011. *Surviving linguistics: A guide for graduate students.* 2nd edn. Somerville, MA: Cascadilla.

Macklovitch, Elliott. 2015. Translation technology in Canada. *Routledge encyclopedia of translation technology,* ed. by Chan Sin-Wai, 267–78. New York: Routledge.

Macnamara, John. 1969. How can one measure the extent of a person's bilingual proficiency? *Description and measurement of bilingualism,* ed. by L. G. Kelly, 80–97. Toronto: University of Toronto Press.

Mallinson, Christine; Becky Childs; Bridget Anderson; and Neal Hutcheson. 2006. If these hills could talk (Smoky Mountains). *American voices: How dialects differ from coast to coast,* ed. by Walt Wolfram and Ben Ward, 22–28. Oxford: Blackwell.

Malotki, Ekkehart. 1983. *Hopi time: A linguistic analysis of the temporal concepts in the Hopi language.* Berlin: Mouton.

Marslen-Wilson, William D. 1984. Function and process in spoken word recognition. *Attention and performance X: Control of language processes,* ed. by Herman Bouma and Don G. Bouwhuis, 125–50. Hillsdale, NJ: Lawrence Erlbaum.

Martin, Joe. 2000. A linguistic comparison: Two notation systems for signed languages: Stokoe Notation and Sutton SignWriting. Available online: http://www.signwriting.org/archive/docs1/sw0032-Stokoe-Sutton.pdf.

McClelland, James L., and Jeffrey L. Elman. 1986. The TRACE model of speech perception. *Cognitive Psychology* 18.1–86.

McConchie, Alan. 2002. The great soda pop controversy. Online: http://www.popvssoda.com/.

McCrum, Robert; Robert MacNeil; and William Cran. 2002. *The story of English.* 3rd revised edn. New York: Viking Penguin.

McGurk, Harry, and John MacDonald. 1976. Hearing lips and seeing voices. *Nature* 264.746–48.

Mendoza-Denton, Norma. 1997. *Chicana/Mexicana identity and linguistic variation: An ethnographic and sociolinguistic study of gang affiliation in an urban high school.* Stanford, CA: Stanford University dissertation.

Mendoza-Denton, Norma. 2002. Language and identity. *The handbook of language variation and change,* ed. by Peter Trudgill, J. K. Chambers, and Natalie Schilling-Estes, 475–99. Malden, MA: Blackwell.

Menzel, Charles R.; E. Sue Savage-Rumbaugh; and Emil W. Menzel, Jr. 2002. Bonobo (*pan paniscus*) spatial memory and communication in a 20-hectare forest. *International Journal of Primatology* 23(3).601–19.

Mervis, Carolyn B., and Angela E. John. 2008. Vocabulary abilities of children with Williams syndrome: Strengths, weaknesses, and relation to visuospatial construction ability. *Journal of Speech, Language, and Hearing Research* 51.967–82.

Miller, George A. 1996. *The science of words.* New York: Scientific American Library.

Millward, Celia M. 1996. *A biography of the English language.* 2nd edn. Orlando, FL: Holt, Rinehart and Winston.

Montgomery, Michael B., and Joseph S. Hall. 2003. *Dictionary of Smoky Mountain English.* Knoxville: University of Tennessee Press.

Motley, Michael T.; Carl T. Camden; and Bernard J. Baars. 1982. Covert formulation and editing in speech production: Evidence from experimentally elicited slips of the tongue. *Journal of Verbal Learning and Verbal Behavior* 21.578–94.

Murray, Thomas E. 1993. Positive *anymore* in the Midwest. *"Heartland" English: Variation and transition in the American Midwest,* ed. by Timothy C. Frazer, 173–86. Tuscaloosa: The University of Alabama Press.

Murray, Thomas E.; Timothy C. Frazer; and Beth L. Simon. 1996. *Needs* + past participle in American English. *American Speech* 71(3).255–71.

Myers-Scotton, Carol. 1990. Intersections between social motivations and structural processing in code-switching. *Papers for the workshop on constraints, conditions, and models,* 57–82. Strasbourg: European Science Foundation.

Newman, Aaron J.; Daphne Bavelier; David Corina; Peter Jezzard; and Helen J. Neville. 2002. A critical period for right hemisphere recruitment in American Sign Language processing. *Nature Neuroscience* 5.76–80.

Newport, Elissa; Henry Gleitman; and Lila R. Gleitman. 1977. Mother, I'd rather do it myself: Some effects and noneffects of maternal speech style. *Talking to children: Language input and acquisition,* ed. by Catherine E. Snow and Charles A. Ferguson, 101–49. Cambridge: Cambridge University Press.

Nic Craith, Máiréad. 2006. *Europe and the politics of language: Citizens, migrants and outsiders.* (Palgrave studies in minority languages and communities.) Basingstoke: Palgrave Macmillan.

Norman, Jerry. 1988. *Chinese.* Cambridge: Cambridge University Press.

Norris, Dennis. 1994. Shortlist: A connectionist model of continuous speech recognition. *Cognition* 52(3).189–234.

Norris, Dennis, and James M. McQueen. 2008. Shortlist B: A Bayesian model of continuous speech recognition. *Psychological Review* 115(2).357–95.

O'Barr, William M., and Bowman K. Atkins. 1980. "Women's language" or "powerless language"? *Women and language in literature and society,* ed. by Sally McConnell-Ginet, Ruth Borker, and Nelly Furman, 93–110. New York: Praeger.

O'Grady, William; John Archibald; Mark Aronoff; and Janie Rees-Miller. 2001. *Contemporary linguistics: An introduction.* 4th edn. New York: St. Martin's Press. [6th edn. 2009.]

Oaks, Dallin D. 1998. *Linguistics at work: A reader of applications.* Fort Worth: Harcourt Brace College Publishers.

Ochs, Elinor. 1993. Indexing gender. *Sex and gender hierarchies,* ed. by Barbara Miller, 146–69. Cambridge: Cambridge University Press.

Odden, David. 2013. *Introducing phonology.* 2nd edn. Cambridge: Cambridge University Press.

Oldfield, R. C, and A. Wingfield. 1965. Response latencies in naming objects. *Quarterly Journal of Experimental Psychology* 17.273–81.

Ong, Walter J. 1982. *Orality and literacy: The technologizing of the world.* London: Routledge.

Padden, Carol A., and David M. Perlmutter. 1987. American Sign Language and the architecture of phonological theory. *Natural Language and Linguistic Theory* 5.335–75.

Pearson, Barbara Z.; Sylvia C. Fernández; Vanessa Lewedeg; and D. Kimbrough Oller. 1997. The relation of input factors to lexical learning by bilingual infants. *Applied Psycholinguistics* 18.41–58.

Penfield, Joyce, and Jacob L. Ornstein-Galicia (eds.). 1985. *Chicano English: An ethnic contact dialect.* Amsterdam: John Benjamins.

Pepperberg, Irene Maxine. 1999. *The Alex studies: Cognitive and communicative abilities of grey parrots.* Cambridge, MA: Harvard University Press.

Phillips, Juliet R. 1973. Syntax and vocabulary of mothers' speech to young children: Age and sex comparisons. *Child Development* 44.182–85.

Postma, Albert, and Catharina Noordanus. 1996. Production and detection of speech errors in silent, mouthed, noise-masked, and normal auditory feedback speech. *Language and Speech* 39(4).375–92.

Purnell, Thomas; William J. Idsardi; and John Baugh. 1999. Perceptual and phonetic experiments on American English dialect identification. *Journal of Language and Social Psychology* 18(1).10–30.

Rickford, John R. 1999. *African-American Vernacular English*. Oxford: Blackwell.

Rickford, John R., and Faye McNair-Knox. 1994. Addressee- and topic-influenced style shift: A quantitative sociolinguistic study. *Sociolinguistic perspectives on register,* ed. by Douglas Biber and Edward Finegan, 235–76. Oxford: Oxford University Press.

Roberts-Kohno, Ruth R. 2000. *Kikamba phonology and morphology.* Columbus: The Ohio State University dissertation.

Rogers, Henry. 2005. *Writing systems: A linguistic approach.* Malden, MA: Blackwell.

Rolheiser, Tyler; Emmanuel A. Stamatakis; and Lorraine K. Tyler. 2011. Dynamic processing in the human language system: Synergy between the arcuate fascicle and extreme capsule. *The Journal of Neuroscience* 31(47).16949–57.

Sachs, Jacqueline, and Marie Johnson. 1976. Language development in a hearing child of deaf parents. *Baby talk and infant speech,* ed. by Walburga von Raffler-Engel and Yvan Lebrun, 246–52. Amsterdam: Swets & Zeitlinger.

Sandler, Wendy, and Diane Lillo-Martin. 2001. Natural sign languages. *Handbook of linguistics,* ed. by Mark Aronoff and Janie Rees-Miller, 533–62. Oxford: Blackwell.

Sapir, Edward. 1949 [1921]. *Language: An introduction to the study of speech.* New York: Harcourt, Brace, and Company.

Savage-Rumbaugh, Sue, and Roger Lewin. 1994. *Kanzi: The ape at the brink of the human mind.* New York: John Wiley & Sons.

Schreuder, Robert, and R. Harald Baayen. 1995. Modeling morphological processing. *Morphological aspects of language processing,* ed. by Laurie Beth Feldman, 131–54. Hillsdale, NJ: Lawrence Erlbaum.

Sedivy, Julie. 2014. *Language in mind: An introduction to psycholinguistics.* Sunderland, MA: Sinauer Associates.

Sedivy, Julie, and Greg Carlson. 2011. *Sold on language: How advertisers talk to you and what this says about you.* Chichester: John Wiley & Sons.

Senghas, Ann, and Marie Coppola. 2001. Children creating language: How Nicaraguan Sign Language acquired a spatial grammar. *Psychological Science* 12(4).323–28.

Shannon, Claude E., and Warren Weaver. 1949. *The mathematical theory of communication.* Urbana-Champaign: University of Illinois Press.

Shroyer, Edgar H., and Susan P. Shroyer. 1984. *Signs across America: A look at regional differences in American Sign Language.* Washington, DC: Gallaudet University Press.

Shuy, Roger W. 2006. *Linguistics in the courtroom: A practical guide.* Oxford: Oxford University Press.

Silva-Corvalán, Carmen. 2004. Spanish in the Southwest. *Language in the USA: Themes for the twenty-first century,* ed. by Edward Finegan and John R. Rickford, 205–29. Cambridge: Cambridge University Press.

Singh, Simon. 1999. *The code book: The science of secrecy from Ancient Egypt to quantum cryptography.* New York: Anchor Books.

Sinkov, Abraham. 1998. *Elementary cryptanalysis: A mathematical approach.* Cambridge: Cambridge University Press.

Slobin, Dan I. 1996. From "thought and language" to "thinking for speaking." *Rethinking linguistic relativity,* ed. by John J. Gumperz and Stephen C. Levinson, 70–96. Cambridge: Cambridge University Press.

Smith, William A. 1989. *The morphological characteristics of verbs in Taiwan Sign Language.* Bloomington: Department of Speech and Hearing Sciences, Indiana University dissertation.

Smith, Wayne H., and Li-fen Ting. 1979. *Shou neng sheng chyau (your hands can become a bridge).* Taipei: Deaf Sign Language Research Association of the Republic of China.

Snow, Catherine E. 1977. The development of conversation between mothers and babies. *Journal of Child Language* 4.1–22.

Snow, Catherine E.; A. Arlman-Rupp; Y. Hassing; J. Jobse; J. Jooksen; and J. Vorster. 1976. Mother's speech in three social classes. *Journal of Psycholinguistic Research* 5.1–20.

Solan, Lawrence M. 1993. *The language of judges.* (Language and Legal Discourse series.) Chicago: University of Chicago Press.

Stephenson, Neal. 2002. *Cryptonomicon.* New York: Harper Perennial.

Stojanovik, Vesna. 2010. Understanding and production of prosody in children with Williams syndrome: A developmental trajectory approach. *Journal of Neurolinguistics* 23(2).112–26.

Stork, David G. (ed.). 1997. *HAL's legacy: 2001's computer as dream and reality.* Cambridge, MA: MIT Press.

Strand, Elizabeth A. 1999. Uncovering the role of gender stereotypes in speech perception. *Journal of Language and Social Psychology* 18(1).86–99.

Taft, Marcus, and Kenneth I. Forster. 1975. Lexical storage and retrieval of prefixed words. *Journal of Verbal Learning and Verbal Behavior* 14.638–47.

Tallal, Paula. 1990. Fine-grained discrimination deficits in language-learning impaired children are specific neither to the auditory modality nor to speech perception. *Journal of Speech, Language, and Hearing Research* 33.616–17.

Tallerman, Maggie. 2005. *Understanding syntax.* London: Hodder Arnold. [3rd edn. published 2013.]

Thomas, Erik R. 1993. The use of the *all the* + comparative structure. *"Heartland" English: Variation and transition in the American Midwest,* ed. by Timothy C. Frazer, 257–65. Tuscaloosa: The University of Alabama Press.

Thomas, Erik R. 2001. *An acoustic analysis of vowel variation in New World English.* Durham, NC: Duke University Press.

Thomason, Sarah Grey. 2001. *Language contact: An introduction.* Washington, DC: Georgetown University Press.

Thomason, Sarah Grey, and Terrence Kaufman. 1988. *Language contact, creolization, and genetic linguistics.* Berkeley: University of California Press.

Thorne, Barrie; Cheris Kramarae; and Nancy Henley (eds.). 1983. *Language, gender, and society.* Rowley, MA: Newbury House.

Todd, Loreto. 1979. *Some day been dey: West African pidgin folktales.* London: Routledge and Kegan Paul.

Trudgill, Peter. 1972. Sex, covert prestige, and linguistic change in the urban British English of Norwich. *Language in Society* 1.179–95.

Trudgill, Peter. 1974. *The social differentiation of English in Norwich.* Cambridge: Cambridge University Press.

Valli, Clayton; Ceil Lucas; Kristin J. Mulrooney; and Miako Villanueva. 2011. *Linguistics of American Sign Language: An introduction.* 5th edn. Washington, DC: Gallaudet University Press.

Velupillai, Viveka. 2015. *Pidgins, creoles and mixed languages: An introduction.* Amsterdam: John Benjamins.

von Wattenwyl, André, and Heinrich Zollinger. 1978. The color lexica of two American Indian languages, Quechi and Misquito: A critical contribution to the application of the Whorf thesis to color naming. *International Journal of American Linguistics* 44.56–68.

Waksler, Rachelle. 2001. A new *all* in conversation. *American Speech* 76(2).128–38.

Warren, Richard M., and Roslyn P. Warren. 1970. Auditory illusions and confusions. *Scientific American* 223(6).30–37.

Watts, Richard J.; Sachiko Ide; and Konrad Ehlich (eds.). 2008. *Politeness in language: Studies in its history, theory and practice.* 2nd edn. Berlin: Mouton de Gruyter.

Weatherholtz, Kodi. 2015. *Perceptual learning of systemic cross-category vowel variation.* Columbus: The Ohio State University dissertation.

West, Candace, and Don H. Zimmerman. 1991. Doing gender. *The social construction of gender,* ed. by Judith Lorber and Susan A. Farrell, 13–37. London: Sage.

Whorf, Benjamin Lee. 1956. *Language, thought, and reality: Selected writings of Benjamin Lee Whorf,* ed. by John B. Carroll. Cambridge, MA: MIT Press.

Williams, Robin. 2005. Cecil B. DeMille Golden Globe Lifetime Achievement Award acceptance speech. Available online: http://www.ruggedelegantliving.com/a/003419.html.

Winford, Donald. 2003. *An introduction to contact linguistics.* Malden, MA: Blackwell.

Wise, Steven M. 2002. *Drawing the line: Science and the case for animal rights.* Cambridge, MA: Perseus.

Wohlgemuth, Jan. 1999. *Grammatical categories and their realisations in Tok Pisin of Papua New Guinea.* Available online: http://www.linguist.de/TokPisin/tp02-en.htm.

Wolfram, Walt. 1969. *A linguistic description of Detroit Negro speech.* Washington, DC: Center for Applied Linguistics.

Wolfram, Walt. 1991. *Dialects and American English.* Englewood Cliffs, NJ: Prentice Hall.

Wolfram, Walt. 2006. From the brickhouse to the swamp (Lumbee Vernacular English). *American voices: How dialects differ from coast to coast,* ed. by Walt Wolfram and Ben Ward, 244–50. Oxford: Blackwell.

Wolfram, Walt, and Donna Christian. 1976. *Appalachian speech.* Washington, DC: Center for Applied Linguistics.

Wolfram, Walt, and Clare Dannenberg. 1999. Dialect identity and a tri-ethnic context: The case of Lumbee American Indian English. *English World-Wide* 20.79–216.

Wolfram, Walt; Clare Dannenberg; Stanley Knick; and Linda Oxendine. 2002. *Fine in the world: Lumbee language in time and place*. Raleigh: North Carolina State University, Humanities Extension/Publications.

Wolfram, Walt, and Natalie Schilling-Estes. 2005. *American English*. 2nd edn. Oxford: Blackwell. [3rd edn. published 2015.]

Wolfram, Walt, and Ben Ward (eds.). 2006. *American voices: How dialects differ from coast to coast*. Oxford: Blackwell.

Wright, Richard Grant. 1882. *Words and their uses, past and present: A study of the English language*. 5th edn. Boston: Houghton Mifflin.

Yule, George. 1996. *The study of language*. 2nd edn. Cambridge: Cambridge University Press. [5th edn. published 2014.]

Zwicky, Ann D. 1981. Styles. *Styles and variables in English,* ed. by Timothy Shopen and Joseph M. Williams, 61–83. Cambridge, MA: Winthrop Publishers (Prentice Hall).

LANGUAGE INDEX

SUBJECT INDEX

....

Examples of Phonetic Symbols Found in Standard American English

Note: Because English spelling does not have a one-to-one correspondence with sounds, underlining the letter in example words can be difficult. For example, we have underlined the <x> in *exceed* to indicate both [k] and [s] because the letter <x> represents a series of two sounds: [ks]. For each symbol, think carefully about how the sound occurs in the example words.

a. Consonants

i. Non-Syllabic Consonants

Symbol	Example Words
[p]	pit, tip, spit, hiccough, appear
[b]	ball, globe, amble, brick, bubble
[t]	tag, pat, stick, pterodactyl, stuffed
[d]	dip, card, drop, loved, batted
[k]	kit, scoot, character, critique, exceed
[g]	guard, bag, finger, designate, Pittsburgh
[ʔ]	uh-oh, hatrack, Batman, button, curtain
[f]	foot, laugh, philosophy, coffee, carafe
[v]	vest, dove, gravel, anvil, average
[θ]	through, wrath, thistle, ether, teeth
[ð]	the, their, mother, either, teethe
[s]	soap, psychology, packs, descent, peace, exceed
[z]	zip, roads, kisses, Xerox, design
[ʃ]	shy, mission, nation, glacial, sure
[ʒ]	measure, vision, azure, casualty, decision
[h]	who, hat, rehash, hole, whole
[tʃ]	choke, match, feature, righteous, constituent
[dʒ]	judge, George, Jell-O, region, residual
[m]	moose, lamb, smack, amnesty, ample
[n]	nap, design, snow, know, mnemonic
[ŋ]	lung, think, finger, singer, ankle
[l]	leaf, feel, Lloyd, mild, applaud
[ɹ]	reef, fear, Harris, prune, carp
[ɾ]	butter, udder, cuter, Adam, bottle, ready
[w]	with, swim, mowing, queen, twilight
[ʍ]	which, where, what, whale, why
[j]	you, beautiful, feud, use, yell

ii. Syllabic Consonants

Symbol	Example Words
[m̩]	possum, chasm, Adam, bottomless
[n̩]	button, chicken, lesson, kittenish
[l̩]	little, single, simple, stabilize
[ɹ̩]	ladder, singer, burp, percent, bird

b. Vowels

i. Monophthongs (Simple Vowels)

Symbol	Example Words
[i]	beat, we, believe, people, money, dean
[ɪ]	bit, consist, injury, malignant, gym, business
[ɛ]	bet, reception, says, guest, bend
[æ]	bat, laugh, anger, bang, comrade, rally, hand
[u]	boot, who, brewer, duty, through, dune
[ʊ]	put, foot, butcher, boogie-woogie, could
[ɔ]	bought, caught, wrong, stalk, core, law
[ɑ]	pot, father, sergeant, honor, hospital, bomb
[ʌ]	but, tough, another, oven, fungus
[ə]	among, Asia, eloquent, famous, harmony

ii. Diphthongs (Complex Vowels)

Symbol	Example Words
[ɑɪ]	I, abide, Stein, aisle, choir, island, fine
[ɑʊ]	bout, brown, doubt, flower, loud
[ɔɪ]	boy, doily, rejoice, perestroika, annoy
[oʊ]	oh, boat, beau, grow, though, over
[eɪ]	bait, reign, great, they, gauge, age

Consonants of Standard American English

The consonants of Standard American English, written with IPA symbols, classified by voicing, place of articulation, and manner of articulation:

		Place of Articulation														
		Bilabial		Labio-dental		Inter-dental		Alveolar		Post-Alveolar		Palatal		Velar		Glottal	
Manner of Articulation	Stop	p	b					t	d					k	g	ʔ	
	Fricative			f	v	θ	ð	s	z	ʃ	ʒ					h	
	Affricate									tʃ	dʒ						
	Flap								ɾ								
	Nasal		m						n						ŋ		
	Lateral Liquid								l								
	Retroflex Liquid								ɹ								
	Glide	w̥	w									j					

State of the Glottis | Voiceless | Voiced

Vowels of Standard American English

The vowels of Standard American English, written with IPA symbols, presented using the traditional American classification system:

Monophthongs:

Diphthongs:

THE INTERNATIONAL PHONETIC ALPHABET (revised to 2005)

CONSONANTS (PULMONIC)

	Bilabial	Labiodental	Dental	Alveolar	Postalveolar	Retroflex	Palatal	Velar	Uvular	Pharyngeal	Glottal
Plosive	p b			t d		ʈ ɖ	c ɟ	k g	q ɢ		ʔ
Nasal	m	ɱ		n		ɳ	ɲ	ŋ	N		
Trill	ʙ			r					R		
Tap or Flap		ⱱ		ɾ		ɽ					
Fricative	ɸ β	f v	θ ð	s z	ʃ ʒ	ʂ ʐ	ç ʝ	x ɣ	χ ʁ	ħ ʕ	h ɦ
Lateral fricative				ɬ ɮ							
Approximant		ʋ		ɹ		ɻ	j	ɰ			
Lateral approximant				l		ɭ	ʎ	ʟ			

Where symbols appear in pairs, the one to the right represents a voiced consonant. Shaded areas denote articulations judged impossible.

CONSONANTS (NON-PULMONIC)

Clicks	Voiced implosives	Ejectives
ʘ Bilabial	ɓ Bilabial	ʼ Examples:
ǀ Dental	ɗ Dental/alveolar	pʼ Bilabial
ǃ (Post)alveolar	ʄ Palatal	tʼ Dental/alveolar
ǂ Palatoalveolar	ɠ Velar	kʼ Velar
ǁ Alveolar lateral	ʛ Uvular	sʼ Alveolar fricative

OTHER SYMBOLS

ʍ Voiceless labial-velar fricative
w Voiced labial-velar approximant
ɥ Voiced labial-palatal approximant
ʜ Voiceless epiglottal fricative
ʢ Voiced epiglottal fricative
ʡ Epiglottal plosive

ɕ ʑ Alveolo-palatal fricatives
ɺ Voiced alveolar lateral flap
ɧ Simultaneous ʃ and x

Affricates and double articulations can be represented by two symbols joined by a tie bar if necessary.

k͡p t͡s

VOWELS

	Front	Central	Back
Close	i • y	ɨ • ʉ	ɯ • u
	ɪ ʏ		ʊ
Close-mid	e • ø	ɘ • ɵ	ɤ • o
		ə	
Open-mid	ɛ • œ	ɜ • ɞ	ʌ • ɔ
	æ	ɐ	
Open	a • ɶ		ɑ • ɒ

Where symbols appear in pairs, the one to the right represents a rounded vowel.

SUPRASEGMENTALS

ˈ Primary stress
ˌ Secondary stress   ˌfoʊnəˈtɪʃən
ː Long   eː
ˑ Half-long   eˑ
˘ Extra-short   ĕ
| Minor (foot) group
‖ Major (intonation) group
. Syllable break   ɹi.ækt
‿ Linking (absence of a break)

DIACRITICS

Diacritics may be placed above a symbol with a descender, e.g. ŋ̊

̥	Voiceless	n̥ d̥	̤	Breathy voiced	b̤ a̤	̪	Dental	t̪ d̪
̬	Voiced	s̬ t̬	̰	Creaky voiced	b̰ a̰	̺	Apical	t̺ d̺
ʰ	Aspirated	tʰ dʰ	̼	Linguolabial	t̼ d̼	̻	Laminal	t̻ d̻
̹	More rounded	ɔ̹	ʷ	Labialized	tʷ dʷ	̃	Nasalized	ẽ
̜	Less rounded	ɔ̜	ʲ	Palatalized	tʲ dʲ	ⁿ	Nasal release	dⁿ
̟	Advanced	u̟	ˠ	Velarized	tˠ dˠ	ˡ	Lateral release	dˡ
̠	Retracted	e̠	ˤ	Pharyngealized	tˤ dˤ	̚	No audible release	d̚
̈	Centralized	ë	̴	Velarized or pharyngealized	ɫ			
̽	Mid-centralized	ě	̝	Raised	e̝ (ɹ̝ = voiced alveolar fricative)			
̩	Syllabic	n̩	̞	Lowered	e̞ (β̞ = voiced bilabial approximant)			
̯	Non-syllabic	e̯	̘	Advanced Tongue Root	e̘			
˞	Rhoticity	ɚ a˞	̙	Retracted Tongue Root	e̙			

TONES AND WORD ACCENTS

LEVEL		CONTOUR	
e̋ or ˥	Extra high	ě or ˩˥	Rising
é ˦	High	ê ˥˩	Falling
ē ˧	Mid	ē̯ ˧˥	High rising
è ˨	Low	è̯ ˩˧	Low rising
ȅ ˩	Extra low	ě̤ ˧˩˧	Rising-falling
↓ Downstep		↗ Global rise	
↑ Upstep		↘ Global fall	